AF856252

Digital Logic Design

CSCE 211

Chin-Tser Huang

UNIV OF SOUTH CAROLINA

COMPUTER SCI & ENGINEERING

McGraw Hill create®

create.mheducation.com

ISBN-13: 9781308693507

ISBN-10: 1308693508

Contents

PREFACE

This book is intended as an introductory logic design book for students in computer science, computer engineering, and electrical engineering. It has no prerequisites, although the maturity attained through an introduction to engineering course or a first programming course would be helpful.

The book stresses fundamentals. It teaches through a large number of examples. The philosophy of the author is that the only way to learn logic design is to do a large number of design problems. Thus, in addition to the numerous examples in the body of the text, each chapter has a set of Solved Problems, that is, problems and their solutions, a large set of Exercises (with answers to selected exercises in Appendix B), and a Chapter Test (with answers in Appendix C). Also, six complete examples (from word problem to circuit design) are included in Appendix E. Three of these are combinational and can be used after Chapter 3, and the others are sequential, to follow Chapter 7. In addition, there is a set of laboratory experiments that tie the theory to the real world. Appendix D provides the background to do these experiments with a standard hardware laboratory (chips, switches, lights, and wires), a breadboard simulator (for the PC or Macintosh), and a schematic capture tool. The course can be taught without the laboratory, but the student will benefit significantly from the addition of 8 to 10 selected experiments.

Although computer-aided tools are widely used for the design of large systems, the student must first understand the basics. The basics provide more than enough material for a first course. The schematic capture laboratory exercises and sections on Hardware Design Languages in Chapters 4 and 8 provide some material for a transition to a second course based on one of the computer-aided tool sets.

Chapter 1, after a brief introduction, gives an overview of number systems as it applies to the material of this book. (Those students who have studied this in an earlier course can skip this chapter.)

Chapter 2 discusses the steps in the design process for combinational systems and the development of truth tables. It then introduces switching algebra and the implementation of switching functions using common gates—AND, OR, NOT, NAND, NOR, Exclusive-OR, and Exclusive-NOR. We are only concerned with the logic behavior of the gates, not the electronic implementation.

Although the Karnaugh map is not introduced until Chapter 3, those who wish to use it in conjunction with algebraic simplification can cover Section 3.1 after Section 2.6, and find a number of examples relating the algebra to the map in Appendix A.

Chapter 3 deals with simplification using the Karnaugh map. It provides methods for solving problems (up to six variables) with both single and multiple outputs.

Chapter 4 introduces two algorithmic methods for solving combinational problems—the Quine-McCluskey method and iterated consensus. Both provide all of the prime implicants of a function or set of functions, and then use the same tabular method to find minimum sum of products solutions.

Chapter 5 is concerned with the design of larger combinational systems. It introduces a number of commercially available larger devices, including adders, comparators, decoders, encoders and priority encoders, and multiplexers. That is followed by a discussion of the use of logic arrays—ROMs, PLAs, and PALs for the implementation of medium-scale combinational systems. Finally, two larger systems are designed.

Chapter 6 introduces sequential systems. It starts by examining the behavior of latches and flip flops. It then discusses techniques to analyze the behavior of sequential systems.

Chapter 7 introduces the design process for sequential systems. The special case of counters is studied next. Finally, the solution of word problems, developing the state table or state diagram from a verbal description of the problem is presented in detail.

Chapter 8 looks at larger sequential systems. It starts by examining the design of shift registers and counters. Then, PLDs (logic arrays with memory) are presented. Three techniques that are useful in the design of more complex systems—ASM diagrams, one-hot encoding, and HDLs—are discussed next. Finally, two examples of larger systems are presented.

Chapter 9 (available on the web site of the book, http://www.mhhe.com/marcovitz) deals with state reduction and state assignment issues. First, a tabular approach for state reduction is presented. Then partitions are utilized both for state reduction and for achieving a state assignment that will utilize less combinational logic.

A feature of this text is the Solved Problems. Each chapter has a large number of problems, illustrating the techniques developed in the body of the text, followed by a detailed solution of each problem. Students are urged to solve each problem (without looking at the solution) and then compare their solution with the one shown.

Each chapter contains a large set of exercises. Answers to a selection of these are contained in Appendix B. Solutions are available to instructors on the website. In addition, each chapter concludes with a Chapter Test; answers are given in Appendix C.

Another unique feature of the book is the laboratory exercises, included in Appendix D. Three platforms are presented—a hardware-based Logic Lab (using chips, wires, etc.); a hardware lab simulator that allows the student to "connect" wires on the computer screen; and a circuit capture program, LogicWorks. Enough information is provided about each to allow the student to perform a variety of experiments. A set of 26 laboratory exercises are presented. Several of these have options, to allow the instructor to change the details from one term to the next.

We teach this material as a four-credit course that includes an average of three and a half hours per week of lecture, plus, typically, eight laboratory exercises. (The lab is unscheduled; it is manned by Graduate Assistants 40 hours per week; they grade the labs.) In that course we cover

Chapter 1: all of it

Chapter 2: all but 2.11

Chapter 3: all of it

Chapter 5: all but 5.8. However, there is a graded design problem based on that material (10 percent of the grade; students usually working in groups of 2 or 3).

Chapter 6: all of it

Chapter 7: all of it

Chapter 8: 8.1, 8.2, 8.3. We sometimes have a second project based on 8.7.

Chapter 9 and Chapter 4: We often have some time to look at one of these. We have never been able to cover both.

With less time, the coverage of Section 2.10 could be minimized. Section 3.5 is not needed for continuity; Section 3.6 is used somewhat in the discussion of PLAs in Section 5.7.2. Chapter 5 is not needed for anything else in the text, although many of the topics are useful to students elsewhere. The instructor can pick and choose among the topics. The *SR* and *T* flip flops could be omitted in Chapters 6 and 7. Sections 7.2 and 7.3 could be omitted without loss of continuity. As is the case for Chapter 5, the instructor can pick and choose among the topics of Chapter 8. With a limited amount of time, Section 9.1 could be covered. With more time, it could be skipped and state reduction taught using partitions (Sections 9.2 and 9.3).

WEBSITE

Teaching and learning resources are available on the website that accompanies this text. For students, these resources include quiz files and sample tests. For instructors, a solutions manual, PowerPoint lecture outlines, and other resources are available. The web address for this site is http://www.mhhe.com/marcovitz.

ELECTRONIC TEXTBOOK OPTIONS

This text is offered through CourseSmart for both instructors and students. CourseSmart is an online resource where students can purchase the complete text online for almost half the cost of a traditional text. Purchasing the eTextbook allows students to take advantage of CourseSmart's web tools for learning, which include full text search, notes and highlighting, and email tools for sharing notes between classmates. To learn more about CourseSmart options, contact your sales representative or visit http://www.CourseSmart.com.

ACKNOWLEDGMENTS

I want to thank my wife, Allyn, for her encouragement and for enduring endless hours when I was closeted in my office working on the manuscript. Several of my colleagues at Florida Atlantic University have read parts of the manuscript and have taught from earlier drafts. I wish to express my appreciation to my chairs, Mohammad Ilyas, Roy Levow, and Borko Fuhrt who made assignments that allowed me to work on the book. Even more importantly, I want to thank my students who provided me with the impetus to write a more suitable text, who suffered through earlier drafts of the book, and who made many suggestions and corrections. The reviewers—

Kurt Behpour, California Polytechnic State University
Noni M. Bohonak, University of South Carolina Lancaster
Frank Candocia, Florida International University
Paula Cheslik, Glendale Community College
William D. Eads, Colorado State University
Nikrouz Faroughi, Sacramento State University
Jose A. Gonzalez-Cueto, Dalhousie University
William M. Jones, Jr., U.S. Naval Academy
Timothy P. Kurzweg, Drexel University
Rod Milbrandt, Rochester Community and Technical College
Shuo Pang, Embry-Riddle Aeronautical University
Martin Reisslein, Arizona State University
Martha Sloan, Michigan Tech
Wei Wang, Indiana University-Purdue University Indianapolis
Xiaohe Wu, Bethune-Cookman University
Tong Zhang, Rensselaer Polytechnic Institute

provided many useful comments and suggestions. The book is much better because of their efforts. Finally, the staff at McGraw-Hill, particularly Darlene Schueller, Raghu Srinivasan, Curt Reynolds, Brenda Rolwes, and Jane Mohr, has been indispensable in producing the final product, as has Emily Pfaff at Lachina Publishing Services.

Alan Marcovitz

CHAPTER 1

Introduction

This book concerns the design of *digital systems,* that is, systems in which all of the signals are represented by discrete values. Internally, digital systems usually are binary, that is, they operate with two-valued signals, which we will label 0 and 1. (Although multivalued systems have been built, two-valued systems are more reliable and thus almost all digital systems use two-valued signals.)

Computers and calculators are obvious examples of digital systems, but most electronic systems contain a large amount of digital logic. The music that we listen to on our CD players or iPods, the individual dots on a computer screen (and on the newer digital televisions), and most cell phone signals are coded into strings of binary digits, referred to as bits.

1.1 LOGIC DESIGN

A digital system, as shown in the Figure 1.1, may have an arbitrary number of inputs (*A*, *B*, . . .) and an arbitrary number of outputs (*W*, *X*, . . .). In addition to the data inputs shown, some circuits require a timing signal, called a clock (which is just another input signal that alternates between 0 and 1 at a regular rate). We will discuss the details of clock signals in Chapter 6.

A simple example of digital systems is described in Example 1.1.

Figure 1.1 A digital system.

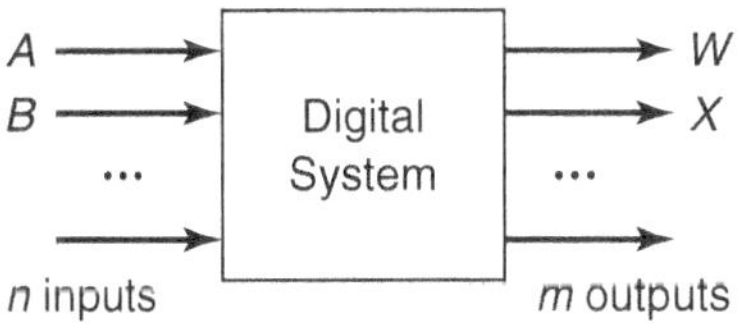

EXAMPLE 1.1

A system with three inputs, *A*, *B*, and *C*, and one output, *Z*, such that $Z=1$ if and only if* two of the inputs are 1.

The inputs and outputs of a digital system represent real quantities. Sometimes, as in Example 1.1, these are naturally binary, that is, they take on one of two values. Other times, they may be multivalued. For example, an input may be a decimal digit or the output might be the letter grade for this course. Each must be represented by a set of binary

*The term *if and only if* is often abbreviated "iff." It means that the output is 1 if the condition is met and is not 1 (which means it must be 0) if the condition is not met.

Table 1.1 A truth table for Example 1.1.

A	*B*	*C*	*Z*
0	0	0	0
0	0	1	0
0	1	0	0
0	1	1	1
1	0	0	0
1	0	1	1
1	1	0	1
1	1	1	1

digits. This process is referred to as coding the inputs and outputs into binary. (We will discuss the details of this later.)

The physical manifestation of these binary quantities may be one of two voltages, for example, 0 volts (V) or ground for logic 0 and 5 V for logic 1. It may also be a magnetic field in one direction or another (as on diskettes), a switch in the up or down position (for an input), or a light on or off (as an output). Except in the translation of verbal descriptions into more formal ones, the physical representation will be irrelevant in this text; we will be concerned with 0's and 1's.

We can describe the behavior of a digital system, such as that of Example 1.1, in tabular form. Since there are only eight possible input combinations, we can list all of them and what the output is for each. Such a table (referred to as a *truth table*) is shown in Table 1.1. We will leave the development of truth tables (including one similar to this) to the next chapter.

Four other examples are given in Examples 1.2 through 1.5.

EXAMPLE 1.2

A system with eight inputs, representing two 4-bit binary numbers, and one 5-bit output, representing the sum. (Each input number can range from 0 to 15; the output can range from 0 to 30.)

EXAMPLE 1.3

A system with one input, *A*, plus a clock, and one output, *Z*, which is 1 iff the input was one at the last three consecutive clock times.

EXAMPLE 1.4

A digital clock that displays the time in hours and minutes. It needs to display four decimal digits plus an indicator for AM or PM. (The first digit display only needs to display a 1 or be blank.) This requires a timing signal to advance the clock every minute. It also requires a means of setting the time. Most digital clocks also have an alarm feature, which requires additional storage and circuitry.

EXAMPLE 1.5

A more complex example is a traffic controller. In the simplest case, there are just two streets, and the light is green on each street for a fixed period of time. It then goes to yellow for another fixed period and finally to red. There are no inputs to this system other than the clock. There are six outputs, one for each color in each direction. (Each output may control multiple bulbs.) Traffic controllers may have many more outputs, if, for example, there are left-turn signals. Also, there may be several inputs to indicate when there are vehicles waiting at a red signal or passing a green one.

The first two examples are *combinational*, that is, the output depends only on the present value of the input. In Example 1.1, if we know the value of *A*, *B*, and *C* right now, we can determine what *Z* is now.* Exam-

*In a real system, there is a small amount of delay between the input and output, that is, if the input changes at some point in time, the output changes a little after that. The time frame is typically in the nanosecond (10^{-9} sec) range. We will ignore those delays almost all of the time, but we will return to that issue in Chapter 5.

ples 1.3, 1.4, and 1.5 are *sequential*, that is, they require *memory*, since we need to know something about inputs at an earlier time (previous clock times).

We will concentrate on combinational systems in the first half of the book and leave the discussion about sequential systems until later. As we will see, sequential systems are composed of two parts: memory and combinational logic. Thus, we need to be able to design combinational systems before we can begin designing sequential ones.

A word of caution about natural language in general, and English in particular, is in order. English is not a very precise language. The previous examples leave some room for interpretation. In Example 1.1, is the output to be 1 if all three of the inputs are 1, or only if exactly two inputs are 1? One could interpret the statement either way. When we wrote the truth table, we had to decide; we interpreted "two" as "two or more" and thus made the output 1 when all three inputs were 1. (In problems in this text, we will try to be as precise as possible, but even then, different people may read the problem statement in different ways.)

The bottom line is that we need a more precise description of logic systems. We will develop that for combinational systems in Chapter 2 and for sequential systems in Chapter 6.

1.1.1 The Laboratory

Although the material in this text can be studied without implementing any of the systems that are designed, hands-on laboratory experimentation greatly aids the learning process. The traditional approach involves wiring logic blocks, connecting inputs from switches or power supplies, and probing the outputs with meters or displaying them with lights. In addition, there are a large number of computer tools available that allow the user to simulate a logic system.

Using whichever platform is available, students should build some of the circuits that they have designed and test them, by applying various inputs and checking that the correct output is produced. For small numbers of inputs, try all input combinations (the complete truth table). For larger numbers of inputs, the 4-bit adder, for example, a sample of the inputs is adequate as long as the sample is chosen in such a way as to exercise all of the circuit. (For example, adding many pairs of small numbers is not adequate, since it does not test the high-order part of the adder.)

We include, in Appendix D, the description of three platforms—one traditional hardware approach and two of the simpler software simulators. Also included is a set of laboratory exercises that can be performed on each, and the pinouts for all of the integrated circuits discussed in the text and the experiments.

In Appendix D.1, we will introduce the features of the IDL-800 Digital Lab.* It provides switches, pulsers, and clock signals for inputs, and a set of lights and two seven-segment displays for outputs. There is a place to put a breadboard and to plug in a number of integrated circuit packages (such as those described throughout the text). Also, power supplies and meters are built in. It is not necessary to have access to this system to execute the experiments, but it does have everything needed in one place (except the integrated circuit packages and the wires for connectors).

We will also introduce, in Appendix D.2, a breadboard simulator (MacBreadboard and WinBreadboard†). It contains switches, pulsers, a clock signal, and lights, very much like the hardware laboratory. Integrated circuits can be placed on the breadboard and wires "connected."

More complex software packages, such as LogicWorks‡ and Altera§, allow us to build a simulation of the circuit on a computer and test it. The circuit can be described as a set of gates or integrated circuits and their connections. In some systems, parts or all of the circuit can be represented in VHDL or other similar design languages. We will introduce the basics of LogicWorks in Appendix D.3, enough to allow us to "build" and test the various circuits discussed in the text. A description of the Altera tool set can be found in Brown & Vranesic, *Fundamentals of Logic with VHDL Design*, 3rd Ed., McGraw-Hill, 2009.

Appendix D.4 contains a set of 26 experiments (keyed to the appropriate chapters) that can be performed on each of the platforms.

Finally, Appendix D.5 contains the pinouts for all of the integrated circuits discussed in the text and the experiments.

1.2 A BRIEF REVIEW OF NUMBER SYSTEMS

This section gives an introduction to some topics in number systems, primarily those needed to understand the material in the remainder of the book. If this is familiar material from another course, skip to Chapter 2.

Integers are normally written using a positional number system, in which each digit represents the coefficient in a power series

$$N = a_{n-1}r^{n-1} + a_{n-2}r^{n-2} + \cdots + a_2r^2 + a_1r + a_0$$

where n is the number of digits, r is the radix or base, and the a_i are the coefficients, where each is an integer in the range

$$0 \le a_i < r$$

For decimal, $r = 10$, and the a's are in the range 0 to 9. For binary, $r = 2$, and the a's are all either 0 or 1. Another commonly used notation in

---

*Manufactured by K & H Mfg. Co., Ltd. (http://www.kandh.com.tw).

†A trademark of Yoeric Software (http://www.yoeric.com).

‡Capilano Computing (http://www.capilano.com).

§Altera Corporation (http://www.altera.com).

computer documentation is hexadecimal, $r = 16$. In binary, the digits are usually referred to as *bits*, a contraction for binary digits.

The decimal number 7642 (sometimes written 7642_{10} to emphasize that it is radix 10, that is, decimal) thus stands for.

$$7642_{10} = 7 \times 10^3 + 6 \times 10^2 + 4 \times 10 + 2$$

and the binary number

$$\begin{aligned} 101111_2 &= 1 \times 2^5 + 0 \times 2^4 + 1 \times 2^3 + 1 \times 2^2 + 1 \times 2 + 1 \\ &= 32 + 8 + 4 + 2 + 1 = 47_{10} \end{aligned}$$

From this example,* it is clear how to convert from binary to decimal; just evaluate the power series. To do that easily, it is useful to know the powers of 2, rather than compute them each time they are needed. (It would save a great deal of time and effort if at least the first 10 powers of 2 were memorized; the first 20 are shown in the Table 1.2.)

We will often be using the first 16 positive binary integers, and sometimes the first 32, as shown in the Table 1.3. (As in decimal, leading 0's are often left out, but we have shown the 4-bit number including leading 0's for the first 16.) When the size of the storage place for a positive binary number is specified, then leading 0's are added so as to obtain the correct number of bits.

Table 1.2 Powers of 2.

n	2^n	n	2^n
1	2	11	2,048
2	4	12	4,096
3	8	13	8,192
4	16	14	16,384
5	32	15	32,768
6	64	16	65,536
7	128	17	131,072
8	256	18	262,144
9	512	19	524,288
10	1,024	20	1,048,576

Table 1.3 First 32 binary integers.

Decimal	Binary	4-bit	Decimal	Binary
0	0	0000	16	10000
1	1	0001	17	10001
2	10	0010	18	10010
3	11	0011	19	10011
4	100	0100	20	10100
5	101	0101	21	10101
6	110	0110	22	10110
7	111	0111	23	10111
8	1000	1000	24	11000
9	1001	1001	25	11001
10	1010	1010	26	11010
11	1011	1011	27	11011
12	1100	1100	28	11100
13	1101	1101	29	11101
14	1110	1110	30	11110
15	1111	1111	31	11111

*Section 1.3, Solved Problems, contains additional examples of each of the types of problems discussed in this chapter. There is a section of Solved Problems in each of the chapters.

Note that the number one less than 2^n consists of n 1's (for example, $2^4 - 1 = 1111 = 15$ and $2^5 - 1 = 11111 = 31$).

An n-bit number can represent the positive integers from 0 to $2^n - 1$. Thus, for example, 4-bit numbers have the range of 0 to 15, 8-bit numbers 0 to 255 and 16-bit numbers 0 to 65,535.

To convert from decimal to binary, we could evaluate the power series of the decimal number, by converting each digit to binary, that is

$$746 = 111 \times (1010)^{10} + 0100 \times 1010 + 0110$$

but that requires binary multiplication, which is rather time-consuming.

There are two straightforward algorithms using decimal arithmetic. First, we can subtract from the number the largest power of 2 less than that number and put a 1 in the corresponding position of the binary equivalent. We then repeat that with the remainder. A 0 is put in the position for those powers of 2 that are larger than the remainder.

EXAMPLE 1.6

For 746, $2^9 = 512$ is the largest power of 2 less than or equal to 746, and thus there is a 1 in the 2^9 (512) position.

746 = 1 _ _ _ _ _ _ _ _ _

We then compute 746 − 512 = 234. The next smaller power of 2 is $2^8 = 256$, but that is larger than 234 and thus, there is a 0 in the 2^8 position.

746 = 1 0 _ _ _ _ _ _ _ _

Next, we compute 234 − 128 = 106, putting a 1 in the 2^7 position.

746 = 1 0 1 _ _ _ _ _ _ _

Continuing, we subtract 64 from 106, resulting in 42 and a 1 in the 2^6 position.

746 = 1 0 1 1 _ _ _ _ _ _

Since 42 is larger than 32, we have a 1 in the 2^5 position, and compute 42 − 32 = 10.

746 = 1 0 1 1 1 _ _ _ _ _

At this point, we can continue subtracting (8 next) or recognize that there is no $2^4 = 16$, and that the binary equivalent of the remainder, 10, is 1010, giving

$$\begin{aligned} 746_{10} &= 1 \times 2^9 + 0 \times 2^8 + 1 \times 2^7 + 1 \times 2^6 + 1 \times 2^5 + 0 \times 2^4 + 1 \\ &\quad \times 2^3 + 0 \times 2^2 + 1 \times 2 + 0 \\ &= 1011101010_2 \end{aligned}$$

The other approach is to divide the decimal number by 2 repeatedly. The remainder each time gives a digit of the binary answer, starting at the least significant bit (a_0). The remainder is then discarded and the process is repeated.

EXAMPLE 1.7

Converting 746 from decimal to binary, we compute

746/2 = 373 with a remainder of 0	0
373/2 = 186 with a remainder of 1	10
186/2 = 93 with a remainder of 0	010
93/2 = 46 with a remainder of 1	1010
46/2 = 23 with a remainder of 0	01010
23/2 = 11 with a remainder of 1	101010
11/2 = 5 with a remainder of 1	1101010
5/2 = 2 with a remainder of 1	11101010
2/2 = 1 with a remainder of 0	011101010
1/2 = 0 with a remainder of 1	1011101010

Do not forget the last division (1/2); it produces the most significant 1. We could continue dividing by 2 and get additional leading 0's. Thus, the answer is 1011101010 as before. In this method, we could also stop when we recognize the number that is left and convert it to binary. Thus, when we had 23, we could recognize that as 10111 (from Table 1.3) and place that in front of the bits we had produced, giving 10111 01010.

EXAMPLE 1.8

Convert 105 to binary

105/2 = 52, rem 1	produces	1
52/2 = 26, rem 0		01
26/2 = 13, rem 0		001
but 13 = 1101		1101 001

The method works because all of the terms in the power series except the last divide evenly by 2. Thus, since

$$746 = 1 \times 2^9 + 0 \times 2^8 + 1 \times 2^7 + 1 \times 2^6 + 1 \times 2^5 + 0 \times 2^4 + 1 \times 2^3 + 0 \times 2^2 + 1 \times 2 + 0$$

$$746/2 = 373 \text{ and remainder of } 0 = 1 \times 2^8 + 0 \times 2^7 + 1 \times 2^6 + 1 \times 2^5 + 1 \times 2^4 + 0 \times 2^3 + 1 \times 2^2 + 0 \times 2 + 1 + \text{rem } 0$$

The last bit became the remainder. If we repeat the process, we get

$$373/2 = 186 \text{ and remainder of } 1 = 1 \times 2^7 + 0 \times 2^6 + 1 \times 2^5 + 1 \times 2^4 + 1 \times 2^3 + 0 \times 2^2 + 1 \times 2 + 0 + \text{rem } 1$$

That remainder is the second digit from the right. On the next division, the remainder will be 0, the third digit. This process continues until the most significant bit is found.

*[SP 1, 2; EX 1, 2]**

*At the end of most sections, a list of solved problems and exercises that are appropriate to that section is given.

1.2.1 Hexadecimal

Hexadecimal, often referred to as *hex* ($r = 16$) is another base that is commonly used in computer documentation. It is just a shorthand notation for binary. In hexadecimal, binary digits are grouped in fours (starting at the least significant). For example, an 8-bit number,

$$\begin{aligned} N &= (b_7 2^7 + b_6 2^6 + b_5 2^5 + b_4 2^4) + (b_3 2^3 + b_2 2^2 + b_1 2^1 + b_0) \\ &= 2^4 (b_7 2^3 + b_6 2^2 + b_5 2^1 + b_4) + (b_3 2^3 + b_2 2^2 + b_1 2^1 + b_0) \\ &= 16h_1 + h_0 \end{aligned}$$

where the h_1 represent the hexadecimal digits and must fall in the range 0 to 15. Each term in parentheses is just interpreted in decimal. If the binary number does not have a multiple of four bits, leading 0's are added. The digits above 9 are represented by the first six letters of the alphabet (uppercase).

10	A
11	B
12	C
13	D
14	E
15	F

EXAMPLE 1.9

(from Examples 1.6 and 1.7)

$$\begin{aligned} 1011101010_2 &= 0010\ 1110\ 1010_2 \\ &= 2EA_{16} \end{aligned}$$

To convert from hex to decimal, we evaluate the power series.

EXAMPLE 1.10

$$\begin{aligned} 2EA_{16} &= 2 \times 16^2 + 14 \times 16 + 10 \\ &= 512 + 224 + 10 = 746_{10} \end{aligned}$$

Finally, to convert from decimal to hex, repeatedly divide by 16, producing the hex digits as the remainder (or convert to binary and then group the bits as in Example 1.9).

EXAMPLE 1.11

746/16 = 46	rem 10	produces	A
46/16 = 2	rem 14		EA
2/16 = 0	rem 2		2EA

[SP 3, 4; EX 3, 4]

1.2.2 Binary Addition

A common operation required in computers and other digital systems is the addition of two numbers. In this section, we will describe the process for adding binary numbers.

To compute the sum of two binary numbers, say

```
0 1 1 0     6
0 1 1 1    +7
```

we add one digit at a time (as we do in decimal), producing a sum and a carry to the next bit. Just as we have an addition table for decimal, we need one for binary (but it is of course much shorter) (Table 1.4). A step-by-step addition is shown in Example 1.12 for adding 6 (0110) and 7 (0111).

Table 1.4 Binary addition.

0 + 0 = 0
0 + 1 = 1
1 + 0 = 1
1 + 1 = 10 (2, or a sum of 0 and a carry of 1 to the next bit)

EXAMPLE 1.12

First, the least significant bits (the rightmost bits) are added, producing a sum of 1 and a carry of 0, as shown in brown.

```
   0
0 1 1 0
0 1 1 1
-------
      1
```

Next, we must add the second digit from the right,

0 + 1 + 1 = 0 + (1 + 1) = 0 + 10 = 10
(a sum of 0 and a carry of 1)

or (0 + 1) + 1 = 1 + 1 = 10
(the order of addition does not matter).

That addition is highlighted in brown.

```
  1 0
0 1 1 0
0 1 1 1
-------
    0 1
```

The final two additions then become

```
1 1          0 1
0 1 1 0        0 1 1 0
0 1 1 1        0 1 1 1
-------        -------
  1 0 1        1 1 0 1
```

Notice that in the third bit of addition, we had three 1's (the carry in plus the two digits). That produced a sum of 3 (11 in binary), that is, a sum bit of 1 and a carry of 1. The answer, of course, comes to 13 (in decimal). In this case, the last addition produced a carry out of 0, and thus the answer was 4-bits long. If the operands were larger (say, 13 + 5), the answer would require 5 bits as shown in the following addition, where the last carry is written as part of the sum. (This is, of course, no different from decimal addition, where the sum of two 4-digit numbers might produce a 4- or 5-digit result.)

```
  1 0 1
  1 1 0 1        1 3
  0 1 0 1          5
---------      -----
1 0 0 1 0        1 8
```

In a computer with n-bit words, when an arithmetic operation produces a result that is out of range [for example, addition of n-bit positive integers produces an $(n + 1)$-bit result], it is called *overflow*. With the addition of 4-bit positive integers, overflow occurs when the sum is greater than or equal to 16 (that is, 2^4). In the previous example, there was overflow since the answer, 18, is greater than 15, the largest 4-bit positive integer.

After the addition of the least significant bits (which only has two operands), each remaining addition is a three-operand problem. We will denote the carry that is added in as c_{in} and the resulting carry from the addition c_{out}. The addition problem then becomes

$$\begin{array}{r} c_{in} \\ a \\ \underline{b} \\ c_{out}\ s \end{array}$$

Table 1.5 shows a truth table of the addition process.

A device that does this 1-bit computation is referred to as a *full adder*. To add 4-bit numbers, we might build four of these and connect them as shown in Figure 1.2. Notice that the carry input of the bit 1 adder

Table 1.5 One-bit adder.

a	b	c_{in}	c_{out}	s
0	0	0	0	0
0	0	1	0	1
0	1	0	0	1
0	1	1	1	0
1	0	0	0	1
1	0	1	1	0
1	1	0	1	0
1	1	1	1	1

[SP 5; EX 5]

Figure 1.2 A 4-bit adder.

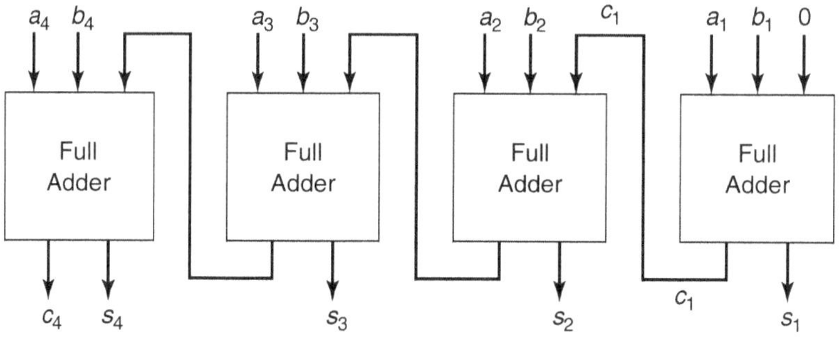

has a 0 on it, since there is no carry into that bit. Sometimes a simpler circuit (called a *half adder*) is built for that bit. We will return to this problem in Chapter 2, when we are prepared to design the full adder.

1.2.3 Signed Numbers

Up to this point, we have only considered positive integers, sometimes referred to as *unsigned numbers*. Computers must deal with *signed numbers*, that is, both positive and negative numbers. The human-friendly notation is referred to as *signed-magnitude* (+ 5 or − 3 as decimal examples). This could be incorporated into a computer, using the first bit of a number as a sign indicator (normally 0 for positive and 1 for negative) and the remaining bits for the magnitude. Thus, in a 4-bit system, we would represent

$$+5 \rightarrow 0101 \qquad -5 \rightarrow 1101 \qquad -3 \rightarrow 1011$$

With 3 bits for magnitude, the range of numbers available would be from −7 to +7. (Of course, most computers use a larger number of bits to store numbers and thus have a much larger range.) Note that such a representation has both a positive (0000) and negative (1000) zero. Although that might cause confusion (or at least complicate the internal logic of the computer), the major problem with signed-magnitude is the complexity of arithmetic. Consider the following addition problems:

$$\begin{array}{cccccc} +5 & -5 & +5 & -5 & -3 & +3 \\ \underline{+3} & \underline{-3} & \underline{-3} & \underline{+3} & \underline{+5} & \underline{-5} \\ +8 & -8 & +2 & -2 & +2 & -2 \end{array}$$

In the first two, where the signs of the two operands are the same, we just add the magnitudes and retain the sign. For these two, the computation is 5 + 3. In each of the other examples, we must determine which is the larger magnitude. (It could be the first operand or the second.) Then, we must subtract the smaller from the larger, and finally, attach the sign of the larger magnitude. For these four, the computation is 5 − 3. Although this could all be done, the complexity of the hardware involved (an adder, a subtractor, and a comparator) has led to another solution.

Signed binary numbers are nearly always stored in *two's complement* format. The leading bit is still the sign bit (0 for positive). Positive numbers (and zero) are just stored in normal binary. The largest number that can be stored is $2^{n-1} - 1$ (7 for $n = 4$). Thus, in a 4-bit system, +5 would be stored as 0101.

The negative number, $-a$, is stored as the binary equivalent of $2^n - a$ in an n-bit system. Thus, for example, −3 is stored as the binary for 16 − 3 = 13, that is, 1101.

The most negative number that can be stored is -2^{n-1} (−8 in a 4-bit system). The largest number available in two's complement is about half that of unsigned numbers with the same number of bits, since half of the 2^n representations are used for negative numbers. This method extends to other bases than binary. It is referred to as *radix complement.* Negative numbers, $-a$, in n digits are stored as $r^n - a$. In decimal for example, this is called ten's complement. In a 2-digit decimal system, -16 would be stored as $100 - 16 = 84$. (Numbers from 0 to 49 would be considered positive and those between 50 and 99 would be representations of negative numbers.)

An easier way to find the storage format for negative numbers in two's complement is the following three-step approach:

1. Find the binary equivalent of the magnitude.
2. Complement each bit (that is, change 0's to 1's and 1's to 0's)
3. Add 1.

EXAMPLE 1.13

		−5		−1		−0
1.	5:	0 1 0 1	1:	0 0 0 1	0:	0 0 0 0
2.		1 0 1 0		1 1 1 0		1 1 1 1
3.		1		1		1
	−5:	1 0 1 1	−1:	1 1 1 1		0 0 0 0
		(a)		(b)		(c)

Note that there is no negative zero; the process of complementing +0 produces an answer of 0000. In two's complement addition, the carry out of the most significant bit is ignored.

Table 1.6 lists the meaning of all 4-bit numbers both as positive (unsigned) numbers and as two's complement signed numbers.

To find the magnitude of a negative number stored in two's complement format (that is, one that begins with a 1), the second and third steps of the negation process are followed.

EXAMPLE 1.14

	−5:	1 0 1 1	−1:	1 1 1 1
2. Bit-by-bit complement		0 1 0 0		0 0 0 0
3. Add 1		1		1
	5:	0 1 0 1	1:	0 0 0 1

(We could subtract 1 and then complement, instead; that will give the same answer.)

The reason that two's complement is so popular is the simplicity of addition. To add any two numbers, no matter what the sign of each is, we just do binary addition on their representations. Three sample computations

Table 1.6 Signed and unsigned 4-bit numbers.

Binary	Positive	Signed (two's complement)
0000	0	0
0001	1	+ 1
0010	2	+ 2
0011	3	+ 3
0100	4	+ 4
0101	5	+ 5
0110	6	+ 6
0111	7	+ 7
1000	8	− 8
1001	9	− 7
1010	10	− 6
1011	11	− 5
1100	12	− 4
1101	13	− 3
1110	14	− 2
1111	15	− 1

are shown in Example 1.15. In each case, the carry out of the most significant bit is ignored.

EXAMPLE 1.15

```
−5        1 0 1 1     −5        1 0 1 1     −5        1 0 1 1
+7        0 1 1 1     +5        0 1 0 1     +3        0 0 1 1
+2   (1)  0 0 1 0      0   (1)  0 0 0 0     −2   (0)  1 1 1 0
```

In the first, the sum is 2. In the second, the sum is 0. In the third, the sum is −2, and, indeed, the representation of −2 is produced.

Overflow occurs when the sum is out of range. For 4-bit numbers, that range is $-8 \le \text{sum} \le +7$.

EXAMPLE 1.16

```
+5        0 1 0 1
+4        0 1 0 0
     (0)  1 0 0 1     (looks like −7)
```

The answer produced is clearly wrong because the correct answer (+9) is out of range.

Indeed, whenever we add two positive numbers (each beginning with a 0) and get a result that looks negative (begins with a 1), there is overflow. Similarly, adding two negative numbers and obtaining a sum more negative than −8 also produces overflow. (Also, we can detect overflow when the carry into the most significant bit [1 in this case] differs from the carry out.)

EXAMPLE 1.17

−5		1 0 1 1	
−4		1 1 0 0	
	(1)	0 1 1 1	(looks like +7)

This time, two negative numbers produced a sum that looks positive.

The addition of two numbers of the opposite sign never produces overflow, since the magnitude of the sum is somewhere between the magnitudes of the two operands. (Although overflow seems rather common when dealing with 4-bit examples, it is an unusual occurrence in most computer applications, where numbers are 16 or 32 bits or longer.)

[SP 6, 7, 8; EX 6, 7, 8, 9]

1.2.4 Binary Subtraction

Subtraction (whether dealing with signed or unsigned numbers) is generally accomplished by first taking the two's complement of the second operand, and then adding. Thus, $a - b$ is computed as $a + (-b)$.

EXAMPLE 1.18

Consider the computation of 7 − 5.

5:	0 1 0 1		
	1 0 1 0	7:	0 1 1 1
	+ 1	−5:	+1 0 1 1
−5:	1 0 1 1	2	(1) 0 0 1 0

The 5 is first complemented. This same process is followed whether the computation involves signed or unsigned numbers. Then, the representation of −5 is added to 7, producing an answer of 2.

For signed numbers, the carry out of the high-order bit is ignored, and overflow occurs if the addition process operates on two numbers of the same sign and produces a result of the opposite sign. For unsigned numbers, the carry out of the high-order bit is the indicator of overflow, as in addition. However, in subtraction, a 0 indicates overflow. In Example 1.18, there was no overflow for either signed or unsigned numbers, since the answer, 2, is within range. The carry out of 1 indicates no overflow, for unsigned numbers. For signed numbers, the addition of a positive number to a negative one never produces overflow.

In most computer applications, the two additions (of the 1 in the complement computation and of the two operands) are done in one step.

The least significant bit of the adder (bit 1) has a zero carry input for addition. The 1 that was added in the process of complementing can be input to that carry input for subtraction. Thus, to compute 7 − 5, we take the bit-by-bit complement of 5 (0101 becomes 1010) and add.

EXAMPLE 1.19

7 − 5

```
         1
      0111
      1010
   (1)0010
```

Of course, we could design a subtractor (in addition to the adder), but that is unnecessary additional hardware for most computers.

Note that this process works for unsigned numbers even if the operands are larger than could be represented in a two's complement system, as shown in Example 1.20, where the difference 14 − 10 is computed.

EXAMPLE 1.20

```
       1
    1110
   +0101
(1) 0100 = 4
```

We see overflow for unsigned numbers in Example 1.21a and for signed numbers in Example 1.21b.

EXAMPLE 1.21

```
      5 − 7       7 − (−5)
          1              1
       0101           0111
       1000           0100
  (0)  1110           1100
       (a)            (b)
```

For unsigned numbers, overflow is indicated by the carry of 0. The result of (a) should be negative (−2), which cannot be represented in an unsigned system. For signed numbers, the result is correct. For signed numbers, overflow may occur if we subtract a negative number from a positive one or a positive number from a negative one, as shown in Example 1.21b. That is overflow because the addition process involved two positive numbers and the result looked negative. (Indeed, the answer should be 12, but that is greater than the largest 4-bit signed number, 7.)

[SP 9, 10; EX 10]

1.2.5 Binary Coded Decimal (BCD)

Internally, most computers operate on binary numbers. However, when they interface with humans, the mode of communication is generally decimal. Thus, it is necessary to convert from decimal to binary on input and from binary to decimal on output. (It is straightforward to write software to do this conversion.) However, even this decimal input and output must be coded into binary, digit by digit. If we use the first 10 binary numbers to represent the 10 decimal digits (as in the first binary column in Table 1.7), then the number 739, for example, would be stored as

0111 0011 1001

Each decimal digit is represented by 4 bits, and thus a 3-digit decimal number requires 12 bits (whereas, if it were converted to binary, it would require only 10 bits because numbers up to 1023 can be represented with 10 bits). In addition to the inefficiency of storage, arithmetic on BCD numbers is much more complex* than that on binary, and thus BCD is only used internally in small systems requiring limited computation.

We have already discussed the simplest code, using the first 10 binary numbers to represent the 10 digits. The remaining 4-bit binary numbers

Table 1.7 Binary-coded decimal codes.

Decimal digit	8421 code	5421 code	2421 code	Excess 3 code	2 of 5 code
0	0000	0000	0000	0011	11000
1	0001	0001	0001	0100	10100
2	0010	0010	0010	0101	10010
3	0011	0011	0011	0110	10001
4	0100	0100	0100	0111	01100
5	0101	1000	1011	1000	01010
6	0110	1001	1100	1001	01001
7	0111	1010	1101	1010	00110
8	1000	1011	1110	1011	00101
9	1001	1100	1111	1100	00011
unused	1010	0101	0101	0000	any of
	1011	0110	0110	0001	the 22
	1100	0111	0111	0010	patterns
	1101	1101	1000	1101	with 0, 1,
	1110	1110	1001	1110	3, 4, or 5
	1111	1111	1010	1111	1's

*See Section 5.8.1 for an example of this.

(1010, 1011, 1100, 1101, 1110, 1111) are unused. This code, and those in the next two columns of Table 1.7 are referred to as *weighted codes* because the value represented is computed by taking the sum of each digit times its weight. This first code is referred to as the 8421 code, since those are the weights of the bits. Each decimal digit is represented by

$$8 \times a_3 + 4 \times a_2 + 2 \times a_1 + 1 \times a_0$$

It is also referred to as straight binary. Two other weighted codes (5421 and 2421) that are occasionally used are shown next.

Two other codes that are not weighted are also shown in Table 1.7. The first is *excess 3* (XS3) where the decimal digit is represented by the binary equivalent of 3 more than the digit. For example, 0 is stored as the binary 3 (0011) and 6 as the binary of 6 + 3 = 9 (1001). The final column shows a 2 of 5 code, where each digit is represented by a 5-bit number, two of which are 1 (and the remaining three bits are 0). This provides some error detection capabilities, because, if an error is made in just one of the bits (during storage or transmission), the result will contain either one or three 1's and can be detected as an error.

Note that in both the 5421 and 2421 codes, other combinations can be used to represent some of the digits (such as 0101 for 5). However, those shown in the table are the standard representations; the others are included in the unused category.

Each of the representations has advantages in various applications. For example, if signed (ten's complement) numbers were stored, the first digit of that number would be in the range 5 to 9 for negative numbers. In the 5421, 2421, and excess 3 codes, that would correspond to the first bit of the number being 1. (We would only need to check 1 bit to determine if a number is negative.) In the 8421 code, however, more complex logic is required, because the first bit might be either 0 or 1 for negative numbers. In both 5421 and excess 3 codes, the ten's complement is computed by complementing each bit and adding 1 (as in two's complement). The process is more complex using the other codes. We will make use of some of these codes in later examples. *[SP 11, 12; EX 11, 12]*

1.2.6 Other Codes

Other codes also appear in the digital world. Alphanumeric information is transmitted using the American Standard Code for Information Interchange (ASCII). Seven digits are used to represent the various characters on the standard keyboard as well as a number of control signals (such as carriage return). Table 1.8 lists the printable codes. (Codes beginning with 00 are for control signals.)

This allows us to code anything that can be printed from the standard keyboard. For example, the word *Logic* would be coded

1001100	1101111	1100111	1101001	1100011
L	o	g	i	c

Table 1.8 ASCII code.

	$a_6a_5a_4$					
$a_3a_2a_1a_0$	**010**	**011**	**100**	**101**	**110**	**111**
0000	space	0	@	P	`	p
0001	!	1	A	Q	a	q
0010	“	2	B	R	b	r
0011	#	3	C	S	c	s
0100	$	4	D	T	d	t
0101	%	5	E	U	e	u
0110	&	6	F	V	f	v
0111	‘	7	G	W	g	w
1000	(	8	H	X	h	x
1001	)	9	I	Y	i	y
1010	*	:	J	Z	j	z
1011	+	;	K	[	k	{
1100	,	<	L	\	l	|
1101		=	M	]	m	}
1110	.	>	N	^	n	~
1111	/	?	O	_	o	delete

In a *Gray code*, consecutive numbers differ in only one bit. Table 1.9 shows a 4-bit Gray code sequence.

Table 1.9 Gray code.

Number	Gray code	Number	Gray code
0	0000	8	1100
1	0001	9	1101
2	0011	10	1111
3	0010	11	1110
4	0110	12	1010
5	0111	13	1011
6	0101	14	1001
7	0100	15	1000

A Gray code is particularly useful in coding the position of a continuous device. As the device moves from one section to the next, only 1 bit of the code changes. If there is some uncertainty as to the exact position, only 1 bit is in doubt. If a normal binary code were used, all 4 bits would change as it moved from 7 to 8.

[SP 13; EX 13]

1.3 SOLVED PROBLEMS

1. Convert the following positive binary integers to decimal.
   a. 110100101
   b. 00010111

   a. 110100101 = 1 + 4 + 32 + 128 + 256 = 421
   Starting the evaluation from right (1's position) to left (2^8 position). (There are 0's in the 2, 8, 16, and 64 bits.)

   b. 00010111 = 1 + 2 + 4 + 16 = 23
   Leading 0's do not change the result.

2. Convert the following decimal integers to binary. Assume all numbers are unsigned (positive) and represented by 12 bits.
   a. 47
   b. 98
   c. 5000

a. 47	47 < 64	Thus no 2^6 bit or greater
	47 − 32 = 15	gives a 2^5 bit
	15 < 16	no 2^4 bit
	15 − 8 = 7	2^3 bit
	7 = 111	thus last 3 bits are 111

47 = 000000101111

b. 98	98/2 = 49	remainder = 0	0
	49/2 = 24	remainder = 1	10
	24/2 = 12	remainder = 0	010
	12/2 = 6	remainder = 0	0010
	6/2 = 3	remainder = 0	00010
	3/2 = 1	remainder = 1	100010
	1/2 = 0	remainder = 1	1100010

We could keep dividing 0 by 2 and getting remainders of 0 until we had 12 bits or recognize that the leading bits must be 0.

98 = 000001100010

As in part a, we could have stopped dividing when we recognized the number, say that 12 = 1100. We would take what we had already found, the three least significant bits of 010, and put the binary for 12 ahead of that, getting the same answer, of course, 1100010 (with enough leading 0's to make up the appropriate number of bits).

c. 5000: cannot represent in 12 bits because 5000 > 2^{12}.

3. Convert the following to hexadecimal

a. 11010110111_2

b. 611_{10}

Leading 0's are added when necessary to make the number of bits a multiple of 4.

a. 0110 1011 0111 = $6B7_{16}$

b. 611/16 = 38	rem	3		3
38/16 = 2	rem	6		63
2/16 = 0	rem	2		263

This equals 0010 0110 0011.

4. Convert the following hexadecimal integers to decimal

a. 263

b. 1C3

a. $3 + 6 \times 16 + 2 \times 16^2 = 3 + 96 + 512 = 611$

b. $3 + 12 \times 16 + 16^2 = 3 + 192 + 256 = 451$

5. Compute the sum of the following pairs of 6-bit unsigned integers. If the answer is to be stored in a 6-bit location, indicate which of the sums produces overflow. Also, show the decimal equivalent of each problem.

a. 0 0 1 0 1 1 + 0 1 1 0 1 0

b. 1 0 1 1 1 1 + 0 0 0 0 0 1

c. 1 0 1 0 1 0 + 0 1 0 1 0 1

d. 1 0 1 0 1 0 + 1 0 0 0 1 1

a.

	0	1 0	0 1	1 0	1 1	1
11	0 0 1 0 1 1	0 0 1 0 1 1	0 0 1 0 1 1	0 0 1 0 1 1	0 0 1 0 1 1	0 0 1 0 1 1
26	0 1 1 0 1 0	0 1 1 0 1 0	0 1 1 0 1 0	0 1 1 0 1 0	0 1 1 0 1 0	0 1 1 0 1 0
37	1	0 1	1 0 1	0 1 0 1	0 0 1 0 1	0 1 0 0 1 0 1 = 37

Note that in this case the last carry result is 0 (it is shown as part of the sum) and thus the answer does fit in 6 bits (there is no overflow).

b.

0 1 1 1 1	(carries)	
1 0 1 1 1 1	47	
0 0 0 0 0 1	1	
0 1 1 0 0 0 0	48	

c.

0 0 0 0 0		
1 0 1 0 1 0	42	
0 1 0 1 0 1	21	
0 1 1 1 1 1 1	63	

d.

0 0 0 1 0		
1 0 1 0 1 0	42	
1 0 0 0 1 1	35	
1 0 0 1 1 0 1	77	overflow (looks like 13)

Note that the answer is larger than 63, which is the largest 6-bit number.

6. The following decimal numbers are to be stored in a 6-bit two's complement format. Show how they are stored.

a. + 14

b. − 20

c. + 37

a. +14 = 001110 Positive numbers are just converted to binary.

b. −20: +20 = 010100

Complement every bit	1 0 1 0 1 1
Add 1	1
−20 is stored as	1 0 1 1 0 0

c. +37: Cannot be stored, the range of 6-bit numbers is $-32 \le n \le 31$. Converting 37 to binary would give 100101, but that represents a negative number.

7. The following 6-bit two's complement numbers were found in a computer. What decimal number do they represent?

a. 001011

b. 111010

a. 001011: Because it begins with 0, it is positive = 1 + 2 + 8 = 11

b. 111010: Because it begins with a 1, it is negative; take two's complement: 0 0 0 1 0 1

1

0 0 0 1 1 0 = 6

Thus, 111010 represents −6.

8. Each of the following pairs of signed (two's complement) numbers are stored in computer words (6 bits). Compute the sum as it is stored in a 6-bit computer word. Show the decimal equivalents of each operand and the sum. Indicate if there is overflow.

a. 1 1 1 1 1 1 + 0 0 1 0 1 1
b. 0 0 1 0 0 1 + 1 0 0 1 0 0
c. 0 0 1 0 0 1 + 0 1 0 0 1 1
d. 0 0 1 0 1 0 + 0 1 1 0 0 0
e. 1 1 1 0 1 0 + 1 1 0 0 0 1
f. 1 0 1 0 0 1 + 1 1 0 0 0 1
g. 1 1 0 1 0 1 + 0 0 1 0 1 1

a.
```
       111111     −1
       001011    +11   The carry out is ignored and will not
    (1)001010    +10   be shown in the remaining examples.
```

b.
```
    001001    +9
    100100   −28
    101101   −19
```

c.
```
    001001    +9
    010011   +19
    011100   +28
```

d.
```
    001010   +10
    011000   +24
    100010   looks like −30; should be +34; overflow
             sum of two positive numbers looks negative
```

e.
```
    111010    −6
    110001   −15
    101011   −21
```

f.
```
    101001   −23
    110001   −15
    011010   looks like +26; should be − 38; overflow
             sum of two negative numbers looks positive
```

g.
```
    110101   −11
    001011   +11
    000000     0
```

9. Subtract each of the following pairs of unsigned integers.

a. 0 0 1 1 0 1 − 0 0 0 1 1 0
b. 1 1 0 1 0 1 − 0 0 0 0 1 1
c. 0 0 0 1 1 1 − 0 1 0 0 1 1

a. (This example is the same for either signed or unsigned numbers.)

	1	
0 0 1 1 0 1	0 0 1 1 0 1	13
−0 0 0 1 1 0	1 1 1 0 0 1	−6
	(1) 0 0 0 1 1 1	7

b.

	1	
1 1 0 1 0 1	1 1 0 1 0 1	53
−0 0 0 0 1 1	1 1 1 1 0 0	−3
	(1) 1 1 0 0 1 0	50

c.

	1	
0 0 0 1 1 1	0 0 0 1 1 1	7
−0 1 0 0 1 1	1 0 1 1 0 0	−19
	(0) 1 1 0 1 0 0	overflow, answer negative

10. Subtract each of the following pairs of signed integers.

a. 1 1 0 1 0 1 − 0 0 0 0 1 1

b. 1 1 0 1 0 1 − 0 1 1 0 0 0

c. 0 1 0 0 0 0 − 1 0 0 1 0 0

a.

	1	
1 1 0 1 0 1	1 1 0 1 0 1	− 11
−0 0 0 0 1 1	1 1 1 1 0 0	−(+3)
	(1) 1 1 0 0 1 0	−14

Note that this is the same binary number as in Solved Problem 9b.

b.

	1	
1 1 0 1 0 1	1 1 0 1 0 1	−11
−0 1 1 0 0 0	1 0 0 1 1 1	−(+24)
	(1) 0 1 1 1 0 1	overflow, answer looks positive

c.

	1	
0 1 0 0 0 0	0 1 0 0 0 0	16
−1 0 0 1 0 0	0 1 1 0 1 1	−(−28)
	(0) 1 0 1 1 0 0	overflow, answer looks negative

11. We have a computer that can store 3 decimal digits. How are the following two numbers stored in each of the five codes?

a. 491

b. 27

a. 8421 0100 1001 0001
5421 0100 1100 0001
2421 0100 1111 0001
XS3 0111 1100 0100
2 of 5 01100 00011 10100
Note that the first four codes require 12-bit words; the 2 of 5 code requires 15-bit words.

b. 8421 0000 0010 0111
5421 0000 0010 1010
2421 0000 0010 1101
XS3 0011 0101 1010
2 of 5 11000 10010 00110

12. We have the following numbers stored in a computer. What is the decimal value represented if the number is stored as

i. BCD 8421
ii. BCD 5421
iii. BCD 2421
iv. BCD excess 3
v. Binary unsigned
vi. Binary signed

a. 1000 0111
b. 0011 0100
c. 1100 1001

a. 1000 0111

i. BCD 8421	87	
ii. BCD 5421	—	0111 not used
iii. BCD 2421	—	1000, 0111 not used
iv. BCD excess 3	54	
v. Binary unsigned	135	
vi. Binary signed	−121	

b. 0011 0100

i. BCD 8421	34
ii. BCD 5421	34
iii. BCD 2421	34
iv. BCD excess 3	01
v. Binary unsigned	52
vi. Binary signed	+52

c. 1100 1001

i. BCD 8421	—	1100 not used
ii. BCD 5421	96	
iii. BCD 2421	—	1001 not used
iv. BCD excess 3	96	
v. Binary unsigned	201	
vi. Binary signed	−55	

13. a. Code the following into ASCII.

i. HELLO

ii. hello

b. Translate the following into English.

i. 1011001 1100101 1110011 0100001

ii. 0110010 0101011 0110001 0111101 0110011

a. i. 1001000 1000101 1001100 1001100 1001111

ii. 1101000 1100101 1101100 1101100 1101111

b. i. Yes!

ii. 2+1=3

1.4 EXERCISES*

1. Convert the following unsigned binary integers to decimal.

*a. 11111	e. 10101010
b. 1000000	f. 000011110000
c. 1001101101	g. 110011001100
*d. 101111	*h. 000000000000

2. Convert the following decimal integers to binary. Assume all numbers are unsigned (positive) and represented by 12 bits.

*a. 73	c. 402	*e. 1000	*g. 4200
b. 127	d. 512	f. 17	h. 1365

3. Convert the following to hexadecimal

*a. 100101101011_2

b. $1011010000010 1_2$

*c. 791_{10}

d. 1600_{10}

4. Convert the following hexadecimal numbers to decimal

a. 1000

b. ABCD

*c. 3FF

5. Compute the sum of the following pairs of 6-bit unsigned integers. If the answer is to be stored in a 6-bit location, indicate which of the sums produce overflow. Also, show the decimal equivalent of both operands and the result.

*a. 000011 + 001100	*e. 001011 + 100111
b. 010100 + 101101	f. 000101 + 000111
c. 011100 + 011010	g. 101100 + 100100
*d. 110011 + 001110	

*Answers to Exercises marked with a star (*) are given in Appendix B.

6. The following decimal integers are to be stored in a 6-bit two's complement format. Show how they are stored.

*a. +25	*c. +32	*e. −15	g. −1
b. 0	d. +15	f. −45	h. −16

7. The following 6-bit two's complement integers were found in a computer. What decimal number do they represent?

a. 000101	*c. 010101	e. 011111	g. 101010
b. 111111	*d. 100100	f. 111001	*h. 100000

8. We have a computer that stores binary signed integers in two's complement form. All numbers are 8 bits long.

a. What decimal number is represented by 01101011?
b. What decimal number is represented by 10101110?
*c. How is the number −113 stored?
*d. How is the number +143 stored?
e. How is the number +43 stored?
f. How is the number −43 stored?

9. Each of the following pairs of signed (two's complement) integers are stored in computer words (6 bits). Compute the sum as it is stored in a 6-bit computer word. Show the decimal equivalents of each operand and the sum. Indicate if there is overflow.

*a. 110101	c. 001100	e. 011010
001111	110100	001100
b. 111010	*d. 101010	*f. 111101
000111	100110	110000

10. For each of the following pairs of integers, subtract the second from the first. Show the operands and the answers in decimal, assuming

i. the numbers are unsigned.
ii. the numbers are signed (two's complement).

Indicate overflow where appropriate.

a. 010101	*c. 111010	e. 110010
001100	000111	110111
*b. 010001	*d. 100100	f. 111010
011000	011000	101101

11. We have a computer that can store 3 decimal digits. How are each of the following numbers stored in each of the five codes?

i. 8421
ii. 5421
iii. 2421
iv. excess 3
v. 2 of 5

*a. 103	b. 999	c. 1	d. 0

12. We have the following numbers stored in a computer. What is the decimal value represented if the number is stored as

i. BCD 8421 iv. BCD excess 3
ii. BCD 5421 v. binary unsigned
iii. BCD 2421 vi. binary signed

a. 1111 1010 *d. 1001 0101
*b. 0001 1011 e. 1110 1101
c. 1000 0011 f. 0100 1000

13. a. Code the following into ASCII

i. Problem 5 iii. 2 + 1 = 3
*ii. "OK" iv. ABM

b. Translate the following into English

i. 1000001 1101100 1100001 1101110
ii. 0100100 0110111 0101110 0111001 0110101
*iii. 0111001 0101111 0110011 0111101 0110011
iv. 1010100 1101000 1100101 0100000 1100101 1101110 1100100

1.5 CHAPTER 1 TEST (30 MINUTES)*

1. Convert the decimal number 347 to
a. binary.
b. hexadecimal.
Show your work.

2. Add the two unsigned binary numbers; show both operands and the result in decimal as well as binary. (Be sure to show the carry as you add.) Indicate if there is overflow.

0 1 0 1 1 1 0 1 0 1 1
0 1 1 1 0 0 1 1 0 0 1

3. Show the decimal equivalent of each of the numbers if they are interpreted as (six answers).

1 0 0 1 0 1 0 1 0 1 1 1 0 0 1 1

a. Unsigned binary
b. Signed binary
c. BCD (8421 code)

*Tests assume students are allowed one sheet of $8\frac{1}{2} \times 11$ paper with any notes they wish on both sides. Solutions to Chapter Tests are given in Appendix C.

4. Add the three pairs of signed (two's complement) numbers. Be sure to show the carry as you add. Show both operands and the result of each addition in decimal as well as binary. Indicate if there is overflow.

1 1 0 0	1 0 1 0	0 1 0 1
1 1 0 1	0 1 1 1	0 0 1 1

5. Subtract the two pairs of numbers. Show the operands and the results in decimal and binary
   a. assuming they are unsigned.
   b. assuming they are signed.

   1 1 0 1 − 1 1 0 0   1 0 1 0 − 0 1 1 0

   Indicate if there is overflow.

CHAPTER 2

Combinational Systems

In this chapter, we will develop the tools to specify combinational systems. Then, we will develop an algebraic approach for the description of these systems, their simplification, and their implementation. We will concentrate on rather small systems, which will enable us to better understand the process. We will look at larger problems in Chapter 5.

2.1 THE DESIGN PROCESS FOR COMBINATIONAL SYSTEMS

In this section, we will outline the process to be used to design combinational systems. (A similar process will be developed in Chapter 7 for sequential systems.) The design process typically starts with a problem statement, a verbal description of the intended system. The goal is to develop a block diagram of that system, utilizing available components and meeting the design objectives and constraints.

We will use the following five examples to illustrate the steps in the design process and, indeed, continue to follow some of them in subsequent chapters, as we develop the tools necessary to do that design.

Continuing Examples (CE)

CE1. A system with four inputs, *A*, *B*, *C*, and *D*, and one output, *Z*, such that $Z = 1$ iff three of the inputs are 1.

CE2. A single light (that can be on or off) that can be controlled by any one of three switches. One switch is the master on/off switch. If it is down, the light is off. When the master switch is up, a change in the position of one of the other switches (from up to down or from down to up) will cause the light to change state.

CE3. A system to do 1 bit of binary addition. It has three inputs (the 2 bits to be added plus the carry from the next lower order bit) and produces two outputs: a sum bit and a carry to the next higher order position.

CE4. A display driver; a system that has as its input the code for a decimal digit and produces as its output the signals to drive a seven-segment display, such as those on most digital watches and numeric displays (more later).

CE5. A system with nine inputs, representing two 4-bit binary numbers and a carry input, and one 5-bit output, representing the sum. (Each input number can range from 0 to 15; the output can range from 0 to 31.)

In addition to these continuing examples, Appendix E will contain some complete examples of the design of small systems, from the verbal description through the design with gates. (There will also be some examples of sequential systems.)

The design process involves each of the following steps (although some may not be necessary in some problems).

Step 1: Represent each of the inputs and outputs in binary.

Sometimes, as in CE1, 3, and 5, the problem statement is already given in terms of binary inputs and outputs. Other times, it is up to the designer. In CE2, we need to create a numeric equivalence for each of the inputs and outputs. We might code the light on as a 1 output and off as 0. (We could just as well have used the opposite definition, as long as we are coordinated with the light designer.) Similarly, we will define a switch in the up position as a 1 input and down as 0. For CE4, the input is a decimal digit. We must determine what BCD code is to be used. That might be provided for us by whoever is providing the input, or we may have the ability to specify it in such a way as to make our system simplest. We must also code the output; we need to know the details of the display and whether a 1 or a 0 lights each segment. (We will discuss those details in Section 2.1.1.) In general, the different input and output representations may result in a significant difference in the amount of logic required.

Step 1.5: If necessary, break the problem into smaller subproblems.

This step is listed here because sometimes it is possible to do this after having developed the truth table and sometimes, we must really break up the problem before we can even begin to do such a table.

It is not possible to apply most of the design techniques that we will develop to very large problems. Even CE5, the 4-bit adder, has nine inputs and would thus require a truth table of $2^9 = 512$ rows with nine input columns and five output columns. Although we can easily produce the entries for any line of that table, the table would spread over several pages and be very cumbersome. Furthermore, the minimization techniques of this chapter and Chapter 3 would be strained. The problem becomes completely unmanageable if we go to a realistic adder for a computer—say one that adds 32-bit numbers. There the table would be 2^{64} lines long, even without a carry input (approximately 1.84×10^{19}). (That means that if we were to write 1 million lines on each page and put 1 million pages in a book, we would still need over 18 million volumes to list the entire truth table. Or, if we had a computer that could process 1 billion lines of the truth table per second (requiring a supercomputer), it would still take over 584 years to process the whole table.)

Obviously, we have been able to solve such problems. In the case of the adder, we can imitate how we do it by hand, namely, add 1 bit at a time, producing 1 bit of the sum and the carry to the next bit. That is the problem proposed in CE3; it only requires an eight-line truth table. We can build 32 such systems and connect them together.

Also, it is often most economical to take advantage of subsystems that already have been implemented. For example, we can buy the 4-bit adder described in CE5 (on a single integrated circuit chip). We might want to use that as a component in our design. We will examine this part of the design process further in Chapter 5.

Step 2: Formalize the design specification either in the form of a *truth table* or of an *algebraic expression*.

We will concentrate on the idea of a truth table here and leave the development of algebraic expressions for later in the chapter. The truth table format is the most common result of step 2 of the design process. We can do this in a digital system because each of the inputs only takes on one of two values (0 or 1). Thus, if we have n inputs, there are 2^n input combinations and thus the truth table has 2^n rows. These rows are normally written in the binary order of the inputs (if, for no other reason, than to make sure that we do not leave any out). The truth table has two sets of columns: n input columns, one for each input variable, and m output columns, one for each of the m outputs.

An example of a truth table with two inputs, A and B, and one output, Y, is shown as Table 2.1, where there are two input columns, one output column, and $2^2 = 4$ rows (not including the title row). We will look at truth tables for some of the continuing examples shortly, after presenting the other steps of the design process.

Table 2.1 A two-input truth table.

A	B	Y
0	0	0
0	1	1
1	0	1
1	1	1

Step 3: Simplify the description.

The truth table will lead directly to an implementation in some technologies (see, for example, the ROM in Chapter 5). More often, we must convert that to an algebraic form to implement it. But the algebraic form we get from the truth table tends to lead to rather complex systems. Thus, we will develop techniques for reducing the complexity of algebraic expressions in this chapter and the next.

Step 4: Implement the system with the available components, subject to the design objectives and constraints.

A *gate* is a network with one output. Most of the implementations of this chapter and the next use gates as the components. The truth table used to illustrate step 2 (see Table 2.1) describes the behavior of one type of gate—a two-input OR gate. The final form of the solution may be a block diagram of the gate implementation, where the OR gate is usually depicted by the symbol of Figure 2.1. We may build the system in the laboratory using integrated circuit packages that contain a few such gates, or we may simulate it on a computer.

Figure 2.1 OR gate symbol.

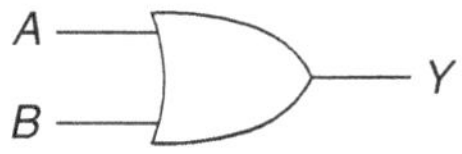

As mentioned earlier, more complex components, such as adders and decoders, may be available as building blocks, in addition to (or in place of) gates. (Of course, when we get to sequential systems, we will introduce storage devices and other larger building blocks.)

The design objective is often to build the least expensive circuit. That usually corresponds to the simplest algebraic expression, although not always. Since gates are usually obtained in packages (say 4 two-input OR gates in a package), the cost may be measured in terms of the number of packages. Thus, whether we need one of the four gates in a package, or all four, the cost would be the same. Sometimes, one of the objectives is speed, that is, to build as fast a circuit as possible. As we will see later, each time a signal passes through a gate, there is a small delay, slowing down the system. Thus, if speed is a factor, we may have a limit on the number of gates any one signal must pass through.

2.1.1 Don't Care Conditions

Table 2.2 A truth table with a don't care.

a	*b*	*f*
0	0	0
0	1	1
1	0	1
1	1	X

Before we can develop the truth table for the display driver example (CE4), we must understand the concept of the *don't care*. In some systems, the value of the output is specified for only some of the input conditions. (Such functions are sometimes referred to as *incompletely specified functions*.) For the remaining input combinations, it does not matter what the output is, that is, we don't care. In a truth table, don't cares are indicated by an X. (Some of the literature uses d, ϕ, or φ.) Table 2.2 is such a truth table.

Table 2.3 Acceptable truth tables.

a	*b*	f_1	f_2
0	0	0	0
0	1	1	1
1	0	1	1
1	1	0	1

This table states that the f must be 0 when a and b are 0, that it must be 1 when $a = 0$ and $b = 1$ or when $a = 1$ and $b = 0$, and that it does not matter what f is when a and b are both 1. In other words, either f_1 or f_2 of Table 2.3 are acceptable.

When we design a system with don't cares, we may make the output either 0 or 1 for each don't care input combination. In the example of Table 2.3, that means that we can implement either f_1 or f_2. One of these might be much less costly to implement. If there are several don't cares, the number of acceptable solutions greatly increases, since each don't care can be either 0 or 1, independently. The techniques we develop in Chapter 3 handle don't cares very easily; they do not require solving separate problems.

In real systems, don't cares occur in several ways. First, there may be some input combinations that never occur. That is the case in CE4, where the input is the code for a decimal digit; there are only 10 possible input combinations. If a 4-bit code is used, then six of the input combinations never occur. When we build a system, we can design it such that the outputs would be either 0 or 1 for each of these don't care combinations, since that input never happens.

A second place where don't cares occur is in the design of one system to drive a second system. Consider the block diagram of Figure 2.2. We are designing System One to make System Two behave in a certain way. On some occasions, for certain values of A, B, and C, System Two will behave the same way whether J is 0 or 1. In that case, the output J of System One is a don't care for that input combination. We will see this behavior arise in Chapter 7, where System Two is a flip flop (a binary storage device).

Figure 2.2 Design example with don't cares.

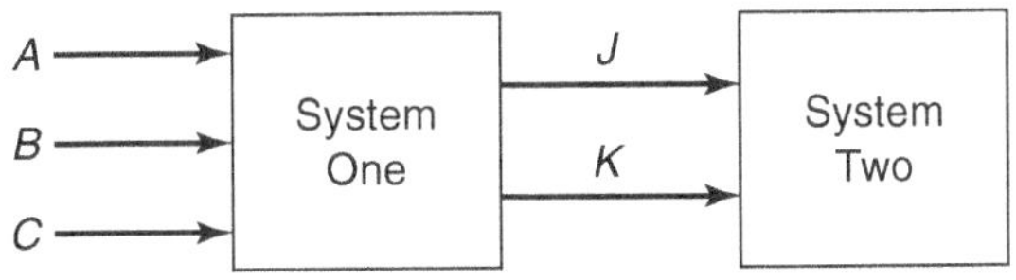

We will see a third kind of don't care in CE4; we may really not care what one output is.

2.1.2 The Development of Truth Tables

Given a word problem, the first step is to decide how to code the inputs. Then, the development of a truth table is usually rather straightforward. The number of inputs determines the number of rows, and the major problem generally revolves about the ambiguity of English (or any natural language).

For CE1, a 16-row truth table is required. There are four input columns and one output column. (In Table 2.4, three output columns are shown Z_1, Z_2, and Z_3 to account for the three interpretations of the problem statement.) There is little room for controversy on the behavior of the system for the first 15 rows of the table. If there are fewer than three 1's on the input lines, the output is 0. If three of the inputs are 1 and the other is 0, then the output is 1. The only question in completing the table is in relation to the last row. Does "three of the inputs are 1" mean *exactly* three or does it mean at *least* three? If the former is true, then the last line of the truth table is 0, as shown for Z_1. If the latter is true, then the last line of the table is 1, as shown in Z_2. Two other options, both shown as Z_3, are that we know that all four inputs will not be 1 simultaneously, and

Table 2.4 Truth table for CE1.

A	B	C	D	Z_1	Z_2	Z_3
0	0	0	0	0	0	0
0	0	0	1	0	0	0
0	0	1	0	0	0	0
0	0	1	1	0	0	0
0	1	0	0	0	0	0
0	1	0	1	0	0	0
0	1	1	0	0	0	0
0	1	1	1	1	1	1
1	0	0	0	0	0	0
1	0	0	1	0	0	0
1	0	1	0	0	0	0
1	0	1	1	1	1	1
1	1	0	0	0	0	0
1	1	0	1	1	1	1
1	1	1	0	1	1	1
1	1	1	1	0	1	X

that we do not care what the output is if all four inputs are 1. In those cases, the last entry is don't care, X.

For CE2, even after coding the inputs and outputs, we do not have a unique solution to the problem. We will label the switches *a, b,* and *c* (where *a* is the master switch) and use a 1 to represent up (and a 0 for down). The light output is labeled *f* (where a 1 on *f* means that the light is on). When $a = 0$, the light is off (0), no matter what the value of *b* and *c*. The problem statement does not specify the output when $a = 1$; it only specifies what effect a change in the other inputs will have. We still have two possible solutions to this problem. If we assume that switches *b* and *c* in the down position cause the light to be off, then the fifth row of the table (100) will have an output of 0, as shown in Table 2.5a. When one of these switches is up (101, 110), then the light must be on. From either of these states, changing *b* or *c* will either return the system to the 100 input state or move it to state 111; for this, the output is 0.

Table 2.5 Truth tables for CE2.

(a)

a	b	c	f
0	0	0	0
0	0	1	0
0	1	0	0
0	1	1	0
1	0	0	0
1	0	1	1
1	1	0	1
1	1	1	0

(b)

a	b	c	f
0	0	0	0
0	0	1	0
0	1	0	0
0	1	1	0
1	0	0	1
1	0	1	0
1	1	0	0
1	1	1	1

We could have started with some other fixed value, such as switches *b* and *c* up means that the light is on or that switches *b* and *c* down means that the light is on. Either of these would produce the truth table of Table 2.5b, which is equally acceptable.

We have already developed the truth table for CE3, the 1-bit binary full adder, in Section 1.2.2, Table 1.5 (although we did not refer to it as a truth table at that time).

Although we could easily construct a truth table for CE5, the 4-bit adder, we would need 512 rows. Furthermore, once we had done this, we would still find it nearly impossible to simplify the function by hand (that is, without the aid of a computer). We will defer further discussion of this problem to Chapter 5.

We will now examine the display driver of CE4. A block diagram of the system is shown in Figure 2.3a. The inputs are a code for the decimal digit and are labeled *W*, *X*, *Y*, and *Z*. The display driver must provide the seven inputs to the display, *a*, *b*, *c*, *d*, *e*, *f*, and *g*. The layout of the display is shown in Figure 2.3b. How each digit is displayed is shown in Figure 2.3c, where a solid line indicates that the segment is lit, and a dashed line that it is not lit. Note that various devices use alternative displays for the digits 6, 7, and 9. For example, segment *a* is sometimes lit for a 6, and sometimes it is not.

The first thing that we must do is to select a code for the decimal digit. That will (obviously) affect the truth table and might make a significant difference in the cost of the implementation. For the sake of this example, we will assume that the digits are stored in 8421 code. (We will look at variations on this in Chapter 4.) The next thing we need to know is whether the display requires a 0 or a 1 on each segment input to light that segment. Both types of displays exist. The design specification must also indicate which of the alternative displays for 6, 7, and 9 should be used, or state that it doesn't matter. Finally, we must decide what to do

Figure 2.3 A seven-segment display.

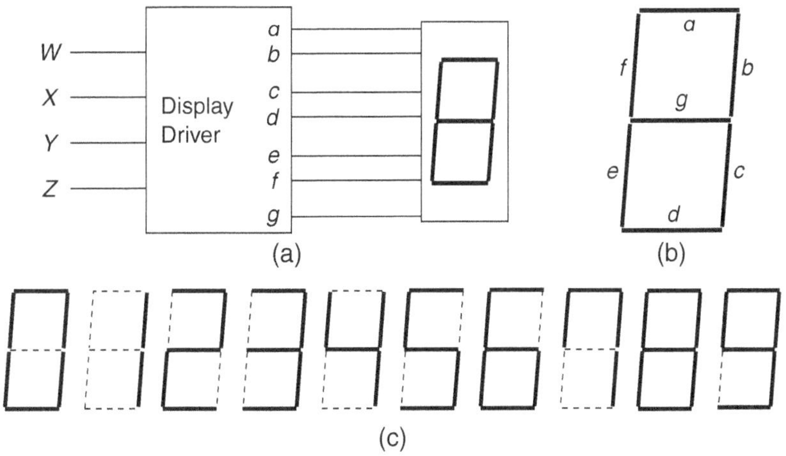

about the inputs that do not correspond to a decimal digit (1010, 1011, . . . , 1111). If we know for sure that they will never happen, then we don't care what the display driver produces for those input combinations. On the other hand, the specifications might state that the display is to be blank (no segment lit) or that it is to display an error code.

The truth table of Table 2.6 assumes 8241 code, a 1 to light a segment, the version of 6, 7, and 9 does not matter, and that the inputs that do not represent a decimal digit never occur.

Table 2.6 A truth table for the seven-segment display driver.

Digit	*W*	*X*	*Y*	*Z*	*a*	*b*	*c*	*d*	*e*	*f*	*g*
0	0	0	0	0	1	1	1	1	1	1	0
1	0	0	0	1	0	1	1	0	0	0	0
2	0	0	1	0	1	1	0	1	1	0	1
3	0	0	1	1	1	1	1	1	0	0	1
4	0	1	0	0	0	1	1	0	0	1	1
5	0	1	0	1	1	0	1	1	0	1	1
6	0	1	1	0	X	0	1	1	1	1	1
7	0	1	1	1	1	1	1	0	0	X	0
8	1	0	0	0	1	1	1	1	1	1	1
9	1	0	0	1	1	1	1	X	0	1	1
–	1	0	1	0	X	X	X	X	X	X	X
–	1	0	1	1	X	X	X	X	X	X	X
–	1	1	0	0	X	X	X	X	X	X	X
–	1	1	0	1	X	X	X	X	X	X	X
–	1	1	1	0	X	X	X	X	X	X	X
–	1	1	1	1	X	X	X	X	X	X	X

EXAMPLE 2.1

We want to develop a truth table for a system with three inputs, *a*, *b*, and *c*, and four outputs, *w*, *x*, *y*, *z*. The output is a binary number equal to the largest integer that meets the input conditions:

a = 0: odd	*a* = 1: even
b = 0: prime	*b* = 1: not prime
c = 0: less than 8	*c* = 1: greater than or equal to 8

Some inputs may never occur; the output is never all 0's.
(A prime is a number that is only evenly divisible by itself and 1.) The following is a truth table for this system.

a	*b*	*c*	*w*	*x*	*y*	*z*
0	0	0	0	1	1	1
0	0	1	1	1	0	1
0	1	0	X	X	X	X
0	1	1	1	1	1	1
1	0	0	0	0	1	0
1	0	1	X	X	X	X
1	1	0	0	1	1	0
1	1	1	1	1	1	0

For the first four rows, we are looking for odd numbers. The odd primes are 1, 3, 5, 7, 11, and 13. Thus, the first row is the binary for 7 (the largest odd prime less than 8) and the second row is the binary for 13. The next two rows contain nonprimes. All odd numbers less than 8 are prime; therefore, the input is never 010 and the outputs are don't cares. Finally, 9 and 15 are odd nonprimes; 15 is larger. For the second half of the table, the only even prime is 2; thus, 101 never occurs. The largest even nonprimes are 6 and 14.

[SP 1, 2; EX 1, 2]

2.2 SWITCHING ALGEBRA

In the last section, we went from a verbal description of a combinational system to a more formal and exact description—a truth table. Although the truth table is sufficient to implement a system using read-only memory (see Chapter 5), we need an algebraic description to analyze and design systems with other components. In this section, we will develop the properties of switching algebra.

We need the algebra for several reasons. Perhaps the most obvious is that if we are presented with a network of gates, we need to obtain a specification of the output in terms of the input. Since each gate is defined by an algebraic expression, we most often need to be able to manipulate that algebra. (We could try each possible input combination and follow the signals through each gate until we reached the output. That, however, is a very slow approach to creating a whole truth table for a system of gates.)

Second, in the design process, we often obtain an algebraic expression that corresponds to a much more complex network of gates than is necessary. Algebra allows us to simplify that expression, perhaps even minimize the amount of logic needed to implement it. When we move on to Chapter 3, we will see that there are other nonalgebraic ways of doing this minimization, methods that are more algorithmic. However, it is still important to understand the algebraic foundation behind them.

Third, algebra is often indispensable in the process of implementing networks of gates. The simplest algebraic expression, found by one of the techniques presented in this chapter or the next, does not always correspond to the network that satisfies the requirements of the problem. Thus, we may need the algebra to enable us to satisfy the constraints of the problem.

In an earlier edition, we introduced the Karnaugh map in the middle of this chapter, to aid in the understanding of the algebraic manipulation. Without loss of continuity, one might study Section 3.1 before Section 2.7 and then refer to some examples in Appendix A, which illustrate the algebra using the map.

One approach to the development of switching algebra is to begin with a set of postulates or axioms that define the more general Boolean algebra. In Boolean algebra, each variable—inputs, outputs, and internal signals—may take on one of k values (where $k \geq 2$). Based on these postulates, we can define an algebra and eventually determine the meaning of the operators. We can then limit them to the special case of switching algebra, $k = 2$. We have deferred a brief discussion of that approach to Section 2.9. Rather, we will define switching algebra in terms of its operators and a few basic properties.

2.2.1 Definition of Switching Algebra

Switching algebra is binary, that is, all variables and constants take on one of two values: 0 and 1. Quantities that are not naturally binary must then be coded into binary format. Physically, they may represent a light off or on, a switch up or down, a low voltage or a high one, or a magnetic field in one direction or the other. From the point of view of the algebra, the physical representation does not matter. When we implement a system, we will choose one of the physical manifestations to represent each value.

We will first define the three operators of switching algebra and then develop a number of properties of switching algebra:

OR (written as +)*

$a + b$ (read a OR b) is 1 if and only if $a = 1$ **or** $b = 1$ or both

AND (written as · or simply two variables catenated)

$a \cdot b = ab$ (read a AND b) is 1 if and only if $a = 1$ **and** $b = 1$.

NOT (written ′)

a' (read NOT a) is 1 if and only if $a = 0$.

The term *complement* is sometimes used instead of NOT. The operation is also referred to as inversion, and the device implementing it is called an inverter.

Because the notation for OR is the same as that for addition in ordinary algebra and that for AND is the same as multiplication, the terminology *sum* and *product* is commonly used. Thus, ab is often referred to as a product term and $a + b$ as a sum term. Many of the properties discussed in this chapter apply to ordinary algebra, as well as switching algebra, but, as we will see, there are some notable exceptions.

Truth tables for the three operators are shown in Table 2.7.

Table 2.7 Truth tables for OR, AND, and NOT.

a	b	$a + b$
0	0	0
0	1	1
1	0	1
1	1	1

a	b	ab
0	0	0
0	1	0
1	0	0
1	1	1

a	a'
0	1
1	0

*OR is sometimes written $\vee$; AND is then written as $\wedge$. NOT x is sometimes written $\sim x$ or $\overline{x}$.

We will now begin to develop a set of properties of switching algebra. (These are sometimes referred to as theorems.) A complete list of the properties that we will use may be found inside the front cover.* The first group of properties follow directly from the definitions (or the truth tables).

P1a. $a + b = b + a$ **P1b.** $ab = ba$ commutative

Note that the values for both OR and AND are the same for the second and third lines of the truth table. This is known as the *commutative* property. It seems obvious because it holds for addition and multiplication, which use the same notation. However, it needs to be stated explicitly, because it is not true for all operators in all algebras. (For example, $a - b \neq b - a$ in ordinary algebra. There is no subtraction operation in switching algebra.)

P2a. $a + (b + c) = (a + b) + c$ **P2b.** $a(bc) = (ab)c$ associative

This property, known as the *associative* law, states that the order in which one does the OR or AND operation doesn't matter, and thus we can write just $a + b + c$ and abc (without the parentheses). It also enables us to talk of the OR or AND of several things. We can thus extend the definition of OR to

$a + b + c + d + \cdots$ is 1 if any of the operands $(a, b, c, d, \ldots)$ is 1 and is 0 only if all are 0

and the definition of AND extends to

$abcd \ldots$ is 1 if all of the operands are 1 and is 0 if any is 0

The most basic circuit element is the gate. A *gate* is a circuit with one output that implements one of the basic functions, such as the OR and AND. (We will define additional gate types later.) Gates are available with two inputs, as well as three, four, and eight inputs. (They could be built with other numbers of inputs, but these are the standard commercially available sizes.) The symbols most commonly used (and which we will use throughout this text) are shown in Figure 2.4. (Note in Figure 2.4 the rounded input for the OR and the flat input for the AND; and the pointed output on the OR and the rounded output on the AND.)

Figure 2.4 Symbols for OR and AND gates.

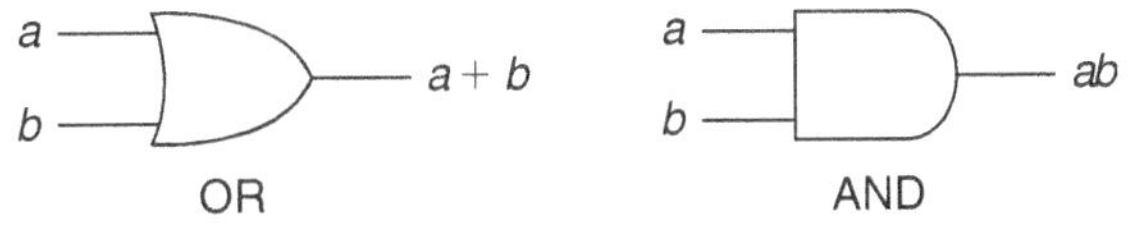

Property 2b states that the three circuits of Figure 2.5 all produce the same output.

*This list is somewhat arbitrary. We are including those properties that we have found useful in manipulating algebraic expressions. Any pair of expressions that are equal to each other could be included on the list. Indeed, other books have a somewhat different list.

Figure 2.5 AND gate implementation of Property 2b.

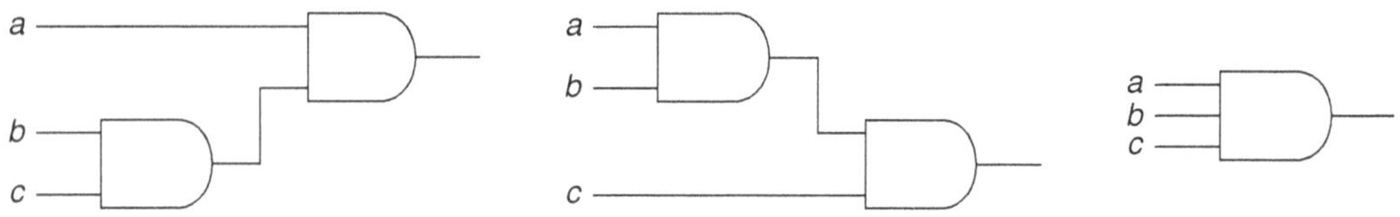

Figure 2.6 A NOT gate.

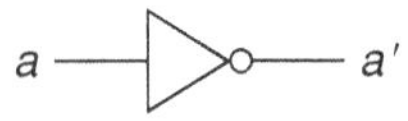

The third gate we will include is the NOT, which has the symbol shown in Figure 2.6. The triangle is just the symbol for an amplifier (from electronics). The circle (sometimes referred to as a bubble) on the output is the symbol for inversion (NOT) and, as we will see later, is often shown attached to other gate inputs and outputs to indicate the NOT function.

Parentheses are used as in other mathematics; expressions inside the parentheses are evaluated first. When evaluating expressions without parentheses, the order of precedence is

NOT
AND
OR

Thus, for example,

$$ab' + c'd = [a(b')] + [(c')d]$$

Even without parentheses, the input b is complemented first and then ANDed with a. Input c is complemented and ANDed with d and then the two product terms are ORed. If the intent is to AND a and b and then complement them, it must be written $(ab)'$ rather than ab' and if the intent is to do the OR before the ANDs, it must be written $a(b' + c')d$.

In each of the properties, we use a single letter, such as $a, b, c, \ldots$ to represent any expression, not just a single variable. Thus, for example, Property 1a also states that

$$xy'z + w' = w' + xy'z$$

One other thing to note is that properties always appear in *dual* pairs. To obtain the dual of a property, interchange OR and AND, and the constants 0 and 1. The first interchange is obvious in P1 and P2; the other will be used in the next three properties. It can be shown that whenever two expressions are equal, the duals of those expressions are also equal. That could save some work later on, since we do not have to prove both halves of a pair of properties.

[SP 3; EX 3]

2.2.2 Basic Properties of Switching Algebra

We will next look at three pairs of properties associated with the constants 0 and 1.

P3a. $a + 0 = a$	**P3b.** $a \cdot 1 = a$	identity
P4a. $a + 1 = 1$	**P4b.** $a \cdot 0 = 0$	null
P5a. $a + a' = 1$	**P5b.** $a \cdot a' = 0$	complement

Properties 3a and 4b follow directly from the first and third lines of the truth tables; Properties 3b and 4a follow from the second and fourth lines. Property 5 follows from the definition of the NOT, namely, that either a or a' is always 1 and the other is always 0. Thus, P5a must be either $0 + 1$ or $1 + 0$, both of which are 1, and P5b must be either $0 \cdot 1$ or $1 \cdot 0$, both of which are 0. Once again, each of the properties comes in dual pairs.

Note that by combining the commutative property (P1a) with 3, 4, and 5, we also have

P3aa. $0 + a = a$	**P3bb.** $1 \cdot a = a$
P4aa. $1 + a = 1$	**P4bb.** $0 \cdot a = 0$
P5aa. $a' + a = 1$	**P5bb.** $a' \cdot a = 0$

Often, as we manipulate expressions, we will use one of these versions, rather than first interchanging the terms using the commutative law (P1).

Another property that follows directly from the first and last lines of the truth tables for OR and AND (see Table 2.7) is

P6a. $a + a = a$ **P6b.** $a \cdot a = a$ idempotency

By repeated application of Property 6a, we can see that

$$a + a + a + a = a$$

In the process of manipulating logic functions, it should be understood that each of these equalities is bidirectional. For example, $xyz + xyz$ can be replaced in an expression by xyz; but, also, it is sometimes useful to replace xyz by $xyz + xyz$.

The final property that we will obtain directly from the truth tables of the operators is the only one we will include on our list that is a self-dual.

P7. $(a')' = a$ involution

If $a = 0$, then $a' = 1$. However, when that is complemented again, that is, $(0')' = 1' = 0 = a$. Similarly, if $a = 1$, $a' = 0$ and $(1')' = 1$. Because there are no ANDs, ORs, 0's, or 1's, the dual is the same property.

The next pair of properties, referred to as the *distributive* law, are most useful in algebraic manipulation.

P8a. $a(b + c) = ab + ac$ **P8b.** $a + bc = (a + b)(a + c)$ distributive

P8a looks very familiar; we use it commonly with addition and multiplication. In right to left order, it is referred to as *factoring*. On the other hand, P8b is not a property of regular algebra. (Substitute 1, 2, 3 for *a, b,*

c, and the computation is $1 + 6 = 7$ on the left and $4 \times 3 = 12$ on the right.) The simplest way to prove these properties of switching algebra is to produce a truth table for both sides of the equality and show that they are equal. That is shown for Property 8b in Table 2.8. The left three columns are the input columns. The left-hand side (LHS) of the equality is constructed by first forming a column for bc. That column has a 1 in each of the rows where both b and c are 1 and 0 elsewhere. Then LHS = $a + bc$ is computed using the column for a and that for bc. LHS is 1 when either of those columns contains a 1 or both are 1 and is 0 when they are both 0. Similarly, the right-hand side (RHS) is computed by first constructing a column for $a + b$, which contains a 1 when $a = 1$ or $b = 1$. The column for $a + c$ is constructed in a similar fashion and finally RHS $= (a + b)(a + c)$ is 1 wherever both of the previous columns are 1.

Table 2.8 Truth table to prove Property 8b.

a	b	c	bc	LHS	$a + b$	$a + c$	RHS
0	0	0	0	0	0	0	0
0	0	1	0	0	0	1	0
0	1	0	0	0	1	0	0
0	1	1	1	1	1	1	1
1	0	0	0	1	1	1	1
1	0	1	0	1	1	1	1
1	1	0	0	1	1	1	1
1	1	1	1	1	1	1	1

The table could have been constructed by evaluating each of the expressions for each row (input combination). For the first row,

$$a + bc = 0 + (0 \cdot 0) = 0 + 0 = 0$$
$$(a + b)(a + c) = (0 + 0)(0 + 0) = 0 + 0 = 0$$

and for the sixth row (101)

$$a + bc = 1 + (0 \cdot 1) = 1 + 0 = 1$$
$$(a + b)(a + c) = (1 + 0)(1 + 1) = 1 \cdot 1 = 1$$

We would need to do this for all eight rows. If we need the whole table, the first method usually requires less work.

This method can also be used to determine whether functions are equal. To be equal, the functions must have the same value for all input combinations. If they differ in any row of the truth table, they are not equal.

EXAMPLE 2.2

Construct a truth table and show which of the three functions are equal. (Be sure to state whether they are equal.)

$$f = y'z' + x'y + x'yz'$$
$$g = xy' + x'z' + x'y$$
$$h = (x' + y')(x + y + z')$$

xyz	$y'z'$	$x'y$	$x'yz'$	f	xy'	$x'z'$	$x'y$	g	$x'+y'$	$x+y+z'$	h
000	1	0	0	1	0	1	0	1	1	1	1
001	0	0	0	0	0	0	0	0	1	0	0
010	0	1	1	1	0	1	1	1	1	1	1
011	0	1	0	1	0	0	1	1	1	1	1
100	1	0	0	1	1	0	0	1	1	1	1
101	0	0	0	0	1	0	0	1	1	1	1
110	0	0	0	0	0	0	0	0	0	1	0
111	0	0	0	0	0	0	0	0	0	1	0

The truth table was constructed for each of the three functions (using the same technique as we did in developing Table 2.8). For input combination 1 0 1, $f = 0$, but $g = h = 1$. Thus, f is not equal to either of the other functions. The columns for g and h are identical; thus, $g = h$.

2.2.3 Manipulation of Algebraic Functions

[SP 4, 5; EX 4, 5]

Before adding some properties that are useful in simplifying algebraic expressions, it is helpful to introduce some terminology that will make the discussion simpler.

A *literal* is the appearance of a variable or its complement. Examples are a and b'. In determining the complexity of an expression, one of the measures is the number of literals. **Each appearance** of a variable is counted. Thus, for example, the expression

$$ab' + bc'd + a'd + e'$$

contains eight literals.

A *product term* is one or more literals connected by AND operators. In the previous example, there are four product terms, ab', $bc'd$, $a'd$, and e'. Notice that a single literal is a product term.

A *standard product term,* also called a *minterm,* is a product term that includes each variable of the problem, either uncomplemented or complemented. Thus, for a function of four variables, w, x, y, and z, the terms $w'xyz'$ and $wxyz$ are standard product terms, but $wy'z$ is not.

A *sum of products* expression (often abbreviated SOP) is one or more product terms connected by OR operators. The previous expression meets this definition as do each of the following:

$w'xyz' + wx'y'z' + wx'yz + wxyz$ (4 product terms)

$x + w'y + wxy'z$ (3 product terms)

$x' + y + z$ (3 product terms)

wy' (1 product term)

z (1 product term)

It is usually possible to write several different SOP expressions for the same function.

A *canonical sum,* or *sum of standard product terms,* is just a sum of products expression where all of the terms are standard product terms. The first example is the only canonical sum (if there are four variables in all of the problems). Often, the starting point for algebraic manipulations is with canonical sums.

A *minimum sum of products* expression is one of those SOP expressions for a function that has the fewest number of product terms. If there is more than one expression with the fewest number of terms, then minimum is defined as one or more of those expressions with the fewest number of literals. As implied by this wording, there may be more than one minimum solution to a given problem. Each of the following expressions are equal (meaning that whatever values are chosen for x, y, and z, each expression produces the same value). Note that the first is a sum of standard product terms.

(1) $x'yz' + x'yz + xy'z' + xy'z + xyz$	5 terms, 15 literals
(2) $x'y + xy' + xyz$	3 terms, 7 literals
(3) $x'y + xy' + xz$	3 terms, 6 literals
(4) $x'y + xy' + yz$	3 terms, 6 literals

Expressions (3) and (4) are the minima. (It should be clear that those are minimum among the expressions shown; it is not so obvious that there is not yet another expression with fewer terms or literals.) (A word of caution: When looking for all of the minimum solutions, do **not** include any solution with more terms or more literals than the best already found.)

Actually, we have enough algebra at this point to be able to go from the first expression to the last two. First, we will reduce the first expression to the second:

$$x'yz' + x'yz + xy'z' + xy'z + xyz$$
$$= (x'yz' + x'yz) + (xy'z' + xy'z) + xyz \quad \text{associative}$$
$$= x'y(z' + z) + xy'(z' + z) + xyz \quad \text{distributive}$$
$$= x'y \cdot 1 + xy' \cdot 1 + xyz \quad \text{complement}$$
$$= x'y + xy' + xyz \quad \text{identity}$$

The first step takes advantage of P2a, which allows us to group terms in any way we wish. We then utilized P8a to factor $x'y$ out of the first two terms and xy' out of the third and fourth terms. Next we used P5aa to replace $z' + z$ by 1. In the final step, we used P3b to reduce the expression.

The last three steps can be combined into a single step. We can add a property

adjacency **P9a.** $ab + ab' = a$ **P9b.** $(a + b)(a + b') = a$

where, in the first case, $a = x'y$ and $b = z'$. Thus, if there are two product terms in a sum that are identical, except that one of the variables is uncomplemented in one and complemented in the other, they can be combined, using P9a. (The proof of this property follows the same three steps we used before—P8a to factor out the a, P5a to replace $b + b'$ by 1, and finally P3b to produce the result.) The dual can be proved using the dual steps, P8b, P5b, and P3a.

The easiest way to get to expression (3), that is, to go to six literals, is to use P6a, and make two copies of $xy'z$, that is,

$$xy'z = xy'z + xy'z$$

The expression becomes

$$\begin{aligned} &x'yz' + x'yz + xy'z' + xy'z + xyz + xy'z \\ &\quad = (x'yz' + x'yz) + (xy'z' + xy'z) + (xyz + xy'z) \\ &\quad = x'y(z' + z) + xy'(z' + z) + xz(y + y') \\ &\quad = x'y \cdot 1 + xy' \cdot 1 + xz \cdot 1 \\ &\quad = x'y + xy' + xz \end{aligned}$$

We added the second copy of $xy'z$ at the end and combined it with the last term (xyz). The manipulation then proceeded in the same way as before. The other expression can be obtained in a similar manner by using P6a on $x'yz$ and combining the second copy with xyz. Notice that we freely reordered the terms in the first sum of products expression when we utilized P6a to insert a second copy of one of the terms.

In general, we may be able to combine a term on the list with more than one other term. If that is the case, we can replicate a term as many times as are needed.

Another property that will allow us to reduce the system to six literals without the need to make extra copies of a term is

P10a. $a + a'b = a + b$ **P10b.** $a(a' + b) = ab$ **simplification**

We can demonstrate the validity of P10a by using P8b, P5a, and P3bb as follows:

$$\begin{aligned} a + a'b &= (a + a')(a + b) && \text{distributive} \\ &= 1 \cdot (a + b) && \text{complement} \\ &= a + b && \text{identity} \end{aligned}$$

P10b can be demonstrated as follows:

$$a(a' + b) = aa' + ab = 0 + ab = ab$$

We can apply this property to the example by factoring x out of the last two terms:

$$\begin{aligned} &x'y + xy' + xyz \\ &\quad = x'y + x(y' + yz) && \text{distributive} \\ &\quad = x'y + x(y' + z) && \text{simplification} \\ &\quad = x'y + xy' + xz && \text{distributive} \end{aligned}$$

We used P10a where $a = y'$ and $b = z$ in going from line 2 to 3. Instead, we could have factored y out of the first and last terms, producing

$$\begin{aligned} &y(x' + xz) + xy' \\ &\quad = y(x' + z) + xy' \\ &\quad = x'y + yz + xy' \end{aligned}$$

which is the other six literal equivalent.

Consider the following example, an expression in canonical form.

EXAMPLE 2.3

$$a'b'c' + a'bc' + a'bc + ab'c'$$

The first two terms can be combined using P9a, producing

$$a'c' + a'bc + ab'c'$$

Now, we can factor a' from the first two terms and use P10a to reduce this to

$$a'c' + a'b + ab'c'$$

and repeat the process with c' and the first and last terms, resulting in the expression

$$a'c' + a'b + b'c'$$

Although this expression is simpler than any of the previous ones, it is not minimum. With the properties we have developed so far, we have reached a dead end, and we have no way of knowing that this is not the minimum. Returning to the original expression, we can group the first term with the last and the middle two terms. Then, when we apply P9a, we get an expression with only two terms and four literals:

$$\begin{aligned} &a'b'c' + a'bc' + a'bc + ab'c' \\ &\quad = b'c' + a'b \end{aligned}$$

Later, we will see a property that allows us to go from the three-term expression to the one with only two terms.

Each terminology defined earlier has a dual that will also prove useful.

A *sum term* is one or more literals connected by OR operators. Examples are $a + b' + c$ and b' (just one literal).

A *standard sum term,* also called a *maxterm,* is a sum term that includes each variable of the problem, either uncomplemented or complemented. Thus, for a function of four variables, w, x, y, and z, the terms $w' + x + y + z'$ and $w + x + y + z$ are standard sum terms, but $w + y' + z$ is not.

A *product of sums* expression (POS) is one or more sum terms connected by AND operators. Examples of product of sums expressions:

$(w + x)(w + y)$	2 terms
$w(x + y)$	2 terms
w	1 term

$w + x$ 1 term

$(w + x' + y' + z')(w' + x + y + z')$ 2 terms

A *canonical product,* or *product of standard sum terms,* is just a POS expression in which all of the terms are standard sum terms. The last example above is the only canonical sum (if there are four variables in all of the problems). Often, the starting point for algebraic manipulations is with canonical sums.

Minimum is defined the same way for both POS and SOP, namely, the expressions with the fewest number of terms, and, among those with the same number of terms, those with the fewest number of literals. A given function (or expression) can be reduced to minimum sum of products form and to minimum product of sums form. They may both have the same number of terms and literals or either may have fewer than the other. (We will see examples later, when we have further developed our minimization techniques.)

An expression may be in sum of products form, product of sums form, both, or neither. Examples are

SOP: $x'y + xy' + xyz$

POS: $(x + y')(x' + y)(x' + z')$

both: $x' + y + z$ or xyz'

neither: $x(w' + yz)$ or $z' + wx'y + v(xz + w')$

We will now look at an example of the simplification of functions in maxterms form. (Later, we will look at methods of going from sum of products to product of sums and from product of sums to sum of products forms.)

$$g = (w' + x' + y + z')(w' + x' + y + z)(w + x' + y + z')$$

The first two terms can be combined, using P9b, where

$$a = w' + x' + y \quad \text{and} \quad b = z'$$

producing

$$g = (w' + x' + y)(w + x' + y + z')$$

That can most easily be reduced further by using P6b, to create a second copy of the first term, which can be combined with the last term, where

$$a = x' + y + z' \quad \text{and} \quad b = w$$

producing the final answer

$$g = (w' + x' + y)(x' + y + z')$$

We could also do the following manipulation (parallel to what we did with the SOP expression)

$$
\begin{aligned}
g &= (w' + x' + y)(w + x' + y + z') \\
&= x' + y + w'(w + z') && \textbf{[P8b]} \\
&= x' + y + w'z' && \textbf{[P10b]} \\
&= (x' + y + w')(x' + y + z') && \textbf{[P8b]}
\end{aligned}
$$

which, after reordering the literals in the first set of parentheses, is the same expression as before.

[SP 6, 7, 8, 9; EX 6, 7, 8, 9]

2.3 IMPLEMENTATION OF FUNCTIONS WITH AND, OR, AND NOT GATES

We will first look at the implementation of switching functions using networks of AND, OR, and NOT gates. (After all, the goal of our design is to produce the block diagram of a circuit to implement the given switching function.) When we defined minimum SOP expressions, we introduced, as an example, the function

$$f = x'yz' + x'yz + xy'z' + xy'z + xyz$$

A block diagram of a circuit to implement this is shown in Figure 2.7. Each of the product terms is formed by an AND gate. In this example, all of the AND gates have three inputs. The outputs of the AND gates are used as inputs to an OR (in this case a five-input OR). This implementation assumes that all of the inputs are available, both uncomplemented and complemented (that is, for example, both x and x' are available as inputs). This is usually the case if the input to the combinational logic circuit comes from a flip flop, a storage device in sequential systems. It is not usually true, however, if the input is a system input.

Figure 2.7 Block diagram of *f* in sum of standard products form.

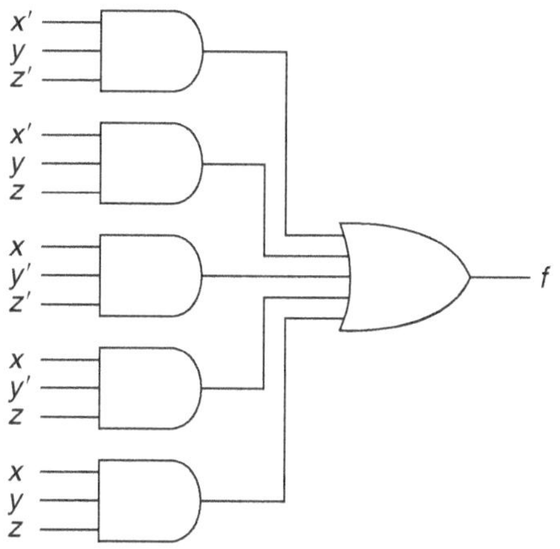

This is an example of a *two-level* circuit. The number of levels is the maximum number of gates through which a signal must pass from the input to the output. In this example, all signals go first through an AND gate and then through an OR. When inputs are available both uncomplemented and complemented, implementations of both SOP and POS expressions result in two-level circuits.

We saw that this same function can be manipulated to a minimum SOP expression, one version of which is

$$f = x'y + xy' + xz$$

This, of course, leads to a less complex circuit, namely, the one shown in Figure 2.8.

Figure 2.8 Minimum sum of product implementation of f.

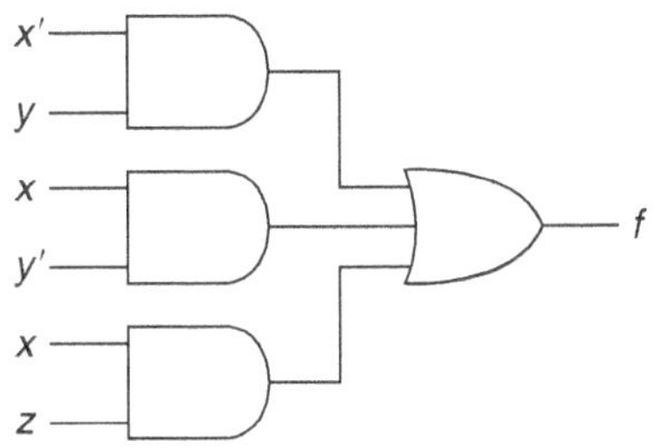

We have reduced the complexity of the circuit from six gates with 20 gate inputs (three to each of the five ANDs and five to the OR) to one with four gates and 9 gate inputs. The simplest definition of minimum for a gate network is minimum number of gates and, among those with the same number of gates, minimum number of gate inputs. For two-level circuits, this always corresponds to minimum sum of products or minimum product of sums functions.

If complemented inputs are not available, then an inverter (a NOT gate) is needed for each input that is required to be complemented (x and y in this example). The circuit of Figure 2.9 shows the NOT gates that must be added to the circuit of Figure 2.8 to implement f. Note that in this version we showed each input once, with that input line connected to whatever gates required it. That is surely what happens when we actually construct the circuit. However, for clarity, we will draw circuits more like the previous one (except, of course, we will only have one NOT gate for each input, with the output of that gate going to those gates that require it). (This is a three-level circuit because some of the paths pass through three gates: a NOT, an AND, and then an OR.)

Figure 2.9 Circuit with only uncomplemented inputs.

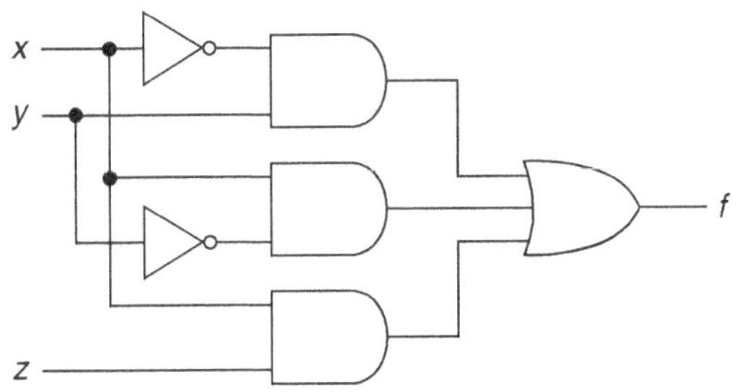

A POS expression (assuming all inputs are available both uncomplemented and complemented) corresponds to a two-level OR–AND network. For this same example, the minimum POS (although that is not obvious based on the algebra we have developed to this point)

$$f = (x + y)(x' + y' + z)$$

is implemented with the circuit of Figure 2.10.

Figure 2.10 A product of sums implementation.

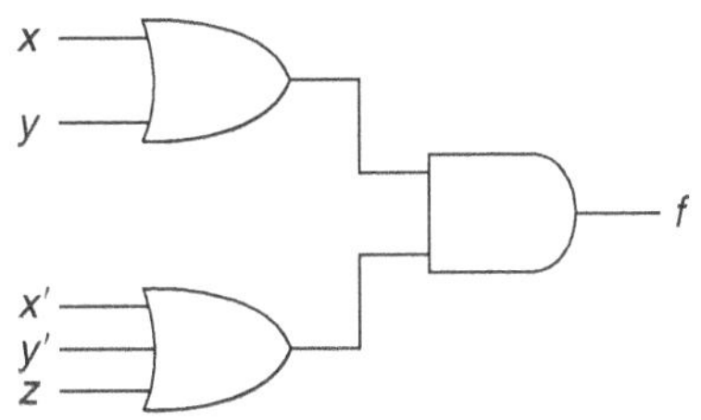

When we implement functions that are in neither SOP nor POS form, the resulting circuits are more than two levels. As an example, consider the following function:

$$h = z' + wx'y + v(xz + w')$$

We begin inside the parentheses and build an AND gate with inputs x and z. The output of that goes to an OR gate, the other input of which is w'. That is ANDed with v, which is ORed with the input z' and the output of the AND gate, producing $wx'y$, which results in the circuit of Figure 2.11.

Figure 2.11 A multilevel circuit.

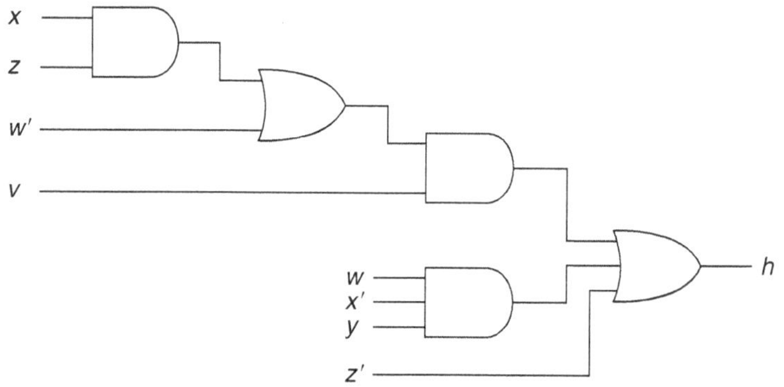

This is a four-level circuit because the signals x and z pass first through an AND gate, then an OR, then an AND, and finally through an OR—a total of four gates.

EXAMPLE 2.4

If we take the version of f used for Figure 2.8, and factor x from the last two terms, we obtain

$$f = x'y + x(y' + z)$$

That would result in the three-level circuit

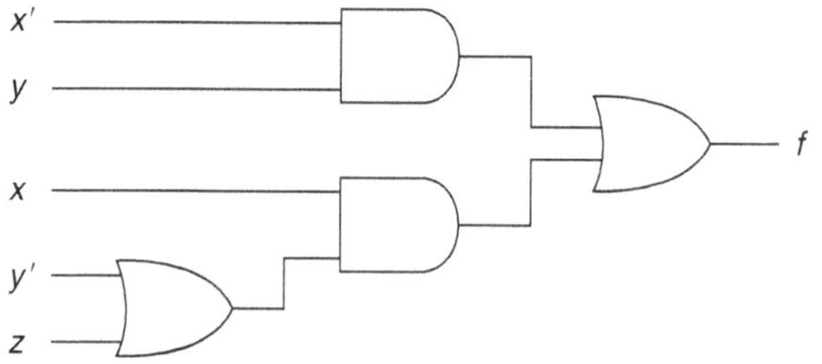

This (three-level) solution uses 4 two-input gates.

Gates are typically available in dual in-line pin packages (DIPs) of 14 connector pins. These packages are often referred to as *chips*. (Larger packages of 16, 18, 22, and more pins are used for more complex logic.) These packages contain *integrated circuits* (ICs). Integrated circuits are categorized as *small-scale integration* (SSI) when they contain just a few gates. Those are the ones that we will refer to in this chapter. Medium-scale (MSI) circuits contain as many as 100 gates; we will see examples of these later. The terminology *large-scale integration* (LSI), *very large-scale integration* (VLSI), and *giga-scale integration* (GSI) is used for even more complex packages, including complete computers.

Two of the connector pins are used to provide power to the chip. That leaves 12 pins for logic connections (on a 14-pin chip). Thus, we can fit 4 two-input gates on a chip. (Each gate has two input connections and one output connection. There are enough pins for four such gates.) Similarly, there are enough pins for 6 one-input gates (NOTs), 3 three-input gates, and 2 four-input gates (with two pins unused). In examples that refer to specific integrated circuits, we will discuss *transistor–transistor logic* (TTL) and, in particular, the 7400 series of chips.* For these chips, the power connections are 5 V and ground (0 V).

A list of the common AND, OR, and NOT integrated circuits that might be encountered in the laboratory is

7404	6 (hex) NOT gates
7408	4 (quadruple) two-input AND gates
7411	3 (triple) three-input AND gates
7421	2 four-input (dual) AND gates
7432	4 (quadruple) two-input OR gates

If a three-input OR (or AND) is needed, and only two-input ones are available, it can be constructed as follows:

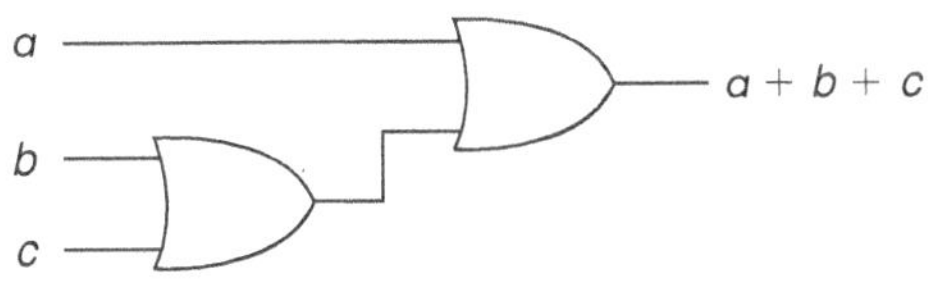

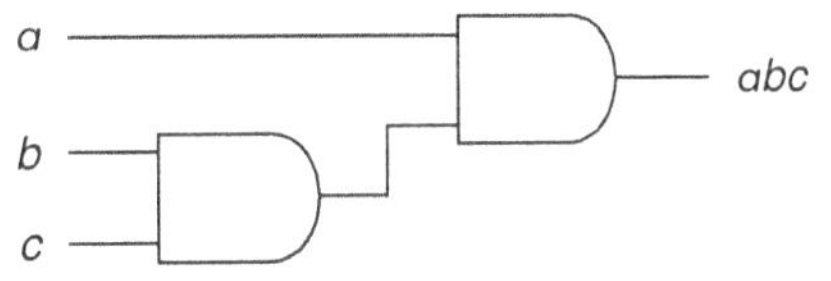

This idea can be extended to gates with larger numbers of inputs.†

Also, if we need a two-input gate and there is a leftover three-input one (because they come three to a package), we can connect the same signal to two of the inputs (since $aa = a$, and $a + a = a$).

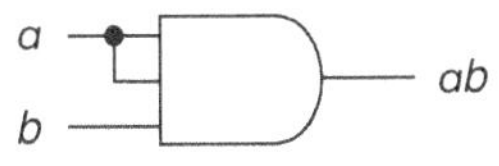

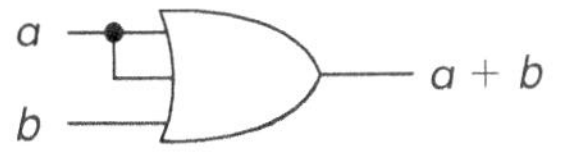

*There are many families of logic circuits on the market, with different electronic characteristics. In each, there are similar packages of gates. Since our primary interest is at the logic level (rather than the electronics level), we chose one of these, TTL, for the examples that involve specific chips. Even within the 7400 series, there are a number of variations, indicated by a letter or letters after the 74 (such as 74H10). We will not be concerned with that detail; it is left for a course on digital electronics.

†Caution: This approach does not work for NAND and NOR gates (which we will introduce in Section 2.6).

Also, we could connect a logic 1 (+5 V) to one of the inputs of an AND or a logic 0 (ground) to one of the inputs of an OR:

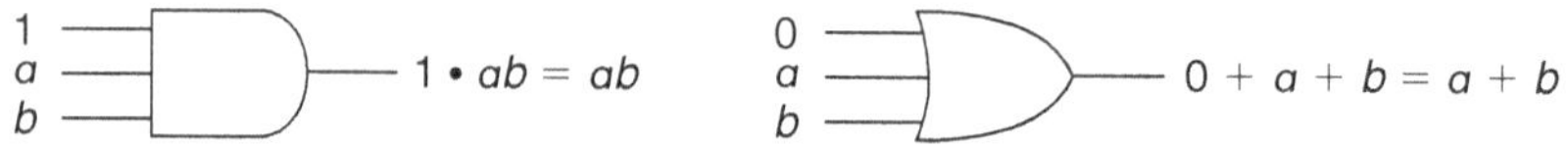

In the laboratory, logic 0 and logic 1 are represented by two voltages: often 0 and 5 V. Most commonly, the higher voltage is used to represent 1 and the lower voltage to represent 0. This is referred to as *positive logic*. The opposite choice is also possible, that is, use the higher voltage to represent 0. That is referred to as *negative logic*. When dealing with 1's and 0's, the concept does not really come up. However, the same electronic circuit has different logic meanings depending on which choice we make.

Consider the truth table of Table 2.9a, where the behavior of the gate is described just in terms of high (H) and low (L). The positive logic interpretation of Table 2.9b produces the truth table for an OR gate. The negative logic interpretation of Table 2.9c is that of an AND gate.

Table 2.9

a. High/Low

a	*b*	*f*
L	L	L
L	H	H
H	L	H
H	H	H

b. Positive logic

a	*b*	*f*
0	0	0
0	1	1
1	0	1
1	1	1

c. Negative logic

a	*b*	*f*
1	1	1
1	0	0
0	1	0
0	0	0

Most implementations use positive logic; we will do that consistently throughout this book. Occasionally, negative logic, or even a mixture of the two, is used.

[SP 10, 11; EX 10, 11; LAB]*

2.4 THE COMPLEMENT

Before we go further, we need to develop one more property. This property is the only one for which a person's name is commonly attached—*DeMorgan's theorem.*

DeMorgan

P11a. $(a + b)' = a'b'$ **P11b.** $(ab)' = a' + b'$

The simplest proof of this property utilizes the truth table of Table 2.10. In Table 2.10, we have produced a column for each of the expressions in the property. (The entries in the table should be obvious because they just involve the AND, OR, and NOT operations on other columns.) Note that the columns (labeled 11a) for $(a + b)'$ and $a'b'$ are the same and those (labeled 11b) for $(ab)'$ and $a' + b'$are the same.

*LAB refers to experiments in Appendix D.

Table 2.10 Proof of DeMorgan's theorem.

a	b	$a + b$	$(a + b)'$	a'	b'	$a'b'$	ab	$(ab)'$	$a' + b'$
0	0	0	1	1	1	1	0	1	1
0	1	1	0	1	0	0	0	1	1
1	0	1	0	0	1	0	0	1	1
1	1	1	0	0	0	0	1	0	0
			11a			11a		11b	11b

The property can be extended to more than two operands easily.

P11aa. $(a + b + c \ldots)' = a'b'c' \ldots$

P11bb. $(abc \ldots)' = a' + b' + c' \ldots$

For P11aa, with three variables, the proof goes

$$(a + b + c)' = [(a + b) + c]' = (a + b)'c' = a'b'c'$$

COMMON MISTAKE: The NOT does not distribute through the parentheses. Thus,

$$(ab)' \neq a'b' \text{ and } (a + b)' \neq a' + b'$$

and, for example,

$$ab + a'b' \neq 1$$

Just look at the $(ab)'$ and $a'b'$ columns of the truth table and compare the expressions for $a = 0$ and $b = 1$ (or for $a = 1$ and $b = 0$):

$$(0 \cdot 1)' = 0' = 1 \quad 0' \cdot 1' = 1 \cdot 0 = 0$$

There will be times when we are given a function and need to find its complement, that is, given $f(w, x, y, z)$, we need $f'(w, x, y, z)$. The straightforward approach is to use DeMorgan's theorem repeatedly.

EXAMPLE 2.5

$$f = wx'y + xy' + wxz$$

then

$$f' = (wx'y + xy' + wxz)'$$
$$= (wx'y)'(xy')'(wxz)' \quad \textbf{[P11a]}$$
$$= (w' + x + y')(x' + y)(w' + x' + z') \quad \textbf{[P11b]}$$

Note that if the function is in SOP form, the complement is in POS form (and the complement of a POS expression is an SOP one).

To find the complement of more general expressions, we can repeatedly apply DeMorgan's theorem or we can follow this set of rules:

1. Complement each variable (that is, a to a' or a' to a).
2. Replace 0 by 1 and 1 by 0.
3. Replace AND by OR and OR by AND, being sure to preserve the order of operations. That sometimes requires additional parentheses.

EXAMPLE 2.6

$$f = ab'(c + d'e) + a'bc'$$

$$f' = [a' + b + c'(d + e')][a + b' + c]$$

Note that in f, the last operation to be performed is an OR of the complex first term with the product term. To preserve the order, parentheses were needed in f'; making the AND the last operation.

We would produce the same result, with much more work, by using P11a and P11b over and over again:

$$\begin{aligned} f' &= [ab'(c + d'e) + a'bc']' \\ &= [ab'(c + d'e)]'[a'bc']' \\ &= [a' + b + (c + d'e)'][a + b' + c] \\ &= [a' + b + c'(d'e)'][a + b' + c] \\ &= [a' + b + c'(d + e')][a + b' + c] \end{aligned}$$

[SP 12; EX 12]

2.5 FROM THE TRUTH TABLE TO ALGEBRAIC EXPRESSIONS

Often, a design problem is stated in terms of the truth table that describes the output in terms of the inputs. Other times, verbal descriptions of systems can most easily be translated into the truth table. Thus, we need the ability to go from the truth table to an algebraic expression. To understand the process, consider the two-variable truth table of Table 2.11.

Table 2.11 A two-variable truth table.

a	b	f
0	0	0
0	1	1
1	0	1
1	1	1

Because this is a two-variable problem, the truth table has $4 (= 2^2)$ rows, that is, there are 4 possible combinations of inputs. (This is the truth table for the OR as we defined it at the beginning of this chapter, but that is irrelevant to this discussion.) What the table says is that

f is 1 if $a = 0$ AND $b = 1$ OR
if $a = 1$ AND $b = 0$ OR
if $a = 1$ AND $b = 1$

However, this is the same as saying

f is 1 if $a' = 1$ AND $b = 1$ OR
if $a = 1$ AND $b' = 1$ OR
if $a = 1$ AND $b = 1$

But $a' = 1$ AND $b = 1$ is the same as saying $a'b = 1$ and thus

f is 1 if $a'b = 1$ OR if $ab' = 1$ OR if $ab = 1$

That finally produces the expression

$$f = a'b + ab' + ab$$

Each row of the truth table corresponds to a product term. An SOP expression is formed by ORing those product terms corresponding to rows of the truth table for which the function is 1. Each product term has each variable included, with that variable complemented when the entry in the input column for that variable contains a 0 and uncomplemented when it contains a 1. Thus, for example, row 10 produces the term ab'. These product terms include all of the variables; they are minterms. Minterms are often referred to by number, by just converting the binary number in the input row of the truth table to decimal. Both of the following notations are common:

$$f(a, b) = m_1 + m_2 + m_3$$
$$f(a, b) = \Sigma m(1, 2, 3)$$

Note: If we use minterm numbers, we must include the variable names in the function name, such as $f(a, b)$. If we write an algebraic expression, such as $f = a'b + ab' + ab$, we can use just f, since the variables are obvious.

We show, in Table 2.12, the minterms and minterm numbers that are used for all functions of the three variables A, B, and C.

For a specific function, those terms for which the function is 1 are used to form an SOP expression for f, and those terms for which the function is 0 are used to form an SOP expression for f'. We can then complement f' to form a POS expression for f.

Table 2.12 Minterms.

ABC	Minterm	Number
0 0 0	$A'B'C'$	0
0 0 1	$A'B'C$	1
0 1 0	$A'BC'$	2
0 1 1	$A'BC$	3
1 0 0	$AB'C'$	4
1 0 1	$AB'C$	5
1 1 0	ABC'	6
1 1 1	ABC	7

EXAMPLE 2.7

ABC	*f*	*f'*
0 0 0	0	1
0 0 1	1	0
0 1 0	1	0
0 1 1	1	0
1 0 0	1	0
1 0 1	1	0
1 1 0	0	1
1 1 1	0	1

where the truth table shows both the function, f, and its complement, f'. We can write

$$f(A, B, C) = \Sigma m(1, 2, 3, 4, 5)$$
$$= A'B'C + A'BC' + A'BC + AB'C' + AB'C$$

Either from the truth table, or by recognizing that every minterm is included in either f or f', we can then write

$$f'(A, B, C) = \Sigma m(0, 6, 7)$$
$$= A'B'C' + ABC' + ABC$$

We can then complement f' to get a sum of maxterms.*

$$f = (f')' = (A + B + C)(A' + B' + C)(A' + B' + C')$$

The two sum of minterm forms are SOP expressions. In most cases, including this one, the sum of minterms expression is not a minimum sum of products expression. We could reduce f from 5 terms with 15 literals to either of two functions with 3 terms and 6 literals as follows:

$$\begin{aligned} f &= A'B'C + A'BC' + A'BC + AB'C' + AB'C \\ &= A'B'C + A'B + AB' && \textbf{[P9a, P9a]} \\ &= A'C + A'B + AB' \\ &= B'C + A'B + AB' \end{aligned}$$

where the final expressions are obtained using P8a and P10a on the first term and either the second or the third. Similarly, we can reduce f' from 3 terms with 9 literals to 2 terms with 5 literals, using P9a:

$$f' = A'B'C' + AB$$

Using P11, we can then obtain the minimum POS expression for f.

$$f = (A + B + C)(A' + B')$$

To find a minimum POS expression, we can either manipulate the previous POS expression (using P9b on the last two terms) or simplify the SOP expression for f' and then use DeMorgan to convert it to a POS expression. Both approaches produce the same result.

In much of the material of Chapter 3, we will specify functions by just listing their minterms (by number). We must, of course, list the variables of the problem as part of that statement. Thus,

$$f(w, x, y, z) = \Sigma m(0, 1, 5, 9, 11, 15)$$

is the simplest way to specify the function

$$f = w'x'y'z' + w'x'y'z + w'xy'z + wx'y'z + wx'yz + wxyz$$

If the function includes don't cares, then those terms are included in a separate sum (Σ).

*It is possible to obtain POS expressions directly from the truth table without first finding the SOP expression. Each 0 of f produces a maxterm in the POS expression. We have omitted that approach here, because it tends to lead to confusion.

EXAMPLE 2.8

$f(a, b, c) = \Sigma m(1, 2, 5) + \Sigma d(0, 3)$

implies that minterms 1, 2, and 5 are included in the function and that 0 and 3 are don't cares, that is the truth table is as follows:

abc	*f*
0 0 0	X
0 0 1	1
0 1 0	1
0 1 1	X
1 0 0	0
1 0 1	1
1 1 0	0
1 1 1	0

Let us now return to the first three of our continuing examples and develop algebraic expressions for them.

EXAMPLE 2.9

Using Z_2 for CE1, we get

$$Z_2 = A'BCD + AB'CD + ABC'D + ABCD' + ABCD$$

directly from the truth table. The last term ($ABCD$) can be combined with each of the others (using P10a). Thus, if we make four copies of it (using P6a repeatedly) and then utilize P10a four times, we obtain

$$Z_2 = BCD + ACD + ABD + ABC$$

No further simplification is possible; this is the minimum sum of products expression. Notice that if we used Z_1, we would have

$$Z_1 = A'BCD + AB'CD + ABC'D + ABCD'$$

No simplification is possible. This expression also has four terms, but it has 16 literals, whereas the expression for Z_2 only has 12.

EXAMPLE 2.10

For CE2, we have either

$$f = ab'c + abc' \quad \text{or} \quad f = ab'c' + abc$$

depending on which truth table we choose. Again, no simplification is possible.

For f', we have (for the first version)

$$\begin{aligned} f' &= a'b'c' + a'b'c + a'bc' + a'bc + ab'c' + abc \\ &= a'b' + a'b + ab'c' + abc && \textbf{[P9a, P9b]} \\ &= a' + ab'c' + abc = a' + b'c' + bc && \textbf{[P9a, P10a]} \end{aligned}$$

Thus, the product of maxterms is

$$f = (a + b + c)(a + b + c')(a + b' + c)(a + b' + c')$$
$$(a' + b + c)(a' + b' + c')$$

and the minimum POS is

$$f = a(b + c)(b' + c')$$

EXAMPLE 2.11

For the full adder, CE3 (using c for the carry in, c_{in}, to simplify the algebraic expressions), we get from the truth table

$$c_{out} = a'bc + ab'c + abc' + abc$$
$$s = a'b'c + a'bc' + ab'c' + abc$$

The simplification of carry out is very much like that of Z_2 in Example 2.9, resulting in

$$c_{out} = bc + ac + ab$$

but s is already in minimum SOP form. We will return to the implementation of the full adder in Section 2.8.

We will next take a brief look at a more general approach to switching functions. How many different functions of n variables are there?

For two variables, there are 16 possible truth tables, resulting in 16 different functions. The truth table of Table 2.13 shows all of these functions. (Each output column of the table corresponds to one of the 16 possible 4-bit binary numbers.)

Table 2.13 All two-variable functions.

a	b	f_0	f_1	f_2	f_3	f_4	f_5	f_6	f_7	f_8	f_9	f_{10}	f_{11}	f_{12}	f_{13}	f_{14}	f_{15}
0	0	0	0	0	0	0	0	0	0	1	1	1	1	1	1	1	1
0	1	0	0	0	0	1	1	1	1	0	0	0	0	1	1	1	1
1	0	0	0	1	1	0	0	1	1	0	0	1	1	0	0	1	1
1	1	0	1	0	1	0	1	0	1	0	1	0	1	0	1	0	1

Some of the functions are trivial, such as f_0 and f_{15}, and some are really just functions of one of the variables, such as f_3. The set of functions, reduced to minimum SOP form, are

$$f_0 = 0 \qquad f_6 = a'b + ab' \qquad f_{12} = a'$$
$$f_1 = ab \qquad f_7 = a + b \qquad f_{13} = a' + b$$
$$f_2 = ab' \qquad f_8 = a'b' \qquad f_{14} = a' + b'$$
$$f_3 = a \qquad f_9 = a'b' + ab \qquad f_{15} = 1$$
$$f_4 = a'b \qquad f_{10} = b'$$
$$f_5 = b \qquad f_{11} = a + b'$$

For n variables, the truth table has 2^n rows, and thus, we can choose any 2^n-bit number for a column. Thus, there are 2^{2^n} different functions of n variables. That number grows very quickly, as can be seen from Table 2.14.

Table 2.14 Number of functions of n variables.

Variables	Terms
1	4
2	16
3	256
4	65,536
5	4,294,967,296

(Thus, we can find a nearly unlimited variety of problems of four or more variables for exercises or tests.)

[SP 13, 14; EX 13, 14, 15, 16]

2.6 NAND, NOR, AND EXCLUSIVE-OR GATES

In this section we will introduce three other commonly used types of gates, the NAND, the NOR, and the Exclusive-OR, and see how to implement circuits using them.

Figure 2.12 NAND gates.

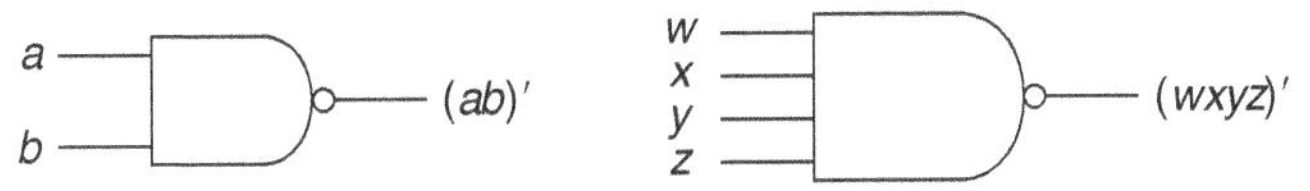

The NAND has the symbol shown in Figure 2.12. Like the AND and the OR, the NAND is commercially available in several sizes, typically two-, three-, four-, and eight-input varieties. When first introduced, it was referred to as an AND-NOT, which perfectly describes its function, but the shorter name, NAND, has become widely accepted. Note that DeMorgan's theorem states that

$$(ab)' = a' + b'$$

and thus an alternative symbol for the two-input NAND is shown in Figure 2.13. The symbols may be used interchangeably; they refer to the same component.

Figure 2.13 Alternative symbol for NAND.

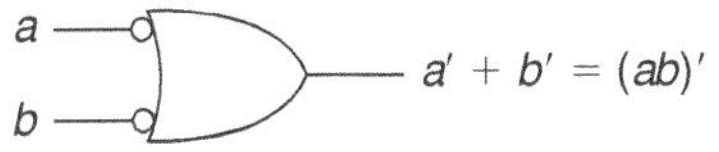

The NOR gate (OR-NOT) uses the symbols shown in Figure 2.14. Of course, $(a + b)' = a'b'$. NOR gates, too, are available with more inputs.

Figure 2.14 Symbols for NOR gate.

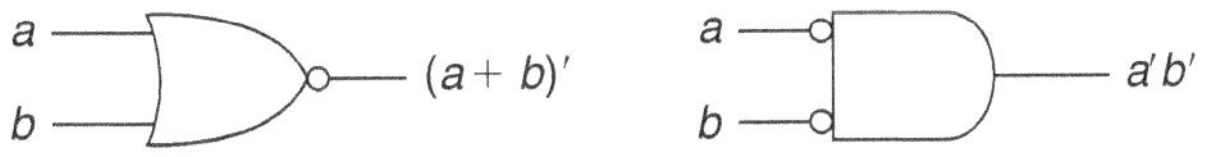

Why use NAND and NOR gates, rather than AND, OR, and NOT gates? After all, the logic expressions are in terms of AND, OR, and NOT operators and thus the implementation with those gates is straightforward. Many electronic implementations naturally invert (complement) signals; thus, the NAND is more convenient to implement than the AND. The most important reason is that with either NAND or NOR, only one type of gate is required. On the other hand, both AND and OR gates are required; and, often, NOT gates are needed, as well. As can be seen from the circuits of Figure 2.15, NOT gates and two-input AND and OR gates can be replaced by just two-input NANDs. Thus, these operators are said to be *functionally complete*. (We could implement gates with more than two inputs using NANDs with more inputs. We could also implement AND, OR, and NOT gates using only NORs; that is left as an exercise.)

Using these gate equivalences, the function, $f = x'y + xy' + xz$, that we first implemented with AND and OR gates in Figure 2.8 (Section 2.3) can now be implemented with NAND gates, as shown in Figure 2.16.

Figure 2.15 Functional completeness of NAND.

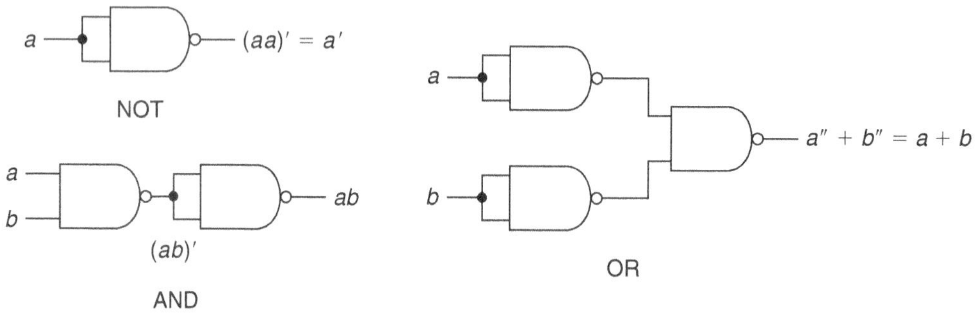

Figure 2.16 NAND gate implementation.

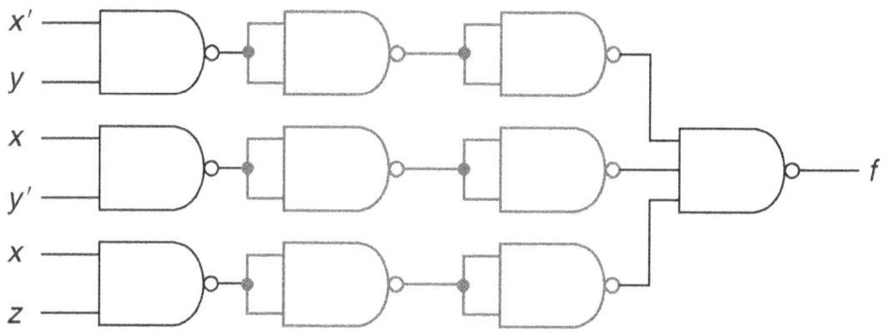

Figure 2.17 Better NAND gate implementation.

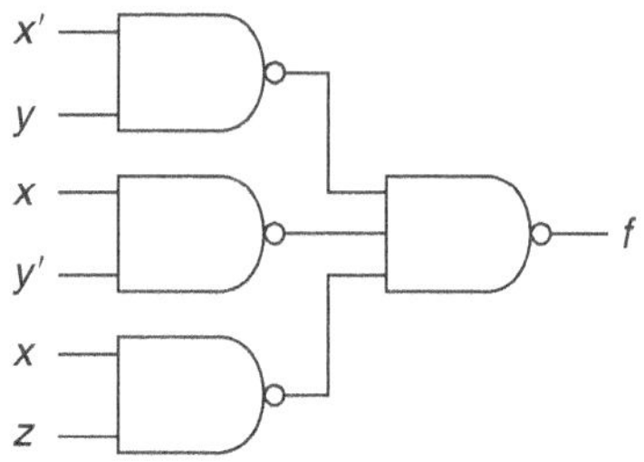

But note that we have two NOT gates in a row in each of the brown paths. They serve no purpose logically (P7 states $(a')' = a$), and thus they can be removed from the circuit, yielding that of Figure 2.17. That is, all of the AND and OR gates of the original circuit became NANDs. Nothing else was changed.

This process can be greatly simplified when we have a circuit consisting of AND and OR gates such that

1. the output of the circuit comes from an OR,
2. the inputs to all OR gates come either from a system input or from the output of an AND, and
3. the inputs to all AND gates come either from a system input or from the output of an OR.

All gates are replaced by NAND gates, and any input coming directly into an OR is complemented.

We can obtain the same result by starting at the output gate and putting a bubble (a NOT) at both ends of each input line to that OR gate. If the circuit is not two-level, we repeat this process at the input of each of the OR gates. Thus, the AND/OR implementation of *f* becomes that of Figure 2.18, where all of the gates have become NAND gates (in one of the two notations we introduced earlier).

This approach works with any circuit that meets these conditions, with only one additional step. If an input comes directly into an OR gate, there is no place for the second NOT; thus, that input must be complemented. For example, the circuit for h

$$h = z' + wx'y + v(xz + w')$$

is shown in Figure 2.19. Again, all of the AND and OR gates become NANDs, but the two inputs that came directly into the OR gates were complemented.

Figure 2.19 A multilevel NAND implementation.

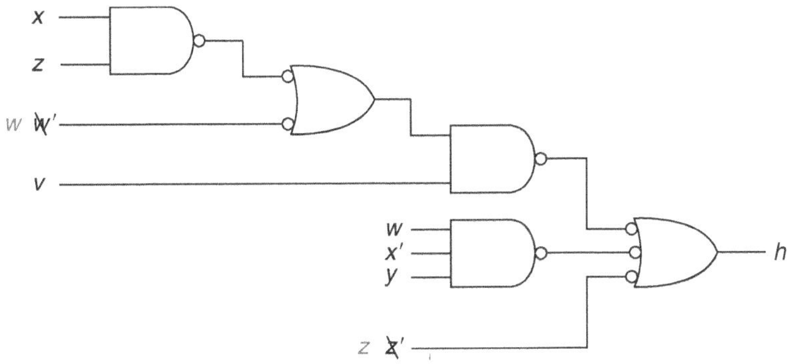

Figure 2.18 Double NOT gate approach.

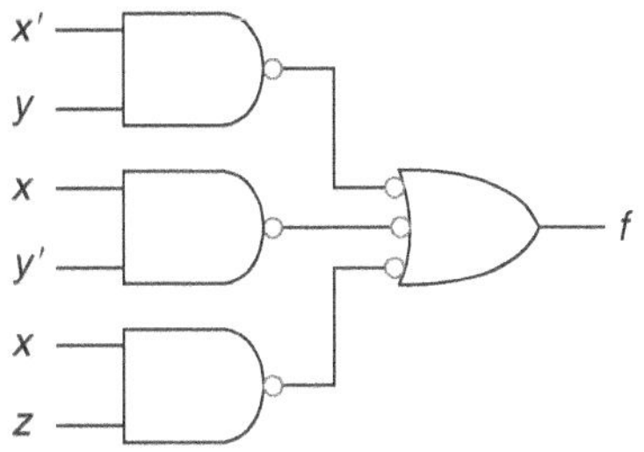

EXAMPLE 2.12

$$f = wx(y + z) + x'y$$

This would be implemented with AND and OR gates in either of two ways.

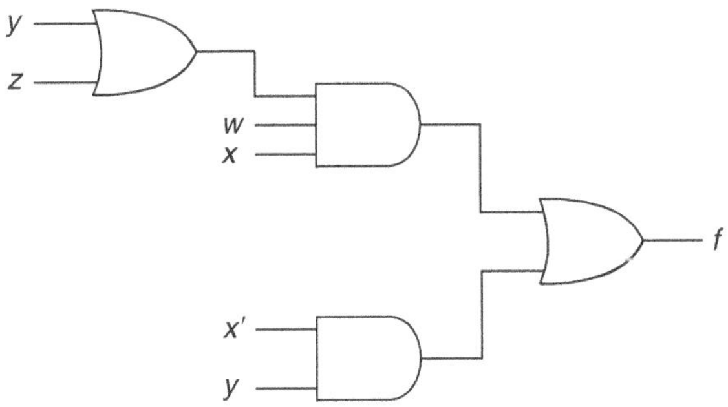

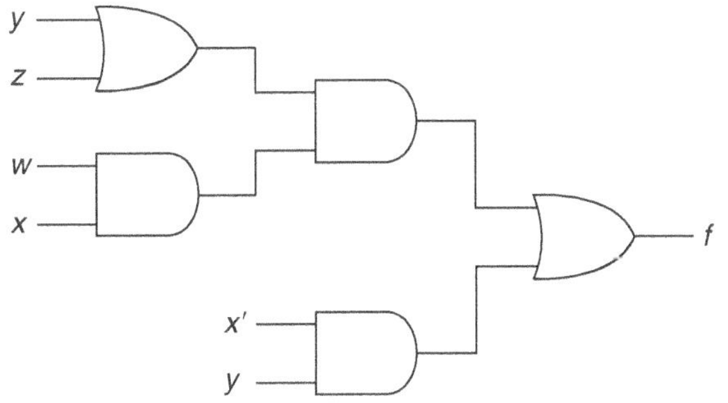

The first version can be directly converted to NAND gates, as follows.

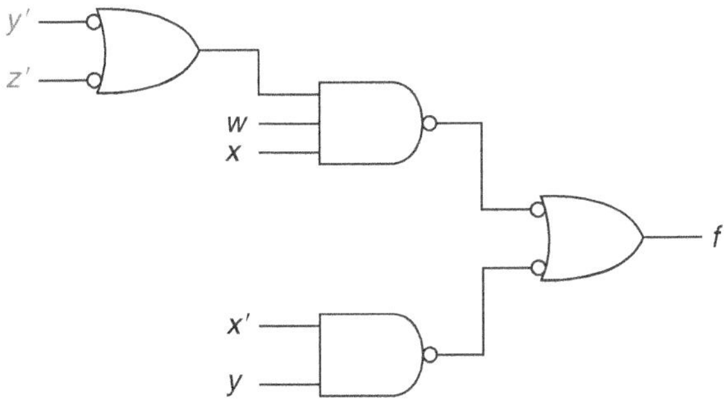

The second version cannot be converted to NAND gates without adding an extra NOT gate, because it violates the third rule—an AND gets an input from another AND. Thus, this circuit would become

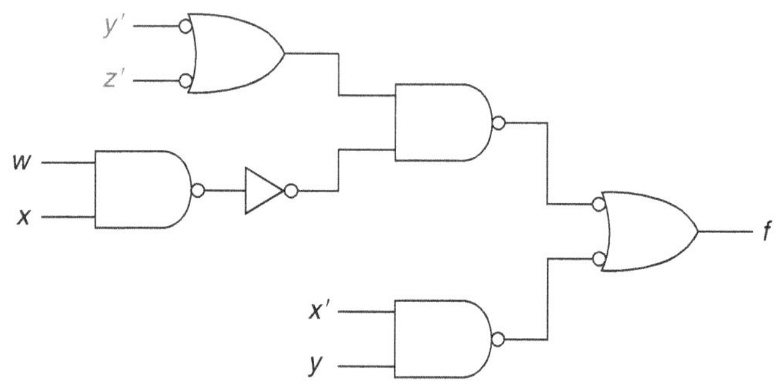

where the NOT is required to implement the AND that forms *wx*. Expressions such as this one are often obtained starting from SOP solutions. We will see some examples of this in Section 2.8.

The dual approach works for implementing circuits with NOR gates. When we have a circuit consisting of AND and OR gates such that

1. the output of the circuit comes from an AND,
2. the inputs to OR gates come either from a system input or from the output of an AND, and
3. the inputs to AND gates come either from a system input or from the output of an OR.

Then all gates can be converted to NOR gates, and, if an input comes directly into an AND gate, that input must be complemented.

EXAMPLE 2.13

$$g = (x + y')(x' + y)(x' + z')$$

is implemented

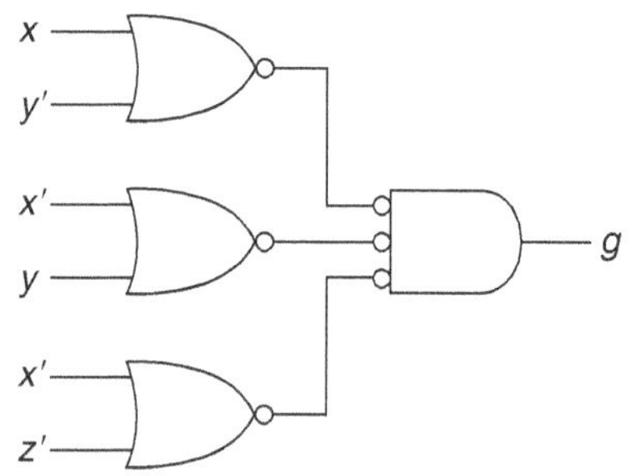

where all gates are NOR gates.

The Exclusive-OR gate implements the expression

$$a'b + ab'$$

which is sometimes written $a \oplus b$. The terminology comes from the definition that $a \oplus b$ is 1 if $a = 1$ (and $b = 0$) **or** if $b = 1$ (and $a = 0$), but not both $a = 1$ and $b = 1$. The operand we have been referring to as OR (+) is sometimes referred to as the Inclusive-OR to distinguish it from the Exclusive-OR. The logic symbol for the Exclusive-OR is similar to that for the OR except that it has a double line on the input, as shown in Figure 2.20a. Also commonly available is the Exclusive-NOR gate, as shown in Figure 2.20b. It is just an Exclusive-OR with a NOT on the output and produces the function

$$(a \oplus b)' = a'b' + ab.$$

This sometimes is referred to as a comparator, since the Exclusive-NOR is 1 if $a = b$, and is 0 if $a \neq b$.

A NAND gate implementation of the Exclusive-OR is shown in Figure 2.21a, where only uncomplemented inputs are assumed.

The two NOT gates (implemented as two-input NANDs) can be replaced by a single gate, as shown in Figure 2.21b, since

$$a(a' + b') + b(a' + b') = aa' + ab' + ba' + bb' = ab' + a'b$$

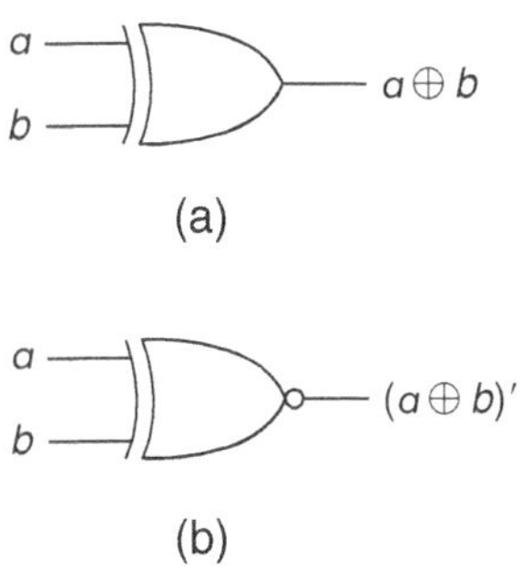

Figure 2.20 (a) An Exclusive-OR gate. (b) An Exclusive-NOR gate.

Figure 2.21 Exclusive-OR gates.

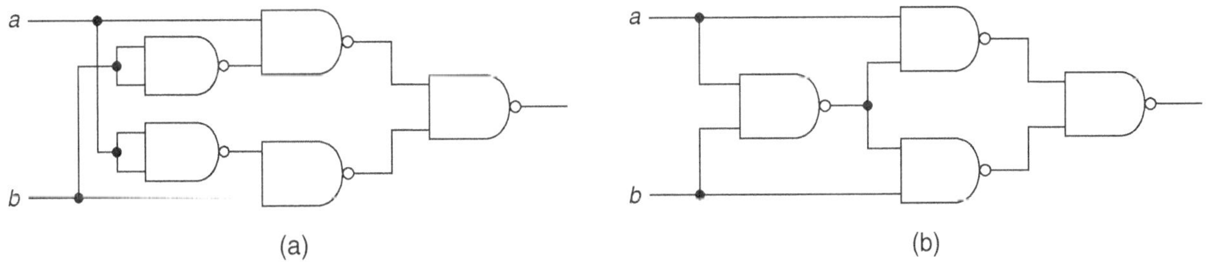

Some useful properties of the Exclusive-OR are

$$(a \oplus b)' = (a'b + ab')' = (a + b')(a' + b) = a'b' + ab$$
$$a' \oplus b = (a')'b + (a')b' = ab + a'b' = (a \oplus b)'$$
$$(a \oplus b') = (a \oplus b)'$$
$$a \oplus 0 = a = (a' \cdot 0 + a \cdot 1)$$
$$a \oplus 1 = a' = (a' \cdot 1 + a \cdot 0)$$

The Exclusive-OR has both the commutative and associative properties, that is,

$$a \oplus b = b \oplus a$$
$$(a \oplus b) \oplus c = a \oplus (b \oplus c)$$

A list of some of the more common NAND, NOR, and Exclusive-OR integrated circuit packages that we may encounter in the laboratory is as follows:

7400 4 (quadruple) two-input NAND gates
7410 3 (triple) three-input NAND gates
7420 2 (dual) four-input NAND gates
7430 1 eight-input NAND gate
7402 4 (quadruple) two-input NOR gates
7427 3 (triple) three-input NOR gates
7486 4 (quadruple) two-input Exclusive-OR gates

To build a circuit, we utilize packages. Even if we only need 1 three-input NAND gate, we must buy a package with three gates on it (a 7410). Recognize, however, that a three-input gate can be used as a two-input gate by connecting two of the inputs together or by connecting one of the inputs to a logic 1.

EXAMPLE 2.14

Consider the following circuit, constructed with ANDs and ORs; the input variables have been omitted because they are irrelevant to the discussion.

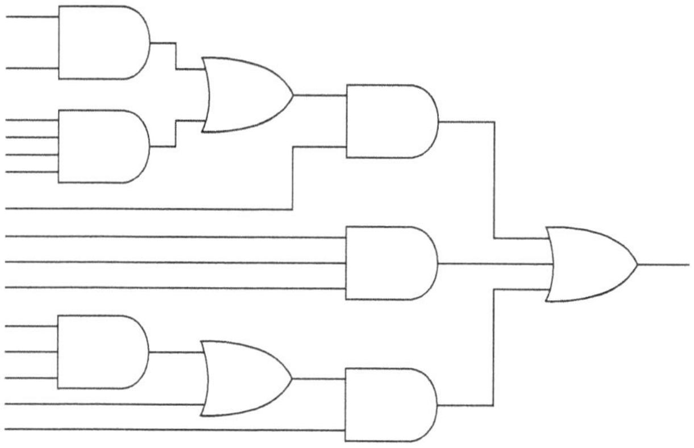

The number of gates and packages are shown in the left part of the following table

	Gates		Packs			
Inputs	AND	OR	AND	OR	NAND	Packs
2	3	2	1		5	1
3	2	1	1	1	3	1
4	1		1		1	1
Total	6	3	3	1	9	3

With AND and OR gates, four packages are needed: three ANDs and one OR package (because the 2 two-input OR gates can be constructed with the leftover three-input gates).

If all of the gates are converted to NANDs (and some of the inputs are complemented) the gate and package count is shown in the right part of the table.

Only three packages are needed. The second four-input gate on the 7420 would be used as the fifth two-input gate (by tying three of the inputs together).

[SP 15, 16, 17; EX 17, 18, 19; LAB]

2.7 SIMPLIFICATION OF ALGEBRAIC EXPRESSIONS*

We have already looked at the process of simplifying algebraic expressions, starting with a sum of minterms or a product of maxterms. The primary tools were

P9a. $ab + ab' = a$ **P9b.** $(a + b)(a + b') = a$

P10a. $a + a'b = a + b$ **P10b.** $a(a' + b) = ab$

although many of the other properties were used, particularly,

P6a. $a + a = a$ **P6b.** $a \cdot a = a$

P8a. $a(b + c) = ab + ac$ **P8b.** $a + bc = (a + b)(a + c)$

If the function is stated in other than one of the standard forms, two other properties are useful. First,

P12a. $a + ab = a$ **P12b.** $a(a + b) = a$ absorption

The proof of P12a uses P3b, P8a, P4aa, and P3b (again).

$$a + ab = a \cdot 1 + ab = a(1 + b) = a \cdot 1 = a$$

Remember that we only need to prove one half of the property, because the dual of a property is always true. However, we could have proven P12b using the duals of each of the theorems we used to prove P12a. Instead, we could distribute the a from the left side of P12b, producing

$$a \cdot a + ab = a + ab$$

However, that is just the left side of P12a, which we have already proved is equal to a.

P10a and P12a look very similar; yet we used two very different approaches to demonstrate their validity. In P10a, we did

$$a + a'b = (a + a')(a + b) = 1 \cdot (a + b) = a + b$$

[P8b, P5a, P3bb]

whereas for P12a, we used P3b, P8a, P4aa, and P3b. How did we know not to start the proof of P11a by using P8b to obtain

$$a + ab = (a + a)(a + b) = a(a + b)?$$

Those steps are all valid, but they do not get us anywhere toward showing that these expressions equal a. Similarly, if we started the proof of P10a by using P3b, that is,

$$a + a'b = a \cdot 1 + a'b$$

*At this point, some instructors prefer to introduce the Karnaugh map. Section 3.1 could be studied next, and the remaining material could be studied along with Appendix A, which shows the relationship between algebraic manipulation and the Karnaugh map.

we also do not get anywhere toward a solution. How does the novice know where to begin? Unfortunately, the answer to that is either trial and error or experience. After solving a number of problems, we can often make the correct guess as to where to start on a new one. If that approach does not work, then we must try another one. This is not much of a problem in trying to demonstrate that two expressions are equal. We know that we can quit when we have worked one side to be the same as the other.

Before proceeding with a number of examples, some comments on the process are in order. There is no algorithm for algebraic simplification, that is, there is no ordered list of properties to apply. On the other hand, of the properties we have up to this point, 12, 9, and 10 are the ones most likely to reduce the number of terms or literals. Another difficulty is that we often do not know when we are finished, that is, what is the minimum. In most of the examples we have worked so far, the final expressions that we obtained appear to be as simple as we can go. However, we will see a number of examples where it is not obvious that there is not a more minimum expression. We will not be able to get around this until Chapter 3 when we develop other simplification methods. (Note that in the Solved Problems and the Exercises, the number of terms and literals in the minimum solution is given. Once that is reached, we know we are done; if we end up with more, we need to try another approach.)

We will now look at several examples of algebraic simplification.

EXAMPLE 2.15

$xyz + x'y + x'y'$

$= xyz + x'$ **[P9a]**

$= x' + yz$ **[P10a]**

where $a = x'$, $a' = x$, and $b = yz$

EXAMPLE 2.16

$wx + wxy + w'yz + w'y'z + w'xyz'$

$= (wx + wxy) + (w'yz + w'y'z) + w'xyz'$

$= wx + w'z + w'xyz'$ **[P12a, P9a]**

$= wx + w'(z + xyz')$

$= wx + w'(z + xy)$ **[P10a]**

$= wx + w'z + w'xy$

$= w'z + x(w + w'y)$

$= w'z + x(w + y)$ **[P10a]**

$= w'z + wx + xy$

P10a could have been used first with wx and $w'xyz'$ (resulting in xyz'). That approach, however, would leave us with an expression

$w'z + wx + xyz'$

for which there are no algebraic clues as to how to proceed. The only way we can now reduce it is to add terms to the expression. Shortly, we will introduce another property that will enable us to go from this expression to the minimum one.

EXAMPLE 2.17

$(x + y)(x + y + z') + y' = (x + y) + y'$ **[P12b]**

$= x + (y + y') = x + 1 = 1$ **[P5a, P4a]**

EXAMPLE 2.18

$(a + b' + c)(a + c')(a' + b' + c)(a + c + d)$

$= (b' + c)(a + c')(a + d)$ **[P9b, P10b]**

where the second simplification really took several steps

$(a + c')(a + c + d) = a + c'(c + d) = a + c'd = (a + c')(a + d)$

One more tool is useful in the algebraic simplification of switching functions. The operator *consensus* (indicated by the symbol ¢) is defined as follows:

For any two product terms where exactly one variable appears uncomplemented in one and complemented in the other, the consensus is defined as the product of the remaining literals. If no such variable exists or if more than one such variable exists, then the consensus is undefined. If we write one term as at_1 and the second as $a't_2$ (where t_1 and t_2 represent product terms), then, if the consensus is defined,

$at_1 \text{ ¢ } a't_2 = t_1t_2$

EXAMPLE 2.19

$ab'c \text{ ¢ } a'd = b'cd$

$ab'c \text{ ¢ } a'cd = b'cd$

$abc' \text{ ¢ } bcd' = abd'$

$b'c'd' \text{ ¢ } b'cd' = b'd'$

$abc' \text{ ¢ } bc'd$ = undefined—no such variable

$a'bd \text{ ¢ } ab'cd$ = undefined—two variables, a and b

We then have the following property that is useful in reducing functions.

P13a. $at_1 + a't_2 + t_1t_2 = at_1 + a't_2$

P13b. $(a + t_1)(a' + t_2)(t_1 + t_2) = (a + t_1)(a' + t_2)$ consensus

P13a states that the consensus term is redundant and can be removed from an SOP expression. (Of course, this property, like all of the others, can be used in the other direction to add a term. We will see an example of that shortly.)

> **COMMON MISTAKE:** The consensus theorem allows you to remove the consensus term (t_1t_2), not the two terms that formed the consensus ($at_1 + a't_2$). For example
>
> $ab + b'c + ac = ab + b'c \neq ac$

A similar kind of simplification can be obtained in POS expressions using the dual (P13b). We will not pursue that further.

First, we will derive this property from the others. Using P12a twice, the right-hand side becomes

$$at_1 + a't_2 = (at_1 + at_1t_2) + (a't_2 + a't_1t_2) \quad \textbf{[P12a]}$$
$$= at_1 + a't_2 + (at_1t_2 + a't_1t_2)$$
$$= at_1 + a't_2 + t_1t_2 \quad \textbf{[P9a]}$$

It is also useful to look at the truth table for this theorem. From Table 2.15, we see that the consensus term, t_1t_2, is 1 only when one of the other terms is already 1. Thus, if we OR that term with RHS, it does not change anything, that is, LHS is the same as RHS.

Table 2.15 Consensus.

a	t_1	t_2	at_1	$a't_2$	RHS	t_1t_2	LHS
0	0	0	0	0	0	0	0
0	0	1	0	1	1	0	1
0	1	0	0	0	0	0	0
0	1	1	0	1	1	1	1
1	0	0	0	0	0	0	0
1	0	1	0	0	0	0	0
1	1	0	1	0	1	0	1
1	1	1	1	0	1	1	1

EXAMPLE 2.20

In Example 2.3 (Section 2.2.3), we reduced the function as

$$f = a'b'c' + a'bc' + a'bc + ab'c'$$

to

$$f_1 = a'c' + a'b + b'c'$$

by combining the first two terms using P9a, and then applying P10a twice. At that point, we were at a dead end. However, we found by starting over with a different grouping that we could reduce this to

$$f_2 = b'c' + a'b$$

Indeed, the term eliminated, $a'c'$, is the consensus of the other terms; we could use P13a to go from f_1 to f_2.

EXAMPLE 2.21

$$g = bc' + abd + acd$$

Because Properties 1 through 12 produce no simplification, we now try consensus. The only consensus term defined is

$$bc' ¢ acd = abd$$

Property 13 now allows us to remove the consensus term. Thus,

$$g = bc' + acd$$

EXAMPLE 2.22

Reduce

$$f = c'd' + ac' + ad + bd' + ab$$

to three terms with six literals. We can use consensus twice.

$$c'd' ¢ ad = ac' \text{ and } ad ¢ bd' = ab$$

Thus, we can remove ac' and ab, leaving

$$f = c'd' + ad + bd'$$

With the following function, there is no way to apply Properties 12, 9 and 10:

$$f = w'y' + w'xz + wxy + wyz'$$

However, we are told that it can be reduced to three terms and eight literals. Next, we try consensus. An approach that ensures that we try to find the consensus of all pairs of terms is to start with consensus of the second term with the first; then try the third with the second and the first; and so forth. Following this approach (or any other) for this example, the only consensus that exists is

$$w'xz ¢ wxy = xyz$$

When a consensus term was part of the SOP expression, P13a allowed us to remove that term and thus simplify the expression. If the consensus term is not one of the terms in the SOP expression, the same property allows us to add it to the expression. Of course, we don't add another term automatically because that makes the expression less minimum. However, we should keep track of such a term, and, as a last resort, consider adding it to the function. Then, see if that term can be used to form other consensus terms and thus reduce the function. In this example, by adding xyz, f becomes

$$f = w'y' + w'xz + wxy + wyz' + xyz$$

Now, however,

$$xyz ¢ wyz' = wxy \quad \text{and} \quad xyz ¢ w'y' = w'xz$$

Thus, we can remove both wxy and $w'xz$, leaving

$$f = w'y' + wyz' + xyz \quad \text{(3 terms, 8 literals)}$$

We will now consider an example making use of consensus, as well as all of the other properties. The usual approach is to try to utilize properties 12, 9, and then 10. When we get as far as we can with these, we then turn to consensus.

EXAMPLE 2.23

$$A'BCD + A'BC'D + B'EF + CDE'G + A'DEF + AB'EF$$
$$= A'BD + B'EF + CDE'G + A'DEF \qquad \text{[P12a, P9a]}$$

But $A'BD ¢ B'EF = A'DEF$ and this reduces to

$$A'BD + B'EF + CDE'G$$

EXAMPLE 2.24

$w'xy + wz + xz + w'y'z + w'xy' + wx'z$

$= wz + w'x + xz + w'y'z$ **[P12a, P9a]**

$= wz + w'x + w'y'z$ since $wz ¢ w'x = xz$ **[P13a]**

But,

$wz + w'y'z = z(w + w'y') = z(w + y')$ **[P10a]**

$= wz + w'x + y'z$

[SP 18; EX 20, 21, 22]

2.8 MANIPULATION OF ALGEBRAIC FUNCTIONS AND NAND GATE IMPLEMENTATIONS

In addition to the need to minimize algebraic expressions, there is sometimes the requirement to put an expression in a certain format, such as SOP, sum of minterms, POS, or product of maxterms. Secondly, to meet design constraints, we sometimes must manipulate the algebra. In this section we will look at some examples and introduce one more property.

If we have an SOP expression and need to expand it to sum of minterms, we have two options. First, we can create a truth table, and, from that, follow the approach of Section 2.5 to produce a sum of minterms. Indeed, this approach will work for an expression in any format. The other approach is to use P9a to add variables to a term.

EXAMPLE 2.25

$f = bc + ac + ab$

$= bca + bca' + ac + ab$

We can repeat the process on the other two terms, producing

$f = bca + bca' + acb + acb' + abc + abc'$

$= abc + a'bc + abc + ab'c + abc + abc'$

$= a'bc + ab'c + abc' + abc$

where P6a was used to remove the duplicate terms.

If two literals were missing from a term, that term would produce four minterms, using P9a repeatedly.

EXAMPLE 2.26

$g = x' + xyz = x'y + x'y' + xyz$

$= x'yz + x'yz' + x'y'z + x'y'z' + xyz$

$g(x, y, z) = \Sigma m(3, 2, 1, 0, 7) = \Sigma m(0, 1, 2, 3, 7)$

since minterm numbers are usually written in numeric order.

To convert to product of maxterms, P9b can be used. For example,

EXAMPLE 2.27

$$f = (A + B + C)(A' + B')$$
$$= (A + B + C)(A' + B' + C)(A' + B' + C')$$

One other property is useful in manipulating functions from one form to another.

P14a. $ab + a'c = (a + c)(a' + b)$

(The dual of this is also true; but it is the same property with the variables b and c interchanged.) This property can be demonstrated by first applying P8a to the right side three times:

$$(a + c)(a' + b) = (a + c)a' + (a + c)b = aa' + a'c + ab + bc$$

However, $aa' = 0$ and $bc = a'c ¢ ab$, and thus, using P3aa and P13a, we get

$$aa' + a'c + ab + bc = a'c + ab$$

which is equal to the left side of the property.

This property is particularly useful in converting POS expressions to SOP and vice versa. We will also use it to manipulate expressions when using NAND gates to implement systems.

In Example 2.7, we found the sum of minterms and the minimum SOP expressions, as well as the product of maxterms and the minimum POS expression for

$$f(A, B, C) = \Sigma m(1, 2, 3, 4, 5)$$

In Example 2.28, we will start with the minimum POS, and use Property 14 to convert it to a SOP.

EXAMPLE 2.28

$$f = (A + B + C)(A' + B') = AB' + A'(B + C) = AB' + A'B + A'C$$

where the a of P14a is A, the b is $B + C$, and the c is B'. This, indeed, is one of the SOP solutions we found in Example 2.7 for this problem. Although the utilization of this property does not always produce a minimum SOP expression (as it does in this case), it does produce a simpler expression than we would get just using P8a.

$$f = AA' + AB' + BA' + BB' + CA' + CB'$$
$$= AB' + A'B + A'C + B'C$$

The term $B'C$ can then be removed because it is the consensus of AB' and $A'C$.

To go from a POS expression (or a more general expression that is neither SOP nor POS) to an SOP expression, we use primarily the following three properties:

P8b. $a + bc = (a + b)(a + c)$

P14a. $ab + a'c = (a + c)(a' + b)$

P8a. $a(b + c) = ab + ac$

We try to apply them in that order, using the first two from right to left.

EXAMPLE 2.29

$$(A + B' + C)(A + B + D)(A' + C' + D')$$
$$= [A + (B' + C)(B + D)](A' + C' + D') \quad \textbf{[P8b]}$$
$$= (A + B'D + BC)(A' + C' + D') \quad \textbf{[P14a]}$$
$$= A(C' + D') + A'(B'D + BC) \quad \textbf{[P14a]}$$
$$= AC' + AD' + A'B'D + A'BC \quad \textbf{[P8a]}$$

The dual of these properties can be used to convert to POS as can be seen in Example 2.30.

EXAMPLE 2.30

$$wxy' + xyz + w'x'z'$$
$$= x(wy' + yz) + w'x'z' \quad \textbf{[P8a]}$$
$$= x(y' + z)(y + w) + w'x'z' \quad \textbf{[P14a]}$$
$$= (x + w'z')[x' + (y' + z)(y + w)] \quad \textbf{[P14a]}$$
$$= (x + w')(x + z')(x' + y' + z)(x' + y + w) \quad \textbf{[P8b]}$$

Another application of P14a and this type of algebraic manipulation comes when we wish to implement functions using only two-input NAND or NOR gates (or two- and three-input gates). (We will only consider examples of NAND gate implementations.) Consider the following problem.

The following expression is the only minimum SOP expression for the function f. Assume all inputs are available both uncomplemented and complemented. Find a NAND gate circuit that uses only two-input gates. No gate may be used as a NOT gate.*

$$f = ab'c' + a'c'd' + bd$$

(A two-level solution would require four gates, three of which would be three-input gates, and 11 gate inputs.)

---

*We could always produce a circuit using two-input gates by replacing a three-input gate by 2 twos and a NOT. For example, a three-input NAND could be implemented as follows:

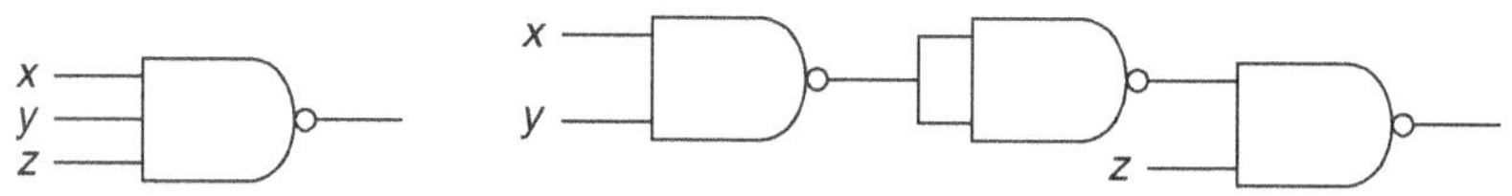

Larger gates could be replaced in a similar fashion. But this approach almost always leads to circuits with more gates than are necessary.

To solve this problem, we must eliminate three-input gates. Thus, the starting point is to attempt to factor something from the three literal terms. In this example, there is a common c' in the first two terms, and we can thus obtain

$$f = c'(ab' + a'd') + bd$$

This, indeed, solves the whole problem in one step because not only did we reduce the 2 three-input product terms to two inputs each, but we also got the final OR to a two-input one. Thus, the resulting circuit is shown in Figure 2.22, where we first implemented it with AND and OR gates and then, starting at the output, added double inverters in each path from the input of an OR back to the output of an AND. (In this example, no inputs came directly into an OR.) This solution requires 6 gates and 12 inputs. It should be noted that either solution, this one or the two-level one mentioned earlier requires two integrated circuit packages. This requires two 7400s (4 two-input NANDs each) and would leave two of the gates unused. The two-level solution would require a 7410 (3 three-input gates) and a 7400 for the remaining two-input gate and would leave three of those gates unused. (If we had replaced each three-input gate by 2 two-input ones plus a NOT, the implementation would require 7 two-input gates plus three NOT gates.)

Figure 2.22 A two-input NAND gate circuit.

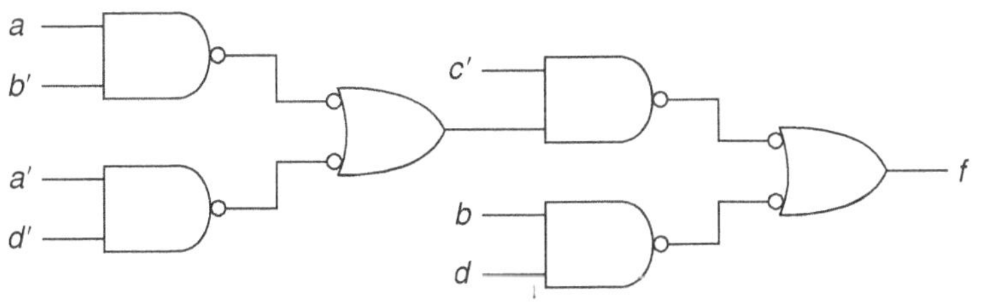

More complex examples of finding a two-input gate implementation often require the use of P14a as well as P8a. Consider the function in Examples 2.31 and 2.32 (already in minimum sum of products form).

EXAMPLE 2.31

$$f = w'y'z + wz' + wx + wy$$

We cannot factor anything from the three-literal term (since there is no w', y', or z in the other terms). We can factor w from any two of the others (not all three because that would leave a term $z' + x + y$).

$$f = (w'y'z + wz') + w(x + y)$$

We can then use Property 14. One of the solutions is

$$f = (w' + z')(w + y'z) + w(x + y)$$

The circuit implementing this is shown below, where the crossed out inputs were those that would have been into an OR.

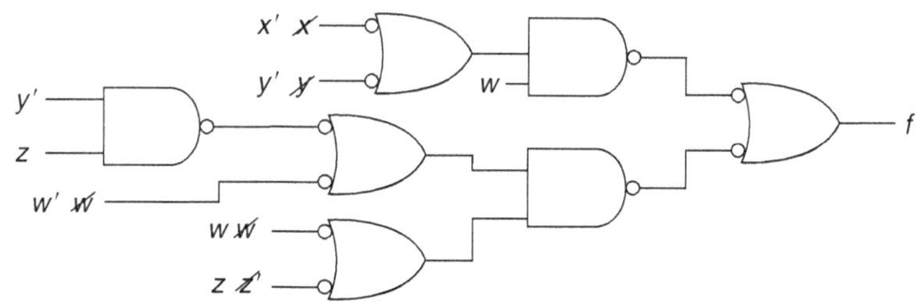

EXAMPLE 2.32

$$G = DE' + A'B'C' + CD'E + ABC'E$$

The four-literal product term is the first place we must attack. We could factor E from the last two terms. That would produce

$$G = DE' + A'B'C' + E(CD' + ABC')$$

But now, there is no way of eliminating the three-input gate corresponding to $A'B'C'$. Instead, we can factor C' from the second and the fourth terms, producing

$$G = C'(A'B' + ABE) + DE' + CD'E$$

We can apply P14a to the expression within the parentheses to get

$$G = C'(A' + BE)(A + B') + DE' + CD'E$$

or, using B instead of A,

$$G = C'(B' + AE)(B + A') + DE' + CD'E$$

In either case, we still have 2 three-input AND terms, that first product and the last one. (We cannot take the output of the OR gate that forms $B' + AE$ and the output of the OR gate that forms $B + A'$ and connect them to a two-input AND gate. We would then need to connect the output of that AND gate to the input of another AND gate with C' as its other input. This would violate the third rule for conversion to NAND gates—the inputs to AND gates may not come from the output of another AND gate.) We can reduce it to all two-input gates by applying P14a again, using the C' from the first complex term and the C from the last product term, producing (from the second version) the following expression:

$$G = (C' + D'E)[C + (B' + AE)(B + A')] + DE'$$

This requires 10 gates, as shown in the following NAND gate circuit.

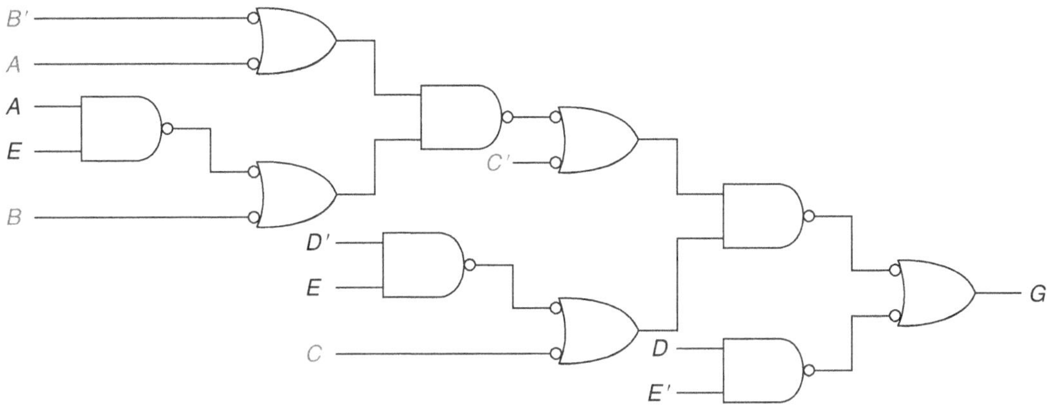

Again, we began by implementing the circuit with ANDs and ORs, starting at the innermost parentheses. Five of the inputs went directly to OR gates and were thus complemented (as shown in brown in the circuit).

There is still another approach to manipulating this algebra.

$$G = C'(A' + BE)(A + B') + DE' + CD'E$$
$$= C'(A' + BE)(A + B') + (D + CE)(D' + E')$$
$$= (A' + BE)(AC' + B'C') + (D + CE)(D' + E')$$

In this case, we eliminated the three-input AND by distributing the C' (P8a) and used P14a on the last two product terms. We will leave the implementation of this as an exercise, but we can count 11 gates (one more than before) from the algebraic expression, as seen from the following count.

$$G = (A' + BE)(AC' + B'C') + (D + CE)(D' + E')$$

1 2 3 4 5 6 7 8 9 10 11

where each gate is numbered below the operator corresponding to that gate.

As an example of sharing a gate, consider the implementation of the following function with two-input NAND gates:

EXAMPLE 2.33

$$G = C'D' + ABC' + A'C + B'C$$
$$= C'(D' + AB) + C(A' + B')$$

The circuit for that expression is shown next.

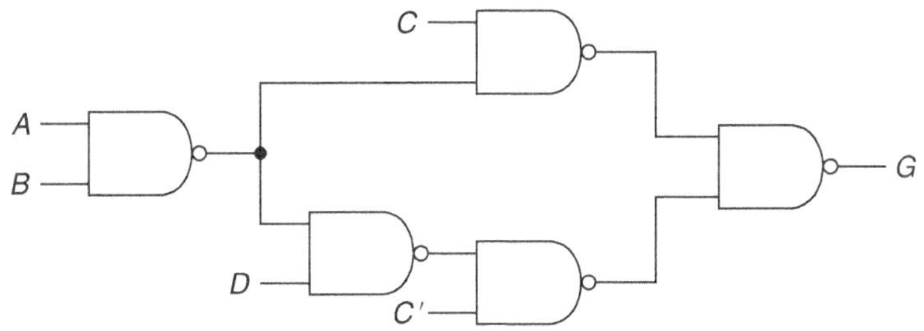

Note that only one NAND gate is needed for the product term AB and for the sum term $A' + B'$ (because inputs coming directly to an OR are complemented).

As a final example, we will return to the implementation of the full adder (CE3). The SOP expressions developed in Example 2.11 are repeated (where the carry input, c_{in}, is represented by just c).

EXAMPLE 2.34

$$s = a'b'c + a'bc' + ab'c' + abc$$

$$c_{out} = bc + ac + ab$$

A two-level implementation of these would require 1 four-input NAND gate (for s), 5 three-input NAND gates (four for s and one for c_{out}), and 3 two-input NANDs (for c_{out}), assuming all inputs are available both uncomplemented and complemented. But this assumption is surely not valid for c because that is just the output of combinational logic just like this (from the next less significant bit of the sum). Thus, we need at least one NOT gate (for c') and possibly three (one for each input). The implementation of this adder would thus require four integrated circuit packages (one 7420, two 7410s, and one 7400). (There would be one gate left over of each size, which could be used to create whatever NOTs are needed.)

Although s and c_{out} are in minimum SOP form, we can manipulate the algebra to reduce the gate requirements by first factoring c from two terms of s and from two terms of c_{out}, and factoring c' from the other two terms of s, yielding*

$$s = c(a'b' + ab) + c'(ab' + a'b)$$

$$c_{out} = c(a + b) + ab$$

This requires 11 two-input NAND gates, not including the three NOTs (because ab need only be implemented once for the two terms and $a + b$ is implemented using the same gate as $a'b'$).

Returning to the expression for sum, note that

$$s = c(a \oplus b)' + c'(a \oplus b) = c \oplus (a \oplus b)$$

Furthermore, we could write

$$c_{out} = c(a \oplus b) + ab$$

(That is a little algebraic trick that is not obvious from any of the properties. However, the difference between $a + b$ and $a \oplus b$ is that the former is

*We could just as easily factor b and b' or a and a' from these expressions; the resulting circuits would have the same layout of gates.

1 when both a and b are 1, but the latter is not. But the expression for c_{out} is 1 for $a = b = 1$ because of the ab term.)

Using these last two expressions, we could implement both the sum and carry using two Exclusive-ORs and 3 two-input NANDs as follows:

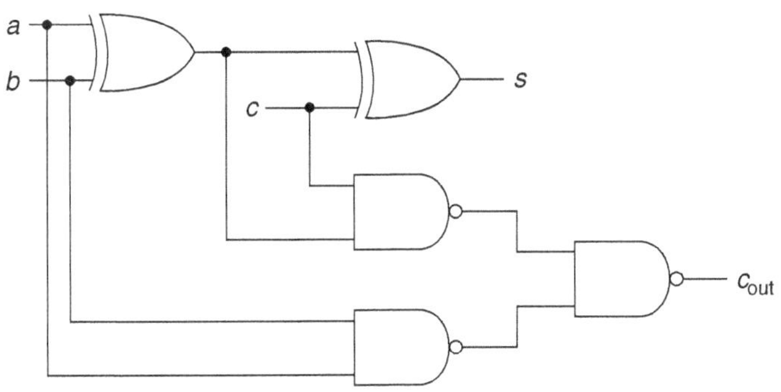

Packages with four Exclusive-OR gates are available (7486) and thus this circuit could be implemented with one of those packages and one 7400. Note that complemented inputs are not necessary for this implementation.

Finally, because we can implement each Exclusive-OR with 4 two-input NAND gates, without requiring complemented inputs, we obtain

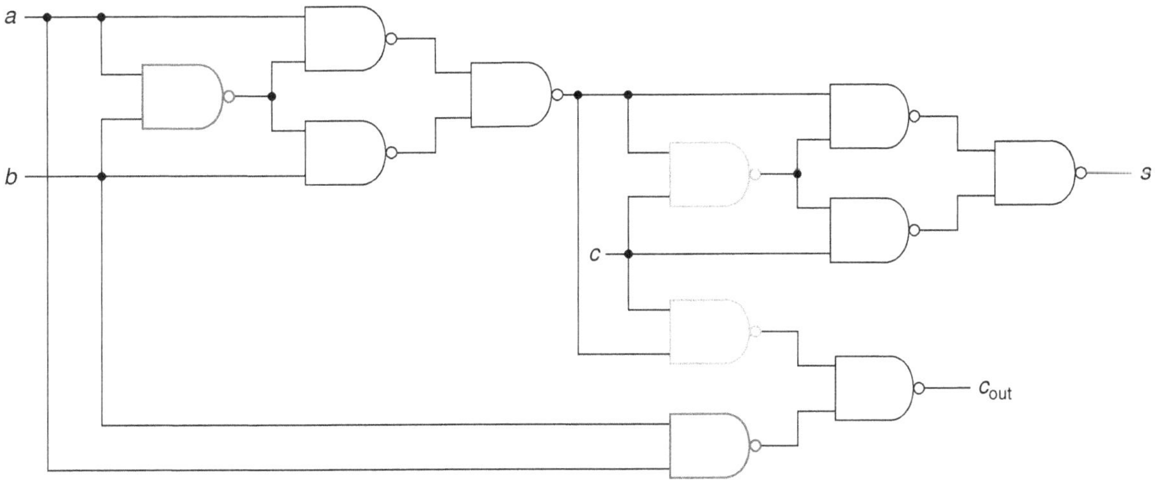

Note that the two brown NAND gates have the same inputs and the two tan ones also have the same inputs. Only one copy of each is necessary, yielding the final circuit with only nine NAND gates.

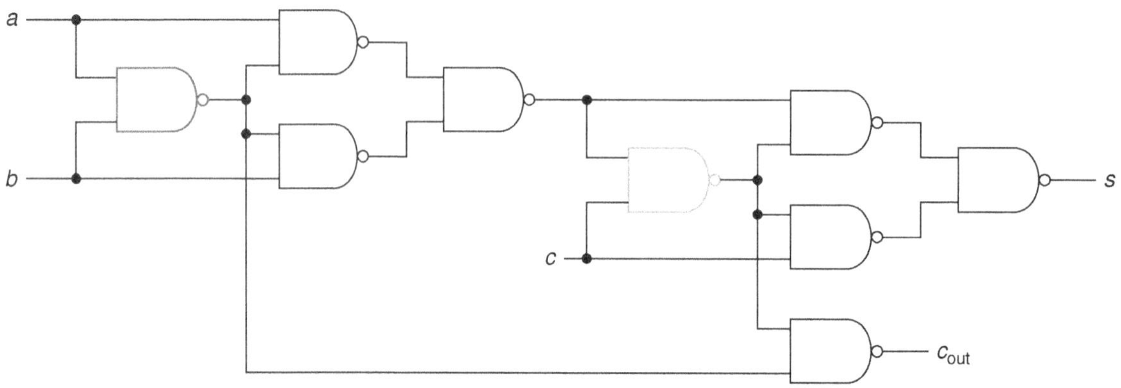

This implementation would require three 7400s if we were only building one bit of an adder. However, a 4-bit adder could be built with nine packages (36 two-input gates).

[SP 19, 20, 21, 22, 23, 24; EX 22, 23, 24, 25, 26, 27; LAB]

2.9 A MORE GENERAL BOOLEAN ALGEBRA

The basis for switching algebra is *Boolean algebra,* first published by George Boole in 1849. It allows more than two elements. It is defined in terms of a set of postulates and then the remaining properties are developed from them as theorems. The postulates have been stated in a variety of ways, but the following development seems most straightforward. Indeed, several of these postulates are identical in form to the properties of switching algebra listed in Sections 2.2.1 and 2.2.2. But there, we began with the definition of the operators (limited to a two-valued algebra) and proved the properties either directly from the definition or by way of a truth table. Here, the operators are not defined, but can be derived from the postulates.

1. A Boolean algebra consists of a set of $k \geq 2$ elements. (For the switching algebra developed in Section 2.2.1, $k = 2$.)
2. There are two binary operators, + and ·, and one unary operator, ′.
3. The algebra is closed, that is, if a and b are members of the set, then

   $$a + b, a \cdot b, a'$$

   are also members of the set. (This property is not true of all operators and all sets in normal algebra. For example, if the set is the set of positive integers, subtraction is not closed since it may result in a negative integer, and division is not closed since the quotient may be a noninteger.)

4. Commutative law (same as P1):
   i. $a + b = b + a$
   ii. $a \cdot b = b \cdot a$

5. Associative law (same as P2):
   i. $a + (b + c) = (a + b) + c$
   ii. $a \cdot (b \cdot c) = (a \cdot b) \cdot c$

6. Distributive law (same as P8):
   i. $a + b \cdot c = (a + b) \cdot (a + c)$
   ii. $a \cdot (b + c) = a \cdot b + a \cdot c$

7. Identity (similar to P3):
   i. There exists a unique element in the set, 0, such that $a + 0 = a$
   ii. There exists a unique element in the set, 1, such that $a \cdot 1 = a$

8. Complement (same as P5): For each element a, there exists a unique element a' such that
   i. $a + a' = 1$
   ii. $a \cdot a' = 0$

We have now defined Boolean algebra. It works for a two-valued system (the switching algebra we have been discussing throughout this chapter) as well as a more general one.

For switching algebra, we can use these postulates to define the operators. First, we can recognize that there are the two elements, 0 and 1, postulated in number 7. Using that postulate and the commutative law, we can complete the first three lines of Table 2.16a for the OR (+) operator and the last three for the AND(·). For the OR, the postulate

Table 2.16a Defining OR and AND.

a	b	$a + b$	$a \cdot b$
0	0	0	
0	1	1	0
1	0	1	0
1	1		1

$$a + 0 = a$$

implies that $0 + 0 = 0$ (first line) and $1 + 0 = 1$ (third line). In addition, using the commutative law, we get

$$0 + a = a$$

and thus the second line is completed ($0 + 1 = 1$).

Using the other part of postulate 7, we get $0 \cdot 1 = 0$, $1 \cdot 1 = 1$, and with the commutative property, $1 \cdot 0 = 0$. For the remaining lines, we need to prove the idempotency property (P6 from before). We can do that in the following steps:

$$a + a = (a + a) \cdot 1 \quad [7ii]$$
$$= (a + a) \cdot (a + a') \quad [8i]$$
$$= a + a \cdot a' \quad [6i]$$
$$= a + 0 \quad [8ii]$$
$$= a \quad [7i]$$

Using this theorem, we can complete the first row of the OR truth table $(0 + 0 = 0)$. We can prove the dual of this theorem,

$$a \cdot a = a$$

using the other half of each of the postulates and thus complete the last line of the AND Table 2.16b $(1 \cdot 1 = 1)$.

Table 2.16b Completed definition of OR and AND.

a	b	$a + b$	$a \cdot b$
0	0	0	0
0	1	1	0
1	0	1	0
1	1	1	1

Finally, we can define the NOT (′) operator from postulate 8. Part i says that either a or a' (or both) is 1; part ii says that either a or a' (or both) is 0. Thus, one of them must be 1 and the other 0, that is, if $a = 0$, then a' must be 1, and if $a = 1$, then a' must be 0.

From here, we can prove all of the properties of switching algebra as before. Most of them are also properties of a general Boolean algebra, but that is beyond the scope of this book.

2.10 SOLVED PROBLEMS

1. For each of the following problems, there are four inputs, A, B, C, and D. Show a truth table for the functions specified. (One truth table with four outputs is shown for the four examples.)
   - **a.** The inputs represent a 4-bit unsigned binary number. The output, W, is 1 if and only if the number is a multiple of 2 or of 3 but not both.
   - **b.** The inputs represent a 4-bit positive binary number. The output, X, is 0 if and only if the input is a prime (where 0 never occurs).
   - **c.** The first two inputs (A, B) represent a 2-bit unsigned binary number (in the range 0 to 3). The last two (C, D) represent a second unsigned binary number (in the same range). The output, Y, is 1 if and only if the two numbers differ by two or more.
   - **d.** The inputs represent a BCD number in Excess-3 code. Those combinations that do not represent one of the digits never occur. The output, Z, is 1 if and only if that number is a perfect square.

The truth table contains the answer to all four parts.

A	B	C	D	W	X	Y	Z
0	0	0	0	0	X	0	X
0	0	0	1	0	0	0	X
0	0	1	0	1	0	1	X
0	0	1	1	1	0	1	1
0	1	0	0	1	1	0	1
0	1	0	1	0	0	0	0
0	1	1	0	0	1	0	0
0	1	1	1	0	0	1	1
1	0	0	0	1	1	1	0
1	0	0	1	1	1	0	0
1	0	1	0	1	1	0	0
1	0	1	1	0	0	0	0
1	1	0	0	0	1	1	1
1	1	0	1	0	0	1	X
1	1	1	0	1	1	0	X
1	1	1	1	1	1	0	X

a. It doesn't matter whether one considers 0 a multiple of 2 or 3 because it is either a multiple of neither or of both. In both cases, $W = 0$. For the next row, 1 is not a multiple of either 2 or 3; thus, $W = 0$. For the next three rows $W = 1$ because 2 and 4 are multiples of 2, but not 3, and 3 is a multiple of 3, but not 2. Both 5 and 7 are multiples of neither and 6 is a multiple of both; thus, for the next three rows, $W = 0$. Then, 8, 10, and 14 are multiples of only 2; 9 and 15 are multiples of only 3; all of these produce an output of 1. The others produce an output of 0 (12 is a multiple of both 2 and 3).

b. A prime number is one that is evenly divisible only by 1 or itself. Note that the problem specifies that the output is 0 for primes and is thus 1 for numbers that are not prime. The first nonprime is 4 (2×2). Indeed, all of the even numbers (other than 2) are nonprimes. Because 0 never occurs, the output for the first row is a don't care.

c. For the first four rows, the first number is 0. It is compared on successive rows with 0, 1, 2, and 3. Only 2 and 3 differ from 0 by 2 or more. In the next group of four rows, the first number is 1; it only differs from 3 by 2 or more. In the next four rows, 2 differs only from 0 by 2 or more. Finally, in the last 4 rows, 3 differs from 0 and 1 by 2 or more.

d. A perfect square is an integer obtained by multiplying some integer by itself. Thus, 0, 1, 4, and 9 are perfect squares. Note that the first three rows and the last three rows are all don't cares because those input combinations never occur.

2. The system is a speed warning device. It receives, on two lines, an indication of the speed limit on the highway. There are three possible values: 45, 55, or 65 mph. It receives from the automobile, on two other lines, an indication of the speed of the vehicle. There are four possible values: under 45, between 46 and 55, between 56 and 65, and over 65 mph. It produces two outputs. The first, *f*, indicates whether the car is going above the speed limit. The second, *g*, indicates that the car is driving at a "dangerous speed"—defined as either over 65 mph or more than 10 mph above the speed limit. Show how each of the inputs and outputs are coded (in terms of binary values) and complete the truth table for this system.

The first step is to code the inputs. We chose (arbitrarily) what is shown in the following tables.

Speed limit	*a*	*b*
45	0	0
55	0	1
65	1	0
unused	1	1

Speed	*c*	*d*
<45	0	0
46–55	0	1
56–65	1	0
>65	1	1

The outputs will be 1 if the car is speeding or driving dangerously.

	a	*b*	*c*	*d*	*f*	*g*
	0	0	0	0	0	0
45	0	0	0	1	1	0
	0	0	1	0	1	1
	0	0	1	1	1	1
	0	1	0	0	0	0
55	0	1	0	1	0	0
	0	1	1	0	1	0
	0	1	1	1	1	1
	1	0	0	0	0	0
65	1	0	0	1	0	0
	1	0	1	0	0	0
	1	0	1	1	1	1
	1	1	0	0	X	X
	1	1	0	1	X	X
	1	1	1	0	X	X
	1	1	1	1	X	X

3. Show a block diagram of a circuit using AND and OR gates for each side of P8b: $a + bc = (a + b)(a + c)$

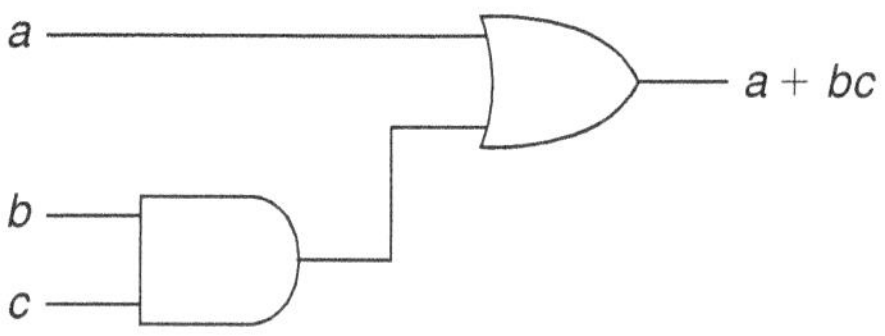

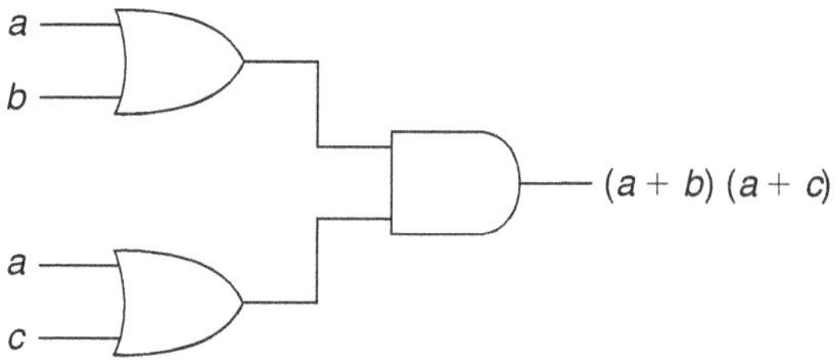

4. Show a truth table for the following functions:

a. $F = XY' + YZ + X'Y'Z'$

b. $G = X'Y + (X + Z')(Y + Z)$

(a)

XYZ	XY'	YZ	$X'Y'Z'$	F
000	0	0	1	1
001	0	0	0	0
010	0	0	0	0
011	0	1	0	1
100	1	0	0	1
101	1	0	0	1
110	0	0	0	0
111	0	1	0	1

(b)

XYZ	$X'Y$	$X + Z'$	$Y + Z$	$()()$	G
000	0	1	0	0	0
001	0	0	1	0	0
010	1	1	1	1	1
011	1	0	1	0	1
100	0	1	0	0	0
101	0	1	1	1	1
110	0	1	1	1	1
111	0	1	1	1	1

5. Determine, using truth tables, whether or not each of the groups of expressions are equal:

a. $f = a'c' + a'b + ac$

$g = bc + ac + a'c'$

b. $f = P'Q' + PR + Q'R$

$g = Q' + PQR$

(a)

abc	$a'c'$	$a'b$	ac	f	bc	ac	$a'c'$	g
000	1	0	0	1	0	0	1	1
001	0	0	0	0	0	0	0	0
010	1	1	0	1	0	0	1	1
011	0	1	0	1	1	0	0	1
100	0	0	0	0	0	0	0	0
101	0	0	1	1	0	1	0	1
110	0	0	0	0	0	0	0	0
111	0	0	1	1	1	1	0	1

The two functions are equal.

(b)

PQR	$P'Q'$	PR	$Q'R$	f	Q'	PQR	g	
000	1	0	0	1	1	0	1	
001	1	0	1	1	1	0	1	
010	0	0	0	0	0	0	0	
011	0	0	0	0	0	0	0	
100	0	0	0	0	1	0	1	←
101	0	1	1	1	1	0	1	
110	0	0	0	0	0	0	0	
111	0	1	0	1	0	1	1	

Note that for row 100 (marked with a brown arrow), $f = 0$ and $g = 1$. Thus, the two functions are different.

6. For each of the following expressions, indicate which (if any) of the following apply (more than one may apply):

i. Product term

ii. Sum of products expression

iii. Sum term

iv. Product of sums expression

a. ab'

b. $a'b + ad$

c. $(a + b)(c + a'd)$

d. $a' + b'$

e. $(a + b')(b + c)(a' + c + d)$

a. i. product of two literals

ii. sum of one product term

iv. product of two sum terms

b. ii. sum of two product terms

c. none; second term is not a sum term

d. ii. sum of two product terms

iii. sum of two literals

iv. product of one sum term

e. iv. product of three sum terms

7. In the expressions of problem 6, how many literals are in each?

a. 2 **b.** 4 **c.** 5 **d.** 2 **e.** 7

8. Using Properties 1 to 10, reduce the following expressions to a minimum SOP form. Show each step (number of terms and number of literals in minimum shown in parentheses).

a. $xyz' + xyz$ (1 term, 2 literals)

b. $x'y'z' + x'y'z + x'yz + xy'z + xyz$ (2 terms, 3 literals)

c. $f = abc' + ab'c + a'bc + abc$ (3 terms, 6 literals)

a. $xyz' + xyz = xy(z' + z) = xy \cdot 1 = xy$ **[P8a, P5aa, P3b]**

or, in one step, using P9a, where $a = xy$ and $b = z'$

b. $x'y'z' + x'y'z + x'yz + xy'z + xyz$

Make two copies of $x'y'z$

$= (x'y'z' + x'y'z) + (x'y'z + x'yz) + (xy'z + xyz)$ **[P6a]**
$= x'y'(z' + z) + x'z(y' + y) + xz(y' + y)$ **[P8a]**
$= x'y' \cdot 1 + x'z \cdot 1 + xz \cdot 1$ **[P5aa]**
$= x'y' + x'z + xz$ **[P3b]**
$= x'y' + (x' + x)z = x'y' + 1 \cdot z$ **[P8a, P5aa]**
$= x'y' + z$ **[P3bb]**

or, without using P6a,

$= (x'y'z' + x'y'z) + x'yz + (xy'z + xyz)$
$= x'y' + x'yz + xz$ **[P9a]**
$= x'(y' + yz) + xz$ **[P8a]**
$= x'(y' + z) + xz$ **[P10a]**
$= x'y' + x'z + xz$ **[P8a]**
$= x'y' + z$ **[P9a]**

Note that we could follow a path that does not lead us to the correct answer, by combining the last two terms in the second line of this second sequence, yielding

$= x'y' + z(x'y + x)$
$= x'y' + z(y + x)$ **[P10a]**
$= x'y' + yz + xz$ **[P8a]**

This is a dead end. It has more terms than the minimum (which was given) and we do not have the tools (in Properties 1 to 10) to reduce this further without backing up to the original expression (or, at least, the first reduction). We should then go back and start again.

c. There are two approaches to this problem. In the first, we note that *abc* can be combined with each of the other terms. Thus, we make three copies of it, using

$abc = abc + abc + abc$ **[P6a]**
$f = (abc' + abc) + (ab'c + abc) + (a'bc + abc)$
$= ab + ac + bc$ **[P9a]**

In the second approach, we just use *abc* to combine with the term next to it, producing

$f = abc' + ab'c + a'bc + abc = abc' + ab'c + bc$ **[P9a]**
$= abc' + c(b + b'a) = abc' + c(b + a)$
$= abc' + bc + ac$ **[P10a]**
$= a(c + c'b) + bc = a(c + b) + bc$
$= ac + ab + bc$ **[P10a]**

or, in place of the last two lines,

$= b(c + c'a) + ac = b(c + a) + ac$

$= bc + ab + ac$ **[P10a]**

In this approach, we used P10a twice to eliminate a literal from the second term and then the first. We could have done it in any order. Indeed, there were two ways to do the last step (as shown on the last two lines).

9. Using Properties 1 to 10, reduce the following expressions to a minimum POS form. Show each step (number of terms and number of literals in parentheses).

a. $(a + b' + c)\,(a + b' + c')\,(a' + b + c)\,(a' + b' + c)$ (2 terms, 4 literals)

b. $(x' + y' + z')\,(x' + y + z')\,(x' + y + z)$ (2 terms, 4 literals)

a. We group the first two and the last two terms, and use Property 9b

$[(a + b' + c)(a + b' + c')][(a' + b + c)(a' + b' + c)] =$
$[a + b'][a' + c]$

b. We can make a second copy of the middle term and group it with each of the others

$(x' + y' + z')(x' + y + z')(x' + y + z)$
$= [(x' + y' + z')(x' + y + z')][(x' + y + z)(x' + y + z')]$
$= [x' + z'][x' + y]$

If we don't make the second copy, we get

$[x' + z'](x' + y + z)$

We can then use P8b to get

$x' + z'(y + z) = x' + yz'$ **[P8a, P5bb, P3a]**

$= (x' + y)(x' + z)$ **[P8b]**

10. Show a block diagram of a system using AND, OR, and NOT gates to implement the following function. Assume that variables are available only uncomplemented. Do not manipulate the algebra.

$F = [A\,(B + C)' + BDE](A' + CE)$

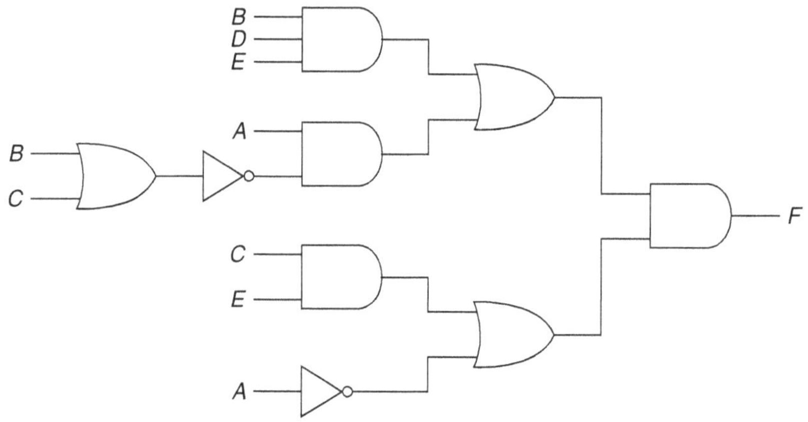

11. For each of the following circuits,

i. find an algebraic expression.

ii. put it in SOP form.

a.

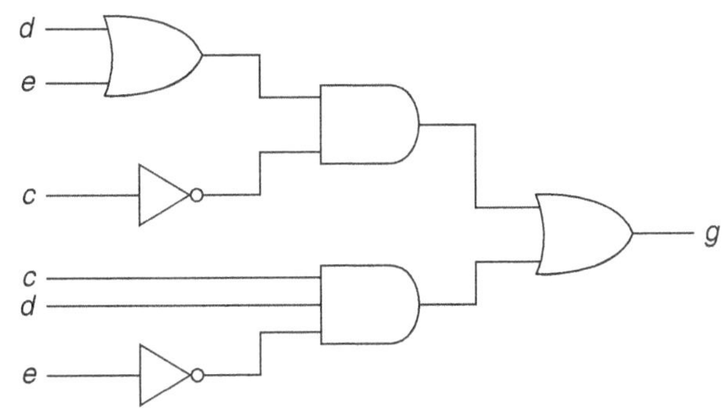

b.

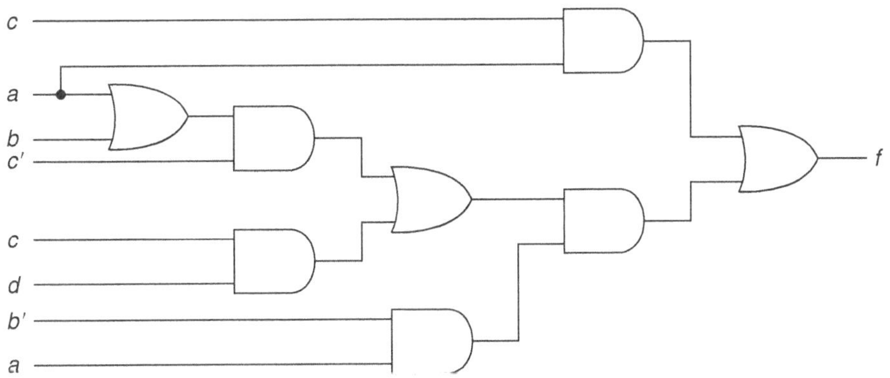

a. i. $g = (d + e)c' + cde'$

ii. $g = c'd + c'e + cde'$

b. i. $f = ac + ab'[cd + c'(a + b)]$

ii. $f = ac + ab'cd + ab'c' + ab'c'b$

$= ac + ab'cd + ab'c'$

$= ac + ab'cd + ab'$* **[P10a]**

12. Find the complement of the following expressions. Only single variables may be complemented in the answer.

a. $f = x'yz' + xy'z' + xyz$

b. $g = (w + x' + y)(w' + x + z)(w + x + y + z)$

c. $h = (a + b'c)d' + (a' + c')(c + d)$

a. $f' = (x + y' + z)(x' + y + z)(x' + y' + z')$

SOP becomes POS.

* We will see later that this can be reduced even further.

b. $g' = w'xy' + wx'z' + w'x'y'z'$

POS becomes SOP.

c. $h' = [a'(b + c') + d][ac + c'd']$

or, step by step

$$
\begin{aligned}
h' &= [(a + b'c)d']'[(a' + c')(c + d)]' \\
&= [(a + b'c)' + d][(a' + c')' + (c + d)'] \\
&= [a'(b'c)' + d][ac + c'd'] \\
&= [a'(b + c') + d][ac + c'd']
\end{aligned}
$$

13. For the following truth table,

a	*b*	*c*	*f*
0	0	0	0
0	0	1	1
0	1	0	0
0	1	1	1
1	0	0	1
1	0	1	0
1	1	0	1
1	1	1	1

a. Show the minterms in numerical form.

b. Show an algebraic expression in sum of minterm form.

c. Show a minimum SOP expression (two solutions, three terms, six literals each).

d. Show the minterms of f' (complement of f) in numeric form.

e. Show an algebraic expression for f in product of maxterm form.

f. Show a minimum POS expression for f (two terms, five literals).

a. $f(a, b, c) + \Sigma m(1, 3, 4, 6, 7)$

b. $f = a'b'c + a'bc + ab'c' + abc' + abc$

c. $f = a'c + ac' + abc$

$= a'c + ac' + ab$ (using P10a on last two terms)

$= a'c + ac' + bc$ (using P10a on first and last term)

d. $f'(a, b, c) = \Sigma m(0, 2, 5)$

e. $f'(a, b, c) = \Sigma m(0, 2, 5)$

$= a'b'c' + a'bc' + ab'c$

$f = (a + b + c)(a + b' + c)(a' + b + c')$

f. Reordering the first two terms of f, we see that adjacency (P9b) is useful.

$$
\begin{aligned}
f &= (a + c + b)(a + c + b')(a' + b + c') \\
&= (a + c)(a' + b + c')
\end{aligned}
$$

Or, we can minimize f' and then use DeMorgan's theorem:

$f' = a'c' + ab'c$

$f = (a + c)(a' + b + c')$

14. For the following function,

$f(x, y, z) = \Sigma m(2, 3, 5, 6, 7)$

a. Show the truth table.

b. Show an algebraic expression for f in sum of minterm form.

c. Show a minimum SOP expression for f (two terms, three literals).

d. Show the minterms of f' (complement of f) in numeric form.

e. Show an algebraic expression for f in product of maxterm form.

f. Show a minimum POS expression for f (two terms, five literals).

a.

$x\ y\ z$	f
0 0 0	0
0 0 1	0
0 1 0	1
0 1 1	1
1 0 0	0
1 0 1	1
1 1 0	1
1 1 1	1

b. $f = x'yz' + x'yz + xy'z + xyz' + xyz$

c. $f = x'y + xy'z + xy$

$= y + xy'z$

$= y + xz$

d. $f'(x, y, z) = \Sigma m(0, 1, 4)$

e. $f' = x'y'z' + x'y'z + xy'z'$

$f = (x + y + z)\,(x + y + z')(x' + y + z)$

f. $f' = x'y'z' + x'y'z + xy'z' + x'y'z'$

$= x'y' + y'z'$

$f = (x + y)\,(y + z)$

15. Show a block diagram corresponding to each of the expressions below using only NAND gates. Assume all inputs are available both uncomplemented and complemented. There is no need to manipulate the functions to simplify the algebra.

a. $f = ab'd' + bde' + bc'd + a'ce$

b. $g = b(c'd + c'e') + (a + ce)\,(a' + b'd')$

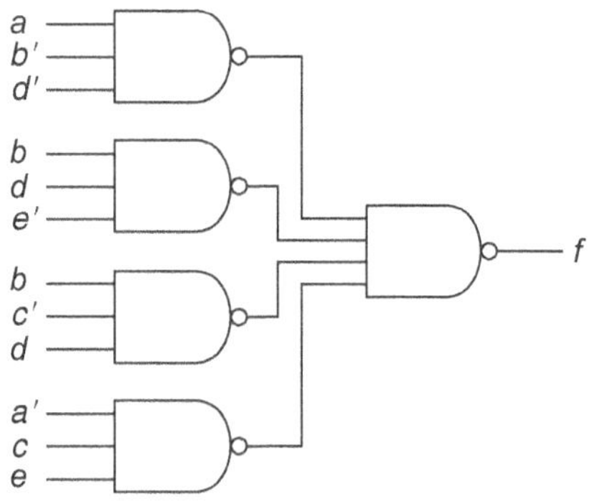

(a)

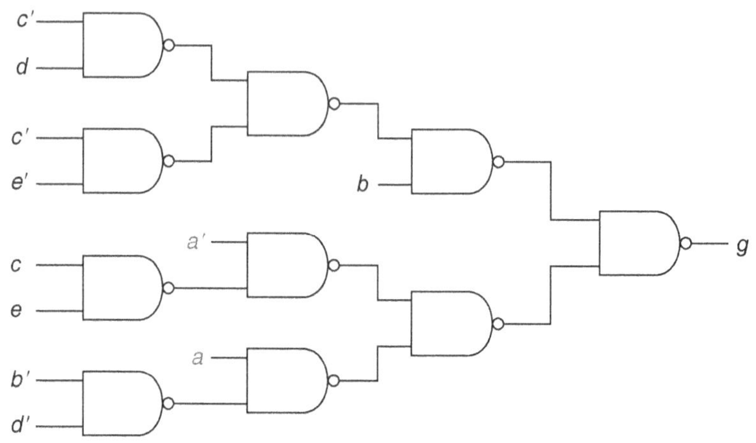

(b)

Note that in part (a), this is a two-level circuit. In part (b), the only inputs that go directly into an OR are a and a'; they are complemented.

16. Show a block diagram corresponding to each of the following expressions using only NOR gates. Assume all inputs are available both uncomplemented and complemented. There is no need to manipulate the functions to simplify the algebra.

a. $f = (a + b')(a' + c + d)(b + d')$

b. $g = [a'b' + a(c + d)](b + d')$

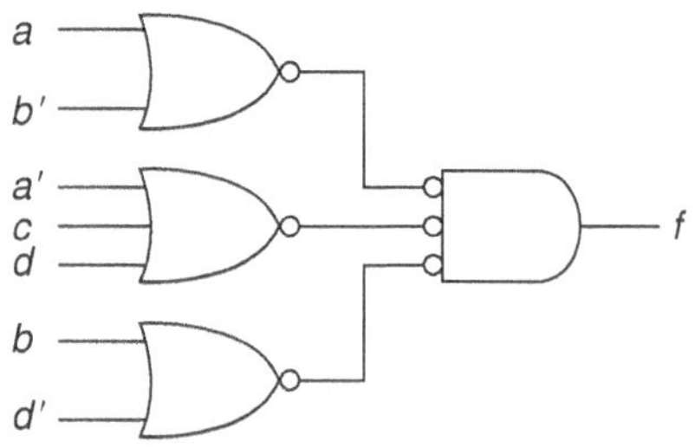

(a)

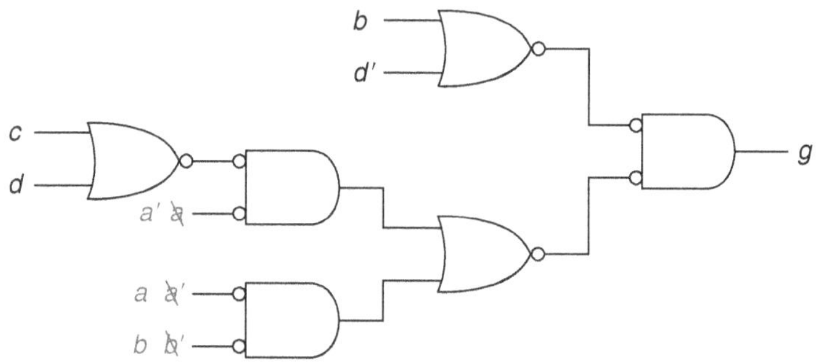

(b)

17. For each of the following circuits,

i. Find an algebraic expression.

ii. Put it in minimum SOP form.

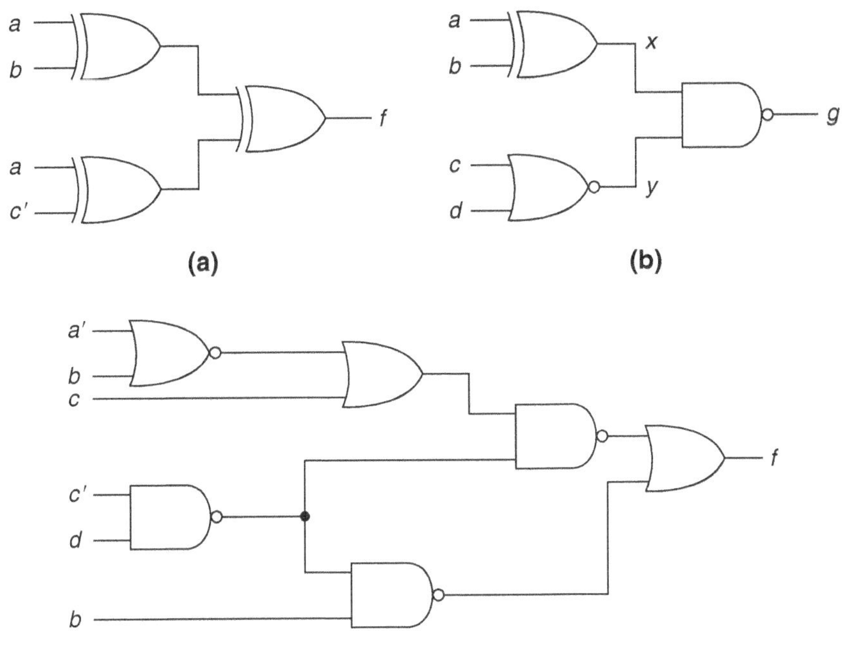

(a) (b) (c)

a. i. $f = (a \oplus b) \oplus (a \oplus c')$

ii. $f = (a'b + ab') \oplus (a'c' + ac)$

$= (a'b + ab')' (a'c' + ac) + (a'b + ab') (a'c' + ac)'$

$= (a'b' + ab) (a'c' + ac) + (a'b + ab')(a'c + ac')$

$= a'b'c' + abc + a'bc + ab'c'$

$= b'c' + bc$

b. i. $g = x' + y' = (a'b + ab')' + c + d$

ii. $g = ab + a'b' + c + d$

c. i. $f = \{[(a' + b)' + c](c'd)'\}' + [(b(c'd)']'$

ii. $f = \{[(a' + b)' + c]' + (c'd)\} + [b' + c'd]$

$= (a' + b)c' + c'd + b' + c'd$

$= a'c' + bc' + c'd + b' = a'c' + c' + c'd + b'$

$= c' + a'c' + c'd + b' = c' + b'$

18. Reduce the following expressions to a minimum SOP form. Show each step (number of terms and number of literals in minimum shown in parentheses).

a. $F = A + B + A'B'C'D$ (3 terms, 4 literals)

b. $f = x'y'z + w'xz + wxyz' + wxz + w'xyz$ (3 terms, 7 literals)

c. $g = wxy' + xyz + wx'yz + xyz' + wy'$ (3 terms, 6 literals)

d. $H = AB + B'C + ACD + ABD' + ACD'$
(2 terms, 4 literals)

e. $G = ABC' + A'C'D + AB'C' + BC'D + A'D$
(2 terms, 4 literals)

f. $f = abc + b'cd + acd + abd'$
(2 solutions, 3 terms, 9 literals)

a. $F = A + B + A'B'C'D$

$= (A + A'B'C'D) + B$

$= (A + B'C'D) + B$ **[P10a]**

$= A + (B + B'C'D)$

$= A + B + C'D$ **[P10a]**

We can also achieve the same result using a different approach.

$A + B + A'B'C'D = (A + B) + (A + B)'C'D$ **[P11a]**

$= (A + B) + C'D$ **[P10a]**

b. $f = x'y'z + w'xz + wxyz' + wxz + w'xyz$

$= x'y'z + w'xz + wxyz' + wxz$ **[P12a]**

$= x'y'z + xz + wxyz'$ **[P9a]**

$= x'y'z + x(z + wyz')$

$= x'y'z + x(z + wy)$ **[P10a]**

$= x'y'z + xz + wxy$

$= z(x'y' + x) + wxy$

$= z(y' + x) + wxy$ **[P10a]**

$= y'z + xz + wxy$

c. There are two ways to apply P10a. If we use it with the first and third terms, we get

$g = w(y' + yx'z) + xy$

$= w(y' + x'z) + xy$

$= wy' + wx'z + xy$

But now, there is nothing further we can do (without a great deal of backtracking or P13a).

However, if we first used P10a with the second and third terms,

$g = wy' + y(x + x'wz)$

$= wy' + y(x + wz)$

$= wy' + xy + wyz$

Now we can apply P10a again to the first and third terms to produce the solution with six literals.

$g = w(y' + yz) + xy = w(y' + z) + xy = wy' + wz + xy$

d. $H = AB + B'C + AC'D + ABD' + ACD'$
$= AB + B'C + AC$ **[P12a, P9a]**
$= AB + B'C$ **[P13a]**

e. $G = ABC' + A'C'D + AB'C' + BC'D + A'D$
$= ABC' + AB'C' + A'D + BC'D$ **[P12a]**
$= AC' + A'D + BC'D$ **[P9a]**

But,

$AC' ¢ A'D = C'D$
$G = AC' + A'D + BC'D + C'D$ **[P13a]**
$= AC' + A'D + C'D$ **[P12a]**
$= AC' + A'D$ **[P13a]**

Note that we used consensus to first add a term and then to remove that same term.

f. $f = abc + b'cd + acd + abd'$

Since

$abc ¢ b'cd = acd$

the consensus term can be removed and thus

$f = abc + b'cd + abd'$

No further reduction is possible; the only consensus that exists among the terms in this reduced expression produces the term *acd*, the one that we just removed. None of the other properties can be used to reduce this function further.

However, if we go back to the original function, we note that another consensus does exist:

$acd ¢ abd' = abc$

and thus the term *abc* can be removed, producing

$f = b'cd + acd + abd'$

That is another equally good minimum solution (because no further minimization is possible). Even though we found two applications of consensus in this function, we cannot take advantage of both of them because no matter which one we use first, the term needed to form the second consensus has been removed.

19. Expand the following function to sum of minterms form

$F(A, B, C) = A + B'C$

We have a choice of two approaches. We could use P3b, P5aa (both from right to left) and P8a repeatedly to produce

$$
\begin{aligned}
A + B'C &= A(B' + B) + (A' + A)B'C \\
&= AB' + AB + A'B'C + AB'C \\
&= AB'(C' + C) + AB(C' + C) + A'B'C + AB'C \\
&= AB'C' + AB'C + ABC' + ABC + A'B'C + AB'C \\
&= AB'C' + AB'C + ABC' + ABC + A'B'C
\end{aligned}
$$

having removed the duplicated term ($AB'C$). Or we could use a truth table, such as

A B C	*B'C*	*F*
0 0 0	0	0
0 0 1	1	1
0 1 0	0	0
0 1 1	0	0
1 0 0	0	1
1 0 1	1	1
1 1 0	0	1
1 1 1	0	1

and thus,

$$F = A'B'C + AB'C' + AB'C + ABC' + ABC$$

which is the same as the previous expression reordered, or

$$F(A, B, C) = \Sigma m(1, 4, 5, 6, 7)$$

20. Convert each of the following expressions to SOP form:

a. $(w + x' + z)(w' + y + z')(x + y + z)$

b. $(a + b + c + d')(b + c + d)(b' + c')$

a. $(w + x' + z)(w' + y + z')(x + y + z)$

$= [z + (w + x')(x + y)](w' + y + z')$ **[P8b]**

$= (z + wx + x'y)(w' + y + z')$ **[P14a]**

$= z(w' + y) + z'(wx + x'y)$ **[P14a]**

$= w'z + yz + wxz' + x'yz'$ **[P8a]**

Note that this is not a minimum SOP expression, even though the original was a minimum POS expression. Using P10a, we could reduce this to

$$w'z + yz + wxz' + x'y$$

b. $(a + b + c + d')(b + c + d)(b' + c')$

$= [b + c + (a + d')d](b' + c')$ **[P8b]**

$= (b + c + ad)(b' + c')$ **[P8b, P5b, P3a]**

$= bc' + b'(c + ad)$ **[P14a]**

$= bc' + b'c + ab'd$ **[P8a]**

or using c instead of b for P14a

$= (b + c + ad)(b' + c')$

$= b'c + c'(b + ad)$

$= b'c + bc' + ac'd$

These are two equally good solutions.

21. Convert the following expression to POS form:

$$a'c'd + a'cd' + bc$$

$a'c'd + a'cd' + bc$

$= c(b + a'd') + c'a'd$ **[P8a]**

$= (c + a'd)(c' + b + a'd')$ **[P14a]**

$= (c + a')(c + d)(c' + b + a')(c' + b + d')$ **[P8b]**

Two comments are in order. This is not in minimum POS form. P12b allows us to manipulate the first and third terms so as to replace the third term by $(a' + b)$. We could have started the process by factoring a' from the first two terms, but that would require more work.

22. Implement each of the following expressions (which are already in minimum SOP form) using only two-input NAND gates. No gate may be used as a NOT. All inputs are available both uncomplemented and complemented. (The number of gates required is shown in parentheses.)

a. $f = w'y' + xyz + wyz' + x'y'z$ (8 gates)

b. $f = abc + abd + a'c'd + a'b'c$ (8 gates)

c. $F = B'C'D' + BD + ACD + ABC$ (7 gates)

d. $g = a'b'c'd' + abcd' + a'ce + ab'd + be$ (12 gates)

a. $f = y'(w' + x'z) + y(xz + wz')$

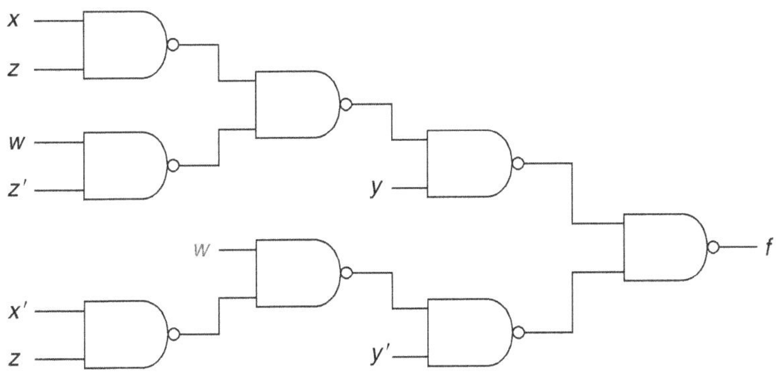

b. $f = abc + abd + a'c'd + a'b'c$

Factoring ab from the first two terms and a' from the second, we get

$$f = ab(c + d) + a'(c'd + b'c)$$

But that would require a three-input AND for the first term. We could distribute the a or b through the parentheses, getting

$$f = a(bc + bd) + a'(c'd + b'c)$$

That requires nine gates. Instead, we can factor c from the first and last term, and d from the middle terms, yielding

$$f = c(ab + a'b') + d(ab + a'c')$$

Since the term ab appears twice, we can share that gate, producing

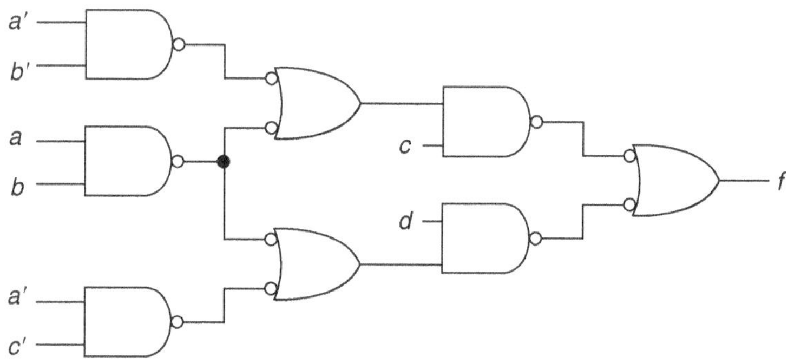

c. $F = AC(B + D) + B'C'D' + BD$
$= (C + B'D')[C' + A(B + D)] + BD$

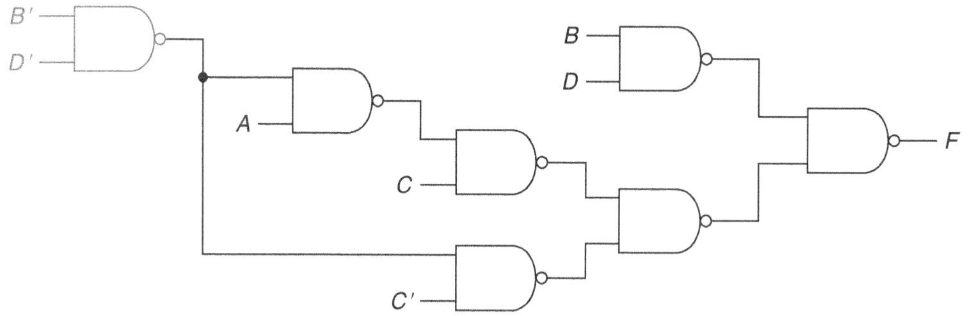

Note that the gate on the left is used to implement both the $B'D'$ term and the $(B + D)$ term.

d. $g = a'b'c'd' + abcd' + a'ce + ab'd + be$

The first attempt at a solution yields one with 13 gates.

$$\begin{aligned} g &= d'(a'b'c' + abc) + e(b + a'c) + ab'd \\ &= (d' + ab')(d + a'b'c' + abc) + e(b + a'c) \\ &= (d' + ab')[d + (a + b'c')(a' + bc)] + e(b + a'c) \end{aligned}$$

1 2 3 4 5 6 7 8 9 10 11 12 13

Another approach is

$$\begin{aligned} g &= a'(b'c'd' + ce) + a(bcd' + b'd) + be \\ &= [a + b'c'd' + ce][a' + bcd' + b'd] + be \\ &= [a + (c + b'd')(c' + e)][a' + (b + d)(b' + cd')] + be \end{aligned}$$

1 2 3 4 5 6 7 3 8 9 10 11 12

where gate three is used twice, as follows.

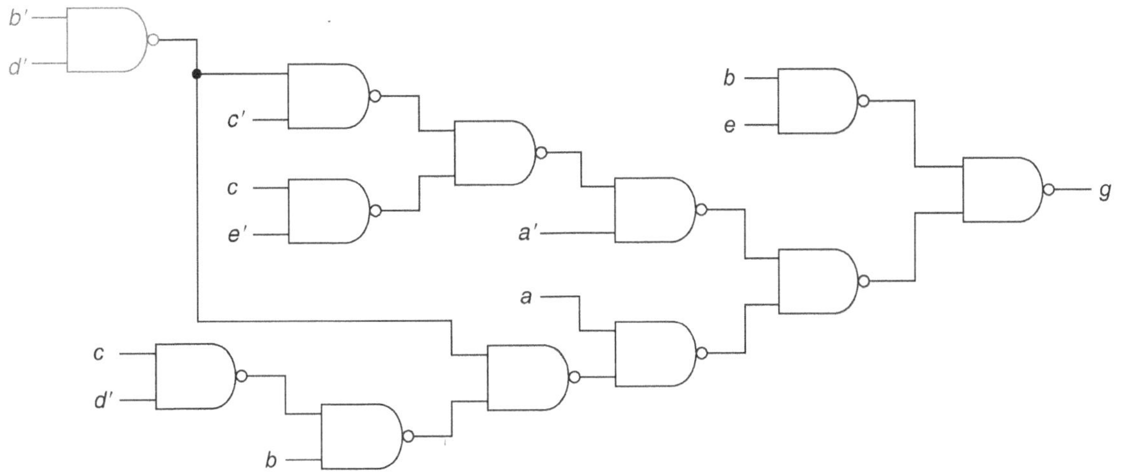

23. For the following function, show the block diagram for a NAND gate implementation that uses only four 7400 series NAND gate modules. No gate may be used as a NOT. Assume that all variables are available both uncomplemented and complemented. (Note that a two-level solution would require 2 six-input gates and a five-input gate (each of which would be implemented with a 7430 module containing 1 eight-input gate), plus a 7420 for the four-input gate and a 7410 for the 2 three-input gates and the 1 two-input gate.)

$$g = abcdef + d'e'f + a'b' + c'd'e' + a'def' + abcd'f'$$

$$g = abc(def + d'f') + d'e'(c' + f) + a'(b' + def')$$

This requires 1 four-input gate (for the first term), 4 three-input gates, and 5 two-input gates (one 7420, with the second gate used as a three-input one, one 7410, and two 7400s with three gates unused). If we required that no four-input gates be used, we could further manipulate the algebra as follows:

$$g = [a' + bc(def + d'f')][a + b' + def'] + d'e'(c' + f)$$

using P14a on the first and last terms, which would require 5 three-input gates and 6 two-input gates (still four modules).

We could also do a completely different factoring, yielding

$$\begin{aligned} g &= de(abcf + a'f') + d'(abcf' + e'f + c'e') + a'b' \\ &= [d' + e(abcf + a'f')][d + abcf' + e'f + c'e'] + a'b' \\ &= [d' + e(a' + f)(f' + abc)] \\ &\qquad \cdot [d + c'e' + (f + abc)(f' + e')] + a'b' \end{aligned}$$

This requires 3 three-input gates and 10 two-input gates (also four modules), as shown below.

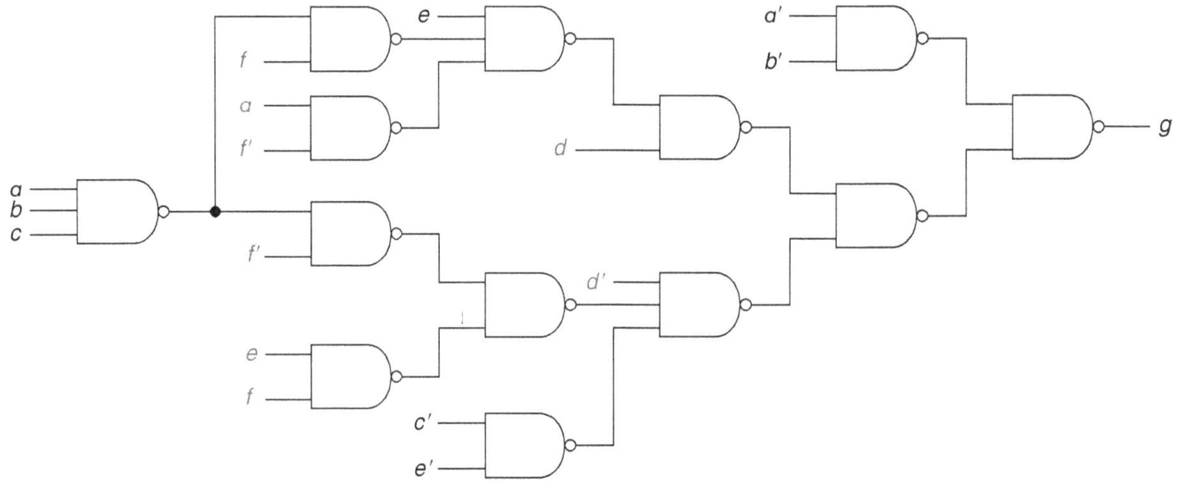

24. The following is already in minimum sum of products form.

$$F = B'DE' + A'B'D + A'BC'D' + ABD'E' + ABDE + ACDE$$

All variables are available both uncomplemented and complemented. Find two solutions, each of which uses no more than three integrated circuit packages of NAND gates (4 two-input or 3 three-input or 2 four-input gates per package). One solution must use only two- and three-input gates; the other must use at least 1 four-input gate package.

The easiest starting point is to factor pairs of terms as follows:

$$F = B'D(A' + E') + BD'(A'C' + AE') + ADE(B + C)$$

This indeed corresponds to a solution that satisfies the problem requirements. There are 3 three-input gates (corresponding to the first AND of $B'D$ ( ), the second AND of BD' ( ), and the output OR). There is 1 four-input gate, corresponding to the last AND, and 5 two-input gates. We thus need one 7420 for the four-input gate; the second gate on that package can be used as the fifth two-input gate. The 3 three-input gates require one 7410, and the remaining 4 two-input gates require one 7400.

By utilizing P14a, we obtain

$$F = B'D(A' + E') + BD'(A' + E')(A + C') + ADE(B + C)$$

Note that the term $A' + E'$ appears twice in the expression, and we can thus share the output of the NAND gate that creates it. This requires 2 four-input gates, 2 three-input gates, and 3 two-input gates, leaving an extra two- and three-input gate unused. (This might be useful if we were building other circuits at the same time and physically close to this one.) A block diagram of this circuit follows.

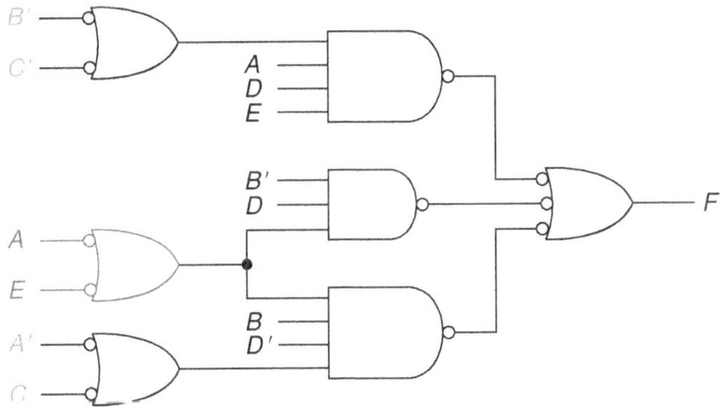

If we wish to find a solution that does not use four-input gates, then we can factor D from the four terms containing it, as follows:

$$F = D[B'(A' + E') + AE(B + C)] + BD'(A'C' + AE')$$
$$\quad 2\;2 \qquad 2 \qquad 2\;3 \qquad 2 \qquad 2\;3 \qquad 2 \qquad 2\;2$$

As can be seen from the listing under the expression, this implementation requires 9 two-input gates and 2 three-input ones, a total of three chips. There are several other solutions which we will not enumerate here (but none of them use only two-input gates).

2.11 EXERCISES

1. Show a truth table for a 1-bit full subtractor that has a borrow input b_{in} and inputs x and y, and produces a difference, d, and a borrow output, b_{out}.

$$\begin{array}{r} b^{in} \\ x \\ \underline{-y} \\ b_{out}\ d \end{array}$$

2. Show truth tables for each of the following.

*a. There are four inputs and three outputs. The inputs, w, x, y, z, are codes for the grade that may be received:

0000 A	0100 B−	1000 D+	1100 Incomplete
0001 A−	0101 C+	1001 D	1101 Satisfactory
0010 B+	0110 C	1010 D−	1110 Unsatisfactory
0011 B	0111 C−	1011 F	1111 Pass

The outputs are

1: a 1 if and only if the grade is C or better (only letter grades; C− is not C or better)

2: a 1 if and only if the university will count it toward the 120 credits required for a degree (passing grade only)

3: a 1 if and only if it will be counted in computing a grade point average (letter grades only).

b. This system has four inputs and three outputs. The first two inputs, a and b, represent a 2-bit binary number (range of 0 to 3). A second binary number (same range) is represented by the other two inputs, c and d. The output f is to be 1 if and only if the two numbers differ by exactly 2. Output g is to be 1 if and only if the numbers are equal. Output h is to be 1 if and only if the second number is larger than the first.

c. The system has four inputs. The first two, a and b, represent a number in the range 1 to 3 (0 is not used). The other two, c and d, represent a second number in the same range. The output, y, is to be 1 if and only if the first number is greater than the second or the second is 2 greater than the first.

*d. A system has one output, F, and four inputs, where the first two inputs (A, B) represent one 2-bit binary number (in the range 0 to 3) and the second two inputs (C, D) represent another binary number (same range). F is to be 1 if and only if the two numbers are equal or if they differ by exactly 1.

e. A system has one output, F, and four inputs, where the first two inputs (A, B) represent one 2-bit binary number (in the range 0 to 3) and the second two inputs (C, D) represent another binary number (same range). F is to be 1 if and only if the sum of the two numbers is odd.

f. The system has four inputs. The first two, a and b, represent a number in the range 0 to 2 (3 is not used). The other two, c and d, represent a second number in the same range. The output, y, is to be 1 if and only if the two numbers do not differ by more than 1.

*g. The months of the year are coded in four variables, $abcd$, such that January is 0000, February is 0001, . . . , and December is 1011. The remaining 4 combinations are never used. (Remember: 30 days has September, April, June, and November. All the rest have 31, except February. . . .) Show a truth table for a function, g, that is 1 if the month has 31 days and 0 if it does not.

h. The months of the year are coded as in 2g, except that February of a leap year is coded as 1100. Show a truth table with five outputs, v, w, x, y, z that indicates the number of days in the selected month.

i. Repeat 2h, except that the outputs are to be in BCD (8421 code). There are now six outputs, u, v, w, x, y, z (where the first decimal digit is coded 0, 0, u, v and the second digit is coded w, x, y, z).

j. The system has four inputs, a, b, c, and d, and one output, f. The last three inputs (b, c, d) represent a binary number, n, in the range 0 to 7; however, the input 0 never occurs. The first input (a) specifies which of two computations is made.

$a = 0$: f is 1 iff n is a multiple of 2
$a = 1$: f is 1 iff n is a multiple of 3

k. The system has four inputs, a, b, c, and d, and one output, f. The first two inputs (a, b) represent one binary number (in the range 0 to 3) and the last two (c, d) represent another number in the range 1 to 3 (0 never occurs). The output, f, is to be 1 iff the second number is at least two larger than the first.

l. Show the truth table for a system with four inputs, a, b, c, and d, and two outputs, f and g. The inputs represent a BCD digit between 1 and 9 (8421 code). All other inputs never happen. The output f is 1 if and only if the input represents an odd number larger than 6 or an even number less than 7. The output g is 1 iff the input represents a perfect square. (A perfect square is a number whose square root is an integer.)

3. Show a block diagram of a circuit using AND and OR gates for each side of each of the following equalities:

*a. P2a: $a + (b + c) = (a + b) + c$

b. P8a: $a(b + c) = ab + ac$

4. Show a truth table for the following functions:

*a. $F = X'Y + Y'Z' + XYZ$

b. $G = XY + (X' + Z)(Y + Z')$

c. $H = WX + XY' + WX'Z + XYZ' + W'XY'$

5. Determine, using truth tables, which expressions in each of the groups are equal:

a. $f = ac' + a'c + bc$
$g = (a + c)(a' + b + c')$

*b. $f = a'c' + bc + ab'$
$g = b'c' + a'c' + ac$
$h = b'c' + ac + a'b$

c. $f = ab + ac + a'bd$
$g = bd + ab'c + abd'$

6. For each of the following expressions, indicate which (if any) of the following apply (more than one may apply):

i. Product term

ii. SOP expression

iii. Sum term

iv. POS expression

a. $abc'd + b'cd + ad'$

*b. $a' + b + cd$

c. $b'c'd'$

*d. $(a + b)c'$

e. $a' + b$

*f. a'

*g. $a(b + c) + a'(b' + d)$

h. $(a + b' + d)(a' + b + c)$

***7.** For the expressions of problem 4, how many literals are in each?

8. Using properties 1 to 10, reduce the following expressions to a minimum SOP form. Show each step (number of terms and number of literals in minimum shown in parentheses).

*a. $x'z + xy'z + xyz$ (1 term, 1 literal)

b. $x'y'z' + x'yz + xyz$ (2 terms, 5 literals)

c. $x'y'z' + x'y'z + xy'z + xyz'$ (3 terms, 7 literals)

*d. $a'b'c' + a'b'c + abc + ab'c$ (2 terms, 4 literals)

e. $x'y'z' + x'yz' + x'yz + xyz$ (2 terms, 4 literals)

*f. $x'y'z' + x'y'z + x'yz + xyz + xyz'$
(2 solutions, each with 3 terms, 6 literals)

g. $x'y'z' + x'y'z + x'yz + xy'z + xyz + xyz'$
(3 terms, 5 literals)

h. $a'b'c' + a'bc' + a'bc + ab'c + abc' + abc$
(3 terms, 5 literals)

9. Using Properties 1 to 10, reduce the following expressions to a minimum POS form. The number of terms and number of literals are shown in parentheses.

a. $(a + b + c)(a + b' + c)(a + b' + c')(a' + b' + c')$
(2 terms, 4 literals)

b. $(x + y + z)(x + y + z')(x + y' + z)(x + y' + z')$
(1 term, 1 literal)

*c. $(a + b + c')(a + b' + c')(a' + b' + c')(a' + b' + c)$
$(a' + b + c)$ (2 solutions, each with 3 terms, 6 literals)

10. Show a block diagram of a system using AND, OR, and NOT gates to implement the following functions. Assume that variables are available only uncomplemented. Do not manipulate the algebra.

a. $P'Q' + PR + Q'R$

b. $ab + c(a + b)$

*c. $wx'(v + y'z) + (w'y + v')(x + yz)'$

11. For each of the following circuits,

i. find an algebraic expression.

ii. put it in sum of product form.

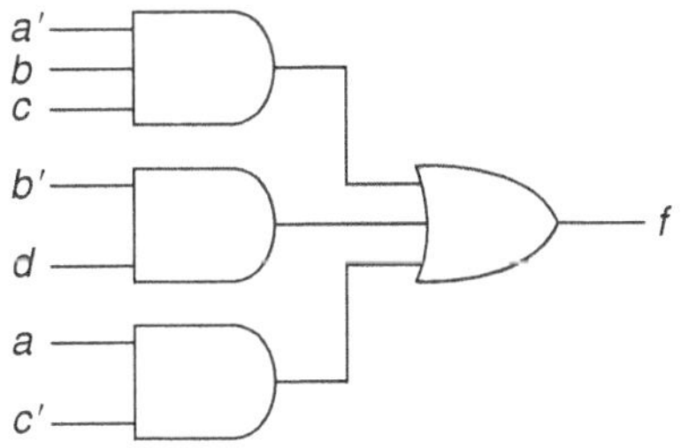

a.

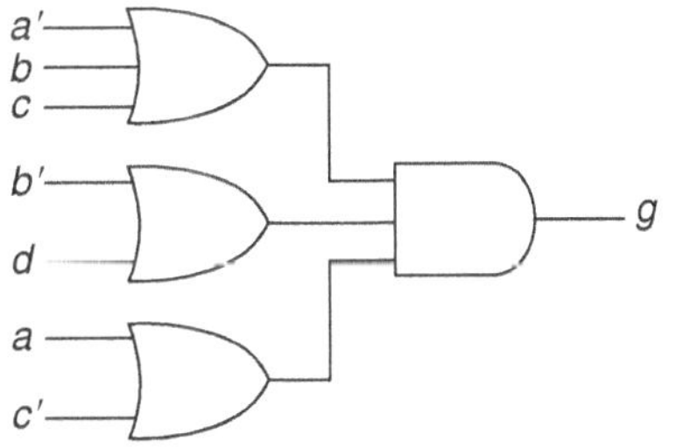

b.

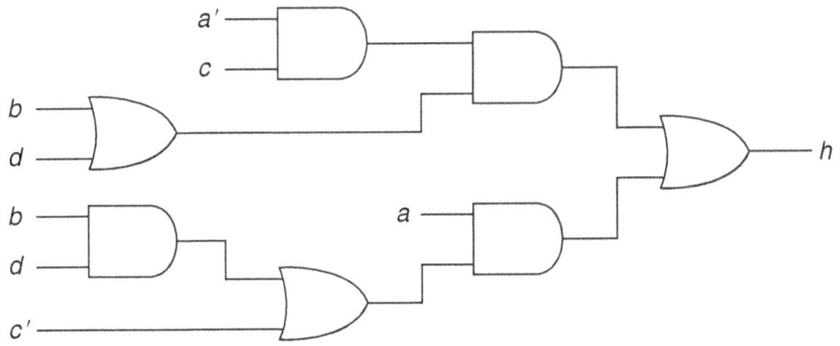

c.

12. Find the complement of the following expressions. Only single variables may be complemented in the answer.

*a. $f = abd' + b'c' + a'cd + a'bc'd$

b. $g = (a + b' + c)(a' + b + c)(a + b' + c')$

c. $h = (a + b)(b' + c) + d'(a'b + c)$

13. For each of the following functions:

$$f(x, y, z) = \Sigma m(1, 3, 6)$$
$$g(x, y, z) = \Sigma m(0, 2, 4, 6)$$

a. Show the truth table.

b. Show an algebraic expression in sum of minterms form.

c. Show a minimum SOP expression (a: 2 terms, 5 literals; b: 1 term, 1 literal).

d. Show the minterms of f' (complement of f) in numeric form.

e. Show an algebraic expression in product of maxterms form.

f. Show a minimum POS expression (f: 2 solutions, 3 terms, 6 literals; g: 1 term, 1 literal)

***14.** For each of the following functions,

a b c	*f*	*g*
0 0 0	0	1
0 0 1	1	1
0 1 0	0	0
0 1 1	0	0
1 0 0	0	1
1 0 1	1	1
1 1 0	1	1
1 1 1	1	0

a. Show the minterms in numerical form.

b. Show an algebraic expression in sum of minterms form.

c. Show a minimum SOP expression (f: 2 terms, 4 literals; g: 2 terms, 3 literals).

d. Show the minterms of f' (complement of f) in numeric form.

e. Show an algebraic expression in product of maxterms form.

f. Show a minimum POS expression (f: 2 terms, 4 literals; g: 2 terms, 4 literals)

15. For each of the following functions:

$$F = AB' + BC + AC$$

$$G = (A + B)(A + C') + AB'$$

a. Show the truth table.

b. Show an algebraic expression in sum of minterms form.

c. Show a minimum sum of products expression (F: 2 terms, 4 literals; G: 2 terms, 3 literals).

d. Show the minterms of the complement of each function in numeric form.

e. Show an algebraic expression in product of maxterms form.

f. Show a minimum POS expression (F: 2 terms, 4 literals; G: 2 terms, 4 literals)

*16. Consider the following function with don't cares:

$$G(X, Y, Z) = \Sigma m(5, 6) + \Sigma d(1, 2, 4)$$

For each of the following expressions, indicate whether it could be used as a solution for G. (Note: It may not be a minimum solution.)

a. $XYZ' + XY'Z$

b. $Z' + XY'Z$

c. $X(Y' + Z')$

d. $Y'Z + XZ' + X'Z$

e. $XZ' + X'Z$

f. $YZ' + Y'Z$

17. Show that the NOR is functionally complete by implementing a NOT, a two-input AND, and a two-input OR using only two-input NORs.

18. For each of the following circuits,

i. find an algebraic expression.

ii. put it in SOP form.

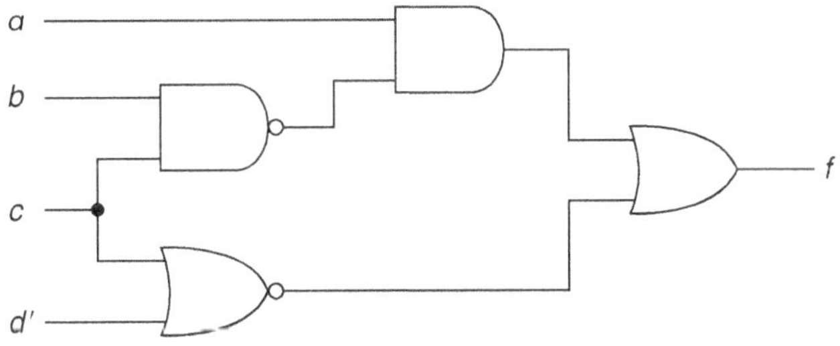

***a.**

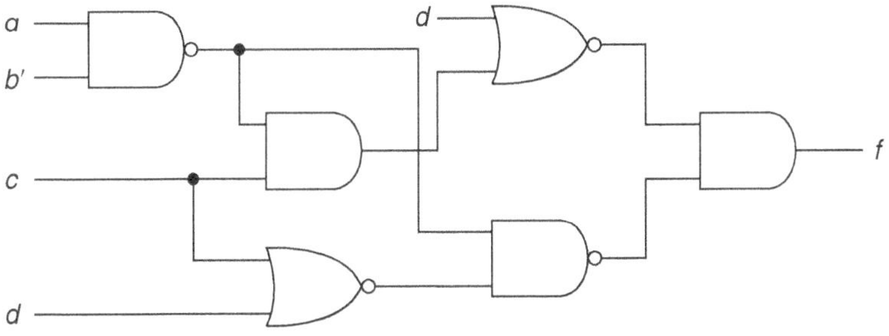

b.

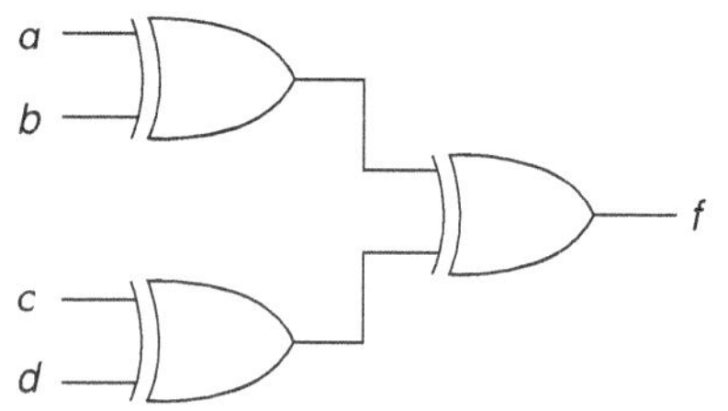

c.

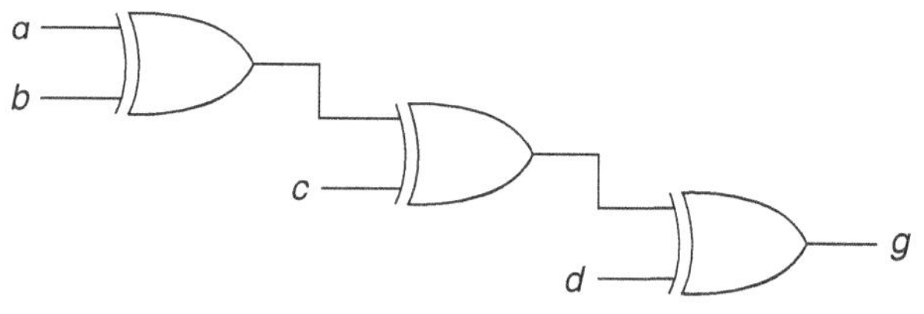

d.

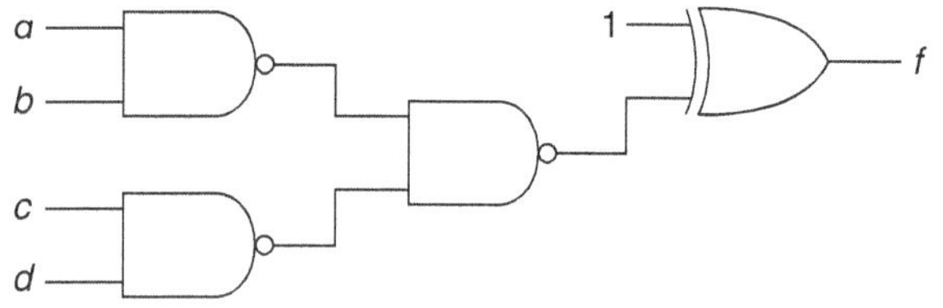

★e.

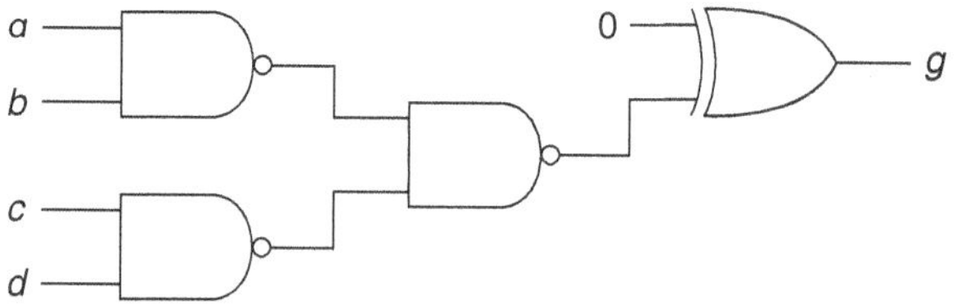

f.

19. Show a block diagram corresponding to each of the expressions below using only NAND gates. Assume all inputs are available both uncomplemented and complemented. Do not manipulate the functions to simplify the algebra.

a. $f = wy' + wxz' + xy'z + w'x'z$

b. $g = wx + (w' + y)(x + y')$

c. $h = z(x'y + w'x') + w(y' + xz')$

★d. $F = D[B'(A' + E') + AE(B + C)] + BD'(A'C' + AE')$

20. Reduce the following expressions to a minimum sum of products form, using P1 through P12. Show each step (number of terms and number of literals in minimum shown in parentheses).

a. $h = ab'c + bd + bcd' + ab'c' + abc'd$ (3 terms, 6 literals)

b. $h = ab' + bc'd' + abc'd + bc$ (3 terms, 5 literals)

★c. $f = ab + a'bd + bcd + abc' + a'bd' + a'c$ (2 terms, 3 literals)

d. $g = abc + abd + bc'd'$ (2 terms, 5 literals)

e. $f = xy + w'y'z + w'xy' + wxyz' + w'yz + wz$ (3 terms, 5 literals)

21. Reduce the following expressions to a minimum sum of products form. Show each step and the property used (number of terms and number of literals in minimum shown in parentheses).

a. $f = x'yz + w'x'z + x'y + wxy + w'y'z$ (3 terms, 7 literals)

b. $G = A'B'C' + AB'D + BCD' + A'BD + CD + A'D$ (4 terms, 9 literals)

★c. $F = W'YZ' + Y'Z + WXZ + WXYZ' + XY'Z + W'Y'Z'$ (3 terms, 7 literals)

d. $g = wxz + xy'z + wz' + xyz + wxy'z + w'y'z'$ (3 terms, 6 literals)

e. $F = ABD' + B'CE + AB'D' + B'D'E + ABCD'E + B'C'D'$ (3 terms, 8 literals)

f. $f = b'c + abc + b'cd + a'b'd + a'c'd$ (3 terms, 7 literals)

★g. $G = B'C'D + BC + A'BD + ACD + A'D$ (3 terms, 6 literals)

h. $f = ab + bcd + ab'c' + abd + bc + abc'$ (2 terms, 4 literals)

i. $h = abc' + ab'd + bcd + a'bc$ (3 terms, 8 literals)

★j. $g = a'bc' + bc'd + abd + abc + bcd' + a'bd'$ (2 solutions, 3 terms, 9 literals)

22. i. For the following functions, use consensus to add as many new terms to the sum of product expression given.

ii. Then reduce each to a minimum sum of products, showing each step and the property used.

★a. $f = a'b'c' + a'bd + a'cd' + abc$ (3 terms, 8 literals)

b. $g = wxy + w'y'z + xyz + w'yz'$ (3 terms, 8 literals)

23. Expand the following functions to sum of minterms form:

a. $f(a, b, c) = ab' + b'c'$

★b. $g(x, y, z) = x' + yz + y'z'$

c. $h(a, b, c, d) = ab'c + bd + a'd'$

24. Convert each of the following expressions to sum of products form:

a. $(a + b + c + d')(b + c' + d)(a + c)$

b. $(a' + b + c')(b + c' + d)(b' + d')$

★c. $(w' + x)(y + z)(w' + y)(x + y' + z)$

d. $(A + B + C)(B' + C + D)(A + B' + D)(B + C' + D')$

25. Convert each of the following expressions to product of sums form:

a. $AC + A'D'$

b. $w'xy' + wxy + xz$

★c. $bc'd + a'b'd + b'cd'$

26. Implement each of the following expressions (which are already in minimum sum of products form) using only two-input NAND gates. No gate may be used as a NOT. All inputs are available both uncomplemented and complemented. (The number of gates required is shown in parentheses.)

★a. $f = wy' + wxz' + y'z + w'x'z$ (7 gates)

b. $ab'd' + bde' + bc'd + a'ce$ (10 gates)

c. $H = A'B'E' + A'B'CD' + B'D'E' + BDE' + BC'E + ACE'$ (14 gates)

★d. $F = A'B'D' + ABC' + B'CD'E + A'B'C + BC'D$ (11 gates)

e. $G = B'D'E' + A'BC'D + ACE + AC'E' + B'CE$ (12 gates, one of which is shared)

f. $h = b'd'e' + ace + c'e' + bcde$ (9 gates)

27. Each of the following is already in minimum sum of products form. All variables are available both uncomplemented and complemented. Find two solutions each of which uses no more than the number of integrated circuit packages of NAND gates (4 two-input or 3 three-input or 2 four-input gates per package) listed. One solution must use only two and three input gates; the other must use at least 1 four-input gate package.

*a. $F = ABCDE + B'E' + CD'E' + BC'D'E + A'B'C + A'BC'E$ (3 packages)

b. $G = ABCDEF + A'B'D' + C'D'E + AB'CE' + A'BC'DF + ABE'F'$ (4 packages)

2.12 CHAPTER 2 TEST (100 MINUTES, OR TWO 50-MINUTE TESTS)

1. The inputs of this system A and B represent one binary number in the range 0:3. The inputs *C* and *D* represent a second binary number (also in the range 0:3). There are three outputs, *X, Y,* and *Z.*

Show a truth table such that *Y* and *Z* represent a number equal to the magnitude of the difference of the two inputs and *X* is 1 if and only if the first is larger. Two lines of the table are filled in.

A	*B*	*C*	*D*	*X*	*Y*	*Z*
0	0	0	0			
0	0	0	1			
0	0	1	0			
0	0	1	1			
0	1	0	0			
0	1	0	1			
0	1	1	0	0	0	1
0	1	1	1			
1	0	0	0			
1	0	0	1	1	0	1
1	0	1	0			
1	0	1	1			
1	1	0	0			
1	1	0	1			
1	1	1	0			
1	1	1	1			

2. Use a truth table to demonstrate whether or not the following functions are equal:

$f = a'b' + a'c' + ab$
$g = (b' + c')(a' + b)$

a b c	f	g
0 0 0		
0 0 1		
0 1 0		
0 1 1		
1 0 0		
1 0 1		
1 1 0		
1 1 1		

3. Reduce the following expression to a SOP expression with two terms and four literals. Show each step.

$a'b'c + a'bc + ab'c + ab'c'$

4. For each part, assume all variables are available both uncomplemented and complemented.

$f = ab'c + ad + bd$

a. Show a block diagram for a two-level implementation of f using AND and OR gates.

b. Show a block diagram for an implementation of f using only two-input AND and OR gates.

5. For the following truth table

x	y	z	f
0	0	0	1
0	0	1	0
0	1	0	1
0	1	1	1
1	0	0	0
1	0	1	1
1	1	0	0
1	1	1	1

a. Write a sum of minterms function in numeric form, for example,

$\Sigma m(0, \ldots)$

b. Write a sum of minterms function in algebraic form, for example,

$x'yz + \cdots$

c. Find one minimum SOP expression (3 terms, 6 literals).

d. Find a POS expression in product of maxterms form.

e. Find a minimum POS form (2 terms, 5 literals).

6. Assume all inputs are available both uncomplemented and complemented. Show an implementation of

$$g = wx + wz + w'x' + w'y'z'$$
$$= (w' + x + z)(w + x' + y')(w + x' + z')$$

a. using NAND gates of any size.

b. using NOR gates of any size.

c. using two-input NAND gates (none of which may be used as a NOT).

7. For each of the following functions find a minimum SOP expression (3 terms, 6 literals). Show each algebraic step.

a. $f = b'd' + bc'd + b'cd' + bcd + ab'd$

5-POINT BONUS: Find a second minimum sum of products.

b. $g = xy'z' + yz + xy'z + wxy + xz$

8. a. Expand the following to sum of minterms (sum of standard product terms). Eliminate any duplicates.

$$g = a' + ac + b'c$$

b. Manipulate the following to a SOP expression.

$$f = (x' + y)(w' + y + z')(y' + z)(w + y' + z')$$

9. Implement the following function using only two-input NAND gates. No gate may be used as a NOT gate. The function is in minimum SOP form. All inputs are available both uncomplemented and complemented.

$f = ac + bcd + a'b'd'$ (7 gates)

10. Implement the following function using only two-input NAND gates. No gate may be used as a NOT gate. The function is in minimum SOP form. All inputs are available both uncomplemented and complemented.

$f = abc + ac'd'e' + a'd'e + ce + cd$

(Full credit for 11 gates, 5-point bonus for 10 gates)

CHAPTER 3

The Karnaugh Map

The algebraic methods developed in Chapter 2 allow us, in theory, to simplify any function. However, there are a number of problems with that approach. There is no formal method, such as first apply Property 10, then P14, etc. The approach is totally heuristic, depending heavily on experience. After manipulating a function, we often cannot be sure whether it is a minimum. We may not always find the minimum, even though it appears that there is nothing else to do. Furthermore, it gets rather difficult to do algebraic simplification with more than four or five variables. Finally, it is easy to make copying mistakes as we rewrite the equations.

In this chapter, we will examine an approach that is easier to implement, the *Karnaugh map** (sometimes referred to as a K-map). This is a graphical approach to finding suitable product terms for use in sum of product expressions. (The product terms that are "suitable" for use in minimum SOP expressions are referred to as *prime implicants*. We will define that term shortly.) The map is useful for problems of up to six variables and is particularly straightforward for most problems of three or four variables. Although there is no guarantee of finding a minimum solution, the methods we will develop nearly always produce a minimum. We will adapt the approach (with no difficulty) to finding minimum POS expressions, to problems with don't cares, and to multiple output problems.

In Chapter 4, we will introduce two other techniques that can be computerized and could be used for more than six variables (although the amount of work required to use them for hand computation is very large).

3.1 INTRODUCTION TO THE KARNAUGH MAP

In this section, we will look at the layout of two-, three-, and four-variable maps. The Karnaugh map consists of one square for each possible minterm in a function. Thus, a two-variable map has 4 squares, a three-variable map has 8 squares, and a four-variable map has 16 squares.

Three views of the two-variable map are shown in Map 3.1. In each, the upper right square, for example, corresponds to $A = 1$ and $B = 0$, minterm 2.

*This tool was introduced in 1953 by Maurice Karnaugh.

Map 3.1 Two-variable Karnaugh maps.

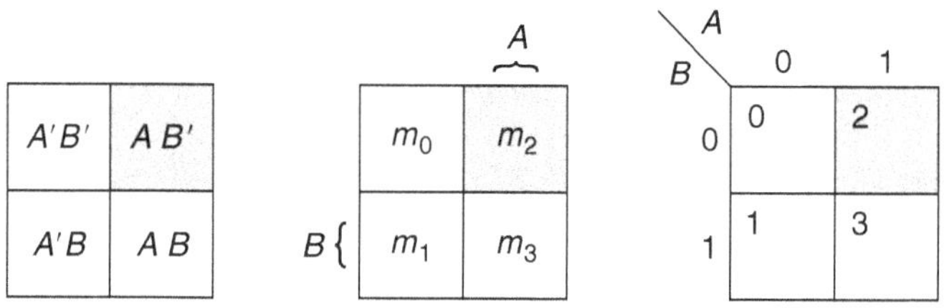

When we plot a function, we put a 1 in each square corresponding to a minterm that is included in the function, and put a 0 in or leave blank those squares not included in the function. For functions with don't cares, an X goes in the square for which the minterm is a don't care. Map 3.2 shows examples of these.

Map 3.2 Plotting functions.

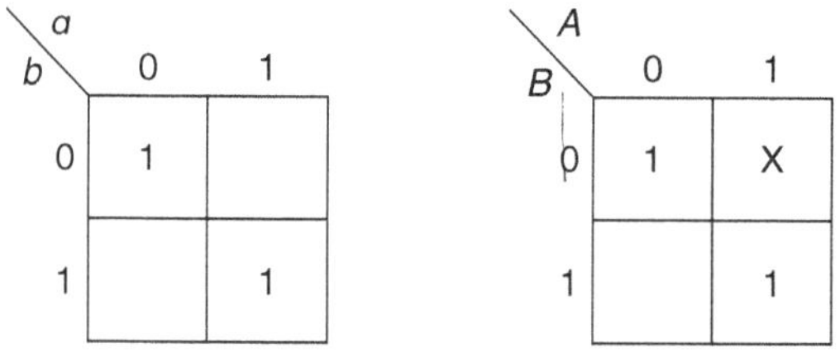

$f(a, b) = \Sigma m\,(0, 3)$ $\quad g(A, B) = \Sigma m\,(0, 3) + \Sigma d\,(2)$

Three-variable maps have eight squares, arranged in a rectangle as shown in Map 3.3.*

Map 3.3 Three-variable maps.

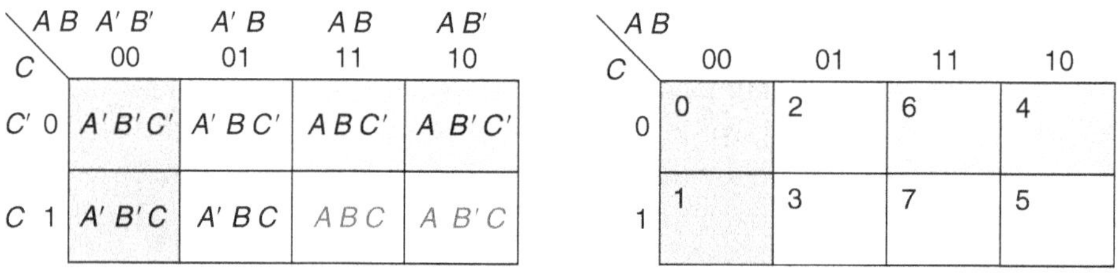

---

*Some people label the row(s) of the map with the first variable(s) and the columns with the others. The three-variable map then looks like

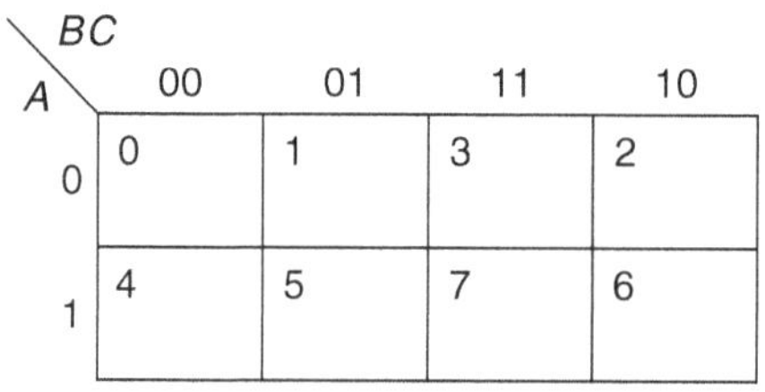

This version of the map produces the same results as the other.

Notice that the last two columns are not in numeric order. That is the key idea that makes the map work. By organizing the map that way, the minterms in adjacent squares can always be combined using the adjacency property,

P9a. $ab + ab' = a$

EXAMPLE 3.1

$m_0 + m_1$: $A'B'C' + A'B'C = A'B'$

$m_4 + m_6$: $AB'C' + ABC' = AC'$

$m_7 + m_5$: $ABC + AB'C = AC$

Also, the outside columns (and the outside rows when there are four rows) are adjacent. Thus,

$m_0 + m_4$: $A'B'C' + AB'C' = B'C'$

$m_1 + m_5$: $A'B'C + AB'C = B'C$

If we had ordered the columns in numeric order, as shown in Map 3.4 (where the algebraic version of the minterms is shown only for m_2 and m_4), we would not be able to combine adjacent squares:

Map 3.4 **Incorrect** arrangement of the map.

C \ AB	00	01	10	11
0	0	2 A' B C'	4 A B' C'	6
1	1	3	5	7

$$m_2 + m_4 = A'BC' + AB'C' = C'(A'B + AB')$$

However, we cannot manipulate that into a single term.

Product terms that correspond to the sum of two minterms appear as two adjacent 1's on the map. The terms of Example 3.1 are shown in Map 3.5.

It is sometimes more convenient to draw the map in a vertical orientation (that is, two columns and four rows) as shown in Map 3.6. Both versions of the map produce the same results.

In reading the map, it is useful to label the pairs of columns (in those arrangements where there are four columns) as shown in Map 3.7. Thus, 1's in squares 4 and 6 are in the A columns and the C' row (that is, not in the C row), producing the AC' term as shown earlier.

Map 3.5 Product terms corresponding to groups of two.

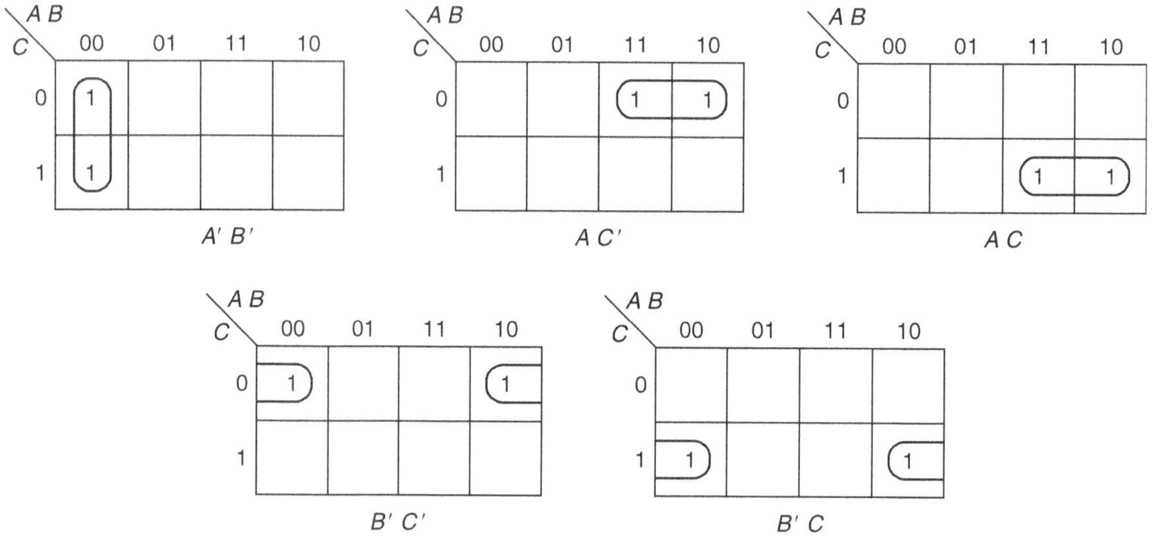

Map 3.6 Vertical orientation of three-variable map.

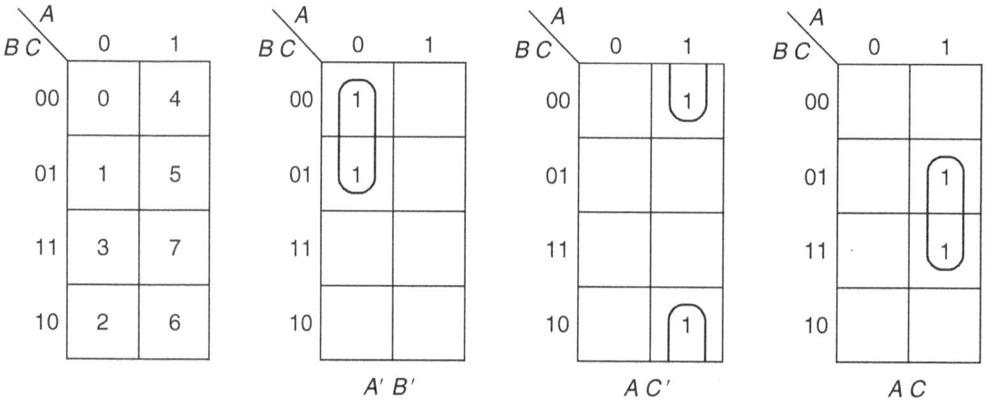

Map 3.7 Map with columns labeled.

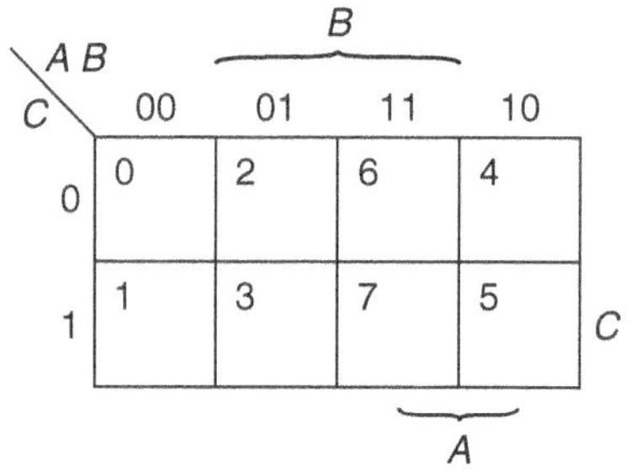

The four-variable map consists of 16 squares in the 4 by 4 arrangement shown in Map 3.8.

As with the three-variable map, 1's in two adjacent squares (where the top and bottom rows as well as the left and right columns are considered to be adjacent) correspond to a single product term (combined using P9a). Example 3.2 shows three such terms.

Map 3.8 The four-variable map.

CD \ AB	00	01	11	10
00	0	4	12	8
01	1	5	13	9
11	3	7	15	11
10	2	6	14	10

CD \ AB	00	01	11	10
00	$A'B'C'D'$	$A'BC'D'$	$ABC'D'$	$AB'C'D'$
01	$A'B'C'D$	$A'BC'D$	$ABC'D$	$AB'C'D$
11	$A'B'CD$	$A'BCD$	$ABCD$	$AB'CD$
10	$A'B'CD'$	$A'BCD'$	$ABCD'$	$AB'CD'$

EXAMPLE 3.2

$m_{13} + m_9$: $ABC'D + AB'C'D = AC'D$

$m_3 + m_{11}$: $A'B'CD + AB'CD = B'CD$

$m_0 + m_2$: $A'B'C'D' + A'B'CD' = A'B'D'$

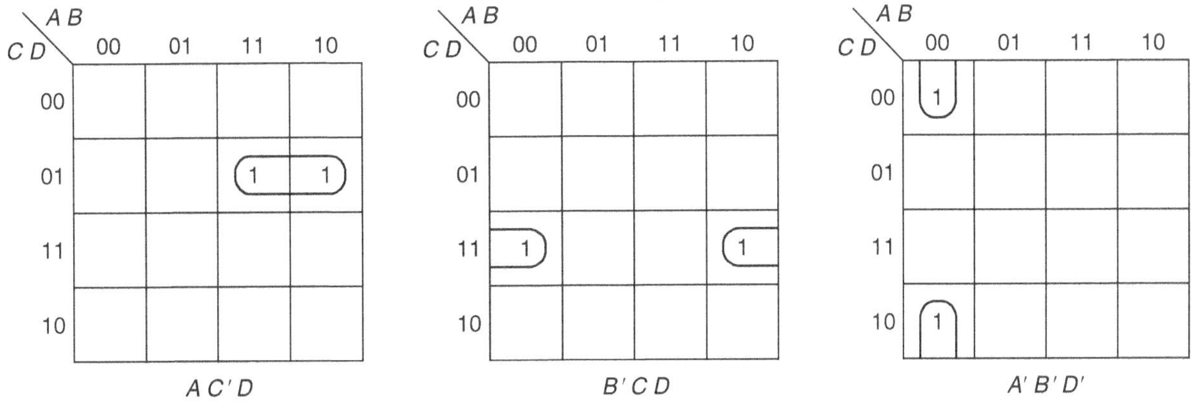

Up to this point, all of the product terms that we have shown correspond to two minterms combined using P9a. These correspond to a product term with one literal missing, that is, with only two literals in a three-variable function and three literals in a four-variable function. Let us next look at the maps of Map 3.9 with a group of four 1's.

On the map to the left, we have circled two groups of two, one forming the term $A'C$ and the other forming the term AC. Obviously, P9a can be applied again to these two terms, producing

$$A'C + AC = C$$

Map 3.9 A group of four 1's.

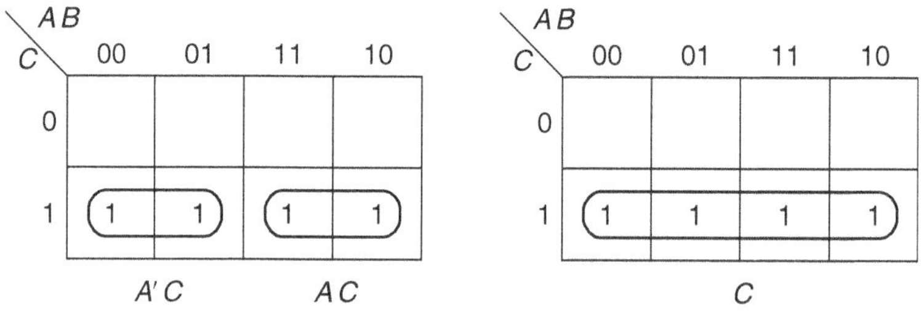

That is shown on the map to the right as a rectangle of four 1's. In general, rectangles of four 1's will correspond to a product term with two of the variables missing (that is, a single literal for three-variable problems and a two-literal term for four-variable problems).

We could have factored C from all of the terms producing

$$A'B'C + A'BC + ABC + AB'C = C(A'B' + A'B + AB + AB')$$

However, the sum inside the parentheses is just a sum of all of the minterms of A and B; that must be 1. Thus, we can get the result in just that one step. Indeed, we could have added a secondary property to P9, namely,

P9aa. $a'b' + a'b + ab + ab' = 1$

P9bb. $(a' + b')(a' + b)(a + b)(a + b') = 0$

These can be proved by repeated application of P9, first to the first two terms, then to the last two terms, and finally to the resulting terms as shown

$$(a'b' + a'b) + (ab + ab') = (a') + (a) = 1$$
$$[(a' + b')(a' + b)][(a + b)(a + b')] = [a'][a] = 0$$

Some examples of such groups for four-variable problems are shown in Map 3.10.

The easiest way to identify the term from the map is by determining in which row(s) and column(s) all of the 1's are located. Thus, on the first map, the 1's in the group on the left are all in the 00 ($A'B'$) column and thus the term is $A'B'$. The other group has its 1's in the 11 and 10 columns; the common feature is the 1 in the A position (which corresponds to A). Furthermore, the 1's are in the 01 and 11 rows; there is a common 1 in the D position. Thus, the term is AD. In the middle map, the

Map 3.10 Examples of groups of four.

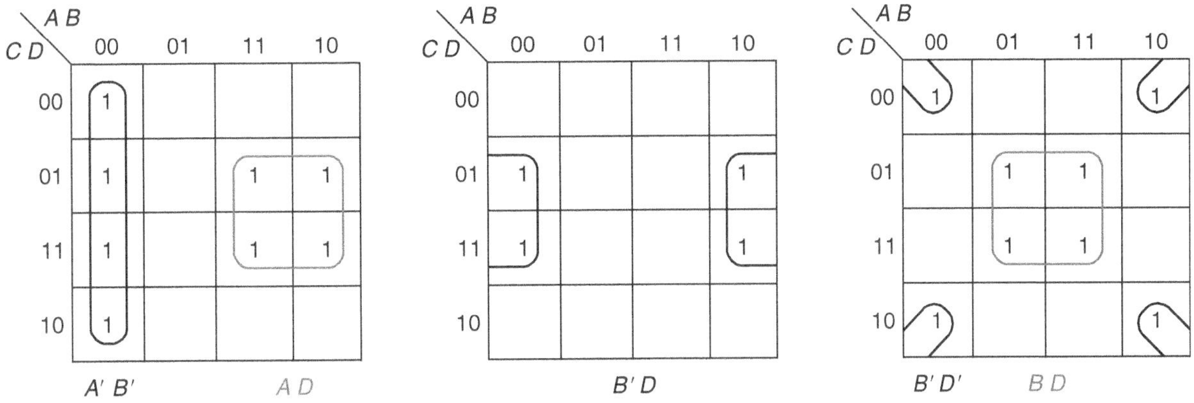

1's are in the 00 and 10 columns, producing B' and the 01 and 11 rows, resulting in D; the term is thus $B'D$. (Notice, by the way, that that term also appears on the first map, even though it was not circled.) On the last map, the four corners produce the term $B'D'$ (since all the 1's are in the 00 or 10 columns and the 00 or 10 rows). The middle group is BD. Any of these terms could also be obtained algebraically by first writing the minterms, then applying P10a to pairs of terms, and then applying it again to the two terms that resulted (as we did for the three-variable example). However, the whole idea of the map is to eliminate the need to do algebra.

Two adjacent groups of four can be combined in a similar way to form a group of eight squares (with three of the literals missing). Two such groups are shown in Map 3.11. The terms are A' for the map on the left and D' for the map on the right.

Map 3.11 Groups of eight.

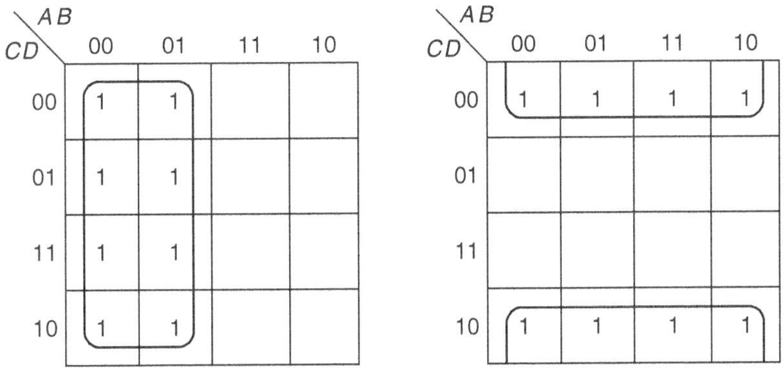

We can plot any function on the map. Either, we know the minterms, and use that form of the map, or we put the function in SOP form and plot each of the product terms.

EXAMPLE 3.3

Map

$$F = AB' + AC + A'BC'$$

The map for F follows, with each of the product terms circled. Each of the two-literal terms corresponds to two squares on the map (since one of the variables is missing). The AB' term is in the 10 column. The AC term is in the $C = 1$ row and in the 11 and 10 columns (with a common 1 in the A position). Finally, the minterm $A'BC'$ corresponds to one square, in the 01 ($A'B$) column and in the $C = 0$ row.

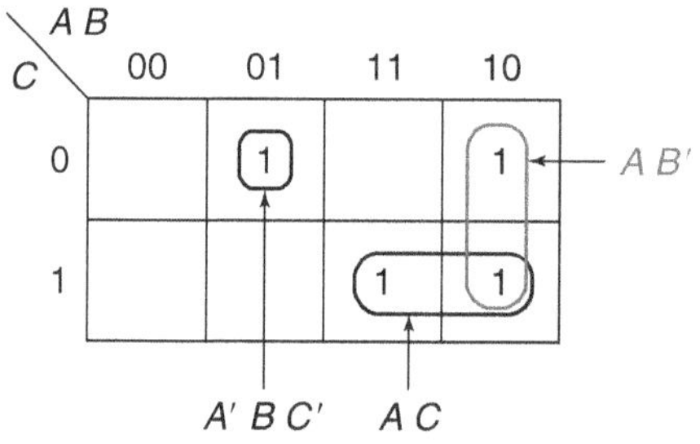

We could have obtained the same map by first expanding F to minterm form algebraically, that is,

$$\begin{aligned} F &= AB'(C' + C) + AC(B' + B) + A'BC' \\ &= AB'C' + AB'C + AB'C + ABC + A'BC' \\ &= m_4 + m_5 + m_5 + m_7 + m_2 \\ &= m_2 + m_4 + m_5 + m_7 \end{aligned}$$

(removing duplicates and reordering)

We can then use the numeric map and produce the same result.

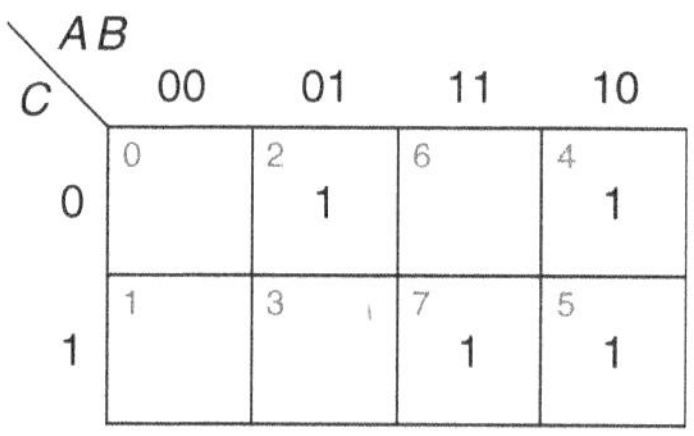

We are now ready to define some terminology related to the Karnaugh map. An *implicant* of a function is a product term that can be used in an SOP expression for that function, that is, the function is 1 whenever the implicant is 1 (and maybe other times, as well). From the point of view of the map, an implicant is a rectangle of 1, 2, 4, 8, . . . (any power of 2) 1's.* That rectangle may not include any 0's. All minterms are implicants.

Consider the function, *F*, of Map 3.12. The second map shows the first four groups of 2; the third map shows the other groups of 2 and the group of 4.

Map 3.12 A function to illustrate definitions.

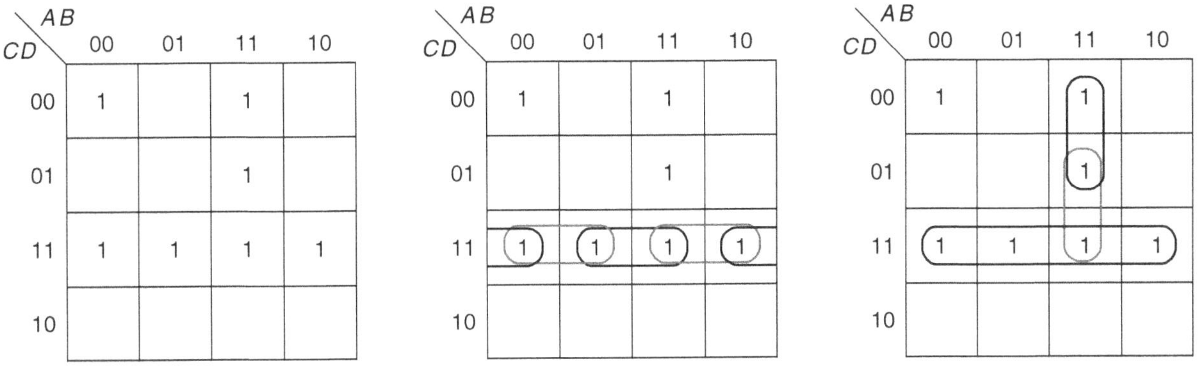

The implicants of *F* are

Minterms	*Groups of 2*	*Groups of 4*
$A'B'C'D'$	$A'CD$	CD
$A'B'CD$	BCD	
$A'BCD$	ACD	
$ABC'D'$	$B'CD$	
$ABC'D$	ABC'	
$ABCD$	ABD	
$AB'CD$		

Any SOP expression for *F* must be a sum of implicants. Indeed, we must choose enough implicants such that each of the 1's of *F* are included in at least one of these implicants. Such an SOP expression is sometimes referred to as a *cover* of *F*, and we sometimes say that an implicant *covers* certain minterms (for example, *ACD* covers m_{11} and m_{15}).

Implicants must be rectangular in shape and the number of 1's in the rectangle must be a power of 2. Thus, neither of the functions whose maps are shown in Example 3.4 are covered by a single implicant, but rather by the sum of two implicants each (in their simplest form).

*We will expand the definition of an implicant to include maps with don't cares in Section 3.3.

EXAMPLE 3.4

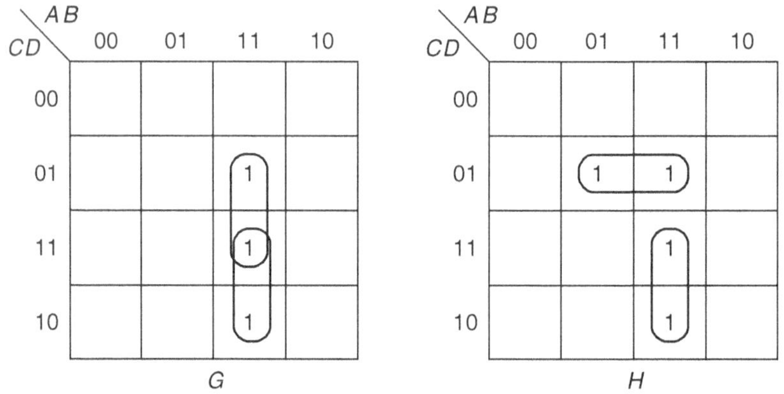

G consists of three minterms, *ABC'D, ABCD,* and *ABCD',* in the shape of a rectangle. It can be reduced no further than is shown on the map, namely, to *ABC* + *ABD*, since it is a group of three 1's, not two or four. Similarly, *H* has the same three minterms plus *A'BC'D*; it is a group of four, but not in the shape of a rectangle. The minimum expression is, as shown on the map, *BC'D* + *ABC*. (Note that *ABD* is also an implicant of *G*, but it includes 1's that are already included in the other terms.)

Map 3.13 Prime implicants.

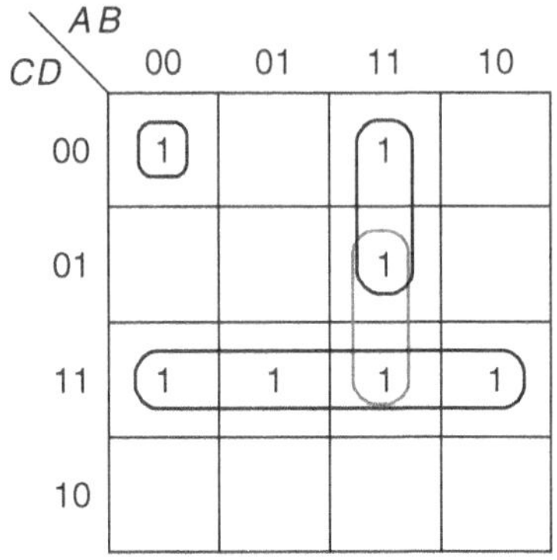

A *prime implicant* is an implicant that (from the point of view of the map) is not fully contained in any one other implicant. For example, it is a rectangle of two 1's that is not part of a single rectangle of four 1's. On Map 3.13, all of the prime implicants of *F* are circled. They are $A'B'C'D'$, ABC', ABD, and CD. Note that the only minterm that is not part of a larger group is m_0 and that the other four implicants that are groups of two 1's are all part of the group of four.

From an algebraic point of view, a prime implicant is an implicant such that if any literal is removed from that term, it is no longer an implicant. From that viewpoint, $A'B'C'D'$ is a prime implicant because $B'C'D'$, $A'C'D'$, $A'B'D'$, and $A'B'C'$ are not implicants (that is, if we remove any literal from that term, we get a term that is 1 for some input combinations for which the function is to be 0). However, ACD is not a prime implicant since when we remove A, leaving CD, we still have an implicant. (Surely, the graphical approach of determining which implicants are prime implicants is easier than the algebraic method of attempting to delete literals.)

The purpose of the map is to help us find minimum SOP expressions, where we defined minimum as being minimum number of product terms (implicants), and among those with the same number of implicants, the ones with the fewest number of literals. However, the only product terms that we need consider are prime implicants. Why? Say we found an implicant that was not a prime implicant. Then, it must be contained in some larger implicant, a prime implicant. But that larger implicant (say four 1's rather than two) has fewer literals. That alone makes a solution using the term that is not a prime implicant not a minimum. (For example, CD has two literals, whereas, ACD has three.) Furthermore, that larger implicant covers more 1's, which often will mean that we need fewer terms.

An *essential prime implicant* is a prime implicant that includes at least one 1 that is not included in any other prime implicant. (If we were to circle all of the prime implicants of a function, the essential prime implicants are those that circle at least one 1 that no other prime implicant circles.) In the example of Map 3.13, $A'B'C'D'$, ABC', and CD are essential prime implicants; ABD is not. The term *essential* is derived from the idea that we must use that prime implicant in any minimum SOP expression. A word of caution is in order. There will often be a prime implicant that is used in a minimum solution (even in all minimum solutions when more than one equally good solution exists) that is not "essential." That happens when each of the 1's covered by this prime implicant could be covered in other ways. We will see examples of that in Section 3.2. [SP 1; EX 1]

3.2 MINIMUM SUM OF PRODUCT EXPRESSIONS USING THE KARNAUGH MAP

In this section, we will describe two methods for finding minimum SOP expressions using the Karnaugh map. Although these methods involve some heuristics, we can all but guarantee that they will lead to a minimum SOP expression (or more than one when multiple solutions exist) for three- and four-variable problems. (It also works for five- and six-variable maps, but our visualization in three dimensions is more limited. We will discuss this in detail in Section 3.6.)

In the process of finding prime implicants, we will be considering each of the 1's on the map starting with the most *isolated* 1's. By isolated, we mean that there are few (or no) adjacent squares with a 1 in it. In an ***n***-variable map, each square has ***n*** adjacent squares. Examples for three- and four-variable maps are shown in Map 3.14.

Map 3.14 Adjacencies on three- and four-variable maps.

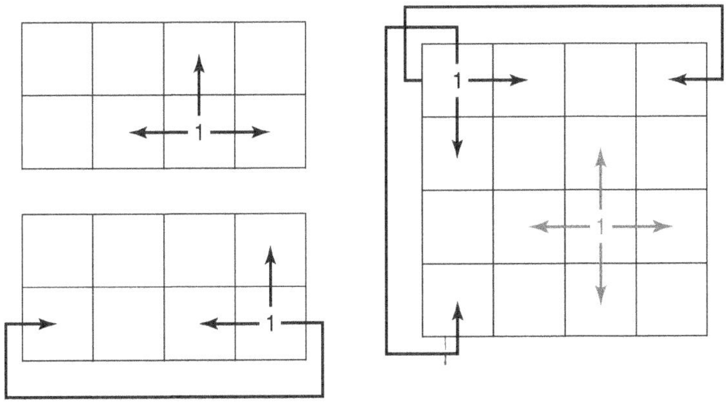

Map Method 1

1. Find all essential prime implicants. Circle them on the map and mark the minterm(s) that make them essential with a star (★). Do this by examining each 1 on the map that has not already been circled. It is usually quickest to start with the most isolated 1's, that is, those that have the fewest adjacent squares with 1's in them.
2. Find *enough* other prime implicants to cover the function. Do this using two criteria:
   a. Choose a prime implicant that covers as many new 1's (that is, those not already covered by a chosen prime implicant).
   b. Avoid leaving isolated uncovered 1's.

It is often obvious what "enough" is. For example, if there are five uncovered 1's and no prime implicants cover more than two of them, then we need at least three more terms. Sometimes, three may not be sufficient, but it usually is.

We will now look at a number of examples to demonstrate this method. First, we will look at the example used to illustrate the definitions.

EXAMPLE 3.5

As noted, m_0 has no adjacent 1's; therefore, it ($A'B'C'D'$) is a prime implicant. Indeed, it is an essential prime implicant, since no other prime implicant covers this 1. (That is always the case when minterms are prime implicants.) The next place that we look is m_{12}, since it has only one adjacent 1. Those 1's are covered by prime implicant ABC'. Indeed, no other prime implicant covers m_{12}, and thus ABC' is essential. (Whenever we have a 1 with only one adjacent 1, that group of two is an essential prime implicant.) At this point, the map has become

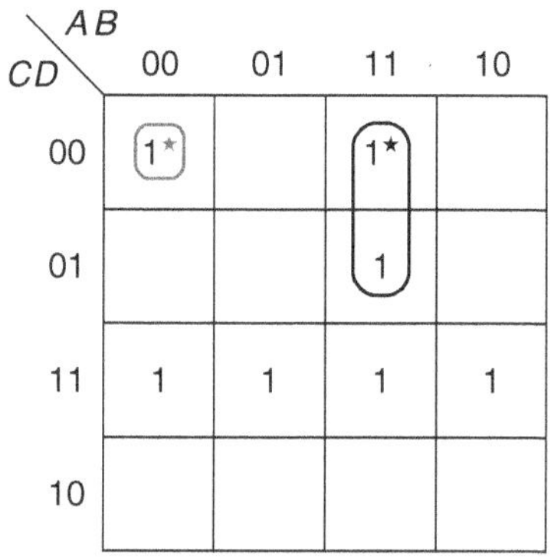

and

$$F = A'B'C'D' + ABC' + \cdots$$

Each of the 1's that have not yet been covered are part of the group of four, *CD*. Each has two adjacent squares with 1's that are part of that group. That will always be the case for a group of four. (Some squares, such as m_{15} may have more than two adjacent 1's.) *CD* is essential because no other prime implicant covers m_3, m_7, or m_{11}. However, once that group is circled, we have covered the function:

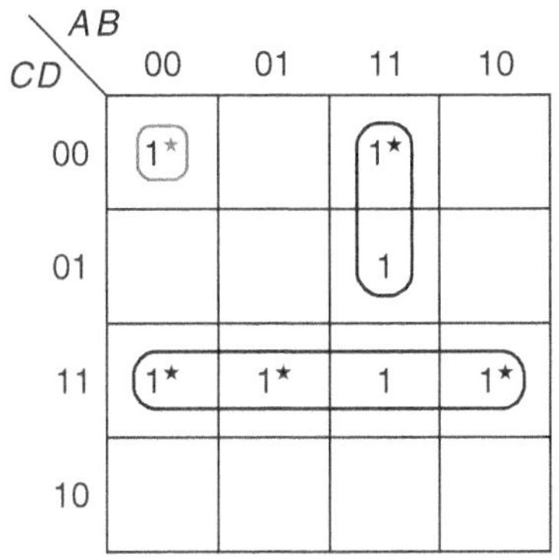

resulting in

$$F = A'B'C'D + ABC' + CD$$

In this example, once we have found the essential prime implicants, we are done; all of the 1's have been covered by one (or more) of the essential prime implicants. We do not need step 2. There may be other prime implicants that were not used (such as *ABD* in this example).

EXAMPLE 3.6

We start looking at the most isolated 1, m_{11}. It is covered only by the group of two shown, *wyz*. The other essential prime implicant is *y′z′* because of m_0, m_8, or m_{12}. None of these are covered by any other prime implicant; each makes that prime implicant essential. The second map shows these two terms circled.

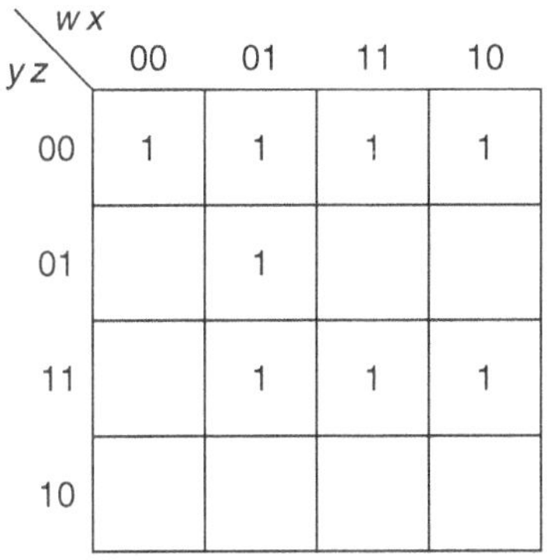

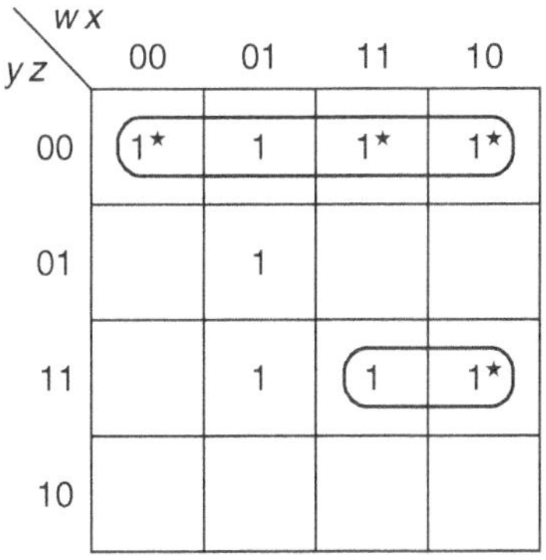

That leaves two 1's uncovered. Each of these can be covered by two different prime implicants, but the only way to cover them both with one term is shown on the first of the maps below.

Thus, the minimum sum of product solution is

$$f = y'z' + wyz + w'xz$$

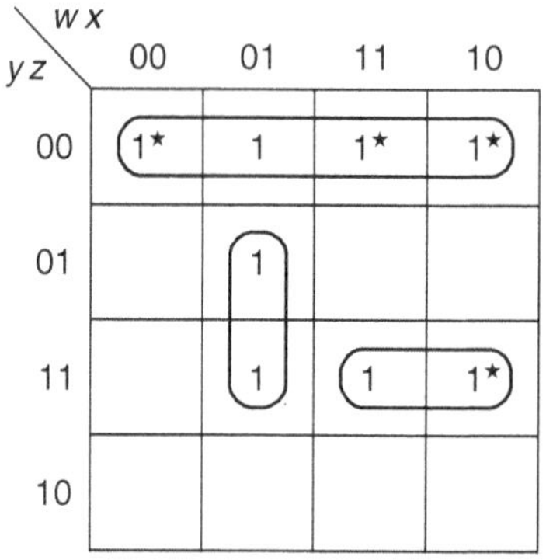

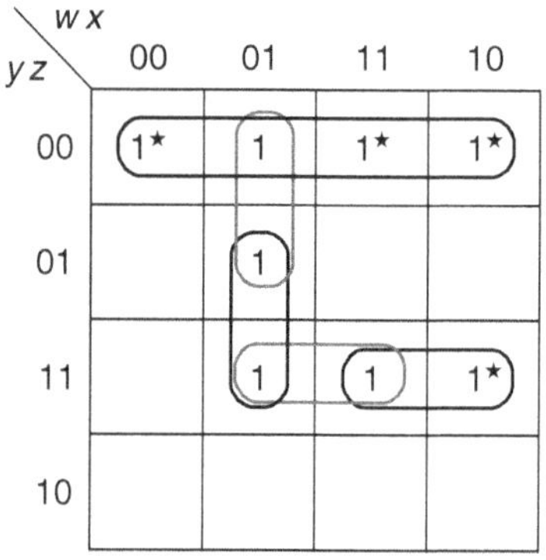

The other two prime implicants are $w'xy'$ and xyz, circled in brown on the last map. They are redundant, however, since they cover no new 1's. Even though $w'xz$ must be used in a minimum solution, it does not meet the definition of an essential prime implicant; each of the 1's covered by it can be covered by other prime implicants.

We will next look at the "dead end" example from Chapter 2 (Example 2.2).

EXAMPLE 3.7

$$f = a'b'c' + a'bc' + a'bc + ab'c'$$

In the first attempt at algebraic manipulation, we grouped the first two minterms. But, as can be seen on the left-hand map below, the two 1's that are left could not be combined and resulted in a three-term solution. Furthermore, $a'c'$ is not an essential prime implicant. If, on the other hand, we used the map, we could see that choosing the two essential prime implicants on the right-hand map includes all of the minterms and produces the solution

$$f = a'b + b'c'$$

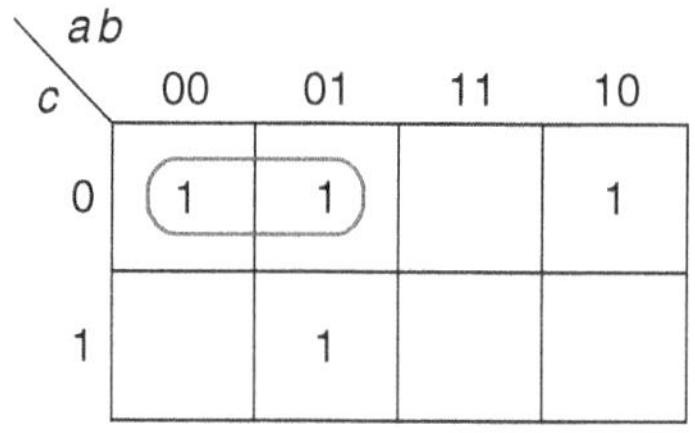

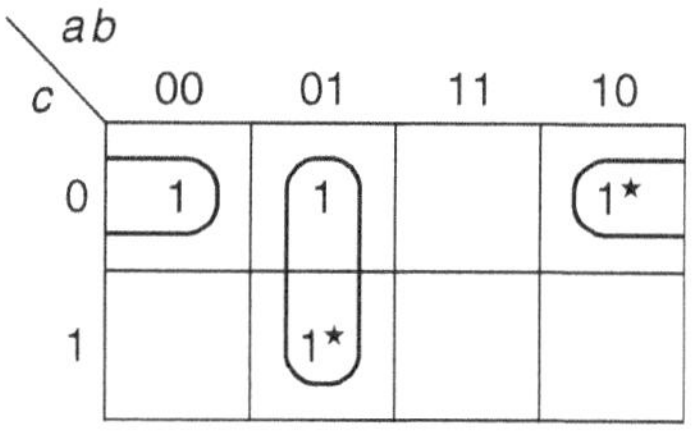

Sometimes, after selecting all of the essential prime implicants, there are two choices for covering the remaining 1's, but only one of these produces a minimum solution, as in Example 3.8.

EXAMPLE 3.8

$f(a, b, c, d) = \Sigma m(0, 2, 4, 6, 7, 8, 9, 11, 12, 14)$

The first map shows the function and the second shows all essential prime implicants circled. In each case, one of the 1's (as indicated with a star, ⋆) can be covered by only that prime implicant. (That is obvious from the last map, where the remaining two prime implicants are circled.)

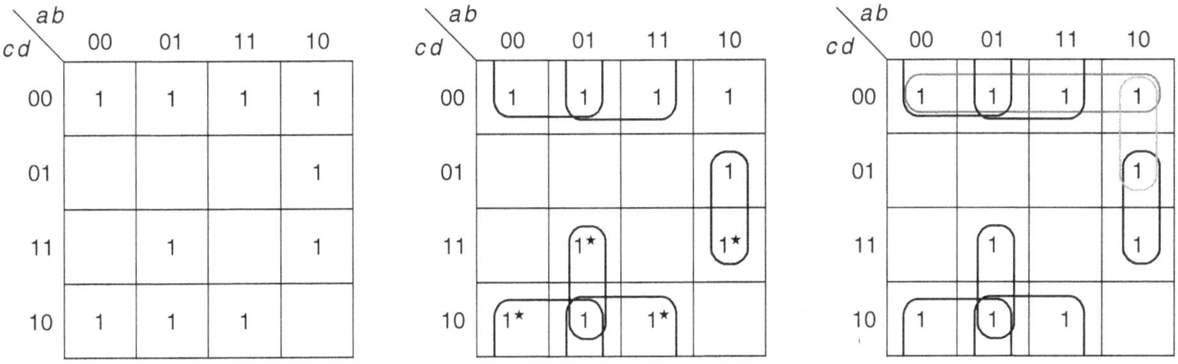

Only one 1 (m_8) is not covered by an essential prime implicant. It can be covered in two ways, by a group of four (in brown) and a group of two (tan). Clearly, the group of four provides a solution with one less literal, namely,

$$f = a'd' + bd' + a'bc + ab'd + c'd'$$

When asking whether a 1 makes a group of four an essential prime implicant on a four-variable map, we need find only two adjacent 0's. If there are fewer than two adjacent 0's, this 1 must be either in a group of eight or part of two or more smaller groups. Note that in Example 3.8, m_2 and m_{14} have two adjacent 0's, and thus each makes a prime implicant essential. In contrast, m_0, m_4, m_8, and m_{12} each have only one adjacent 0 and are each covered by two or three prime implicants.

We will now consider some examples with multiple minimum solutions, starting with the three-variable function used to illustrate the definition of terminology in Section 2.2.3.

EXAMPLE 3.9

$$x'yz' + x'yz + xy'z' + xy'z + xyz$$

A map of that function is shown on the left. The two essential prime implicants are shown on the map on the right.

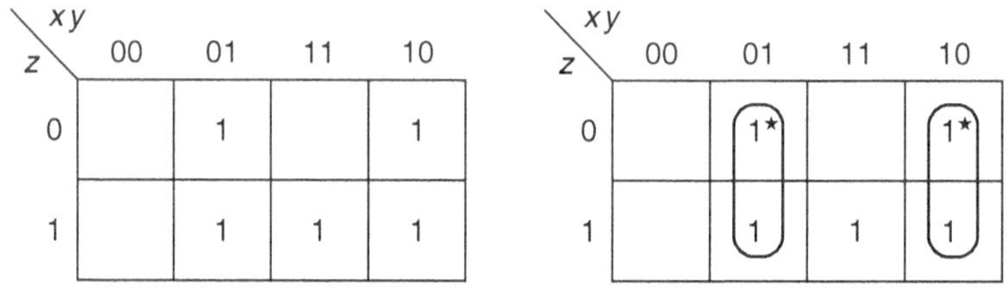

After finding the two essential prime implicants, m_7 is still uncovered. The following maps show the two solutions.

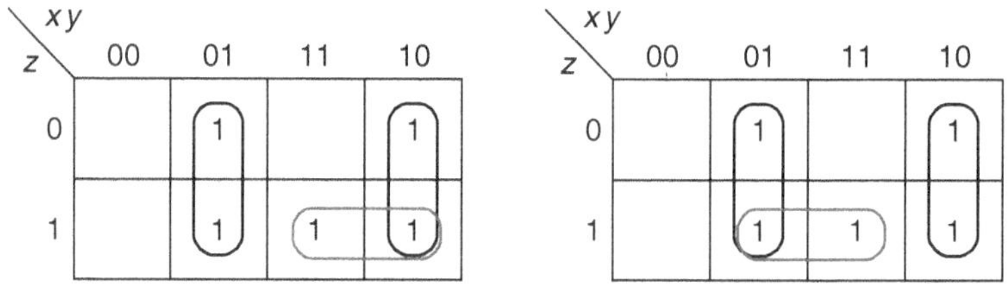

$x'y + xy' + xz$ $\qquad$ $x'y + xy' + yz$

EXAMPLE 3.10

This example is one we call "don't be greedy."

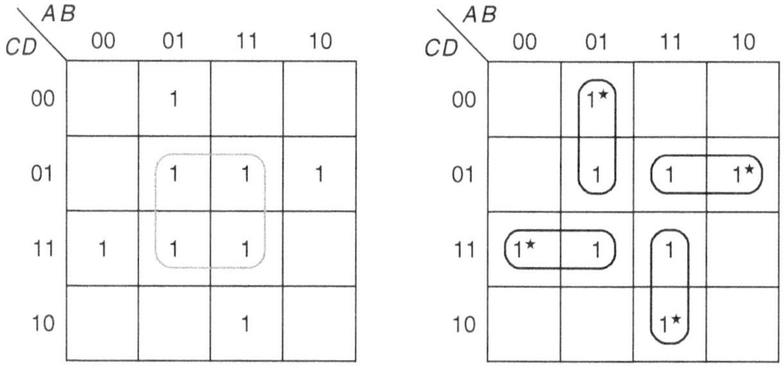

At first glance, one might want to take the only group of four (circled in tan). However, that term is not an essential prime implicant, as is obvious once we circle all of the essential prime implicants and find that the four 1's in the center are covered. Thus, the minimum solution is

$$G = A'BC' + A'CD + ABC + AC'D$$

EXAMPLE 3.11

$$g(w, x, y, z) = \Sigma m(2, 5, 6, 7, 9, 10, 11, 13, 15)$$

The function is mapped first, and the two essential prime implicants are shown on the second map, giving

$$g = xz + wz + \cdots$$

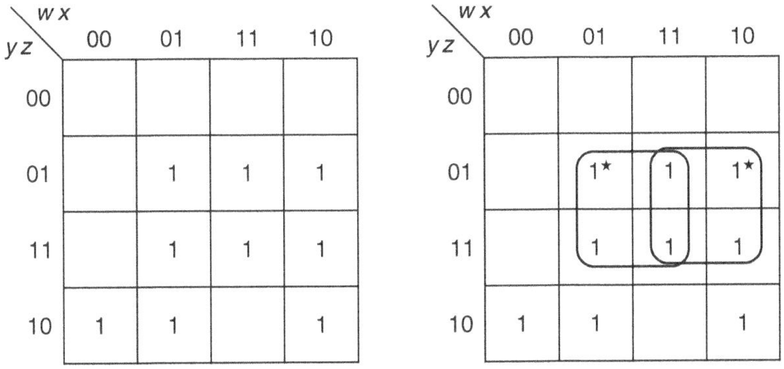

Although m_2 looks rather isolated, it can indeed be covered by $w'yz'$ (with m_6) or by $x'yz'$ (with m_{10}). After choosing the essential prime implicants, the remaining three 1's can each be covered by two different prime implicants. Since three 1's still need to be covered (after choosing the essential prime implicants), and since all the remaining prime implicants are groups of two and thus have three literals, we need at least two more of these prime implicants. Indeed, there are three ways to cover the remaining 1's with two more prime implicants. Using the first criteria, we choose one of the prime implicants that covers two new 1's, $w'yz'$, as shown on the left-hand map.

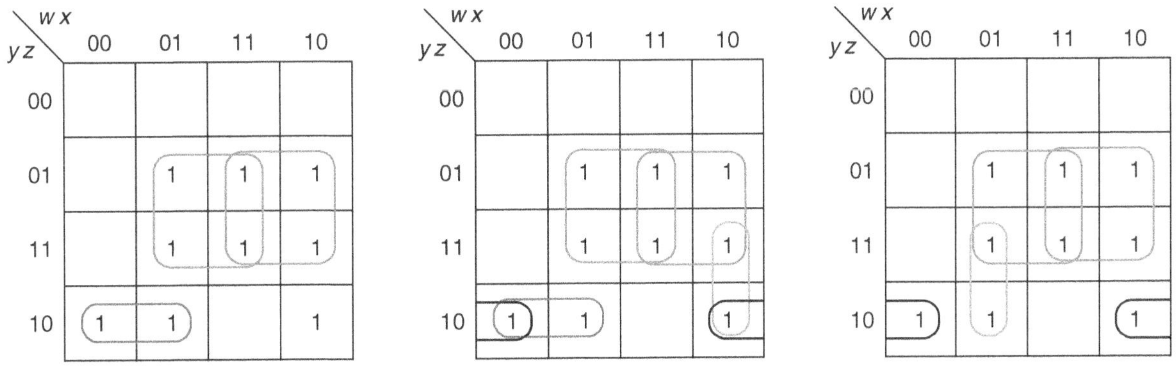

Then, only m_{10} remains, and it can be covered either by $wx'y$ or by $x'yz'$, as shown on the center map. Similarly, we could have started with $x'yz'$, in which case we could use $w'xy$ to complete the cover, as on the right-hand map. (We could also have chosen $w'yz'$, but that repeats one of the answers from before.) Thus, the three solutions are

$$g = xz + wz + w'yz' + wx'y'$$
$$g = xz + wz + w'yz' + x'yz'$$
$$g = xz + wz + x'yz' + w'xy$$

All three minimum solutions require four terms and 10 literals.

At this point, it is worth stating the obvious.

> **COMMON MISTAKE:** If there are multiple solutions, all minimum solutions must have the same number of terms and literals. If, for example, you find a minimum solution with three terms and seven literals, no solution with four terms is minimum, and no solution with three terms and eight literals is minimum.

EXAMPLE 3.12

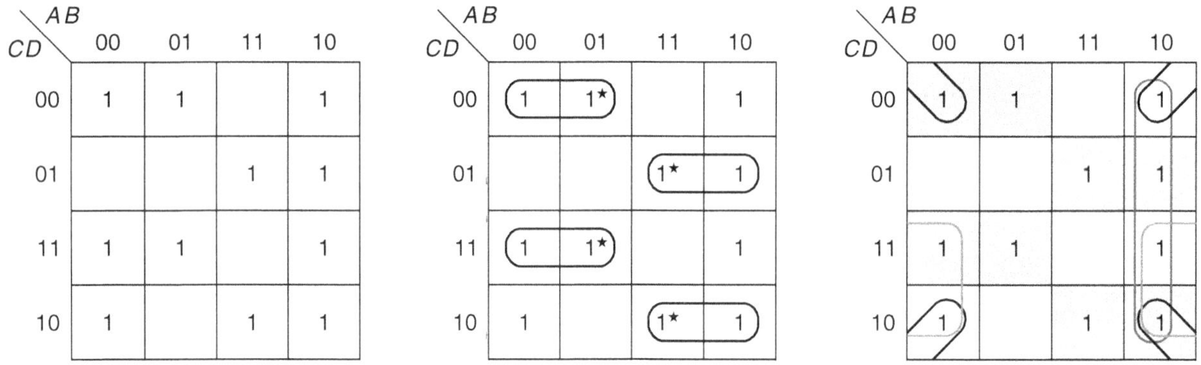

The four essential prime implicants are shown on the second map, leaving three 1's to be covered:

$$F = A'C'D' + AC'D + A'CD + ACD' + \cdots$$

These squares are shaded on the right-hand map. The three other prime implicants, all groups of four, are also shown on the right-hand map. Each of these covers two of the remaining three 1's (no two the same). Thus, any two of $B'D'$, AB', and $B'C$ can be used to complete the minimum SOP expression. The resulting three equally good answers are

$$F = A'C'D' + AC'D + A'CD + ACD' + B'D' + AB'$$
$$F = A'C'D' + AC'D + A'CD + ACD' + B'D' + B'C$$
$$F = A'C'D' + AC'D + A'CD + ACD' + AB' + B'C$$

EXAMPLE 3.13

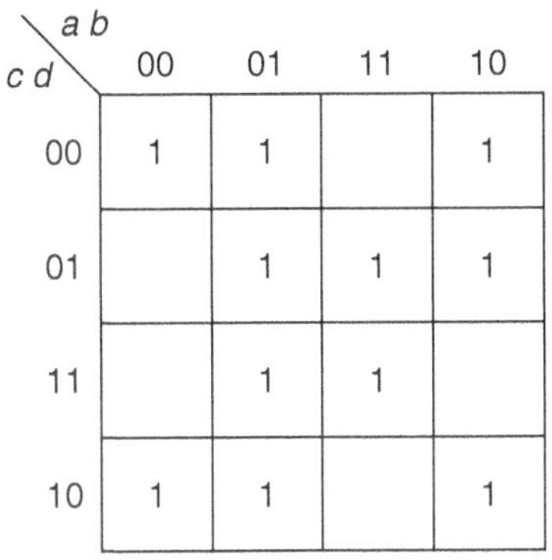

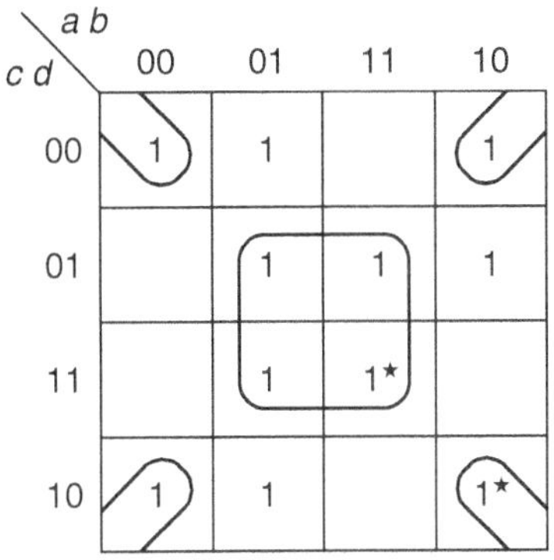

Once again there are two essential prime implicants, as shown on the right-hand map. The most isolated 1's are m_{10} and m_{15}. Each has only two adjacent 1's. But all of the 1's in groups of four have at least two adjacent 1's; if there are only two, then that minterm will make the prime implicant essential. (Each of the other 1's in those groups of four has at least three adjacent 1's.) The essential prime implicants give us

$$f = b'd' + bd + \cdots$$

There are three 1's not covered by the essential prime implicants. There is no single term that will cover all of them. However, the two in the 01 column can be covered by either of two groups of four, as shown on the map on the left ($a'd'$ circled in brown, $a'b$ in tan). And, there are two groups of two that cover m_9 ($ac'd$ circled in brown, $ab'c'$ in tan), shown on the map to the right.

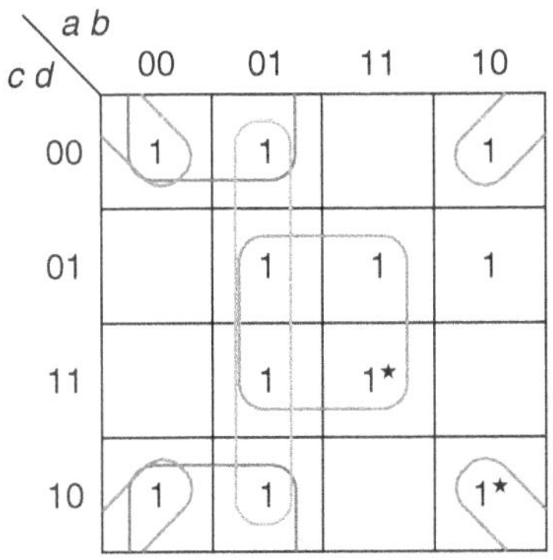

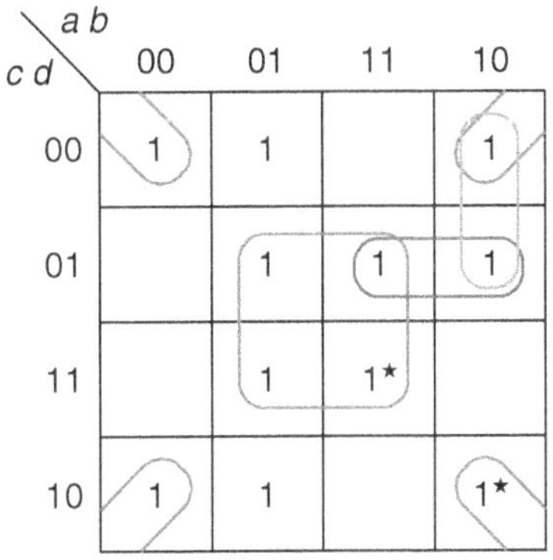

We can choose one term from the first pair and (independently) one from the second pair. Thus, there are four solutions. We can write the solution as shown, where we take one term from within each bracket

$$f = b'd' + bd + \begin{Bmatrix} a'd' \\ a'b \end{Bmatrix} + \begin{Bmatrix} ac'd \\ ab'c' \end{Bmatrix}$$

or we can write out all four expressions

$$
\begin{aligned}
f &= b'd' + bd + a'd' + ac'd \\
&= b'd' + bd + a'd' + ab'c' \\
&= b'd' + bd + a'b + ac'd \\
&= b'd' + bd + a'b + ab'c'
\end{aligned}
$$

EXAMPLE 3.14

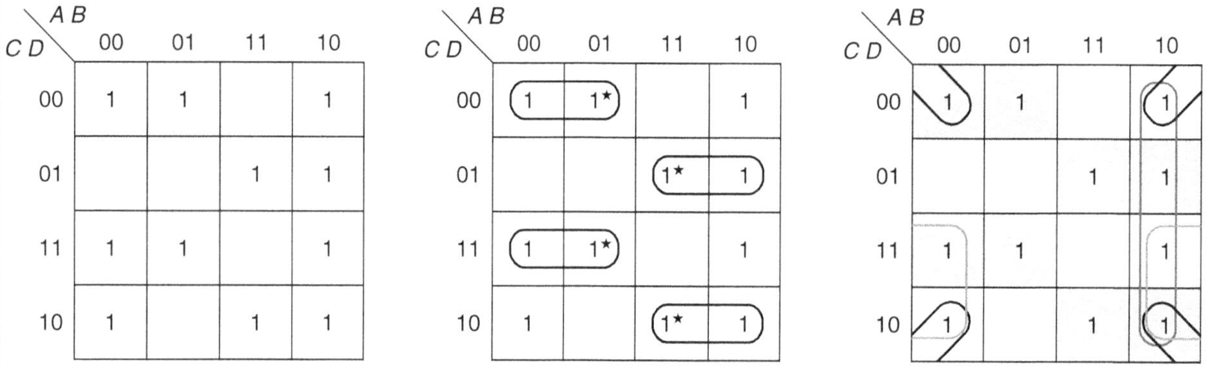

The four essential prime implicants are shown on the second map, leaving three 1's to be covered:

$$F = A'C'D' + AC'D + A'CD + ACD' + \cdots$$

These squares are shaded on the third map. The three other prime implicants, all groups of four, are also shown on the third map. Each of these covers two of the remaining three 1's (no two the same). Thus any two of $B'D'$, AB', and $B'C$ can be used to complete the minimum sum of products expression. The resulting three equally good answers are

$$
\begin{aligned}
F &= A'C'D' + AC'D + A'CD + ACD' + B'D' + AB' \\
F &= A'C'D' + AC'D + A'CD + ACD' + B'D' + B'C \\
F &= A'C'D' + AC'D + A'CD + ACD' + AB' + B'C
\end{aligned}
$$

Before doing additional (more complex) examples, we will introduce a somewhat different method for finding minimum sum of products expressions.

Map Method 2

1. Circle all of the prime implicants.
2. Select all essential prime implicants; they are easily identified by finding 1's that have only been circled once.
3. Then choose enough of the other prime implicants (as in Method 1). Of course, these prime implicants have already been identified in step 1.

EXAMPLE 3.15

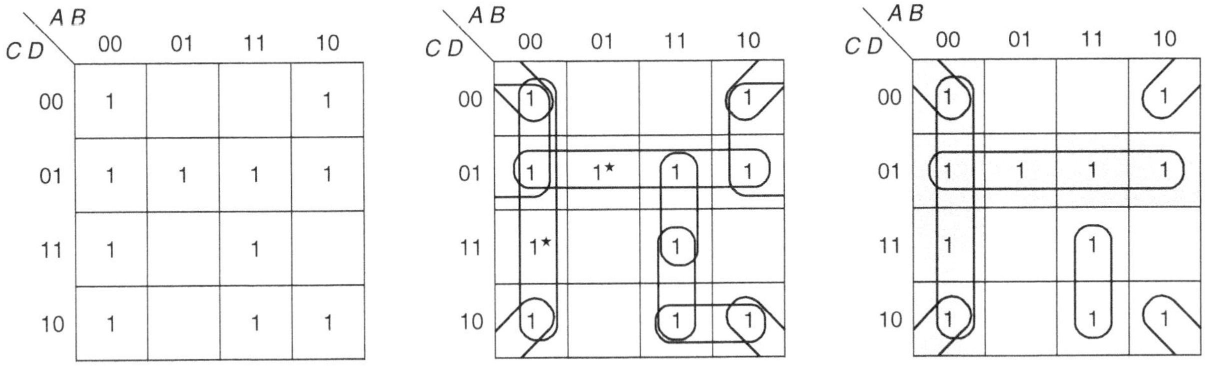

All of the prime implicants have been circled on the center map. Note that m_0 has been circled three times and that several minterms have been circled twice. However, m_3 and m_5 have only been circled once. Thus, the prime implicants that cover them, $A'B'$ and $C'D$ are essential. On the third map, we have shaded the part of the map covered by essential prime implicants to highlight what remains to be covered. There are four 1's, each of which can be covered in two different ways, and five prime implicants not used yet. No prime implicant covers more than two new 1's; thus, we need at least two more terms. Of the groups of four, only $B'D'$ covers two new 1's; $B'C'$ covers only one. Having chosen the first group, we must use ABC to cover the rest of the function, producing

$$F = A'B' + C'D + B'D' + ABC$$

Notice that this is the only set of four prime implicants (regardless of size) that covers the function.

EXAMPLE 3.16

$$G(A, B, C, D) = \Sigma m(0, 1, 3, 7, 8, 11, 12, 13, 15)$$

This is a case with more 1's left uncovered after finding the essential prime implicant. The first map shows all the prime implicants circled. The only essential prime implicant is YZ; there are five 1's remaining to be covered. Since all of the other prime implicants are groups of two, we need three more prime implicants. These 1's are organized in a chain, with each prime implicant linked to one on either side. If we are looking for just one solution, we should follow the guidelines from Method 1, choosing two terms that

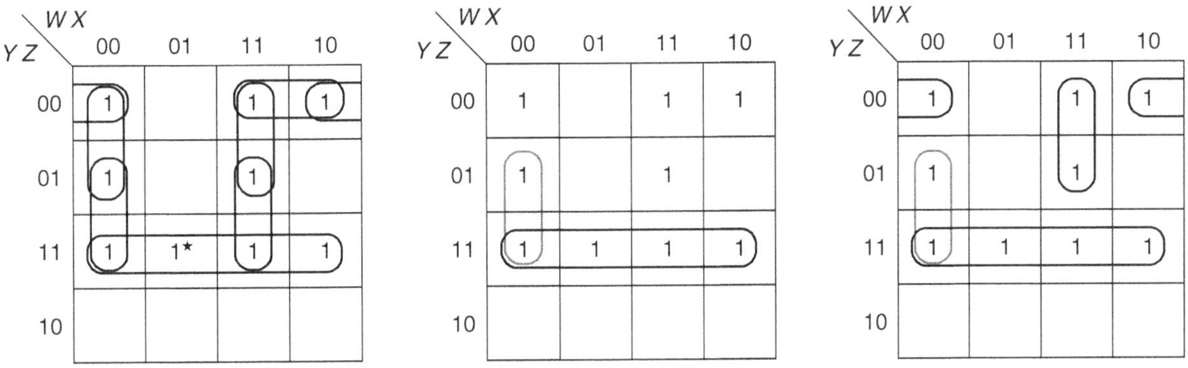

each cover new 1's and then select a term to cover the remaining 1. One such example is shown on the third map, starting with *WXY'* and *X'Y'Z'*. If we wish to find all of the minimum solutions, one approach is to start at one end of the chain (as shown in the second map). (We could have started at the other end, with m_{13}, and achieved the same results.) To cover m_1, we must either use *W'X'Z*, as shown in brown above, or *W'X'Y'* (as shown on the maps below). Once we have chosen *W'X'Z*, we have no more freedom, since the terms shown on the third map above are the only way to cover the remaining 1's in two additional terms. Thus, one solution is

$$F = YZ + W'X'Z + X'Y'Z' + WXY'$$

The next three maps show the solutions using *W'X'Y'* to cover m_0.

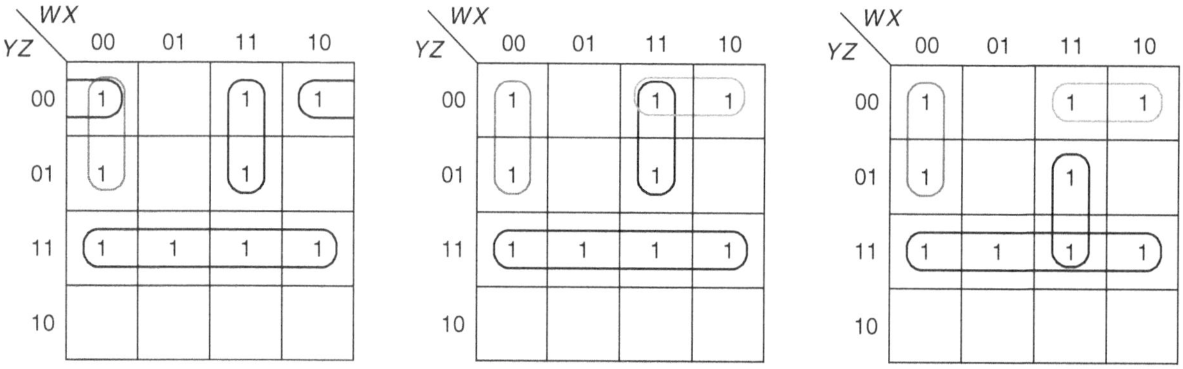

After choosing *W'X'Y'*, there are now three 1's to be covered. We can use the same last two terms as before (left) or use *WY'Z'* to cover m_8 (right two maps). The other three solutions are thus

$$F = YZ + W'X'Y' + X'Y'Z' + WXY'$$
$$F = YZ + W'X'Y' + WY'Z' + WXY'$$
$$F = YZ + W'X'Y' + WY'Z' + WXZ$$

We will now look at some examples with no essential prime implicants. A classic example of such a function is shown in Example 3.17.

EXAMPLE 3.17

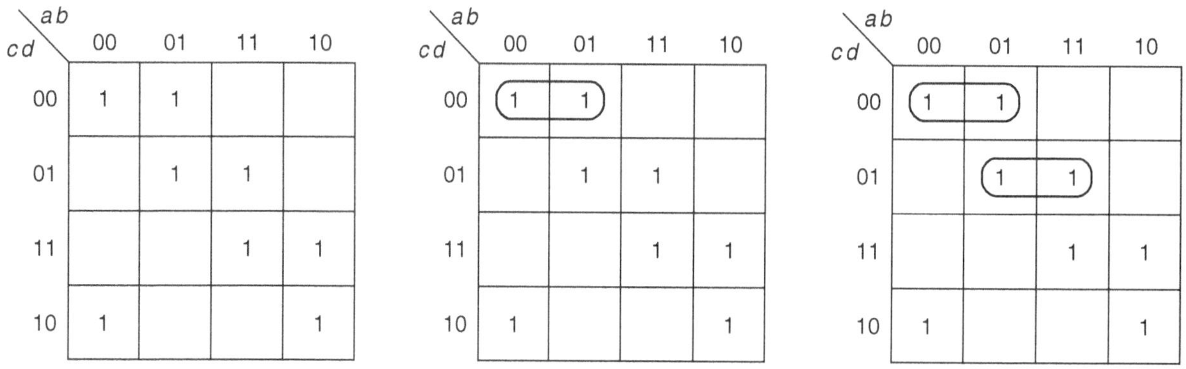

There are eight 1's; all prime implicants are groups of two. Thus, we need at least four terms in a minimum solution. There is no obvious place to start; thus, in the second map, we arbitrarily chose one of the terms, $a'c'd'$. Following the guidelines of step 2, we should then choose a second term that covers two new 1's, in such a way as not to leave an isolated uncovered 1. One such term is $bc'd$, as shown on the third map. Another possibility would be $b'cd'$ (the group in the last row). As we will see, that group will also be used. Repeating that procedure, we get the cover on the left-hand map below,

$$f = a'c'd' + bc'd + acd + b'cd'$$

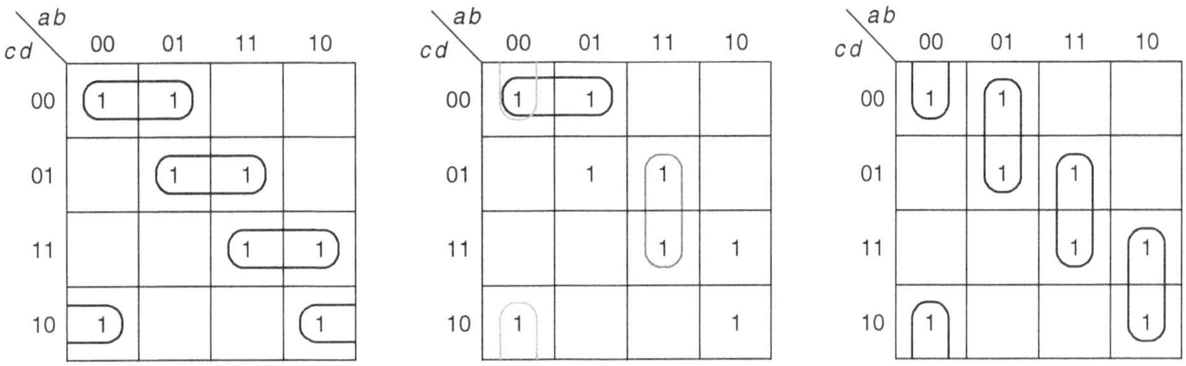

Notice that if, after starting with $a'c'd'$, we chose one of the prime implicants not included in this solution above, such as abd, shown on the middle map, we leave an isolated uncovered 1 (which would require a third term) plus three more 1's (which would require two more terms). A solution using those two terms would require five terms (obviously not minimum since we found one with four). Another choice would be a term such as $a'b'd'$, which covers only one new 1, leaving five 1's uncovered. That, too, would require at least five terms.

The other solution to this problem starts with $a'b'd'$, the only other prime implicant to cover m_0. Using the same process, we obtain the map on the right and the expression

$$f = a'b'd' + a'bc' + abd + ab'c$$

EXAMPLE 3.18

$$G(A, B, C, D) = \Sigma m(0, 1, 3, 4, 6, 7, 8, 9, 11, 12, 13, 14, 15)$$

All of the prime implicants are groups of four. Since there are 13 1's, we need at least four terms. The first map shows all of the prime implicants circled; there are nine. There are no 1's circled only once, and thus, there are no essential prime implicants.

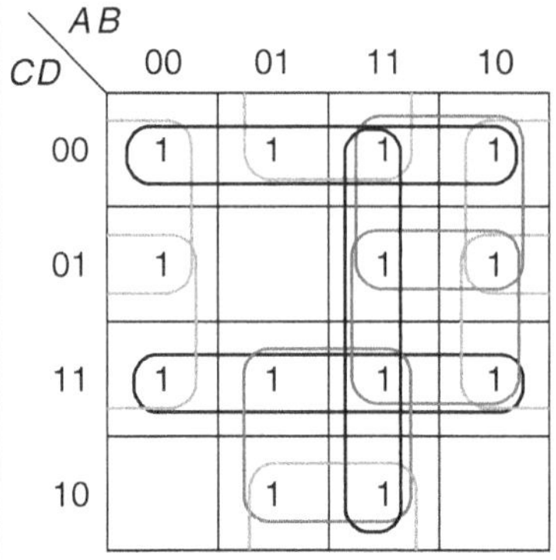

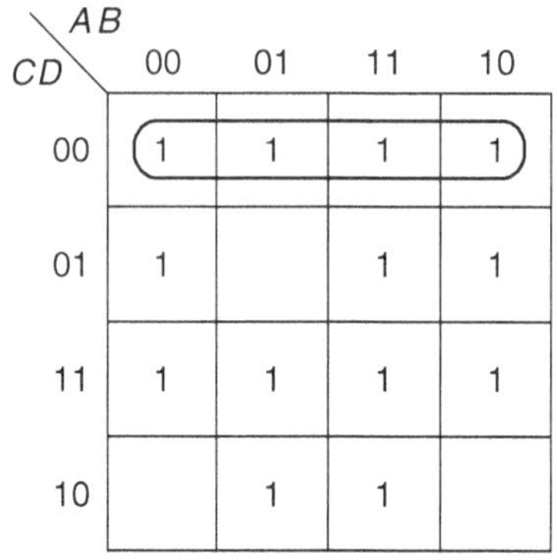

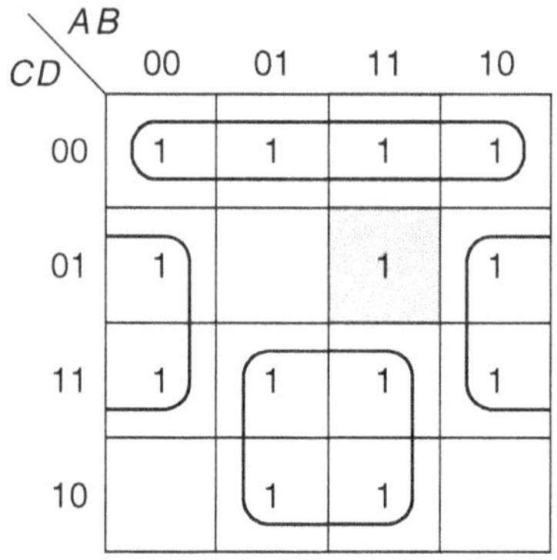

As a starting point, we choose one of the minterms covered by only two prime implicants, say m_0. On the second map, we used $C'D'$ to cover it. Next, we found two additional prime implicants that cover four new 1's each, as shown on the third map. That leaves just m_{13} to be covered. As can be seen on the fourth map (shown below), there are three different prime implicants that can be used. Now, we have three of the minimum solutions.

$$F = C'D' + B'D + BC + \{AB \quad \text{or} \quad AC' \quad \text{or} \quad AD\}$$

If, instead of using $C'D'$ to cover m_0, we use $B'C'$ (the only other prime implicant that covers m_0), as shown on the next map, we can find two other groups of four that each cover four new 1's and leave just m_{13} to be covered. Once again, we have three different ways to complete the cover (the same three terms as before).

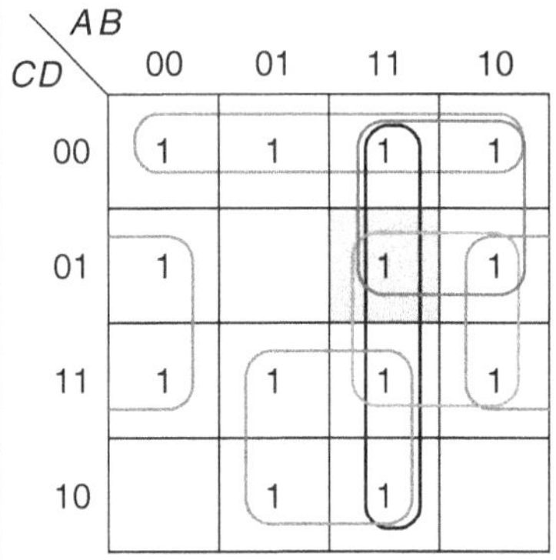

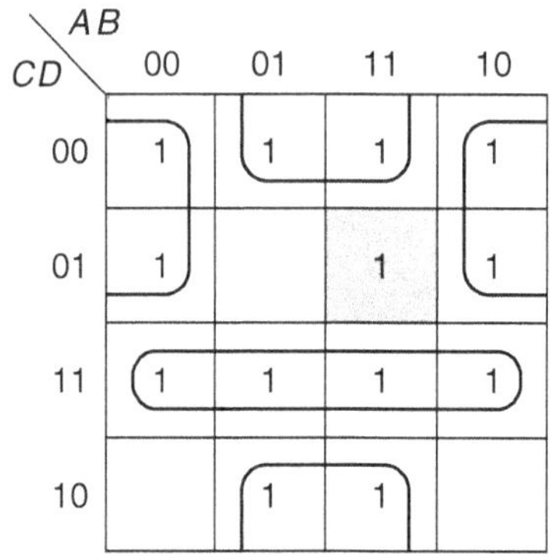

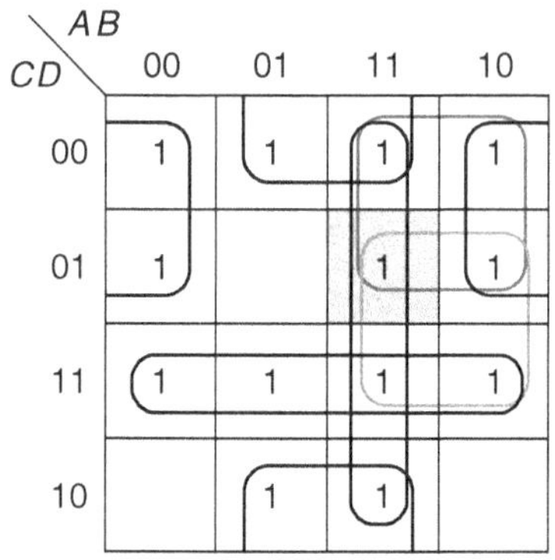

Thus, there are six equally good solutions

$$F = \begin{Bmatrix} C'D' + B'D + BC \\ B'C' + BD' + CD \end{Bmatrix} + \begin{Bmatrix} AB \\ AC' \\ AD \end{Bmatrix}$$

where one group of terms is chosen from the first bracket and an additional term from the second. We are sure that there are no better solutions, since each uses the minimum number of prime implicants, four. Although it may not be obvious without trying other combinations, there are no additional minimum solutions.

A number of other examples are included in Solved Problems 1 and 2. Example 3.19 is one of the most complex four-variable problems, requiring more terms than we might estimate at first.

EXAMPLE 3.19

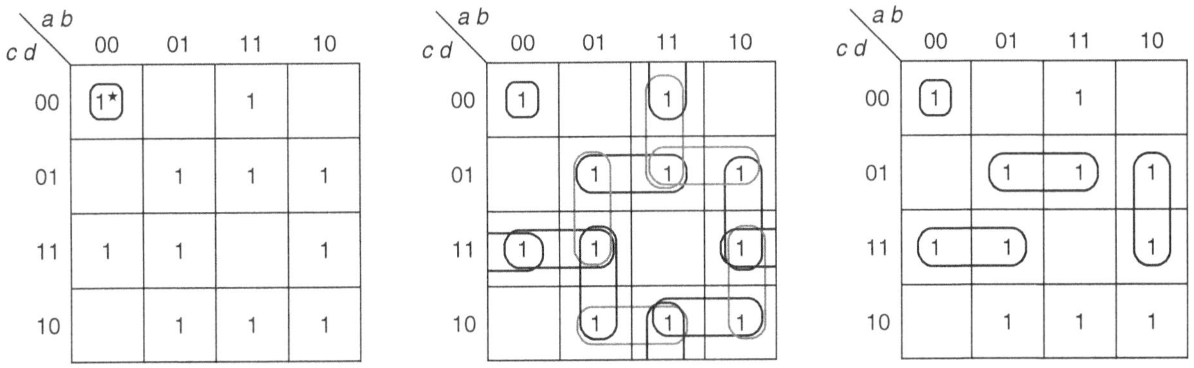

This function has one essential prime implicant (a minterm) and ten other 1's. All of the other prime implicants are groups of two. The second map shows all 13 prime implicants. The prime implicants of this function are

$a'b'c'd'$ $a'cd$ $b'cd$ $ac'd$ $bc'd$ bcd' acd'
$a'cd$ $a'bd$ abc' abd' $ab'c$ $ab'd$

Note that every 1 (other than m_0) can be covered by two or three different terms.

Since there are ten 1's to be covered by groups of two, we know that we need at least five terms, in addition to $a'b'c'd'$. The third map shows the beginnings of an attempt to cover the function. Each term covers two new 1's without leaving any isolated uncovered 1. (The 1 at the top could be combined with m_{14}.) The four 1's that are left require three additional terms. After trying several other groupings, we can see that it is not possible to cover this function with less than seven terms. There are 32 different minimum solutions to this problem. A few of the solutions are listed below. The remainder are left as an exercise (Exercise 1p).

$$\begin{aligned} f &= a'b'c'd' + a'cd + bc'd + ab'd + abc' + a'bc + acd' \\ &= a'b'c'd' + a'cd + bc'd + ab'd + abd' + bcd' + ab'c \\ &= a'b'c'd' + b'cd + a'bd + ac'd + abd' + acd' + bcd' \\ &= a'b'c'd' + b'cd + abc' + bcd' + a'bd + ab'c + ab'd \end{aligned}$$

[SP 2, 3, 4; EX 2, 3, 4]

3.3 DON'T CARES

Finding minimum solutions for functions with don't cares does not significantly change the methods we developed in the last section. We need to modify slightly the definitions of an implicant and a prime implicant, and clarify the definition of an essential prime implicant.

An *implicant* is a rectangle of 1, 2, 4, 8, . . . 1's or X's (containing no 0's).

A *prime implicant* is an implicant not included in any one larger rectangle. Thus, from the point of view of finding prime implicants, X's (don't cares) are treated as 1's.

An *essential prime implicant* is a prime implicant that covers at least one 1 not covered by any other prime implicant (as always). Don't cares (X's) do not make a prime implicant essential.

Now, we just apply either of the methods of the last section. When we are done, some of the X's may be included and some may not. But we *don't care* whether or not they are included in the function.

EXAMPLE 3.20

$F(A, B, C, D) = \Sigma m(1, 7, 10, 11, 13) + \Sigma d(5, 8, 15)$

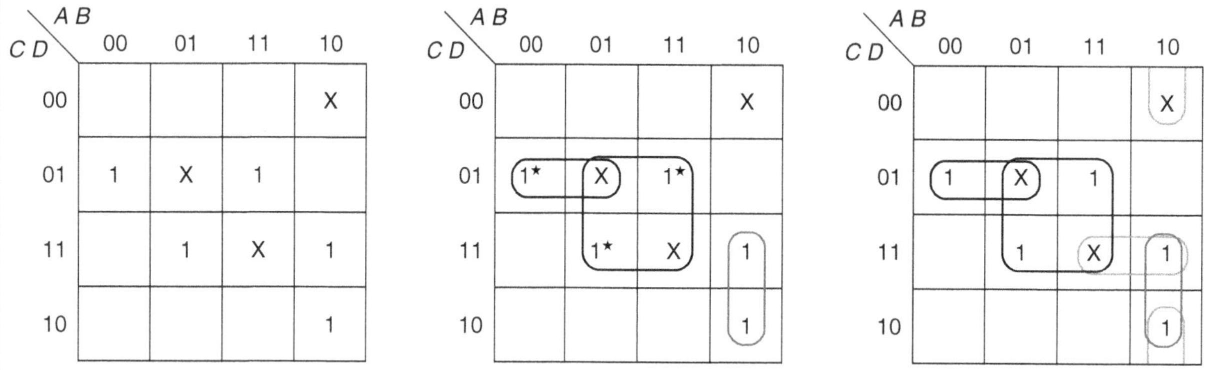

We first mapped the function, entering a 1 for those minterms included in the function and an X for the don't cares. We found two essential prime implicants, as shown on the center map. In each case, the 1's with a star cannot be covered by any other prime implicant. That left the two 1's circled in brown to cover the rest of the function. That is not an essential prime implicant, since each of the 1's could be covered by another prime implicant (as shown in tan on the third map). However, if we did not use $AB'C$, we would need two additional terms, instead of one. Thus, the only minimum solution is

$$F = BD + A'C'D + AB'C$$

and terms $AB'D'$ and ACD are prime implicants not used in the minimum solution. Note that if all of the don't cares were made 1's, we would need a fourth term to cover m_8, making

$$F = BD + A'C'D + AB'C + AB'D' \quad \text{or}$$
$$F = BD + A'C'D + ACD + AB'D'$$

and that if all of the don't cares were 0's, the function would become

$$F = A'B'C'D + A'BCD + ABC'D + AB'C$$

In either case, the solution is much more complex then when we treated those terms as don't cares (and made two of them 1's and the other a 0).

EXAMPLE 3.21

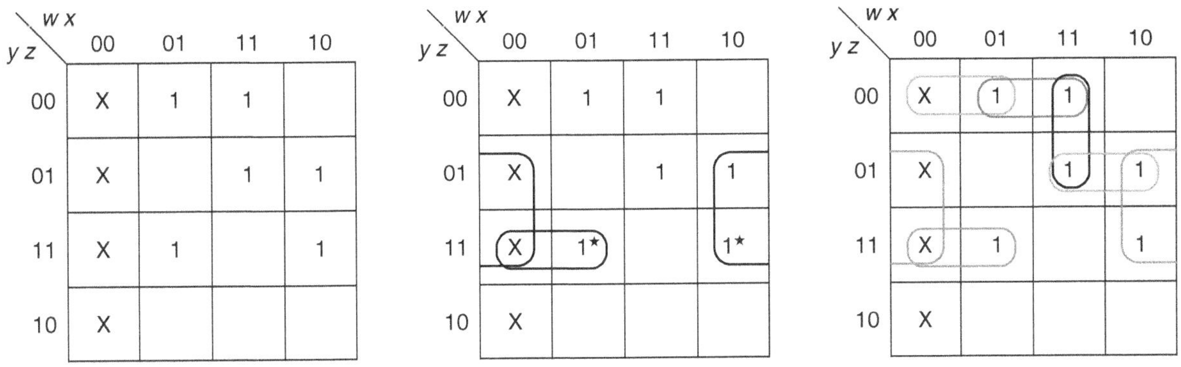

There are two essential prime implicants, as shown on the center map, $x'z$ and $w'yz$. The group of four don't cares, $w'x'$, is a prime implicant (since it is a rectangle of four 1's or X's) but it is not essential (since it does not cover any 1's not covered by some other prime implicant). Surely, a prime implicant made up of all don't cares would never be used, since that would add a term to the sum without covering any additional 1's. The three remaining 1's require two groups of two and thus there are three equally good solutions, each using four terms and 11 literals:

$$g_1 = x'z + w'yz + w'y'z' + wxy'$$
$$g_2 = x'z + w'yz + xy'z' + wxy'$$
$$g_3 = x'z + w'yz + xy'z' + wy'z$$

An important thing to note about Example 3.21 is that the three algebraic expressions are not all equal. The first treats the don't care for m_0 as a 1, whereas the other two (which are equal to each other) treat it as a 0. This will often happen with don't cares. They must treat the specified part of the function (the 1's and the 0's) the same, but the don't cares may take on different values in the various solutions. The maps of Map 3.15 show the three functions.

Map 3.15 The different solutions for Example 3.21.

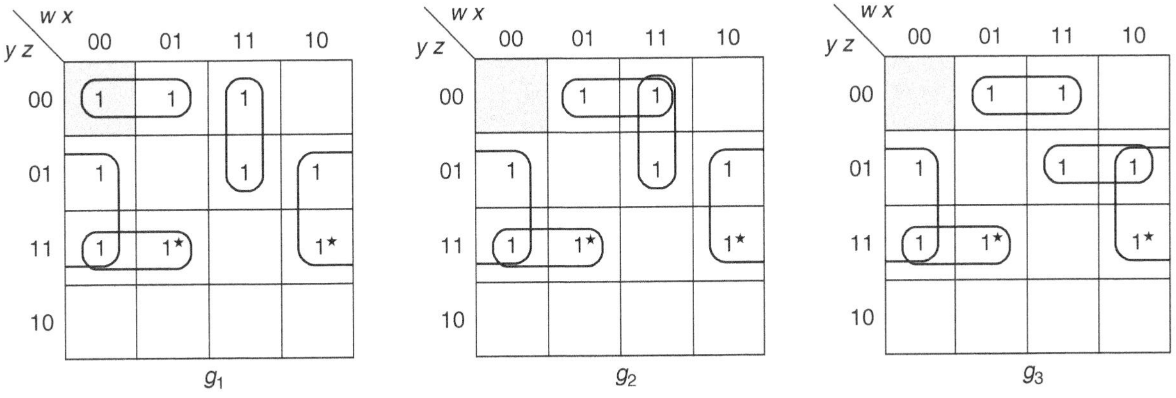

EXAMPLE 3.22

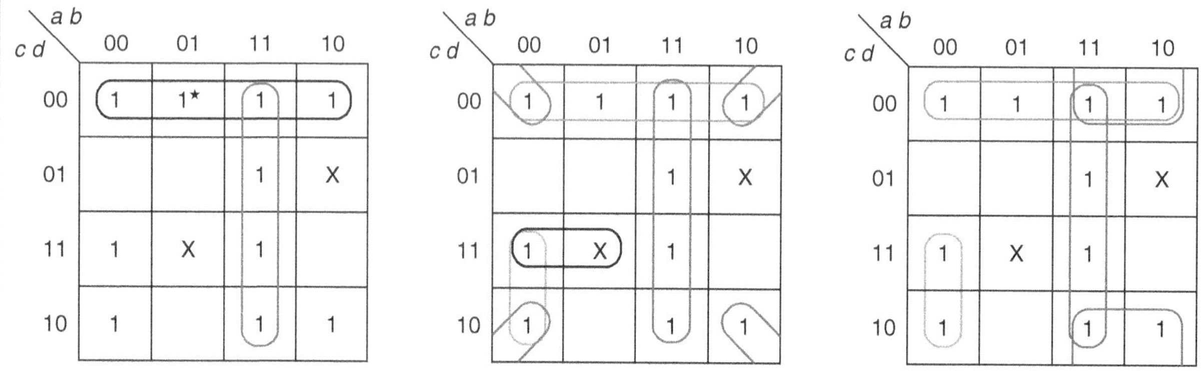

On the first map, we have shown the only essential prime implicant, $c'd'$, and the other group of four that is used in all three solutions, ab. (This must be used since the only other prime implicant that would cover m_{15} is bcd, which requires one more literal and does not cover any 1's that are not covered by ab.) The three remaining 1's require two terms, one of which must be a group of two (to cover m_3) and the other must be one of the groups of four that cover m_{10}. On the second map, we have shown two of the solutions, those that utilize $b'd'$ as the group of four. On the third map, we have shown the third solution, utilizing ad'. Thus, we have

$$g_1 = c'd' + ab + b'd' + a'cd$$
$$g_2 = c'd' + ab + b'd' + a'b'c$$
$$g_3 = c'd' + ab + ad' + a'b'c$$

We can now ask if these solutions are equal to each other. We can either map all three solutions as we did for Example 3.21, or we can make a table of the behavior of the don't cares—one column for each don't care and one row for each solution.

	m_7	m_9
g_1	1	0
g_2	0	0
g_3	0	0

From the table, it is clear that $g_2 = g_3$, but neither is equal to g_1. A more complex example is found in the solved problems.

Don't cares give us another option for solving map problems for functions with or without don't cares. At any point in the process of using either Map Method 1 or 2, we can replace all 1's covered by the terms already chosen by don't cares. That highlights the 1's remaining to be covered. We then need to choose enough terms to cover the remaining

1's. This works because the 1's already covered can be used again (as part of a term covering some new 1's), but need not be.

EXAMPLE 3.23

$F(A, B, C, D) = \Sigma m(0, 3, 4, 5, 6, 7, 8, 10, 11, 14, 15)$

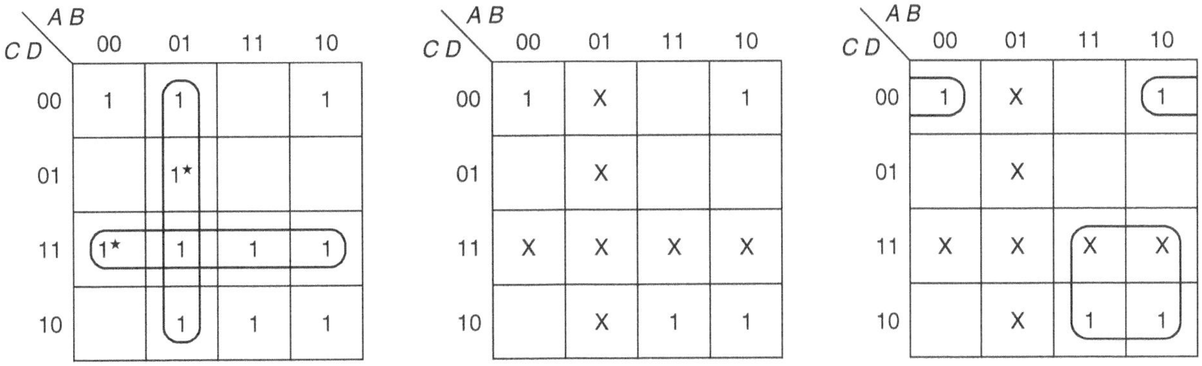

We first found the two essential prime implicants, $A'B$ and CD. On the second map, we converted all of the 1's covered to don't cares. Finally, we can cover the remaining 1's with AC and $B'C'D'$, producing

$$F = A'B + CD + AC + B'C'D'$$

Replacing covered minterms by don't cares accomplishes the same thing as the shading that we did in Examples 3.14 and 3.15; it highlights the 1's that remain to be covered.

EXAMPLE 3.24

The essential prime implicants, xy' and $x'y$, are circled on the first map. The 1's covered by them are changed to don't cares on the second map. It is now clear that the two 1's in the 10 column can be covered by either $w'y$ or $w'x$ and that the other 1 can be covered by $wx'z'$ or $wy'z'$.

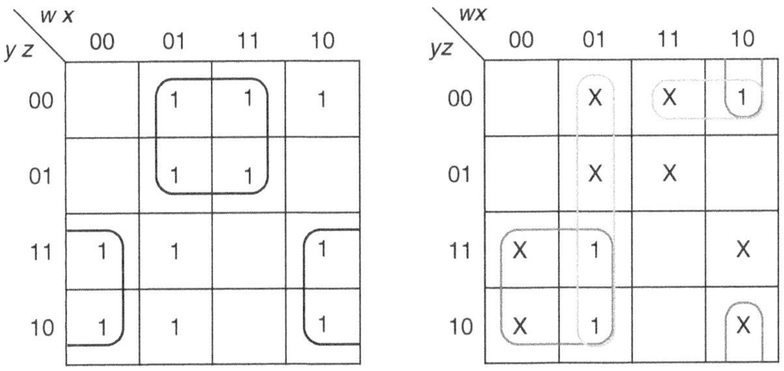

Thus, the four minimum solutions are

$$xy' + x'y + \begin{Bmatrix} w'y \\ x'y \end{Bmatrix} + \begin{Bmatrix} wx'z' \\ wy'z' \end{Bmatrix}$$

[SP 5, 6; EX 5, 6]

3.4 PRODUCT OF SUMS

Finding a minimum product of sums expression requires no new theory. The following approach is the simplest:

1. Map the complement of the function. (If there is already a map for the function, replace all 0's by 1's, all 1's by 0's, and leave X's unchanged.)
2. Find the minimum sum of products expression for the complement of the function (using the techniques of the last two sections).
3. Use DeMorgan's theorem (P11) to complement that expression, producing a product of sums expression.

Another approach, which we will not pursue here, is to define the dual of prime implicants (referred to as prime implicates) and develop a new method.

EXAMPLE 3.25

$$f(a, b, c, d) = \Sigma m(0, 1, 4, 5, 10, 11, 14)$$

Since all minterms must be either minterms of f or of f', then f' must be the sum of all of the other minterms, that is

$$f'(a, b, c, d) = \Sigma m(2, 3, 6, 7, 8, 9, 12, 13, 15)$$

Maps of both f and f' are shown below:

cd \ ab	00	01	11	10
00	1	1		
01	1	1		
11				1
10			1	1

f

cd \ ab	00	01	11	10
00			1	1
01			1	1
11	1	1	1	
10	1	1		

f'

We did not need to map f, unless we wanted both the sum of products expression and the product of sums expression. Once we mapped f, we did not need to write out all the minterms of f'; we could have just replaced the 1's by 0's and 0's by 1's. Also, instead of mapping f', we could look for rectangles of 0's on the map of f. This function is rather straightforward. The maps for the minimum sum of product expressions for both f and f' are shown next:

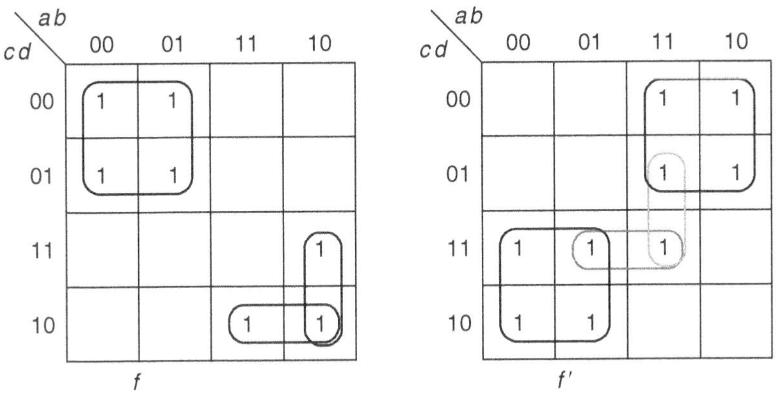

There is one minimum solution for f and there are two equally good solutions for the sum of products for f':

$$f = a'c' + ab'c + acd' \qquad f' = ac' + a'c + abd$$
$$f' = ac' + a'c + bcd$$

We can then complement the solutions for f' to get the two minimum product of sums solutions for f:

$$f = (a' + c)(a + c')(a' + b' + d')$$
$$f = (a' + c)(a + c')(b' + c' + d')$$

The minimum sum of products solution has three terms and eight literals; the minimum product of sums solutions have three terms and seven literals. (There is no set pattern; sometimes the sum of products solution has fewer terms or literals, sometimes the product of sums does, and sometimes they have the same number of terms and literals.)

EXAMPLE 3.26

Find all of the minimum sum of products and all minimum product of sums solutions for

$$g(w, x, y, z) = \Sigma m(1, 3, 4, 6, 11) + \Sigma d(0, 8, 10, 12, 13)$$

We first find the minimum sum of products expression by mapping g. However, before complicating the map by circling prime implicants, we also map g' (top of next page). Note that the X's are the same on both maps.

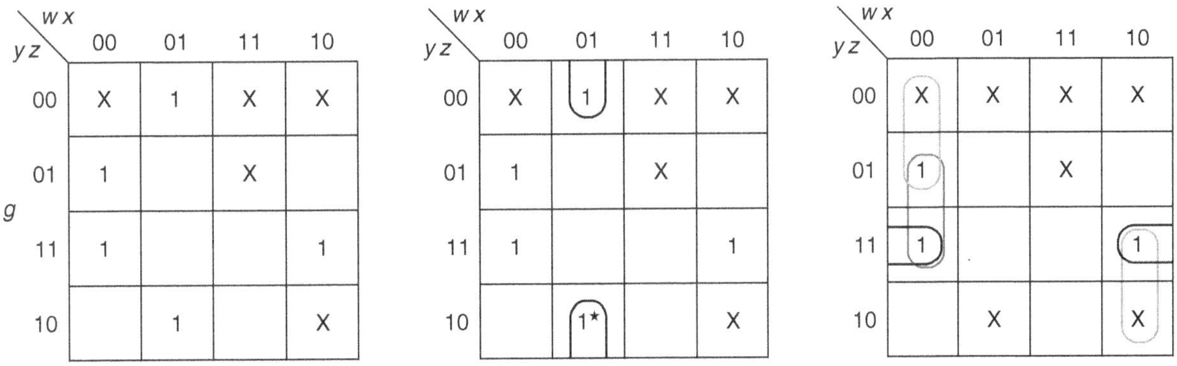

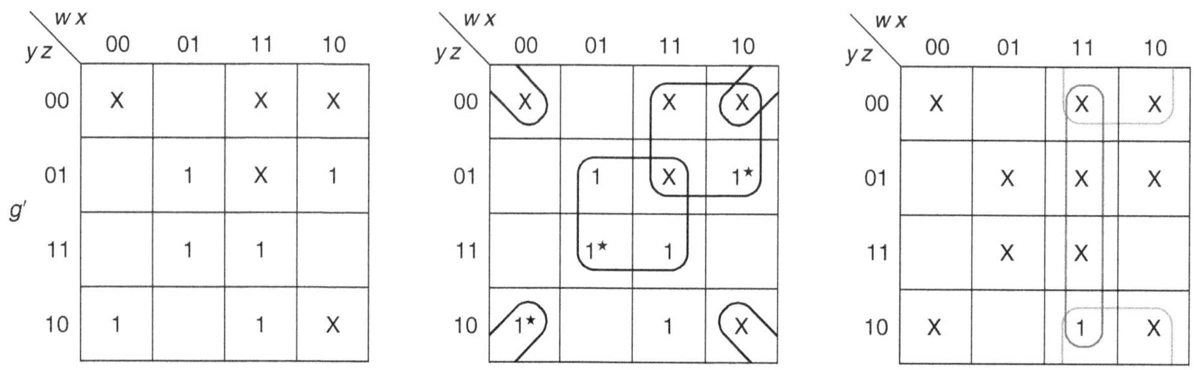

For g, the only essential prime implicant, $w'xz'$ is shown on the center map. The 1's covered by it are made don't cares on the right-hand map, and the remaining useful prime implicants are circled. We have seen similar examples before, where we have three 1's to be covered in groups of two. There are three equally good solutions:

$$g = w'xz' + \begin{Bmatrix} w'x'y' + x'yz \\ w'x'z + x'yz \\ w'x'z + wx'y \end{Bmatrix}$$

For g', there are three essential prime implicants, as shown on the center map. Once all of the 1's covered by them have been made don't cares, there is only one 1 left; it can be covered in two ways as shown on the right map:

$$g' = x'z' + xz + wy' + \begin{Bmatrix} wx \\ wz' \end{Bmatrix}$$

$$g = (x + z)(x' + z')(w' + y)\begin{Bmatrix} (w' + x') \\ (w' + z) \end{Bmatrix}$$

Note that in this example, the sum of products solutions each require only three terms (with nine literals), whereas the product of sums solutions each require four terms (with eight literals).

Finally, we want to determine which, if any, of the five solutions are equal. The complication (compared to this same question in the last section) is that when we treat a don't care as a 1 for g', that means that we are treating it as a 0 of g. Labeling the three sum of product solutions as g_1, g_2, and g_3, and the two product of sums solutions as g_4 and g_5, we produce the following table:

	0	**8**	**10**	**12**	**13**
g_1	1	0	0	0	0
g_2	0	0	0	0	0
g_3	0	0	1	0	0
g_4'	1	1	1	1	1
g_4	0	0	0	0	0
g_5'	1	1	1	1	1
g_5	0	0	0	0	0

The product of sum solutions treat all of the don't cares as 1's of g' since each is circled by the essential prime implicants of g'. (Thus, they are 0's of g.) We then note that the three solutions that are equal are

$$g_2 = w'xz' + w'x'z + x'yz$$

$$g_4 = (x + z)(x' + z')(w' + y)(w' + x')$$

$$g_5 = (x + z)(x' + z')(w' + y)(w' + z)$$

[SP 7, 8; EX 7, 8]

3.5 FIVE- AND SIX-VARIABLE MAPS

A five-variable map consists of $2^5 = 32$ squares. Although there are several arrangements that have been used, we prefer to look at it as two layers of 16 squares each. The top layer (on the left below) contains the squares for the first 16 minterms (for which the first variable, A, is 0) and the bottom layer contains the remaining 16 squares, as pictured in Map 3.16:

Map 3.16 A five-variable map.

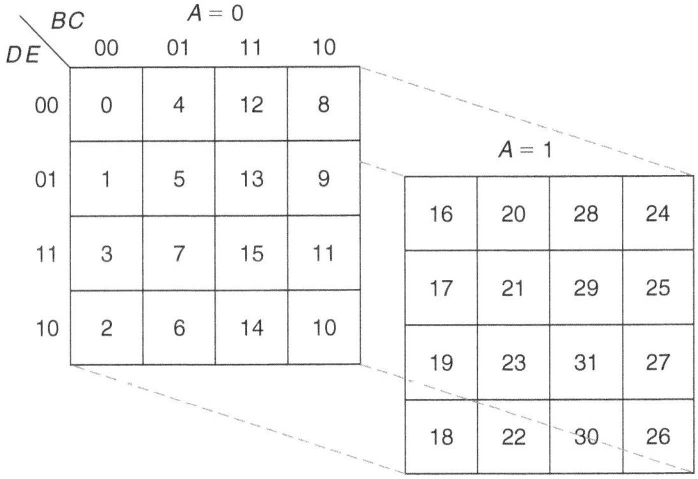

Each square in the bottom layer corresponds to the minterm numbered 16 more than the square above it. Product terms appear as rectangular solids of 1, 2, 4, 8, 16, . . . 1's or X's. Squares directly above and below each other are adjacent.

EXAMPLE 3.27

$$m_2 + m_5 = A'B'C'DE' + AB'C'DE' = B'C'DE'$$

$$m_{11} + m_{27} = A'BC'DE + ABC'DE = BC'DE$$

$$m_5 + m_7 + m_{21} + m_{23} = B'CE$$

These terms are circled on the following map.

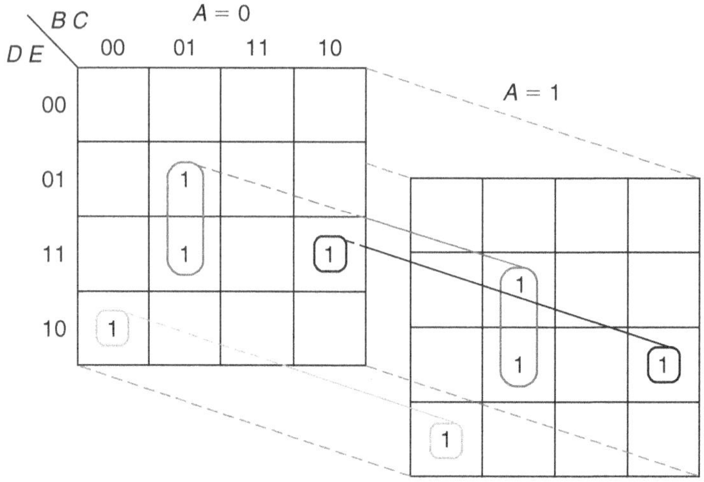

In a similar manner, six-variable maps are drawn as four layers of 16-square maps, where the first two variables determine the layer and the other variables specify the square within the layer. The layout, with minterm numbers shown, is given in Map 3.17. Note that the layers are ordered in the same way as the rows and the columns, that is 00, 01, 11, 10.

In this section, we will concentrate on five-variable maps, although we will also do an example of six-variable maps at the end. The techniques are the same as for four-variable maps; the only thing new is the need to visualize the rectangular solids. Rather than drawing the maps to look like three dimensions, we will draw them side by side. The function, F, is mapped in Map 3.18.

$$F(A, B, C, D, E) = \Sigma m(4, 5, 6, 7, 9, 11, 13, 15, 16, 18, 27, 28, 31)$$

Map 3.17 A six-variable map.

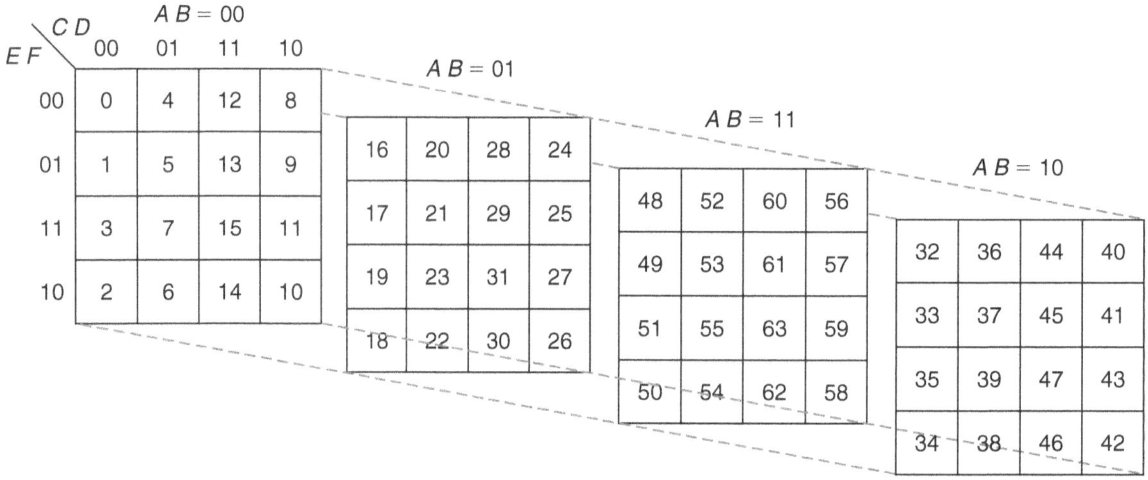

Map 3.18 A five-variable problem.

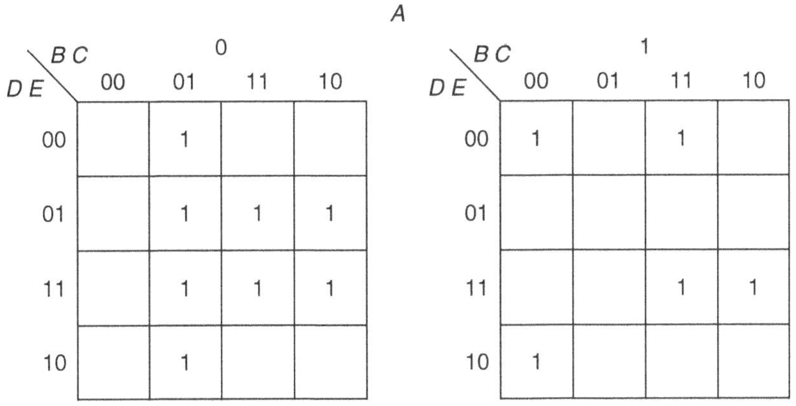

As always, we first look for the essential prime implicants. A good starting point is to find 1's on one layer for which there is a 0 in the corresponding square on an adjoining layer. Prime implicants that cover that 1 are contained completely on that layer (and thus, we really only have a four-variable map problem). In this example, m_4 meets this criteria (since there is a 0 in square 20 below it). Thus, the only prime implicants covering m_4 must be on the first layer. Indeed, $A'B'C$ is an essential prime implicant. (Note that the A' comes from the fact that this group is contained completely on the $A = 0$ layer of the map and the $B'C$ from the fact that this group is in the second column.) Actually, all four 1's in this term have no counterpart on the other layer and m_6 would also make this prime implicant essential. (The other two 1's in that term are part of another prime implicant, as well.) We also note that m_9, m_{16}, m_{18}, and m_{28} have 0's in the corresponding square on the other layer and make a prime implicant essential. Although m_{14} has a 0 beneath it (m_{30}), it does not make a prime implicant on the A' layer essential. Thus, Map 3.19 shows each of these circled, highlighting the essential prime implicants that are contained on one layer.

Map 3.19 Essential prime implicants on one layer.

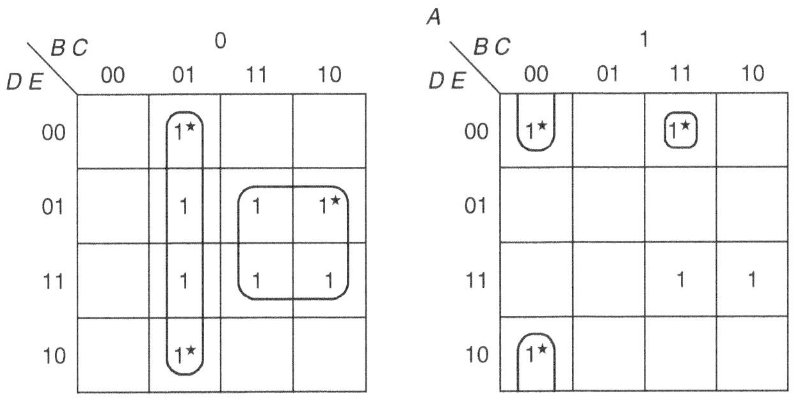

So far, we have

$$F = A'B'C + A'BE + AB'C'E' + ABCD'E' + \cdots$$

The two 1's remaining uncovered do have counterparts on the other layer. However, the only prime implicant that covers them is BDE, as shown on Map 3.20 in brown. It, too, is an essential prime implicant. (Note that prime implicants that include 1's from both layers do not have the variable A in them. Such prime implicants must, of course, have the same number of 1's on each layer; otherwise, they would not be rectangular.)

Map 3.20 A prime implicant covering 1's on both layers.

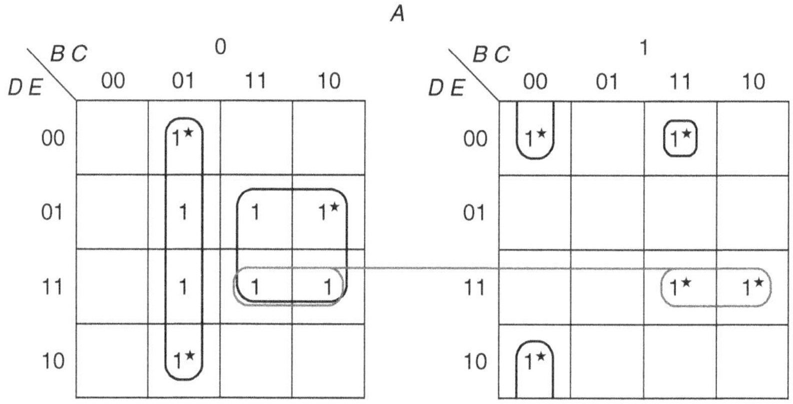

The complete solution is thus

$$F = A'B'C + A'BE + AB'C'E' + ABCD'E' + BDE$$

Groups of eight 1's are not uncommon in five-variable problems, as illustrated in Example 3.28.

EXAMPLE 3.28

$$G(A, B, C, D, E) = \Sigma m(1, 3, 8, 9, 11, 12, 14, 17, 19, 20, 22, 24, 25, 27)$$

The first map shows a plot of that function. On the second map, to the right, we have circled the two essential prime implicants that we found by considering 1's on one layer with 0's in the corresponding square on the other layer, $A'BCE'$ and $AB'CE'$. The group of eight 1's, $C'E$ (also an essential prime implicant), is shown in brown on the third map (where the essential prime implicants found on the second map are shown as don't cares). Groups of eight have three literals missing (leaving only two). At this point, only two 1's are left uncovered; that requires the essential prime implicant, $BC'D'$, shown on the fourth map in tan.

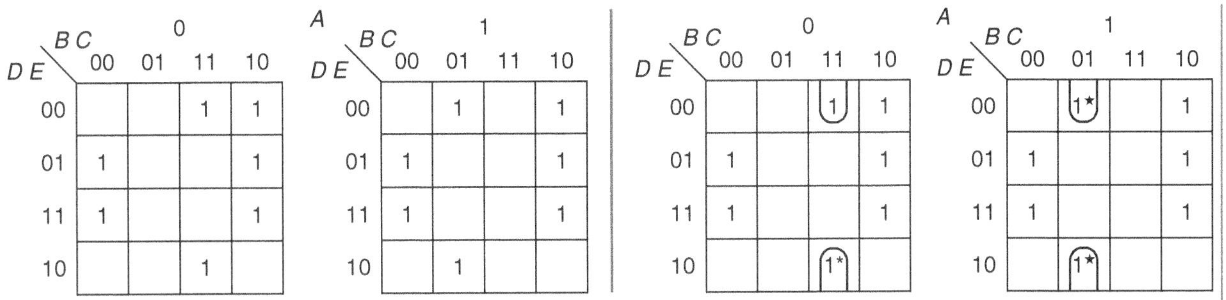

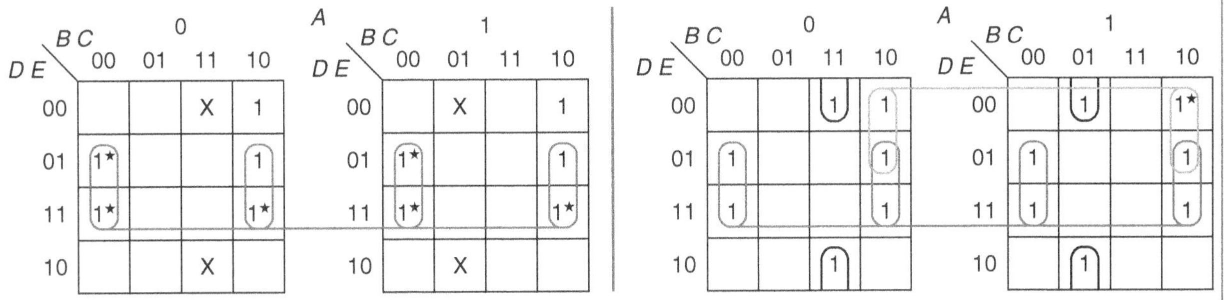

The solution is thus

$$G = A'BCE' + AB'CE' + C'E + BC'D'$$

Note that there is only one other prime implicant in this function, $A'BD'E'$; it covers no 1's not already covered.

EXAMPLE 3.29

The next problem is shown on the maps below. Once again, we start by looking for 1's that are on one layer, with a corresponding 0 on the other layer. Although there are several such 1's on the $A = 0$ layer, only m_{10} makes a prime implicant essential. Similarly, on the $A = 1$ layer, m_{30} is covered by an essential prime implicant. These terms, $A'C'E'$ and $ABCD$, are shown on the second map. The 1's covered are shown as don't cares on the next map.

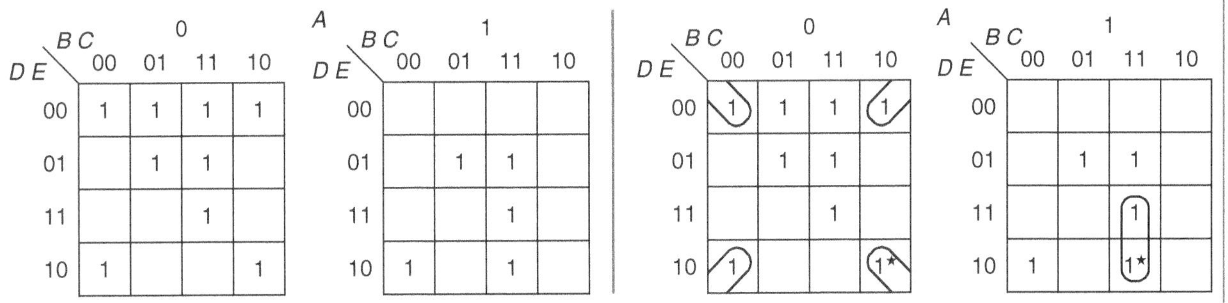

Three other essential prime implicants include 1's from both layers of the map; they are $CD'E$, BCE and $B'C'DE'$, as shown on the left-hand map below. These were found by looking for isolated 1's, such as m_{21}, m_{15}, and m_{18}.

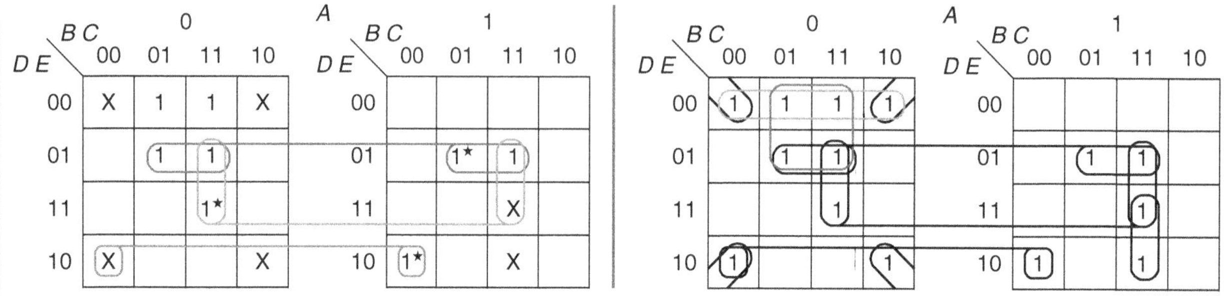

Finally, the remaining two 1's (m_4 and m_{12}) can be covered in two ways, as shown on the right-hand map above, $A'CD'$ and $A'D'E'$. Thus, the two solutions are

$$F = A'C'E' + ABCD + CD'E + BCE + B'C'DE' + A'CD'$$

$$F = A'C'E' + ABCD + CD'E + BCE + B'C'DE' + A'D'E'$$

EXAMPLE 3.30

$$H(A, B, C, D, E) = \Sigma m(1, 8, 9, 12, 13, 14, 16, 18, 19, 22, 23, 24, 30) + \Sigma d(2, 3, 5, 6, 7, 17, 25, 26)$$

A map of H is shown below on the left with the only essential prime implicant, $B'D$ (a group of eight, including four 1's and four don't cares), circled.

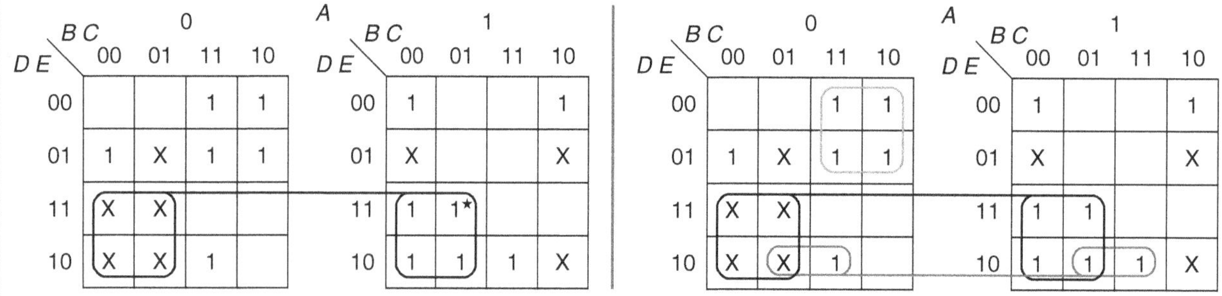

Next, we choose CDE', since otherwise separate terms would be needed to cover m_{14} and m_{30}. We also chose $A'BD'$ since it covers four new 1's. Furthermore, if that were not used, a group of two ($A'BCE'$) would be needed to cover m_{12}. That leaves us with three 1's (m_1, m_{16}, and m_{24}) to be covered. On the maps below, we have replaced all covered 1's by don't cares (X's) to highlight the remaining 1's. No term that covers m_1 also covers either of the other terms. However, m_{16} and m_{24} can be covered with one term in either of two ways ($AC'E'$ or $AC'D'$) as shown on the first map below, and m_1 can

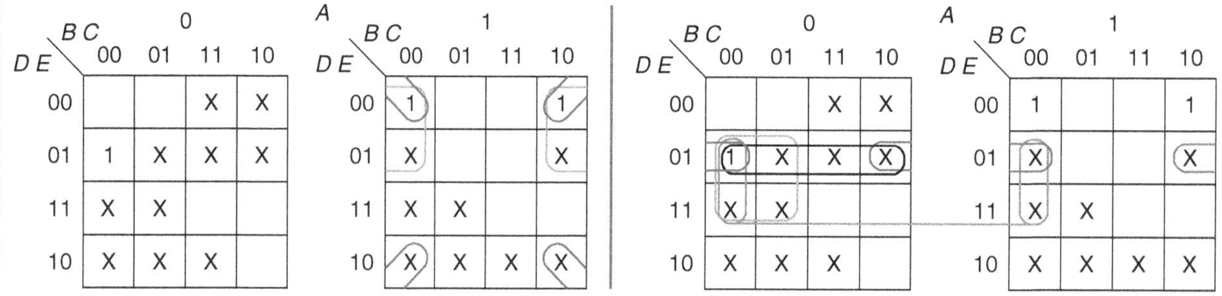

be covered by four different groups of four, as shown on the second map ($A'D'E$, $A'B'E$, $B'C'E$, or $C'D'E$), yielding the eight solutions shown.

$$H = B'D + CDE' + A'BD' + \begin{Bmatrix} AC'E' \\ AC'D' \end{Bmatrix} + \begin{Bmatrix} A'D'E \\ A'B'E \\ B'C'E \\ C'D'E \end{Bmatrix}$$

Finally, we will look at one example of a six-variable function.

EXAMPLE 3.31

$G(A, B, C, D, E, F) = \Sigma m(1, 3, 6, 8, 9, 13, 14, 17, 19, 24, 25, 29, 32, 33, 34, 35, 38, 40, 46, 49, 51, 53, 55, 56, 61, 63)$

The map is drawn horizontally, with the first two variables determining the 16-square layer (numbered, of course 00, 01, 11, 10).

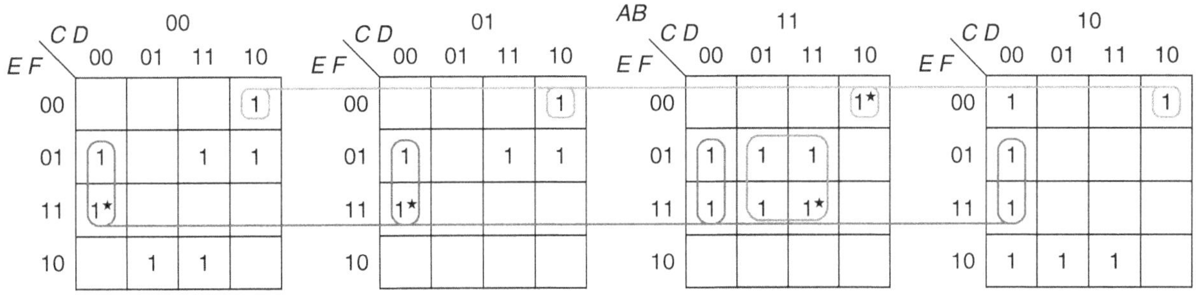

The first map shows three of the essential prime implicants. The only one that is confined to one layer is on the third layer, $ABDF$. The 1's in the upper right-hand corner of each layer form another group of four (without the first two variables), $CD'E'F'$. The brown squares form a group of eight, $C'D'F$. The next map shows 1's covered by the first three prime implicants as don't cares.

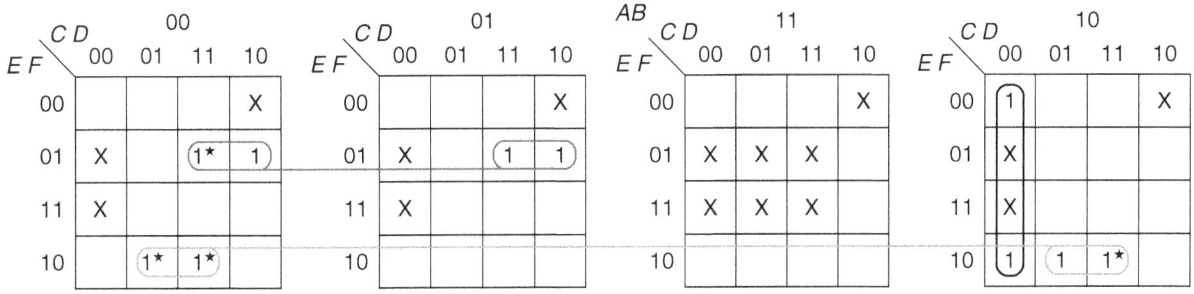

The other two essential prime implicants are $A'CE'F$ and $B'DEF'$. (Remember that the top and bottom layers are adjacent.) Finally, m_{32} and m_{34} (on the fourth layer) remain uncovered; they are covered by the term, $AB'C'D'$. (Each of them could have been covered by a group of two, but that would take two terms.) Thus, the minimum expression is

$$G = ABDF + CD'E'F' + C'D'F + A'CE'F + B'DEF' + AB'C'D'$$

[SP 9, 10; EX 9, 10]

3.6 MULTIPLE OUTPUT PROBLEMS

Many real problems involve designing a system with more than one output. If, for example, we had a problem with three inputs, *A*, *B*, and *C* and two outputs, *F* and *G*, we could treat this as two separate problems (as shown on the left in Figure 3.1). We would then map each of the functions, and find minimum solutions. However, if we treated this as a single system with three inputs and two outputs (as shown on the right), we may be able to economize by sharing gates.

Figure 3.1 Implementation of two functions.

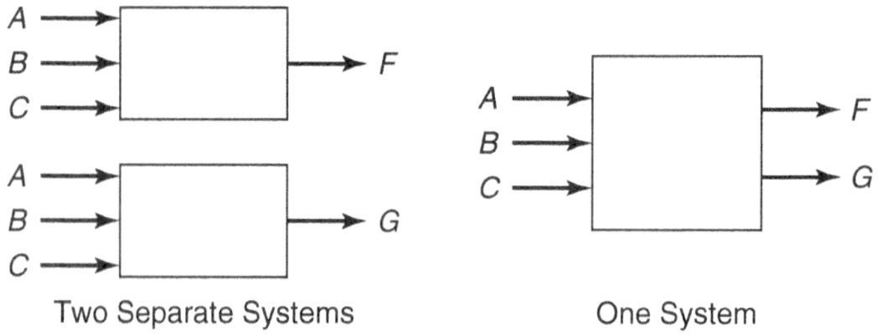

In this section, we will illustrate the process of obtaining minimum two-level solutions using AND and OR gates (sum of products solutions), assuming all variables are available both uncomplemented and complemented.* We could convert each of these solutions into NAND gate circuits (using the same number of gates and gate inputs). We could also find product of sums solutions (by minimizing the complement of each of the functions and then using DeMorgan's theorem).

We will illustrate this by first considering three very simple examples.

EXAMPLE 3.32

$$F(A, B, C) = \Sigma m(0, 2, 6, 7) \qquad G(A, B, C) = \Sigma m(1, 3, 6, 7)$$

If we map each of these and solve them separately,

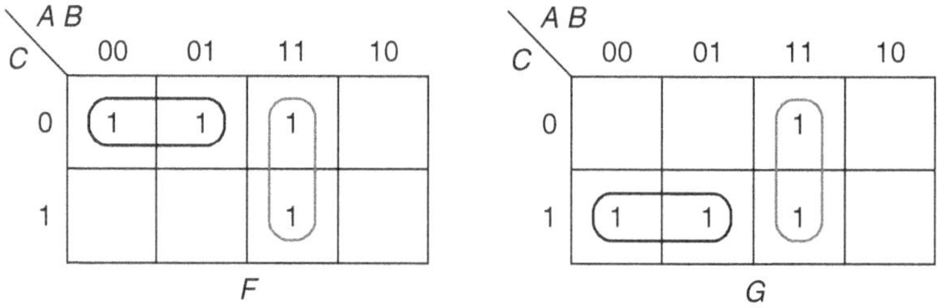

we obtain

$$F = A'C' + AB \qquad G = A'C + AB$$

Looking at the maps, we see that the same term (AB) is circled on both. Thus, we can build the circuit on the left, rather than the two circuits on the right.

*We will use as the definition for *minimum* a circuit containing the minimum number of gates, and among those with the same number of gates, the minimum number of gate inputs.

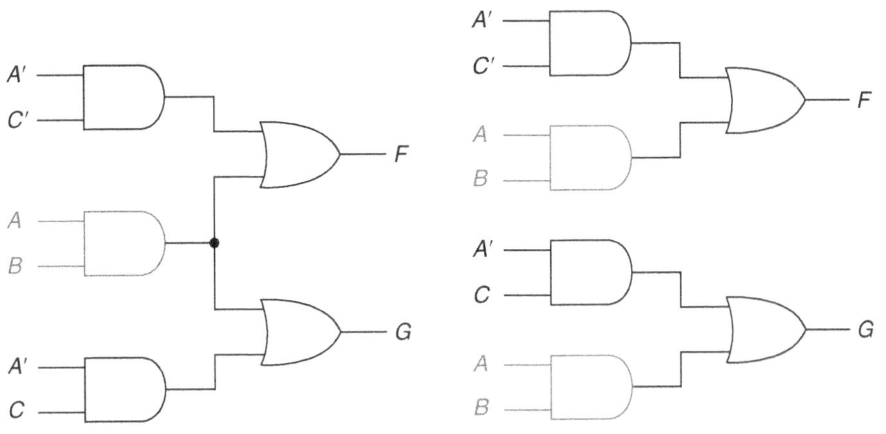

Obviously, the version on the left requires only five gates, whereas the one on the right uses six.

This example is the simplest. Each of the minimum sum of products expressions contains the same term. It would take no special techniques to recognize this and achieve the savings.

Even when the two solutions do not have a common prime implicant, we can share as illustrated in the following example:

EXAMPLE 3.33

$F(A, B, C) = \Sigma m(0, 1, 6) \qquad G(A, B, C) = \Sigma m(2, 3, 6)$

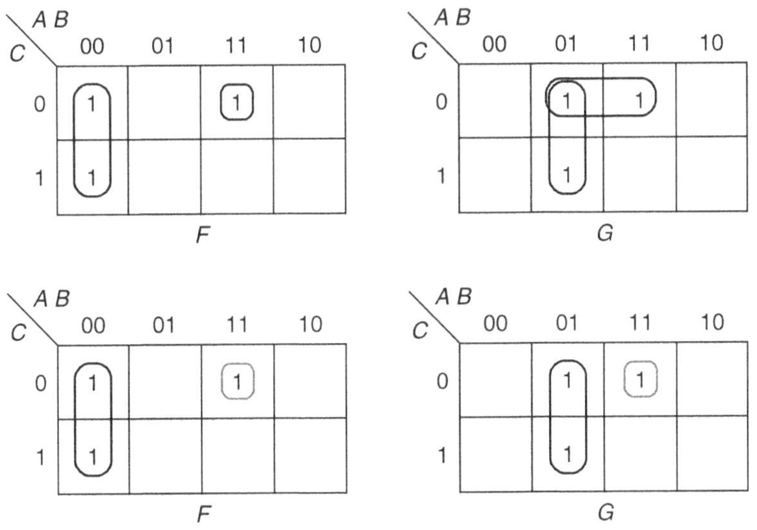

In the top maps, we considered each function separately and obtained

$F = A'B' + ABC' \qquad G = A'B + BC'$

This solution requires six gates (four ANDs and two ORs) with 13 inputs. However, as can be seen from the second pair of maps, we can share the term ABC' and obtain

$$F = A'B' + ABC' \qquad G = A'B + ABC'$$

(To emphasize the sharing, we have shown the shared term in brown, and will do that in other examples that follow.) As can be seen from the circuit below, this only requires five gates with 11 inputs.

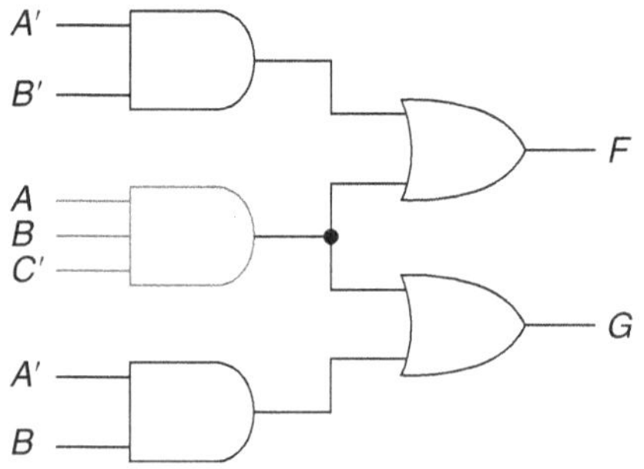

This example illustrates that a shared term in a minimum solution need not be a prime implicant. (In Example 3.33, ABC' is a prime implicant of F but not of G; in Example 3.34, we will use a term that is not a prime implicant of either function.)

EXAMPLE 3.34

$$F(A, B, C) = \Sigma m(2, 3, 7) \qquad G(A, B, C) = \Sigma m(4, 5, 7)$$

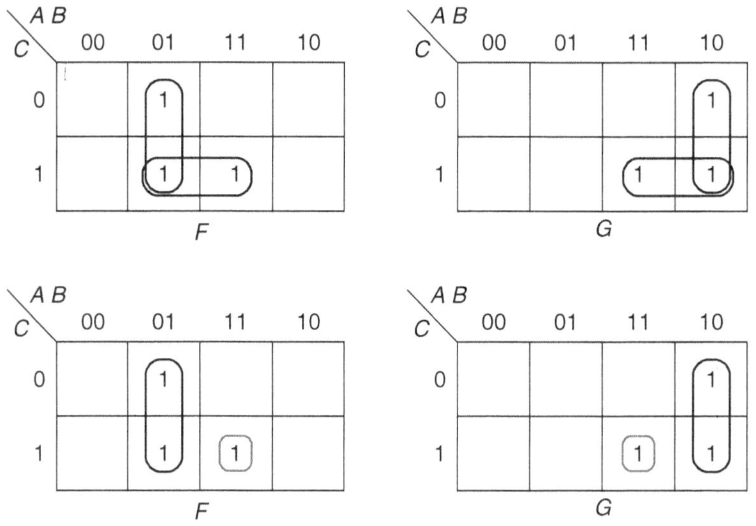

In the first pair of maps, we solved this as two problems. Using essential prime implicants of each function, we obtained

$$F = A'B + BC \qquad G = AB' + AC$$

However, as can be seen in the second set of maps, we can share the term ABC, even though it is not a prime implicant of either function, and once again get a solution that requires only five gates:

$$F = A'B + ABC \qquad G = AB' + ABC$$

The method for solving this type of problem is to begin by looking at the 1's of each function that are 0's of the other function. They must be covered by prime implicants of that function. Only the shared terms need not be prime implicants. In this last example, we chose $A'B$ for F since m_2 makes that an essential prime implicant of F and we chose AB' for G since m_4 makes that an essential prime implicant of G. That left just one 1 uncovered in each function—the same 1—which we covered with ABC. We will now look at some more complex examples.

EXAMPLE 3.35

$$F(A, B, C, D) = \Sigma m(4, 5, 6, 8, 12, 13)$$
$$G(A, B, C, D) = \Sigma m(0, 2, 5, 6, 7, 13, 14, 15)$$

The maps of these functions are shown below. In them, we have shown in brown the 1's that are included in one function and not the other.

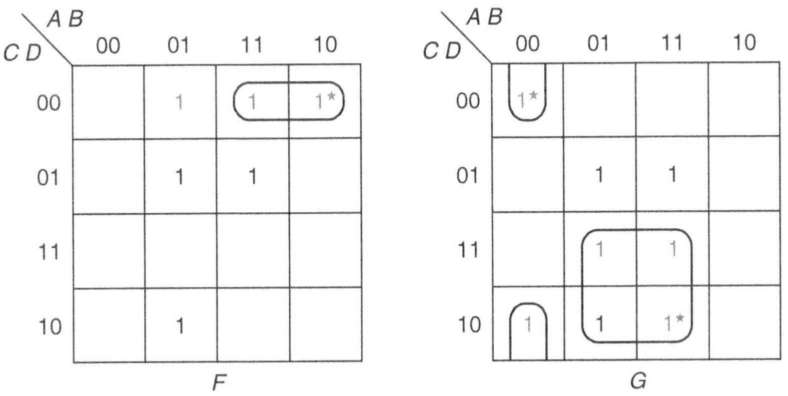

We then circled each of those prime implicants that was made essential by a brown 1. The only brown 1 that was not circled in F is m_4 because that can be covered by two prime implicants. Even though one of the terms would have fewer literals, we must wait. Next, we will use $A'BD'$ for F. Since m_6 was covered by an essential prime implicant of G, we are no longer looking for a term to share. Thus, m_6 will be covered in F by the prime implicant, $A'BD'$. As shown on the maps below, that leaves m_4 and m_{12} to be covered in both functions, allowing us to share the term $BC'D$, as shown on the following maps circled in brown.

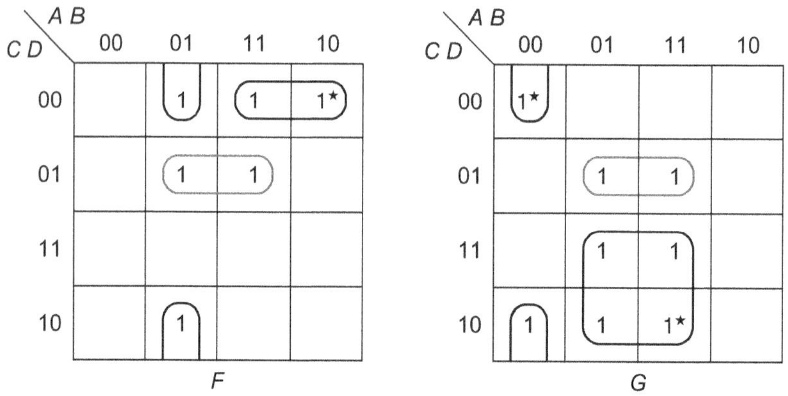

leaving

$$F = AC'D' + A'BD' + BC'D$$
$$G = A'B'D' + BC + BC'D$$

for a total of seven gates with 20 gate inputs. Notice that if we had minimized the functions individually, we would have used two separate terms for the third term in each expression, resulting in

$$F = AC'D' + A'BD' + BC'$$
$$G = A'B'D' + BC + BD$$

for a total of eight gates with 21 gate inputs. Clearly, the shared circuit costs less.

The shared version of the circuit is shown below.*

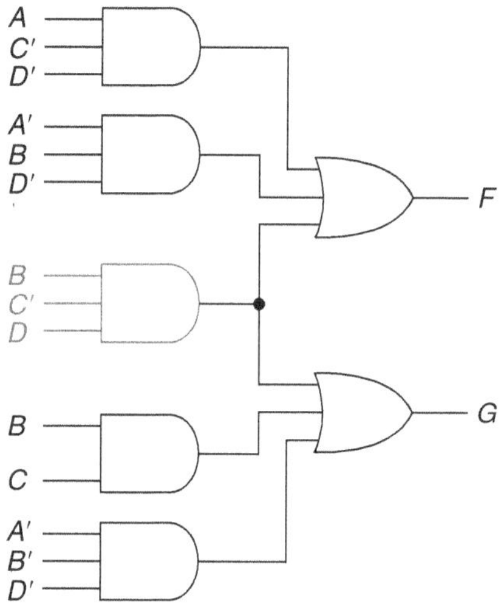

*All of these gates can be changed to NAND gates, even though the output of $BC'D$ goes to two places. There are still two bubbles (NOTs) in each path.

EXAMPLE 3.36

$F(A, B, C, D) = \Sigma m(0, 2, 3, 4, 6, 7, 10, 11)$

$G(A, B, C, D) = \Sigma m(0, 4, 8, 9, 10, 11, 12, 13)$

Once again the maps are shown with the unshared 1's in brown and the prime implicants made essential by one of those 1's circled.

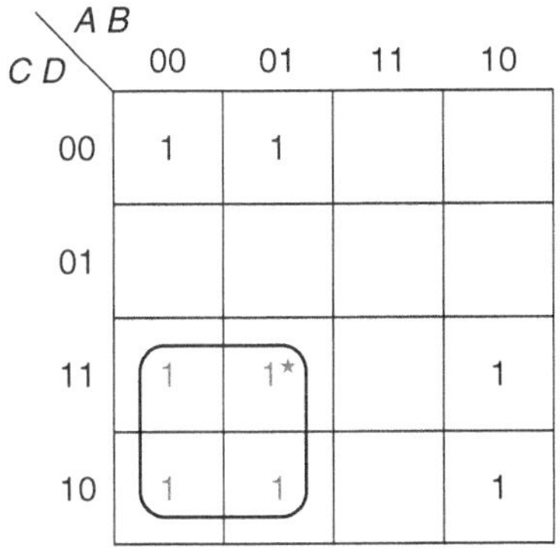

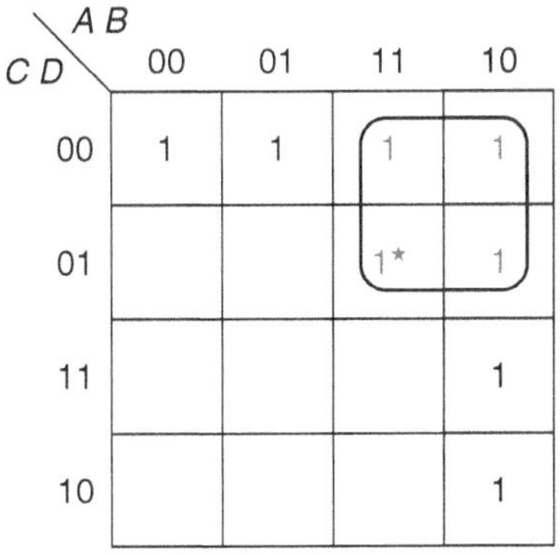

Each of the functions can be solved individually with two more groups of four, producing

$$F = A'C + A'D' + B'C \qquad G = AC' + C'D' + AB'$$

That would require eight gates with 18 gate inputs. However, sharing the groups of two as shown on the next set of maps reduces the number of gates to six and the number of gate inputs to 16. If these functions were implemented with NAND gates, the individual solutions would require a total of three packages, whereas the shared solution would require only two.

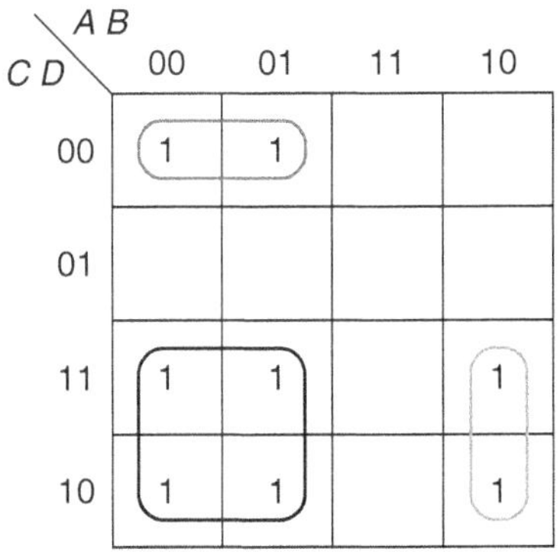

F

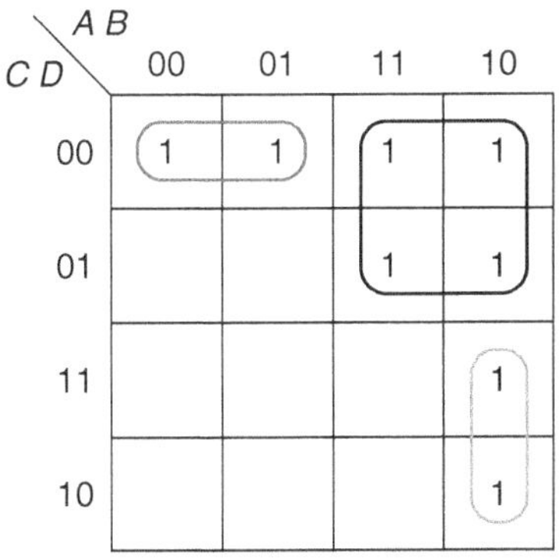

G

leaving the equations and the resulting AND/OR circuit.

$$F = A'C + A'C'D' + AB'C \qquad G = AC' + A'C'D' + AB'C$$

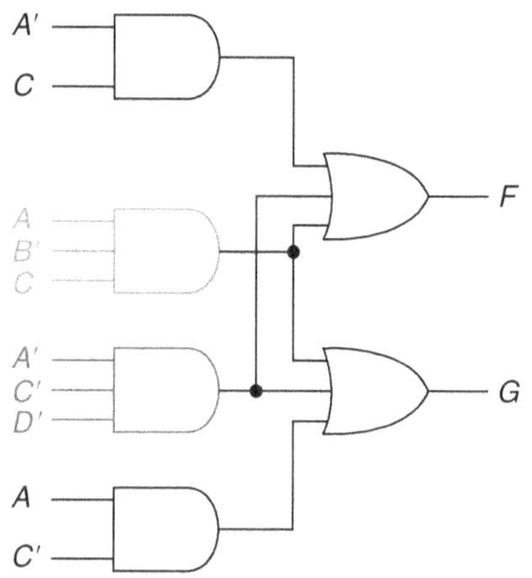

EXAMPLE 3.37

$$F(W, X, Y, Z) = \Sigma m(2, 3, 7, 9, 10, 11, 13)$$

$$G(W, X, Y, Z) = \Sigma m(1, 5, 7, 9, 13, 14, 15)$$

On the maps below, the 1's that are not shared are shown in brown and the essential prime implicants that cover these 1's are circled.

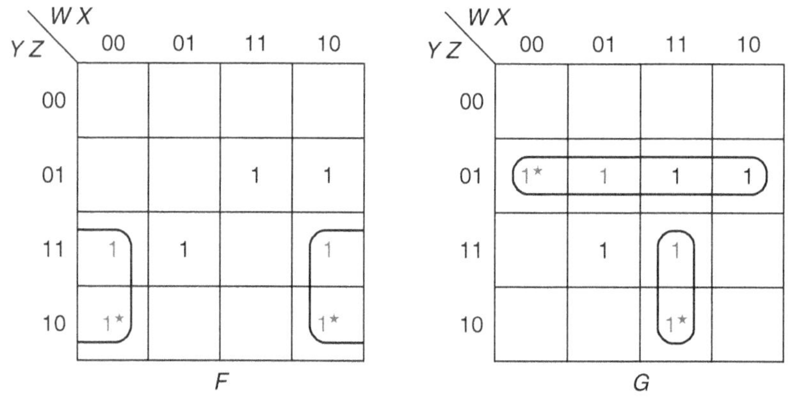

$$F = X'Y + \cdots$$

$$G = Y'Z + WXY + \cdots$$

Now, there are three 1's left in F. Since m_9 and m_{13} have been covered in G by an essential prime implicant, no sharing is possible for these terms in F. Thus, $WY'Z$, a prime implicant of F, is used in the minimum cover. Finally, there is one uncovered 1 in each function, m_7; it can be covered by a shared term, producing the solution

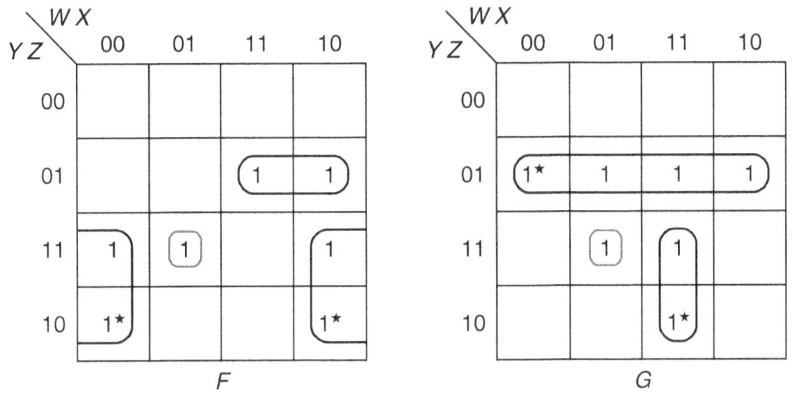

$F = X'Y + WY'Z + W'XYZ$

$G = Y'Z + WXY + W'XYZ$

This requires seven gates and 20 inputs, compared to the solution we obtain by considering these as separate problems

$F = X'Y + WY'Z + W'YZ$

$G = Y'Z + WXY + XZ$

which requires eight gates with 21 inputs.

The same techniques can be applied to problems with three or more outputs.

EXAMPLE 3.38

First, we show the solution obtained if we considered them as three separate problems.

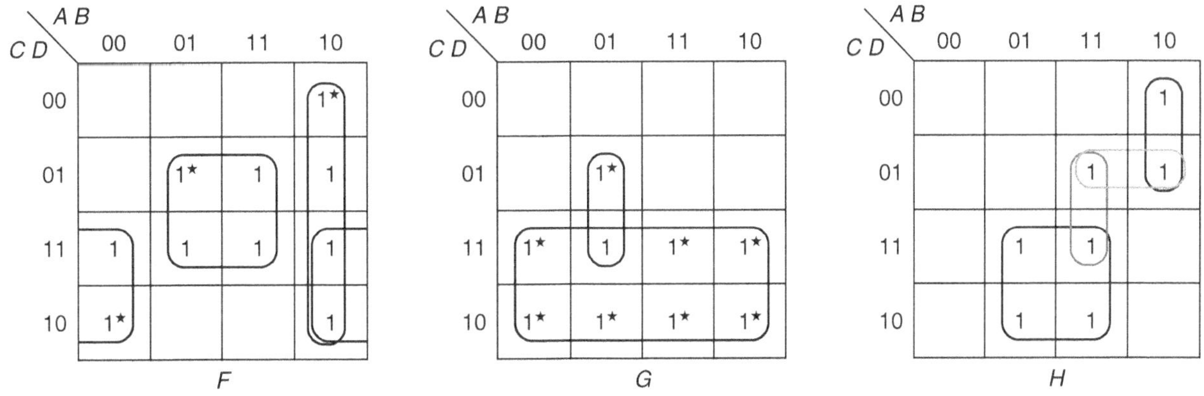

$F = AB' + BD + B'C$

$G = C + A'BD$

$H = BC + AB'C' + (ABD \text{ or } AC'D')$

This solution requires 10 gates and 25 gate inputs. (Note that the term C in function G does not require an AND gate.)

The technique of first finding 1's that are only minterms of one of the functions does not get us started for this example, since each of the 1's is a minterm of at least two of the functions. The starting point, instead, is to choose C for function G. The product term with only one literal does not require an AND gate and uses only one input to the OR gate. Any other solution, say sharing $B'C$ with F and BC with H, requires at least two inputs to the OR gate. Once we have made that choice, however, we must then choose $B'C$ for F and BC for H because of the 1's shown in brown on the following maps. There is no longer any sharing possible for those 1's and they make those prime implicants essential in F and H.

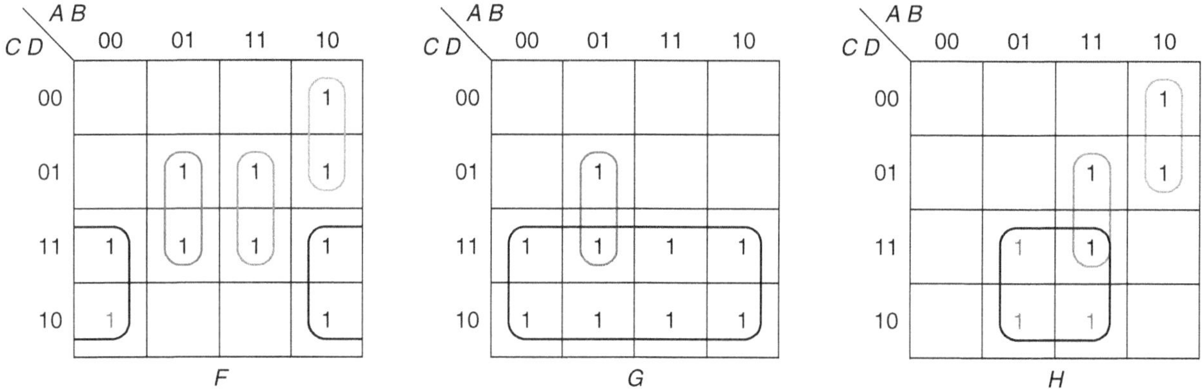

The term $AB'C'$ (circled in tan) was chosen next for H since it is an essential prime implicant of H and it can be shared (that is, all of the 1's in that term are also 1's of F, the only place where sharing is possible). $AB'C'$ is also used for F, since it covers two 1's and we would otherwise require an additional term, AB', to cover m_8. In a similar fashion, the term $A'BD$ is used for G (it is the only way to cover m_5) and can then be shared with F. Finally, we can finish covering F and H with ABD (a prime implicant of H, one of the choices for covering H when we treated that as a separate problem). It would be used also for F, rather than using another AND gate to create the prime implicant BD. The solution then becomes

$$F = B'C + AB'C' + A'BD + ABD$$
$$G = C + A'BD$$
$$H = BC + AB'C' + ABD$$

which requires only eight gates and 22 gate inputs (a savings of two gates and three-gate inputs).

EXAMPLE 3.39

$$F(A, B, C, D) = \Sigma m(0, 2, 6, 10, 11, 14, 15)$$
$$G(A, B, C, D) = \Sigma m(0, 3, 6, 7, 8, 9, 12, 13, 14, 15)$$
$$H(A, B, C, D) = \Sigma m(0, 3, 4, 5, 7, 10, 11, 12, 13, 14, 15)$$

The map on the next page shows these functions; the only 1 that is not shared and makes a prime implicant essential is m_9 in G. That prime implicant, AC', is shown circled.

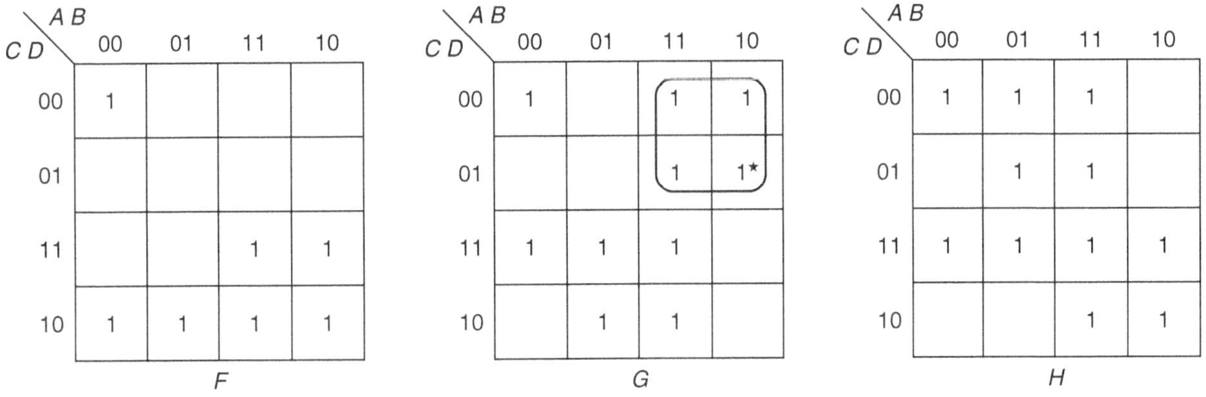

Next, we note that *AC* is an essential prime implicant of *F* (because of m_{11} and m_{15}) and of *H* (because of m_{10}). Furthermore, neither m_{10} nor m_{11} are 1's of *G*. Thus, that term is used for both *F* and *H*. Next, we chose *BC′* for *H* and *BC* for *G*; each covers four new 1's, some of which can no longer be shared (since the 1's that correspond to other functions have already been covered).

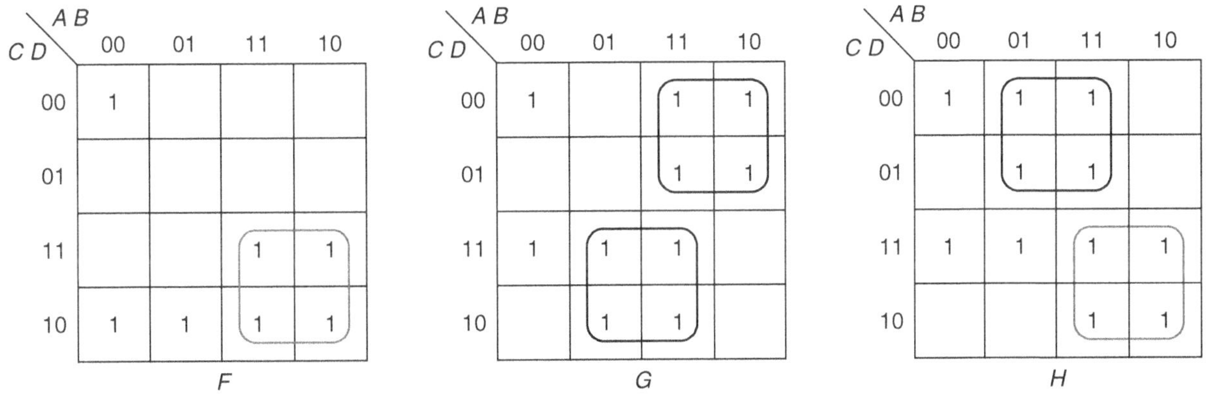

At this point, we can see that *A′B′C′D′* can be used to cover m_0 in all three functions; otherwise, we would need three different three-literal terms. *A′CD* can be used for *G* and *H*, and, finally, *CD′* is used for *F*, producing the following map and algebraic functions.

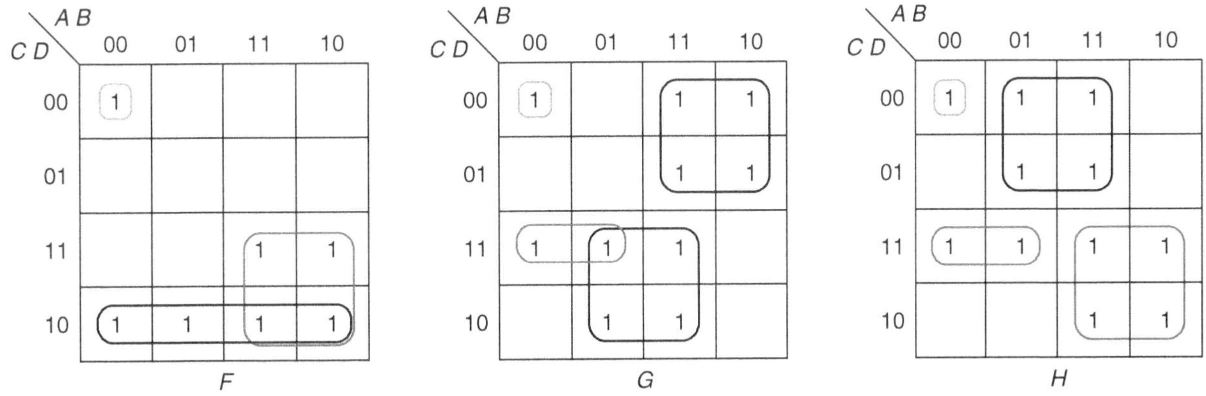

$$F = AC + A'B'C'D' + CD'$$
$$G = AC' + BC + A'B'C'D' + A'CD$$
$$H = AC + BC' + A'B'C'D' + A'CD$$

This solution requires 10 gates with 28 inputs, compared to 13 gates and 35 inputs if these were implemented separately.

EXAMPLE 3.40

Finally, we will consider an example of a system with don't cares:

$$F(A, B, C, D) = \Sigma m(2, 3, 4, 6, 9, 11, 12) + \Sigma d(0, 1, 14, 15)$$
$$G(A, B, C, D) = \Sigma m(2, 6, 10, 11, 12) + \Sigma d(0, 1, 14, 15)$$

A map of the functions, with the only prime implicant made essential by a 1 that is not shared circled, $B'D$, is shown below.

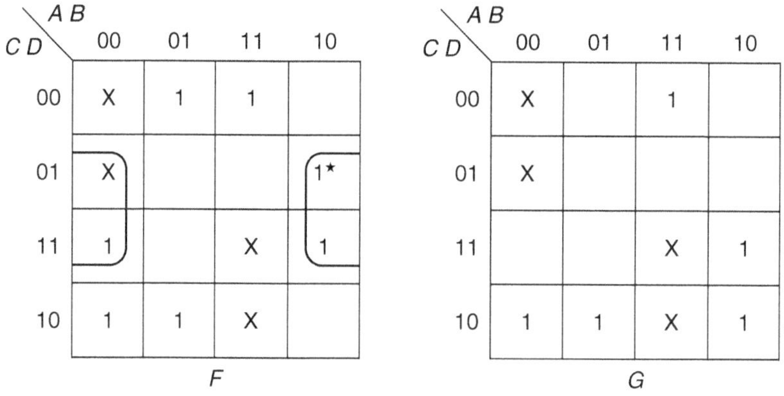

Since m_{11} has now been covered in F, we must use the essential prime implicant of G, AC, to cover m_{11} there. Also, as shown on the next maps, ABD' is used for G, since that is an essential prime implicant of G, and the whole term can be shared. (We will share it in the best solution.)

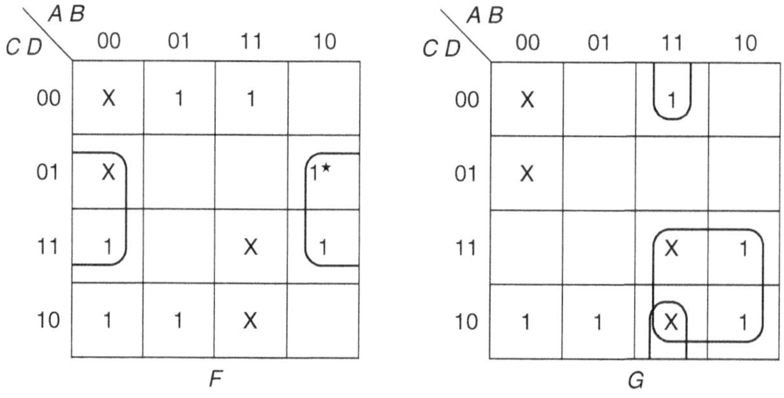

Since we need the term *ABD'* for *G*, one approach is to use it for *F* also. (That only costs a gate input to the OR gate.) If we do that, we could cover the rest of *F* with *A'D'* and the rest of *G* with *CD'*, yielding the map and equations that follow.

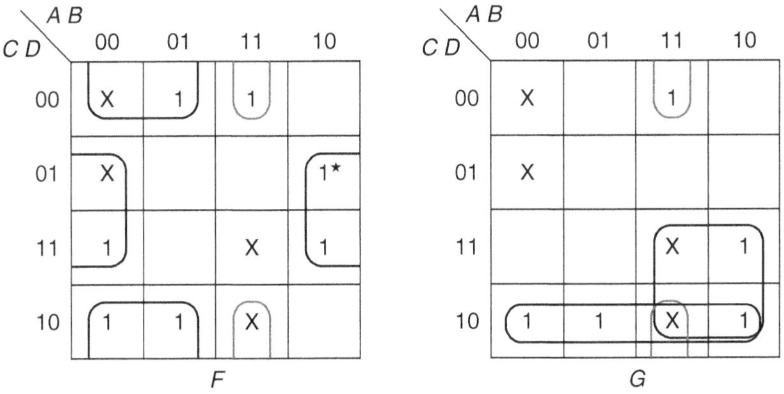

$$F = B'D + ABD' + A'D'$$
$$G = AC + ABD' + CD'$$

That solution uses seven gates and 17 inputs. Another solution using the same number of gates but one more input shares *A'CD'*. That completes *G*, and then the cover of *F* is completed with *BD'*. The maps and equations are thus:

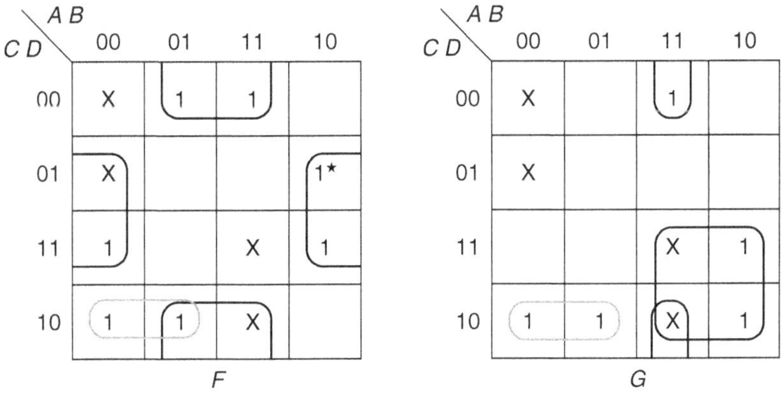

$$F = B'D + A'CD' + BD'$$
$$G = AC + ABD' + A'CD'$$

That, too, requires seven gates, but using a three-input AND gate instead of a two-input one, bringing the total number of inputs to 18. Thus, this solution is not minimum.

[SP 11; EX 11, 12]

3.7 SOLVED PROBLEMS

1. Plot the following functions on a Karnaugh map:
   a. $f(a, b, c) = \Sigma m(0, 1, 3, 6)$
   b. $g(w, x, y, z) = \Sigma m(3, 4, 7, 10, 11, 14) + \Sigma d(2, 13, 15)$
   c. $F = BD' + ABC + AD + A'B'C$

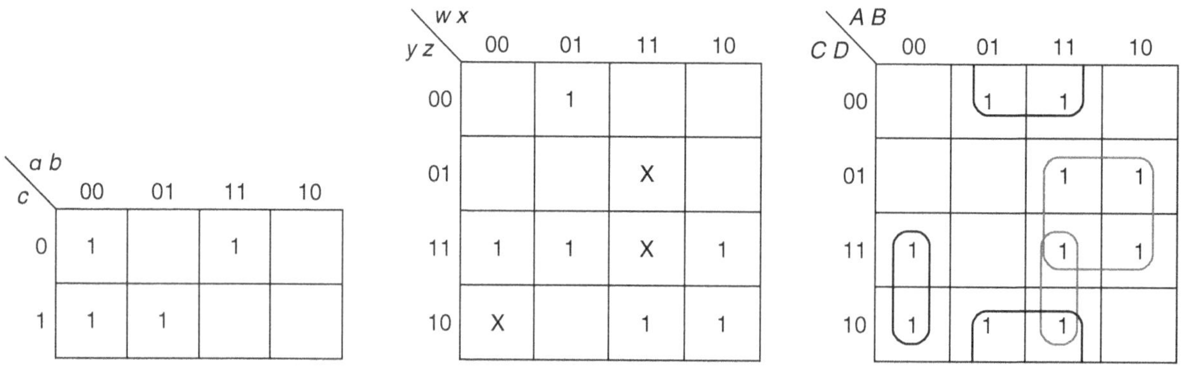

a. **b.** **c.**

2. For each of the following, find all minimum sum of products expressions. (If there is more than one solution, the number of solutions is given in parentheses.)
   a. $G(X, Y, Z) = \Sigma m(1, 2, 3, 4, 6, 7)$
   b. $f(w, x, y, z) = \Sigma m(2, 5, 7, 8, 10, 12, 13, 15)$
   c. $g(a, b, c, d) = \Sigma m(0, 6, 8, 9, 10, 11, 13, 14, 15)$ (2 solutions)
   d. $f(a, b, c, d) = \Sigma m(0, 4, 5, 6, 7, 8, 9, 10, 11, 13, 14, 15)$ (2 solutions)
   e. $f(a, b, c, d) = \Sigma m(0, 1, 2, 4, 6, 7, 8, 9, 10, 11, 12, 15)$
   f. $g(a, b, c, d) = \Sigma m(0, 2, 3, 5, 7, 8, 10, 11, 12, 13, 14, 15)$ (4 solutions)

   a. All of the prime implicants are essential, as shown on the map to the right.

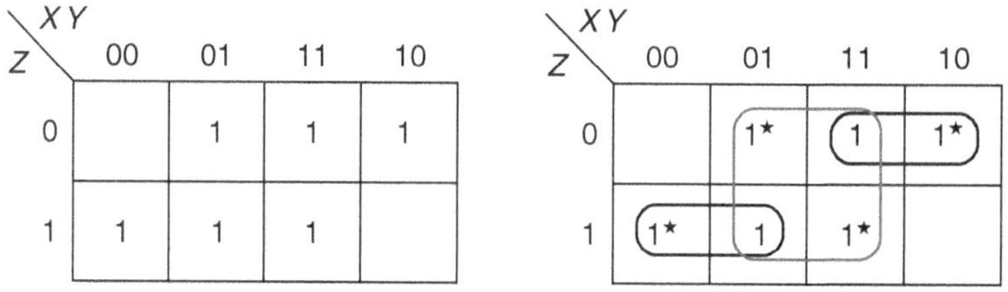

$G = Y + XZ' + X'Z$

b.

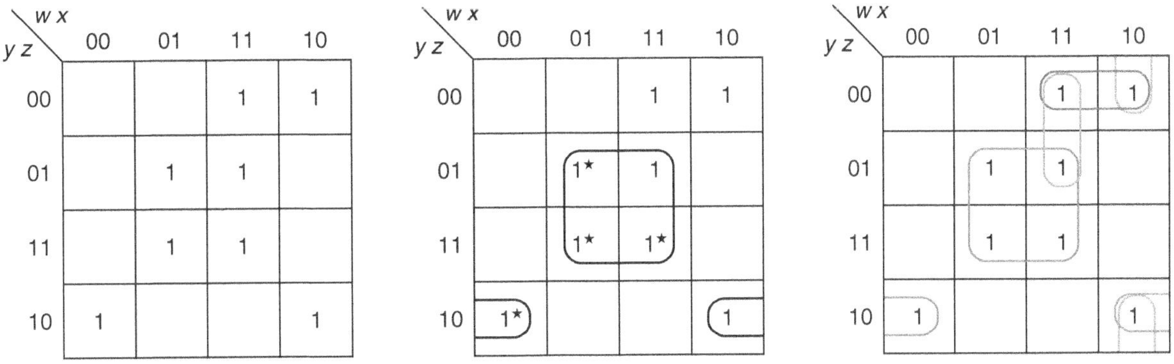

The essential prime implicants are shown on the second map, leaving two 1's to be covered. The third map shows that each can be covered by two different prime implicants, but the brown group shown is the only one that covers both with one term. We would require both tan terms. The minimum is

$$f = xz + x'yz' + wy'z'$$

c.

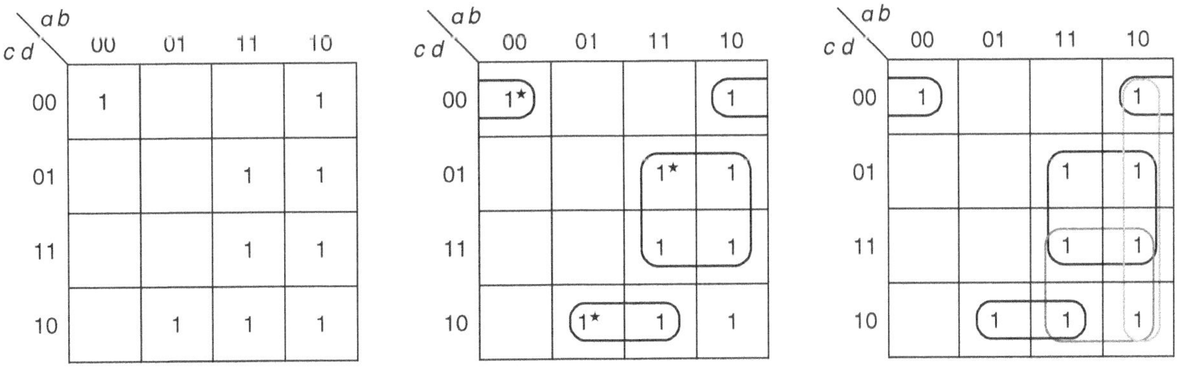

The three essential prime implicants are shown on the center map. The only 1 left to be covered can be covered by either of two groups of four, as shown circled in brown on the third map, producing

$$g = b'c'd' + bcd' + ad + ab'$$
$$g = b'c'd' + bcd' + ad + ac$$

d.

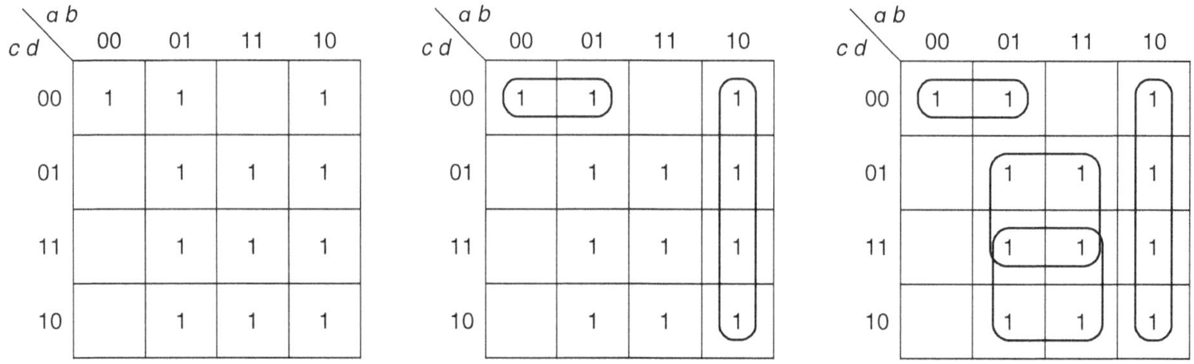

There are no essential prime implicants. We need one group of two to cover m_0; all other 1's can be covered by groups of four. Once we have chosen $a'c'd'$ to cover m_0 (center map), we would choose ab' to cover m_8. (Otherwise, we must use $b'c'd'$, a group of two, to cover that 1. Not only is that more literals, but it covers nothing else new; ab' covered three additional uncovered 1's.) Once that has been done, the other two prime implicants become obvious, giving

$$f = a'c'd' + ab' + bc + bd$$

In a similar fashion (on the next map), once we choose $b'c'd'$ (the other prime implicant that covers m_0), $a'b$ is the appropriate choice to cover m_4:

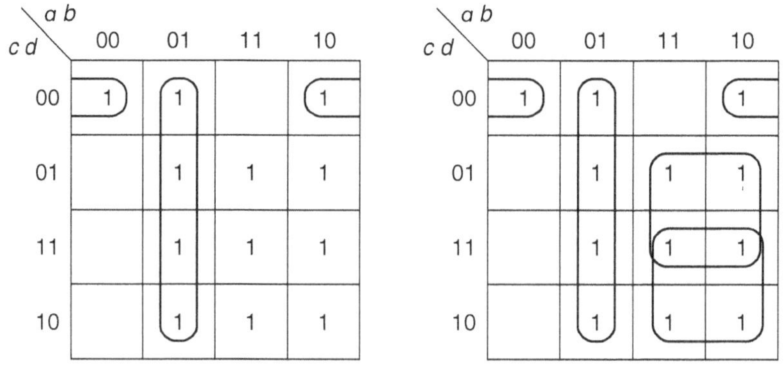

The only way to cover the remaining 1's in two terms is with ac and ad, as shown on the second map, leaving

$$f = b'c'd' + a'b + ac + ad$$

e. There are two essential prime implicants, as indicated on the first map, leaving six 1's to be covered. The essential prime implicants are shaded on the second map.

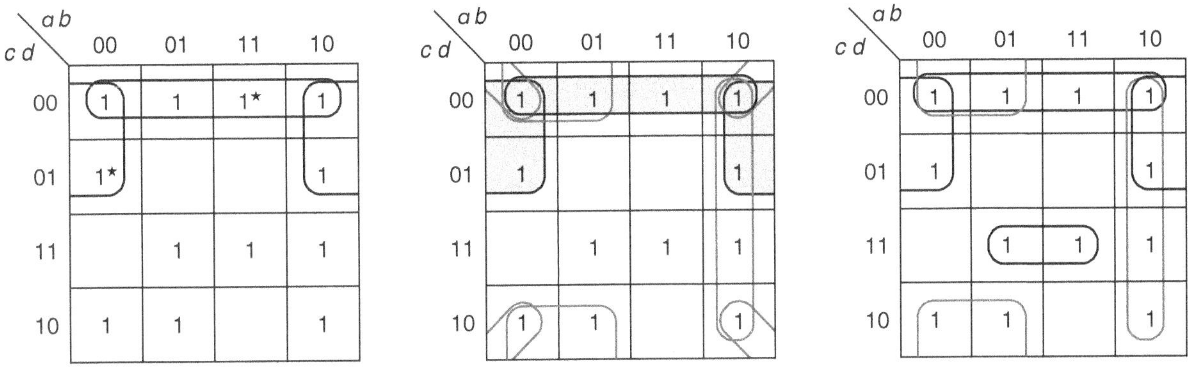

No prime implicant covers more than two of the remaining 1's; thus, three more terms are needed. The three groups of four (two literal terms) are circled in brown on the second map. We can cover four new 1's only using $a'd'$ and ab'. Note that m_7 and m_{15} are uncovered; they require a group of two, bcd. The only minimum solution, requiring five terms and 11 literals,

$$f = c'd' + b'c' + a'd' + ab' + bcd$$

is shown on the third map. There is another solution that uses five terms, but it requires 12 literals, namely,

$$f = c'd' + b'c' + b'd' + a'bc + acd$$

Obviously, it is not minimum (since it has an extra literal); it only used one of the groups of four instead of two.

f. On the second map, the two essential prime implicants have been highlighted ($b'd' + bd$), leaving four 1's uncovered. On the third map, we have shown the 1's covered by these prime implicants shaded.

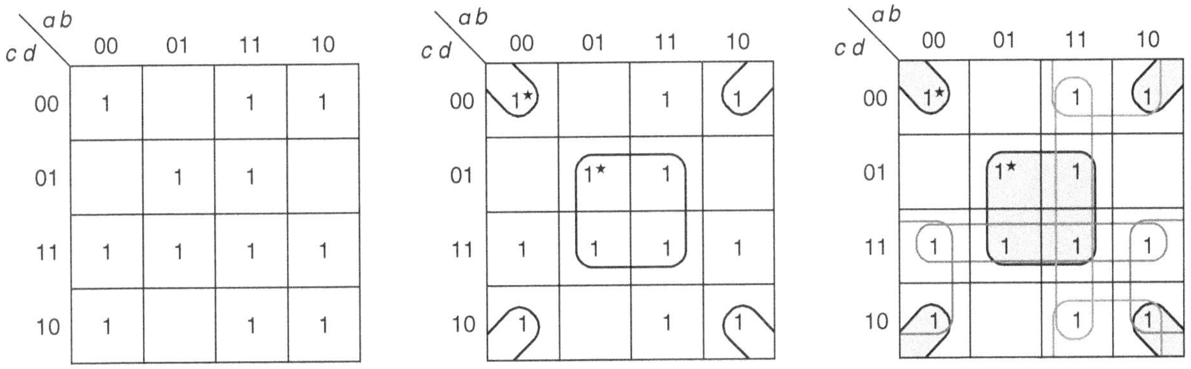

We can cover m_3 and m_{11} by either cd or $b'c$ (shown with brown lines), and we can cover m_{12} and m_{14} by either ab or ad' (shown in gray lines). Thus, there are four solutions:

$$f = b'd' + bd + cd + ab$$
$$f = b'd' + bd + cd + ad'$$
$$f = b'd' + bd + b'c + ab$$
$$f = b'd' + bd + b'c + ad'$$

The term ac is also a prime implicant. However, it is not useful in a minimum solution since it leaves two isolated 1's to be covered, resulting in a five-term solution.

3. For each of the following functions, find the minimum SOP expression(s). There are two solutions for z.

cd \ ab	00	01	11	10
00			1	1
01		1	1	
11			1	1
10		1	1	

w

cd \ ab	00	01	11	10
00	1		1	1
01		1	1	
11			1	1
10		1	1	

x

cd \ ab	00	01	11	10
00	1		1	1
01	1	1	1	
11			1	1
10		1	1	

y

cd \ ab	00	01	11	10
00	1		1	1
01	1	1	1	
11	1		1	1
10	1	1	1	

z

All of the 1's of w are also 1's of the other functions. For x, we added one 1; for y, we added a second 1; and for z, we added two more. Only essential prime implicants are used for w (and the group of four is not needed).

$$w = ac'd' + bc'd + acd + bcd'$$

For x, the last three terms of w are still essential prime implicants, as is $b'c'd'$. As can be seen on the next map, that leaves only m_{12} uncovered.

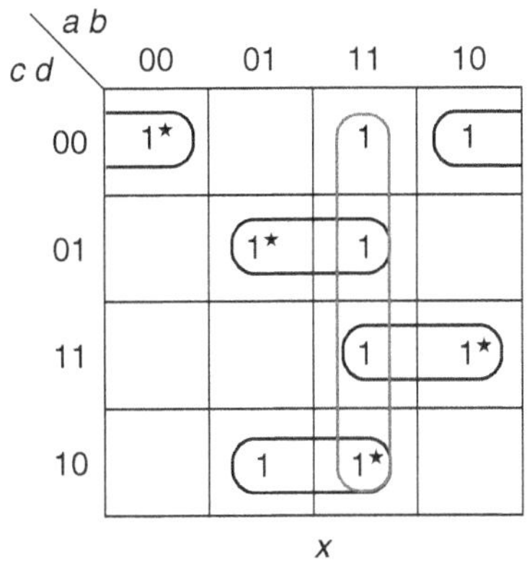

That leaves a choice between ab and $ac'd'$. Obviously, the former has one less literal, leaving the minimum solution:

$$x = bc'd + acd + bcd' + b'c'd' + ab$$

For y, there are only two essential prime implicants, leaving six 1's to cover.

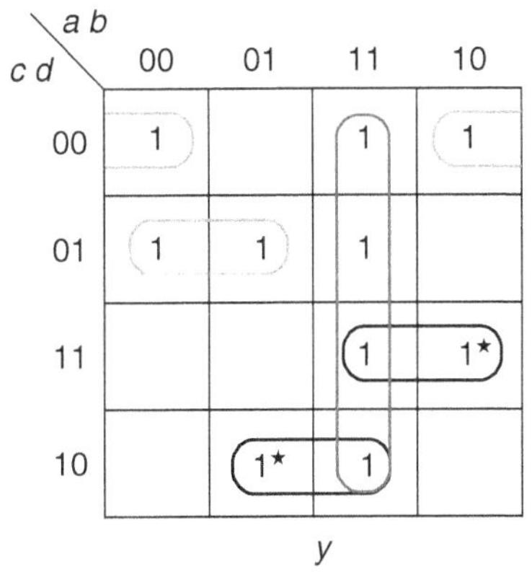

No term covers more than two of them. We must then use the group of four, giving

$$y = acd + bcd' + ab + b'c'd' + a'c'd$$

Finally, for z, we need 4 three-literal terms to cover the 1's in columns 01 and 10.

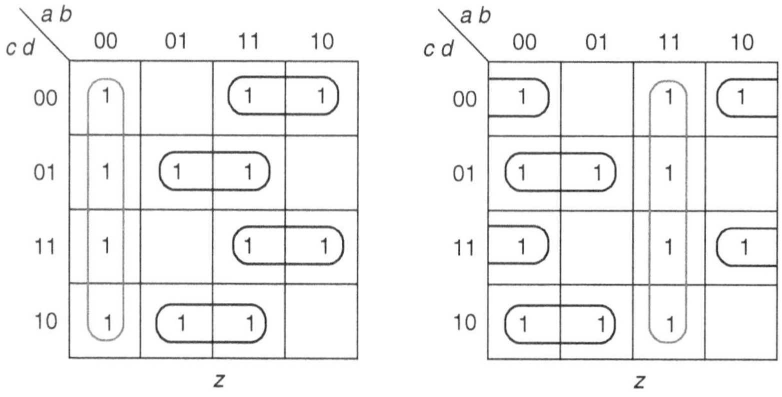

We can either use the solution for w and add $a'b'$ (as shown on the left) or use the other 4 three-literal terms along with ab (as shown on the right).

$$f = ac'd' + bc'd + acd + bcd' + a'b'$$
$$= ab + b'c'd' + a'c'd + b'cd + a'cd'$$

4. For the following functions,

i. List all prime implicants, indicating which are essential.

ii. Show the minimum sum of products expression(s).

a. $G(A, B, C, D) = \Sigma m(0, 1, 4, 5, 7, 8, 10, 13, 14, 15)$ (3 solutions)

b. $f(w, x, y, z) = \Sigma m(2, 3, 4, 5, 6, 7, 9, 10, 11, 13)$

c. $h(a, b, c, d) = \Sigma m(1, 2, 3, 4, 8, 9, 10, 12, 13, 14, 15)$ (2 solutions)

a. The first map shows all of the prime implicants circled; the 1's that have been covered only once are indicated with a star.

Essential prime implicants: $A'C'$, BD

Other prime implicants: $B'C'D'$, $AB'D'$, ACD', ABC

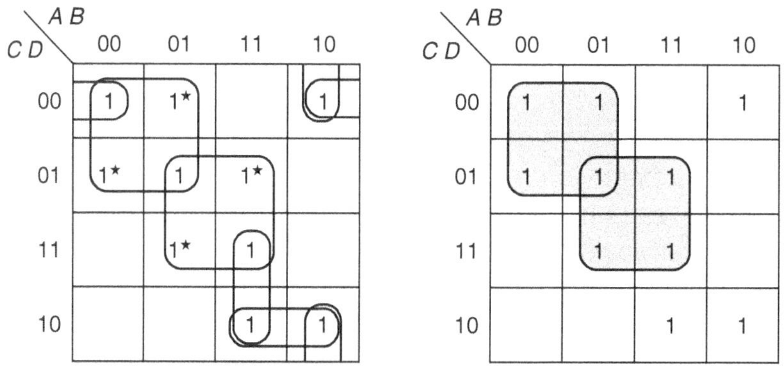

On the second map, the essential prime implicants have been shaded, highlighting the three 1's remaining to be covered. We need two terms to cover them, at least one of which must cover two of these remaining 1's. The three solutions are thus

$$F = A'C' + BD + ACD' + B'C'D'$$
$$F = A'C' + BD + AB'D' + ACD'$$
$$F = A'C' + BD + AB'D' + ABC$$

b.

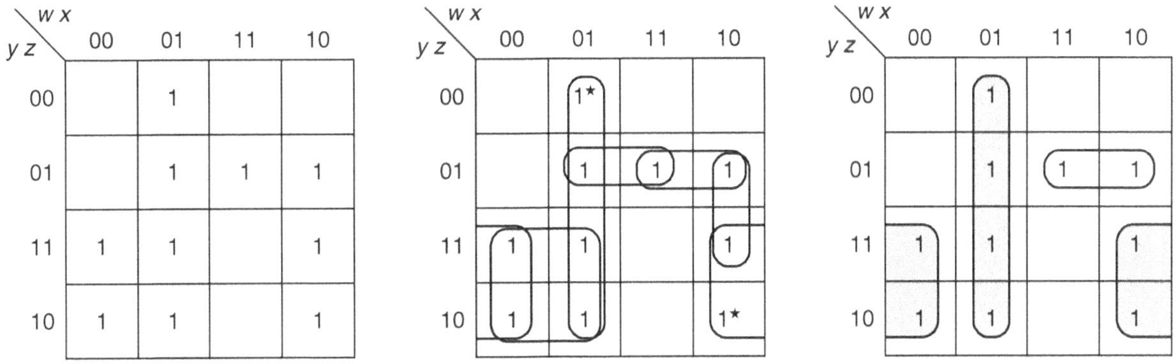

The second map shows all of the prime implicants circled and the 1's that have been covered only once are indicated with a star:

Essential prime implicants: $w'x$, $x'y$
Other prime implicants: $w'y$, $xy'z$, $wy'z$, $wx'z$

With the essential prime implicants shaded on the third map, it is clear that the only minimum solution is

$$f = w'x + x'y + wy'z$$

c. All of the prime implicants are circled on the first map, with the essential prime implicants shown in brown.

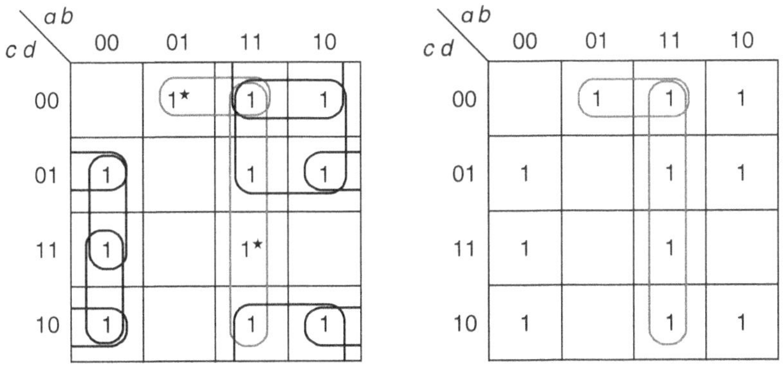

Essential prime implicants: $ab, bc'd'$

Other prime implicants: $ac', ad', b'c'd, b'cd', a'b'c, a'b'd$

Once we chose the essential prime implicants, there are six 1's left to be covered. We can only cover two at a time. There are two groups of four 1's, either of which can be used. (We cannot use both, since that would only cover three 1's.) The two solutions are shown on the maps below.

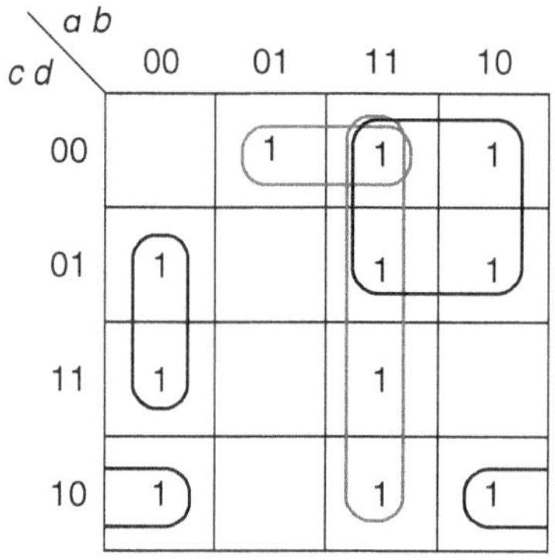

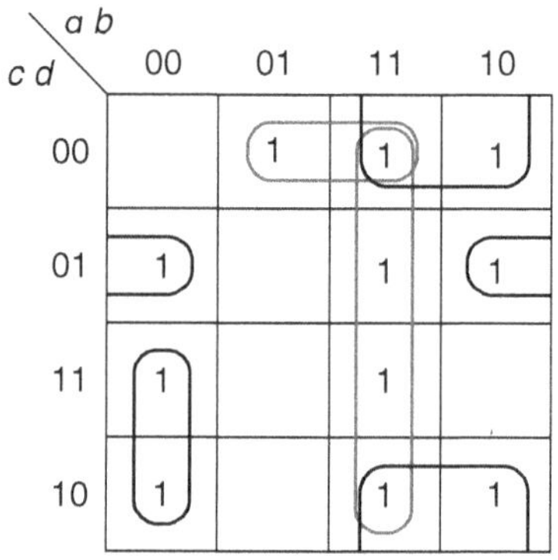

$$h = ab + bc'd' + ac' + a'b'd + b'cd'$$
$$h = ab + bc'd' + ad' + b'c'd + a'b'c$$

5. For each of the following, find all minimum sum of products expressions. (If there is more than one solution, the number of solutions is given in parentheses.)

a. $f(a, b, c, d) = \Sigma m(0, 2, 3, 7, 8, 9, 13, 15) + \Sigma d(1, 12)$

b. $F(W, X, Y, Z) = \Sigma m(1, 3, 5, 6, 7, 13, 14) + \Sigma d(8, 10, 12)$ (2 solutions)

c. $f(a, b, c, d) = \Sigma m(3, 8, 10, 13, 15) + \Sigma d(0, 2, 5, 7, 11, 12, 14)$ (8 solutions)

a.

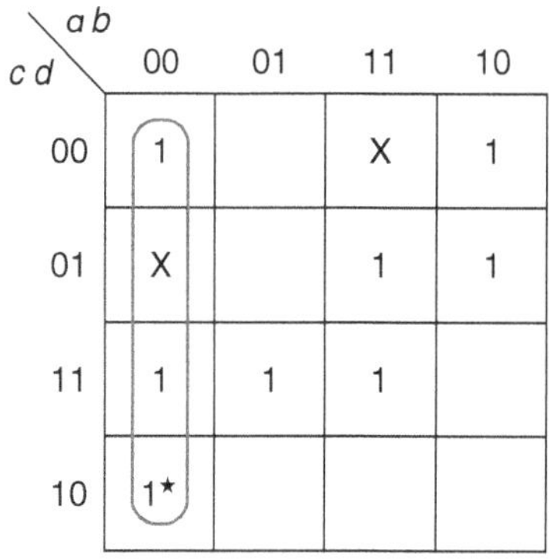

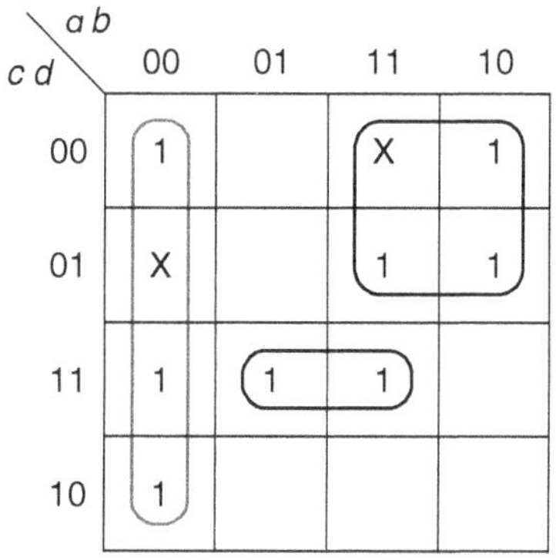

The first map shows the one essential prime implicant, $a'b'$. The remaining 1's can be covered by two additional terms, as shown on the second map. In this example, all don't cares are treated as 1's. The resulting solution is

$$f = a'b' + ac' + bcd$$

Although there are other prime implicants, such as $b'c'$, abd, and $a'cd$, three prime implicants would be needed in addition to $a'b'$ if any of them were chosen.

b.

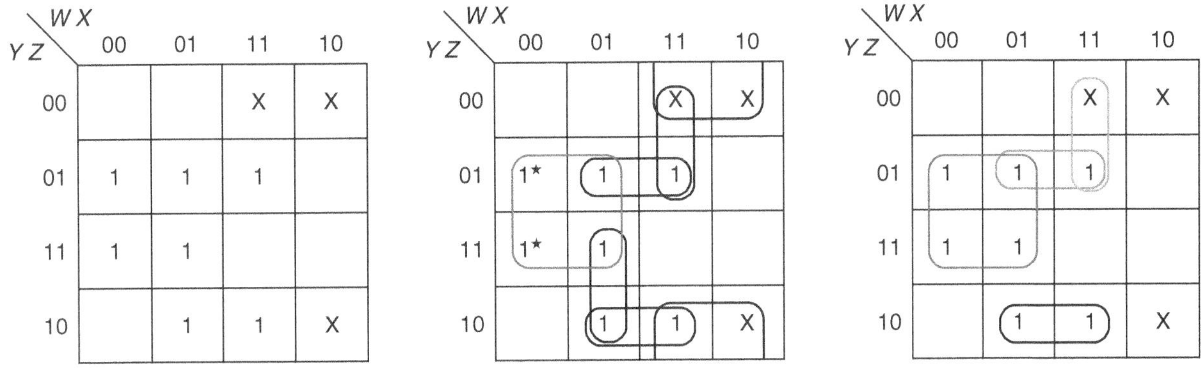

The second map shows all of the prime implicants circled. It is clear that only $W'Z$ is essential, after which three 1's remain uncovered. The prime implicant XYZ' is the only one that can cover two of these and thus appears in both minimum solutions. That leaves a choice of two terms to cover the remaining one—either WXY' (tan) or $XY'Z$ (gray). Note that they treat the don't care at m_{12} differently, and, thus, although the two solutions shown below both satisfy the requirements of the problem, they are not equal:

$$F = W'Z + XYZ' + WXY'$$
$$F = W'Z + XYZ' + XY'Z$$

Also, the group of four (WZ') is not used; that would require a four-term solution.

c. There are no essential prime implicants in this problem. The left map shows the only two prime implicants that cover m_8; they also cover m_{10}. We must choose one of these. The next map shows the only prime implicants that cover m_{13}; both also cover m_{15}. We must choose one of these also. Finally, the last map shows the only two prime implicants that cover m_3.

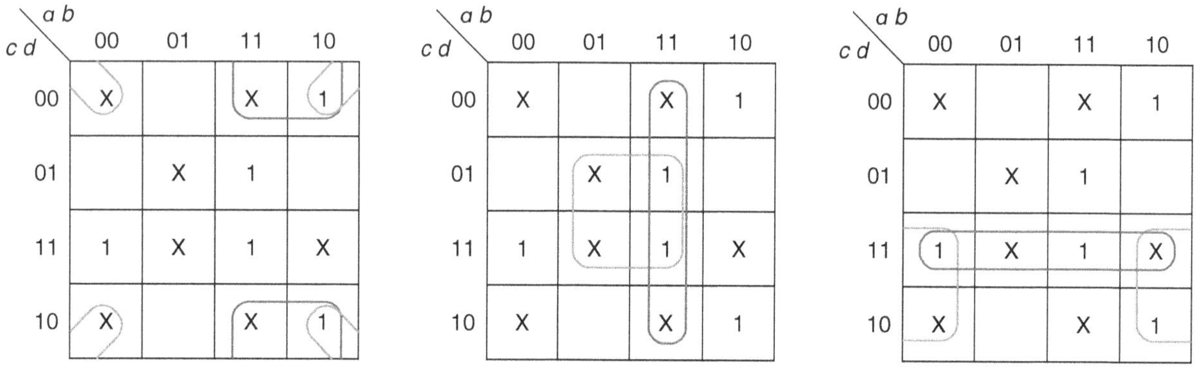

So, our final solution takes one from each group, giving us a total of eight solutions:

$$f = \begin{Bmatrix} ad' \\ b'd' \end{Bmatrix} + \begin{Bmatrix} ab \\ bd \end{Bmatrix} + \begin{Bmatrix} cd \\ b'c \end{Bmatrix}$$

or, written out

$$f = ad' + ab + cd$$
$$f = ad' + ab + b'c$$
$$f = ad' + bd + cd$$
$$f = ad' + bd + b'c$$
$$f = b'd' + ab + cd$$
$$f = b'd' + ab + b'c$$
$$f = b'd' + bd + cd$$
$$f = b'd' + bd + b'c$$

6. For each of the following, find all minimum sum of products expressions. Label the solutions $f_1, f_2, \ldots$ and indicate which solutions are equal.

   a. $F(A, B, C, D) = \Sigma m(4, 6, 9, 10, 11, 12, 13, 14) + \Sigma d(2, 5, 7, 8)$ (3 solutions)

   b. $f(a, b, c, d) = \Sigma m(0, 1, 4, 6, 10, 14) + \Sigma d(5, 7, 8, 9, 11, 12, 15)$ (13 solutions)

a.

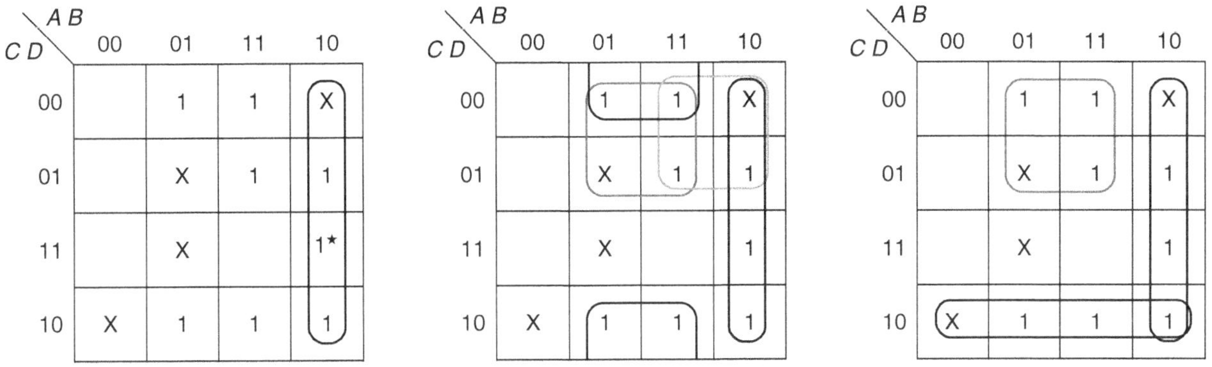

On the first map, we have shown the one essential prime implicant, AB'. Neither $A'B$ nor CD' are essential, since the 1's covered by them can each be covered by some other prime implicant. (That there is a don't care that can only be covered by one of these terms does not make that term essential.) With five 1's left to be covered, we need two additional terms. The first that stands out is BD', circled on the middle map, since it covers four of the remaining 1's. If that is chosen, it leaves only m_{13}, which can be covered by BC' or AC'. However, the third map shows still another cover, utilizing BC' and CD'. Thus, the three solutions are

$$F_1 = AB' + BD' + BC'$$
$$F_2 = AB' + BD' + AC'$$
$$F_3 = AB' + BC' + CD'$$

Notice that none of the solutions utilize the remaining prime implicant, $A'B$.

Next is the question of whether or not these three solutions are equal. The answer can be determined by examining how the don't cares are treated by each of the functions. The following table shows that:

	2	**5**	**7**	**8**
F_1	0	1	0	1
F_2	0	0	0	1
F_3	1	1	0	1

In all functions, m_7 is treated as 0 (that is, it is not included in any prime implicant used) and m_8 as 1 (since it is included in the essential prime implicant, AB'); but the first two columns show that no two functions treat m_2 and m_5 the same. Thus, none of these is equal to any other.

b. There are no essential prime implicants. The best place to start is with a 1 that can only be covered in two ways; in this problem there is only one, m_1. Any solution must contain either the term $a'c'$ (as shown on the first four maps) or the term $b'c'$ (as shown on the remaining two maps). There is no reason to use both, since $b'c'$ does not cover any 1's that are not already covered by $a'c'$. The first map shows $a'c'$. Note that there are three 1's left, requiring two more terms. At least one of these terms must cover two of the remaining 1's.

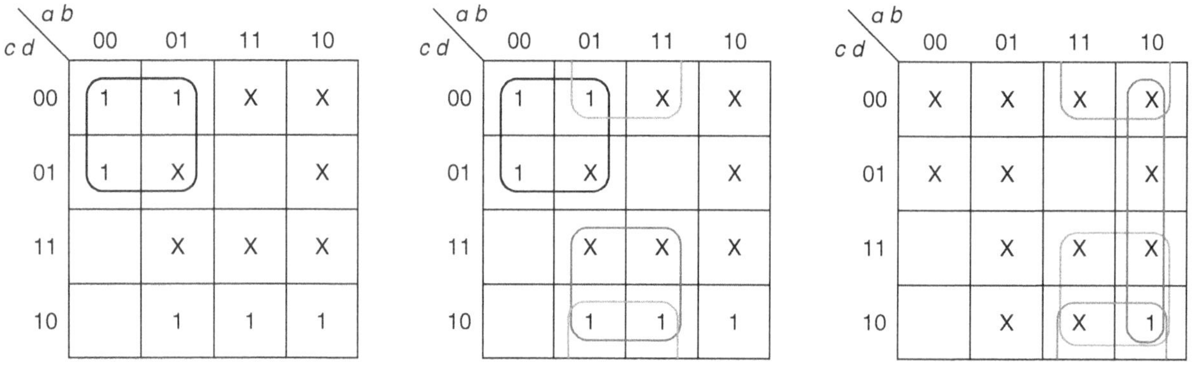

The second map shows two ways of covering m_6 and m_{14}, bc and bd'. In either case, only one 1 is left to be covered. The third map shows the previously covered 1's as don't cares and three ways of covering the last 1, m_{10}. Thus, we have as the first six solutions

$$f_1 = a'c' + bc + ab'$$
$$f_2 = a'c' + bc + ac$$
$$f_3 = a'c' + bc + ad'$$
$$f_4 = a'c' + bd' + ab'$$
$$f_5 = a'c' + bd' + ac$$
$$f_6 = a'c' + bd' + ad'$$

Next, we consider how we may cover both m_{10} and m_{14} with one term (in addition to those already found). That provides two more solutions shown on the left map below. (Other solutions that use these terms have already been listed.)

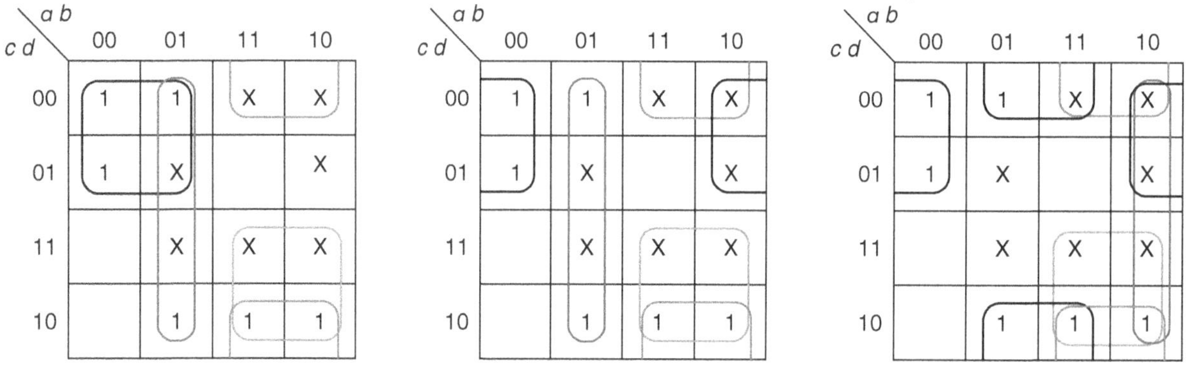

$f_7 = a'c' + a'b + ad'$
$f_8 = a'c' + a'b + ac$

We next consider the solutions that use $b'c'$. The middle map shows two of these, utilizing $a'b$. The last map shows the final three, utilizing bd', instead; it has the same three last terms as in the first series. Thus, we have

$f_9 = b'c' + a'b + ad'$
$f_{10} = b'c' + a'b + ac$
$f_{11} = b'c' + bd' + ab'$
$f_{12} = b'c' + bd' + ac$
$f_{13} = b'c' + bd' + ad'$

Finally, the table below shows how each of the functions treats the don't cares:

	5	7	8	9	11	12	15
f_1	1	1	1	1	1	0	1
f_2	1	1	0	0	1	0	1
f_3	1	1	1	0	0	1	1
f_4	1	0	1	1	1	1	0
f_5	1	0	0	0	1	1	1
f_6	1	0	1	0	0	1	0
f_7	1	1	1	0	0	1	0
f_8	1	1	0	0	1	0	1
f_9	1	1	1	1	0	1	0
f_{10}	1	1	1	1	1	0	1
f_{11}	0	0	1	1	1	1	0
f_{12}	0	0	1	1	1	1	1
f_{13}	0	0	1	1	0	1	0

Comparing the rows, the only two pairs that are equal are

$f_1 = f_{10}$ and $f_2 = f_8$.

7. For each of the following functions, find all of the minimum sum of products expressions and all of the minimum product of sums expressions:
   a. $f(w, x, y, z) = \Sigma m(2, 3, 5, 7, 10, 13, 14, 15)$
   (1 SOP, 1 POS solution)
   b. $f(a, b, c, d) = \Sigma m(3, 4, 9, 13, 14, 15) + \Sigma d(2, 5, 10, 12)$
   (1 SOP, 2 POS solutions)
   c. $f(a, b, c, d) = \Sigma m(4, 6, 11, 12, 13) + \Sigma d(3, 5, 7, 9, 10, 15)$
   (2 SOP and 8 POS solutions)

a. The map of f is shown below.

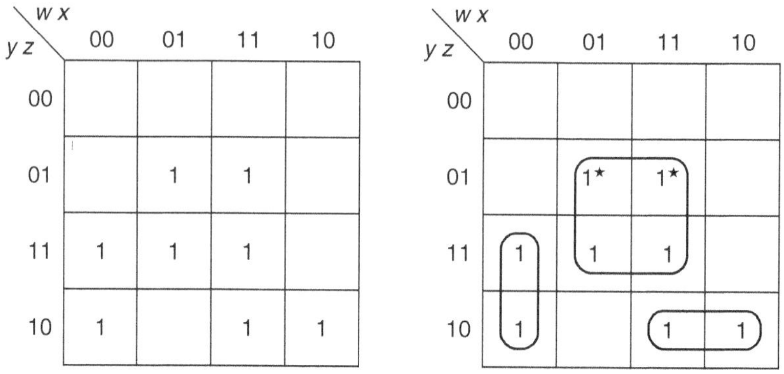

Although there is only one essential prime implicant, there is only one way to complete the cover with two more terms, namely,

$$f = xz + w'x'y + wyz'$$

By replacing all the 1's with 0's and 0's with 1's, or by plotting all the minterms not in f, we get the map for f'

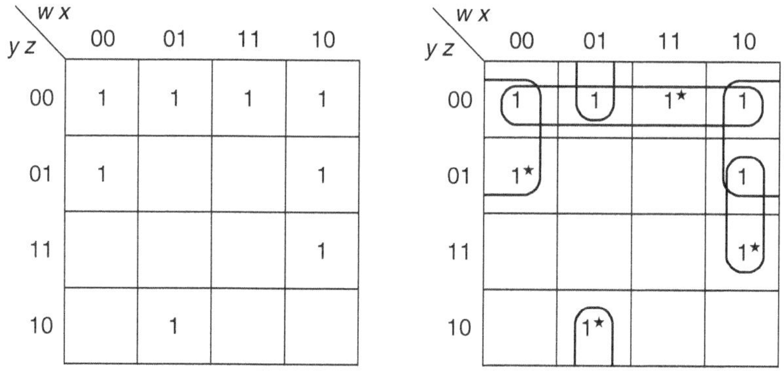

There are four essential prime implicants, covering all of f', giving

$$f' = x'y' + y'z' + w'xz' + wx'z$$

Using DeMorgan's theorem, we get

$$f = (x + y)(y + z)(w + x' + z)(w' + x + z')$$

In this case, the sum of products solution requires fewer terms.

b. As indicated on the map below, all of the 1's are covered by essential prime implicants, producing the minimum sum of products expression.

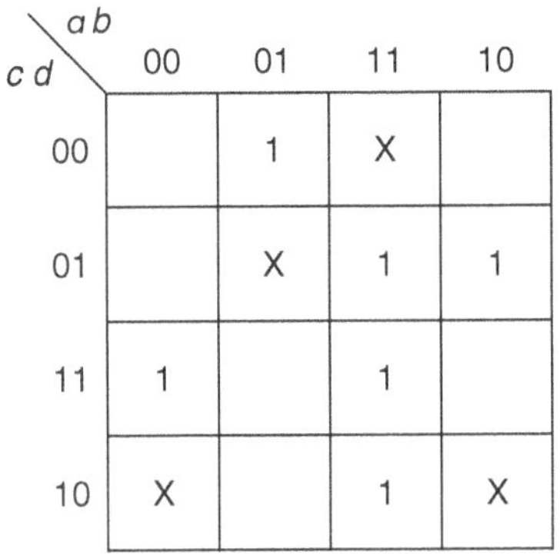

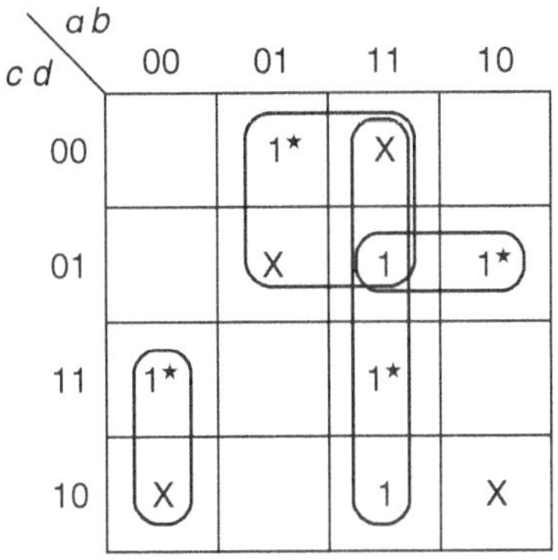

$$f_1 = bc' + ab + a'b'c + ac'd$$

Now, replacing all of the 1's by 0's and 0's by 1's and leaving the X's unchanged, we get the map for f'.

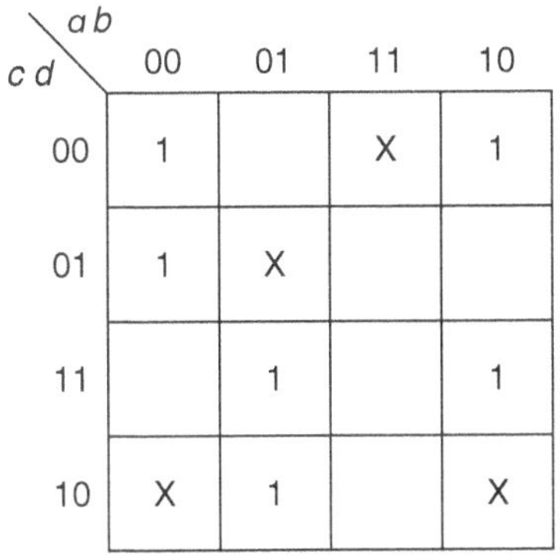

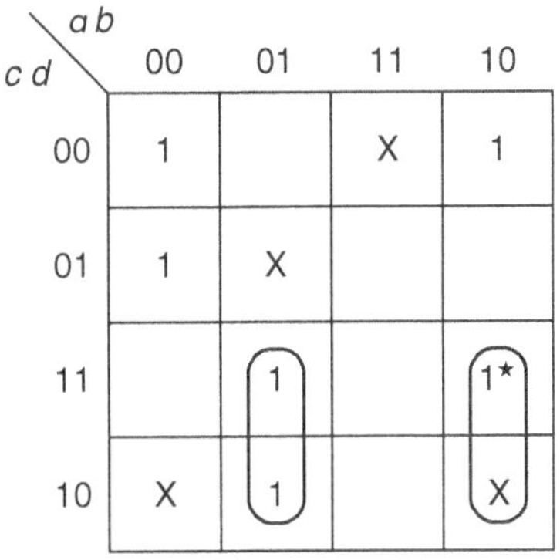

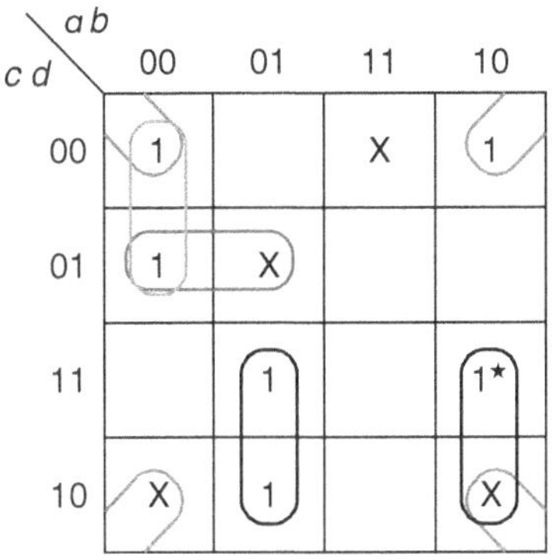

There is one essential prime implicant, $ab'c$. Although m_6 and m_7 can each be covered in two ways, only $a'bc$ covers them both (and neither of the other terms cover additional 1's). The middle map shows each of these terms circled, leaving three 1's to be covered. There is a group of four, covering two of the 1's (as shown on the third map), $b'd'$. That leaves just m_1, which can be covered in two ways, as shown on the third map in brown and tan lines. Thus, the two minimum sum of product expressions for f' are

$$f_2' = ab'c + a'bc + b'd' + a'c'd$$
$$f_3' = ab'c + a'bc + b'd' + a'b'c'$$

producing the two minimum product of sums solutions

$$f_2 = (a' + b + c')(a + b' + c')(b + d)(a + c + d')$$
$$f_3 = (a' + b + c')(a + b' + c')(b + d)(a + b + c)$$

c. The map for f is shown next (on the left). There are two essential prime implicants, leaving only m_{11} to be covered. There are two groups of four that can be used, as indicated on the right-hand map.

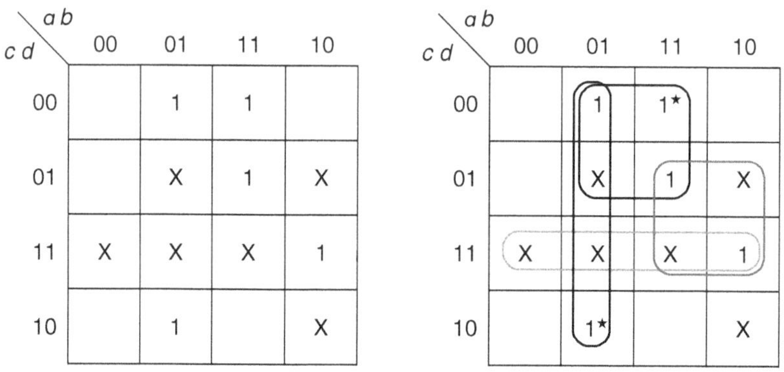

Thus the two sum of products solutions are

$$f_1 = a'b + bc' + ad$$
$$f_2 = a'b + bc' + cd$$

We then mapped f' and found no essential prime implicants.

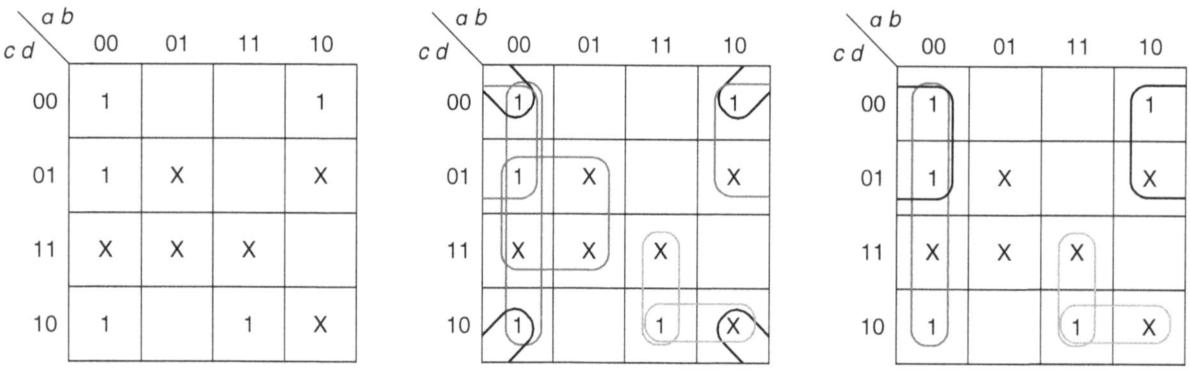

We chose as a starting point m_8. It can be covered either by the four corners, $b'd'$ (as shown on the second map) or by $b'c'$, as shown on the third map. Whichever solution we choose, we need a group of two to cover m_{14} (as shown in tan); neither covers any other 1. After choosing one of these (and $b'd'$), all that remains to be covered is m_1. The three brown lines show the covers. (Notice that one of those is $b'c'$.) If we don't choose $b'd'$, then we must choose $b'c'$ to cover m_0 and $a'b'$ to cover m_2 (since the only other prime implicant that covers m_2 is $b'd'$, and we have already found all of the solutions using that term). Thus, the eight solutions for f' are

$$f_3' = b'd' + abc' + a'b'$$
$$f_4' = b'd' + abc' + a'd$$
$$f_5' = b'd' + abc' + b'c'$$

$$f_6' = b'd' + acd' + a'b'$$
$$f_7' = b'd' + acd' + a'd$$
$$f_8' = b'd' + acd' + b'c'$$
$$f_9' = b'c' + abc + a'b'$$
$$f_{10}' = b'c' + acd' + a'b'$$

The product of sums solutions for f are thus

$$f_3 = (b + d)(a' + b' + c')(a + b)$$
$$f_4 = (b + d)(a' + b' + c')(a + d')$$
$$f_5 = (b + d)(a' + b' + c')(b + c)$$
$$f_6 = (b + d)(a' + c' + d)(a + b)$$
$$f_7 = (b + d)(a' + c' + d)(a + d')$$
$$f_8 = (b + d)(a' + c' + d)(b + c)$$
$$f_9 = (b + c)(a' + b' + c')(a + b)$$
$$f_{10} = (b + c)(a' + c' + d)(a + b)$$

8. Label the solutions of each part of problem 7 as $f_1, f_2, \ldots,$ and indicate which solutions are equal.

a. Since this problem does not involve don't cares, all solutions are equal.

b.

	2	5	10	12
f_1	1	1	0	1
f_2'	1	1	1	0
f_2	0	0	0	1
f_3'	1	0	1	0
f_3	0	1	0	1

All of the solutions are unique. The sum of products solution treats m_2 as a 1; the product of sums treats it as a 0. The two product of sums solutions treat m_5 differently.

c.

	3	5	7	9	10	15
f_1	0	1	1	1	0	1
f_2	1	1	1	0	0	1
f_3'	1	0	0	0	1	1
f_4'	1	1	1	0	1	1
f_5'	0	0	0	1	1	1
f_6'	1	0	0	0	1	0
f_7'	1	1	1	0	1	0
f_8'	0	0	0	1	1	0
f_9'	1	0	0	1	0	1
f_{10}'	1	0	0	1	1	0

For one of the sum of products expressions to be equal to one of the product of sums expressions, the pattern must be opposite (since we are showing the values of the don't cares for f' for the POS forms). Thus, $f_1 = f_6$, and $f_2 = f_8$, that is

$$a'b + bc' + ad = (b + d)(a' + c' + d)(a + b)$$
$$a'b + bc' + cd = (b + d)(a' + c' + d)(b + c)$$

9. Find the minimum sum of products solution(s) for each of the following:

a. $F(A, B, C, D, E) = \Sigma m(0, 5, 7, 9, 11, 13, 15, 18, 19, 22, 23, 25, 27, 28, 29, 31)$

b. $F(A, B, C, D, E) = \Sigma m(0, 2, 4, 7, 8, 10, 15, 17, 20, 21, 23, 25, 26, 27, 29, 31)$

c. $G(V, W, X, Y, Z) = \Sigma m(0, 1, 4, 5, 6, 7, 10, 11, 14, 15, 21, 24, 25, 26, 27)$ (3 solutions)

d. $G(V, W, X, Y, Z) = \Sigma m(0, 1, 5, 6, 7, 8, 9, 14, 17, 20, 21, 22, 23, 25, 28, 29, 30)$ (3 solutions)

e. $H(A, B, C, D, E) = \Sigma m(1, 3, 10, 14, 21, 26, 28, 30) + \Sigma d(5, 12, 17, 29)$

a. We begin by looking at 1's for which the corresponding position on the other layer is 0. On the first map, all of the essential prime implicants that are totally contained on one layer of the map, $A'B'C'D'E'$, $A'CE$, $AB'D$, and $ABCD'$, are circled.

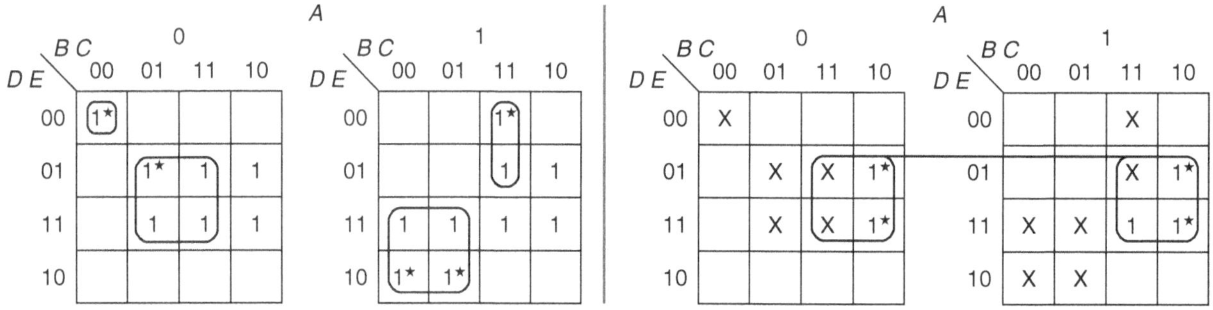

The 1's covered by these essential prime implicants are shown as don't cares on the second map. The remaining 1's are all part of the group of eight, BE, shown on the second map. Thus, the minimum solution is

$$F = A'B'C'D'E' + A'CE + AB'D + ABCD' + BE$$

b. On the left-hand map below, the essential prime implicants are circled. Note that $A'C'E'$ is on the top layer, $AD'E$ is on the lower layer, and CDE is split between the layers.

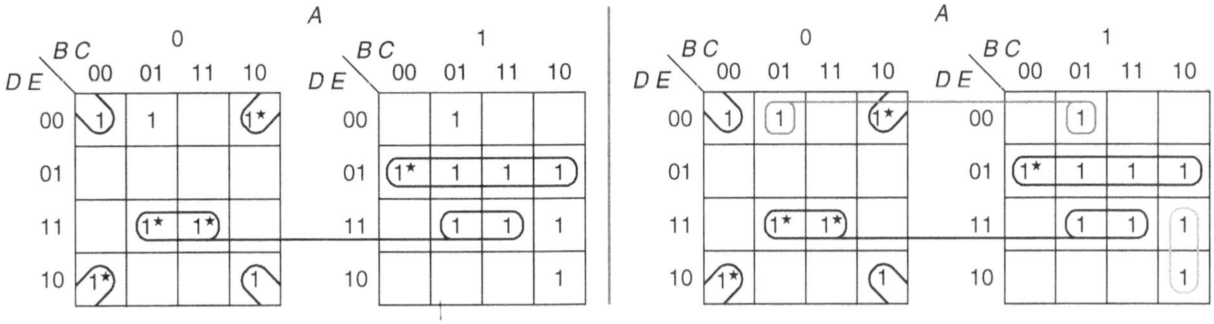

That leaves four 1's to be covered, using two groups of two as shown on the right map. The minimum is thus

$$F = A'C'E' + AD'E + CDE + B'CD'E' + ABC'D$$

c. The map, with essential prime implicants circled, is shown on the left. After choosing $V'W'Y' + VWX' + W'XY'Z$, there are still six 1's uncovered. On the right-hand map, the minterms covered by essential prime implicants are shown as don't cares. Each of the 1's can be covered by two different groups of four, which are shown on the map on the right.

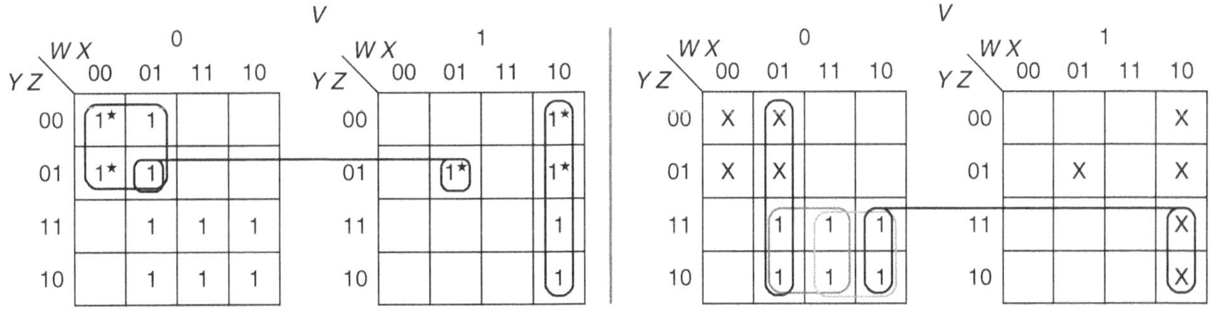

One group that covers four new 1's must be used (or both of them may be used), giving the following solutions:

$$G = V'W'Y' + VWX' + W'XY'Z + V'XY + V'WY$$
$$G = V'W'Y' + VWX' + W'XY'Z + V'XY + WX'Y$$
$$G = V'W'Y' + VWX' + W'XY'Z + V'WY + V'W'X$$

d. On the first map, the two essential prime implicants, $V'X'Y'$ and XYZ', are circled. The term $W'XZ$ is circled on the second map; if it is not used, $W'XY$ would be needed to cover m_7 and m_{23}. But then, three more terms would be needed to cover the function.

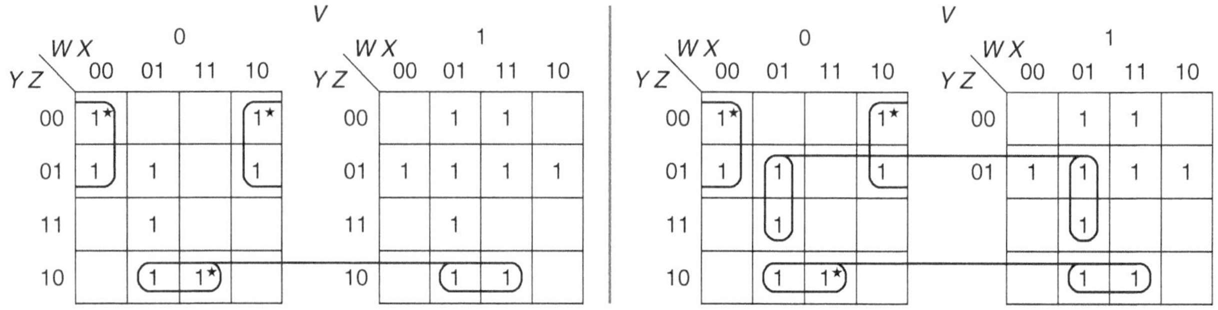

The following maps show the covered terms as don't cares and three ways of covering the remaining 1's. On the left map, the brown term, $VY'Z$, is used with either of the other terms, VXY' or VXZ'. On the right map, VXY' and $X'Y'Z$ are used.

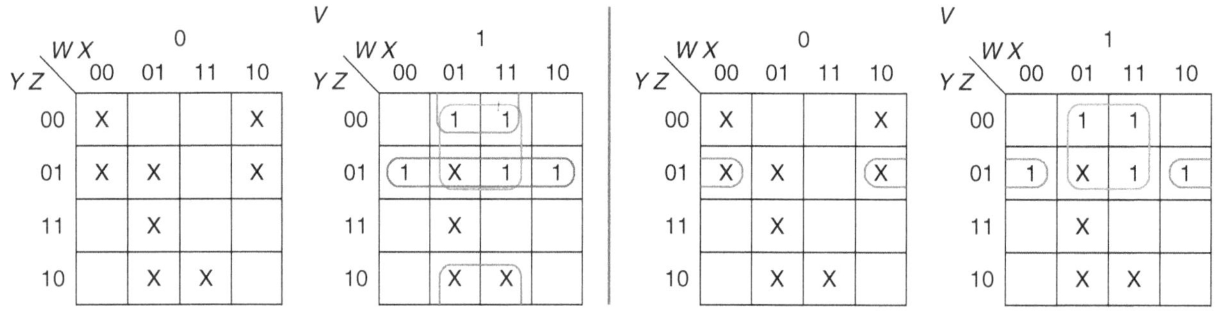

The three minimum solutions are thus

$$G = V'X'Y' + XYZ' + W'XZ + VY'Z + VXY'$$
$$G = V'X'Y' + XYZ' + W'XZ + VY'Z + VXZ'$$
$$G = V'X'Y' + XYZ' + W'XZ + VXY' + X'Y'Z$$

e. The two essential prime implicants, $A'B'C'E$ and BDE', are circled on the first map. Each of the remaining 1's can be covered in two ways, by a group of two contained completely on one layer or by the group of four shown.

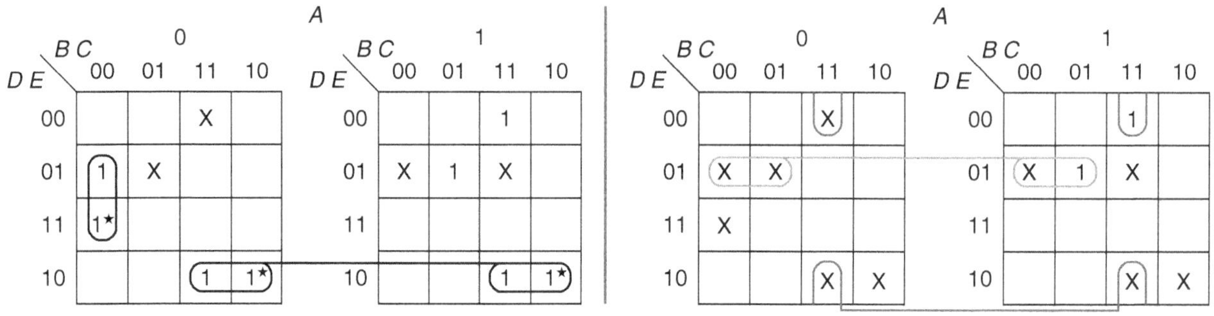

Thus, the minimum solution is

$$H = A'B'C'E + BDE' + BCE' + B'D'E$$

10. Find the four minimum sum of products expressions for the following six-variable function

$$G(A, B, C, D, E, F) = \Sigma m(0, 4, 6, 8, 9, 11, 12, 13, 15, 16, 20, 22, 24, 25, 27, 28, 29, 31, 32, 34, 36, 38, 40, 41, 42, 43, 45, 47, 48, 49, 54, 56, 57, 59, 61, 63)$$

On the first map, the three essential prime implicants, $ABD'E'$, CF, and $C'DEF'$, are circled in black. The first is on just the third layer. The other two include 1's on all four layers (and thus do not involve the variable A and B). Also circled (in brown) is a group of eight, $A'E'F'$, that is not essential (since each of the 1's is part of some other prime implicant). If that is not used, however, at least two terms would be needed to cover those 1's.

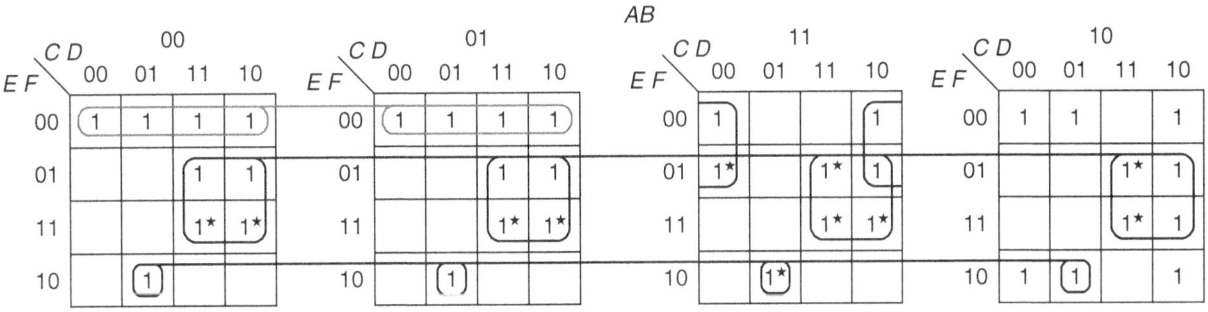

On the next map, the 1's that have been covered are shown as don't cares. The remaining 1's are all on the bottom (10) layer. The four corners, $AB'D'F'$, covers four of the five remaining 1's. Then, either $AB'C'F'$ (on the bottom layer) or $B'C'E'F'$ or $B'C'DF'$ (both half on the top layer and half on the bottom) can be used to cover the remaining 1's. These terms are circled below.

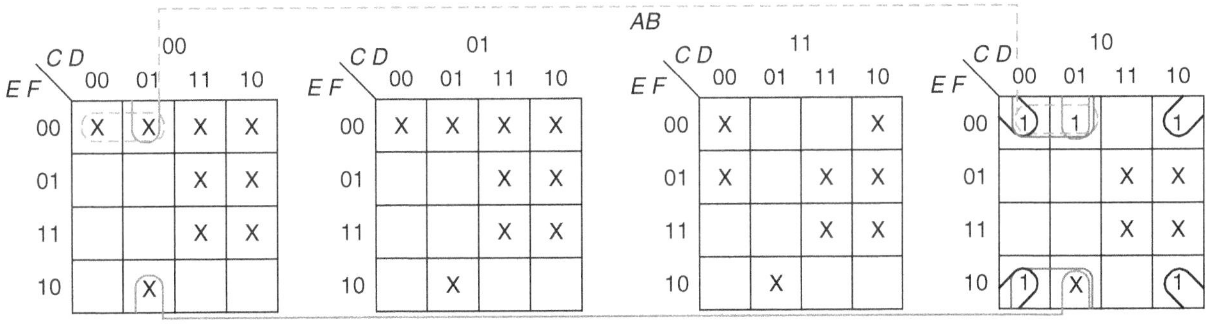

Also, as shown on the map below, $AB'C'F'$ could be used with $AB'CD'$.

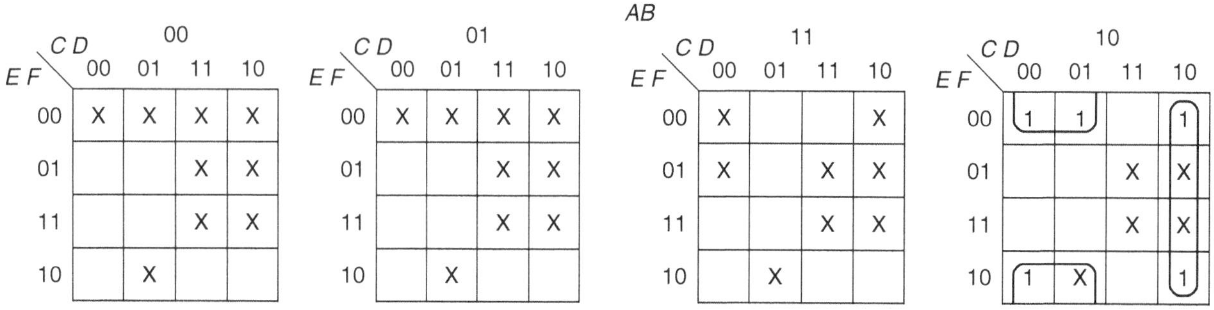

Thus, we have the following four solutions

$$H = ABD'E' + CF + C'DEF' + A'E'F' + AB'D'F' + AB'C'F'$$

$$H = ABD'E' + CF + C'DEF' + A'E'F' + AB'D'F' + B'C'E'F'$$

$$H = ABD'E' + CF + C'DEF' + A'E'F' + AB'D'F' + B'C'DF'$$

$$H = ABD'E' + CF + C'DEF' + A'E'F' + AB'C'F' + AB'CD'$$

11. Find a minimum two-level circuit (corresponding to sum of products expressions) using AND gates and one OR gate per function for each of the following sets of functions:

a. $f(a, b, c, d) = \Sigma m(0, 1, 2, 3, 5, 7, 8, 10, 11, 13)$
$g(a, b, c, d) = \Sigma m(0, 2, 5, 8, 10, 11, 13, 15)$
(7 gates, 19 inputs)

b. $f(a, b, c, d) = \Sigma m(1, 2, 4, 5, 6, 9, 11, 13, 15)$
$g(a, b, c, d) = \Sigma m(0, 2, 4, 8, 9, 11, 12, 13, 14, 15)$
(8 gates, 23 inputs)

c. $F(W, X, Y, Z) = \Sigma m(2, 3, 6, 7, 8, 9, 13)$
$G(W, X, Y, Z) = \Sigma m(2, 3, 6, 7, 9, 10, 13, 14)$
$H(W, X, Y, Z) = \Sigma m(0, 1, 4, 5, 9, 10, 13, 14)$
(8 gates, 22 inputs)

d. $f(a, b, c, d) = \Sigma m(0, 2, 3, 8, 9, 10, 11, 12, 13, 15)$
$g(a, b, c, d) = \Sigma m(3, 5, 7, 12, 13, 15)$
$h(a, b, c, d) = \Sigma m(0, 2, 3, 4, 6, 8, 10, 14)$
(10 gates, 28 inputs)

e. $f(a, b, c, d) = \Sigma m(0, 3, 5, 7) + \Sigma d(10, 11, 12, 13, 14, 15)$
$g(a, b, c, d) = \Sigma m(0, 5, 6, 7, 8) + \Sigma d(10, 11, 12, 13, 14, 15)$
(7 gates, 19 inputs)

a. The maps below show the prime implicant $a'd$ in f, that covers a 1 not part of the other function.

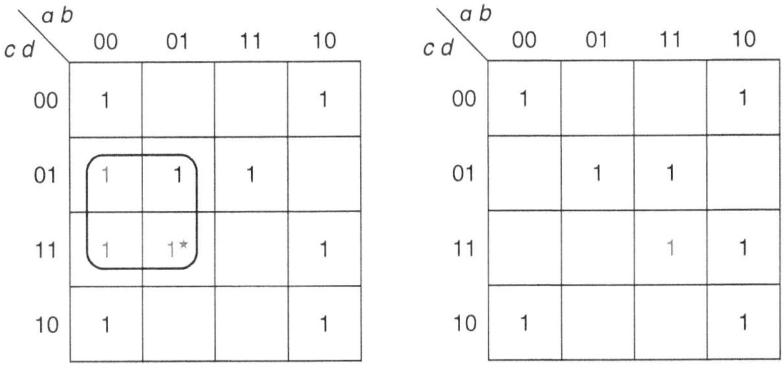

f g

No other 1 (of either f or g) that is not shared makes a prime implicant essential (m_1 or m_3 in f or m_{15} in g). Two other terms, $b'd'$ and $bc'd$, are essential prime implicants of both f and g and have been thus chosen in the maps below.

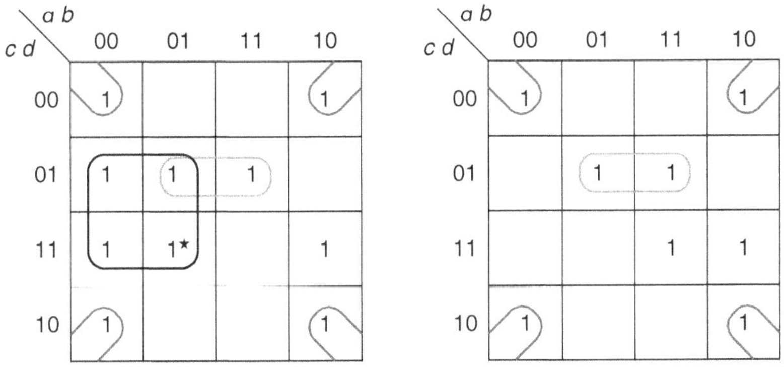

f g

Although the term $ab'c$ could be shared, another term would be needed for g (either abd or acd). This would require seven gates and 20 gate inputs (one input too many). But, if acd is used for g, we could then complete covering both functions using $b'c$ for f as shown on the maps below.

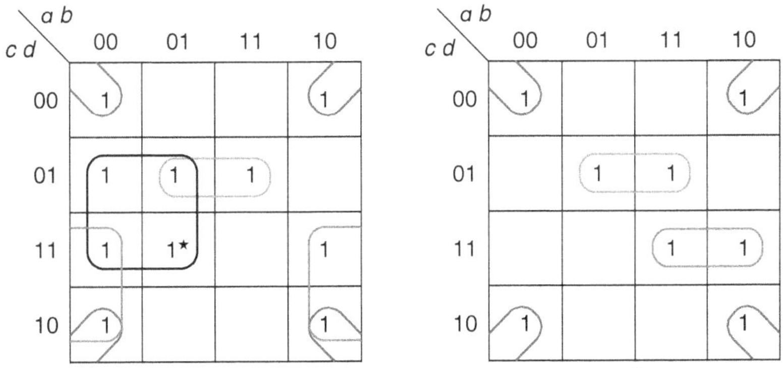

f g

Thus,

$$f = a'd + b'd' + bc'd + b'c$$
$$g = b'd' + bc'd + acd$$

requiring seven gates and 19 inputs.

---

b. Scanning each function for 1's that are not part of the other function, we find m_1, m_5, and m_6 in f and m_0, m_8, m_{12}, and m_{14} in g. The only ones that make a prime implicant essential are indicated on the map below.

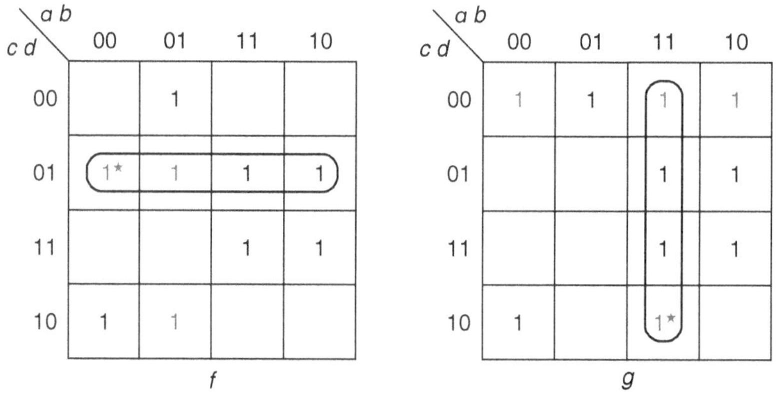

Next, we note that ad is an essential prime implicant of both functions, producing the following maps:

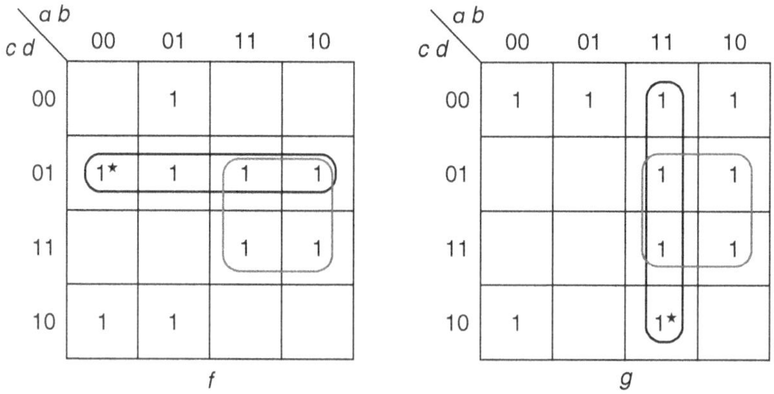

Unless we choose $c'd'$ to cover the remaining three 1's in the first row of g, we will need an extra term. Once we have done that, we see that the last 1 (m_2) of g can be covered by the minterm and shared with f. That leaves just two 1's of f that can be covered with the term $a'bd'$. The functions and the maps are shown next:

$$f = c'd + ad + a'b'cd' + a'bd'$$
$$g = ab + ad + c'd' + a'b'cd'$$

for a total of eight gates and 23 inputs.

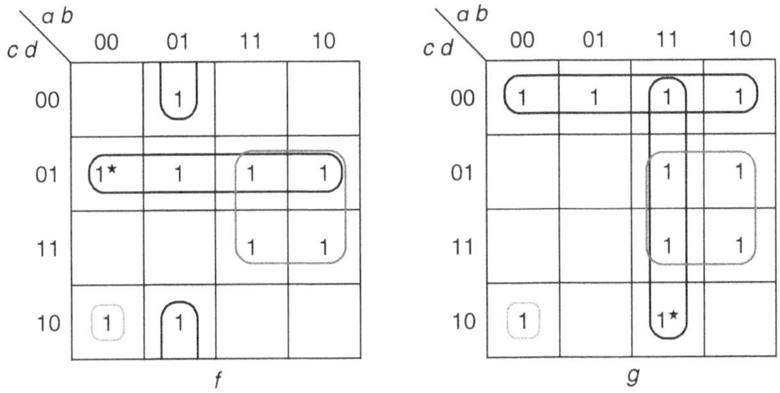

c. When minimizing three functions, we still look for 1's that are only included in one of the functions and that make a prime implicant essential. In this problem, the only ones that satisfy these conditions are m_8 in F and m_0 and m_4 in H, as shown on the map below.

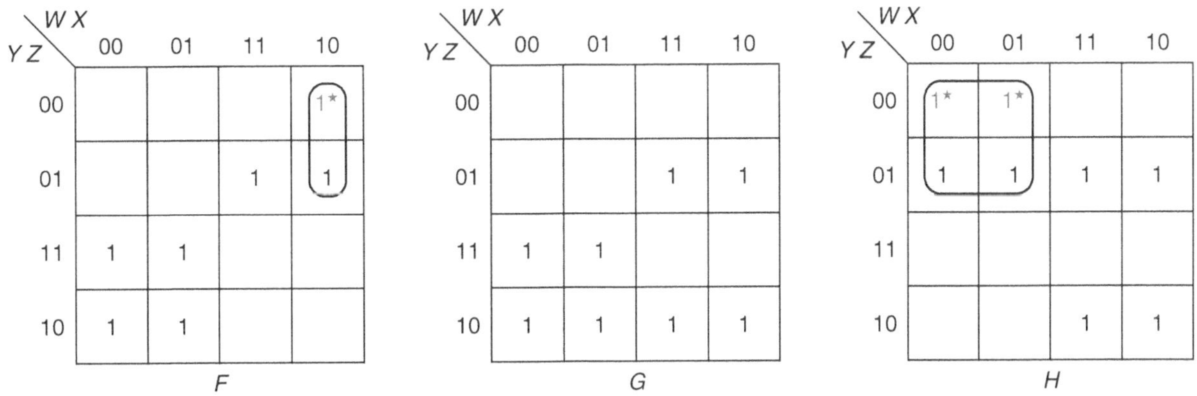

Next, notice that $W'Y$ is an essential prime implicant of both F and G. Once that is chosen, the term $WY'Z$ covers the remaining 1 of F and two 1's in G and H. (That term would be used for both F and G in any case since it is an essential prime implicant of both and is shareable. It is used for H since the remaining 1's in the prime implicant $Y'Z$ are already covered.) Finally, WYZ', an essential prime implicant of H, finishes the cover of G and H. The maps and functions below show the final solution, utilizing eight gates and 22 inputs.

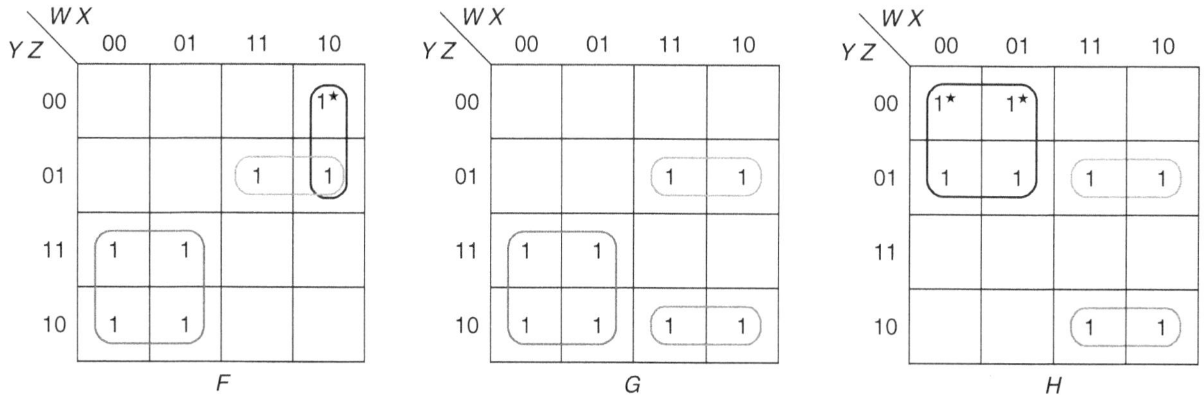

$$F = WX'Y' + W'Y + WY'Z$$
$$G = W'Y + WY'Z + WYZ'$$
$$H = W'Y' + WY'Z + WYZ'$$

d. On the maps below, the essential prime implicants that cover 1's not part of any other function are circled. In f, m_9 and m_{11} can be covered with any of three prime implicants.

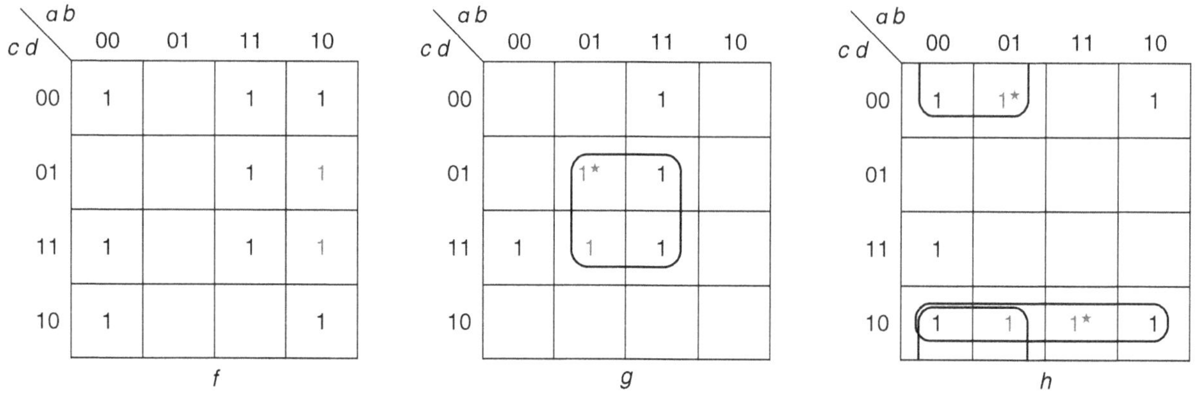

Next, we note that m_8 can only be covered by $b'd'$ in h and that $b'd'$ is also an essential prime implicant of f. That leaves only m_3 uncovered in h; by using the minterm for that, it can be shared with both f and g. (Otherwise, a new term would be required in each of those functions.) The resulting maps are shown below.

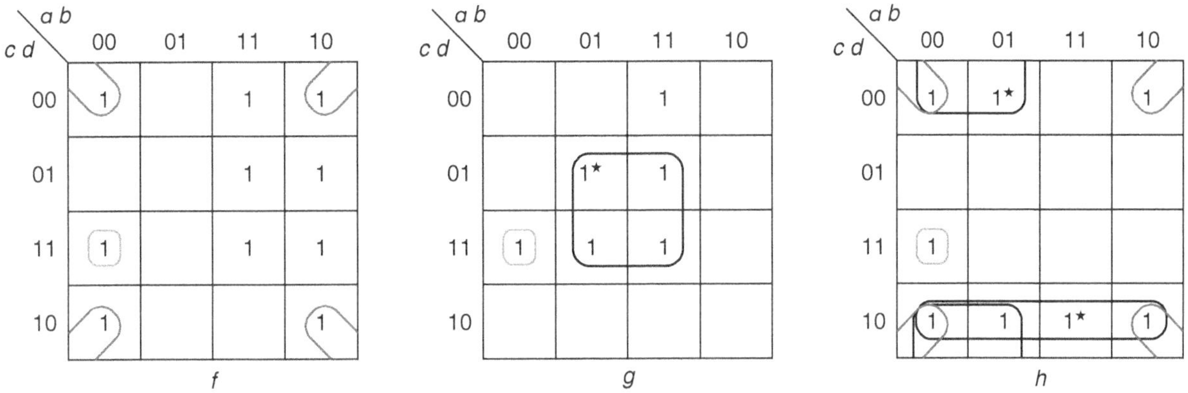

The only uncovered 1 in g is m_{12}. By using abc' for both that and for f, we can cover the three remaining 1's in f with ad, yielding the maps and equations below.

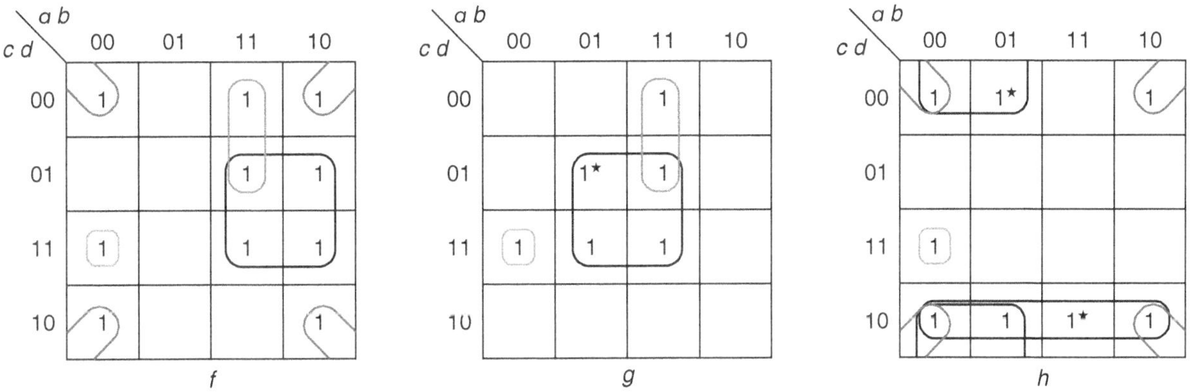

$$f = b'd' + a'b'cd + abc' + ad$$
$$g = bd + a'b'cd + abc'$$
$$h = a'd' + cd' + b'd' + a'b'cd$$

---

e. This example includes a number of don't cares, but that does not change the process significantly. There are two essential prime implicants, cd in f and bc in g, that cover 1's that cannot be shared. In addition, $a'b'c'd'$ must be used in f since it is the only prime implicant that covers m_0. (If a minterm is a prime implicant, we have no choice but to use it.) The following maps show these terms circled.

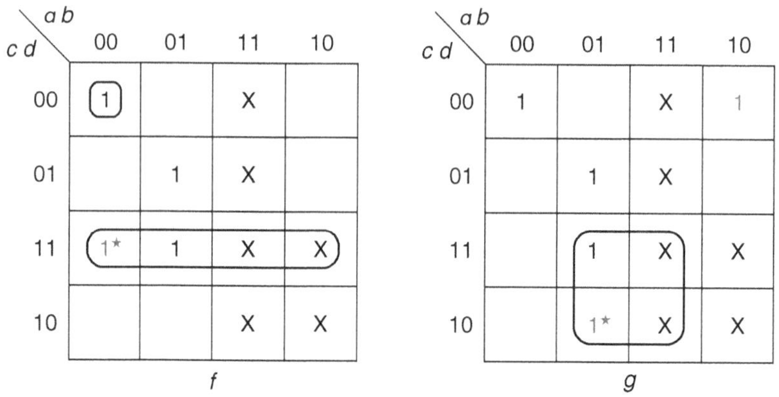

Next, we use bd to cover m_5 in both functions, and complete the cover of f. The obvious choice is to use $b'c'd'$ for the remaining 1's of g, producing the following maps and equations:

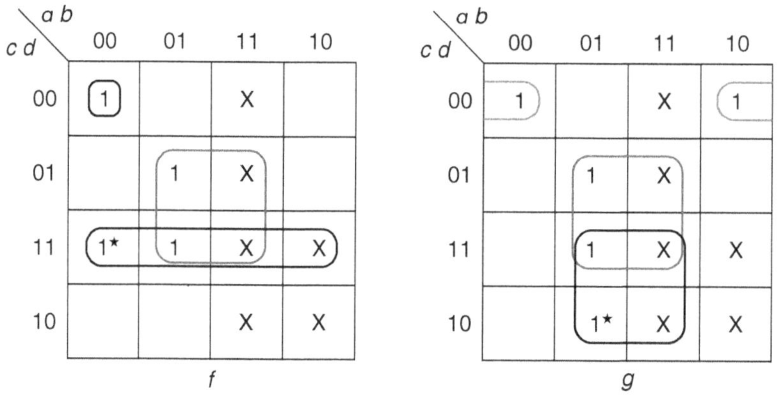

$$f = cd + a'b'c'd' + bd$$
$$g = bc + bd + b'c'd'$$

But, there is another solution, as illustrated below. By using $a'b'c'd'$ to cover m_0 in g (we already needed that term for f), we can cover the remaining 1 in g with a group of four, ad', producing the solution

$$f = cd + a'b'c'd' + bd$$
$$g = bc + bd + a'b'c'd' + ad'$$

as shown on the following maps. Both solutions require seven gates and 19 inputs.

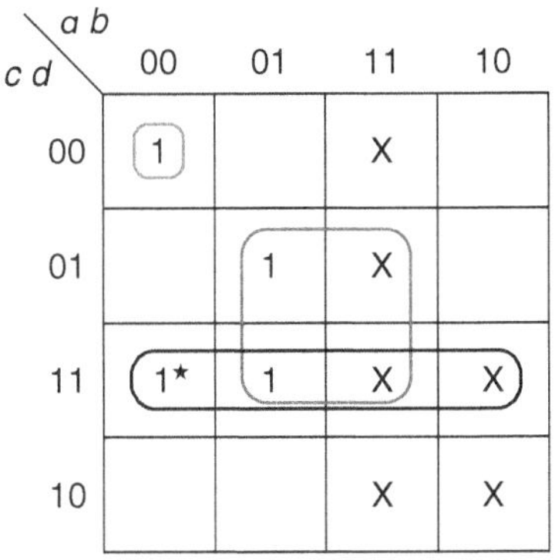

f

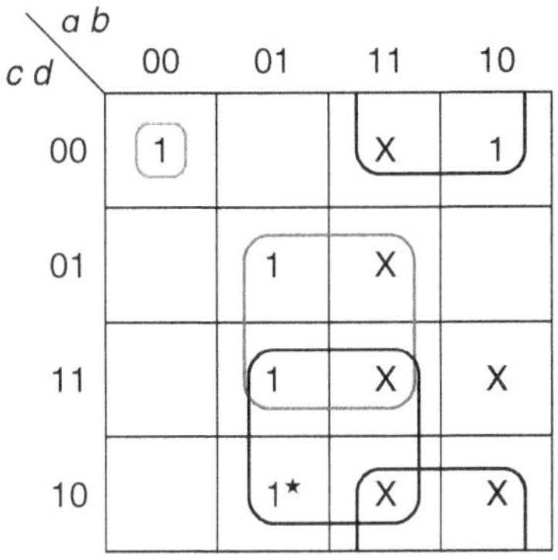

g

3.8 EXERCISES

1. Plot the following functions on the Karnaugh map:

a. $f(a, b, c) = \Sigma m(1, 2, 3, 4, 6)$

*b. $g(w, x, y, z) = \Sigma m(1, 3, 5, 6, 7, 13, 14) + \Sigma d(8, 10, 12)$

c. $F = WX'Y'Z + W'XYZ + W'X'Y'Z' + W'XY'Z + WXYZ$

*d. $g = a'c + a'bd' + bc'd + ab'd + ab'cd'$

e. $h = x + yz' + x'z$

2. For each of the following, find all minimum sum of products expressions. (If there is more than one solution, the number of solutions is given in parentheses.)

a. $f(a, b, c) = \Sigma m(1, 2, 3, 6, 7)$

*b. $g(w, x, y) = \Sigma m(0, 1, 5, 6, 7)$ (2 solutions)

c. $h(a, b, c) = \Sigma m(0, 1, 2, 5, 6, 7)$ (2 solutions)

d. $f(a, b, c, d) = \Sigma m(1, 2, 3, 5, 6, 7, 8, 11, 13, 15)$

*e. $G(W, X, Y, Z) = \Sigma m(0, 2, 5, 7, 8, 10, 12, 13)$

f. $h(a, b, c, d) = \Sigma m(2, 4, 5, 6, 7, 8, 10, 12, 13, 15)$ (2 solutions)

g. $f(a, b, c, d) = \Sigma m(1, 3, 4, 5, 6, 11, 12, 13, 14, 15)$ (2 solutions)

h. $g(w, x, y, z) = \Sigma m(2, 3, 6, 7, 8, 10, 11, 12, 13, 15)$ (2 solutions)

*i. $h(p, q, r, s) = \Sigma m(0, 2, 3, 4, 5, 8, 11, 12, 13, 14, 15)$ (3 solutions)

j. $F(W, X, Y, Z) = \Sigma m(0, 2, 3, 4, 5, 8, 10, 11, 12, 13, 14, 15)$ (4 solutions)

k. $f(w, x, y, z) = \Sigma m(0, 1, 2, 4, 5, 6, 9, 10, 11, 13, 14, 15)$ (2 solutions)

l. $g(a, b, c, d) = \Sigma m(0, 1, 2, 3, 4, 5, 6, 8, 9, 10, 12, 15)$

*m. $H(W, X, Y, Z) = \Sigma m(0, 2, 3, 5, 7, 8, 10, 12, 13)$ (4 solutions)

★n. $f(a, b, c, d) = \Sigma m(0, 1, 2, 4, 5, 6, 7, 8, 9, 10, 11, 13, 14, 15)$ (6 solutions)

o. $g(w, x, y, z) = \Sigma m(0, 1, 2, 3, 5, 6, 7, 8, 9, 10, 13, 14, 15)$ (6 solutions)

★p. $f(a, b, c, d) = \Sigma m(0, 3, 5, 6, 7, 9, 10, 11, 12, 13, 14)$ (32 solutions)

3. For the following functions,

i. List all prime implicants, indicating which are essential.

ii. Show the minimum sum of products expression(s).

a. $f(a, b, c, d) = \Sigma m(0, 3, 4, 5, 8, 11, 12, 13, 14, 15)$

★b. $g(w, x, y, z) = \Sigma m(0, 3, 4, 5, 6, 7, 8, 9, 11, 13, 14, 15)$

4. Map each of the following functions and find the minimum sum of products expression:

a. $F = AD + AB + A'CD' + B'CD + A'BC'D'$

★b. $g = w'yz + xy'z + wy + wxy'z' + wz + xyz'$

5. For each of the following, find all minimum sum of products expressions. (If there is more than one solution, the number of solutions is given in parentheses.) Label the solutions $f_1, f_2, \ldots$.

a. $f(w, x, y, z) = \Sigma m(1, 3, 6, 8, 11, 14) + \Sigma d(2, 4, 5, 13, 15)$ (3 solutions)

b. $f(a, b, c, d) = \Sigma m(0, 3, 6, 9, 11, 13, 14) + \Sigma d(5, 7, 10, 12)$

★c. $f(a, b, c, d) = \Sigma m(0, 2, 3, 5, 7, 8, 9, 10, 11) + \Sigma d(4, 15)$ (3 solutions)

d. $f(w, x, y, z) = \Sigma m(0, 2, 4, 5, 10, 12, 15) + \Sigma d(8, 14)$ (2 solutions)

e. $f(a, b, c, d) = \Sigma m(5, 7, 9, 11, 13, 14) + \Sigma d(2, 6, 10, 12, 15)$ (4 solutions)

★f. $f(a, b, c, d) = \Sigma m(0, 2, 4, 5, 6, 7, 8, 9, 10, 14) + \Sigma d(3, 13)$ (3 solutions)

g. $f(w, x, y, z) = \Sigma m(1, 2, 5, 10, 12) + \Sigma d(0, 3, 4, 8, 13, 14, 15)$ (7 solutions)

6. For each of the functions of problem 5, indicate which solutions are equal.

7. For each of the following functions, find all of the minimum sum of products expressions and all of the minimum product of sums expressions:

★a. $f(A, B, C, D) = \Sigma m(1, 4, 5, 6, 7, 9, 11, 13, 15)$

b. $f(W, X, Y, Z) = \Sigma m(2, 4, 5, 6, 7, 10, 11, 15)$

c. $f(A, B, C, D) = \Sigma m(1, 5, 6, 7, 8, 9, 10, 12, 13, 14, 15)$ (1 SOP and 2 POS solutions)

*d. $f(a, b, c, d) = \Sigma m(0, 2, 4, 6, 7, 9, 11, 12, 13, 14, 15)$ (2 SOP and 1 POS solutions)

e. $f(w, x, y, z) = \Sigma m(0, 4, 6, 9, 10, 11, 14) + \Sigma d(1, 3, 5, 7)$

f. $f(a, b, c, d) = \Sigma m(0, 1, 2, 5, 7, 9) + \Sigma d(6, 8, 11, 13, 14, 15)$ (4 SOP and 2 POS solutions)

g. $f(w, x, y, z) = \Sigma m(4, 6, 9, 10, 11, 13) + \Sigma d(2, 12, 15)$ (2 SOP and 2 POS solutions)

h. $f(a, b, c, d) = \Sigma m(0, 1, 4, 6, 10, 14) + \Sigma d(5, 7, 8, 9, 11, 12, 15)$ (13 SOP and 3 POS solutions)

*i. $f(w, x, y, z) = \Sigma m(1, 3, 7, 11, 13, 14) + \Sigma d(0, 2, 5, 8, 10, 12, 15)$ (6 SOP and 1 POS solutions)

j. $f(a, b, c, d) = \Sigma m(0, 1, 6, 15) + \Sigma d(3, 5, 7, 11, 14)$ (1 SOP and 2 POS solutions)

8. Label the solutions of each part of problem 7 as $f_1, f_2, \ldots$ and indicate which solutions are equal.

9. For each of the following five-variable functions, find all minimum sum of products expressions. (If there is more than one solution, the number of solutions is given in parentheses.)

a. $F(A, B, C, D, E) = \Sigma m(0, 1, 5, 7, 8, 9, 10, 11, 13, 15, 18, 20, 21, 23, 26, 28, 29, 31)$

b. $G(A, B, C, D, E) = \Sigma m(0, 1, 2, 4, 5, 6, 10, 13, 14, 18, 21, 22, 24, 26, 29, 30)$

*c. $H(A, B, C, D, E) = \Sigma m(5, 8, 12, 13, 15, 17, 19, 21, 23, 24, 28, 31)$

d. $F(V, W, X, Y, Z) = \Sigma m(2, 4, 5, 6, 10, 11, 12, 13, 14, 15, 16, 17, 18, 21, 24, 25, 29, 30, 31)$

e. $G(V, W, X, Y, Z) = \Sigma m(0, 1, 4, 5, 8, 9, 10, 15, 16, 18, 19, 20, 24, 26, 28, 31)$

*f. $H(V, W, X, Y, Z) = \Sigma m(0, 1, 2, 3, 5, 7, 10, 11, 14, 15, 16, 18, 24, 25, 28, 29, 31)$ (2 solutions)

g. $F(A, B, C, D, E) = \Sigma m(0, 4, 6, 8, 12, 13, 14, 15, 16, 17, 18, 21, 24, 25, 26, 28, 29, 31)$ (6 solutions)

h. $G(A, B, C, D, E) = \Sigma m(0, 3, 5, 7\ 12, 13, 14, 15, 19, 20, 21, 22, 23, 25, 26, 29, 30)$ (3 solutions)

*i. $H(A, B, C, D, E) = \Sigma m(0, 1, 5, 6, 7, 8, 9, 14, 17, 20, 21, 22, 23, 25, 28, 29, 30)$ (3 solutions)

j. $F(V, W, X, Y, Z) = \Sigma m(0, 4, 5, 7, 10, 11, 14, 15, 16, 18, 20, 21, 23, 24, 25, 26, 29, 31)$ (4 solutions)

k. $G(V, W, X, Y, Z) = \Sigma m(0, 2, 5, 6, 8, 10, 11, 13, 14, 15, 16, 17, 18, 19, 20, 21, 22, 24, 26, 29, 31)$ (3 solutions)

l. $H(V, W, X, Y, Z) = \Sigma m(0, 1, 2, 3, 5, 8, 9, 10, 13, 17, 18, 19, 20, 21, 26, 28, 29)$
(3 solutions)

m. $F(A, B, C, D, E) = \Sigma m(1, 2, 5, 8, 9, 10, 12, 13, 14, 15, 16, 18, 21, 22, 23, 24, 26, 29, 30, 31)$
(18 solutions)

*n. $G(V, W, X, Y, Z) = \Sigma m(0, 1, 5, 7, 8, 13, 24, 25, 29, 31) + \Sigma d(9, 15, 16, 17, 23, 26, 27, 30)$
(2 solutions)

o. $H(A, B, C, D, E) = \Sigma m(0, 4, 12, 15, 27, 29, 30) + \Sigma d(1, 5, 9, 10, 14, 16, 20, 28, 31)$
(4 solutions)

p. $F(A, B, C, D, E) = \Sigma m(8, 9, 11, 14, 28, 30) + d(0, 3, 4, 6, 7, 12, 13, 15, 20, 22, 27, 29, 31)$
(8 solutions)

10. For each of the following six-variable functions, find all minimum sum of products expressions. (The number of terms and literals, and, if there is more than one solution, the number of solutions is given in parentheses.)

a. $G(A, B, C, D, E, F) = \Sigma m(4, 5, 6, 7, 8, 10, 13, 15, 18, 20, 21, 22, 23, 26, 29, 30, 31, 33, 36, 37, 38, 39, 40, 42, 49, 52, 53, 54, 55, 60, 61)$
(6 terms, 21 literals)

*b. $G(A, B, C, D, E, F) = \Sigma m(2, 3, 6, 7, 8, 12, 14, 17, 19, 21, 23, 25, 27, 28, 29, 30, 32, 33, 34, 35, 40, 44, 46, 49, 51, 53, 55, 57, 59, 61, 62, 63)$
(8 terms, 30 literals)

c. $G(A, B, C, D, E, F) = \Sigma m(0, 1, 2, 4, 5, 6, 7, 9, 13, 15, 17, 19, 21, 23, 26, 27, 29, 30, 31, 33, 37, 39, 40, 42, 44, 45, 46, 47, 49, 53, 55, 57, 59, 60, 61, 62, 63)$
(8 terms, 28 literals, 2 solutions)

11. Find a minimum two-level circuit (corresponding to sum of products expressions) using AND and one OR gate per function for each of the following sets of functions.

*a. $f(a, b, c, d) = \Sigma m(1, 3, 5, 8, 9, 10, 13, 14)$
$g(a, b, c, d) = \Sigma m(4, 5, 6, 7, 10, 13, 14)$ (7 gates, 21 inputs)

b. $f(a, b, c, d) = \Sigma m(0, 1, 2, 3, 4, 5, 8, 10, 13)$
$g(a, b, c, d) = \Sigma m(0, 1, 2, 3, 8, 9, 10, 11, 13)$
(6 gates, 16 inputs)

c. $f(a, b, c, d) = \Sigma m(5, 8, 9, 12, 13, 14)$
$g(a, b, c, d) = \Sigma m(1, 3, 5, 8, 9, 10)$
(3 solutions, 8 gates, 25 inputs)

d. $f(a, b, c, d) = \Sigma m(1, 3, 4, 5, 10, 11, 12, 14, 15)$
$g(a, b, c, d) = \Sigma m(0, 1, 2, 8, 10, 11, 12, 15)$
(9 gates, 28 inputs)

*e. $F(W, X, Y, Z) = \Sigma m(1, 5, 7, 8, 10, 11, 12, 14, 15)$
$G(W, X, Y, Z) = \Sigma m(0, 1, 4, 6, 7, 8, 12)$ (8 gates, 23 inputs)

f. $F(W, X, Y, Z) = \Sigma m(0, 2, 3, 7, 8, 9, 13, 15)$
$G(W, X, Y, Z) = \Sigma m(0, 2, 8, 9, 10, 12, 13, 14)$
(2 solutions, 8 gates, 23 inputs)

g. $f(a, b, c, d) = \Sigma m(1, 3, 5, 7, 8, 9, 10)$
$g(a, b, c, d) = \Sigma m(0, 2, 4, 5, 6, 8, 10, 11, 12)$
$h(a, b, c, d) = \Sigma m(1, 2, 3, 5, 7, 10, 12, 13, 14, 15)$
(2 solutions, 12 gates, 33 inputs)

*h. $f(a, b, c, d) = \Sigma m(0, 3, 4, 5, 7, 8, 12, 13, 15)$
$g(a, b, c, d) = \Sigma m(1, 5, 7, 8, 9, 10, 11, 13, 14, 15)$
$h(a, b, c, d) = \Sigma m(1, 2, 4, 5, 7, 10, 13, 14, 15)$
(2 solutions, 11 gates, 33 inputs)

i. $f(a, b, c, d) = \Sigma m(0, 2, 3, 4, 6, 7, 9, 11, 13)$
$g(a, b, c, d) = \Sigma m(2, 3, 5, 6, 7, 8, 9, 10, 13)$
$h(a, b, c, d) = \Sigma m(0, 4, 8, 9, 10, 13, 15)$
(2 solutions for f and g, 10 gates, 32 inputs)

*j. $f(a, c, b, d) = \Sigma m(0, 1, 2, 3, 4, 9) + \Sigma d(10, 11, 12, 13, 14, 15)$
$g(a, c, b, d) = \Sigma m(1, 2, 6, 9) + \Sigma d(10, 11, 12, 13, 14, 15)$
(3 solutions for f, 6 gates, 15 inputs)

k. $f(a, c, b, d) = \Sigma m(5, 6, 11) + \Sigma d(0, 1, 2, 4, 8)$
$g(a, c, b, d) = \Sigma m(6, 9, 11, 12, 14) + \Sigma d(0, 1, 2, 4, 8)$
(2 solutions for g, 7 gates, 18 inputs)

12. In each of the following sets, the functions have been minimized individually. Find a minimum two-level circuit (corresponding to sum of products expressions) using AND and one OR gate per function for each.

a. $F = B'D' + CD' + AB'C$
$G = BC + ACD$ (6 gates, 15 inputs)

*b. $F = A'B'C'D + BC + ACD + AC'D'$
$G = A'B'C'D' + A'BC + BCD'$
$H = B'C'D' + BCD + AC' + AD$
(2 solutions for H, 10 gates, 35 inputs)

c. $f = a'b' + a'd + b'c'd'$
$g = b'c'd' + bd + acd + abc$
$h = a'd' + a'b + bc'd + b'c'd'$ (10 gates, 31 inputs)

3.9 CHAPTER 3 TEST (100 MINUTES, OR TWO 50-MINUTE TESTS)

1. Map each of the following functions (be sure to label the maps):

a. $f(x, y, z) = \Sigma m(1, 2, 7) + \Sigma d(4, 5)$

	00	01	11	10
0				
1				

b. $g = a'c + ab'c'd + a'bd + abc'$

Circle each of the terms.

	00	01	11	10
00				
01				
11				
10				

2. Find the minimum sum of products expression for each of the following functions (that is, circle the terms on the map and write the algebraic expressions).

a.

yz \ wx	00	01	11	10
00		1		1
01		1		
11		1	1	1
10		1		

b.

cd \ ab	00	01	11	10
00	1	1	1	
01	1	1	1	
11			1	1
10	1	1	1	

3. Find all four minimum sum of products expressions for the following function. (Two copies of the map are given for your convenience.)

cd \ ab	00	01	11	10
00	1	1	1	
01	1		1	1
11	1		1	1
10		1	1	1

cd \ ab	00	01	11	10
00	1	1	1	
01	1		1	1
11	1		1	1
10		1	1	1

4. For the following function (three copies of the map are shown),

a. List all prime implicants, indicating which, if any, are essential.

b. Find all four minimum solutions.

yz \ wx	00	01	11	10
00		1	1	X
01	X	X		X
11	X			1
10			1	1

yz \ wx	00	01	11	10
00		1	1	X
01	X	X		X
11	X			1
10			1	1

yz \ wx	00	01	11	10
00		1	1	X
01	X	X		X
11	X			1
10			1	1

5. For the following four-variable function, *f*, find both minimum sum of products expressions and both minimum product of sums expressions.

cd \ ab	00	01	11	10
00			X	
01	X	1	X	1
11	1	1		X
10		X		

6. For the following function, *f*, find all four minimum sum of products expressions and all four minimum product of sums expressions.

yz \ wx	00	01	11	10
00	X		1	
01	X	1	1	
11	X		X	1
10	X		X	

7. For the following five-variable problem, find both minimum sum of products expressions.

A = 0

DE \ BC	00	01	11	10
00	1		1	
01	1	1		
11	1			
10	1			

A = 1

DE \ BC	00	01	11	10
00			1	
01		1	1	
11		1	1	1
10				1

8. For the following five-variable problem, find both minimum sum of products expressions. (5 terms, 15 literals)

A = 0

DE \ BC	00	01	11	10
00	1			1
01				1
11		1	1	1
10	1			1

A = 1

DE \ BC	00	01	11	10
00	1	1	1	
01	1			1
11	1	1	1	1
10	1	1	1	

9. a. For the following two functions, find the minimum sum of products expression for each (treating them as two separate problems).

yz \ wx	00	01	11	10
00		1	1	1
01				1
11				1
10			1	1

f

yz \ wx	00	01	11	10
00				
01	1	1		1
11	1	1		1
10		1		

g

b. For the same two functions, find a minimum sum of products solution (corresponding to minimum number of gates, and among those with the same number of gates, minimum number of gate inputs). (7 gates, 19 inputs)

10. Consider the three functions, the maps of which are shown below.

yz \ wx	00	01	11	10
00				1
01	1	1		
11	1	1	1	1
10	1	1		1

f

yz \ wx	00	01	11	10
00		1	1	1
01				
11			1	
10	1	1	1	

g

yz \ wx	00	01	11	10
00		1		1
01	1	1		
11	1	1	1	
10		1		

h

a. Find the minimum sum of products expression (individually) for each of the three functions. Indicate which, if any, prime implicants can be shared.

b. Find a minimum two-level NAND gate solution. Full credit for a solution using 10 gates and 32 inputs. All variables are available both uncomplemented and complemented. Show the equations *and* a block diagram.

CHAPTER 4

Function Minimization Algorithms

In this chapter, we will look at two approaches to finding all of the prime implicants of a function and then algorithms for finding minimum sum of products solutions. We will then extend the approaches to problems with multiple outputs.

The first approach to finding prime implicants is referred to as the *Quine-McCluskey method.* It starts with minterms and uses, repeatedly, the adjacency property

$$ab + ab' = a$$

The second approach is *iterated consensus.* It starts with any set of terms that covers the function and uses the consensus operation and the absorption property

$$a + ab = a$$

Each of these methods has been computerized and is effective for a larger number of variables than the Karnaugh map, although the amount of computing becomes excessive for many practical problems.

4.1 QUINE-McCLUSKEY METHOD FOR ONE OUTPUT*

In this section, we will use the Quine-McCluskey method to find all of the prime implicants of a function. In Section 4.3, we will use that set of prime implicants to find the minimum sum of products expression(s) for that function. We start with a list of minterms, in numerical form (that is, 1 for an uncomplemented variable and 0 for a complemented one). If we start with minterm numbers, this is just the binary equivalent of the minterm number. We order this list by the number of 1's in each term. We will use the function of Example 3.6:

$$f(w, x, y, z) = \Sigma m(0, 4, 5, 7, 8, 11, 12, 15)$$

*The Quine-McCluskey algorithm was developed by W. V. Quine and Edward J. McCluskey in the 1950s.

Our initial list, grouped by the number of 1's, is

A 0 0 0 0

B 0 1 0 0
C 1 0 0 0

D 0 1 0 1
E 1 1 0 0

F 0 1 1 1
G 1 0 1 1

H 1 1 1 1

where we have labeled the terms for easy reference.

We now apply the adjacency property to each pair of terms. Since that property requires all the variables to be the same except for one, we need only consider terms in consecutive groups. We produce a second column of terms with one variable missing:

$A + B = J = 0 - 0\ 0$ (where the dash represents a missing variable)
$A + C = K = -\ 0\ 0\ 0$
$B + D = L = 0\ 1\ 0\ -$
$B + E = M = -\ 1\ 0\ 0$
$C + D =$ none
$C + E = N = 1 - 0\ 0$
$D + F = O = 0\ 1 - 1$
$D + G =$ none
$E + F =$ none
$E + G =$ none
$F + H = P = -\ 1\ 1\ 1$
$G + H = Q = 1 - 1\ 1$

Of course, some pairs of terms, even in adjacent groups, cannot be combined because they differ in more than one place, such as terms C and D. Whenever a term is used to produce another term, it is checked off; it is not a prime implicant. These (three literal) terms are placed in a second column as shown in Table 4.1. All of the minterms have been used to form at least one term in the second column; thus, no minterms are prime implicants.

We now repeat the process with the second column. Again, we need only consider terms in consecutive sections of that column (number of

Table 4.1 Quine-McCluskey prime implicant computation.

A 0 0 0 0 √	*J* 0 – 0 0 √	*R* – – 0 0
-------------	*K* – 0 0 0 √	
B 0 1 0 0 √	-------------	
C 1 0 0 0 √	*L* 0 1 0 –	
-------------	*M* – 1 0 0 √	
D 0 1 0 1 √	*N* 1 – 0 0 √	
E 1 1 0 0 √	-------------	
-------------	*O* 0 1 – 1	
F 0 1 1 1 √	-------------	
G 1 0 1 1 √	*P* – 1 1 1	
-------------	*Q* 1 – 1 1	
H 1 1 1 1 √		

1's differing by only one). Also, we need only consider terms with dashes in the same position, since they are the only ones with the same three variables. Thus, we find

$$J + N = R = --00$$

$$K + M = R \quad \text{(same term)}$$

Each term in this column is always formed by two different pairs of terms. In this example, $y'z'$ is formed by the computation $w'y'z' + wy'z'$ as well as by $x'y'z' + xy'z'$, as shown on the map below. (Note that only these terms of the function are shown.)

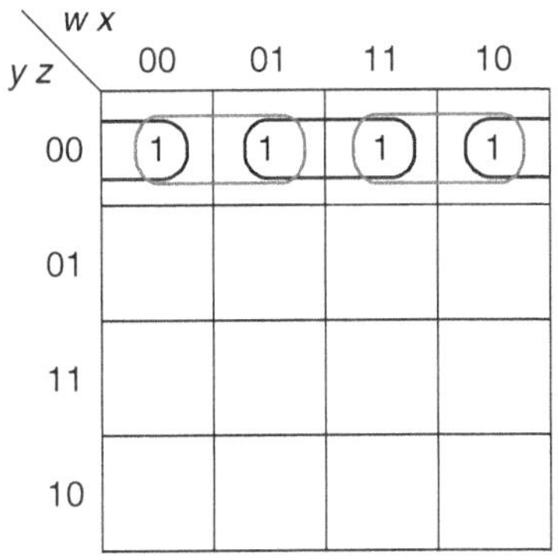

There are no adjacencies between the second and third group or between the third and fourth group.

Since there is only one term in the third column, we are done. If there were more terms, we would repeat the process, forming a column with three literals missing (corresponding to a group of eight minterms). The prime implicants are

L	0 1 0 –	$w'xy'$
O	0 1 – 1	$w'xz$
P	– 1 1 1	xyz
Q	1 – 1 1	wyz
R	– – 0 0	$y'z'$

If there are don't cares in the problem, all of them must be included in the first column of the table, since don't cares are part of prime implicants.

EXAMPLE 4.1

$$g(w, x, y, z) = \Sigma m(1, 3, 4, 6, 11) + \Sigma d(0, 8, 10, 12, 13)$$

The process proceeds as before

0 0 0 0 √	0 0 0 –	– – 0 0
--------	0 – 0 0 √	
0 0 0 1 √	– 0 0 0 √	
0 1 0 0 √	--------	
1 0 0 0 √	0 0 – 1	
--------	0 1 – 0	
0 0 1 1 √	– 1 0 0 √	
0 1 1 0 √	1 0 – 0	
1 0 1 0 √	1 – 0 0 √	
1 1 0 0 √	--------	
--------	– 0 1 1	
1 0 1 1 √	1 0 1 –	
1 1 0 1 √	1 1 0 –	

Thus, the prime implicants are

$w'x'y'$	$x'yz$
$w'x'z$	$wx'y$
$w'xz'$	wxy'
$wx'z'$	$y'z'$

Although wxy' and $wx'z'$ are prime implicants, they consist of all don't cares and would never be used in a minimum solution.

This process works for larger number of variables, but the number of minterms and other implicants can increase rapidly. We will see one example with five variables in the solved problems. This process has been computerized.

[SP 1; EX 1]

4.2 ITERATED CONSENSUS FOR ONE OUTPUT

In this section, we will use the iterated consensus algorithm to list all of the prime implicants of a function. In the next section, we will use that list to find the minimum sum of products expression(s).

To simplify the discussion, we will first define the relationship *included in.*

Product term t_1 is *included in* product term t_2 (written $t_1 \leq t_2$) if t_2 is 1 whenever t_1 is 1 (and elsewhere, too, if the two terms are not equal).*

*The relationship *included in* is also applied to more complex functions than product terms, but that will not be important here.

All this really means for product terms is that either $t_1 = t_2$, or $t_1 = xt_2$, where x is a literal or a product of literals. From the perspective of the map, it means that t_1 is a subgroup of t_2. If an implicant, t_1, is included in another implicant, t_2, then t_1 is not a prime implicant since

$$t_1 + t_2 = xt_2 + t_2 = t_2 \qquad \textbf{[P12a]}$$

The iterated consensus algorithm for single functions is as follows:

1. Find a list of product terms (implicants) that cover the function. Make sure that no term is equal to or included in any other term on the list. (The terms on the list could be prime implicants or minterms or any other set of implicants. However, the rest of the algorithm proceeds more quickly if we start with prime implicants.)
2. For each pair of terms, t_i and t_j (including terms added to the list in step 3), compute $t_i \text{ ¢ } t_j$.
3. If the consensus is defined, and the consensus term is not equal to or included in a term already on the list, add it to the list.
4. Delete all terms that are included in the new term added to the list.
5. The process ends when all possible consensus operations have been performed. The terms remaining on the list are ALL of the prime implicants.

Consider the following function (Example 3.6 from Chapter 3 and the function we used to describe the Quine-McCluskey method in Section 4.1).

$$f(w, x, y, z) = \Sigma m(0, 4, 5, 7, 8, 11, 12, 15)$$

We chose as a starting point a set of product terms that cover the function; they include some prime implicants and a minterm, as well as other implicants.

$A \quad w'x'y'z'$
$B \quad w'xy'$
$C \quad wy'z'$
$D \quad xyz$
$E \quad wyz$

We labeled the terms for reference and go in the order, B ¢ A, C ¢ B, C ¢ A, D ¢ C, . . . , omitting any computation when the term has been removed from the list. When a term is removed, we cross it out. The first consensus, B ¢ A, produces $w'y'z'$; A is included in that term and can thus be removed. After the first step, the list becomes

~~$A \quad w'x'y'z'$~~
$B \quad w'xy'$
$C \quad wy'z'$
$D \quad wyz$
$E \quad wyz$
$F \quad w'y'z'$

We next find C ¢ B, which creates term G, $xy'z'$; it is not included in any other term and no other term is included in it. There is no need to compute C ¢ A, since term A has already been removed from the list.

The complete computation is shown in Table 4.2, where each possible consensus is listed on a separate line.

Table 4.2 Computing the prime implicants.

~~A~~	~~$w'x'y'z'$~~		
B	$w'xy'$		
~~C~~	~~$wy'z'$~~		
D	xyz		
E	wyz		
~~F~~	~~$w'y'z'$~~	B ¢ A ≥ A (remove A)	
~~G~~	~~$xy'z'$~~	C ¢ B	
		D ¢ C	undefined
H	$w'xz$	D ¢ B	
		E ¢ D	undefined
		E ¢ C	undefined
		E ¢ B	undefined
		F ¢ E	undefined
		F ¢ D	undefined
J	$y'z'$	F ¢ C ≥ G, F, C (remove G, F, C)	
		H ¢ E = D (do not add)	
		H ¢ D	undefined
		H ¢ B	undefined
		J ¢ H = B (do not add)	
		J ¢ E	undefined
		J ¢ D	undefined
		J ¢ B	undefined

The terms that remain, B, D, E, H, and J, that is, $w'xy$, xyz, wyz, $w'xz$, and $y'z'$, are all the prime implicants. The minimum sum of products expression(s) will use some of these, typically not all of them.

The process can be simplified by using a numeric representation of the terms. As in the truth table, a 0 represents a complemented variable, and a 1 represents an uncomplemented variable. If a variable is missing from a term, as we did in Quine-McCluskey, a dash (–) is used in its place so that each term has four entries. A consensus exists if there is a 1 for exactly one variable in one term and a 0 for that variable in the other. The consensus term has a 1 for a variable if one term has a 1 and the other either a 1 or a –; it has a 0 if one term has a 0 and the other a 0 or a –, and a – if one term has a 0 and the other a 1 or if both terms have a –. For the function of Table 4.2, the process becomes that of Table 4.3 (where we have not left lines for consensus operations that are undefined).

The five terms remaining in Table 4.3 are the same as those in Table 4.2.

Table 4.3 Numeric computation of prime implicants.

~~A~~	~~0~~	~~0~~	~~0~~	~~0~~		
B	0	1	0	–		
~~C~~	~~1~~	~~–~~	~~0~~	~~0~~		
D	–	1	1	1		
E	1	–	1	1		
~~F~~	~~0~~	~~–~~	~~0~~	~~0~~	B ¢ A ≥ A	
~~G~~	~~–~~	~~1~~	~~0~~	~~0~~	C ¢ B	
H	0	1	–	1	D ¢ B	(D ¢ C undefined)
					(E ¢ D, E ¢ C, E ¢ B, F ¢ E, F ¢ D undefined)	
J	–	–	0	0	F ¢ C ≥ G, F, C	
					(H ¢ E = D; H ¢ D, H ¢ B undefined; J ¢ H = B; J ¢ E, J ¢ D, J ¢ B undefined)	

If there are don't cares in the function, all of them must be included in at least one of the terms to start the process. The resulting list of prime implicants will then include all possible prime implicants (including possibly some that are made up of only don't cares). The prime implicant table will then allow us to choose the minimum cover.

EXAMPLE 4.2

$g(w, x, y, z) = \Sigma m(1, 3, 4, 6, 11) + \Sigma d(0, 8, 10, 12, 13)$

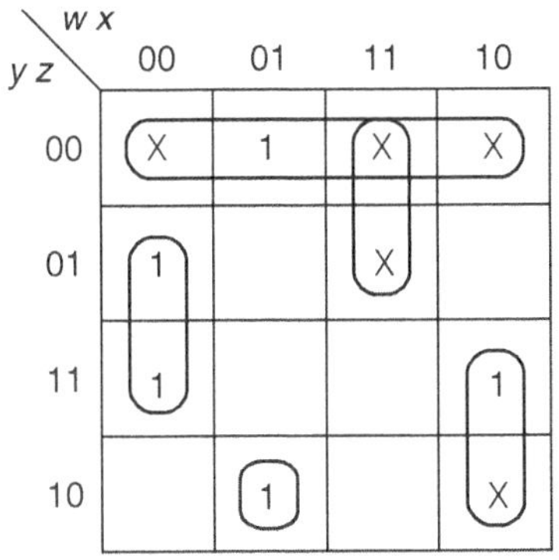

Using the map above, we chose the following list of implicants as a starting point:

A	$y'z'$	–	–	0	0
B	$w'x'z$	0	0	–	1
C	$w'xyz'$	0	1	1	0
D	wxy'	1	1	0	–
E	$wx'y$	1	0	1	–

All of these, except the third, are prime implicants. It does not matter what set of terms we start with (as long as all of the 1's and don't cares are included in at least one term); we will get the same result. By choosing a pretty good cover, we will create few if any extraneous terms. The process then proceeds:

A	–	–	0	0	
B	0	0	–	1	
~~C~~	~~0~~	~~1~~	~~1~~	~~0~~	
D	1	1	0	–	
E	1	0	1	–	
F	0	0	0	–	B ¢ A C ¢ B undefined
G	0	1	–	0	C ¢ A ≥ C D ¢ B, D ¢ A, E ¢ D undefined
H	–	0	1	1	E ¢ B
J	1	0	–	0	E ¢ A

F ¢ E, F ¢ D, F ¢ B, F ¢ A undefined, G ¢ F = 0 – 0 0 ≤ A;
G ¢ E undefined; G ¢ D ≤ A; G ¢ B, G ¢ A, H ¢ G undefined;
H ¢ F = B; H ¢ E, H ¢ D, H ¢ B, H ¢ A, undefined; J ¢ H = E;
J ¢ G, J ¢ E, J ¢ B, J ¢ A undefined; J ¢ F ≤ A, J ¢ D ≤ A

Thus, all terms but term C are prime implicants.

4.3 PRIME IMPLICANT TABLES FOR ONE OUTPUT

Once we have a complete list of prime implicants, using either Quine-McCluskey or iterated consensus, a table is constructed with one row for each prime implicant and one column for each minterm included in the function (not don't cares). An X is entered in the column of a minterm that is covered by that prime implicant. Thus, for the prime implicants of the first function, *f*, in both Sections 4.1 and 4.2, the prime implicant table is shown in Table 4.4.

Table 4.4 A prime implicant (PI) table.

PI	Numeric	$	Label	0	4	5	7	8	11	12	15
$w'xy'$	0 1 0 –	4	*A*		X	X					
xyz	– 1 1 1	4	*B*				X				X
wyz	1 – 1 1	4	*C*						X		X
$w'xz$	0 1 – 1	4	*D*			X	X				
$y'z'$	– – 0 0	3	*E*	X	X			X		X	

The first column is the list of prime implicants in algebraic form; the second is in numeric form.* The latter makes it easy to find a list of minterms that are covered by this term, since each – can represent either a 0 or a 1. For example, term 010– covers minterms 0100 (4) and 0101 (5). The third column is the number of gate inputs when that term is used in a two-level circuit, that is, just one for each literal plus one for the input to the output gate (OR). The fourth column is just the label (to save writing the whole term later). We will label terms in alphabetic order. (They may differ from the labeling of these terms in Sections 4.1 and 4.2.)

Our job is to find a minimum set of rows such that using only these rows, every column has at least one X, that is, all of the minterms are included in the expression. If there is more than one set, the total number of gate inputs ($ column) is minimized. The first step in the process is to find essential prime implicants. They correspond to rows where the X is the only one in at least one column. Those squares are shaded; the minterms covered by each of the essential prime implicants are checked off; and an asterisk is placed next to the prime implicant as shown in Table 4.5.

*The order of the list is not important. The two methods used to find prime implicants produced the same list but in different order.

Table 4.5 Finding essential prime implicants.

				√	√			√	√	√	√
PI	**Numeric**	**$**	**Label**	**0**	**4**	**5**	**7**	**8**	**11**	**12**	**15**
$w'xy'$	0 1 0 –	4	A		X	X					
xyz	– 1 1 1	4	B				X				X
wyz*	1 – 1 1	4	C						X		X
$w'xz$	0 1 – 1	4	D			X	X				
$y'z'$*	– – 0 0	3	E	X	X			X		X	

Note that all of the minterms covered by the essential prime implicants are checked, not just those columns with shaded X's. The table is now reduced to that of Table 4.6 by eliminating the essential prime implicant rows and the covered minterms.

In this simple example, the answer is apparent. Prime implicant H covers the remaining 1's; any other solution would require at least two more terms, for a total of four. Thus, the solution is

$$C + E + D = wyz + y'z' + w'xz$$

Before looking at some more complex examples that will require us to develop additional techniques, we will complete Examples 4.1 and 4.2 (with don't cares), for which we have already developed a list of prime implicants. The only thing that is different from the first example is that we only have columns for minterms included in the function—not for don't cares. That is really what happened in the reduced table above; the columns that were eliminated correspond to minterms that became don't cares after having chosen the essential prime implicants (as in Map Method 3).

Table 4.6 The reduced table.

$	**Label**	**5**	**7**
4	A	X	
4	B		X
4	D	X	X

EXAMPLE 4.3

						√	√	
PI		**$**	**Label**	**1**	**3**	**4**	**6**	**11**
$y'z'$	– – 0 0	3	A			X		
$w'x'z$	0 0 – 1	4	B	X	X			
wxy'	1 1 0 –	4	C					
$wx'y$	1 0 1 –	4	D					X
$w'x'y'$	0 0 0 –	4	E	X				
$w'xz'$*	0 1 – 0	4	F			X	X	
$x'yz$	– 0 1 1	4	G		X			X
$wx'z'$	1 0 – 0	4	H					

The first thing to note about this table is that rows *C* and *H* have no X's in them; they correspond to prime implicants that cover only don't cares. *F* is essential, as indicated by the shading. We can now eliminate rows *C*, *H*, and *F* and columns 4 and 6, producing the reduced table:

$	**Label**	**1**	**3**	**11**
3	*A*			
4	*B*	X	X	
4	*D*			X
4	*E*	X		
4	*G*		X	X

Note that row *A* has no X's; the minterm that it covered was already covered by the essential prime implicant. There are several ways to proceed from here. By looking at the table, we can see that we need at least one prime implicant that covers two minterms (either *B* or *G*). In either case, one minterm is left. There are three solutions:

$$F + B + D = w'xz' + w'x'z + wx'y$$
$$F + B + G = w'xz' + w'x'z + x'yz$$
$$F + G + E = w'xz' + x'yz + w'x'y'$$

All of these are equal cost, since each of the prime implicants used have the same number of literals. (We will see in other examples that some of the covers that use the same number of terms may have a different number of literals.)

If we are looking for only one of the minimum solutions, instead of all of them, we can often reduce a prime implicant table by removing *dominated* or equal rows. A row dominates another if the term it represents costs no more than the other and has X's in every column that the dominated row does (and possibly more).

EXAMPLE 4.4

In Example 4.3, row *E* is dominated by *B*, and row *D* is dominated by *G*. Removing the dominated rows, the table reduces to

$	**Label**	**1**	**3**	**11**
4	*B*	X	X	
4	*G*		X	X

and the only solution produced is

$$F + B + G = w'xz' + w'x'z + x'yz$$

Finally, a third approach, called *Petrick's method*, utilizes the table we have obtained after removing the essential prime implicants, but before removing dominated and equal rows. Create a product of sums expression by producing one term for each column. For the last example, the expression is

$$(B + E)(B + G)(D + G)$$

Minterm 1 must be covered by B or E, minterm 3 by B or G, and minterm 11 by E or G. Expanding that expression to sum of products form, we get

$$\begin{aligned}(B + EG)(D + G) &= BD + BG + DEG + EG \\ &= BD + BG + EG\end{aligned}$$

Each product term corresponds to a set of prime implicants that could be used to cover the function. These are, of course, the solutions that we found.

We are now ready to look at some more complex examples.

EXAMPLE 4.5

$f(a, b, c, d) = \Sigma m(1, 3, 4, 6, 7, 9, 11, 12, 13, 15)$

From the map, Quine-McCluskey, or iterated consensus,* we could find all of the prime implicants and construct the following table:

		$		√ **1**	√ **3**	**4**	**6**	**7**	√ **9**	√ **11**	**12**	**13**	**15**
*b'd**	– 0 – 1	3	*A*	X	X				X	X			
cd	– – 1 1	3	*B*		X			X		X			X
ad	1 – – 1	3	*C*						X	X		X	X
abc'	1 1 0 –	4	*D*								X	X	
bc'd'	– 1 0 0	4	*E*			X					X		
a'bd'	0 1 – 0	4	*F*			X	X						
a'bc	0 1 1 –	4	*G*				X	X					

There is one essential prime implicant, $b'd$, as shown in the table above. The table is then reduced, by eliminating that row and the terms that have been covered.

$		**4**	**6**	**7**	**12**	**13**	**15**
3	*B*			X			X
3	*C*					X	X
4	*D*				X	X	
4	*E*	X			X		
4	*F*	X	X				
4	*G*		X	X			

*An effective approach is to map the function and find as many prime implicants as possible. Then, use iterated consensus to check that none have been left out.

The reduced table has two X's in each column and two X's in each row. Since there are six minterms to be covered, we need at least three prime implicants. Also, since *B* and *C* cost less than the other terms, we should try to use them. A careful study of the table will show that there are two covers that use three terms, each of which uses one of the less costly terms, namely,

$$A + B + D + F = b'd + cd + abc' + a'bd'$$
$$A + C + E + G = b'd + ad + bc'd' + a'bc$$

(We cannot complete the cover with three terms in addition to *A* by using both of the less costly rows, since they only cover three 1's between them.) The more systematic approach is to choose one of the minterms that can be covered in the fewest number of ways, for example, 4. We then recognize that we must choose either *E* or *F* in order to cover minterm 4. We will next derive a minimum solution using each of those and compare them. After we choose *E*, the table reduces to

$		**6**	**7**	**13**	**15**
3	*B*		X		X
3	*C*			X	X
4	*D*			X	
4	*F*	X			
4	*G*	X	X		

Note that row *D* is dominated by *C* and costs more than *C*. It can be removed. (This row is shaded in the table above.) If that is eliminated, *C* is needed to cover minterm 13. (It also covers minterm 15.) Now, only minterms 6 and 7 need to be covered; the only way to do that with one term is with *G*. That produces the solution

$$A + C + E + G$$

Row *F* is also dominated (by *G*); but those two terms cost the same. In general (although not in this example), we risk losing other equally good solutions if we delete dominated rows that are not more expensive.

If, instead, we chose prime implicant *F* to cover minterm 4, we would have

$		**7**	**12**	**13**	**15**
3	*B*	X			X
3	*C*			X	X
4	*D*		X	X	
4	*E*		X		
4	*G*	X			

Row G is dominated by row B and costs more. Thus, prime implicant B is needed to cover the function. With only minterms 12 and 13 left, we must choose term D, giving the other solution

$$A + F + B + D$$

Finally, we could go back to the second table (with six minterms) and consider the prime implicants needed to cover each minterm. Petrick's method produces the following expression

$$\begin{aligned}&(E + F)(F + G)(B + G)(D + E)(C + D)(B + C)\\&\quad = (F + EG)(B + CG)(D + CE)\\&\quad = (BF + BEG + CFG + CEG)(D + CE)\\&\quad = \underline{BDF} + BDEG + CDFG + CDEG + BCEF\\&\qquad + BCEG + CEFG + \underline{CEG}\end{aligned}$$

Any of these eight combinations could be used; but only the two underlined correspond to three terms (in addition to A). This approach produces the same two minimum solutions.

EXAMPLE 4.6

$$f(w, x, y, z) = \Sigma m(1, 2, 3, 4, 8, 9, 10, 11, 12)$$

The prime implicants are

$x'z$
$x'y$
wx'
$xy'z'$
$wy'z'$

The prime implicant table is

				√	√	√	√		√	√	√	√
		$		**1**	**2**	**3**	**4**	**8**	**9**	**10**	**11**	**12**
$x'z$★	– 0 – 1	3	A	X		X			X		X	
$x'y$★	– 0 1 –	3	B		X	X				X	X	
wx'	1 0 – –	3	C					X	X	X	X	
$xy'z'$★	– 1 0 0	4	D				X					X
$wy'z'$	1 – 0 0	4	E					X				X

There are three essential prime implicants, A, B, and D, which cover all but one of the 1's. The reduced table is thus

	$	**8**
C	3	X
E	4	X

Although either prime implicant could cover m_8, C is less expensive. Thus, the only minimum solution is

$$f = x'z + x'y + xy'z' + wx'$$

EXAMPLE 4.7

$$g(a, b, c, d) = \Sigma m(0, 1, 3, 4, 6, 7, 8, 9, 11, 12, 13, 14, 15)$$

From Example 3.18 we came up with the list of nine prime implicants shown in the table below. (We can check that this list is complete and that all of these are prime implicants by using them as the starting point for iterated consensus. If we do that, no new terms are produced in this example.) We do not need a cost column since all terms consist of two literals.

		0	**1**	**3**	**4**	**6**	**7**	**8**	**9**	**11**	**12**	**13**	**14**	**15**
– – 0 0	*A*	X			X			X			X			
– 0 0 –	*B*	X	X					X	X					
– 0 – 1	*C*		X	X					X	X				
– 1 – 0	*D*				X	X					X		X	
– 1 1 –	*E*					X	X						X	X
– – 1 1	*F*			X			X			X				X
1 1 – –	*G*										X	X	X	X
1 – 0 –	*H*							X	X		X	X		
1 – – 1	*J*								X	X		X		X

All of the minterms are covered by at least two prime implicants (some by as many as four). We will choose one of the columns that has only two X's and try to minimize the function first using one term, and then using the other. For this example, we will use either term *A* or term *B* to cover m_0; first we will use *A* and reduce the table by removing the minterms covered by *A*.

		√ **1**	√ **3**	√ **6**	√ **7**	√ **9**	√ **11**	**13**	√ **14**	√ **15**
– 0 0 –	*B*	X				X				
– 0 – 1*	*C*	X	X			X	X			
– 1 – 0	*D*			X					X	
– 1 1 –	*E*			X	X				X	X
– – 1 1	*F*		X		X		X			X
1 1 – –	*G*							X	X	X
1 – 0 –	*H*					X		X		
1 – – 1	*J*					X	X	X		X

Row *B* is dominated by *C*; and row *D* is dominated by *E*. Although row *H* is dominated by *J*, we will leave that for now. Thus, we will choose terms *C* and *E*. Reducing the table once more, we get

		13
– – 1 1	*F*	
1 1 – –	*G*	X
1 – 0 –	*H*	X
1 – – 1	*J*	X

Obviously, any of *G*, *H*, or *J* could be used to cover minterm 13. Notice that row *H*, even though it was dominated, is used in one of the minimum solutions. We must now ask if that might be true of row *B* or row *D*. To be sure, we must go back to the previous table and see what happens if we don't eliminate them. We will choose *B* (rather than *C* to cover m_1 and m_4) and *E* and leave it to the reader to do it for *D* (rather than *E*) and *C*. The reduced table now becomes

		3	11	13
– 0 – 1	*C*	X	X	
– – 1 1	*F*	X	X	
1 1 – –	*G*			X
1 – 0 –	*H*			X
1 – – 1	*J*		X	X

Now, however, we need two more prime implicants to complete the cover, a total of five. Those solutions cannot be minimum, since we found three (so far) with only four terms. Thus, the three minimum solutions using term *A* are

$$f = c'd' + b'd + bc + ab$$
$$f = c'd' + b'd + bc + ac'$$
$$f = c'd' + b'd + bc + ad$$

We will now go back and repeat the process, starting with term *B*. We can eliminate row *A*, since we already found all minimum solutions using row *A*.

			√	√			√		√	
		3	4	6	7	11	12	13	14	15
– 0 – 1	*C*	X				X				
– 1 – 0*	*D*		X	X			X		X	
– 1 1 –	*E*			X	X				X	X
– – 1 1	*F*	X			X	X				X
1 1 – –	*G*						X	X	X	X
1 – 0 –	*H*						X	X		
1 – – 1	*J*					X		X		X

Row D is now required. We will reduce the table one more time.

		3	7	11	13	15
– 0 – 1	C	X		X		
– 1 1 –	E		X			X
– – 1 1	F	X	X	X		X
1 1 – –	G				X	X
1 – 0 –	H				X	
1 – – 1	J			X	X	X

It is clear now that F is necessary, covering all the remaining minterms except m_{13}. (Otherwise, we would need both C and E and would still leave m_{13} uncovered.) As before, prime implicants G, H, and J could be used to complete the function. The three solutions using term B are thus

$$f = b'c' + bd' + cd + ab$$
$$f = b'c' + bd' + cd + ac'$$
$$f = b'c' + bd' + cd + ad$$

giving a total of six solutions.

[SP 3; EX 3]

4.4 QUINE-McCLUSKEY FOR MULTIPLE OUTPUT PROBLEMS

The Quine-McCluskey method can be expanded to include multiple output systems by adding a tag section to each product term. The tag indicates for which functions that term can be used. We will include a bit for each function, with a – if the term is included in that function and a 0 if not. Terms can be combined if they have a common –. When combining terms (using the adjacency property), each tag is 0 if either term had a 0 and is – if both terms had a dash. We will develop the technique for finding all useful terms in this section and defer to Section 4.6 the method for finding minimum sum of products expressions.

To illustrate the process, consider the following functions (the same functions as in Example 3.34):

$$f(a, b, c) = \Sigma m(2, 3, 7)$$
$$g(a, b, c) = \Sigma m(4, 5, 7)$$

We begin, by grouping the terms based on the number of 1's (where letters are added for easy identification).

A	0 1 0	– 0
B	1 0 0	0 –

C	0 1 1	– 0
D	1 0 1	0 –

E	1 1 1	– –

We now apply the adjacency property to each pair of terms in adjacent groups that have at least one – in common.

$A + C = F =$	0 1 –	– 0
$B + D = G =$	1 0 –	0 –

$C + E = H =$	– 1 1	– 0
$D + E = J =$	1 – 1	0 –

When we continue to another column, terms are checked off only if they are covered in all functions. Thus, for example, term *E* is not checked because no term covers it in both *F* and *G*.

Table 4.7 Multiple output Quine-McCluskey method.

A	0 1 0	– 0 √	*F*	0 1 –	– 0
B	1 0 0	0 – √	*G*	1 0 –	0 –
------			------		
C	0 1 1	– 0 √	*H*	– 1 1	– 0
D	1 0 1	0 – √	*J*	1 – 1	0 –

E	1 1 1	– –			

There are no adjacencies in the second column. At the end of the process, there are 2 two-literal terms for each function and 1 three-literal term that can be shared.

Before completing the solution of this problem using multiple output prime implicant tables (in Section 4.6), we will consider two additional examples.

EXAMPLE 4.8

$f(a, b, c, d) = \Sigma m(2, 3, 4, 6, 9, 11, 12) + \Sigma d(0, 1, 14, 15)$*

$g(a, b, c, d) = \Sigma m(2, 6, 10, 11, 12) + \Sigma d(0, 1, 14, 15)$

*This is the same problem as Example 3.40.

We begin by listing all of the minterms, with tags, including the don't cares, grouping terms by the number of 1's:

A	0000	--√	*AA*	000-	--	*BA*	00--	-0
	--------------		*AB*	00-0	--	*BB*	0--0	-0
B	0001	--√	*AC*	0-00	-0√		--------------	
C	0010	--√		--------------		*BC*	-0-1	-0
D	0100	-0√	*AD*	00-1	-0√	*BD*	--10	0-
	--------------		*AE*	-001	-0√	*BE*	-1-0	-0
E	0011	-0√	*AF*	001-	-0√		--------------	
F	0110	--√	*AG*	0-10	--	*BF*	1-1-	0-
G	1001	-0√	*AH*	-010	0-√			
H	1010	0-√	*AI*	01-0	-0√			
I	1100	--√	*AJ*	-100	-0√			
	--------------			--------------				
J	1011	--√	*AK*	-011	-0√			
K	1110	--√	*AL*	-110	--			
	--------------		*AM*	10-1	-0√			
L	1111	--√	*AN*	101-	0-√			
			AO	1-10	0-√			
			AP	11-0	--			

			AQ	1-11	--			
			AR	111-	--			

Thus, the terms that can be shared are $a'b'c'$, $a'b'd'$, $a'cd'$, bcd', abd', acd, and abc. The prime implicants of f are $a'b'$, $a'd'$, $b'd$, and bd'. The prime implicants of g are cd' and ac.

Note that some sums, such as $AF + AN$ exist, but the two terms belong to different functions (and would have a tag of 00); they are not included.

EXAMPLE 4.9

Last, we will consider a small example with three outputs:

$$f(x, y, z) = \Sigma m(0, 2, 5, 6, 7)$$

$$g(x, y, z) = \Sigma m(2, 3, 5, 6, 7)$$

$$h(x, y, z) = \Sigma m(0, 2, 3, 4, 5)$$

The tag now has three bits, but otherwise the process is as before:

```
A  000  -0-√      H  0-0  -0-       R  -1-  0-0
--------------    J  -00  00-
B  010  ---       --------------
C  100  00-√      K  01-  0--
--------------    L  -10  --0
D  011  0--√      M  10-  00-
E  101  ---       --------------
F  110  --0√      N  -11  0-0√
--------------    P  1-1  --0
G  111  --0√      Q  11-  --0
```

The terms that can be used for all three functions are $x'yz'$ and $xy'z$. For f and g, we can use yz', xz, and xy. For f and h, we can use $x'z'$. For g and h, we can use $x'y$. For h, we can use $y'z'$ and xy'. For g, we can use y.

[SP 4; EX 4]

4.5 ITERATED CONSENSUS FOR MULTIPLE OUTPUT PROBLEMS

The iterated consensus algorithm needs only minor modifications to produce all of the terms that may be used for sum of products expressions for multiple output problems. Candidates are terms that are prime implicants of any one function or prime implicants of the product of functions. (Although we did not make use of this property in other approaches, if we look back, we will find that all terms that were shared between two functions were indeed prime implicants of the product of those two functions, and terms that were shared among three functions were prime implicants of the product of the three functions.) In this section, we will find all prime implicants. We will find minimum solutions in Section 4.6.

To begin the iterated consensus procedure, we must either start with minterms or include not only a cover of each function but also a cover of all possible products of functions. We will follow the first approach in this example and use the second in some of the Solved Problems. To each product term on our list for iterated consensus, we add a tag section with a dummy variable for each output. That tag contains a 0 (complemented output variable) if the term is not an implicant of that function and a blank if it is. We will illustrate the process using the same functions as those of Section 4.4.

$$f(a, b, c) = \Sigma m(2, 3, 7)$$

$$g(a, b, c) = \Sigma m(4, 5, 7)$$

The initial list then becomes

a'	b	c'	g'	0	1	0	– 0
a'	b	c	g'	0	1	1	– 0
a	b'	c'	f'	1	0	0	0 –
a	b'	c	f'	1	0	1	0 –
a	b	c		1	1	1	– –

We now proceed as before, taking the consensus of each pair of terms (including the tag), adding new terms and deleting terms included in others. The only new rule is that terms that have an all 0 tag section are also deleted. (They correspond to a grouping made of a 1 from one function with a 1 from the other function; they are not implicants of either function.) Note that the tag never affects whether or not a consensus exists, since there are no 1's in the tag section.

We now proceed, as in Table 4.8.

Table 4.8 Iterated consensus for multiple output functions.

~~*A*~~	~~0 1 0~~	~~– 0~~		
~~*B*~~	~~0 1 1~~	~~– 0~~		
~~*C*~~	~~1 0 0~~	~~0 –~~		
~~*D*~~	~~1 0 1~~	~~0 –~~		
E	1 1 1	– –		
F	0 1 –	– 0	*B* ¢ *A* ≥ *B*, *A*	
G	1 0 –	0 –	*D* ¢ *C* ≥ *D*, *C*	
H	– 1 1	– 0	*F* ¢ *E*	
J	1 – 1	0 –	*G* ¢ *E*	(*G* ¢ *F* undefined)
		H ¢ *G* zero tag; *H* ¢ *F*, *H* ¢ *E* undefined		
		J ¢ *H*, *J* ¢ *F* zero tag; *J* ¢ *G*, *J* ¢ *E* undefined		

The term that can be shared is abc; $a'b$ and bc are prime implicants of f; ab' and ac are prime implicants of g.

EXAMPLE 4.10

We will consider the functions from Example 4.8, a two-output problem with don't cares.

$$f(a, b, c, d) = \Sigma m(2, 3, 4, 6, 9, 11, 12) + \Sigma d(0, 1, 14, 15)$$
$$g(a, b, c, d) = \Sigma m(2, 6, 10, 11, 12) + \Sigma d(0, 1, 14, 15)$$

To obtain the list of prime implicants to include in the prime implicant table, we can start with minterms, treating all don't cares as 1's and work the iterated consensus algorithm. It is very time-consuming and prone to error (although it would be fairly straightforward to write a computer routine to process it).* The other approach is to map fg (the product of the two functions), find all of the prime implicants of that plus those terms that are only prime implicants of one of the functions. The following maps show the

*Another example of this approach is given in Solved Problem 5a.

prime implicants of *fg* and those of *f* and *g* that are not prime implicants of both functions, where all don't cares have been made 1 on the maps, since we must include all prime implicants that cover don't cares, as well.

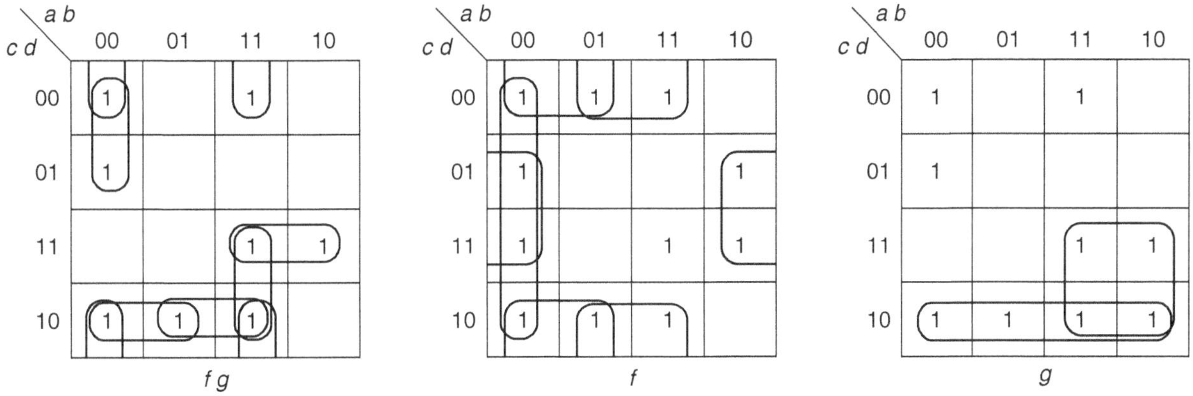

The product terms (with their tag) are

0 0 0 –	– –	0 0 – –	– 0	– – 1 0	0 –
0 0 – 0	– –	0 – – 0	– 0	1 – 1 –	0 –
0 – 1 0	– –	– 1 – 0	– 0		
– 1 1 0	– –	– 0 – 1	– 0		
1 1 1 –	– –				
1 1 – 0	– –				
1 – 1 1	– –				

We could try iterated consensus on this list but would find no new terms.

EXAMPLE 4.11

$f(x, y, z) = \Sigma m(0, 2, 5, 6, 7)$
$g(x, y, z) = \Sigma m(2, 3, 5, 6, 7)$
$h(x, y, z) = \Sigma m(0, 2, 3, 4, 5)$

We start by listing all of the minterms used for any of the functions, including the tag, and then perform the iterated consensus algorithm to find all of the prime implicants.

~~*A*~~	~~0 0 0~~	~~– 0 –~~	*H*	0 – 0	– 0 –	*B* ¢ *A* ≥ *A*
B	0 1 0	– – –	*J*	0 1 –	0 – –	*C* ¢ *B* ≥ *C*
~~*C*~~	~~0 1 1~~	~~0 – –~~	*K*	1 0 –	0 0 –	*E* ¢ *D* ≥ *D*
~~*D*~~	~~1 0 0~~	~~0 0 –~~	*L*	– 1 0	– – 0	*F* ¢ *B* ≥ *F*
E	1 0 1	– – –	*M*	1 – 1	– – 0	*G* ¢ *E* ≥ *G*
~~*F*~~	~~1 1 0~~	~~– – 0~~	*N*	– 0 0	0 0 –	*K* ¢ *H*
~~*G*~~	~~1 1 1~~	~~– – 0~~	*P*	1 1 –	– – 0	*M* ¢ *L*
			~~*Q*~~	~~– 1 1~~	~~0 – 0~~	*M* ¢ *J*
			R	– 1 –	0 – 0	*Q* ¢ *L* ≥ *Q*

We did not show any term that produced an all 0 tag section, and we did not list the consensus operations that led to undefined terms or to terms included in other terms already on the list. This leaves a total of 10 prime implicants (of one of the functions or the product of functions). Note that two of the minterms remain, since they can be used for all three functions and are not part of any one larger group in all three.

4.6 PRIME IMPLICANT TABLES FOR MULTIPLE OUTPUT PROBLEMS

Having found all of the product terms, we create a prime implicant table with a separate section for each function. The prime implicant table for the first set of functions of the last two sections

$$f(a, b, c) = \Sigma m(2, 3, 7)$$
$$g(a, b, c) = \Sigma m(4, 5, 7)$$

is shown in Table 4.9. An X is only placed in the column of a function for which the term is an implicant. (For example, there is no X in column 7 of g or for term D.) Essential prime implicants are found as before ($a'b$ for f and ab' for g).

Table 4.9 A multiple output prime implicant table.

				f			*g*	
			√	√		√	√	
	$		2	3	7	4	5	7
1 1 1	4	*A*			X			X
0 1 –*	3	*B*	X	X				
1 0 –*	3	*C*				X	X	
– 1 1	3	*D*		X	X			
1 – 1	3	*E*					X	X

The table is then reduced as in Table 4.10.

Table 4.10 A reduced prime implicant table.

			f	*g*
	$		7	7
1 1 1	4	*A*	X	X
– 1 1	3	*D*	X	
1 – 1	3	*E*		X

Now, it is clear that we can use term E to cover both functions, rather than two separate terms, even though E costs 4 and the others cost 3. Indeed, the cost to use a term in each function after the first is only 1, the input to another OR gate. (We only build one AND gate for that term.) The solution using A thus costs 5, compared to 6 for a solution that uses both D and E. (The latter solution requires an extra gate.) The solution is thus,

$$f = a'b + abc$$
$$g = ab' + abc$$

EXAMPLE 4.12

The prime implicant table for the functions of Example 4.8 and 4.10

$$f(a, b, c, d) = \Sigma m(2, 3, 4, 6, 9, 11, 12) + \Sigma d(0, 1, 14, 15)$$

$$g(a, b, c, d) = \Sigma m(2, 6, 10, 11, 12) + \Sigma d(0, 1, 14, 15)$$

is shown below.

			f							**g**				
				√			√	√						√
			2	**3**	**4**	**6**	**9**	**11**	**12**	**2**	**6**	**10**	**11**	**12**
0 0 0 –	*A*	4												
0 0 – 0	*B*	4	X							X				
0 – 1 0	*C*	4	X			X				X	X			
– 1 1 0	*D*	4				X					X			
1 – 1 1	*E*	4						X					X	
1 1 1 –	*F*	4												
1 1 – 0*	*G*	4							X					X
– 1 – 0	*H*	3			X	X			X					
0 – – 0	*J*	3	X		X	X								
0 0 – –	*K*	3	X	X										
– 0 – 1*	*L*	3		X			X	X						
– – 1 0	*M*	3								X	X	X		
1 – 1 –	*N*	3										X	X	

Note that the table is divided into three sections of rows. The first (*A* to *G*) includes the terms that are eligible for sharing. The second section contains the prime implicants of *f* that are not also implicants of *g*, and the last section contains those of *g* that are not implicants of *f*. Notice that rows *A* and *F* have no *X*'s; they are prime implicants made up of only don't cares. (Of course, there are no columns corresponding to the don't cares.)

Row *L*, $b'd$, is an essential prime implicant of *f* and row *G*; abd' is an essential prime implicant of *g*. Although the latter is also useful for *f*, it is not essential, and we may or may not want to use it. The reduced table is shown next.

			f				**g**			
									√	√
			2	**4**	**6**	**12**	**2**	**6**	**10**	**11**
0 0 – 0	*B*	4	X				X			
0 – 1 0	*C*	4	X		X		X	X		
– 1 1 0	*D*	4			X			X		
1 – 1 1	*E*	4								X
1 1 – 0*	*G*	1				X				
– 1 – 0	*H*	3		X	X	X				
0 – – 0	*J*	3	X	X	X					
0 0 – –	*K*	3	X							
– – 1 0	*M*	3					X	X	X	
1 – 1 –	*N*	3							X	X

Note that the cost for term *G* has been reduced to 1, since the AND gate has already been built; we only need an input to the OR gate. Term *E* is dominated by and costs more than term *N*, and can be eliminated. (It will never be part of a minimum solution, since it is less expensive to use term *N*.) That makes term *N*, *ac*, necessary for *g*. With these two terms and the minterms they cover removed, the table reduces to

			f				**g**	
			2	**4**	**6**	**12**	**2**	**6**
0 0 – 0	*B*	4	X				X	
0 – 1 0	*C*	4	X		X		X	X
– 1 1 0	*D*	4			X			X
1 1 – 0	*G*	1				X		
– 1 – 0	*H*	3		X	X	X		
0 – – 0	*J*	3	X	X	X			
0 0 – –	*K*	3	X					
– – 1 0	*M*	3					X	X

Neither *B* nor *D* would be used, since term *C* covers all of the 1's of *B* and *D*. That leaves us with a choice of using either *C* or *M* for function *g*. If we use *C*, we would use it for both functions, since *M* is less expensive if we were not sharing. That would require us to use *H* to complete the cover of *f*. The cost would be 5 (for *C*) plus 3, or 8. The alternative is to use *M* (at a cost of 3) for *g*, and then use *J* and *G* to cover *f*, at a total cost of only 7. Either solution requires two new gates.

Thus, the minimum solution is the second one, as we found in Example 3.36,

$$f = b'd + abd' + a'd'$$
$$g = ac + abd' + cd'$$

EXAMPLE 4.13

For the functions of Example 4.9 and 4.11, we have the following prime implicant table:

			f					g					h				
			√	√				√	√		√	√		√	√		
			0	**2**	**5**	**6**	**7**	**2**	**3**	**5**	**6**	**7**	**0**	**2**	**3**	**4**	**5**
0 1 0	4	*A*		X				X						X			
1 0 1	4	*B*			X					X							X
0 – 0*	3	*C*	X	X									X	X			
0 1 –*	3	*D*						X	X						X	X	
1 0 –	3	*E*														X	X
– 1 0	3	*F*		X		X		X			X						
1 – 1	3	*G*			X		X			X		X					
– 0 0	3	*H*											X			X	
1 1 –	3	*J*				X	X				X	X					
– 1 –*	1	*K*						X	X		X	X					

We see that term *C* is an essential prime implicant of *f*, but not of *h*. (We will thus check off the terms in *f* and leave those in *h*, but reduce the cost of this term to 1 in the reduced table, since the AND gate is already accounted for; only the input to the *h* OR gate needs to be charged.) Similarly, term *D* is an essential prime implicant of *h*, but not of *g*. Finally, term *K* will be used for *g*, since it only costs 1 (the OR gate input). Even if we could cover that with two shared terms, that would cost two inputs to the OR gate. The table thus reduces to

			f			g	h		
			5	**6**	**7**	**5**	**0**	**4**	**5**
0 1 0	4	*A*							
1 0 1	4	*B*	X			X			X
0 – 0	1	*C*					X		
0 1 –	1	*D*							
1 0 –	3	*E*						X	X
– 1 0	3	*F*		X					
1 – 1	3	*G*	X		X	X			
– 0 0	3	*H*					X	X	
1 1 –	3	*J*		X	X				

We can see that terms A and D no longer cover any terms; those rows can be eliminated. We seem to have two choices now. First, we can use B for all three functions, at a cost of 6. We would then use J for f and H for h, for a cost of 12 (on this table). This solution requires eight gates and 19 inputs.

$$f = x'z' + xy'z + xy$$
$$g = y + xy'z$$
$$h = x'y + xy'z + y'z'$$

The other choice is to use G for f and g (at a cost of 4). Then F or J can be used for f; and C (since it costs only 1) and E for h. The total cost is 11 inputs and three gates (G, F or J, and E), and thus this second solution is best. (Note that the gate to create term C is not included in the gate count here, since it was already built.) The equations are

$$f = x'z' + xz + (yz' \quad \text{or} \quad xy)$$
$$g = y + xz$$
$$h = x'y + x'z' + xy'$$

It also uses eight gates, but has only 18 inputs.

[SP 6; EX 6]

4.7 SOLVED PROBLEMS

1. For each of the following functions, find all of the prime implicants using the Quine-McCluskey method. (The first three functions have been minimized using the Karnaugh map in Solved Problems 2b, 2d, and 5b of Chapter 3.)

a. $f(w, x, y, z) = \Sigma m(2, 5, 7, 8, 10, 12, 13, 15)$

b. $f(a, b, c, d) = \Sigma m(0, 4, 5, 6, 7, 8, 9, 10, 11, 13, 14, 15)$ (2 solutions)

c. $F(W, X, Y, Z) = \Sigma m(1, 3, 5, 6, 7, 13, 14) + \Sigma d(8, 10, 12)$ (2 solutions)

d. $f(a, b, c, d, e) = \Sigma m(0, 2, 4, 5, 6, 7, 8, 9, 10, 11, 13, 15, 21, 23, 26, 28, 29, 30, 31)$

a. We organize the minterms by the number of 1's

A	0 0 1 0 √	J	– 0 1 0	R	– 1 – 1
B	1 0 0 0 √	K	1 0 – 0		
	--------	L	1 – 0 0		
C	0 1 0 1 √		--------		
D	1 0 1 0 √	M	0 1 – 1 √		
E	1 1 0 0 √	N	– 1 0 1 √		
	--------	O	1 1 0 –		
F	0 1 1 1 √		--------		
G	1 1 0 1 √	P	– 1 1 1 √		
	--------	Q	1 1 – 1 √		
H	1 1 1 1 √				

Only sums that produce a product term are shown

$A + D = J$	$E + G = O$
$B + D = K$	$F + H = P$
$B + E = L$	$G + H = Q$
$C + F = M$	$M + Q = N + P = R$
$C + G = N$	

The prime implicants are thus $x'yz'$, $wx'z'$, $wy'z'$, wxy', and xz.

b.

0 0 0 0 √	0 – 0 0	0 1 – –
--------	– 0 0 0	1 0 – –
0 1 0 0 √	--------	--------
1 0 0 0 √	0 1 0 – √	– 1 – 1
--------	0 1 – 0 √	– 1 1 –
0 1 0 1 √	1 0 0 – √	1 – – 1
0 1 1 0 √	1 0 – 0 √	1 – 1 –
1 0 0 1 √	--------	
1 0 1 0 √	0 1 – 1 √	
--------	– 1 0 1 √	
0 1 1 1 √	0 1 1 – √	
1 0 1 1 √	– 1 1 0 √	
1 1 0 1 √	1 0 – 1 √	
1 1 1 0 √	1 – 0 1 √	
--------	1 0 1 – √	
1 1 1 1 √	1 – 1 0 √	

	– 1 1 1 √	
	1 – 1 1 √	
	1 1 – 1 √	
	1 1 1 – √	

The prime implicants are $a'c'd'$, $b'c'd'$, $a'b$, ab', bd, bc, ad, and ac.

c.

0 0 0 1 √	0 0 – 1 √	0 – – 1
1 0 0 0 √	0 – 0 1 √	1 – – 0
--------	1 0 – 0 √	
0 0 1 1 √	1 – 0 0 √	
0 1 0 1 √	--------	
0 1 1 0 √	0 – 1 1 √	
1 0 1 0 √	0 1 – 1 √	
1 1 0 0 √	– 1 0 1	
--------	0 1 1 –	
0 1 1 1 √	– 1 1 0	
1 1 0 1 √	1 – 1 0 √	
1 1 1 0 √	1 1 0 –	
	1 1 – 0 √	

The prime implicants are $XY'Z$, $W'XY$, XYZ', WXY', $W'Z$, and WZ'.

d.

0 0 0 0 0 √	0 0 0 – 0 √	0 0 – – 0	– – 1 – 1
----------	0 0 – 0 0 √	0 – 0 – 0	
0 0 0 1 0 √	0 – 0 0 0 √	----------	
0 0 1 0 0 √	----------	0 0 1 – –	
0 1 0 0 0 √	0 0 – 1 0 √	0 1 0 – –	
----------	0 – 0 1 0 √	----------	
0 0 1 0 1 √	0 0 1 0 – √	0 – 1 – 1 √	
0 0 1 1 0 √	0 0 1 – 0 √	– – 1 0 1 √	
0 1 0 0 1 √	0 1 0 0 – √	– 0 1 – 1 √	
0 1 0 1 0 √	0 1 0 – 0 √	0 1 – – 1	
----------	----------	----------	
0 0 1 1 1 √	0 0 1 – 1 √	– – 1 1 1 √	
0 1 0 1 1 √	0 – 1 0 1 √	– 1 1 – 1 √	
0 1 1 0 1 √	– 0 1 0 1 √	1 – 1 – 1 √	
1 0 1 0 1 √	0 0 1 1 – √	1 1 1 – –	
1 1 0 1 0 √	0 1 0 – 1 √		
1 1 1 0 0 √	0 1 – 0 1 √		
----------	0 1 0 1 – √		
0 1 1 1 1 √	– 1 0 1 0		
1 0 1 1 1 √	----------		
1 1 1 0 1 √	0 – 1 1 1 √		
1 1 1 1 0 √	– 0 1 1 1 √		
----------	0 1 – 1 1 √		
1 1 1 1 1 √	0 1 1 – 1 √		
	– 1 1 0 1 √		
	1 0 1 – 1 √		
	1 – 1 0 1 √		
	1 1 – 1 0		
	1 1 1 0 – √		
	1 1 1 – 0 √		

	– 1 1 1 1 √		
	1 – 1 1 1 √		
	1 1 1 – 1 √		
	1 1 1 1 – √		

Note that terms in the fourth column are formed in three ways. The prime implicants are $bc'de'$, $abde'$, $a'b'e'$, $a'c'e'$, $a'b'c$, $a'bc'$, $a'be$, abc, and ce.

2. For each of the functions of Solved Problem 1, find all of the prime implicants using iterated consensus.

   a. We will start with the minterms for this solution, listing only those consensus terms that are to be added to the list.

~~*A*~~	~~0 0 1 0~~	~~*J*~~	~~0 1 – 1~~	$C ¢ B \geq C, B$
~~*B*~~	~~0 1 0 1~~	*K*	1 0 – 0	$E ¢ D \geq D, E$
~~*C*~~	~~0 1 1 1~~	*L*	1 1 0 –	$G ¢ F \geq F, G$
~~*D*~~	~~1 0 0 0~~	~~*M*~~	~~– 1 1 1~~	$J ¢ H \geq H$
~~*E*~~	~~1 0 1 0~~	*N*	– 0 1 0	$K ¢ A \geq A$
~~*F*~~	~~1 1 0 0~~	*P*	1 – 0 0	$L ¢ K$
~~*G*~~	~~1 1 0 1~~	~~*Q*~~	~~– 1 0 1~~	$L ¢ J$
~~*H*~~	~~1 1 1 1~~	~~*R*~~	~~1 1 – 1~~	$M ¢ L$
		S	– 1 – 1	$Q ¢ M \geq J, M, Q, R$

All other consensus operations are either undefined or produce a term that is already on the list. The terms remaining on the list are all the prime implicants—$wx'z'$, wxy', $x'yz'$, $wy'z'$, and xz.

b. We first map the function (as in Solved Problem 2d of Chapter 3) and find four prime implicants that cover the function. We then use iterated consensus to generate the rest.

A	0 – 0 0	~~*E*~~	~~0 1 0 –~~	$B ¢ A$
B	– 1 – 1	~~*F*~~	~~0 1 – 0~~	$C ¢ A$
C	– 1 1 –	*G*	1 – 1 –	$D ¢ C$
D	1 0 – –	*H*	1 – – 1	$D ¢ B$
		J	– 0 0 0	$D ¢ A$
		K	0 1 – –	$E ¢ C \geq E, F$

No other consensus terms are formed.

c. First, we took the map of the function and converted all of the don't cares to 1's. We then found a set of prime implicants that covered the function. (We could have used any set of product terms that covered the function, but starting with prime implicants usually reduces the amount of work.)

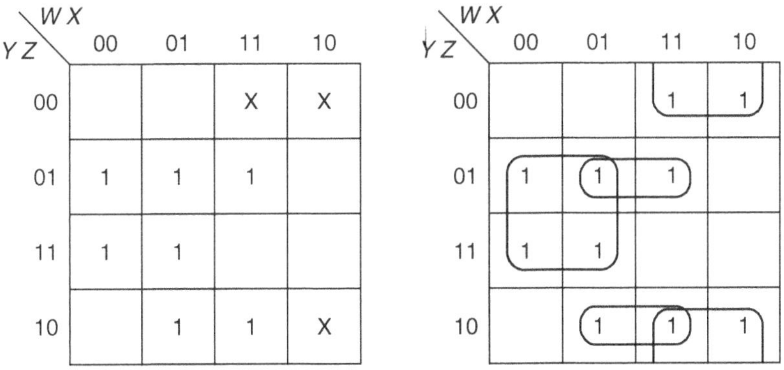

Iterated consensus then proceeds very smoothly

A	0	–	–	1	
B	1	–	–	0	
C	–	1	0	1	
D	–	1	1	0	
E	1	1	0	–	$C \not c B$
F	0	1	1	–	$D \not c A$

No other new terms are formed. The only other consensus terms formed are

$$E \not c D = 1\,1 - 0 \leq B$$
$$E \not c A = C$$
$$F \not c C \leq A$$
$$F \not c B = D$$

d. We will first map the function and cover the function with product terms on one layer.

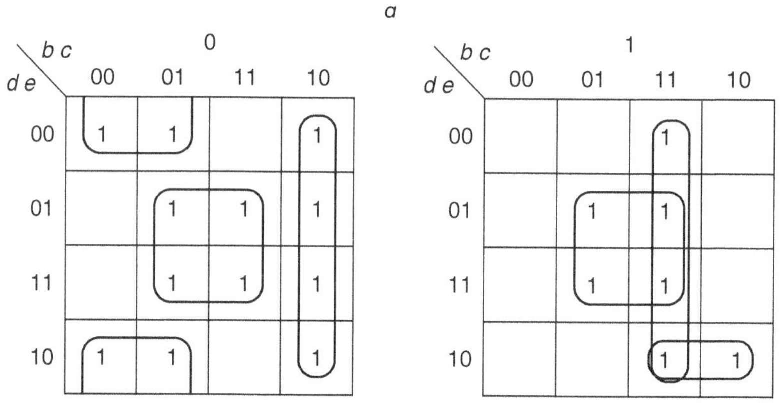

Those product terms are shown in the first column. We then perform the consensus algorithm, which creates some new terms (in the second column) and eliminates others. There are a total of nine terms.

0 0 – – 0	0 0 1 – –
~~0 – 1 – 1~~	0 1 – – 1
0 1 0 – –	0 – 0 – 0
1 1 1 – –	~~– 1 1 – 1~~
~~1 – 1 – 1~~	– – 1 – 1
1 1 – 1 0	– 1 0 1 0

3. For each of the functions of Solved Problems 1 and 2, find all minimum sum of product solutions (one solution for a, two for each of the others).

a. The prime implicant table is

				√	√	√		√		√	√
			$	**2**	**5**	**7**	**8**	**10**	**12**	**13**	**15**
$wx'z'$	1 0 – 0	*A*	4				X	X			
wxy'	1 1 0 –	*B*	4						X	X	
$x'yz'$*	– 0 1 0	*C*	4	X				X			
$wy'z'$	1 – 0 0	*D*	4				X		X		
xz*	– 1 – 1	*E*	3		X	X				X	X

The 1's that make two prime implicants essential, $x'yz'$ and xz, are shaded, and the minterms covered by them are checked. The table then reduces to

		$	**8**	**12**
$wx'z'$	*A*	4	X	
wxy'	*B*	4		X
$wy'z'$	*D*	4	X	X

Clearly, term *D* must be used; otherwise, two more terms would be necessary. The solution becomes

$$f = x'yz' + xz + wy'z'$$

b. The prime implicant table is

		$	**0**	**4**	**5**	**6**	**7**	**8**	**9**	**10**	**11**	**13**	**14**	**15**
A	0 – 0 0	4	X	X										
B	– 1 – 1	3			X		X					X		X
C	– 1 1 –	3				X	X						X	X
D	1 0 – –	3						X	X	X	X			
E	1 – 1 –	3								X	X		X	X
F	1 – – 1	3							X		X	X		X
G	– 0 0 0	4	X					X						
H	0 1 – –	3		X	X	X	X							

There are no essential prime implicants. The starting point should be one of the columns in which there are only two X's. We will choose minterm 5, since both terms will cover four 1's (but we could have used minterm 0, 4, 5, 6, 8, 9, 10, 13, or 14). We will first try prime implicant *B*; then we will try prime implicant *H*. If we choose *B*, the table reduces to

						√	√	√	√	
		$	**0**	**4**	**6**	**8**	**9**	**10**	**11**	**14**
A	0 – 0 0	4	X	X						
C	– 1 1 –	3			X					X
D	1 0 – –*	3				X	X	X	X	
E	1 – 1 –	3						X	X	X
F	1 – – 1	3					X		X	
G	– 0 0 0	4	X			X				
H	0 1 – –	3		X	X					

Row *F* is dominated by row *D*. If row *D* is chosen, the table reduces to

		$	**0**	**4**	**6**	**14**
A	0 – 0 0	4	X	X		
C	– 1 1 –	3			X	X
E	1 – 1 –	3				X
G	– 0 0 0	4	X			
H	0 1 – –	3		X	X	

At this point, the only way to cover the function with two terms is to choose *A* and *C*, giving a solution of

$$f = bd + ab' + a'c'd' + bc$$

Notice that if the dominated term *F* had been chosen instead of *D*, three additional terms would be required to cover the function, since minterms 8 and 10 are not covered by *F*.

Now, we must consider what happens if we choose term *H* instead of *B*. The resulting table is

			√	√		√	√		√	√
		$	**0**	**8**	**9**	**10**	**11**	**13**	**14**	**15**
A	0 – 0 0	4	X							
B	– 1 – 1	3						X		X
C	– 1 1 –	3							X	X
D	1 0 – –	3		X	X	X	X			
E	1 – 1 –⋆	3				X	X		X	X
F	1 – – 1	3			X		X	X		X
G	– 0 0 0⋆	4	X	X						

Prime implicant *A* is dominated by *G*, and *C* is dominated by *E*. Eliminating them, we must choose *G* and *E*, leaving only minterms 9 and 13 uncovered. They can both be covered by term *F*. No other solution (that used *H*) requires as few as four terms (even those using one of the dominated terms, *A* or *C*). The resulting function, the second equally good solution, is

$$f = a'b + ac + b'c'd' + ad$$

c. The prime implicant table is

			√	√	√		√		
		$	**1**	**3**	**5**	**6**	**7**	**13**	**14**
0 – – 1⋆	*A*	3	X	X	X		X		
1 – – 0	*B*	3							X
– 1 0 1	*C*	4			X			X	
– 1 1 0	*D*	4				X			X
1 1 0 –	*E*	4						X	
0 1 1 –	*F*	4				X	X		

Note that there are no columns for the don't cares; they do not need to be covered. There is one essential prime implicant, $A(W'Z)$, and the table can then be reduced to

		$	6	13	14
1 – – 0	*B*	3			X
– 1 0 1	*C*	4		X	
– 1 1 0	*D*	4	X		X
1 1 0 –	*E*	4		X	
0 1 1 –	*F*	4	X		

A study of the reduced table reveals that row *D* must be chosen; otherwise, it would take both terms *B* and *F* to cover minterms 6 and 14. That leaves us two choices to conclude the cover, *C* or *E*. Thus, the two solutions to the problem are

$$F = W'Z + XYZ' + XY'Z$$
$$F = W'Z + XYZ' + WXY'$$

d. The prime implicant table is

						√		√					√	√	√	√		√	√	√	√
			0	2	4	5	6	7	8	9	10	11	13	15	21	23	26	28	29	30	31
–1010	*A*	4									X						X				
11–10	*B*	4															X			X	
00––0	*C*	3	X	X	X		X														
0–0–0	*D*	3	X	X					X		X										
001––	*E*	3			X	X	X	X													
010––	*F*	3							X	X	X	X									
01––1	*G*	3								X		X	X	X							
111––	*H**	3																X	X	X	X
––1–1	*J**	2				X		X					X	X	X	X			X		X

The two essential prime implicants are *H* and *J*. The table is then reduced to

			0	2	4	6	8	9	10	11	26
–1010	*A*	4							X		X
11–10	*B*	4									X
00––0	*C*	3	X	X	X	X					
0–0–0	*D*	3	X	X			X		X		
001––	*E*	3			X	X					
010––	*F*	3					X	X	X	X	
01––1	*G*	3						X		X	

At this point, there are nine minterms left to be covered. Either A or B must be used for m_{26}. C and F must be used to cover the remaining 1's, producing the solutions

$$f = abc + ce + a'b'e' + a'bc' + bc'de'$$
$$= abc + ce + a'b'e' + a'bc' + abde'$$

4. For each of the sets of functions, find all terms that may be used in a minimum two-level AND/OR gate (or NAND gate) solution using the Quine-McCluskey method.

a. $f(a, b, c, d) = \Sigma m(0, 1, 2, 3, 5, 7, 8, 10, 11, 13)$
$g(a, b, c, d) = \Sigma m(0, 2, 5, 8, 10, 11, 13, 15)$

b. $f(w, x, y, z) = \Sigma m(5, 7, 9, 11, 13, 15)$
$g(w, x, y, z) = \Sigma m(1, 5, 7, 9, 10, 11, 14)$

c. $f(a, b, c, d) = \Sigma m(0, 3, 5, 7) + \Sigma d(10, 11, 12, 13, 14, 15)$
$g(a, b, c, d) = \Sigma m(0, 5, 6, 7, 8) + \Sigma d(10, 11, 12, 13, 14, 15)$

d. $f(a, b, c, d) = \Sigma m(0, 2, 3, 8, 9, 10, 11, 12, 13, 15)$
$g(a, b, c, d) = \Sigma m(3, 5, 7, 12, 13, 15)$
$h(a, b, c, d) = \Sigma m(0, 2, 3, 4, 6, 8, 10, 14)$

a. We first form a column of minterms, organized by the number of 1's in each term. We then produce a second column of three-literal terms and a third of two-literal terms.

0000	--√	000-	-0√	00--	-0
---------------		00-0	--√	-0-0	--
0001	-0√	-000	--√	---------------	
0010	--√	---------------		0--1	-0
1000	--√	00-1	-0√	-01-	-0
---------------		0-01	-0√		
0011	-0√	001-	-0√		
0101	--√	-010	--√		
1010	--√	10-0	--√		
---------------		---------------			
0111	-0√	0-11	-0√		
1011	--√	-011	-0√		
1101	--√	01-1	-0√		
---------------		-101	--		
1111	0-√	101-	--		

		1-11	0-		
		11-1	0-		

The unshared prime implicants of f are $a'b'$, $a'd$, and $b'c$; those of g are acd and abd. The shared terms are $b'd'$, $bc'd$, and $ab'c$.

b.

0001 0–√	0–01 0–	–1–1 –0
---------------	–001 0–	1––1 –0
0101 ––√	---------------	
1001 ––√	01–1 ––	
1010 0–√	–101 –0√	
---------------	10–1 ––	
0111 ––√	1–01 –0√	
1011 ––√	101– 0–	
1101 –0√	1–10 0–	
1110 0–√	---------------	
---------------	–111 –0√	
1111 –0√	1–11 –0√	
	11–1 –0√	

The prime implicants of *f* are xz and wz; those of *g* are $w'y'z$, $x'y'z$, $wx'y$, and wyz'. The terms that can be shared are $w'xz$ and $wx'z$.

c. We must include all of the don't cares

0000 ––	–000 0–	1––0 0–
---------------	---------------	---------------
1000 0–√	10–0 0–√	––11 –0
---------------	1–00 0–√	–1–1 ––
0011 –0√	---------------	–11– 0–
0101 ––√	0–11 –0√	1–1– ––
0110 0–√	–011 –0√	11–– ––
1010 ––√	01–1 ––√	
1100 ––√	–101 ––√	
---------------	011– 0–√	
0111 ––√	–110 0–√	
1011 ––√	101– ––√	
1101 ––√	1–10 ––√	
1110 ––√	110– ––√	
---------------	11–0 ––√	
1111 ––√	---------------	
	–111 ––√	
	1–11 ––√	
	11–1 ––√	
	111– ––√	

The unshared prime implicant of *f* is *cd*; those of *g* are *b′c′d′*, *ad′*, and *bc*. The shared terms are *a′b′c′d′*, *bd*, *ac*, and *ab*.

d. The tag has three terms

0000	-0-√	00-0	-0-√	0--0	00-
-----------------		0-00	00-√	-0-0	-0-
0010	-0-√	-000	-0-√	-----------------	
0100	00-√	-----------------		-01-	-00
1000	-0-√	001-	-0-	--10	00-
-----------------		0-10	00- √	10--	-00
0011	---	-010	-0-√	1-0-	-00
0101	0-0√	01-0	00-√	-----------------	
0110	00-√	100-	-00√	-1-1	0-0
1001	-00√	10-0	-0-√	1--1	-00
1010	-0-√	1-00	-00√		
1100	--0√	-----------------			
-----------------		0-11	0-0		
0111	0-0 √	-011	-00 √		
1011	-00√	01-1	0-0√		
1101	--0√	-101	0-0√		
1110	00-√	-110	00-√		
-----------------		10-1	-00√		
1111	--0√	1-01	-00√		
		101-	-00√		
		1-10	00-√		
		110-	--0		

		-111	0-0√		
		1-11	-00√		
		11-1	--0		

The unshared prime implicants of *f* are *b′c*, *ab′*, *ac′*, and *ad*; those of *g* are *a′bc* and *bd*; those of *h* are *a′d′* and *cd′*. Terms shared by *f* and *g* are *abc′* and *abd*; those shared by *f* and *h* are *a′b′c* and *b′d′*; the one shared by all three functions is *a′b′cd*.

5. Repeat Solved Problem 4 using iterated consensus.

a. The maps of *f*, *g*, and *fg* are shown below

cd \ ab	00	01	11	10
00	1			1
01	1	1	1	
11	1	1		1
10	1			1

f

cd \ ab	00	01	11	10
00	1			1
01		1	1	
11			1	1
10	1			1

g

cd \ ab	00	01	11	10
00	1			1
01		1	1	
11				1
10	1			1

fg

We will start by finding all of the prime implicants of the product, *fg*, and then those that are prime implicants of the individual functions but not of the product. (Of course, we will add the appropriate tag section, – if it is included in the function, 0 if it is not.)

A	– 0 – 0	– –
B	1 0 1 –	– –
C	– 1 0 1	– –
D	0 0 – –	– 0
E	0 – – 1	– 0
F	1 1 – 1	0 –
G	1 – 1 1	0 –

After "completing" the list, it is a good idea to try the consensus of all pairs of terms, in case we missed one. In this case, we did.

H	– 0 1 –	– 0	*D* ¢ *B*

Note that in trying the consensus, there is no need to take the consensus of *F* or *G* with *D* or *E* (or *H*) since the tag would be 0 0, indicating that the term is in neither function.

The unshared prime implicants of *f* are $a'b'$, $a'd$, and $b'c$; those of *g* are *abd* and *acd*. The terms that can be shared are $b'd'$, $ab'c$, and $bc'd$.

b. We will solve this problem by starting with minterms and finding all of the prime implicants.

~~1 0 0 0 1 0 –~~	*A* 0 – 0 1 0 –	5 ¢ 1 ≥ 1
~~5 0 1 0 1 – –~~	*B* 0 1 – 1 – –	7 ¢ 5 ≥ 7, 5
~~7 0 1 1 1 – –~~	*C* 1 0 1 – 0 –	11 ¢ 10 ≥ 10
~~9 1 0 0 1 – –~~	*D* 1 0 – 1 – –	11 ¢ 9 ≥ 11, 9
~~10 1 0 1 0 0 –~~	~~*E* 1 1 – 1 – 0~~	15 ¢ 13 ≥ 15, 13
~~11 1 0 1 1 – –~~	*F* 1 – 1 0 0 –	*C* ¢ 14 ≥ 14
~~13 1 1 0 1 – 0~~	*G* – 0 0 1 0 –	*D* ¢ *A*
~~14 1 1 1 0 0 –~~	*H* 1 – – 1 – 0	*E* ¢ *D* ≥ *E*
~~15 1 1 1 1 – 0~~	*J* – 1 – 1 – 0	*H* ¢ *B*

Each of the new terms that is created by consensus is shown; all of the original terms and one of the groups of 2 are included in a larger prime implicant.

The unshared prime implicants of *f* are *wz* and *xz*; those of *g* are *w'y'z*, *wx'y*, *wyz'*, and *x'y'z*. The product terms that can be shared are *w'xz* and *wx'z*.

c. In finding the prime implicants, we must treat all don't cares as 1's. We first map *f*, *g*, and *fg*, converting all X's to 1's to find the prime implicants. (Once again, it is a good idea to check that none have been missed by using the iterated consensus algorithm on the result.)

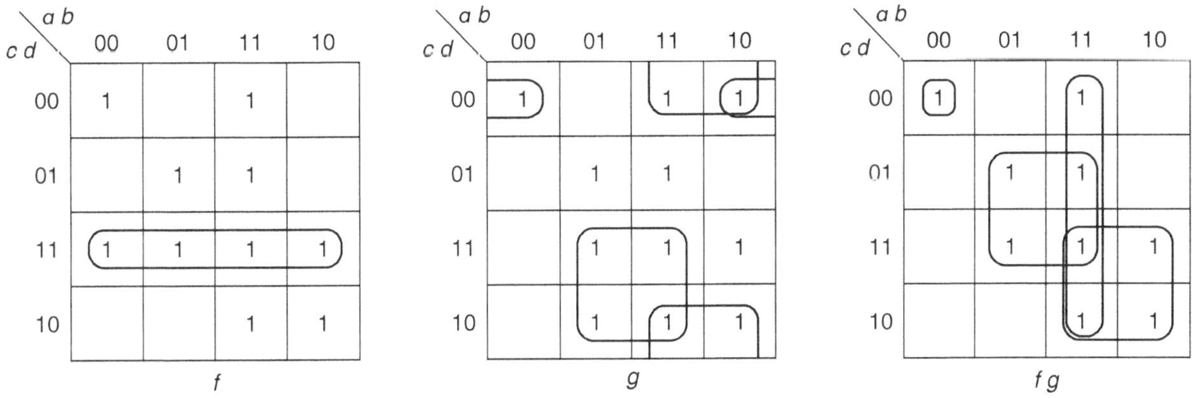

The unshared prime implicant of *f* is *cd*; those of *g* are *bc*, *ad'*, and *b'c'd'*. The shared terms are *a'b'c'd'*, *bd*, *ab*, and *ac*.

d. We first map the functions and all the products of pairs of functions. (We do not need a separate map for *fgh*, since it equals *gh*.)

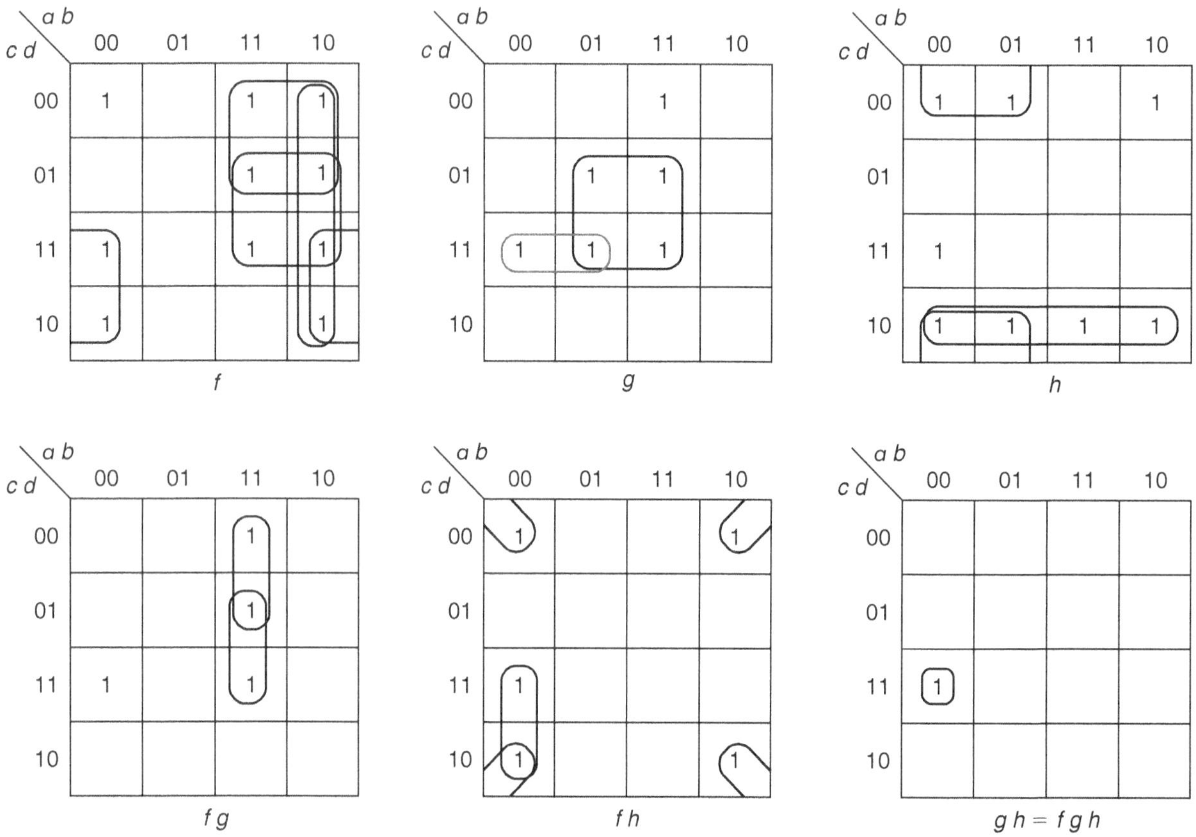

We started with the products and listed the circled terms (*A* through *E*) and then listed the prime implicants of the individual functions (*F* through *M*). When we finished, we applied the iterated consensus algorithm and found that we had missed term *N* (circled in brown),

A	0 0 1 1	– – –
B	1 1 0 –	– – 0
C	1 1 – 1	– – 0
D	0 0 1 –	– 0 –
E	– 0 – 0	– 0 –
F	– 0 1 –	– 0 0
G	1 0 – –	– 0 0
H	1 – 0 –	– 0 0
J	1 – – 1	– 0 0
K	– 1 – 1	0 – 0
L	– – 1 0	0 0 –
M	0 – – 0	0 0 –
N	0 – 1 1	0 – 0

6. For each of the sets of functions of Solved Problems 4 and 5, find a set of minimum sum of products expressions, corresponding to a two-level AND/OR gate (or NAND gate) system (a. 1 solution, b. 6 solutions, c. 2 solutions, d. 2 solutions).

a. The prime implicant table is

			f										*g*							
			√	√	√	√	√	√	√	√		√	√	√	√	√	√		√	
			0	**1**	**2**	**3**	**5**	**7**	**8**	**10**	**11**	**13**	**0**	**2**	**5**	**8**	**10**	**11**	**13**	**15**
– 0 – 0*	3	*A*	X		X				X	X			X	X		X	X			
1 0 1 –	4	*B*								X	X						X	X		
– 1 0 1*	4	*C*					X					X			X				X	
0 0 – –	3	*D*	X	X	X	X														
0 – – 1*	3	*E*		X		X	X	X												
1 1 – 1	4	*F*																	X	X
1 – 1 1	4	*G*																X		X
– 0 1 –	3	*H*			X	X				X	X									

Terms *A* and *C* are essential prime implicants of both *f* and *g*, and *E* is an essential prime implicant of *f*. The reduced table thus becomes

			f	*g*	
			11	**11**	**15**
1 0 1 –	4	*B*	X	X	
0 0 – –	3	*D*			
1 1 – 1	4	*F*			X
1 – 1 1	4	*G*		X	X
– 0 1 –	3	*H*	X		

Term *G* completes the cover of *g* and term *H* would then be used for *f* since it is less expensive than *B*. The other option, using *B* for both *f* and *g*, and then using either *F* or *G* to cover m_{15} in *g*, would cost an extra input. The solution thus becomes

$$f = b'd' + bc'd + a'd + b'c$$
$$g = b'd' + bc'd + acd$$

---

b. The prime implicant table is

			f						*g*						
										√	√		√		√
			5	**7**	**9**	**11**	**13**	**15**	**1**	**5**	**7**	**9**	**10**	**11**	**14**
0 – 0 1	*A*	4							X	X					
0 1 – 1*	*B*	4	X	X						X	X				
1 0 1 –	*C*	4											X	X	
1 0 – 1	*D*	4			X	X						X		X	
1 – 1 0*	*E*	4											X		X
– 0 0 1	*F*	4							X			X			
1 – – 1	*G*	3			X	X	X	X							
– 1 – 1	*H*	3	X	X			X	X							

The two essential prime implicants of g, $w'xz$ and wyz', are shown. The table is then reduced (and the cost of B is made 1, since the AND gate was already built).

			f						*g*		
			5	**7**	**9**	**11**	**13**	**15**	**1**	**9**	**11**
0 – 0 1	*A*	4							X		
0 1 – 1	*B*	1	X	X							
1 0 1 –	*C*	4									X
1 0 – 1	*D*	4			X	X				X	X
– 0 0 1	*F*	4							X	X	
1 – – 1	*G*	3			X	X	X	X			
– 1 – 1	*H*	3	X	X			X	X			

We have two sharing possibilities. We could share B, using it with G to cover f. Then, we have three choices for g: $A + D$, $F + D$, and $F + C$, costing 1 for B, 3 for G, and 8 for any of the pair of terms covering g, costing a total of 12. If not, we could choose D to share. In that case, we could cover f with one more term, H, and cover g with either A or F. That would cost 5 for D, 3 for H, and 4 for A or F, also a total of 12.

The three solutions that share B, $w'x\,z$, are

$$f_1 = w'xz + wz$$
$$g_1 = w'xz + wyz' + w'y'z + wx'z$$
$$g_2 = w'xz + wyz' + wx'y + x'y'z$$
$$g_3 = w'xz + wyz' + wx'z + x'y'z$$

The two that share D, $wx'z$, are

$$f_2 = wx'z + xz$$
$$g_4 = w'xz + wyz' + wx'z + w'y'z$$
$$g_5 = w'xz + wyz' + wx'z + x'y'z$$

c. This produces the following prime implicant table.

			f				*g*				
			√	√	√	√		√	√	√	
			0	**3**	**5**	**7**	**0**	**5**	**6**	**7**	**8**
1 1 – –	*A*	3									
– 1 – 1*	*B*	3			X	X		X		X	
1 – 1 –	*C*	3									
0 0 0 0*	*D*	5	X				X				
– – 1 1*	*E*	3		X		X					
– 0 0 0	*F*	4					X				X
– 1 1 –*	*G*	3							X	X	
1 – – 0	*H*	3									X

Notice that prime implicants A and C cover no minterms; they are both groups of four don't cares. The function f is covered by essential prime implicants; only minterms 0 and 8 of g are left. The reduced prime implicant table (for g) becomes

			g	
			0	**8**
0 0 0 0	*D*	1	X	
– 0 0 0	*F*	4	X	X
1 – – 0	*H*	3		X

There are two equally good solutions. Prime implicant F covers both minterms, but requires one AND gate and four inputs. Prime implicant D was an essential prime implicant of *f* and thus does not require a new AND gate and only one gate input. Thus, *D* and *H* also produce a solution that requires one new gate and four inputs. The two solutions are

$$f = bd + a'b'c'd' + cd$$

and

$$g_1 = bd + bc + b'c'd'$$

or

$$g_2 = bd + bc + a'b'c'd' + ad'$$

d. When we map the various products and find all of the prime implicants, we come up with the following prime implicant table. Note that because of its size, we have broken it into two parts. We show all of the prime implicants in each part of the table, although some of the rows are empty in one part of the table. After finding essential prime implicants, we will be able to combine the tables and complete the problem.

f

			√	√		√		√				
			0	**2**	**3**	**8**	**9**	**10**	**11**	**12**	**13**	**15**
0 0 1 1	*A*	5			X							
1 1 0 –	*B*	4								X	X	
1 1 – 1	*C*	4									X	X
– 0 – 0*	*D*	3	X	X		X		X				
0 0 1 –	*E*	4		X	X							
1 0 – –	*F*	3				X	X	X	X			
1 – 0 –	*G*	3				X	X			X	X	
1 – – 1	*H*	3					X		X		X	X
– 0 1 –	*J*	3		X	X			X	X			
– 1 – 1	*K*	3										
0 – 1 1	*L*	4										
0 – – 0	*M*	3										
– – 1 0	*N*	3										

			g						*h*							
				√	√	√	√	√	√	√		√	√	√	√	√
			3	**5**	**7**	**12**	**13**	**15**	**0**	**2**	**3**	**4**	**6**	**8**	**10**	**14**
0 0 1 1	*A*	5	X								X					
1 1 0 –*	*B*	4				X	X									
1 1 – 1	*C*	4					X	X								
– 0 – 0*	*D*	3							X	X				X	X	
0 0 1 –	*E*	4								X	X					
1 0 – –	*F*	3														
1 – 0 –	*G*	3														
1 – – 1	*H*	3														
– 0 1 –	*J*	3														
– 1 – 1*	*K*	3		X	X		X	X								
0 – 1 1	*L*	4	X		X											
0 – – 0*	*M*	3							X	X		X	X			
– – 1 0*	*N*	3								X			X		X	X

The table can be reduced, and the two halves combined as shown below. Note that all of *g* and *h* other than minterm 3 have already been covered and that the cost of prime implicant *B* has been reduced to 1, since it is an essential prime implicant of *g*.

			f						*g*	*h*
				√	√		√	√		
			3	**9**	**11**	**12**	**13**	**15**	**3**	**3**
0 0 1 1	*A*	5	X						X	X
1 1 0 –	*B*	1				X	X			
1 1 – 1	*C*	4					X	X		
0 0 1 –	*E*	4	X							X
1 0 – –	*F*	3		X	X					
1 – 0 –	*G*	3		X		X	X			
1 – – 1	*H*	3		X	X		X	X		
– 0 1 –	*J*	3	X		X					
0 – 1 1	*L*	4							X	

Clearly, prime implicant *A* should be used to cover m_3 in both *g* and *h* (at a cost of $5 + 1 = 6$), since otherwise we would need both E and L at a cost of 8. For f, we can eliminate prime implicant C, since that row is dominated by row H and costs more. That requires us to choose H to cover m_{15}. Once H is chosen, all that remains to be covered are m_3 and m_{12}, which can be covered by A and B (respectively), each at a cost of 1. (J or G could have been used, but they would cost 3 each.) The final functions are

$$f = b'd' + ad + a'b'cd + abc'$$
$$g = abc' + bd + a'b'cd$$
$$h = b'd' + a'd' + cd' + a'b'cd$$

4.8 EXERCISES*

1. For each of the following functions, find all prime implicants using the Quine-McCluskey method.

a. $f(a, b, c) = \Sigma m(1, 2, 3, 6, 7)$

*b. $g(w, x, y) = \Sigma m(0, 1, 5, 6, 7)$

c. $g(w, x, y, z) = \Sigma m(2, 3, 6, 7, 8, 10, 11, 12, 13, 15)$

*d. $h(p, q, r, s) = \Sigma m(0, 2, 3, 4, 5, 8, 11, 12, 13, 14, 15)$

e. $f(a, b, c, d) = \Sigma m(5, 7, 9, 11, 13, 14) + \Sigma d(2, 6, 10, 12, 15)$

*f. $f(a, b, c, d) = \Sigma m(0, 2, 4, 5, 6, 7, 8, 9, 10, 14) + \Sigma d(3, 13)$

g. $G(V, W, X, Y, Z) = \Sigma m(0, 1, 4, 5, 8, 9, 10, 15, 16, 18, 19, 20, 24, 26, 28, 31)$

*h. $H(V, W, X, Y, Z) = \Sigma m(0, 1, 2, 3, 5, 7, 10, 11, 14, 15, 16, 18, 24, 25, 28, 29, 31)$

2. For the functions of Exercise 1, find all prime implicants using iterated consensus.

3. For the functions of Exercises 1 and 2, find all minimum sum of products expressions (b. 2 solutions, c. 2 solutions, d. 4 solutions, e. 4 solutions, f. 3 solutions, h. 2 solutions, all others, 1 solution).

4. For the following sets of functions, find all product terms that could be used in a minimum two-level AND/OR system using the Quine-McCluskey algorithm.

a. $f(a, b, c, d) = \Sigma m(5, 8, 9, 12, 13, 14)$

$g(a, b, c, d) = \Sigma m(1, 3, 5, 8, 9, 10)$

*b. $F(W, X, Y, Z) = \Sigma m(1, 5, 7, 8, 10, 11, 12, 14, 15)$

$G(W, X, Y, Z) = \Sigma m(0, 1, 4, 6, 7, 8, 12)$

---

*Each of the functions and sets of functions was included in the exercises of Chapter 3. Other exercises from that chapter could also be used here.

c. $f(a, b, c, d) = \Sigma m(1, 3, 5, 7, 8, 9, 10)$
$g(a, b, c, d) = \Sigma m(0, 2, 4, 5, 6, 8, 10, 11, 12)$
$h(a, b, c, d) = \Sigma m(1, 2, 3, 5, 7, 10, 12, 13, 14, 15)$

*d. $f(a, b, c, d) = \Sigma m(0, 3, 4, 5, 7, 8, 12, 13, 15)$
$g(a, b, c, d) = \Sigma m(1, 5, 7, 8, 9, 10, 11, 13, 14, 15)$
$h(a, b, c, d) = \Sigma m(1, 2, 4, 5, 7, 10, 13, 14, 15)$

5. For each of the sets of functions of Solved Problem 4, find all product terms that could be used in a minimum two-level AND/OR system using iterated consensus.

6. For each of the sets of functions of Solved Problems 4 and 5, find a set of minimum sum of products expressions, corresponding to a two-level AND/OR gate (or NAND gate) system.

a. 3 solutions, 8 gates, 25 inputs
b. 8 gates, 23 inputs
c. 2 solutions, 12 gates, 33 inputs
d. 2 solutions, 11 gates, 33 inputs

4.9 CHAPTER 4 TEST (50 MINUTES)*

1. For the following function, find all of the prime implicants using

a. the Quine-McCluskey method.
b. iterated consensus.

$$f(w, x, y, z) = \Sigma m(0, 2, 3, 6, 8, 12, 15) + \Sigma d(1, 5)$$

2. For the following function,

$$g(a, b, c, d) = \Sigma m(3, 4, 5, 6, 7, 8, 9, 12, 13, 14)$$

we have found the complete list of prime implicants

$a'cd$	bd'
$a'b$	ac'
bc'	

Find both of the minimum sum of products solutions.

3. For the following set of functions, find all terms that can be used in a minimum two-level AND/OR system using

a. the Quine-McCluskey method.
b. iterated consensus.

$$f(w, x, y, z) = \Sigma m(1, 2, 5, 7, 10, 11, 13, 15)$$
$$g(w, x, y, z) = \Sigma m(0, 2, 3, 4, 5, 7, 8, 10, 11, 12)$$

*The timing assumes that the student will solve either 1a. or 1b. and either 3a. or 3b.

4. For the following set of functions,

$$f(a, b, c, d) = \Sigma m(2, 3, 4, 6, 7) + \Sigma d(0, 1, 14, 15)$$
$$g(a, b, c, d) = \Sigma m(2, 3, 5, 7, 8, 10, 13) + \Sigma d(0, 1, 14, 15)$$

We found the possible shared terms: $a'b'$, $a'cd$, bcd, abc.

Other prime implicants of f are $a'd'$, $a'c$, bc.

Other prime implicants of g are $a'd$, $b'd'$, bd, acd'.

Find a set of minimum sum of products expressions, corresponding to a two-level AND/OR gate (or NAND gate) system.

CHAPTER 5

Designing Combinational Systems

Until now, we have concentrated on rather small systems—mostly systems with five or fewer inputs and three or fewer outputs. In this chapter, we want to expand our horizons. Large systems are usually designed by breaking them up into smaller subsystems. Indeed, these subsystems may need to be broken down still further.

In this chapter, we will first look at systems that consist of a number of identical blocks. (These are sometimes referred to as *iterative systems.*) Adders and other arithmetic functions are examples of this type of system.

Because signals in large systems pass through many layers of logic, the small delay encountered as a signal passes through a single gate adds up. We will use the design of a multibit adder to illustrate this.

Next, we will look at some common types of circuit—the binary decoder and encoder, and the multiplexer. Each of these have many applications in digital system design and are available commercially in a variety of forms.

Another class of circuits used in the design of medium- and large-size systems is *gate arrays*, sometimes referred to as *programmable logic devices* (*PLDs*). As we will discuss in Chapter 7, some PLDs also contain memory. Gate arrays consist of a set of AND gates and a set of OR gates connected to form SOP expressions. The basic structure is standard; some of the connections can be specified by the user. Gate arrays are commonly available in three forms: *read only memory* (*ROM*), *programmable logic array* (*PLA*), and *programmable array logic* (*PAL*).

We will also look at issues of testing and simulation of combinational circuits.

We will then look at the design of a decimal adder and a driver for a seven-segment display. We will use a variety of the techniques of this chapter and Chapter 3 in these designs. A large number of exercises (Exercises 20–25) fall into this category.

5.1 ITERATIVE SYSTEMS

We will first look at adders as an example of a system that can be implemented with multiple copies of a smaller circuit. We will use the adder to illustrate the issue of delay in multiple-level circuits and then discuss other iterative circuits.

When we add two numbers by hand, we add the two least significant digits (plus possibly a carry-in) to produce one bit of the sum and a carry to the next bit. Such a one-bit adder (referred to as a full adder) is defined as CE3 and was designed with NAND gates in Example 2.34 (Section 2.8). If we wish to build an n-bit adder, we need only connect n of these. A 4-bit version is shown in Figure 5.1.

Figure 5.1 A 4-bit adder.

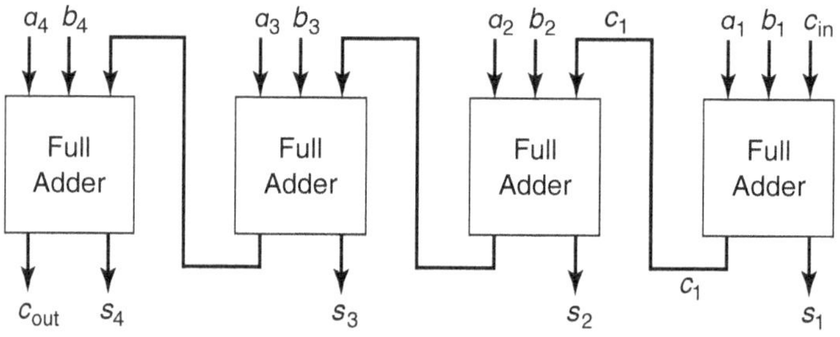

5.1.1 Delay in Combinational Logic Circuits

When the input to a gate changes, the output of that gate does not change instantaneously, but there is a small delay, Δ. If the output of one gate is used as the input to another, the delays add. A block diagram of a simple circuit is shown in Figure 5.2a and the timing diagram associated with it in Figure 5.2b.

Figure 5.2 Illustration of gate delay.

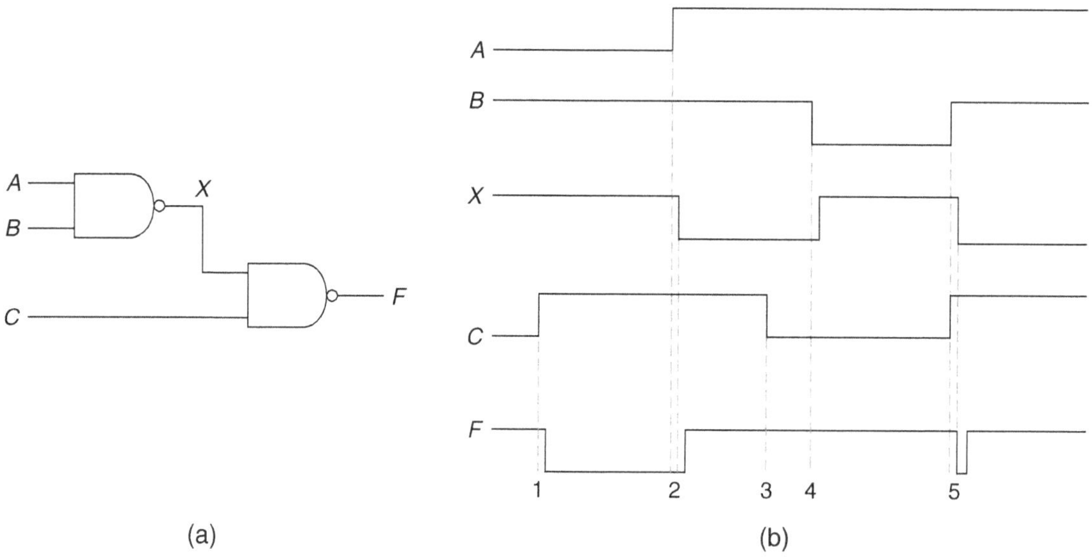

When a change in C causes F to change, F changes one delay time, Δ, later, as shown at time 1. If A or B changes, then point X changes one delay time later, and F changes one time after that, as indicated at time 2. At time 3, a change in C does not cause a change in F, and at time 4, a change in B causes a change in X, but not the output. Finally, at time 5, both B and C change simultaneously. The output F goes to 0 briefly when the change in C is recognized (Δ after the change in C), and then F returns to 1 when the change in B is propagated (2Δ after the change in B). This situation is known as a *hazard* or a *glitch*.

The output is stable after the longest delay path. We are not usually interested in the output until it is stable. In this case, that time is 2Δ. As a more complex example of delay, we will consider the *full adder*, the system of CE3. It adds two 1-bit numbers and a carry input from the next less significant digit and produces a sum bit and a carry out to the next more significant digit.

We will now look at the time it takes for the result of an addition to be available at the two outputs of the full adder. We will assume that all inputs are available at the same time. Figure 5.3 repeats the adder circuit of Example 2.34 (from Section 2.8), with the delay (from when inputs a and b change) indicated at various points in the circuit. Of course, if two inputs to a gate change at different times, the output may change as late as Δ after the last input change.

As shown, the delay from the time inputs a or b change to the time that the sum is available is 6Δ and to the time that the carry-out is available is 5Δ. If a and b are established,* the delay from the carry-in to the

Figure 5.3 Delay through a 1-bit adder.

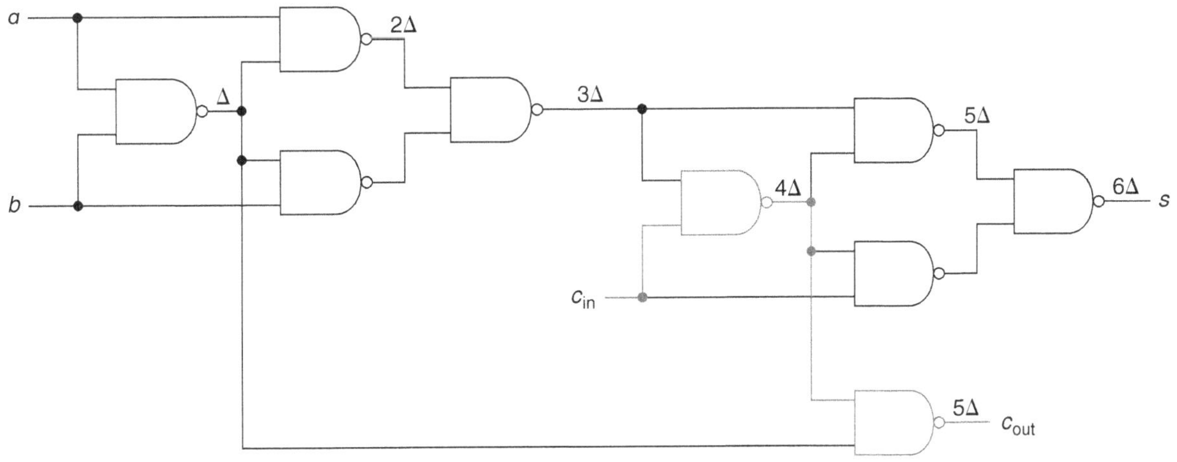

*All of the bits of the two multidigit numbers to be added are normally available at one time. Thus, after the least significant digit, all of the a's and b's are established before c_{in} arrives.

carry-out is only 2Δ, since c_{in} passes through only two gates on the way to c_{out}, as shown in the brown path. This latter time is most critical, as we will see shortly. (Also, the delay from carry-in to sum is 3Δ.)

We can build an n-bit adder with n copies of the full adder; as shown in Figure 5.1. The total time required is calculated as the delay from the inputs to c_{out} (for the least significant bit) plus $n - 2$ times the delay from c_{in} to c_{out} (for the middle full adders), plus the longer of the delay from c_{in} to c_{out} or from c_{in} to s (for the most significant bit). For the multilevel adder, that equals $5\Delta + 2(n - 2)\Delta + 3\Delta = (2n + 4)\Delta$. For a 64-bit adder, the delay would be 132Δ.

5.1.2 Adders

As indicated in the previous section, one approach to building an n-bit adder is to connect together n 1-bit adders. This is referred to as a *carry-ripple adder*. The time for the output of the adder to become stable may be as large as $(2n + 4)\Delta$. It does not always take that long for all the outputs to be set, because, for any bit, if a_i and b_i are both 1, then a carry-out is always 1 (independent of the carry-in from lower order bits) and if a_i and b_i are both 0, then a carry-out is always 0.

To speed this up, several approaches have been attempted. One approach is to implement a multibit adder with an SOP expression. After all, an n-bit adder (with a carry-in to the least significant bit) is just a $2n + 1$ variable problem. In theory, we can construct a truth table for that and get an SOP (or POS) expression.

The truth table for a 2-bit adder is shown in Table 5.1, where bit 1 is the low order bit. This can be implemented by an SOP expression. The (five-variable) maps are shown in Map 5.1. The prime implicants are not circled because that would make the map unreadably cluttered.

The minimum SOP expressions are

$$c_{out} = a_2b_2 + a_1b_1a_2 + a_1b_1b_2 + c_{in}b_1b_2 + c_{in}b_1a_2 + c_{in}a_1b_2 + c_{in}a_1a_2$$

$$\begin{aligned} s_2 = {} & a_1b_1a_2'b_2' + a_1b_1a_2b_2 + c_{in}'a_1'a_2'b_2 + c_{in}'a_1'a_2b_2' \\ & + c_{in}'b_1'a_2'b_2 + c_{in}'b_1'a_2b_2' + a_1'b_1'a_2b_2' \\ & + a_1'b_1'a_2'b_2 + c_{in}b_1a_2'b_2' + c_{in}b_1a_2b_2 \\ & + c_{in}a_1a_2'b_2' + c_{in}a_1a_2b_2 \end{aligned}$$

$$s_1 = c_{in}'a_1'b_1 + c_{in}'a_1b_1' + c_{in}a_1'b_1' + c_{in}a_1b_1$$

The equations are very complex, requiring 23 terms with 80 literals. A two-level solution would require a 12-input gate for s_1. Clearly, we could repeat this process for a 3-bit or 4-bit adder, but the algebra gets very complex, and the number of terms increases drastically. (We do not have seven- or nine-variable maps; other methods would work, although it

Table 5.1 Two-bit adder truth table.

a_2	b_2	a_1	b_1	c_{in}	c_{out}	s_2	s_1
0	0	0	0	0	0	0	0
0	0	0	0	1	0	0	1
0	0	0	1	0	0	0	1
0	0	0	1	1	0	1	0
0	0	1	0	0	0	0	1
0	0	1	0	1	0	1	0
0	0	1	1	0	0	1	0
0	0	1	1	1	0	1	1
0	1	0	0	0	0	1	0
0	1	0	0	1	0	1	1
0	1	0	1	0	0	1	1
0	1	0	1	1	1	0	0
0	1	1	0	0	0	1	1
0	1	1	0	1	1	0	0
0	1	1	1	0	1	0	0
0	1	1	1	1	1	0	1
1	0	0	0	0	0	1	0
1	0	0	0	1	0	1	1
1	0	0	1	0	0	1	1
1	0	0	1	1	1	0	0
1	0	1	0	0	0	1	1
1	0	1	0	1	1	0	0
1	0	1	1	0	1	0	0
1	0	1	1	1	1	0	0
1	1	0	0	0	1	0	0
1	1	0	0	1	1	0	1
1	1	0	1	0	1	0	1
1	1	0	1	1	1	1	0
1	1	1	0	0	1	0	1
1	1	1	0	1	1	1	0
1	1	1	1	0	1	1	0
1	1	1	1	1	1	1	1

would be a lengthy process by hand.) We could also manipulate the algebra to produce multilevel solutions with fewer large gates, but that would increase the delay. Another problem that we would encounter in that implementation in the real world is that there is a limitation on the number of inputs (called *fan-in*) for a gate. Gates with 12 inputs may not be practical or may encounter delays of greater than Δ.

For the 2-bit adder, c_{out} can be implemented with two-level logic (with a maximum fan-in of seven). Thus, the delay from carry-in to carry-out of every two bits is only 2Δ (other than the first 2 and the last 2 bits) producing a total delay of

$$2\Delta + 2(n/2 - 2)\Delta + 3\Delta = (n + 1)\Delta$$

about half that of the previous solution.

Map 5.1 2-bit adder.

c_{out}, $a_2 = 0$:

$c_{in}b_1 \backslash b_2a_1$	00	01	11	10
00				
01			1	
11			1	1
10			1	

c_{out}, $a_2 = 1$:

$c_{in}b_1 \backslash b_2a_1$	00	01	11	10
00			1	1
01		1	1	1
11	1	1	1	1
10		1	1	1

s_2, $a_2 = 0$:

$c_{in}b_1 \backslash b_2a_1$	00	01	11	10
00			1	1
01		1		1
11	1	1		
10		1		1

s_2, $a_2 = 1$:

$c_{in}b_1 \backslash b_2a_1$	00	01	11	10
00	1	1		
01	1		1	
11			1	1
10	1		1	

s_1, $a_2 = 0$:

$c_{in}b_1 \backslash b_2a_1$	00	01	11	10
00		1	1	
01	1			1
11		1	1	
10	1			1

s_1, $a_2 = 1$:

$c_{in}b_1 \backslash b_2a_1$	00	01	11	10
00		1	1	
01	1			1
11		1	1	
10	1			1

There have been some compromises, where the carry is implemented with a two-level circuit and the sum is a less complex multilevel circuit. This only increases the delay by a few Δ (for the last sum), independent of $\boldsymbol{n}$.

There are commercially available 4-bit adders: the 7483, 7483A, and 74283. Each is implemented differently, with a three-level circuit for the carry-out. The 7483A and 74283 differ only in pin connections; each produces the sum with a four-level circuit, using a mixture of NAND, NOR, AND, NOT, and Exclusive-OR gates. Thus, the delay from carry-in to carry-out is 3Δ for each four bits, producing a total delay of $(3/4\,\boldsymbol{n} + 1)\Delta$ (an extra delay for the last sum). The 7483 ripples the carry internally (although it has a three-level chip carry out); it uses an eight-level circuit for s_4.

When larger adders are needed, these 4-bit adders can be *cascaded*. For example, a 12-bit adder, using three 4-bit adders (such as the one of Figure 5.1 or the 7483) is shown in Figure 5.4, where each block represents a 4-bit adder.

Figure 5.4 Cascading 4-bit adders.

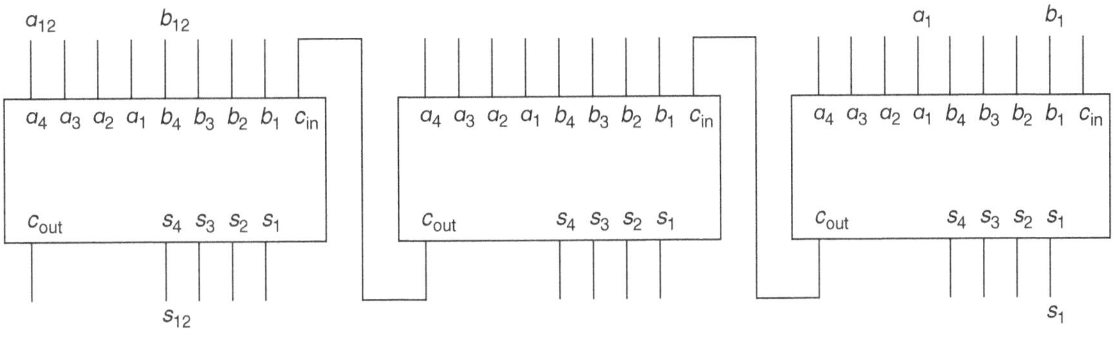

Still another approach is to build a *carry-look-ahead adder*. Each stage of the adder produces two outputs: a carry *generate* signal, g, and a carry *propagate* signal, p. The generate signal is 1 if that stage of the adder has a carry-out of 1, whether or not there was a carry-in. The propagate signal is 1 if that state produces a carry-out of 1 if the carry-in is 1. For a 1-bit adder,

$$g = ab \qquad p = a + b$$

We could build a three-level circuit for the carry-out of any stage. For example, the carry-out of the 4-bit adder we discussed earlier would be

$$c_{out} = g_4 + p_4 g_3 + p_4 p_3 g_2 + p_4 p_3 p_2 g_1 + p_4 p_3 p_2 p_1 c_{in}$$

The carry-out is 1 if the last bit generated a carry, or if it propagated a carry and the stage below it generated a carry, and so forth. This could be extended to any number of bits, limited only by the fan-in capabilities of the logic. (In the 4-bit example, we required a fan-in of five.)*

*For a more detailed discussion of carry-look-ahead adders, see Brown and Vranesic, *Fundamentals of Digital Logic with VHDL Design*, 3rd ed., McGraw-Hill, 2009.

5.1.3 Subtractors and Adder/Subtractors

To do subtraction, we could develop the truth table for a 1-bit full subtractor (See Solved Problem 3) and cascade as many of these as are needed, producing a borrow-ripple subtractor.

Most of the time, when a subtractor is needed, an adder is needed as well. In that case, we can take advantage of the approach to subtraction we developed in Section 1.2.4. There, we complemented each bit of the subtrahend and added 1.

To build such an adder/subtractor, we need a signal line that is 0 for addition and 1 for subtraction. We will call that a'/s (short for *add'/subtract*).* Remembering that

$$1 \oplus x = x' \quad \text{and} \quad 0 \oplus x = x$$

we can now build the circuit of Figure 5.5, using the 4-bit adder we have already designed. There needs to be an Exclusive-OR on each input. The carry-out from one stage is connected directly to the carry-in of the next. The b_i of all stages are connected through Exclusive-OR gates enabled by a'/s.

Figure 5.5 A 4-bit adder/subtractor.

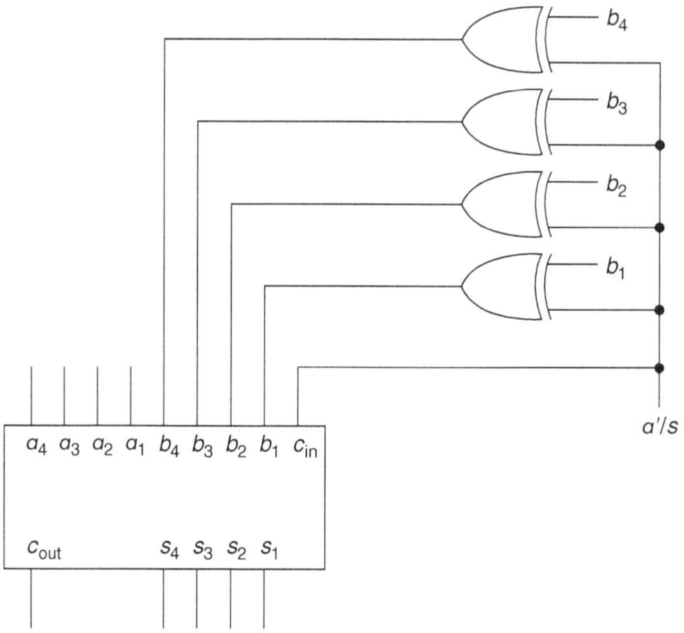

5.1.4 Comparators

A common arithmetic requirement is to compare two numbers, producing an indication if they are equal or if one is larger than the other. The

*This notation is quite common. The a' indicates that a 0 on this line calls for addition and the s implies that a 1 on this line calls for subtraction.

Exclusive-OR produces a 1 if the two inputs are unequal and a 0, otherwise. Multibit numbers are unequal if any of the input pairs are unequal. The circuit of Figure 5.6a shows a 4-bit comparator. The output of the NOR is 1 if the numbers are equal. In Figure 5.6b, we accomplished the same thing with Exclusive-NORs and an AND gate.

Figure 5.6 Two 4-bit comparators.

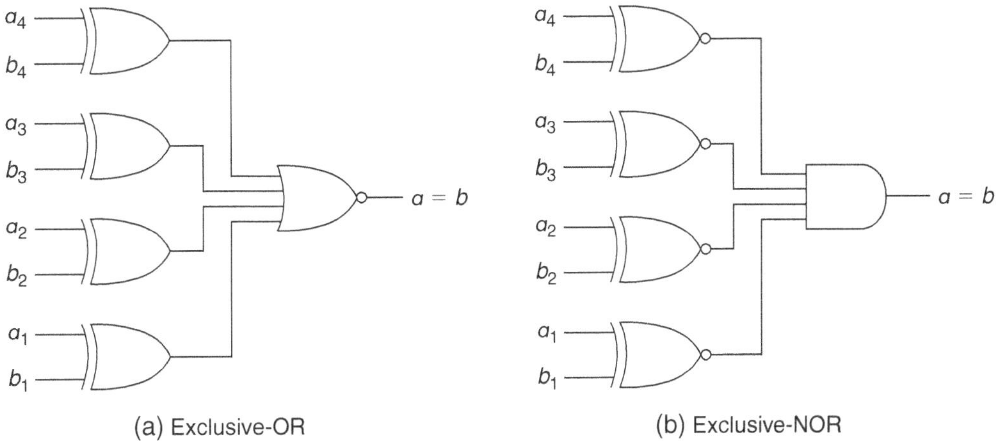

These comparators can be extended to any number of bits.

To build a 4-bit comparator that will indicate greater than and less than, as well as equal to (for unsigned numbers), we recognize that, starting at the most significant bit (a_4 and b_4),

$a > b$ if $a_4 > b_4$ or ($a_4 = b_4$ and $a_3 > b_3$) or ($a_4 = b_4$ and $a_3 = b_3$ and $a_2 > b_2$) or ($a_4 = b_4$ and $a_3 = b_3$ and $a_2 = b_2$ and $a_1 > b_1$)

$a < b$ if $a_4 < b_4$ or ($a_4 = b_4$ and $a_3 < b_3$) or ($a_4 = b_4$ and $a_3 = b_3$ and $a_2 < b_2$) or ($a_4 = b_4$ and $a_3 = b_3$ and $a_2 = b_2$ and $a_1 < b_1$)

$a = b$ if $a_4 = b_4$ and $a_3 = b_3$ and $a_2 = b_2$ and $a_1 = b_1$

This can, of course, be extended to any size, or 4-bit comparators can be cascaded, passing on the three signals, greater than, less than, and equal to. A typical bit of such a comparator is shown in Figure 5.7.

The 7485 is a 4-bit comparator, with cascading inputs and outputs. Like the adder, the cascading signals go from lower order module to higher order module (as opposed to the previous example). It thus computes the greater output as 1 if the a inputs to this module are greater than the b inputs or if they are equal and the cascading input is greater.

Figure 5.7 Typical bit of a comparator.

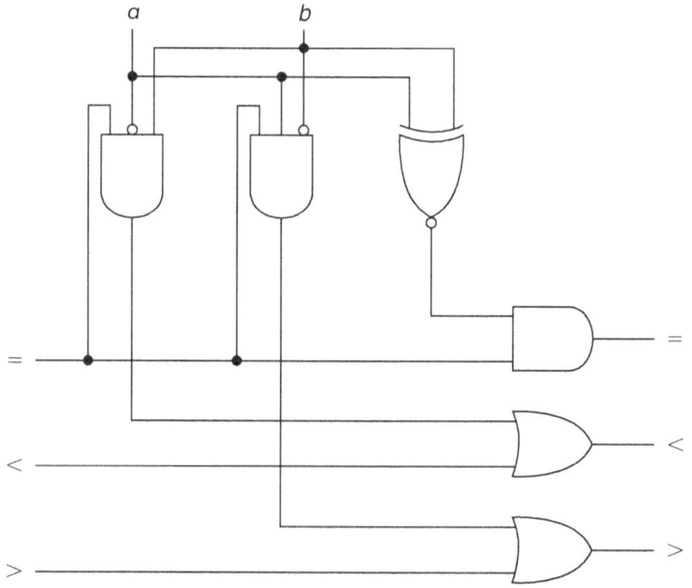

[SP 1, 2, 3, 4; EX 1, 2, 3, 4, 5, 6; LAB]

5.2 BINARY DECODERS

A *binary decoder* is a device that, when activated, selects one of several output lines, based on a coded input signal. Most commonly, the input is an ***n***-bit binary number, and there are up to 2^n output lines.* (Some decoders have an enable signal that activates it; we will get to that shortly.)

The truth table for a two-input (four-output) decoder is shown in Table 5.2a. The inputs are treated as a binary number, and the output selected is made active. In this example, the output is *active high*, that is, the active output is 1 and the inactive ones are 0. (We will use the terms *active high* and *active low* (active value is 0) to refer both to inputs and outputs.) This decoder just consists of an AND gate for each output, plus NOT gates to invert the inputs. (We assume only *a* and *b* are available, not their complements.) The block diagram is given in Figure 5.8a. Output 0 is just $a'b'$; output 1 is $a'b$; output 2 is ab'; and output 3 is ab. Each output corresponds to one of the minterms for a two-variable function.

An active low output version of the decoder has one 0 corresponding to the input combination; the remaining outputs are 1. The circuit and the truth table describing it are shown in Figure 5.8b and Table 5.2b. The AND gates in the previous circuit are just replaced by NANDs.

Most decoders also have one or more enable inputs. When such an input is active, the decoder behaves as described. When it is inactive, all of the outputs of the decoder are inactive. In most systems with a single

*Although 4 inputs have 16 combinations, some decoders only have 10 outputs.

Figure 5.8a An active high decoder.

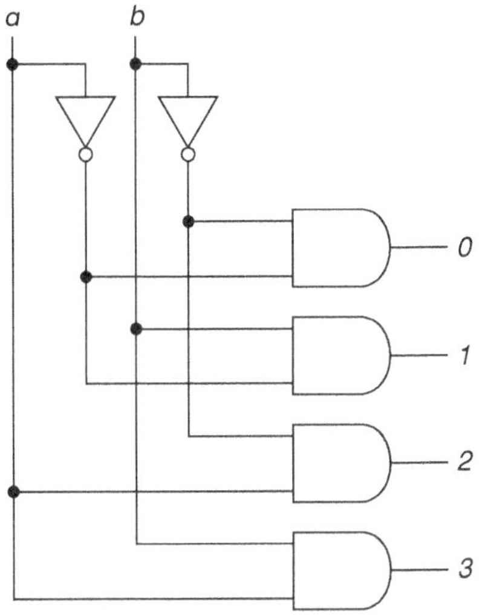

Table 5.2a An active high decoder.

a	*b*	*0*	*1*	*2*	*3*
0	0	1	0	0	0
0	1	0	1	0	0
1	0	0	0	1	0
1	1	0	0	0	1

Figure 5.8b An active low decoder.

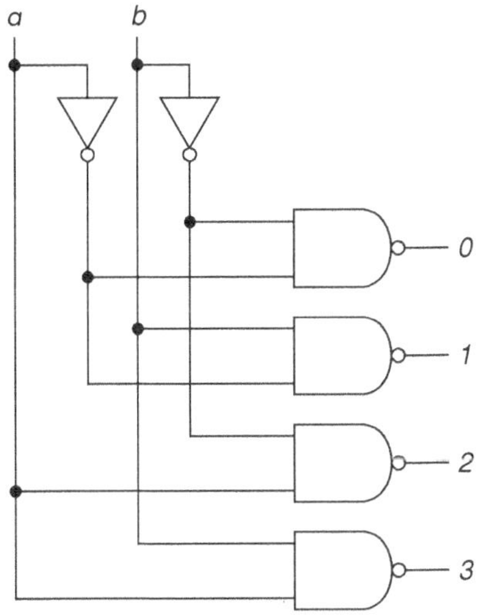

Table 5.2b An active low decoder.

a	*b*	*0*	*1*	*2*	*3*
0	0	0	1	1	1
0	1	1	0	1	1
1	0	1	1	0	1
1	1	1	1	1	0

enable input (not just decoders), that input is active low. The truth table, a block diagram, and the circuit for an active high output decoder with an active low enable input is shown in Figure 5.9. Note that the enable input is inverted and connected to each AND gate. When $EN' = 1$, a 0 is on the input to each AND gate, and, thus, all of the AND gate outputs are 0. When $EN' = 0$, the additional input (beyond those for the circuit without an enable) is 1, and, thus, the output selected by a and b is 1, as before. Active low signals are often indicated with a circle (bubble), as shown in the block diagram in Figure 5.9. In most commercial literature, such signals are labeled with an overbar ($\overline{EN}$), rather than as EN'.

Figure 5.9 Decoder with enable.

EN'	*a*	*b*	*0*	*1*	*2*	*3*
1	X	X	0	0	0	0
0	0	0	1	0	0	0
0	0	1	0	1	0	0
0	1	0	0	0	1	0
0	1	1	0	0	0	1

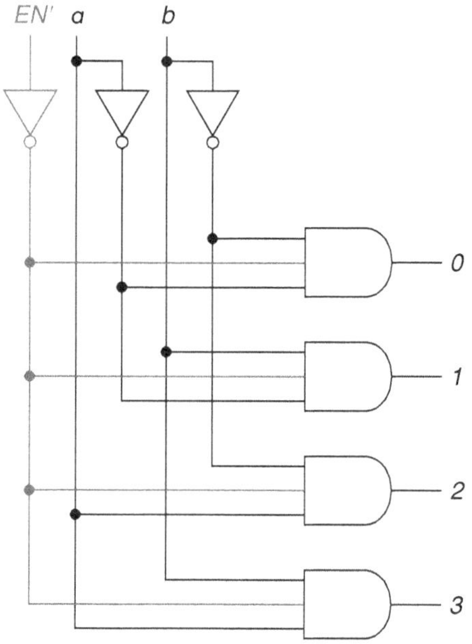

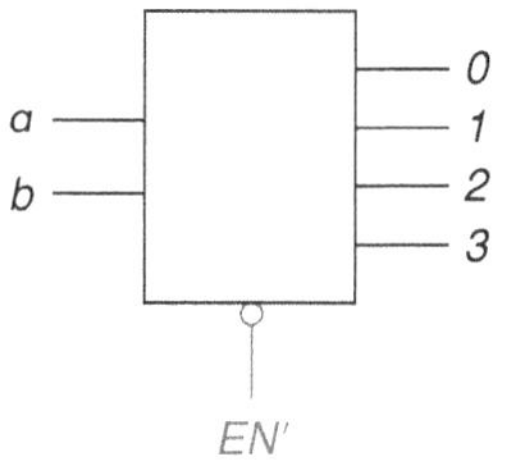

Notice that we have shortened the truth table (from eight rows to five) by the notation in the first row. That row says that if $EN' = 1$, we don't care what a and b are (X's); all outputs are 0. That notation will appear in many places where we discuss commercial circuits.

Larger decoders can be built; 3-input, 8-output as well as 4-input, 16-output decoders are commercially available. The limitation on size is based on the number of connections to the integrated circuit chip that is required. A 3-input decoder uses 11 logic connections (three inputs and eight outputs) in addition to two power connections and one or more enable inputs.

Figure 5.10 The 74138 decoder.

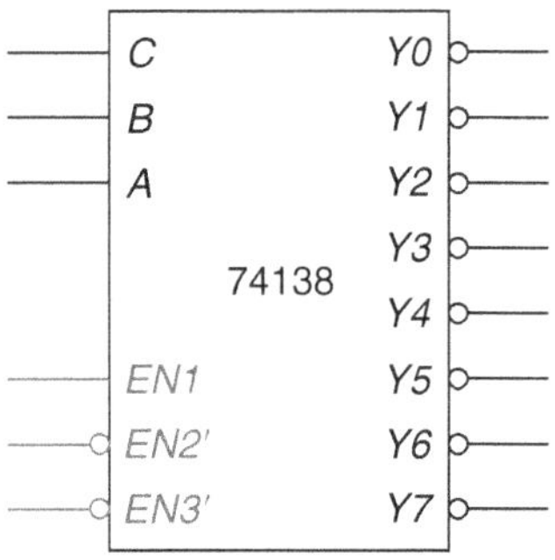

A truth table for the 74138 one of eight decoders is shown in Table 5.3 and the block diagram is shown in Figure 5.10. This chip has active low outputs and three enable inputs (thus requiring a 16-pin chip), one of which is active high ($EN1$) and the other two are active low. Only when all three ENABLES are active, that is, when

$$EN1 = 1, \quad EN2' = 0, \quad \text{and} \quad EN3' = 0$$

is the chip enabled. Otherwise, all outputs are inactive, that is, 1.

Notice that in this circuit (and this is true in many of the commercial integrated circuit packages) the inputs are labeled C, B, A (with C the high-order bit). In previous examples, we have made A the

Table 5.3 The 74138 decoder.

Enables			Inputs			Outputs							
EN1	*EN2'*	*EN3'*	***C***	***B***	***A***	***Y0***	***Y1***	***Y2***	***Y3***	***Y4***	***Y5***	***Y6***	***Y7***
0	X	X	X	X	X	1	1	1	1	1	1	1	1
X	1	X	X	X	X	1	1	1	1	1	1	1	1
X	X	1	X	X	X	1	1	1	1	1	1	1	1
1	0	0	0	0	0	0	1	1	1	1	1	1	1
1	0	0	0	0	1	1	0	1	1	1	1	1	1
1	0	0	0	1	0	1	1	0	1	1	1	1	1
1	0	0	0	1	1	1	1	1	0	1	1	1	1
1	0	0	1	0	0	1	1	1	1	0	1	1	1
1	0	0	1	0	1	1	1	1	1	1	0	1	1
1	0	0	1	1	0	1	1	1	1	1	1	0	1
1	0	0	1	1	1	1	1	1	1	1	1	1	0

high-order bit. When using such a device, be sure which input has which meaning.

Two other commercially available decoder chips are the 74154, which is a four-input (plus two active low enables), 16-output decoder (implemented in a 24-pin package), and the 74155, which contains dual two-input, four-output decoders with common inputs and separate enables (such that it can be used as a three-input, eight-output decoder).

One application of decoders is to select one of many devices, each of which has a unique address. The address is the input to the decoder; one output is active, to select the one device that was addressed. Sometimes, there are more devices than can be selected with a single decoder. We will consider two such examples.

EXAMPLE 5.1

We have available 74138 decoders and wish to select one of 32 devices. We would need four such decoders. Typically, one of these would select one of the first eight addressed devices; another would select one of the next eight, and so forth. Thus, if the address were given by bits a, b, c, d, e, then c, d, e would be the inputs (to C, B, A in order) for each of the four decoders, and a, b would be used to enable the appropriate one. Thus, the first decoder would be enabled when $a = b = 0$, the second when $a = 0$ and $b = 1$, the third when $a = 1$ and $b = 0$, and the fourth when $a = b = 1$. Since we have two active low enable inputs and one active high enable, only the fourth decoder would require a NOT gate for the enable input assuming a' and b' are not available. The circuit is shown next.

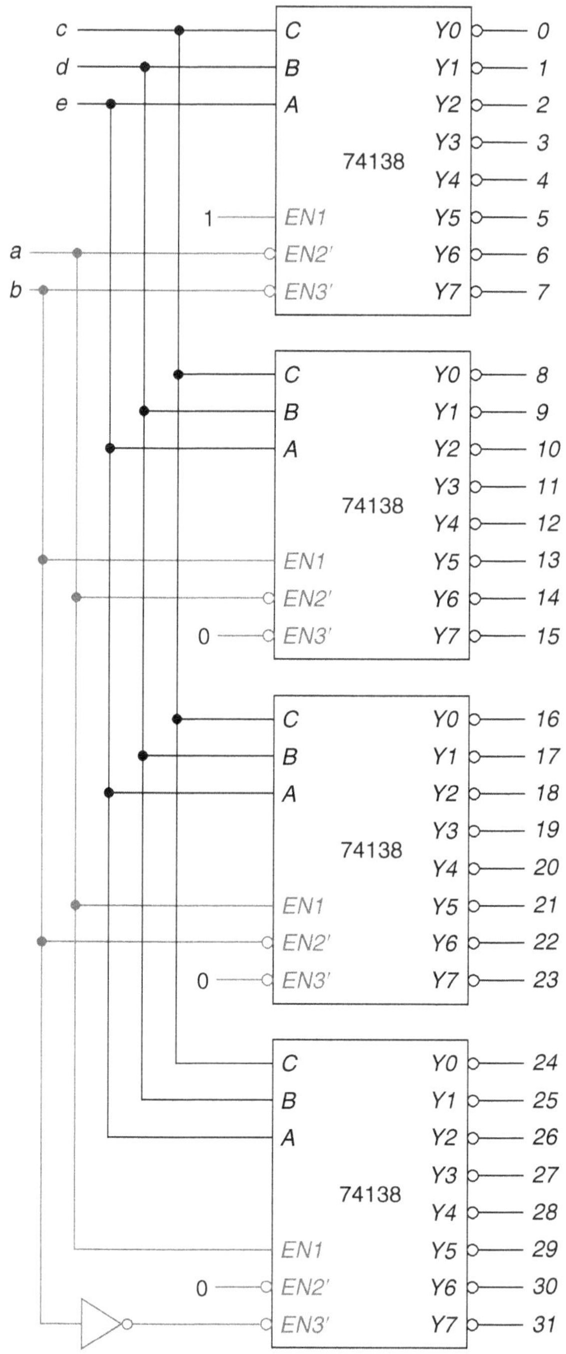

EXAMPLE 5.2

Sometimes, an extra decoder is used to enable other decoders. If, for example, we had a two-input, four-output active low decoder with an active low enable, and needed to select one of 16 devices, we could use one decoder to choose among four groups of devices, based on two of the inputs. Most commonly, the first two (highest order) inputs are used, so that the groupings are devices *0–3*, *4–7*, *8–11*, and *12–15*. Then, for each group, one decoder is used to choose among the four devices in that group. Such an arrangement is shown below.

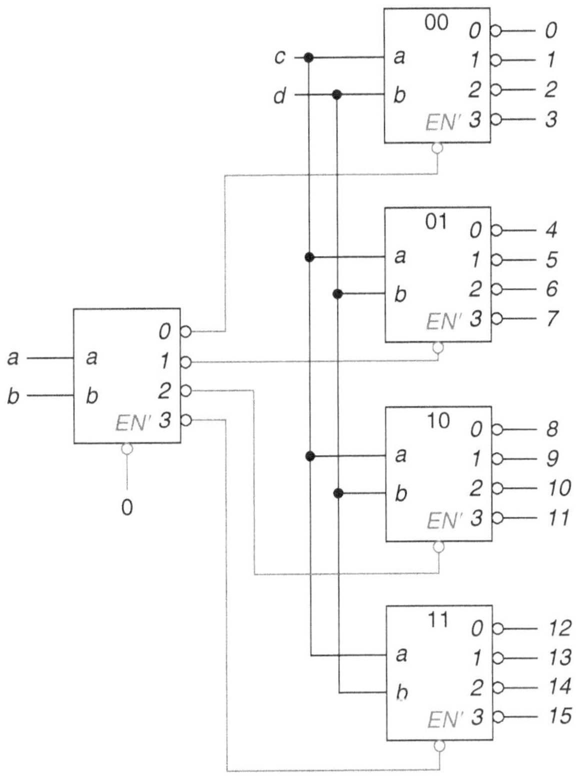

Another application of decoders is the implementation of logic functions. Each active high output of a decoder corresponds to a minterm of that function. Thus, all we need is an OR gate connected to the appropriate outputs. With an active low output decoder, the OR gate is replaced by a NAND (making a NAND-NAND circuit from an AND-OR). With more than one such function of the same set of inputs, we still only need one decoder, but one OR or NAND for each output function.

EXAMPLE 5.3

$f(a, b, c) = \Sigma m(0, 2, 3, 7)$

$g(a, b, c) = \Sigma m(1, 4, 6, 7)$

It could be implemented with either of the decoder circuits shown here.

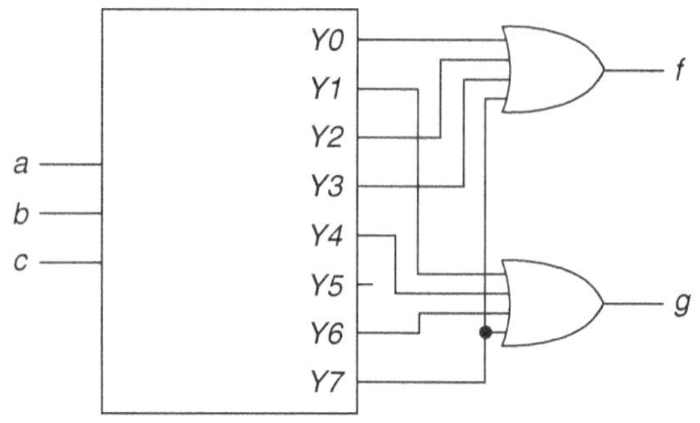

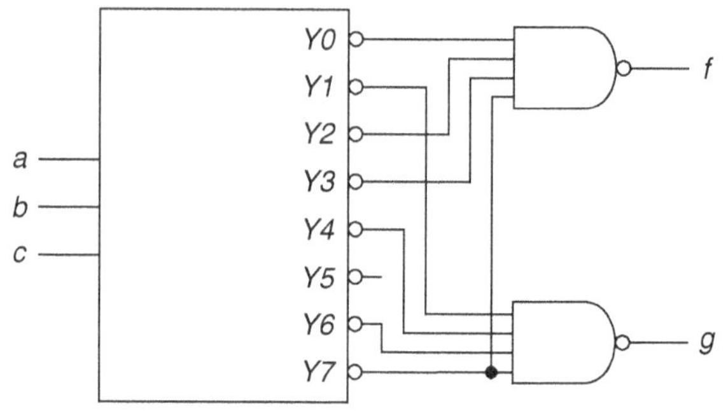

EXAMPLE 5.4

For the following functions, implement them using only the decoders shown below and three NAND gates (with as many inputs as necessary). Try to do it with no NAND gate larger than 8 inputs and only four decoders; it would be even better to do it with only 4-input NANDs.

cd \ ab	00	01	11	10
00	1	1		1
01				
11	1	1	1	1
10	1			1

f

cd \ ab	00	01	11	10
00	1		1	1
01	1	1	1	1
11			1	
10	1			1

g

cd \ ab	00	01	11	10
00		1	1	1
01				
11			1	
10	1	1	1	1

h

EN'	*a*	*b*	*0*	*1*	*2*	*3*
1	X	X	1	1	1	1
0	0	0	0	1	1	1
0	0	1	1	0	1	1
0	1	0	1	1	0	1
0	1	1	1	1	1	0

If we use the layout of Example 5.2, we would need a 9-input NAND for *f* and a 10-input gate for *g*. By using *c* and *d* for the inputs to the first decoder, we get the layout that follows.

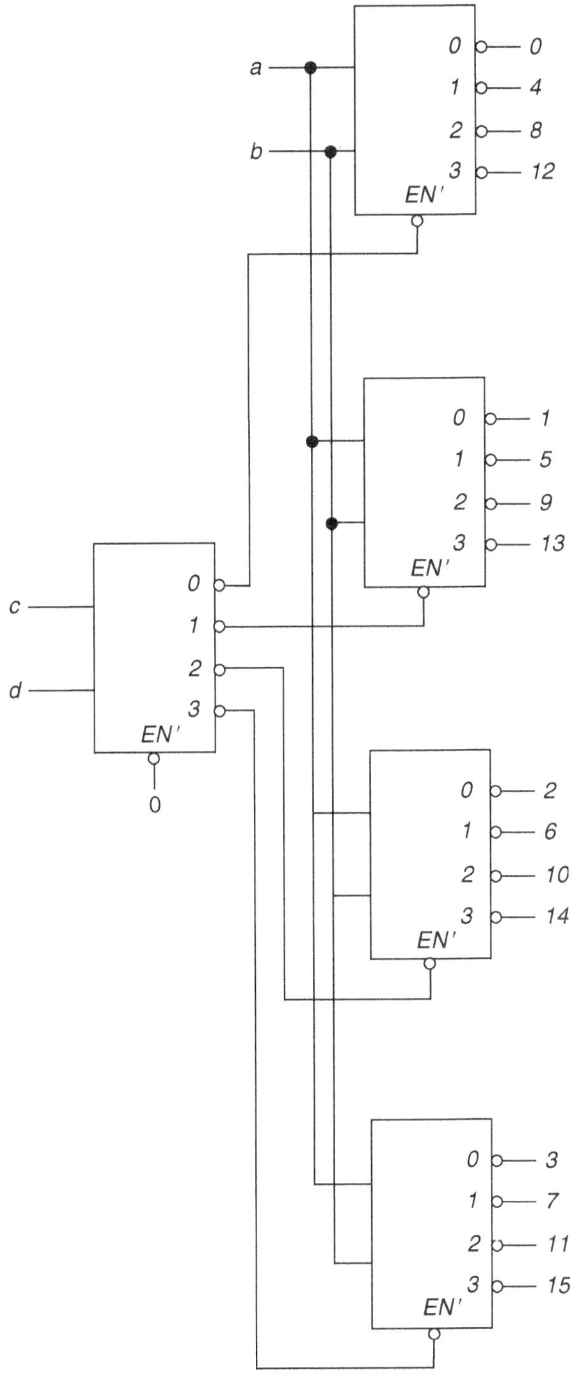

This would still require the same set of NAND gates if we did not take advantage of the fact that for *f*, minterms 3, 7, 11, and 15 are all included. Thus, we can connect the enable input to the fourth decoder directly to the *f* output gate. In the next diagram, we can see that the same approach can be taken for *g* and *h*. All NAND gates now have less than 8 inputs. Also, one of the decoders is not necessary (shown in dashed lines), since its outputs are not used. That is because the 01 row of the maps either have no 1's or all 1's.

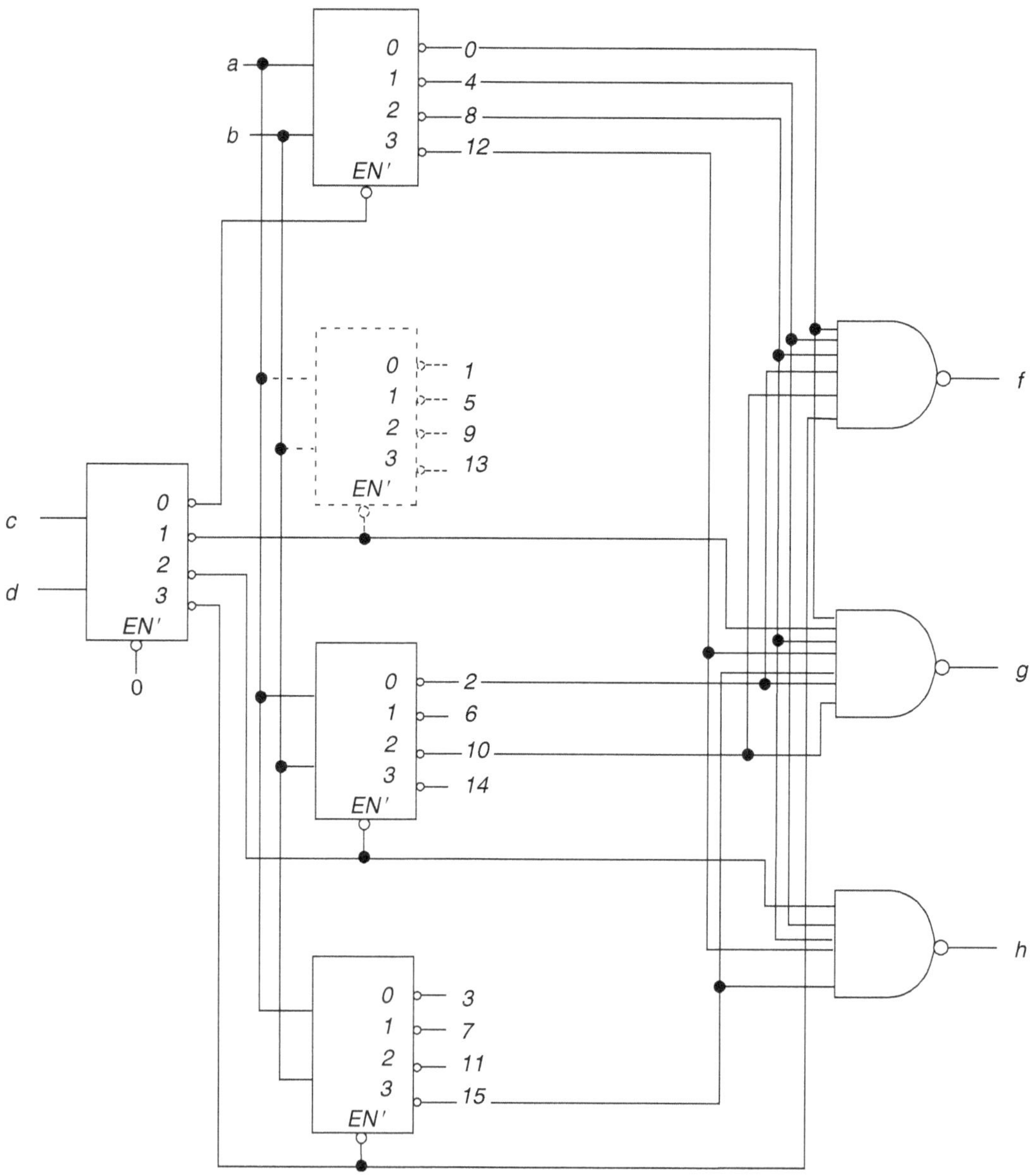

To implement this with only 4-input NAND gates, we must take a different approach. The next set of maps shows several groups of four.

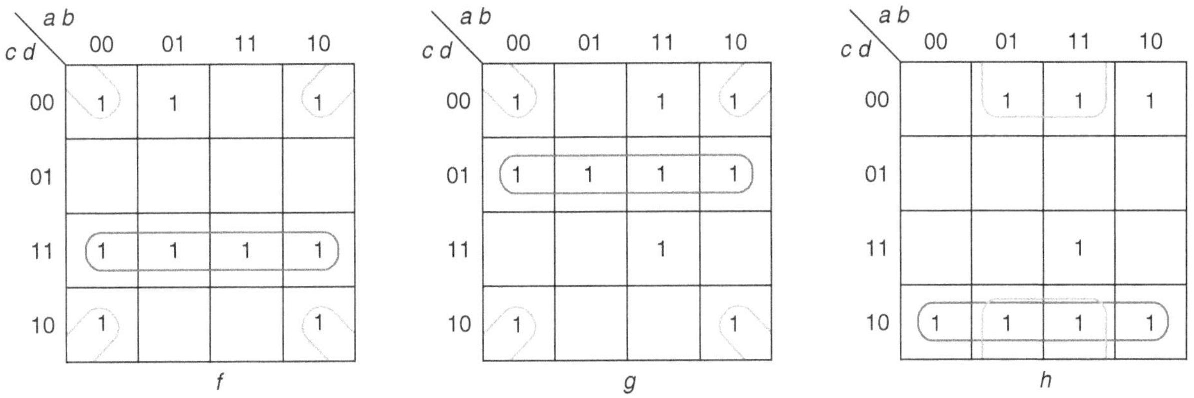

The brown terms correspond to *cd*, *c′d*, and *cd′*, the *3*, *1*, and *2* outputs, respectively, from a decoder with inputs *c* and *d*. Similarly, the tan outputs correspond to *b′d′* and *bd′*, the *0* and *2* outputs from a decoder with inputs *b* and *d*. The remaining 1's are covered as before, by adding a second-level decoder for the *0* and *3* outputs of the *cd* decoder.

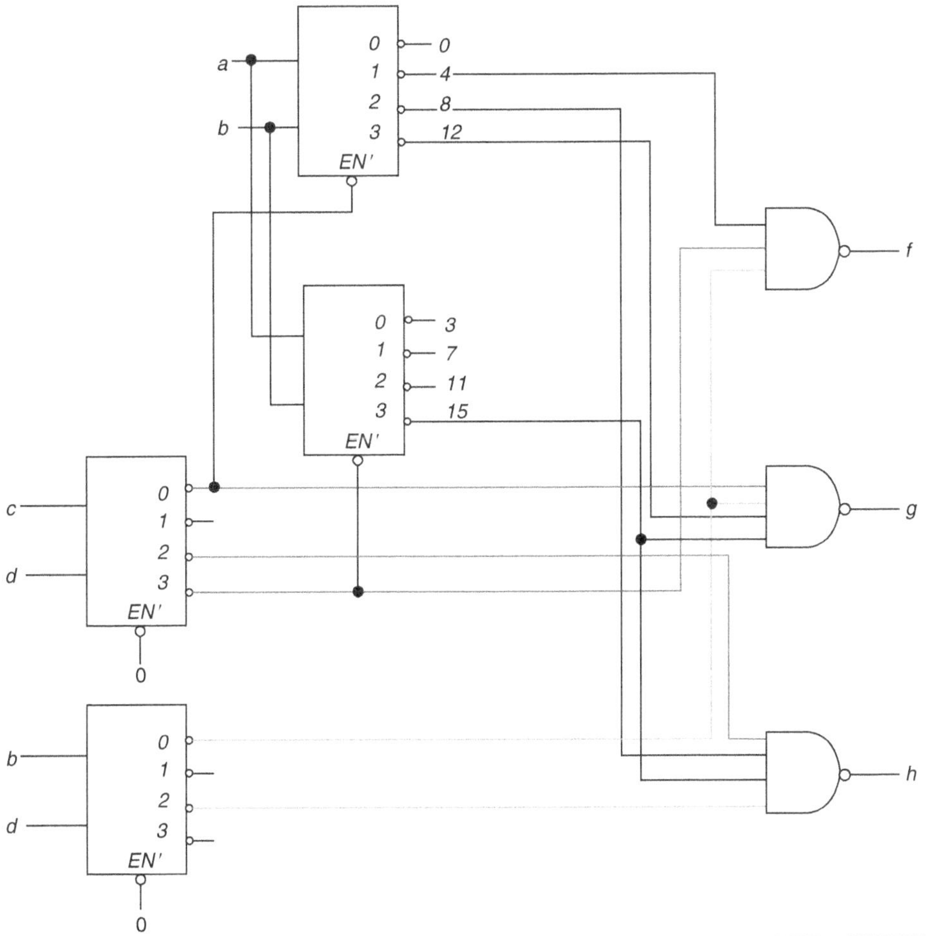

[SP 5, 6, 7, 8, 14c; EX 7, 8, 9, 10, 16c; LAB]

5.3 ENCODERS AND PRIORITY ENCODERS

A *binary encoder* is the inverse of a binary decoder. It is useful when one of several devices may be signaling a computer (by putting a 1 on a wire from that device); the encoder then produces the device number. If we can assume that exactly one input (of A_0, A_1, A_2, A_3) is 1, then the truth table of Table 5.4 describes the behavior of the device.

Table 5.4 A four-line encoder.

A_0	A_1	A_2	A_3	Z_0	Z_1
1	0	0	0	0	0
0	1	0	0	0	1
0	0	1	0	1	0
0	0	0	1	1	1

If, indeed, only one of the inputs can be 1, then this table is adequate and

$$Z_0 = A_2 + A_3$$
$$Z_1 = A_1 + A_3$$

This arrangement does not differentiate between device 0 and no device signaling. (If there is no device numbered 0, this is not a problem.) Otherwise, we could add another output, N, which indicates that no input is active.

$$N = A_0'A_1'A_2'A_3' = (A_0 + A_1 + A_2 + A_3)'$$

If more than one input can occur at the same time, then some priority must be established. The output would then indicate the number of the highest priority device with an active input. The priorities are normally arranged in descending (or ascending) order with the highest priority given to the largest (smallest) input number. The truth table for an eight-input priority encoder is shown in Table 5.5, where device 7 has the highest priority.

Table 5.5 A priority encoder.

A_0	A_1	A_2	A_3	A_4	A_5	A_6	A_7	Z_0	Z_1	Z_2	NR
0	0	0	0	0	0	0	0	X	X	X	1
X	X	X	X	X	X	X	1	1	1	1	0
X	X	X	X	X	X	1	0	1	1	0	0
X	X	X	X	X	1	0	0	1	0	1	0
X	X	X	X	1	0	0	0	1	0	0	0
X	X	X	1	0	0	0	0	0	1	1	0
X	X	1	0	0	0	0	0	0	1	0	0
X	1	0	0	0	0	0	0	0	0	1	0
1	0	0	0	0	0	0	0	0	0	0	0

The output NR indicates that there are no requests. In that case, we don't care what the other outputs are. If device 7 has an active signal (that is, a 1), then the output is the binary for 7, regardless of what the other inputs are (as shown on the second line of the table). Only when $A_7 = 0$ is any other input recognized. The equations describing this device are

$$NR = A_0'A_1'A_2'A_3'A_4'A_5'A_6'A_7'$$
$$Z_0 = A_4 + A_5 + A_6 + A_7$$

$$Z_1 = A_6 + A_7 + (A_2 + A_3)A_4'A_5'$$
$$Z_2 = A_7 + A_5A_6' + A_3A_4'A_6' + A_1A_2'A_4'A_6'$$

The 74147 is a commercial BCD encoder, taking nine active low input lines and encoding them into four active low outputs. The input lines are numbered *9'* to *1'* and the outputs are *D'*, *C'*, *B'*, and *A'*. Note that all outputs of 1 (inactive) indicate that no inputs are active; there is no *0'* input line. The truth table describing its behavior is shown in Table 5.6.

Table 5.6 The 74147 priority encoder.

1'	*2'*	*3'*	*4'*	*5'*	*6'*	*7'*	*8'*	*9'*	*D'*	*C'*	*B'*	*A'*
1	1	1	1	1	1	1	1	1	1	1	1	1
X	X	X	X	X	X	X	X	0	0	1	1	0
X	X	X	X	X	X	X	0	1	0	1	1	1
X	X	X	X	X	X	0	1	1	1	0	0	0
X	X	X	X	X	0	1	1	1	1	0	0	1
X	X	X	X	0	1	1	1	1	1	0	1	0
X	X	X	0	1	1	1	1	1	1	0	1	1
X	X	0	1	1	1	1	1	1	1	1	0	0
X	0	1	1	1	1	1	1	1	1	1	0	1
0	1	1	1	1	1	1	1	1	1	1	1	0

[SP 9; EX 11]

5.4 MULTIPLEXERS AND DEMULTIPLEXERS

A *multiplexer*, often referred as a *mux*, is basically a switch that passes one of its data inputs through to the output, as a function of a set of select inputs. Often, sets of multiplexers are used to choose among several multibit input numbers.

A two-way multiplexer and its logic symbol are shown in Figure 5.11.

Figure 5.11 Two-way multiplexer.

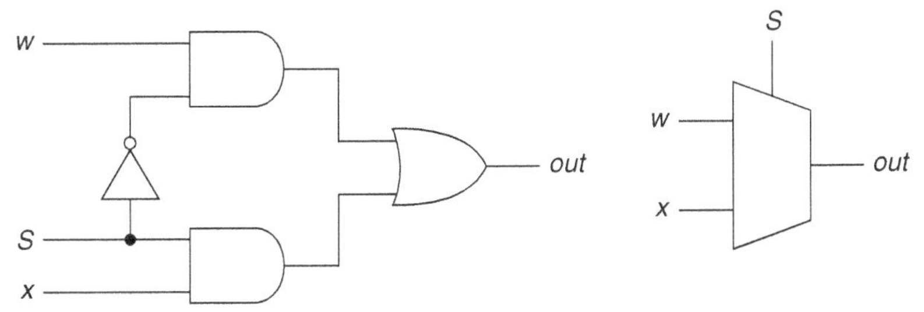

The output, *out*, equals *w* if $S = 0$, and equals *x* if $S = 1$.

A four-way multiplexer can be implemented with AND and OR gates, as shown in Figure 5.12a, or with three two-way multiplexers, as shown in Figure 5.12b. The logic symbol is shown in Figure 5.12c.

Figure 5.12 (a) A four-way multiplexer. (b) From two-way multiplexers. (c) Logic symbol.

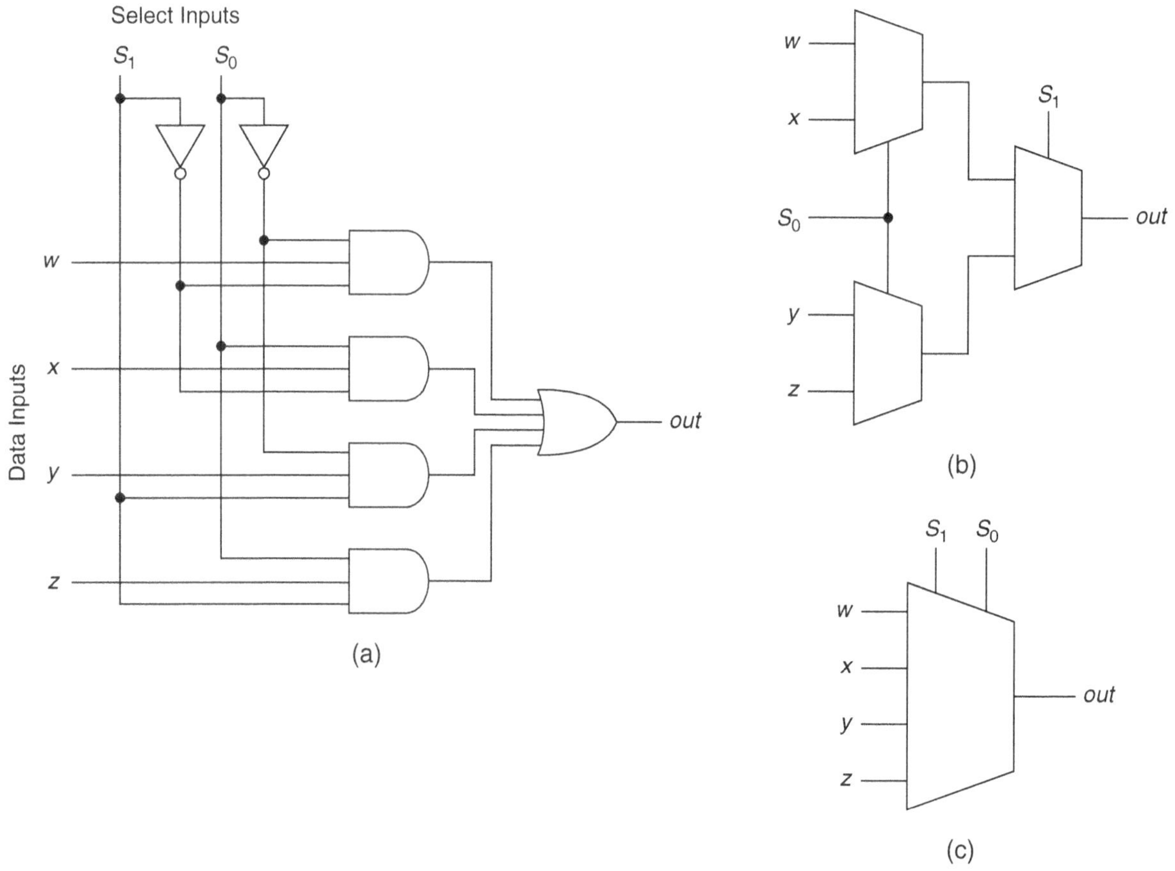

The output equals input *w* if the select inputs (S_1, S_0) are 00, *x* if they are 01, *y* if they are 10, and *z* if they are 11. The circuit is very similar to that of the decoder, with one AND gate for each select input combination. Some multiplexers also have enable inputs, such that *out* is 0 unless the enable is active.

If the inputs consist of a set of 16-bit numbers, and the control inputs choose which of these numbers is to be passed on, then we would need 16 multiplexers, one for each bit. We could build 16 of the circuits of Figure 5.12a, utilizing 64 three-input AND gates and 16 four-input OR gates. (Of course, all of the gates could be replaced by NAND gates.)

The alternative is to use one decoder to drive all the multiplexers. The first 3 bits of such a circuit are shown in Figure 5.13.

There are still 16 four-input OR gates, but now the AND gates in the multiplexers require only two inputs. There are, of course, 4 two-input AND gates in the decoder. The total is then 68 two-input gates for a 16-bit multiplexer. If we were to implement this with 7400 series integrated circuits, this implementation would require 17 packages of two-input AND gates (four to a package), whereas the previous solution would require 22 packages of three-input AND gates (three to a package).

Figure 5.13 A multibit multiplexer.

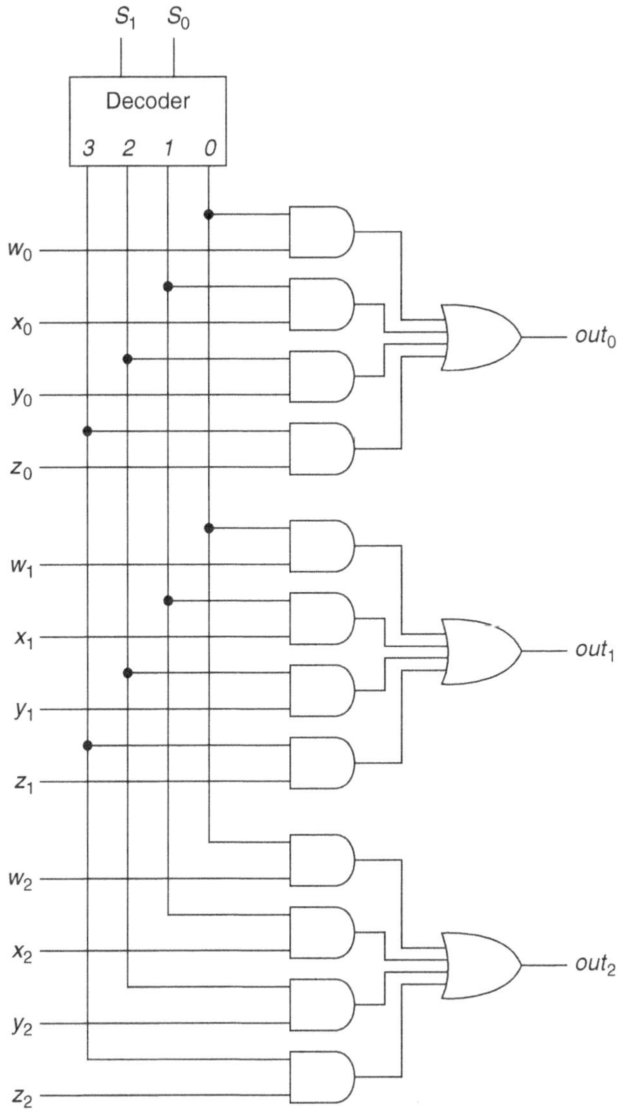

Multiplexers can be used to implement logic functions. The simplest approach is to use the select inputs to make a decoder and connect the constants 0 and 1 to the data inputs.

EXAMPLE 5.5

A three-variable function can be directly implemented with an eight-way multiplexer. The three variables go to the control inputs. The truth table for the function is then connected to the data inputs.

For $f(a, b, c) = \Sigma m(0, 1, 2, 5)$, the truth table is

a b c	*f*
0 0 0	1
0 0 1	1
0 1 0	1
0 1 1	0
1 0 0	0
1 0 1	1
1 1 0	0
1 1 1	0

With a mux, it would be implemented by

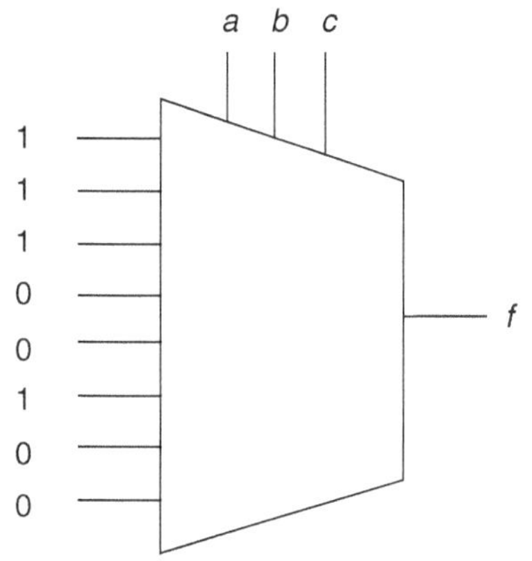

We could also use a four-way multiplexer. To do this, we would rewrite the truth table as follows.

a b	*f* (*c* = 0)	*f* (*c* = 1)	*f*
0 0	1	1	1
0 1	1	0	*c'*
1 0	0	1	*c*
1 1	0	0	0

First, we took the third variable, c (it could have been any of them), and made an output column for $c = 0$ and one for $c = 1$. Then, considering each row, we created a single output column that was a function of c. For the first row, $f = 1$ for both $c = 0$ and $c = 1$; thus, $f = 1$. For the second row, $f = c'$ since f is only 1 when $c = 0$. This leads to the following implementation.

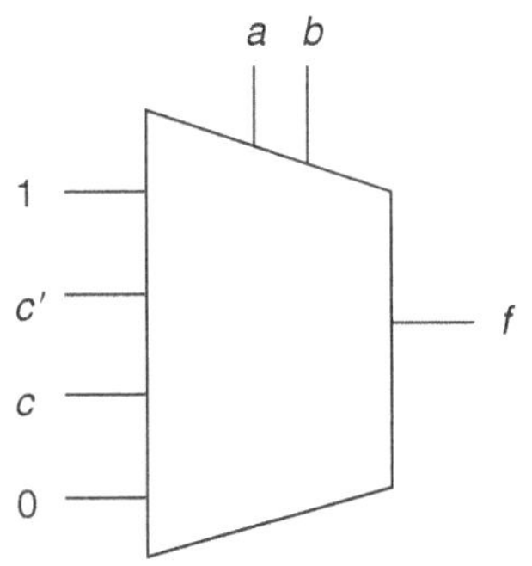

We will briefly describe three of the commercially available multiplexer packages. The 74151 is a 1-bit eight-way multiplexer with one active low enable input, EN', and both an uncomplemented (active high) and a complemented (active low) output. The data inputs are labeled *A7* through *A0* (corresponding to the binary select) and the outputs are *Y* and Y'. The select inputs are labeled *S2*, *S1*, and *S0*, in that order.

The 74153 contains two (dual) four-way multiplexers, *A* and *B*, each with its own active low enable (ENA' and ENB'). The inputs to the first are labeled *A3* to *A0* and its output is *YA*; the inputs to the second are *B3* to *B0*, with output *YB*. There are two select lines (labeled *S1* and *S0*). The same select signal is used for both multiplexers. This would provide 2 bits of multiplexer for choosing among four input words.

The 74157 contains four (quad) two-way multiplexers, with a common active low enable (EN') and a single common select input (*S*). The multiplexers are labeled *A*, *B*, *C*, and *D*, with inputs *A0* and *A1* and output *YA* for the first multiplexer. This provides 4 bits of a two-way selection system.

A *demultiplexer* (*demux*) is the inverse of a mux. It routes a signal from one place to one of many. Figure 5.14 shows one bit of a four-way demux, where *a* and *b* select which way the signal, *in*, is directed. The circuit is the same as for a four-way decoder with the signal *in* replacing *EN*.

Figure 5.14 A four-way demux.

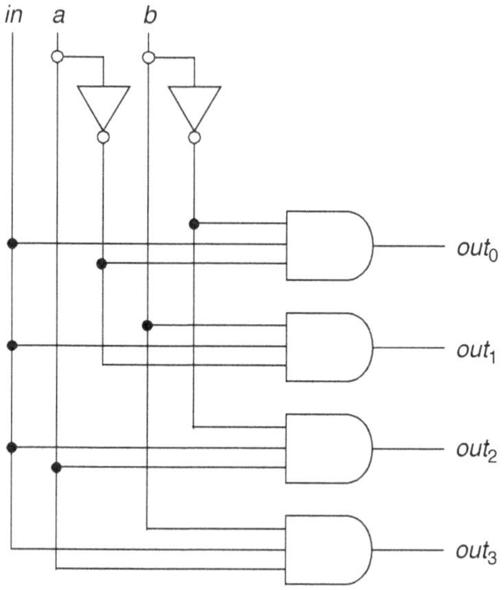

[SP 10, 11, 12; EX 12, 13, 14; LAB]

5.5 THREE-STATE GATES

Up to this point, we assumed that all logic levels were either 0 or 1. Indeed, we also encountered don't care values, but in any real circuit implementation, each don't care took on either the value 0 or 1. Furthermore, we never connected the output of one gate to the output of another gate, since if the two gates were producing opposite values, there would be a conflict. (In some technologies, it is possible to connect the output of two AND gates and achieve a "wired AND" or a "wired OR," but in others, there is a real possibility that one or more of the gates would be destroyed. Thus, we have not suggested this option in anything we have discussed so far.)

Some design techniques have been used that do allow us to connect outputs to each other. The more commonly used one today is referred to as *three-state* (or tristate) output gates. (We will not discuss other similar implementations, such as transmission gates and open-collector gates.)

In a three-state gate, there is an enable input, shown on the side of the gate. If that input is active (it could be active high or active low), the gate behaves as usual. If the control input is inactive, the output behaves as if it is not connected (as an open circuit). That output is typically represented by a *Z*. The truth table and the circuit representation of a three-state buffer (with an active high enable) is shown in Figure 5.15.

Figure 5.15 A three-state buffer.

EN	*a*	*f*
0	0	Z
0	1	Z
1	0	0
1	1	1

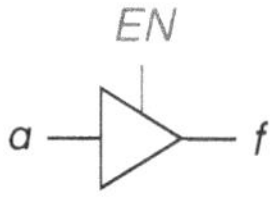

Three-state buffers with active low enables and/or outputs exist; in the latter case, it is a three-state NOT gate. Three-state outputs also exist on other more complex gates. In each case, they behave normally when the enable is active and produce an open circuit output when it is not. With three-state gates, we can build a multiplexer without the OR gate. For example, the circuit of Figure 5.16 is a two-way multiplexer. The enable is the control input, determining whether $f = a$ ($EN = 0$) or $f = b$ ($EN = 1$). The three-state gate is often used for signals that travel between systems.

A *bus* is a set of lines over which data are transferred. Sometimes, that data may travel in either direction between devices located physically at a distance. The bus itself is really just a set of multiplexers, one for each bit in the set.

Figure 5.16 A multiplexer using three-state gates.

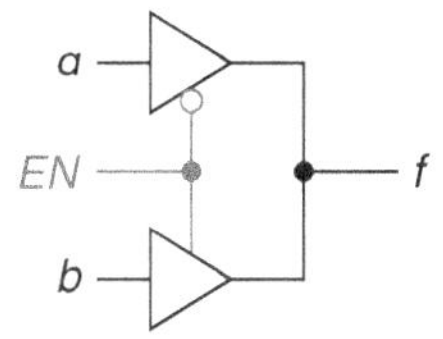

EXAMPLE 5.6

The following circuits show a bit of two implementations of the bus—one using AND and OR gates and the other using three-state gates.

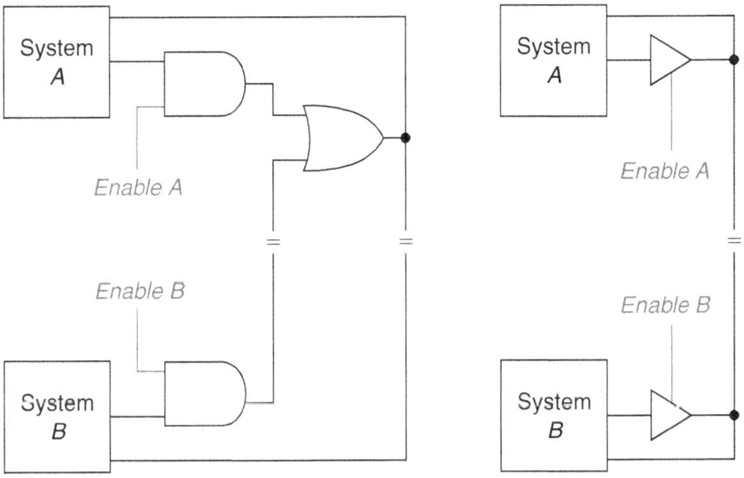

(a) Using AND/OR Gates (b) Using Three-State Gates

The major difference is the two long wires per bit between the systems for the AND-OR multiplexer compared to only one for the three-state version. The difference is even greater if what is being transferred between systems is 32-bit words. In that case, there would be 32 multiplexers. The AND–OR system would require 64 wires between systems, whereas the three-state version would require only 32. Further, if the enable signal came from one of the systems (instead of being generated internally in each), that would only add one wire, no matter how long the words are.

When we discuss gate arrays, both in this chapter and in Chapter 8, we will see that many systems have three-state output buffers.

5.6 GATE ARRAYS*—ROMs, PLAs, AND PALs

Gate arrays are one approach to the rapid implementation of fairly complex systems. They come in several varieties, but all have much in common. The basic concept is illustrated in Figure 5.17 for a system with three inputs and three outputs where the dashed lines indicate possible connections. (This is much smaller than most real gate arrays.)

Figure 5.17 Structure of a gate array.

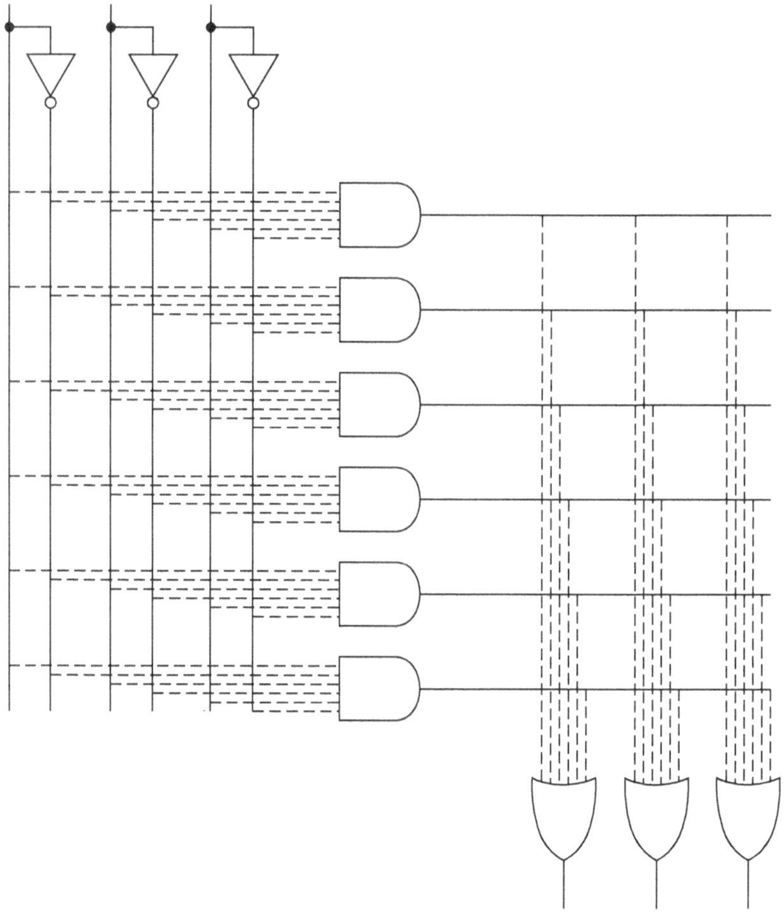

*A more general term is a *programmable logic device* (*PLD*). That includes all of these, as well as devices that include gate arrays and memory. The term *field programmable gate array* (*FPGA*) is also commonly used for such devices.

What these devices implement are SOP expressions. (In this case, three functions of three variables can be implemented. However, since there are only six AND gates, a maximum of six different product terms can be used for the three functions.) The array only requires uncomplemented inputs; there is internal circuitry that produces the complement.

EXAMPLE 5.7a

The following circuit shows the implementation of

$$f = a'b' + abc$$
$$g = a'b'c' + ab + bc$$
$$h = a'b' + c$$

using such an array, where the solid lines show the actual connections.

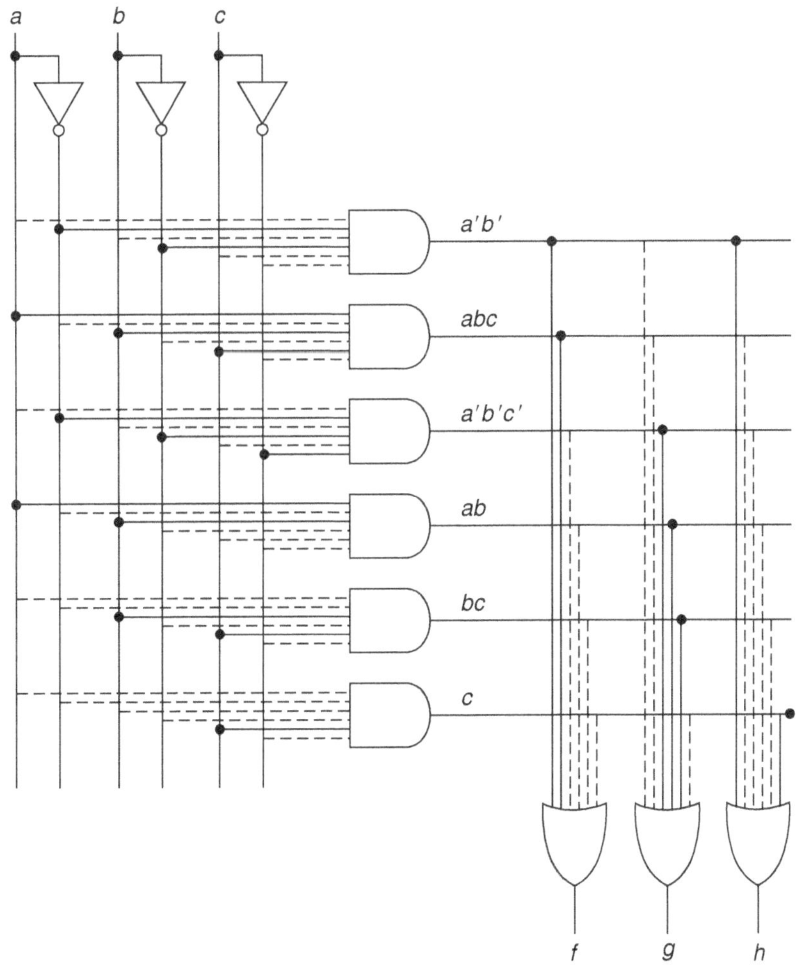

Two things should be noted in this diagram. First, the output of the AND gate that produces the *a′b′* is connected to the inputs of two of the OR gates. That is just sharing the term. Second, the term *c*, which does not require a gate in a NAND gate implementation (or in an AND/OR implementation), does require a term in a logic array. There is no other way to get *c* to the output.

This version of the diagram is rather cumbersome, particularly as the number of inputs and the number of gates increase. Thus, rather than showing all of the wires, only a single input line is usually shown for each gate, with X's or dots shown at the intersection where a connection is made. Thus, the previous circuit can be redrawn as in Example 5.7b.

EXAMPLE 5.7b

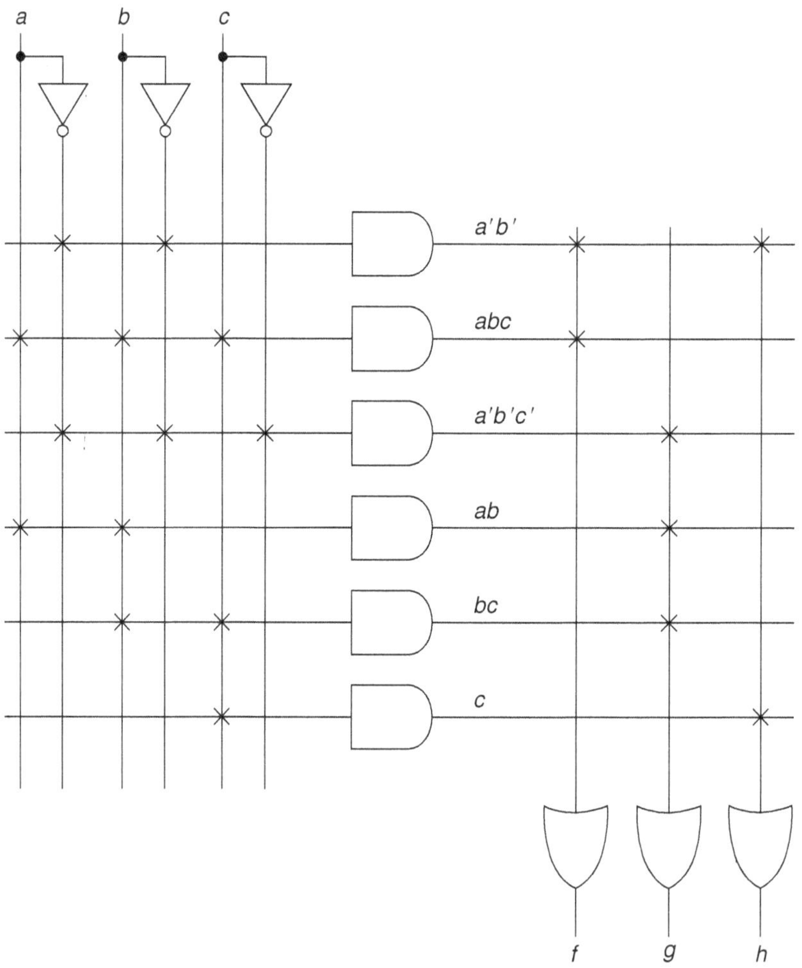

Sometimes, the AND and OR gates are not shown but are understood. (We will see examples of this shortly.)

There are three common types of combinational logic arrays. (We will discuss those with memory in Chapter 8.) The most general type (the one we have illustrated so far) is the *Programmable Logic Array* (*PLA*). In the PLA, the user specifies all of the connections (in both the AND array and in the OR array). Thus, we can create any set of SOP expressions (and share common terms). The second type is the *Read-Only Memory* (*ROM*). In a ROM, the AND array is fixed. It is just a decoder, consisting of 2^n AND gates for an n-input ROM. The user can only specify the connections to the OR gate. Thus, he produces a sum of minterms solution. The third type is the *Programmable Array Logic* (*PAL*), where the connections to the OR gates are specified; the user can determine the AND gate inputs. Each product term can be used only for one of the sums. We will discuss each of these in more detail in the sections that follow.

In each case, the base array is manufactured first, with the connections added later. One option is to have them added by the manufacturer on the user's specifications. There are also *field programmable* versions, where the user can enter the connections using a special programming device. The concept behind field programmable devices is to include a fuse in each connection line. If the user does not want the connection, he blows the fuse. (A blown fuse produces a 1 input to the AND gates and a 0 input to the OR gates. That fuse may be electronic, in which case it may be reset.) This sounds more complicated and time consuming than it is; the programming device does all of this automatically from inputs describing the desired array. This idea is carried one step further in the case of ROMs; there are *Erasable Programmable Read-Only Memories* (*EPROMs*). (This does sound like an oxymoron, to have a writable read-only device, but they do exist.) One type of fuse can be reset by exposing the device to ultraviolet light for several minutes; another type can be reset electronically.

In addition to the logic shown above, many field programmable devices make the output available in either active high or active low form. (By active low, we really mean the complement of the output, that is, f' instead of f.) This just requires an Exclusive-OR gate on the output with the ability to program one of the inputs to 0 for f and to 1 for f'. The output logic for such a case is shown in Figure 5.18.

Figure 5.18 A programmable output circuit.

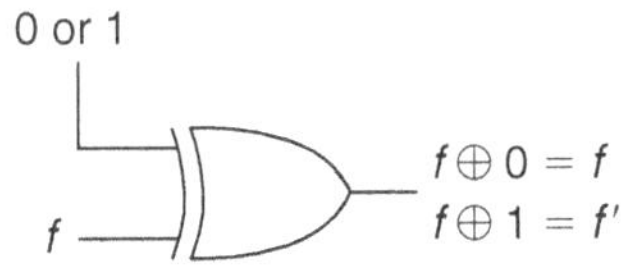

Some programmable devices have a three-state buffer at the output, which may be enabled either by an enable input line or one of the logic AND gates. This allows the output to be easily connected to a bus.

Sometimes, the output is fed back as another input to the AND array. This allows for more than two-level logic (most commonly in PALs, as we will discuss later). It also allows that output to be used as an input instead of an output, if a three-state output gate is added, as shown in Figure 5.19.

Figure 5.19 Three-state output.

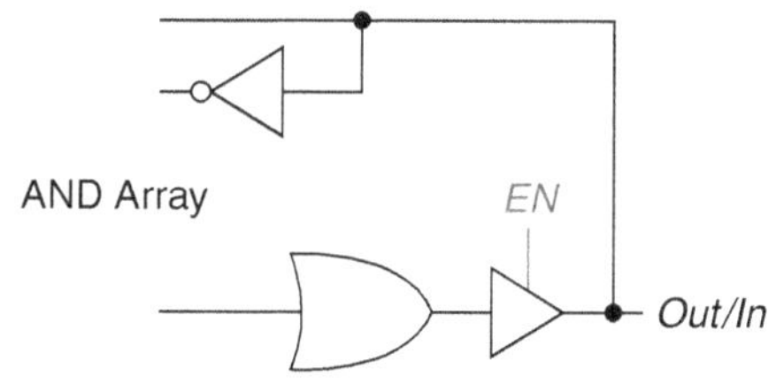

Note that if the three-state gate is enabled, the connection from the OR array to the output and back as an input to the AND array is established. If the three-state gate is not enabled, the logic associated with that OR is disconnected, and this *Out/In* can be used as just another input to the AND array.

5.6.1 Designing with Read-Only Memories

To design a system using a ROM, you need only to have a list of minterms for each function. A ROM has one AND gate for each minterm; you connect the appropriate minterm gates to each output. This is really the same type of circuitry as the decoder implementation of a sum of product expression presented in Example 5.3.

EXAMPLE 5.8

$$W(A, B, C, D) = \Sigma m(3, 7, 8, 9, 11, 15)$$
$$X(A, B, C, D) = \Sigma m(3, 4, 5, 7, 10, 14, 15)$$
$$Y(A, B, C, D) = \Sigma m(1, 5, 7, 11, 15)$$

The rows of the ROM are numbered (in order) from 0 to 15 for the four-input ROM shown here. An X or a dot is then placed at the appropriate intersection. In the following circuit, the connections shown as X's are built into the ROM; the user supplied the ones shown as dots to implement the functions above.

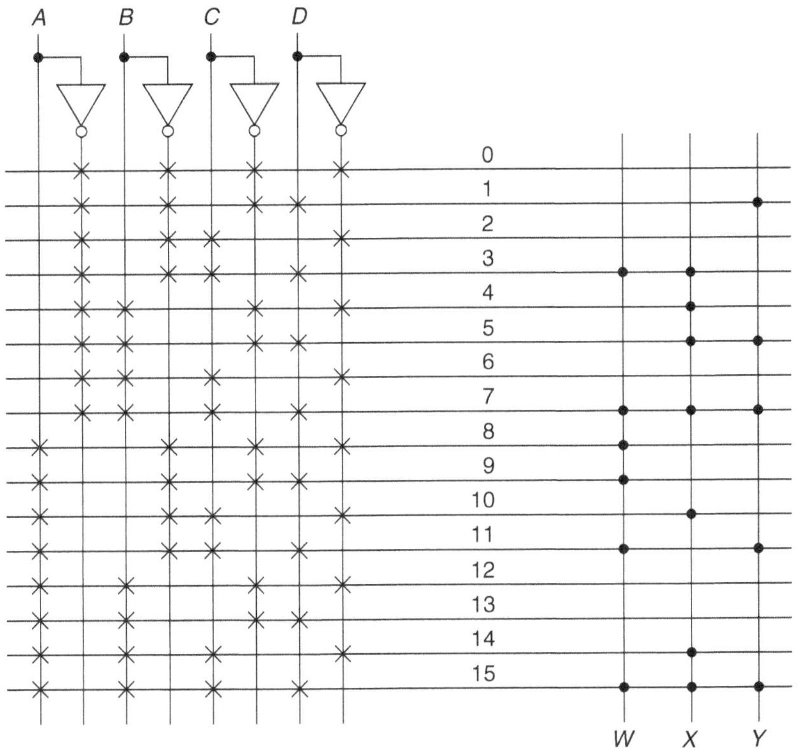

In spite of the terminology, that is, referring to this device as a memory, it is really a combinational logic device, as used in a circuit. The outputs are just a function of the present inputs. In Chapter 8, we will see programmable devices that do have memory in them. Typical commercial programmable ROMs have 8 to 12 inputs and 4 to 8 outputs.

5.6.2 Designing with Programmable Logic Arrays

To design a system using a PLA, you need only find SOP expressions for the functions to be implemented. The only limitation is the number of AND gates (product terms) that are available. Any SOP expression for each of the functions will do, from just a sum of minterms to one that minimizes each function individually to one that maximizes sharing (uses the techniques of Section 3.6).

EXAMPLE 5.9

Consider the same example we used to illustrate the ROM design:

$$W(A, B, C, D) = \Sigma m(3, 7, 8, 9, 11, 15)$$
$$X(A, B, C, D) = \Sigma m(3, 4, 5, 7, 10, 14, 15)$$
$$Y(A, B, C, D) = \Sigma m(1, 5, 7, 11, 15)$$

The first set of maps shows the solution considering these as individual functions. *X* and *Y* have two solutions.

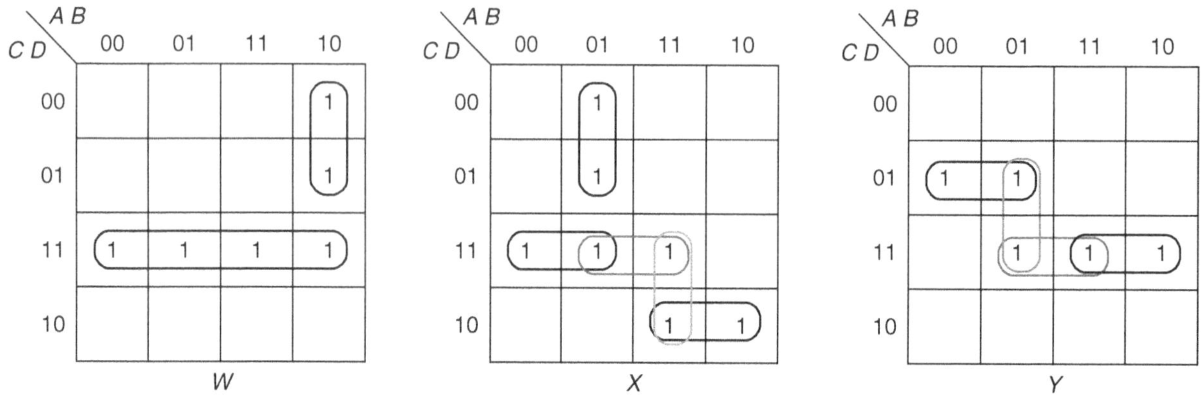

$$W = AB'C' + CD$$

$$Y = A'BC' + A'CD + ACD' + \{BCD \text{ or } ABC\}$$

$$Z = A'C'D + ACD + \{A'BD \text{ or } BCD\}$$

If we choose *BCD* for both *Y* and *Z*, this solution requires eight terms. Otherwise, it requires nine terms.

We can use fewer terms, by treating this as a multiple-output problem, as shown in the following maps:

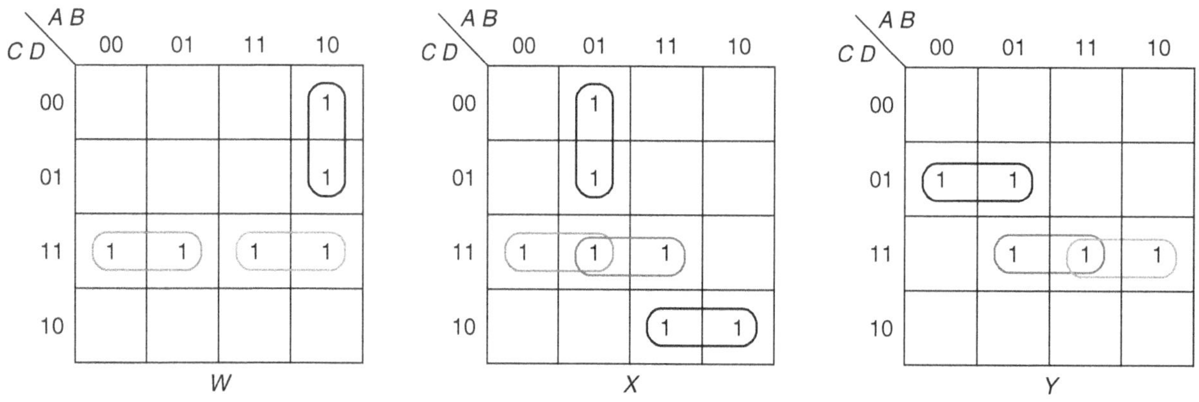

$$W = AB'C' + A'CD + ACD$$

$$X = A'BC' + ACD' + A'CD + BCD$$

$$Y = A'C'D + ACD + BCD$$

This solution only uses seven terms instead of eight or nine.

The following PLA shows both solutions. In the first set of output columns, we show the first solution. The first eight terms are used or the term *BCD* (brown dots) can be replaced by *ABC* in *X* and *A'BD* in *Z* (as shown with X's), using a total of nine terms. In the second solution, the second term, *CD*, is not used; only seven product terms are needed. If the PLA to be used is as big as the one shown, it does not matter which solution is chosen.

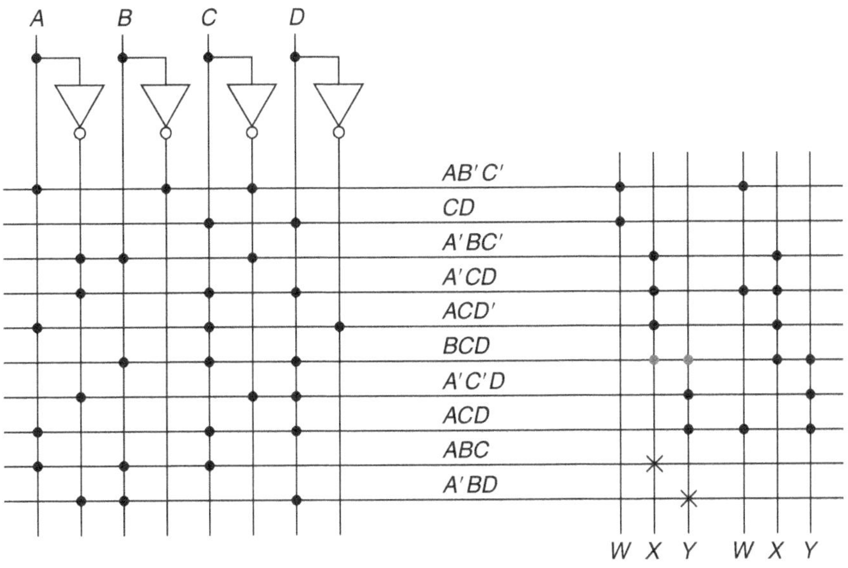

EXAMPLE 5.10

We will look at one other example to illustrate what happens when there is a term with a single literal. In Example 3.38 (Section 3.6), we saw the following maps:

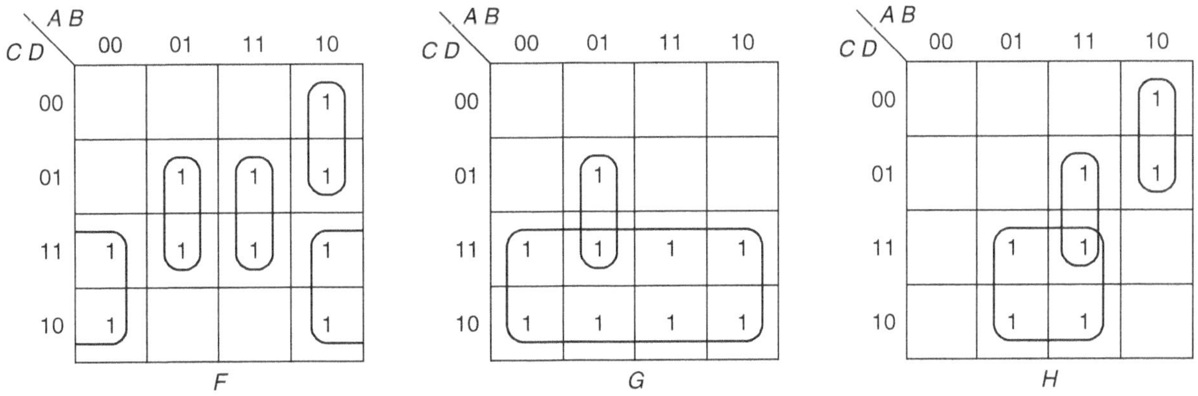

We chose the group of eight, *C* for *G*, because it did not require an AND gate and used only one input to the OR. In a PLA, however, even a single literal term requires a gate, and we are not counting gate inputs. We could reduce the number of terms needed by using $BC + B'C$ for G, since $B'C$ was required for F and BC was required for H. Thus, either set of output columns in the following PLA diagram would be a solution. Note that the term C is only used in the first implementation; the second requires one less term.

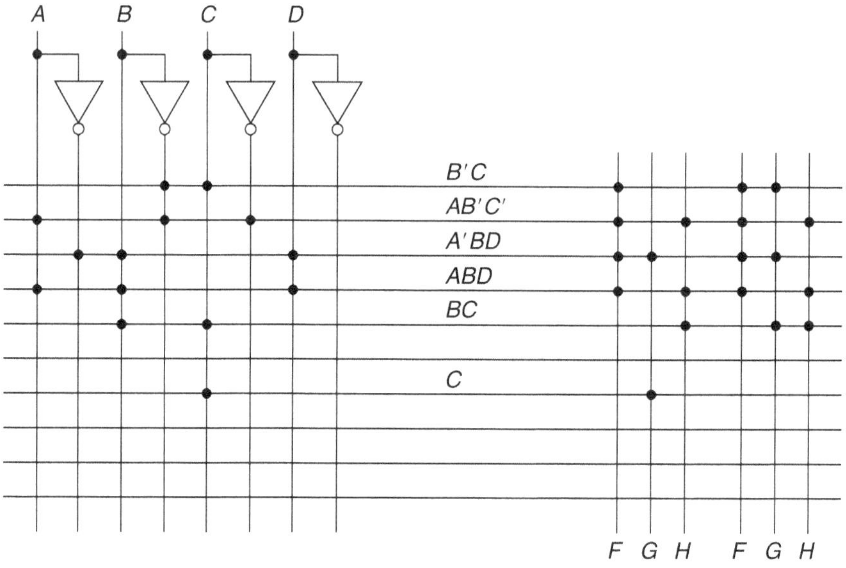

A typical commercially available PLA (PLS100) has 16 inputs, 48 product terms, and 8 outputs. Each output is programmable to be active high or low and has a three-state buffer, controlled by a common active low enable input. Note that this is less than one thousandth the number of product terms that would be required for a ROM with 16 inputs.

5.6.3 Designing with Programmable Array Logic

In a PAL, each output comes from an OR that has its own group of AND gates connected to it. The layout of a small PAL is shown in Figure 5.20.

For this PAL, there are six inputs and four outputs, with each OR gate having four input terms. When using a PAL, the output of each AND gate goes to only one OR. Thus, there is no sharing of terms, and we would solve each function individually. However, most PALs provide for the possible feedback of some or all of the outputs to an input. Sometimes this is internal, that is, the output of some of the OR gates is available as another input to all of the AND gates. In other cases, an external connection is made (as implied in Example 5.12). This allows for more terms (more than

Figure 5.20 A PAL.

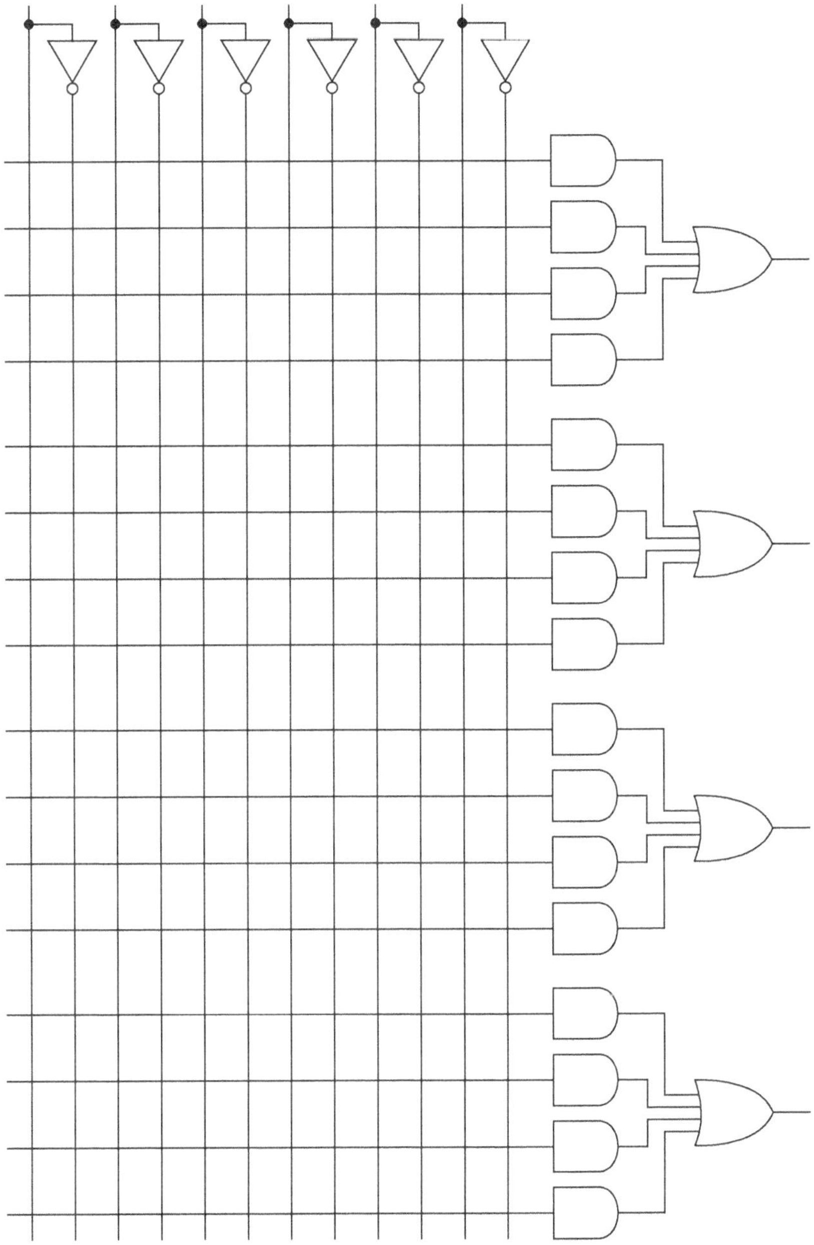

four in this example) in a sum of products expression, or for expressions that are not sum of product, or for sharing a group of terms. Many PALs have a three-state buffer on the output (before the feedback to the inputs), allowing that output to be used as an input as well.

EXAMPLE 5.11

We will first return to the example we used for ROMs and PLAs, namely,

$$W = AB'C' + CD$$
$$X = A'BC' + A'CD + ACD' + \{BCD \text{ or } ABC\}$$
$$Y = A'C'D + ACD' + \{A'BD \text{ or } BCD\}$$

There is no reason to consider sharing. Choosing the first of each of the optional terms, the implementation is

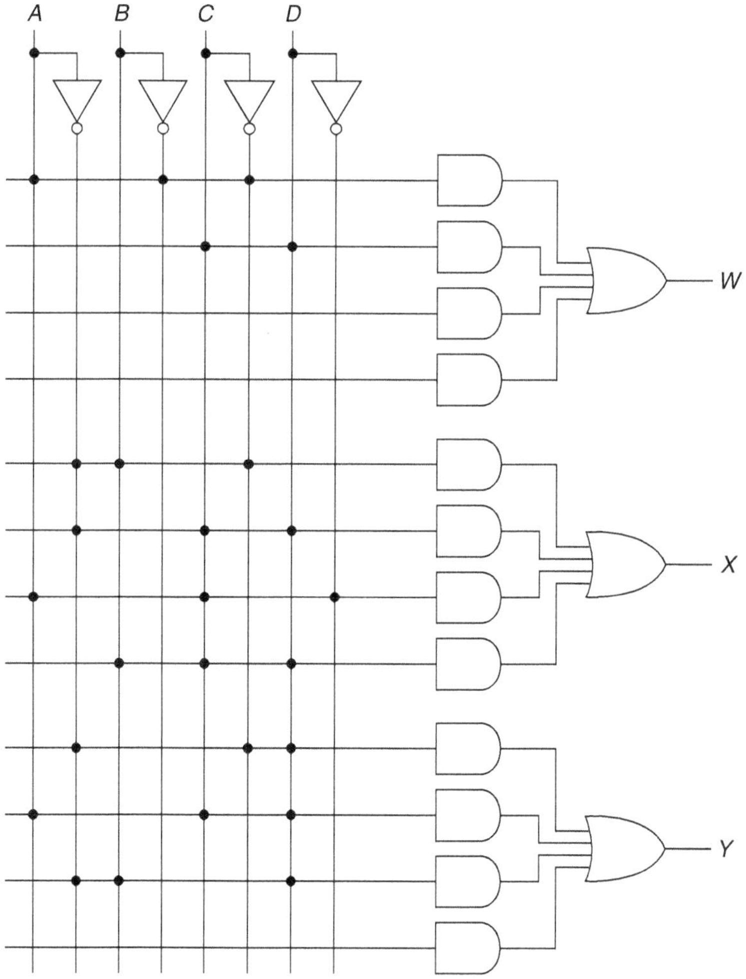

EXAMPLE 5.12

As an example of a system where feedback is useful, consider the functions shown in the following maps:

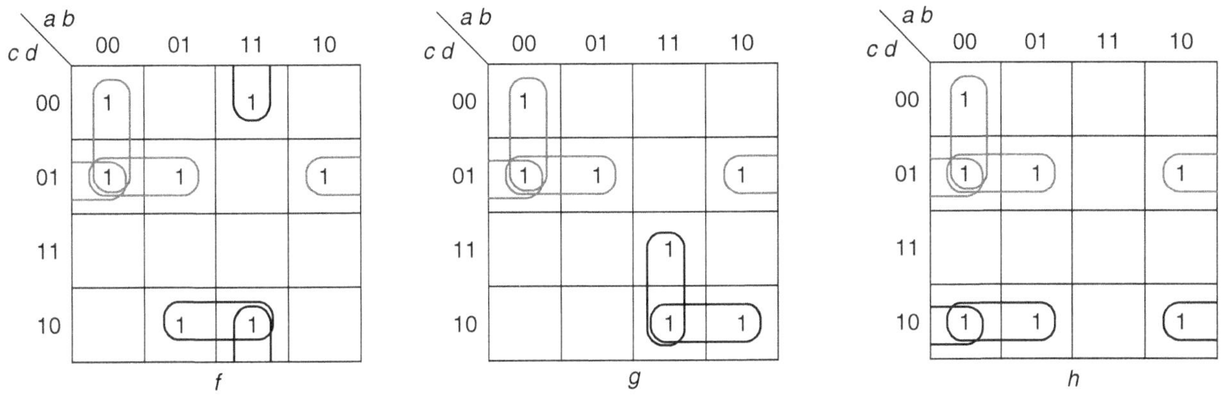

Note that the three brown terms are essential prime implicants of each function; the other two are not. This results in the following equations:

$$f = a'b'c' + a'c'd + b'c'd + abd' + bcd'$$
$$g = a'b'c' + a'c'd + b'c'd + abc + acd'$$
$$h = a'b'c' + a'c'd + b'c'd + a'cd' + b'cd'$$

(This solution was obtained by considering each function individually. If we treated this as a multiple-output problem, we would use the term $ab'cd'$ in both g and h, rather than acd' in g and $b'cd'$ in h. That would reduce the number of different terms in the algebraic solution, but it would not change the number of gates used in the PAL.) The PAL implementation is shown in the following circuit. The first three terms are implemented in the first OR gate, the output of which, t, is fed back to the input of one of the AND gates in each of the other three circuits. Note that the fourth AND gate of the t circuit has both a and a' connected at its input. Obviously, the output of that AND gate is 0. Some implementations require the user to connect unused AND gates in that way. (We did not do that for the other unused AND gates.)

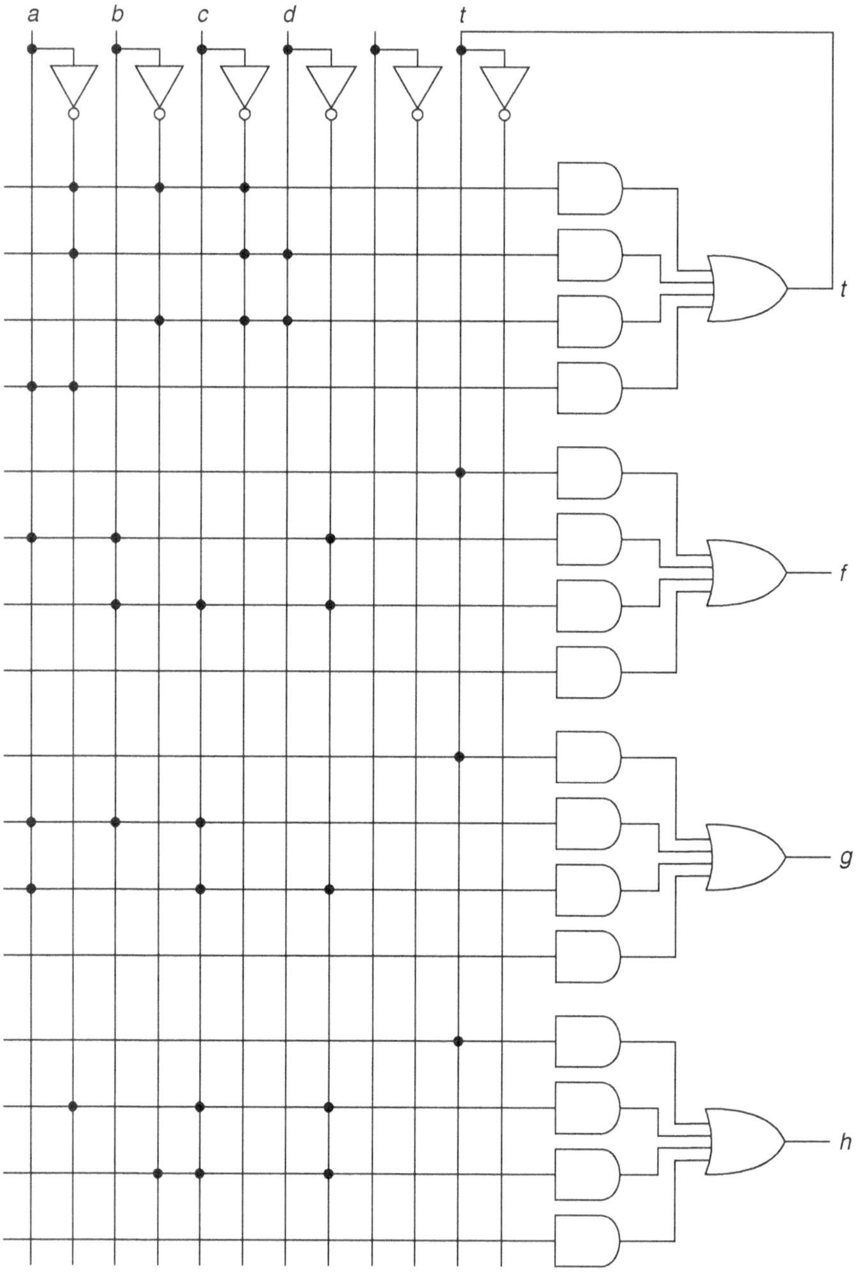

[SP 13, 14; EX 15, 16, 17]

5.7 TESTING AND SIMULATION OF COMBINATIONAL SYSTEMS

After designing a system, it is necessary to test it to make sure that it does what it was intended to do. For a small system, this means applying all possible input combinations and comparing the output with what was expected. As systems get a little larger, that process becomes very time-consuming. For example, if we are testing the behavior of a 4-bit adder (with carry input), there are 2^9 input combinations to test. We can be sure that it works by trying many fewer input sets, as long as we are careful to make sure that all parts of the circuit are tested (each sum circuit and each carry circuit).

When building a large system, it is often necessary to break it into several smaller systems and design and test each subsystem separately. If you are building a large number of a particular system, you would normally design an integrated circuit. Before committing to that design, you must test the design, either by building a circuit using small-scale components or simulating it.

5.7.1 An Introduction to Verilog

Most design of significant digital systems is done with computer-aided tools. They allow the user to specify either the behavior of the system or the structure of the system (or a mixture of the two) using a notation similar to a programming language. The two most widely used systems are *Verilog* and *VHDL*. They have many similarities, but differ in detail. In this section, we will show examples of Verilog code, both structural and behavioral, but a discussion adequate to allow the user to design using any HDL is beyond the scope of this book.*

We will first illustrate a structural Verilog description, using the full adder first discussed in Example 2.34 and shown here as Figure 5.21.

Figure 5.21 A full adder.

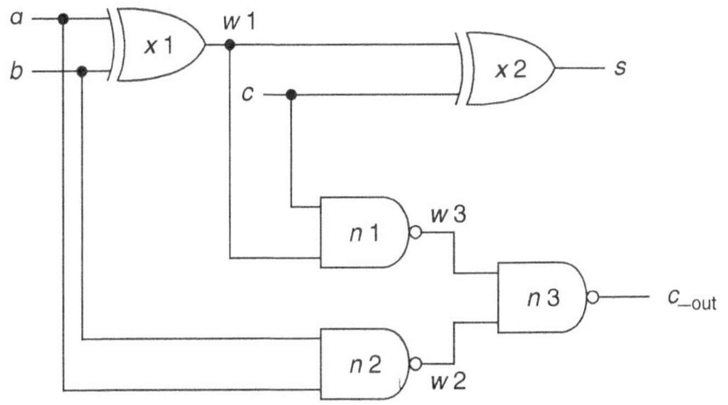

*For a detailed discussion of Verilog or VHDL, see Brown and Vranesic, *Fundamentals of Digital Logic with Verilog Design*, 2nd ed. McGraw-Hill, 2008 or Brown and Vranesic, *Fundamentals of Digital Logic with VHDL Design*, 3rd ed. McGraw-Hill, 2009.

The corresponding Verilog code (description) is shown in Figure 5.22.

Figure 5.22 Verilog structural description of a full adder.

```
module full_adder (c_out, s, a, b, c);
     input a, b, c;
     wire a, b, c;
     output c_out, s;
     wire c_out, s;
     wire w1, w2, w3;
     xor x1 (w1, a, b);
     xor x2 (s, w1, c);
 nand n1 (w2, a, b);
     nand n2 (w3, w1, c);
     nand n3 (c_out, w3, w2);
endmodule
```

The first line includes the key word `module` followed by the name of the module and the parameters, that is, the outputs and the inputs. Names may include characters other than spaces; Verilog is case-sensitive, that is x1 means something different from X1. (The symbol _ is used to connect multiple word names.) Each module ends with the statement `endmodule`. Statements within Verilog are ended with a semicolon (;), other than `endmodule`. A list of inputs and outputs must be included, and each gate output must be declared a `wire`. Structural Verilog includes most standard gate types, such as `and`, `or`, `not`, `nand`, `nor`, `xor`. They are indicated by listing the key word (such as `xor`), a unique name for each copy of that device, their output wire name, and their inputs, as shown in Figure 5.22. The connections for the circuit are made exactly as in Figure 5.21. The order in which the logic statements are written does not matter. (That is not true in behavioral Verilog.)

A 4-bit adder can be built using the full adder as a building block, as shown in Figure 5.23. (We will use a full adder for the least significant bit, although a half adder would do.)

Figure 5.23 A 4-bit adder.

```
module  adder_4_bit (c, sum, a, b);
     input a, b;
     output c, sum;
     wire [3:0] a, b, sum;
     wire c0, c1, c2, c;
     full_adder f1 (c0, sum[0], a[0], b[0], 'b0);
     full_adder f2 (c1, sum[1], a[1], b[1], c0);
     full_adder f3 (c2, sum[2], a[2], b[2], c1);
     full_adder f4 (c, sum[3], a[3], b[3], c2);
endmodule
```

Some additional notation appears in this example. Multibit wires are labeled with brackets. The `wire [3:0] a, b, sum` declaration states that each of the inputs and the sum output are 4 bits (with the highest number on the left. When a module is used, such as `full_adder`, the order of the parameters is what matters, not the name. Thus, the first copy of the full adder adds the least significant bits, `a[0]` and `b[0]`, with a 0 in the carry position (denoted as `'b0`, where the `'b` indicates that the number following it is binary).

Verilog also provides for the description of the behavior of a system, without specifying the details of the structure. This is often the first step in the design of a complex system, made up of a number of modules. The behavioral description of each module can be completed and tested. That is often much more straightforward. Once that works, the individual modules can be designed and described structurally. The structural description can then replace the behavioral one, one module at a time. Behavioral Verilog uses notation very similar to the C programming language. The normal mathematics operators (such as +, −, *, and /) are available, as are the bitwise logical operators (not: ~, and: &, or: |, and exclusive or: ^). Two behavioral Verilog descriptions of the full adder are shown in Figure 5.24.

Figure 5.24 Behavioral Verilog for the full adder.

```
module full_adder (c_out, s, a, b, c);
     input a, b, c;
     wire a, b, c;
     output c_out, s;
     reg c_out, s;
     always
          begin
               s = a ^ b ^ c;
               c_out = (a & b) | (a & c_in) | (b & c_in);
          end
endmodule
```

(a) With logic equations.

```
module full_adder (c_out, s, a, b, c);
     input a, b, c;
     wire a, b, c;
     output c_out, s;
     reg c_out, s;
     always
          {c_out, s} = a + b + c;
endmodule
```

(b) With algebraic equations.

Note that values set in behavioral models are referred to as `reg`, rather than `wire`.

5.8 LARGER EXAMPLES

In this section, we will look at the design of three systems that are somewhat larger than any we have considered so far.

5.8.1 A One-Digit Decimal Adder

We want to design an adder to add two decimal digits (plus a carry-in), where the digits are stored in 8421 code. This system would have nine inputs (two coded digits plus the carry-in) and five outputs (the one digit and the carry-out). Rather than trying to solve a nine-input problem, we can break it up into smaller parts, using the 4-bit binary adder that we already designed (or obtained on a single chip). We will assume that none of the unused inputs ever occur.

Decimal addition can be performed by first doing binary addition. Then, if the sum is greater than 9, a carry is generated and 6 is added to this digit. (That is to make up for the six combinations that are not used). For example,

		0		1	1
0011	3	0111	7	1000	8
0101	5	0101	5	1001	9
0 1000	8	0 1100	--	1 0010	1 2
sum $\leq$ 9		0110	6	0110	6
no correction		1 0010	1 2	1 1000	1 8

We add the two numbers using a binary adder and detect whether the sum is greater than 10. If it is, we must add six (0110) to the result. A block diagram of the decimal adder, using two binary adders, is shown in Figure 5.25.

The carry detect circuit takes the output of the first adder (including the carry) and produces a 1 output if that number is greater than 9. That is the carry output from the decimal adder, as well as the correction indicator. When there is a carry-out, 6 is added to the answer from the first adder; otherwise, 0 is added. A map for the carry detect circuit is shown as Map 5.2.

Figure 5.25 A decimal adder.

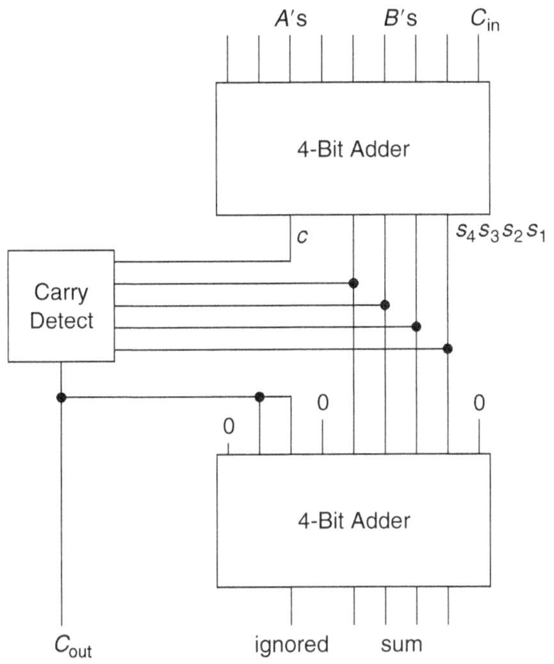

Map 5.2 Carry detect.

$c = 0$

$s_2 s_1$ \ $s_4 s_3$	00	01	11	10
00			1	
01			1	
11			1	1
10			1	1

$c = 1$

$s_2 s_1$ \ $s_4 s_3$	00	01	11	10
00	1	X	X	X
01	1	X	X	X
11	1	X	X	X
10	1	X	X	X

$c_{out} = c + s_4 s_3 + s_4 s_2$

5.8.2 A Driver for a Seven-Segment Display

In Chapter 2 (CE4), we introduced the seven-segment display commonly used for decimal digits. A block diagram of that display system is repeated as Figure 5.26.

Figure 5.26 A seven-segment display and driver.

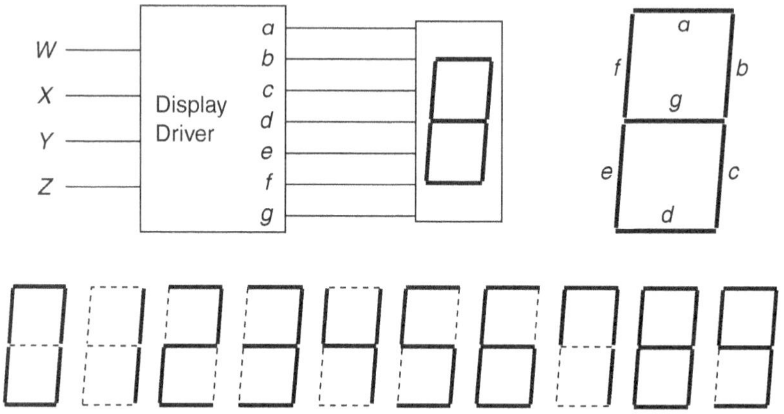

where the solid lines represent segments to be lit and the dashed ones segments that are not lit. For digits 6, 7, and 9, two alternative representations are shown (that is, one segment of each may or may not be lit).

This display driver is a problem with four inputs, *W*, *X*, *Y*, and *Z* and seven outputs, *a*, *b*, *c*, *d*, *e*, *f*, and *g*. If, indeed, the system is to display only a decimal digit, and the inputs are limited to only proper codes for those digits, then only 10 of the possible 16 input combinations can occur. The others can be treated as don't cares. In Section 2.1.2, we chose the 8421 code (straight binary) to represent the decimal digits and showed the truth table under the assumption that a 1 input to the display would cause that segment to be lit. Although this seems like a natural assumption, displays are available that require a 0 on a segment input to light that segment.

There are several approaches to this design. There are BCD-to-seven-segment converters available, such as the 7449, that could be used for this problem. (There are also chips that produce an active low output.)

We could solve each of these as individual functions (as in Section 3.3), or we could treat them as multiple-output problems, as in Section 3.6. We could also use a ROM, a PLA, or a PAL to complete the design. We will design the ROM and PLA solution for this problem.

Solving each as an individual function is very straightforward. There are several prime implicants that can be shared. The minimum is obtained by choosing one of the multiple solutions for *g* that takes advantage of sharing. A minimum solution, shown in Map 5.3, is

$$a = W + Y + XZ + X'Z'$$
$$b = X' + YZ + Y'Z'$$
$$c = X + Y' + Z$$
$$d = X'Z' + YZ' + X'Y + XY'Z$$
$$e = X'Z' + YZ'$$
$$f = W + X + Y'Z'$$
$$g = W + X'Y + XY' + \{XZ' \text{ or } YZ'\}$$

Map 5.3 Seven-segment display driver.

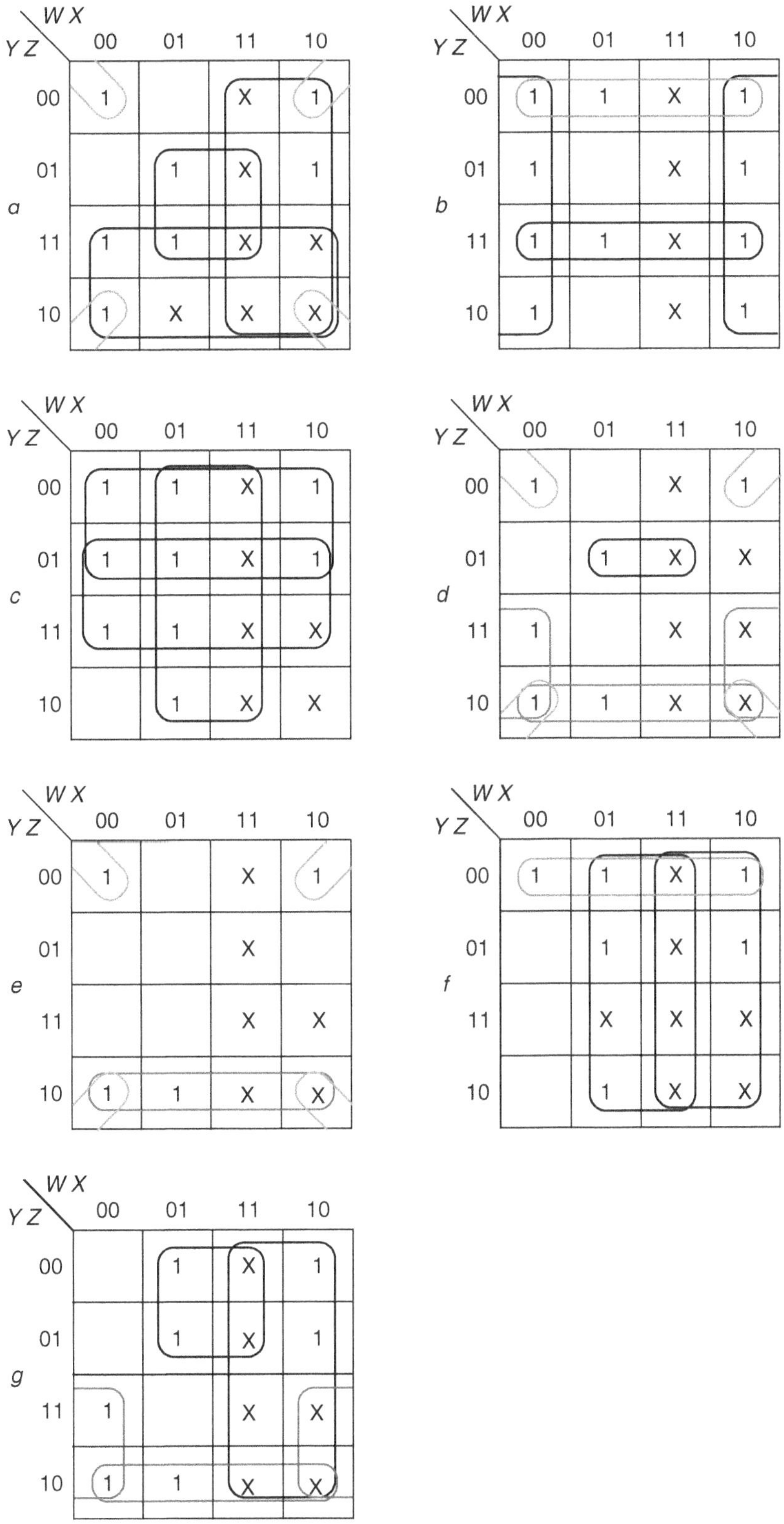

where the shared terms are shown in brown, tan, and gray. There are eight unique terms requiring gates (since single literal terms do not require a gate). Thus, this would require a total of 15 gates, assuming all inputs are available both uncomplemented and complemented. (Otherwise, four additional NOT gates would be required.) If these were implemented with 7400 series NAND gates, then we would use

Type	Number	Number of modules	Chip number
2-in	8	2	7400
3-in	4	1	7410
4-in	3	2	7420

where only one 7410 is required since the extra four-input gate would be used as the fourth three-input gate. Treating this as a multiple-output problem, we could save one gate by using $XY'Z$ in function a in place of XZ.

A more interesting problem (in the sense that there is more of an advantage to treating the problem as a multiple-output one) results if we demand that all segments be unlit if the code is not one of those used for a decimal digit. The maps for this, with the minimum solutions circled, are shown in Map 5.4. All of the don't cares for minterms 10 to 15 have become 0's. (The don't cares for the alternative representations of 6, 7, and 9 remain.) The shared prime implicants are shown circled in brown, tan, and gray. (There are multiple solutions to several of the functions; the one that provides the maximum sharing is shown.)

One way to display the answer is shown in Table 5.7, with a row for each product term and a column for each function. An X is placed in the column if that product term is used in the function.

Table 5.7 Seven-segment display driver (prime implicants only).

	a	b	c	d	e	f	g
$X'Y'Z'$	X			X	X		
$WX'Y'$	X					X	X
$W'Y$	X						
$W'XZ$	X						
$W'Y'Z'$		X				X	
$W'X'$		X					
$W'YZ$		X					
$X'Y'$		X	X				
$W'X$			X			X	
$W'Z$			X				
$W'YZ'$				X	X		X
$W'X'Y$				X			X
$W'XY'Z$				X			
$W'XY'$							X

Map 5.4 Seven-segment display driver (individual).

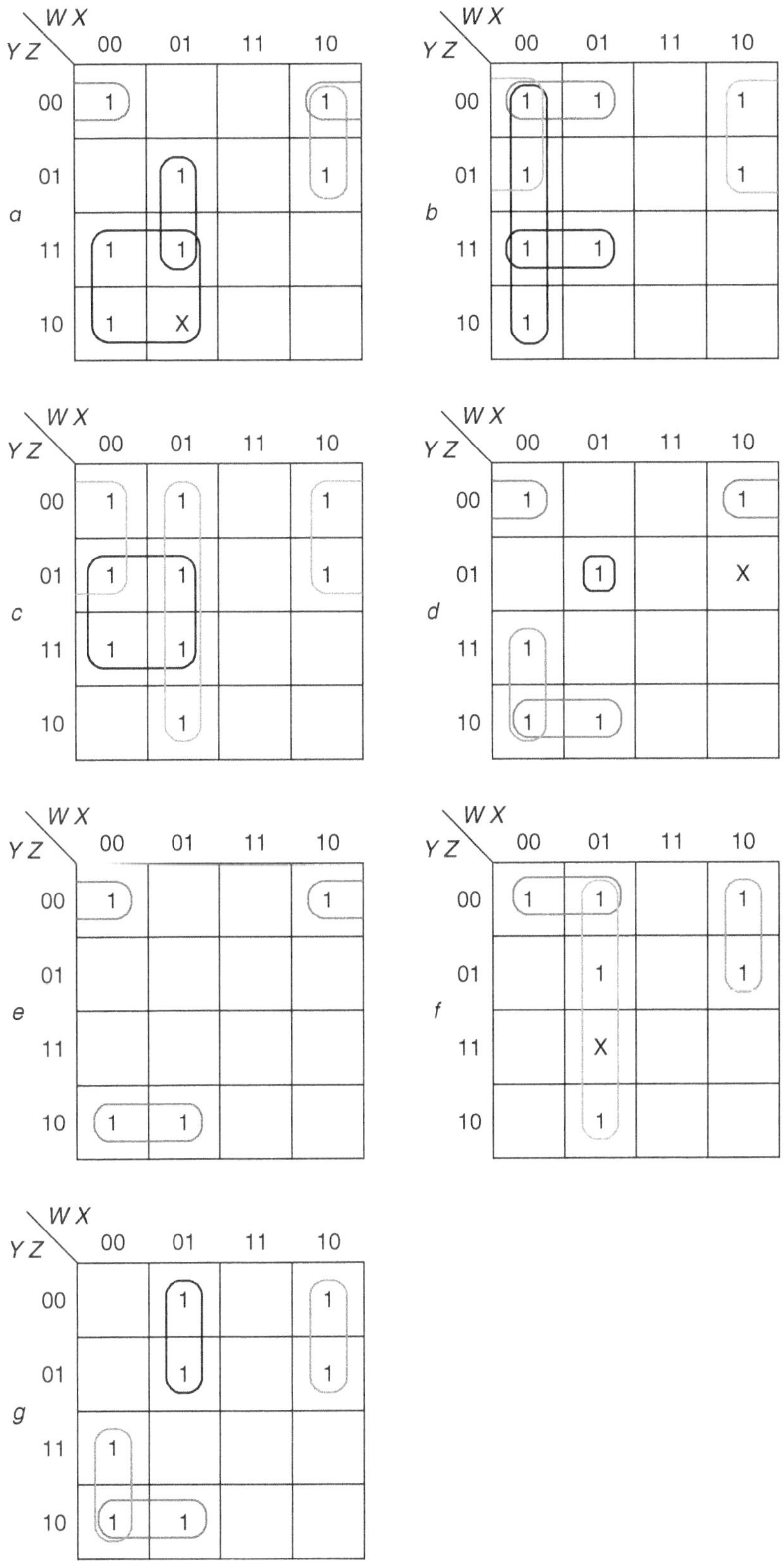

The algebraic expressions can be obtained by just ORing the terms included in each function. We can count the number of gates (one for each term, that is, each row and one for each output column). The number of gate inputs is also easy to compute, since we just add the number of literals in each term and the number of X's in each function (corresponding to OR gate inputs). For this example, the total is 21 gates and 62 gate inputs.

We next attempt to solve this by sharing terms wherever possible, even if the term is not a prime implicant. The first obvious spot is in a, where the prime implicant $W'XZ$ can be replaced by the term $W'XY'Z$, a term we already need for d. Map 5.5 shows a minimum solution, where terms that are shared are shown circled in brown, tan, and gray. This results in the solution of Table 5.8.

Table 5.8 Seven-segment display driver (maximum sharing).

	a	***b***	***c***	***d***	***e***	***f***	***g***
$X'Y'Z'$	X			X	X		
$WX'Y'$	X					X	X
$W'XY'Z$	X			X			
$W'YZ$	X	X	X				
$W'X'Y$	X	X		X			X
$W'Y'Z'$		X				X	
$X'Y'$		X	X				
$W'X$			X			X	
$W'YZ'$				X	X		X
$W'XY'$							X

This solution requires only 10 terms and thus 17 gates, a savings of 4 gates, and 54 inputs, a savings of 8 gate inputs. The corresponding equations are thus

$$a = X'Y'Z' + WX'Y' + W'XY'Z + W'YZ + W'X'Y$$

$$b = W'YZ + W'X'Y + W'Y'Z' + X'Y'$$

$$c = W'YZ + X'Y' + W'X$$

$$d = X'Y'Z' + W'XY'Z + W'X'Y + W'YZ'$$

$$e = X'Y'Z' + W'YZ'$$

$$f = WX'Y' + W'Y'Z' + W'X$$

$$g = WX'Y' + W'X'Y + W'YZ' + W'XY'$$

If we are to implement each of these with 7400 series NAND gates, the system would require

Map 5.5 Seven-segment display driver (maximum sharing).

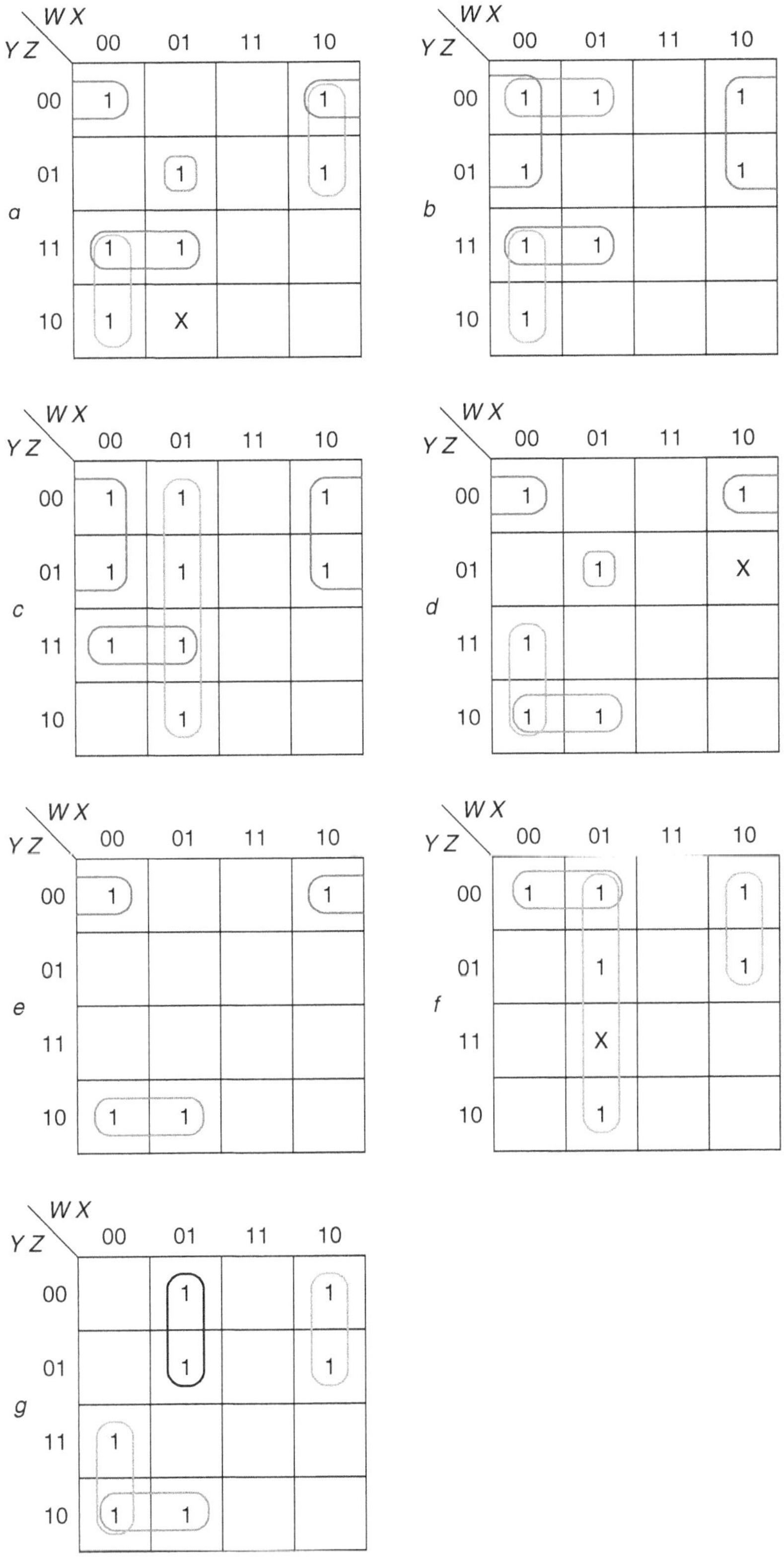

		Individually		Multiple output	
Type	**Chip number**	**Number**	**Number of modules**	**Number**	**Number of modules**
2-in	7400	6	2	3	1
3-in	7410	10	3	9	3
4-in	7420	5	3	4	2
8-in	7430	0		1	1
Total		21	8	17	7

Thus, we save four gates and one module by treating this as a multiple-output problem.

Notice that these two solutions are not equal. The first treats the don't care in *d* as 0 and the don't cares in *a* and *f* as 1's; the second treats the don't cares in *a* and *d* as 0's and only the one in *f* as a 1.

We could also implement this problem using the ROM shown in Figure 5.27. Note that we did not include any of the don't cares; we could have made any or all of them 1's. Notice that this solution is not equal to either of the other ones, since each of them treat at least one of the don't cares as 1.

Figure 5.27 ROM implementation of seven-segment display driver.

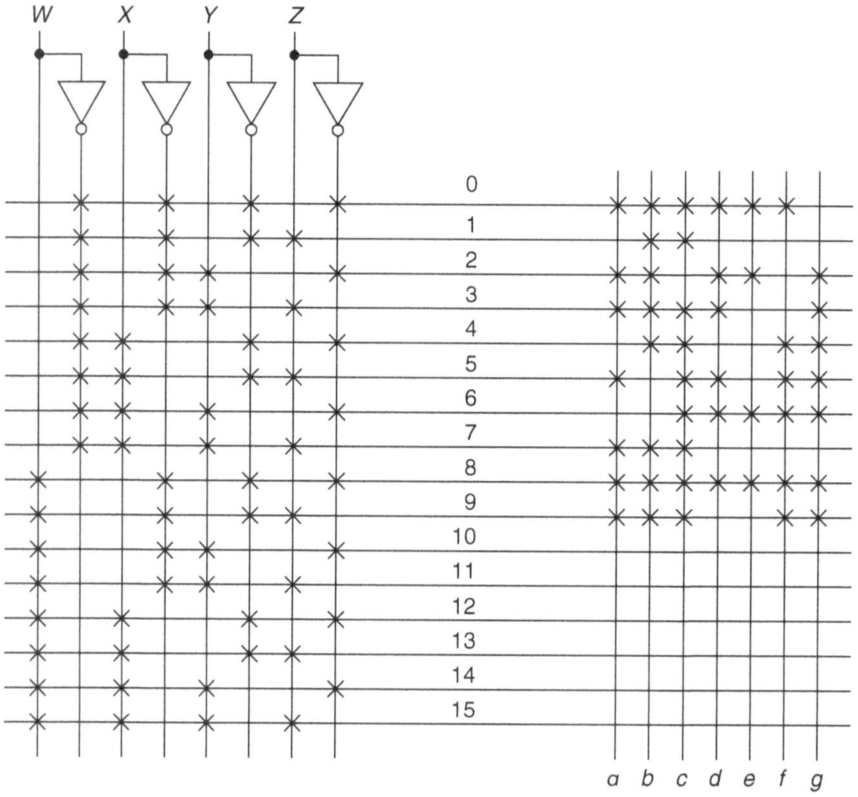

We could implement this system with the PLA of Figure 5.28 with four inputs, seven outputs, and 14 product terms. If all we had were 10 product terms, then we must use the minimum solution we found for the NAND implementation. If we have more terms, then a less minimum solution could be utilized.

Figure 5.28 PLA implementation of seven-segment display driver.

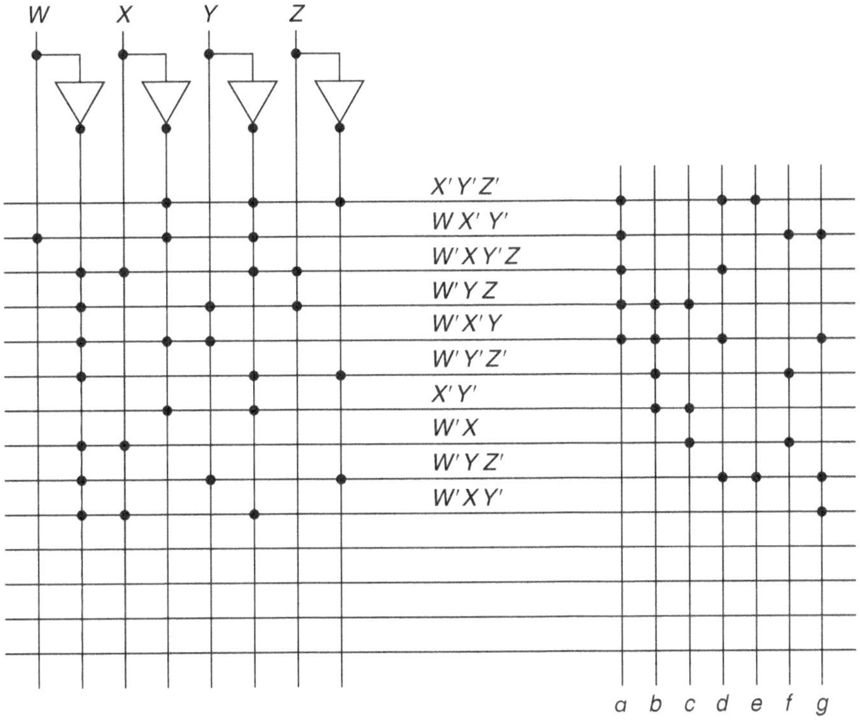

If we wished to implement this with a PAL, we would need seven OR gates (two of the circuits we discussed in the previous section). There are a number of variations to this problem, each of which creates a totally new problem. We could require 0's to light a segment, in which case the complement of each of these functions must be found. That would create a whole new set of maps. Once again, we could demand that the unused conditions be unlit, or we could allow them to be don't cares. We could specify the form for 6, 7, and/or 9, thus eliminating those don't cares. That would change the problem slightly. We could make this into a hexadecimal display, in which case the last six codes would represent *A*, *B*, *C*, *D*, *E*, and *F*. Finally, one of the other codes could have been used for the decimal digits, with each of the variations described earlier. Some of these are included in the Solved Problems and Exercises.

5.8.3 An Error Coding System

We are designing two systems that are to be used in conjunction with an error detection and correction system. When data are transmitted (or stored), errors occur. Richard Hamming developed a technique for coding data (by adding extra digits) so that a single error (that is, an error in 1 bit) can be corrected. (This can be extended to double error detection and even multiple error correction.) To detect an error in a set of bits, a *check bit* is created so that the total number of 1's in the word, including the check bit, is even.* That bit is referred to as a *parity* bit. If one error is made, either a 1 will become a 0, or a 0 will become a 1, making the total number of 1's odd.

The parity bit can be computed by using the Exclusive-OR function on the bits to be checked. On the receiving end, the checked bits and the parity bit are Exclusive-ORed; if the result is 0, then the answer is assumed to be correct.† For error correction, multiple parity bits are required, each checking a different set of information bits. Data are coded in such a way that a single error from any transmitted word will not produce another transmitted word or a word that has a single error from another transmitted word. (The *Hamming distance* between words is the number of digits in which they differ. For single error correction, transmitted words must be at distance 3.) For a single data bit, two check bits are required. The two transmitted words would be 000 for data 0 and 111 for data 1. A single error from 000 would produce a word with one 1; thus, all words with zero or one 1 would be decoded as 0 and all words with two or three 1's would be decoded as 1.

Hamming showed that for three check bits, we could have up to four data bits, and that for four check bits, we can have up to 11 data bits. As an example, we will consider three data bits and three check bits, which provide for the correction of all single errors and the detection of some double errors (since some of the possible received words may not correspond to a transmitted word or a single error from one of those words). A block diagram is shown in Figure 5.29.

Figure 5.29 Error detection and correction system.

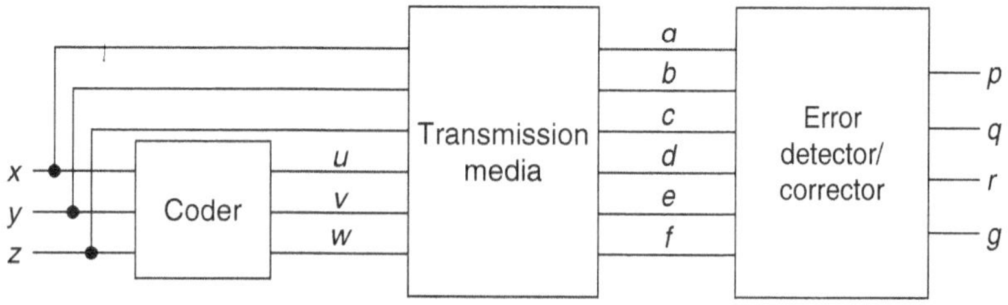

The first check bit, u, checks x and y; v checks x and z; and w checks y and z. Thus, the coder is just

$$u = x \oplus y \qquad v = x \oplus z \qquad w = y \oplus z$$

The list of transmitted words is shown in Table 5.9.

Table 5.9 Transmitted words.

Data			Check		
x	y	z	u	v	w
0	0	0	0	0	0
0	0	1	0	1	1
0	1	0	1	0	1
0	1	1	1	1	0
1	0	0	1	1	0
1	0	1	1	0	1
1	1	0	0	1	1
1	1	1	0	0	0

*The parity bit could be chosen so as to make the total number of 1's odd, instead.

†This method is not foolproof. If two errors are made, there will once again be an even number of 1's, and it will look like the received word is correct. This approach is used when the likelihood of multiple errors is very small.

For each transmitted word, there are six single errors that will be decoded to that word (plus the correct word). For example, single errors from the first word are 100000, 010000, 001000, 000100, 000010, and 000001. Each of these, plus 000000, should be decoded as 000. Map 5.6 shows the maps for p, q, and r—the corrected word—and for g, which is 1 if a multiple error is detected (in which case, p, q, and r are not

Map 5.6 Error detector/corrector.

p, *ab* = 00

ef \ cd	00	01	11	10
00	0	0	X	0
01	0	0	1	0
11	0	X	0	0
10	0	1	0	0

p, *ab* = 01

ef \ cd	00	01	11	10
00	0	0	0	1
01	0	0	0	X
11	1	0	0	0
10	X	0	0	0

p, *ab* = 11

ef \ cd	00	01	11	10
00	1	X	1	1
01	1	0	1	1
11	1	1	X	1
10	1	1	0	1

p, *ab* = 10

ef \ cd	00	01	11	10
00	0	1	1	1
01	X	1	1	1
11	1	1	1	0
10	1	1	1	X

q, *ab* = 00

ef \ cd	00	01	11	10
00	0	0	X	0
01	0	1	0	0
11	0	X	0	0
10	0	0	1	0

q, *ab* = 01

ef \ cd	00	01	11	10
00	0	1	1	1
01	1	1	1	X
11	1	1	1	0
10	X	1	1	1

q, *ab* = 11

ef \ cd	00	01	11	10
00	1	X	1	1
01	1	1	0	1
11	1	1	X	1
10	1	0	1	1

q, *ab* = 10

ef \ cd	00	01	11	10
00	0	0	0	1
01	X	0	0	0
11	1	0	0	0
10	0	0	0	X

r, *ab* = 00

ef \ cd	00	01	11	10
00	0	0	X	0
01	0	0	1	1
11	1	X	1	1
10	0	0	1	1

r, *ab* = 01

ef \ cd	00	01	11	10
00	0	0	1	1
01	0	0	0	X
11	0	0	1	1
10	X	1	1	1

r, *ab* = 11

ef \ cd	00	01	11	10
00	1	X	1	1
01	0	0	1	1
11	0	0	X	0
10	0	0	1	1

r, *ab* = 10

ef \ cd	00	01	11	10
00	0	0	1	1
01	X	1	1	1
11	0	0	1	1
10	0	0	0	X

g, *ab* = 00

ef \ cd	00	01	11	10
00			1	
01				
11		1		
10				

g, *ab* = 01

ef \ cd	00	01	11	10
00				
01				1
11				
10	1			

g, *ab* = 11

ef \ cd	00	01	11	10
00		1		
01				
11			1	
10				

g, *ab* = 10

ef \ cd	00	01	11	10
00				
01	1			
11				
10				1

reliable). The shaded squares correspond to the words with no errors. The outputs that produce $uvw = 000$ are shown in brown. Squares that do not correspond to correct words or single errors are shown as don't cares on the first three maps, and as 1's on the map for g (which indicates multiple errors). Sum of products expressions for these functions are very complex, requiring 30 product terms. If implemented with NAND gates, 22 integrated circuit packages would be needed.

However, the code has been set up in such a way that the correct outputs can be determined more easily. Computing the Exclusive-OR of each check bit with the bits that formed it, we get

$$t_1 = a \oplus b \oplus d$$
$$t_2 = a \oplus c \oplus e$$
$$t_3 = b \oplus c \oplus f$$

That test word indicates which bit is in error (if a single error was made), as described in Table 5.10.

Table 5.10 Bit error.

t_1	t_2	t_3	Error
0	0	0	none
0	0	1	f
0	1	0	e
0	1	1	c
1	0	0	d
1	0	1	b
1	1	0	a
1	1	1	multiple

The decoder circuit can then be built with three 7486 (quad Exclusive-OR) packages and one three-input/eight-output decoder (such as the one used in Example 5.3), as shown in Figure 5.30.

Figure 5.30 Error decoder.

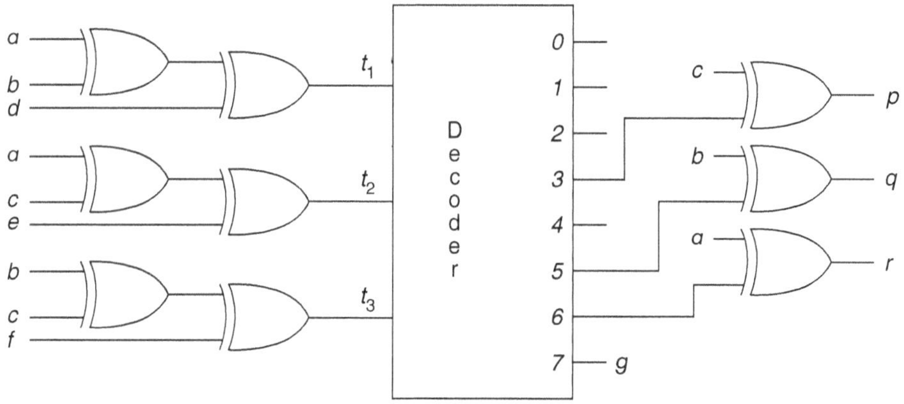

[SP 15, 16, 17, 18; EX 18, 19, 20, 21, 22, 23, 24, 25; LAB]

5.9 SOLVED PROBLEMS

1. For the following circuit

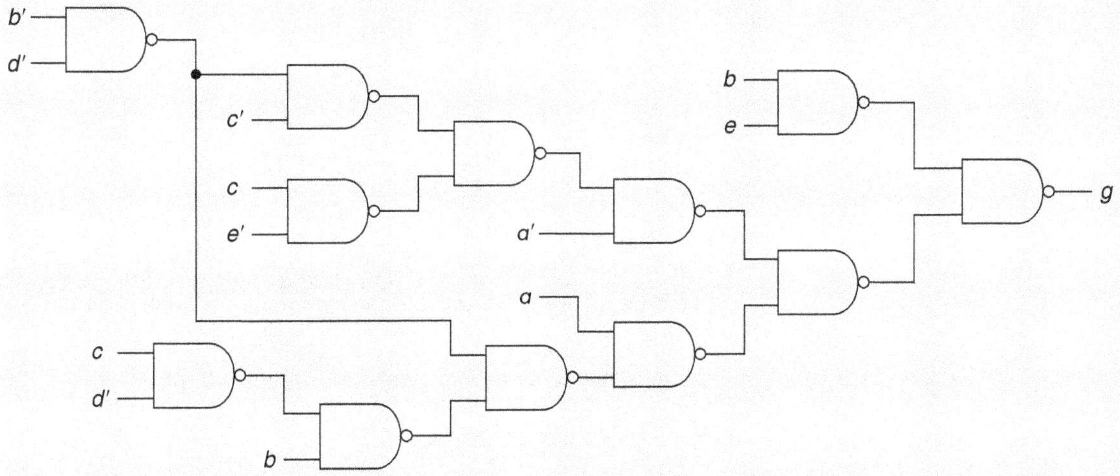

   a. Compute the maximum delay,
      i. Assuming that all inputs are available both uncomplemented and complemented.
      ii. Assuming only uncomplemented inputs are available and an additional gate must be added to complement each input.

   b. Compute the maximum delay from input *a* to the output, assuming that all inputs are available both uncomplemented and complemented.

   a. i. The signal from the gate whose inputs are *b*′ and *d*′ must pass through six gates.
      ii. Both *b* and *d* must be complemented and thus there is a seventh delay.

   b. Signal *a* passes through only three gates.

2. We want to build a NAND gate circuit to compute the parity of an ***n***-bit number. The parity is defined as 1 if and only if there are an odd number of 1's in the number.* One way of doing this is to build the circuit 1 bit at a time (as in the adder), such that the circuit computes the parity after that bit as a function of the

*This is sometimes referred to as odd parity. However, the terminology is used in two different ways. Some use odd parity to mean an odd number of 1's in the word plus the parity bit (which is, of course, the opposite of what we defined). For our purposes, we will stick to the definition above.

parity up to that bit and the one input bit. A block diagram of the first few bits of such a circuit is shown below.

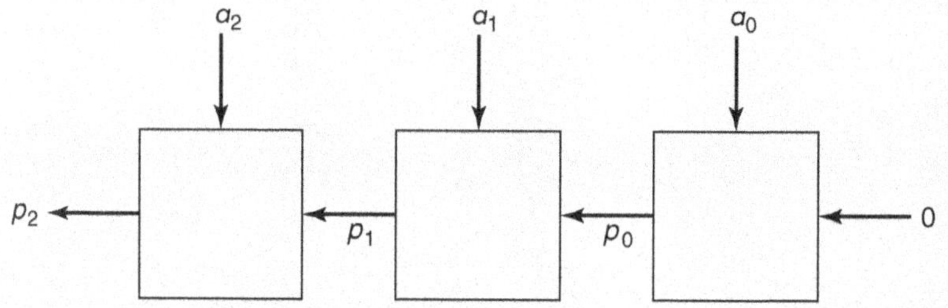

a. Show a NAND gate circuit to implement 1 bit and compute the delay for ***n*** bits. Assume that inputs are available only uncomplemented.

b. Reduce the delay by implementing 2 bits at a time.

a. Each block has a truth table

p_{i-1}	a_i	p_i
0	0	0
0	1	1
1	0	1
1	1	0

that is, the output parity indicates an odd number of 1's so far if the input indicated there were an even number of 1's ($p_{i-1} = 0$) and this bit (a_i) is 1, or if the input indicated there were an odd number of 1's ($p_{i-1} = 1$) and this bit (a_i) is 0. The logic expression is

$$p_i = p'_{i-1}a_i + p_{i-1}a'_i$$

This requires a three-level NAND circuit; it is just an Exclusive-OR, as shown here

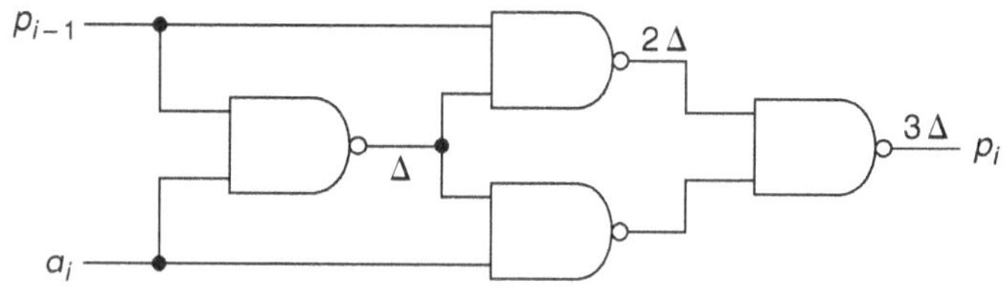

The delay from either input to the output is 3Δ. If we had an ***n***-bit number, the total delay would then be $3n\Delta$.

b. We can build a block that computes 2 bits of parity at a time. We will call the inputs a, b, and p_{in} and the output p_{out}. The truth table is thus*

a	b	p_{in}	p_{out}
0	0	0	0
0	0	1	1
0	1	0	1
0	1	1	0
1	0	0	1
1	0	1	0
1	1	0	0
1	1	1	1

The equation for p_{out} is thus

$$p_{out} = a'b'p_{in} + a'bp'_{in} + ab'p'_{in} + abp_{in}$$

and the NAND circuit is

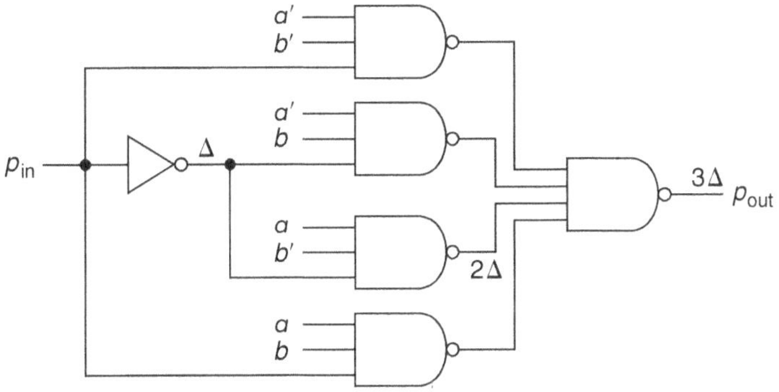

where the NOT gate required for p_{in} is shown (but not those for a and b). The total delay for the 2 bits is 3Δ and thus the n-bit delay is 1.5 nΔ. We could reduce the delay by building a separate circuit for p'_{out} in each box. It would also require five NAND gates, since

$$p'_{out} = a'b'p'_{in} + a'bp_{in} + ab'p_{in} + abp'_{in}$$

However, now we do not need the NOT gate for the parity input, and, thus, these circuits are all two-level. The delay per two bits is 2Δ, and the total delay for n bits is nΔ.

3. Design a full subtractor, that is, a circuit that computes $a - b - c$, where c is the borrow from the next less significant digit and produces a difference, d, and a borrow from the next more significant bit, p.

*Notice that this is the same truth table as the sum in a full adder if we replace p_{in} by c_{in}.

The truth table for the full subtractor is as follows:

a	b	c	p	d
0	0	0	0	0
0	0	1	1	1
0	1	0	1	1
0	1	1	1	0
1	0	0	0	1
1	0	1	0	0
1	1	0	0	0
1	1	1	1	1

Note that the difference bit is the same as the sum bit for the adder. The borrow is 1 if there are more 1's in b and c than in a. Thus, the equations become

$$d = a'b'c + a'bc' + ab'c' + abc$$
$$p = bc + a'c + a'b$$

The eight-NAND gate circuit used for the adder could be used for d. However, the p circuit would be different from c_{out}.

$$p = bc + a'c + a'b = c(b + a') + a'b = c(a' \oplus b) + a'b$$
$$= c(a \oplus b)' + a'b$$

This would require two NAND gates and two NOT gates for the borrow (in addition to the eight NAND gates for the difference). The timing would be the same as for the adder, except that the first borrow out delay would now be 6Δ (an increase of 1).

If we wish to use the minimum number of gates, we would need to factor a from both functions, rather than c, producing the equation

$$p = a'(b \oplus c) + bc$$

An extra NAND and a NOT is needed (compared with the adder). One solution would be

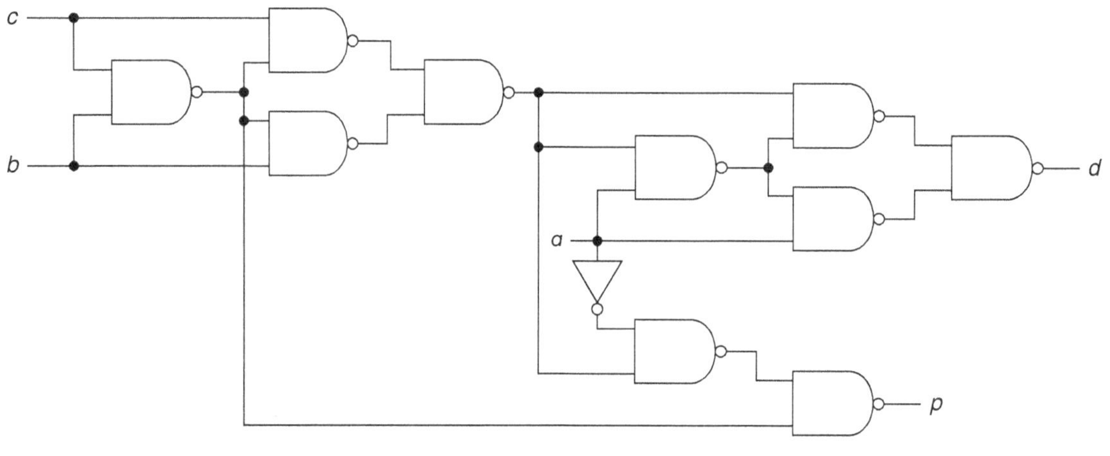

The disadvantage of this approach is that the delay from borrow in to borrow out is 5Δ.

4. We have two 4-bit comparators that produce greater than (>), equal (=), and less than (<) outputs. Show the external logic that can be used to cascade them.

The output indicates equal if both comparators show equal. It is greater than if the high-order one is greater than or if it is equal and the low-order one is greater than. Finally, it shows less than if the high-order one shows less than or if the high-order one is equal and the low-order one is less than. (This is how the internal logic of the 7485 works, although the details of the circuit are quite different.)

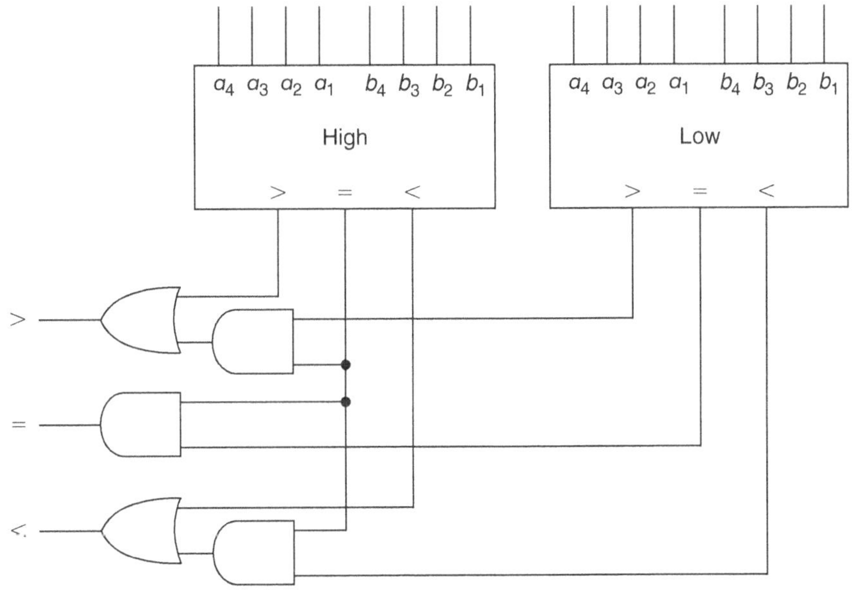

5. We have a decoder with three inputs, a, b, and c, and eight active low outputs, labeled 0 through 7. In addition, there is an active low enable input EN'. We wish to implement the following function using the decoder and as few NAND gates as possible. Show a block diagram.

$$f(a, b, c, e) = \Sigma m(1, 3, 7, 9, 15)$$

Note that all of the minterms are odd; thus, variable e is 1 for each of these. If we enable the decoder when $e = 1$, that is, connect e' to the enable input, and connect a, b, and c to the control inputs, the outputs of the decoder will correspond to minterms 1, 3, 5, 7, 9, 11, 13, and 15. Thus, the following circuit solves the problem:

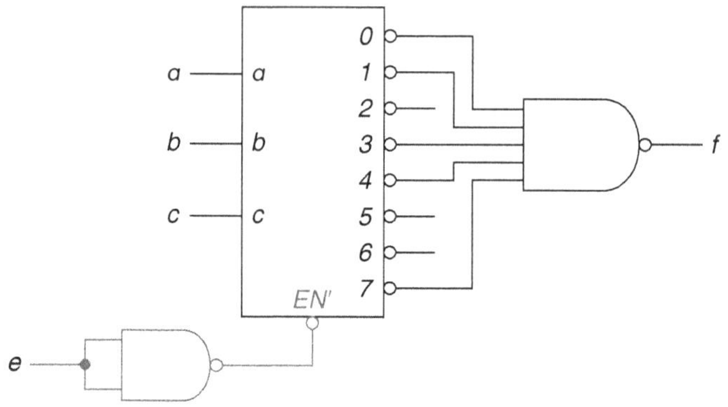

6. We wish to build a 32-way active high decoder, using only the four-way decoders shown here.

EN	*a*	*b*	*0*	*1*	*2*	*3*
0	X	X	0	0	0	0
1	0	0	1	0	0	0
1	0	1	0	1	0	0
1	1	0	0	0	1	0
1	1	1	0	0	0	1

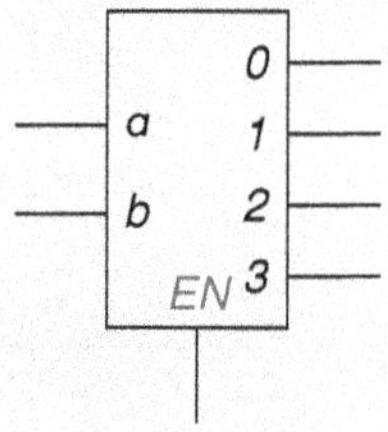

The inputs are *v*, *w*, *x*, *y*, and *z*; the outputs are numbered 0 to 31.

We need eight of these decoders at the output. Each is enabled based on the first 3 bits of the input. Thus, we need an eight-way decoder for the enabling. That must be built in two levels, as shown in the following diagram.

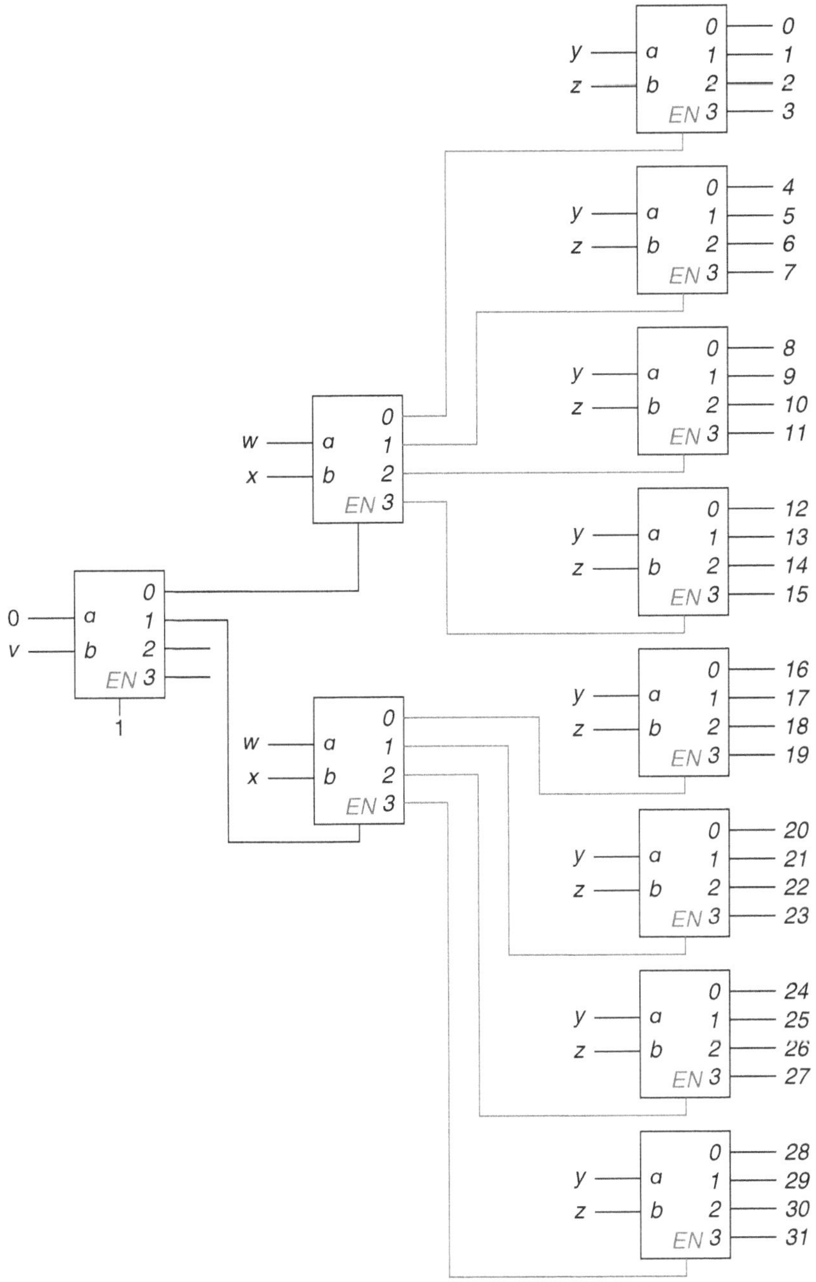

7. Professor Smith computes grades as follows: He uses only the first digit (that is, 9 for averages between 90 and 99). He never has an average of 100. He gives a P (pass) to anyone with an average of 60 or above and an F to anyone with an average below 60. That first digit is coded in 8421 code (that is, straight binary, 5 as 0101, for example); these are inputs w, x, y, and z.

Design a circuit using up to two of the decoders with active high outputs and an active low enable shown below, one NOT gate, and one OR gate to produce an output of 1 iff the student passes.

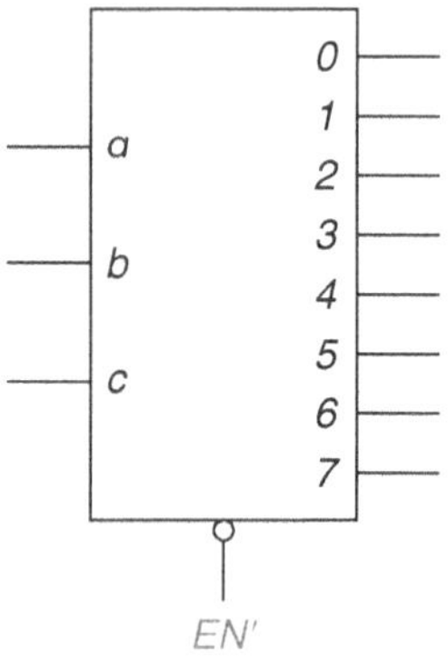

EN'	a	b	c	0	1	2	3	4	5	6	7
1	X	X	X	0	0	0	0	0	0	0	0
0	0	0	0	1	0	0	0	0	0	0	0
0	0	0	1	0	1	0	0	0	0	0	0
0	0	1	0	0	0	1	0	0	0	0	0
0	0	1	1	0	0	0	1	0	0	0	0
0	1	0	0	0	0	0	0	1	0	0	0
0	1	0	1	0	0	0	0	0	1	0	0
0	1	1	0	0	0	0	0	0	0	1	0
0	1	1	1	0	0	0	0	0	0	0	1

This problem has two solutions. The more straightforward one uses two decoders, where one is enabled when $w = 0$ and has outputs corresponding to minterms 0 to 7 and the other is enabled when $w = 1$ and has outputs corresponding to minterms 8 to 15 (although only 8 and 9 ever occur). The output is 1 for minterms 6, 7, 8, and 9.

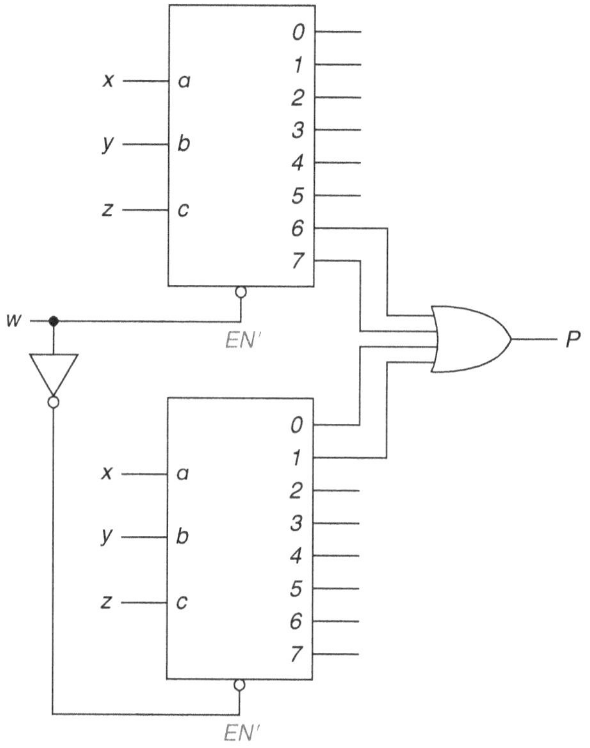

Another approach is to recognize that the only inputs that will lead to $P = 0$ are minterms 0, 1, 2, 3, 4, and 5. Thus, we can use just one decoder and the following circuit:

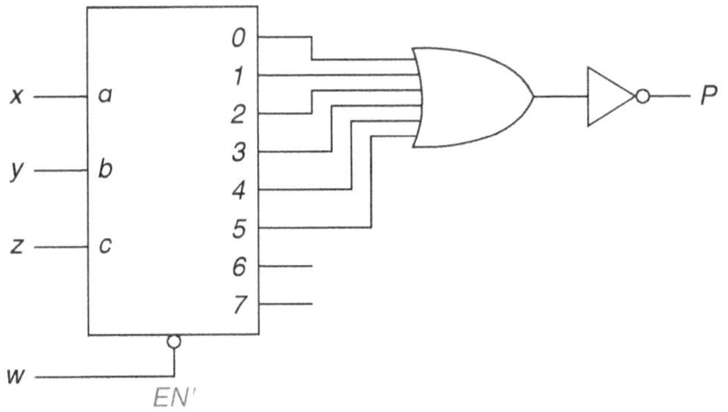

In this case, we OR together the first six outputs of the decoder, which produces a 1 for grades between 0 and 59 (and a 0 for passing grades).We then complement it to get the desired output.

8. For the following functions, implement them only using as many of the decoders shown below as needed and three OR gates (with as many inputs as necessary). If possible, limit the OR gates to less than eight inputs and use only four decoders.

yz \ wx	00	01	11	10
00	1			1
01	1			1
11	1	1		1
10	1			

f

yz \ wx	00	01	11	10
00	1	1		1
01		1		1
11		1		
10	1	1		1

g

yz \ wx	00	01	11	10
00	1		1	1
01			1	
11		1	1	1
10	1		1	1

h

EN	*a*	*b*	*0*	*1*	*2*	*3*
0	X	X	0	0	0	0
1	0	0	1	0	0	0
1	0	1	0	1	0	0
1	1	0	0	0	1	0
1	1	1	0	0	0	1

Since each function has a column of all 1's, we can save OR gate inputs by using the first two variables on the first decoder, the one that enables the others. Also, since the 11 column has either all 0's or all 1's, we do not need the 11 decoder. Thus, the circuit becomes

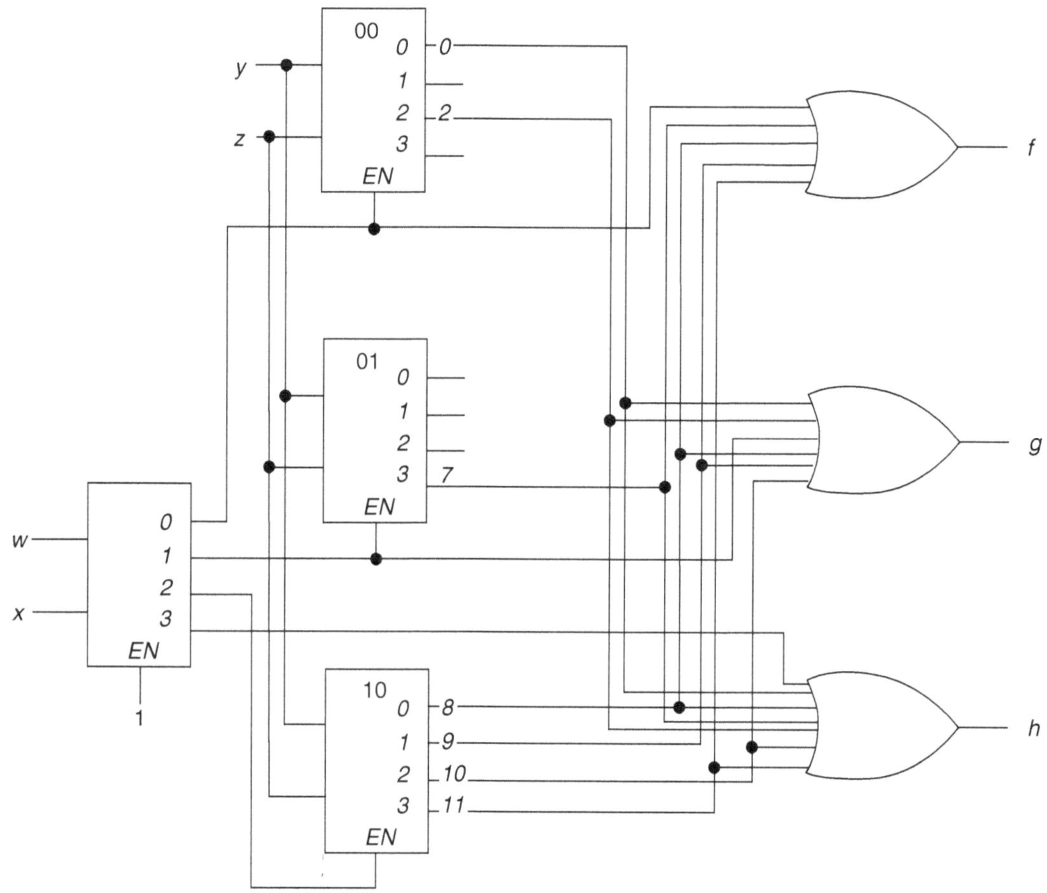

9. Design a priority encoder with four active high inputs *0*, *1*, *2*, and *3* and three active high outputs, *A* and *B*, indicating the number of the highest priority device requesting service, and *N*, indicating no active requests. Input *0* is the highest priority (and *3* the lowest).

0	*1*	*2*	*3*	*A*	*B*	*N*
0	0	0	0	X	X	1
1	X	X	X	0	0	0
0	1	X	X	0	1	0
0	0	1	X	1	0	0
0	0	0	1	1	1	0

N is clearly just

$$N = 0'\ 1'\ 2'\ 3'$$

We can map A and B to obtain

23 \ 01	00	01	11	10
00	X			
01	1			
11	1			
10	1			

A

23 \ 01	00	01	11	10
00	X	1		
01	1	1		
11		1		
10		1		

B

$A = 0'\ 1'$

$B = 0'\ 1 + 0'\ 2'$

10. We have four 3-bit numbers: $w_2 - w_0$, $x_2 - x_0$, $y_2 - y_0$, and $z_2 - z_0$. We want to select one of these, based on the input s and t (where $st = 00$ selects w, $st = 01$ selects x, and so forth). The answer is to appear on output lines $f_2 - f_0$. Use the 74153 multiplexer chip to do this.

The 74153 contains two 4-way multiplexers. Since we need three, we will use two such circuits as shown below. Note that one-half of the second 74153 is unused.

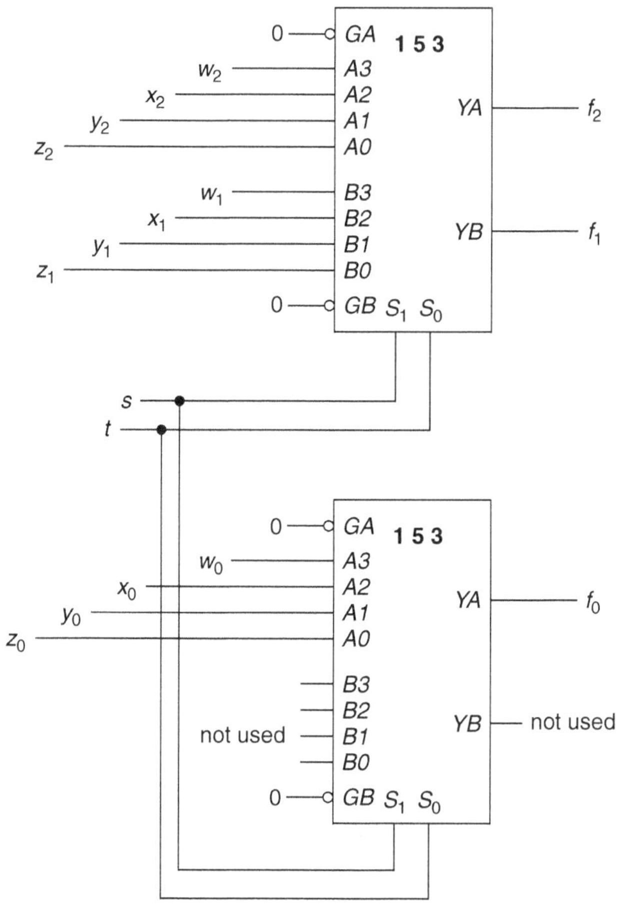

11. Create an eight-way multiplexer using some of the 2-way multiplexers of Figure 5.11.

We build two 4-way multiplexers as in Figure 5.12b and use a third layer of multiplexer to switch those two outputs. Assume S_2 is the high-order select bit.

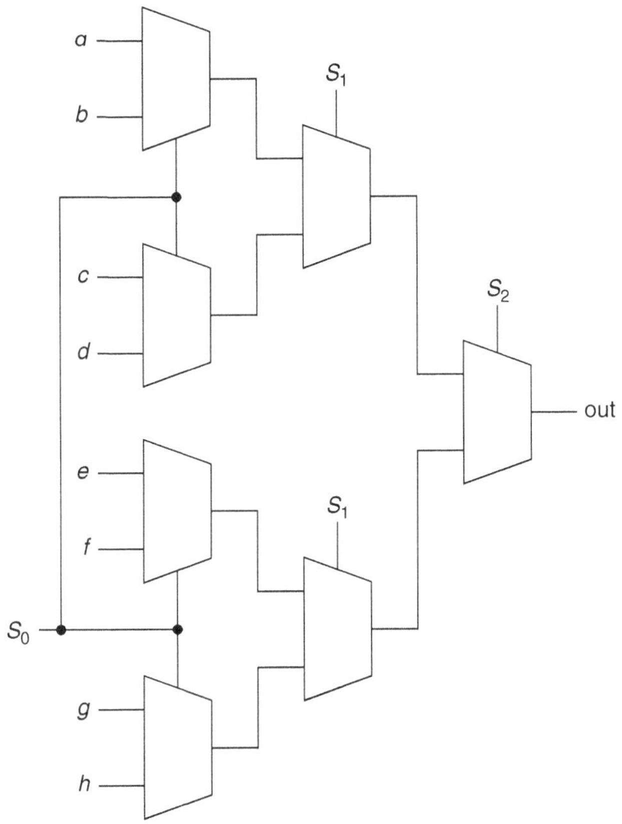

12. Implement the function

$f(w, x, y, z) = \Sigma m(0, 1, 5, 7, 8, 10, 13, 14, 15)$

a. Using two 8-way multiplexers with an active low enable, plus an OR gate

b. Using one 8-way multiplexer

a. We will enable the first multiplexer if $w = 0$ and the second if $w = 1$. Thus, the inputs to the first correspond to the first eight minterms, and those to the second correspond to the second eight.

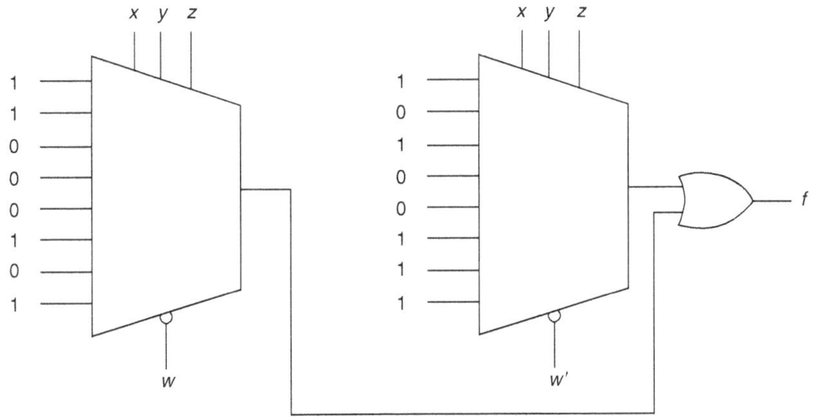

b. We can construct an 8-line truth table with columns for w' and w. Finally, we add a column that is a function of w.

	f		f
$x\,y\,z$	$w = 0$	$w = 1$	
0 0 0	1	1	1
0 0 1	1	0	w'
0 1 0	0	1	w
0 1 1	0	0	0
1 0 0	0	0	0
1 0 1	1	1	1
1 1 0	0	1	w
1 1 1	1	1	1

That produces the circuit (with no need for an enable):

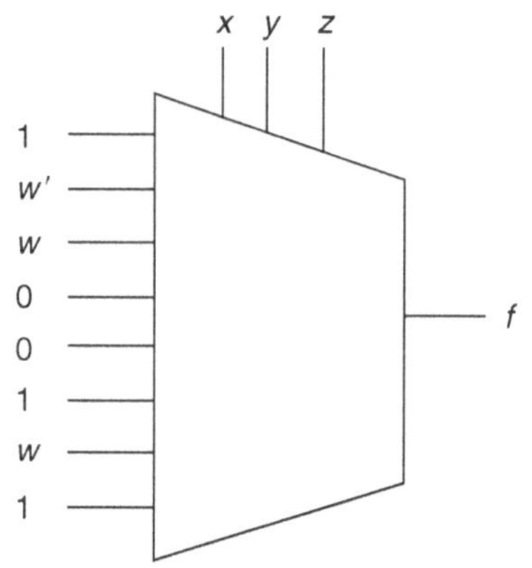

13. For the three functions of four variables shown on the maps below,

a. Implement it with the ROM.

b. Find a minimum cost two-level NAND circuit (where minimum cost is minimum number of gates, and among those with the same number of gates, minimum number of gate inputs). Assume all inputs are available both complemented and uncomplemented. (Minimum is 10 gates.)

c. Implement with a PAL similar to the one in the text.

d. Implement it with the PLA with eight product terms available (less may be used).

CD \ AB	00	01	11	10
00				1
01	1	1		1
11	1	1		1
10				

X

CD \ AB	00	01	11	10
00	1	1	1	1
01		1		
11		1		1
10	1			1

Y

CD \ AB	00	01	11	10
00			1	
01	1	1	1	
11	1	1	1	
10	1		1	1

Z

a. For the ROM, we need a list of minterms, namely,

$$X(A, B, C, D) = \Sigma m(1, 3, 5, 7, 8, 9, 11)$$
$$Y(A, B, C, D) = \Sigma m(0, 2, 4, 5, 7, 8, 10, 11, 12)$$
$$Z(A, B, C, D) = \Sigma m(1, 2, 3, 5, 7, 10, 12, 13, 14, 15)$$

We can then complete the ROM diagram below.

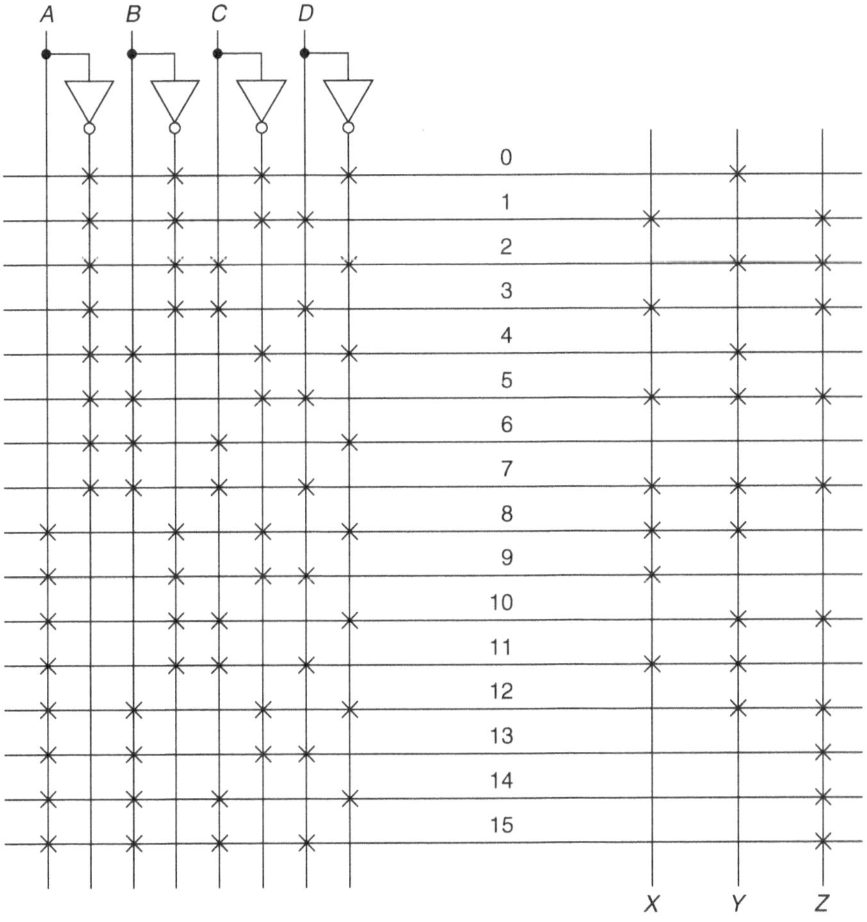

b. The maps below show the minimum cost two-level solution.

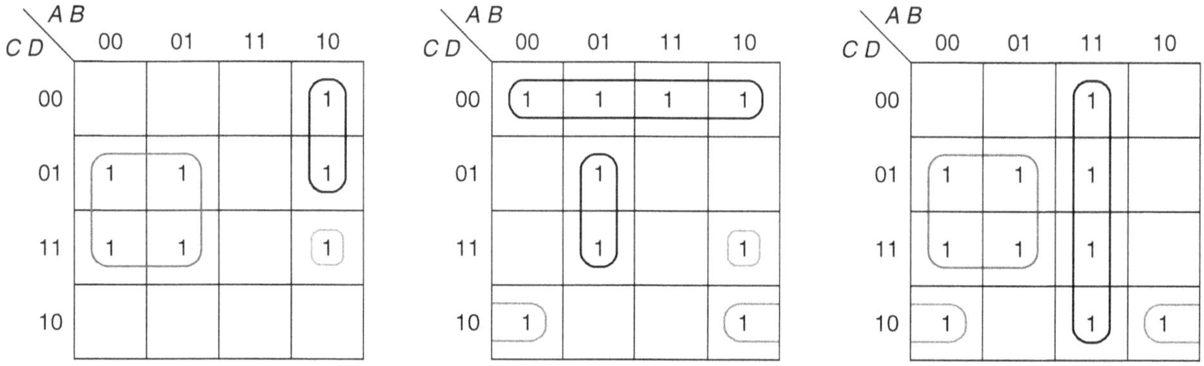

where the terms circled in brown and gray are shared. The resulting equations are

$$X = A'D + AB'C' + AB'CD$$
$$Y = C'D' + A'BD + B'CD' + AB'CD$$
$$Z = A'D + AB + B'CD'$$

The resulting circuit is

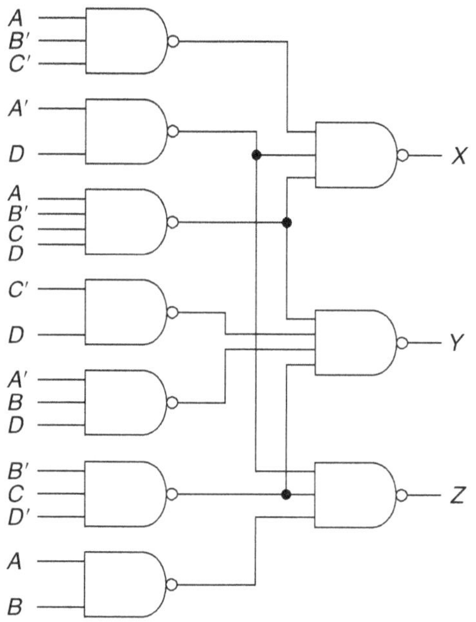

c. For the PAL, nothing is gained by treating this as a multiple output problem. Thus, the equations we get solving each function individually are implemented.

$$X = B'D + A'D + AB'C'$$
$$Y = C'D' + B'D' + A'BD + AB'C$$
$$Z = AB + A'D + B'CD'$$

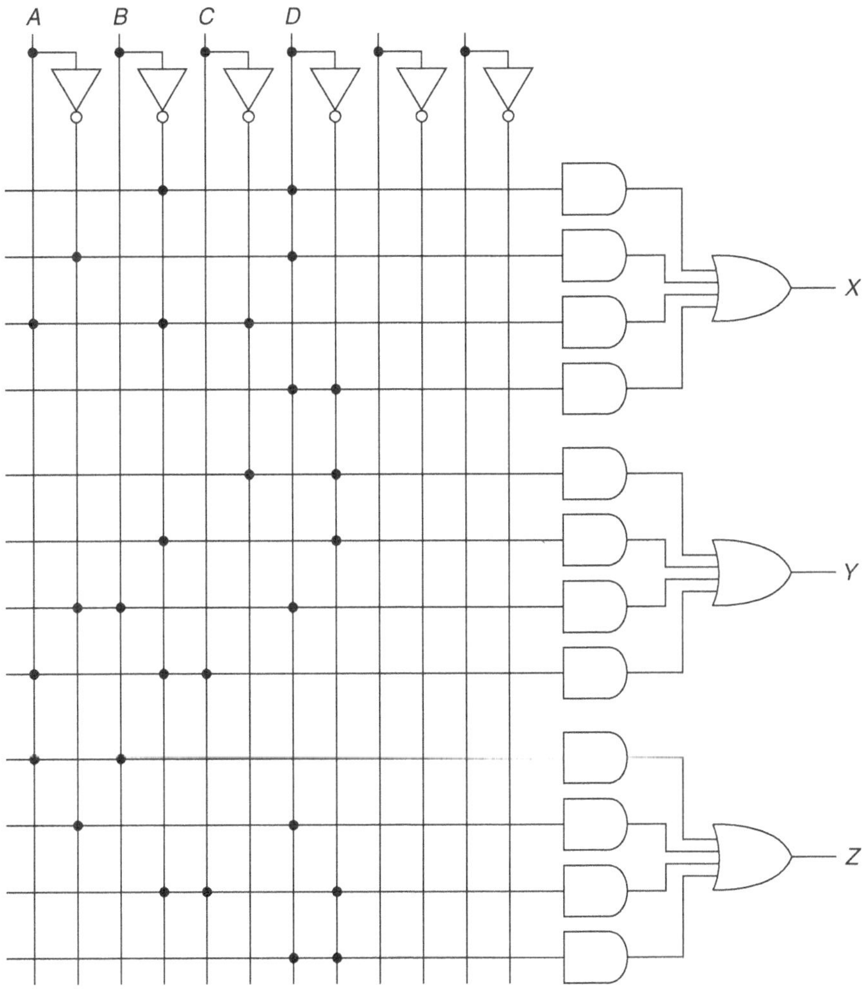

Two of the inputs are not used; the fourth output is not shown. AND gates that are not used have D and D' connected to their inputs to produce a 0 output.

d. For the PLA, we also need sum of products expressions, but are limited to eight terms. The solution used for part c uses nine terms. We could use $B'CD'$ (which is required for Z) in place of $B'D'$ in Y, or we could use the solution to part b; that solution is shown on the next page.

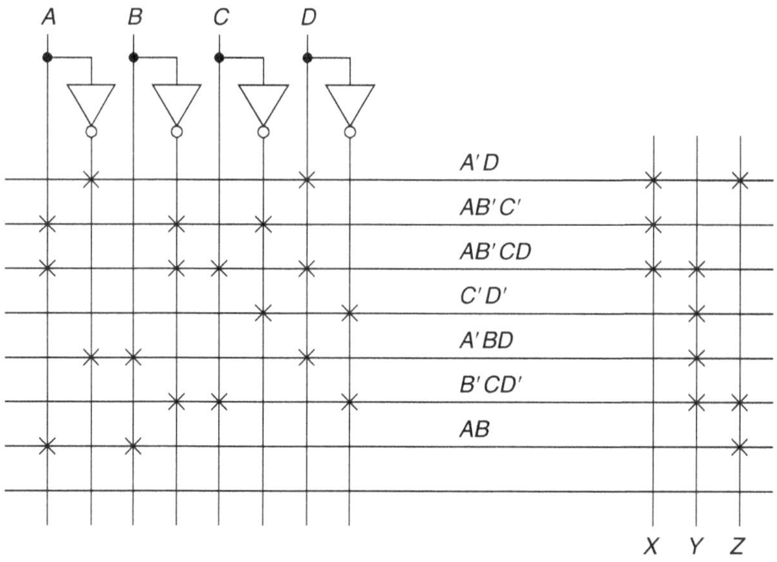

14. We have found a minimum sum of products expression for each of two functions, F and G, minimizing them individually (no sharing):

$$F = WY' + XY'Z$$
$$G = WX'Y' + X'Z + W'Y'Z$$

a. Implement them with a ROM.

b. Implement them with a PLA using no more than four terms.

c. For the same functions, we have available as many of the decoders described below as we need plus 2 eight-input OR gates. Show a block diagram for this implementation. All inputs are available both uncomplemented and complemented.

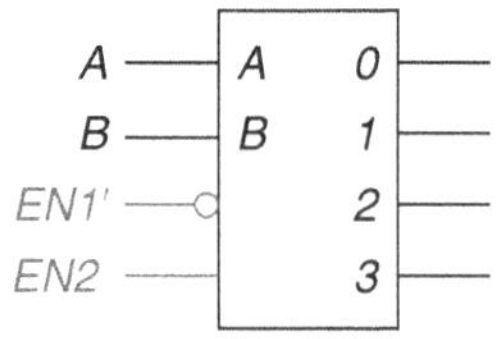

EN1'	*EN2*	*A*	*B*	*0*	*1*	*2*	*3*
X	0	X	X	0	0	0	0
1	X	X	X	0	0	0	0
0	1	0	0	1	0	0	0
0	1	0	1	0	1	0	0
0	1	1	0	0	0	1	0
0	1	1	1	0	0	0	1

Note that this chip is enabled only when $EN1' = 0$ and $EN2 = 1$.

a. The first step is to find the minterm numbers. Since we will need to map the functions for part b, that is the easiest thing to do now. (We could, of course, expand the functions algebraically to sum of minterm form.)

YZ \ WX	00	01	11	10
00			1	1
01		1	1	1
11				
10				

F

YZ \ WX	00	01	11	10
00				1
01	1	1		1
11	1			1
10				

G

From this, we get

$$F(W, X, Y, Z) = \Sigma m(5, 8, 9, 12, 13)$$
$$G(W, X, Y, Z) = \Sigma m(1, 3, 5, 8, 9, 11)$$

This produces the following ROM diagram:

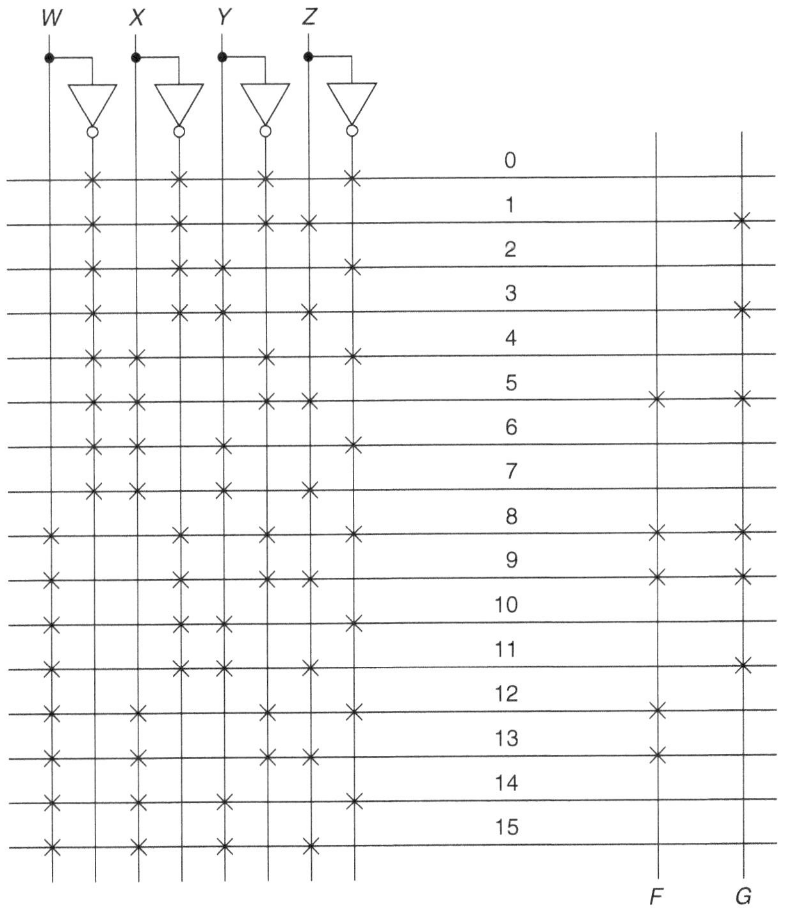

b. For the PLA, we need to find a sum of products solution that uses only four different terms. The maps below show such a solution.

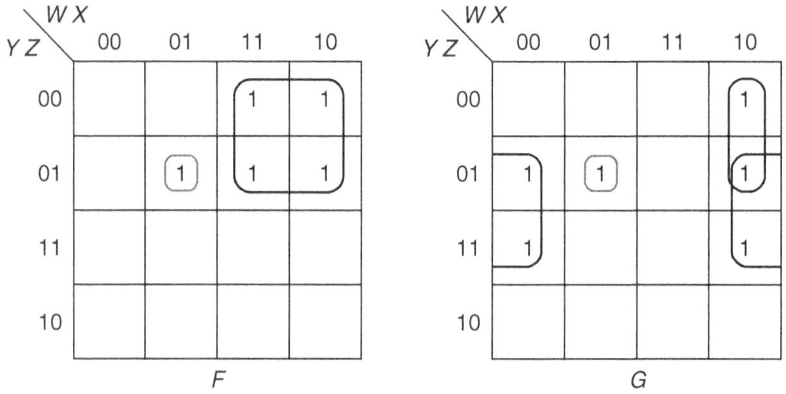

$F = WY' + W'XY'Z$
$G = X'Z + WX'Y' + W'XY'Z$

The PLA below implements this four-term solution.

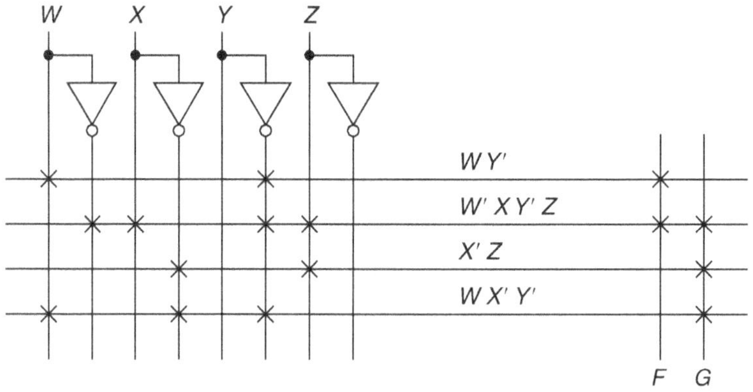

c. The straightforward approach is to use *W* and *X* to enable each of four decoders. However, looking at the maps, we see that the last row of each map contains no 1's. If we use *Y* and *Z* to enable the decoders, we only need three, enabled on 00,

01, and 11. The first decoder has active outputs for all of the minterms that end in 00, that is, 0, 4, 8, and 12. The circuit then becomes

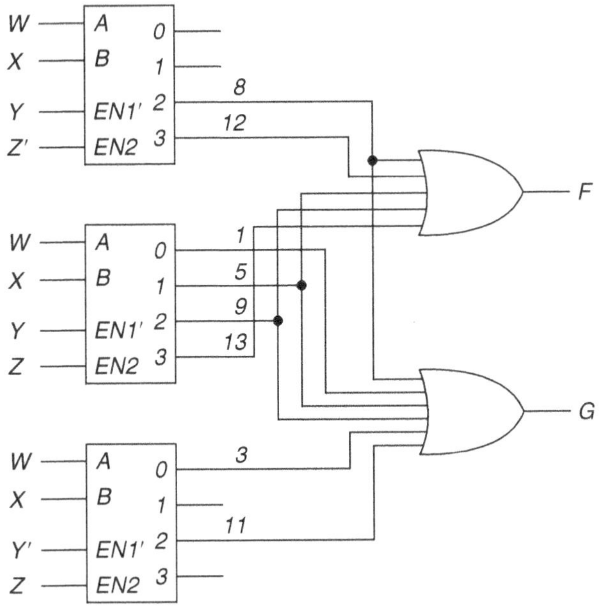

15. Design a 1-bit decimal adder, where decimal digits are stored in excess 3 code.

When you add the two codes using a binary adder, the carry is always correct. The sum must be corrected by adding +3 if there is no carry or −3 if there is a carry.

	0011	0		1010	7
	<u>0100</u>	<u>1</u>		<u>1001</u>	<u>6</u>
0	0111		1	0011	
−3	<u>1101</u>		+3	<u>0011</u>	
(1)	0100	1		0110	13

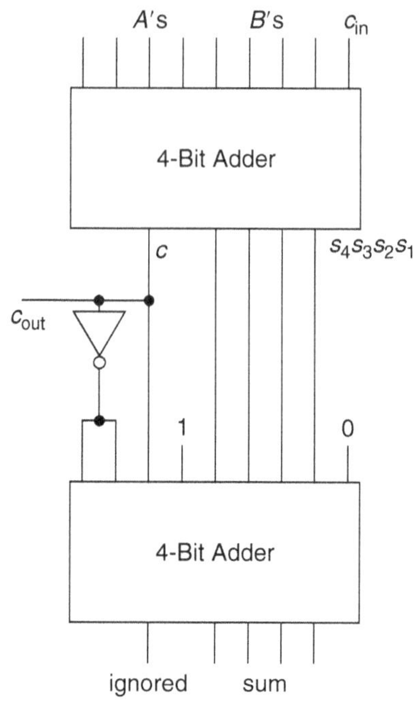

16. We have two different codes for the decimal digits that we sometimes use—the excess 3 code and the 2 of 5 code, shown below.

Digit	*Excess 3* *wxyz*	*2 of 5* *abcde*
0	0011	11000
1	0100	10100
2	0101	10010
3	0110	10001
4	0111	01100
5	1000	01010
6	1001	01001
7	1010	00110
8	1011	00101
9	1100	00011

All other combinations of input bits never occur. We wish to build a box that converts excess 3 code to 2 of 5 code. It thus has four inputs—*w*, *x*, *y*, and *z*—and has five outputs—*a*, *b*, *c*, *d*, and *e*. All inputs are available both complemented and uncomplemented.

a. Map each of the five functions and find all minimum sum of products and product of sums solutions for each of the five functions individually.

b. Our building blocks consist of integrated circuit chips. We can buy any of the following chips:

7404:	6 inverters		
7400:	4 two-input NAND gates	7402:	4 two-input NOR gates
7410:	3 three-input NAND gates	7427:	3 three-input NOR gates
7420:	2 four-input NAND gates	7425:	2 four-input NOR gates

All chips cost the same, 25¢ each.

Find one of the least expensive ($1.25) implementations of the five outputs. (The gates on any chip may be used as part of the implementation of more than one of the outputs.) Show the algebraic expression and the block diagram for the solution.

c. Find three solutions, one of which uses only 7400 and 7410 packages, one of which uses 7420s also (it must use at least one four-input gate), and a solution that uses only NOR gates. Each of these must cost no more than $1.25. (Of course, one of these is the solution to part b.)

d. Implement this with a ROM.

e. Implement this with a PLA.

a. The maps of the five functions and their complements are shown next.

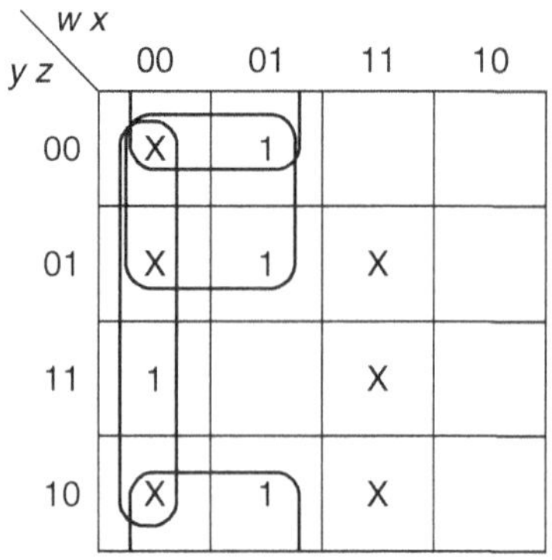

$a = w'x' + w'y' + w'z'$

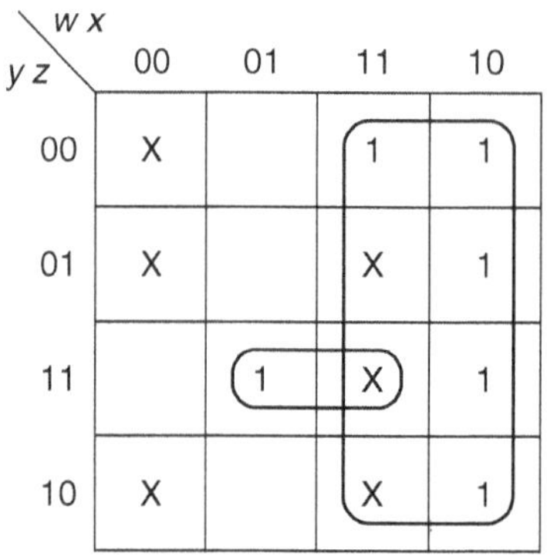

$a' = w + xyz$

$a = w'(x' + y' + z')$

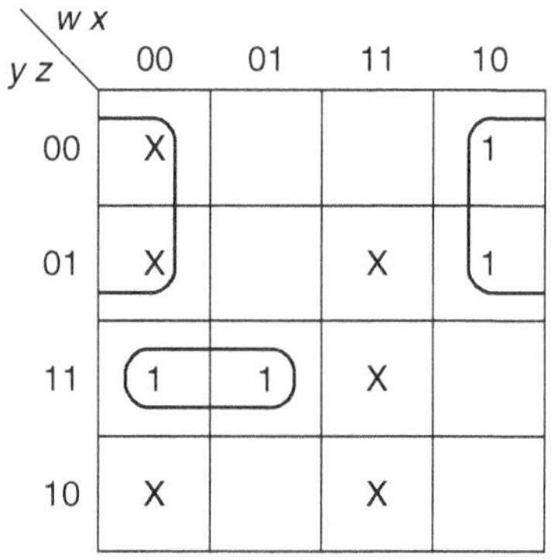

$b = x'y' + w'yz$

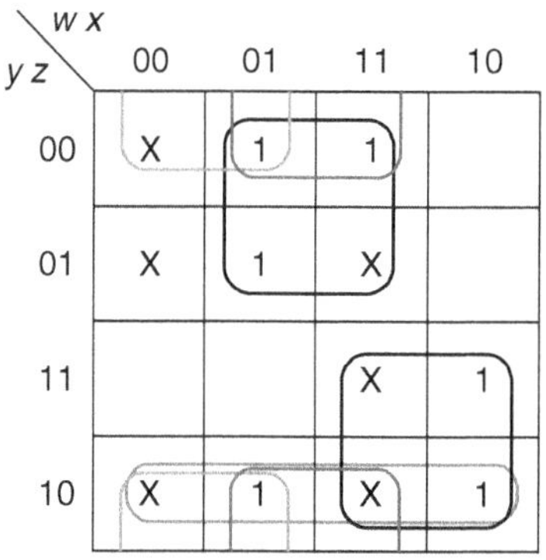

$$b' = wy + xy' + \left\{\begin{matrix} xz' \\ w'z' \\ yz' \end{matrix}\right\}$$

$$b = (w' + y')(x' + y)\left\{\begin{matrix} (x' + z) \\ (w + z) \\ (y' + z) \end{matrix}\right\}$$

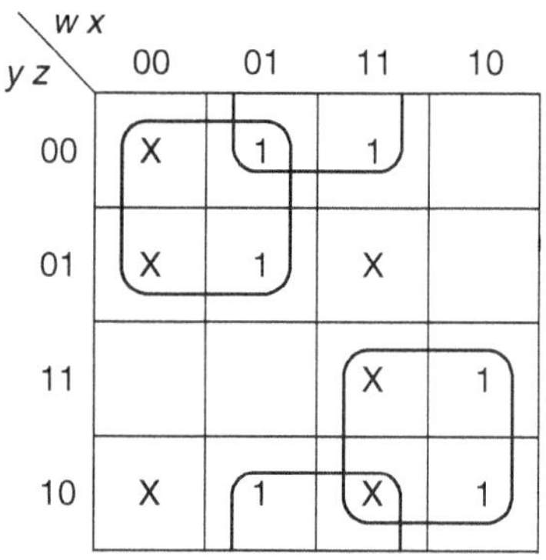

$b' = wy + xz' + w'y'$

$b = (w' + y')(x' + z)(w + y)$

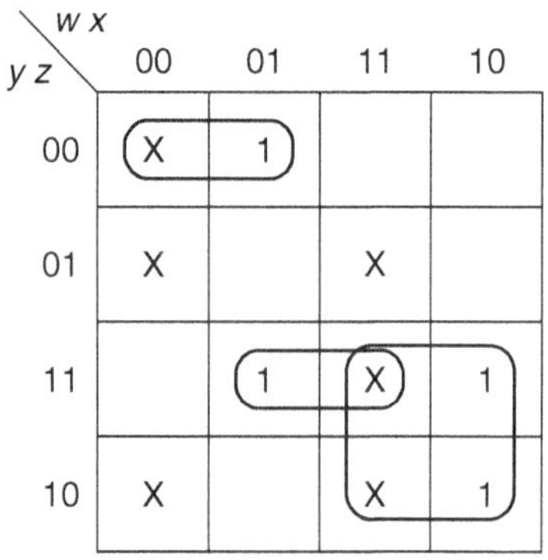

$c = w'y'z' + xyz + wy$

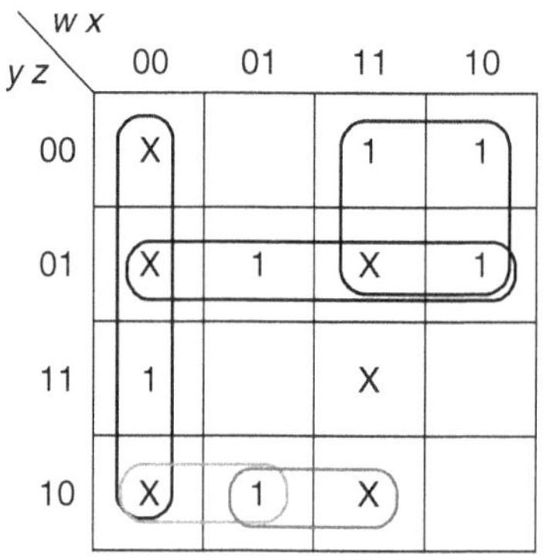

$$c' = w'x' + wy' + y'z + \left\{\begin{matrix} xyz' \\ w'yz' \end{matrix}\right\}$$

$$c = (w + x)(w' + y)(y + z')\left\{\begin{matrix} (x' + y' + z) \\ (w + y' + z) \end{matrix}\right\}$$

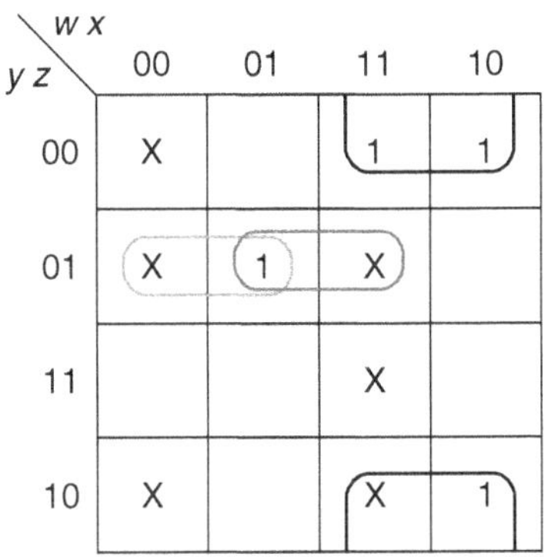

$$d = wz' + \left\{\begin{matrix} xy'z \\ w'y'z \end{matrix}\right\}$$

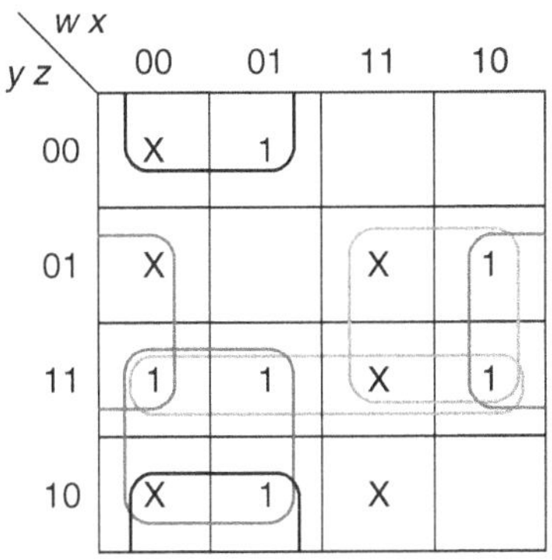

$$d' = w'z' + \left\{\begin{matrix} x'z \\ wz \end{matrix}\right\} + \left\{\begin{matrix} w'y \\ yz \end{matrix}\right\}$$

$$d = (w + z) \left\{\begin{matrix} (x + z') \\ (w' + z') \end{matrix}\right\} \left\{\begin{matrix} (w + y') \\ (y' + z') \end{matrix}\right\}$$

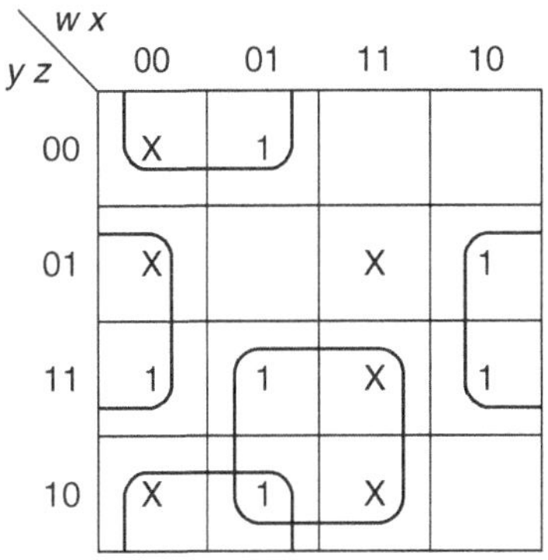

$$d' = w'z' + x'z + xy$$
$$d = (w + z)(x + z')(x' + y')$$

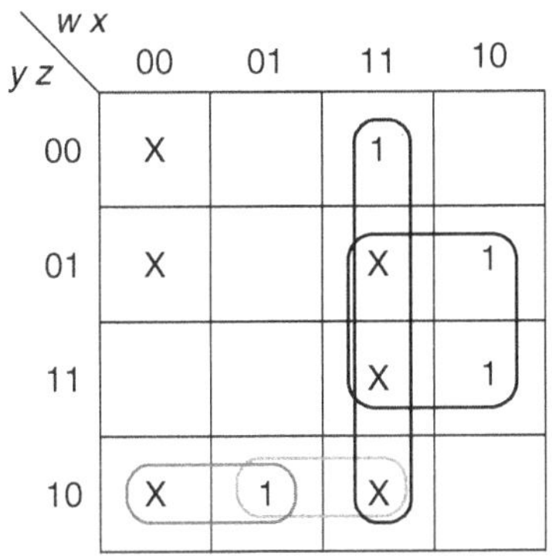

$$e = wz + wx + \left\{\begin{matrix} w'yz' \\ xyz' \end{matrix}\right\}$$

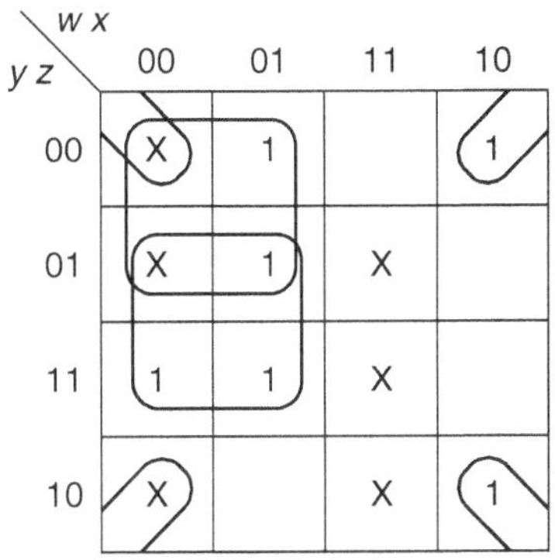

$$e' = x'z' + w'y' + w'z$$
$$e = (x + z)(w + y)(w + z')$$

Note that there are two SOP solutions for d and e, and that there are four POS solutions for b, two for c, and five for d.

b. If we were to use the solutions that we found in part a, there are no common product terms and thus no sharing is possible in the NAND gate implementation. We would need 10 two-input gates and 8 three-input gates, for a total of three 7400s and three 7410s (at a total cost of $1.50). For the NOR gate solution, we would use the product of sums. There is only one term that can be shared, $w + y$, in b and e. There would be a total of 1 four-input gate, 5 three-input gates, and 12 two-input gates, once again requiring six integrated circuit packages.

We must then attempt to do sharing. The following maps show that for the sum of product solutions.

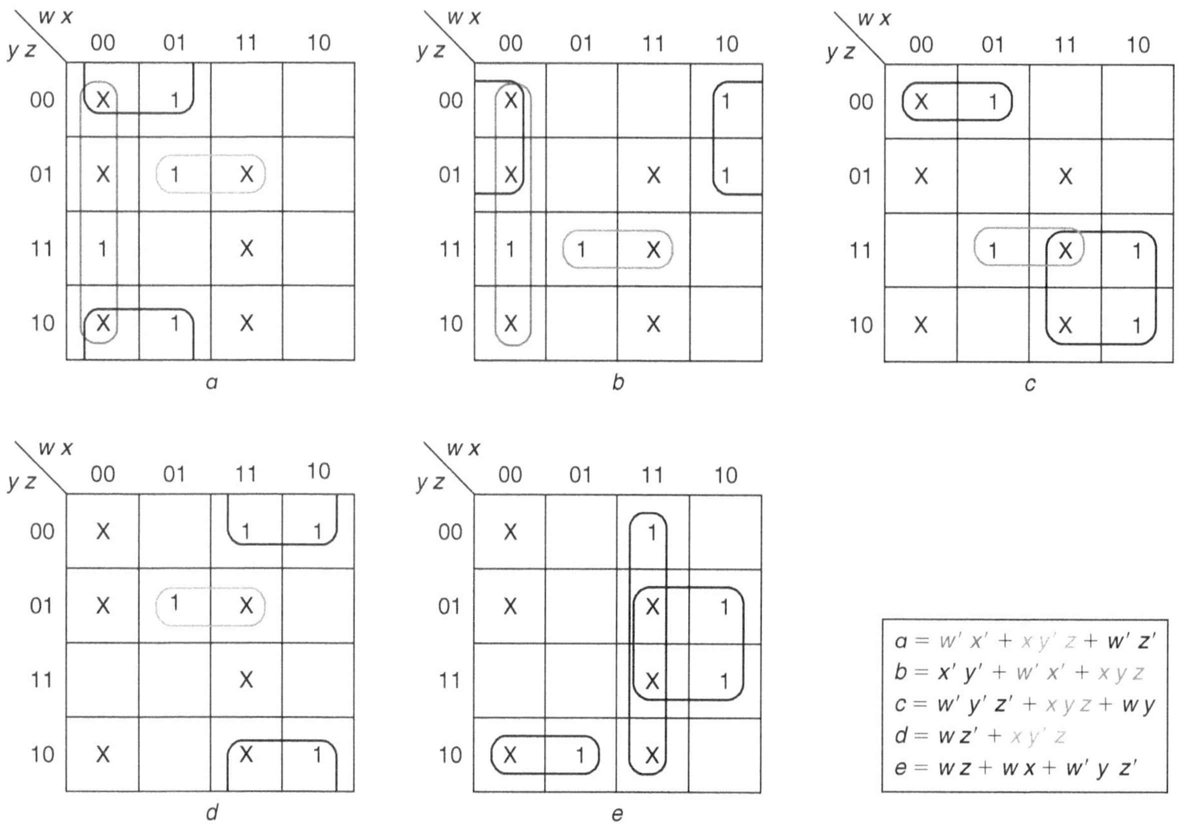

$a = w'x' + xy'z + w'z'$
$b = x'y' + w'x' + xyz$
$c = w'y'z' + xyz + wy$
$d = wz' + xy'z$
$e = wz + wx + w'yz'$

In this solution, three terms have been shared (as indicated by the colored circling and terms). There are some other choices ($w'y'z$ in place of $xy'z$ in a and d, and xyz' in place of $w'yz'$ in e), but they would not alter the gate count. This solution requires 8 two-input gates and 8 three-input gates and utilizes two 7400s and three 7410s (total cost $1.25).

c. The solution to part b could be used as one of the three solutions to part c, and any of those shown here could have been used for part b. A solution that requires one less new product term is

$$a = w'x' + xy'z + w'y'z' + w'yz'$$

where the last two terms are required for (and shared with) c and e, respectively. This saves 1 two-input gate, but replaces a three-input gate with a four-input one (all in the implementation of a). This solution requires 1 four-input gate and 7 each of three-input and two-input gates. It utilizes one 7420, two 7430s (using the extra four-input gate for the seventh three-input one) and two 7400s (total cost \$1.25).

There is also a solution using NOR gates, based on the product of sums solutions. The maps of the complements below produce one solution that almost works:

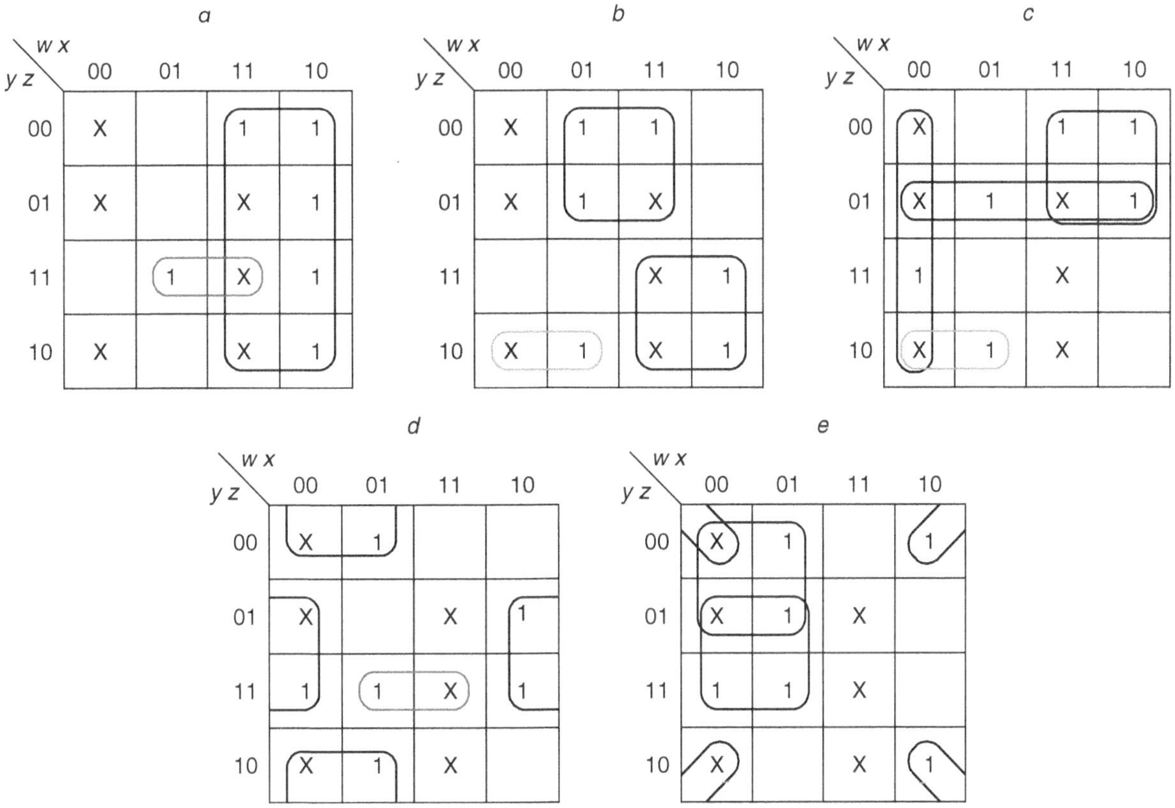

$a = w'(x' + y' + z')$

$b = (x' + y)(w' + y')(w + y' + z)$

$c = (w + x)(w' + y)(y + z')(w + y' + z)$

$d = (w + z)(x + z')(x' + y' + z')$

$e = (x + z)(w + y)(w + z')$

This solution requires 1 four-input gate, 5 three-input gates, and 11 two-input gates (utilizing six packages).

However, if we do not restrict ourselves to two-level solutions, we could eliminate the four-input gate, by rewriting c as

$c = (w + x)(y + w'z')(w + y' + z)$

Now, the gate count becomes 6 three-input gates and 10* two-input gates (utilizing five packages). (Similar manipulation could be done on *e*, replacing a three-input gate by a two-input one, but that would not change the package count.) A block diagram of the circuit is shown below.

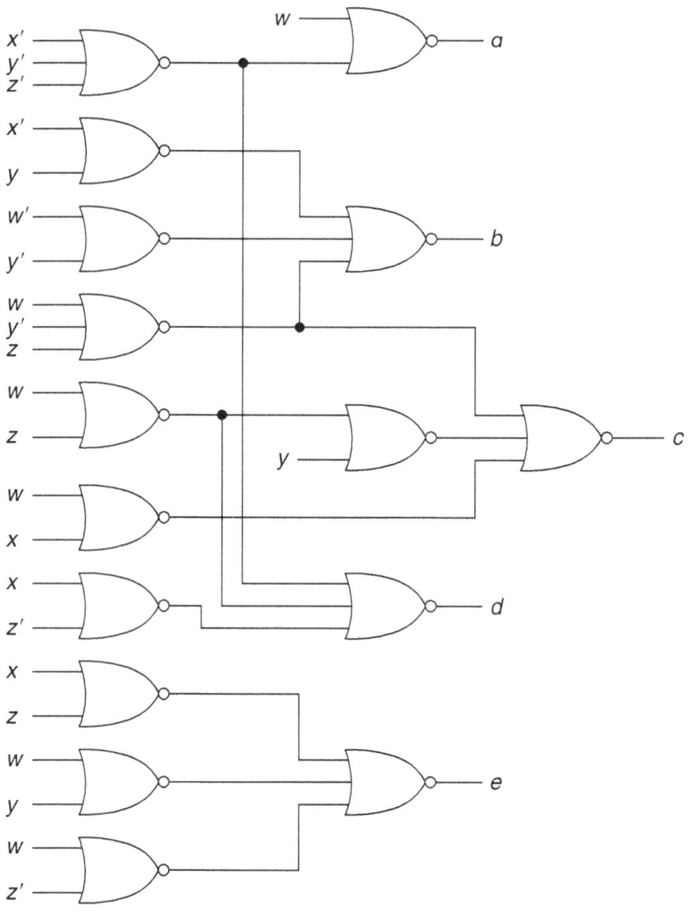

d, e. The implementation with a ROM and a PLA are rather straightforward. For the ROM, all we need is the minterms; the don't cares are ignored. For the PLA, any of the sum of product solutions can be used, as long as we have enough terms. The two solutions are shown below.

*By doing this, we have saved a two-input gate, since the term $w'z'$ uses the same NOR gate as the term $w + z$.

d.

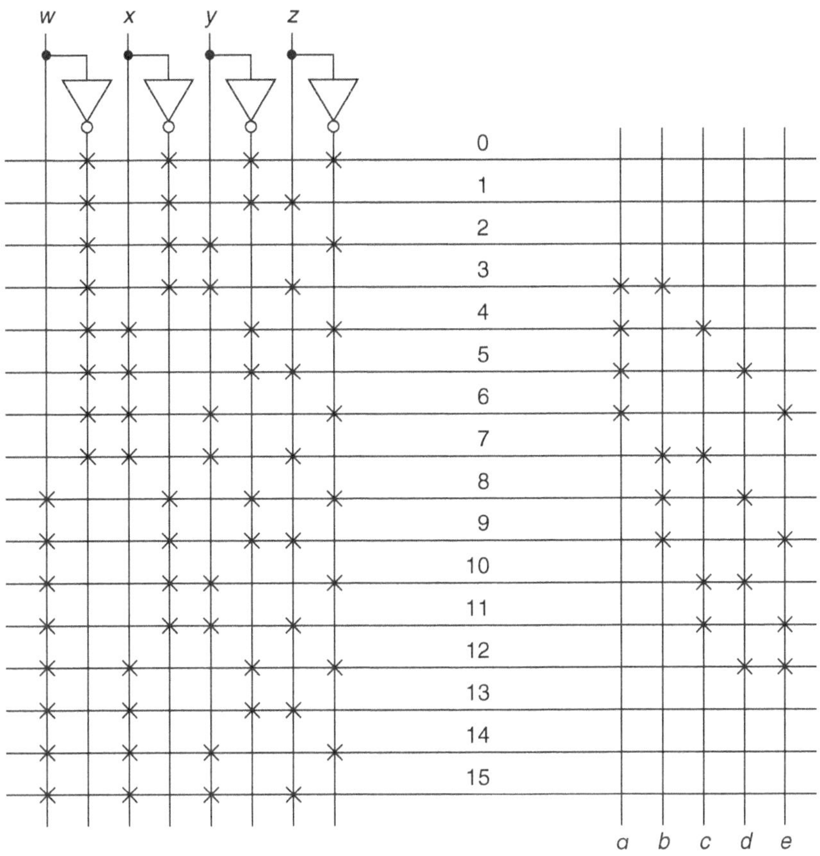

e.

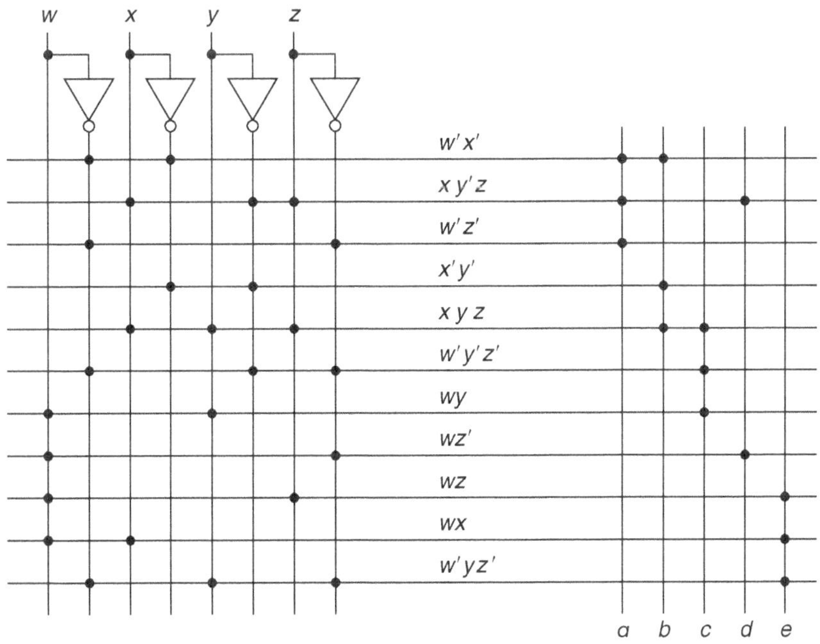

17. Design a controller to display an electronic nine-dotted die as shown next. A set of these could be used to display decimal numbers and some mathematical equations.

The inputs to the controller represent a 4-bit number, *W*, *X*, *Y*, *Z*, which indicates what is to be displayed. They are all available both uncomplemented and complemented. There are nine outputs, *A*, *B*, *C*, *D*, *E*, *F*, *G*, *H*, *J*, one for each of the dots.

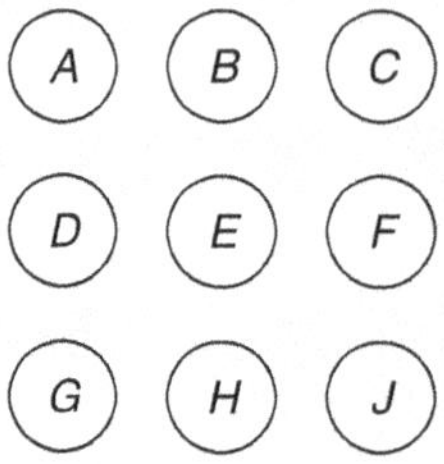

The display comes in two types. The first type requires a 1 to light the display. The second type requires a 0 to light the display. For the second version, the outputs of the controller are the complement of the outputs required for the first type of display.

The diagram below shows each of the inputs and the display that results. A black dot indicates that the bit is lit; a circle indicates not lit. Note that 0 lights none of the lights; 9 lights all of them.

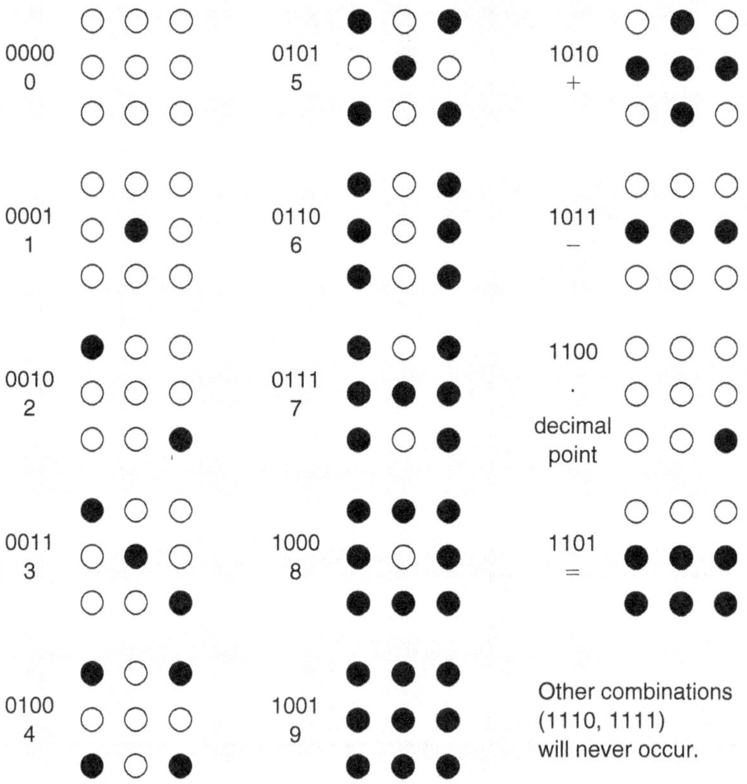

a. Show the truth table for the controller.

b. Write a minimum sum of products expression for each of the outputs, treating each output as a separate problem. Show both maps and algebraic expressions. For each expression, all terms must be prime implicants of that function. Sharing is possible only if a product term is a prime implicant of more than one function.

c. Assume that the functions found in part b are to be implemented with a two-level NAND gate circuit. Do not build two gates with the same inputs. How many two-input and how many three-input gates are used? (No gates may be used as NOT gates; there is no need for any gates with more than three inputs.) If 7400 and 7410 integrated circuit packages were used, how many of each are used?

d. Show the equations and a block diagram of a minimum cost two-level NAND gate implementation. (Of course, there will be sharing, and some of the terms will not be prime implicants of one or more of the functions for which they are used.) No gates may be used as NOT gates. How many integrated circuit packages are needed?

e. We went to implement this but ran into a problem. All we could find was one 7410 package of three-input NAND gates (three gates in the package). There were plenty of 7400 packages of two-input gates. Show the equations and a block diagram for an implementation this way. No gates may be used as NOT gates. (It is possible to start with either the solution to part b or d above, or some other set of equations.) Use as few 7400s as possible.

a. The truth table for the controller with active high outputs is shown below. (In the output columns of the version with active low outputs, there would be 0's where this one has 1's and 1's where this has 0's. The don't cares would be the same.)

W	*X*	*Y*	*Z*	*A*	*B*	*C*	*D*	*E*	*F*	*G*	*H*	*J*
0	0	0	0	0	0	0	0	0	0	0	0	0
0	0	0	1	0	0	0	0	1	0	0	0	0
0	0	1	0	1	0	0	0	0	0	0	0	1
0	0	1	1	1	0	0	0	1	0	0	0	1
0	1	0	0	1	0	1	0	0	0	1	0	1
0	1	0	1	1	0	1	0	1	0	1	0	1
0	1	1	0	1	0	1	1	0	1	1	0	1
0	1	1	1	1	0	1	1	1	1	1	0	1
1	0	0	0	1	1	1	1	0	1	1	1	1
1	0	0	1	1	1	1	1	1	1	1	1	1
1	0	1	0	0	1	0	1	1	1	0	1	0
1	0	1	1	0	0	0	1	1	1	0	0	0
1	1	0	0	0	0	0	0	0	0	0	0	1
1	1	0	1	0	0	0	1	1	1	1	1	1
1	1	1	0	X	X	X	X	X	X	X	X	X
1	1	1	1	X	X	X	X	X	X	X	X	X

We can see from the truth table (or from the maps below) that *D* and *F* are identical; obviously, we only need to build the function once.

b. We construct the nine maps (although we only will simplify the eight unique ones). In *B*, where there are two equally good solutions, we chose the one that could share a term with *H*.

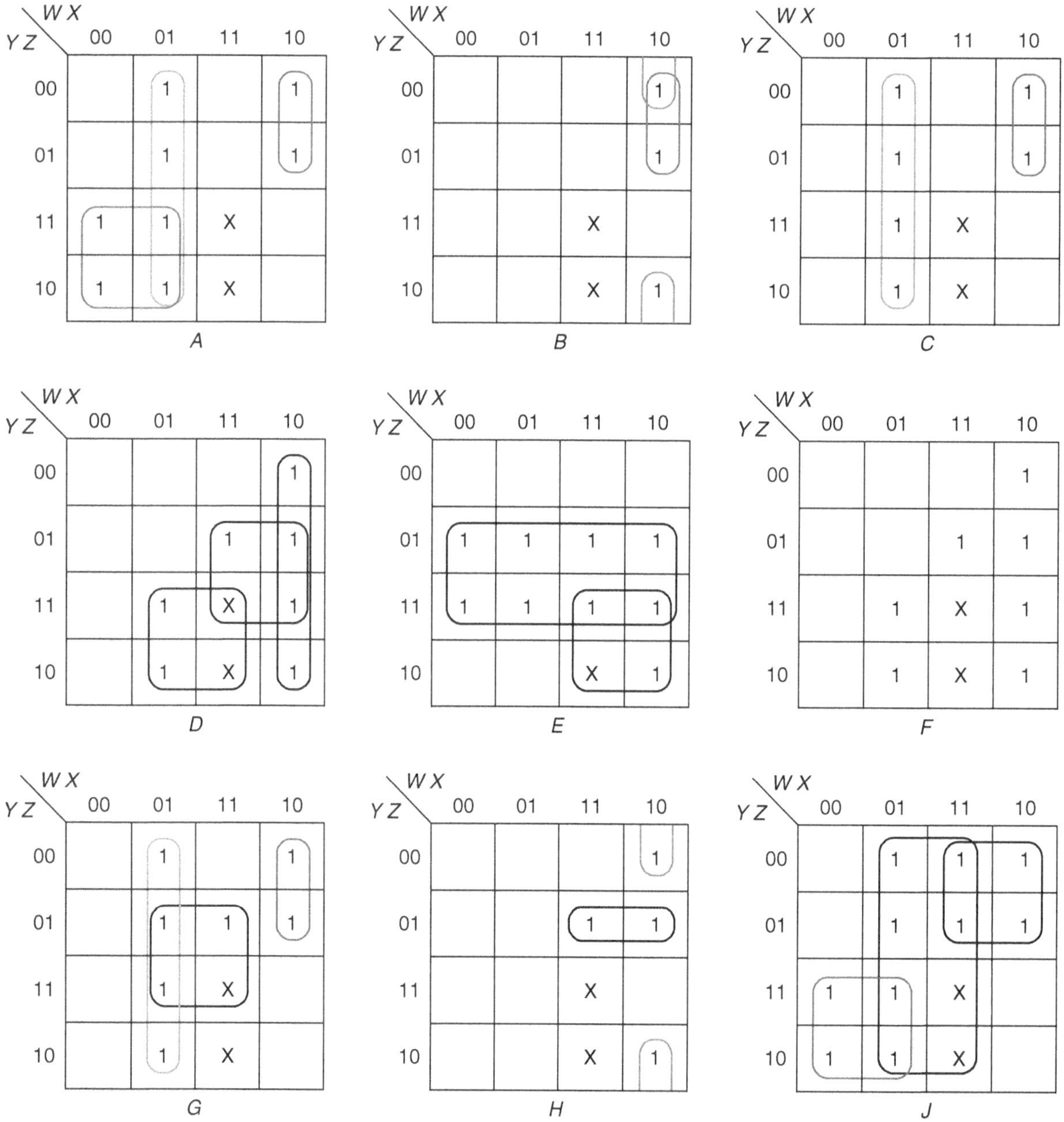

The equations for the eight functions are

$$A = W'X + W'Y + WX'Y'$$
$$B = WX'Y' + WX'Z'$$
$$C = W'X + WX'Y'$$
$$D = XY + WX' + WZ$$
$$E = Z + WY$$
$$G = W'X + WX'Y' + XZ$$
$$H = WX'Z' + WY'Z$$
$$J = X + WY' + W'Y$$

---

c. Note that there are four terms that are shared. This solution requires 12 two-input gates and 7 three-input gates (three 7400s and three 7410s).

---

b, c. The maps for the complementary outputs are shown next. The equations for this active low controller (where we are implementing the complements) are

$$A' = W'X'Y' + WX + WY$$
$$B' = W' + X + YZ$$
$$C' = WX + WY + W'X'$$
$$D' = W'X' + W'Y' + WXZ'$$
$$E' = Y'Z' + W'Z'$$
$$G' = WY + W'X' + WXZ'$$
$$H' = W' + YZ + XZ'$$
$$J' = W'X'Y' + WY$$

They require 10 two-input gates and 8 three-input gates (three 7400s and three 7410s). There is a lot more sharing, but still six integrated circuit packages are required.

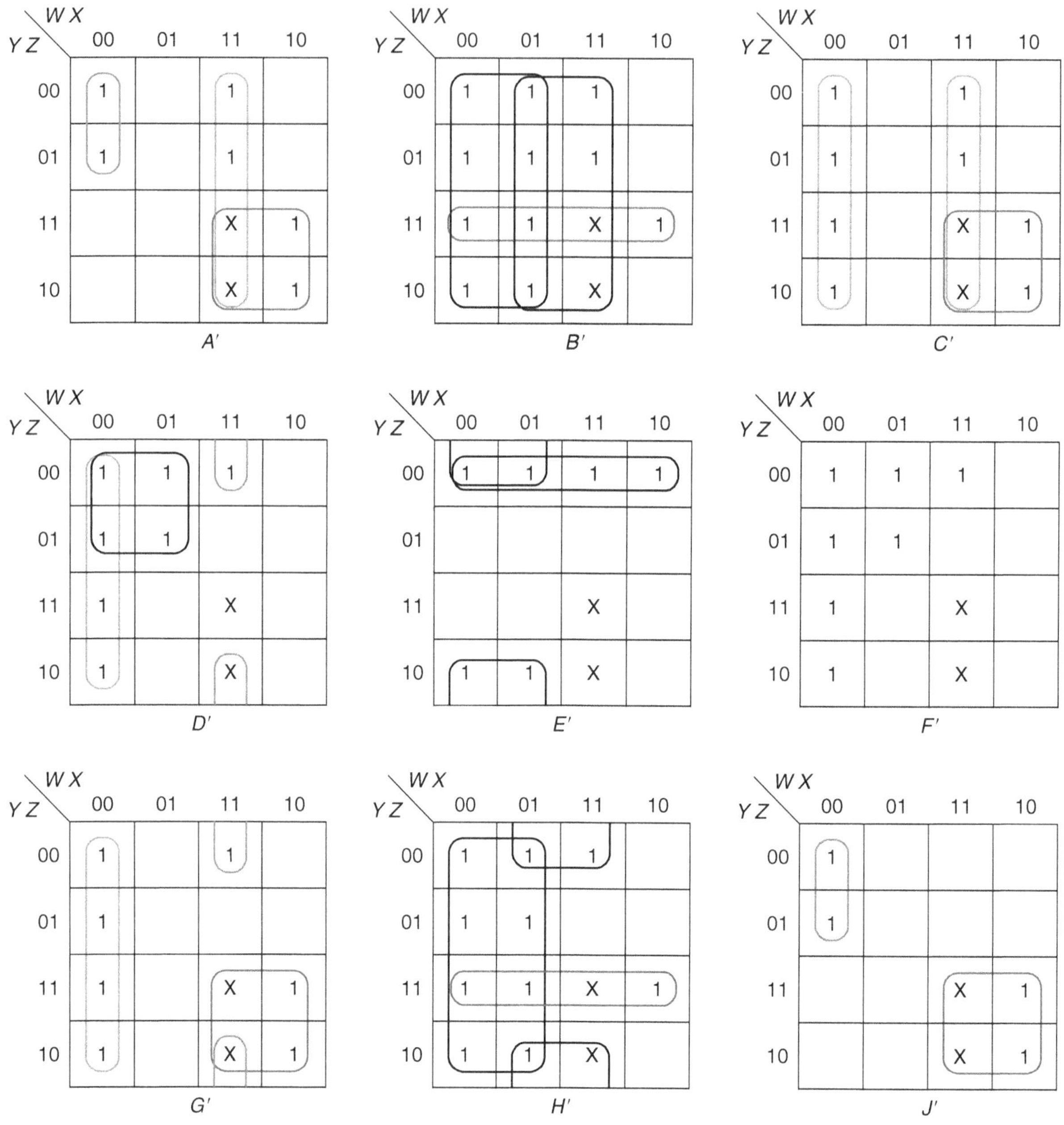

d. Both versions can be reduced to five packages by treating this as a multiple output problem. The active low version has only one small adjustment. In the equation for H', we can use the term WXZ', which has already been implemented for D' and G', in place of XZ'. That saves a two-input gate, reducing the count to nine. Now the ninth three-input gate on the 7410 packages can be used as a two-input gate and only two 7400s are needed.

For the active high version, a considerable amount of sharing can be achieved. The maps for a minimum solution are shown below.

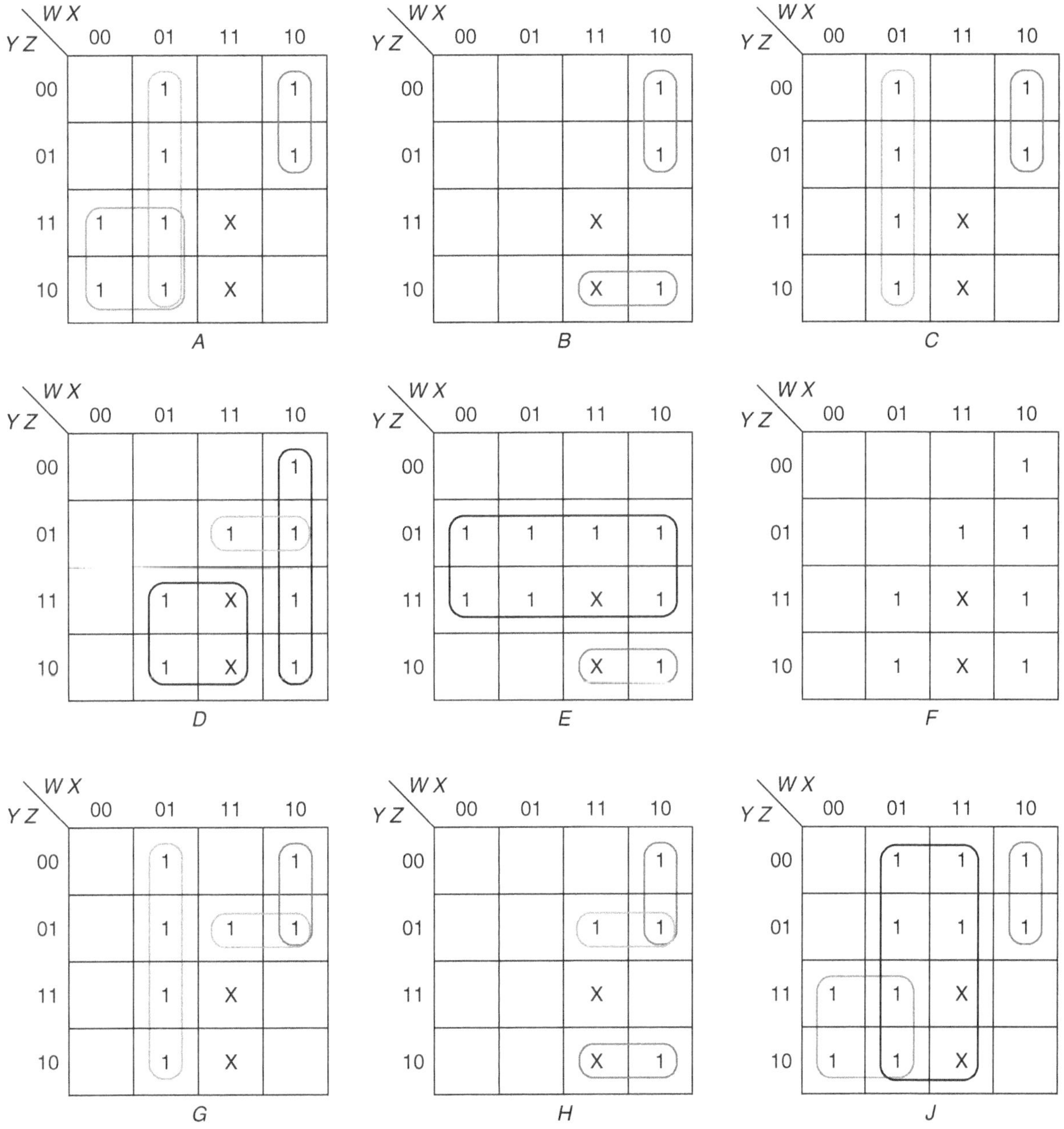

As can be seen on the maps, a number of terms are used that are not prime implicants of a particular function. Also, three terms are used for H, rather than two, to avoid building a new gate for that term. The solution is shown in tabular form below. Each row corresponds to a product term; each column to one of the functions. Also shown is the size of the gate to create the term in each row and to combine the terms in each column.

		A	B	C	D, F	E	G	H	J
$W'X$	2	X		X			X		
$W'Y$	2	X							X
$WX'Y'$	3	X	X	X			X	X	X
WYZ'	3		X			X		X	
XY	2				X				
$WY'Z$	3				X		X	X	
WX'	2				X				
Z	0					X			
X	0								X
Inputs		3	2	2	3	2	3	3	3

There are 8 three-input gates and 7 two-input gates, requiring 5 modules.

e. We need to go back to the part b solution, since it has fewer terms and fewer three-literal terms. An active high solution is

$$A = W'(X + Y) + WX'Y'$$
$$B = WX'Y' + WY'Z'$$
$$C = W'X + WX'Y'$$
$$D = W(X' + Z) + XY$$
$$E = Z + WY$$
$$G = WX'Y' + X(W' + Z)$$
$$H = WX'Z' + WY'Z$$
$$J = X + (W + Y)(W' + Y')$$

Of the 3 three-input gates, two are shared. Note that in the NAND gate realization shown below, that WY and $(W' + Y')$ are implemented by the same gate. In addition to the package of three-input gates, this realization uses 19 two-input gates.

The active low solution is

$$A' = WX'Y' + W(X + Y)$$
$$B' = W' + X + YZ$$
$$C' = W(X + Y) + W'X'$$

$$D' = W'X' + (W' + XZ')(W + Y')$$
$$E' = Y'Z' + W'Z'$$
$$G' = W(Y + XZ') + W'X'$$
$$H' = W' + (X + Z)(Y + Z')$$
$$J' = WX'Y' + WY$$

It uses seven modules. The circuits are shown below.

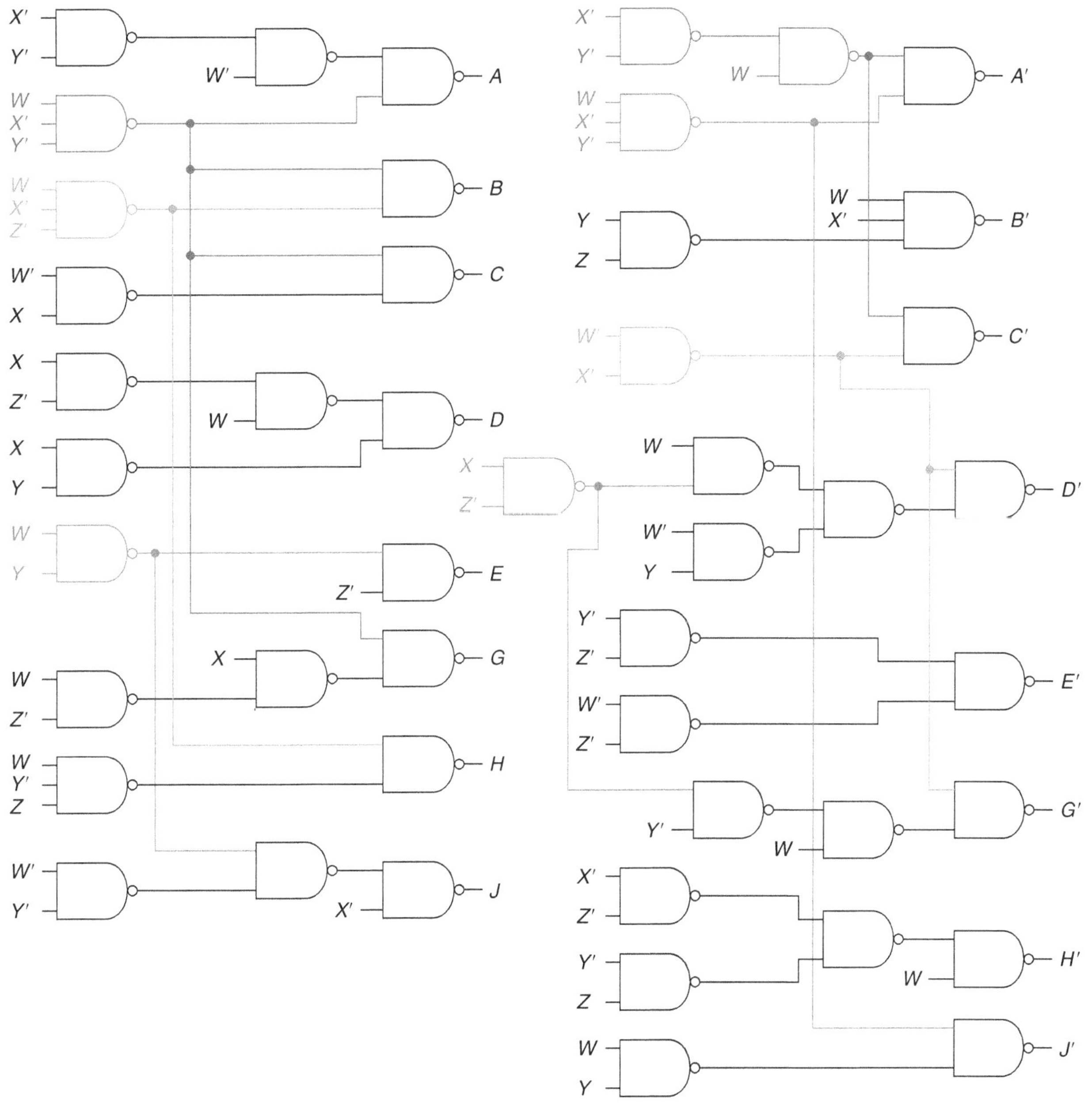

18. You are to design a driver for an eight-segment display as described below. It has four inputs, *a*, *b*, *c*, *d* and eight outputs, *X1*, . . . , *X8*.

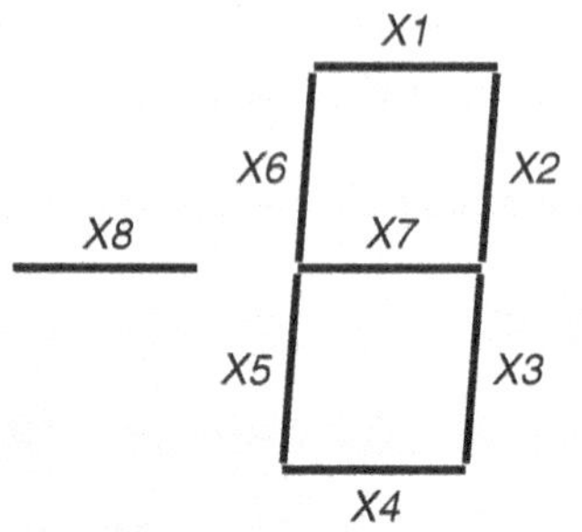

This is to display the decimal equivalent of a 4-bit binary number that is in one's complement format. In one's complement, the following values are coded:

0000	0	1000	−7
0001	1	1001	−6
0010	2	1010	−5
0011	3	1011	−4
0100	4	1100	−3
0101	5	1101	−2
0110	6	1110	−1
0111	7	1111	0

(Note that the minus sign (*X8*) is lit for −1 to −7, but not for either 0 or for 1 to 7.) Segment *X1* may or may not be lit for the digit 6; segment *X6* is not lit for digit 7. All inputs are available both complemented and uncomplemented.

a. Show the maps, equations, and a block diagram for a minimum two-level NAND gate solution that treats this as eight separate problems and uses only prime implicants of each of the functions. However, the gate implementation should share gates whenever possible. (Minimum is 36 gates, 107 inputs.)

b. Show the maps, equations, and a block diagram for a minimum two-level NAND gate solution—but this time gates are to be shared wherever possible. Restriction: There are no gates with more than eight inputs. Also, indicate how many modules you have used.

c. *X4* requires at least eight terms and thus an eight-input NAND gate for a two-level solution. Find a minimum solution for *X4* that uses only two-input gates. (This must, of course, be more than two levels.) Note: This part has nothing to do with part b. No gate may be used as a NOT.

d. Implement these functions using a PLA with as few terms as possible. Show a PLA diagram.

a. All but *X3* and *X7* have unique solutions. There are six solutions for *X3*, the first three of which can share two terms with other solutions. The maps for one of the best solutions, requiring 36 gates and 107 gate inputs, are shown on the next page. Shared terms are in brown. The list of solutions is given below. The underlined subscripted terms are shared in this solution. Other terms that could be shared in a different solution are underlined:

$$X1 = b'd' + bd + \underline{ac'}_7 + a'c$$
$$X2 = a'b' + ab + \underline{c'd'}_6 + \underline{cd}$$
$$X3 = \underline{ab'}_5 + \underline{c'd'}_6 + a'd + bc$$
$$= \underline{ab'} + bd' + \underline{cd} + a'c'$$
$$= a'b + \underline{cd} + \underline{ad'} + b'c'$$
$$= b'd + \underline{c'd'} + a'b + ac$$
$$= a'c' + \underline{ad'} + b'd + bc$$
$$= b'c' + ac + bd' + a'd$$
$$X4 = \underline{a'b'd'}_4 + b'cd' + a'b'c + \underline{a'cd'}_3 + abc' + \underline{abd}_2 + bc'd + \underline{ac'd}_1$$
$$X5 = \underline{ac'd}_1 + \underline{abd}_2 + \underline{a'cd'}_3 + \underline{a'b'd'}_4$$
$$X6 = a'c'd' + a'bc' + \underline{a'bd'} + \underline{ab'd} + ab'c + acd$$
$$X7 = bc' + b'c + \{\underline{a'cd'}_3 \text{ or } \underline{a'bd'}\} + \{\underline{ac'd}_1 \text{ or } \underline{ab'd}\}$$
$$X8 = \underline{ab'}_5 + \underline{ac'}_7 + \underline{ad'}$$

The gate count for this solution is

X1:	2	2	2	2					4
X2:	2	2	2	2					4
X3:	2	(2)	2	2					4
X4:	3	3	3	3	3	3	3	3	8
X5:	(3)	(3)	(3)	(3)					4
X6:	3	3	3	3	3	3			6
X7:	2	2	(3)	(3)					4
X8:	(2)	(2)	2						3

2′s:	14	7430s:	2	36 gates/107 inputs
3′s:	15	7420s:	3	
4′s:	5	7410s:	5	
6′s:	1	7400s:	4	
8′s:	1			

14 chips

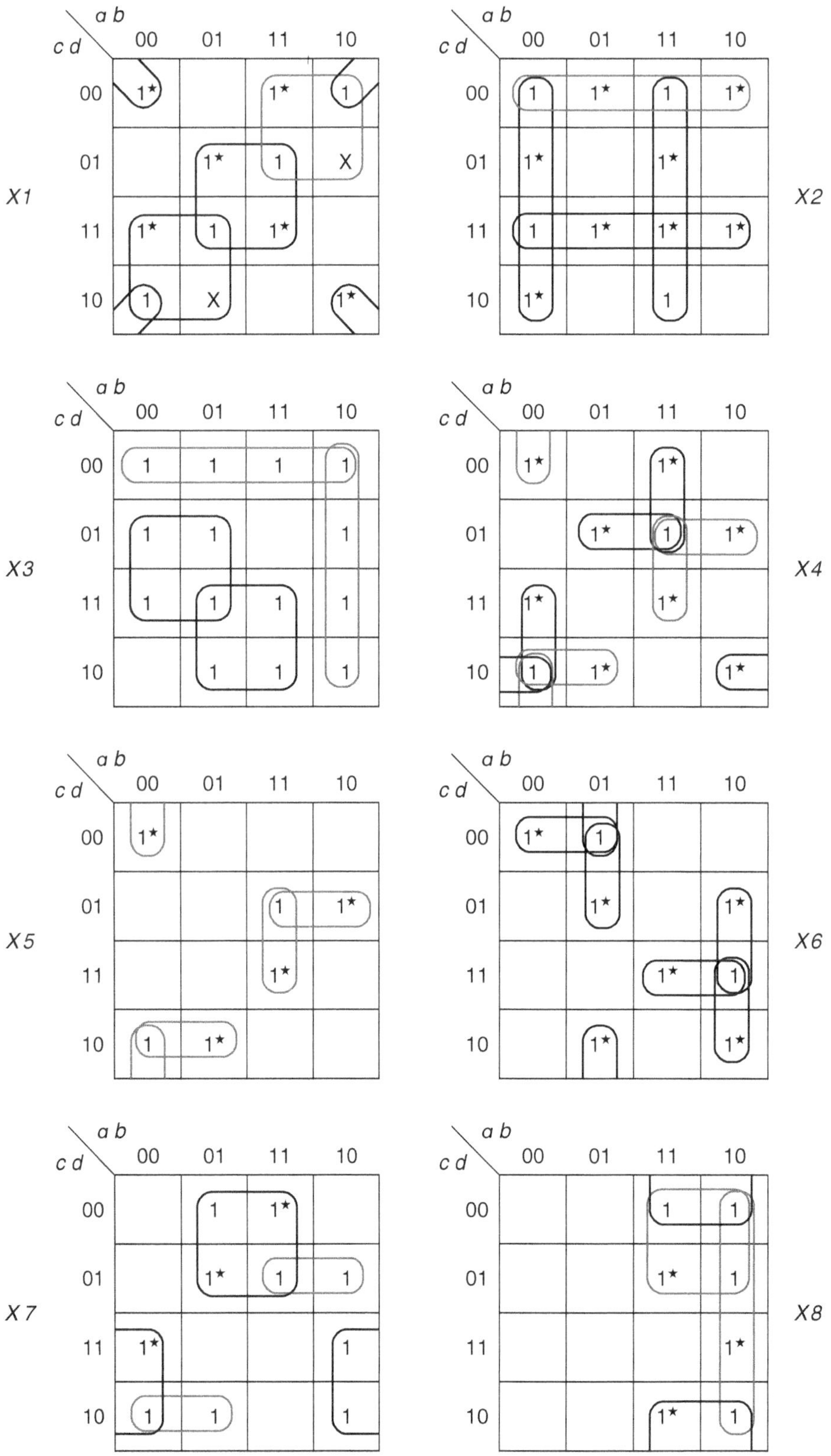
X1
X2
X3
X4
X5
X6
X7
X8

b. The best solution is shown in the following table and maps. It requires 24 gates with 95 inputs and only 13 chips.

	X1	*X2*	*X3*	*X4*	*X5*	*X6*	*X7*	*X8*	
a′b′c′d′	X			X	X	X			4
abc′	X	X		X			X	X	3
a′b′c	X	X		X			X		3
bd	X								2
ab′d′	X		X					X	3
a′b′c′		X	X						3
abd′		X	X					X	3
c′d′		X							2
cd		X	X						2
a′bd′			X			X	X		3
a′bc′d			X	X		X	X		4
ab′d			X			X	X	X	3
ac′d				X	X				3
a′cd′				X	X				3
abcd				X	X	X			4
ab′cd′				X		X	X		4
	5	6	7	8	4	6	6	4	

8-in	1	1	
7-in	1	1	
6-in	3	3	
5-in	1	1	
4-in	6	3	
3-in	9	3	
2-in	3	1	
Total	24	13	95 inputs

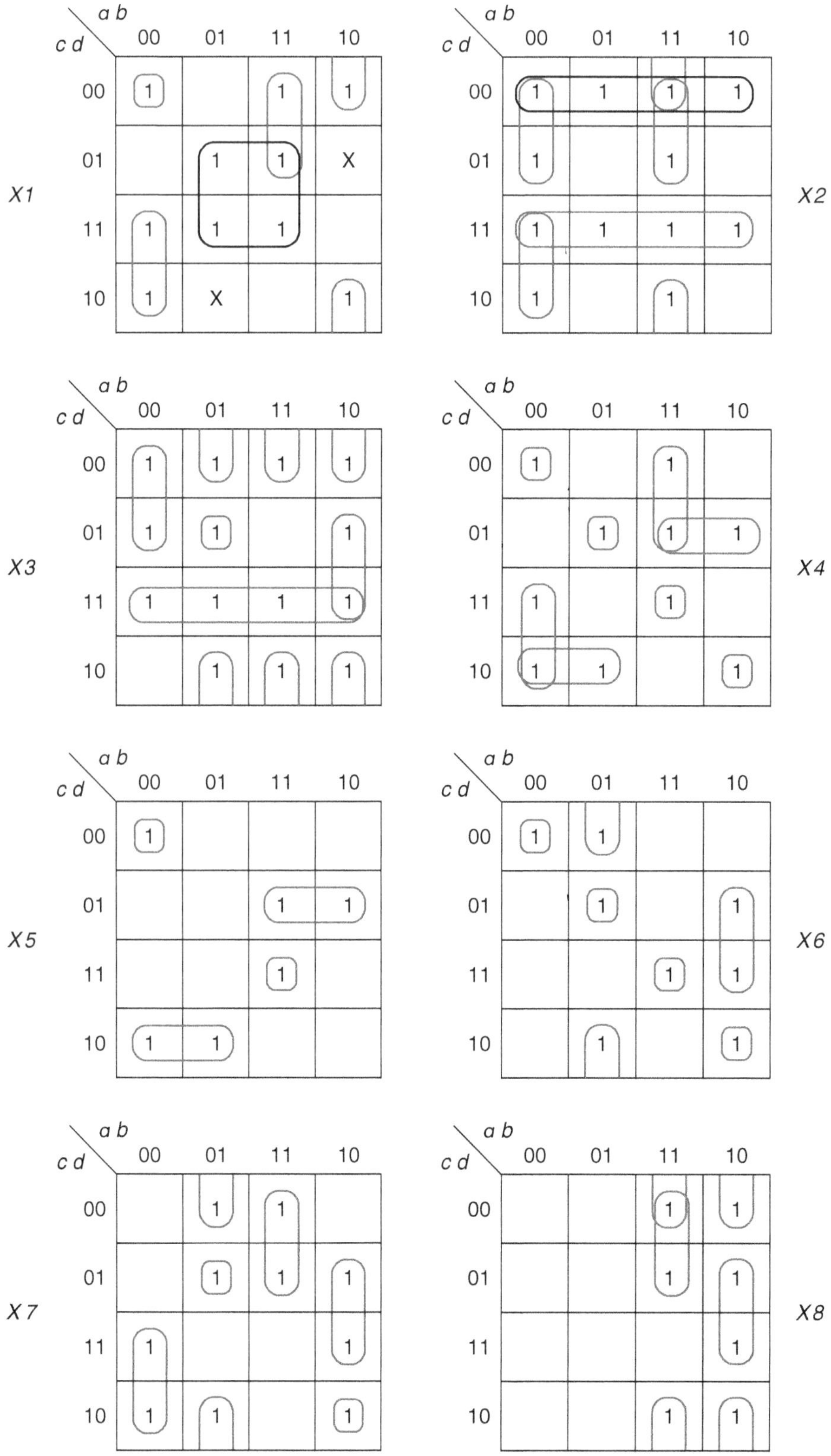
X1
X2
X3
X4
X5
X6
X7
X8
a b
c d
00
01
11
10

c.

$$\begin{aligned} X4 &= a'b'd' + b'cd' + a'b'c + a'cd' + abc' + abd + bc'd + ac'd \\ &= a'b'(c + d') + ab(c' + d) + cd'(a' + b') + c'd(a + b) \\ &= [a' + b(c' + d)][a + b'(c + d')] \\ &\quad + [c + d(a + b)][c' + d'(a' + b')] \end{aligned}$$

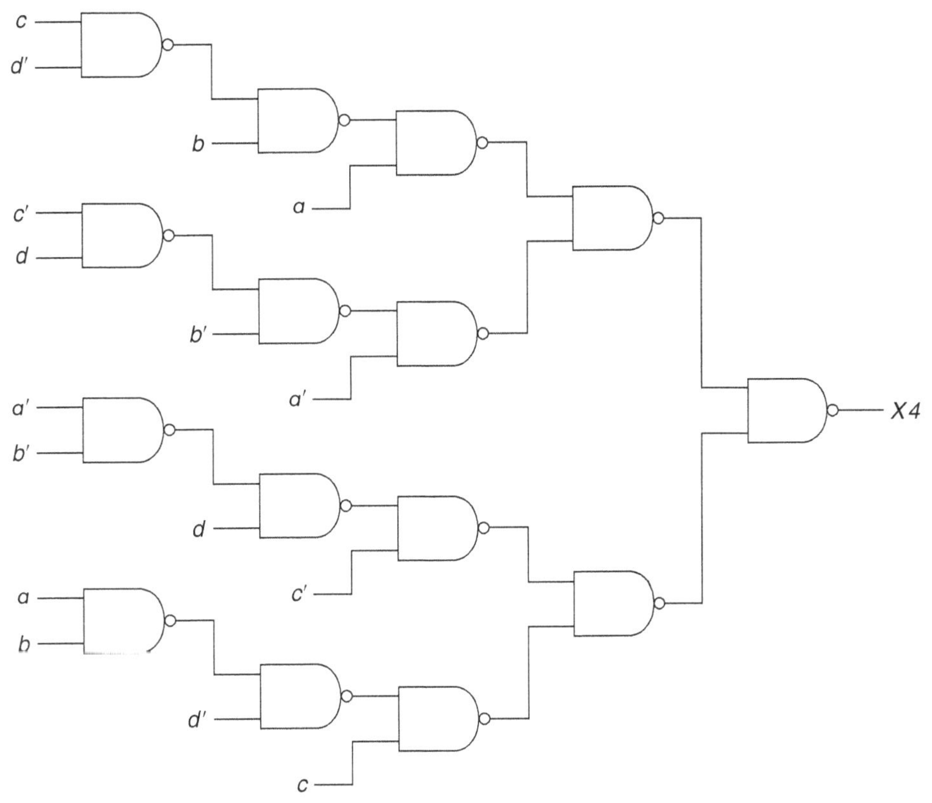

d. The solution to part b translates directly into a PLA with 16 product terms (where each row corresponds to a product term). An equally good solution would be to design the PLA as a ROM. It, too, would have 16 terms. (Note: The ROM solution does not work for part b since it would require a 14-input gate for *X3*.)

5.10 EXERCISES

1. For the following circuit:

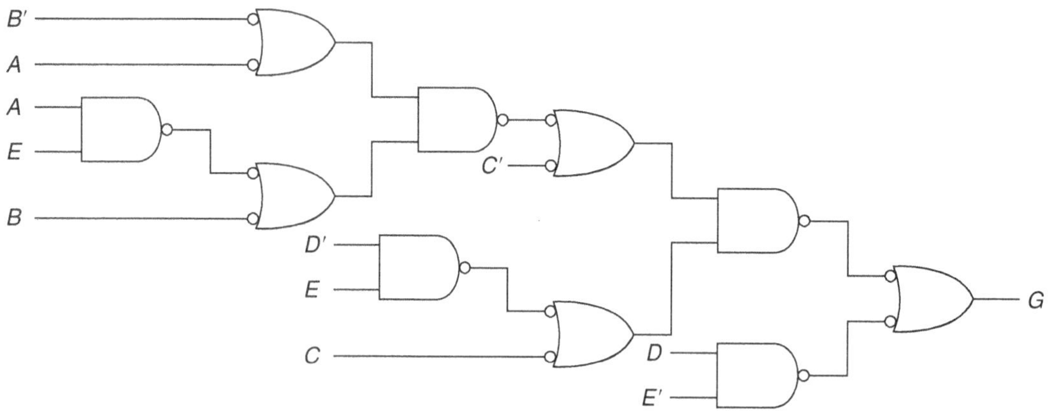

a. Compute the maximum delay,

   i. Assuming that all inputs are available both uncomplemented and complemented

   ii. Assuming only uncomplemented inputs are available and an additional gate must be added to complement each input

b. Compute the maximum delay from input *C* to the output, assuming that all inputs are available both uncomplemented and complemented.

*__2.__ We are building an adder to add the 32-bit constant

10101010101010101010101010101010

to an arbitrary 32-bit number. We will implement this with 16 identical adder modules, each of which will add 2 bits of the number to the constant (10) and a carry from the next lower pair of bits and produce 2 bits of the sum and the carry to the next bits. A block diagram of part of this is shown below:

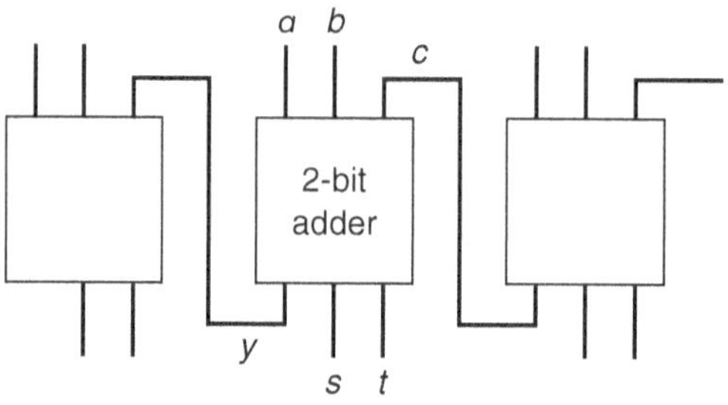

The problem each 2-bit adder solves is

		c
	a	b
	1	0
y	s	t

a. Show a truth table for that 2-bit adder (it has three inputs, a, b, and c, and it has three outputs, y, s, and t), and find minimum SOP expressions for each output.

b. Compute the delay from the c input of each module to the y output of that module and the total delay for the 32 bits.

3. We want to build a circuit to compute the two's complement of an $\boldsymbol{n}$-bit number. We will do this with $\boldsymbol{n}$ modules, each of which complements that bit and then adds the carry from the next lower bit. Thus, the first three bits of a block diagram of the circuit will look like

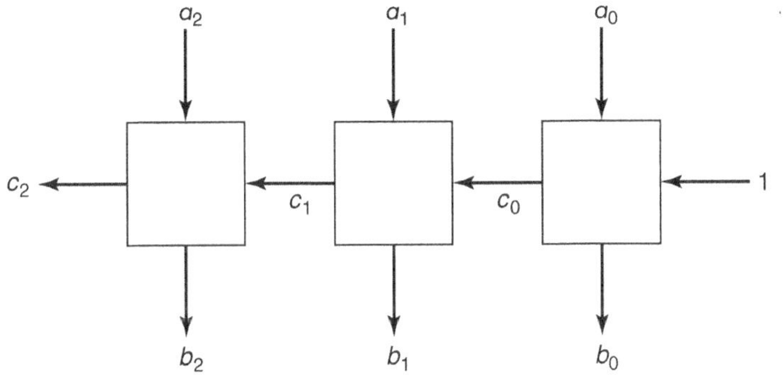

a. Show a block diagram for each of the boxes using NAND gates. (Design the first—on the right—box specially.)

b. Compute the delay for $\boldsymbol{n}$ bits.

c. Improve the speed by designing 2 bits at a time. Show a NAND gate circuit and compute the total delay.

4. We want to build an adder to simultaneously add three multidigit binary numbers. Design a single bit of that adder. It has three inputs for that digit, x, y, and z, plus two carry inputs, u and v (since you may have a carry of 0, 1, or 2). There are three outputs, a sum, s, and two carries, f and g. Show a truth table and find the minimum sum of products expressions for the three outputs.

5. Design a circuit to multiply two 2-bit numbers—a, b and c, d and produce a 4-bit product—w, x, y, z. Show a truth table and the equations.

6. We need to determine whether a three-bit number, a_3, a_2, a_1, is equal to another number, b_3, b_2, b_1, or if it is greater than that number. (We do not need an output for less than.)

a. Show how the 7485 would be connected to accomplish this.

b. Implement this with AND and OR gates.

c. Assuming that the 7485 costs \$1, what must 7400 series AND and OR gate packages cost to make the AND/OR implementation less expensive?

★7. Consider the following circuit with an active high output decoder. Draw a truth table for *X* and *Y* in terms of *a*, *b*, and *c*.

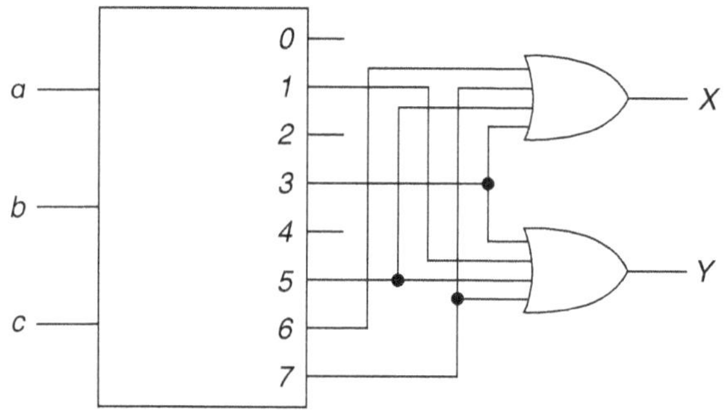

8. We wish to design a decoder, with three inputs, *x*, *y*, *z*, and eight active high outputs, labeled *0*, *1*, *2*, *3*, *4*, *5*, *6*, *7*. There is no enable input required. (For example, if $xyz = 011$, then output *3* would be 1 and all other outputs would be 0.)

The **only** building block is a two-input, four-output decoder (with an active high enable), the truth table for which is shown below.

EN	*A*	*B*	*0*	*1*	*2*	*3*
0	X	X	0	0	0	0
1	0	0	1	0	0	0
1	0	1	0	1	0	0
1	1	0	0	0	1	0
1	1	1	0	0	0	1

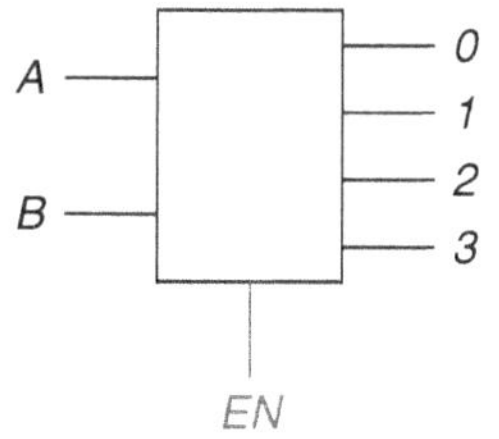

Draw a block diagram of the system using as many of these building blocks as are needed.

★9. We want to implement a full adder; we'll call the inputs *a*, *b*, and *c* and the outputs *s* and c_{out}. As always, the adder is described by the following equations:

$$s(a, b, c) = \Sigma m(1, 2, 4, 7)$$
$$c_{out}(a, b, c) = \Sigma m(3, 5, 6, 7)$$

To implement this, all we have available are two decoders (as shown below) and two OR gates. Inputs *a* and *b* are available both uncomplemented and complemented; *c* is available only uncomplemented. Show a block diagram for this system. Be sure to label all of the inputs to the decoders.

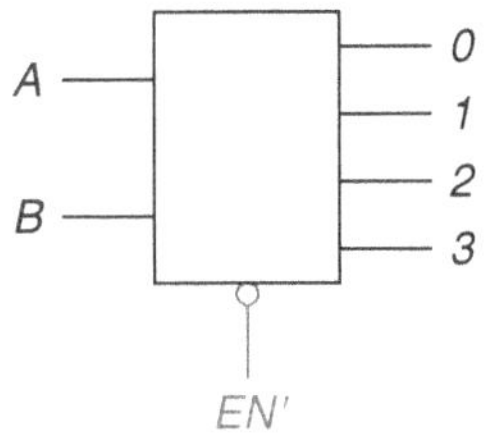

EN'	*A*	*B*	*0*	*1*	*2*	*3*
1	X	X	0	0	0	0
0	0	0	1	0	0	0
0	0	1	0	1	0	0
0	1	0	0	0	1	0
0	1	1	0	0	0	1

10. Show the block diagram for a decoder, the truth table for which is shown below. The available components are one-, two-, and three-input NAND gates. (A one-input NAND is an inverter.)

Inputs				**Outputs**		
E1	*E2*	*a*	*b*	*1*	*2*	*3*
0	X	X	X	1	1	1
X	0	X	X	1	1	1
1	1	0	0	1	1	1
1	1	0	1	0	1	1
1	1	1	0	1	0	1
1	1	1	1	1	1	0

11. Design, using AND, OR, and NOT gates, a priority encoder with seven active low inputs, *1'*, . . . , *7'* and three active high outputs, *CBA* that indicate which is the highest priority line active. Input *1'* is highest priority; *7'* is lowest. If none of the inputs are active, the output is 000. There is a fourth output line, *M*, which is 1 if there are multiple active inputs.

★**12.** Implement the function

$$f(x, y, z) = \Sigma m(0, 1, 3, 4, 7)$$

using two-way multiplexers.

13. In the following circuit, the decoder (DCD) has two inputs and four (active high) outputs (such that, for example, output 0 is 1 if and only if inputs *A* and *B* are both 0). The three multiplexers each have two select inputs (shown on the top of the box), four data inputs (shown on the left) and an active high enable input (shown on the bottom). Inputs *A*, *B*, *C*, and *D* are select inputs; inputs *N* through *Z* are data inputs. Complete a truth giving the value of *F* for each of the 16 possible select input combinations. (Comment: For some values, *F* = 0; for one value, *F* = *W*.)

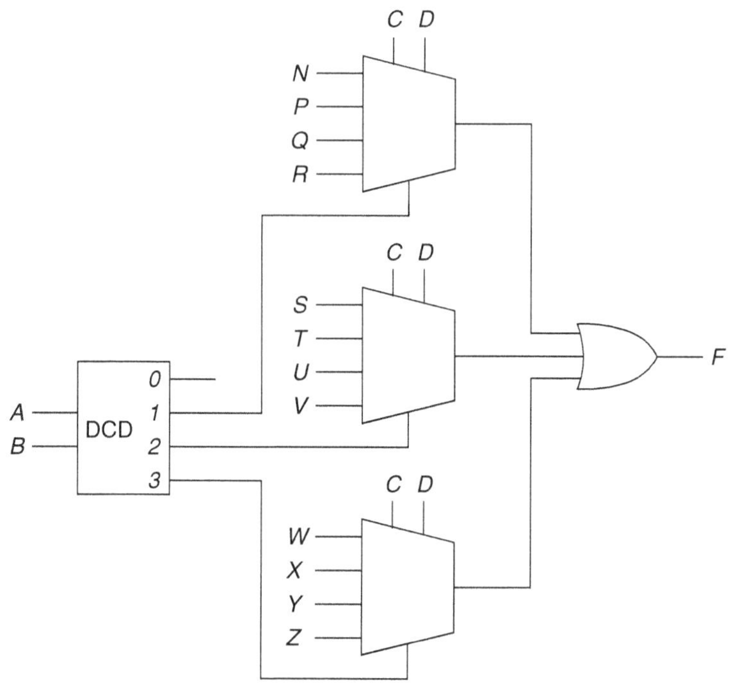

14. The following circuit includes a multiplexer with select inputs, *A* and *B*, and data inputs, *W*, *X*, *Y*, and *Z*:

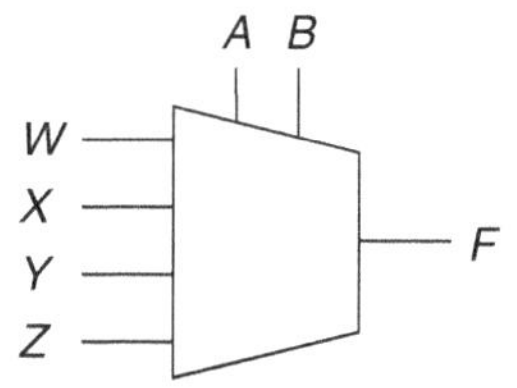

Write an algebraic equation for *F*.

15. For the following sets of functions, design a system

i. Using a ROM

ii. Using a PLA with the number of product terms shown

iii. Using a PAL

a. $F(A, B, C) = \Sigma m(3, 4, 5, 7)$

$G(A, B, C) = \Sigma m(1, 3, 5, 6, 7)$

$H(A, B, C) = \Sigma m(1, 4, 5)$ (4 product terms)

b. $W(A, B, C) = \Sigma m(0, 1, 4)$

$X(A, B, C) = \Sigma m(0, 3, 4, 7)$

$Y(A, B, C) = \Sigma m(1, 2, 6)$

$Z(A, B, C) = \Sigma m(2, 3, 6, 7)$ (4 product terms)

c. $f(a, b, c, d) = \Sigma m(3, 5, 6, 7, 8, 11, 13, 14, 15)$
$g(a, b, c, d) = \Sigma m(0, 1, 5, 6, 8, 9, 11, 13, 14)$
(6 product terms)

d. $F(A, B, C, D) = \Sigma m(1, 2, 6, 7, 8, 9, 12, 13)$
$G(A, B, C, D) = \Sigma m(1, 8, 9, 10, 11, 13, 15)$
$H(A, B, C, D) = \Sigma m(1, 6, 7, 8, 11, 12, 14, 15)$
(8 product terms)

16. We have found a minimum sum of products expression for each of two functions, *F* and *G*, minimizing them individually (no sharing):

$$F = W'X'Y' + XY'Z + W'Z$$
$$G = WY'Z + X'Y'$$

a. Implement them with a ROM.

b. Implement them with a PLA with four terms.

c. For the same functions, we have available as many of the decoders described below as are needed plus 2 eight-input OR gates. Show a block diagram for this implementation. All inputs are available both uncomplemented and complemented.

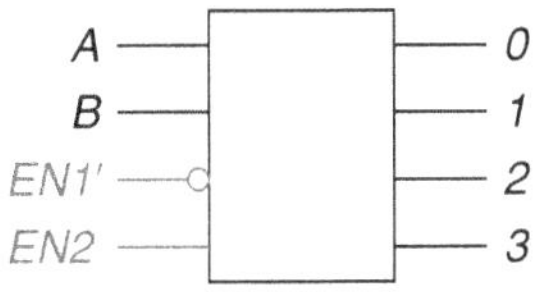

EN1'	*EN2*	*A*	*B*	*0*	*1*	*2*	*3*
X	0	X	X	0	0	0	0
1	X	X	X	0	0	0	0
0	1	0	0	1	0	0	0
0	1	0	1	0	1	0	0
0	1	1	0	0	0	1	0
0	1	1	1	0	0	0	1

Note that this chip is enabled only when $EN1' = 0$ and $EN2 = 1$.

17. Consider the following three functions, *f*, *g*, and *h* of the four variables, *a*, *b*, *c*, and *d*, whose minimum solutions (treating each as a separate problem) are listed below. Throughout, all variables are available *only uncomplemented:*

$$f = b'c'd' + bd + a'cd$$
$$g = c'd' + bc' + bd' + a'b'cd$$
$$h = bd' + cd + ab'd$$

a. Implement them with a ROM.

b. Implement them on a PLA with six terms.

c. Implement them using only decoders of the type shown below (as many as needed) and three OR gates (each with as many inputs as you need). (No other gates are allowed.) Logic 0 and logic 1 are available.

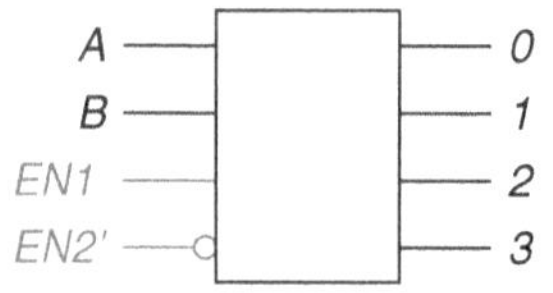

EN1	*EN2'*	*A*	*B*	*0*	*1*	*2*	*3*
0	X	X	X	0	0	0	0
X	1	X	X	0	0	0	0
0	1	0	0	1	0	0	0
0	1	0	1	0	1	0	0
0	1	1	0	0	0	1	0
0	1	1	1	0	0	0	1

★18. We have three functions, X, Y, Z of the four variables, A, B, C, D. Note: Each part can be solved without the other:

$$X(A, B, C, D) = \Sigma m(0, 2, 6, 7, 10, 13, 14, 15)$$
$$Y(A, B, C, D) = \Sigma m(2, 6, 7, 8, 10, 12, 13, 15)$$
$$Z(A, B, C, D) = \Sigma m(0, 6, 8, 10, 13, 14, 15)$$

a. Implement with a two-level NAND gate circuit. This can be done using only prime implicants of the individual functions with 13 gates. With sharing, it can be done with 10 gates. Assume that all variables are available both complemented and uncomplemented.

b. Implement these functions using a ROM.

c. Implement this with 2 three-input (plus active low enable) decoders as shown below, plus a minimum number of AND, OR, and NOT gates.

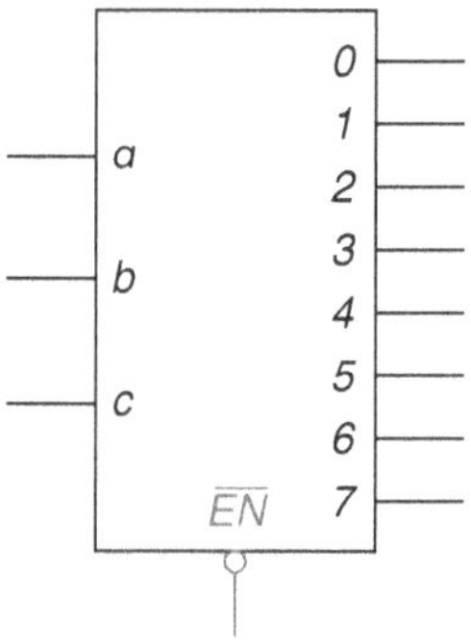

d. Implement it with a PLA with eight terms. (You may not need to use all of them.)

e. Implement them with the PAL shown in the text.

19. Implement the 2-bit adder of Section 5.1.2 using the PAL of Section 5.6.3. The problem is that one of the output functions requires 7 terms and another 12. This can be overcome by building the carry between the 2 bits and using that output as another input to compute s_1 and c_{out}.

20. In Solved Problem 16, we designed a converter from excess 3 to 2 of 5 code. In this exercise, we want to do the reverse, that is design a converter from 2 of 5 code to excess 3. There will be four functions of five variables. We will assume that only legitimate digit codes are input; thus, there will be 22 don't cares on each map. All inputs are available both uncomplemented and complemented.

a. Map each of the four functions and find all minimum sum of products and product of sums solutions for each of the four functions individually.

b. Our building blocks consist of integrated circuit chips. We can buy any of the following chips:

7404: 6 inverters	
7400: 4 two-input NAND gates	7402: 4 two-input NOR gates
7410: 3 three-input NAND gates	7427: 3 three-input NOR gates
7420: 2 four-input NAND gates	7425: 2 four-input NOR gates

All chips cost the same, 25¢ each.

Find one of the least expensive ($1.00) implementations of the four outputs. (The gates on any chip may be used as part of the implementation of more than one of the outputs.) Show the algebraic expression and the block diagram for the solution.

c. Find two solutions, one of which uses only 7400 and 7410 packages, and a solution that uses only NOR gates. Each of these must cost no more than $1.00. (Of course, one of these is the solution to part b.)

d. Implement this with a ROM.

e. Implement this with a PLA.

f. Implement this with the PAL described in the text.

★**21.** We have a special eight-segment display, as shown below.

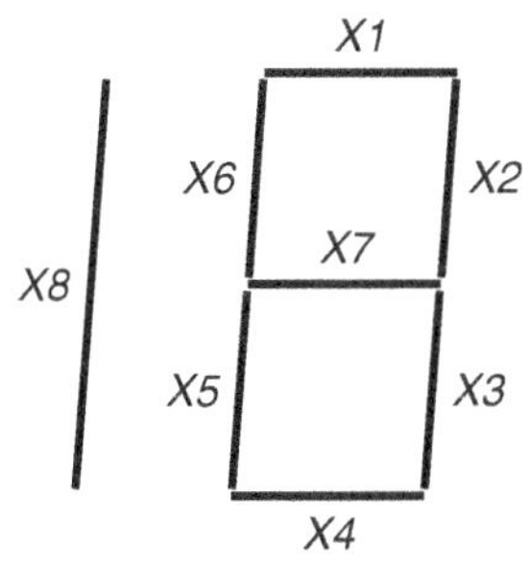

We want to display the numbers from 0 to 15, as shown on the next figure, where a dashed line means an unlit segment and a solid line a lit one. Note that for 6 and 9, one segment each may be lit or unlit, as you wish.

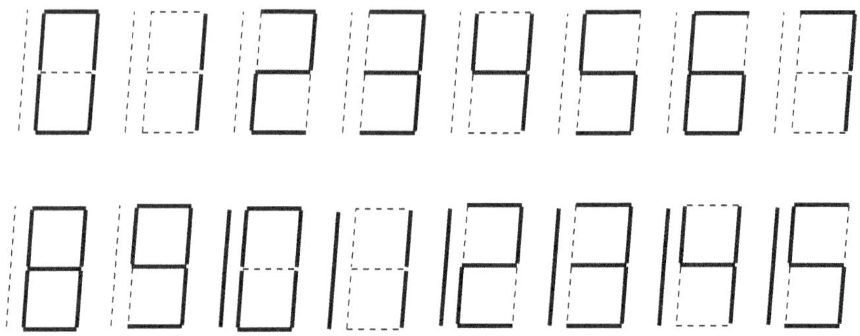

Design three versions of a system that accepts as an input a 4-bit number, *A*, *B*, *C*, *D* and produces the eight outputs, *X1*, *X2*, . . . , *X8* under each of the following constraints. (All inputs are available both complemented and uncomplemented.)

a. Each output is minimized independently using a two-level NAND gate circuit, where minimum is minimum number of gates, and among those with the same number of gates, minimum number of gate inputs. (Each function must be a sum of prime implicants of that function. A gate can be shared among functions only if it implements a prime implicant of each function.) (Minimum solution: 32 gates, 95 inputs.)

b. Two-level NAND gates, using a minimum number of the following modules:

   Type 7400: 4 two-input NAND gates
   Type 7410: 3 three-input NAND gates
   Type 7420: 2 four-input NAND gates
   Type 7430: 1 eight-input NAND gate

   (There is a solution that uses 11 modules.) (Note: The solution to part a uses 13 modules.)

c. A PLA with the minimum number of terms.
   For parts a and b, show the maps, the equations, and a block diagram.

22. We have a decimal digit stored in excess 3 code. The bits of the code are labeled *w*, *x*, *y*, *z* (from left to right). We wish to display that digit on a seven-segment display. The layout follows. Note that there are two ways to display a 6, a 7, and a 9; choose whichever is most convenient. The display requires a 1 to light a segment and a 0 for it not to be lit.

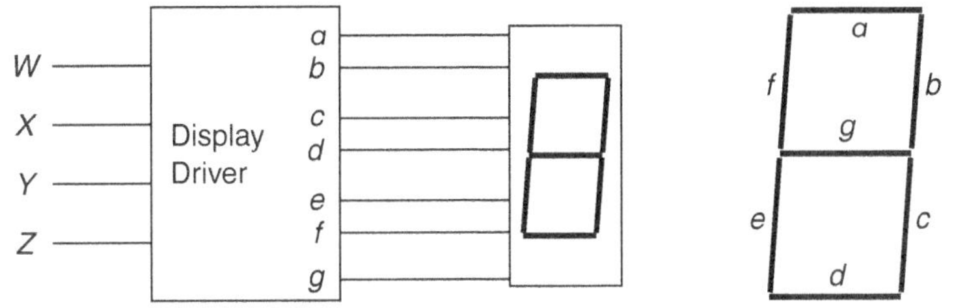

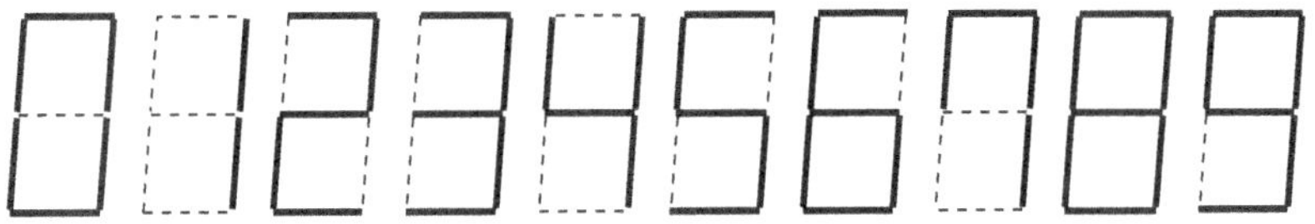

Design the four-input, seven-output device that takes the code for the digit produces the signals to drive the display. If any of the unused input combinations are applied to your device, the display is to be blank, that is all the outputs from the device are to be 0. Assume that the four inputs are available both uncomplemented and complemented.

We are looking for three different designs for this. For each, show the maps, the algebraic equations, and a block diagram. Please use color to make your solutions readable. For the first two parts, indicate how many of each type of package you need (7400, 7410, 7420, 7430). But minimum is defined as minimum number of gates, and among those with the same number of gates, minimum number of gate inputs.

a. First, find a minimum cost two-level NAND gate solution such that all terms are prime implicants of the individual functions. Only terms that are prime implicants of each function are to be shared. When there are multiple solutions, one answer will often lead to more sharing than others.

b. Second, reduce the number of gates by doing more sharing (including terms that are not prime implicants).

c. Third, implement this with a PLA, which has four inputs, seven outputs, and 12 product terms.

23. For the following three functions (of five variables)

$$f(a, b, c, d, e) = \Sigma m(0, 2, 5, 7, 8, 10, 13, 15, 16, 21, 23, 24, 29, 31)$$

$$g(a, b, c, d, e) = \Sigma m(2, 5, 7, 10, 13, 15, 16, 18, 20, 21, 22, 23, 25, 27)$$

$$h(a, b, c, d, e) = \Sigma m(2, 9, 10, 12, 13, 14, 16, 18, 20, 22, 28, 29, 30, 31)$$

a. Find a minimum sum of products solution for each. Show the maps and the algebraic equations for each.

b. Find a minimum solution, assuming a two-level NAND gate circuit. All variables are available both uncomplemented and complemented. Show the maps, the equations and a block diagram of the circuit. Also, indicate how many 7400 series packages you need (that is 7400, 7410, 7420, 7430). (It can be done with no more than 12 gates.)

c. Find an implementation that uses as few two-input NAND gates as possible. No gate may be used as a NOT. Show the equations and a block diagram of the circuit. (Comment: The solution may be derived from part a or from part b or some combination thereof.)

d. Show an implementation with a PLA with five inputs, three outputs, and 10 product terms.

24. Consider the following three functions:

$$f(a, b, c, d, e) = \Sigma m(2, 3, 4, 5, 8, 9, 12, 20, 21, 24, 25, 31)$$

$$g(a, b, c, d, e) = \Sigma m(2, 3, 4, 5, 6, 7, 10, 11, 12, 20, 21, 26, 27, 31)$$

$$h(a, b, c, d, e) = \Sigma m(0, 2, 3, 4, 5, 8, 10, 12, 16, 18, 19, 20, 21, 22, 23, 24, 28, 31)$$

All variables are available both uncomplemented and complemented.

a. Consider each as a separate problem and find all the minimum SOP expression(s). Both f and h have multiple solutions.

b. Assume that 7400, 7410, 7420, and 7430 packages are available at 25¢ each. Show the number of each size gate, how many of each package is required, and the total cost for a two-level solution. (Take advantage of sharing ONLY if the same term is a prime implicant of more than one function.)

c. For each function (again using the solutions of part a), find a solution that only uses 7400 and 7410 packages (25¢ each) (no four- or eight-input gates). Show the maps, the equations, indicating sharing, and a block diagram. Show the number of each size gate, how many of each package is required and the total cost for a two-level solution.

d. Take maximum advantage of sharing to try to reduce the cost of a two-level solution. Use 7400, 7410, 7420, and 7430 packages (25¢ each). Show the maps, the equations, indicating sharing, and a block diagram. Show the number of each size gate, how many of each package is required, and the total cost for a two-level solution.

e. Implement this using a ROM and also using a PLA with five inputs, 12 product terms, and three outputs.

25. Design a system that has as its inputs a number from 1 to 10 and provides as its outputs (eight of them) the signals to drive the display described below. The inputs are labeled *W*, *X*, *Y*, and *Z* and are normal binary. The input combinations 0000, 1011, 1100, 1101, 1110, and 1111 will never occur; they are to be treated as don't cares. The available building blocks are 7400, 7410, and 7420 integrated circuits. The design should use the minimum number of packages (which is five for all cases). The solution should include the maps for each of the functions and a block diagram of the circuit.

The display allows for the representation of Roman numerals (except that IIX is used to represent 8, whereas it is normally written as VIII).

There are a total of eight segments in the display, labeled *A* through *H*, as shown below.

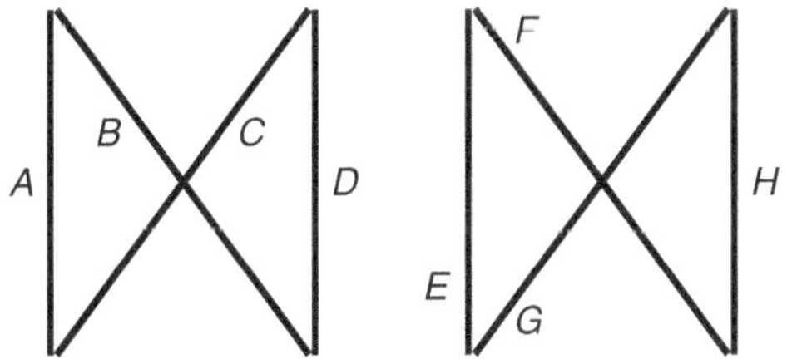

Version High: To light a segment, a 1 is placed on the appropriate display input (*A*, *B*, . . . , *H*).

Version Low: To light a segment, a 0 is placed on the appropriate display input (*A*, *B*, . . . , *H*). Note that for this version, each input is just the complement of the one for Version High.

There are two ways to represent a 5 on this display.

Left: Light segments *A* and *C* (or *E* and *G*).

Right: Light segments *B* and *D* (or *F* and *H*).

The following illustration shows all digits as they should be coded for each of these, with a lit segment represented by a bold line and an unlit segment represented by a dashed line.

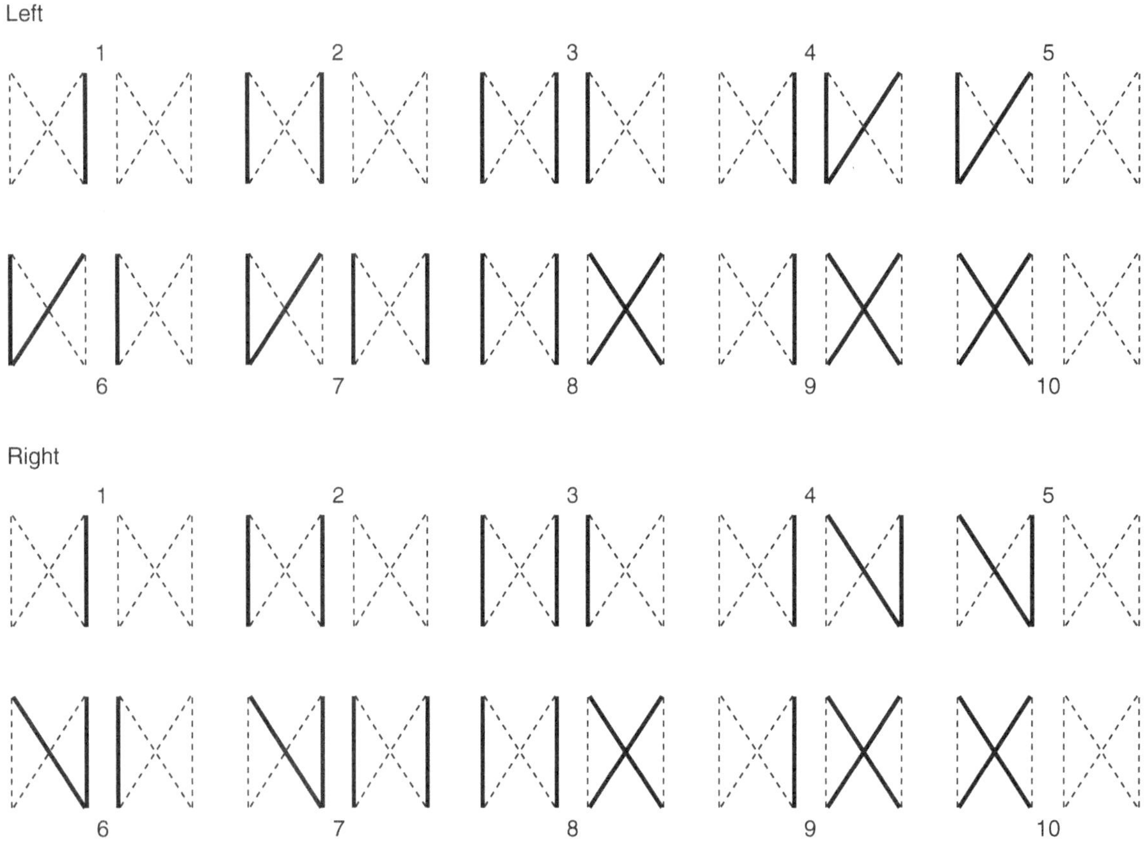

This is really four separate problems, one for each version of the design.

5.11 CHAPTER 5 TEST (60 MINUTES)

1. Implement the following functions using only two of the decoders described below and two 8-input OR gates.

$$f(w, x, y, z) = \Sigma m(0, 4, 5, 6, 7, 12, 15)$$
$$g(w, x, y, z) = \Sigma m(1, 3, 12, 13, 14, 15)$$

EN1	*EN2'*	*a*	*b*	*c*	*0*	*1*	*2*	*3*	*4*	*5*	*6*	*7*
0	X	X	X	X	0	0	0	0	0	0	0	0
X	1	X	X	X	0	0	0	0	0	0	0	0
1	0	0	0	0	1	0	0	0	0	0	0	0
1	0	0	0	1	0	1	0	0	0	0	0	0
1	0	0	1	0	0	0	1	0	0	0	0	0
1	0	0	0	1	0	0	0	1	0	0	0	0
1	0	1	0	0	0	0	0	0	1	0	0	0
1	0	1	0	1	0	0	0	0	0	1	0	0
1	0	1	1	0	0	0	0	0	0	0	1	0
1	0	1	0	1	0	0	0	0	0	0	0	1

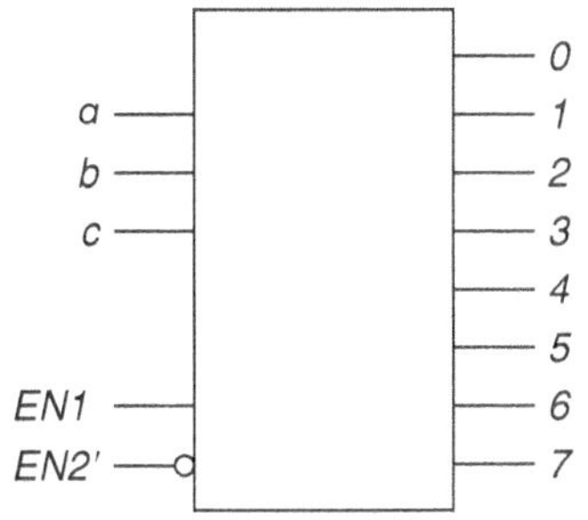

2. Consider the three functions, the maps of which are shown below:

yz \ wx	00	01	11	10
00				1
01	1	1		
11	1	1	1	1
10	1	1		1

f

yz \ wx	00	01	11	10
00		1	1	1
01				
11			1	
10	1	1	1	

g

yz \ wx	00	01	11	10
00		1		1
01	1	1		
11	1	1	1	
10		1		

h

Implement them on the PLA shown here. Be sure to label the inputs and the outputs. Full credit if you use eight terms or less.

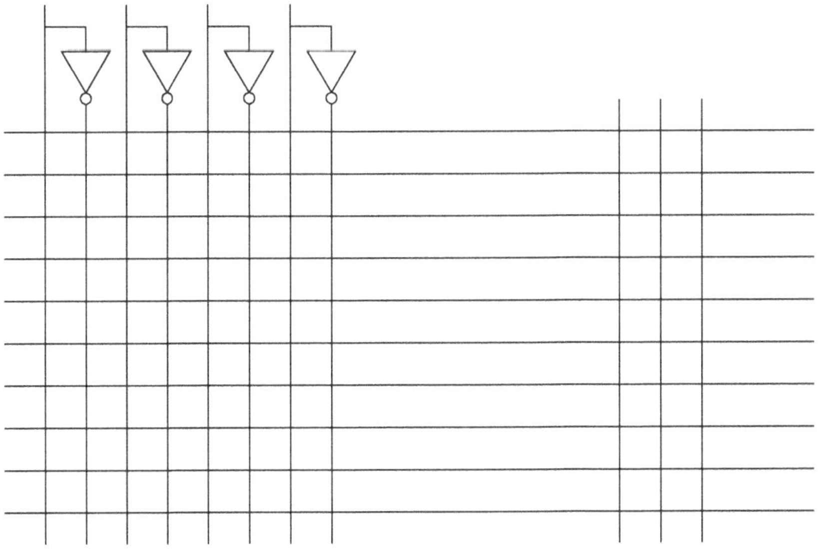

3. For the same set of functions, implement them with the ROM shown. Be sure to label the inputs and the outputs.

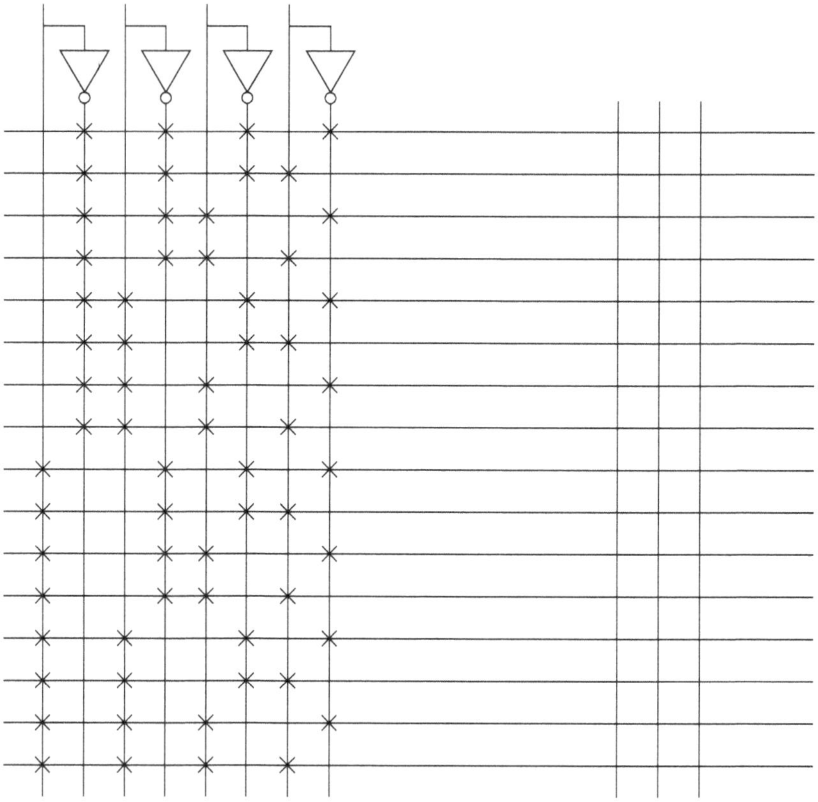

4. For the same set of functions, implement them with the PAL that follows. Be sure to label the inputs and the outputs.

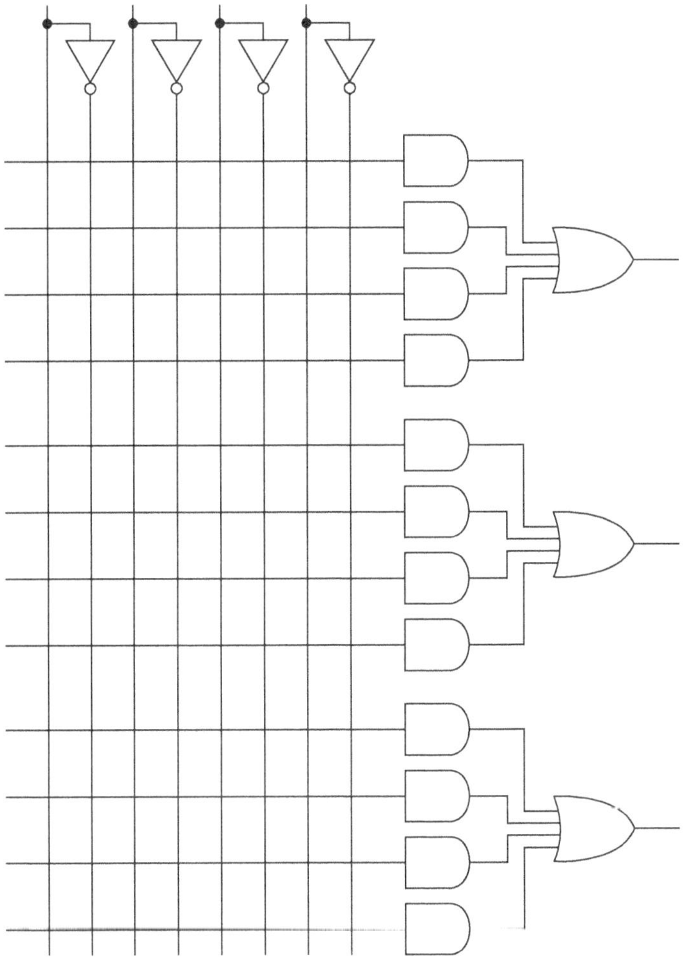

CHAPTER TEST

5. For the same set of functions, we have available as components three NAND gates (as many inputs as you need) and some active low input, active low enable decoders, as shown below (as many as you need).

EN	*a*	*b*	*0*	*1*	*2*	*3*
1	X	X	1	1	1	1
0	0	0	0	1	1	1
0	0	1	1	0	1	1
0	1	0	1	1	0	1
0	1	1	1	1	1	0

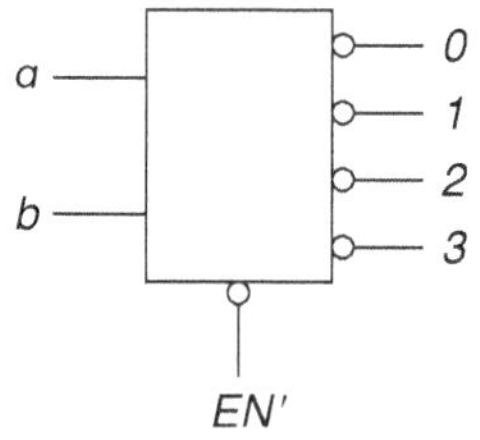

Show a diagram of a circuit to implement these functions with only these components.

5 points extra credit: Show a diagram that uses only 3 eight-input NAND gates and 4 of these decoders.

CHAPTER 6

Analysis of Sequential Systems

Up to now everything has been combinational—that is, the output at any instant of time depends only on what the inputs are at that time. (This ignores the small delay between the time the input of a circuit changes and when the output changes.)

We will now focus on systems that have memory, referred to as *sequential systems* or as *finite state machines*. Thus, the output will depend not only on the present input but also on the past history—what has happened earlier.

We will deal primarily with *clocked* systems (sometimes referred to as *synchronous*). A clock is just a signal that alternates (over time) between 0 and 1 at a regular rate.* Two versions of a clock signal are shown in Figure 6.1. In the first, the clock signal is 0 half of the time and 1 half of the time. In the second, it is 1 for a shorter part of the cycle. The same clock is normally connected to all flip flops.

The period of the signal (T on the diagram) is the length of one cycle. The frequency is the inverse ($1/T$). A frequency of 200 MHz (megahertz, million cycles per second) corresponds to a period of 5 nsec† (5 nanoseconds, 5 billionths of a second). The exact values are not important in most of the discussion that follows.

Figure 6.1 Clock signals.

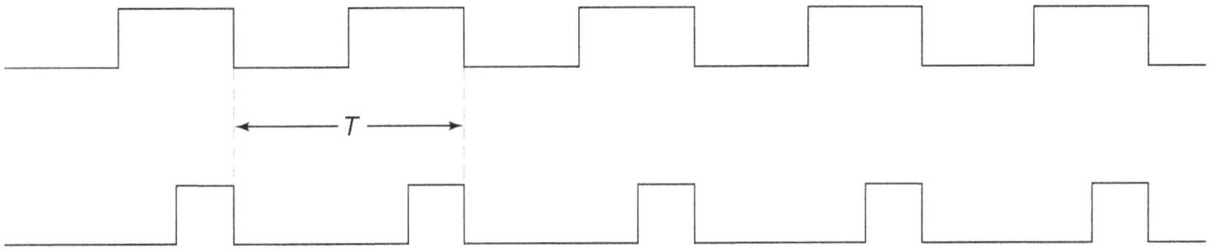

*Although the clock is usually a regular waveform as shown, the regularity of the clock is not crucial to the operation of most sequential systems.

†$1/(200 \times 10^6) = (1000/200) \times 10^{-9} = 5 \times 10^{-9} = 5$ nsec.

In most synchronous systems, change occurs on the transition of the clock signal. We will look at this in more detail as we introduce the several types of *flip flops*, clocked binary storage devices.

The block diagram of Figure 6.2 is a conceptual view of a synchronous sequential system. A sequential system consists of a set of memory devices and some combinational logic. This diagram depicts a system with n inputs (x's), in addition to the clock, k outputs (z's), and m binary storage devices (q's). Each memory device may need one or two input signals. Many systems have only one input and one output, although we will see examples with several of each, and some where there is no input, other than the clock. Many memory devices provide the complemented output (q') as well as q.

Figure 6.2 Conceptual view of a sequential system.

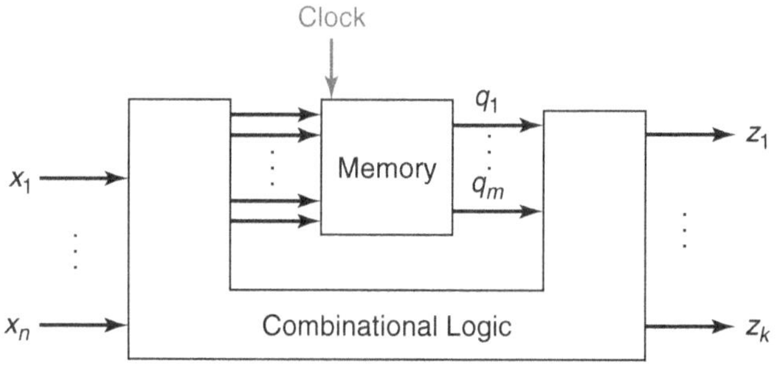

The inputs to the combinational logic are the system inputs and the contents of memory; the combinational logic outputs are the system outputs and signals to update the memory.

In Section 6.2, we will introduce the simplest storage device, the *latch*. It is a static device constructed of gates. The output changes immediately whenever the input changes; there is no clock involved. Latches are used primarily for temporary (buffer) storage.

In Section 6.3, we will develop the most common binary storage device, the flip flop. A flip flop almost always has two outputs, q and q'; that is, both the bit stored and its complement. It may have one or two inputs (indeed, they used to make one with three); we will describe several types of flip flops.

In Section 6.1, we will introduce state table, state diagrams, and timing traces. In Section 6.4, we will discuss the analysis of sequential systems.

6.1 STATE TABLES AND DIAGRAMS

A simple example of a sequential system is the first of a set of continuing examples for sequential systems. (Others will be introduced in Chapter 7.)

CE6. A system with one input x and one output z such that $z = 1$ iff x has been 1 for at least three consecutive clock times.*

For this example, the system must store in its memory information about the last three inputs and produce an output based on that. What is stored in memory is the *state* of the system. Memory consists of a set of binary devices. They may just store the last few inputs, but it is often more economical to code the information in a different way. Sometimes, a finite number of recent inputs is not adequate.

A *timing trace* is a set of values for the input and the output (and sometimes the state or other variables of the system, as well) at consecutive clock times. It is often used to clarify the definition of system behavior or to describe the behavior of a given system. The inputs are an arbitrary set of values that might be applied to the system, chosen so as to demonstrate the behavior of the system. For CE6, the timing trace is shown in Trace 6.1.

Trace 6.1 Three consecutive 1's.

x	0	1	1	0	1	1	1	0	0	1	0	1	1	1	1	1	0	0			
z	?	0	0	0	0	0	0	1	0	0	0	0	0	0	1	1	1	0	0	0	0

For CE6, the output depends only on the state of the system (not the present input) and, thus, occurs after the desired input pattern has occurred. Such a system is called a *Moore model*, named after E. F. Moore. The output for the first input is shown as unknown because we have no history of what happened before. (If the system were initialized to indicate that no 1's had yet occurred, then that output would be 0.) After three consecutive inputs are 1, the system goes to a state where the output is 1, and remains there as long as the input remains 1.

Several designs are possible for this system. We will defer until Chapter 7 our discussion of the techniques for designing a system from a verbal description. At this point, we will introduce two tools for describing sequential systems.

A *state table* shows, for each input combination and each state, what the output is and what the *next state* is, that is, what is to be stored in memory after the next clock.

A *state diagram* (or *state graph*) is a graphical representation of the behavior of the system, showing for each input combination and each state what the output is and what the *next state* is, that is, what is to be stored in memory after the next clock.

Table 6.1 shows an example of a state table, one that does describe CE6, although that is not obvious at this point.

*In Section 6.3, we will define exactly when during the clock that the input matters.

Table 6.1 A state table.

Present state	Next state $x = 0$	Next state $x = 1$	Present output
A	A	B	0
B	A	C	0
C	A	D	0
D	A	D	1

We will refer to the present state as q and the next state as $q^\star$. (Some books use Q or $q+$ or $q(t + \Delta)$ to represent the next state.) The next state is what will be stored in memory after this clock transition. That will then become the present state at the next clock time. The next state is a function of the present state and the input, x. The output, in this example, depends on the present state, but not the present input. The output only changes when the state changes, at the time of a clock transition. The first row of the table signifies that if the system is in state A, that is, fact A is stored in memory and the input is a 0, then the next state is A (that is, A is to be stored in memory again); and if fact A is stored in memory and the input is a 1, then the next state is B. Whenever the system is in state A (or B or C), the output is 0.

The state diagram that corresponds to this state table is shown in Figure 6.3. Each state is represented by a circle. Also included in the circle is the output for that state. Each line coming out of a circle represents a possible transition. The label on the line indicates the input that causes that transition. There must be one path from each state for each possible input combination. (In this example, there is only one input; thus, there are two paths.) Sometimes, the same next state is reached for both input combinations and a single line is shown either with two labels or with a don't care (X). This state diagram contains the identical information as the state table.

Figure 6.3 A state diagram.

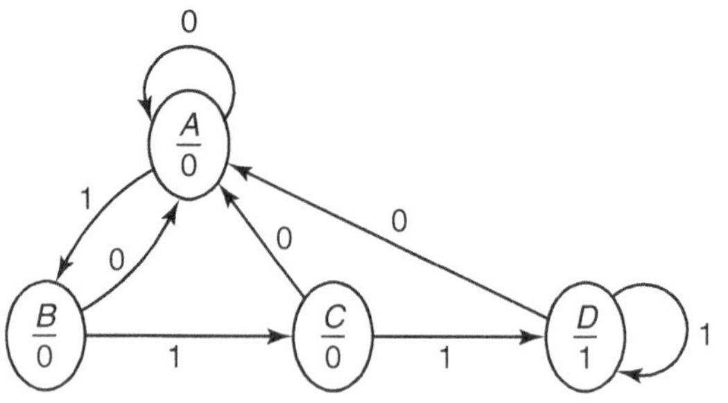

If we were given the state table or diagram, we can construct the timing trace. In Trace 6.2, we repeat the previous trace but include the state.

Trace 6.2 Trace with state.

x	0	1	1	0	1	1	1	0	0	1	0	1	1	1	1	1	0	0		
q	?	A	B	C	A	B	C	D	A	A	B	A	B	C	D	D	D	A	A	?
z	?	0	0	0	0	0	0	1	0	0	0	0	0	0	1	1	1	0	0	0	0

Whether we know the initial state or not, the state table and the state diagram both show that a 0 input takes the system to state A from all states. From state A, a 1 input takes the system to state B; from B, it goes to C; from C, it goes to D; and from D, it remains in D.

In some systems, the output depends not only on the present state of the machine, but also on the present input. This type of system is referred to as a *Mealy model* (after G. B. Mealy). The state table has as many output columns as the next state portion (one for each possible input combination). An example (which we will return to in the next chapter) is shown in Table 6.2.

Table 6.2 State table for a Mealy model system.

	$q^\star$		z	
q	$x = 0$	$x = 1$	$x = 0$	$x = 1$
A	A	B	0	0
B	A	C	0	0
C	A	C	0	1

The Mealy model state diagram is different from the Moore model. The output is associated with the transition, rather than the state, as shown in Figure 6.4. Each path has a double label: the input causing the transition, followed by a slash and the output that occurs when the system is in that state and that is the input. Thus, from state A, the path to state B is labeled 1/0, meaning that that path is followed when $x = 1$, and the output produced is 0.

Figure 6.4 State diagram for the Mealy system of Table 6.2.

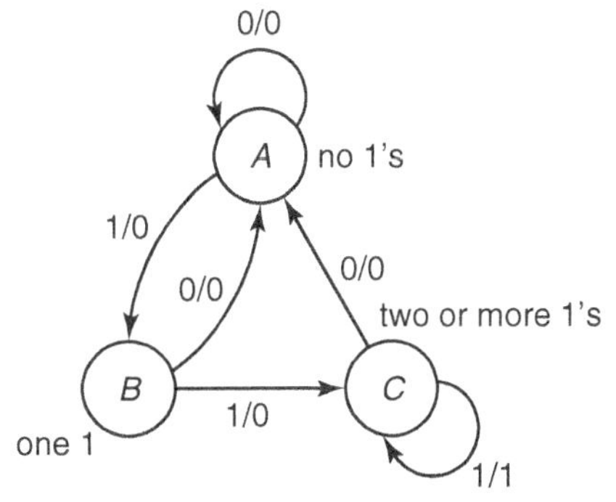

The timing trace (Trace 6.3) is constructed in much the same way as for a Moore model, except that the present output depends on the present input as well as the present state.

Trace 6.3 Timing trace.

x	0	1	1	0	1	1	1	0	0	1	0	1	0	1	1	1	1	1	0	0		
q	?	A	B	C	A	B	C	C	A	A	B	A	B	A	B	C	C	C	C	A	A	
z	0	0	0	0	0	0	1	0	0	0	0	0	0	0	0	0	1	1	0	0	0	0

The analysis and design process for Moore and Mealy machines are very similar. We will return to that issue in Section 6.4 and again in Chapter 7.

[SP 1; EX 1]

6.2 LATCHES

A *latch* is a binary storage device, composed of two or more gates, with feedback—that is, for the simplest two-gate latch, the output of each gate is connected to the input of the other gate. Figure 6.5 shows such a latch, constructed with two NOR gates.

Figure 6.5 A NOR gate latch.

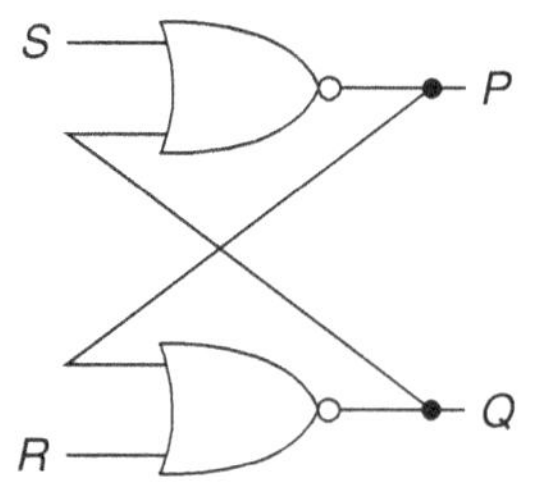

We can write the equations for this system:

$$P = (S + Q)'$$
$$Q = (R + P)'$$

The normal storage state is both inputs 0 (inactive). If S and R are 0, then both equations state that P is the opposite of Q, that is,

$$P = Q' \qquad Q = P'$$

The latch can store either a 0 ($Q = 0$ and $P = 1$) or a 1 ($Q = 1$ and $P = 0$). Thus, the P output is usually just labeled Q'. The letter S is used to indicate *set*, that is, store a 1 in the latch. If $S = 1$ and $R = 0$, then

$$P = (1 + Q)' = 1' = 0$$
$$Q = (0 + 0)' = 0' = 1$$

Thus, a 1 is stored in the latch (on line Q). Similarly, if the *reset* line, R, is made 1 and $S = 0$,

$$Q = (1 + P)' = 1' = 0$$
$$P = (0 + 0)' = 0' = 1$$

Finally, the latch is not operated with both S and R active, since, if $S = 1$ and $R = 1$,

$$P = (1 + Q)' = 1' = 0$$
$$Q = (1 + P)' = 1' = 0$$

Both outputs would be 0 (not the complement of each other). Further, if both S and R became inactive (went to 0) simultaneously, it is not clear to which state the latch would go (since either $Q = 0$ or $Q = 1$ would satisfy the logic equations). What happens would depend on such issues as whether they go to 0 at exactly the same time or one input goes to 0 ahead of the other, in which case the last 1 will dominate. Otherwise, such factors that are beyond the normal interest of the logic designer (such as the stray capacitance or the gain of the individual transistors) will determine the final state. To avoid this problem, we ensure that both inputs are not active simultaneously.

More complex latches can also be built. We will look at a gated latch, as shown in Figure 6.6. When the *Gate* signal is inactive (= 0), *SG* and *RG* are both 0, and the latch remains unchanged. Only when *Gate* goes to 1, can a 0 or 1 be stored in the latch, exactly as in the simpler latch of Figure 6.5.

Figure 6.6 A gated latch.

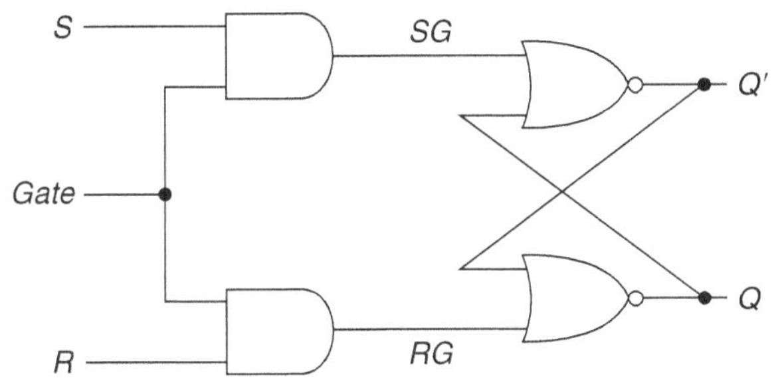

[SP 2; EX 2]

6.3 FLIP FLOPS

A *flip flop* is a clocked binary storage device, that is, a device that stores either a 0 or a 1. Under normal operation, that value will only change on the appropriate transition of the clock.* The state of the system (that is, what is in memory) changes on the transition of the clock. For some flip flops, that change takes place when the clock goes from 1 to 0; that is referred to as *trailing-edge triggered.* For others, that change takes place when the clock goes from 0 to 1; that is referred to as *leading-edge triggered.* What is stored after the transition depends on the flip flop data inputs and what was stored in the flip flop prior to the transition.

Flip flops have one or two outputs. One output is the state of the flip flop. If there are two, the other output is the complement of the state.

---

*Many flip flops also have asynchronous clear and/or preset inputs that override the clock and put a 0 (clear) or a 1 (preset) in the flip flop immediately, in much the same way as in the simple *SR* latch. We will address that issue shortly.

Individual flip flops almost always have both outputs. However, when several flip flops are contained in one integrated circuit package, pin limitations may make only the uncomplemented output available.

A simple SR *master/slave* flip flop can be constructed with two gated latches, as shown in Figure 6.7. When the clock is 1, the S and R inputs establish the values for the first flip flop, the *master.* During that time, the *slave* is not enabled. As soon as the clock goes to 0, the master is disabled and the slave enabled. The values of the master's outputs, X and X', are determined by the value of S and R just before the trailing edge. These are the inputs of the slave. Thus, the slave (and the flip flop output) changes as the clock goes to 0 (on the trailing edge) and remains that way until the next clock cycle. We could get a leading-edge triggered flip flop by connecting the clock to the slave and its complement to the master. The change in the output of the flip flop is delayed from the edge of the clock (a somewhat longer delay than that through a gate). Commercial flip flops use a more complex but faster circuit.

We will concentrate on two types of flip flops, the D and the JK. The D flip flop is the most straightforward and is commonly found in programmable logic devices (Chapter 8). The JK flip flop almost always produces the simplest combinational logic. We will also introduce the SR and T flip flops, in between the discussion of the D and JK, since they naturally lead to the JK.

Figure 6.7 A master/slave flip flop.

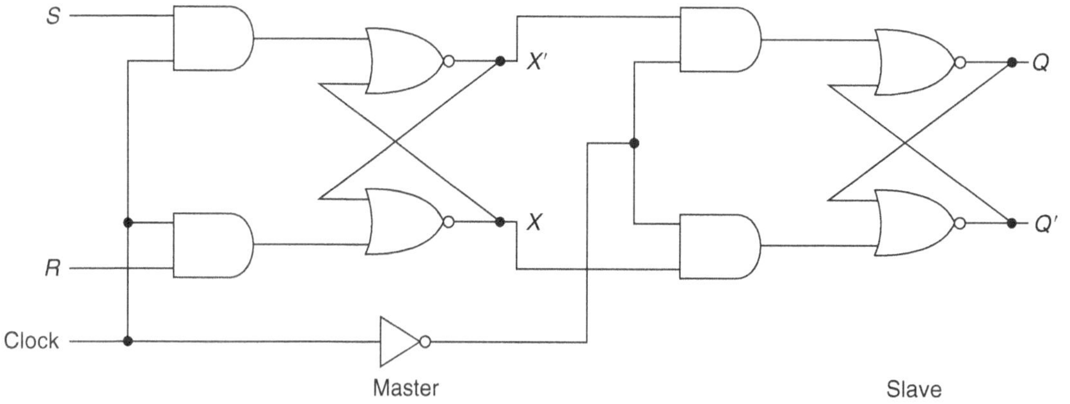

The simplest flip flop is the D flip flop. The name comes from **D**elay, since the output is just the input delayed until the next active clock transition. The next state of the D flip flop is the value of D before the clock transition. Block diagrams of D flip flops, both trailing-edge triggered and leading-edge triggered, are shown in Figure 6.8. The triangle is used to indicate which input is the clock. A circle is usually shown on the clock input of a trailing-edge triggered flip flop. (We will do that consistently.) Caution is in order, however, since some publications do not differentiate in the diagram.

Figure 6.8 *D* flip flop diagrams.

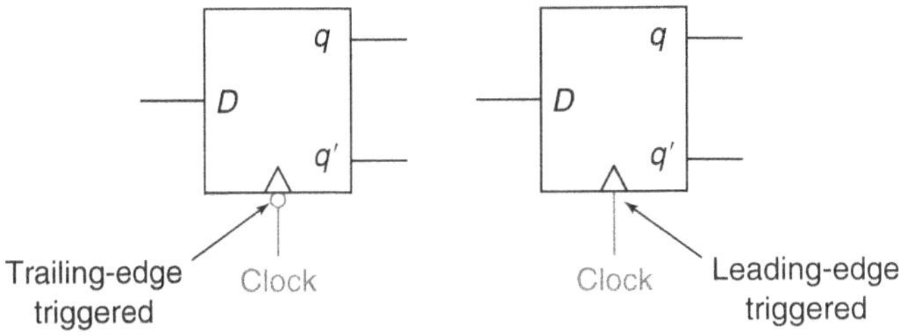

We will use two forms of a truth table (Table 6.3) and a state diagram to describe the behavior of each type of flip flop. Although these are particularly simple for the *D* flip flop, we will show them here as well. In the first form of the truth table, the flip flop input(s) and the present state are in the input columns; in the second, only the flip flop input(s) are needed. The state diagram for a *D* flip flop is shown in Figure 6.9. It has two states (for all types of flip flops). The transition paths are labeled with the input that causes that transition. The output is not shown in the circle since it is the same as the state.

Figure 6.9 *D* flip flop state diagram.

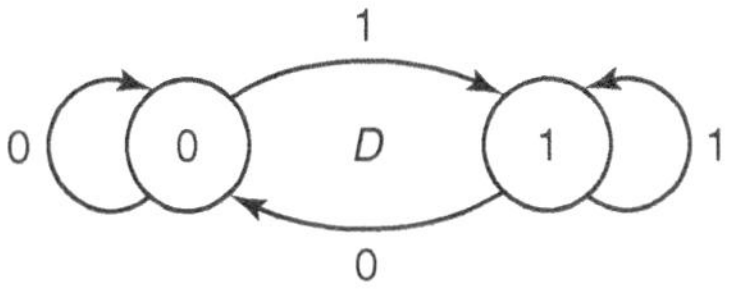

Table 6.3 The *D* flip flop behavioral tables.

D	q	$q^\star$
0	0	0
0	1	0
1	0	1
1	1	1

D	$q^\star$
0	0
1	1

The next state of a flip flop can be described algebraically as a function of its inputs and present state (by obtaining an equation directly from the first truth table). In the case of the *D* flip flop, the equation is

$$q^\star = D$$

The behavior of a trailing-edge triggered *D* flip flop is illustrated in the timing diagram of Figure 6.10a. Unless we know the initial value of q, that is, what was stored in the flip flop before we started to look, then q is unknown until after the first negative-going clock transition. That is indicated by the slashed section on the timing diagram. When the first trailing edge of the clock occurs, the state of the flip flop is established.

Figure 6.10 *D* flip flop timing diagram.

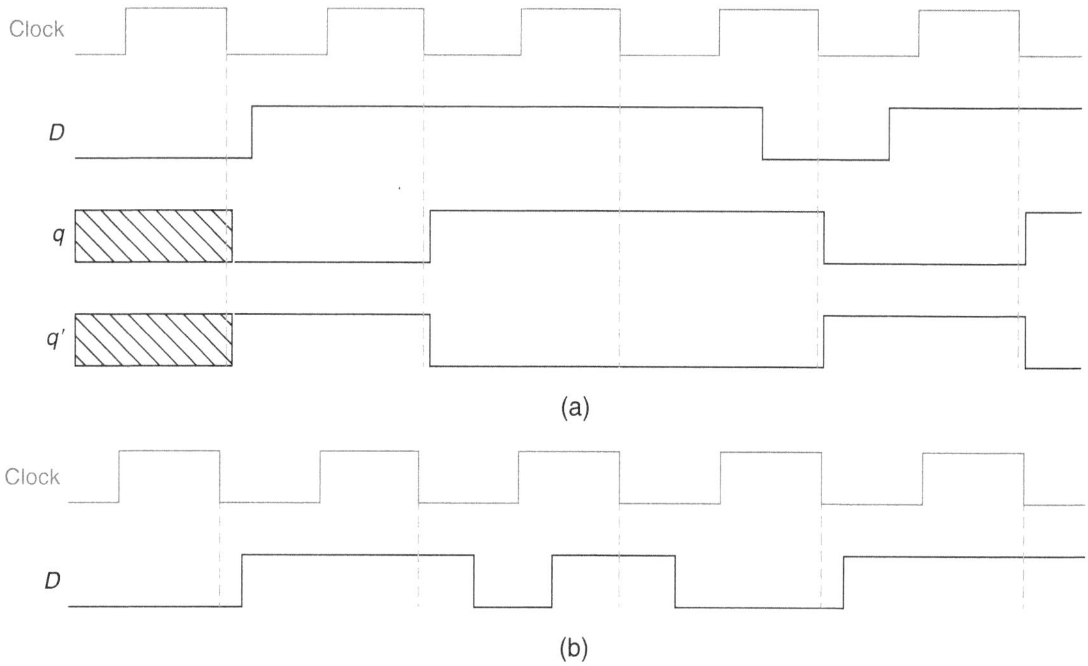

Since D is 0 at that time, q goes to 0 (and, of course, q' goes to 1). Note that there is a slight delay in the output. The input, D, usually changes shortly after the transition, as shown for the first change, but may change at any time, as long as it has reached the correct value well before the next active transition. (Note that the second and third changes in D come later in the clock cycle.) As shown, the q' output is (as the name implies) the opposite of the q output. At the second trailing edge, D is 1; thus, q is 1 for the next clock period. At the third trailing edge, D is still 1, and q remains 1 for another clock period. Note that if the D input were to go back and forth between clock transitions, as shown in Figure 6.10b, the output would not be affected, since the value of D is only relevant near the time of a trailing edge. It would be the same as in Figure 6.10a.*

Next, we will look at the behavior of a leading-edge triggered version of that flip flop. The tables describing the flip flop need not be modified; the only difference is when the output changes relative to the clock. A timing diagram for a leading-edge triggered D flip flop, using the same input as before, is shown in Figure 6.11. The output (the state of the flip

*In some flip flops, the input must be established by the preceding leading edge. We will not discuss those further.

flop) changes shortly after the clock goes from 0 to 1 (based on the input just before that transition).

Figure 6.11 Leading-edge triggered D flip flop.

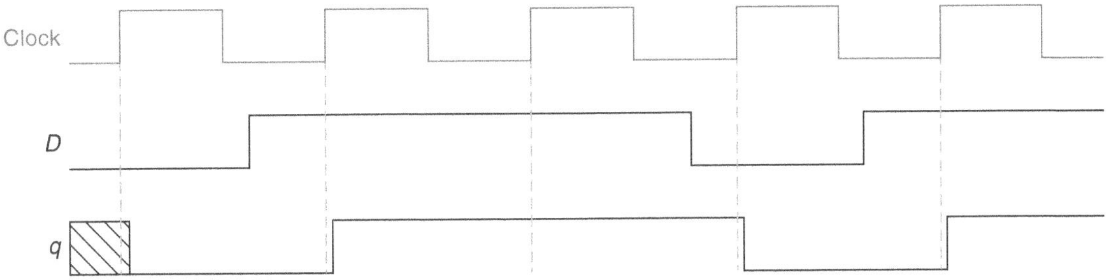

Since the behavior of the flip flop at a clock transition depends on the value of the flip flop inputs prior to that transition, we can connect the output of one flip flop to the input of another, as shown in Figure 6.12 (with trailing-edge triggered flip flops), and clock them simultaneously. At a clock transition when flip flop q changes, the old value of q is used to compute the behavior of r, as indicated in the timing diagram of Figure 6.13. The input to the first flip flop has not changed from the last example, and thus, q is the same as it was before. (We have not shown q' on this diagram.) At the first trailing edge, the input to r (the output of the q flip flop) is unknown; thus, the output remains unknown after that clock. At the second trailing edge, the input to r is 0 and thus r goes to 0. That flip flop q changes from 0 to 1 as a result of this clock edge is not relevant; it is the value of the input *before* the clock edge that determines the behavior of r. The new value of q will be used to determine the

Figure 6.12 Two flip flops.

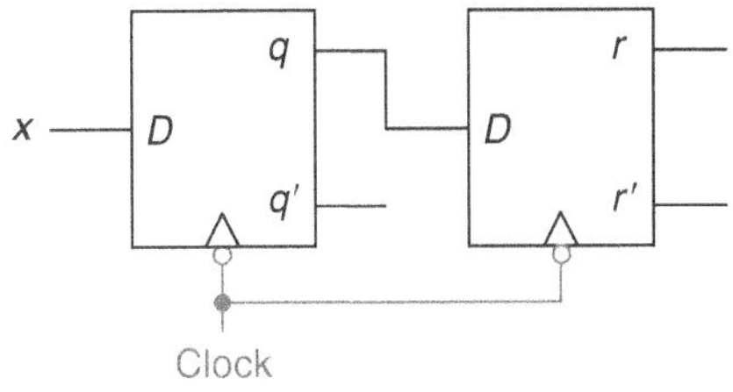

Figure 6.13 Timing for two flip flops.

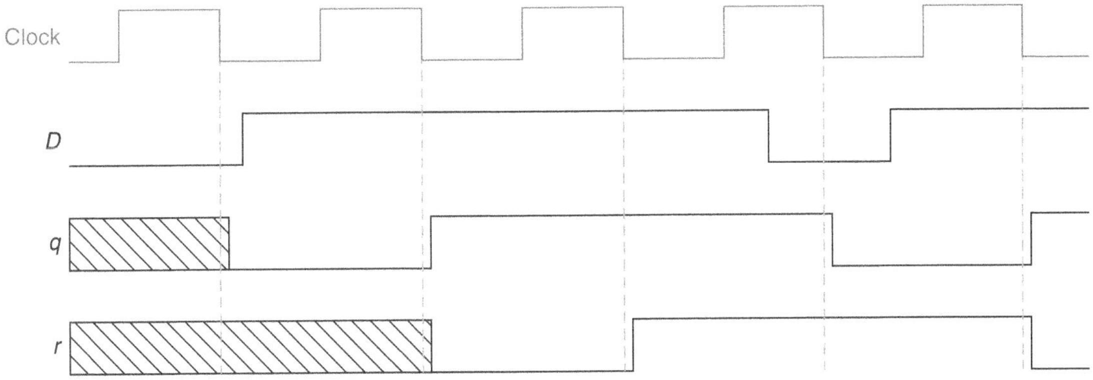

behavior of r at the next clock transition. The output of flip flop r is a replica of that of q, delayed by one clock period.

This type of behavior is common throughout sequential systems. Usually, all flip flops in the system are triggered by the same clock. Often, the inputs to flip flops are a function of the contents of the flip flops of the system, as was shown in the global view of a sequential system at the beginning of this chapter.

Before going on to look at other types of flip flops, we will examine the behavior of flip flops with *static (asynchronous) clear** and preset inputs. Any type of flip flop may have one or both of these available. A D flip flop with active low (the most common arrangement) clear and preset inputs is shown in Figure 6.14. The version on the left uses overbars for the complement (the most common notation in the integrated circuit literature); we will continue to use primes, as on the right, where the behavior of the flip flop is described by the truth table of Table 6.4. The clear and preset inputs act immediately (except for circuit delay) and override the clock, that is, they force the output to 0 and 1, respectively. Only when both of these static inputs are 1, does the flip flop behave as before, with the clock transition and the D input determining the behavior. A timing example is shown in Figure 6.15. The clear input becomes active near the beginning of the time shown, forcing q to 0. As long as that input remains 0, the clock and D are ignored; thus, nothing changes at the first trailing edge of the clock that is shown. Once the clear returns to 1, then the clock and D take over; but they have no effect until the next trailing edge of the clock. The D input determines the behavior of the flip flop at the next four trailing edges. When the preset input goes to 0, the flip flop output goes to 1. When the preset input goes back to 1, the clock and D once again take over.

Figure 6.14 Flip flop with clear and preset inputs.

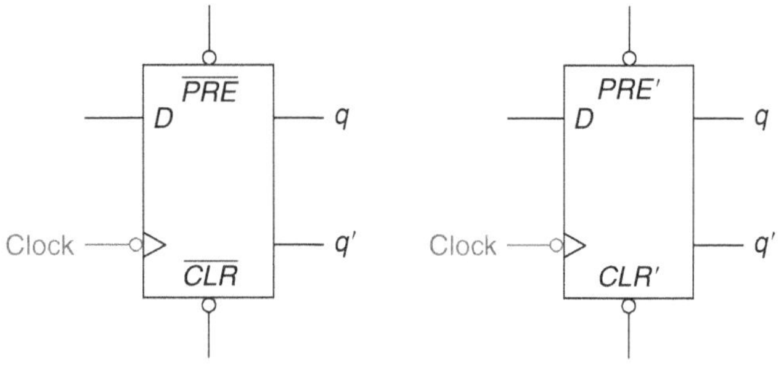

Table 6.4 D flip flop with clear and preset inputs behavioral table.

PRE'	*CLR'*	*D*	*q*	$q^\star$	
0	1	X	X	1	static
1	0	X	X	0	immediate
0	0	X	X	—	not allowed
1	1	0	0	0	
1	1	0	1	0	clocked
1	1	1	0	1	(as before)
1	1	1	1	1	

*Preset is sometimes referred to as *set,* in which case, clear may be referred to as *reset.*

Figure 6.15 Timing for flip flop with clear and preset.

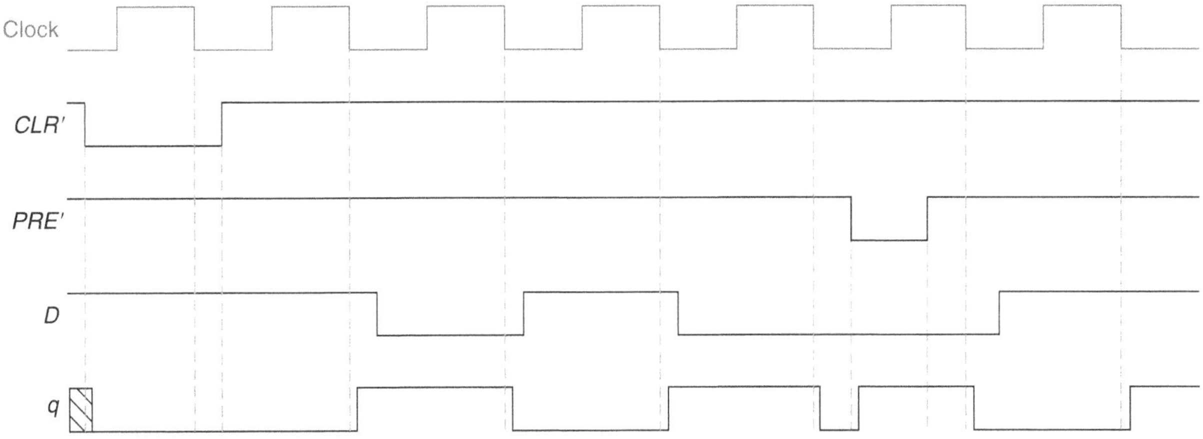

Table 6.5 *SR* flip flop behavioral tables.

S	*R*	*q*	$q^\star$	
0	0	0	0	
0	0	1	1	
0	1	0	0	
0	1	1	0	
1	0	0	1	
1	0	1	1	
1	1	0	—	not
1	1	1	—	allowed

S	*R*	$q^\star$	
0	0	*q*	
0	1	0	
1	0	1	
1	1	—	not allowed

Figure 6.16 *SR* flip flop state diagram.

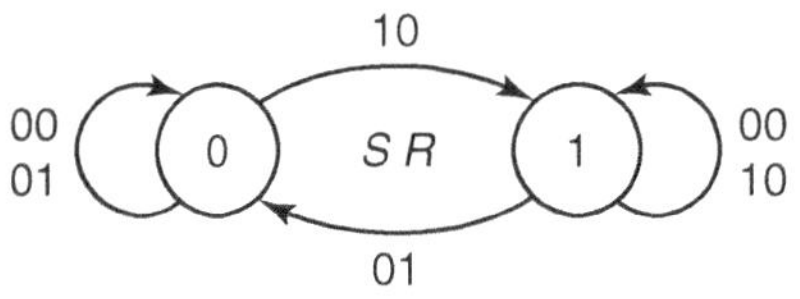

Next, we will look at the *SR* (**S**et-**R**eset) flip flop. It has two inputs, *S* and *R*, which have the same meaning as those for the *SR* latch. Its behavior is described by the truth tables of Table 6.5 and state diagram of Figure 6.16. The Set (*S*) input causes a 1 to be stored in the flip flop at the next active clock edge; the Reset (*R*) input causes a 0 to be stored. The *S* and *R* inputs are never made 1 at the same time. Although that would not damage the flip flop, as in the case of the latch, it is not certain what happens when *S* and *R* both go back to 0. Note that in the diagram, each label is two digits; the first is the value of *S* and the second the value of *R*. Two labels are on the path from 0 to 0 since either 00 or 01 will cause the flip flop to return to state 0. (There are also two input combinations that cause the flip flop to go from state 1 to 1.)

In Map 6.1, we map $q^\star$ (from the first truth table). Notice that two of the squares are don't cares, since we will never make both *S* and *R* equal to 1 at the same time. This allows us to write an equation for the next

Map 6.1 *SR* flip flop behavioral map.

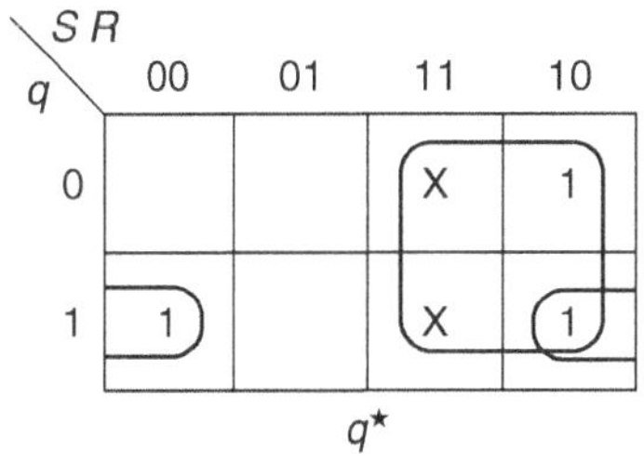

state of the flip flop, $q^\star$, in terms of the present state, q, and the inputs, S and R:

$$q^\star = S + R'q$$

The equation says that after the clock, there will be a 1 in the flip flop if we set it ($S = 1$) or if there was already a 1 and we don't reset it ($R = 0$). A timing example (where there is only a clear input, not a preset one) is given in Figure 6.17. Note that we never made both S and R equal to 1 at the same time. Also, when both S and R are 0, q does not change.

Figure 6.17 *SR* flip flop timing diagram.

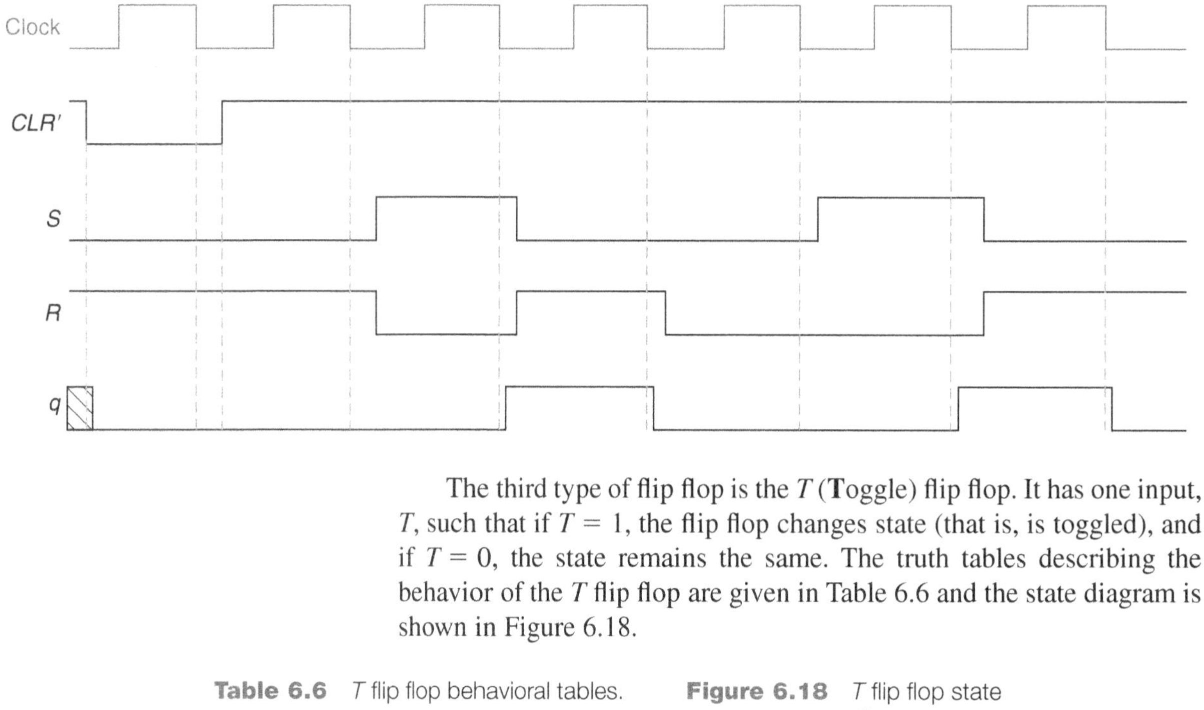

The third type of flip flop is the T (**T**oggle) flip flop. It has one input, T, such that if $T = 1$, the flip flop changes state (that is, is toggled), and if $T = 0$, the state remains the same. The truth tables describing the behavior of the T flip flop are given in Table 6.6 and the state diagram is shown in Figure 6.18.

Table 6.6 *T* flip flop behavioral tables.

T	q	$q^\star$
0	0	0
0	1	1
1	0	1
1	1	0

T	$q^\star$
0	q
1	q'

Figure 6.18 *T* flip flop state diagram.

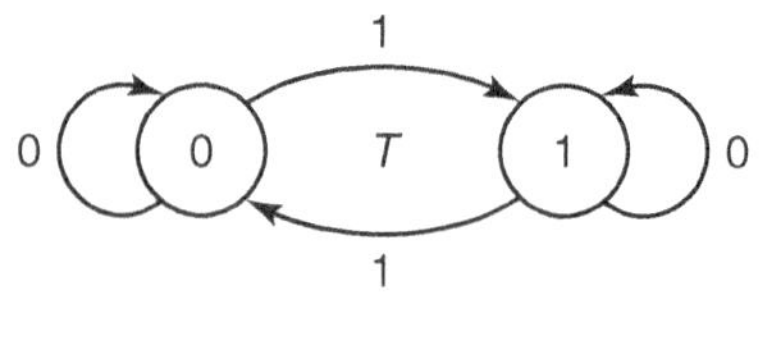

The behavioral equation is

$$q^\star = T \oplus q$$

and a timing example is shown in Figure 6.19.*

*The T flip flop must have static clear or preset, since the next state always depends on the previous one. For each of the other types of flip flops, there is at least one input combination that will force the flip flop to state 0.

Figure 6.19 *T* flip flop timing diagram.

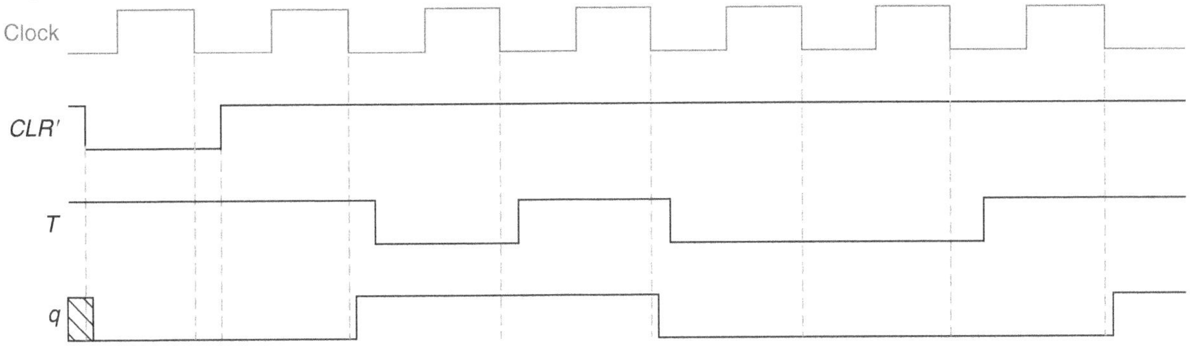

The last type of flip flop we will present is the *JK* (where the letters are not an acronym), which is a combination of the *SR* and *T*, in that it behaves like an *SR* flip flop, except that $J = K = 1$ causes the flip flop to change states (as in $T = 1$). The truth tables are given in Table 6.7 and the state diagram is shown in Figure 6.20.

Table 6.7 *JK* flip flop behavioral tables.

J	K	q	$q^\star$
0	0	0	0
0	0	1	1
0	1	0	0
0	1	1	0
1	0	0	1
1	0	1	1
1	1	0	1
1	1	1	0

J	K	$q^\star$
0	0	q
0	1	0
1	0	1
1	1	q'

Figure 6.20 *JK* flip flop state diagram.

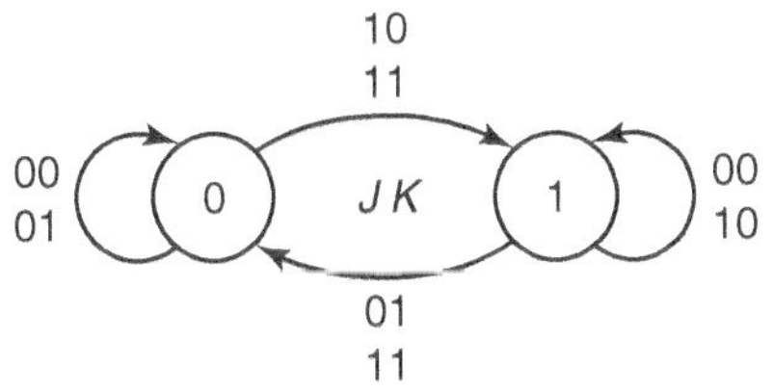

From the first truth table, we can derive Map 6.2 and the equation for $q^\star$:

$$q^\star = Jq' + K'q$$

A timing example for the *JK* flip flop is shown in Figure 6.21. Note that there are times when both *J* and *K* are 1 simultaneously; the flip flop just changes state at those times.

We now have the behavioral aspects of all of the flip flops and can begin to analyze more complex systems. Before we continue with that, we will look at some of the commercially available flip flop packages. *D* and *JK* flip flops are the most common. We will look at four packages, all of which are available in LogicWorks and in the Breadboard simulator (although the latter two are listed under registers in the simulator).

Map 6.2 *JK* flip flop behavioral map.

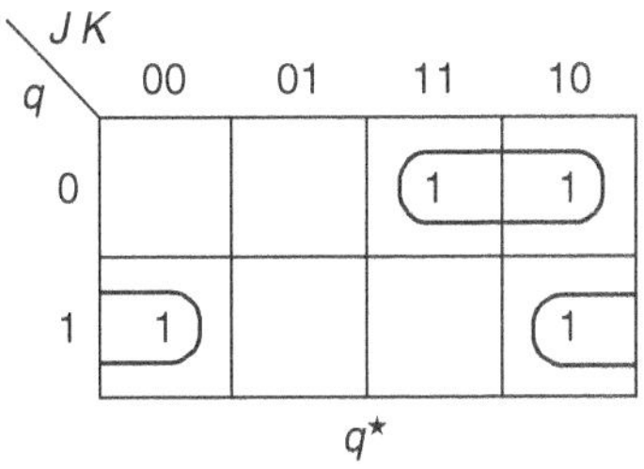

Figure 6.21 Timing diagram for *JK* flip flop.

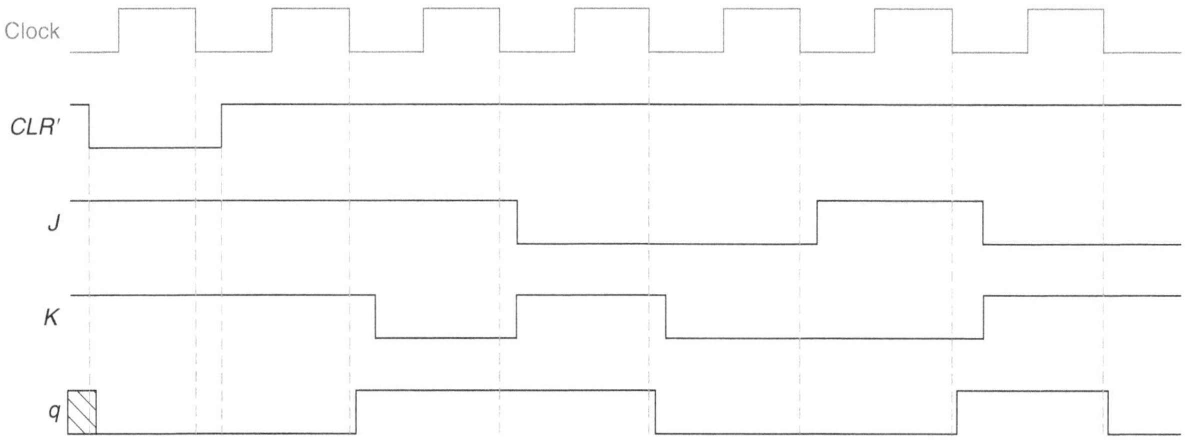

The 7473 is a dual *JK* flip flop package. It contains two independent *JK* flip flops, each of which has an active low clear input, and both q and q' outputs. It is trailing-edge triggered (with separate clock inputs for each of the flip flops). (Each flip flop has four inputs—*J*, *K*, clear, and clock—and two outputs—q and q'; it fits in a 14-pin integrated circuit package.)

The 7474 is a dual *D* flip flop, also in a 14-pin package. Since there is only one data input per flip flop, there are two available pins; they are used for active low preset inputs. It is leading-edge triggered (with separate clock inputs for each of the flip flops).

There are packages of *D* flip flops with four or six flip flops. The 74174 is a hex (six) *D* flip flop package, with only a q output for each flip flop and a common leading-edge triggered clock. There is a common active low clear (sometimes referred to as a Master Reset). This is a 16-pin package.

Lastly, we have the 74175, a quad (four) *D* flip flop package. Each flip flop has both a q and q' output. There is a common leading-edge triggered clock and a common active low clear. Once again, this is a 16-pin package. The pin connections for these are shown in Appendix A.6.

[SP 3, 4; EX 3, 4, 5, 6; LAB]

6.4 ANALYSIS OF SEQUENTIAL SYSTEMS

In this section, we will examine some small state machines (consisting of flip flops and gates) and analyze their behavior, that is, produce timing diagrams, timing traces, state tables, and state diagrams. We will also look at the relationship between the state table and the timing.

The first example, the circuit of Figure 6.22, is a circuit with two trailing-edge triggered *D* flip flops. (We will call the flip flops q_1 and q_2; sometimes we will use names, such as *A* and *B*.)

Figure 6.22 A D flip flop Moore model circuit.

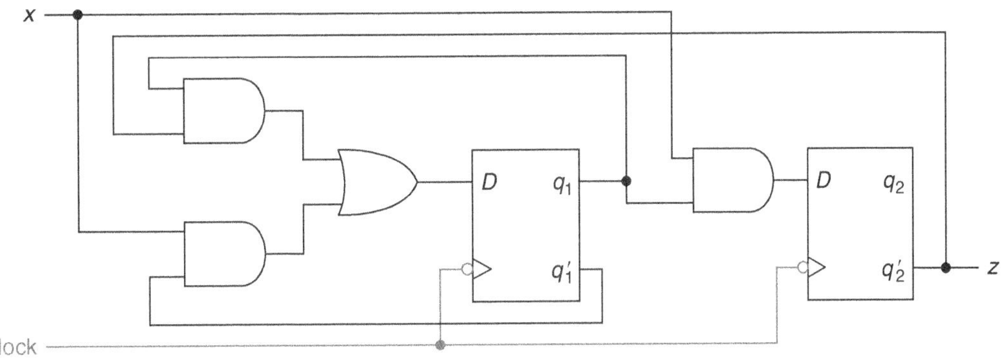

From the circuit, we find

$$D_1 = q_1 q_2' + x q_1'$$
$$D_2 = x q_1$$
$$z = q_2'$$

We will first construct the state table. Since this is a Moore model, there is only one output column. The next state part is particularly easy for a D flip flop $q^\star = D$. We first complete the output (z) column and the $q_1^\star$ ($= D_1$) part of the table as shown in Table 6.8a.

Finally, we add $q_2^\star(D_2)$ to produce the complete state table of Table 6.8b.

Table 6.8a Partial state table.

	$q_1^\star$ $q_2^\star$		
q_1q_2	$x = 0$	$x = 1$	z
0 0	0	1	1
0 1	0	1	0
1 0	1	1	1
1 1	0	0	0

Table 6.8b Complete state table.

	$q_1^\star$ $q_2^\star$		
q_1q_2	$x = 0$	$x = 1$	z
0 0	0 0	1 0	1
0 1	0 0	1 0	0
1 0	1 0	1 1	1
1 1	0 0	0 1	0

Figure 6.23 A Moore state diagram.

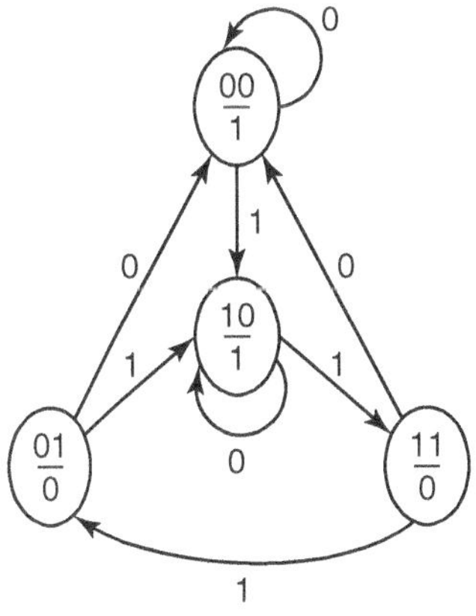

The corresponding state diagram is shown in Figure 6.23.

We will now look at a Moore model circuit with JK flip flops (See Figure 6.24).

Figure 6.24 A Moore model circuit.

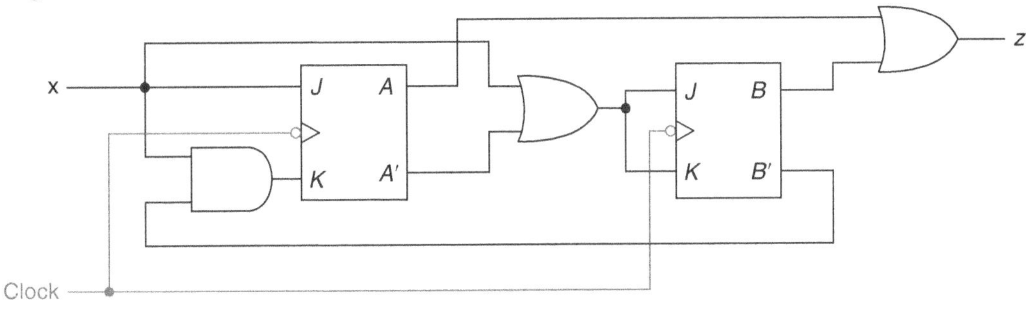

This is a Moore model, since the output z, which equals $A + B$, is a function of the state (that is, the contents of the flip flops) and not of the input x.

We will now write equations for the flip flop inputs and the output, and, from them, construct a state table:

$$J_A = x \qquad K_A = xB'$$
$$J_B = K_B = x + A'$$
$$z = A + B$$

The output column comes directly from the z equation. We can now fill in the next state section one entry at a time. For the first entry, since $x = A = B = 0$, $J_A = K_A = 0$ and $J_B = K_B = 1$. From the flip flop behavioral table of Table 6.7 (Section 6.3), we can see that A does not change state, but B does. Thus, the next state is 0 1. Next, for $x = A = 0$ and $B = 1$ (the second row of the first column), $J_A = K_A = 0$ and $J_B = K_B = 1$. Again, A does not change state, but once again B does. The resulting next state is 00. At this point, we have the state table of Table 6.9a.

Table 6.9a State table with first two entries.

	$A^\star B^\star$		
$A\ B$	$x = 0$	$x = 1$	z
0 0	0 1		0
0 1	0 0		1
1 0			1
1 1			1

We can continue through the remaining entries, or we can look at the equations for one flip flop at a time (as we did with the D flip flops). When $x = 0$ (no matter what A and B are), $J_A = K_A = 0$ and flip flop A does not change state. Thus, we can complete $A^\star$ for $x = 0$, as in Table 6.9b. When $x = 1$, $J_A = 1$ and $K_A = B'$. For the two rows where $B = 0$ (the first and third), J_A and K_A are both 1 and A toggles. For the two rows where $B = 1$ (the second and fourth), $J_A = 1$ and $K_A = 0$, putting a 1 in flip flop A. That results in the partial table (where $A^\star$ has been filled in) of Table 6.9b.

Table 6.9b State table with $A^\star$ entered.

	$A^\star B^\star$		
$A\ B$	$x = 0$	$x = 1$	z
0 0	0	1	0
0 1	0	1	1
1 0	1	0	1
1 1	1	1	1

Now we can complete the $B^\star$ section of the table. When $A = 0$ (the first two rows of both columns), $J_B = K_B = 1$ and B changes state. When $A = 1$, $J_B = K_B = x$. For $x = 0$ (the first column, last two rows), B remains unchanged. Finally, for $A = 1$ and $x = 1$, $J_B = K_B = 1$ and B changes, producing the completed Table 6.9c.

Table 6.9c Completed state table.

	$A^\star B^\star$		
A B	**x = 0**	**x = 1**	z
0 0	0 1	1 1	0
0 1	0 0	1 0	1
1 0	1 0	0 1	1
1 1	1 1	1 0	1

Another technique to construct the state table is to use the equations we developed in the last section for the next state, namely,

$$q^\star = Jq' + K'q$$

Using the values from this problem, we obtain

$$A^\star = J_A A' + K'_A A = xA' + (xB')'A = xA' + x'A + AB$$
$$B^\star = J_B B' + K'_B B = (x + A')B' + (x + A')'B$$
$$= xB' + A'B' + x'AB$$

We can now construct the state table as we did with D flip flops. These equations give exactly the same results as before.

For this example, we will produce a timing trace and a timing diagram if we are given the input x and the initial state.* The values of x and the initial values of A and B in Trace 6.4 are given.

Trace 6.4 Trace for Table 6.9.

x	[0]	0	1	0	1	1	0		
A	[0] →	[0]	0	1	1	1	0	0	
B	[0]	[1]	0	1	1	0	1	0	1
	↓								
z	[0]	1	0	1	1	1	1	0	1

*The process is really a repetition of what we did in Trace 6.2. The major differences are that there we had state names and here we have the values of the state variables (flip flops).

At the first clock edge, the values in the shaded box determine the next state (the box to the right) and the present output (the box below). The next state is obtained from the first row ($AB = 00$) and the first column ($x = 0$), the shaded square in Table 6.9c. The output is just the value of z in the first row. (Only the state is needed to determine the output.) For the next column of the timing trace, we start the process over again; this is effectively a new problem. The state is 01 (second row of the state table) and the input is 0, giving a next state of 00. This continues through successive inputs. The last input shown, a 0 when the system is in state 01 takes the system to state 00. We know that state and that output, even though we do not know the input any longer. Finally, for this example, we can determine the output and the value of B for one more clock time, since, from state 00, the next state is either 01 or 11, both of which have $B = 1$ and a 1 output. (We cannot go any further.)

In Figure 6.25, we will next look at a timing diagram for the same system with the same input sequence. We must look at the value of the variables (A, B, and x) just before the trailing edge. From that, we know the present state and the input, and can determine what the values for A and B must be during the next clock period. At any time that we know A and B, we can determine z.

Figure 6.25 Timing diagram for Table 6.9.

We did not need to construct the state table to obtain either the timing diagram or the trace. We could, at each clock trailing edge, determine the behavior of each flip flop. The output can then be constructed last, since it is just the OR of the two state variables (A and B). Thus, when the first clock edge arrives, $A = B = x = 0$ and, thus, $J_A = K_A = 0$, leaving A at 0. At the same time, $J_B = K_B = 1$ and thus B toggles, that is, goes to 1. We can now shift our attention to the next clock time and repeat the computations.

At this point, a word is in order about the initial value. For this example, we assumed that we knew what was stored in A and B when the first clock arrived. That may have been achieved using a static clear input, which was not shown to simplify this problem. In some cases, we can determine the behavior of the system after one or two clock periods even if we did not know the initial value. (That will be the case in the next example.) But, in this problem, we must initialize the system. (Try the other initial states and note that each follows a completely different sequence over the time period shown.) Finally, for this problem (a Moore model), the state diagram is given in Figure 6.26.

Figure 6.26 State diagram for Table 6.9.

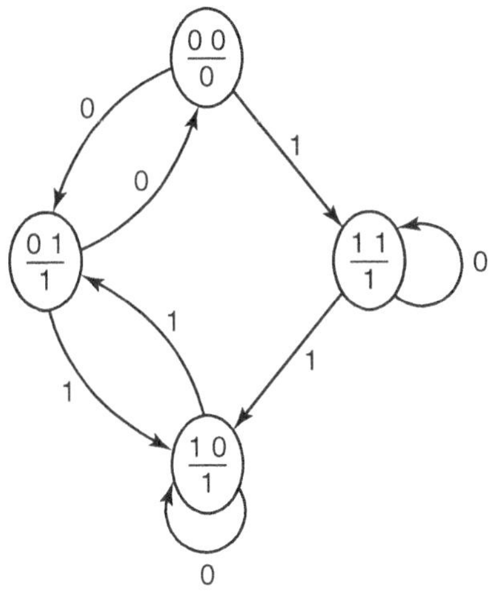

In some systems, the output depends on the present input, as well as the state. From a circuit point of view, that just means that z is a function of x, as well as the state variables. This type of circuit is referred to as a *Mealy model.* An example of such a system is shown in Figure 6.27.

Figure 6.27 A Mealy model.

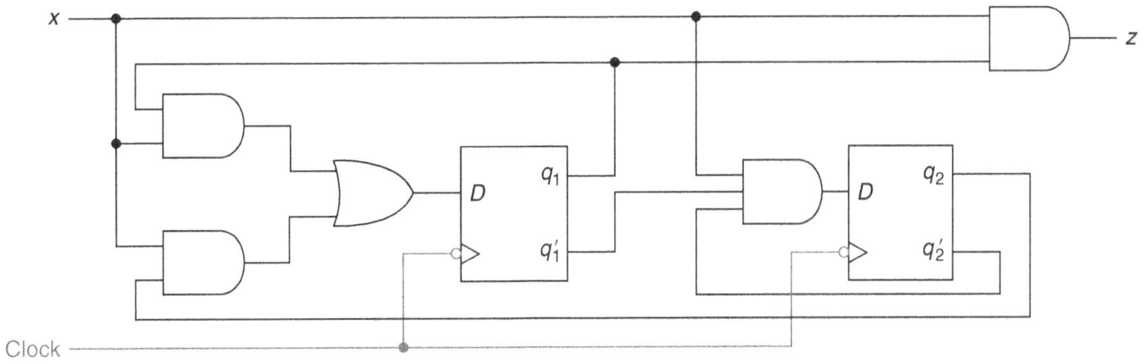

The flip flop input and the output equations are

$$D_1 = xq_1 + xq_2$$
$$D_2 = xq_1'q_2'$$
$$z = xq_1$$

Of course, with D flip flops, $q^\star = D$. Thus,

$$q_1^\star = xq_1 + xq_2$$
$$q_2^\star = xq_1'q_2'$$

From that, we obtain the state table of Table 6.10. Notice that we need two output columns, one for $x = 0$ and one for $x = 1$.

Table 6.10 State table for the Mealy system.

	$q^\star$		z	
q	$x = 0$	$x = 1$	$x = 0$	$x = 1$
0 0	0 0	0 1	0	0
0 1	0 0	1 0	0	0
1 0	0 0	1 0	0	1
1 1	0 0	1 0	0	1

Note that state 11 is never reached; this problem really only has 3 states (although when the system is first turned on, it could start in state 11). But after the first clock, it will leave that state and never return. That becomes obvious from the state diagram of Figure 6.28.

Figure 6.28 State diagram for a Mealy model.

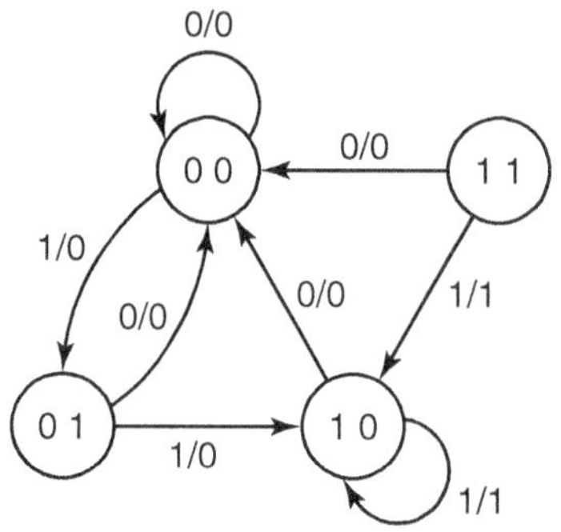

Notice that there is no path into state 11. Also note that whenever there is a 0 input, we return to state 00. Thus, even if we do not initialize this system, it will behave properly after the first 0 input.

We will next look at the timing trace (see Trace 6.5, where the input is given and shown in tan) and then at the timing diagram for this system.

Trace 6.5 Mealy model timing.

x	0	1	1	0	1	1	1	1	0		
q_1	?	0	→ 0	1	0	0	1	1	1	0	
q_2	?	0	1	0	0	1	0	0	0	0	
		↓									
z	0	0	0	0	0	0	1	1	0	0	0

Even though we do not know the initial state (the ? for q_1 and q_2), the 0 input forces the system to state 00 at the next clock time and we complete the trace. Note that the output is known for two clock periods after the input is not, since the system cannot reach state 10 (the only state for which there is a 1 output) any sooner than that. A word of caution: The present state and the present input determine the *present* output and the *next* state, as indicated.

The timing diagram for this example is shown in Figure 6.29. It illustrates a peculiarity of Mealy systems.* Note that there is a *false output* (sometimes referred to as a *glitch*), that is, the output goes to 1 for a short period even though that is not indicated in the timing trace nor in the state table.

Figure 6.29 Illustration of false output.

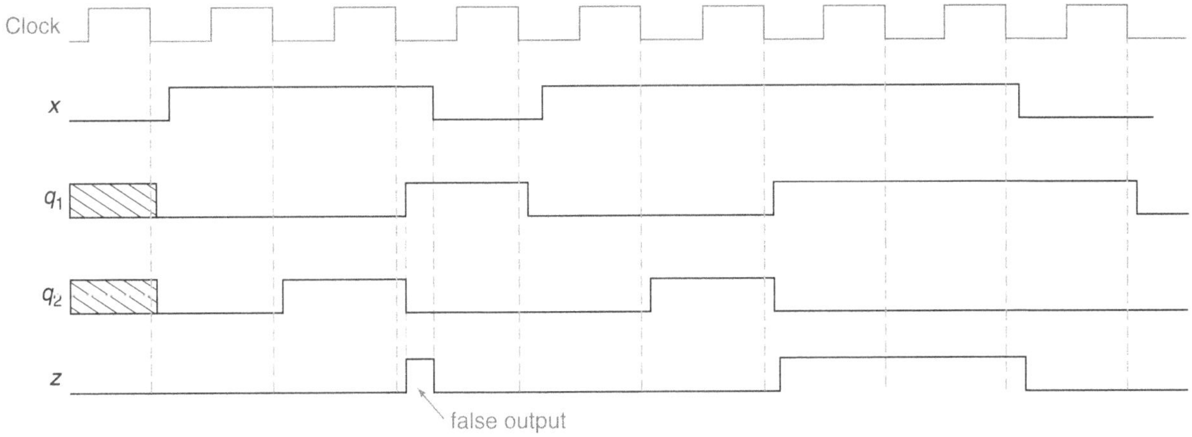

The output comes from combinational logic; it is just xq_1. If the input x does not change simultaneously with the trailing edge of the clock (as is the case here), and it remains 1 after q_1 goes to 1, the output will go to 1. But the output indicated by the state table or the timing trace is based on the value of q_1 at the time of the next clock. The false output is not usually important, since the output of a Mealy system is mainly of interest at clock times (that is, just before the edge on which flip flops might change state). Furthermore, it is often the case that system inputs change

*In the timing diagram, the delay through the output AND gate is ignored since it is typically shorter than that of the flip flop.

simultaneously with the trailing edge of the clock.* The glitch occurred only because x changed well after the flip flop change. As the change in x gets closer (in time) to the changes in q (that is, the clock edge), the glitch gets narrower and if x goes to 0 at the same time that q_1 goes to 1, the false output disappears.

EXAMPLE 6.1a

Consider the following circuit with one JK and one D flip flop:

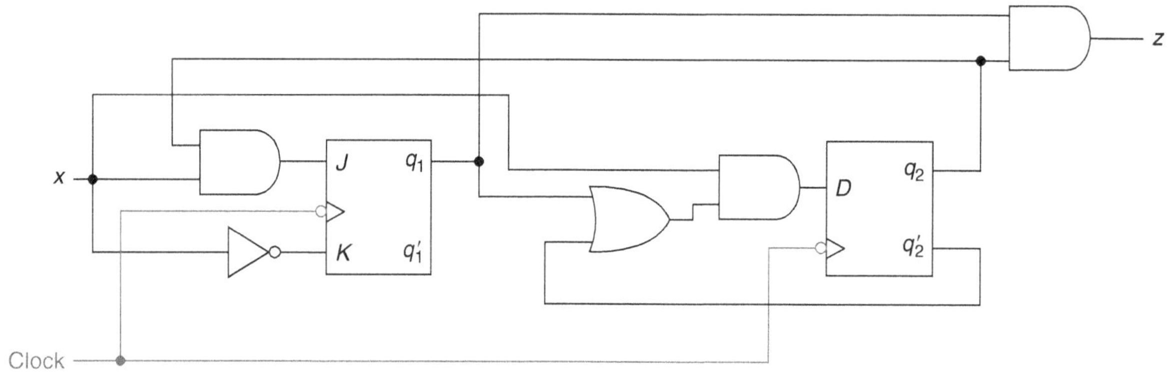

The output, $z = q_1q_2$, does not depend on the input x; thus, this is a Moore model. (This system also produces an output of 1 if the input is 1 for three or more consecutive clock periods [CE 6]).

The input equations for the system are

$$J_1 = xq_2 \qquad K_1 = x'$$
$$D_2 = x(q_1 + q_2')$$

Notice that when $x = 0$, J_1 is 0, K_1 is 1, and D_2 is 0; thus the system goes to state 00. When $x = 1$,

$$J_1 = q_2 \qquad K_1 = 0 \qquad D_2 = q_1 + q_2'$$

Flip flop q_1 goes to 1 when $q_2 = 1$ and is unchanged otherwise. (Of course, q_1 remains at 1 in state 10.) Flip flop q_2 goes to 1 when $q_1 = 1$ or $q_2 = 0$ and to 0 only if $q_1 = 0$ and $q_2 = 1$.

We could also use, for q_1, the equation

$$q^\star = Jq' + K'q$$

and obtain

$$q_1^\star = xq_2q_1' + xq_1 = x(q_2 + q_1)$$

From either approach, we get the following state table:

$q_1 q_2$	$q_1^\star q_2^\star$ $x = 0$	$x = 1$	z
0 0	0 0	0 1	0
0 1	0 0	1 0	0
1 0	0 0	1 1	0
1 1	0 0	1 1	1

*Sometimes, circuitry is added to synchronize the input changes with the clock edge.

This is the same state table as in Table 6.1 if we note that *A* has been coded as 00, *B* as 01, *C* as 10, and *D* as 11.

This system produces the following timing diagram:

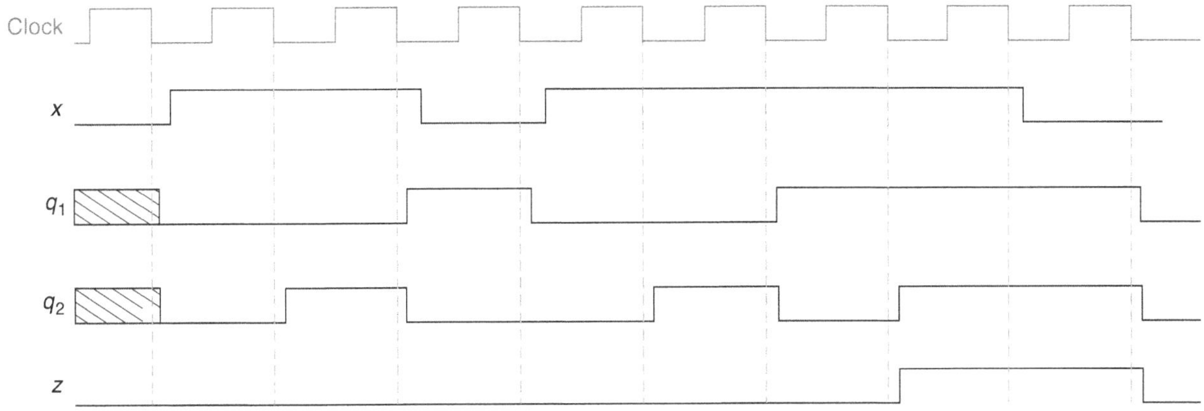

There is never a false output in a Moore model, since the output depends only on the state of the flip flops, and they all change simultaneously, on the trailing edge of the clock. The output is valid for a whole clock period, from just after one negative-going transition to just after the next.

EXAMPLE 6.1b

If the AND gate of Example 6.1a had a third input, x', then $z = x'q_1q_2$ and this would be a Mealy model. The next state portion of the state table and of the timing diagram would be unchanged. There would be two columns in the state table.

$q_1 q_2$	$q_1^\star q_2^\star$ $x = 0$	$x = 1$	z $x = 0$	$x = 1$
0 0	0 0	0 1	0	0
0 1	0 0	1 0	0	0
1 0	0 0	1 1	0	0
1 1	0 0	1 1	1	0

The *z* in the timing diagram would remain 0 until after *x* goes to 0 (one clock time later than in Example 6.1a).

EXAMPLE 6.2

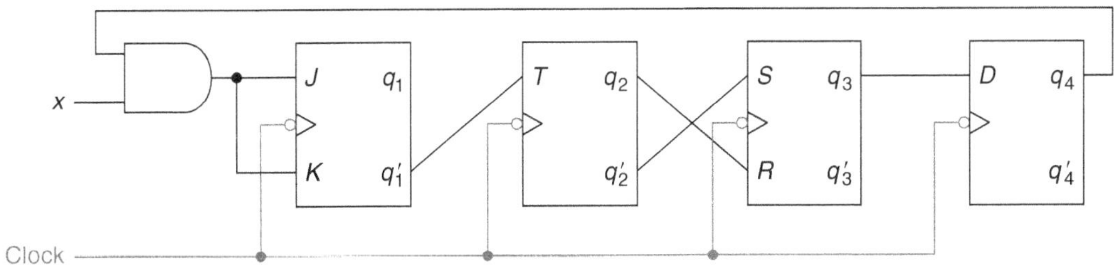

Complete the timing trace as far as possible. Assume that the system is initially in state 0000. The given values are shown in brown.

$$J_1 = K_1 = xq_4$$
$$T_2 = q_1'$$
$$S_2 = q_2' \qquad R_2 = q_2$$
$$D_4 = q_3$$

Therefore,

q_1 changes state only when $xq_4 = 1$
q_2 changes state only when $q_1 = 0$
$q_3^\star = q_2'$
$q_4^\star = q_3$

x	1 1 1 0 1 1
q_1	0 0 0 1 1 0 0 0 0
q_2	0 1 0 1 1 1 0 1 1 0
q_3	0 1 0 1 0 0 0 1 0 0 1
q_4	0 0 1 0 1 0 0 0 1 0 0 1

After the first clock, q_1 remains at 0, q_2 toggles, q_3 is loaded with 1 (q_2'), and q_4 goes to 0 (from q_3). After the last input is known for this circuit, we can determine the next value of q_1 as long as the present value of q_4 is 0 (since xq_4 will be 0). The next state of each of the other flip flops depends only on the present state of the one to its left. Thus, we can find a value for q_2 one clock time after q_1 is known, for q_3 one clock time after that, and for q_4 one additional clock time later.

[SP 5, 6, 7, 8; EX 7, 8, 9; LAB]

6.5 SOLVED PROBLEMS

1. For each of the following state tables, show a state diagram and complete the timing trace as far as possible (even after the input is no longer known).

a.

	$q_1^\star q_2^\star$		z	
q_1q_2	$x = 0$	$x = 1$	$x = 0$	$x = 1$
0 0	0 0	1 0	0	1
0 1	0 0	0 0	0	0
1 0	1 1	0 1	1	1
1 1	1 0	1 0	1	0

x	0 1 0 0 1 1 1 0
q_1	0
q_2	0
z	

b.

q	$q^\star$ $x = 0$	$x = 1$	z
A	A	B	1
B	D	C	1
C	D	C	0
D	A	B	0

x	0 1 0 1 0 1 1 1 0 1 0 0 0 0
q	A
z	

a.

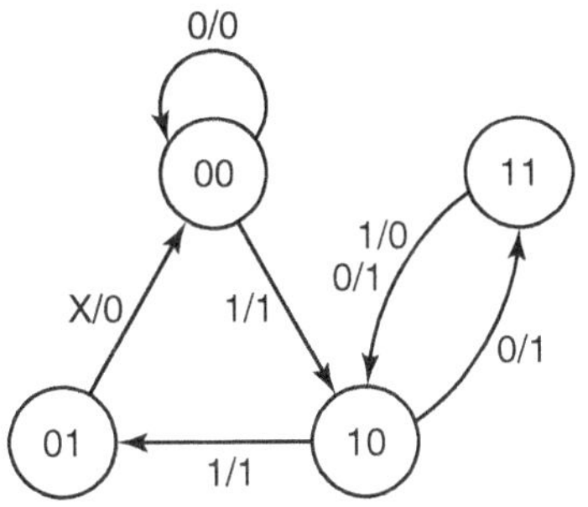

b.

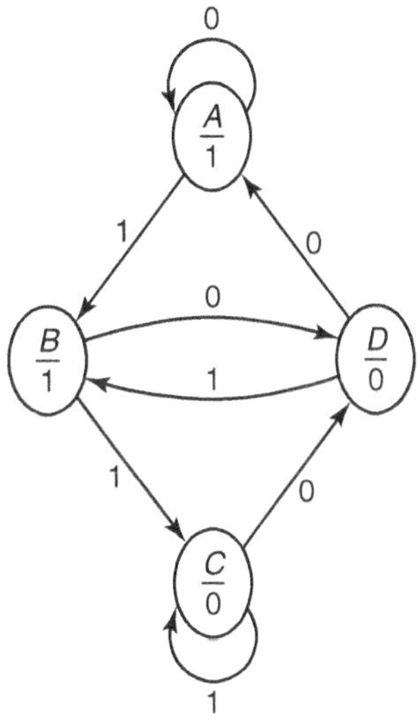

Note that in part a, state 01 goes to 00 always (input is don't care), and the output is always 0. State 11 always goes to 10, but the outputs are different for the two different inputs; thus two labels are shown on that path.

The timing traces are as follows:

a. x	0	1	0	0	1	1	1	0				
q_1	0	0	1	1	1	0	0	1	1	1		
q_2	0	0	0	1	0	1	0	0	1	0	1	0
z	0	1	1	1	1	0	1	1	?	1		

Since state 11 always goes to state 10 (independent of the input), we can determine the next state for the second clock after the input is no longer known. At the first clock after the last input, the output is unknown, but at the next one, we know that it must be 1, since the output is 1 from state 10, no matter what the input is. Note that we can determine q_2 for two additional clock times.

b. x 0 1 0 1 0 1 1 1 0 1 0 0 0 0
q A A B D B D B C C D B D A A A
z 1 1 1 0 1 0 1 0 0 0 1 0 1 1 1 1

Since state A goes to either A or B, and the output in each of those states is 1, we can determine the output for one extra clock time.

2. Analyze the following latch; give the appropriate inputs and outputs meaningful labels.

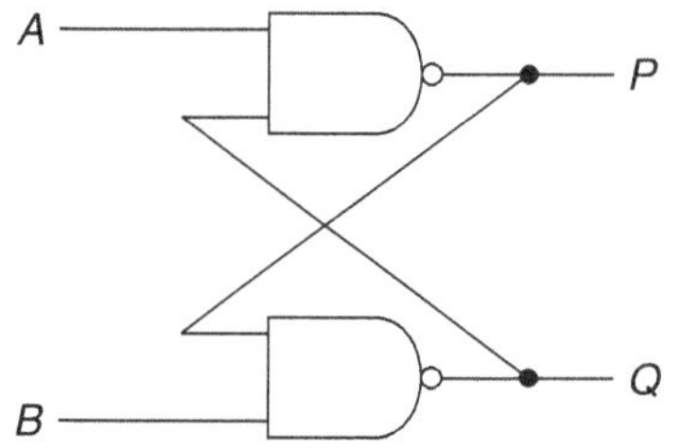

$$P = (AQ)' \qquad Q = (BP)'$$

If $A = B = 0$,

$$P = Q = 1$$

If $A = B = 1$,

$$P = Q' \qquad Q = P'$$

If $A = 0$ and $B = 1$,

$$P = 1 \qquad Q = 0$$

If $A = 1$ and $B = 0$,

$$Q = 1 \qquad P = 0$$

This is an active low input latch, where both inputs active ($A = B = 0$) is not allowed. The store state is $A = B = 1$ (inactive), where the outputs are the complement of each other. When A is active, P is made 1 (and $Q = 0$). When B is active, $Q = 1$ and $P = 0$. Thus, we could label the latch as follows:

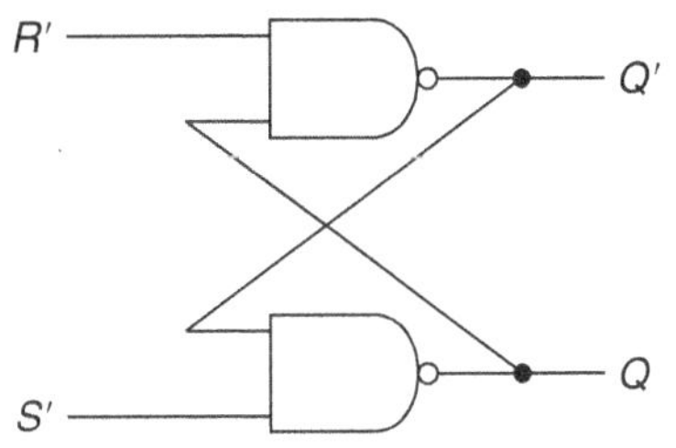

3. Consider the trailing-edge triggered flip flops shown.

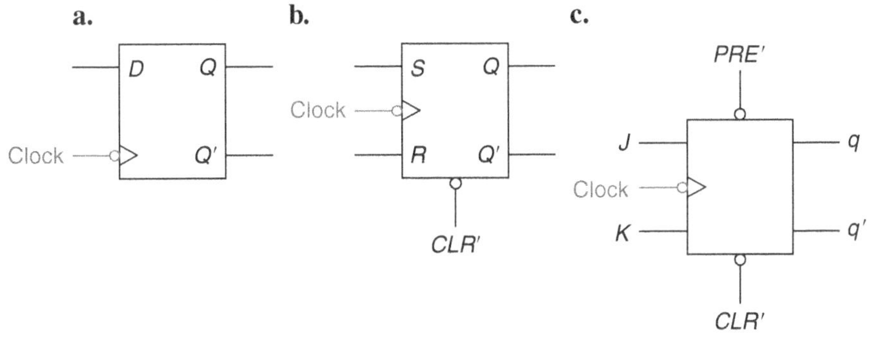

a. Show a timing diagram for Q.

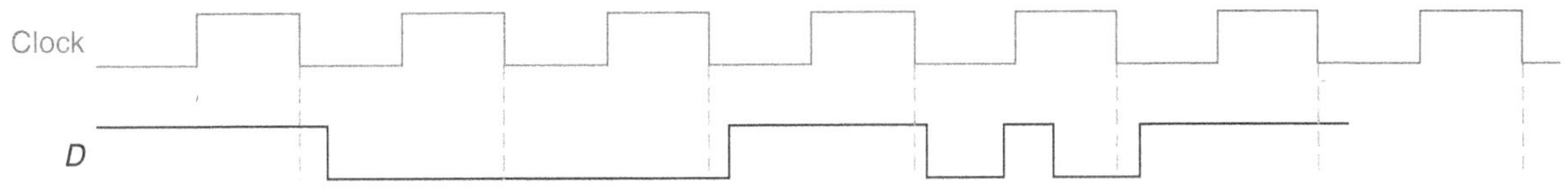

b. Show a timing diagram for Q if

i. there is no CLR' input.

ii. the CLR' input is as shown.

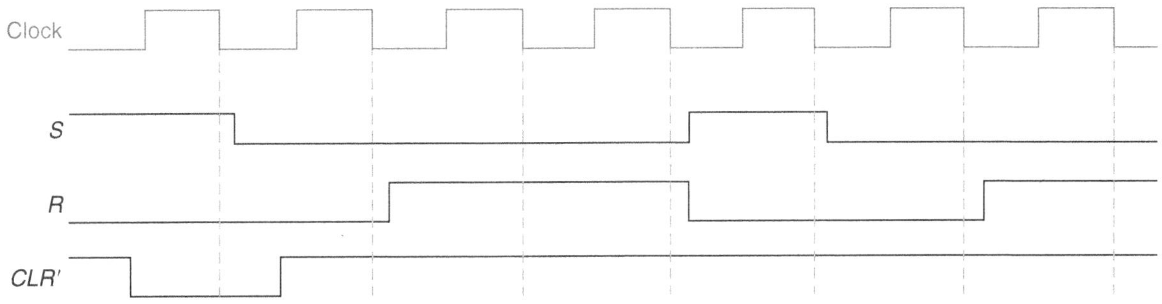

c. Show a timing diagram for Q if

i. there is no PRE' input.

ii. the PRE' input is as shown (in addition to the CLR' input).

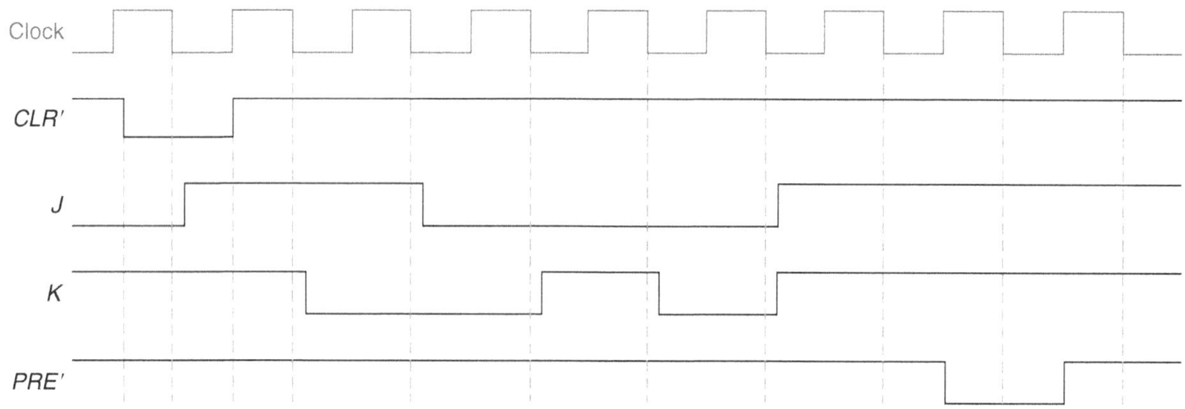

a.

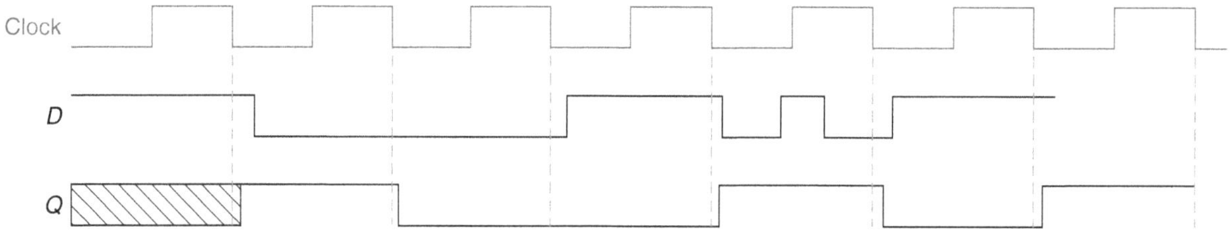

The state of the flip flop is not known until the first trailing edge. At that point, D determines what is to be stored. Thus, the first time, Q goes to 1; the second time, Q goes to 0; the third time, Q goes to (stays at) 0. When D changes between clock times, that does not affect the behavior; it is the value just before the trailing edge that matters.

b.

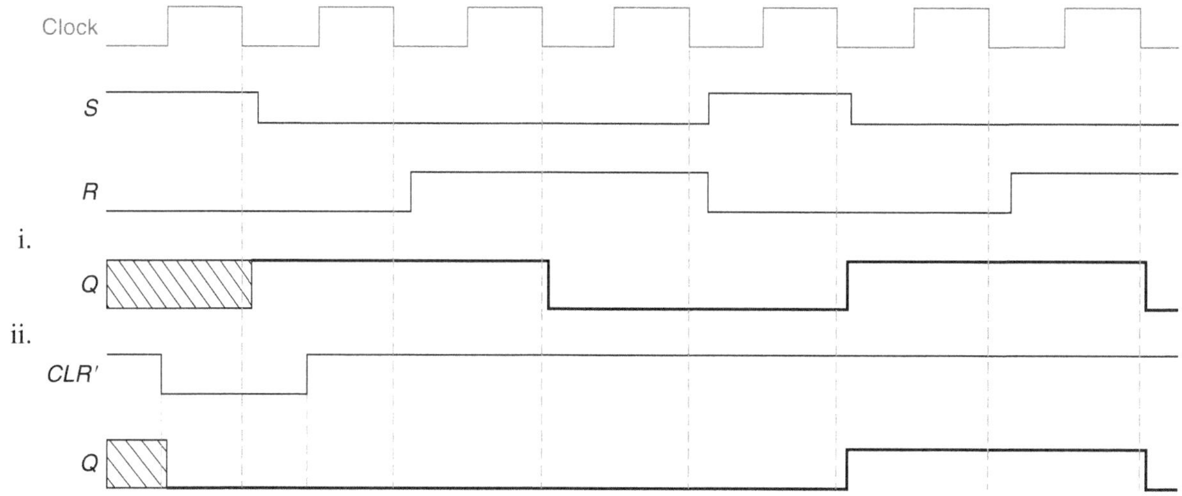

Without the clear, we do not know what Q is until after the first trailing edge. At that point, since $S = 1$, Q goes to 1. At the next clock, both S and R are 0; thus, Q does not change. Since $R = 1$ for the next two clock times, Q goes to 0. Then $S = 1$, making $Q = 1$; both are 0 leaving Q at 1; and finally $R = 1$, returning Q to 0. With the clear, Q goes to 0 earlier and the first clock edge is ignored. Thus, Q remains at 0 for the next three clock times. Then, this part behaves like the first part. (Once the Q from the second part is the same as that from the first, the behavior is identical.)

c.

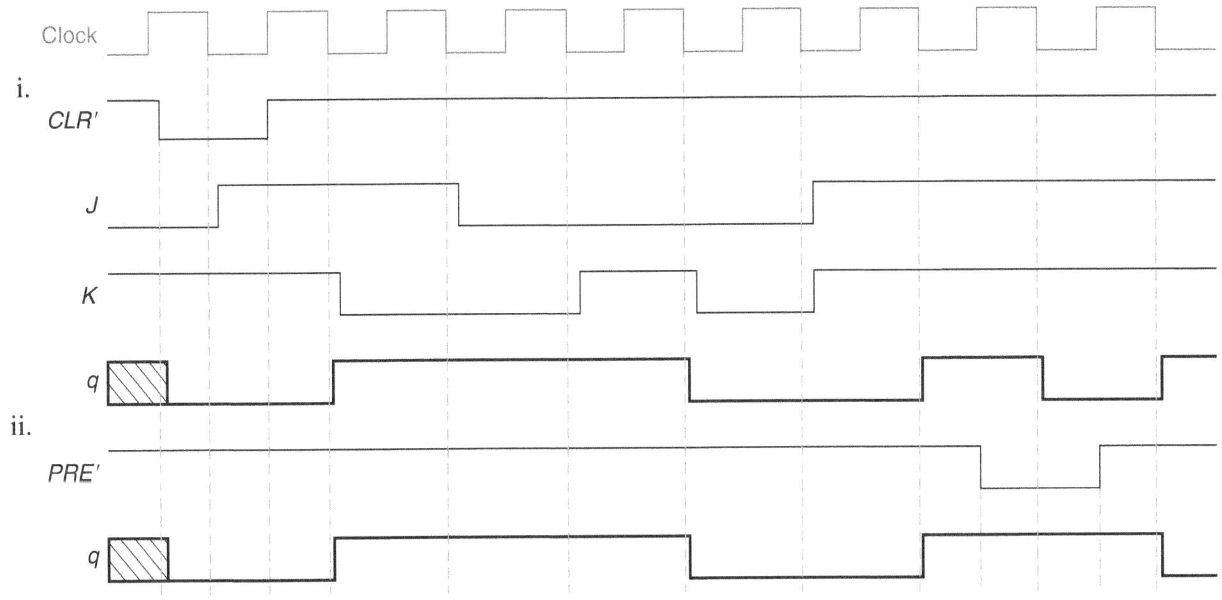

The two parts are the same up to the time of the active preset input. In the second case, the preset overrides the clock and keeps the output at 1. Then, when the outputs start toggling (since J and K are 1), the two timing pictures are the opposite of each other.

4. We have a new flip flop with three inputs, S, R, and T (in addition to a trailing-edge triggered clock input). No more than one of these inputs may be 1 at any time. The S and R inputs behave exactly as they do in an SR flip flop (that is, S puts a 1 into the flip flop and R puts a 0 in the flip flop). The T input behaves as it does in a T flip flop (that is, it causes the flip flop to change state).

a. Show a state graph for this flip flop.

b. Write an equation for $Q^\star$ in terms of S, R, T, and Q.

a.

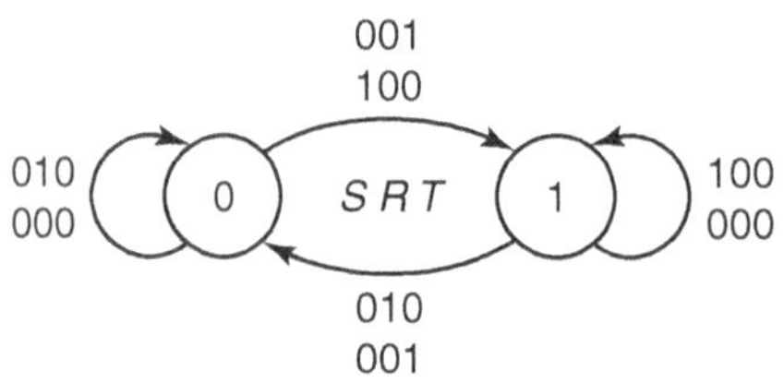

b.

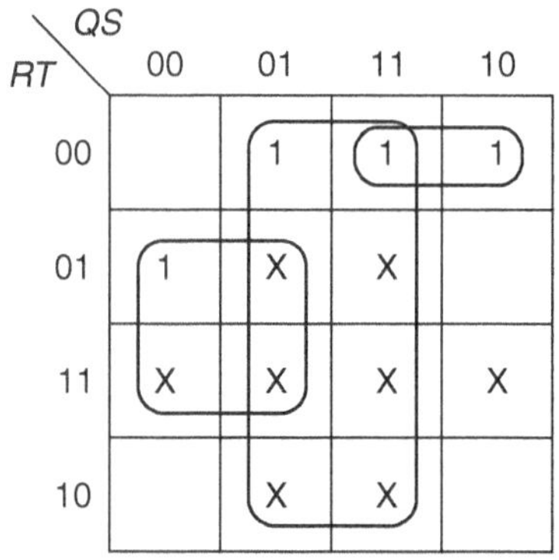

$Q^\star = S + Q'T + QR'T'$

5. For the following circuit,

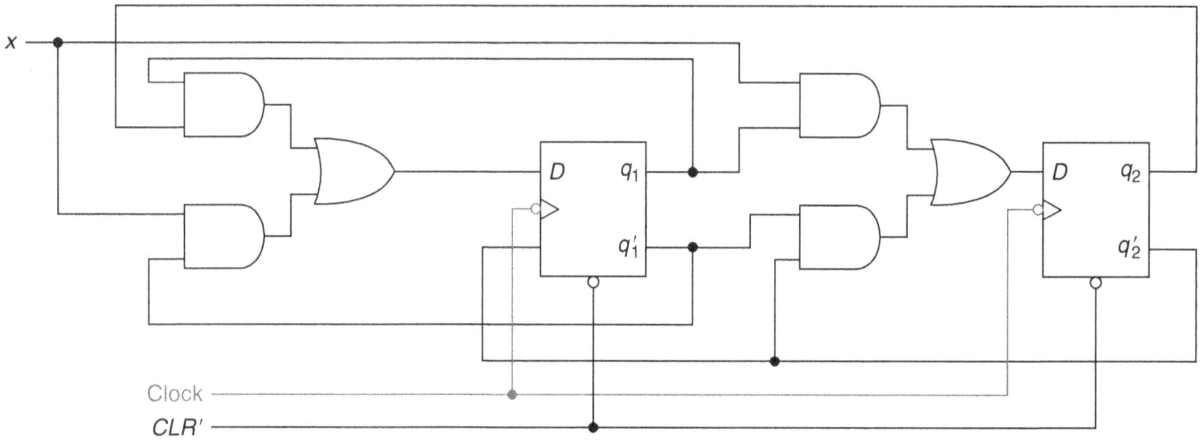

a. Ignore the CLR' input. Find a state diagram and a state table.

b. Assume that the flip flops are each initially in state 0 (and there is no CLR'), complete the timing trace for the states of the flip flops as far as possible.

x 1 0 1 1 1 0

c. For the following inputs (both x and CLR'), complete the timing diagram for the state of each flip flop.

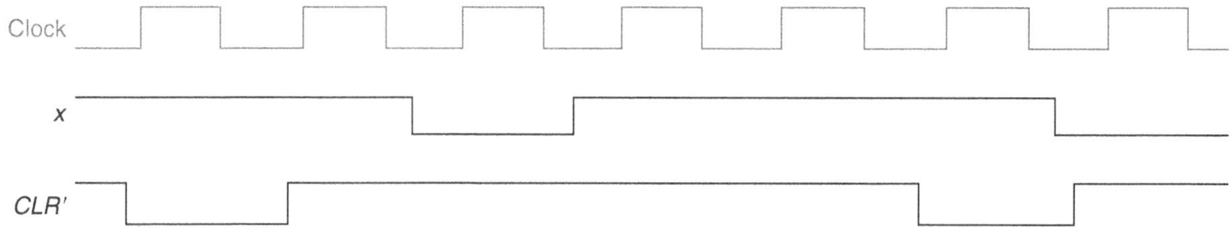

a. For this circuit,

$$D_1 = q_1q_2 + xq_1' \qquad D_2 = xq_1 + q_1'q_2'$$

The state table is

$q_1 q_2$	$q_1^\star q_2^\star$ $x = 0$	$x = 1$
0 0	0 1	1 1
0 1	0 0	1 0
1 0	0 0	0 1
1 1	1 0	1 1

Since no outputs are shown, we will assume that the state is the only output. The state diagram becomes

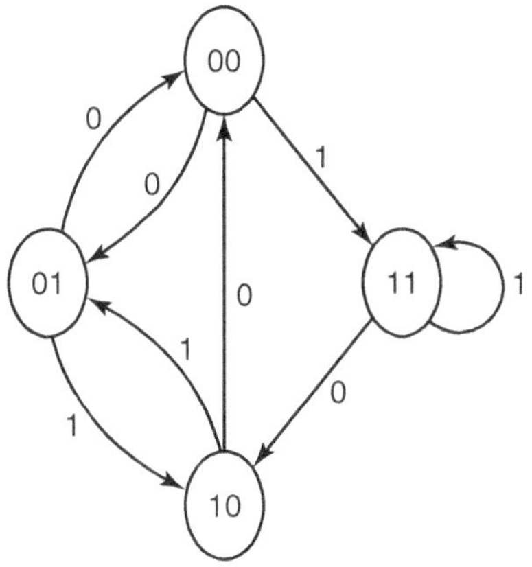

b. The timing trace for the given string is

x	1 0 1 1 1 0
q_1	0 1 1 0 1 0 0
q_2	0 1 0 1 0 1 0 1

c. The timing diagram is

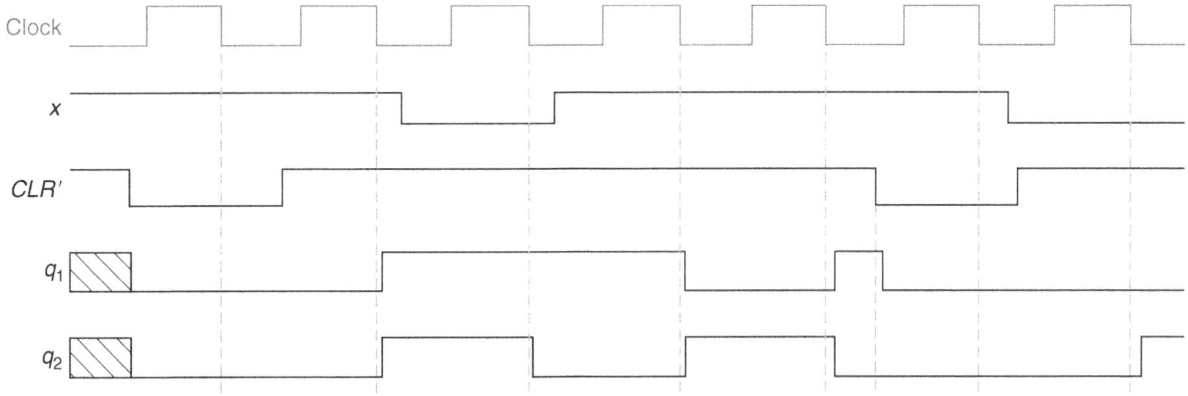

The flip flop contents are unknown until the CLR' signal goes to 0. The first transition of the clock has no effect. At the second negative-going transition of the clock, $x = 1$. Both flip flops go to 1. We can evaluate the flip flop inputs at the next three clock trailing edges and produce the balance of the timing, until CLR' goes to 0 again. At that time, q_1 and q_2 go to 0. The clock takes over again at the last transition.

6. For each of the following circuits, complete the timing diagram for the state of each flip flop and the output, where shown. All flip flops are trailing-edge triggered.

a.

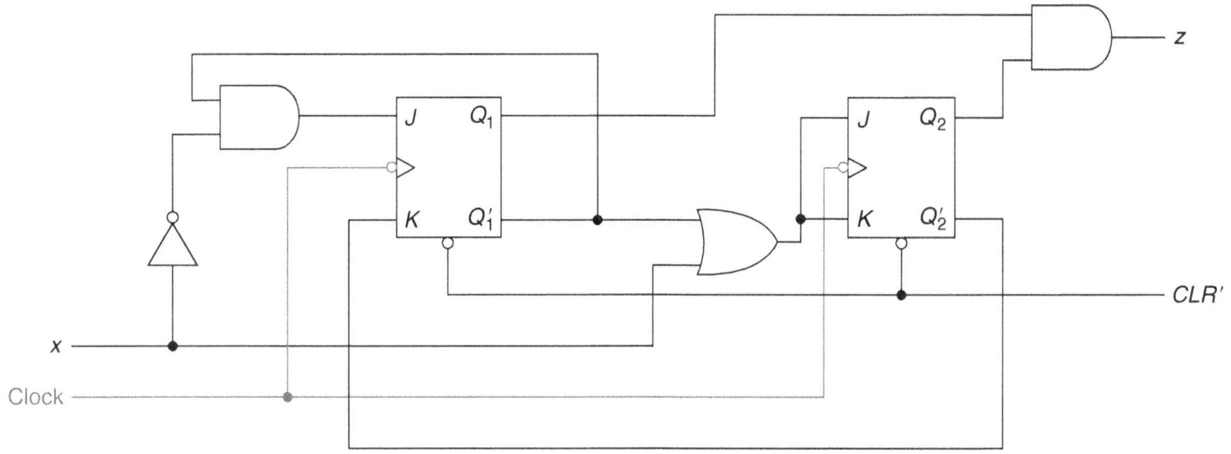

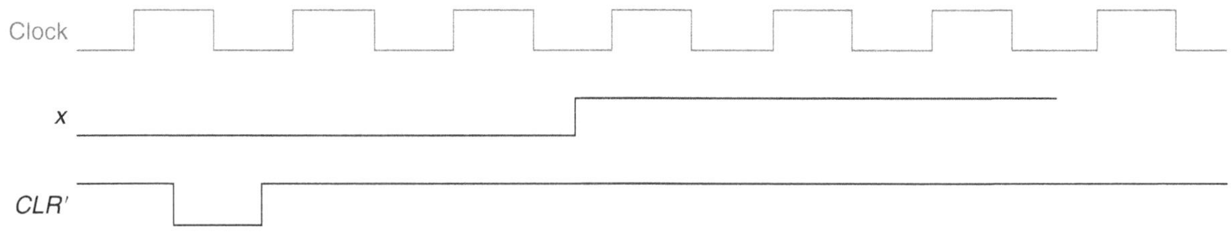

b. Assume that the three flip flops are all initially 0.

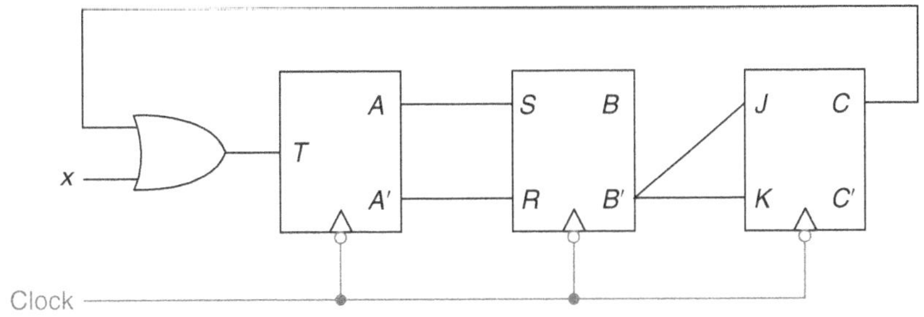

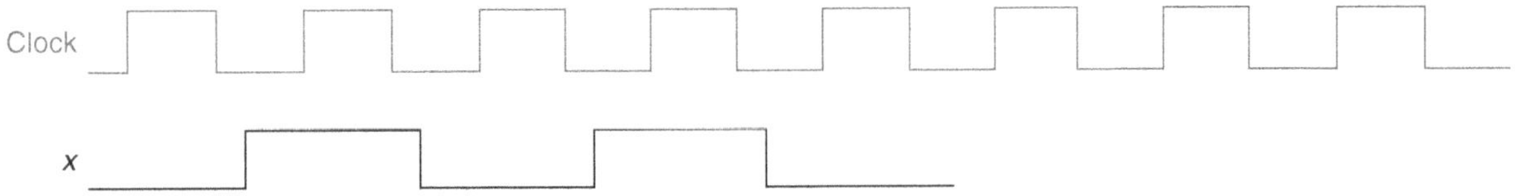

a. For this circuit,

$$J_1 = x'Q_1' \quad K_1 = Q_2' \quad J_2 = K_2 = x + Q_1' \quad z = Q_1Q_2$$

The output z is just a function of the state of the flip flops. It can be determined last (after completing the flip flop outputs). At the last clock transition, the input is not known and thus J_1 is unknown (since $Q_1' = 1$). Thus, we cannot determine the next value of Q_1. But, $J_2 = K_2 = 1$ (no matter what x is) and thus we can determine the value for Q_2.

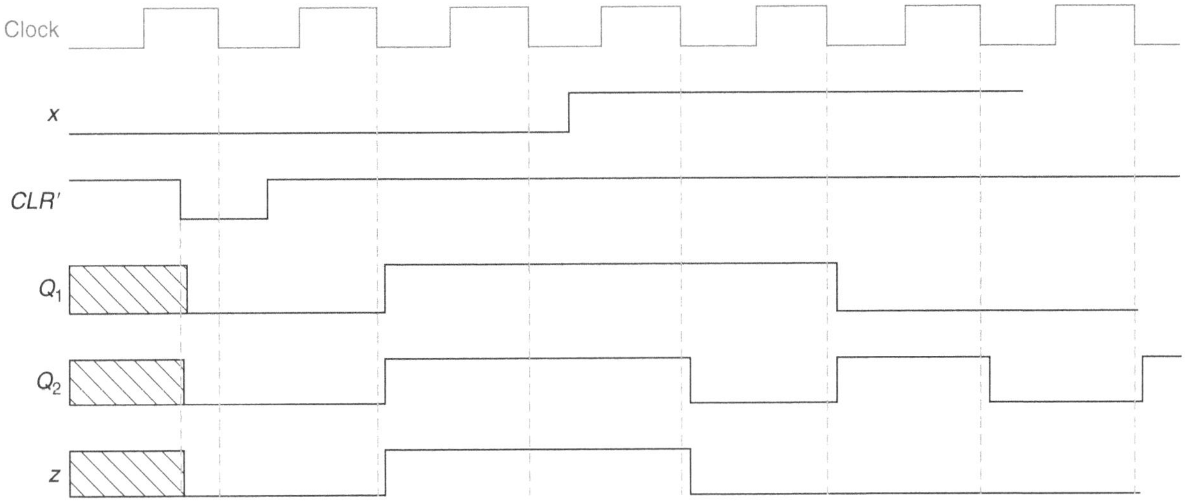

b. For this circuit,

$$T = x + C \quad S = A \quad R = A' \quad J = K = B'$$

We really do not need to think of S and R, since $B^{\star} = A$. The resulting timing diagram is thus

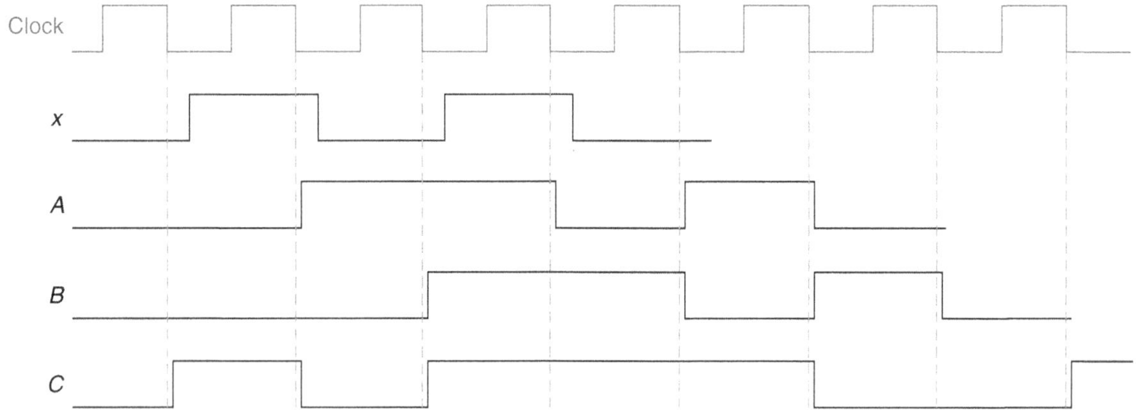

After we no longer know x, we can still determine the value for A for one more clock, since

$$T = x + C = ? + 1 = 1$$

But, once C goes to 0, then T is unknown. Since the inputs to B only depend on A, we can determine B for one more clock than A. Similarly, the input to C depends only on B and thus C is known for still another clock time.

7. For each of the following circuits and input strings,

i. Construct a state table (calling the states 00, 01, 10, 11).

ii. Show a timing trace for the values of the flip flops and the output for as far as possible. Assume all flip flops are initially in state 0.

a.

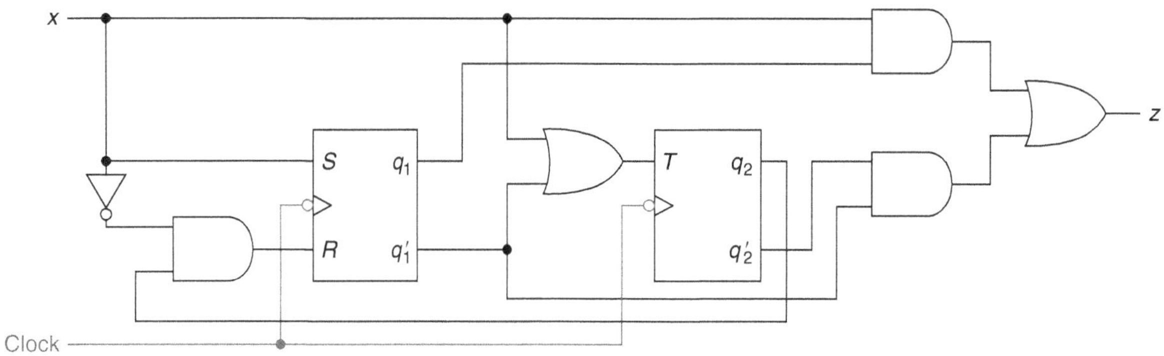

x   0 0 1 1 0 0 1 0 0

b.

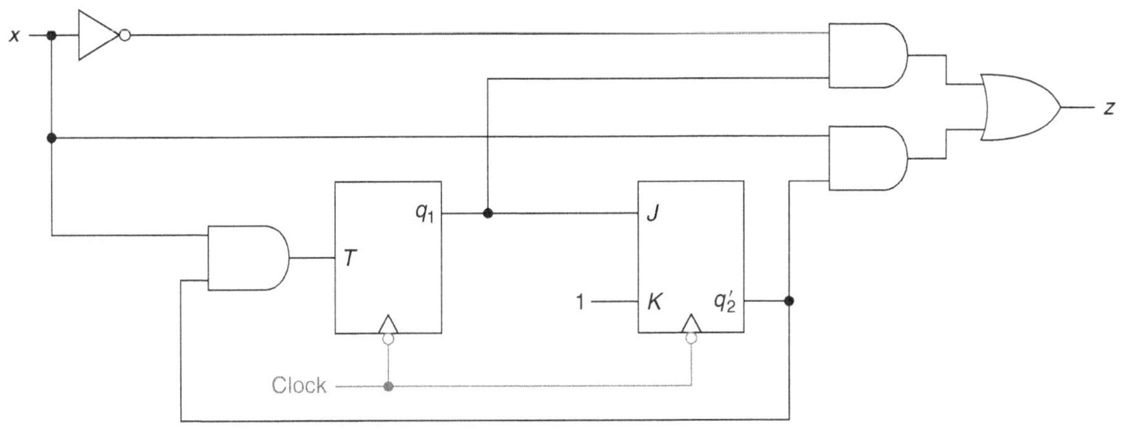

x 1 1 0 0 1 0 0 0 1

a. $S = x \quad R = x'q_2 \quad T = q_1' + x \quad z = xq_1 + q_1'q_2'$

For $x = 0$, $S = 0$ and $R = q_2$. Thus, q_1 is unchanged when $q_2 = 0$ and cleared otherwise. For $x = 1$, q_1 is set. When $x = 1$ or $q_1 = 0$, q_2 toggles; otherwise, it remains unchanged. That produces the following state table:

q_1q_2	$q_1^\star q_2^\star$ $x = 0$	$x = 1$	z $x = 0$	$x = 1$
0 0	0 1	1 1	1	1
0 1	0 0	1 0	0	0
1 0	1 0	1 1	0	1
1 1	0 1	1 0	0	1

x	0	0	1	1	0	0	1	0	0	
q_1	0	0	0	1	1	1	1	1	0	0
q_2	0	1	0	1	0	0	0	1	1	0	1
z	1	0	1	1	0	0	1	0	0	1

Note that at the first clock time when the input is unknown, we can determine the output even though we do not know the input, since $z = 1$ in state 00, for both $x = 0$ and $x = 1$. We know q_2 one additional clock time, since 00 goes to states **01** or 1**1**, both of which give $q_2 = 1$.

b. $T = xq_2' \quad J = q_1 \quad K = 1 \quad z = x'q_1 + xq_2'$

Note that q_1 toggles only when $x = 1$ and $q_2 = 0$; and that q_2 toggles when $q_1 = 1$, and goes to 0, otherwise.

q_1q_2	$q_1^\star q_2^\star$ $x = 0$	$x = 1$	z $x = 0$	$x = 1$
0 0	0 0	1 0	0	1
0 1	0 0	0 0	0	0
1 0	1 1	0 1	1	1
1 1	1 0	1 0	1	0

x	1	1	0	0	1	0	0	0	1	1			
q_1	0	1	0	0	0	1	1	1	1	1	0	0	
q_2	0	0	1	0	0	0	1	0	1	0	1	0	0
z	1	1	0	0	1	1	1	1	0	1	0		

In this example, we can determine the state for two clocks after the input is no longer known, the value of q_2 for a third (since from state 00, we go either to **0**0 or **1**0) and the output for one clock after the last known input.

8. For the following circuits, complete the timing trace as far as possible. The state of some flip flops can be determined as many as five or six clocks after the input is no longer known. Assume that all flip flops are initially 0.

a.

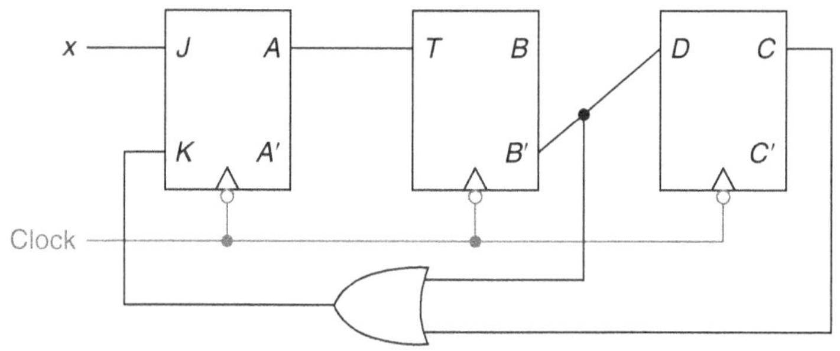

x 0 1 1 1

b.

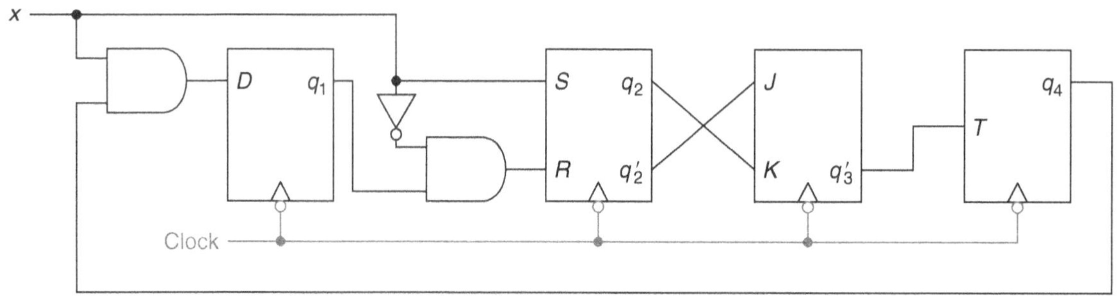

x 0 1 1 1 0 0 1

a. $J = x \quad K = B' + C \quad T = A \quad D = C^\star = B'$

x	0	1	1	1					
A	0	0	1	0	1	1	0		
B	0	0	0	1	1	0	1	1	
C	0	1	1	1	0	0	1	0	0

Since flip flop B depends only on A, and C depends only on B, we know the value of C one clock time after B, and B one clock time after A. At the first clock time when x (and, thus, J) is unknown, A contains a 1. If K is 0 (independent of J), flip flop A will still have a 1; if K is 1, it will go to 0. Thus, for this sequence, we are able to determine A for two clock times when x is unknown.

b. $D = xq_4 \quad S = x \quad R = x'q_1 \quad q_3^\star = q_2' \quad T = q_3'$

x	0	1	1	1	0	0	1						
q_1	0	0	1	1	1	0	0	0	0	0			
q_2	0	0	1	1	1	0	0	1	1	1	1		
q_3	0	1	1	0	0	0	1	1	0	0	0	0	
q_4	0	1	1	1	0	1	0	0	0	1	0	1	0

6.6 EXERCISES

1. For each of the following state tables, show a state diagram and complete the timing trace as far as possible (even after the input is no longer known).

a.

	$q_1^\star q_2^\star$		z	
q_1q_2	$x = 0$	$x = 1$	$x = 0$	$x = 1$
0 0	0 1	0 0	0	1
0 1	1 0	1 1	0	0
1 0	0 0	0 0	1	1
1 1	0 1	0 1	1	0

x	1	0	1	1	0	0	0	1
q_1	0							
q_2	0							
z								

★b.

q	$q^{\star}$ $x = 0$	$x = 1$	z
A	A	B	0
B	C	B	0
C	A	D	0
D	C	B	1

x 1 1 0 1 0 1 0 1 0 0 1 0 1 1
q A
z

c.

q	$q^{\star}$ $x = 0$	$x = 1$	z $x = 0$	$x = 1$
A	B	C	0	1
B	C	A	0	0
C	A	B	1	0

x 0 0 1 1 1 0 0 0 0 0 1 0
q A
z

d.

q	$q^{\star}$ $x = 0$	$x = 1$	z $x = 0$	$x = 1$
A	A	B	1	0
B	C	D	0	0
C	A	B	0	0
D	C	D	1	0

x 0 1 0 0 0 1 1 1 1 0 1
q A
z

2. Show the block diagram for a gated latch that behaves similarly to the one of Figure 6.6, but uses only NAND gates.

3. For the input shown below, show the flip flop outputs.

a. Assume that the flip flop is a D flip flop without a clear or preset.

b. Assume that the flip flop is a D flip flop with an active low clear.

c. Assume that the flip flop is a D flip flop with active low clear and preset inputs.

d. Assume that the flip flop is a T flip flop with the same input as part a, and that Q is initially 0.

e. Assume that the flip flop is a T flip flop with an active low clear and the same inputs as part b.

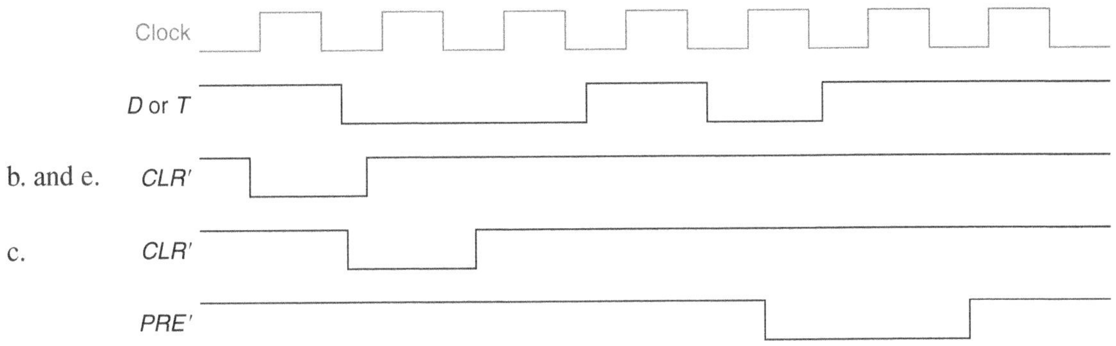

4. For the following JK flip flops, complete each of the timing diagrams. First, assume that CLR' and PRE' are inactive (1). Then, use the values shown.

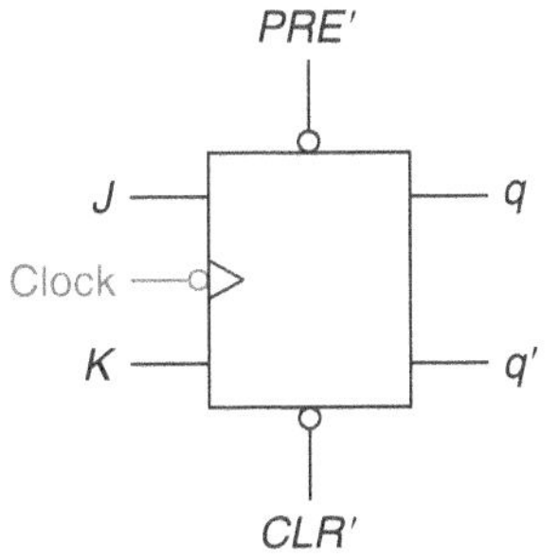

a.

b.

*c.

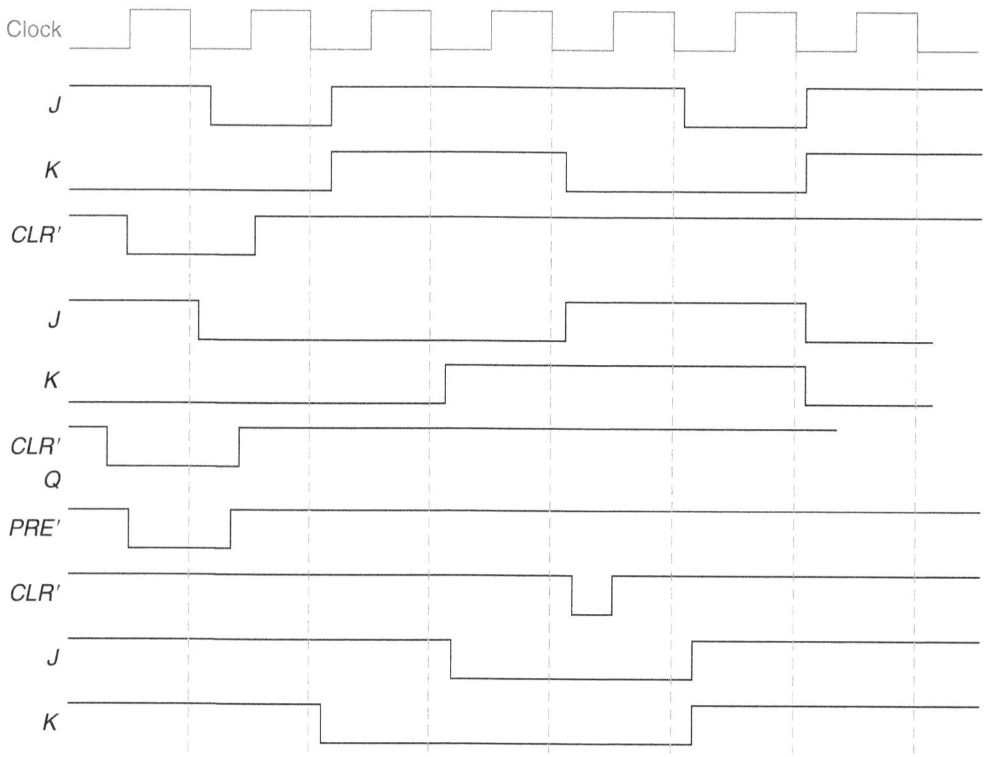

5. Consider the following flip flop circuit

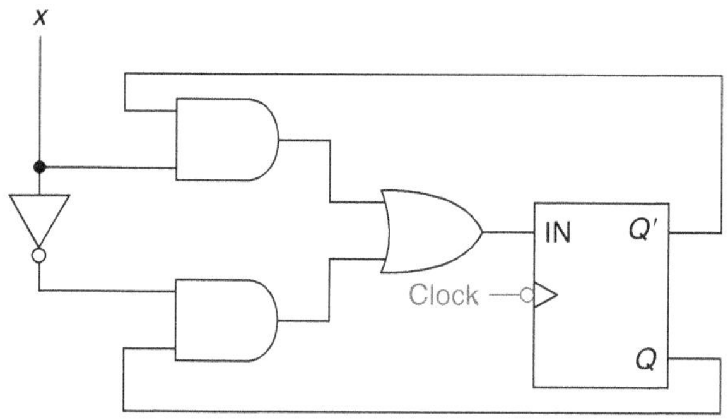

Complete the timing diagram below if that flip flop is

a. a *D* flip flop

b. a *T* flip flop

In both cases, the flip flop starts with a 0 in it.

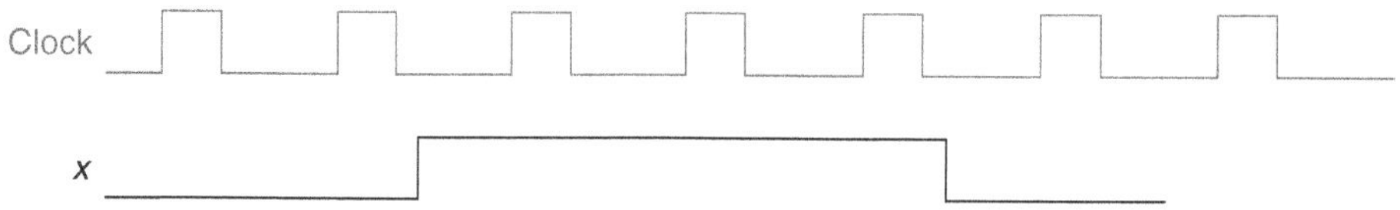

6. We have a new type of flip flop, with inputs A and B. If $A = 0$, then $Q^\star = B$; if $A = 1$, $Q^\star = B'$.

a. Show a state diagram for this flip flop.

b. Write an equation for $Q^\star$ in terms of A, B, and Q.

7. For each of the following circuits, complete the timing diagram for the state of each flip flop and the output, where shown. All flip flops are trailing-edge triggered. For those circuits in which there is no clear input, assume each flip flop starts at 0.

a.

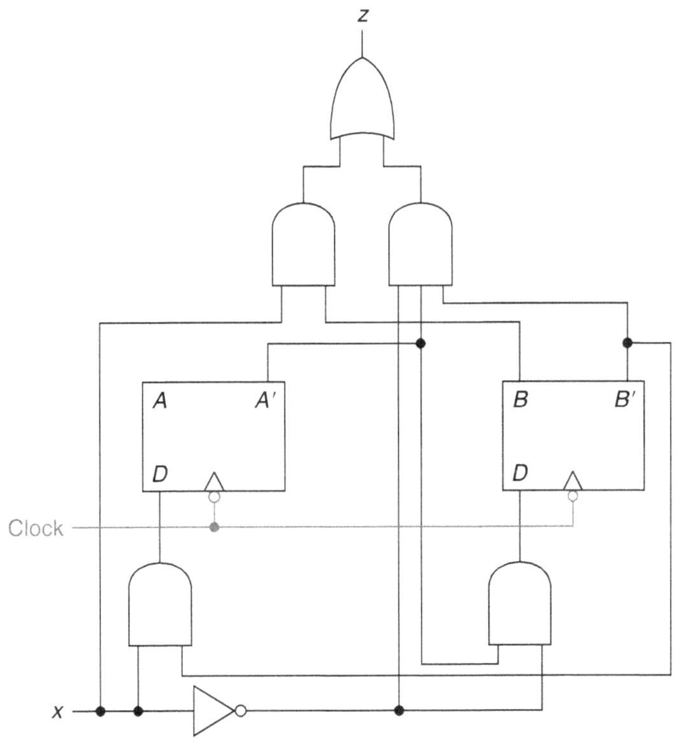

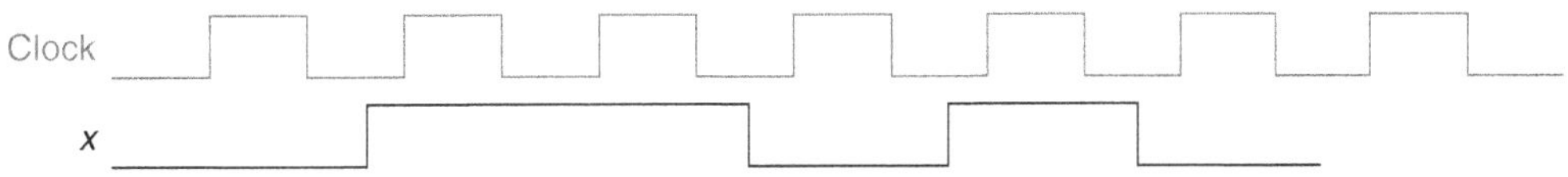

*b.

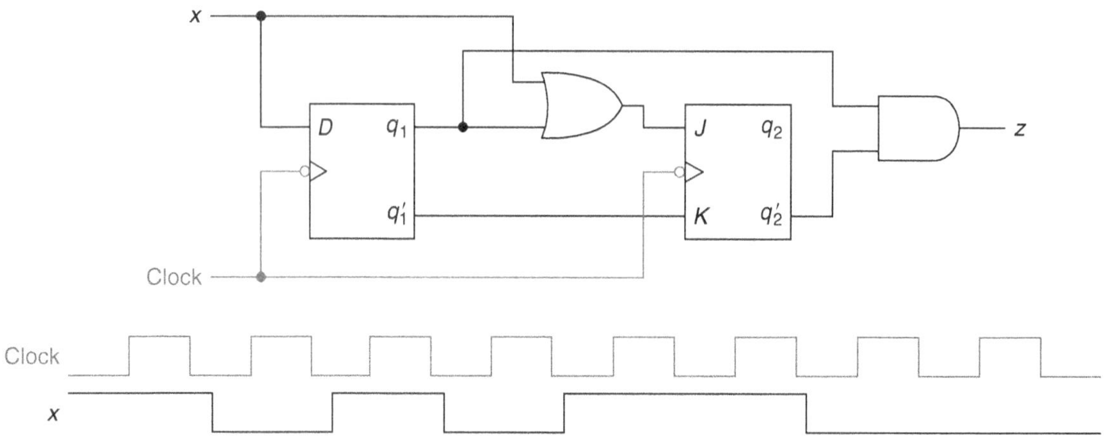
x
D
q_1
q_1'
J
K
q_2
q_2'
z
Clock
Clock
x

c.

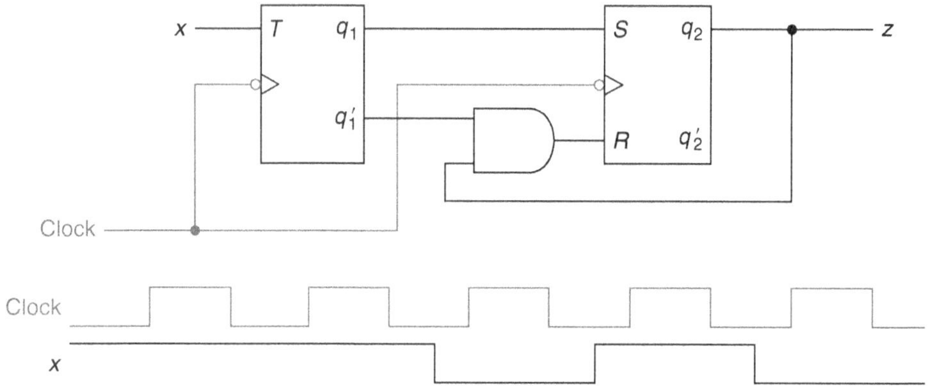
x
T
q_1
q_1'
S
R
q_2
q_2'
z
Clock
Clock
x

d.

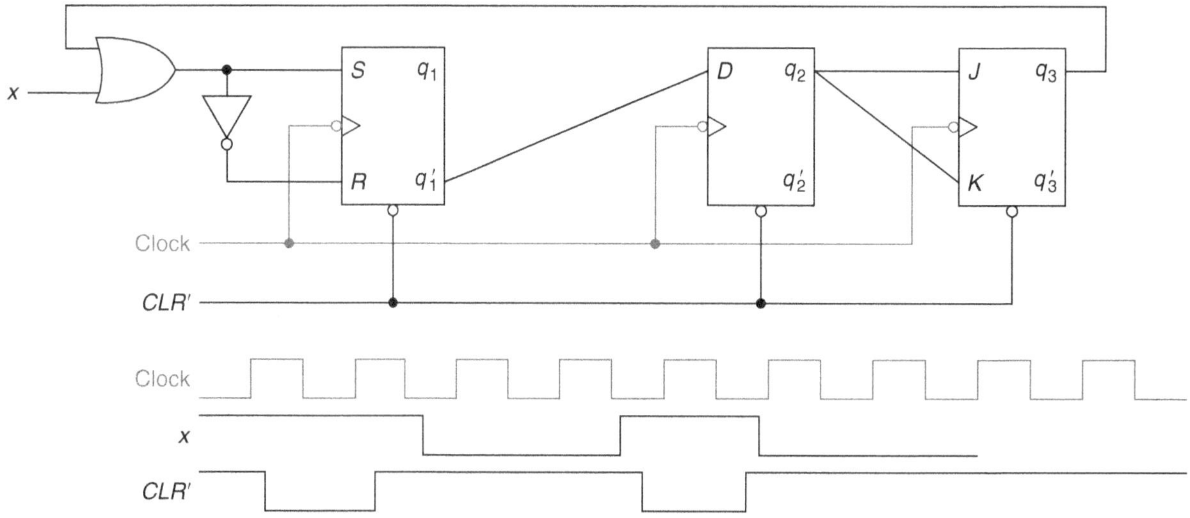
x
S
R
q_1
q_1'
D
q_2
q_2'
J
K
q_3
q_3'
Clock
CLR'
Clock
x
CLR'

8. For each of the following circuits and input strings

i. Construct a state table (calling the states 00, 01, 10, 11).

ii. Show a timing trace for the values of the flip flops and the output for as far as possible. Assume that the initial value of each flip flop is 0.

★a.

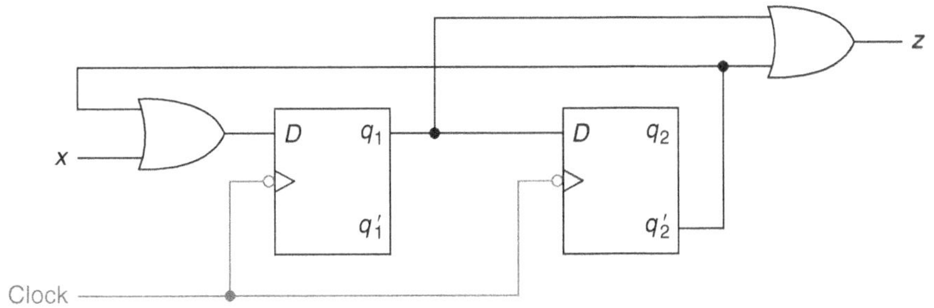

x 0 0 1 1 0 0 1 1 0

b.

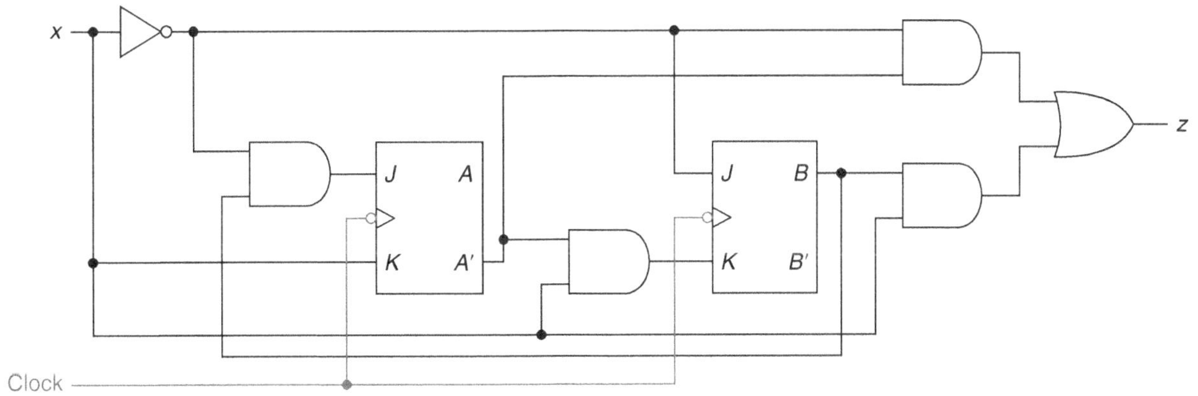

x 0 0 1 1 0 0 1 1 0

c.

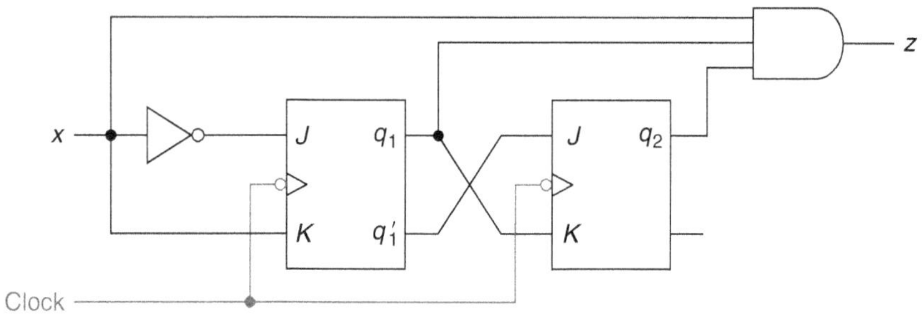

x 0 1 1 0 1 1 1 1 1

d.

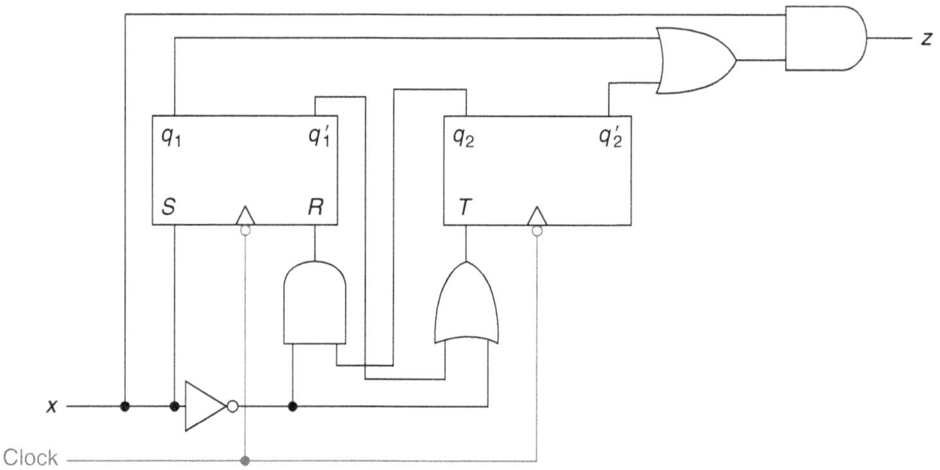

x 0 0 1 1 0 0 1 1 0

9. For the following circuits, complete the timing trace as far as possible. The state of some flip flops and the output can be determined for as many as three clocks after the input is no longer known. Assume that all flip flops are initially 0.

a.

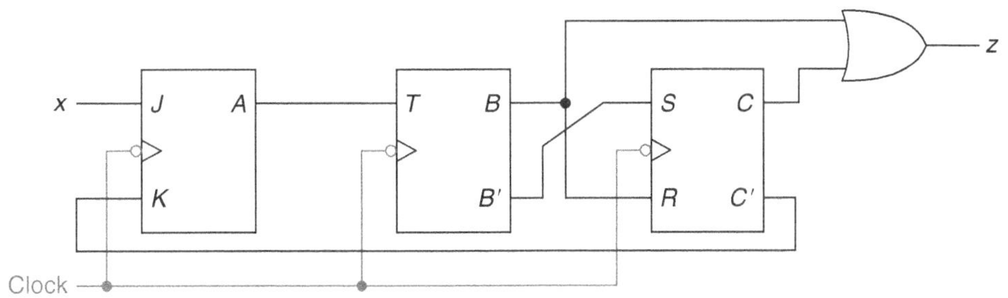

x 0 1 1 0 1 0 1

b.

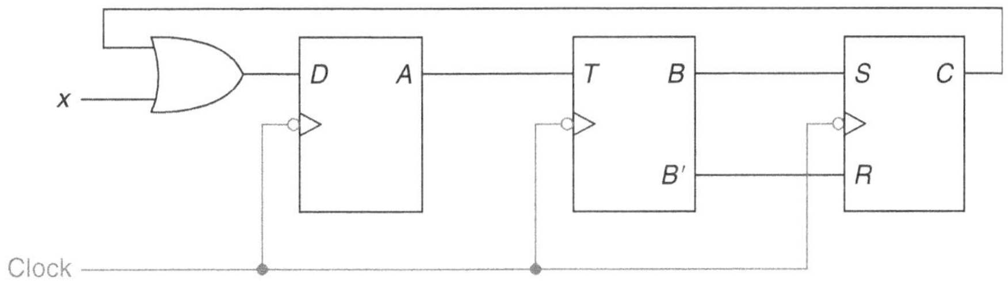

x 0 1 0 1 0 1 0

EXERCISES

*c.

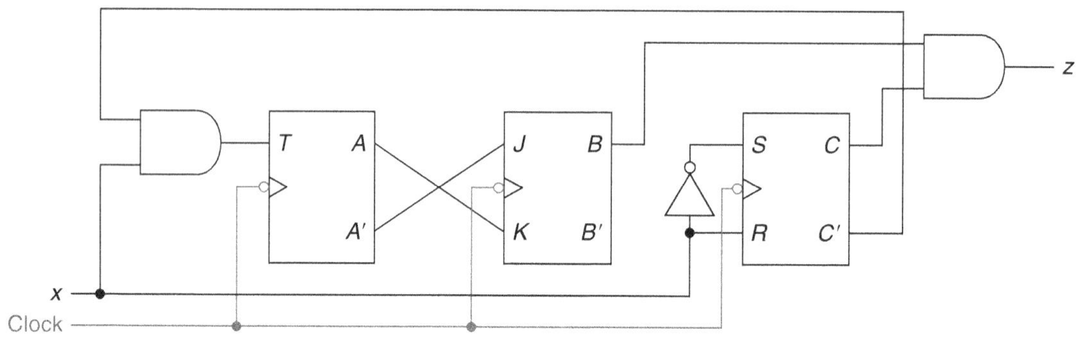

x 0 1 1 0 0 1 1 1 0

d.

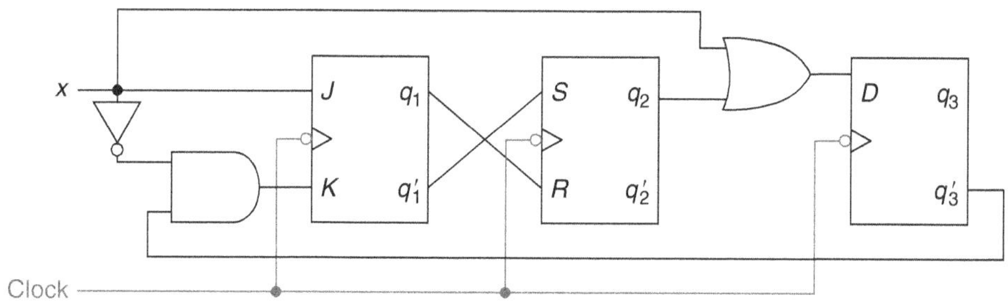

x 0 0 1 0 0 0

CHAPTER TEST

6.7 CHAPTER 6 TEST (50 MINUTES)

1. For the following state table, complete the timing trace as far as you can.

q	$q^\star$ $x = 0$	$q^\star$ $x = 1$	z $x = 0$	z $x = 1$
A	C	A	0	0
B	A	D	1	1
C	B	C	0	1
D	B	B	0	0

x 0 0 1 1 0 0 0 1 0 1

q A

z

2. For the following *JK* trailing-edge triggered flip flop with an active low clear, show the timing diagram for *Q*.

a. Assuming no *CLR′* input.

b. With the *CLR′* input shown.

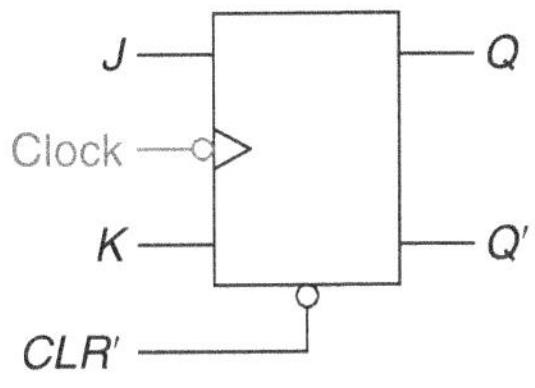

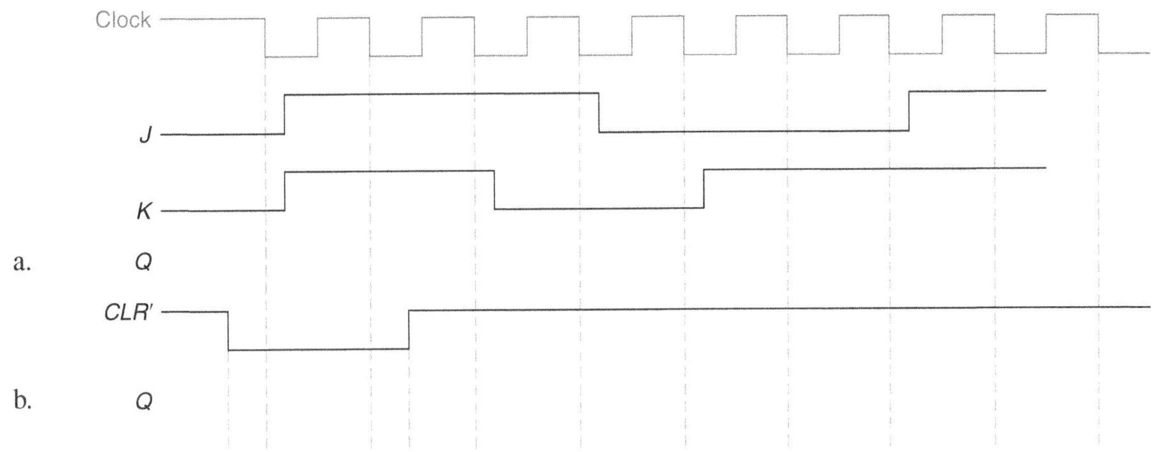

3. For the following circuit, construct the state table.

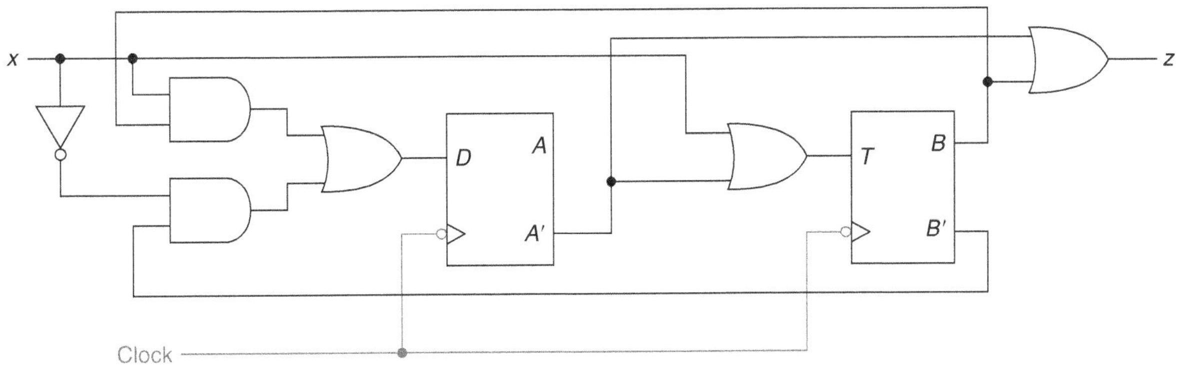

4. For the following circuit, complete the timing diagram.

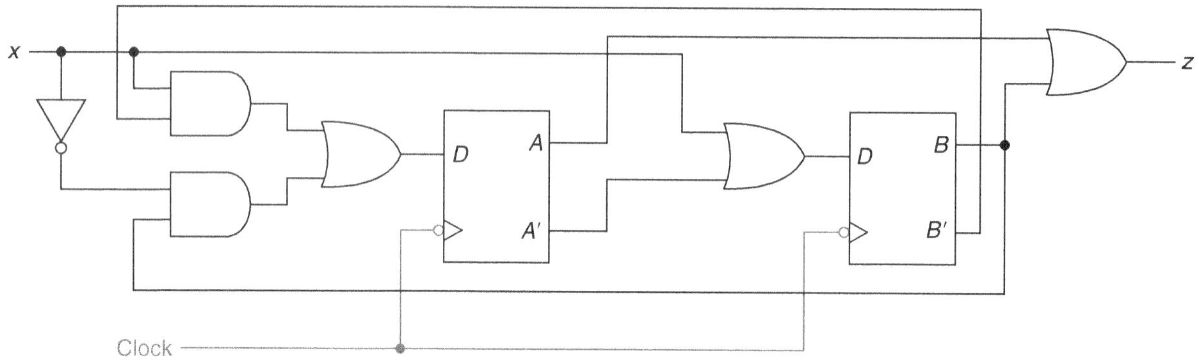

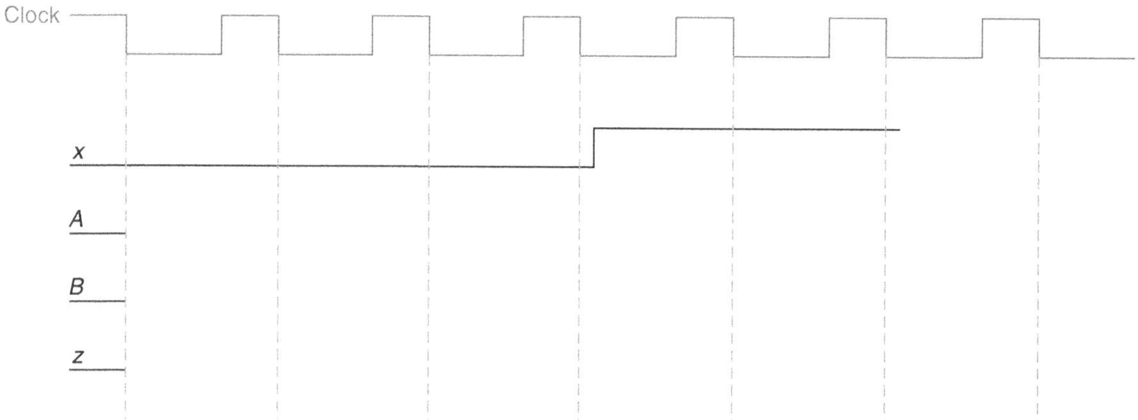

CHAPTER 7

The Design of Sequential Systems

As in the case of combinational systems, the design process typically starts with a problem statement, a verbal description of the intended behavior of the system. The goal is to develop a block diagram of the system utilizing the available components and meeting the design objectives and constraints.

We will first present five additional Continuing Examples, which we will use throughout the chapter to illustrate the design techniques.

Continuing Examples (CE)

CE7. A Mealy system with one input x and one output z such that $z = 1$ at a clock time iff x is currently 1 and was also 1 at the previous two clock times.*

CE8. A Moore system with one input x and one output z, the output of which is 1 iff three consecutive 0 inputs occurred more recently than three consecutive 1 inputs.

CE9. A system with no inputs and three outputs, that represent a number from 0 to 7, such that the outputs cycle through the sequence 0 3 2 4 1 5 7 and repeat on consecutive clock inputs.

CE10. A system with two inputs, x_1 and x_2, and three outputs, z_1, z_2, and z_3, that represent a number from 0 to 7, such that the output counts up if $x_1 = 0$ and down if $x_1 = 1$, and recycles if $x_2 = 0$ and saturates if $x_2 = 1$. Thus, the following output sequences might be seen

$x_1 = 0, x_2 = 0$:	0 1 2 3 4 5 6 7 0 1 2 3 4 5 6 7 . . .
$x_1 = 0, x_2 = 1$:	0 1 2 3 4 5 6 7 7 7 7 7 7 7 7 7 . . .
$x_1 = 1, x_2 = 0$:	7 6 5 4 3 2 1 0 7 6 5 4 3 2 1 0 . . .
$x_1 = 1, x_2 = 1$:	7 6 5 4 3 2 1 0 0 0 0 0 0 0 0 0 . . .

*This is very similar to CE6 (introduced in Chapter 6), except that the output goes to 1 simultaneously with the third consecutive 1 (whereas in CE6, the system went to a state with a 1 output when it received the third 1).

(Of course, x_1 and x_2 may change at some point so that the output would switch from one sequence to another.)

CE11. A bus controller that receives requests on separate lines, R_0 to R_3, from four devices desiring to use the bus. It has four outputs, G_0 to G_3, only one of which is 1, indicating which device is granted control of the bus for that clock period. (We will consider, in Section 7.4, the design for such a priority controller, where the low number device has the highest priority, if more than one device requests the bus at the same time. We look at both interrupting controllers, where a high priority device can preempt the bus, and one where a device keeps control of the bus once it gets control until it no longer needs the bus.)

In addition to these Continuing Examples, there are three additional complete examples (from verbal description to final design) in Appendix E.2.

We will next look at the design process for systems similar to those that we just described. In Chapter 8, we will look at some other techniques that are suitable for larger systems.

> **Step 1:** From a word description, determine what needs to be stored in memory. That is, what are the possible states?

Sometimes there may be different ways of storing the necessary information. For CE7, we could just store the last two values of the input. If we know that and we know the current input, then we know if all three have been 1. But we could also store how many consecutive 1's there have been—none, one, or two or more. We can develop the state table either way; each will produce a properly working circuit. However, the cost might be quite different. Just consider what would have been the case if we wanted an output of 1 iff the input was now 1 and was also 1 for the last 27 consecutive clocks. The first approach would require us to store the last 27 inputs—in 27 flip flops. The second approach would require us to keep track of only 28 things, 0 consecutive 1's through 27 or more consecutive 1's. But 28 facts can be stored using only five binary storage devices, coding none as 00000, through 27 or more as 11011 (the binary equivalent of 27).

> **Step 2:** If necessary, code the inputs and outputs in binary.

This is the same problem as for combinational systems. Many problems are stated in such a way that this step is not necessary.

> **Step 3:** Derive a state table or state diagram to describe the behavior of the system.

In Moore systems, such as CE6 and CE8, the output depends only on the present state of the system. (The combinational logic that produces the output is just a function of the contents of the various flip flops.) (The output does, of course, depend on the input, since the state depends on the input, but the effect on the output is delayed until after the next clock.) In other examples, such as CE7, the output depends on the current input as well as the contents of memory.

Step 4: Use state reduction techniques (see Chapter 9)* to find a state table that produces the same input/output behavior but has fewer states.

Fewer states may mean fewer storage devices. By reducing the number of flip flops, we also reduce the number of inputs to the combinational logic. Thus, for example, a system with one input and three flip flops requires four-variable combinational logic, whereas one with two flip flops would use only three-variable logic. This usually means a less expensive circuit. (This step could be omitted and a correctly working system designed.)

Step 5: Choose a state assignment, that is, code the states in binary.

Any coding will do, that is, will produce a correct solution. However, a good choice will often lead to simpler combinational logic (see Chapter 9).

Step 6: Choose a flip flop type and derive the flip flop input maps or tables.

The state table and state assignment produce a table that tells what is to be stored in each flip flop as a function of what is in memory now and the system input. This part of the problem is to determine what input must be applied to each flip flop to get that transition to take place. In this chapter, we will look at the technique that is required for the various types of flip flops commonly used.

Step 7: Produce the logic equation and draw a block diagram (as in the case of combinational systems).

*Chapter 9 is available on the student side of the book's Web site, http://www.mhhe.com/marcovitz.

In this chapter, we will be concerned first with Steps 6 and 7; then, we will return to Step 1. In Chapter 9, we will develop techniques for state reduction (Step 4) and state assignment (Step 5).

The state table of Table 6.1 and the state diagram of Figure 6.3 are repeated here as Figure 7.1.

Figure 7.1 Design example.

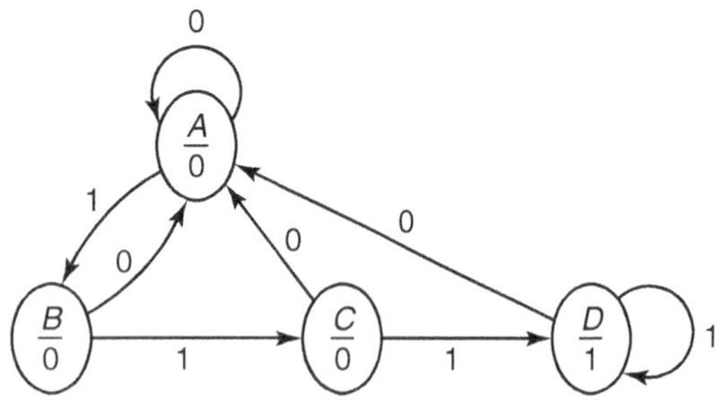

q	$q^\star$ $x = 0$	$x = 1$	z
A	A	B	0
B	A	C	0
C	A	D	0
D	A	D	1

Three state assignments are shown in Table 7.1.*

Table 7.1 State assignments.

q	q_1	q_2
A	0	0
B	0	1
C	1	0
D	1	1

(a)

q	q_1	q_2
A	0	0
B	1	1
C	1	0
D	0	1

(b)

q	q_1	q_2
A	0	0
B	0	1
C	1	1
D	1	0

(c)

These assignments were chosen arbitrarily. It is not clear which choice might lead to the least combinational logic.

From either the state diagram or the state table, we construct the *design truth table* of Table 7.2 for the next state. For this first example, we will use the state assignment of Table 7.1a.

Table 7.2 Design truth table.

q	x	q_1	q_2	$q_1^\star$	$q_2^\star$
A	0	0	0	0	0
B	0	0	1	0	0
C	0	1	0	0	0
D	0	1	1	0	0
A	1	0	0	0	1
B	1	0	1	1	0
C	1	1	0	1	1
D	1	1	1	1	1

Although the q column is not really needed, it is helpful in the development of the truth table, particularly if the states are assigned in some order other than numerical (such as in Tables 7.1b and 7.1c). The first half of the design truth table corresponds to the first column of the state table ($x = 0$). The next state is 00 for the first four rows, since each of the states go to state A on a 0 input. The second half of the table corresponds to $x = 1$.

For a Moore system, we construct a separate table for the output (Table 7.3), since it depends only on the two state variables. (As we will

*We will demonstrate in Chapter 9 that all of the other possible state assignments result in the same amount of combinational logic as one of these. Each can be obtained either by a renumbering of the flip flops or the replacement of variables by their complement or both.

see shortly, the z column would be included as another column in the design truth table for a Mealy system.)

We can now map $q_1^\star$, $q_2^\star$, and z, as shown in Map 7.1. We prefer to draw the Karnaugh maps in the vertical orientation for such problems since the columns correspond to the input and the rows to the states.

Table 7.3 Output truth table.

q	q_1	q_2	z
A	0	0	0
B	0	1	0
C	1	0	0
D	1	1	1

Map 7.1 Next state and output maps.

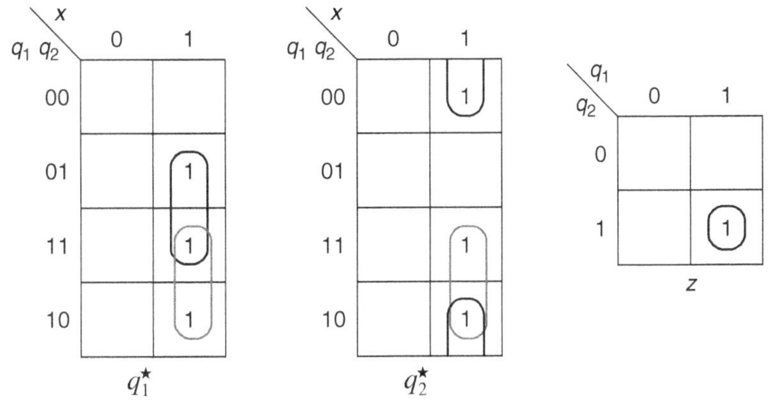

We thus have the equations

$$q_1^\star = xq_2 + xq_1$$
$$q_2^\star = xq_2' + xq_1$$
$$z = q_1q_2$$

(Although we took advantage of the obvious sharing available in this example, we will not emphasize sharing in the development of flip flop input equations.) Note that this sum of products solution requires 4 two-input AND gates and 2 two-input OR gates (or 6 two-input NAND gates plus a NOT, since z comes from an AND, requiring a NAND followed by a NOT).*

EXAMPLE 7.1

If we use the state assignment of Table 7.1b, we get the following design truth table:

	x	q_1	q_2	$q_1^\star$	$q_2^\star$
A	0	0	0	0	0
D	0	0	1	0	0
C	0	1	0	0	0
B	0	1	1	0	0
A	1	0	0	1	1
D	1	0	1	0	1
C	1	1	0	0	1
B	1	1	1	1	0

q	q_1	q_2	z
A	0	0	0
D	0	1	1
C	1	0	0
B	1	1	0

*We assumed that q_1 and q_2 are available both uncomplemented and complemented, but x is only available uncomplemented (although the latter is irrelevant in this example).

The resulting maps for $q_1^\star$ and $q_2^\star$ are

$q_1^\star$:

$q_1 q_2$ \ x	0	1
00		1
01		
11		1
10		

$q_2^\star$:

$q_1 q_2$ \ x	0	1
00		1
01		1
11		
10		1

$$q_1^\star = xq_1'q_2' + xq_1q_2$$
$$q_2^\star = xq_1' + xq_2'$$
$$z = q_1'q_2$$

Note that this implementation requires an extra gate and three extra gate inputs.

[SP 1]

What we have done so far does not depend on the type of flip flop we will use to implement the system. We will use these results to complete the design in Section 7.2.

7.1 FLIP FLOP DESIGN TECHNIQUES

Table 7.4 Flip flop design table.

q	$q^\star$	Input(s)
0	0	
0	1	
1	0	
1	1	

The design truth table that we developed for the next state will be used in conjunction with the appropriate *flip flop design table* to obtain a truth table for the flip flop inputs. We will present this approach first and then look at a map approach that does not require the truth table and finally a *quick method* that saves a great deal of work but applies only to *JK* flip flops.

The flip flop design table is most readily obtained from the state diagram. Its general form is shown in Table 7.4. For each line of the truth table equivalent of the state table, and for each flip flop, we know its present value and the desired next state. This table allows us to then determine the inputs.

Figure 7.2 *D* flip flop state diagram.

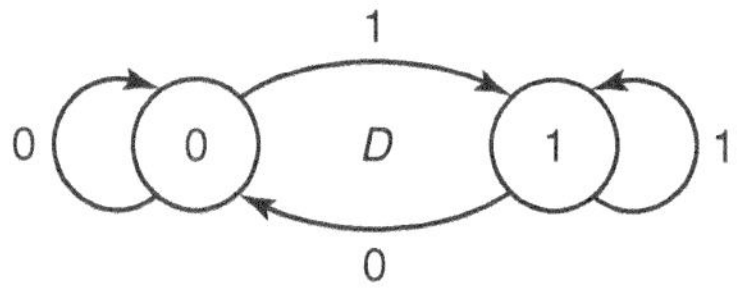

Although the *D* flip flop is trivial, we will use that to illustrate the process. The state diagram for the *D* flip flop is repeated as Figure 7.2. The diagram indicates that if the flip flop is in state 0 and the desired next state is also 0, the only path is $D = 0$. Similarly, to go from 0 to 1, *D* must be 1; from 1 to 0, *D* must be 0; and from 1 to 1, *D* must be 1. That produces the flip flop design table of Table 7.5 for the *D* flip flop.

For the D flip flop, we do not need separate columns in the truth table for D_1 and D_2, since they are identical to the $q_1^\star$ and $q_2^\star$ columns. We will use the design table of Table 7.2 as an example throughout this section. Thus, for D flip flops,

$$D_1 = x\,q_2 + x\,q_1$$
$$D_2 = x\,q_2' + x\,q_1$$

A block diagram of the solution, using D flip flops and AND and OR gates, is shown in Figure 7.3.

Table 7.5 *D* flip flop design table.

q	$q^\star$	D
0	0	0
0	1	1
1	0	0
1	1	1

Figure 7.3 Implementation using *D* flip flops.

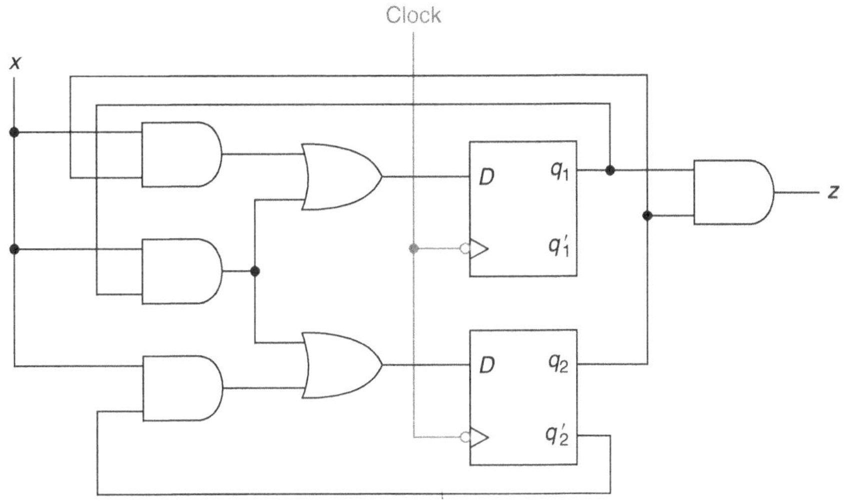

We will now repeat the process for the JK flip flop. The state diagram for the JK flip flop is repeated as Figure 7.4. To go from state 0 to state 0, we have two choices; we can make $J = 0$ and $K = 0$, or $J = 0$ and $K = 1$. In other words, J must be 0 and it does not matter what K is, that is, K is a don't care. Similarly, to go from 1 to 1, K must be 0 and J is a don't care. To go from 0 to 1, J must be 1 and K is a don't care and to go from 1 to 0, K must be 1 and J is a don't care. This results in the JK flip flop design table of Table 7.6. The truth table for the system design is thus shown in Table 7.7. Now, the truth table for the design requires four more columns for the four flip flop inputs. (The q column with state names has been omitted since the first five columns of this table are identical to the corresponding columns of Table 7.2.) The shaded columns, q_1 and $q_1^\star$, produce the shaded flip flop input columns, using Table 7.6. The unshaded columns (for flip flop 2) produce the unshaded flip flop inputs. In each of the first two rows, q_1 goes from 0 to 0; thus, from the first row of the flip flop design table, $J_1 = 0$ and $K_1 = \text{X}$. In the first row, q_2 also goes from 0 to 0, producing $J_2 = 0$ and $K_2 = \text{X}$.

Figure 7.4 *JK* flip flop state diagram.

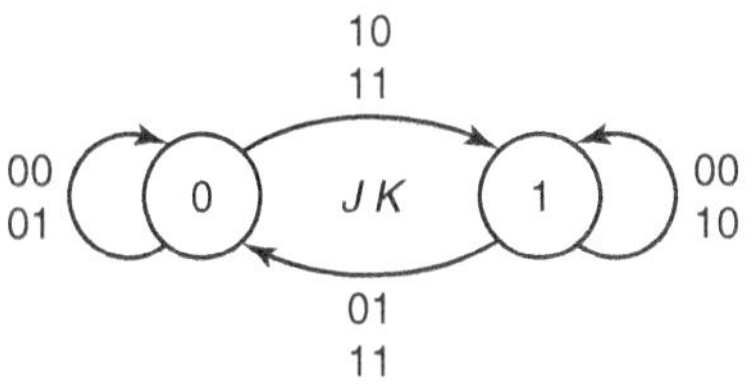

Table 7.6 *JK* flip flop design table.

q	$q^\star$	J	K
0	0	0	X
0	1	1	X
1	0	X	1
1	1	X	0

Table 7.7 Flip flop input table.

x	q_1	q_2	$q_1^\star$	$q_2^\star$	J_1	K_1	J_2	K_2
0	0	0	0	0	0	X	0	X
0	0	1	0	0	0	X	X	1
0	1	0	0	0	X	1	0	X
0	1	1	0	0	X	1	X	1
1	0	0	0	1	0	X	1	X
1	0	1	1	0	1	X	X	1
1	1	0	1	1	X	0	1	X
1	1	1	1	1	X	0	X	0

In the second row, q_2 goes from 1 to 0; thus, from the third row of the flip flop design table, $J_2 = \text{X}$ and $K_2 = 1$. The rest of the table can be completed in a similar manner.

The resulting maps are shown in Map 7.2.

Map 7.2 *JK* input maps.

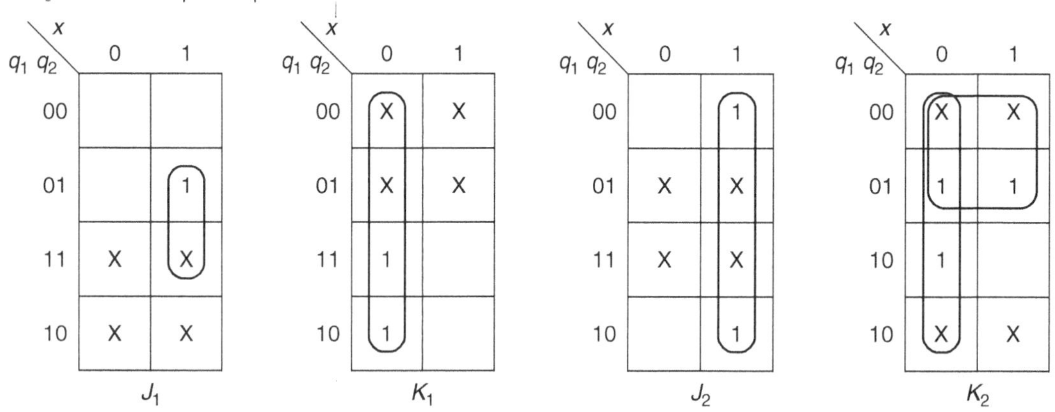

The flip flop input equations are

$$J_1 = xq_2 \qquad K_1 = x' \qquad z = q_1q_2$$
$$J_2 = x \qquad K_2 = x' + q_1'$$

This requires just 2 two-input AND gates (including the output gate), 1 two-input OR gate, and a NOT for x', by far the least expensive solution. (For NAND gates, we would need 3 two-input gates and 2 NOTs.)

Looking at the *JK* flip flop input equations, we note that J_1 and K_1 do not depend on q_1, and J_2 and K_2 do not depend on q_2. That is not just a property of this particular problem, but there is always a minimum solution for which this is true (no matter how big the system). This can be seen by looking at the maps for J and K, repeated in Map 7.3. Note that half of each map contains don't cares (shown in brown). (Indeed, sometimes, when all combinations of state variables are not used, there are even more don't cares. We will see an example of that later.) Each of the 1's on the map has a don't care in such a position that the 1 can be combined with the don't care to eliminate the variable involved. These are shown circled on the maps and the terms listed below. These terms are not necessarily prime implicants, but those for J_1 and K_1 do not involve q_1, and those for J_2 and K_2 do not involve q_2.

Map 7.3 Pairing of 1's and don't cares in *JK* flip flop inputs.

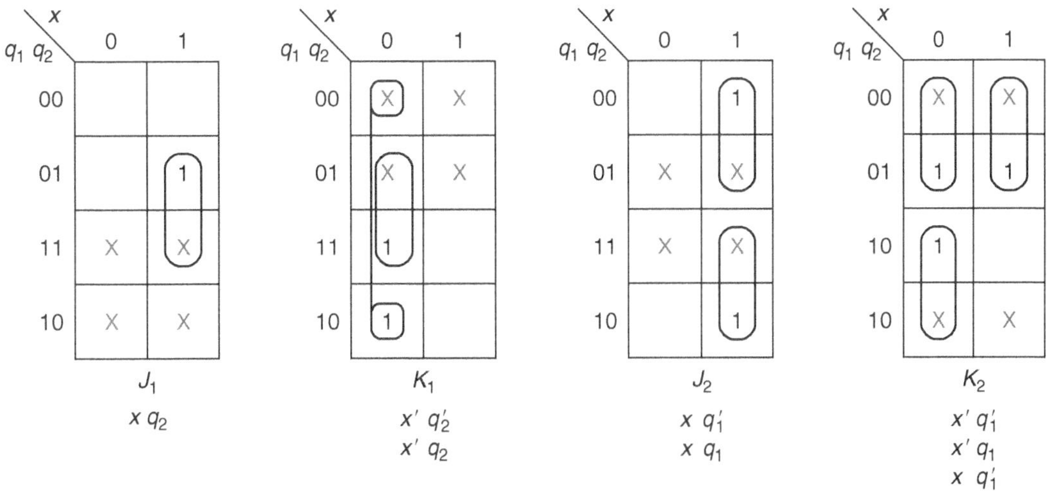

In Examples 7.2 and 7.3, we will repeat this process for the *SR* and *T* flip flops.

EXAMPLE 7.2

The state diagram for the *SR* flip flop is repeated below.

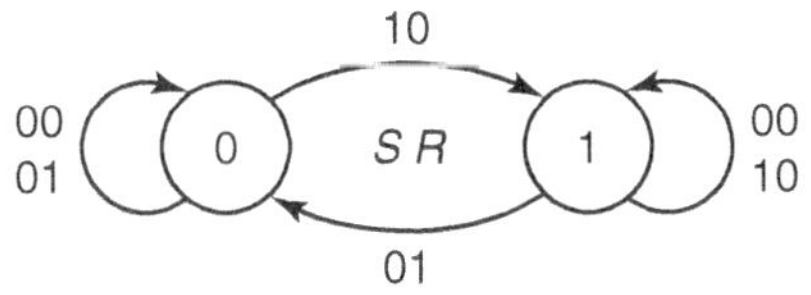

To go from state 0 to state 0 or from state 1 to state 1, we have the same two choices as for the *JK*. To go from 0 to 1, *S* must be 1 and *R* must be 0, and to go from 1 to 0, *R* must be 1 and *S* must be 0. The resulting *SR* flip flop design table is

q	$q^\star$	S	R
0	0	0	X
0	1	1	0
1	0	0	1
1	1	X	0

Note that *S* and *R* will never both be made 1 (whatever values we choose for the don't cares). Following the same technique as for *JK* flip flops, we get

x	q_1	q_2	$q_1^\star$	$q_2^\star$	S_1	R_1	S_2	R_2
0	0	0	0	0	0	X	0	X
0	0	1	0	0	0	X	0	1
0	1	0	0	0	0	1	0	X
0	1	1	0	0	0	1	0	1
1	0	0	0	1	0	X	1	0
1	0	1	1	0	1	0	0	1
1	1	0	1	1	X	0	1	0
1	1	1	1	1	X	0	X	0

The maps for the flip flops inputs (the output z is still q_1q_2) become

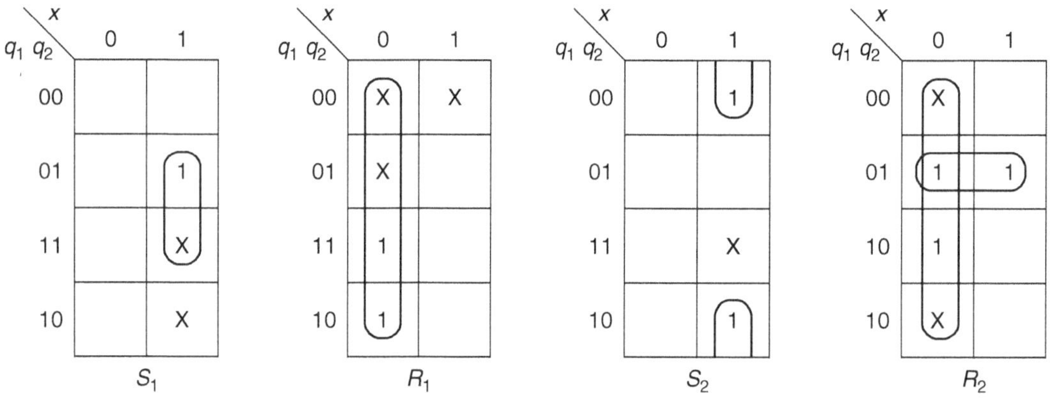

and the input equations are

$$S_1 = xq_2 \qquad R_1 = x' \qquad z = q_1q_2$$
$$S_2 = xq_2' \qquad R_2 = x' + q_1'q_2$$

This requires 4 two-input AND gates (including the one for the output), 1 two-input OR gate, and 1 NOT gate for x'. (The NAND solution would require 3 additional NOT gates, for S_1, S_2, and for z.)

EXAMPLE 7.3

The state diagram for the T flip flop is

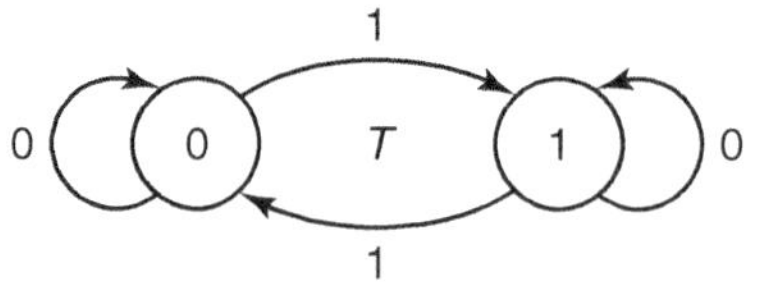

There is only one way to get from any state to any other state. The flip flop design table is thus

q	$q^\star$	T
0	0	0
0	1	1
1	0	1
1	1	0

and the truth table for the system design becomes

x	q_1	q_2	$q_1^\star$	$q_2^\star$	T_1	T_2
0	0	0	0	0	0	0
0	0	1	0	0	0	1
0	1	0	0	0	1	0
0	1	1	0	0	1	1
1	0	0	0	1	0	1
1	0	1	1	0	1	1
1	1	0	1	1	0	1
1	1	1	1	1	0	0

The maps for T and the equations are shown below.

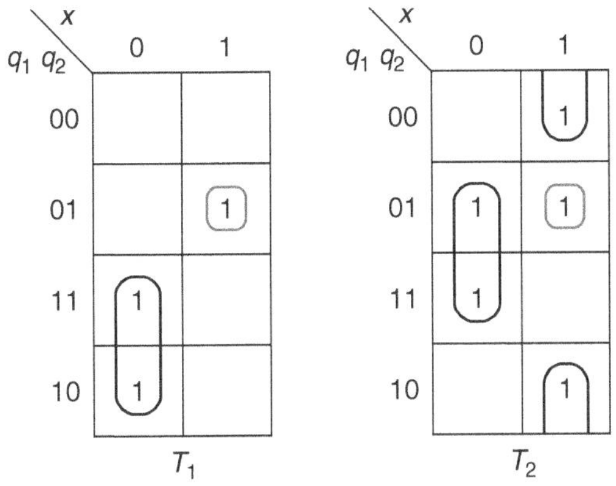

$$T_1 = x'q_1 + xq_1'q_2$$
$$T_2 = x'q_2 + xq_2' + xq_1'q_2$$
$$z = q_1q_2$$

This requires 4 two-input AND gates, 1 three-input AND gate, 1 two-input and 1 three-input OR gate, and a NOT for x. This is the most expensive solution for this example. (But, there are systems for which the T will result in a less expensive circuit than D or SR.)

The JK solution never requires more logic than either the SR or the T. Comparing the maps for the SR and the JK solutions, we see that both maps have 1's in exactly the same places. Further, all of the X's in the SR solution are also X's on the JK maps. The JK maps have additional don't cares. We could always choose to make those don't cares 0 and arrive at the SR solution. But, as we saw above, some of those X's were useful to make larger groupings and thus simplify the logic. From a different point of view, say we were to design a system for SR flip flops and build the combinational logic. If we then found that all we had available with which to build it was JK flip flops, we could use the logic and it would work. Similarly, if we designed for T flip flops, we could connect that logic to both J and K; the JK flip flop would behave like a T. (As in the case of the SR, there is often more logic required this way.) The relationship between the D and JK design is not quite so clear. However, if the logic for D is connected to J and the complement of that to K, the circuit will work. (Again, this might not be the best design for the JK flip flop; it certainly was not in this example.)

An important point to note is that the input equations for any flip flop are derived from the q and $q^\star$ columns for *that* flip flop. Thus, if two (or more) different types of flip flops were used, the same truth table would be developed as we have just done. Then the appropriate flip flop design table would be used for each flip flop. If, for example, a JK flip flop were used for q_1 and a D for q_2, then the logic equations would be

$$J_1 = xq_2 \qquad K_1 = x'$$
$$D_2 = xq_2' + xq_1$$
$$z = q_1 q_2$$

These are the same equations that we obtained for J_1, K_1, and D_2 earlier in this section.

Let us now go back and look at another approach to solving these problems without the use of the truth table. If the states are coded in binary, we can get maps for $q_1^\star$ and $q_2^\star$ directly from the state table as shown in Figure 7.5.

The columns of the state table shaded in tan produce the map for $q_1^\star$ and the gray columns on the truth table produce the map for $q_2^\star$. A word of caution is in order (although it does not come into play in this problem). The state table has the present state numbered in binary order; the map, of course, has them numbered appropriately. The last two rows of the state table must be interchanged when they are copied onto the map. (Some people prefer to draw the state table in map order to avoid this problem, that is, 00, 01, 11, 10; that also works.)

Figure 7.5 State table to maps.

$q_1\,q_2$	$q_1^\star\,q_2^\star$ $x = 0$	$q_1^\star\,q_2^\star$ $x = 1$	z
00	0 0	0 1	0
01	0 0	1 0	0
10	0 0	1 1	0
11	0 0	1 1	1

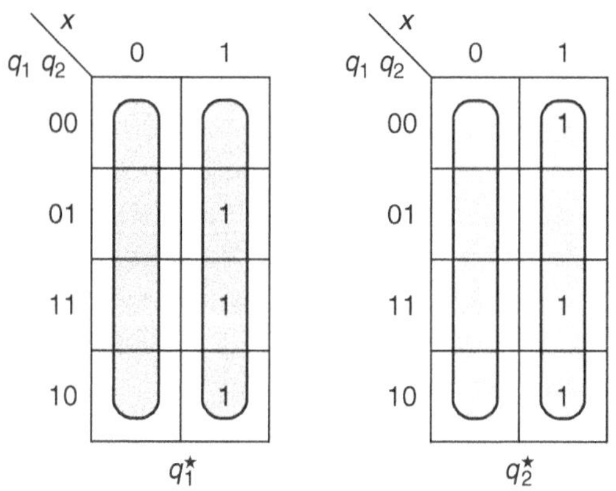

For D flip flops, we are done, since the maps for $q_1^\star$ and $q_2^\star$ are also the maps for D_1 and D_2. Map 7.4a contains the maps for $q_1^\star$, J_1, and K_1 (from earlier in the section).

Map 7.4a First column of J_1 and K_1.

$q_1^\star$

$q_1\ q_2 \backslash x$	0	1
0 0		
0 1		1
1 1		1
1 0		1

J_1

$q_1\ q_2 \backslash x$	0	1
00		
01		1
11	X	X
10	X	X

K_1

$q_1\ q_2 \backslash x$	0	1
00	X	X
01	X	X
11	1	
10	1	

The shaded columns on the $q_1^\star$ map, together with the JK flip flop design table (Table 7.6) are used, row by row, to produce the shaded columns on the J_1 and K_1 maps. For example, the first two rows have q_1 going from 0 to 0, producing $J = 0$, $K = \text{X}$. The last two rows have q_1 going from 1 to 0, producing $J = \text{X}$, $K = 1$. To get the second column of the J_1 and K_1 maps, we use the second column of the $q_1^\star$ map but still the q_1 column (the first column) as shown shaded in Map 7.4b.

Map 7.4b Second column of J_1 and K_1.

$q_1^\star$

$q_1\ q_2 \backslash x$	0	1
0 0		
0 1		1
1 1		1
1 0		1

J_1

$q_1\ q_2 \backslash x$	0	1
00		
01		1
11	X	X
10	X	X

K_1

$q_1\ q_2 \backslash x$	0	1
00	X	X
01	X	X
11	1	
10	1	

In the first row, 0 goes to 0, producing $JK = 0\text{X}$; in the second row, 0 goes to 1, producing $JK = 1\text{X}$; in the third and fourth rows, 1 goes to 1, producing $JK = \text{X}0$. The results are, of course, the same as before.

To find J and K for flip flop q_2, we map $q_2^\star$ and use the q_2 column, as shown in the shading for the first column of J_2 and K_2 in Map 7.4c. We then use the same column of q_2 with the other column of the $q_2^\star$ map to form the second columns of the J_2 and K_2 maps.

This same technique can be used with the other type of flip flops (using the appropriate flip flop design table). Caution: The q_1 input (the first input column) is used with both the first and second columns of $q_1^\star$ to obtain the inputs to the first flip flop. The q_2 input (the second input column) is used with both the first and second columns of $q_2^\star$ to obtain the inputs to the second flip flop.

Map 7.4c Computation of J_2 and K_2.

$q_2^\star$:

q_1 q_2 \ x	0	1
0 0		1
0 1		
1 1		1
1 0		1

J_2:

q_1 q_2 \ x	0	1
00		1
01	X	X
11	X	X
10		1

K_2:

q_1 q_2 \ x	0	1
00	X	X
01	1	1
10	1	
10	X	X

The *quick* method for *JK* flip flop design (it does not apply to the other types of flip flop) takes advantage of a property of the *JK* flip flop input equations, where J_1 and K_1 do not depend on q_1, and J_2 and K_2 do not depend on q_2. That is not just a property of this particular problem, but there is always a minimum solution for which this is true (no matter how big the system).

We can take advantage of this property by utilizing the equation we developed in Section 6.3,

$$q^\star = Jq' + K'q$$

Notice that when $q = 0$,

$$q^\star = J \cdot 1 + K' \cdot 0 = J$$

and when $q = 1$,

$$q^\star = J \cdot 0 + K' \cdot 1 = K'.$$

Thus, the part of the map of $q^\star$ (for each variable) for which that variable is 0 is the map for J and the part for which that variable is 1 is the map for K'. On Map 7.5a, we show $q_1^\star$ with the $q_1 = 0$ section shaded in tan and the $q_1 = 1$ section shaded in gray. The two smaller maps are then copied separately to the right. (That is not really necessary; we could work on the separate sections of the larger map.)

Map 7.5a Computing J_1 and K_1 using the quick method.

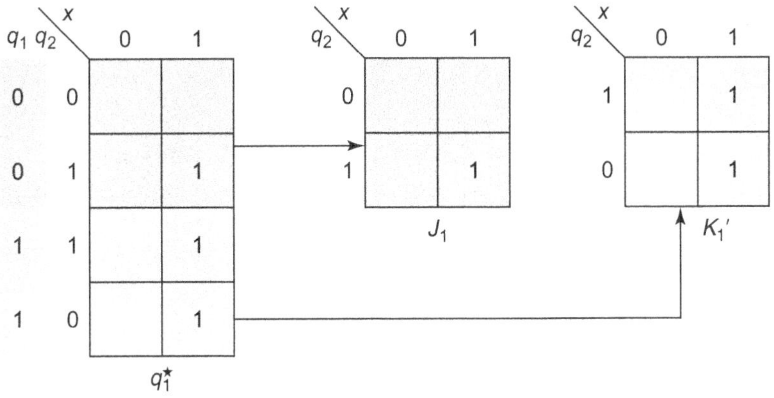

The three variable map has been reduced to 2 two-variable maps, one for J and the other for K'. The variable q_1 has been eliminated; that was used to choose the section of the original map. (We could have drawn the map for K; it would just require replacing 0's by 1's and 1's by 0's.) From these maps, we see

$$J_1 = xq_2 \qquad K_1' = x \quad \text{or} \quad K_1 = x'$$

These are, of course, the same answer we obtained using the other methods as in Map 7.2 and Maps 7.4a and 7.4b. Be careful in using the map for K_1'; the two rows are reversed, that is, the $q_2 = 1$ row is on the top. That does not affect this problem and just requires care in reading the map in other problems. (We could redraw the map and interchange the rows.)

We will repeat this process for the second flip flop on Map 7.5b, since the map geometry is somewhat different.

Map 7.5b Computing J_2 and K_2 using the quick method.

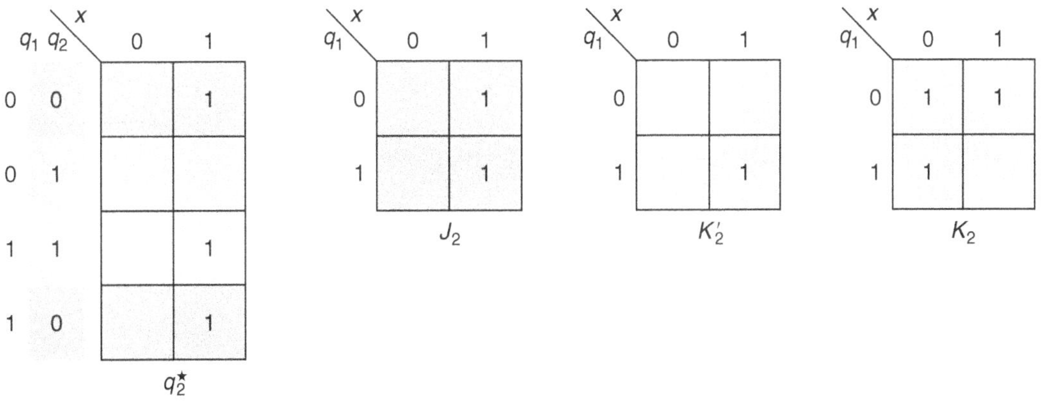

The $q_2 = 0$ portion of the map consists of the first and last rows; the $q_2 = 1$ portion is made up of the middle two rows. The maps for J_2, K'_2 and then K_2 are shown in Map 7.5b. As we found with the other methods,

$$J_2 = x \qquad K_2 = x' + q_1'$$

For this approach, it is really only necessary to plot maps of $q^\star$ for each variable. We do not need the system truth table nor maps for each of the flip flop inputs.

EXAMPLE 7.4

We will now look at a complete example. The state table and the state assignment are shown below.

q	$q^\star$ x = 0	$q^\star$ x = 1	z x = 0	z x = 1
A	B	C	1	1
B	A	B	1	0
C	B	A	1	0

q	q_1	q_2
A	1	1
B	1	0
C	0	1

From these, we create the truth table below, including a column with the state name.

	x	q_1	q_2	$q_1^\star$	$q_2^\star$	z
–	0	0	0	X	X	X
C	0	0	1	1	0	1
B	0	1	0	1	1	1
A	0	1	1	1	0	1
–	1	0	0	X	X	X
C	1	0	1	1	1	0
B	1	1	0	1	0	0
A	1	1	1	0	1	1

The resulting maps for the output and for *D* flip flop inputs are shown below.

$q_1 q_2$ \ x	0	1
00	X	X
01	1	
11	1	1
10	1	

z

$q_1 q_2$ \ x	0	1
00	X	X
01	1	1
11	1	
10	1	1

$q_1^\star$

$q_1 q_2$ \ x	0	1
00	X	X
01		1
11		1
10	1	

$q_2^\star$

The resulting equations are

$$z = x' + q_1 q_2$$
$$D_1 = x' + q_1' + q_2'$$
$$D_2 = x q_2' + x' q_2$$

Notice that even the maps for D have don't cares, since one of the combinations of state variables is unused.

Columns for J and K are now added to the truth table, producing

	x	q_1	q_2	$q_1^\star$	$q_2^\star$	z	J_1	K_1	J_2	K_2
–	0	0	0	X	X	X	X	X	X	X
C	0	0	1	1	0	1	1	X	X	1
B	0	1	0	1	1	1	X	0	1	X
A	0	1	1	1	0	1	X	0	X	1
–	1	0	0	X	X	X	X	X	X	X
C	1	0	1	1	1	0	1	X	X	0
B	1	1	0	1	0	0	X	0	0	X
A	1	1	1	0	1	1	X	1	X	0

Even without mapping the functions, we can see that $J_1 = 1$. It is not unusual for one (or both) of the inputs to a JK flip flop to be 1. It is also noteworthy that more than half of the entries in the truth table are don't cares. The equations for the flip flop inputs follow. (The output is the same for all types of flip flops.)

$J_1 = 1 \qquad K_1 = xq_2$

$J_2 = x' \qquad K_2 = x'$

We could have used the quick method to obtain the JK equations. The maps for $q_1^\star$ and $q_2^\star$ are repeated, with the shading for the quick method.

$q_1 q_2$ \ x	0	1
00	X	X
01	1	1
11	1	
10	1	1

$q_1^\star$

$q_1 q_2$ \ x	0	1
00	X	X
01		1
11		1
10	1	

$q_2^\star$

Of course, we get the same answers.

EXAMPLE 7.5

To conclude this section, we will look at one larger example. We wish to design the following system:

q	$q^\star$ $x = 0$	$q^\star$ $x = 1$	z
S_1	S_2	S_1	0
S_2	S_3	S_1	0
S_3	S_4	S_1	0
S_4	S_4	S_5	1
S_5	S_4	S_6	1
S_6	S_4	S_1	1

The first issue is to make a state assignment. We will consider two different ones, as shown below.

1.

q	*A*	*B*	*C*
S_1	0	0	0
S_2	0	0	1
S_3	0	1	0
S_4	0	1	1
S_5	1	0	0
S_6	1	0	1

2.

q	*A*	*B*	*C*
S_1	0	0	0
S_2	1	0	1
S_3	1	0	0
S_4	1	1	1
S_5	0	1	1
S_6	0	1	0

The first assignment just uses the first six binary numbers; the second uses an assignment meant to reduce the combinational logic (based on ideas we will develop in Chapter 9).

For the first assignment, we will consider the use of *D* and *JK* flip flops. It is easy to produce the maps for the three next states, $A^\star$, $B^\star$, and $C^\star$, without first drawing the truth table. The squares on each map correspond to the present state, as shown below (S_1 is 000; S_6 is 101; 110 and 111 are not used.) The left half of the map corresponds to $x = 0$, and the right half to $x = 1$.

BC \ *xA*	00	01	11	10
00	S_1	S_5	S_5	S_1
01	S_2	S_6	S_6	S_2
11	S_4	—	—	S_4
10	S_3	—	—	S_3

We can now complete the next state maps directly from the state table. Since S_1 goes to S_2 when $x = 0$, the upper left square for the maps become 0, 0, and 1. The complete maps are shown next.

BC \ *xA*	00	01	11	10
00			1	
01				
11		X	X	1
10		X	X	

$A^\star$

BC \ *xA*	00	01	11	10
00		1		
01	1	1		
11	1	X	X	
10	1	X	X	

$B^\star$

BC \ *xA*	00	01	11	10
00	1	1	1	
01		1		
11	1	X	X	
10	1	X	X	

$C^\star$

These are not only the maps of the next state, but also the D inputs. The map of the output, which is only a function of the state (since this is a Moore model), is shown next.

BC \ A	0	1
00		1
01		1
11	1	X
10		X

We can now find the input equations and the output.

$D_A = xAC' + xBC$

$D_B = x'A + x'B + x'C$

$D_C = x'A + x'B + x'C' + AC'$

$z = A + BC$

Using AND and OR gates requires 13 gates (including the NOT for x') with 30 inputs (including 1 four-input gate and 3 three-input gates).

To implement this with JK flip flops, we will first use the quick method. On the maps below, the part of the map used for J is shaded.

BC \ xA	00	01	11	10
00			1	
01				
11		X	X	1
10		X	X	

$A^\star$

BC \ xA	00	01	11	10
00		1		
01	1	1		
11	1	X	X	
10	1	X	X	

$B^\star$

BC \ xA	00	01	11	10
00	1	1	1	
01		1		
11	1	X	X	
10	1	X	X	

$C^\star$

From the shaded parts, we can find the J's:

$J_A = xBC \qquad J_B = x'A + x'C \qquad J_C = x' + A$

For J_A, A determines which part of the map is shaded; thus, the first column is only x' and the last x. Similarly, for B, the first row of the shaded part corresponds to C' and the second to C. From the 0's (and X's) of the unshaded part, we can find the K's, or from the 1's and X's, we can find K' and then complement it:

$K_A = x' + C \qquad K_B = x \qquad K_C = x + A'B'$

Of course, the output does not depend on the flip flop type and thus

$z = A + BC$

This requires 11 gates (including the NOT for x') and 22 inputs (only 1 three-input gate).

Next, we will go directly from the maps for $Q^\star$ of each flip flop to the maps for J and K.

BC \ xA	00	01	11	10
00			1	
01				
11		X	X	1
10		X	X	

$A^\star$

BC \ xA	00	01	11	10
00		X	X	
01		X	X	
11		X	X	1
10		X	X	

J_A

BC \ xA	00	01	11	10
00	X	1		X
01	X	1	1	X
11	X	X	X	X
10	X	X	X	X

K_A

BC \ xA	00	01	11	10
00		1		
01	1	1		
11	1	X	X	
10	1	X	X	

$B^\star$

BC \ xA	00	01	11	10
00		1		
01	1	1		
11	X	X	X	X
10	X	X	X	X

J_B

BC \ xA	00	01	11	10
00	X	X	X	X
01	X	X	X	X
11		X	X	1
10		X	X	1

K_B

BC \ xA	00	01	11	10
00	1	1	1	
01		1		
11	1	X	X	
10	1	X	X	

$C^\star$

BC \ xA	00	01	11	10
00	1	1	1	
01	X	X	X	X
11	X	X	X	X
10	1	X	X	

J_C

BC \ xA	00	01	11	10
00	X	X	X	X
01	1		1	1
11		X	X	1
10	X	X	X	X

K_C

As we can see, the map for J_A has don't cares in the two columns for which A is 1, and the map for K_A has X's in the two columns for which A is 0. Rows of don't cares are seen in the maps for $B^\star$ and $C^\star$. Of course, the equations are the same.

Before considering the other state assignment, we will look at a related problem to this. Say we designed the system as above and found that we had only one package of two D flip flops and one package of two

JK flip flops. We already have done all the design work necessary; we can use the equation we found for *D* or those for *JK* for any of the flip flops. The table below shows the number of gates and gate inputs used in each of these arrangements (as well as those using only *D* or *JK* flip flops), including the output gates.

A	B	C	Gates	Inputs
D	D	JK	13	28
D	JK	D	13	29
JK	D	D	12	27
D	JK	JK	12	25
JK	D	JK	12	25
JK	JK	D	12	26
D	D	D	13	30
JK	JK	JK	11	22

As one might guess, the best solution uses two *JK* flip flops. Even the sharing provided by using *D*'s for *B* and *C* requires more gate inputs. The *D* can be used equally well for *A* or *B*; other arrangements would require an extra gate and/or gate input(s).

Next, we will consider the solution using the second state assignment. For this, we will use the truth table approach. When dealing with state assignments that are not in numeric order, it is still best to list the truth table in binary order, but to list the state name next to the binary name. In that way, we can map the appropriate functions most directly.

	x	A	B	C	z	$A^\star$	$B^\star$	$C^\star$	J_A	K_A	J_B	K_B	J_C	K_C
S_1	0	0	0	0	0	1	0	1	1	X	0	X	1	X
—	0	0	0	1	X	X	X	X	X	X	X	X	X	X
S_6	0	0	1	0	1	1	1	1	1	X	X	0	1	X
S_5	0	0	1	1	1	1	1	1	1	X	X	0	X	0
S_3	0	1	0	0	0	1	1	1	X	0	1	X	1	X
S_2	0	1	0	1	0	1	0	0	X	0	0	X	X	1
—	0	1	1	0	X	X	X	X	X	X	X	X	X	X
S_4	0	1	1	1	1	1	1	1	X	0	X	0	X	0
S_1	1	0	0	0		0	0	0	0	X	0	X	0	X
—	1	0	0	1		X	X	X	X	X	X	X	X	X
S_6	1	0	1	0		0	0	0	0	X	X	1	0	X
S_5	1	0	1	1		0	1	0	0	X	X	0	X	1
S_3	1	1	0	0		0	0	0	X	1	0	X	0	X
S_2	1	1	0	1		0	0	0	X	1	0	X	X	1
—	1	1	1	0		X	X	X	X	X	X	X	X	X
S_4	1	1	1	1		0	1	1	X	1	X	0	X	0

The truth table above shows the next state and the *JK* inputs for each of the flip flops. Note that only the first eight rows are completed for the output column *z*, since *z* is not a function of the input *x*.

We can now find expressions for the output (with a three-variable map) and for the *D* inputs (using the $A^\star$, $B^\star$, and $C^\star$ columns) or for the *JK* inputs. First, the output map and equation are shown, since they apply to a solution using any type of flip flop (with this state assignment).

BC \ A	0	1
00		
01	X	
11	1	1
10	1	X

$z = B$

BC \ xA	00	01	11	10
00	1	1		
01	X	1		X
11	1	1		
10	1	X	X	

$A^{\star}$

BC \ xA	00	01	11	10
00		1		
01	X			X
11	1	1	1	1
10	1	X	X	

$B^{\star}$

BC \ xA	00	01	11	10
00	1	1		
01	X			X
11	1	1	1	
10	1	X	X	

$C^{\star}$

$$D_A = x'$$
$$D_B = x'B + BC + x'AC'$$
$$D_C = AB + x'C' + \{x'B \text{ or } x'A'\}$$

This requires a total of 9 gates with 20 inputs (including the NOT for x').

We could have solved the *JK* version using the quick method, but for this example, we have completed the truth table for *J* and *K*. We will leave the maps as an exercise for the reader; the equations are

$$J_A = x' \qquad K_A = x$$
$$J_B = x'AC' \qquad K_B = xC'$$
$$J_C = x' \qquad K_C = B' + xA'$$
$$z = B$$

This requires 5 gates with 10 inputs, significantly better than the *D* solution. Both the *D* and the *JK* solution for this assignment are considerably less expensive than the corresponding ones for the first state assignment.

[SP 2, 3, 4; EX 1, 2, 3, 4; LAB]

7.2 THE DESIGN OF SYNCHRONOUS COUNTERS

In this section, we will look at the design of a type of synchronous sequential system referred to as a *counter*. In the next section, we will look briefly at asynchronous counters, that is, those that do not require a clock input. In the next chapter, we will discuss some of the commercially available counters and the application of counters as part of a larger system.

Most counters are devices with no data input that go through a fixed sequence of states on successive clocks. The output is often just the state of the system, that is, the contents of all of the flip flops. (Thus, no output column is required in the state table.) We will also investigate counters with one or two control inputs that will, for example, determine whether the sequence is up (to the next larger number) or down.

Our first example, a 4-bit binary counter, has four flip flops that cycle through the sequence

0 1 2 3 4 5 6 7 8 9 10 11 12 13 14 15 0 1 . . .

There are really no new techniques required for this design. The state table and the truth table are the same; they have 16 rows, 4 input columns, and 4 output columns, as shown in Table 7.8. Note that the flip flops are labeled D, C, B, and A, which is the common practice.

As can be seen, the next state for state 0 (0000) is 1 (0001), for 1 is 2, and so forth, until the next state for 15 (1111) is 0 (0000).

Table 7.8 A base-16 counter.

D	C	B	A	$D^\star$	$C^\star$	$B^\star$	$A^\star$
0	0	0	0	0	0	0	1
0	0	0	1	0	0	1	0
0	0	1	0	0	0	1	1
0	0	1	1	0	1	0	0
0	1	0	0	0	1	0	1
0	1	0	1	0	1	1	0
0	1	1	0	0	1	1	1
0	1	1	1	1	0	0	0
1	0	0	0	1	0	0	1
1	0	0	1	1	0	1	0
1	0	1	0	1	0	1	1
1	0	1	1	1	1	0	0
1	1	0	0	1	1	0	1
1	1	0	1	1	1	1	0
1	1	1	0	1	1	1	1
1	1	1	1	0	0	0	0

The maps for the four next state functions are shown in Map 7.6.

Map 7.6 *D* flip flop inputs for 16-state counter.

$D^\star$

BA \ DC	00	01	11	10
00			1	1
01			1	1
11		1		1
10			1	1

$C^\star$

BA \ DC	00	01	11	10
00		1	1	
01		1	1	
11	1			1
10		1	1	

$B^\star$

BA \ DC	00	01	11	10
00				
01	1	1	1	1
11				
10	1	1	1	1

$A^\star$

BA \ DC	00	01	11	10
00	1	1	1	1
01				
11				
10	1	1	1	1

That produces

$$
\begin{aligned}
D_D &= DC' + DB' + DA' + D'CBA \\
D_C &= CB' + CA' + C'BA \\
D_B &= B'A + BA' \\
D_A &= A'
\end{aligned}
$$

This solution would require 12 gates with 30 gate inputs. If we have Exclusive-OR gates available, we could simplify the expressions to

$$
\begin{aligned}
D_D &= D(C' + B' + A') + D'CBA = D(CBA)' + D'(CBA) \\
&= D \oplus CBA \\
D_C &= C(B' + A') + C'BA = C(BA)' + C'(BA) = C \oplus BA \\
D_B &= B'A + BA' = B \oplus A \\
D_A &= A'
\end{aligned}
$$

This would only require two AND gates and three Exclusive-OR gates.

Next, we will look at the *JK* design, using Map 7.7. (The *SR* design is left as an exercise.) Using the quick method, the maps for *J* are the shaded parts of the next state maps (and those of *K'* are unshaded).

Map 7.7 Maps for *JK* flip flop design.

$D^\star$

BA \ DC	00	01	11	10
00			1	1
01			1	1
11		1		1
10			1	1

$C^\star$

BA \ DC	00	01	11	10
00		1	1	
01		1	1	
11	1			1
10		1	1	

$B^\star$

BA \ DC	00	01	11	10
00				
01	1	1	1	1
11				
10	1	1	1	1

$A^\star$

BA \ DC	00	01	11	10
00	1	1	1	1
01				
11				
10	1	1	1	1

This produces the equations

$$J_D = K_D - CBA$$
$$J_C = K_C = BA$$
$$J_B = K_B = A$$
$$J_A = K_A = 1$$

Note that since $J = K$ for each of the flip flops, they are being used as T flip flops (that is, either they remain unchanged or they toggle). We could extend the design to 5 flip flops, counting to 31 by adding flip flop E with inputs

$$J_E = K_E = DCBA$$

A circuit to implement this system using JK flip flops is shown in Figure 7.6.

Figure 7.6 A 4-bit counter.*

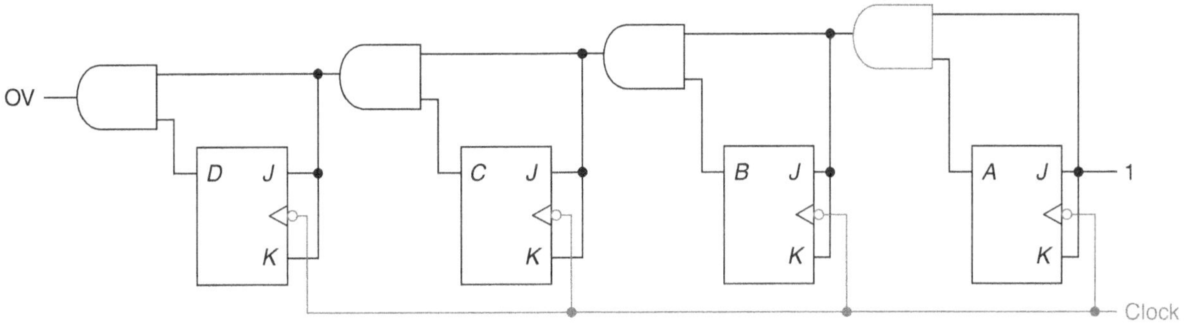

The brown AND gate is not necessary if this is a stand-alone counter; the output of the A flip flop would be connected directly to J_B and K_B. The OV output is 1 when the counter is in state 15 (1111). OV could be connected to the JK inputs of another flip flop or, if we built two 4 flip flop circuits like the one above, we could connect the OV output of one to the input where a 1 is now connected to construct an 8-bit counter.

We will next look at an up/down counter, that is, one that can count in either direction, depending upon a control input. We will label that control input x, such that the counter counts up when $x = 0$ and down when $x = 1$.† The state table for such a counter is shown as Table 7.9.

Table 7.9 An up/down counter.

x	C	B	A	$C^\star$	$B^\star$	$A^\star$
0	0	0	0	0	0	1
0	0	0	1	0	1	0
0	0	1	0	0	1	1
0	0	1	1	1	0	0
0	1	0	0	1	0	1
0	1	0	1	1	1	0
0	1	1	0	1	1	1
0	1	1	1	0	0	0
1	0	0	0	1	1	1
1	0	0	1	0	0	0
1	0	1	0	0	0	1
1	0	1	1	0	1	0
1	1	0	0	0	1	1
1	1	0	1	1	0	0
1	1	1	0	1	0	1
1	1	1	1	1	1	0

*Note that the combinational logic is multilevel. The term CBA is produced by using the output of the BA AND gate. In this way, we could extend the counter to any number of bits by adding as many flip flop/AND gate pairs as are needed.

†In commercial counters, this input is often labeled D/U', where the notation implies that down is active high and up is active low, just as we defined x.

The maps for $C^\star$, $B^\star$, and $A^\star$ are shown in Map 7.8, with the $q = 0$ section shaded for the quick method with JK flip flops.

Map 7.8 An up/down counter.

$C^\star$

BA \ xC	00	01	11	10
00		1		1
01		1	1	
11	1		1	
10		1	1	

$B^\star$

BA \ xC	00	01	11	10
00			1	1
01	1	1		
11			1	1
10	1	1		

$A^\star$

BA \ xC	00	01	11	10
00	1	1	1	1
01				
11				
10	1	1	1	1

From these maps, we can see that

$$J_A = K_A = 1$$
$$J_B = K_B = x'A + xA'$$
$$J_C = K_C = x'BA + xB'A'$$

Just as in the case of the 4- and 5-bit up counters, this pattern continues, yielding (if we had two more flip flops)

$$J_D = K_D = x'CBA + xC'B'A'$$
$$J_E = K_E = x'DCBA + xD'C'B'A'$$

A block diagram for the 3-bit counter is shown in Figure 7.7.

Figure 7.7 An up/down counter.

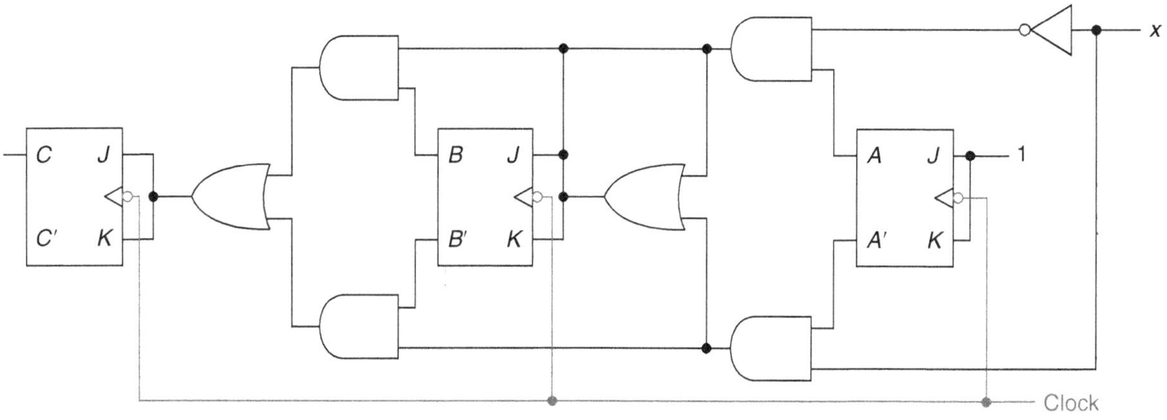

EXAMPLE 7.6

We will look next at a decimal or decade counter, one that goes through the sequence

0 1 2 3 4 5 6 7 8 9 0 1 . . .

The state (truth) table is similar to that for the binary counter, as seen below

D	*C*	*B*	*A*	$D^\star$	$C^\star$	$B^\star$	$A^\star$
0	0	0	0	0	0	0	1
0	0	0	1	0	0	1	0
0	0	1	0	0	0	1	1
0	0	1	1	0	1	0	0
0	1	0	0	0	1	0	1
0	1	0	1	0	1	1	0
0	1	1	0	0	1	1	1
0	1	1	1	1	0	0	0
1	0	0	0	1	0	0	1
1	0	0	1	0	0	0	0
1	0	1	0	X	X	X	X
1	0	1	1	X	X	X	X
1	1	0	0	X	X	X	X
1	1	0	1	X	X	X	X
1	1	1	0	X	X	X	X
1	1	1	1	X	X	X	X

The next state for the 9 (1001) row is 0 (0000) and the remaining next states are don't cares, since states 10 through 15 are never reached. We have included rows in this table for the unused states because they are needed to produce don't cares on the maps. Some may write the state table without these rows and then convert it to this truth table (as we did in the last section). The maps for the next state, with the *J* section shaded for finding *J* and *K* using the quick method, are shown next.

$D^\star$

BA \ DC	00	01	11	10
00			X	1
01			X	
11		1	X	X
10			X	X

$C^\star$

BA \ DC	00	01	11	10
00		1	X	
01		1	X	
11	1		X	X
10		1	X	X

$B^\star$

BA \ DC	00	01	11	10
00			X	
01	1	1	X	
11			X	X
10	1	1	X	X

$A^\star$

BA \ DC	00	01	11	10
00	1	1	X	1
01			X	
11			X	X
10	1	1	X	X

From this we can see that

$J_D = CBA \qquad K_D = A$

$J_C = K_C = BA$

$J_B = D'A \qquad K_B = A$

$J_A = K_A = 1$

EXAMPLE 7.7

We will next design a counter that goes through some sequence of states that are not in numeric order

0 3 2 4 1 5 7 and repeat

(This is CE9.) Note that the cycle is 7 states; it never goes through state 6. We can now draw the state table (in any order) or go directly to the truth table, including a row for the unused state.

q_1	q_2	q_3	$q_1^\star$	$q_2^\star$	$q_3^\star$
0	0	0	0	1	1
0	0	1	1	0	1
0	1	0	1	0	0
0	1	1	0	1	0
1	0	0	0	0	1
1	0	1	1	1	1
1	1	0	X	X	X
1	1	1	0	0	0

The table can be completed either by going through it row by row and seeing that state 0 goes to 3, state 1 goes to 5, and so forth, or by following the sequence, first filling in the next state for row 0 as 3, then a next state of 2 for state 3, and so forth. In the first approach, when we get to state 6, we find that it is not in the sequence, and thus the next state is don't cares. In the second approach, when we get to state 7, we must be sure to enter the next state as 0. Then, when we get done with the cycle, we find that row 6 is empty and also put in don't cares. We surely write the truth table in numeric order.

The table is repeated below with columns for inputs to *SR* and *T* flip flops; we will use the quick method for *JK* flip flops.

q_1	q_2	q_3	$q_1^\star$	$q_2^\star$	$q_3^\star$	S_1	R_1	S_2	R_2	S_3	R_3	T_1	T_2	T_3
0	0	0	0	1	1	0	X	1	0	1	0	0	1	1
0	0	1	1	0	1	1	0	0	X	X	0	1	0	0
0	1	0	1	0	0	1	0	0	1	0	X	1	1	0
0	1	1	0	1	0	0	X	X	0	0	1	0	0	1
1	0	0	0	0	1	0	1	0	X	1	0	1	0	1
1	0	1	1	1	1	X	0	1	0	X	0	0	1	0
1	1	0	X	X	X	X	X	X	X	X	X	X	X	X
1	1	1	0	0	0	0	1	0	1	0	1	1	1	1

For *D* flip flops, we just use the $q_1^\star$, $q_2^\star$, and $q_3^\star$ columns, producing the following maps and equations.

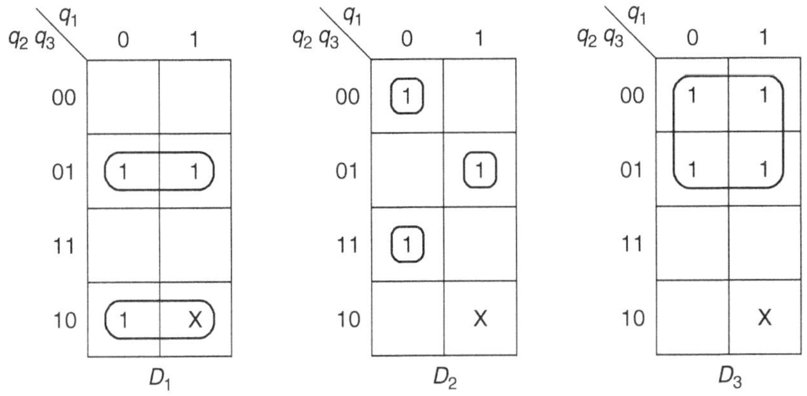

$$D_1 = q_2'q_3 + q_2q_3'$$
$$D_2 = q_1'q_2'q_3' + q_1'q_2q_3 + q_1q_2'q_3$$
$$D_3 = q_2'$$

This solution requires 4 three-input gates and 3 two-input gates.

The maps and equations for the *SR* solution follow. Note that for state 6, where we don't care what the next state is, we then don't care what the inputs are. *S* and *R* are both don't cares for all three flip flops.

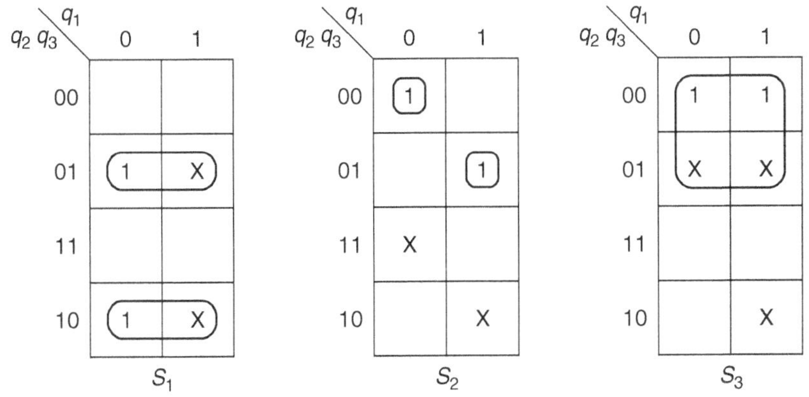

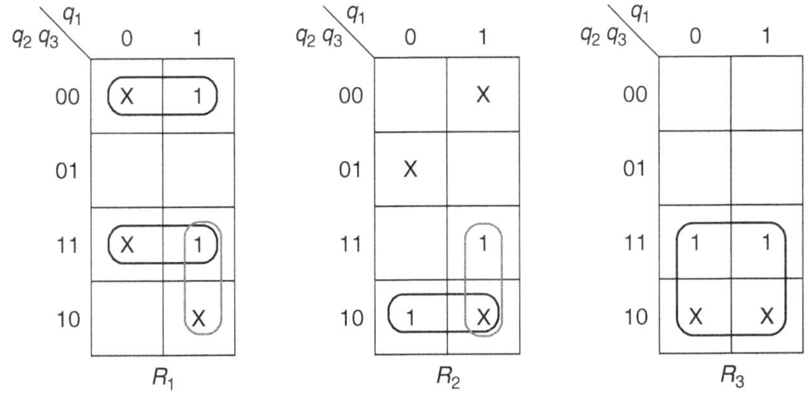

$$S_1 = q_2'q_3 + q_2q_3' \qquad R_1 = q_2'q_3' + q_2q_3 = S_1'$$
$$= q_2'q_3' + q_1q_2$$
$$S_2 = q_1'q_2'q_3' + q_1q_2'q_3 \qquad R_2 = q_1q_2 + q_2q_3'$$
$$S_3 = q_2' \qquad R_3 = q_2$$

Even taking advantage of the sharing or using a NOT for R_1, this requires more logic than the D solution (10 or 11 gates).

We will compute the T solution; the maps and the equations are shown next.

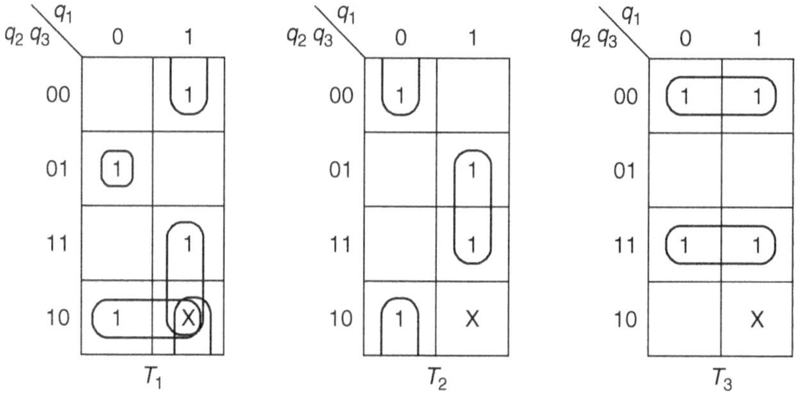

$$T_1 = q_1'q_2'q_3 + q_2q_3' + q_1q_2 + q_1q_3'$$
$$T_2 = q_1'q_3' + q_1q_3$$
$$T_3 = q_2'q_3' + q_2q_3$$

This solution requires 11 gates.

Finally, we will solve this system using the quick method for JK flip flops as shown on the maps and equations below.

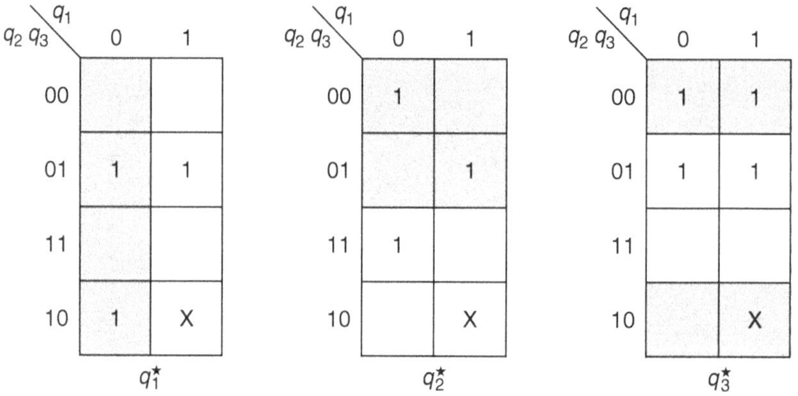

$$J_1 = q_2'q_3 + q_2q_3' \qquad K_1 = q_3' + q_2$$
$$J_2 = q_1'q_3' + q_1q_3 \qquad K_2 = q_1 + q_3'$$
$$J_3 = q_2' \qquad K_3 = q_2$$

This solution requires 8 two-input gates, although the gate for K_1 could be replaced by a NOT gate and the gate for K_2 could be eliminated, since by choosing the don't cares as 1's in both places, we get

$$K_1 = J_1' \quad \text{and} \quad K_2 = J_2$$

If we do not have a static clear (or do not use it) and turn the system on, we do not know in what state each flip flop will be initially. If we care, we should clear the flip flops or use some combination of clears and presets to get the system into the proper initial state. Often, all we care about is that once this is turned on, it goes through the desired sequence after one or two clocks. That will always happen if it is initialized to one of the states in the sequence. But, if it is initialized to one of the unused states, it is not obvious what will happen. When we designed the systems of the last two examples, we assumed that that state never happened and thus made the next state a don't care.

Once we complete the design, there are no longer any don't cares. The algebraic expressions (or the block diagrams) specify what happens for all possible combinations of variables.

EXAMPLE 7.7 (Cont.)

We can determine what would happen by assuming we are in state 110. Thus, we would make $q_1 = 1$, $q_2 = 1$, and $q_3 = 0$ in the equations. For D flip flops, we would get

$$D_1 = q_2'q_3 + q_2q_3' = 00 + 11 = 1$$
$$D_2 = q_1'q_2'q_3' + q_1'q_2q_3 + q_1q_2'q_3 = 001 + 011 + 100 = 0$$
$$D_3 = q_2' = 0$$

In that case, the system would go to state 4 (100) on the first clock and continue through the sequence from there. (With the design shown, we would also go to state 4 with *SR* flip flops, to state 2 with *T* flip flops, and to state 0 with *JK* flip flops.)

If this were not satisfactory, we could go back and redesign the system by replacing the don't cares in row 110 of the truth table by the desired next state.

A state diagram, showing the behavior of the system designed with *D* or *SR* flip flops, including what happens if the system starts in the unused state, is shown next.

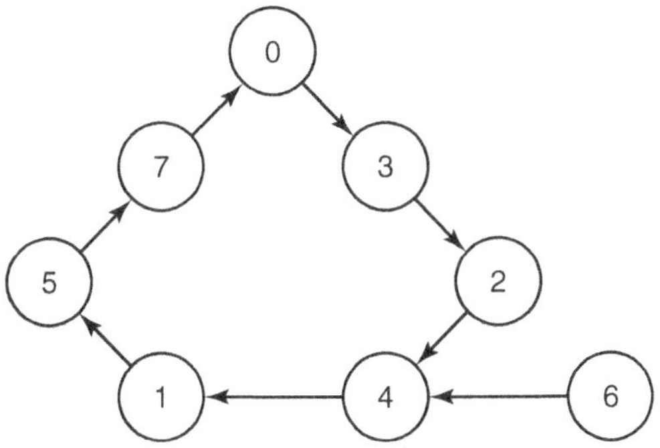

Note that there are no labels on the paths, since there is no input to the system, and the output is just equal to the state. (It is a Moore system.)

EXAMPLE 7.8

As a final example in this section, we will consider the design of a 2-bit up/down, cycling/saturating counter. This counter has two flip flops, A and B, and thus only four states. It has two control inputs, x and y. If $x = 0$, it counts up and if $x = 1$, it counts down. If $y = 0$, it cycles, that is, goes 0 1 2 3 0 1 . . . or 3 2 1 0 3 2 . . . , and if $y = 1$, it saturates, that is, it goes 0 1 2 3 3 3 . . . or 3 2 1 0 0 0 . . . . (This is a two-flip flop version of CE10.) The state table for this counter is

	$A^\star B^\star$			
A B	**xy = 00**	**xy = 01**	**xy = 10**	**xy = 11**
0 0	0 1	0 1	1 1	0 0
0 1	1 0	1 0	0 0	0 0
1 0	1 1	1 1	0 1	0 1
1 1	0 0	1 1	1 0	1 0

Since this is a problem with two inputs, there are four input combinations and thus four columns in the next state section. (If this were a Mealy system, there would also be four output columns.) This can easily be converted into a 16-row truth table or directly to maps. The latter is easiest if we are to implement this with either D or JK flip flops. In going to the maps, care must be taken since both the rows and columns are in binary order, not map order. The maps for D_A ($A^\star$) and D_B ($B^\star$) are shown below.

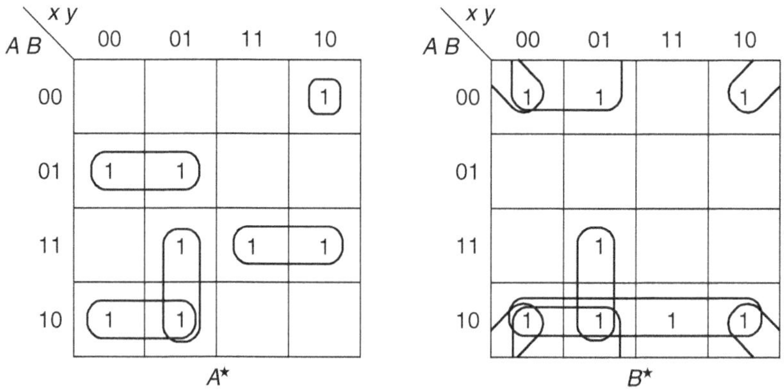

The functions are rather complex.

$$D_A = x'A'B + x'AB' + x'yA + xAB + xy'A'B'$$

$$D_B = x'yA + AB' + x'B' + y'B'$$
$$= x'yA + AB' + x'B' + xy'A'B'$$

Even if we were to implement this counter with *JK* flip flops, there is a great deal of combinational logic, as can be seen from the maps and equations below.

A*

AB \ xy	00	01	11	10
00				1
01	1	1		
11		1	1	1
10	1	1		

B*

AB \ xy	00	01	11	10
00	1	1		1
01				
11		1		
10	1	1	1	1

$J_A = x'B + xy'B'$ $\quad K_A = xB' + x'y'B$

$J_B = x' + y' + A$ $\quad K_B = x + y' + A'$

[SP 5, 6, 7; EX 5, 6, 7, 8, 9, 10, 11; LAB]

7.3 DESIGN OF ASYNCHRONOUS COUNTERS

Binary counters are sometimes designed without a clock input. They are constructed from the same clocked flip flops (typically *JK*) as synchronous counters, but each flip flop is triggered by the transition of the previous one. Consider the circuit of Figure 7.8 with two flip flops.

Figure 7.8 A 2-bit asynchronous counter.

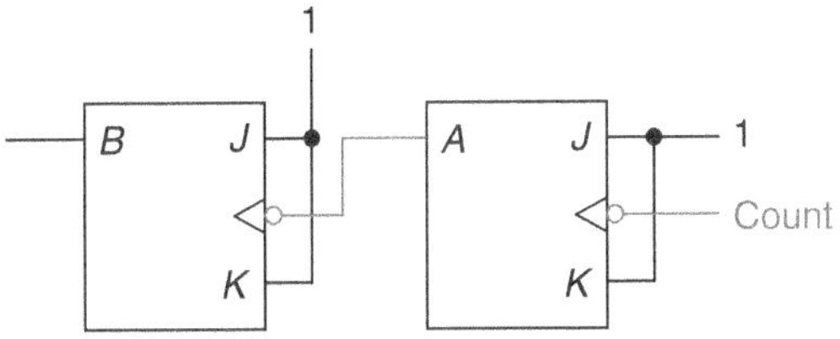

When the Count signal goes from 1 to 0, flip flop *A* is triggered. If it started out at 0, it goes to 1. The 0 to 1 transition on the output of *A*, and thus on the clock input of *B*, has no effect. When the next negative transition on Count occurs, *A* will go from 1 to 0 causing the clock input to *B* to do the same. Since *J* and *K* are 1, flip flop *B* will change states. Since there is a delay from the clock edge to the output change, flip flop *B* is clocked somewhat later than *A* and thus its output changes later. This is emphasized in the timing diagram of Figure 7.9. We assume in this diagram that flip flops *A* and *B* both start at 0.

Figure 7.9 Timing delay in an asynchronous counter.

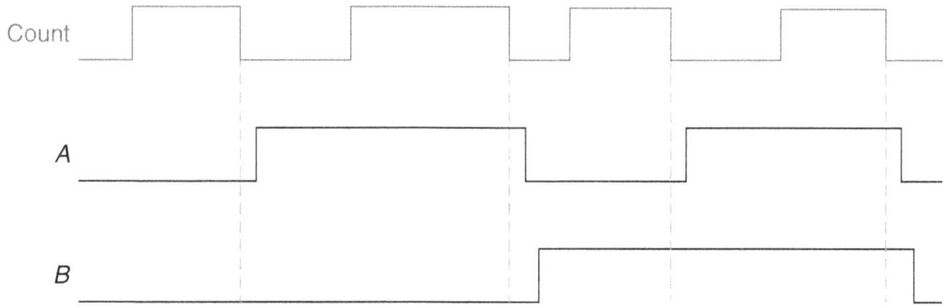

There are two things that are different about this timing diagram from the previous ones. Since the Count signal is not necessarily a clock, it might be rather irregular.* Second, the first flip flop (*A*) changes shortly after the negative edge of the Count (the dashed line), but the second flip flop (*B*) does not change until somewhat after *A* changes, and thus the delay from the clock is much greater. This becomes more significant as the changes ripple through several flip flops.

Note that the flip flops (*BA*) go through the sequence 00, 01, 10, 11, and repeat. Thus, this is a 2-bit counter. We can obtain a 4-bit counter by connecting four flip flops in the same fashion. A block diagram is shown in Figure 7.10.

Figure 7.10 A 4-bit asynchronous counter.

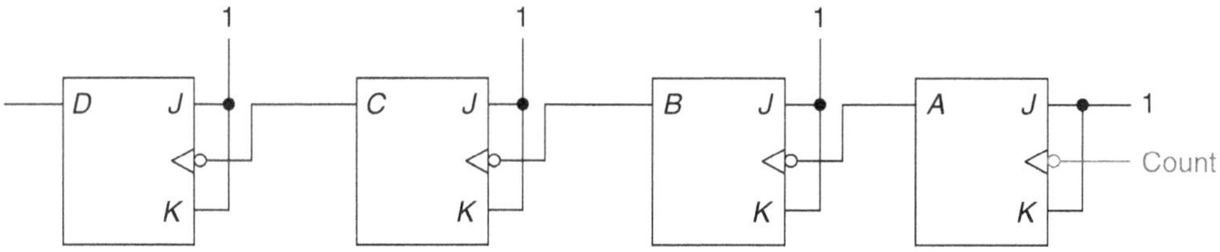

The timing is shown in Figure 7.11, where there is one unit of delay through each flip flop and the clock period is 10 units.

Figure 7.11 Timing for the 4-bit counter.

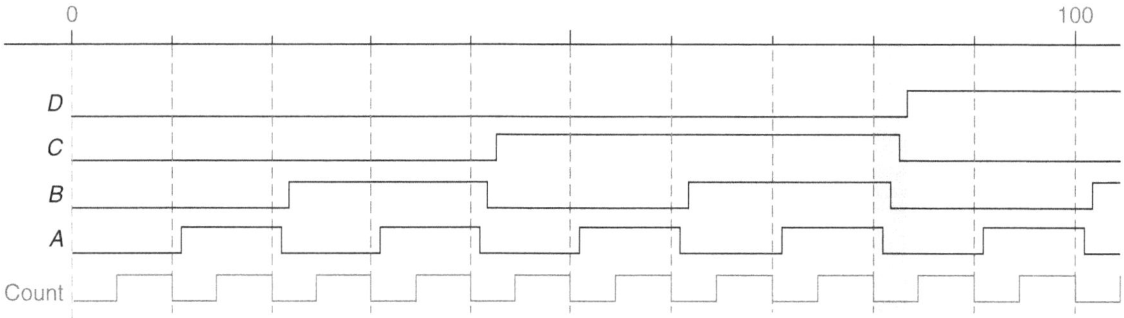

*The Clock input for synchronous counters is really a Count input also. Although the clock is usually regular, it need not be. The counter will change states on each negative transition.

Notice that A changes one unit of time after the trailing edge of the clock, B one unit after a trailing edge of A, C after B, and D after C. Thus, the change in D occurs 4 units after the clock (almost at the next leading edge in this example).

Notice also that this counter does go through the sequence 0 1 2 3 4 5 6 7 8 9 10 (as far as the timing diagram goes) and would continue through 11 12 13 14 15 0 . . . .

The advantage of the asynchronous counter is the simplicity of the hardware. There is no combinational logic required. The disadvantage is speed. The state of the system is not established until all of the flip flops have completed their transition, which, in this case, is four flip flop delays. If the counter were larger or the clock faster, it might not reach its final state until after the next negative clock transition. In that case, its value would not be available for other parts of the system at the next clock. Also, care must be taken when using outputs from this counter since it goes through unintended states. For example, a close inspection of the timing diagram as the counter moves from state 7 to state 8, the shaded area in Figure 7.11, shows that it is in state 6, state 4, and then state 0 before flip flop D goes to 1 and it reaches state 8. These short periods are not important if the outputs are used to light a display or as the inputs to a clocked flip flop, but they could produce spikes that would trigger a flip flop if used as a clock or Count input.

EXAMPLE 7.9

Design an asynchronous base-12 counter using *JK* flip flops with active low clears and NAND gates.

The easiest way to do this is to take the 4-bit binary counter and reset it when it reaches 12. Thus, the circuit below computes (*DC*)′ and uses that to reset the counter.

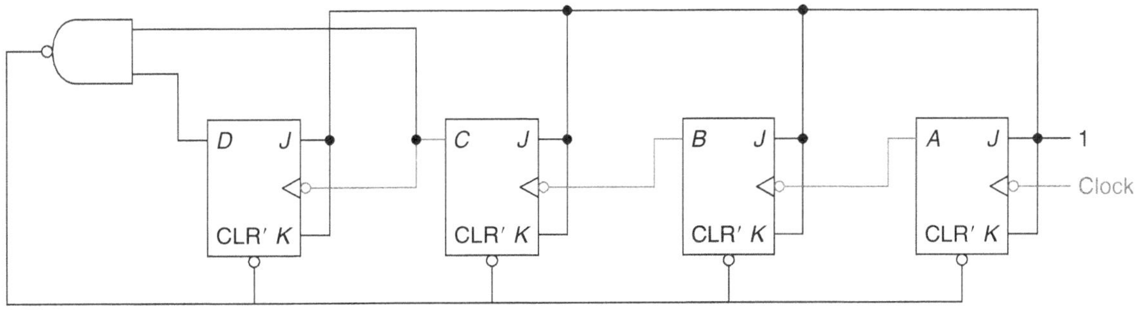

As can be seen from the timing diagram below, the counter cycles

0 1 2 3 4 5 6 7 8 9 10 11 (12) 0

where it remains in state 12 for a short time. Note that there is a delay from the time that *A* changes to when *B* changes and so forth. The count is only valid after the last flip flop settles down.

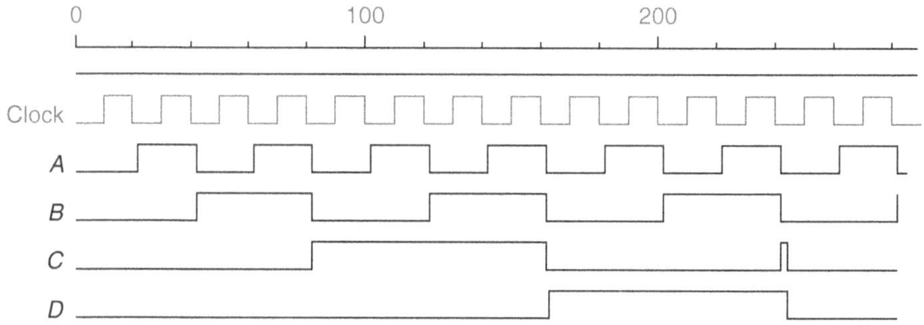

[SP 8; EX 12; LAB]

7.4 DERIVATION OF STATE TABLES AND STATE DIAGRAMS

In this section, we will start with verbal descriptions of sequential systems and develop state diagrams or tables. In some cases, we will carry the design further; but that is just a review of the material of earlier sections.

We will first look at Continuing Examples 6 and 7. Although the statement of CE6 does not include the term Moore, the wording of the problem implies a Moore system. That of CE7 is a Mealy model. We repeat CE6 here.

CE6. A system with one input x and one output z such that $z = 1$ iff x has been 1 for at least three consecutive clock times.

The timing trace of Trace 6.1 is repeated as Trace 7.1.

Trace 7.1 Three consecutive 1's.

x	0	1	1	0	1	1	1	0	0	1	0	1	1	1	1	1	0	0			
z	?	0	0	0	0	0	0	1	0	0	0	0	0	0	1	1	1	0	0	0	0

The first step in this problem (as it is in many word problems) is to determine what needs to be stored in memory. In this case, the question is: What do we need to know about previous inputs to determine whether the output should be 1 or not, and to update memory?

There are two approaches to step 1 for this problem. First, we could store the last three inputs. Knowing them, we could determine the output. For memory, we would just discard the oldest input stored and save the last two plus the present one. The inputs are already coded in binary (step 2). If we store the oldest input in q_1, the next oldest in q_2, and the most recent one in q_3, we get the state table of Table 7.10.

The new value of q_3, $q_3^\star = x$; it will hold the most recent input. Similarly, $q_2^\star = q_3$ and $q_1^\star = q_2$. The output is only 1 when the system is in state 111.

For the second approach, we store in memory the number of consecutive 1's, as follows:*

- *A* none, that is, the last input was 0
- *B* one
- *C* two
- *D* three or more

That, too, is sufficient information, since the output is 1 if and only if there have been three or more.

The state diagram and the state table are the same as those in Figure 7.1 and are repeated here as Figure 7.12.

Table 7.10 Three flip flop state table.

$q_1\ q_2\ q_3$	$q_1^\star q_2^\star q_3^\star$ $x = 0$	$x = 1$	z
0 0 0	0 0 0	0 0 1	0
0 0 1	0 1 0	0 1 1	0
0 1 0	1 0 0	1 0 1	0
0 1 1	1 1 0	1 1 1	0
1 0 0	0 0 0	0 0 1	0
1 0 1	0 1 0	0 1 1	0
1 1 0	1 0 0	1 0 1	0
1 1 1	1 1 0	1 1 1	1

Figure 7.12 State diagram and state table.

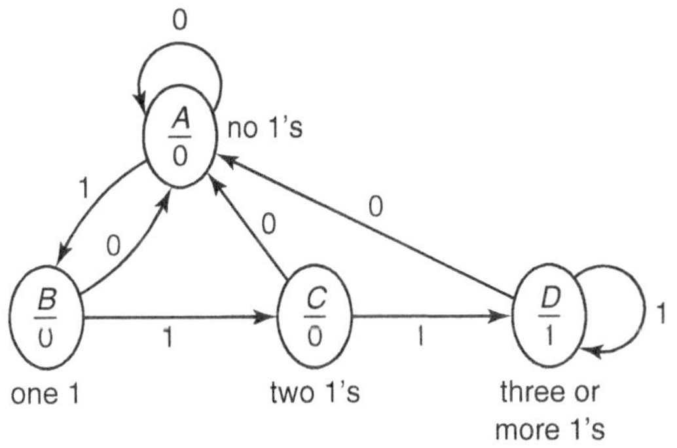

q	$q^\star$ $x = 0$	$x = 1$	z
A	*A*	*B*	0
B	*A*	*C*	0
C	*A*	*D*	0
D	*A*	*D*	1

This approach required only four states, whereas the first approach required eight. The first approach uses three flip flops, whereas the second uses only two. This is not much of a difference. Consider, however, what happens if the problem required a 1 output iff the input has been 1 for 25 or more consecutive clock times. For the first approach, we would need to save the last 25 inputs, using 25 flip flops. The state table would have 2^{25} rows. The second approach requires 26 states (no 1's through 25 or more 1's). They could be coded with just five flip flops.

The next step in the process is to reduce the state table, if possible, to one with fewer states. Although we will not be prepared to consider this step until Chapter 9, it is clear that Table 7.10 has some redundant states. For example, both states 000 and 100 go to state 000 if the input is 0; they go to state 001 if the input is 1; both have the same output.

*We will just name the memory contents, that is, the state with letters *A*, *B*, *C*, . . . and deal with coding these into binary later.

Thus, only one of them is needed. Indeed, this table can be reduced to one with only four states. The state table obtained using the second approach cannot be reduced.

Even if we do not reduce the table, we can proceed to choose a state assignment (whether we take advantage of the techniques in Chapter 9 to choose a "good" assignment or just pick any convenient one) and then complete the design. The system might be more expensive than one we would have obtained, but it will still work correctly.

For the first design, the state assignment has already been made. We labeled the flip flops q_1, q_2, and q_3. The flip flop inputs require no logic for *D* flip flops.

$$D_1 = q_2 \qquad D_2 = q_3 \qquad D_3 = x$$

For *JK* flip flops,

$$J_1 = q_2 \qquad J_2 = q_3 \qquad J_3 = x$$
$$K_1 = q_2' \qquad K_2 = q_3' \qquad K_3 = x'$$

A NOT gate is needed for x' if we use *JK* flip flops. For either type of flip flop, one AND gate is needed for z:

$$z = q_1 q_2 q_3$$

For the second approach, we have already constructed the design truth table for one state assignment in Table 7.2 and found that

$$D_1 = q_1^\star = xq_2 + xq_1 \quad \text{or} \quad J_1 = xq_2 \qquad K_1 = x$$
$$D_2 = q_2^\star = xq_2' + xq_1 \quad \text{or} \quad J_2 = x \qquad K_2 = x' + q_1$$
$$z = q_1 q_2$$

The corresponding Mealy example is CE7.

CE7. A system with one input x and one output z such that $z = 1$ at a clock time iff x is currently 1 and was also 1 at the previous two clock times.

Another way of wording this same problem is

CE7#. A Mealy system with one input x and one output z such that $z = 1$ iff x has been 1 for three consecutive clock times.

The timing trace corresponding to this problem is shown in Trace 7.2.

Trace 7.2 Timing trace for CE7.

x	0	1	1	0	1	1	1	0	0	1	0	1	1	1	1	1	0	0		
z	0	0	0	0	0	0	1	0	0	0	0	0	0	1	1	1	0	0	0	0

There are two approaches for this problem, as well. We need only store the last two inputs (rather than three for the Moore model). This produces the state table of Table 7.11.

Table 7.11 State table for saving last two inputs.

	$q_1^\star\ q_2^\star$		z	
$q_1\ q_2$	$x = 0$	$x = 1$	$x = 0$	$x = 1$
0 0	0 0	0 1	0	0
0 1	1 0	1 1	0	0
1 0	0 0	0 1	0	0
1 1	1 0	1 1	0	1

For the second approach, we store in memory the number of consecutive 1's, as follows:

A none, that is, the last input was 0

B one

C two or more

That, too, is sufficient information since the output is 1 if and only if there were previously two or more 1's and the present input is a 1. If the present input is a 0, the next state is *A*; otherwise, we move from *A* to *B* and from *B* to *C*. The state diagram is shown in Figure 7.13.

Figure 7.13 State diagram for three consecutive 1's.

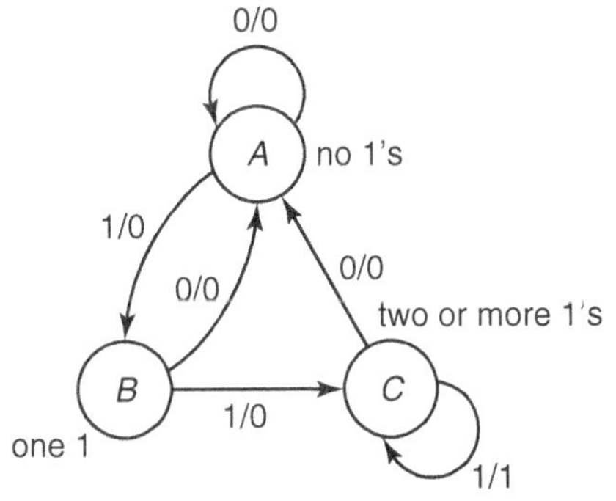

The description can also be written as a state table, as shown in Table 7.12.

Table 7.12 State table for three consecutive 1's.

	$q^\star$		z	
q	$x = 0$	$x = 1$	$x = 0$	$x = 1$
A	*A*	*B*	0	0
B	*A*	*C*	0	0
C	*A*	*C*	0	1

To compare the behavior of the Mealy and Moore models, we will look at the timing diagram for each (using the four-state Moore model and the three-state Mealy model).

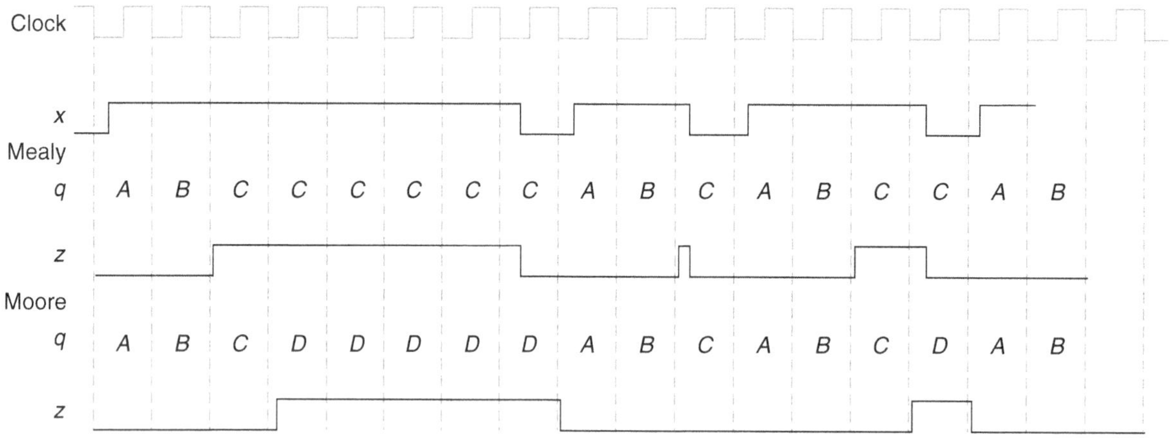

Basically, the Moore model output is the same as the Mealy, but delayed by one clock period. It does not have any false outputs, since z depends only on the flip flops, all of which change at the same time.

EXAMPLE 7.10

Design both a Moore and a Mealy system with one input x and one output z such that $z = 1$ iff x has been 1 for *exactly* three consecutive clock times.

A sample input/output trace for such a system is

x	0	1	1	1	1	1	1	1	0	1	1	0	1	1	1	0	1		
z-Mealy	0	0	0	0	0	0	0	0	0	0	0	0	0	0	0	1	0	0	0*
z-Moore	0	0	0	0	0	0	0	0	0	0	0	0	0	0	0	0	1	0	0	0
				↑											↑				

We cannot tell whether there should be a 1 output when the third consecutive 1 input occurs. The past history and the present input are the same at the two places indicated with arrows. It is not until the next input arrives that we know that there have been exactly three 1's in a row. For the Mealy model we now need five states,

A none, that is, the last input was 0

B one 1 in a row

C two 1's in a row

D three 1's in a row

E too many (more than 3) 1's in a row

*Notice that, in this example, we can determine the output for two or three clocks after the input is no longer known, since even if both inputs were 1, the output would remain 0 at least until the clock time after the one shown.

The state diagram begins like that of the previous solution. However, when we get a third 1 input, we go to state *D*. From *D*, a 0 input produces a 1 output; a 1 input gets us to a new state, *E*. Sometimes, we think of state *A* as nowhere, that is, we are looking for the first 1 to get started on the successful path to a 1 output. In that case, state *E* is worse than nowhere, since we must first get a 0 before we can even begin to look for three 1's. The complete state diagram is shown next.

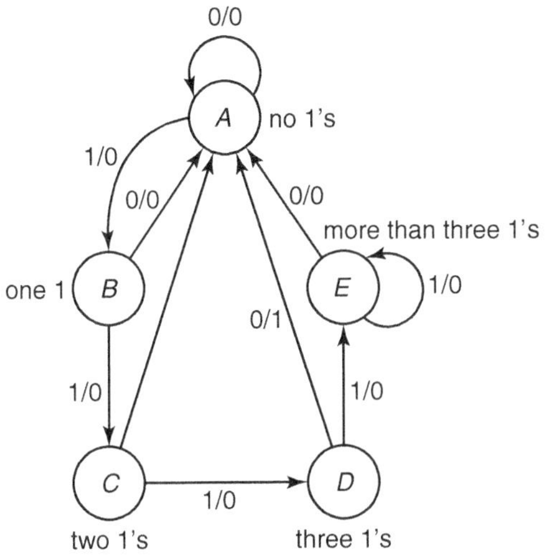

The implementation of this system requires three flip flops. The design is left as an exercise.

For the Moore model, we need a state *D* to indicate exactly three 1's. From there, it goes to *E* on another 1, indicating too many 1's. State *F* is reached on a 0 input; it is the state with a 1 output. The state table is shown below. (We could have constructed a state diagram for this version or a state table for the Mealy model.)

q	$q^\star$ $x = 0$	$x = 1$	z
A	A	B	0
B	A	C	0
C	A	D	0
D	F	E	0
E	A	E	0
F	A	B	1

EXAMPLE 7.11

Design a Mealy system whose output is 1 iff the input has been 1 for three consecutive clocks, but inputs are nonoverlapping. (That means that a 1 input can only be used toward one 1 output.)

A sample input/output trace for such a system is

x	0 1 1 1 1 1 1 1 0 1 1 0 1 1 1 0 1
z	0 0 0 1 0 0 1 0 0 0 0 0 0 0 1 0 0 0

As in CE7, only three states are needed. From state *C*, the system returns to state *A* whether the input is 0 or 1; the output is 1 if the input is 1 (third in a row) and 0 if the input is 0.

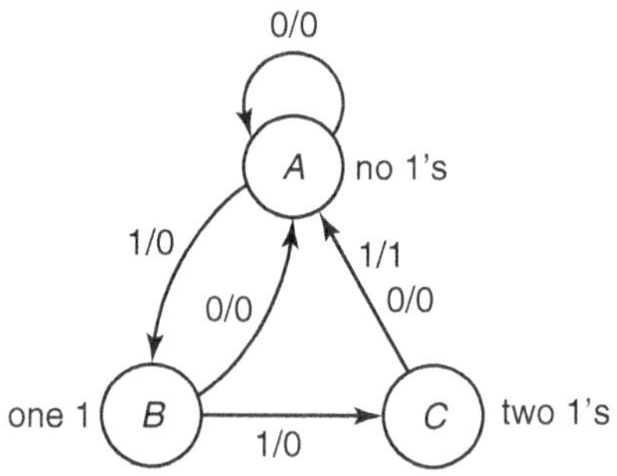

When the third 1 input occurs, we are, once again, nowhere; we need three more 1's to get a 1 output.

In each of the systems that we have considered so far, we have not worried about initializing the system. They all produce the correct output, once the first 0 input is received. If we are willing to ignore the output prior to that, we do not need to be concerned with initialization. If we need to know the output from the first input, then we must initialize the system to state *A* (or 000 in the first example). The next two examples do depend upon initializing the system to state *A*, that is, we need to know where the starting point is.

EXAMPLE 7.12

Design a Mealy system where the inputs are considered in blocks of three. The output is 1 iff the input is 1 for all three inputs in a block; obviously, that 1 output cannot occur until the third input is received.

A sample input/output trace for such a system is

x	0 1 1	1 1 1	1 0 1	1 1 0	1 1 1	0 1
z	0 0 0	0 0 1	0 0 0	0 0 0	0 0 1	0 0 0

where the blocks are indicated by extra space.

The initial state, *A*, is reached when the system is first turned on and before each new block (as the next state when the third input in a block is received). After receiving the first input in a block, the system goes to *B* if the input is 1 and *C* if it is 0; in either case, the output is 0. We could now have four states after the second input, *D* and *E* from *B* (on a 1 and a 0, respectively) and *F* and *G* from *C* (on a 1 and a 0, respectively).

A state table for this version, with seven states, is shown below.

q	$q^\star$		z	
	$x = 0$	$x = 1$	$x = 0$	$x = 1$
A	C	B	0	0
B	E	D	0	0
C	G	F	0	0
D	A	A	0	1
E	A	A	0	0
F	A	A	0	0
G	A	A	0	0

But that creates two extra states. We only need *D* for the case where the first two inputs have been 1, and *E* for all of the other cases, as shown in the state diagram below.

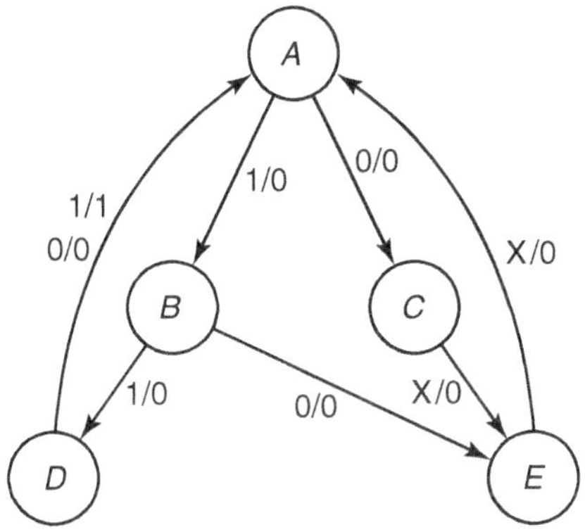

Note that the paths out of *C* and of *E* are denoted as X/0, meaning that we don't care what the input is; that path is followed, and the output is 0.

Notice that the next state and output sections of the last three rows of the state table are identical. That indicates that it does not matter whether the system is in state *E*, *F*, or *G*; it behaves the same in all three cases. As we will see in Chapter 9, we will be able to reduce the state table by combining these three rows into one. (Indeed, that is what the state diagram solution did.)

EXAMPLE 7.13

Design a Mealy system whose output is 1 for every third 1 input (not necessarily consecutive).

The initial state, *A*, is used for no 1's or a multiple of three 1's. When a 0 is received, the system stays where it is, rather than returning to the initial state, since a 0 does not interrupt the count of three 1's. A sample input/output trace for such a system is

x	0	1	1	1	1	1	1	1	0	1	1	0	1	0	1	0	0	1	0	1
z	0	0	0	1	0	0	1	0	0	0	1	0	0	0	0	0	0	1	0	0	0

The state diagram is thus

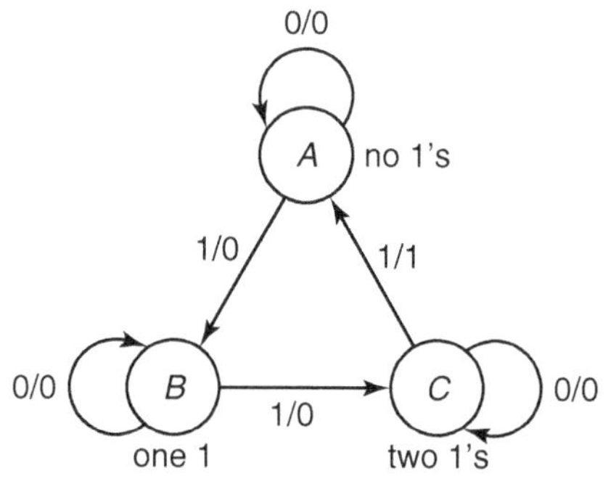

EXAMPLE 7.14

CE8. Design a Moore system whose output is 1 iff three consecutive 0 inputs occurred more recently than three consecutive 1 inputs.* A sample input/output trace for such a system is

x 1 1 1 0 0 1 0 1 1 1 0 0 1 0 0 0 0 1 1 1 1 0 1
z ? ? ? 0 0 0 0 0 0 0 0 0 0 0 0 0 1 1 1 1 0 0 0 0 0

We showed the first three outputs as unknown, assuming that we started looking at some time when the system was running or that we turned it on and did not know what state it came up in. The wording implies that when first turned on, the system should have a 0 output, since there have not recently been three consecutive 1's. (This is the same example that we did at the end of Section 7.1.)

We will call the initial state S_1. The first path to develop is to get the output to change from 0 to 1. That part of the state diagram is shown below.

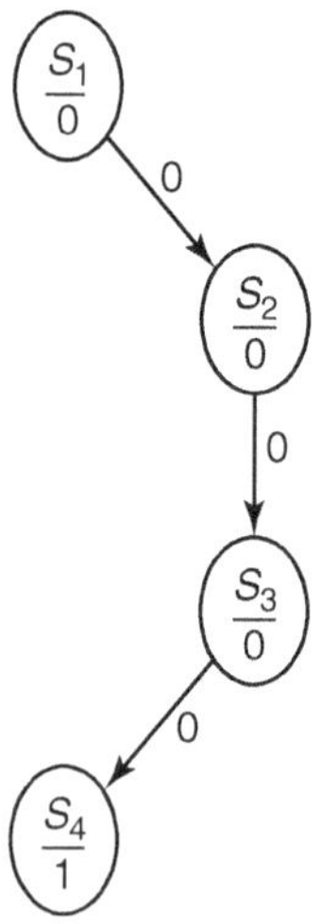

*We are assuming that three means three or more, not exactly three.

We had reached S_1 whenever the input was a 1 and the output was to be 0. To get the output to change to 1, we need three consecutive 0's, leading us to S_4. From there, three 1's will lead us back to S_1 as shown below on the left. On the right, we complete the state diagram, by showing that we return to S_1 when we are looking for 0's and get a 1 input and return to S_4 when we are looking for 1's and get a 0 input.

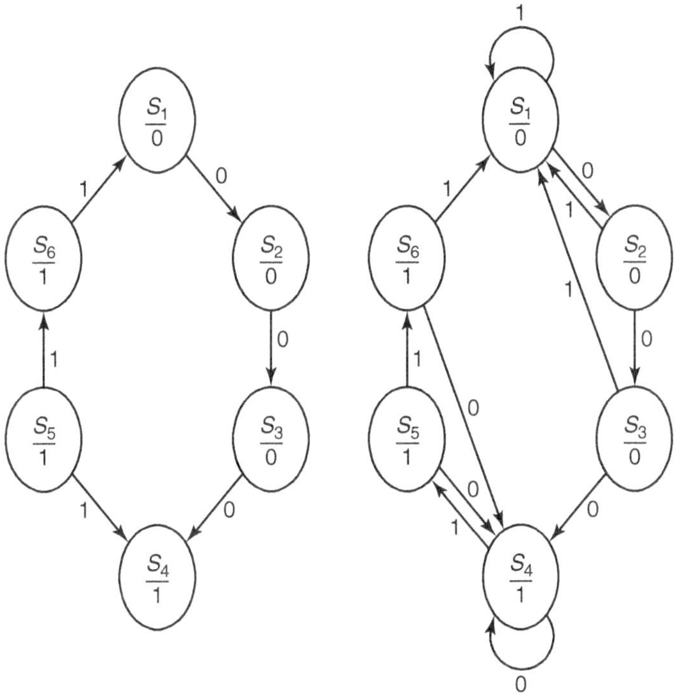

EXAMPLE 7.15

Design a Mealy system whose output is 1 iff there have been exactly two 1's followed by a 0 and then a 1.

a. Assume overlapping is allowed.
b. Assume overlapping is not allowed.

The following timing trace depicts the expected behavior for the overlapped case:

a.

x	0 0 1 1 0 1 1 0 1 1 0 1 1 1 0 1 1 0 1 1 0 1
z	0 0 0 0 0 1 0 0 1 0 0 1 0 0 0 0 0 0 1 0 0 1 0 0

The underlines indicate the 1101 pattern that is being searched for; the double underline is not an acceptable pattern since it does not begin with exactly two 1's. The behavior in the overlapping case is quite clear. When the final 1 input that produces a 1 output occurs, that 1 also counts as the first of two consecutive 1 inputs for the next 1 output. The two brown underlines indicate overlapping patterns.

It is often easiest to begin the state diagram by following a success path, that is, one leading to the desired output, as shown below.

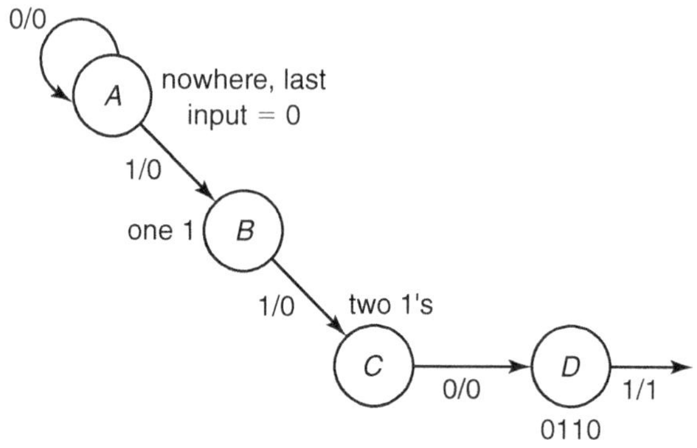

State *A* is the nowhere state, where we are looking for the first 1. On successive 1's, we move to *B* and *C*; a 0 takes us to *D* and then a 1 produces the 1 output. Since overlapping is allowed, that 1 is the first 1 toward a new sequence, and we return to state *B* from *D*. We must also complete the failed paths. A 0 in any state other than *C* (where we are looking for a 0) returns us to state *A*. If, after getting two consecutive 1's, we get a third, we need another state, *E*, which indicates that we have too many 1's and are waiting for a 0 before we can go back to state *A* and start again. The complete state diagram for the overlapped solution is thus shown below.

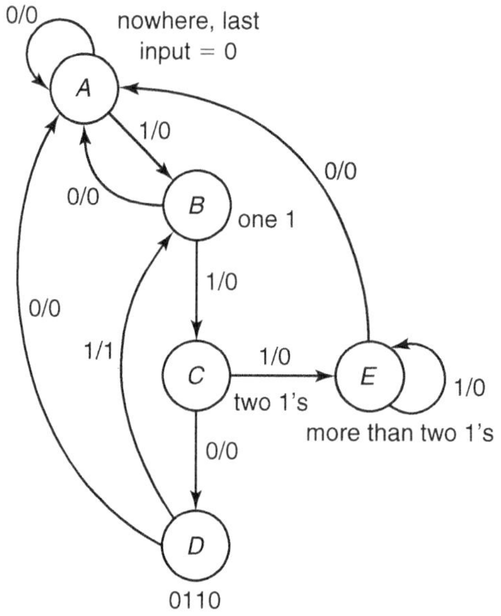

There are two interpretations to consider in the nonoverlapping case. The first is shown as *b-1*. In that case, when a 1 output occurs, there must be a 0 input before we can have exactly two 1's. Thus, after the first 1 output, we do not get started toward another 1 output until after a 0 input.

x	0 0 1 1 0 1 1 0 1 1 0 1 1 1 0 1 1 0 1 1 0 1
b-1	0 0 0 0 0 1 0 0 0 0 0 1 0 0 0 0 0 0 1 0 0 0 0 0

A second interpretation (perhaps a little far-fetched) is that once we have completed a pattern, we need exactly two more 1's followed by a 10; that is what accepts the double-underlined sequence.

x	0 0 1 1 0 1 1 0 1 1 0 1 1 1 0 1 1 0 1 1 0 1
b-2	0 0 0 0 0 1 0 0 0 0 0 1 0 0 0 1 0 0 0 0 0 1 0 0 0

The two solutions for the nonoverlapping versions are shown next. They begin exactly like the overlapping version but behave differently when we get the input that produces a 1 output.

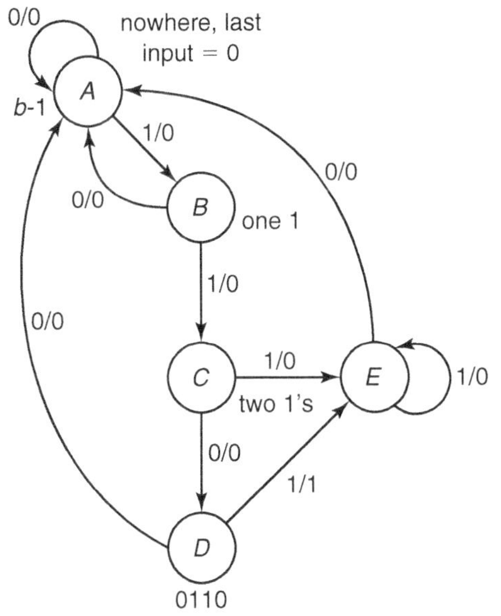

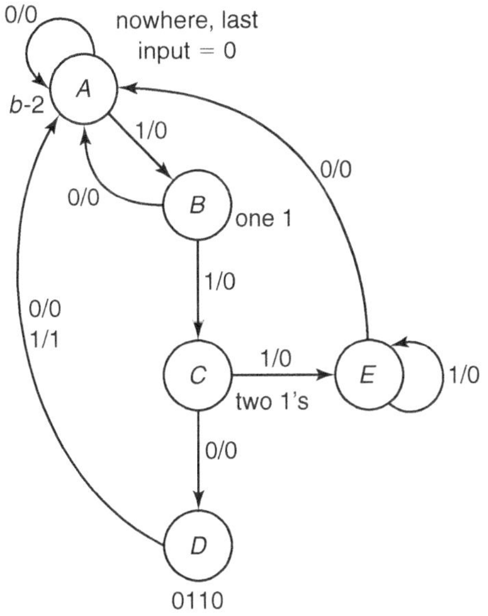

EXAMPLE 7.16

Finally, we will look at the design of the bus controller CE11.

CE11. Design a Moore model bus controller that receives requests on separate lines, R_0 to R_3, from four devices desiring to use the bus. It has four outputs, G_0 to G_3, only one of which is 1, indicating which device is granted control of the bus for that clock period. The low number device has the highest priority, if more than one device requests the bus at the same time. We look at both interrupting controllers (where a high priority device can preempt the bus) and one where a device keeps control of the bus once it gets it until it no longer needs it.

The bus controller has five states:

A: idle, no device is using the bus
B: device 0 is using the bus
C: device 1 is using the bus
D: device 2 is using the bus
E: device 3 is using the bus

We will first consider the case where once device *j* gets control of the bus ($G_j = 1$), it retains that control until it is no longer requesting it (until $R_j = 0$). Further, we will assume that it must return to the idle state for one clock period between allocations. This results in the following state diagram.

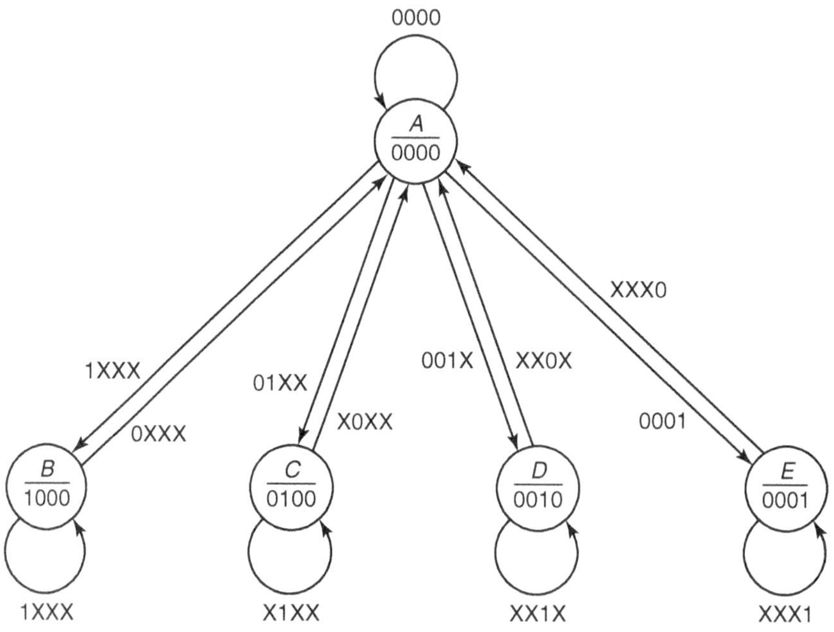

The system remains in the idle state if there are no requests. It goes to the highest priority state when there are one or more requests. Thus, it goes to state *B* if $R_0 = 1$, no matter what the other *R*'s are. Once it has granted the bus, it remains in that state if that device is still requesting the bus and returns to the idle state otherwise. If there is another request pending, it is idle for one clock period before granting the next highest priority request.

If the idle period is not necessary, the state diagram becomes much more complex. When any device no longer needs the bus, the controller will return to state *A* if no other device is requesting it; but it proceeds directly to granting the highest priority request. A state table for such a system is shown below.

q	$q^\star$																$G_0\ G_1\ G_2\ G_3$
R_0	0	0	0	0	0	0	0	0	1	1	1	1	1	1	1	1	
R_1	0	0	0	0	1	1	1	1	0	0	0	0	1	1	1	1	
R_2	0	0	1	1	0	0	1	1	0	0	1	1	0	0	1	1	
R_3	0	1	0	1	0	1	0	1	0	1	0	1	0	1	0	1	
A	*A*	*E*	*D*	*D*	*C*	*C*	*C*	*C*	*B*	*B*	*B*	*B*	*B*	*B*	*B*	*B*	0 0 0 0
B	*A*	*E*	*D*	*D*	*C*	*C*	*C*	*C*	*B*	*B*	*B*	*B*	*B*	*B*	*B*	*B*	1 0 0 0
C	*A*	*E*	*D*	*D*	*C*	*C*	*C*	*C*	*B*	*B*	*B*	*B*	*C*	*C*	*C*	*C*	0 1 0 0
D	*A*	*E*	*D*	*D*	*C*	*C*	*D*	*D*	*B*	*B*	*D*	*D*	*B*	*B*	*D*	*D*	0 0 1 0
E	*A*	*E*	*D*	*E*	*C*	*E*	*C*	*E*	*B*	*E*	*B*	*E*	*B*	*E*	*B*	*E*	0 0 0 1

Note that in this version, we can go from any state to any other state. There would be 20 paths on the state diagram. The partial diagram below shows just the paths to and from state *C*.

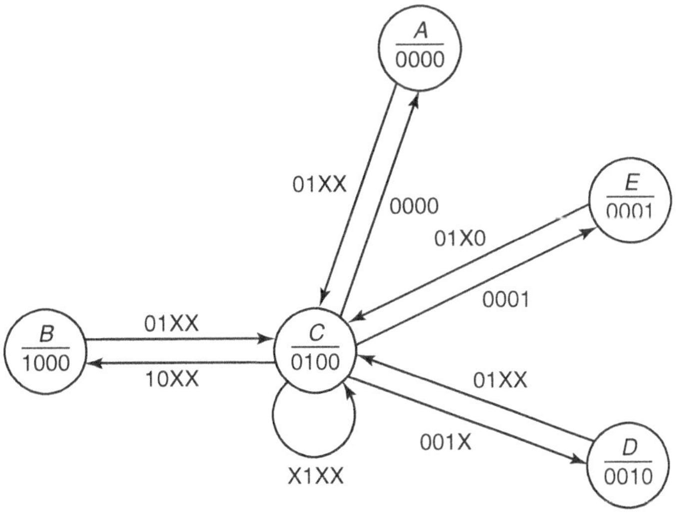

Finally, we will look at a preemptive controller, where a high priority device will take control from a lower priority one, even if the lower priority one is still using the bus. For this case (whether we must return to state 0 or not), we remain in states *C*, *D*, and *E* only if that device is requesting the bus and no higher priority device is simultaneously requesting it. The state diagram for the system that must return to idle for one clock period is shown first and then the state table for the system that can go directly to the next state having use of the bus.

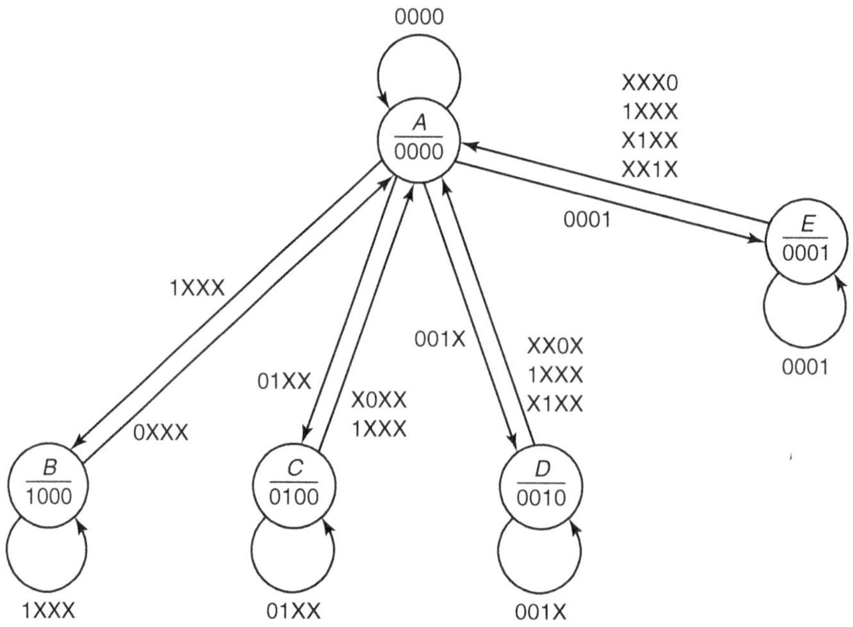

q	$q^\star$																$G_0\ G_1\ G_2\ G_3$
R_0	0	0	0	0	0	0	0	0	1	1	1	1	1	1	1	1	
R_1	0	0	0	0	1	1	1	1	0	0	0	0	1	1	1	1	
R_2	0	0	1	1	0	0	1	1	0	0	1	1	0	0	1	1	
R_3	0	1	0	1	0	1	0	1	0	1	0	1	0	1	0	1	
A	A	E	D	D	C	C	C	C	B	B	B	B	B	B	B	B	0 0 0 0
B	A	E	D	D	C	C	C	C	B	B	B	B	B	B	B	B	1 0 0 0
C	A	E	D	D	C	C	C	C	B	B	B	B	B	B	B	B	0 1 0 0
D	A	E	D	D	C	C	C	C	B	B	B	B	B	B	B	B	0 0 1 0
E	A	E	D	D	C	C	C	C	B	B	B	B	B	B	B	B	0 0 0 1

Although the state diagram for this version would require the same 20 paths as was needed for the second version, the logic is much simpler. The condition for going to state *B*, from each state is 1XXX (R_1), to *C* is 01XX ($R_1'R_2$), to *D* is 001X ($R_1'R_2'R_3$), and to *E* is 0001 ($R_1'R_2'R_3'R_4$) (the same as the condition from state *A* in all of the versions).

7.5 SOLVED PROBLEMS

1. For the following state table and state assignment, show equations for the next state and the output.

	$q^\star$		z	
q	$x = 0$	$x = 1$	$x = 0$	$x = 1$
A	C	A	1	0
B	B	A	0	1
C	B	C	1	0

q	q_1	q_2
A	0	1
B	1	1
C	0	0

We will first construct a truth table and map the functions.

q	x	q_1	q_2	z	$q_1^\star$	$q_2^\star$
C	0	0	0	1	1	1
A	0	0	1	1	0	0
—	0	1	0	X	X	X
B	0	1	1	0	1	1
C	1	0	0	0	0	0
A	1	0	1	0	0	1
—	1	1	0	X	X	X
B	1	1	1	1	0	1

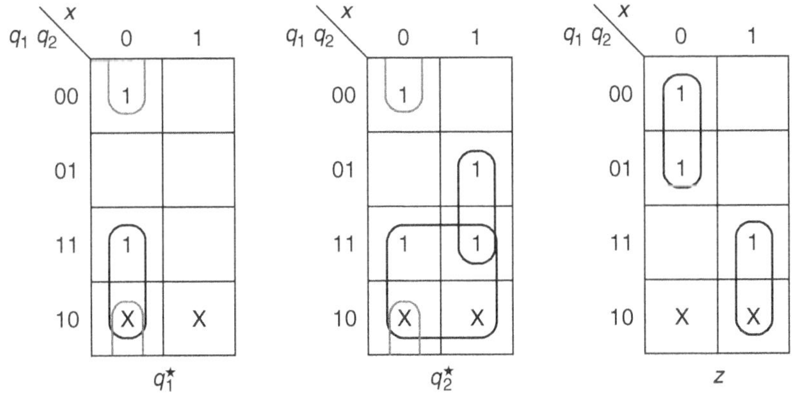

$$q_1^\star = x'q_2' + x'q_1$$

$$q_2^\star = q_1 + x'q_2' + xq_2$$

$$z = x'q_1' + xq_1$$

2. For each of the following state tables, design the system using

i. *D* flip flops

ii. *SR* flip flops

iii. *T* flip flops
iv. *JK* flip flops
Show the equations for each and a block diagram for the *JK* design (using AND, OR, and NOT gates).

a.

	$A^\star B^\star$		z	
$A\,B$	$x = 0$	$x = 1$	$x = 0$	$x = 1$
0 0	0 1	0 0	1	0
0 1	1 1	0 0	1	1
1 1	1 1	0 1	0	1

b.

	$A^\star B^\star$		
$A\,B$	$x = 0$	$x = 1$	z
0 0	1 0	0 0	0
0 1	0 0	1 1	1
1 0	0 1	1 1	1
1 1	1 0	0 1	1

a. We can map $A^\star$, $B^\star$, and z directly from the state table, where the last row of the maps are don't cares, since state 10 is not used.

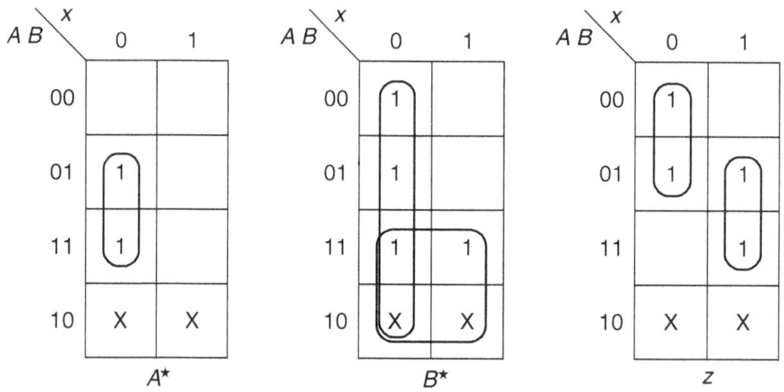

For all types of flip flops, z is the same, namely,

$$z = x'A' + xB$$

i. For the *D* flip flop,

$$D_A = A^\star = x'B \qquad D_B = B^\star = x' + A$$

ii. For the *SR* flip flop, we will use the truth table and the flip flop design table as follows:

x	A	B	$A^\star$	$B^\star$	S_A	R_A	S_B	R_B
0	0	0	0	1	0	X	1	0
0	0	1	1	1	1	0	X	0
0	1	0	X	X	X	X	X	X
0	1	1	1	1	X	0	X	0
1	0	0	0	0	0	X	0	X
1	0	1	0	0	0	X	0	1
1	1	0	X	X	X	X	X	X
1	1	1	0	1	0	1	X	0

The resulting maps are

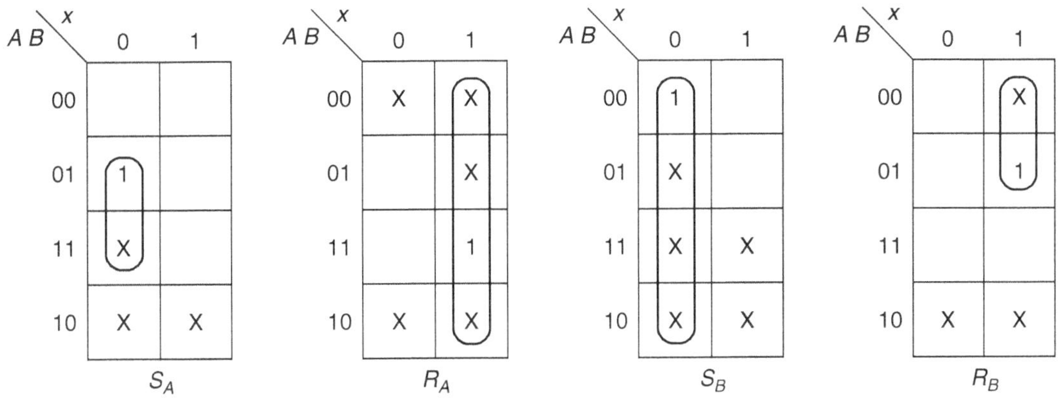

$$S_A = x'B \quad R_A = x \quad S_B = x' \quad R_B = xA'$$

We will develop the *T* maps directly from the next state maps. If the flip flop is to change, *T* is 1; otherwise, *T* is 0.

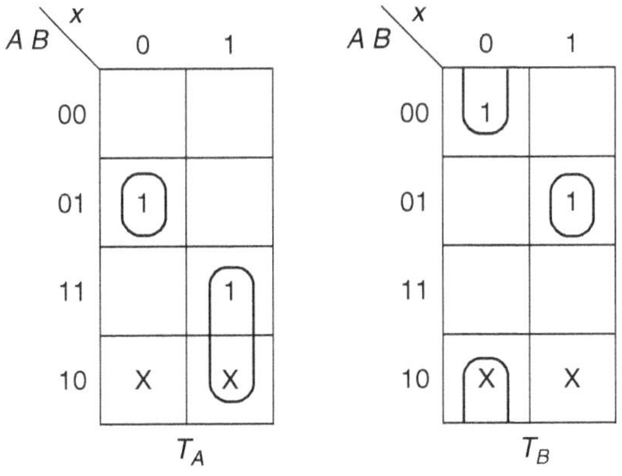

$T_A = x'\,A'\,B + x\,A$ $\qquad$ $T_B = x'\,B' + x\,A'\,B$

Finally, we will derive the *JK* inputs using the quick method. The maps below show the *J* section of the map shaded.

AB \ x	0	1
00		
01	1	
11	1	
10	X	X

$A^\star$

AB \ x	0	1
00	1	
01	1	
11	1	1
10	X	X

$B^\star$

$$J_A = x'B \quad K_A = x \quad J_B = x' \quad K_B = xA'$$

Note that these are the same equations as those for the *SR* flip flop and the same amount of logic as is required for the *D* flip flop. Only the *T* flip flop requires significantly more logic.

A block diagram of the system with *JK* flip flops follows.

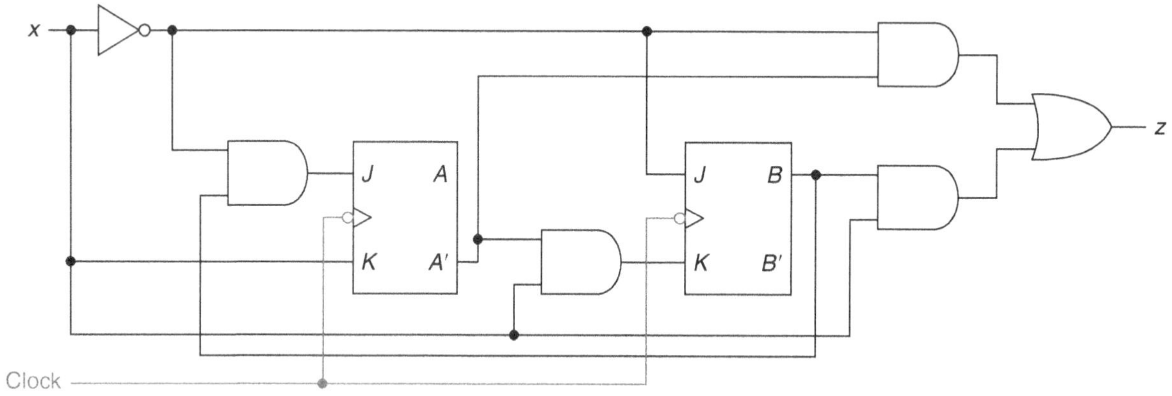

b. We can go to the truth table or we can first map $A^\star$ and $B^\star$ to find the *D* inputs. The output is only a two-variable problem. We do not need to map that to recognize that

$$z = A + B$$

The truth table is shown (with columns for all types of flip flops).

x	A	B	$A^\star$	$B^\star$	S_A	R_A	S_B	R_B	T_A	T_B	J_A	K_A	J_B	K_B
0	0	0	1	0	1	0	0	X	1	0	1	X	0	X
0	0	1	0	0	0	X	0	1	0	1	0	X	X	1
0	1	0	0	1	0	1	1	0	1	1	X	1	1	X
0	1	1	1	0	X	0	0	1	0	1	X	0	X	1
1	0	0	0	0	0	X	0	X	0	0	0	X	0	X
1	0	1	1	1	1	0	X	0	1	0	1	X	X	0
1	1	0	1	1	X	0	1	0	0	1	X	0	1	X
1	1	1	0	1	0	1	X	0	1	0	X	1	X	0

Maps for each of the functions are shown below (where D_A is just $A^\star$).

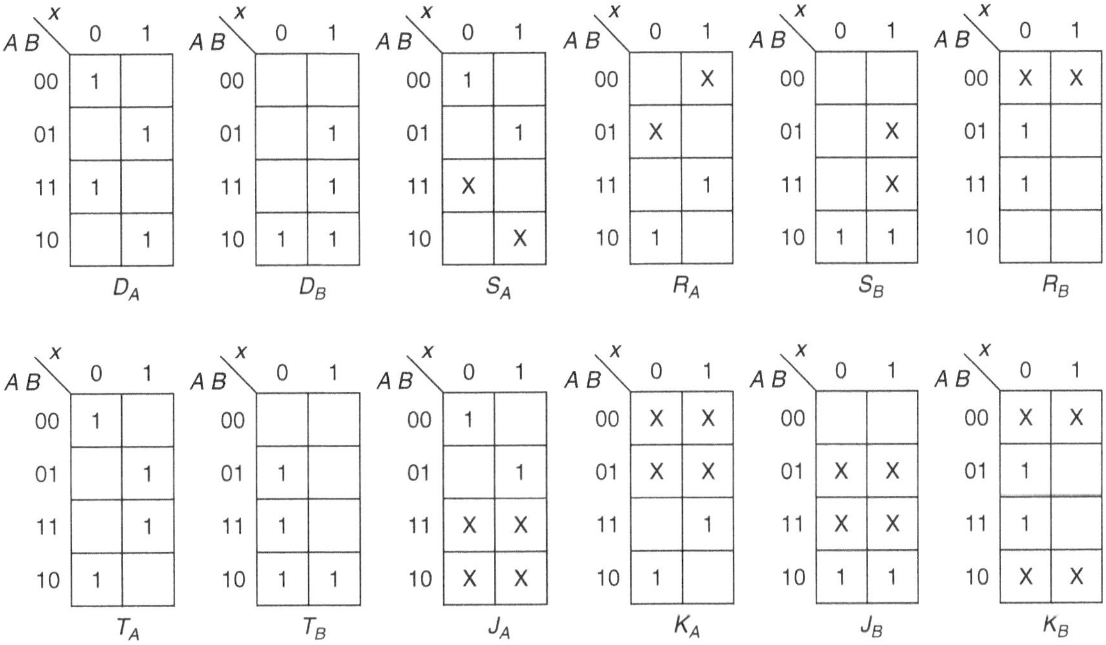

The corresponding equations are

$$z = A + B$$

$$D_A = x'A'B' + x'AB + xA'B + xAB'$$

$$D_B = xB + AB'$$

$$S_A = x'A'B' + xA'B \qquad R_A = x'AB' + xAB$$

$$S_B = AB' \qquad R_B = x'B$$

$$T_A = x'B' + xB \qquad T_B = x'B + AB'$$

$$J_A = K_A = x'B' + xB \qquad J_B = A \qquad K_B = x'$$

Note that the logic required to implement the *JK* flip flop solution is the least, followed by the *T* and the *SR*, with the *D* requiring the most. A block diagram of the *JK* solution is shown below. To make the drawing clearer, we put flip flop *B* on the left.

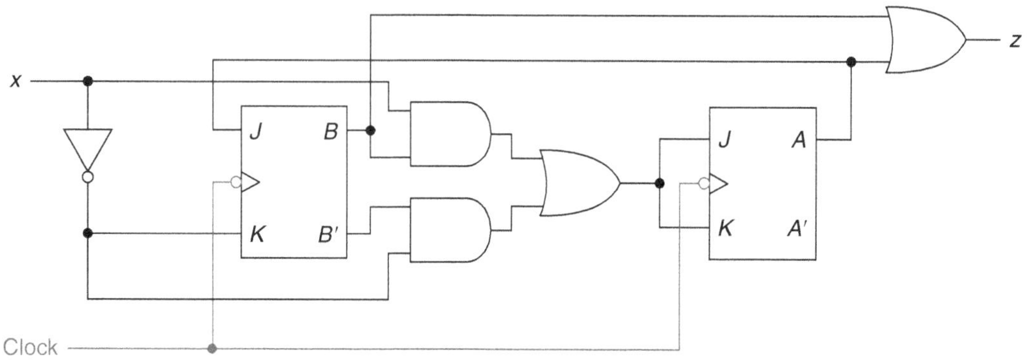

Comment: In either part of this problem, we could have specified that flip flop *A* was one type (say a *T*) and the other was a different type (say a *JK*). The solutions we have obtained are correct for each of the flip flops.

3. For each of the following state tables and state assignments, find the flip flop input equations and the system output equation for an implementation using

i. *D* flip flops

ii. *JK* flip flops

a.

	$q^\star$		z	
q	$x = 0$	$x = 1$	$x = 0$	$x = 1$
A	B	C	1	1
B	A	B	1	0
C	B	A	1	0

q	q_1	q_2
A	1	1
B	1	0
C	0	1

b.

	$q^\star$		z	
q	$x = 0$	$x = 1$	$x = 0$	$x = 1$
A	A	B	0	0
B	C	B	0	0
C	A	D	0	0
D	C	B	1	0

q	q_1	q_2
A	0	0
B	1	1
C	0	1
D	1	0

a. We will first produce the truth table.

q	x	q_1	q_2	z	$q_1^\star$	$q_2^\star$
—	0	0	0	X	X	X
C	0	0	1	1	1	0
B	0	1	0	1	1	1
A	0	1	1	1	1	0
—	1	0	0	X	X	X
C	1	0	1	0	1	1
B	1	1	0	0	1	0
A	1	1	1	1	0	1

i. We can now map z, D_1 ($q_1^\star$) and D_2 ($q_2^\star$)

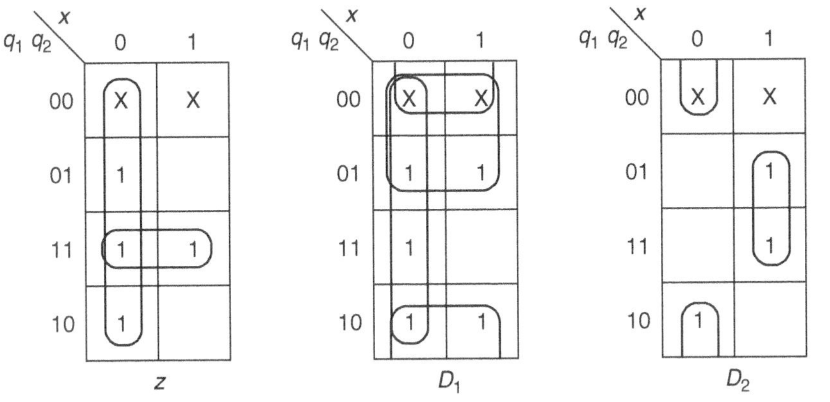

$z = x' + q_1 q_2$ $\quad$ $D_1 = x' + q_1' + q_2'$ $\quad$ $D_2 = x' q_2' + x q_2$

ii. Using the quick method, we look at the shaded part of the maps for J and the unshaded parts for K. (z is unchanged.)

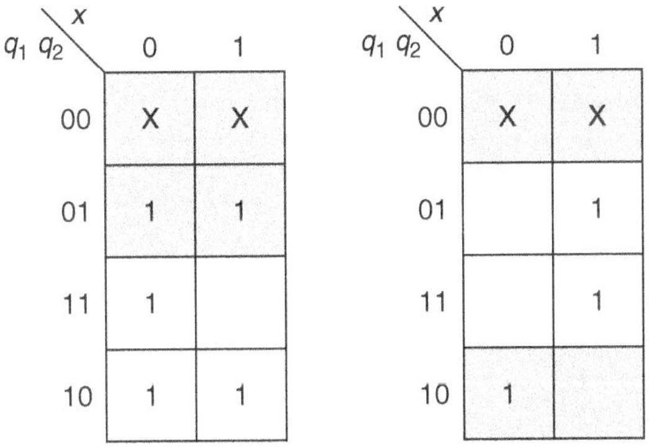

$J_1 = 1$ $\quad$ $K_1 = x q_2$ $\quad$ $J_2 = x'$ $\quad$ $K_2 = x'$

---

b. We will first produce the truth table.

q	x	q_1	q_2	z	$q_1^\star$	$q_2^\star$
A	0	0	0	0	0	0
C	0	0	1	0	0	0
D	0	1	0	1	0	1
B	0	1	1	0	0	1
A	1	0	0	0	1	1
C	1	0	1	0	1	0
D	1	1	0	0	1	1
B	1	1	1	0	1	1

We do not need to map z, since it is clear from the truth table that

$$z = x' q_1 q_2'$$

i. We can now map $D_1(q_1^\star)$ and $D_2(q_2^\star)$

$q_1 q_2$ \ x	0	1
00		1
01		1
11		1
10		1

D_1

$q_1 q_2$ \ x	0	1
00		1
01		
11	1	1
10	1	1

D_2

$D_1 = x$ $\qquad$ $D_2 = x\, q_2' + q_1$

ii. For *JK* flip flops, we get

$$J_1 = x \qquad K_1 = x' \qquad J_2 = x + q_1 \qquad K_2 = q_1'$$

4. For the state table and each of the state assignments shown, design a system using *D* flip flops.

q	$q^\star$ $x = 0$	$x = 1$	z $x = 0$	$x = 1$
A	B	C	1	0
B	D	A	0	0
C	B	C	1	1
D	D	A	1	0

a.

q	q_1	q_2
A	0	0
B	0	1
C	1	0
D	1	1

b.

q	q_1	q_2
A	0	0
B	0	1
C	1	1
D	1	0

c.

y	q_1	q_2
A	0	0
B	1	1
C	1	0
D	0	1

Each part of this is really a separate problem. (As we will see in Chapter 9, these are the only three assignments that produce significantly different hardware. Each of the other possible state assignments involve either interchanging variables or complementing variables or both.) Compare the amount of combinational logic for each state assignment.

a. Since the assignment is in normal binary order, it is easy to go directly to the maps.

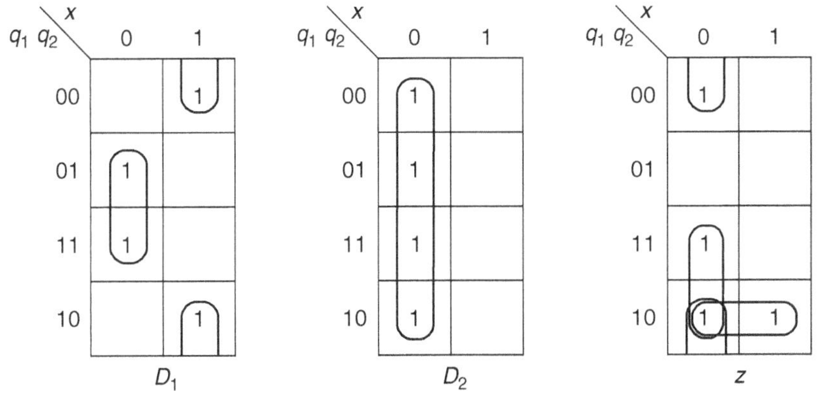

$D_1 = x'\,q_2 + x\,q_2'$ $\qquad D_2 = x'$ $\qquad z = x'\,q_1 + x'\,q_2' + q_1\,q_2'$

b. This assignment is in map order and once again we will go directly to the maps without first producing a truth table.

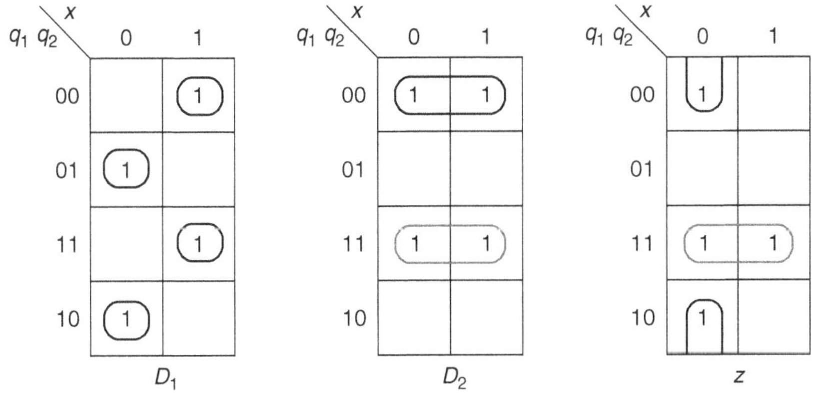

$D_1 = x'\,q_1'\,q_2 + x'\,q_1\,q_2' + x\,q_1'\,q_2' + x\,q_1\,q_2$

$D_2 = q_1'\,q_2' + q_1\,q_2$ $\qquad z = x'\,q_2' + q_1\,q_2$

where the brown terms are shared between D_2 and z.

c. For this part, we will first construct the truth table and then go to the maps.

q	x	q_1	q_2	z	$q_1^\star$	$q_2^\star$
A	0	0	0	1	1	1
D	0	0	1	1	0	1
C	0	1	0	1	1	1
B	0	1	1	0	0	1
A	1	0	0	0	1	0
D	1	0	1	0	0	0
C	1	1	0	1	1	0
B	1	1	1	0	0	0

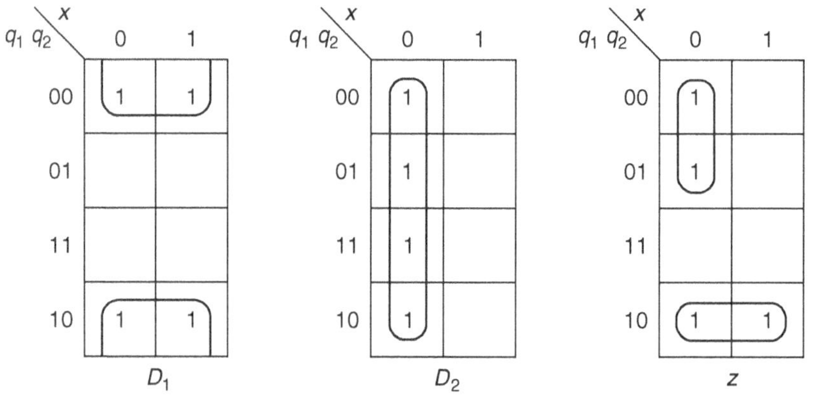

$D_1 = q_2'$ $D_1 = x'$ $z = x' q_1' + q_1 q_2'$

We really did not need to map D_1 and D_2; we should be able to see those from the truth table.

Comparing the three solutions we see a major difference, based on the three state assignments.

a. 8 gates 16 inputs
b. 11 gates 27 inputs
c. 4 gates 7 inputs

5. Design a synchronous counter that goes through the sequence

1 3 5 7 4 2 0 6 and repeat

using *D* flip flops.

The truth table is shown below.

A	*B*	*C*	$A^\star$	$B^\star$	$C^\star$
0	0	0	1	1	0
0	0	1	0	1	1
0	1	0	0	0	0
0	1	1	1	0	1
1	0	0	0	1	0
1	0	1	1	1	1
1	1	0	0	0	1
1	1	1	1	0	0

The maps for the *D* inputs are shown next, with the possible shared terms circled in brown and tan.

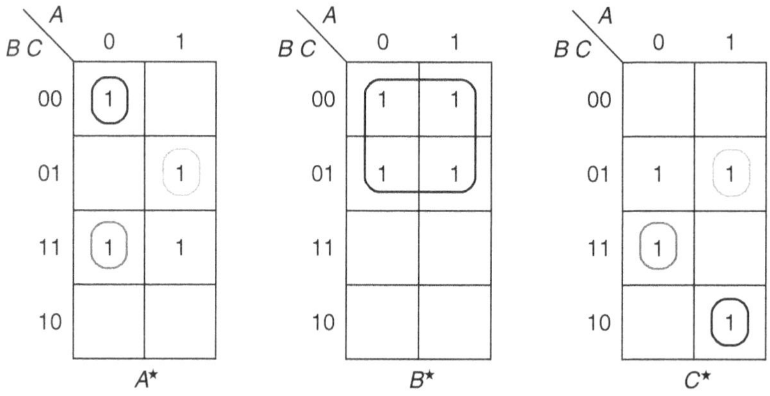

D_B is clearly B'. If we solve for the other two inputs independently, we get

$$D_A = AC + BC \qquad D_C = A'C + B'C$$

But, we can save a gate by sharing in either of two ways:

$$D_A = AC + A'BC \qquad D_C = A'BC + B'C \qquad \text{or}$$
$$D_A = AB'C + BC \qquad D_C = A'C + AB'C$$

6. Design a synchronous counter that goes through the sequence

2 6 1 7 5 and repeat

using

i. D flip flops
ii. JK flip flops

Show a state diagram, indicating what happens if it initially is in one of the unused states (0, 3, 4) for each of the designs.

The truth table is shown below. The next state for unused states is shown as don't cares.

A	B	C	$A^\star$	$B^\star$	$C^\star$
0	0	0	X	X	X
0	0	1	1	1	1
0	1	0	1	1	0
0	1	1	X	X	X
1	0	0	X	X	X
1	0	1	0	1	0
1	1	0	0	0	1
1	1	1	1	0	1

The maps and equations for the D inputs are shown next.

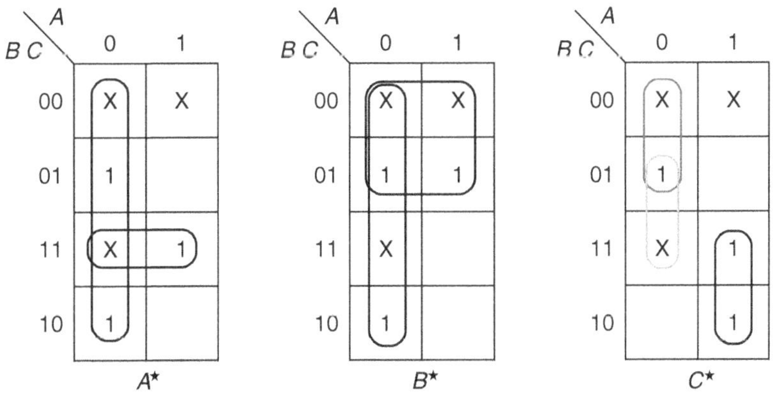

$$D_A = A' + BC$$
$$D_B = A' + B'$$
$$D_C = AB + \{A'B' \text{ or } A'C\}$$

There are two equally good solutions for D_C; as we will see shortly, the behavior of the system is different for those choices if it is initialized to one of the unused states.

Substituting the values for the three states not in the cycle:

0 (000): $D_A = 1, D_B = 1, D_C = 1$ or $D_C = 0$

3 (011): $D_A = 1, D_B = 1, D_C = 0$ or $D_C = 1$

4 (100): $D_A = 0, D_B = 1, D_C = 0$

where the color indicates that the next state depends upon the choice for the second term of D_C.

The state diagrams for the two solutions are shown below.

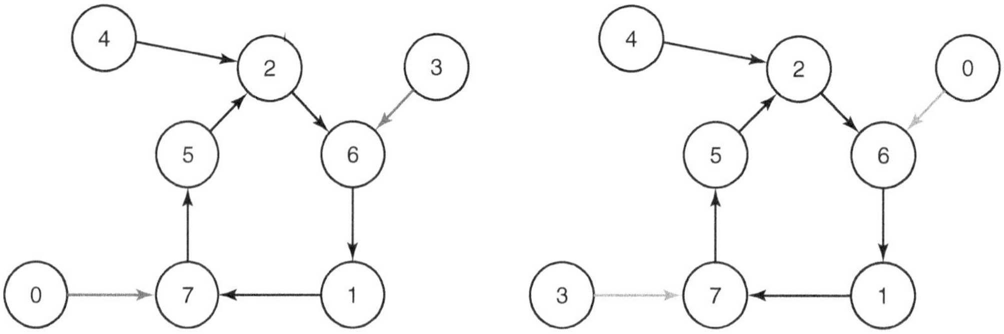

ii. The maps for the JK solution, with the J section shaded, and the equations are shown below.

$A^\star$

BC \ A	0	1
00	X	X
01	1	
11	X	1
10	1	

$B^\star$

BC \ A	0	1
00	X	X
01	1	1
11	X	
10	1	

$C^\star$

BC \ A	0	1
00	X	X
01	1	
11	X	1
10		1

$J_A = 1 \qquad K_A = B' + C'$

$J_B = 1 \qquad K_B = A$

$J_C = A \qquad K_C = AB'$

Substituting the values for the three states not in the cycle:

0 (000): $J_A = K_A = 1, J_B = 1, K_B = 0,$
$J_C = K_C = 0 \Rightarrow 110$

3 (011): $J_A = 1, K_A = 0, J_B = 1, K_B = 0,$
$J_C = K_C = 0 \Rightarrow 111$

4 (100): $J_A = K_A = 1, J_B = K_B = 1,$
$J_C = K_C = 1 \Rightarrow 011$

This is still a different behavior for the unused states. Now, state 4 goes to 3 and then, on the next clock, it will get back into the cycle. The state diagram is shown below.

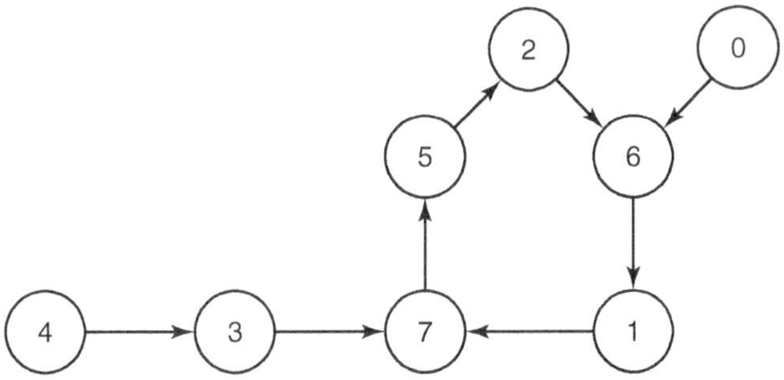

7. Design a counter with two *JK* flip flops, *A* and *B*, and one input, *x*. If $x = 0$, it counts 0, 1, 2, 3, 3, . . . ; if $x = 1$, it counts 3, 2, 1, 0, 0, ...

This is an up/down saturating counter. The truth table is shown below.

x	*A*	*B*	$A^\star$	$B^\star$
0	0	0	0	1
0	0	1	1	0
0	1	0	1	1
0	1	1	1	1
1	0	0	0	0
1	0	1	0	0
1	1	0	0	1
1	1	1	1	0

From this we can develop the maps for the quick method and the equations for *J* and *K*.

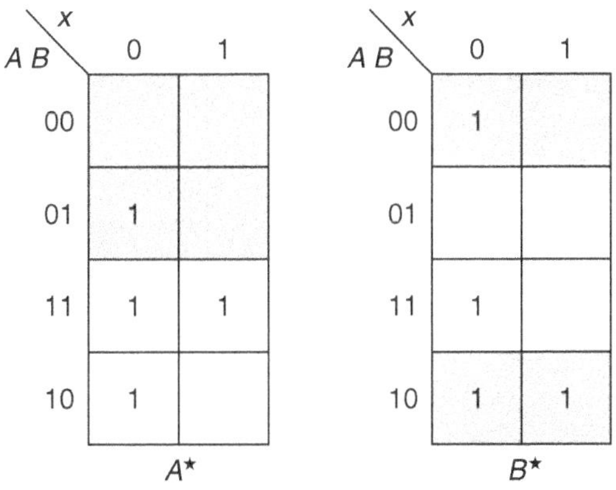

$J_A = x'B \quad K_A = xB' \qquad J_B = x' + A \quad K_B = x + A'$

8. Construct a base 60 (0 to 59) asynchronous counter using *JK* flip flops.

We need six flip flops and must detect when the count reaches 60 and reset the counter. (That occurs when *FEDC* = 1.)

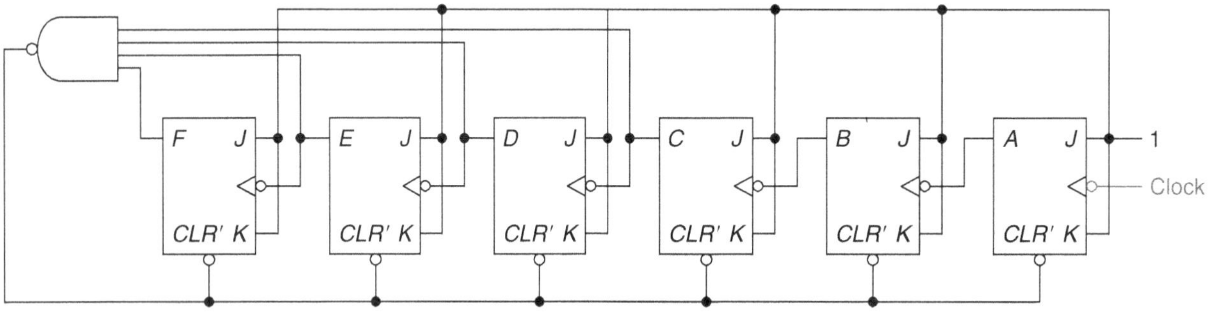

9. For each of the following problems show a state table or a state diagram. (A sample input/output trace is shown for each.)

a. A Mealy system that produces a 1 output iff there have been four or more consecutive 1 inputs or two or more consecutive 0 inputs. (4 states)

x 0 1 1 0 0 1 0 0 1 1 1 1 1 0 0 0 1
z ? 0 0 0 1 0 0 1 0 0 0 1 1 0 1 1 0 0

b. A Mealy system whose output is 1 iff the last three inputs were 010. (3 states)

i. assuming overlapping is allowed
ii. assuming overlapping is not allowed

x 1 1 0 1 0 1 0 1 0 0 1 0 0 1 0 0 1 1 0
z-i 0 0 0 0 1 0 1 0 1 0 0 1 0 0 1 0 0 0 0 0
z-ii 0 0 0 0 1 0 0 0 1 0 0 1 0 0 1 0 0 0 0 0

c. A Mealy system whose output is 1 iff the last four inputs were 1100 or the last output was a 1 and it is continuing on that pattern. (7 states)

x 1 0 1 1 0 0 1 0 1 1 0 0 1 1 0 0 1 1 1 0 0 1 0
z ? ? 0 0 0 1 1 0 0 0 0 1 1 1 1 1 1 0 0 1 1 0 0 0 0

d. A Moore system whose output changes whenever it detects a sequence 110. (Assume that initially the output is 0.) (6 states)

x 0 0 1 0 1 1 1 0 1 1 0 0 1 1 0 1 0 1
z 0 0 0 0 0 0 0 0 0 1 1 1 0 0 0 0 1 1 1 1 1

e. A Moore system whose output is 1 iff the input has been alternating for at least four clock periods. (8 states)

x 0 0 1 0 1 1 0 1 0 1 0 1 0 0
z ? ? 0 0 0 1 0 0 0 1 1 1 1 1 0

f. Show a state table or a state diagram for *either* a Mealy (6 states) or a Moore (7 states) system with one input, x, and one output, z, such that $z = 1$ if and only if the input has been exactly one or two 1's followed immediately by exactly one or two 0's.

x	0 1 1 0 1 1 0 0 0 1 0 0 1 1 0 0 1 0 1 1 1 0
Mealy z	? ? 0 0 1 0 0 0 0 0 0 0 1 0 0 0 1 0 1 0 0 0 0 0
Moore z	? ? ? 0 0 1 0 0 0 0 0 0 0 1 0 0 0 1 0 1 0 0 0 0 0 0

a.

	$q^\star$		z	
q	$x = 0$	$x = 1$	$x = 0$	$x = 1$
A	A	B	1	0
B	A	C	0	0
C	A	D	0	0
D	A	D	0	1

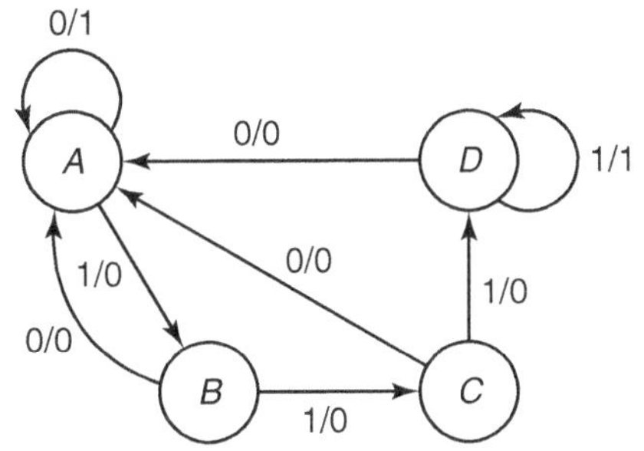

We start with a state for which the last input is 0. From there, we need four consecutive 1's to get a 1 output or another 0. Thus, on additional 0's, we loop back to state A. On a 1, we go to B; on a second 1, we go to C; and on a third 1, we go to D. In D, additional 1's produce a 1 output; 0's return the system to state A.

---

b. i.

	$q^\star$		z	
q	$x = 0$	$x = 1$	$x = 0$	$x = 1$
A	B	A	0	0
B	B	C	0	0
C	B	A	0	1

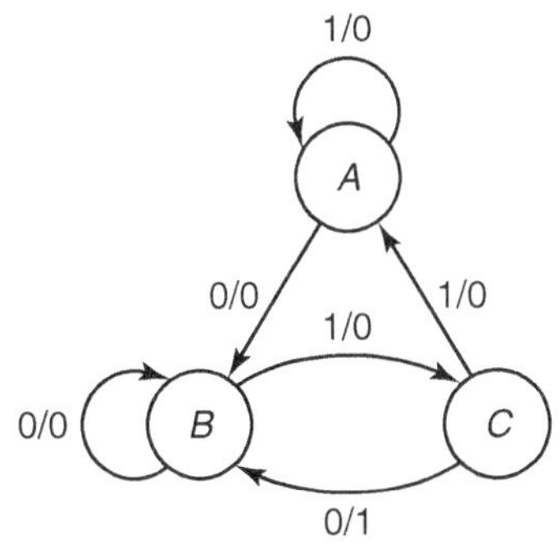

State *A* is the "nowhere" state, where we are looking for the first 0 in the pattern. A 0 gets us to *B* and then a 1 gets us to *C*. From there, a 0 input produces a 1 output. Since overlapping is allowed, that 0 input is the first 0 in a new string, and, thus, we return to state *B*.

In the case where overlapping is not allowed, we go from state *C* back to state *A* on a 0 input, since we are now nowhere, looking for a 010 pattern, as shown on the state diagram below.

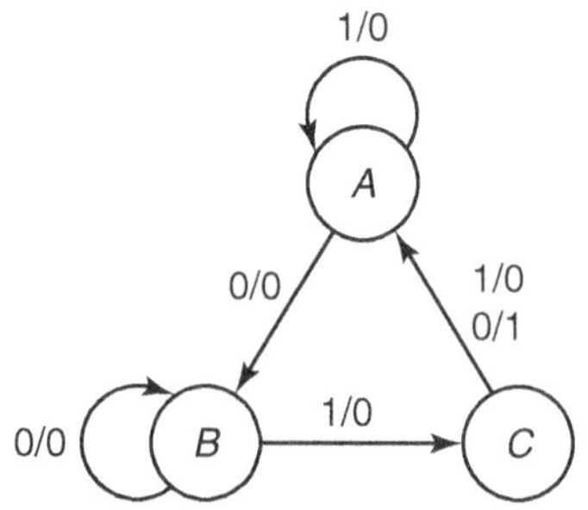

c. If we start with the "nowhere" state, that is, where the output is to be 0 and we are looking for the first 1, the success path consists of 1 1 0 0, at which point the output goes to 1. If that is followed by a 1, the output remains 1. It also remains 1 if there is another 1 input and then a 0 input (which gets the system back to state *D*). That produces the following start for the state diagram.

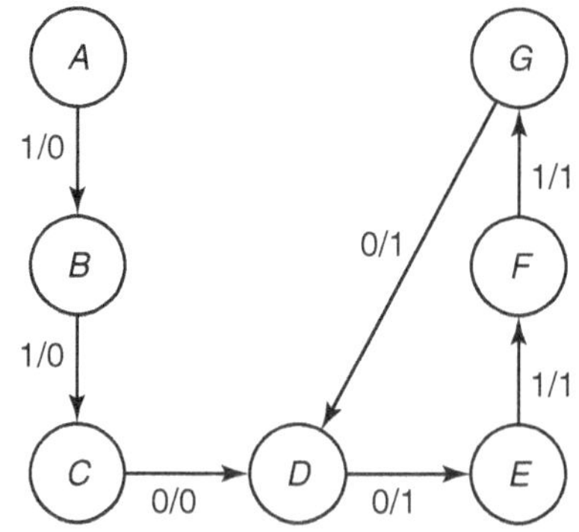

Now we can complete the failed paths. When we get a 0 while we are looking for 1's in states *A*, *B*, *E*, and *F*, we return to state *A*. We go next to state *C* on a 1 from either *C* or *G* (when there are more than two 1's in a row) and we go to *B* from *D* on a 1. Of course, all of these failed inputs produce a 0 output. The state diagram and then the state table are shown below.

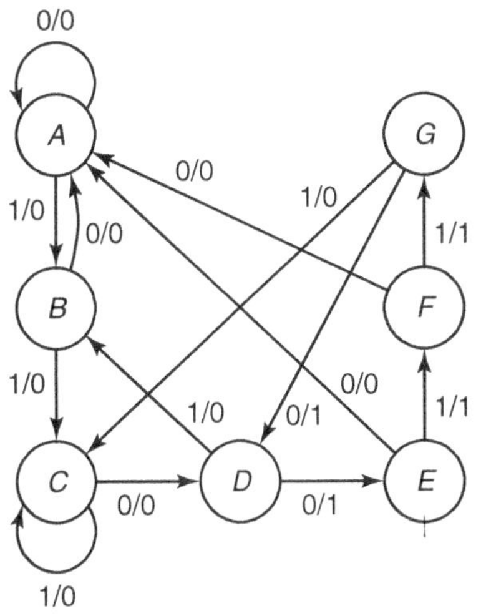

q	$q^\star$ x = 0	x = 1	z x = 0	x = 1
A	A	B	0	0
B	A	C	0	0
C	D	C	0	0
D	E	B	1	0
E	A	F	0	1
F	A	G	0	1
G	D	C	1	0

d. For a Moore system, the output is associated with the state. There are two "nowhere" states, *A* and *D*, one for which the output is 0 and another for which the output is 1. The state diagram and table are as follows:

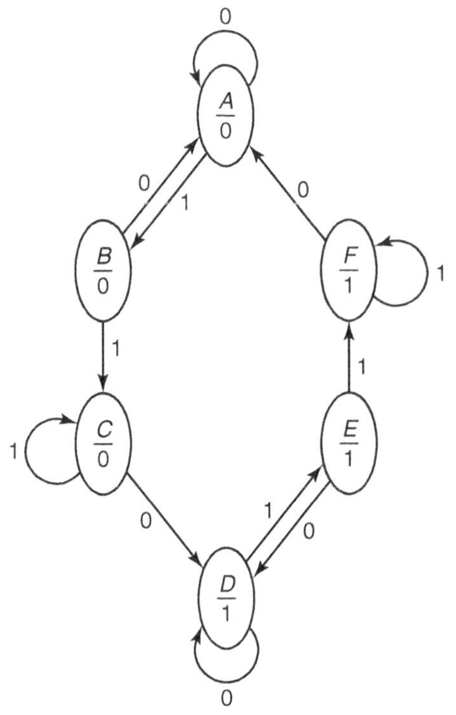

q	$q^\star$ x = 0	x = 1	z
A	A	B	0
B	A	C	0
C	D	C	0
D	D	E	1
E	D	F	1
F	A	F	1

When in the "nowhere" state and the input is 0, the system remains there. It progresses on the first 1 to B or E and on the second 1 to C or F. The system remains in C or F if 1's continue, and goes to the "nowhere" state with the opposite output on a 0 input.

e. We start with two "nowhere" states: A when the input has been 0 for two or more consecutive inputs, and B when it has been 1 for two or more consecutive inputs. From each of these there is a separate success path (from A to C to E to G or from B to D to F to H). States G and H have a 1 output. If the input continues to alternate, the system goes back and forth between these two states.

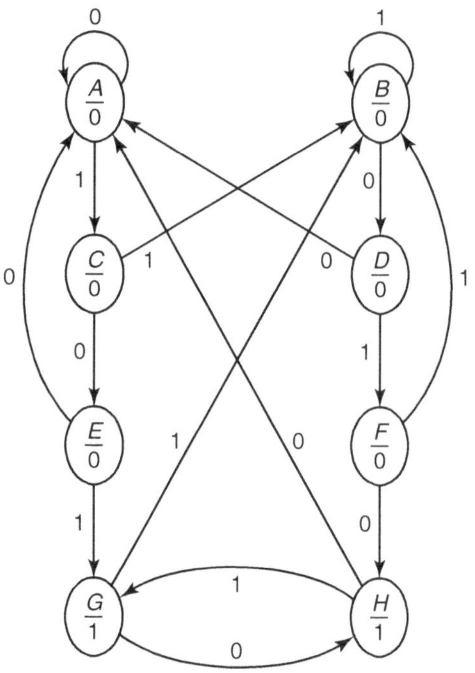

f. For both versions, the "nowhere" state, A, is when we are looking for the first 1 input. The first 1 gets us to B, and the second, to C. State D is reached when we have had exactly one or two 1's (from B or C). In the Mealy version (on the left), the output is 1 when the system is in state D and the input is 1 or is 0 followed by a 1. That 1 is treated as the first 1 of a new input sequence. The Moore version gets to state F after the same sequence, where the output is 1. After too many 0's (from state C), they go to F (Mealy) or G (Moore); after more than two 0's in a row, the systems return to state A.

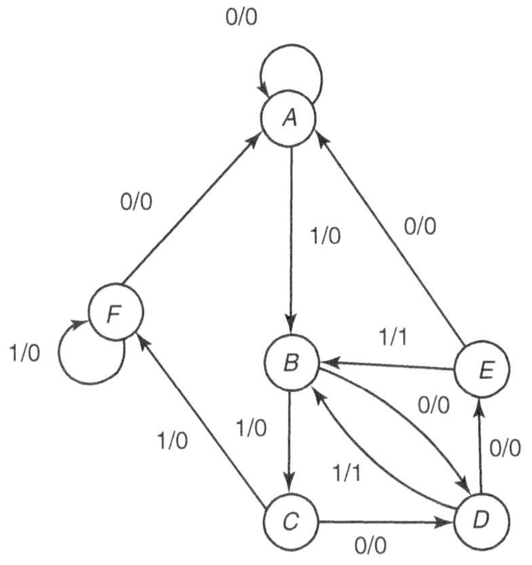

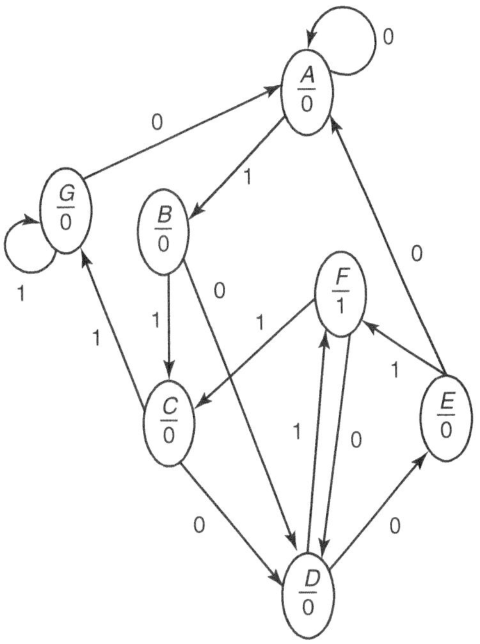

7.6 EXERCISES

1. Find equations for $q_1^\star$, $q_2^\star$, and Z for the state table of Figure 7.1, using the state assignment of Table 7.1c.

2. For each of the following state tables, design the system using
   i. *D* flip flops
   ii. *SR* flip flops
   iii. *T* flip flops
   iv. *JK* flip flops

   Show the equations for each and a block diagram for the *JK* design (using AND, OR, and NOT gates).

★a.

	$A^\star B^\star$		z	
$A\ B$	$x = 0$	$x = 1$	$x = 0$	$x = 1$
0 0	1 1	0 0	0	1
0 1	0 1	0 0	1	0
1 1	0 1	1 1	1	0

b.

	$A^\star B^\star$		z	
$A\ B$	$x = 0$	$x = 1$	$x = 0$	$x = 1$
0 0	1 0	1 1	0	0
0 1	0 0	0 1	0	0
1 0	0 1	1 1	1	0
1 1	0 0	0 0	1	1

c.

	$A^\star B^\star$		
$A\ B$	$x = 0$	$x = 1$	z
0 0	0 1	0 0	0
0 1	1 1	0 0	1
1 1	0 0	0 1	1

d.

	$A^\star B^\star$		
$A\ B$	$x = 0$	$x = 1$	z
0 0	1 0	0 0	0
0 1	0 0	1 1	1
1 0	0 1	0 1	1
1 1	0 0	0 1	1

e.

	$A^\star B^\star$		
$A\ B$	$x = 0$	$x = 1$	z
0 0	1 1	1 0	0
0 1	1 0	1 0	1
1 0	1 1	0 0	1
1 1	0 1	1 1	1

★f.

	$A^\star B^\star$		
$A\ B$	$x = 0$	$x = 1$	z
0 0	1 0	0 1	1
0 1	1 1	0 0	1
1 0	0 0	1 1	0
1 1	0 1	0 0	0

g.

	$A^\star B^\star C^\star$		z	
$A\ B\ C$	$x = 0$	$x = 1$	$x = 0$	$x = 1$
0 0 0	0 0 1	0 0 0	1	1
0 0 1	0 1 0	0 0 0	1	1
0 1 0	0 1 1	0 0 0	1	1
0 1 1	1 0 0	0 0 0	1	1
1 0 0	1 0 1	0 0 0	1	1
1 0 1	1 0 1	0 0 0	0	1

3. For each of the following state tables and state assignments, find the flip flop input equations and the system output equation for an implementation using
   i. *D* flip flops
   ii. *JK* flip flops

a.

q	$q^\star$ $x = 0$	$x = 1$	z
A	C	B	1
B	C	A	1
C	A	C	0

q	$q_1 q_2$
A	1 1
B	0 1
C	1 0

b.

q	$q^\star$ $x = 0$	$x = 1$	z $x = 0$	$x = 1$
A	C	B	1	1
B	A	A	1	0
C	C	A	1	0

q	$q_1 q_2$
A	0 0
B	1 1
C	0 1

★c.

q	$q^\star$ $x = 0$	$x = 1$	z
A	B	C	1
B	A	B	0
C	B	A	0

q	$q_1 q_2$
A	0 0
B	1 0
C	0 1

d.

q	$q^\star$ $x = 0$	$x = 1$	z $x = 0$	$x = 1$
A	B	B	0	0
B	D	A	1	0
C	D	B	0	0
D	C	D	1	0

q	$q_1 q_2$
A	0 0
B	1 1
C	1 0
D	0 1

e.

q	$q^\star$ $x = 0$	$x = 1$	z $x = 0$	$x = 1$
A	B	D	0	0
B	D	C	1	0
C	A	B	0	0
D	C	A	1	0

q	$q_1 q_2$
A	0 0
B	0 1
C	1 1
D	1 0

4. a. For the state table and each of the state assignments shown, design a system using *D* flip flops.

q	$q^\star$ $x = 0$	$x = 1$	z
A	B	D	0
B	C	A	1
C	B	B	1
D	D	C	1

i.

q	q_1	q_2
A	0	0
B	0	1
C	1	0
D	1	1

ii.

q	q_1	q_2
A	0	0
B	0	1
C	1	1
D	1	0

iii.

q	q_1	q_2
A	0	0
B	1	1
C	1	0
D	0	1

b, c. For each of the state tables and each of the state assignments shown, design a system using *D* flip flops.

★b.

q	$q^\star$ $x = 0$	$x = 1$	z $x = 0$	$x = 1$
A	B	C	1	0
B	A	B	0	1
C	B	B	0	0

c.

q	$q^\star$ $x = 0$	$x = 1$	z $x = 0$	$x = 1$
A	A	C	0	0
B	C	B	1	1
C	A	B	1	0

i.

q	q_1	q_2
A	0	0
B	0	1
C	1	0

ii.

q	q_1	q_2
A	0	0
B	0	1
C	1	1

iii.

q	q_1	q_2
A	0	0
B	1	1
C	1	0

5. Complete the design of the 4-bit binary counter (from the beginning of Section 7.2) with *SR* flip flops.

6. If we build the decade counter using *JK* flip flops, show a state diagram, including what happens if it initially is in one of the unused states (10, 11, 12, 13, 14, 15).

7. Design, using

i. *D* flip flops

ii. *JK* flip flops

★a. a synchronous base-12 counter, one that goes through the sequence

0 1 2 3 4 5 6 7 8 9 10 11 . . .

b. a synchronous binary down counter, one that goes through the sequence

15 14 13 12 11 10 9 8 7 6 5 4 3 2 1 0 . . .

8. Design synchronous counters that go through each of the following sequences

a. 6 5 4 3 2 1 and repeat

★b. 1 3 4 7 6 and repeat

c. 6 5 4 1 2 3 and repeat

d. 6 5 1 3 7 and repeat

e. 7 4 3 6 1 2 and repeat

f. 1 3 5 7 6 4 2 0 and repeat

using

i. *JK* flip flops

ii. *D* flip flops

Show a state diagram, indicating what happens if it initially is in one of the unused states for each of the designs.

9. Design a counter with two *JK* flip flops, *A* and *B*, and one input, *x*. If $x = 0$, it counts 1 3 0 and repeat; if $x = 1$, it counts 1 2 3 and repeat.

a. Assume that *x* changes only when it is in state 1 or 3 (in which case there are two combinations which never occur—state 2 and $x = 0$, and state 0 and $x = 1$).

b. After building the design of part a (with the two don't cares), what happens if somehow *x* is 0 in state 2 and what happens if somehow *x* is 1 in state 0?

★**10.** a. Design a counter with two *JK* flip flops (*A* and *B*) and an input (*x*) that counts 0 1 2 3 and repeat when $x = 0$ and counts 0 1 2 and repeat when $x = 1$. Design this assuming that *x* never is 1 when the count is 3. Show the minimum equations for each.

b. What does happen when *x* goes to 1 when the count is 3?

11. Design the system of CE10, using *JK* flip flops.
12. Design an asynchronous base-10 counter, using *T* flip flops with a static active high clear.
13. Complete the design of CE6 using *JK* flip flops for the three different state assignments of Table 7.1.
14. Design the three-state version of CE7, using *D* flip flops and each of the following state assignments.

q	q_1	q_2
A	0	0
B	0	1
C	1	0

(a)

q	q_1	q_2
A	0	0
B	0	1
C	1	1

(b)

q	q_1	q_2
A	0	0
B	1	1
C	0	1

(c)

15. Design a system using *JK* flip flops that produces a 1 output iff there have been exactly three 1's in a row. (See Example 7.10.)
    a. Using the Mealy state diagram.
    b. Using the Moore state table.
16. For each of the following problems show a state table or a state diagram. (A sample input/output trace and the minimum number of states required is shown for each.)
    a. A Moore system that produces a 1 output iff the input has been 0 for at least two consecutive clocks followed immediately by two or more consecutive 1's. (5 states)

    x 0 1 0 0 1 0 0 1 1 0 0 0 1 0 1 0 0 0 1 1 1 1 0
    z 0 0 0 0 0 0 0 0 0 1 0 0 0 0 0 0 0 0 0 0 1 1 1 0 0

    ★b. A Moore system, the output of which is 1 iff there have been two or more consecutive 1's or three or more consecutive 0's. (5 states)

    x 0 0 0 0 1 0 1 1 0 0 1 1 1 0 0 0 1 0
    z ? ? ? 1 1 0 0 0 1 0 0 0 1 1 0 0 1 0 0 0

    c. A Mealy system that produces a 1 output iff the input has been 1 for three or more consecutive clock times or 0 for three or more consecutive clock times. When first turned on, it is in an initial state *A*. (There are four additional states.)

    x 0 0 0 0 1 0 1 1 0 0 0 1 1 1 1 1 0 0 1
    z 0 0 1 1 0 0 0 0 0 0 0 1 0 0 1 1 1 0 0 0 0

    d. A Mealy system that produces a 1 output iff the input has been either 0 1 0 or 1 0 1. Overlapping is allowed. When first turned on, it is in an initial state *A*. (There are four additional states.)

x 0 0 1 0 0 1 0 1 0 0 1 1 0 1 1 0 1 0 0
z 0 0 0 1 0 0 1 1 1 0 0 0 0 1 0 0 1 1 0 0

e. A Mealy system that produces a 1 output iff the input is 0 for the first time after it has been 1 for at least two consecutive clocks or when it is 1 after having been 0 for at least two consecutive clocks. Overlapping is allowed. When first turned on, it is in an initial state *A*. (There are four additional states.)

x 0 1 0 0 0 1 1 1 1 1 0 0 1 1 0
z 0 0 0 0 0 1 0 0 0 0 1 0 1 0 1 0

★f. A Mealy system, the output of which is 1 iff the input had been at least two 0's followed by exactly two 1's followed by a 0. Overlapping is not allowed. (5 states)

x 1 1 1 0 0 0 1 1 0 0 1 1 0 0 1 1 1 0 0 0 0 1 1 0 0
z 0 0 0 0 0 0 0 0 1 0 0 0 0 0 0 0 0 0 0 0 0 0 0 1 0 0 0

g. A Mealy system, the output of which is 1 iff there have been exactly two consecutive 1's followed by at least two consecutive 0's. (5 states)

x 0 1 1 0 0 0 1 1 0 0 1 1 0 0 1 1 1 0 0 0 0 1 1 0 0
z ? 0 0 0 1 1 0 0 0 1 0 0 0 1 0 0 0 0 0 0 0 0 0 0 1

h. A Mealy system, the output of which is 1 iff there have been exactly two consecutive 0's or exactly two consecutive 1's.
   i. Overlapping is allowed (6 states)
   ii. Overlapping is not allowed (6 states)

x 0 1 1 1 0 1 1 0 0 1 1 0 1 0 1 0 0 1
z-i ? ? 0 0 0 0 0 1 0 1 0 1 0 0 0 0 0 1 0
z-ii ? ? 0 0 0 0 0 1 0 0 0 1 0 0 0 0 0 1 0 0

i. A Mealy system, the output of which is 1 iff there has been a pattern of 1 0 1 1.
   i. Overlapping is allowed (4 states)
   ii. Overlapping is not allowed (4 states)

x 0 0 1 0 1 1 0 1 1 0 1 1 1 0 0 1 0 1 0 1 1
z-i 0 0 0 0 0 1 0 0 1 0 0 1 0 0 0 0 0 0 0 0 1 0 0
z-ii 0 0 0 0 0 1 0 0 0 0 0 1 0 0 0 0 0 0 0 0 1 0 0 0

j. A Mealy system, the output of which is 0 iff there has been a pattern of 1 1 0 1. (The output is 1 most of the time.)
   i. Overlapping is allowed (4 states)
   ii. Overlapping is not allowed (4 states)

x	0 0 1 0 1 1 0 1 1 0 1 1 1 0 0 1 0 1 1 0 1 1
z-i	1 1 1 1 1 1 1 0 1 1 0 1 1 1 1 1 1 1 1 0 1 1
z-ii	1 1 1 1 1 1 1 0 1 1 1 1 1 1 1 1 1 1 1 0 1 1 1

*k. A Mealy system, the output of which is 1 iff the input has contained an even number of 0's (including no 0's) and a multiple of four 1's (including no 1's). When first turned on, the system is initialized to a state indicating no 0's and no 1's (but that state is reached again later). (8 states)

x	0 1 1 0 1 1 0 0 0 0 1 0 1 0 0 0 1 0 1 0
z	0 0 0 0 0 1 0 1 0 1 0 0 0 0 0 0 0 0 0 1 0

*l. A Moore system, the output of which is 1 iff the pattern 1 0 1 has occurred more recently than 1 1 1. (6 states)

x	1 0 1 0 1 1 0 1 0 1 1 1 1 0 0 1 0 1 1 1
z	? ? ? 1 1 1 1 1 1 1 1 1 0 0 0 0 0 1 1 1 0 0

Determine from the sample whether overlapping is allowed.

m. A Mealy system, the output of which is 1 iff the input is exactly two 1's followed immediately by exactly one or two 0's. Full credit for solutions with six or less states.

x	1 0 0 1 1 0 0 1 1 0 1 1 1 0 0 1 1 0 0 0 0 0
z	? 0 0 0 0 0 0 1 0 0 1 0 0 0 0 0 0 0 0 0 0 0 0 0 0

n. A Mealy system, the output of which is 1 iff there has been a pattern of 1 1 0 0 0. (5 states)

x	0 0 0 0 1 0 1 1 0 0 0 0 1 1 1 1 0 0 0 1
z	? ? ? 0 0 0 0 0 0 0 1 0 0 0 0 0 0 0 1 0 0 0 0

o. In this Mealy system, there are two inputs, *a* and *b*; they are to be treated as a binary number, that is 00 is 0, 01 is 1, 10 is 2, and 11 is 3. The output is to be 1 if the current number is greater than or equal to the previous one AND the previous one is greater than or equal to the one before that. It is to be 0 otherwise. There is an initial state for which there have been no previous numbers. Be sure to explain the meaning of each state. (8 states in addition to the initial one)

a	0 0 1 0 1 0 0 0 1 1 1 0 1 1
b	1 0 0 1 1 0 0 1 0 1 0 0 1 1
z	0 0 0 0 0 0 0 1 1 1 0 0 0 1

7.7 CHAPTER 7 TEST (75 MINUTES)

1. For the following state table, design a system using a D flip flop for A, a JK flip flop for B, and AND, OR, and NOT gates. Show the flip flop input equations and the output equation; you do NOT need to draw a block diagram.

	$A^\star B^\star$		z	
A B	$x = 0$	$x = 1$	$x = 0$	$x = 1$
0 0	1 1	0 1	0	1
0 1	0 0	1 0	0	0
1 0	1 0	0 1	1	1
1 1	0 1	1 0	1	0

2. For the following state table and state assignment, design a system using an SR flip flop for q_1 and a JK flip flop for q_2. Show the flip flop input equations and the output equation; you do NOT need to draw a block diagram.

	$q^\star$		
q	$x = 0$	$x = 1$	z
A	A	B	1
B	B	C	1
C	A	C	0

q	q_1	q_2
A	0	0
B	1	0
C	1	1

3. For the following state table, design a system using D flip flops for each of the state assignments. Show equations for D_1, D_2, and z.

	$q^\star$		
q	$x = 0$	$x = 1$	z
A	C	B	1
B	D	D	0
C	A	D	0
D	C	B	0

a.

q	q_1	q_2
A	0	0
B	0	1
C	1	0
D	1	1

b.

q	q_1	q_2
A	0	0
B	1	1
C	0	1
D	1	0

c. Show a block diagram for the solution to part b, using AND, OR, and NOT gates.

4. Design a counter that goes through the sequence

1 4 3 6 2 5 and repeat

using a *D* flip flop for *A*, a *JK* flip flop for *B*, and a *T* flip flop for *C*. *Five-point bonus:* Show a state diagram, including what happens if the system is initially in state 0 or 7.

5. a. Show the state table or state diagram for a Mealy system that produces a 1 output if and only if the input has been 1 0 1 0 for the last four clock times. Overlapping is allowed. (4 states)

b. Show the state table or state diagram for a Mealy system that produces a 1 output if and only if the input has been 1 0 1 0 for the last four clock times. Overlapping is not allowed. (4 states)

Example:

x	1	1	0	1	0	1	1	1	0	1	0	1	0	1	0	0
z-a	0	0	0	0	1	0	0	0	0	0	1	0	1	0	1	0
z-b	0	0	0	0	1	0	0	0	0	0	1	0	0	0	1	0

6. Show the state table or state diagram for a Moore system that produces a 1 output if and only if the input has been 0 1 1 for the last three clock times. (4 states)

Example:

x	0	0	1	0	1	1	1	0	0	1	1	0	1	1	
z	?	0	0	0	0	0	1	0	0	0	0	1	0	0	1

CHAPTER 8

Solving Larger Sequential Problems

As we get to larger problems, data are often stored in *registers,* rather than individual flip flops. A register is just a collection of flip flops, often with a common name (using subscripts to indicate the individual flip flops) and usually with a common clock. For example, in a computer, the two inputs to the adder (say 16 bits each) may come from two registers, each of which consists of 16 flip flops. It is nearly impossible to show a block diagram of such a system with all of the individual flip flops and gates.

In this chapter, we will look first at two classes of commercial medium-scale integrated circuits*—shift registers and counters. We will introduce programmable logic devices with memory to implement more complex problems such as CPLDs and FPGAs. We will then look briefly at two tools for dealing with these larger systems, ASM (Algorithmic State Machine) diagrams and HDL (Hardware Design Languages). Lastly, we will then look at some larger design problems than we could manage in Chapter 7. We will concentrate on synchronous (clocked) systems.

8.1 SHIFT REGISTERS

A shift register, in its simplest form, is a set of flip flops, such that the data moves one place to the right on each clock or shift input. A simple 4-bit shift register is shown in Figure 8.1, using SR flip flops. (Although shift registers are most commonly implemented with *SR* flip flops, *JK* flip flops could be used in place of the *SR*'s in the same circuit. *D* flip flops could also be used; the q output of one flip flop would be connected to the D input of the next.) At each clock, the input, x, is moved into q_1, and the contents of each of the flip flops is shifted one place to the right.

*When we look at the details of some of these circuits, we will simplify the logic somewhat by looking at just one bit and by eliminating some of the double NOT gates that are used for reducing load.

Figure 8.1 A simple shift register.

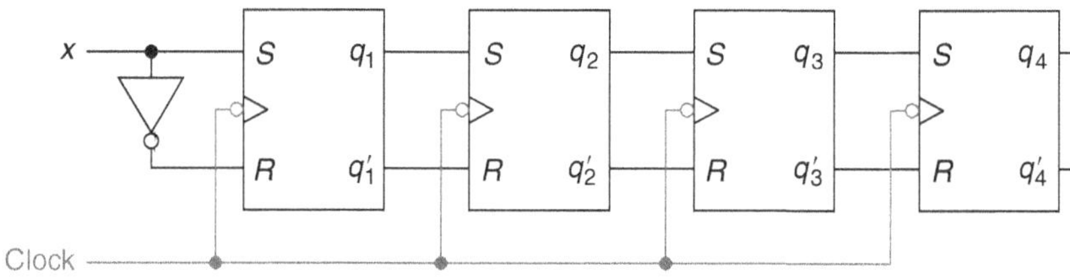

A sample timing trace is shown in Trace 8.1, assuming that all flip flops are initially 0. The sample input is shown in brown.

Trace 8.1 Shift register timing.

x	1	0	1	1	1	0	1	1	1	1	0	0	0				
q_1	0	1	0	1	1	1	0	1	1	1	1	0	0	0			
q_2	0	0	1	0	1	1	1	0	1	1	1	1	0	0	0		
q_3	0	0	0	1	0	1	1	1	0	1	1	1	1	0	0	0	
q_4	0	0	0	0	1	0	1	1	1	0	1	1	1	1	0	0	0

In some commercial shift registers, a NOT gate is added at the clock input, as shown in Figure 8.2.

Figure 8.2 Leading-edge triggered shift register.

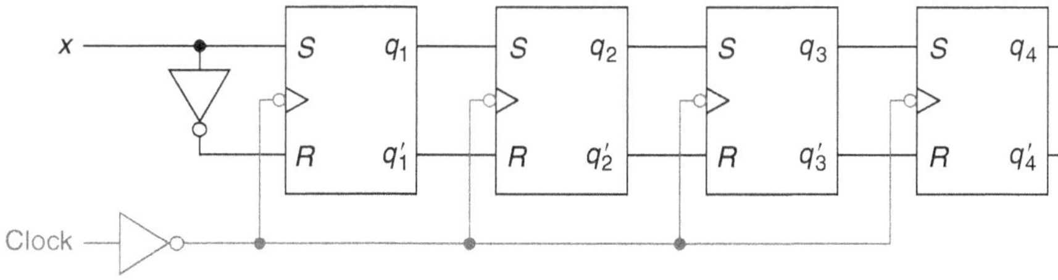

This accomplishes two things. The shift register is now leading-edge triggered (since the leading edge of the clock is the trailing edge of the flip flop input). Also, the clock input signal only goes to the NOT gate. Thus, this circuit presents a load of 1 to the clock, rather than a load of 4 (if the signal went to all four flip flops). When a trailing-edge triggered shift register is desired, a second NOT gate is added in series with the one shown. Sometimes, the x input is first inverted to present only a load of 1. Both of these changes are shown in the circuit of Figure 8.3.

Figure 8.3 Shift register with load-reducing NOT gates.

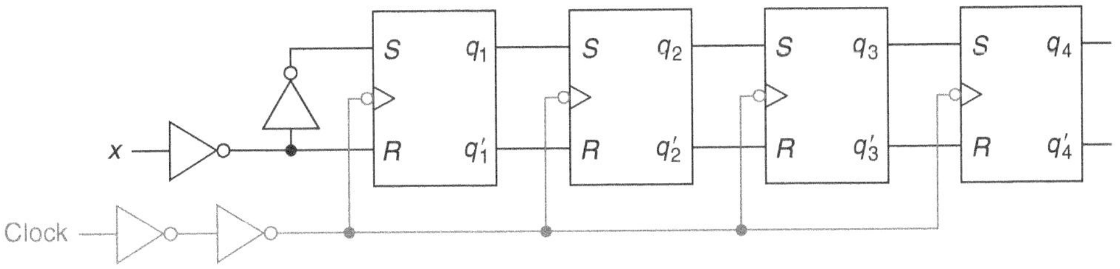

This version of the shift register is referred to as *serial-in, serial-out* in that only 1 bit (the left bit) may be loaded into the register at a time and, as shown, only 1 bit (the right bit) may be read. (Only the uncomplemented value, q_4, may be available or both the uncomplemented and complemented, q_4 and q_4', may be outputs.) The main limitation on the amount of logic that can fit on a single chip is the number of input and output connections. Thus, one could build a serial-in, serial-out shift register with a nearly unlimited number of bits on a chip, since there are only three or four logic connections.

One application of a large serial-in, serial-out shift register is a memory similar to a disk. If the output bit is connected back to the input as shown in Figure 8.4, when *Load* is 0, the data circulate around the n flip flops. It is available only when it is in q_n, once every n clock cycles. At that time it can be modified, by making *Load* = 1 and supplying the new value on x. If we needed a series of 8-bit numbers, we could build eight such shift registers, storing 1 bit in each. As we clocked all the shift registers, we would obtain 1 byte (8 bits) at a time.

Figure 8.4 Shift register storage.

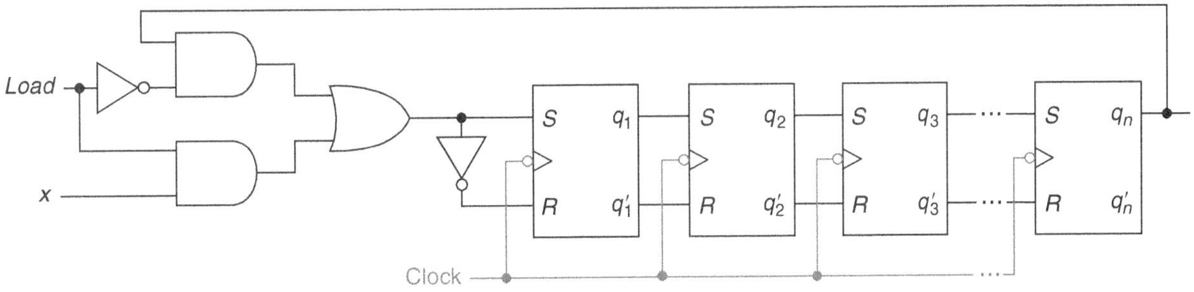

To initialize a 4-bit serial-in, serial-out shift register to all 0's, we would have to clock it four times, with 0 on input x each time. To avoid this, most shift registers have an active low (usually static) clear input. Many shift registers have a *parallel* output, that is, the contents of each of the flip flops is available. (Obviously, if we were building this with independent flip flops, this would just require connecting a wire to each flip flop output. If, however, the whole shift register were contained on a single integrated circuit, each output would require a pin.) There is an 8-bit serial-in, parallel-out shift register on one chip, using *D* flip flops (74164); it uses the 12 logic connections for 8 outputs, the clock, the clear, and 2 for serial input, as shown in Figure 8.5. (The *x* is replaced by *A B*, two inputs into a built-in AND gate.)

Figure 8.5 74164 serial-in parallel-out shift register.

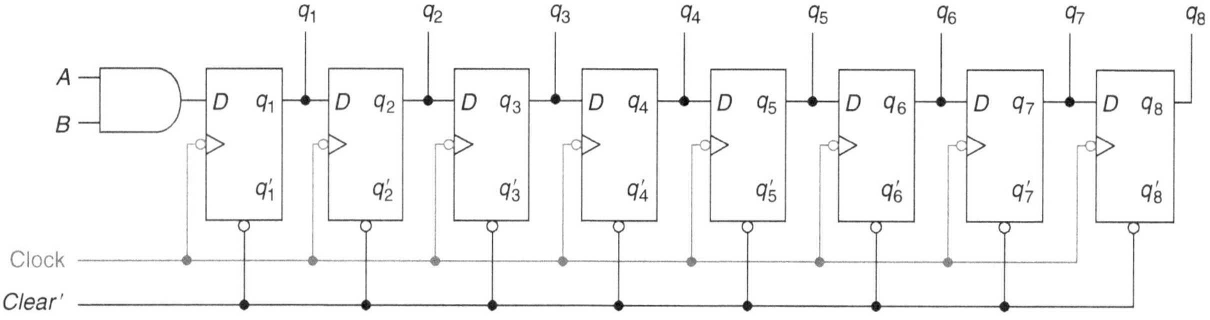

One application of a serial-in, parallel-out shift register is an input port from a modem. Data are transmitted serially over telephone lines. It is clocked into a shift register until a whole byte or word is received. Only then is there interaction with the computer's memory; the group of bits are read in parallel from the shift register and loaded into memory.

A *parallel-in* shift register allows the register to be loaded in one step. That, of course, requires an input line for each flip flop, as well as a control line to indicate load. Sometimes the loading is done statically (74165), as demonstrated for a typical bit (q_2) in Figure 8.6a. Sometimes it is done synchronously (74166), as shown in Figure 8.6b. Both of these are serial-out, that is, there is only one output connection, from the right flip flop. There is a serial input to the left bit for shift operations (going to the same place in the first flip flop logic that q_1 goes to in the typical bit in Figure 8.6).

For the 74165, the clock input to the flip flops is inverted from the input to the chip and passed through only when *Load'* is high (don't load) and *Enable'* is low (enable shift). When *Load'* is high, both *CLR'* and *PRE'* are high, and the shift works. When *Load'* is low, the clock is disabled, IN_2' appears on *PRE'*, and IN_2 appears on *CLR'*, thus loading IN_2 into the flip flop.

For the 74166, there is an active low static clear, independent of the load. The clock is inverted when *Enable'* is 0; otherwise, the flip flops are not clocked and nothing changes. When enabled and *Load'* is 0, IN_2 is stored in q_2; when *Load'* is 1 (inactive), q_1 is shifted into q_2.

Figure 8.6 Parallel-in shift registers.

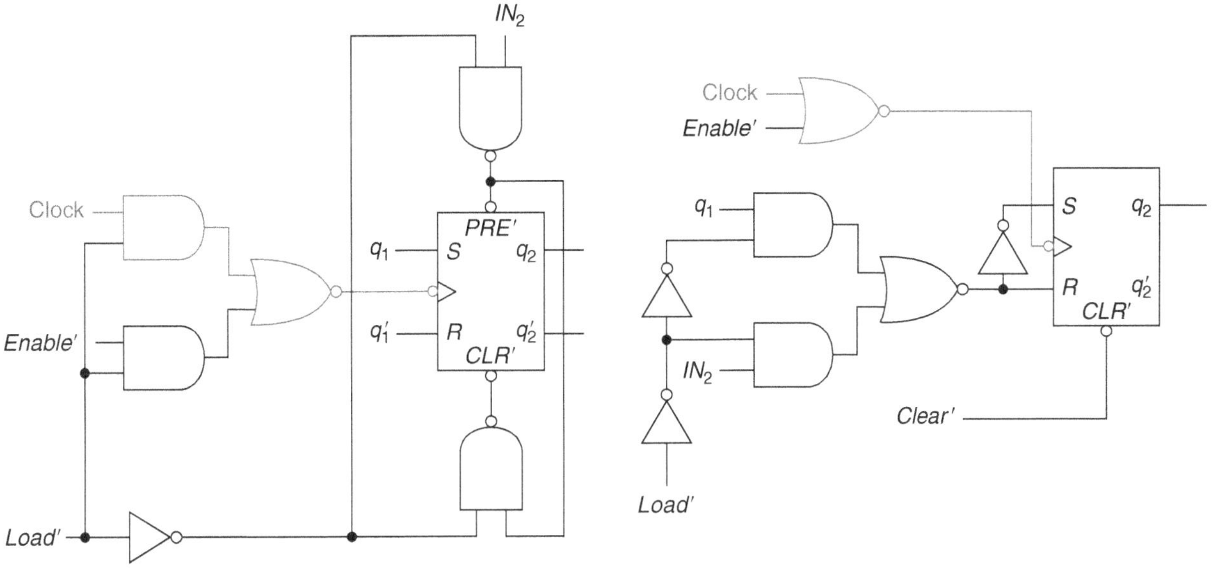

(a) 74165

(b) 74166

The parallel-in, serial-out shift register is used in the output process for serial data. A word is loaded (all at once) into the shift register from the computer. Then, bits are sent to the modem from the right end of the shift register one at a time.

Parallel-in, parallel-out shift register chips are limited to 4 or 5 bits because of the number of connections required. The 7495 is very similar to the 74166 in control structure, except that it has a separate clock input for shifting and for loading.

In most computers, there are both left and right shift and rotate* instructions. To implement these, we might use a right/left shift register (such as the 74194, a synchronous parallel-in, parallel-out 4-bit shift register). For this, a three-way multiplexer is needed at each bit, since that bit can receive the bit to its left, the bit to its right, or the input bit. A truth table describing the behavior of the shift register is shown in Table 8.1. Bits are numbered 1 to 4 from left to right.

Table 8.1 Right/left shift register.

	Clear'	S_0	S_1	$q_1^\star$	$q_2^\star$	$q_3^\star$	$q_4^\star$
Static clear	0	X	X	0	0	0	0
Hold	1	0	0	q_1	q_2	q_3	q_4
Shift left	1	0	1	q_2	q_3	q_4	LS
Shift right	1	1	0	RS	q_1	q_2	q_3
Load	1	1	1	IN_1	IN_2	IN_3	IN_4

*A one place right rotate moves every bit one place to the right and moves the right-most bit back into the left flip flop.

Where the IN_i are the inputs for parallel load, *RS* is the serial input for a right shift, and *LS* is the serial input for a left shift. The hold combination is really the "don't shift, don't load" input. A typical bit (with the control circuitry) is shown in Figure 8.7.

Figure 8.7 Right/left shift register.

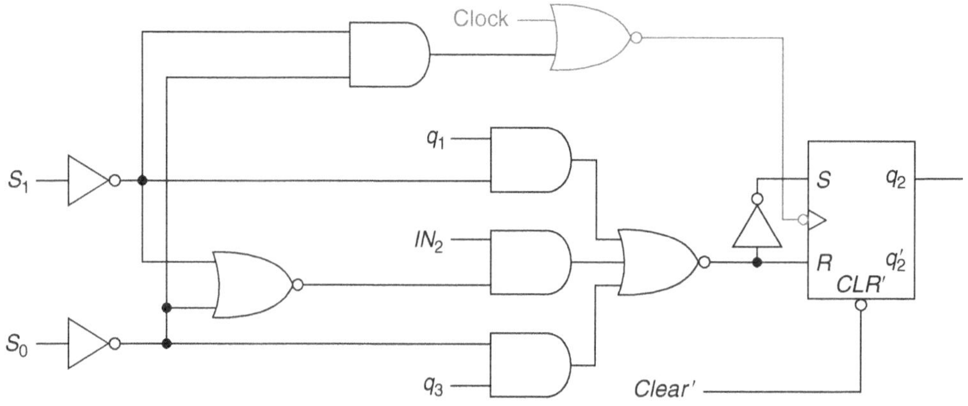

Note that when S_0 and S_1 are both 0, the clock input to the flip flop is 0; there is no edge, and thus the flip flop holds. Otherwise, the clock is inverted and thus this is a leading-edge triggered shift register. (Note that for q_1, the left flip flop, *RS* comes into the top input of the multiplexer, and for q_4, *LS* comes into the bottom input.)

As an example of an application of shift registers, consider the following problem.

EXAMPLE 8.1

We want to design a system with one output, *z*, which is 1 if the input, *x*, has been alternating for seven clock times (including the present). We have available an 8-bit serial-in, parallel-out shift register as shown below:

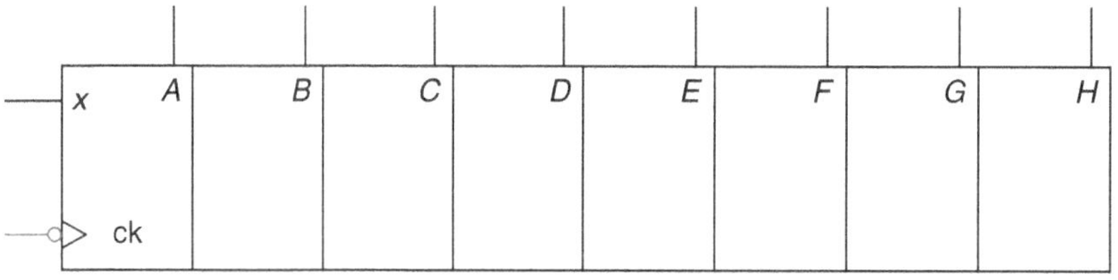

(The shift register probably also has a static clear input, but it is not needed for this problem.)

At any time, the register contains the value of *x* at the eight most recent clocks, with the most recent in *A* and the oldest in *H*. For this problem, we only need six of these. The circuit below computes the answer.

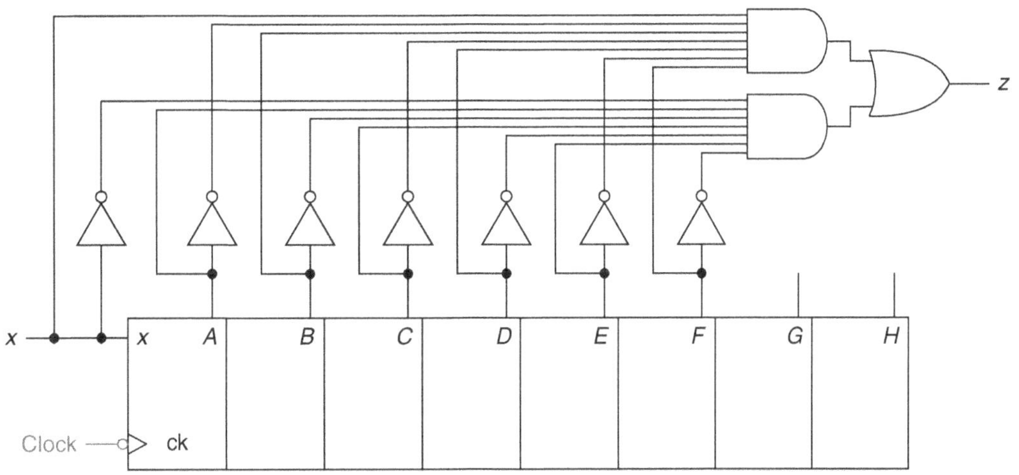

[SP 1, 2, 4a; EX 1, 2, 4b; LAB]

8.2 COUNTERS

In Chapter 7, we discussed the design of counters. In this section, we will look at some of the commercially available counters and applications of counters. A counter consists of a register and the associated logic.

Counters may be synchronous or asynchronous and may be base 10, 12, or 16 (that is, cycle through 10, 12, or 16 states on consecutive clock pulses). Most synchronous counters have parallel loads; they may be preset to a value, using the load signal and an input line for each bit. Many also have a clear (or Master Reset) signal to load the register with all 0's. These control signals are usually active low; they may be synchronous or asynchronous. Most asynchronous counters just have a static clear. In addition, some synchronous counters count both up and down. Most counters have a carry or overflow output, which indicates that the counter has reached its maximum and is returning to 0 (for up counters). That may be a logic 1, or it may be a clock pulse coincident with the pulse that causes the transition back to 0.

We will first look at the 74161 counter, which does synchronous counting and loading and has an asynchronous (active low) clear. It has two count enables, *ENT* and *ENP** (both of which must be 1 to enable

*Only *ENT* enables the overflow output.

counting). Labeling the bits *D* (high), *C*, *B*, and *A*, a block representation of the counter and the logic for a typical bit, bit *C*, is shown in Figure 8.8. Since the clock is inverted before going to the trailing-edge triggered flip flop, the counter is leading-edge triggered. The only difference between bits is the inputs to the brown AND gate. That is the value for the *J* and *K* inputs to each bit when counting (ANDed with the enable). (Thus, *D*'s input is *A B C*, *C*'s input is *A B*, *B*'s input is *A*, and *A*'s input is 1.) When loading ($Load' = 0$), point *x* is 1, point *y* is 1, point *z* equals IN'_C, and point *w* equals IN_C. Thus, the flip flop is loaded with the value on IN_C. When $Load' = 1$, then point *x* equals 0, points *w* and *z* equal 1, and point *y* is just the output of the brown AND gate. Thus, *J* and *K* are 1 when the brown gate output is 1, that is, when this flip is to change during the count.

Figure 8.8 The 74161 counter.

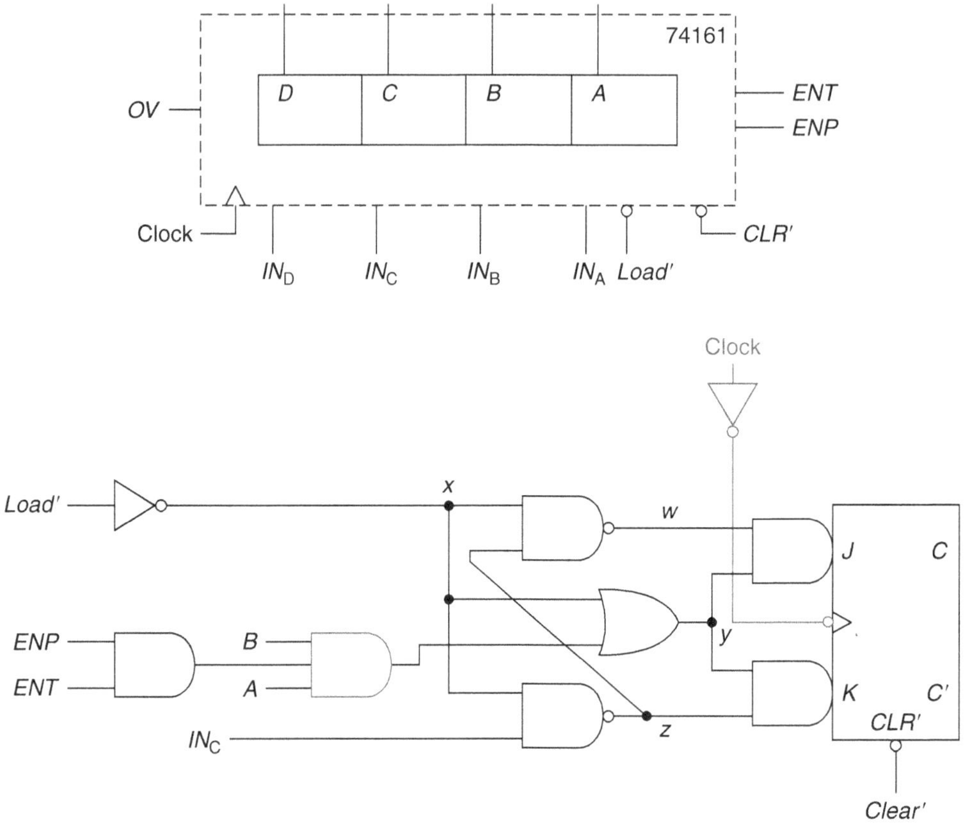

We could use two of these counters to count to 255 ($2^8 - 1$) or three to count to 4095 ($2^{12} - 1$). The block diagram of Figure 8.9 illustrates the 8-bit counter, where no parallel load inputs are shown.

If the counter is cleared initially, only the low-order counter (the one on the right) is enabled for the first 15 clocks. When that counter reaches

Figure 8.9 8-bit counter.

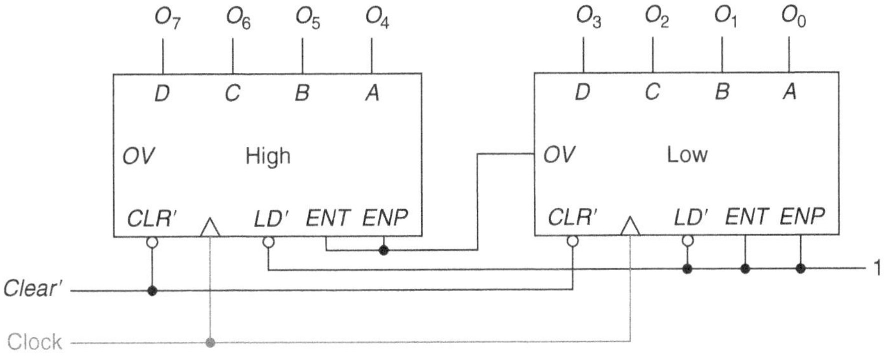

15 (1111), the overflow output (OV) becomes 1. That enables the second counter. On the next clock, the right counter goes to 0 (returning OV to 0) and the left counter increases by 1. (Thus, the count reaches 16.) Only the low-order counter increments on the next 15 clocks, as the count reaches 31. On the 32nd clock, the high-order counter is enabled again.

EXAMPLE 8.2

If we wanted to count through a number of states other than a power of 16, we would need to reset the counter when we reached the desired maximum. Since the 74161 counter has a static clear (similar to the asynchronous counter example in Example 7.9), we must count one beyond the desired maximum and use that to clear the counter. We will thus reach the extra state for a brief time (before the clear is effective), but that is well before the next clock time. For example, the counter of Figure 8.9 could be used to count through 120 states (0 to 119) by adding the NAND gate shown to clear it when it reaches 120 (01111000).

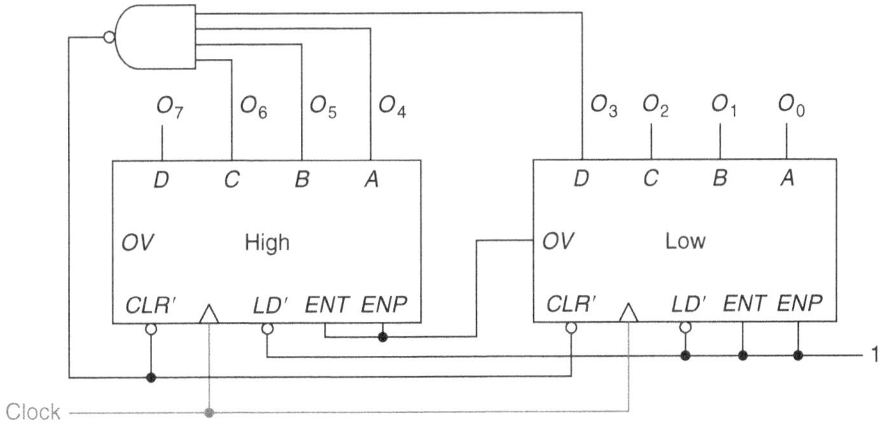

We do not need to AND O_2', O_1', O_0', or O_7', since we never reach a count over 120, and thus these are never 1 when O_6, O_5, O_4, and O_3 are all 1.

EXAMPLE 8.3

The 74163 is similar to the 74161, except that the clear is clocked. The internal structure of the circuit is modified so that an active clear input loads a 0 into each flip flop on the clock. To use it in a 120 state counter, we need to detect 119 and reset it on the next clock pulse, as shown below. The advantage of this approach is that there is no period (not even a short one) where the counter reaches 120.

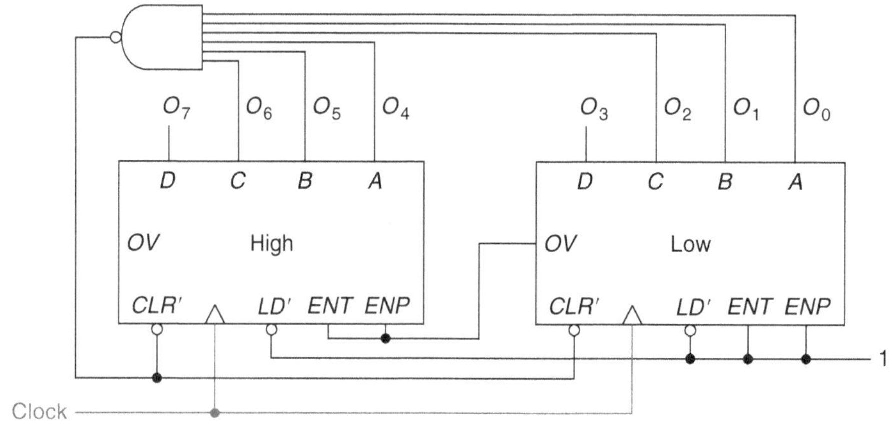

There are decade counters (counting 0 to 9) similar to the two binary counters we just described (74160 with a static clear and 74162 with a clocked clear).

There are both binary (74191 and 74193) and decade (74190 and 74192) up/down counters. The first of each type has a single clock input and a Down/Up′ input (where a 1 indicates down and a 0 indicates up). The second has two separate clock inputs, one for counting down and the other for counting up; one of those must be a logic 1 for the other to work. All of these have static load inputs. Bit *C* of the 74191 binary counter is shown in Figure 8.10. When *Load*′ is 0, the preset input is low

Figure 8.10 Typical bit of the 74191 Down/Up′ counter.

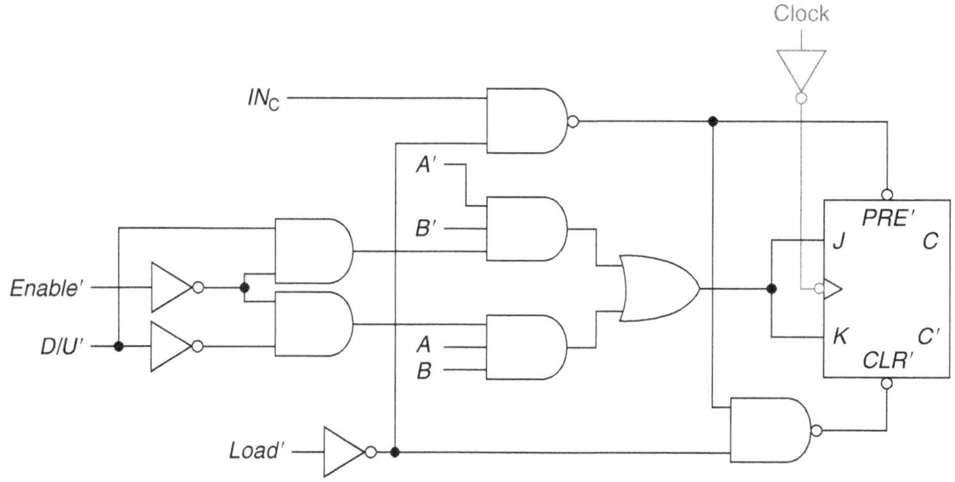

(active) if IN_C is 1 and the clear input is low (active) if IN_C is 0. (There is no clear input to the counter; that is accomplished by loading 0 into each bit.) If *Load'* is 1, then both preset and clear are 1 (inactive) and the clock controls the counter. Note that *J* and *K* are *B A* when counting up and *B' A'* when counting down.

A block diagram and a truth table for the 74191 counter are shown in Figure 8.11.

Figure 8.11 The 74191 Down/Up′ counter.

LD′	*EN′*	*D/U′*	
0	X	X	Static load
1	1	X	Do nothing
1	0	0	Clocked count up
1	0	1	Clocked count down

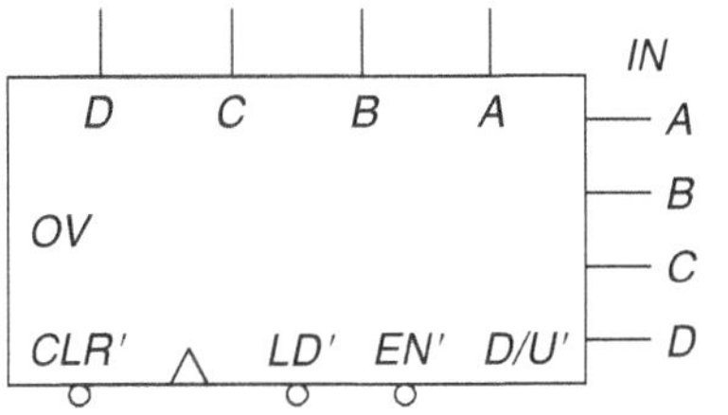

The final group of counter we will discuss are asynchronous counters

7490 Base 10 (2 × 5)
7492 Base 12 (2 × 6)
7493 Base 16 (2 × 8)

Each of these is trailing-edge triggered and consists of a single flip flop and then a 3-bit counter (base 5, 6, and 8, respectively). The output from the single flip flop must be externally connected to the clock of the 3-bit counter to achieve the full count. Each has two static clear inputs, both of which must be 1 to clear all four flip flops. The decade counter also has a pair of static set inputs, which (when both are 1) sets the counter to 9 (1001); the set overrides the clear.

A simplified block diagram of the 7493 is shown in Figure 8.12.

Figure 8.12 7493 asynchronous binary counter.

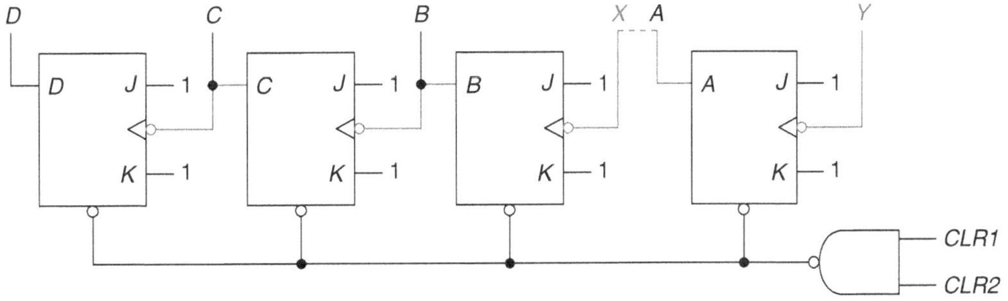

Note that to count to 8, the clock is connected to point *X*, and the outputs are from *D*, *C*, and *B*. To count to 16, the clock is connected to point *Y*, and points *A* and *X* must be connected (externally from the integrated circuit, as shown dashed).

EXAMPLE 8.4

We will now look at four solutions, each using a binary counter, to the following problem:

> Design a system the output of which is a clock pulse for every ninth input clock pulse.

For this, the counter must go through nine states. The output is obtained by ANDing the clock with a circuit that detects any one of the nine states. One solution is to have the counter sequence

0 1 2 3 4 5 6 7 8 0 . . .

If we use a 74163, which has a clocked clear, the circuit is

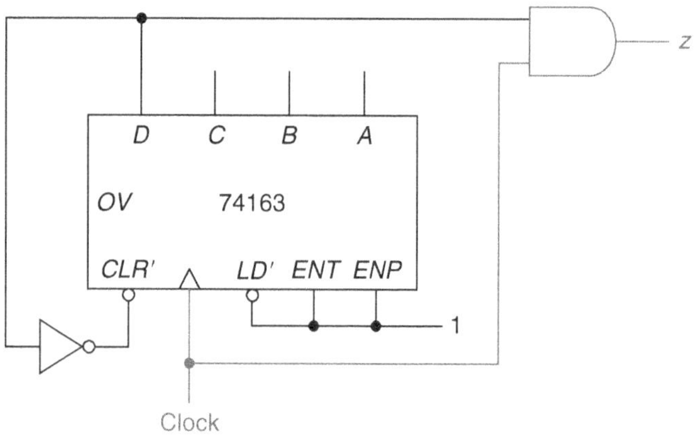

D is only 1 in state 8; thus it can be used to reset the counter to 0 and for the output.

If we use a 74161 with a static clear, then we must count to 9 before clearing it, as shown below.

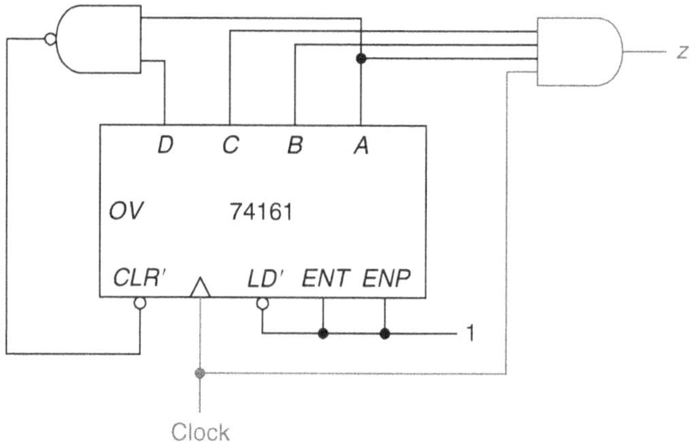

It will remain in state 9 for a short time (depending on the delays in the circuit). We cannot not use the same output circuit, because we would get a short output pulse at the beginning of state 9 (as well as the one in state 8), as shown in the timing diagram below. Instead, we made the output 1 when the counter was at 7.

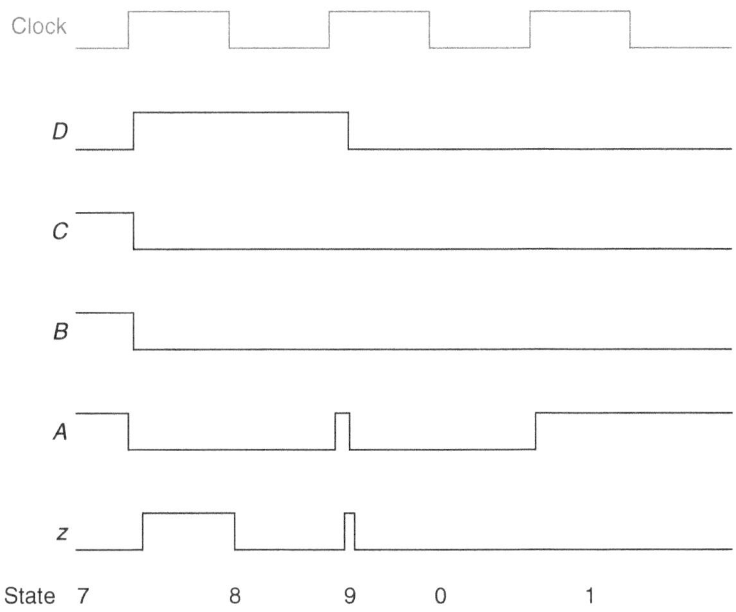

Another approach to this problem, using the first counter (74163), is to count

8 9 10 11 12 13 14 15 0 8 . . .

As before, this counter cycles through 9 states. When the count reaches 0, we load an 8 into the counter. Since the load is synchronous, this occurs on the next clock pulse. The output can be coincident with the time we are in state 0 (or any other state). This results in the following circuit, where the load inputs, IN_D, IN_C, IN_B, and IN_A, are shown down the right side of the block. The only state for which $D = 0$ is state 0; thus, the load is activated in that state and the output coincides with the clock pulse during that state.

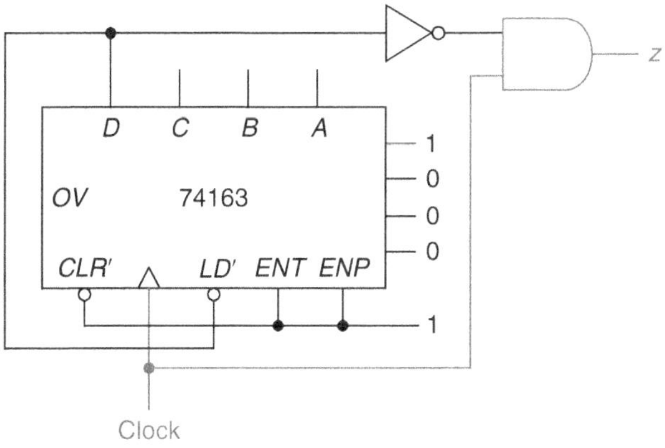

Finally, with the 74163, we could implement this to count the sequence

7 8 9 10 11 12 13 14 15 7 . . .

using the *OV* output. Since that indicates when the count is 15, we can invert it to create an active low load signal and connect 0111 to the parallel input lines, as shown below.

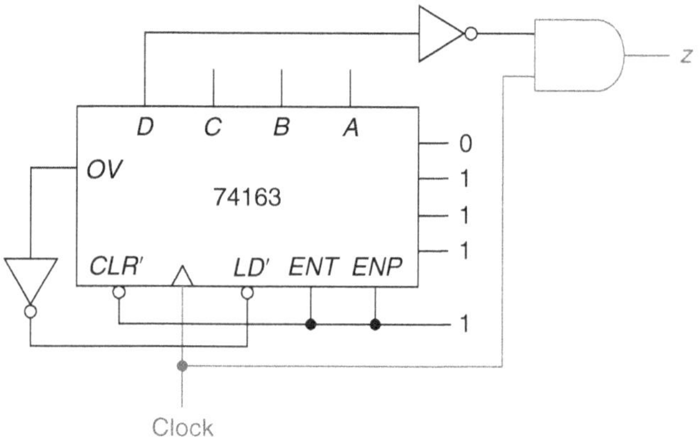

[SP 3, 4b; EX 3, 4a, 5, 6; LAB]

8.3 PROGRAMMABLE LOGIC DEVICES (PLDs)

Since a sequential system consists of a combination of memory and combinational logic, one approach to its implementation is to use a PAL (or other logic array described in Chapter 5) and some flip flops (for the memory). There are a variety of devices that combine a PAL and some *D* flip flops. One family of these devices is the 16R8,* 16R6, and 16R4. A simplified schematic of a portion of the 16R4 is shown in Figure 8.13. There are eight external inputs (two of which are shown). The *registered* outputs (all eight in the 16R8 and four in the 16R4) come from a flip flop, driven by a PAL (as shown for the first two outputs in Figure 8.13). Each PAL has eight AND gates (four of which are shown). There is a common clock and a common (active low) output enable, providing active low flip flop outputs (since the three-state gate inverts). Note that Q' is fed back to the AND array; but, it is then provided both uncomplemented and

*The 16 is the number of inputs to the AND array, the R indicates that at least some of the outputs are registered, that is, come from flip flops, and the 8 is the number of flip flops.

Figure 8.13 A PLD.

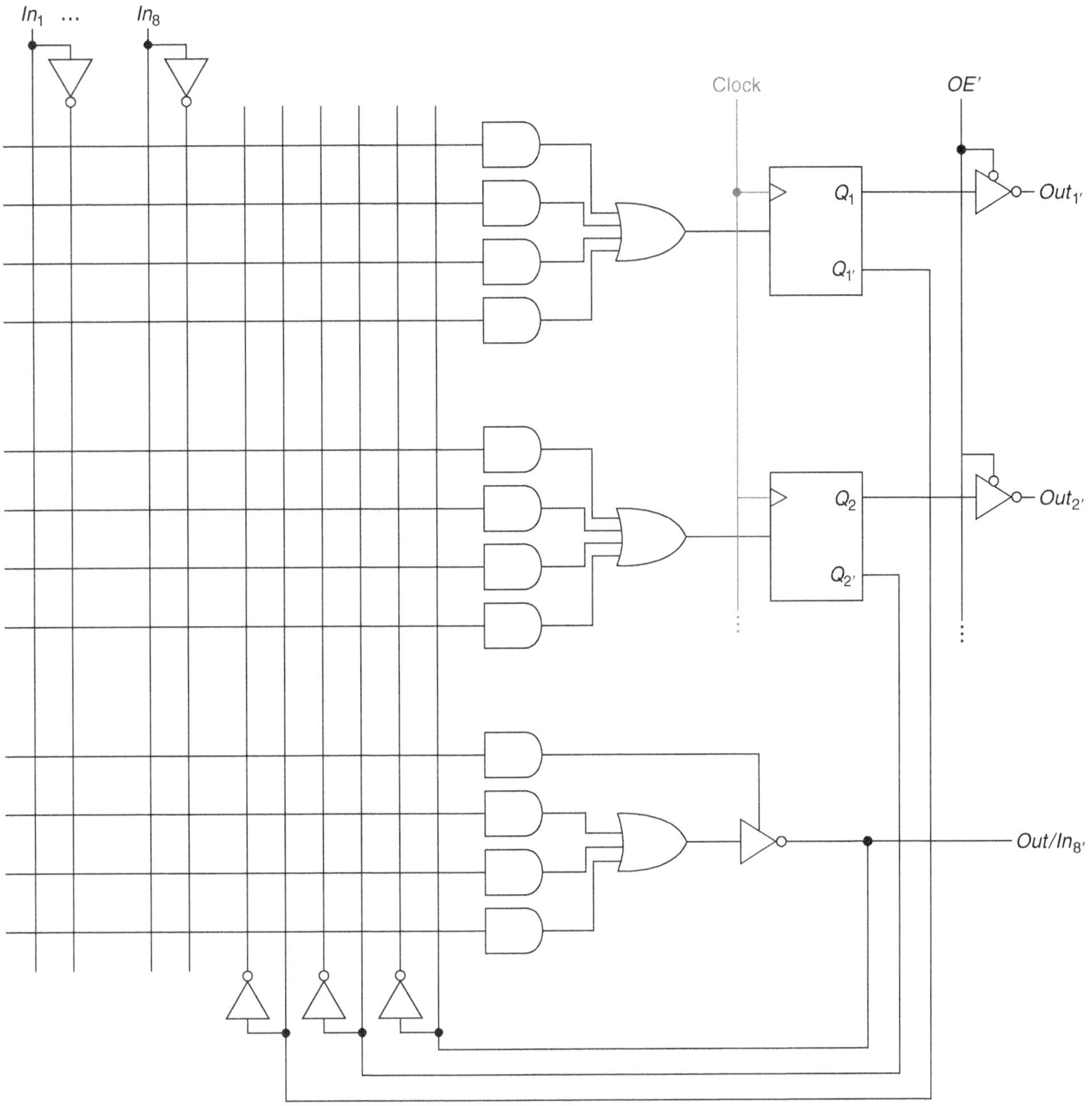

complemented, just as are the external AND array inputs. Thus, all the inputs to the combinational logic are available both uncomplemented and complemented.

This 16R8, by itself, is sufficient to implement only those sequential systems whose output is the state of the flip flops, such as counters.

Those outputs that are not registered (as shown in the bottom of Figure 8.13) are enabled by one of the AND gates (and the PAL has only seven terms). If it is not enabled, that pin can be used as an additional input (making as many as 12 inputs for the 16R4).

EXAMPLE 8.5

As an example, we will look at the design of the up/down counter from Example 7.8, where we have added two outputs, *F* and *G*, where *F* indicates that the counter is saturated and *G* indicates that the counter is recycling (that is, going from 3 back to 0 or from 0 back to 3). The state table is shown below.

	$A^\star B^\star$				*F G*			
A B	***xy* = 00**	***xy* = 01**	***xy* = 10**	***xy* = 11**	***xy* = 00**	***xy* = 01**	***xy* = 10**	***xy* = 11**
0 0	0 1	0 1	1 1	0 0	0 0	0 0	0 1	1 0
0 1	1 0	1 0	0 0	0 0	0 0	0 0	0 0	0 0
1 0	1 1	1 1	0 1	0 1	0 0	0 0	0 0	0 0
1 1	0 0	1 1	1 0	1 0	0 1	1 0	0 0	0 0

We developed the following equations for the *D* inputs in Example 7.8:

$$D_A = x'A'B + x'AB' + x'yA + xAB + xy'A'B'$$
$$D_B = x'yA + AB' + x'B' + y'B'$$

(There is no point in considering sharing, since the PAL does not permit it.) We can obtain the output equations from the state table (or we could construct maps):

$$F = x'yAB + xyA'B'$$
$$G = x'y'AB + xy'A'B'$$

A block diagram of that PAL, with only the gates that are used included, is shown next. Note that we did not show the output gates for the flip flops. We used five of the eight input lines (including one for a 1 to enable the two outputs). We used only two of the flip flops. This could be implemented with either a 16R6 or a 16R4.

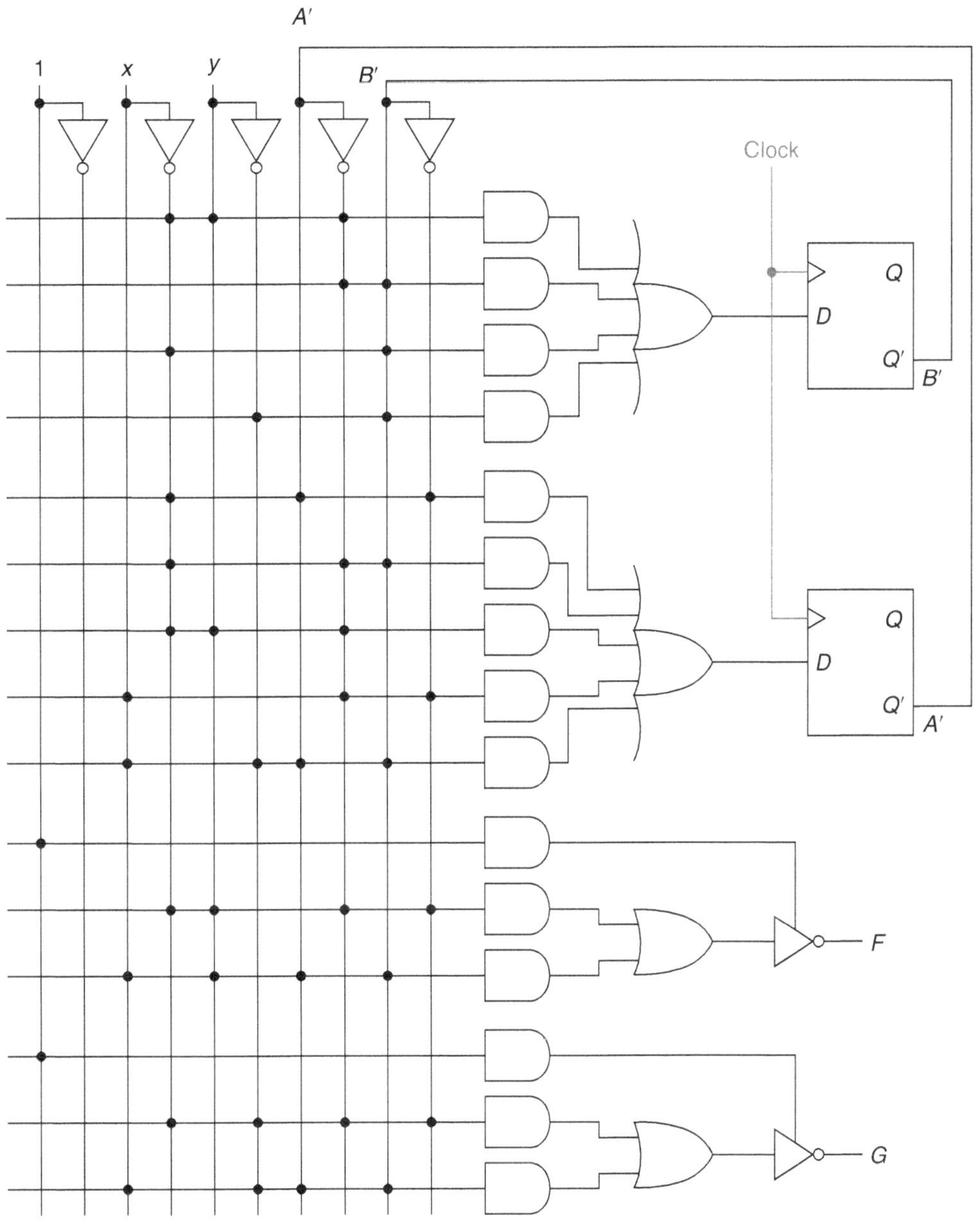

The PLDs we have described are useful for relatively small circuits—typically no more than a total of 32 inputs and outputs. Although it would theoretically be possible to build them much larger, other approaches are used.

A *complex programmable logic device* (CPLD)* incorporates an array of PLD-like blocks and a programmable interconnection network. Commercially available CPLDs have as many as a few hundred PLD blocks.

For larger circuits, *field programmable gate arrays* (FPGA) are used. Rather than containing PALs, FPGAs have as their basic building block a general purpose logic generator (typically three to five variables), with multiplexers and a flip flop. These blocks are connected by a programmable routing network, which also connects to input/output blocks. The logic generator is effectively a *lookup table* (LUT), often with a flip flop. A three-variable LUT is shown in Figure 8.14, with a flip flop that may be bypassed if Control is 0. Each cell can be programmed to a 0 or a 1; thus, any three-variable function can be created.

Figure 8.14 A three-input lookup table.

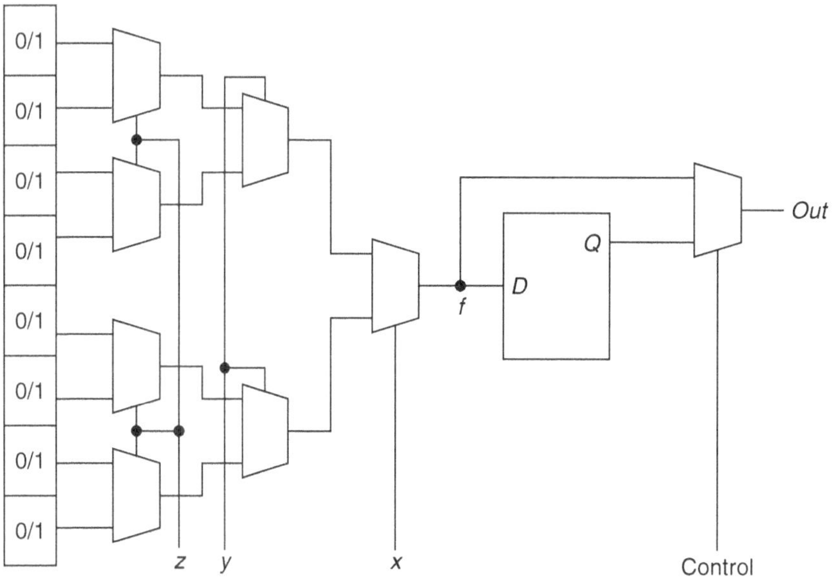

If, for example, the cells are programmed to 0, 0, 0, 1, 0, 0, 1, 1, then the function represented is $f = x'yz + xyz' + xyz = yz + xy$. To illustrate the interconnection network, Figure 8.15 shows an implementation of the function

$$f = x_1x_2' + x_2x_3$$

using two-input LUTs. The brown input/output connectors, connections (X), and LUTs are active. All of the others are inactive. One LUT produces $f_1 = x_1x_2'$, the second produces $f_2 = x_2x_3$, and the third produces $f = f_1 + f_2$.

*For a more complete discussion of CPLDs and FPGAs, see Brown and Vranesic, *Fundamentals of Digital Logic with VHDL Design*, 3rd ed., McGraw-Hill, 2009.

Figure 8.15 A section of a programmed FPGA.

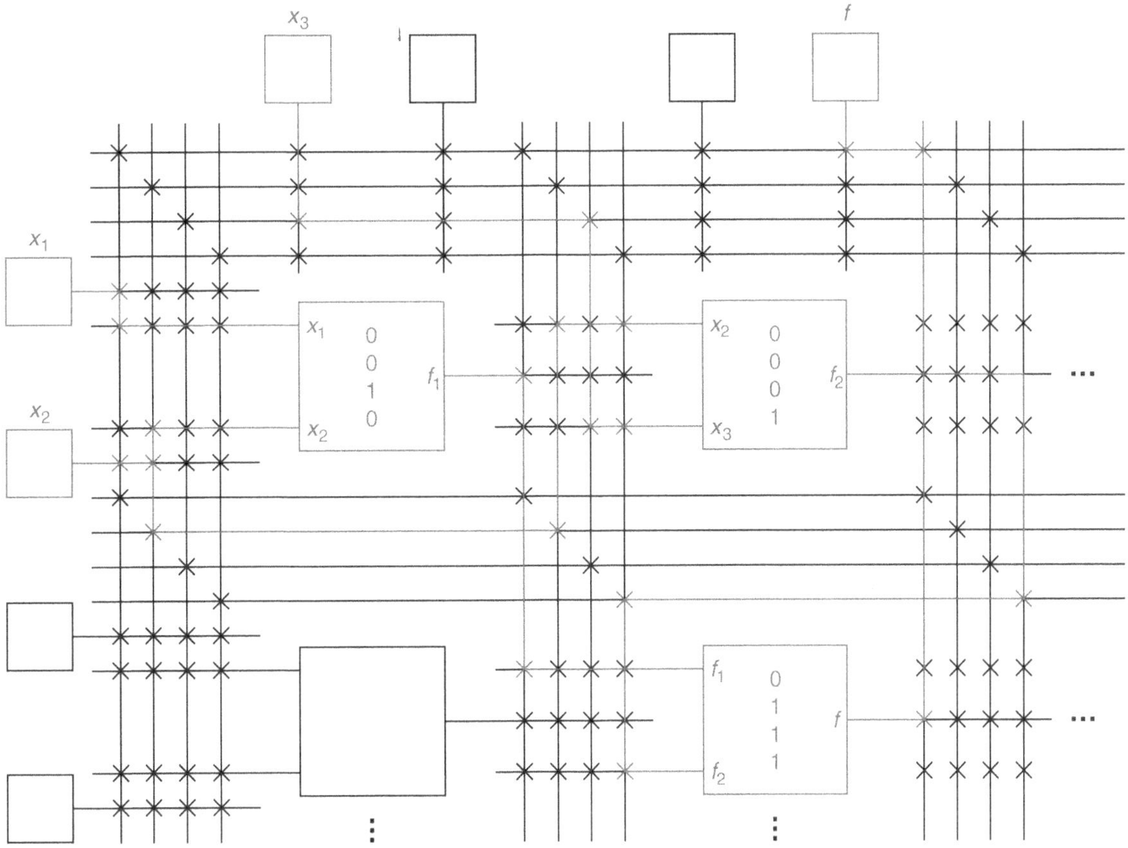

[SP 5]

8.4 DESIGN USING ASM DIAGRAMS

As we indicated in Chapter 6, the term state machine, also called finite state machine or *algorithmic state machine (ASM)* is the same as *sequential system.* A tool that is a cross between a state diagram and a flow chart is the ASM diagram (sometimes referred to as an ASM chart). We will first describe the basic elements and compare its structure to that of a state diagram. Then, we will apply this tool to a controller for a small system of registers (the place where this tool is most useful).

There are three types of blocks in an ASM diagram. The first is the state box. It is a rectangle, with one entry point and one exit point, as shown in Figure 8.16a.

The name of the state is shown above the box, and the output(s) corresponding to that state is shown in the box. (This is a Moore type output, one that occurs whenever the system is in that state. We will see how to indicate a Mealy output shortly.) When an output is listed, it indicates that the output is 1; any output not listed is 0.

The second type of box is the decision box, as shown in Figure 8.16b, which allows a two-way branch based on a switching expression.

Figure 8.16a State box.

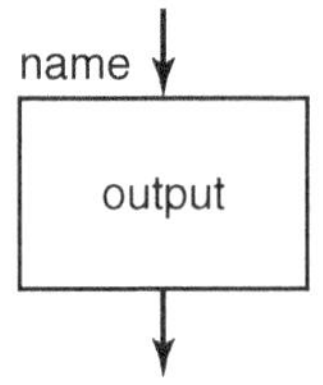

Figure 8.16b Decision box.

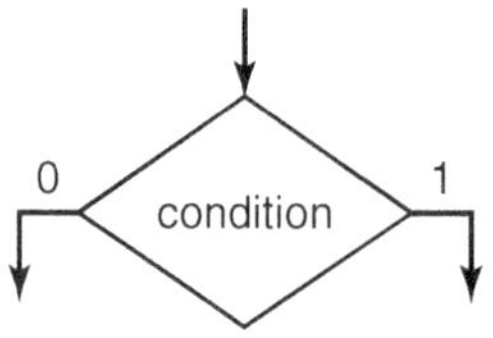

Figure 8.16c Mealy output box.

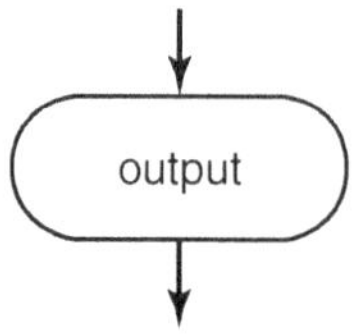

It has one entry point and two exit points, one corresponding to the expression equal to 0, the other corresponding to a 1. If more than a two-way branch is needed, the exit of a decision box can go to the entry of another decision box.

The third type of box is the conditional output box (Figure 8.16c). It has one entry and one exit. It specifies the output that occurs when that state transition takes place. (It is the Mealy output.)

An ASM block consists of the state box and all the decision boxes and conditional output boxes connected to it. There is one entry to the block, but there may be one or more exits; each of these goes to the entry of a state box.

There is no symbol for a merge point; two or more exit paths may go to the same entry point, as will be seen in some examples below. A typical ASM block (associated with state A) is shown in Figure 8.17. The output, z, of this system is 1 when the system is in state A and the input, x, is 1. The system goes to state B when $x = 1$, and back to state A when $x = 0$.

Figure 8.17 An ASM block.

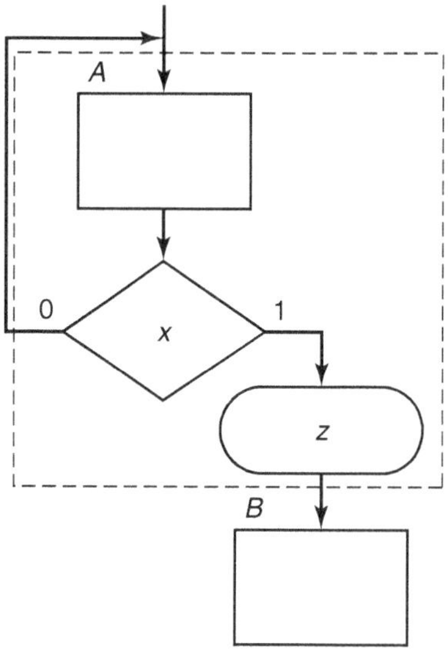

We will now look at the ASM diagram for the Moore system with an output of 1 iff the input has been 1 for at least three consecutive clocks (as first presented in Section 6.1). The state diagram is shown first in Figure 8.18 and then the corresponding ASM diagram.

Figure 8.18 Moore state diagram and ASM diagram.

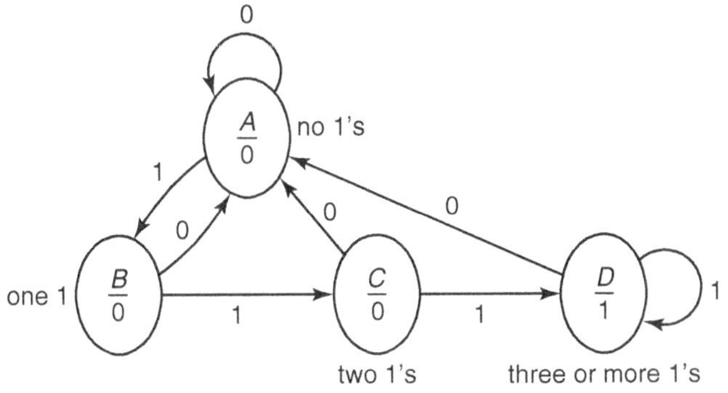

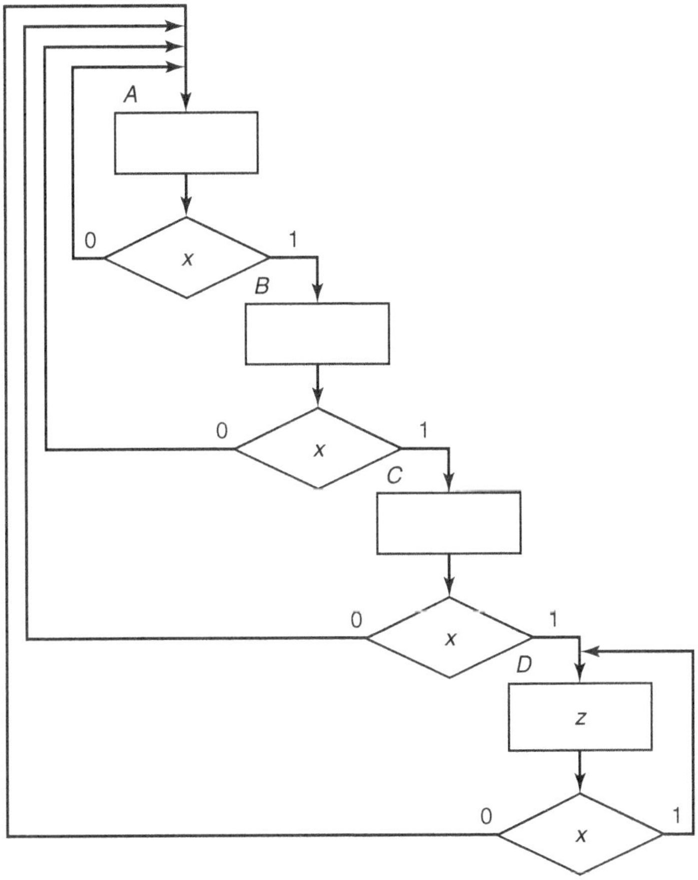

For the similar Mealy problem, with one input, x, and one output, z, such that $z = 1$ iff x has been 1 for three consecutive clock times, the state diagram (Figure 7.13) and the corresponding ASM diagram is shown in Figure 8.19. Note that the state assignment may be shown to the right of the state name, outside the state box.

Figure 8.19 Mealy state diagram and ASM diagram.

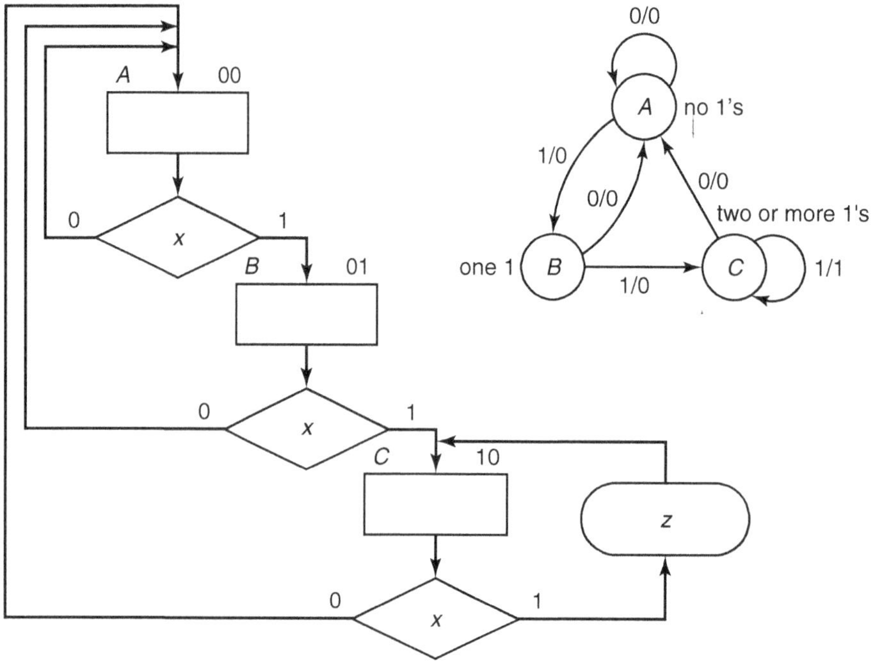

EXAMPLE 8.6

Finally, we will look at the design for a controller for a serial adder. The numbers are each stored in an 8-bit register (with shifting capability), and the answer is returned to one of those registers, as shown in the diagram below (a simplified version of this is given in Experiment 24). We will assume that the two operands are already loaded into registers *A* and *B*.

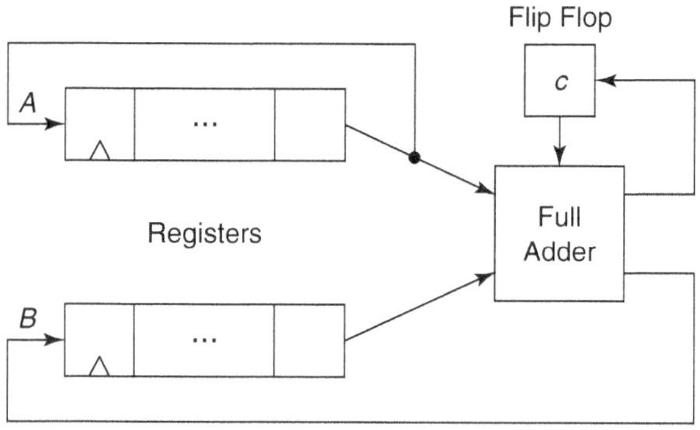

A signal of 1 on line *s* indicates that the system is to start the addition process. A 1 (for one clock period) on line *d* indicates that it is done. An ASM diagram for a controller for this system follows. The bits of the register are numbered 7 (left, most significant) to 0. Bits 0 of the numbers and the carry (*c*) are added, and the result is loaded into the left bit (bit 7) of *B* as both registers are shifted to the right.

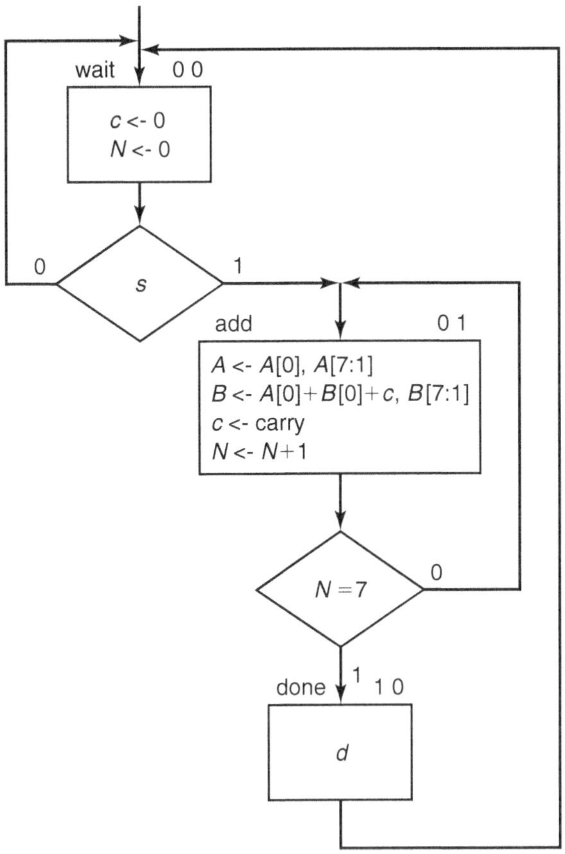

This controller can be implemented by a sequential machine with three states. It requires a 3-bit register, N, and an incrementer to count through the eight add/shift steps. This controller goes from state 00 to state 01 when $s = 1$ (and remains in state 00, otherwise). It goes from state 01 to 10 when register N contains three 1's (and returns to state 01, otherwise). It always goes from state 10 to 00 on the next clock. The design of the sequential circuit is left as an exercise.

[SP 6; EX 7, 8]

8.5 ONE-HOT ENCODING

Up until now, we have encoded states using the minimum number of flip flops. Another approach, particularly simple when designing from an ASM diagram, is to use one flip flop for each state. That flip flop is 1 (or *hot*) and all others are 0 when the system is in that state.

For the Moore system of Figure 8.18, we have four states and would thus have four flip flops. If we labeled them A, B, C, and D, we can see by inspection that

$$A^{\star} = x'(A + B + C + D) = x'$$

(since one of the state variables must be 1).

$$B^\star = x A$$

(since the condition box indicates that we go to state B when $x = 1$)

$$C^\star = x B$$
$$D^\star = x(C + D)$$

This produces very simple combinational logic for the next state (although the savings there is typically not adequate to make up for the cost of extra flip flops).

The output is 1 only when in state D; thus the output equation is

$$z = D$$

This approach is sometimes used in designing large controllers, where most states produce an output signal. As in the example above, the output signal comes directly from a flip flop, rather than from combinational logic that decodes the state.

8.6 VERILOG FOR SEQUENTIAL SYSTEMS*

In Section 5.7.1, we introduced Verilog constructs for combinational systems. Here, we will give examples of the use of Verilog for sequential systems.

We will now look at the structural model for a trailing-edge triggered D flip flop with an active low input, CLR' in Figure 8.20.

Figure 8.20 Structural model of a *D* flip flop.

```
module D_ff (q, ck, D, CLR);
     input ck, D, CLR;
     output q;
     reg q;
     always @ (negedge ck or negedge CLR)
          begin
               if (!CLR)
                    q <= 0;
               else
                    q <= D;
          end
endmodule
```

*For a detailed discussion of Verilog, see Brown and Vranesic, *Fundamentals of Digital Logic with Verilog Design*, 2nd ed., McGraw-Hill, 2008, or for VHDL, see Brown and Vranesic, *Fundamentals of Digital Logic with VHDL Design*, 3rd ed., McGraw-Hill, 2009.

Note that q is referred to as a register (reg) rather than a wire, since it is storage. The symbol @ indicates the time when the following steps are executed. Only on the trailing edge (negedge) of the clock or the CLR input will anything happen. The symbol ! indicates *not*, and the arrowed equal (<=) is used to indicate time dependence. In the combinational models, an equal sign (=) was used since it did not matter in what order things happened.

We can use the flip flop we just described to build an 8-bit trailing-edge triggered shift register (shift right), as shown in Figure 8.21a.

Figure 8.21a Shift register using flip flop module.

```
module shift (Q, x, ck, CLR);
     input x, clock, CLR;
     output [7:0]Q;
     wire [7:0]Q;
     D_ff Stage 7 (Q[7], x, ck, CLR);
     D_ff Stage 6 (Q[6], Q[7], ck, CLR);
     D_ff Stage 5 (Q[5], Q[6], ck, CLR);
     D_ff Stage 4 (Q[4], Q[5], ck, CLR);
     D_ff Stage 3 (Q[3], Q[4], ck, CLR);
     D_ff Stage 2 (Q[2], Q[3], ck, CLR);
     D_ff Stage 1 (Q[1], Q[2], ck, CLR);
     D_ff Stage 0 (Q[0], Q[1], ck, CLR);
endmodule
```

Another approach is to define the shift register in a single module.

Figure 8.21b Single module shifter.

```
module shift (Q, x, ck, CLR);
     input x, clock, CLR;
     output [7:0]Q;
     wire [7:0]Q;
     reg [7:0]Q;
always (@ negedge ck)
     begin
          Q[0] <= Q[1];
          Q[1] <= Q[2];
          Q[2] <= Q[3];
          Q[3] <= Q[4];
          Q[4] <= Q[5];
          Q[5] <= Q[6];
          Q[6] <= Q[7];
          Q[7] <= x;
     end
endmodule
```

8.7 DESIGN OF A VERY SIMPLE COMPUTER

In this section, we will look at the design of an overly simplified computer. It includes a memory of 256 (2^8) registers often just referred to as *words*, 12 bits each, and a rudimentary instruction set. Although this computer will not solve any real problems, there is enough capability to understand the basic process of executing a set of instructions.

The memory* stores both instructions and data. To read from it, the address of the register (an 8-bit number) is connected to the set of eight input lines, $A_0, \ldots, A_7$, and a 0 is placed on line r'/w. The contents of that register are available on the 12-bit bus, $D_0, \ldots, D_{11}$. To write to it, the register address is connected to A, the data to be stored to D, and the line r'/w is made 1.

There are two 12-bit user addressable registers, B and C. In addition, there are a few internal registers needed to implement the machine:

R—a 12-bit register to hold the instruction while it is being decoded and executed
P—an 8-bit register to keep track of the address of the next instruction
T—a 12-bit register to temporarily hold data

Each instruction fits into one word, and has the following format:

0 1	2	3	4 … 11
OP	*N*	*M*	*Address*

where *OP* specifies one of four operations, *N* indicates one of two internal registers, and *M* specifies (with *Address*) how the effective address (the actual location in memory) is computed.

Two addressing modes are included—direct ($M = 0$), where *Address* is the effective address, and indirect ($M = 1$), where *Address* contains the memory location where the effective address is found (in the right 8 bits).

The four instructions are

00 Load register (from the memory location)
01 Store register (in the memory location)
10 Add the number from memory to the one in the register
11 Jump to (get next instruction from) the location

To execute a sequence of instructions, the computer follows this step-by-step procedure (returning to step 1 after completing each instruction):

*More information about memory design can be found in Marcovitz, Alan B., *Introduction to Logic and Computer Design*, McGraw-Hill, 2008.

1. Send the address of the instruction (from the *Program Counter*, *P* in what follows) to memory to fetch the instruction. Save that word in an internal register of the CPU, sometimes called the *Instruction Register*, *I*, in the description that follows.
2. Update the Program Counter so that it points to the (first word of the) next instruction.
3. Decode the instruction, that is, determine what operation is to be performed and what operands, if any, are needed.
4. Obtain the operands. Some may be in registers and others in memory. In the latter case, the address may need to be computed and the data fetched from memory into a CPU register.
5. Execute the instruction, that is, do the computation (if any) required.
6. Store the result, if any, either in memory or in a register. (For jump instructions, the result may be the address of the next instruction to be stored in the Program Counter.)

An ASM diagram for the controller of this computer is shown in Figure 8.22. Rather than showing output boxes, we have labeled each state box with the steps that are to be performed. In the first step, the program counter (which contains the address of the instruction about to be executed) is connected to the address input and the instruction is read into *I*. If I_3 is 1, this is indirect addressing, and the right 8 bits of *I* are replaced by the contents of the memory location. The Program Counter, *P*, is incremented to point to the next instruction, and, based on I_1, the flow branches. To the left, we read data from memory into the temporary register, *T*. For Load, it is moved to the appropriate register; for Add, *T* is added* to either register *B* or *C*. For the right branch, *P* is changed to the address portion of *I* for a jump. For store, the appropriate register is connected to *D*, the address to *A*, and r'/w is made 1 (to write the data into memory).

This controller implies that the bus *D* has inputs from memory and registers *B* and *C*. Its contents can be clocked into registers *I* (or the right 8 bits of *I*) and *T*. There is a 12-bit adder, with neither a carry-in nor a carry-out, that takes one input from *T* and the other either from *B* or *C* (implying a multiplexer on the second input). The internal transfers implied are from the right 8 bits of *I* to *P*, and from *T* to *B* and *C*.

The state boxes in the ASM diagram have been numbered, and we then implemented the controller using a one-hot design (where each state corresponds to a 1 in just one of the flip flops) in Figure 8.23. The clock inputs have not been connected to the clock in that figure to make it more readable.

*We have used the notation ++ to indicate addition (as opposed to OR).

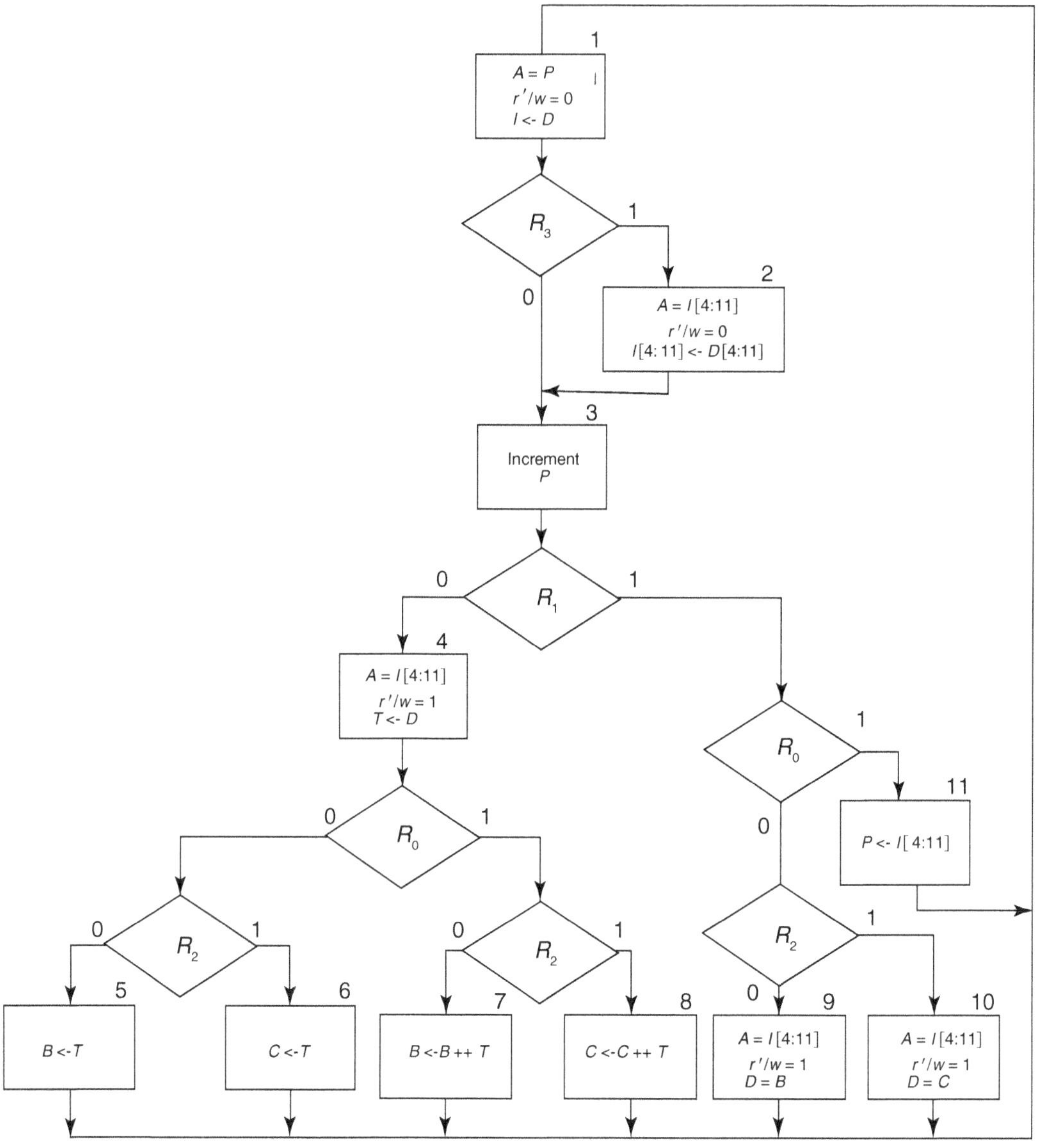

Figure 8.22 ASM diagram for very simple computer.

8.8 OTHER COMPLEX EXAMPLES

As the first example, consider the design of the following system:

> The system keeps track of how many consecutive 1 inputs occur on input line ***x*** and then, starting at the first time that the input ***x*** is 0, it outputs on line *z* that same number of 1's at consecutive clocks (*z* is 0 at all other times).

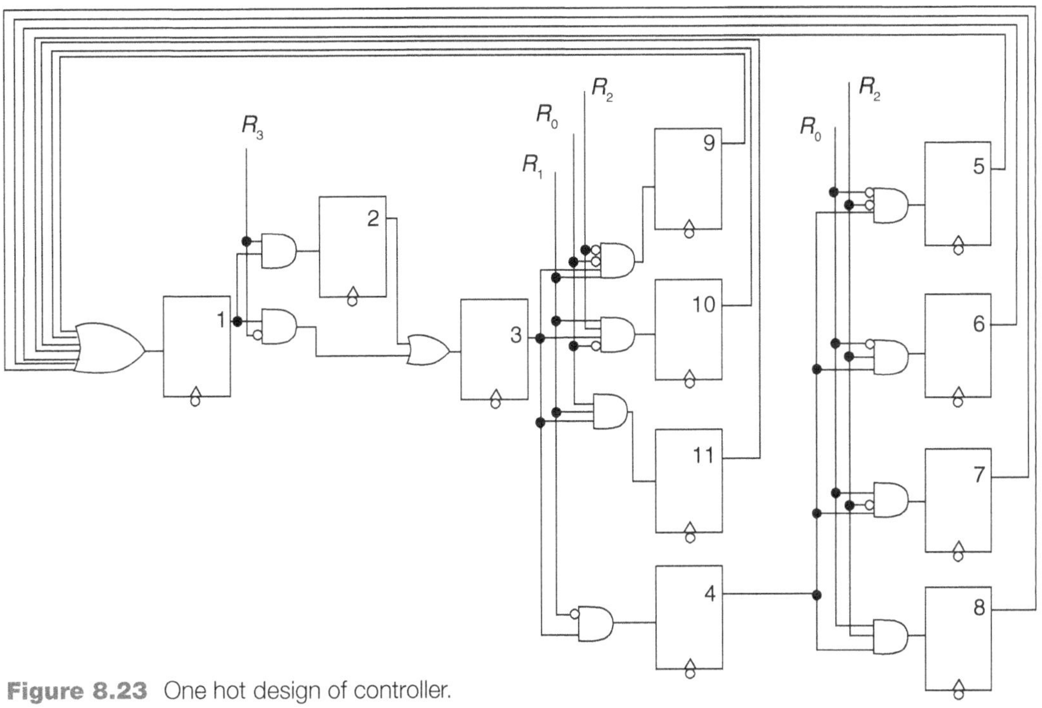

Figure 8.23 One hot design of controller.

A sample timing trace of the input and output of such a system is shown in Trace 8.2.

Trace 8.2

x	0 0 0 1 0 0 0 0 1 1 1 1 0 0 0 0 0 0 0 1 1 0 0 0
z	0 0 0 0 1 0 0 0 0 0 0 0 1 1 1 1 0 0 0 0 0 1 1 0

We will first assume that the available components are AND, OR, and NOT gates, a *JK* flip flop and a 74191 up/down counter with four outputs, labeled *D*, *C*, *B*, *A* (with *D* the high-order output). We will use the counter to count the number of consecutive 1's (counting up) and then count down to 0 as the 1's are output.

We will first look at the simplest solution and then examine the assumptions that must be made for this to be valid. We will then add circuitry so as to make the system work for a more general case. The circuit of Figure 8.24 is our first attempt at a solution. No clear was provided. Once the system produces its last 1 output, the counter will be left with 0 in it; so there is no need to clear it. When x is 1, the D/U' is set to 0, and the counter is enabled; thus, it counts up. When x returns to 0, it will count down, as long as it is enabled, that is, as long as there

Figure 8.24 A simple solution with a counter.

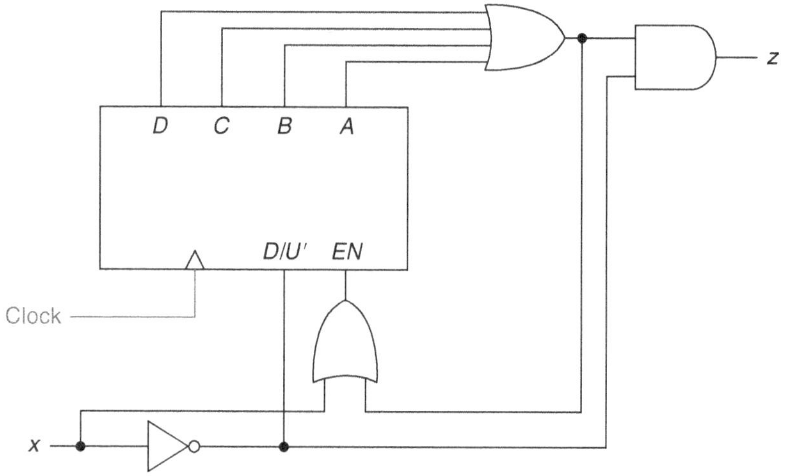

is a nonzero value in the counter. The output is 1 when x is 0 and there is a nonzero count. This solution works only if the count never exceeds 15, since on the 16th consecutive 1 input, the counter goes back to 0. If a larger number were required, we would need one or more additional counters so as to be able to count higher than 15. An alternative to that would be to limit the output to a maximum of 15 1's, even if the input included more than 15 consecutive 1's. In that case, we would disable the counter when we reached 15, if x remains 1. That would require the circuit of Figure 8.25.

Figure 8.25 Example with maximum of 16 outputs of 1.

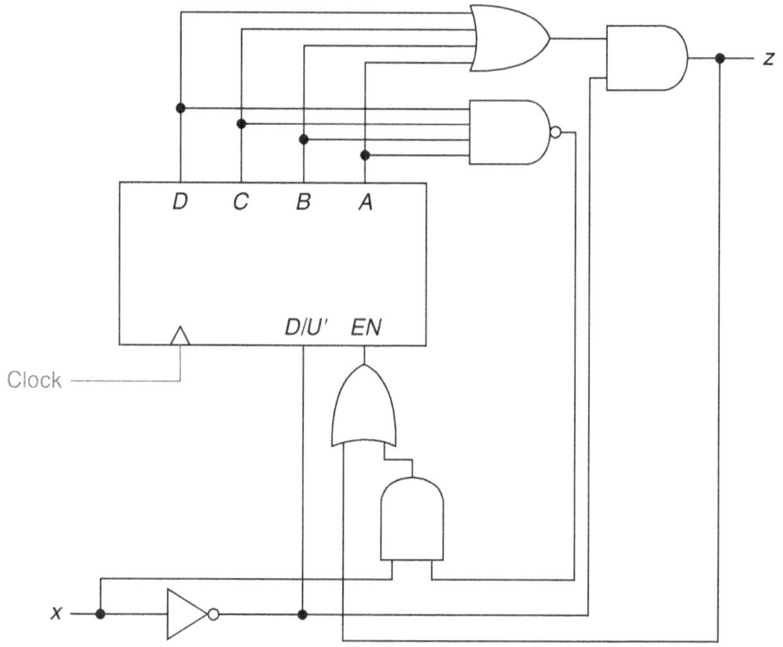

Now the counter is not enabled when the count is 15 (1111) and x is 1. Thus, if there are a large number of consecutive 1's, it will count to 15 and stop until x goes to 0; then it will count down, outputting fifteen 1's.

The other unstated assumption that we made was that x remains 0 until the 1 outputs are completed. That was the case in the sample trace. If that is not true, the counter will start counting up again as soon as x returns to 1 and the output will be 0. Assuming that we want to ignore the input until the 1 outputs are completed, we need a flip flop, Q, to keep track of when the system is counting down and we should ignore x. We must then consider the following possibilities.

$x = 0$	$Q = 0$	count = 0	$EN = 0$	$z = 0$	$D/U' = X$*	
$x = 0$	$Q = 0$	count = 1†	$EN = 1$	$z = 1$	$D/U' = 1$	
$x = 0$	$Q = 0$	count > 1	$EN = 1$	$z = 1$	$D/U' = 1$	$Q \leftarrow 1$
$x = 1$	$Q = 0$	count ≠ 15	$EN = 1$	$z = 0$	$D/U' = 0$	
$x = 1$	$Q = 0$	count = 15	$EN = 0$	$z = 0$	$D/U' = X$	
$x = X$‡	$Q = 1$	count > 1	$EN = 1$	$z = 1$	$D/U' = 1$	
$x = X$	$Q = 1$	count = 1	$EN = 1$	$z = 1$	$D/U' = 1$	$Q \leftarrow 0$

Flip flop Q will be turned on when x is 0 and the count is not 0 or 1, and it will be turned off when it is 1 and the output gets down to 1. Thus,

$$J = x'(D + C + B) \qquad K = D'C'B'A$$

The output is 1 when Q is 1 or when x is 0 and Q is 0 but the count is not 0. Thus,

$$z = Q + x'Q'(D + C + B + A) = Q + x'(D + C + B + A)$$

The counter is enabled when $x = 1$ and the count is not at 15 (as in the last example, to allow for more than 15 consecutive 1 inputs) or when $z = 1$. Thus,

$$EN = x(ABCD)' + z$$

*Since the counter is not enabled, it does not matter whether it is set to count up or down.

†If there is only one 1, that will cause the counter to increase to 1, but Q will not be set at the next clock time, since that is the last time the output is to be 1. The condition to set Q is just that the count is between 2 and 15, which yields, from the map, $D + C + B$.

‡When it is counting down (and the output is 1), the input is ignored; it does not matter.

Finally,

$$D/U' = Q + x'(D + C + B + A)$$

the same as z, since at the only places where they differ, D/U' is a don't care (since the counter is not enabled).

We will now look at the same example, utilizing shift registers instead of a counter. We need some right/left shift registers (more than 1 if we are to allow more than four consecutive 1 outputs). If we set the limit at 12, we could use three 74194 shift registers. They would be connected as shown in Figure 8.26, where the parallel inputs are not shown, since they are not used.

Figure 8.26 Circuit using three right/left shift registers.

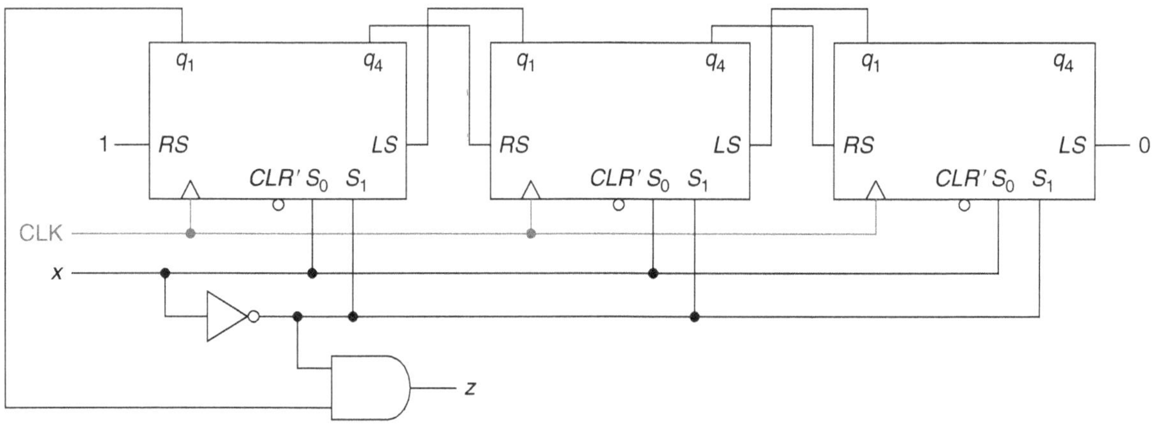

The three shift registers are connected to form one 12-bit shift register. When $x = 1$, $S_0 = 1$, and $S_1 = 0$, making the registers shift right. A 1 is shifted into the leftmost bit. When $x = 0$, the register shifts left, loading 0's from the right. After the input has been 0 for several clocks (or if the shift register is cleared), all bits will be 0. The output is 1 whenever there is a 1 in the left bit of the shift register and x is 0. Note that if there are more than 12 consecutive 1 inputs, the shift register will contain all 1's. When the input goes to 0, the output will be 1 for 12 clock times. Thus, this solution handles the situation where there are more 1 inputs than the register can hold (similar to the second counter design).

If the input could go to 1 again while the output is still 1, we need an extra flip flop, Q, here, as well. This flip flop is set ($J = 1$) when $x = 0$ and q_2 of the left shift register is 1 (indicating that there have been at least two 1's). It is cleared ($K = 1$) when q_2 is 0 (indicating that there are no more than one more 1 to be output). S_0 becomes xQ' and S_1 becomes $x' + Q$.

EXAMPLE 8.7

Design a counter that goes through the following sequence of 16 states

1 2 4 7 11 0 6 13 5 14 8 3 15 12 10 9, and repeat

It does not matter where it starts. For the combinational logic, there are packages of NAND gates (7400, 7404, 7410, 7420, and 7430) available at 50¢ each. We will consider two alternative designs and compare them. The first uses four *JK* flip flops at a total cost of $2.00. The second uses a 4-bit synchronous counter (such as the 74161) and a combinational decoder block. This block takes the output of the counter that goes 0, 1, 2, 3, 4, . . . and translates the 0 to 1, the 1 to 2, the 2 to 4, and so forth.

First, we will design the counter using *JK* flip flops. The state table is shown below.

D	**C**	**B**	**A**	$D^\star$	$C^\star$	$B^\star$	$A^\star$
0	0	0	0	0	1	1	0
0	0	0	1	0	0	1	0
0	0	1	0	0	1	0	0
0	0	1	1	1	1	1	1
0	1	0	0	0	1	1	1
0	1	0	1	1	1	1	0
0	1	1	0	1	1	0	1
0	1	1	1	1	0	1	1
1	0	0	0	0	0	1	1
1	0	0	1	0	0	0	1
1	0	1	0	1	0	0	1
1	0	1	1	0	0	0	0
1	1	0	0	1	0	1	0
1	1	0	1	0	1	0	1
1	1	1	0	1	0	0	0
1	1	1	1	1	1	0	0

We can map these functions and use the quick method to find the *JK* flip flop input equations, as shown next.

BA \ DC	00	01	11	10
00			1	
01		1		
11	1	1	1	
10		1	1	1

$D^\star$

BA \ DC	00	01	11	10
00	1	1		
01		1	1	
11	1		1	
10	1	1		

$C^\star$

BA \ DC	00	01	11	10
00	1	1	1	1
01	1	1		
11	1	1		
10				

$B^\star$

BA \ DC	00	01	11	10
00		1		1
01				1
11	1	1	1	
10		1		1

$A^\star$

$J_D = CA + CB + BA \qquad K_D = C'B' + C'A + B'A$

$J_C = D'A' + D'B \qquad K_C = DA' + D'BA$

$J_B = D' + A' \qquad K_B = D + A'$

$J_A = D'C + DC' \qquad K_C = D'B' + CB' + DC'B$

This would require 18 two-input gates and 5 three-input gates or a total of 7 integrated circuit packages at 50¢ each. Thus, the total cost is \$5.50.

For the other approach, we construct the following truth table for the decoder block:

D	*C*	*B*	*A*	*W*	*X*	*Y*	*Z*
0	0	0	0	0	0	0	1
0	0	0	1	0	0	1	0
0	0	1	0	0	1	0	0
0	0	1	1	0	1	1	1
0	1	0	0	1	0	1	1
0	1	0	1	0	0	0	0
0	1	1	0	0	1	1	0
0	1	1	1	1	1	0	1
1	0	0	0	0	1	0	1
1	0	0	1	1	1	1	0
1	0	1	0	1	0	0	0
1	0	1	1	0	0	1	1
1	1	0	0	1	1	1	1
1	1	0	1	1	1	0	0
1	1	1	0	1	0	1	0
1	1	1	1	1	0	0	1

The output maps are then shown below.

BA \ *DC*	00	01	11	10
00		1	1	
01			1	1
11		1	1	
10			1	1

W

BA \ *DC*	00	01	11	10
00			1	1
01			1	1
11	1	1		
10	1	1		

X

BA \ *DC*	00	01	11	10
00		1	1	
01	1			1
11	1			1
10		1	1	

Y

BA \ *DC*	00	01	11	10
00	1	1	1	1
01				
11	1	1	1	1
10				

Z

$W = CB'A' + DB'A + CBA + DBA'$

$X = DB' + D'B$

$Y = C'A + CA'$

$Z = B'A' + BA$

This requires 9 two-input gates, 4 three-input gates, and 1 four-input gate. In addition, we need four NOT gates (a 7404 package), since only the uncomplemented outputs from the counter (*D*, *C*, *B*, and *A*) are available.

The total required is six packages. Thus, this approach costs \$3.00 plus the cost of the counter and is less expensive if the counter costs less than \$2.50.

It is interesting to note that if we built the counter using four *JK* flip flops, we would only need to create the functions *BA* and *CBA*. That would require just two NOT gates, since $(BA)'$ and $(CBA)'$ are used in *W* and *Z*. Thus, we end up with only six packages and a total cost of \$5.00, which is less expensive than the first solution. This solution is best if the counter costs more than \$2.00.

[SP 5, 6; EX 6, 9, 10, 11, 12, 13, 14, 15; LAB]

8.9 SOLVED PROBLEMS

1. Design a Mealy system using a 74164 shift register and whatever gates are needed to produce an output of 1 when the last six inputs have been 1, and 0 otherwise.

The shift register stores the previous eight inputs; we only need the five most recent ones. The circuit is shown below.

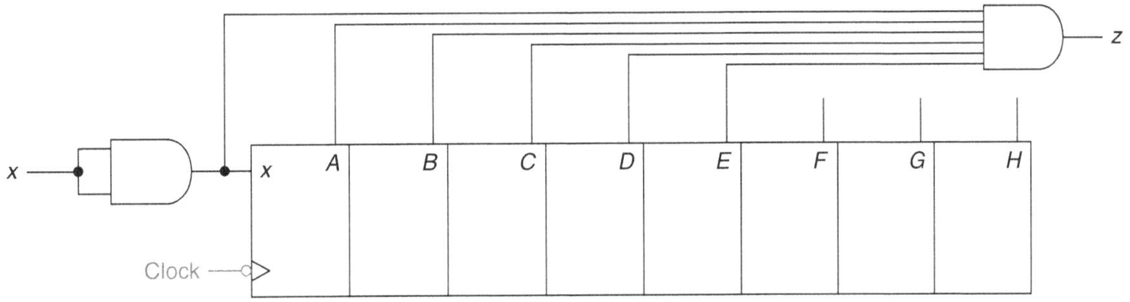

(We really only needed a 5-bit shift register, but it is easier and less expensive to use an 8-bit one than to build a 5-bit one with flip flops.)

2. Design a Moore circuit, using a 74164 shift register and AND, OR, and NOT gates to produce a 1 output for every eighth 1 input (not necessarily consecutive). We are not concerned about when the first output comes, as long as there is a 1 for every eight 1 inputs thereafter.

We will input a 1 to the shift register, clocking it only when the input is 1. When a 1 reaches the last flip flop, *H*, the shift register will be cleared. We can take the output from *G* (or from any of the first seven flip flops); it goes to 1 on the seventh 1 input and is cleared shortly after the eighth. A block diagram is as follows:

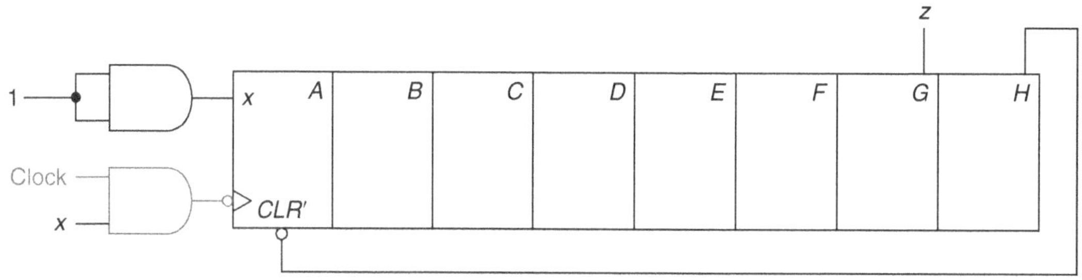

3. Design a Mealy system, using a 74161 counter and AND, OR, and NOT gates that produces a 1 output when the input has been 1 for at least 12 consecutive clock times.

The counter will be reset whenever the input is 0 and will be allowed to count when the input is 1 until the count reaches 11. At that point, if the input is 1, there will be a 1 output. A block diagram is shown below.

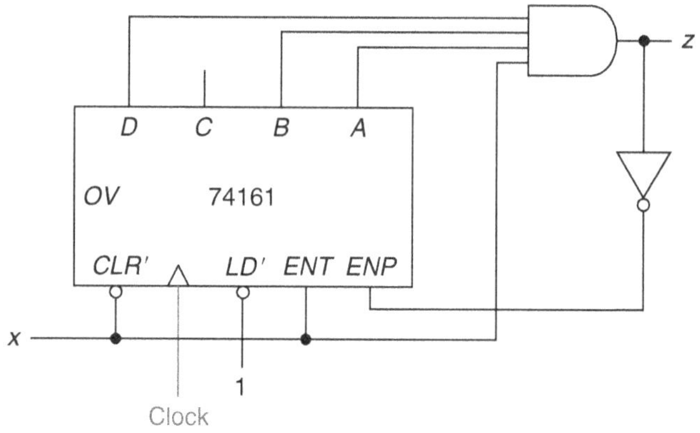

Note that the counter is enabled whenever $x = 1$ and the output is not already 1; that keeps it from counting beyond 11.

4. Design a system such that when the input, x, goes to 1 during one clock period, the output, z, will be the next eight consecutive clocks. z will be 0 at all other times. Assume that x remains 0 throughout the period of nonzero output. Show the block diagram.

Example:

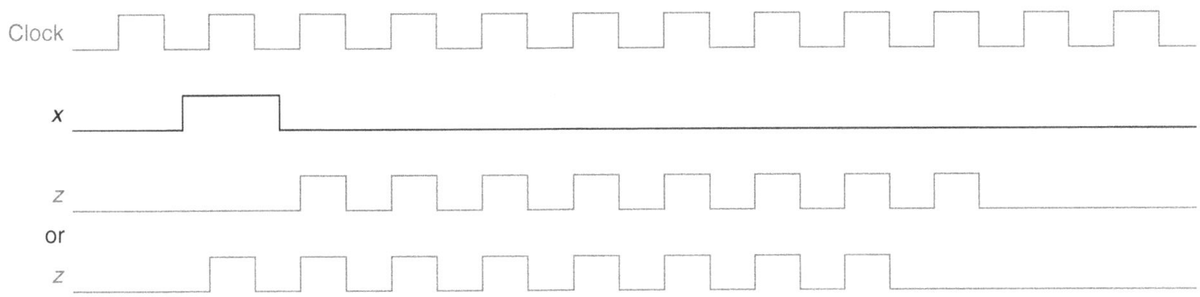

Use AND, OR, and NOT gates plus either

a. a trailing-edge triggered 8-bit serial-in, serial-out shift register with a static, active low clear, *CLR*′, or

b. a trailing-edge triggered 4-bit counter with a static, active low clear, *CLR*′.

Assume either that this has been running for a while or that we don't look at the output before the first time $x = 1$.

a. We will use x to clear the shift register and will clock a 1 into the leftmost bit at each clock time thereafter. The output will be taken from the right bit; when it is 0, there will be a clock pulse.

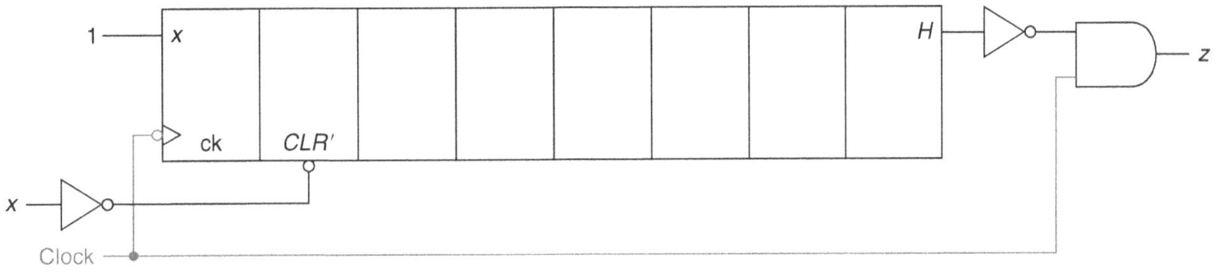

This circuit produces the second timing picture, since the first output occurs during the time x is 1. Note that this only uses the serial output; if H' is available, we do not need the output NOT gate.

b. For the counter design, we will use x to clear the counter and let it count as long as the count is less than 8 (that is, $D = 0$). Either of the following circuits could be used.

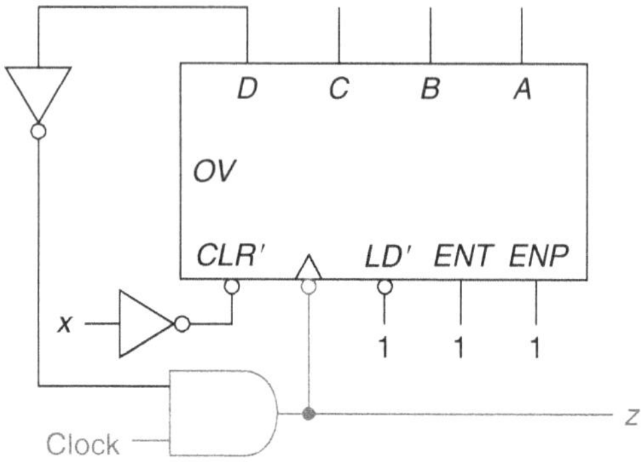

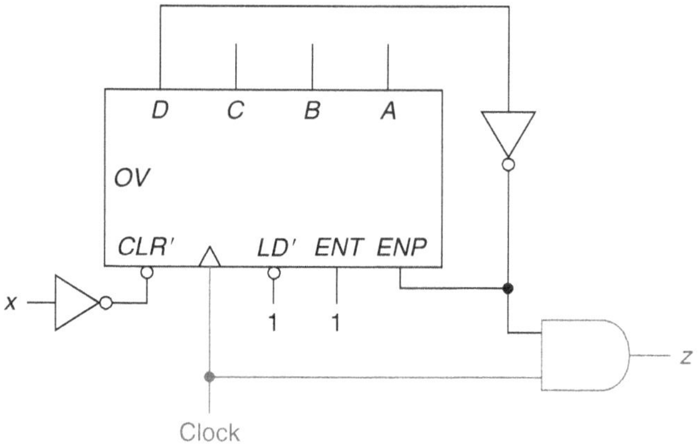

In both cases, the timing is that of the second drawing.

5. Design a system that counts up from 1 to 6 (and repeat) when input x is 0 and down from 6 to 1 when $x = 1$ and displays the results on a die. The die has seven lights (as shown in the diagram below).

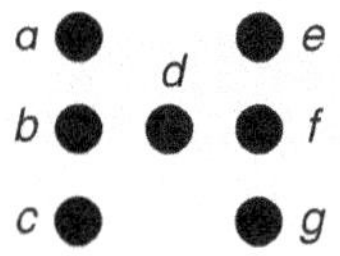

A 1 for each segment (a, b, c, d, e, f, g) indicates that it is lit; a 0 that it is not. The arrangement for the six numbers on a die are shown below, where the darkened circles are to be lit.

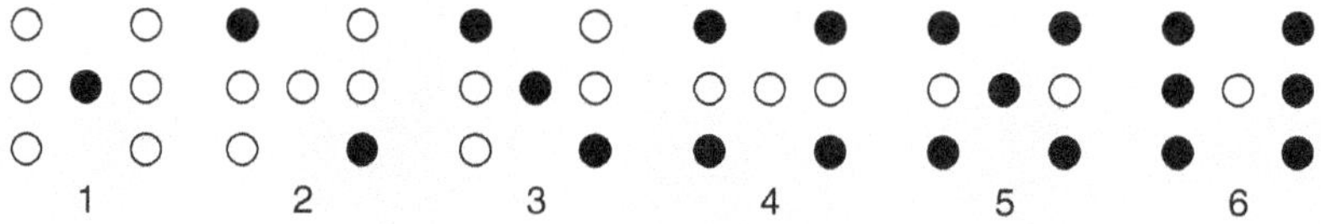

Design the counter, using three D flip flops to count from 1 (001) to 6 (110) and repeat. Then, design a decoder/driver that takes the outputs from the counter and produces the seven signals (a, b, c, d, e, f, g) to drive the display. Use a 16R4 PLD. (That works since there are really only four distinct outputs; a and g, b and f, and c and e are always the same.)

Labeling the flip flops F, G, and H, we get the following truth table for the system. There are only eight rows for the display inputs, since they do not depend on x.

x	F	G	H	D_F	D_G	D_H	$a = g$	$b = f$	$c = e$	d
0	0	0	0	X	X	X	X	X	X	X
0	0	0	1	0	1	0	0	0	0	1
0	0	1	0	0	1	1	1	0	0	0
0	0	1	1	1	0	0	1	0	0	1
0	1	0	0	1	0	1	1	0	1	0
0	1	0	1	1	1	0	1	0	1	1
0	1	1	0	0	0	1	1	1	1	0
0	1	1	1	X	X	X	X	X	X	X
1	0	0	0	X	X	X				
1	0	0	1	1	1	0				
1	0	1	0	0	0	1				
1	0	1	1	0	1	0				
1	1	0	0	0	1	1				
1	1	0	1	1	0	0				
1	1	1	0	1	0	1				
1	1	1	1	X	X	X				

The maps for the seven functions are shown below.

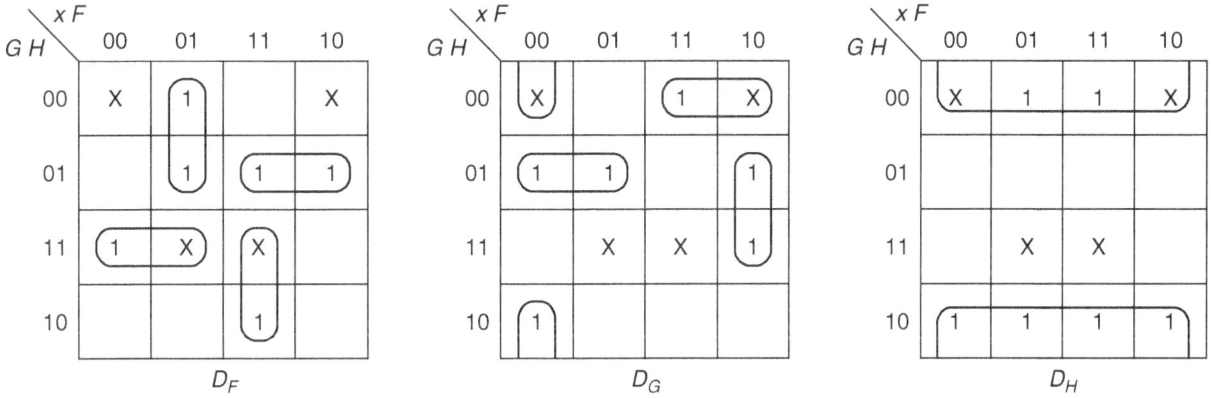

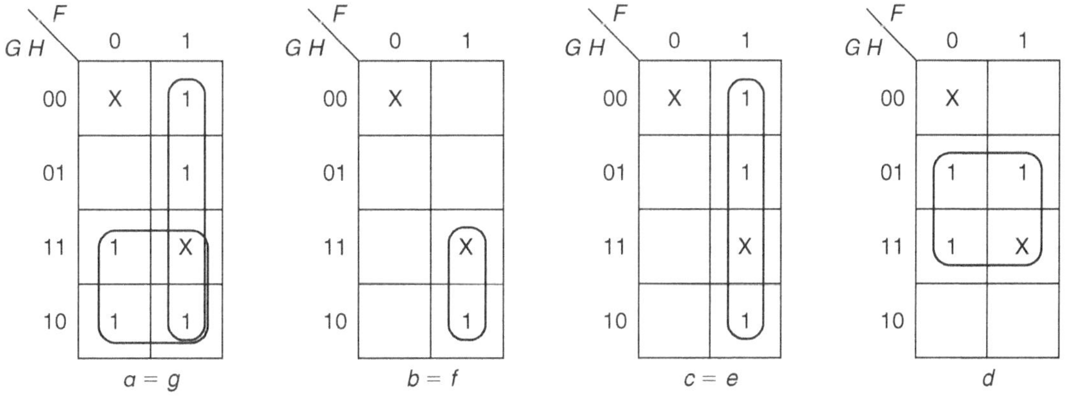

$$D_F = x'FG' + xG'H + xFG + x'GH$$
$$D_G = x'F'H' + x'G'H + xG'H' + xF'H$$
$$D_H = H'$$
$$a = g = F + G \qquad c = e = F$$
$$b = f = FG \qquad d = H$$

The PLD diagram is shown next. (Only those gates that are used are shown.)

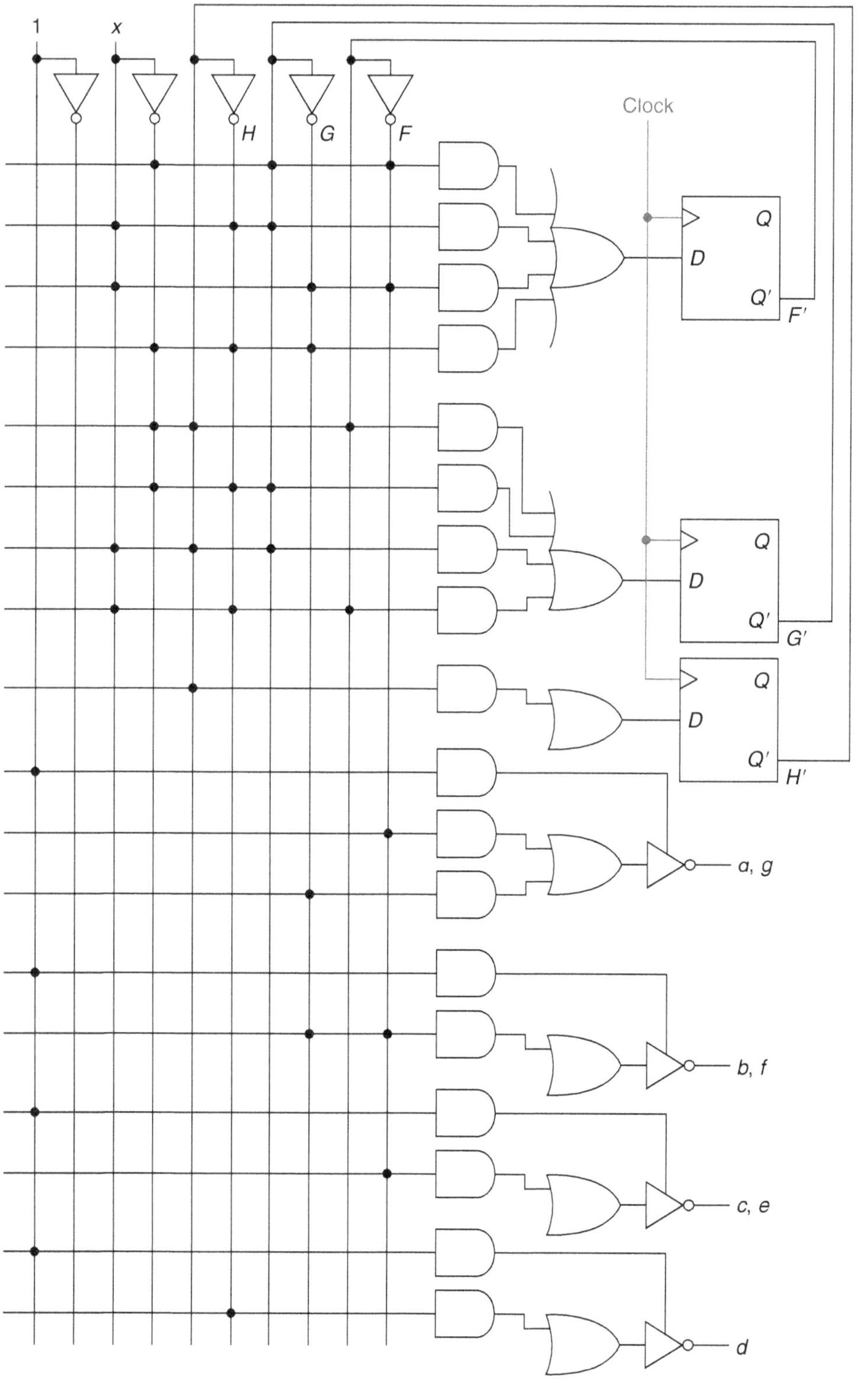

6. We are designing a rather rudimentary alarm system. The first part of the system includes a flip flop *A* that is 1 if the alarm is set (armed) and 0 if it is not, and a keypad (with 10 keys and 4 output lines). It produces an output of all 1's if no key is pushed or 0000 to 1001 if one of keys 0 to 9 are pushed. (You may assume that two keys are never pushed at the same time and that the keypad never produces one of the other five combinations.)

   To set or clear the alarm, a 3-digit combination must be entered. Hidden away in the control box is a set of three 10-position switches (that contains the 3-digit alarm code). The switches each produce a 4-bit number, $R_{1:4}$, $S_{1:4}$, and $T_{1:4}$. As one pushes the buttons to enter the alarm code, the first digit will appear on the keypad output for several clock periods, followed by a hexadecimal F (indicating that no key is pushed) for several more clock periods, followed by the second digit, and so on. We must design a system that watches the keypad and, if the right code is received, complements *A*. (Note: Like many alarms, the same code is used to arm the alarm, that is, put a 1 in *A*, as to disarm it.) Assume that there is at least one clock period when no key is pushed between digits. However, if another key is not depressed within 100 clocks, the system goes back to looking for the first digit.

   The second part of the system is used to sound the alarm. There is an input signal, *D*, indicating that a door is open (1) or closed (0) and an output, *N*, indicating that the alarm is sounded (1) or not (0). (Of course, *A* is also an input to this part of the system.) When the alarm is first armed, the door must be closed within 1000 clock pulses or the alarm will sound. (Note that this gives the user the chance to set the alarm and go out without the alarm sounding.) Also, if thc alarm has been armed for more than 1000 clock periods and the door is opened, the alarm will sound if it is not disarmed within 1000 clock periods.

   Design both parts of this system. Available components include trailing-edge triggered *JK* flip flops, synchronous 4-bit binary or decimal counters, and whatever gates that are needed. Show a modular diagram that shows various parts, also a detailed block diagram or the equations for each part, and an ASM diagram for the first part.

   One approach to the first part uses the following set of states:

   1. Waiting for first input digit.
   2. Have first input digit, waiting for key to be released.
   3. Nothing pushed, but have first digit—waiting for second.
   4. Have first two input digits, waiting for key to be released.
   5. Nothing pushed, have two digits—waiting for third.
   6. Have third input digit, waiting for key to be released.

An ASM diagram, ignoring the 100 clock timeout, is shown below.

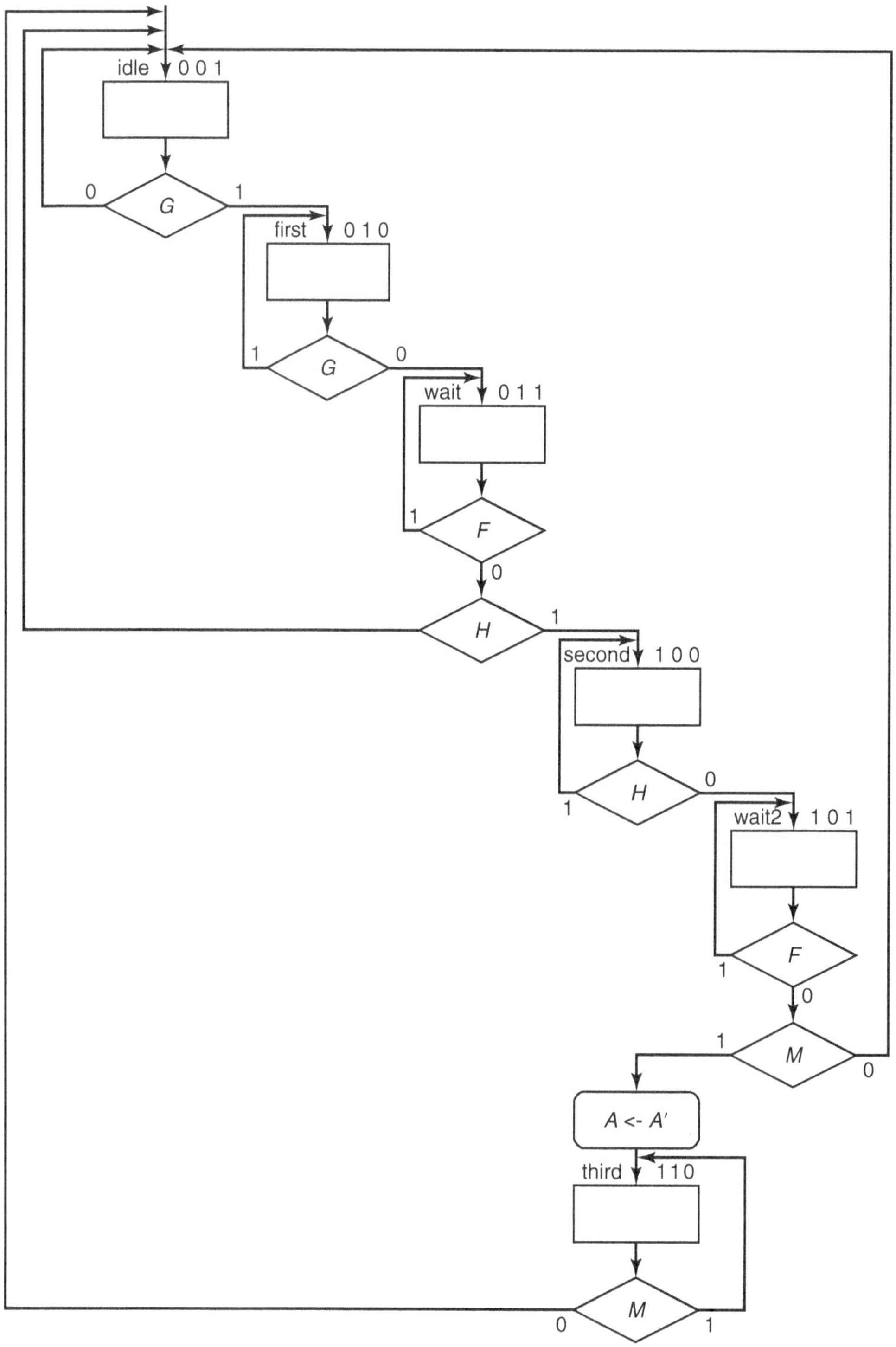

If we call the inputs from the keyboard $X_{1:4}$, then

$$\text{Nothing pushed} = X_1X_2X_3X_4 = F$$
$$\text{First Digit} = (X_1 \oplus R_1)'(X_2 \oplus R_2)'(X_3 \oplus R_3)'(X_4 \oplus R_4)' = G$$
$$\text{Second digit} = (X_1 \oplus S_1)'(X_2 \oplus S_2)'(X_3 \oplus S_3)'(X_4 \oplus S_4)' = H$$
$$\text{Third digit} = (X_1 \oplus T_1)'(X_2 \oplus T_2)'(X_3 \oplus T_3)'(X_4 \oplus T_4)' = M$$

This is a seven-variable problem—the three states q_1, q_2, and q_3, and the functions produced by the inputs, F, G, H, and M. We will code the states in binary (for example, 3 will be 011). We will then produce a table in binary, separating the three flip flop next state sections.

			$q_1^\star$					$q_2^\star$					$q_3^\star$				
q_1	q_2	q_3	F	G	H	M	#	F	G	H	M	#	F	G	H	M	#
0	0	0	X	X	X	X	X	X	X	X	X	X	X	X	X	X	X
0	0	1	0	0	0	0	0	0	1	0	0	0	1	0	1	1	1
0	1	0	0	0	X	X	X	1	1	X	X	X	1	0	X	X	X
0	1	1	0	0	1	0	0	1	0	0	0	0	1	1	0	1	1
1	0	0	1	X	1	X	X	0	X	0	X	X	1	X	0	X	X
1	0	1	1	0	0	1	0	0	0	0	1	0	1	1	1	0	1
1	1	0	0	X	X	1	X	0	X	X	1	X	1	X	X	0	X
1	1	1	X	X	X	X	X	X	X	X	X	X	X	X	X	X	X

where $\# = F'G'H'M'$. Note, only one of F, G, H, or M can be 1.

We found expressions for the next state by considering one column of the table at a time. Although this might not be minimum, it is close.

$$q_1^\star = Fq_1q_2' + H(q_2 + q_3') + Mq_1$$
$$q_2^\star = Fq_1'q_2 + G(q_1'q_2' + q_3') + Mq_1$$
$$q_3^\star = F + G(q_1 + q_2q_3) + H(q_1'q_2' + q_1q_3) + Mq_1' + F'G'H'M'$$

The control flip flop, A, is complemented when this controller goes from state 5 to 6, that is, on $q_1q_2'q_3M$. The one thing that has been omitted so far is the time out. A base 100 counter is built with two decade counters. It is cleared when going from state 2 to 3 or from 4 to 5 and is enabled whenever the controller is in state 2 or 4. It uses the static clear and preset inputs of the controller flip flops to set the controller to state 1 as the counter rolls over, that is, goes from 99 to 00.

Next we will design the alarm control. When A goes to 1, a three-digit decade counter will be cleared. When that reaches 1000, a second flip flop, B, will be set. When B is set and D

goes to 1, we will start to count to 1000 again. If, by the time the counter gets to 1000, *A* does not go to 0, the alarm will sound; flip flop *N* will go to 1. Both *B* and *N* are cleared when *A* goes to 0. A diagram of the system is shown below.

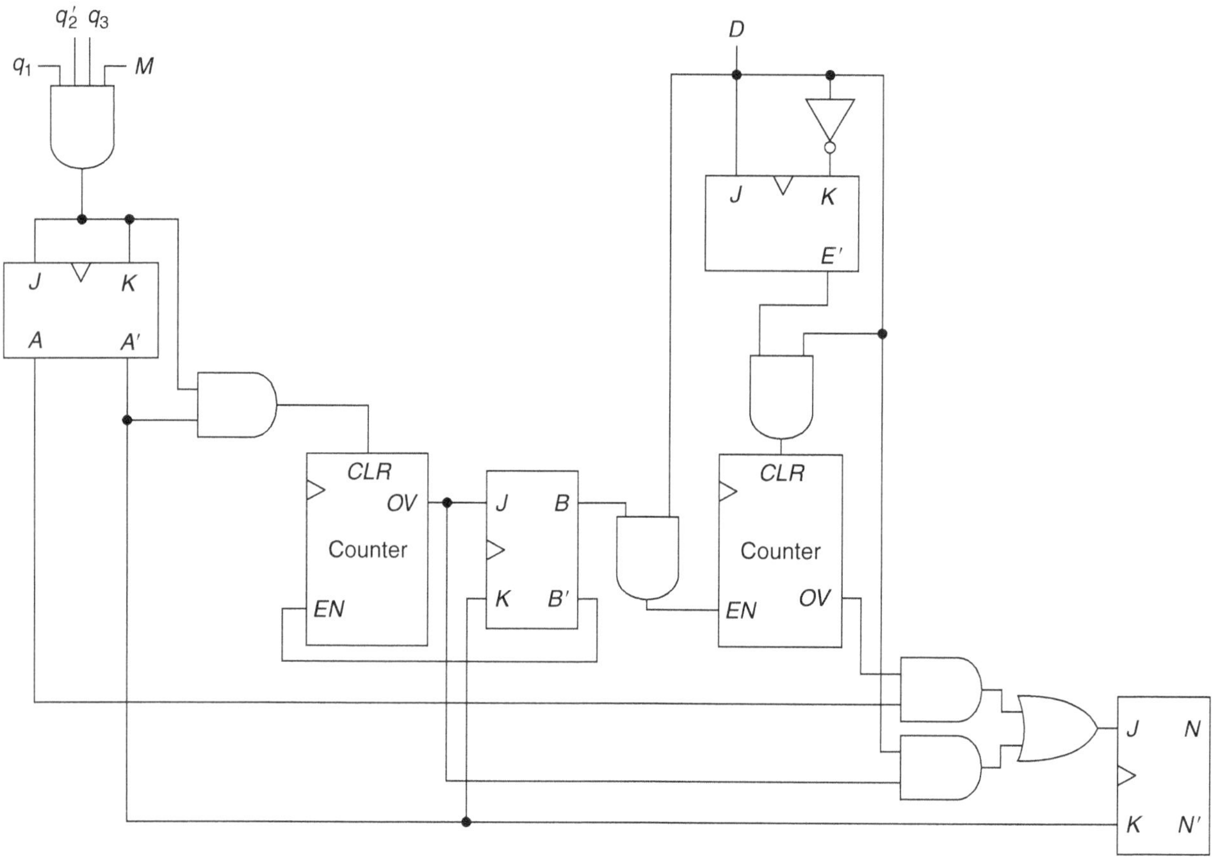

In this diagram, all of the clock inputs are connected to the system clock (but not shown to simplify the diagram). The two counters are base 1000 (that is, three decade counters cascaded); all inputs are assumed to be active high. When *A* goes to 1, the first counter is cleared. Flip flop *B* is 0, since it is cleared whenever *A* has been 0. It will be set when the counter reaches 1000. However, the alarm will be sounded if the door is still open (first counter overflows and door is open). The alarm flip flop (*N*) remains set until the code is entered to clear *A*. The *E* flip flop is used to produce a clear signal for the second counter when the door is first opened. That counter is enabled when the door is open and *B* = 1. The alarm will sound if it has not been disarmed (causing *A* and *B* to go to 0) within 1000 clocks.

8.10 EXERCISES

1. Using a 74164 shift register, design a Mealy system that produces an output of 1 when the last nine inputs were 0.
2. Using two 74164 shift registers, design a Moore system whose output is 1 when there have been exactly six 1's followed by exactly eight 0 inputs.
3. Design a system using a counter that produces a 1 output when the input has been 1 for eight or more consecutive clock times.
   a. Use a counter with a clocked active low clear and no enable input.
   b. Use a counter with a static active low clear and an active high enable.
*4. Design a system that has an output of 1 when the input has been 0 for exactly seven clock times. In addition to combinational logic blocks, one of the following is available:
   a. A 4-bit counter
   b. An 8-bit shift register
5. Design a sequential system that has a clock pulse input and produces a pulse that is coincident with every 25th clock pulse. (We do not care about initializing the system.)

   The only available components are

      1. AND gates (any number of inputs)
      2. Inverters (NOT gates)
      3. Two base 16-counters (as described below)

   The counter is trailing-edge triggered. It has four outputs—*D* (high-order bit), *C*, *B*, and *A*. It has a clock input and an active low static *Clear'* input. There is also an active low static *Load'* input, along with data input lines, *IND*, *INC*, *INB*, and *INA*. (Assume that *Clear'* and *Load'* are never both 0 at the same time. When either is 0, it overrides the clock.)

   a. Design a system using these components that uses the *Clear'* input, but not the *Load'* input.
   b. Design a system using these components that uses the *Load'* input, but not the *Clear'* input.
6. Design a system using
   a. a 74190
   b. a 74192

   plus whatever other logic that is needed (including a flip flop) to go through the sequence

   0 1 2 3 4 5 6 7 8 9 8 7 6 5 4 3 2 1 (0 1) and repeat
7. Implement the controller for the system of Example 8.6 using *D* flip flops and NAND gates.

★8. Show the ASM diagram for the controller of a system that has a 16-bit register, *A*, and a 4-bit register, *N*. When a signal of 1 appears on input line *s*, the register *A* is shifted right the number of places (0 to 15) as specified by *N* (with 0's put in the left bits). The register *A* can be shifted only one place at a time. The register *N* can be decremented (decreased by 1). When shifting is complete, a 1 is to appear on output line *d* for two clock periods.

★9. Design a system that consists of three components, a counter, a display driver, and a seven-segment display, as shown below.

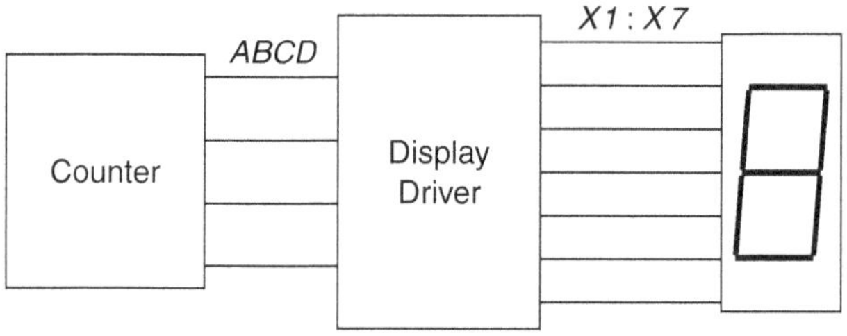

a. Design the counter using four *JK* flip flops, *A*, *B*, *C*, and *D*, and a minimum number of NOR gates. The counter is binary coded decimal, using 2421 code (as described in Table 1.7) and is to go through the sequence:

0 3 6 9 2 5 8 1 4 7 and repeat

Thus, the counter sequences 0000, 0011, 1100, 1111, 0010, and so on. After completing the design of this counter, draw a state graph. Make sure that it shows what happens if the counter is turned on and comes up in one of the unused states (for example, 0101).

b. The outputs of the counter are inputs to the display driver. It is just a four-input, seven-output combinational circuit. If one of the unused codes turns up (for example, the counter is turned on and *ABCD* = 0111), the display should be blank (that is, all seven inputs should be 0). Find a near minimum sum of products implementation of *X1*, *X2*, *X3*, *X4*, *X5*, *X6*, and *X7*. (Use the versions of 6, 7, and 9 without the extra segment lit.) (There is a solution with 17 gates and 56 inputs.)

10. We already have a decimal counter that sequences

0000 0001 0010 0011 0100 0101 0110 0111 1000 1001 and repeat

It has flip flops *W*, *X*, *Y*, and *Z*. We still want the display to cycle through 0, 3, 6, 9, 2, 5, 8, 1, 4, 7, and repeat (as in Exercise 9). Accomplish this by designing another box to go between the counter and the display driver of Exercise 9b. Note that this means, for example, that when the counter has *WXYZ* = 0010, the display is to be 6 and thus *ABCD* = 1100 (6 in 2421 code). Implement this box with a PLA with four inputs and four outputs.

11. Show a block diagram of a system whose output, z, is 1 if and only if at least two of the latest three inputs (including the present one) are 0. There is no need to show a state table or state diagram. Any kind of flip flops and gates may be used.

***12.** Design a sequential system (a counter) with one input line, x, and three flip flops, A, B, and C. When $x = 0$, the system sequences through the states (0, 1, 2, 3, 4), 0, . . . and when $x = 1$, the system sequences through the states (2, 3, 4, 5, 6, 7), 2, ... If, at any time, x is 0 when the system is in states 5, 6, or 7, or if x is 1 when the system is in states 0 or 1, it should go to state 3 on the next clock.

a. The available components are

7400, 7404, 7410, 7420, and 7430 (NAND gate packages)	25¢ each
Dual *JK* trailing-edge triggered flip flop packages	\$1.00 each
Dual *D* flip flop packages	cost to be determined

Design the system two ways:

i. First, using *JK* flip flops

ii. Second, using *D* flip flops

Show the equations for both designs and a block diagram of one of them.

b. Determine the price range for the *D* flip flop packages for which it would be more economical to use

all *JK* flip flops

one package of *JK* and one of *D*

all *D* flip flops.

c. We would like to add an output that is 1 whenever the system is in state 3 and got there because it was out of sequence (when x is 0 and the system is in states 5, 6, or 7, or if x is 1 and the system is in states 0 or 1). This requires another flip flop.

d. Design the system of part c using a PLD. (Any of the ones we described will do.)

13. Design a clock display to show the time in hours, minutes, and seconds. Assume that we have a clock of exactly 1 KHz (1000 clock pulses per second). It will use 6 seven-segment displays and operate either in military time (hours 00 to 23) or regular time (1 to 12, with AM and PM). An input line, x, differentiates between the two. A seventh display is used to show A or P in the latter case; it is blank otherwise. Assume that there is a BCD-to-seven-segment decoder driver available; one is needed for each display other than the AM/PM one.

a. Design this using asynchronous counters (utilizing the 7490 and 7492). The problem with these is that they can not be set arbitrarily.

b. Design this using synchronous counters with static load inputs. (They would require a large number of switches to set this to some arbitrary time, four for each digit.)

c. For either design, provide a set function for minutes and hours as follows:

When input f is 0, the clock operates normally; when $f = 1$, we can adjust the time.

When $f = 1$ and $g = 1$, the hour advances once every second.

When $f = 1$ and $h = 1$, the minute advances once every second.

Also, when $f = 1$, the seconds go to 00.

14. Design a counter that goes through the following sequence of 12 states

10 4 5 1 2 8 11 3 9 12 13 0 and repeat

It is not important where it starts. The available packages are NAND gates (7400, 7404, 7410, 7420, and 7430) at 50¢ each, plus the storage devices described below.

Consider three alternate designs and compare them. For each, show the equations and a block diagram. Label the four outputs in each design W (high-order bit), X, Y, Z.

a. The available storage devices are four JK flip flops at a total cost of $2.50.

b. The available storage devices are four D flip flops at a cost to be determined.

c. There is a 74161 4-bit synchronous counter, and we must build a combinational decoder block. This block takes the output of the counter that goes 0, 1, 2, 3, 4, . . . and translates the 0 to 10, the 1 to 4, the 2 to 5, the 3 to 1, the 4 to 2, and so forth. It must also go back to state 0 from state 11.

Comparing the three designs, how much must the D flip flops cost for design b to be less expensive than design a, and how much must the counter cost for design c to be less expensive than design a?

15. a. Repeat Solved Problem 5, so that we can count to 7, where a 7 lights all of the dots on the die display.

b. Repeat Solved Problem 5, so that we can count from 0 (no lights lit) to 7, but the counter saturates (that is, it remains at 7 counting up or 0 counting down, rather than recycling).

8.11 CHAPTER 8 TEST (50 MINUTES)

1. Show two designs for a Mealy system that produces an output of 1 if and only if the input is 0 for exactly seven consecutive clock times. In addition to AND, OR, and NOT gates, we have available an 8-bit serial-in, parallel-out shift register, with an active low, clocked clear (that works whether or not the counter is enabled) for one and a 4-bit counter with an active low, static clear, and an active low enable for the other.

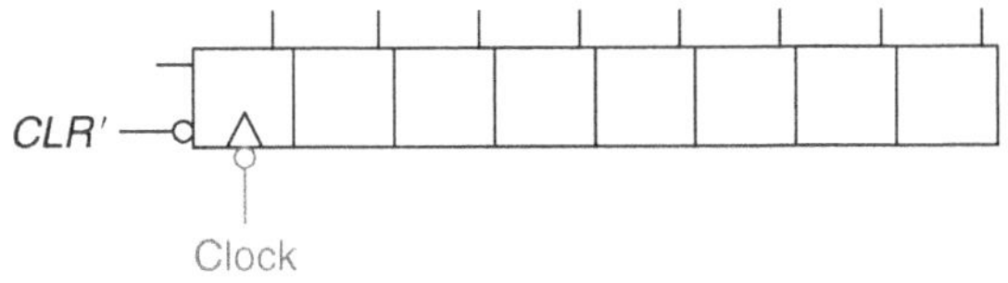

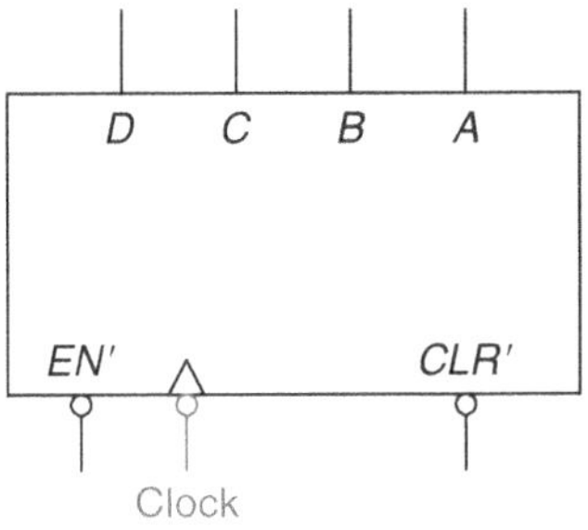

2. We wish to implement the following state table.

AB	$A^\star B^\star$		*z*	
	$x = 0$	$x = 1$	$x = 0$	$x = 1$
0 0	1 1	0 1	1	0
0 1	1 0	0 1	0	0
1 0	0 1	1 1	1	1
1 1	0 0	1 1	0	1

To implement this, we have the PAL shown. Two of the outputs are connected to the input of a *D* flip flop; the third is available for an output. Label the diagram and show the connections either with dots or X's. Note that the PAL has more inputs and gates than you need; you can ignore the extras.

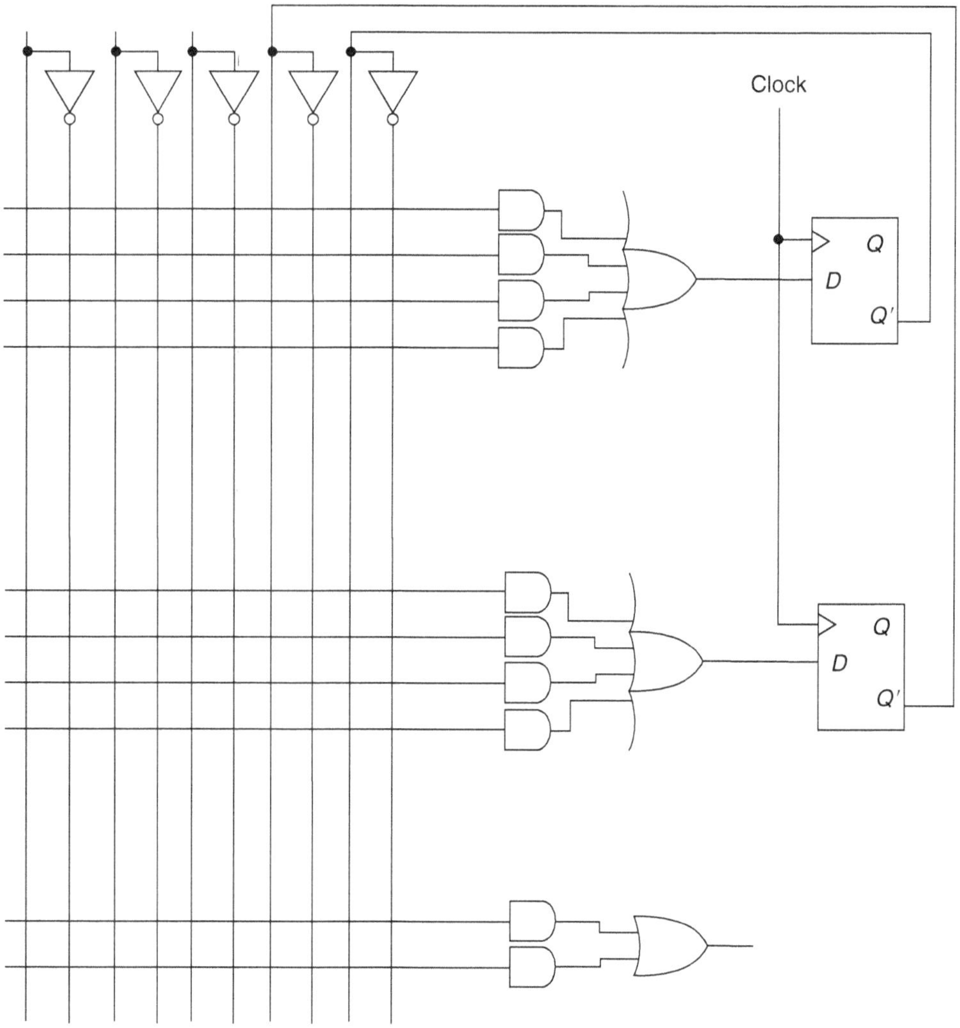
Clock
Q
D
Q′
Q
D
Q′

CHAPTER 9

Simplification of Sequential Circuits

In this chapter, we will first look at a technique to remove redundant states from sequential systems. We will then introduce the concept of partitions as another approach to reducing the number of states and as a technique to find state assignments that reduce the amount of combinational logic.

Two states of a sequential system are said to be *equivalent* if every input sequence will produce the same output sequence starting in either state. If the output sequence is the same, then we don't need to know in which of the two states we started. That definition is rather hard to apply, since we must try a very long input sequence or a large number of shorter sequences to be sure that we satisfied the definition.

A more practical definition is:

> Two states of a sequential system are *equivalent* if, starting in either state, any one input produces the same output and equivalent next states.

If two states are equivalent, we can remove one of them and have a system with fewer states. Usually, systems with fewer states are less expensive to implement. This is particularly true if the reduced system requires fewer state variables. For example, reducing a system from six states to four states reduces the number of flip flops required to store the state from three to two. If the system is built with *JK* flip flops and there is one input, x, and one output, z, we have only five functions to implement instead of seven. Furthermore, the J and K inputs are two-variable functions rather than three and the output is also a function of one less variable (three for a Mealy and two for a Moore system). Fewer variables usually means less combinational logic.

Occasionally, we can tell states are equivalent by just inspecting the state table. We will look at the simple example of Table 9.1 to illustrate this approach.

Table 9.1 A state table.

q	$q^{\star}$ $x = 0$	$x = 1$	z $x = 0$	$x = 1$
A	C	B	0	0
B	E	D	0	0
C	A	D	0	1
D	A	B	0	1
E	A	B	0	1

Note that for states D and E, the next state is the same (A) for $x = 0$ and is also the same (B) for $x = 1$. Also, the outputs are the same for each state, for both $x = 0$ and $x = 1$. Thus, we can delete one of the states. We will remove state E and obtain Table 9.2.

Table 9.2 Reduced state table.

q	$q^{\star}$ $x = 0$	$x = 1$	z $x = 0$	$x = 1$
A	C	B	0	0
B	D	D	0	0
C	A	D	0	1
D	A	B	0	1

We replaced each appearance of E in the state table by D. Although it is not obvious, no further reduction is possible. Often, we cannot see the equivalences so easily.

EXAMPLE 9.1

q	$q^{\star}$ $x = 0$	$x = 1$	z $x = 0$	$x = 1$
A	C	B	0	0
B	D	D	0	0
C	A	D	0	1
D	A	C	0	1

States C and D are equivalent. They both have a 0 output for $x = 0$, and a 1 output for $x = 1$. Both go to A when $x = 0$, and they go to either C or D when $x = 1$. We could say that C and D are equivalent if D is equivalent to C; but that is a truism. Thus, this system can be reduced to three states:

q	$q^{\star}$ $x = 0$	$x = 1$	z $x = 0$	$x = 1$
A	C-D	B	0	0
B	C-D	C-D	0	0
C-D	A	C-D	0	1

where we have named the state resulting from the equivalence of *C* and *D* by a compound name *C-D*. (We will do that some of the time, but it often gets cumbersome, and we will name the state in the reduced system using the name of the first state in the group.)

More commonly, equivalences are not so obvious. Therefore, we will develop two algorithmic methods in the next two sections.

9.1 A TABULAR METHOD FOR STATE REDUCTION

In this section, we will develop a technique using a chart with one square for each possible pairing of states. We will enter in that square an X if those states cannot be equivalent because the outputs are different, a √ if the states are equivalent (because they have the same output and go to the same state or to each other for each input), and otherwise the conditions that must be met for those two states to be equivalent (that is, which states must be equivalent to make these equivalent).

The chart has one row for each state except the first and one column for each state except the last; only the lower half of the chart is necessary to include all pairs of states. For the state table of Table 9.1, we first get the chart of Figure 9.1.

Figure 9.1 Chart for Table 9.1.

B	*C E*, *B D*			
C	X	X		
D	X	X	*B D*	
E	X	X	*B D*	√
	A	*B*	*C*	*D*

In order for states *A* and *B* to be equivalent, they must have the same output for both $x = 0$ and $x = 1$ (which they do) and must go to equivalent states. Thus, *C* must be equivalent to *E* and *B* must be equivalent to *D*, as shown in the first square. Each square in the balance of that column and the whole next column contains an X since states *A* and *B* have a 0 output for $x = 1$ and states *C*, *D*, and *E* have a 1 output. In the *CD* square, we place *BD* since *C* goes to *D* and *D* goes to *B* when $x = 1$. That is also the case in the *CE* square. Finally, in the *DE* square, we place a check (√), since both states have the same output and next state for each input. We must now go back through the table to see if the conditions are met. Since *B* cannot be equivalent to *D* (there is already an X in the *BD* square), none of the three pairs can be equivalent. We thus cross out those squares, leaving only one check, as shown in Figure 9.2.

Figure 9.2 Reduced chart with states crossed out.

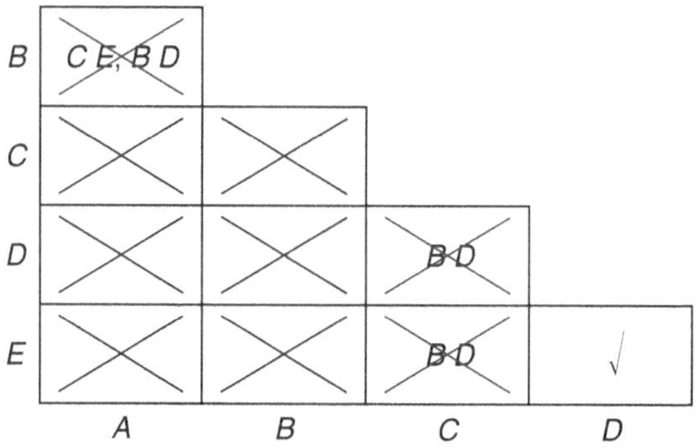

The states D and E can be combined. The reduced table can then be produced. In the process of doing that, there is a check that there was no mistake in the first part. As entries are made for combined states (such as D-E), each of the original states must go to the same state in the reduced table and they must have the same output. The reduced table was shown in the last section (Table 9.2).

The process is not always as easy as this. Example 9.2 will illustrate some further steps that are necessary.

EXAMPLE 9.2

	$q^\star$		
q	$x = 0$	$x = 1$	z
A	B	D	1
B	D	F	1
C	D	A	0
D	D	E	0
E	B	C	1
F	C	D	0

The chart for this table is

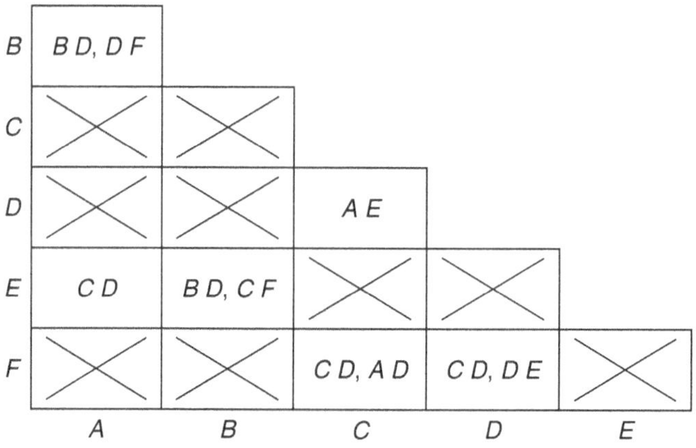

Note that the first entry could have been written *BDF*, that is, all three states must be equivalent. (Indeed, since this is the condition for *A* and *B* to be equivalent, we then require that *A*, *B*, *D*, and *F* all be equivalent.) Going through the table, we see that *B* and *D* cannot be equivalent; neither can *A* and *D*, nor *D* and *E*. That reduces the table to the following:

B	~~B D; D F~~				
C	X	X			
D	X	X	A E		
E	C D	~~B D; C F~~	X	X	
F	X	X	~~C D; A D~~	~~C D; D E~~	X
	A	B	C	D	E

What remains is that *A* is equivalent to *E* if *C* is equivalent to *D* and that *C* is equivalent to *D* if *A* is equivalent to *E*. That allows us to check off both of these, producing the reduced table:

q	q* x = 0	q* x = 1	z
A-E	B	C-D	1
B	C-D	F	1
C-D	C-D	A-E	0
F	C-D	C-D	0

Before looking at some more complex examples, we want to emphasize the effect that the output column has on the process. The state table and chart of Example 9.3 correspond to a system with the same next state behavior as that of Example 9.2, but a different output column.

EXAMPLE 9.3

q	q* x = 0	q* x = 1	z
A	B	D	1
B	D	F	1
C	D	A	1
D	D	E	0
E	B	C	0
F	C	D	0

The chart is different, because the pairings that are automatically X'd (due to the output) are different.

	A	B	C	D	E
B	B D F				
C	A B D	A F			
D	X	X	X		
E	X	X	X	B D, C E	
F	X	X	X	C D E	B C D

None of the conditions can be satisfied, and thus, no states can be combined and the state table cannot be reduced.

Sometimes, when the obvious unequivalences are crossed off, there may be some doubt as to whether the remaining states can be combined. We could try to combine them all and develop the reduced state table. If we were mistaken, it will quickly become evident. Also, if we find one or more equivalences before completing the process, we can reduce the table and start the process over. That is somewhat more work, but the chart for the reduced table is much smaller and may be easier to work with.

EXAMPLE 9.4

	$q^\star$		z	
q	$x = 0$	$x = 1$	$x = 0$	$x = 1$
A	F	B	0	0
B	E	G	0	0
C	C	G	0	0
D	A	C	1	1
E	E	D	0	0
F	A	B	0	0
G	F	C	1	1

The chart for this table is

	A	B	C	D	E	F
B	E F, B G					
C	B G, C F	C E				
D	X	X	X			
E	E F, B D	D G	D G	X		
F	√	A E, B G	A C, B G	X	A E, B D	
G	X	X	X	A F	X	X

Note that we checked *AF*, since the requirement that *A* is equivalent to *F* is just that *F* is equivalent to *A*. That is always true. We first go through the chart to find which conditions cannot be met, crossing them out. We also note that condition *AF* has already been checked and therefore *D* and *G* are equivalent. During this pass, we may take advantage of the new equivalences and the cross outs or we may wait until the next pass. Waiting until the next pass, the table becomes

B	~~*E F*, *B G*~~					
C	~~*B G*, *C F*~~	*C E*				
D	X	X	X			
E	~~*E F*, *B D*~~	*D G*	*D G*	X		
F	√	~~*A E*, *B G*~~	~~*A C*, *B G*~~	X	~~*A E*, *B D*~~	
G	X	X	X	√ *A F*	X	X
	A	*B*	*C*	*D*	*E*	*F*

We now have *A* equivalent to *F* and *D* equivalent to *G*. The latter satisfies the condition for *C* being equivalent to *E* and *B* being equivalent to *E*. Finally, since *C* and *E* are equivalent, *B* is equivalent to *C*. That makes *B*, *C*, and *E* all equivalent. Thus, the reduced table has three states—*A* (*A-F*), *B* (*B-C-E*), and *D* (*D-G*).

	$q^\star$		z	
q	$x = 0$	$x = 1$	$x = 0$	$x = 1$
A	*A*	*B*	0	0
B	*B*	*D*	0	0
D	*A*	*B*	1	1

With the last chart above, we could have reduced the system to one with five states, just using the equivalences checked (*A-F* and *D-G*). That would produce the new table

	$q^\star$		z	
q	$x = 0$	$x = 1$	$x = 0$	$x = 1$
A	*A*	*B*	0	0
B	*E*	*D*	0	0
C	*C*	*D*	0	0
D	*A*	*C*	1	1
E	*E*	*D*	0	0

We can now construct a new chart

B	*A E*, *B D*			
C	*B D*	*C E*		
D	X	X	X	
E	*B D*	√	√	X
	A	*B*	*C*	*D*

However, *B* and *D* cannot be equivalent; *C* and *E* are. Thus, states *B*, *C*, and *E* can be replaced by one state, *B*; that will allow us to reduce this table to the three-state one we have already obtained.

EXAMPLE 9.5

	$q^\star$		z	
q	$x = 0$	$x = 1$	$x = 0$	$x = 1$
A	*B*	*D*	0	0
B	*E*	*D*	1	0
C	*B*	*C*	0	0
D	*F*	*A*	0	0
E	*A*	*B*	1	1
F	*E*	*C*	1	0

We first construct the chart

B	X				
C	*C D*	X			
D	*B F*	X	*B F*, *A C*		
E	X	X	X	X	
F	X	*C D*	X	X	X
	A	*B*	*C*	*D*	*E*

None of the conditions in the squares are contradicted. The chart says that for *A* to be equivalent to *C*, *C* must be equivalent to *D*. That would make *A*, *C*, and *D* one group. For *A* to be equivalent to *D*, *B* must be equivalent to *F*, and for *B* to be equivalent to *F*, *C* must be equivalent to *D*. Finally, *C* is equivalent to *D* if *B* is equivalent to *F* and *A* is equivalent to *C*. All of these can be true, producing a reduced state table with only three states, *A* (*A*-*C*-*D*), *B* (*B*-*F*), and *E*. (As we construct that table, we can check our conclusions from the chart by making sure that all states in one group go to a state in a single group for each input.)

	$q^\star$		z	
q	$x = 0$	$x = 1$	$x = 0$	$x = 1$
A	*B*	*A*	0	0
B	*E*	*A*	1	0
E	*A*	*B*	1	1

EXAMPLE 9.6

As our last example of this technique, we will consider a system with two inputs, $x\,y$. Thus, there are four columns in the next state section of the table.

	$x\,y$	$q^\star$			
q	0 0	0 1	1 0	1 1	z
A	*B*	*A*	*F*	*D*	1
B	*E*	*A*	*D*	*C*	1
C	*A*	*F*	*D*	*C*	0
D	*A*	*A*	*B*	*C*	1
E	*B*	*A*	*C*	*B*	1
F	*A*	*F*	*B*	*C*	0

The charting problem is really no different than before; we just have more conditions, since equivalent states must go to equivalent states for all four input combinations (that is, all four columns). The chart then becomes

B	*B E* *C D F*				
C	X	X			
D	*A B F* *C D*	*A E*	X		
E	*C F* *B D*	*B C D*	X	*A B C*	
F	X	X	*B D*	X	X
	A	*B*	*C*	*D*	*E*

None of the groups of three states shown in the chart can be equivalent; one of each has a different output than the other two. Crossing out those squares, we have

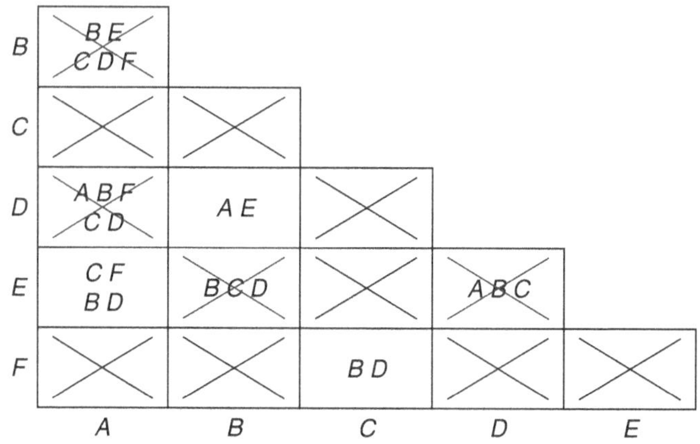

That leaves three pairings intact, *A E*, *B D*, and *C F*. The only requirement for any of these is that one of the others be equivalent. Thus, we can reduce this to three states as follows:

q	**x y** 00	01	$q^\star$ 10	11	**z**
A	*B*	*A*	*C*	*B*	1
B	*A*	*A*	*B*	*C*	1
C	*A*	*C*	*B*	*C*	0

[SP 1; EX 1]

9.2 PARTITIONS

A *partition* on the states of a system is a grouping of the states of that system into one or more blocks. Each state must be in one and only one block. For a system with four states, *A*, *B*, *C*, and *D*, the complete list of partitions is

$P_0 = (A)(B)(C)(D)$ $\quad P_8 = (AC)(BD)$
$P_1 = (AB)(C)(D)$ $\quad P_9 = (AD)(BC)$
$P_2 = (AC)(B)(D)$ $\quad P_{10} = (ABC)(D)$
$P_3 = (AD)(B)(C)$ $\quad P_{11} = (ABD)(C)$
$P_4 = (A)(BC)(D)$ $\quad P_{12} = (ACD)(B)$
$P_5 = (A)(BD)(C)$ $\quad P_{13} = (A)(BCD)$
$P_6 = (A)(B)(CD)$ $\quad P_N = (ABCD)$
$P_7 = (AB)(CD)$

This list of partitions does not depend on the details of the state table, only on the list of states. P_0 is the partition with each state in a separate block; P_N is the partition with all of the states in the same block. We will be concerned with partitions that have special properties for a particular state table. There are three categories of partitions that will be of interest. To illustrate these, we will use Table 9.3.

Any partition with two blocks can be used to assign one of the state variables. Those states in the first block would be assigned 0 and those in the second block 1 (or vice versa). P_7 through P_{13} meet that requirement. (We write partitions in alphabetic order; thus, state A will usually be assigned all 0's.) In a four-state system, there are only three pairs of partitions that can be used for a two-variable state assignment, P_7 and P_8, P_7 and P_9, and P_8 and P_9. The three are shown in Table 9.4.

Table 9.3 State table to illustrate types of partitions.

q	$q^\star$ $x = 0$	$x = 1$	z
A	C	A	1
B	D	B	0
C	A	B	1
D	B	A	0

Table 9.4 State assignments for four states.

q	q_1	q_2
A	0	0
B	0	1
C	1	0
D	1	1
	P_7	P_8

(a)

q	q_1	q_2
A	0	0
B	0	1
C	1	1
D	1	0
	P_7	P_9

(b)

q	q_1	q_2
A	0	0
B	1	1
C	0	1
D	1	0
	P_8	P_9

(c)

If we try any other pair of two-block partitions, we do not have an adequate state assignment. For example, using P_8 and P_{11}, we get the assignment of Table 9.5. Note that states B and D have the same assignment.

Table 9.5 An unsuccessful assignment.

q	q_1	q_2
A	0	0
B	1	0
C	0	1
D	1	0
	P_8	P_{11}

A second useful class of partitions are those for which all of the states in each block have the same output for each of the inputs. Such partitions are referred to as *output consistent*. P_0 is always output consistent; for Table 9.3, the other output consistent partitions are

$$P_2 = (AC)(B)(D)$$
$$P_5 = (A)(BD)(C)$$
$$P_8 = (AC)(BD)$$

Knowing the block of an output consistent partition and the input is enough information to determine the output (without having to know which state within a block).

For some partitions, knowing the block of the partition and the input is enough information to determine the block of the next state. Such a partition is said to have the *substitution property* and is referred to as an *SP partition*. P_N is always SP since all states are in the same block, and P_0 is always SP since knowing the block is the same as knowing the state. Others may be SP, depending on the details of the state table. For this state table, there are two nontrivial SP partitions (those other than P_0 and P_N), namely,

$$P_7 = (AB)(CD)$$
$$P_9 = (AD)(BC)$$

If a partition other than P_0 is both SP and output consistent, then we can reduce the system to one having just one state for each block of that partition. (That should be obvious since knowing the input and the block of the partition is all we need to know to determine the output, since it is output consistent, and to determine the next state, since it is SP). For this example, neither of the SP partitions is also output consistent. In Example 9.1, the partition

$$(A)(B)(CD)$$

is both SP and output consistent; thus, we were able to reduce the system to one with only three states.

Before developing a method for finding all SP partitions, we will look at Example 9.7. It will help us understand the application of the various categories of partitions.

EXAMPLE 9.7

q	$q^\star$ $x = 0$	$q^\star$ $x = 1$	z
A	C	D	0
B	C	E	1
C	A	D	1
D	B	E	1
E	B	E	0

Assignment 1

q	q_1	q_2	q_3
A	0	0	0
B	0	0	1
C	0	1	0
D	0	1	1
E	1	0	0

For this state assignment, we obtain the output equation and the inputs to D flip flops

$$z = q_2 + q_3$$
$$D_1 = xq_1 + xq_3$$
$$D_2 = x'q_1'q_2' + xq_1'q_3'$$
$$D_3 = x'q_2q_3 + x'q_1 + xq_1'q_3'$$

This requires 11 gates and 25-gate inputs (for either AND and OR or NAND, including a NOT for x'). We would need four 7400 series integrated circuit packages to implement the combinational logic with NAND gates. (The development of the equations and the gate count is left as an exercise.)

If we make the state assignment using the following three partitions:

$P_1 = (ABC)(DE)$ SP
$P_2 = (AB)(CDE)$ SP
$P_3 = (AE)(BCD)$ output consistent

we have

Assignment 2

q	q_1	q_2	q_3
A	0	0	0
B	0	0	1
C	0	1	1
D	1	1	1
E	1	1	0

Logic Equations

$$z = q_3$$
$$D_1 = x$$
$$D_2 = x + q_2'$$
$$D_3 = x'q_1 + x'q_2' + \{q_2'q_3 \text{ or } q_1'q_3\} + xq_1'q_2$$

This requires only seven gates, 16 inputs, and three 7400 series NAND gate integrated circuit packages. D_3 is the only complex function.

We saw the advantage of using an output consistent partition, that the output is just equal to that variable or its complement. Thus, z is only a function of q_3.

We saw the advantage of using an SP partition to assign a state variable, that the next state of that variable is only a function of the input, x, and that variable (no matter how many flip flops are needed to implement that system). Since q_1 and q_2 are assigned using SP partitions, D_1 is only a function of x (could also depend on q_1), and D_2 is only a function of x and q_2. For JK flip flops, the inputs are functions only of x (x, x', and 1 are the only possibilities). Indeed, we do not need to deal with the whole state table for the implementation of flip flops assigned according to SP partitions; we only need a block table. Thus, for the flip flops assigned according to partition $P_1 = (ABC)(DE)$, where the first block is assigned 0, we would have Table 9.6, which gives

$$D_1 = q_1^\star = x \qquad J_1 = x \qquad K_1 = x'$$

Table 9.6 Truth table for q_1.

	x	q_1	$q_1^\star$	J	K
(ABC)	0	0	0	0	X
(DE)	0	1	0	X	1
(ABC)	1	0	1	1	X
(DE)	1	1	1	X	0

This is, of course, the same answer we got for D_1 before. We could follow this approach for D_2 or J_2 and K_2 as well, but would need the full four-variable truth table to solve for the inputs to q_3.

9.2.1 Properties of Partitions

First, we will define, for pairs of partitions, the relationship *greater than or equal* ($\geq$) and two operators, the product and the sum.

- $P_a \geq P_b$ if and only if all states in the same block of P_b are also in the same block of P_a.

For example,

$$P_{10} = (ABC)(D) \geq P_2 = (AC)(B)(D)$$

since the only states in the same block of P_2 (A and C) are also in the same block of P_{10}. P_0 is the smallest partition; all other partitions are greater than it. P_N is the largest partition; it is greater than all others. Not all partitions are ordered. For example, P_1 is neither $\geq$ nor $\leq$ P_2.

- The *product* of two partitions is written $P_c = P_a P_b$.

  Two states are in the same block of the product P_c if and only if they are in the same block of both P_a and P_b.

For example,

$$P_{12}P_{13} = \{(ACD)(B)\}\{(A)(BCD)\} = (A)(B)(CD) = P_6$$

The only states that are in the same block of both P_{12} and P_{13} are C and D; they are then together in the product. The partitions P_a and P_b are always greater than or equal to the product P_c. If the two partitions are ordered, the product is equal to the smaller one. For example, $P_6 < P_{13}$ and thus, $P_6 P_{13} = P_6$. It is also clear from the definitions that, for any partition, P_a

$$P_a P_0 = P_0 \quad \text{and} \quad P_a P_N = P_a$$

- The *sum* of two partitions is written $P_c = P_a + P_b$.

  Two states are in the same block of the sum P_d if they are in the same block of either P_a or P_b or both.

For example,

$$P_2 + P_5 = \{(AC)(B)(D)\} + \{(A)(BD)(C)\} = P_8 = (AC)(BD)$$

The sum sometimes brings together states that are not in the same block of either since whole blocks are combined. Consider the following example:

$$P_a = (AB)(C)(DF)(EG)$$
$$P_b = (ACD)(BG)(E)(F)$$
$$P_a + P_b = (ABCDEFG) = P_N$$

Since A and B are in the same block of P_a and A, C, and D are in the same block of P_b, then $ABCD$ are in one block of the sum. But F is in the same block as D in P_a and G is in the same block as B of P_b; so they must be included with $ABCD$. Finally, E is in the same block as G in P_a, producing a sum of P_N. The sum P_c is always greater than or equal to both P_a and P_b. If P_a and P_b are ordered, the sum equals the greater. Thus, $P_6 + P_{13} = P_{13}$. Also,

$$P_a + P_0 = P_a \quad \text{and} \quad P_a + P_N = P_N$$

9.2.2 Finding SP Partitions

The process of finding all SP partitions has two steps.

Step 1: For each pair of states, find the smallest SP partition that puts those two states in the same block.

We must ask what is required to make a partition SP if these two states are in the same block, that is, what makes these two states equivalent. They must go to equivalent states for each input. We must then follow through, determining what groupings are forced.

We will use the state table of Table 9.3, repeated here without the output columns (since that has no relevance to finding SP partitions) as Table 9.7.

Table 9.7 A state table for finding SP partitions.

q	$q^\star$ $x = 0$	$x = 1$
A	C	A
B	D	B
C	A	B
D	B	A

For A to be equivalent to B, C must be equivalent to D. We continue by checking what conditions are required to make C equivalent to D. In this example, the only requirement is that A be equivalent to B. Thus, we have our first SP partition

$$(AB) \rightarrow (CD) \qquad \rightarrow\rightarrow (AB)(CD) = P_1$$

where the right arrow ($\rightarrow$) is used to indicate requires, and the double arrow indicates the smallest SP partition that results. Sometimes, we find no new conditions and other times the conditions force all of the states into one block, producing P_N.

The next step is

$$(AC) \rightarrow (AB) \rightarrow (CD) \rightarrow (ABCD) = P_N$$

(Since C must be with A and B must be with A, then A, B, and C must all be together. But then D must be with C, resulting in P_N.) The balance of step 1 produces

$$(AD) \rightarrow (BC) \qquad \rightarrow\rightarrow (AD)(BC) = P_2$$
$$(BC) \rightarrow (AD) \qquad \rightarrow\rightarrow (AD)(BC) = P_2$$
$$(BD) \rightarrow (AB) \qquad \rightarrow\rightarrow P_N$$
$$(CD) \rightarrow (AB) \qquad \rightarrow\rightarrow (AB)(CD) = P_1$$

Step 2: Find the sum of all of the SP partitions found in step 1 and, if new ones are found, repeat step 2 on these new ones.

In this process, we do not need to find the sum of another partition with any two-block partition since that always results in either the two-block partition or P_N. Also, if one partition is greater than another, its sum is always the greater partition. We can omit those additions, too.

For the first example, there are no sums to compute, since the only two unique nontrivial (that is, other than P_0 and P_N) SP partitions formed by step 1 are both two-block.

EXAMPLE 9.8

q	$q^\star$ $x = 0$	$x = 1$	z
A	C	D	1
B	C	D	0
C	B	D	1
D	C	A	1

Step 1 produces five SP partitions.

$(AB) \to \surd$* $\to\to P_1 = (AB)(C)(D)$
$(AC) \to (BC)$, $(BC) \to$ ok $\to\to P_2 = (ABC)(D)$
$(AD) \to \surd$ $\to\to P_3 = (AD)(B)(C)$
$(BC) \to \surd$ $\to\to P_4 = (A)(BC)(D)$
$(BD) \to (AD) \to (ABD)$ $\to\to P_5 = (ABD)(C)$
$(CD) \to (BC), (AD)$ $\to\to P_N$

Step 2 really only requires three sums, although we will show all 10 below:

$P_1 + \mathbf{P_2} = (ABC)(D)$ $\to\to P_2$ not needed
$P_1 + P_3 = (ABD)(C)$ $\to\to P_5$
$P_1 + P_4 = (ABC)(D)$ $\to\to P_2$
$P_1 + \mathbf{P_5} = (ABD)(C)$ $\to\to P_5$ not needed
$\mathbf{P_2} + P_3$ $\to\to P_N$ not needed
$\mathbf{P_2} + P_4 = (ABC)(D)$ $\to\to P_2$ not needed
$\mathbf{P_2} + \mathbf{P_5}$ $\to\to P_N$ not needed
$P_3 + P_4 = (AD)(BC)$ $\to\to P_6 = (AD)(BC)$
$P_3 + \mathbf{P_5} = (ABD)(C)$ $\to\to P_5$ not needed
$P_4 + \mathbf{P_5}$ $\to\to P_N$ not needed

Those partitions shown in bold are two-block and thus never produce anything new. Only one new SP partition is found by step 2.

EXAMPLE 9.9

	$q^\star$		
q	$x = 0$	$x = 1$	z
A	C	D	0
B	D	A	0
C	E	D	0
D	B	A	1
E	C	D	1

Step 1 of the process produces five SP partitions, as follows:

$(AB) \to (CD)(AD) \to (ACD) \to (BCE)$ $\to\to P_N$
$(AC) \to (CE)$ $\to\to (ACE)(B)(D) = P_1$
$(AD) \to (BC) \to (DE)$ $\to\to (ADE)(BC) = P_2$
$(AE) \to \surd$ $\to\to (AE)(B)(C)(D) = P_3$
$(BC) \to (ADE)$ $\to\to P_2$
$(BD) \to \surd$ $\to\to (A)(BD)(C)(E) = P_4$
$(BE) \to (ACD) \to (BCE)$ $\to\to P_N$
$(CD) \to (BE)(AD) \to (BC)$ $\to\to P_N$
$(CE) \to \surd$ $\to\to (A)(B)(CE)(D) = P_5$
$(DE) \to (BC)(AD) \to (ADE)$ $\to\to P_2$

*Here is the first example of a pairing that requires no other states to be combined. It results in a partition where these two states are in one block and all others are by themselves.

For step 2, we add each of the pairs of partitions found in step 1, except that we do not need to add P_2 to anything (since it is two-block) and P_1 need not be added to P_3 or P_5 (since it is greater than each of them).

$$P_1 + P_4 = (ACE)(BD) \quad = P_6$$
$$P_3 + P_4 = (AE)(BD)(C) \quad = P_7$$
$$P_3 + P_5 = (ACE)(B)(D) \quad = P_1$$
$$P_4 + P_5 = (A)(BD)(CE) \quad = P_8$$

We now add pairs of these new partitions (with the same exceptions as above); there is only one sum (which does not produce anything new):

$$P_7 + P_8 = (ACE)(BD) \quad = P_6$$

If there were new partitions of more than two blocks, they must also be added.

For this example, there are eight nontrivial SP partitions, of which two are two-block and none are output-consistent. We will return to this state table in the next sections when we discuss state reduction and how to make good state assignments.

[SP 2, EX 2]

9.3 STATE REDUCTION USING PARTITIONS

Any partition that is both output consistent and SP can be used to reduce the system to one with one state for each block of that partition. Just as there is always a unique largest SP partition (P_N), there is always a unique largest output consistent SP partition. That is the one with the fewest blocks and thus corresponds to the reduced system with the fewest number of states.*

For the state table of Example 9.8, repeated here as Table 9.8, the only SP partition that is output consistent is $P_3 = (AD)(B)(C)$; thus, this state table can be reduced to one with three states (one for each block of P_3).

We will call the combined state A (rather than A-D); the reduced table is shown in Table 9.9.

We do not need to recalculate all of the SP partitions (although for this small example, that would be very easy). Any SP partition of the original system that is greater than (>) the one used to reduce the system is still SP. For this example, only $P_5 \geq P_3$. Thus, we get one nontrivial SP partition for the reduced system, namely,

$$P_5^{\star} = (AB)(C)$$

where AD of the original P_5 has been replaced by the new state A.

The last state table of the previous section, Example 9.9, did not have any output consistent SP partitions. Thus, it can not be reduced.

Table 9.8 A reducible state table.

q	$q^\star$ $x = 0$	$q^\star$ $x = 1$	z
A	C	D	1
B	C	D	0
C	B	D	1
D	C	A	1

Table 9.9 Reduced state table.

q	$q^\star$ $x = 0$	$q^\star$ $x = 1$	z
A	C	A	1
B	C	A	0
C	B	A	1

*It is possible that P_N is output consistent; but that is a combinational system, where the output does not depend on the state.

We will now look at two state tables with the same next state section, but different output columns.

EXAMPLE 9.10

q	$q^\star$ x = 0	x = 1	z
A	C	D	0
B	D	A	1
C	E	D	0
D	B	A	0
E	C	D	0

q	$q^\star$ x = 0	x = 1	z
A	C	D	0
B	D	A	1
C	E	D	0
D	B	A	1
E	C	D	0

The set of SP partitions for these two is the same as those for Example 9.9, since the substitution property does not depend on the output. Repeating the complete list here, we have

$P_1 = (ACE)(B)(D)$
$P_2 = (ADE)(BC)$
$P_3 = (AE)(B)(C)(D)$
$P_4 = (A)(BD)(C)(E)$
$P_5 = (A)(B)(CE)(D)$
$P_6 = (ACE)(BD)$
$P_7 = (AE)(BD)(C)$
$P_8 = (A)(BD)(CE)$

In the first table, P_1, P_3, and P_5 are the only output consistent partitions. Since

$P_1 = (ACE)(B)(D)$

is greater than either of the others, we will use it to reduce the system to one with three states, as follows:

q	$q^\star$ x = 0	x = 1	z
A-C-E	A-C-E	D	0
B	D	A-C-E	1
D	B	A-C-E	0

(We labeled the combined state with a compound name; we could have just called it *A*.) Note that only $P_6 > P_1$; thus, the only SP partition of the reduced system is

$P_6^\star = (A\text{-}C\text{-}E)(BD)$

For the second state table, P_1, P_3, P_4, P_5, P_6, and P_8 are all output consistent. The largest is

$P_6 = (ACE)(BD)$

as can be seen from the chart below, where the smaller ones are on the left.

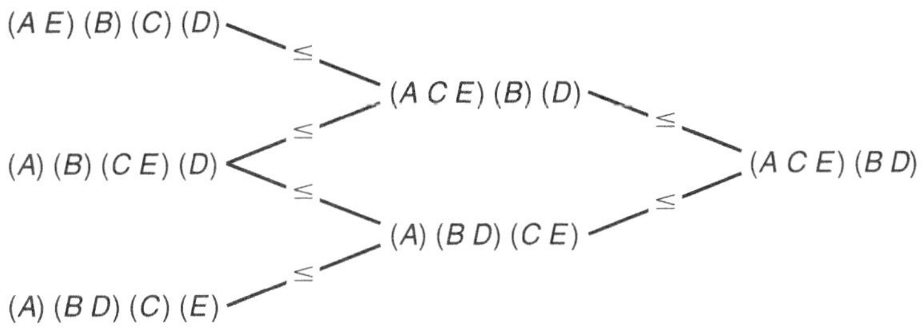

We can thus reduce the system to one with only two states, *A* (*ACE*) and *B* (*BD*), as shown below. This system requires only one flip flop.

q	$q^\star$ $x = 0$	$x = 1$	*z*
A	A	B	0
B	B	A	1

The computation of all of the SP partitions for a fairly large system can be quite time-consuming. If our interest is in reducing the system to one with the minimum number of states, we can do that immediately when we find an output consistent SP partition. Consider the following example.

EXAMPLE 9.11

q	$q^\star$ $x = 0$	$x = 1$	*z*
A	B	E	0
B	D	A	1
C	G	A	0
D	F	G	1
E	B	C	0
F	D	G	1
G	D	E	1

As we begin the process of finding SP partitions, we get

$(AB) \rightarrow (BD)(AE) \rightarrow (DF)(AG)(CE) \quad \rightarrow \rightarrow P_N$

$(AC) \rightarrow (BG)(AE) \rightarrow (ACE) \quad \rightarrow \rightarrow (ACE)(BG)(D)(F)$

This SP partition is also output consistent. Therefore, we could stop and reduce the system to one with four states (one for each block) and find the SP partitions of that smaller system.

q	$q^\star$ $x = 0$	$x = 1$	*z*
A	B	A	0
B	D	A	1
D	F	B	1
F	D	B	1

We can now find the SP partitions of this smaller system

$(AB) \to (BD) \to (DF) \quad \to \to P_N$
$(AD) \to (AB)^*(BF) \quad \to \to P_N$
$(AF) \to (BD)(AB) \quad \to \to P_N$
$(BD) \to (DF)(AB) \quad \to \to P_N$
$(BF) \to (AB) \quad \to \to P_N$
$(DF) \to \surd \quad \to (A)(B)(DF)$

This system can be reduced further, to one with three states, since the SP partition is also output consistent. The smallest equivalent system is thus

q	**q★** x = 0	x = 1	**z**
A	B	A	0
B	D	A	1
D	D	B	1

As a final example, consider the following state table, where five different output columns are shown. (This is a Moore system with an output that does not depend on the input; we will consider the different outputs as five different problems.)

EXAMPLE 9.12

q	**q★** x = 0	x = 1	z_1	z_2	z_3	z_4	z_5
A	D	B	0	0	0	1	1
B	E	C	0	0	1	0	1
C	A	B	1	1	0	0	1
D	E	C	1	1	1	1	1
E	D	B	1	0	0	1	1

We will start by finding all of the SP partitions. That, of course, does not depend upon which output column is used.

$(AB) \to (BC)(DE) \to (AE) \quad \to \to P_N$
$(AC) \to (AD) \to (AE)(BC) \quad \to \to P_N$
$(AD) \to (DE)(BC) \quad \to \to (ADE)(BC) = P_1$
$(AE) \to \surd \quad \to \to (AE)(B)(C)(D) = P_2$
$(BC) \to (AE) \quad \to \to (AE)(BC)(D) = P_3$
$(BD) \to \surd \quad \to \to (A)(BD)(C)(E) = P_4$
$(BE) \to (BC)(DE) \to (AE) \quad \to \to P_N$
$(CD) \to (AE)(BC) \quad \to \to (AE)(BCD) = P_5$
$(CE) \to (AD) \to (DE)(BC) \quad \to \to P_N$
$(DE) \to (BC) \to (AE) \quad \to \to P_1$

*Since we found that the only SP partition that combines *A* and *B* is P_N, we can stop looking; this must also produce P_N.

Now, forming sums, we obtain only one new partition

$$P_2 + P_4 = (AE)(BD)(C) = P_6$$

Thus, there are six nontrivial SP partitions.

For the first output column, none of the SP partitions are output consistent. Thus, the state table cannot be reduced. (We will return to this example in the next section and determine a good state assignment.)

For the second output column, only P_2 is output consistent. Thus, this system can be reduced to one with four states (replacing *A* and *E* by a state called *A*).

	$q^\star$		
q	***x* = 0**	***x* = 1**	z_2
A	*D*	*B*	0
B	*A*	*C*	0
C	*A*	*B*	1
D	*A*	*C*	1

Since any SP partition that is greater than P_2 is an SP partition of the reduced table (with states *A* and *E* shown as one, just *A*), we can see that the SP partitions are

$$P_1^\star = (AD)(BC)$$
$$P_3^\star = (A)(BC)(D)$$
$$P_5^\star = (A)(BCD)$$
$$P_6^\star = (A)(BD)(C)$$

For the third output column, P_2, P_4, and P_6 are all output consistent. Since P_6 is the largest of these, it is used to reduce the system to one with only three states.

	$q^\star$		
q	***x* = 0**	***x* = 1**	z_3
A	*B*	*B*	0
B	*A*	*C*	0
C	*A*	*B*	1

The only nontrivial SP partition for this system is

$$P_5^\star = (A)(BC)$$

For the fourth output column, P_1 is output consistent, reducing the state table to one with only two states.

q	$q^\star$ $x = 0$	$x = 1$	z_4
A	A	B	0
B	A	B	1

Finally, for the last output column, there was no need to find the SP partitions; P_N is output consistent; the system is combinational. It does not depend on the state.

$z = 1$

[SP 3, EX 3]

9.4 CHOOSING A STATE ASSIGNMENT

In this section, we will look at a strategy for making a "good" state assignment. We will first find all of the SP partitions, then reduce the system if possible, and finally make a state assignment to solve the problem. We have three levels of work, depending upon how important it is to reduce the cost of the combinational logic. If an absolute minimum is required, we must try all possible sets of two-block partitions for which the product is P_0. For three or four states, there are only three such assignments, and it is fairly easy to do that. For five states, however, that number goes up to 140, and this method is not practical. (It rises to 420 for six states, to 840 for seven or eight states, and to over 10 million for nine states.) If we can use two-block SP partitions for one or more of the variables, that is almost always preferable (as long as we do not increase the number of variables). We can then try to group states that are in the same block of multiblock SP partitions or to use partitions that correspond to one or more of the output columns for the other variables. This will usually lead to a pretty good solution. Last, and least likely to produce good results, we could choose an assignment at random, say using 000 for A, 001 for B, and so forth. Sometimes, that will lead to a good solution. But more often, it will result in a more costly system.

To illustrate this, we will consider the example in Table 9.10. The SP partitions are

Table 9.10 State assignment example.

q	$q^\star$ $x = 0$	$x = 1$	z
A	B	C	0
B	A	D	1
C	A	D	0
D	B	C	1

$$P_1 = (AB)(CD)$$
$$P_2 = (AD)(B)(C)$$
$$P_3 = (A)(BC)(D)$$
$$P_2 + P_3 = P_4 = (AD)(BC)$$

There are no output consistent SP partitions. There are two SP partitions that could be used for state assignment, namely, P_1 and P_4. That would produce the assignment of Table 9.11 and the D flip flop input equations shown.

Table 9.11 State assignment.

q	q_1	q_2
A	0	0
B	0	1
C	1	1
D	1	0

$$z = q_1'q_2 + q_1q_2'$$
$$D_1 = x$$
$$D_2 = q_2'$$

Since both flip flops were assigned according to an SP partition, the input equations are very simple.

If we repeat the design, using the output consistent partition for q_2, we get the state assignment of Table 9.12 and the equations shown beside it.

Table 9.12 State assignment.

q	q_1	q_2
A	0	0
B	0	1
C	1	0
D	1	1

$$z = q_2'$$
$$D_1 = x$$
$$D_2 = x'q_1'q_2' + x'q_1q_2 + xq_1'q_2 + xq_1q_2'$$

Notice that D_1 is unchanged. Since it was assigned according to the same SP partition as before, its behavior does not depend on the rest of the assignment. Also, z becomes simple, since q_2 is assigned according to an output consistent partition. This is an extreme case; D_2 is particularly complex. If, on the other hand, we assigned q_1 according to the output consistent partition and q_2 according to P_4 (as in the first example), we would get the assignment of Table 9.13 and the equations shown below.

Table 9.13 State assignment.

q	q_1	q_2
A	0	0
B	1	1
C	0	1
D	1	0

$$z = q_1$$
$$D_1 = x'q_2' + xq_2$$
$$D_2 = q_2'$$

Now, D_1 is more complex, although the total cost of combinational logic is the same as for the first assignment. Costs do not vary as much in two flip flop circuits as they do in larger ones.

We will illustrate the procedure with two of the output columns from Example 9.12.

EXAMPLE 9.13

We will first consider the table of Example 9.12 with output column z_2.

q	$q^\star$ $x = 0$	$x = 1$	z_2
A	D	B	0
B	E	C	0
C	A	B	1
D	E	C	1
E	D	B	0

The first step is to see if the system can be reduced. The SP partition, $(AE)(B)(C)(D)$ is output consistent, and thus this system can be reduced to one with four states, as shown below.

q	$q^\star$ $x = 0$	$x = 1$	z_2
A	D	B	0
B	A	C	0
C	A	B	1
D	A	C	1

The SP partitions for this are (as we found earlier)

$P_1^\star = (AD)(BC)$ $\quad P_5^\star = (A)(BCD)$

$P_3^\star = (A)(BC)(D)$ $\quad P_6^\star = (A)(BD)(C)$

The best assignment seems to be the one that uses $P_1^\star$ and the output consistent partition ($P_{OC} = (AB)(CD)$). That produces

$$z = q_2$$
$$D_1 = x$$
$$D_2 = q_1'q_2' + xq_2$$

If, instead, we used output column z_1, there could be no reduction, and three flip flops would be needed. However, there are 2 two-block SP partitions, in addition to the output consistent one, that can be used for the state assignment.

$$P_1 = (ADE)(BC)$$
$$P_5 = (AE)(BCD)$$
$$P_{OC} = (AB)(CDE)$$

This produces the state assignment

q	q_1	q_2	q_3
A	0	0	0
B	1	1	0
C	1	1	1
D	0	1	1
E	0	0	1

and the equations

$z = q_3$
$D_1 = x$
$D_2 = x + q_2'$
$D_3 = \{x'q_1' \text{ or } x'q_2'\} + q_1'q_2 + \{q_2q_3' \text{ or } q_1q_3'\}$

This requires only five gates plus the NOT gate for x'.

EXAMPLE 9.14

q	$q^\star$ x = 0	$q^\star$ x = 1	z x = 0	z x = 1
A	D	C	0	1
B	F	C	0	0
C	E	A	0	0
D	A	C	1	0
E	C	B	1	0
F	B	C	1	1

The nontrivial SP partitions are

$P_1 = (AB)(C)(DF)(E)$ $\quad P_6 = (AB)(CE)(DF)$
$P_2 = (ABC)(DEF)$ $\quad P_7 = (ABDF)(C)(E)$
$P_3 = (AD)(B)(C)(E)(F)$ $\quad P_8 = (ABDF)(CE)$
$P_4 = (AF)(BD)(C)(E)$ $\quad P_9 = (AD)(BF)(C)(E)$
$P_5 = (A)(BF)(C)(D)(E)$

As can be seen, none of these are output consistent; thus the table cannot be reduced.

For the first two variables, we will use the 2 two-block SP partitions, P_2 and P_8. The product of these are

$P_1 = (AB)(C)(DF)(E)$

For the third variable, we need a partition that separates A from B and D from F. There are many that will do that; we chose

$P_9 = (AF)(BCDE)$

because that corresponds to the second output column and will simplify somewhat the expression for z.

First, we will construct next block tables for q_1 and q_2.

q_1	$q_1^\star$ x = 0	$q_1^\star$ x = 1
0	1	0
1	0	0

q_2	$q_2^\star$ x = 0	$q_2^\star$ x = 1
0	0	1
1	1	0

This produces

$D_1 = x'q_1' \qquad D_2 = xq_2' + x'q_2$

For q_3 and z, we will need the state assignment and truth table:

q	q_1	q_2	q_3
A	0	0	1
B	0	0	0
C	0	1	0
D	1	0	0
E	1	1	0
F	1	0	1
	P_2	P_8	P_9

	x	q_1	q_2	q_3	$q_3^\star$	z
B	0	0	0	0	1	0
A	0	0	0	1	0	0
C	0	0	1	0	0	0
—	0	0	1	1	X	X
D	0	1	0	0	1	1
F	0	1	0	1	0	1
E	0	1	1	0	0	1
—	0	1	1	1	X	X
B	1	0	0	0	0	0
A	1	0	0	1	0	1
C	1	0	1	0	1	0
—	1	0	1	1	X	X
D	1	1	0	0	0	0
F	1	1	0	1	0	1
E	1	1	1	0	0	0
—	1	1	1	1	X	X

(We do not need columns for $q_1^\star$ and $q_2^\star$, since we already computed the inputs for those flip flops from the next block table.) The resulting maps are

$q_2 q_3$ \ $x q_1$	00	01	11	10
00	1	1		
01				
11	X	X	X	X
10				1

$q_3^\star$

$q_2 q_3$ \ $x q_1$	00	01	11	10
00		1		
01		1	1	1
11	X	X	X	X
10		1		

z

From this, we can find

$$D_3 = x'q_2'q_3' + xq_1'q_2 \qquad z = x'q_1 + xq_3$$

The advantage of using SP partitions is even more dramatic with JK flip flops (since J and K do not depend on the state of that flip flop). Thus, for this example,

$$J_1 = x' \qquad K_1 = 1$$
$$J_2 = x \qquad K_2 = x$$
$$J_3 = x'q_2' + xq_1'q_2 \qquad K_3 = 1$$

If, instead, we used the state assignment

q	q_1	q_2	q_3
A	0	0	0
B	0	0	1
C	0	1	0
D	0	1	1
E	1	0	0
F	1	0	1

we would obtain the equations

$$z = x'q_1 + q_1q_3 + xq_1'q_2'q_3' + x'q_2q_3$$
$$D_1 = x'q_1'q_2'q_3 + x'q_2q_3'$$
$$D_2 = xq_3 + x'q_2'q_3' + q_1'q_2'q_3'$$
$$D_3 = x'q_1'q_2' + xq_1q_3' + x'q_1q_3$$

These equations are much more complex than the previous solution.

EXAMPLE 9.15

q	q* x = 0	q* x = 1	z
A	B	C	0
B	D	C	1
C	A	E	0
D	A	C	0
E	A	C	1

The SP partitions are

$P_1 = (ABD)(C)(E)$ $P_4 = (A)(B)(CE)(D)$
$P_2 = (ABDE)(C)$ $P_5 = (A)(B)(C)(DE)$
$P_3 = (A)(B)(CDE)$ $P_6 = (ABD)(CE)$

None of these is output consistent; therefore, the system cannot be reduced. Although there are 2 two-block partitions, we cannot use both of them, since their product is P_1, which has three states in the same block. One more two-block partition cannot separate these three states. We can use P_6 and the output consistent partition,

$P_7 = (ACD)(BE)$

for two of the variables. Their product is

$(AD)(B)(C)(E)$

We now need to choose one more partition to separate A and D. From the list of SP partitions, P_3 is attractive. It groups C, D, and E. We could use either

$P_8 = (AB)(CDE)$ or $P_9 = (A)(BCDE)$

The two state assignments are

q	q_1	q_2	q_3
A	0	0	0
B	0	1	0
C	1	0	1
D	0	0	1
E	1	1	1

q	q_1	q_2	q_3
A	0	0	0
B	0	1	1
C	1	0	1
D	0	0	1
E	1	1	1

The resulting sets of equations for the first assignment are

$$J_1 = x \qquad K_1 = x'$$
$$J_2 = x'q_3' + xq_1 \qquad K_2 = 1$$
$$J_3 = x + q_2 \qquad K_3 = x'$$
$$z = q_2$$

For the second assignment, J_1, K_1, J_2, K_2, and z are unchanged; the others become

$$J_3 = 1 \qquad K_3 = x'q_2' + x'q_1$$

If, instead, we use the first five combinations for the five states, the equations become

$$J_1 = q_2q_3' \qquad K_1 = 1$$
$$J_2 = x + q_3 \qquad K_2 = x' + q_3'$$
$$J_3 = x'q_1'q_2' \qquad K_3 = x + q_2$$
$$z = q_1 + q_2'q_3$$

The cost of this combinational logic is about double that of the first solution.

The choice of state assignment is more of an art than a science. Surely, we want to use two-block SP partitions when possible. But when we run out of those, we use the output consistent partition and the groupings suggested by other SP partitions (if there are any).

This approach does not guarantee a minimum solution. The only way to do that is to try *all* possible sets of partitions. (In some unusual circumstances, it may even be possible to find a less costly solution with an extra flip flop or without reducing the number of states to a minimum.)

[SP 4; EX 4, 5, 6, 7]

9.5 SOLVED PROBLEMS

1. Reduce each of the following systems to ones with the minimum number of states using the tabular method.

a.

q	$q^\star$ $x = 0$	$x = 1$	z
A	C	B	0
B	D	A	1
C	A	B	0
D	B	B	1

b.

q	$q^\star$ $x = 0$	$x = 1$	z
A	C	D	1
B	C	C	1
C	E	B	0
D	E	A	0
E	A	B	1

c.

q	$q^\star$ $x = 0$	$x = 1$	z
A	E	B	0
B	D	A	1
C	F	B	0
D	E	B	1
E	D	C	1
F	D	A	1

d.

q	$q^\star$ $x = 0$	$x = 1$	z
A	D	G	0
B	C	E	1
C	B	G	0
D	A	B	1
E	F	E	0
F	G	B	1
G	F	A	0

a. We will first construct the chart

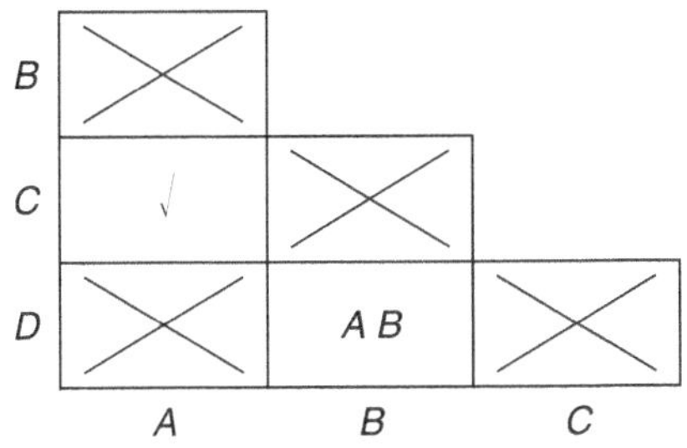

Since the *AB* box already has an X in it, the only equivalent states are *A* and *C*. The state table can be reduced to one with three states, as follows:

q	$q^\star$ $x = 0$	$x = 1$	z
A-C	A-C	B	0
B	D	A-C	1
D	B	B	1

b. The chart for this table is

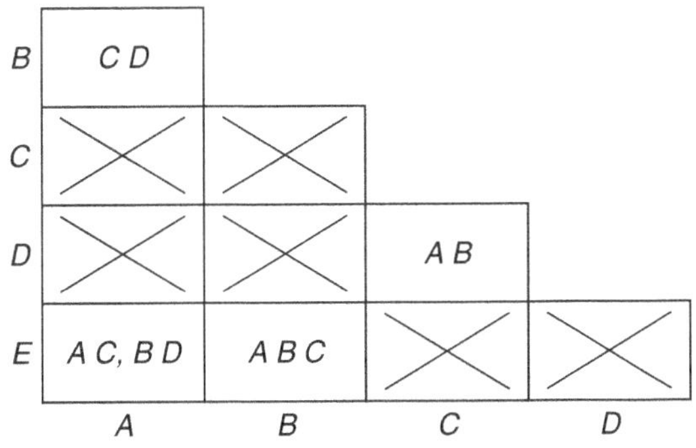

Since for *A* to be together with *B* requires *C* to be grouped with *D*, and the *CD* grouping requires *A* and *B* to be together, both of those can be checked off. *A* and *C* cannot be in the same block of a partition; thus, the other two are crossed off, resulting in

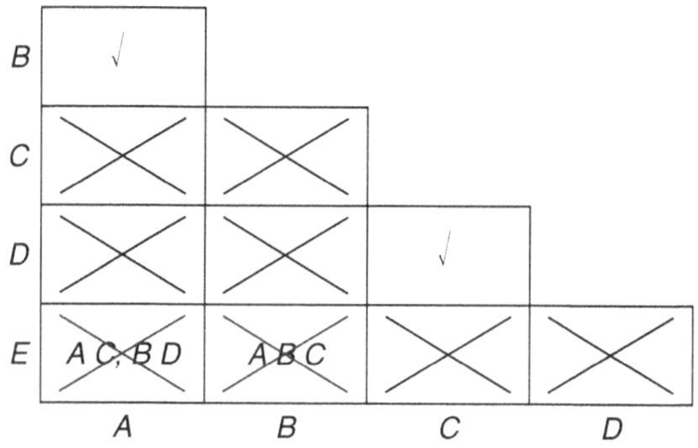

The reduced state table is thus (where *A*-*B* has been called *A*, and *C*-*D* has been called *C*)

q	$q^\star$ $x = 0$	$x = 1$	z
A	C	C	1
C	E	A	0
E	A	A	1

c. We get the following chart:

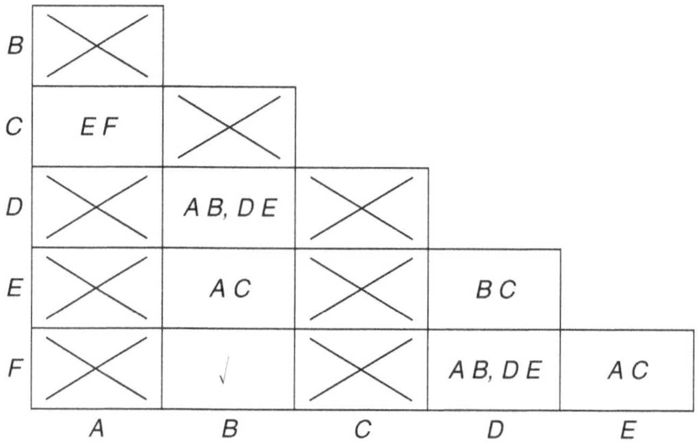

B and *F* are already grouped; *AC* and *EF* also group. That produces a group with *B*, *E*, and *F*, reducing the table to one with only three states (since *AB* and *BC* cannot be grouped):

q	$q^\star$ $x = 0$	$x = 1$	z
A	*B*	*B*	0
B	*D*	*A*	1
D	*B*	*B*	1

---

d. The chart becomes

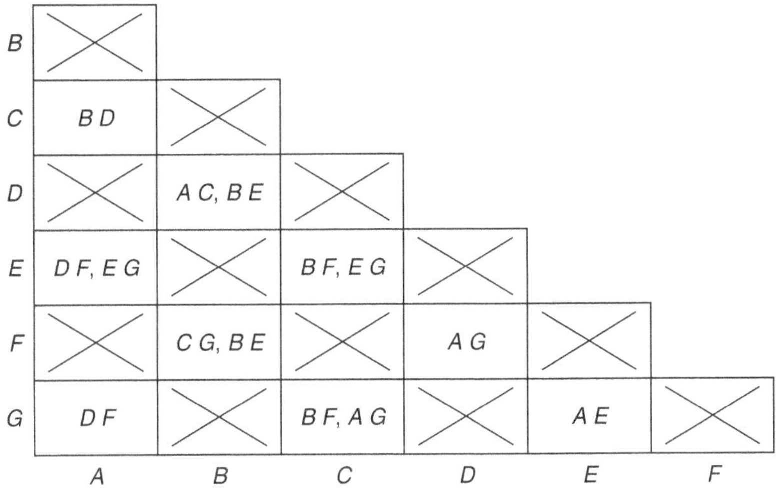

We can cross out a few squares and obtain

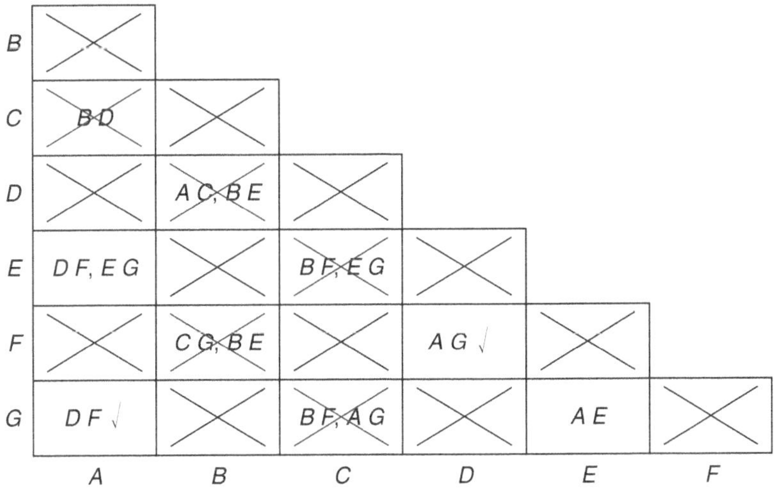

On the first pass, we were able to cross out *BE*, which then allowed us to cross out *BD* and *BF*. Since those pairs could not be equivalent, we were then able to eliminate *AC*, *CE*, and *EG*. At this point, we note that for *A* and *G* to be equivalent, *D* and *F* must be equivalent and for *D* and *F* to be equivalent, *A* and *G* must be equivalent. We can thus reduce the number of states by two, reduce the state table and repeat the process, as follows:

	$q^\star$		
q	$x = 0$	$x = 1$	z
A	D	A	0
B	C	E	1
C	B	A	0
D	A	B	1
E	D	E	0

The new smaller chart is thus

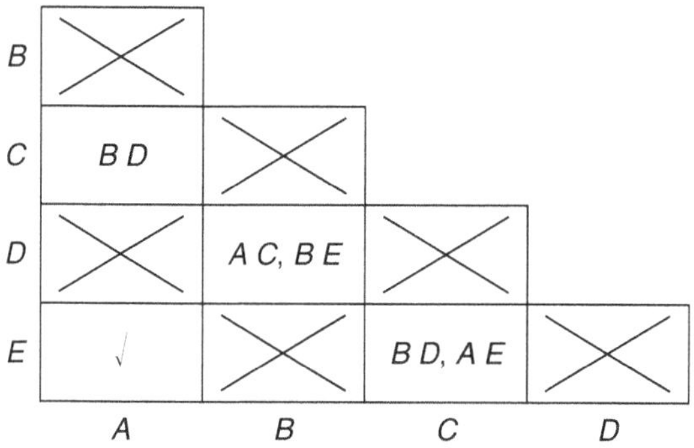

Only *A* and *E* can be equivalent, since *B* and *E* are not equivalent, making *B* and *D* not equivalent. Thus, we can reduce this further to four states, namely,

	$q^\star$		
q	$x = 0$	$x = 1$	z
A	D	A	0
B	C	A	1
C	B	A	0
D	A	B	1

Of course, we could have determined this from the original chart, where we have replaced the crossed out squares with X's and the two equivalences we had previously determined with checks.

B	X					
C	X	X				
D	X	X	X			
E	D F, G E	X	X	X		
F	X	X	X	√	X	
G	√	X	X	X	A E	X
	A	B	C	D	E	F

From this table, we can see that *G* and *E* are equivalent if *A* and *E* are equivalent, grouping *A*, *G*, and *E*. That would directly produce the same table with four states as above.

2. For the same state tables as in Solved Problem 1, find all of the nontrivial SP partitions. (Of course, the output columns are not used.)

a. $(AB) \rightarrow (CD)$ $\rightarrow\rightarrow (AB)(CD) = P_1$
(AC) √ $\rightarrow\rightarrow (AC)(B)(D) = P_2$
$(AD) \rightarrow (BC) \rightarrow (AB)$ $\rightarrow\rightarrow (ABCD) = P_N$
$(BC) \rightarrow (ABD)$ $\rightarrow\rightarrow P_N$
$(BD) \rightarrow (AB)$ $\rightarrow\rightarrow P_N$
$(CD) \rightarrow (AB)$ $\rightarrow\rightarrow (AB)(CD) = P_1$

b. $(AB) \rightarrow (CD)$ $\rightarrow\rightarrow (AB)(CD)(E) = P_1$
$(AC) \rightarrow (CE)(BD)$ $\rightarrow\rightarrow (ACE)(BD) = P_2$
$(AD) \rightarrow (CE) \rightarrow (AE)$ $\rightarrow\rightarrow P_N$
$(AE) \rightarrow (AC)(BD)$ $\rightarrow\rightarrow P_2$
$(BC) \rightarrow (CE)(ABCE)$ $\rightarrow\rightarrow P_N$
$(BD) \rightarrow (ACE)$ $\rightarrow\rightarrow P_2$
$(BE) \rightarrow (ABC)$ $\rightarrow\rightarrow P_N$
$(CD) \rightarrow (AB)$ $\rightarrow\rightarrow P_1$
$(CE) \rightarrow (AE) \rightarrow (BD)$ $\rightarrow\rightarrow P_2$
$(DE) \rightarrow (ABE)$ $\rightarrow\rightarrow P_N$

c. $(AB) \rightarrow (DE) \rightarrow (BC) \rightarrow (DF)$ $\rightarrow\rightarrow (ABC)(DEF) = P_1$
$(AC) \rightarrow (EF)$ $\rightarrow\rightarrow (AC)(B)(EF)(D) = P_2$
(AD) √ $\rightarrow\rightarrow (AD)(B)(C)(E)(F) = P_3$
$(AE) \rightarrow (DE)(BC)$ $\rightarrow\rightarrow P_N$

$(AF) \rightarrow (DE)(AB) \rightarrow (BC) \quad \rightarrow\rightarrow P_N$
$(BC) \rightarrow (DF)(AB)$
$\quad \rightarrow (ABC)(DEF) \quad \rightarrow\rightarrow P_1$
$(BD) \rightarrow (DE)(AB) \rightarrow (BC) \quad \rightarrow\rightarrow P_N$
$(BE) \rightarrow (AC) \rightarrow (EF) \quad \rightarrow\rightarrow (AC)(BEF)(D) = P_4$
$(BF) \rightarrow \surd \quad \rightarrow\rightarrow (A)(BF)(C)(D)(E) = P_5$
$(CD) \rightarrow (EF)(AC) \quad \rightarrow\rightarrow (ACD)(B)(EF) = P_6$
$(CF) \rightarrow (DF)(AB) \rightarrow (DE) \quad \rightarrow\rightarrow P_N$
$(DE) \rightarrow (BC) \rightarrow (DF)(AB) \quad \rightarrow\rightarrow P_1$
$(DF) \rightarrow (DE)(AB) \quad \rightarrow\rightarrow P_1$
$(EF) \rightarrow (AC) \quad \rightarrow\rightarrow P_2$

At this point, we have found six SP partitions. We must now add each pair, since the sum of SP partitions is also SP. The only new partitions are

$$P_3 + P_4 = P_7 = (ACD)(BEF)$$
$$P_3 + P_5 = P_8 = (AD)(BF)(C)(E)$$

No new sums are formed from these two (since P_7 is two-block). (We will return to this example in later solved problems.)

---

d. $(AB) \rightarrow (CD)(EG) \rightarrow (ABEG)$
$\quad \rightarrow (CDF) \quad \rightarrow\rightarrow (ABEG)(CDF) = P_1$
$(AC) \rightarrow (BD) \rightarrow (BE) \rightarrow (CF) \rightarrow (BDG) \quad \rightarrow\rightarrow P_N$
$(AD) \rightarrow (BG) \rightarrow (CF)(AE) \quad \rightarrow\rightarrow P_N$
$(AE) \rightarrow (DF)(EG) \rightarrow (AEG) \quad \rightarrow\rightarrow (AEG)(B)(C)(DF) = P_2$
$(AF) \rightarrow (BDG) \rightarrow (ACF)(ABE) \quad \rightarrow\rightarrow P_N$
$(AG) \rightarrow (DF) \quad \rightarrow\rightarrow (AG)(B)(C)(DF)(E) = P_3$
$(BC) \rightarrow (GE) \rightarrow (AE) \rightarrow (DF) \quad \rightarrow\rightarrow (AEG)(BC)(DF) = P_4$
$(BD) \rightarrow (AC)(BE) \quad \rightarrow\rightarrow P_N$
$(BE) \rightarrow (CF) \rightarrow (BG) \rightarrow (AE) \quad \rightarrow\rightarrow P_1$
$(BF) \rightarrow (CG)(BE) \rightarrow (BF)(AG) \quad \rightarrow\rightarrow P_N$
$(BG) \rightarrow (CF)(AE) \rightarrow (DF)(EG) \quad \rightarrow\rightarrow P_1$
$(CD) \rightarrow (ABG) \quad \rightarrow\rightarrow P_1$
$(CE) \rightarrow (BF)(EG) \quad \rightarrow\rightarrow P_N$
$(CF) \rightarrow (BG) \rightarrow (AE) \rightarrow (DF)(EG) \quad \rightarrow\rightarrow P_1$
$(CG) \rightarrow (BF)(AG) \quad \rightarrow\rightarrow P_N$
$(DE) \rightarrow (AF)(BE) \quad \rightarrow\rightarrow P_N$
$(DF) \rightarrow (AG) \quad \rightarrow\rightarrow P_3$
$(DG) \rightarrow (ABF) \quad \rightarrow\rightarrow P_N$
$(EF) \rightarrow (FG)(BE) \rightarrow (AB) \quad \rightarrow\rightarrow P_N$

$(EG) \to (AE)$ $\to \to P_2$

$(FG) \to (AB)$ $\to \to P_N$

The sums produce nothing new. Thus, there are four nontrivial SP partitions.

3. a. Reduce the system of Solved Problem 2a to one with a minimum number of states if the output column is

	(i)	(ii)	(iii)
A	0	1	0
B	1	0	0
C	0	0	1
D	1	1	1

b. Reduce the system of Solved Problem 2c to one with a minimum number of states and find all of the SP partitions of the reduced system if the output column is

	(i)	(ii)	(iii)
A	0	1	0
B	1	0	0
C	0	1	1
D	0	0	1
E	0	0	1
F	1	0	0

a. (i) $P_2 = (AC)(B)(D)$ is the only output consistent SP partition. Thus, the system can be reduced to one with three states:

q	$q^\star$ $x = 0$	$x = 1$	z
A	A	B	0
B	D	A	1
D	B	B	1

(ii) There are no output consistent SP partitions; therefore, the system cannot be reduced for this output column.

(iii) $P_1 = (AB)(CD)$ is the only output consistent SP partition. Thus, we can reduce the system to one with just two states:

q	$q^\star$ $x = 0$	$x = 1$	z
A	C	A	0
C	A	A	1

b. (i) The output consistent SP partitions are

$$P_3 = (AD)(B)(C)(E)(F)$$
$$P_5 = (A)(BF)(C)(D)(E)$$
$$P_8 = (AD)(BF)(C)(E)$$

Clearly, P_8 is larger than either of the others; it can be used to reduce the system to one with only four states. None of the SP partitions is larger than P_8; therefore, the reduced system has no nontrivial SP partitions.

q	$q^\star$ $x = 0$	$x = 1$	z
A	E	B	0
B	A	A	1
C	B	B	0
E	A	C	0

(ii) The output consistent SP partitions are

$$P_2 = (AC)(B)(D)(EF)$$
$$P_4 = (AC)(BEF)(D)$$
$$P_5 = (A)(BF)(C)(D)(E)$$

P_4 is larger than either of the others and can be used to reduce this to a system with three states:

q	$q^\star$ $x = 0$	$x = 1$	z
A	B	B	1
B	D	A	0
D	B	B	0

Since $P_7 > P_4$, then $P_7^\star = (AD)(B)$ is SP.

(iii) The only output consistent SP partition is

$$P_5 = (A)(BF)(C)(D)(E)$$

Thus, the minimum system requires five states, namely,

q	$q^\star$ $x = 0$	$x = 1$	z
A	E	B	0
B	D	A	0
C	B	B	1
D	E	B	1
E	D	C	1

There are three SP partitions for this reduced system,

$P_4^\star = (AC)(BE)(D)$
$P_7^\star = (ACD)(BE)$
$P_8^\star = (AD)(B)(C)(E)$

4. Find good state assignments for each of the following state tables. (Each of the first four correspond to one of the state tables from Solved Problem 2.) Compute the input equations for either *D* or *JK* flip flops and the output equation.

a.

q	$q^\star$ $x = 0$	$q^\star$ $x = 1$	z
A	C	B	0
B	D	A	1
C	A	B	0
D	B	B	0

b.

q	$q^\star$ $x = 0$	$q^\star$ $x = 1$	z
A	C	B	1
B	D	A	1
C	A	B	0
D	B	B	1

c.

q	$q^\star$ $x = 0$	$q^\star$ $x = 1$	z
A	E	B	0
B	D	A	0
C	F	B	1
D	E	B	1
E	D	C	1
F	D	A	1

d.

q	$q^\star$ $x = 0$	$q^\star$ $x = 1$	z
A	E	B	0
B	D	A	0
C	F	B	1
D	E	B	1
E	D	C	0
F	D	A	1

e.

q	$q^\star$ $x = 0$	$q^\star$ $x = 1$	z $x = 0$	z $x = 1$
A	C	D	0	0
B	E	A	1	1
C	A	D	0	0
D	B	A	1	0
E	B	C	1	1

f.

q	$q^\star$ $x = 0$	$q^\star$ $x = 1$	z $x = 0$	z $x = 1$
A	C	D	0	1
B	E	A	1	1
C	A	D	0	0
D	B	A	1	0
E	B	C	1	1

a. $P_2 = (AC)(B)(D)$ is output consistent; therefore, this system can be reduced to one with three states, namely,

q	$q^\star$ $x = 0$	$x = 1$	z
A	A	B	0
B	D	A	1
D	B	B	0

Since the other SP partition is not larger than P_2, this system has no nontrivial SP partitions. There is not a good clue as to how to choose partitions for a state assignment, other than choosing the output consistent one to minimize the output logic. We can try both

i.

q	q_1	q_2
A	0	0
B	0	1
D	1	0

ii.

q	q_1	q_2
A	0	0
B	1	1
D	1	0

For assignment i, we get

$$D_1 = x'q_2 \quad D_2 = q_1 + xq_2' \quad z = q_2$$

and for assignment ii, we obtain

$$D_1 = x'q_1 + xq_2' \qquad D_2 = q_1q_2' + xq_2' \qquad z = q_2$$

The first assignment requires the least amount of logic. If we tried the third assignment, we would find that it needs about the same amount of logic as the second (but uses 2 three-input gates).

---

b. This, of course, is the same next state behavior as part a, but the new output column is such that there are no output consistent SP partitions. We will implement it with JK flip flops. We do have one two-block SP partition,

$$P_1 = (AB)(CD)$$

The two-block output consistent partition is not useful, since its product with P_1 is not P_0. We will use for the second variable

$$P_3 = (AC)(BD)$$

which takes advantage of the other SP partition, $P_2 = (AC)(B)(D)$, by putting A and C in the same block. This results in

$$J_1 = x' \quad K_1 = 1 \quad J_2 = x \quad K_2 = xq_1' \quad z = q_1' + q_2$$

Each of the other solutions requires very little logic as well. That will normally be the case with only two flip flops.

---

c. There are no output consistent SP partitions; thus, this system cannot be reduced. There are 2 two-block SP partitions,

$$P_1 = (ABC)(DEF)$$
$$P_7 = (ACD)(BEF)$$

which will be used for the first two variables. The output consistent two-block partition is not useful, since its product with P_1 and P_7 is not P_0; states E and F would have the same assignment. We need a partition to separate A from C and E from F. P_3 indicates that A and D should be together; P_5 indicates that B and F should be together. One of the partitions that accomplishes these goals and still produces a product of P_0 with P_1 and P_7 is

$$P_9 = (ABDF)(CE)^*$$

The resulting state assignment is

q	q_1	q_2	q_3
A	0	0	0
B	0	1	0
C	0	0	1
D	1	0	0
E	1	1	1
F	1	1	0

The equations for q_1 and q_2 can be obtained from just the block tables; the equation for D_3 requires a 16-row truth table and those for z require an 8-row table. (The work is left as an exercise for the reader.)

$$D_1 = x' \quad D_2 = q_2' \quad z = q_1 + q_3$$
$$D_3 = x'q_2'q_3' + \{xq_1q_3 \text{ or } xq_2q_3\}$$

This solution requires four gates plus the NOT gate. If we used the straight binary assignment (A: 000, B: 001, . . .), we would need 13 gates.

---

d. The next state portion of the table (and thus the list of SP partitions) is the same as for part c. But, in this case, the product of the output consistent partition

$$P_{OC} = (ABE)(CDF)$$

---

*There are others; you should try them as an exercise to see if one of them produces a less costly solution.

with the other two is P_0, and we can use it for the third variable. The inputs to the first two flip flops would be the same as for part c; the inputs for the third flip flop and the output would be

$$D_3 = x'q_1'q_2 + x'q_2 + q_1'q_3' \quad z = q_3$$

This requires seven gates. As in part c, the straight binary assignment would be much more expensive (14 gates).

e. The SP partitions are found as follows (ignoring the output section, of course):

$$\begin{array}{ll}
(AB) \rightarrow (AD)(CE) \rightarrow (BC)(CD) \rightarrow & \rightarrow P_N \\
(AC) \rightarrow \surd & \rightarrow (AC)(B)(D)(E) \\
 & = P_1 \\
(AD) \rightarrow (BC) \rightarrow (ADE) \rightarrow (AC) & \rightarrow P_N \\
(AE) \rightarrow (BCD) & \rightarrow P_N \\
(BC) \rightarrow (ADE) \rightarrow (AC) & \rightarrow P_N \\
(BD) \rightarrow (BE) \rightarrow (AC) & \rightarrow (AC)(BDE) = P_2 \\
(BE) \rightarrow (AC) & \rightarrow (AC)(BE)(D) = P_3 \\
(CD) \rightarrow (ABD) & \rightarrow P_N \\
(CE) \rightarrow (AB)(CD) & \rightarrow P_N \\
(DE) \rightarrow (AC) & \rightarrow (AC)(B)(DE) = P_4
\end{array}$$

Note that both

$$P_N \geq P_2 \geq P_3 \geq P_1 \geq P_0$$
$$P_N \geq P_2 \geq P_4 \geq P_1 \geq P_0$$

No additional SP partitions are found by taking the sum of these.

An inspection of the state table shows that P_1 and P_3 are output consistent; thus the system can be reduced (using the larger of these) to one with three states (combining A with C and B with E), as follows:

	$q^\star$		z	
q	$x = 0$	$x = 1$	$x = 0$	$x = 1$
A	A	D	0	0
B	B	A	1	1
D	B	A	1	0

The only SP partition for this reduced table is

$$P_3^\star = (A)(BD)$$

It can be used for one variable, q_1, in the state assignment. For that variable, we just need a next block table, namely,

q	$q^\star$ $x = 0$	$x = 1$
0(A)	0	1
1(B-D)	1	0

Either directly from the state table or by converting it to a truth table or directly to maps, we can determine

$$J_1 = K_1 = x$$

The first row of $q^\star$ is the map for J and the second row is that for K'. (We can always do a block table for variables assigned using SP partitions.)

There is no clue from the next state portion as to which partition to choose for the other variable. However, if we use

$$P_4 = (AD)(B)$$

(which corresponds to the second column of the output section), we are assured of a fairly simple output equation, namely,

$$z = x'q_1 + xq_2$$

If we choose P_4 for q_2, then the state assignment and the truth table for the next value of q_2 and the output become

q	q_1	q_2
A	0	0
B	1	1
D	1	0

q	x	q_1	q_2	z	$q_2^\star$
A	0	0	0	0	0
—	0	0	1	X	X
D	0	1	0	1	1
B	0	1	1	1	1
A	1	0	0	0	0
—	1	0	1	X	X
D	1	1	0	0	0
B	1	1	1	1	0

The maps for z and q_2 (with the J portion for the quick method shaded) are

$q_1 q_2$ \ x	0	1
00		
01	X	X
11	1	1
10	1	

z

$q_1 q_2$ \ x	0	1
00		
01	X	X
11	1	
10	1	

$q_2^\star$

The resulting equations are

$$z = q_2 + x'q_1 \qquad J_2 = x'q_1 \qquad K_2 = x$$

Note that we have an even simpler version of z than expected.

If we retain the SP partition for assigning the first variable and use the other two-block partition, $P_5 = (AB)(D)$, for q_2, we get

$$z = x'q_2 + q_1q_2' \qquad J_2 = xq_1' \qquad K_2 = 1$$

There is not much difference. Finally, if we do not use the SP partition, but rather use the state assignment

q	q_1	q_2
A	0	0
B	0	1
D	1	0

we will get

$$z = q_2 + x'q_1 \qquad J_1 = xq_2' \qquad K_2 = 1 \qquad J_2 = x'q_1$$
$$K_2 = x$$

For this simple problem, the state assignment does not make a major difference.

---

f. The table of part f has one small change in the output section, so that there are no longer any output consistent SP partitions. We now need three variables, only one of which can use an SP partition. The only two-block SP partition is P_2, and we will use it to assign q_1. We will then use P_3 to help with the second variable; it keeps A and C together, and B and E together. We must group D with AC; otherwise, we would just repeat the same partition as before. Thus, we use

$P_5 = (ACD)(BE)$

The product of these two is P_3 and we must now find a two-block partition, the product of which with P_3 is P_0. There are several possibilities, such as

$P_6 = (ABD)(CE)$
$P_7 = (AB)(CDE)$
$P_8 = (AE)(BCD)$
$P_9 = (ADE)(BC)$

Any of these might lead to a good solution. Using P_2, P_5, and P_6, we have the following state assignment and design tables:

q	q_1	q_2	q_3
A	0	0	0
B	1	1	0
C	0	0	1
D	1	0	0
E	1	1	1

q_1	$q_1^\star$ $x = 0$	$q_1^\star$ $x = 1$
0	0	1
1	1	0

	x	q_1	q_2	q_3	$q_2^\star$	$q_3^\star$	z
A	0	0	0	0	0	1	0
C	0	0	0	1	0	0	0
—	0	0	1	0	X	X	X
—	0	0	1	1	X	X	X
D	0	1	0	0	1	0	1
—	0	1	0	1	X	X	X
B	0	1	1	0	1	1	1
E	0	1	1	1	1	0	1
A	1	0	0	0	0	0	1
C	1	0	0	1	0	0	0
—	1	0	1	0	X	X	X
—	1	0	1	1	X	X	X
D	1	1	0	0	0	0	0
—	1	1	0	1	X	X	X
B	1	1	1	0	0	0	1
E	1	1	1	1	0	1	1

The block table is used to solve for q_1 and the truth table allows us to solve for the other two flip flop inputs and the system output. The resulting equations are

$$D_1 = xq_1' + x'q_1$$
$$D_2 = x'q_1$$
$$D_3 = x'q_1'q_3' + x'q_2q_3' + \{xq_1q_3 \text{ or } xq_2q_3\}$$
$$z = q_2 + x'q_1 + xq_1'q_3'$$

requiring nine gates (since $x'q_1$ need only be built once) (plus a NOT gate to form x').

If, instead, we used the assignment (just the first five binary numbers)

q	q_1	q_2	q_3
A	0	0	0
B	0	0	1
C	0	1	0
D	0	1	1
E	1	0	0

we get the equations

$$D_1 = x'q_2'q_3$$
$$D_2 = xq_3' + q_1'q_2'q_3$$
$$D_3 = x'q_1 + xq_1'q_3' + q_2q_3'$$
$$z = q_1 + x'q_3 + xq_2'$$

This requires 11 gates (plus the NOT for x'), significantly more logic than required for the other assignment. The other assignments with P_7, P_8, and P_9 are left as an exercise.

9.6 EXERCISES

1. Reduce each of the following systems to ones with the minimum number of states using the tabular method.

a.

q	$q^\star$ $x = 0$	$q^\star$ $x = 1$	z
A	C	B	0
B	D	A	0
C	A	B	1
D	B	B	1

b.

q	$q^\star$ $x = 0$	$q^\star$ $x = 1$	z
A	C	B	0
B	D	C	1
C	A	B	0
D	A	B	0

★c.

q	$q^\star$ $x = 0$	$q^\star$ $x = 1$	z
A	C	B	0
B	D	A	0
C	E	A	1
D	E	B	1
E	D	B	1

d. Same table as c, except that the output for state B is 1.

e.

q	$q^\star$ $x = 0$	$q^\star$ $x = 1$	z
A	F	B	0
B	E	C	0
C	D	C	1
D	C	A	0
E	B	C	1
F	A	B	0

f.

q	$q^\star$ $x = 0$	$q^\star$ $x = 1$	z
A	B	B	0
B	F	D	0
C	D	A	1
D	C	E	0
E	F	E	0
F	E	A	1

g.

q	$q^\star$ $x = 0$	$q^\star$ $x = 1$	z
A	B	C	0
B	D	E	1
C	D	F	0
D	B	E	1
E	F	C	0
F	D	A	0

★h.

q	$q^\star$ $x = 0$	$q^\star$ $x = 1$	z $x = 0$	z $x = 1$
A	B	D	0	0
B	E	G	1	0
C	G	F	0	0
D	A	C	1	1
E	B	D	0	0
F	G	D	0	0
G	A	B	1	0

i.

q	$q^\star$ $x = 0$	$q^\star$ $x = 1$	z
A	E	B	0
B	C	C	1
C	D	E	1
D	F	B	0
E	A	F	1
F	D	F	1

j.

q	$q^\star$ $x = 0$	$q^\star$ $x = 1$	z
A	B	G	0
B	A	E	1
C	A	F	1
D	G	B	1
E	C	D	0
F	B	D	0
G	G	B	1

★k.

q	$q^\star$ $x = 0$	$q^\star$ $x = 1$	z
A	G	B	0
B	E	C	0
C	E	B	1
D	A	B	0
E	F	D	0
F	E	D	1
G	A	B	1

l.

q	$q^\star$ $x = 0$	$q^\star$ $x = 1$	z
A	G	B	0
B	E	C	1
C	E	B	1
D	A	B	1
E	F	D	1
F	E	D	1
G	A	B	0

2. For each of the state tables of Exercise 1, find all of the nontrivial SP partitions.

3. a. For state tables a and b of Exercise 2, reduce the system to one with a minimum number of states if the output column is

A	(i) 0	(ii) 1	(iii) 0	(iv) 0
B	1	0	0	1
C	0	0	1	0
D	1	1	1	0

b. Reduce the system of Exercises 1e and 1g to ones with a minimum number of states if the output column is

A	(i) 0	(ii) 1	(iii) 0	(iv) 1
B	1	0	0	0
C	0	1	0	0
D	1	1	1	0
E	0	0	1	0
F	1	1	1	0

★c. Reduce the system of Exercises 1k to one with a minimum number of states if the output column is

A	(i) 0	(ii) 1	(iii) 0	(iv) 1
B	1	0	0	0
C	1	1	1	0
D	1	1	1	1
E	0	0	1	0
F	0	1	0	0
G	0	1	0	1

4. a. For Solved Problem 4c,

i. Find the *D*'s and z for the straight binary assignment.

ii. Find D_3 and z using the two SP partitions for q_1 and q_2 and using $P_9 = (ABDE)(CF)$ for q_3.

iii. Find D_3 and z using the two SP partitions for q_1 and q_2 and using $P_{10} = (ADE)(BCF)$ for q_3.

b. Continue the example of Solved Problem 4f, using

$$P_2 = (AC)(BDE)$$
$$P_5 = (ACD)(BE)$$

and each of

i. $P_7 = (AB)(CDE)$

ii. $P_8 = (AE)(BCD)$

iii. $P_9 = (ADE)(BC)$

5. For each of the state tables shown below, find a good state assignment and design the system using *JK* flip flops. Compare that design with the state assignment that just uses the binary numbers in order for the states (that is, *A*: 000, *B*: 001, *C*: 010, . . .).*

a.

q	$q^{\star}$ $x = 0$	$q^{\star}$ $x = 1$	z
A	D	B	1
B	C	D	1
C	E	D	1
D	A	B	0
E	C	D	0

b.

q	$q^{\star}$ $x = 0$	$q^{\star}$ $x = 1$	z $x = 0$	z $x = 1$
A	D	G	1	0
B	C	E	1	1
C	B	G	0	1
D	A	B	0	0
E	F	E	1	0
F	G	B	1	1
G	F	A	1	1

★c. Exercise 1e with output column
1
0
0
1
1
0

d. Exercise 1k.

6. For each of the following output columns, reduce the system if possible and find a good state assignment

q	$q^{\star}$ $x = 0$	$q^{\star}$ $x = 1$	z_1	z_2	z_3	z_4
A	E	B	0	0	1	0
B	C	D	0	0	0	0
C	E	F	1	1	0	0
D	E	A	1	0	0	1
E	C	F	0	1	0	1
F	C	D	1	0	1	0

*Note that part b has the same next state portion as Solved Problem 2d.

7. Consider the following state table, where the next state is not specified. Complete the next state portion such that the system can be reduced to four states (not any smaller) and it is possible to get from any state to any other state with an appropriate input sequence.

q	$q^\star$ $x = 0$	$q^\star$ $x = 1$	z $x = 0$	z $x = 1$
A			0	0
B			0	1
C			1	1
D			0	0
E			1	1
F			1	0

9.7 CHAPTER 9 TEST (50 MINUTES)

1. Using the techniques of Section 7.1, reduce the following state table to one with the minimum number of states.

q	$q^\star$ $x = 0$	$q^\star$ $x = 1$	z
A	C	B	0
B	D	A	0
C	E	A	0
D	E	B	0
E	D	B	1

2. For the state table of Problem 1,
   a. For each of the following partitions, indicate whether or not it is SP and whether or not it is output consistent.

      $P_1 = (ABCD)(E)$
      $P_2 = (ABE)(CD)$
      $P_3 = (AC)(BE)(D)$
      $P_4 = (AB)(CD)(E)$
      $P_5 = (AB)(CDE)$
      $P_6 = (A)(B)(C)(D)(E)$

   b. Using one of these partitions, reduce the system to the one with the smallest number of states, showing a new state table.

3. For the following state table, find all of the nontrivial SP partitions.

q	$q^\star$ $x = 0$	$x = 1$	z
A	C	B	
B	D	C	
C	A	B	
D	B	C	

4. For the following state table,

q	$q^\star$ $x = 0$	$x = 1$	z
A	D	B	1
B	F	D	0
C	A	D	1
D	E	D	0
E	C	B	1
F	D	C	0

The following are all of the SP partitions,

$P_1 = (AE)(CD)(B)(F)$
$P_2 = (AF)(BC)(D)(E)$
$P_3 = (AEF)(BCD)$

Make a "good" state assignment and show the output equation and the input equations for D flip flops.

APPENDIX A

Relating the Algebra to the Karnaugh Map

Although we use the map without worrying about the algebra, it is useful to see how some of the properties appear on the map.

Property 9a. $ab + ab' = a$

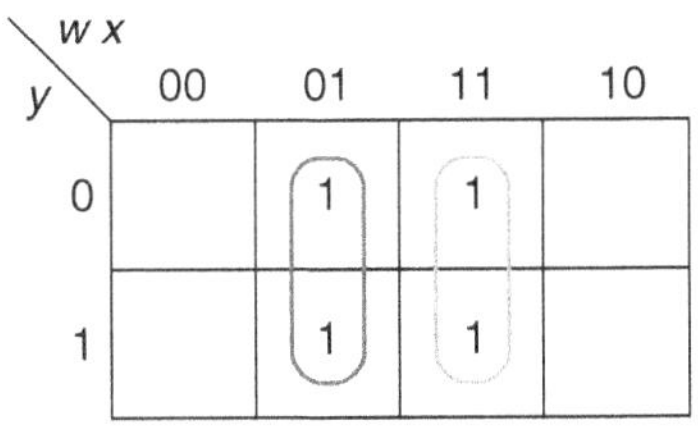

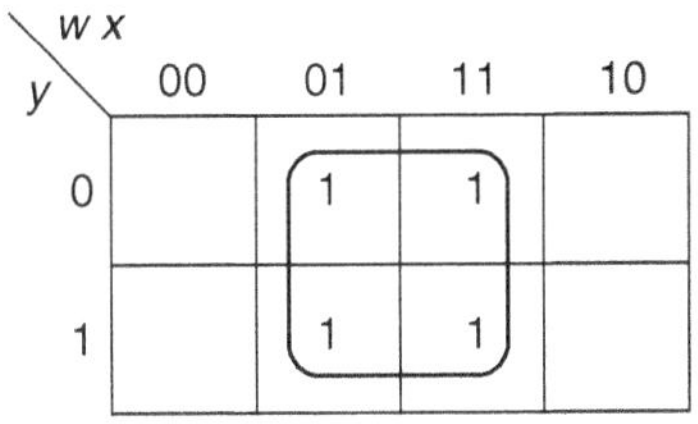

On the left, we have circled $w'x$ and wx. They combine to form the term x. Two adjacent rectangles combine to form one larger rectangle. Another geometry is shown next.

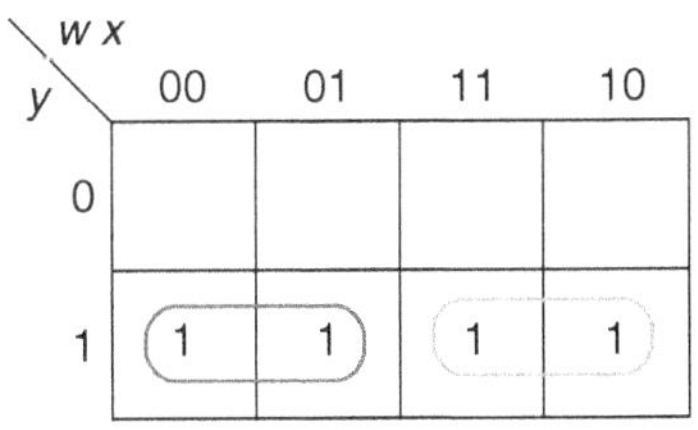

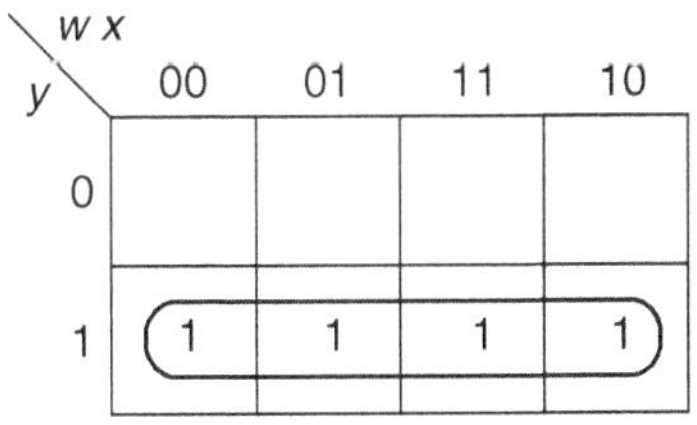

Here, $w'y + wy = y$.

Property 10a. $a + a'b = a + b$

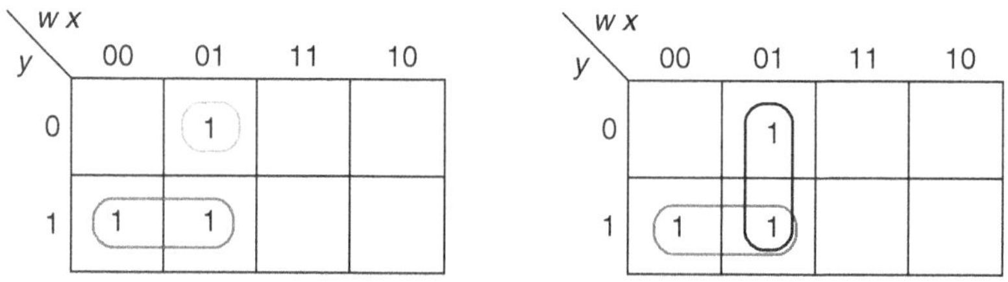

On the left, we have $w'y$ and $w'xy'$. Algebraically, we would factor w' from both terms, leaving $w'(y + xy') = w'(y + y'x)$. For Property 10a, a is y, and b is x. Thus, we have $w'y + w'x$, as shown on the right map. On the map, this involves one group adjacent to a smaller group. A four-variable example is shown below.

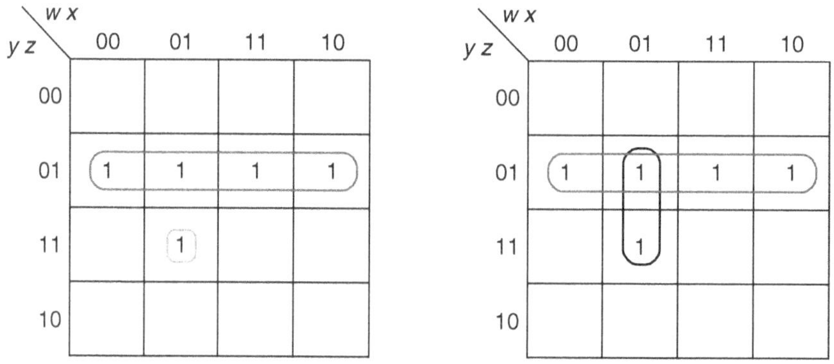

where $y'z + w'xyz = y'z + w'xz$. After factoring out the common z, we have $z(y' + yw'x)$. Thus, the a of P10 is y', and the b is $w'x$.

Property 12a. $a + ab = a$

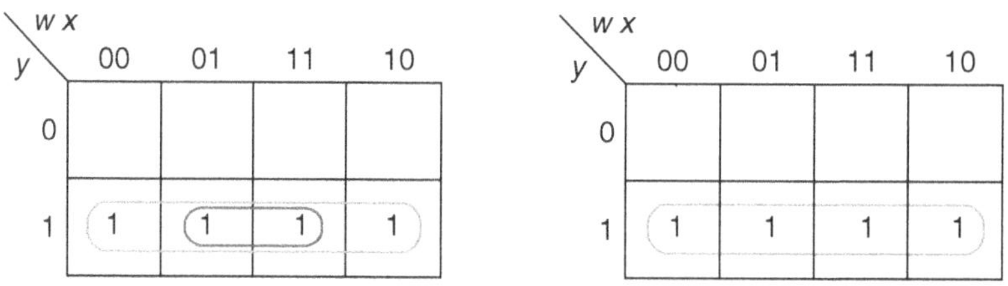

where the term xy on the left map is completely contained in the term y, and can thus be deleted.

Property 13a. $at_1 + a't_2 + t_1t_2 = at_1 + a't_2$

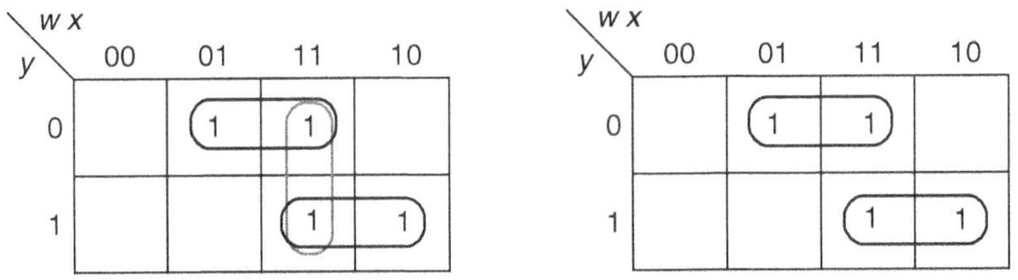

The term *wx* on the left map is the consensus of *xy*′ and *wy*, and is thus removed on the right map. The 1's of the consensus term are half from one group and half from the other. A larger example is shown next,

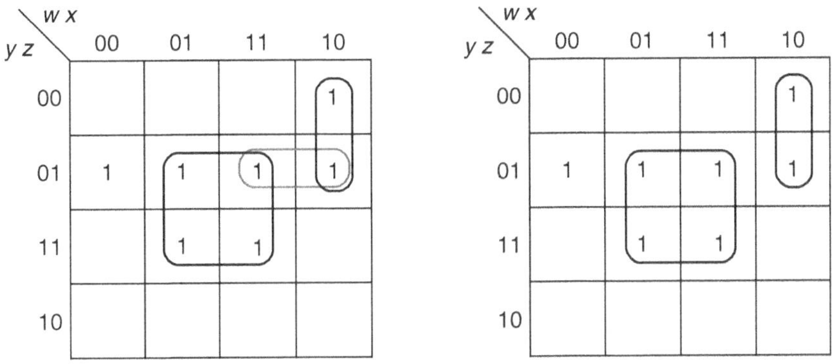

where *wy*′*z* is the consensus of *xz* and *wx*′*y*′ and has been removed on the right map.

We will now look at some examples of algebraic reduction, showing the corresponding maps.

EXAMPLE A.1

Reduce the following to two terms with four literals.

$$f = wxy' + yz + xz + w'xy' + w'xy'z'$$

The function is shown on the first map. After using Property 9a on the first and fourth term and Property 12a on the last two terms, we get the second map.

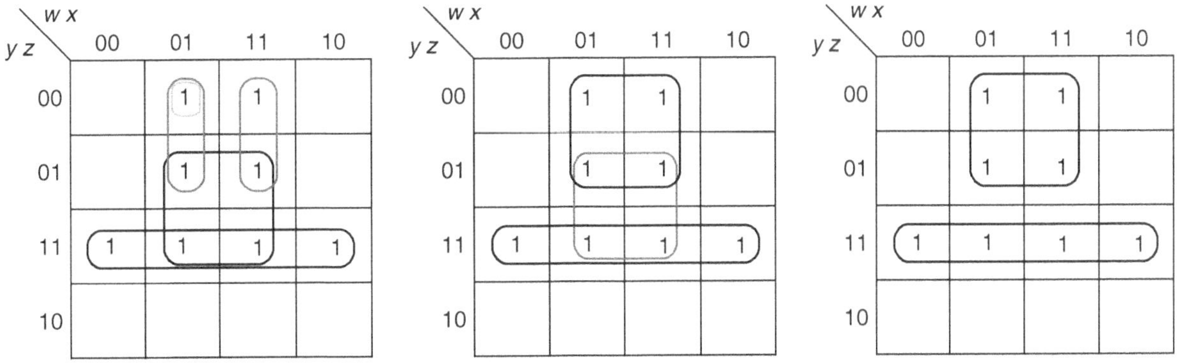

$$f = xy' + xz + yz$$

But xz is the consensus of xy' and yz, producing

$$f = xy' + yz$$

and the third map.

EXAMPLE A.2

Reduce the following to three terms and seven literals.

$$G = BC + AC'D + AB'D + A'C'D'$$

This function is plotted on the first map.

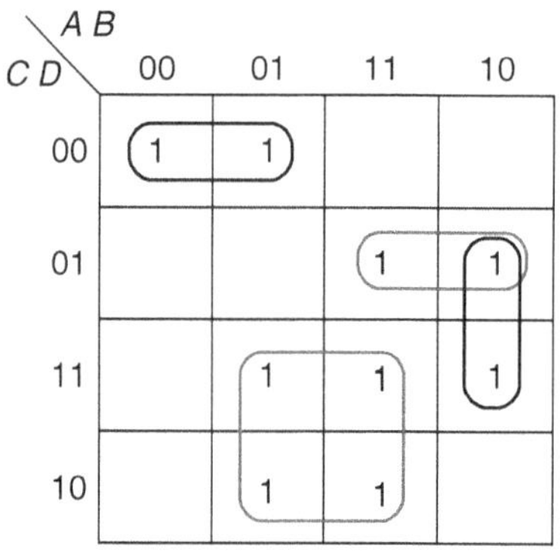

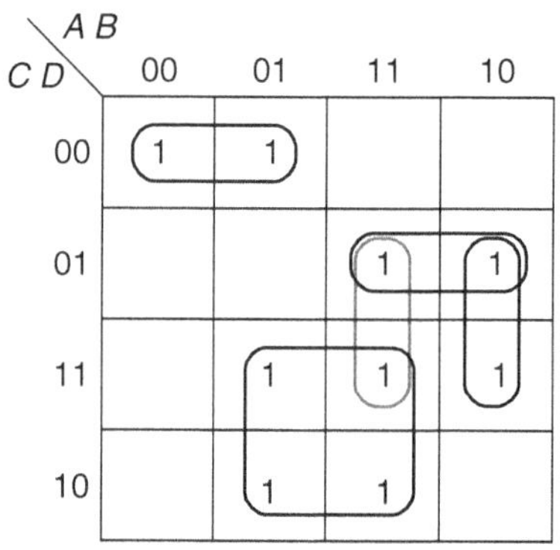

The consensus of the first two terms gives us ABD, as shown on the second map. Property 9a then allows us to replace $AB'D + ABD$ by AD (as shown on the next map) and Property 12a allows us to remove $AC'D$, finally reducing the expression to

$$G = BC + AD + A'C'D'$$

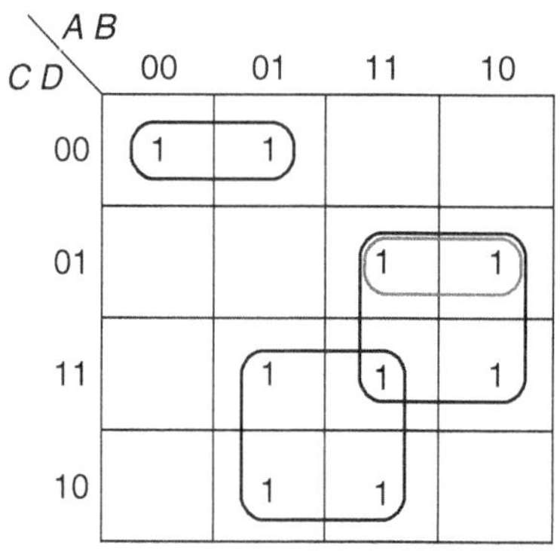

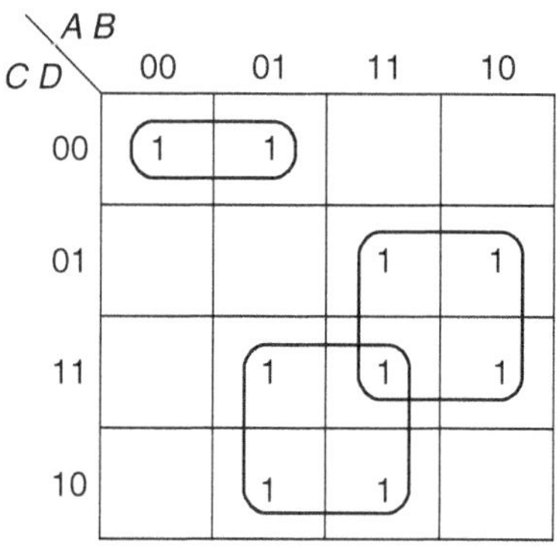

EXAMPLE A.3

Reduce the following to three terms and seven literals.

$$h = wx + wz + w'xz' + x'yz + w'yz'$$

The first map shows the original terms. Using Property 10a on the first and third terms produces xz'. Then, wx ¢ $xz' = wx$ and allows us to remove that term, producing the second map.

$$h = wz + xz' + x'yz + w'yz'$$

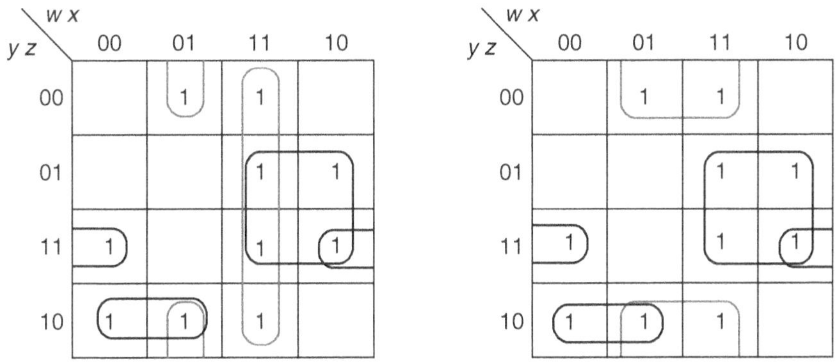

None of the properties other than consensus help, and the only consensus that exists is

$$x'yz \text{ ¢ } w'yz' = w'x'y$$

If we add that term, as on the next map, we can then compute

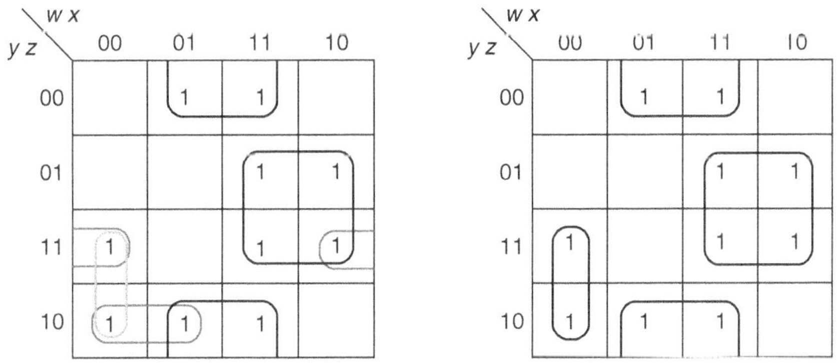

wz ¢ $w'x'y = x'yz$ and xz' ¢ $w'x'y = w'yz'$

Thus, we can remove $x'yz$ and $w'yz'$, leaving

$$h = wz + xz' + w'x'y$$

as shown on the fourth map.

APPENDIX B: ANSWERS TO SELECTED EXERCISES

B.1 Chapter 1 Answers

1. a. 31 d. 47 h. 0

2. a. 000001001001
e. 001111101000
g. $4200 > 2^{12} = 4096$ Thus, can't represent in 12 bits

3. a. 96B
c. 317

4. c. 1023

5. a. 001111 $3 + 12 = 15$
d. 000001 $51 + 14 = 65$ overflow
e. 110010 $11 + 39 = 50$

6. a. 011001 c. cannot be stored
e. 110001

7. c. +21 d. −28 h. −32

8. c. 10001111
d. cannot store numbers larger than +127

9. a. 000100 $-11 + (+15) = +4$
d. 010000 $-22 + (-26) =$ overflow
f. 101101 $-3 + (-16) = -19$

10. b. 111001 i. $17 - 24 =$ overflow
ii. $+17 - (+24) = -7$
c. 110011 i. $58 - 7 = 51$
ii. $-6 - (+7) = -13$
d. 001100 i. $36 - 24 = 12$
ii. $-28 - (+24) =$ overflow

11. a. i. 0001 0000 0011
ii. 0001 0000 0011
iii. 0001 0000 0011
iv. 0100 0011 0110
v. 10100 11000 10001

12.

	i.	ii.	iii.	iv.	v.	vi.
b.	no	18	15	no	27	+27
d.	95	no	no	62	149	−107

13. a. ii. 0100010 1001111 1001011 0100010
b. iii. $9/3 = 3$

B.2 Chapter 2 Answers

2. a.

w	*x*	*y*	*z*	1	2	3
0	0	0	0	1	1	1
0	0	0	1	1	1	1
0	0	1	0	1	1	1
0	0	1	1	1	1	1
0	1	0	0	1	1	1
0	1	0	1	1	1	1
0	1	1	0	1	1	1
0	1	1	1	0	1	1
1	0	0	0	0	1	1
1	0	0	1	0	1	1
1	0	1	0	0	1	1
1	0	1	1	0	0	1
1	1	0	0	0	0	0
1	1	0	1	0	1	0
1	1	1	0	0	0	0
1	1	1	1	0	1	0

d.

A	*B*	*C*	*D*	*F*
0	0	0	0	1
0	0	0	1	1
0	0	1	0	0
0	0	1	1	0
0	1	0	0	1
0	1	0	1	1
0	1	1	0	1
0	1	1	1	0
1	0	0	0	0
1	0	0	1	1
1	0	1	0	1
1	0	1	1	1
1	1	0	0	0
1	1	0	1	0
1	1	1	0	1
1	1	1	1	1

g.

a	*b*	*c*	*d*	*g*
0	0	0	0	1
0	0	0	1	0
0	0	1	0	1
0	0	1	1	0
0	1	0	0	1
0	1	0	1	0
0	1	1	0	1
0	1	1	1	1
1	0	0	0	0
1	0	0	1	1
1	0	1	0	0
1	0	1	1	1
1	1	0	0	X
1	1	0	1	X
1	1	1	0	X
1	1	1	1	X

3. a.

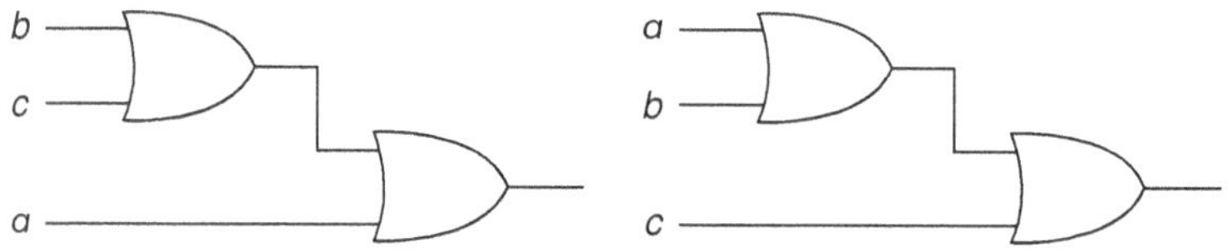

4. a.

X	*Y*	*Z*	*F*
0	0	0	1
0	0	1	0
0	1	0	1
0	1	1	1
1	0	0	1
1	0	1	0
1	1	0	0
1	1	1	1

5. b. $f = h$, but $\neq g$ because of row 011

6. b. ii. sum of three product terms

d. iv. product of two sum terms

f. i. product of 1 literal iii. sum of 1 literal

ii. sum of 1 product term iv. product of 1 sum term

g. none

7. b. 4 d. 3 f. 1 g. 6

8. a. $= z$

d. $= a'b' + ac$

f. $= x'y' + x'z + xy$

also $= x'y' + yz + xy$

9. c. $(a + c')(a' + c)(a' + b') = (a + c')(a' + c)(b' + c')$

10. c.

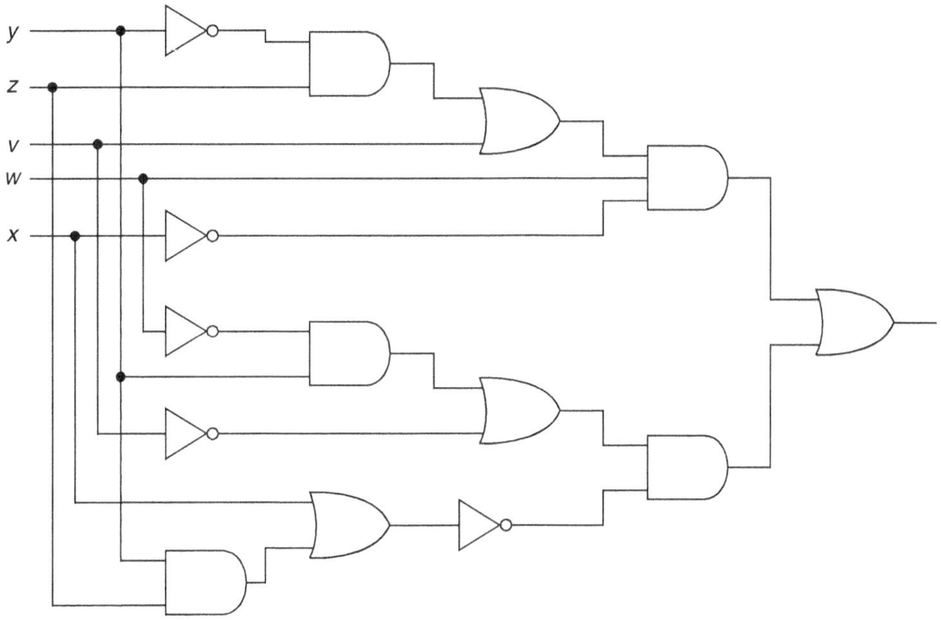

11. c. i. $h = a'c(b + d) + a(c' + bd)$

ii. $= a'bc + a'cd + ac' + abd$

12. a. $f' = (a' + b' + d)(b + c)(a + c' + d')(a + b' + c + d')$

14. a. $f(a, b, c) = \Sigma m(1, 5, 6, 7)$

$g(a, b, c) = \Sigma m(0, 1, 4, 5, 6)$

b. $f = a'b'c + ab'c + abc' + abc$

$g = a'b'c' + a'b'c + ab'c' + ab'c + abc'$

c. $f = b'c + ab$

$g = b' + ac'$

d. $f'(a, b, c) = \Sigma m(0, 2, 3, 4)$

$g'(a, b, c) = \Sigma m(2, 3, 7)$

e. $f = (a + b + c)(a + b' + c)(a + b' + c')(a' + b + c)$

$g = (a + b' + c)(a + b' + c')(a' + b' + c')$

f. $f = (b + c)(a + b')$

$g = (a + b')(b' + c')$

16. a. yes b. no c. yes d. no e. no f. yes

18. a. $f = a(bc)' + (c + d')' = ab' + ac' + c'd$

e. $f = 1 \oplus (ab + cd) = a'c' + a'd' + b'c' + b'd'$

19. d.

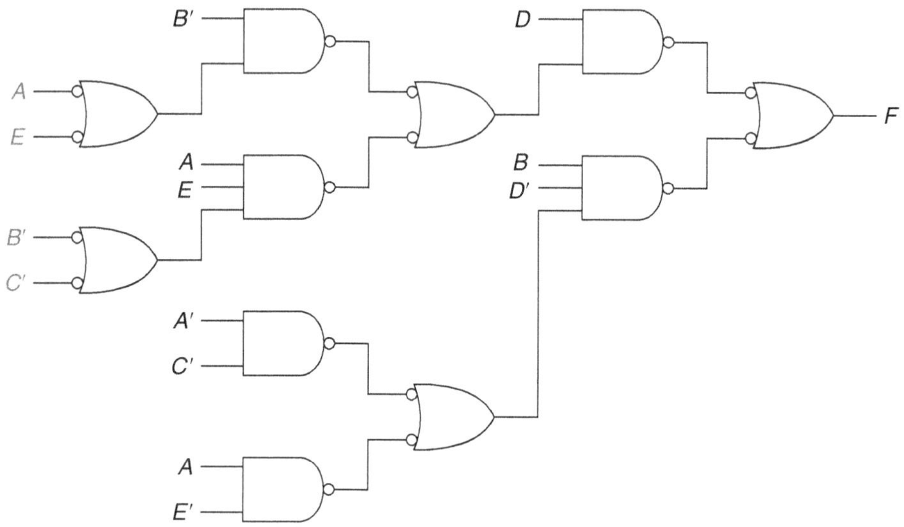

20. c. $f = b + a'c$

21. c. $F = W'Z' + Y'Z + WXY$

e. $G = B'D + BC + A'D$

g. $g = bc'd + abc + a'bd'$

$= a'bc' + abd + bcd'$

22. a. $f = a'b'c' + a'bd + a'cd' + abc + a'c'd$
$+ a'b'd' + a'bc + bcd + bcd'$
$= bc + a'c'd + a'b'd'$

23. b. $g = x'y'z' + x'y'z + x'yz' + x'yz + xyz + xy'z'$

$g(w, x, y, z) = \Sigma m(0, 1, 2, 3, 4, 7)$

24. c. $xy + w'z$

25. c. $(b' + d)(c + d)(a' + b + d')(b' + c' + d')$

26. a. $f = w(y' + xz') + z(y' + w'x')$

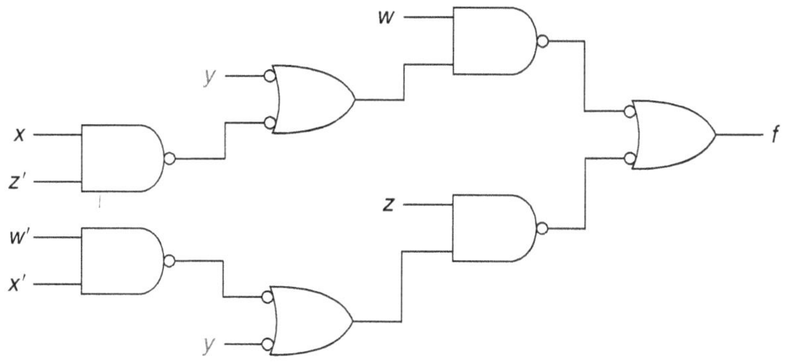

d. $F = B'[D'(A' + CE) + A'C] + B(AC' + C'D)$

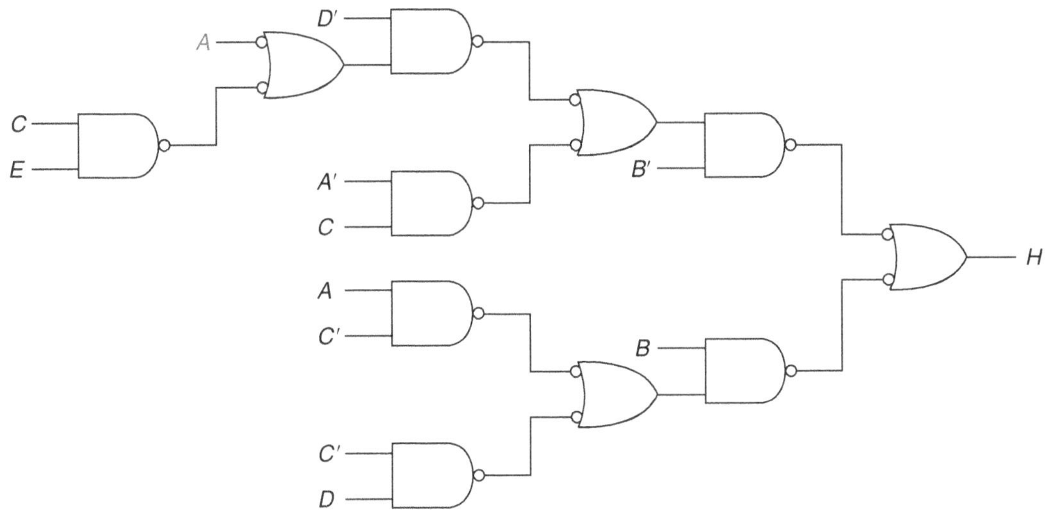

27. a. $F = BE(ACD + C'D' + A'C') + B'(E' + A'C) + CD'E'$

3 3 3 2 2 3 2 2 2 3 3 packs

$= BE(C'(A' + D') + ACD) + B'E' + CD'E' + A'B'C$

3 2 2 2 3 4 2 3 3 3 packs

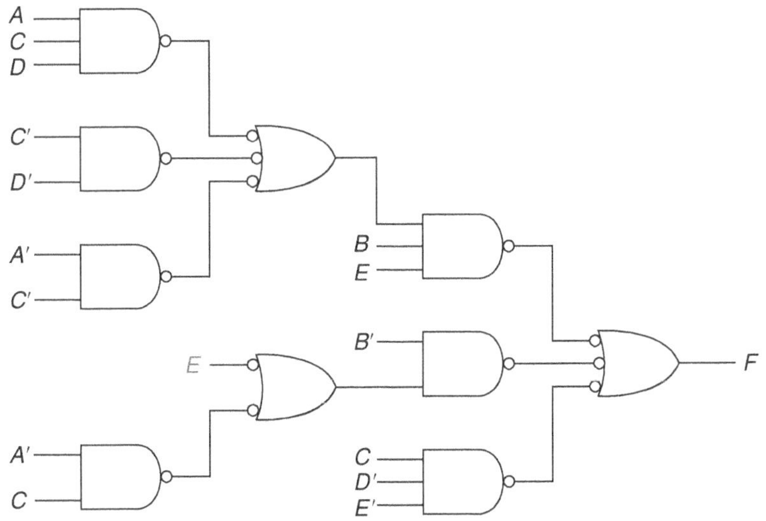

B.3 Chapter 3 Answers

1. b.

yz \ wx	00	01	11	10
00			X	X
01	1	1	1	
11	1	1		
10		1	1	X

c.

cd \ ab	00	01	11	10
00		1		
01		1	1	1
11	1	1		1
10	1	1		1

2. b. $g = w'x' + wx + wy \qquad g = w'x' + wx + x'y$

e. $G = X'Z' + W'XZ + WXY'$

i. $h = pq + qr' + r's' + p'q'r + prs$

$h = pq + qr' + r's' + p'q'r + q'rs$

$h = pq + qr' + r's' + q'rs + p'q's'$

l. Prime Implicants: xy, yz, xz, wz, $w'x$, $w'y'z'$, $x'y'z'$, $wx'y'$

Minimum: $g = yz + xy + w'x + wz + x'y'z'$

m. $H = X'Z' + W'X'Y + W'XZ + WXY'$

$H = X'Z' + W'YZ + W'XZ + WXY'$

$H = X'Z' + W'YZ + XY'Z + WXY'$

$H = X'Z' + W'YZ + XY'Z + WY'Z'$

n. $f = a'c' + ab' + cd' + bd$

$f = b'c' + a'b + cd' + ad$

$f = c'd + ac + a'b + b'd'$

$f = a'c' + ad + bc + b'd'$

$f = b'c' + bd + ac + a'd'$

$f = c'd + bc + ab' + a'd'$

p. $f_1 = a'b'c'd' + a'cd + a'bc + acd' + ab'd + abc' + a'bd$
$f_2 = a'b'c'd' + a'cd + a'bc + acd' + ab'd + abc' + bc'd$
$f_3 = a'b'c'd' + a'cd + a'bc + acd' + ab'd + ac'd + a'bd$
$f_4 = a'b'c'd' + a'cd + a'bc + abd' + ab'c + ac'd + a'bd$
$f_5 = a'b'c'd' + a'cd + a'bc + abd' + ab'c + ac'd + bc'd$
$f_6 = a'b'c'd' + a'cd + a'bc + abd' + ab'c + ab'd + a'bd$
$f_7 = a'b'c'd' + a'cd + bcd' + acd' + ab'd + ac'd + a'bd$
$f_8 = a'b'c'd' + a'cd + bcd' + acd' + ab'd + abc' + a'bd$
$f_9 = a'b'c'd' + a'cd + bcd' + acd' + ab'd + abc' + bc'd$
$f_{10} = a'b'c'd' + a'cd + bcd' + ab'c + ab'd + abc' + a'bd$
$f_{11} = a'b'c'd' + a'cd + bcd' + ab'c + ab'd + abc' + bc'd$
$f_{12} = a'b'c'd' + a'cd + bcd' + ab'c + ab'd + abd' + bc'd$
$f_{13} = a'b'c'd' + a'cd + bcd' + ab'c + ac'd + abd' + a'bd$
$f_{14} = a'b'c'd' + a'cd + bcd' + ab'c + ac'd + abd' + bc'd$
$f_{15} = a'b'c'd' + a'cd + bcd' + ab'c + ac'd + abc' + a'bd$
$f_{16} = a'b'c'd' + a'cd + bcd' + ab'c + ac'd + abc' + bc'd$
$f_{17} = a'b'c'd' + b'cd + ab'c + bcd' + a'bd + abc' + ac'd$
$f_{18} = a'b'c'd' + b'cd + ab'c + bcd' + a'bd + abc' + ab'd$
$f_{19} = a'b'c'd' + b'cd + ab'c + bcd' + a'bd + abd' + ac'd$
$f_{20} = a'b'c'd' + b'cd + ab'c + abd' + a'bc + bc'd + ac'd$
$f_{21} = a'b'c'd' + b'cd + ab'c + abd' + a'bc + bc'd + ab'd$
$f_{22} = a'b'c'd' + b'cd + ab'c + abd' + a'bc + ac'd + a'bd$
$f_{23} = a'b'c'd' + b'cd + acd' + a'bc + a'bd + abc' + ab'd$
$f_{24} = a'b'c'd' + b'cd + acd' + a'bc + a'bd + abc' + ac'd$
$f_{25} = a'b'c'd' + b'cd + acd' + a'bc + a'bd + abd' + ac'd$
$f_{26} = a'b'c'd' + b'cd + acd' + a'bc + bc'd + abc' + ac'd$
$f_{27} = a'b'c'd' + b'cd + acd' + a'bc + bc'd + abc' + ab'd$
$f_{28} = a'b'c'd' + b'cd + acd' + a'bc + bc'd + abd' + ac'd$
$f_{29} = a'b'c'd' + b'cd + acd' + a'bc + bc'd + abd' + ab'd$
$f_{30} = a'b'c'd' + b'cd + acd' + bcd' + a'bd + abc' + ac'd$
$f_{31} = a'b'c'd' + b'cd + acd' + bcd' + a'bd + abc' + bc'd$
$f_{32} = a'b'c'd' + b'cd + acd' + bcd' + a'bd + abd' + ac'd$

3. b. Prime Implicants: $xy, yz, xz, wz, w'x, w'y'z', x'y'z', wx'y'$
Minimum: $g = yz + xy + w'x + wz + x'y'z'$

4. b. $g = wx + yz + xy + xz + wy + wz$

5. c. $f_1 = ab' + b'd' + cd + a'bc'$
$f_2 = ab' + b'd' + cd + a'bd$
$f_3 = ab' + b'd' + b'c + a'bd$

f. $f_1 = cd' + a'b + b'd' + ac'd$
$f_2 = cd' + a'b + b'd' + ab'c'$
$f_3 = cd' + a'b + a'd' + ab'c'$

6. c. All are different.

f. f_2 and f_3 are equal; f_1 treats m_{13} differently

7. a. $f = A'B + C'D + AD$

$f = (B + D)(A + B + C')(A' + D)$

d. $f_1 = a'd' + ad + bc + ab$

$f_2 = a'd' + ad + bc + bd'$

$f_3 = (a' + b + d)(a + c + d')(a + b + d')$

i. $f_1 = w'z + wy + xz$

$f_2 = w'z + wy + wx$

$f_3 = w'z + wx + x'z$

$f_4 = w'z + wx + yz$

$f_5 = w'x' + wx + yz$

$f_6 = w'x' + wy + xz$

$f_7 = (w + z)(w' + x + y)$

8. a, d. Since there are no don't cares, all solutions to each problem are equal.

i. All are different.

9. c. $H = AB'E + BD'E' + BCDE + A'CD'E$

f. $H = V'W'Z + V'WY + VWY' + W'X'Z' + VWXZ$

$H = V'W'Z + V'WY + VWY' + W'X'Z' + WXYZ$

i. $H = A'C'D' + CDE' + B'CE + AD'E + \{ACD' \text{ or } ACE'\}$

$H = A'C'D' + CDE' + B'CE + ACD' + C'D'E$

n. $G = X'Y' + V'XZ + \{VWZ \text{ or } WXZ\}$

10. b. $G = B'C'E'F' + BD'F + AB'C'D' + CDEF' + A'B'C'E + ABF + BC'F + A'BCDE'$

11. a. $f = a'b'd + ab'c' + bc'd + acd'$

$g = a'b + bc'd + acd'$

e. $F = WY + WZ' + W'XZ + W'X'Y'Z$

$G = Y'Z' + W'XY + W'X'Y'Z$

h. $f = c'd' + a'cd + bd$

$g = bd + a'c'd + ab' + \{abc \text{ or } acd'\}$

$h = b'cd' + bd + a'c'd + a'bc' + \{abc \text{ or } acd'\}$

j. $f = b'c'd + a'b' + a'c'd'$ or

$f = b'c'd + a'b' + bc'd'$ or

$f = b'c'd + b'c + a'c'd'$

$g = b'c'd + cd'$

12. b. $F = A'B'C'D + AC'D' + ACD + BCD' + A'BCD$

$G = A'B'C'D' + BCD' + A'BCD$

$H = AC'D' + AD + A'BCD + A'B'C'D'$

$F = A'B'C'D + AC'D' + ACD + BCD' + A'BCD$

$G = A'B'C'D' + BCD' + A'BCD$

$H = ACD + AC' + A'BCD + A'B'C'D'$

B.4 Chapter 4 Answers

1., 2.

b.	d.	f.	h.
$w'x'$	$r's'$	$a'b$	$V'W'X'$
wx	qr'	$b'd'$	$W'X'Z'$
$x'y$	pq	cd'	$V'W'Z$
wy	$p'q's'$	$a'c$	$V'YZ$
	$p'q'r$	$a'd'$	$V'WY$
	prs	$ac'd$	$V'X'Y$
	$q'rs$	$bc'd$	$VX'Y'Z'$
		$ab'c'$	VWY'
			$VWXZ$
			$WXYZ$

3. b. $g = w'x' + wx + wy$
$g = w'x' + wx + x'y$

d. $h = pq + qr' + r's' + p'q'r + prs$
$h = pq + qr' + r's' + p'q'r + q'rs$
$h = pq + qr' + r's' + q'rs + p'q's'$

f. $f_1 = cd' + a'b + b'd' + ac'd$
$f_2 = cd' + a'b + b'd' + ab'c'$
$f_3 = cd' + a'b + a'd' + ab'c'$

h. $H = V'W'Z + V'WY + VWY' + W'X'Z' + VWXZ$
$H = V'W'Z + V'WY + VWY' + W'X'Z' + WXYZ$

4., 5. b. Prime implicants of F: $W'Y'Z, XYZ, WY, WZ', W'XZ$
Prime implicants of G: $Y'Z', W'X'Y', W'XY, W'XZ'$
Shared terms: $W'XYZ, W'X'Y'Z, WY'Z'$

d. Terms for f only: $a'cd, c'd', bc'$
Terms for g only: $c'd, ab', ac, ad$
Term for h only: $b'cd'$
Term for f and g: $ab'c'd'$
Term for f and h: $a'bc'$
Terms for g and h: $a'c'd, abc, acd'$
Term for all three: bd

6. b. $F = WY + WZ' + W'XZ + W'X'Y'Z$
$G = Y'Z' + W'XY + W'X'Y'Z$

d. $f = c'd' + a'cd + bd$
$g = bd + a'c'd + ab' + \{abc \text{ or } acd'\}$
$h = b'cd' + bd + a'c'd + a'bc' + \{abc \text{ or } acd'\}$

B.5 Chapter 5 Answers

2. a. The truth table for this module is

a	b	c	y	s	t
0	0	0	0	1	0
0	0	1	0	1	1
0	1	0	0	1	1
0	1	1	1	0	0
1	0	0	1	0	0
1	0	1	1	0	1
1	1	0	1	0	1
1	1	1	1	1	0

$y = a + bc \qquad s = a'b' + a'c' + abc \qquad t = b'c + bc'$

b. The delay from c to y is 2 for each module. The total delay is 32 + 1.

7.

a	b	c	X	Y
0	0	0	0	0
0	0	1	0	1
0	1	0	0	0
0	1	1	1	1
1	0	0	0	0
1	0	1	1	1
1	1	0	1	0
1	1	1	1	1

9.

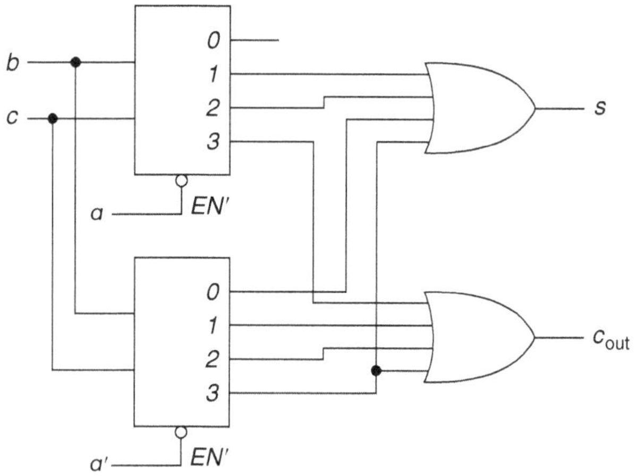

12.

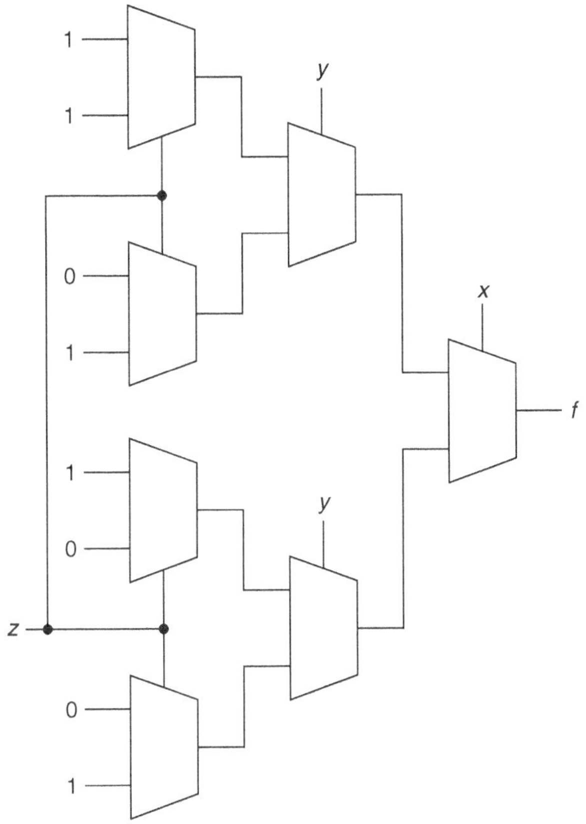

18. a.

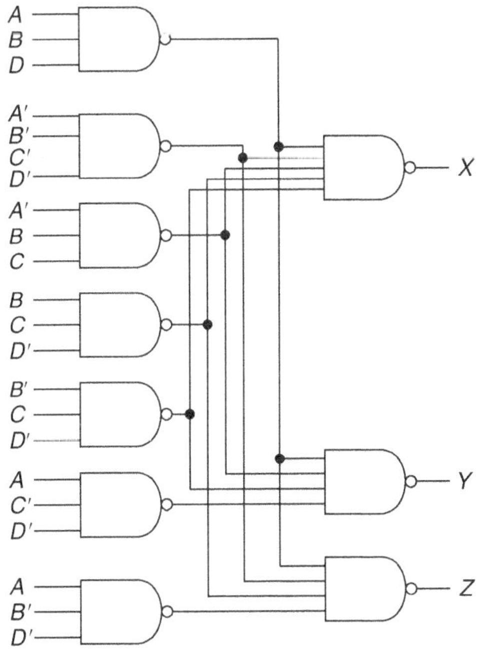

b. The solution is straightforward; the diagram is not shown.

c. We need two decoders. A is connected to the enable of the first. The outputs correspond to the first eight minterms. A' is used to enable the second, producing the other eight minterms. Only three OR gates are needed.

d. The solution of part a is implemented on a PLA with seven terms:

$$X = ABD_1 + A'B'C'D'_2 + A'BC_3 + BCD'_4 + B'CD'_5$$
$$Y = AC'D' + ABD_1 + A'BC_3 + B'CD'_5$$
$$Z = ABD_1 + A'B'C'D'_2 + AB'D' + BCD'_4$$

e. The PAL would be implemented with a solution using only prime implicants of individual functions:

$$X = A'B'D' + CD' + ABD + BC$$
$$Y = AC'D' + ABD + A'BC + B'CD' \quad \text{or}$$
$$= A'CD' + BCD + ABC' + AB'D'$$
$$Z = B'C'D' + ABD + BCD' + \{AB'D' + ACD'\}$$

21. a. $X1 = B'D'_2 + BD + AC'_1 + A'C$

$X2 = B' + C'D' + AD' + AC'_1 + A'CD$

$X3 = D + B'C' + A'B + AC_4$ ***

or

$= D + A'C' + BC + AB'$

$X4 = B'D'_2 + A'B'C_5 + A'CD'_6 + BC'D + ABD + AC'_1$

$X5 = B'D'_2 + A'CD'_6 + AC'D'$

$X6 = A'BC' + ABC + AB'C' + \{B'C'D' \text{ or } A'C'D'\}$
$\quad + \{ACD' \text{ or } AB'D'\} + \{BCD' \text{ or } A'BD'\}$

$X7 = BC' + AC'_1 + AB_3 + A'B'C_5 + \{A'CD'^{*}_6 \text{ or } BD'\}$

$X8 = AB_7 + AC_3$

Package Count

X1:	2	2	2	2			4
X2:	0	2	2	(2)	3		5
X3:	0	2	2	2			4
X4:	(2)	3	3	3	3	(2)	6
X5:	(2)	(3)	3				3
X6:	3	3	3	3	3	3	6
X7:	2	(2)	2	(3)	2		5
X8:	(2)	(2)					2

2's:	13	7430s:	4	32 gates/95 inputs
3's:	13	7420s:	1	
4's:	2	7410s:	5	(2 left over)
5's:	2	7400s:	3	(use one 3-input)
6's:	2		Total: 13 packages	

*Solving $X7$ alone, you would use BD' in place of $A'CD'$. But, the latter is also a prime implicant and can be shared, saving one gate and three inputs. Gate count is based on BD'.

b. $X1 = B'D'_1 + AC'_3 + A'CD_2 + BD$
$X2 = B' + A'CD_2 + AC'_3 + C'D' + ACD'_8$
$X3 = D + ACD'_8 + B'C'D'_{10} + A'BD'_5$
$X4 = A'B'C_4 + B'D'_1 + AC'_3 + A'CD'_7 + A'BC'D_6 + ABCD_9$
$X5 = B'D'_1 + A'CD'_7 + AC'D'$
$X6 = ACD'_8 + B'C'D'_{10} + ABCD_9 + A'BC'D_6 + AB'C' + A'BD'_5$
$X7 = A'B'C_4 + AC'_3 + A'BC'D_6 + AB_{11} + A'BD'_5$
$X8 = AC + AB_{11}$

Package Count

X1:	2	2	3	2			4
X2:	0	(3)	(2)	2	3		5
X3:	0	(3)	3	3			4
X4:	3	(2)	(2)	3	4	4	6
X5:	(2)	(3)	3				3
X6:	(3)	(3)	(4)	(4)	3	(3)	6
X7:	(3)	(2)	(4)	2	(3)		5
X8:	2	(2)					2

2's:	7	7430s:	4	24 gates /79 inputs
3's:	9	7420s:	2	
4's:	4	7410s:	3	
5's:	2	7400s:	2	
6's:	2	Total: 11 packages		

c. The PLA implementation of part b would require 18 product terms, one for each of the product terms shown, including the single literal terms (B' in $X2$ and D in $X3$). We could do this with only 16 product terms if we treated the PLA as a ROM (that is, created the 16 minterms). This would not have worked for part b, since it requires gates of more than eight inputs for those functions with more than 8 minterms (all but $X5$ and $X8$).

B.6 Chapter 6 Answers

1. b.

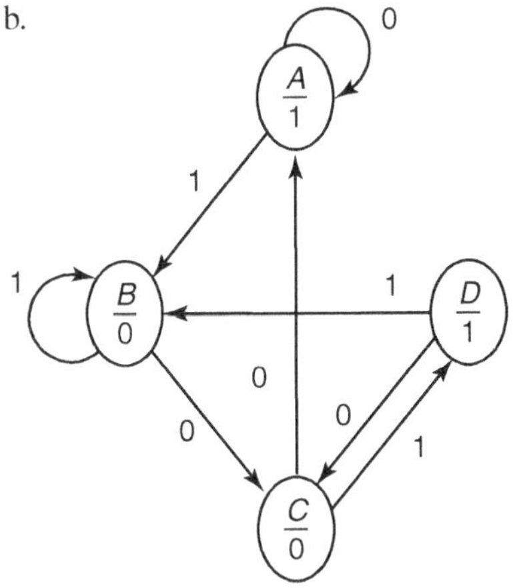

x	1	1	0	1	0	1	0	1	0	0	1	0	1	1	
q	*A*	*B*	*B*	*C*	*D*	*C*	*D*	*C*	*D*	*C*	*A*	*B*	*C*	*D*	*B*
z	0	0	0	0	1	0	1	0	1	0	0	0	0	1	0	0

4. c.

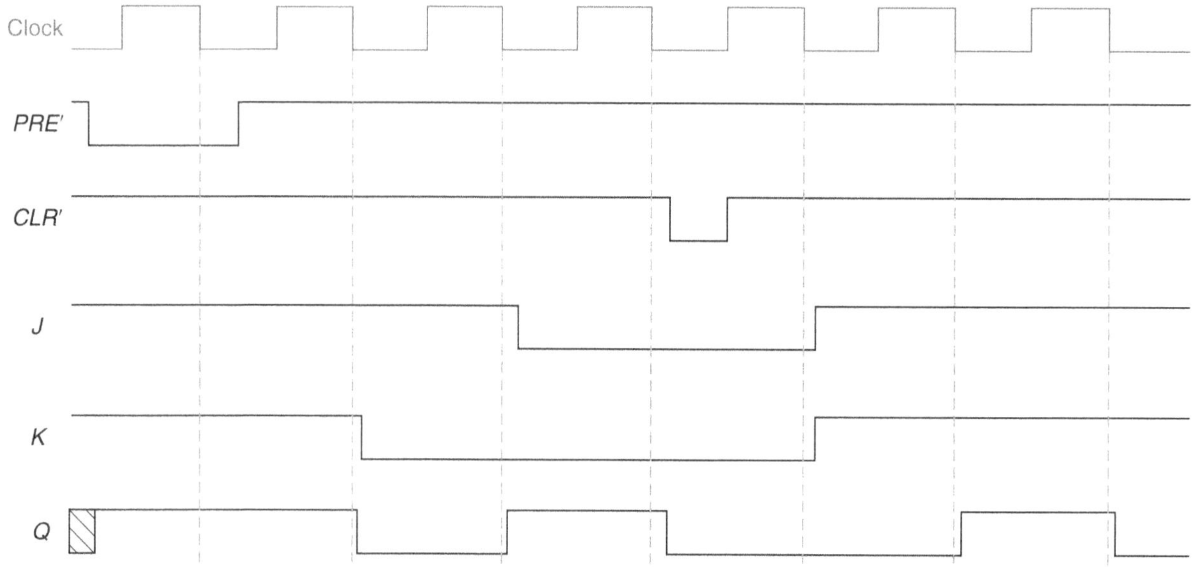

7. b.

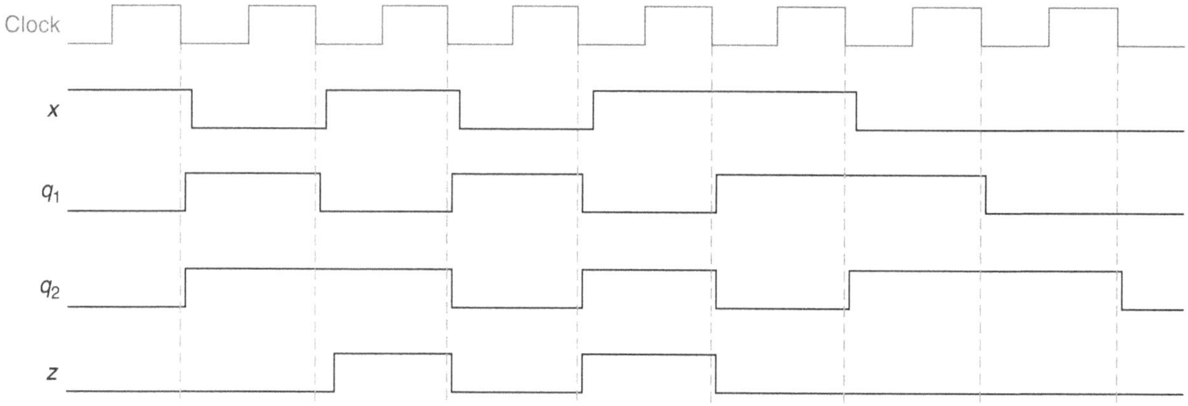

8. a.

q_1q_2	$q_1^\star q_2^\star$ $x = 0$	$x = 1$	z
0 0	1 0	1 0	1
0 1	0 0	1 0	0
1 0	1 1	1 1	1
1 1	0 1	1 1	1

x 0 0 1 1 0 0 1 1 0
q_1 0 1 1 1 1 0 0 1 1 0 ? 1 ?
q_2 0 0 1 1 1 1 0 0 1 1 0 ? 1
z 1 1 1 1 1 0 1 1 1 0 1 1 ?

9. c.
x 0 1 1 0 0 1 1 1 0
A 0 0 0 1 1 1 1 0 1 1 1
B 0 1 1 1 0 0 0 0 1 0 0 0
C 0 1 0 0 1 1 0 0 0 1
z 0 1 0 0 0 0 0 0 0 0 0 0

B.7 Chapter 7 Answers

2. a. The output equation is the same for all types of flip flop:

$z = x'B + xB'$

$D_A = x'B' + xA \qquad D_B = x' + A$

$S_A = x'B' \qquad R_A = x'B$ (or $x'A$) $\qquad S_B = x' \qquad R_B = xA'$

$T_A = x'A + x'B' \qquad T_B = x'B' + xA'B$

$J_A = x'B' \qquad K_A = x' \qquad J_B = x' \qquad K_B = xA'$

f. $z = A'$

$D_A = x'A' + xAB' \qquad D_B = x'B + xB'$

$J_A = x' \qquad K_A = x' + B \qquad J_B = x \qquad K_B = x$

$S_A = x'A' \qquad R_A = x'A + AB \qquad S_B = xB' \qquad R_B = xB$

$T_A = x' + AB \qquad T_B = x$

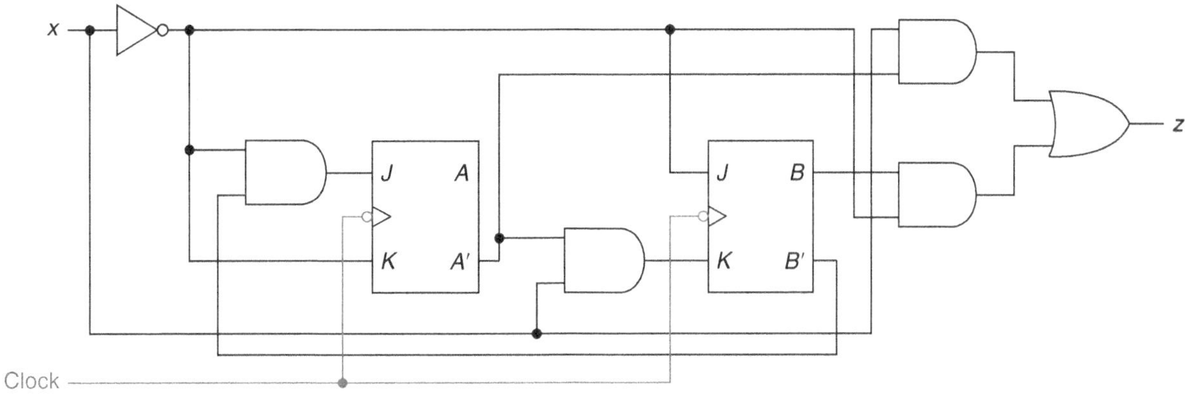

3. c. $z = q_1'q_2'$

$D_1 = x'q_1' + xq_1 \qquad D_2 = xq_1'q_2'$

$J_1 = x' \quad K_1 = x' \qquad J_2 = xq_1' \quad K_2 = 1$

4. b. (i) $D_1 = xq_1'q_2'$

$D_2 = q_1 + x'q_2' + xq_2 = q_1 + x'q_1'q_2' + xq_2$

$z = x'q_1'q_2' + xq_2 = x'q_1'q_2' + xq_2$

(ii) $D_1 = xq_2'$

$D_2 = q_1 + q_2' + x$

$z = x'q_2' + xq_1'q_2$

(iii) $D_1 = x' + q_1' + q_2'$

$D_2 = xq_1 + xq_2'$

$z = xq_2 + x'q_1'$

7. a. $D_D = CBA + DB' + DA'$ $\quad J_D = CBA$ $\quad K_D = BA$

$D_C = D'C'BA + CB' + CA'$ $\quad J_C = D'BA$ $\quad K_C = BA$

$D_B = B'A + BA'$ $\quad J_B = K_B = A$

$D_A = A'$ $\quad J_A = K_A = 1$

8. b. $D_C = BA + \{CB' \text{ or } B'A'\}$ $\quad J_C = B$ $\quad K_C = BA'$

$D_B = B' + CA$ $\quad J_B = 1$ $\quad K_B = C' + A'$

$D_A = B' + A'$ $\quad J_A = 1$ $\quad K_A = B$

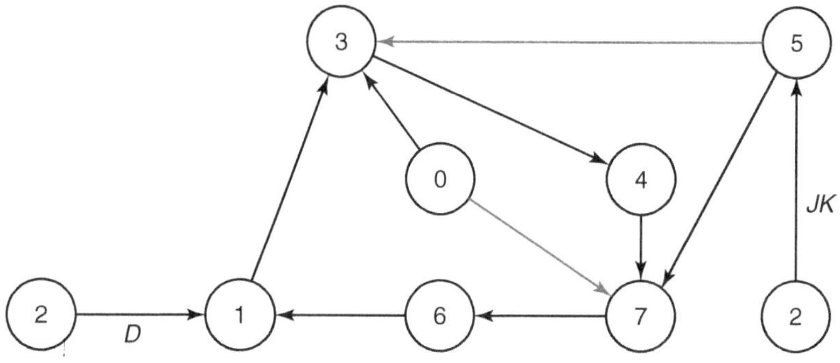

Brown path from 0 and 5 when $D_C = BA + B'A'$

10. a. $J_A = B$ $\quad K_A = x + B$ $\quad J_B = x' + A'$ $\quad K_B = 1$

b. $11 \rightarrow 00$

16. b.

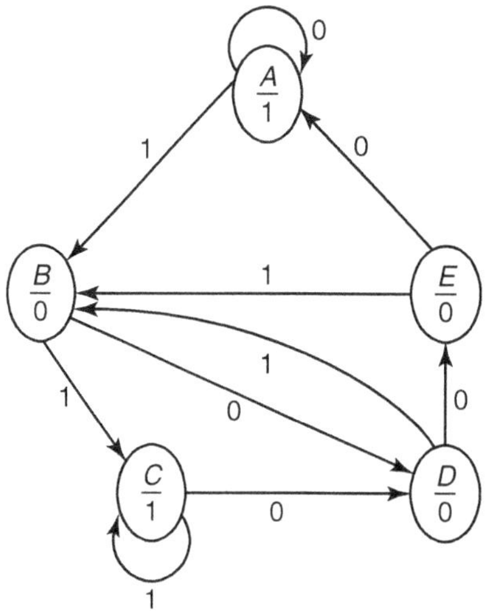

f.

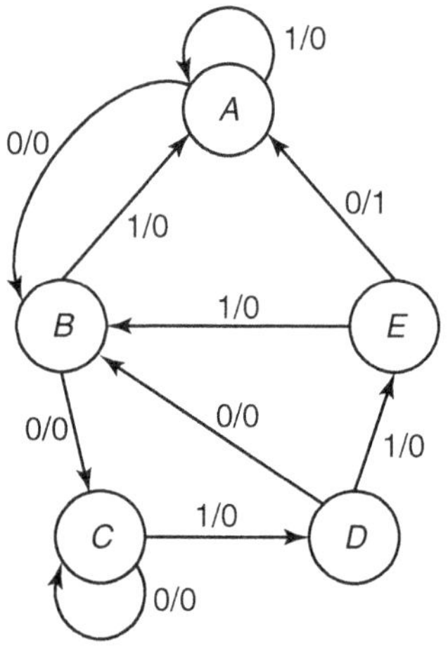

k.

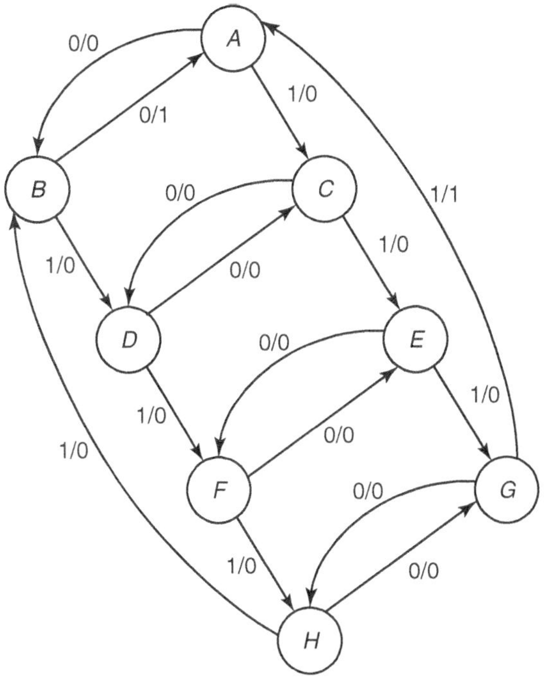

l.

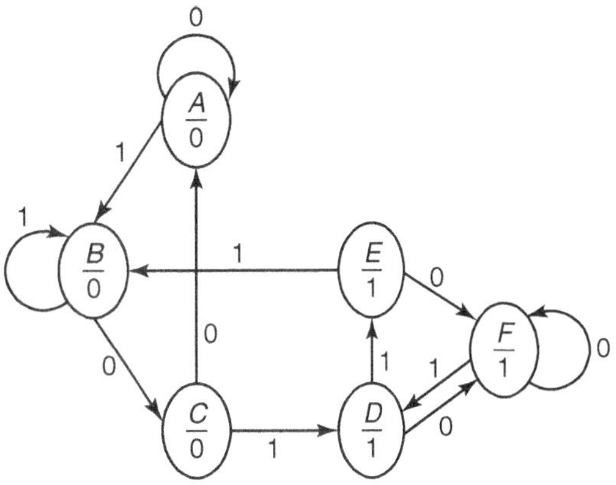

B.8 Chapter 8 Answers

4. a. Assume *CLR′* is clocked, but does not require counter to be enabled.

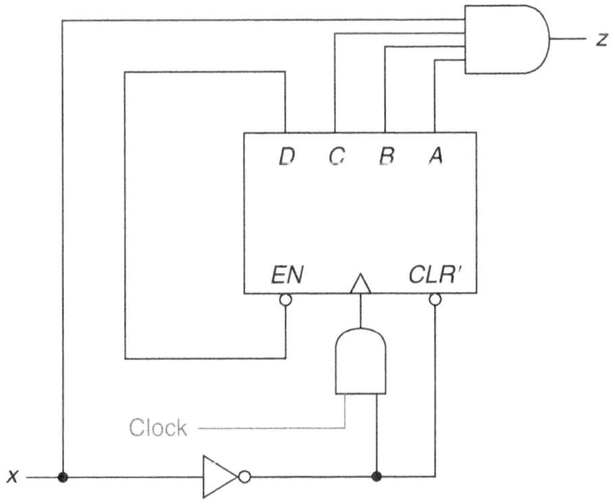

b. $z = x\, q_1'\, q_2'\, q_3'\, q_4'\, q_5'\, q_6'\, q_7'\, q_8$
$= x(q_1 + q_2 + q_3 + q_4 + q_5 + q_6 + q_7)'\, q_8$

8.

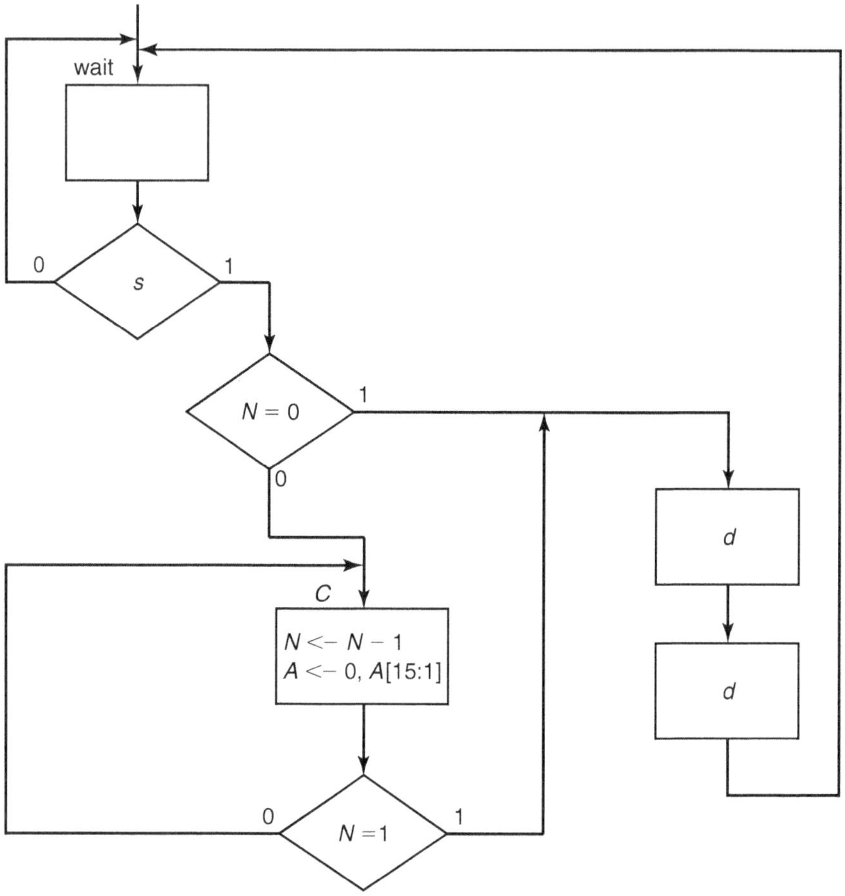

9. a. $J_A = B + C$ $K_A = \{BD + BC \text{ or } BD + CD' \text{ or } BC + C'D\}$
$J_B = D$ $K_B = C + D$
$J_C = AD' + B'D'$ $K_C = A'D + \{AD' \text{ or } BD'\}$
$J_D = 1$ $K_D = 1$

In some cases, the next state depends on the choice for K_A or K_C. Those transitions are shown with dashed lines. In any case, the sequence is reached within three clocks.

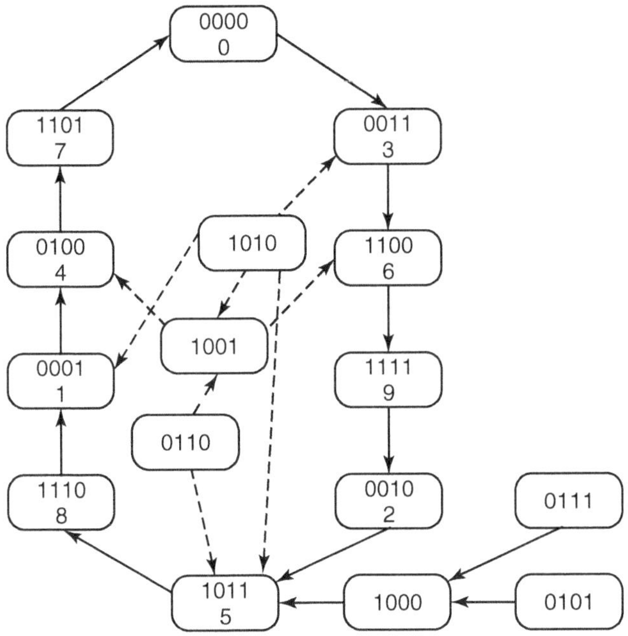

b. A table for the minimal sum of product expressions is shown.

	X1	*X2*	*X3*	*X4*	*X5*	*X6*	*X7*
$A'B'D'$	X			X	X		
$B'CD$	X		X	X			X
ABC	X	X					X
ABD	X	X	X				
$A'C'D'$		X	X			X	
$A'B'C'$		X	X				
$A'B'C$		X					X
ABD'			X	X	X	X	
ACD						X	
$BC'D'$							X
or inputs	4	5	5	3	2	3	4

12. The state table for this counter follows:

a. i. For the D flip flop, we have

$$D_A = A'BC + xAB' + xAC'$$
$$D_B = B'C + BC' + xA'B' + \{AB \text{ or } AC\}$$
$$D_C = x'AC + xA'B' + xAC' + BC' + A'C'$$

The NAND gate requirements are

Size	Number	Packages
1	1 (x')	0 (from 4)
2	4	1
3	6	2
4	1	1
5+	1	1

The cost is thus $1.25 for gates plus the flip flops.

ii. Using *JK* flip flops, we get

$J_A = BC$ $\quad K_A = x' + BC$
$J_B = C + xA'$ $\quad K_B = A'C$
$J_C = x + A' + B$ $\quad K_C = x'A' + xA + \{xB \text{ or } A'B\}$

For this, the NAND gate requirements are

Size	Number	Packages
1	3	1
2	8	2
3	2	1

The two extra NOT gates (1-input) are needed to create the AND for J_A and K_B. The cost is thus \$1.00 for gates plus \$2.00 for the flip flops, a total of \$3.00.

b. Thus, if the *D* flip flop packages cost less than \$0.875, the first solution is less expensive.

If we can use one *D* package and one *JK* package, the best option is to use the *JK* package for *B* and *C*, and one of the *D*s for *A* (using xB and a shared xAB' in place of xA in K_C). That would require

Size	Number	Packages
1	2	0 (from 2's)
2	5	2
3	6	2

This solution would cost \$2.00 plus the cost of the *D* package. If the *D* package cost between \$0.75 and \$0.875, this solution would be better.

c. This flip flop will be set when the system is in state 5, 6, or 7 and *x* is 0, or when in state 0 or 1 and the input is 1. It can be cleared whenever the system is in state 3. Thus, for the new flip flop,

$J = xA'B' + x'AB + x'AC$
$K = A'BC$

and the output is just the state of that flip flop.

d. All of the outputs come from flip flops. We can compute the inputs for a *D* flip flop for *Q* using

$$D = Q^{\star} = JQ' + K'Q$$

and then simplifying the algebra. The result is

$$D = AQ + B'Q + C'Q + xA'B' + x'AB + x'AC$$

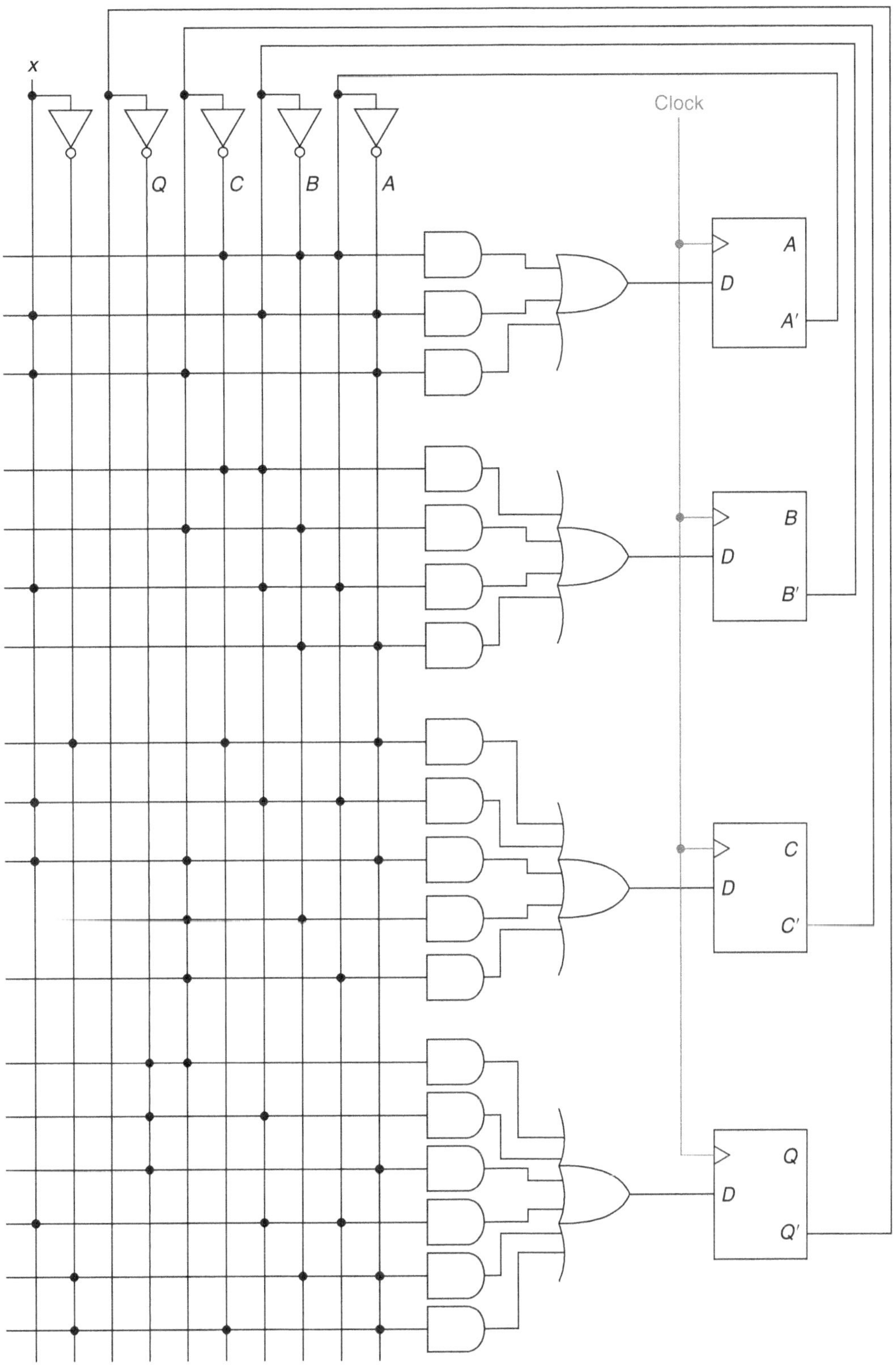
x
Q
C
B
A
Clock
A
D
A′
B
D
B′
C
D
C′
Q
D
Q′

B.9 Chapter 9 Answers

1. c.

q	$q^{\star}$ $x = 0$	$x = 1$	z
A	C	A	0
C	C	A	1

h.

q	$q^{\star}$ $x = 0$	$x = 1$	z $x = 0$	$x = 1$
A	B	D	0	0
B	A	B	1	0
C	B	A	0	0
D	A	C	1	1

k. The system cannot be reduced.

2. c. $P_1 = (AB)(CD)(E)$
$P_2 = (ABE)(CD)$
$P_3 = (A)(BC)(DE)$
$P_4 = (AB)(CDE)$
$P_5 = (A)(B)(C)(DE)$

h. $P_1 = (AE)(B)(C)(D)(F)(G)$
$P_2 = (AEF)(BG)(C)(D)$
$P_3 = (AE)(BG)(C)(D)(F)$

k. $P_1 = (ADG)(B)(C)(E)(F)$
$P_2 = (AE)(BCD)(FG)$
$P_3 = (AEFG)(BCD)$
$P_4 = (AG)(B)(C)(D)(E)(F)$
$P_5 = (A)(BC)(D)(E)(F)(G)$
$P_6 = (AE)(BCDFG)$
$P_7 = (A)(B)(C)(DG)(E)(F)$
$P_8 = (A)(B)(C)(D)(EF)(G)$
$P_9 = (ADG)(BC)(E)(F)$
$P_{10} = (ADG)(B)(C)(EF)$
$P_{11} = (AG)(BC)(D)(E)(F)$
$P_{12} = (AG)(B)(C)(D)(EF)$
$P_{13} = (A)(BC)(DG)(E)(F)$
$P_{14} = (A)(BC)(D)(EF)(G)$
$P_{15} = (A)(B)(C)(DG)(EF)$
$P_{16} = (ADG)(BC)(EF)$
$P_{17} = (AG)(BC)(D)(EF)$
$P_{18} = (A)(BC)(DG)(EF)$

3. c. i.

q	$q^\star$ $x = 0$	$x = 1$	z
A	A	B	0
B	A	B	1

ii.

q	$q^\star$ $x = 0$	$x = 1$	z
A	A	B	1
B	E	C	0
C	E	B	1
E	F	A	0
F	E	A	1

iii.

q	$q^\star$ $x = 0$	$x = 1$	z
A	A	B	0
B	E	C	0
C	E	B	1
D	A	B	1
E	F	D	1
F	E	D	0

iv.

q	$q^\star$ $x = 0$	$x = 1$	z
A	A	B	0
B	E	B	0
E	E	A	1

5. c. The three SP partitions are

$P_1 = (ABC)(DEF)$
$P_2 = (AF)\,(B)\,(C)\,(D)\,(E)$
$P_3 = (A)\,(BE)\,(C)\,(D)\,(F)$

P_1 is the only two-block SP partition; it can be used for the first variable. If we use the output consistent partition, $P_{OC} = (ADE)(BCF)$, for q_3, we need another partition that separates D from E, and B from C. Using P_2, we should keep A and F together, and using P_3, we should keep B and E together. Two such partitions for q_2 use

$P_4 = (ACDF)(BE)$
$P_5 = (ABEF)(CD)$

producing the assignments

q	q_1	q_2	q_3
A	0	0	0
B	0	1	1
C	0	0	1
D	1	0	0
E	1	1	0
F	1	0	1

q	q_1	q_2	q_3
A	0	0	0
B	0	0	1
C	0	1	1
D	1	1	0
E	1	0	0
F	1	0	1

For the first assignment, the equations are

$$J_1 = x' \qquad K_1 = 1$$
$$J_2 = xq_1q_3 + xq_1'q_3' \qquad K_2 = x$$
$$J_3 = x' + q_1' + q_2 \qquad K_3 = x'$$
$$z = q_3'$$

using four gates with 11 inputs (plus a NOT).

For the second assignment, the equations are

$$J_1 = x' \qquad K_1 = 1$$
$$J_2 = xq_1q_3' + xq_1'q_3 \qquad K_2 = xq_1$$
$$J_3 = x' + q_2' \qquad K_3 = x'$$
$$z = q_3'$$

using five gates with 12 inputs (plus a NOT).

Using the first six binary numbers, the solution requires 11 gates with 24 inputs (plus a NOT).

$$J_1 = x'q_2' \qquad K_1 = 1$$
$$J_2 = xq_1q_3' + xq_1'q_3 \qquad K_2 = xq_3$$
$$J_3 = x' + q_1'q_2' \qquad K_3 = x' + q_1'$$
$$z = q_2'q_3' + q_2q_3$$

APPENDIX C: CHAPTER TEST ANSWERS

APPENDIX C: CHAPTER TEST ANSWERS

C.1 Chapter 1

1. a. 101011011 b. 533

2.

	1 1 1 0			1 1 0 1 1	
	0 1 0 1 1	1 1		1 0 1 0 1 1	4 3
	0 1 1 1 0	1 4		0 1 1 0 0 1	2 5
0	1 1 0 0 1	2 5	1	0 0 0 1 0 0	looks like 4—overflow

3. a. 149 115 b. −107 +115 c. 95 73

4.

	1 0 0			1 1 0			1 1 1	
	1 1 0 0	−4		1 0 1 0	−6		0 1 0 1	+5
	1 1 0 1	−3		0 1 1 1	+7		0 0 1 1	+3
(0)	1 0 0 1	−7	(1)	0 0 0 1	+1	(0)	1 0 0 0	overflow

5. a. 13 − 12 = 1 10 − 6 = 4

b. −3 − (−4) = +1 −6 − (+6) = overflow

C.2 Chapter 2

1.

A	*B*	*C*	*D*	*X*	*Y*	*Z*
0	0	0	0	0	0	0
0	0	0	1	0	0	1
0	0	1	0	0	1	0
0	0	1	1	0	1	1
0	1	0	0	1	0	1
0	1	0	1	0	0	0
0	1	1	0	0	0	1
0	1	1	1	0	1	0
1	0	0	0	1	1	0
1	0	0	1	1	0	1
1	0	1	0	0	0	0
1	0	1	1	0	0	1
1	1	0	0	1	1	1
1	1	0	1	1	1	0
1	1	1	0	1	0	1
1	1	1	1	0	0	0

2.

a	b	c	f	g
0	0	0	1	1
0	0	1	1	1
0	1	0	1	1
0	1	1	0	0
1	0	0	0	0
1	0	1	0	0
1	1	0	1	1
1	1	1	1	0

NOT equal

3. $a'c + ab'$

4. a.

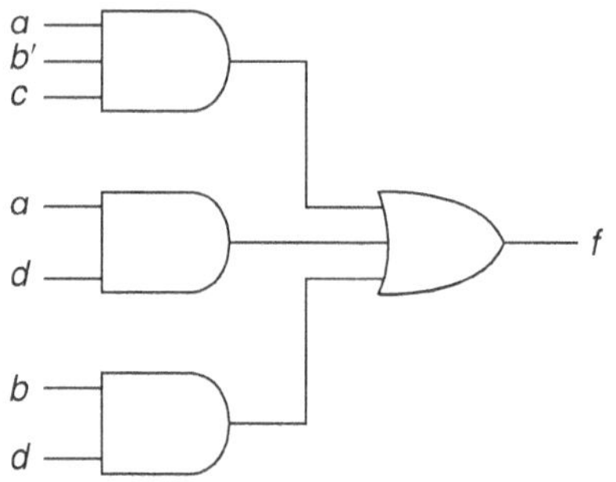

b.

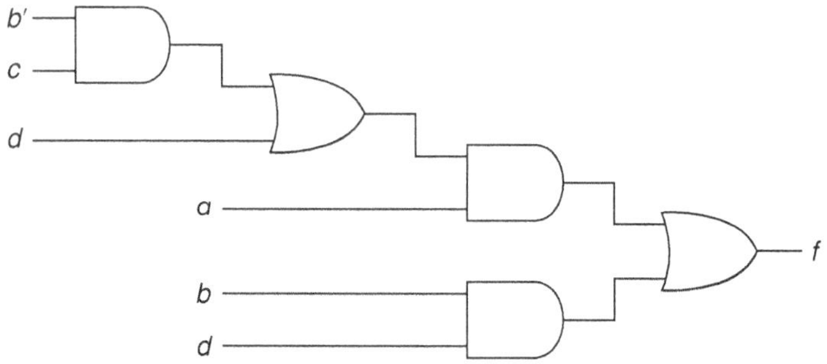

5. a. $f(x, y, z) = \Sigma m(0, 2, 3, 5, 7)$
   b. $f = x'y'z' + x'yz' + x'yz + xy'z + xyz$
   c. $f = x'z' + x'y + xz = x'z' + xz + yz$
   d. $f = (x + y + z')(x' + y + z)(x' + y' + z)$
   e. $f = (x + y + z')(x' + z)$

6. a.

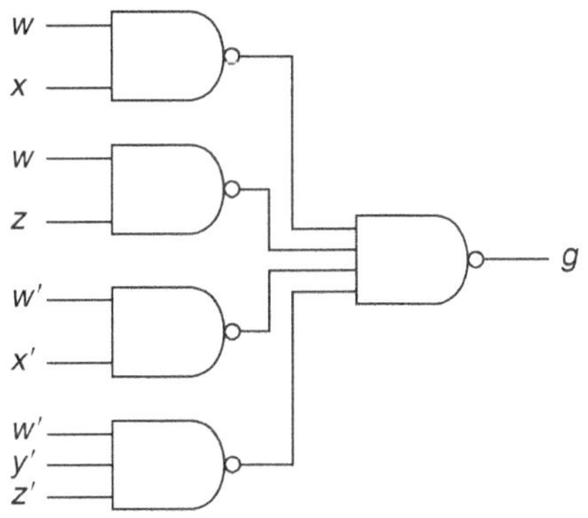

b.

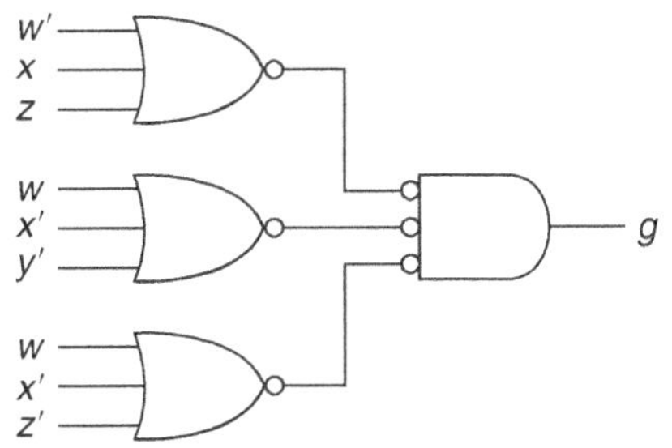

c.

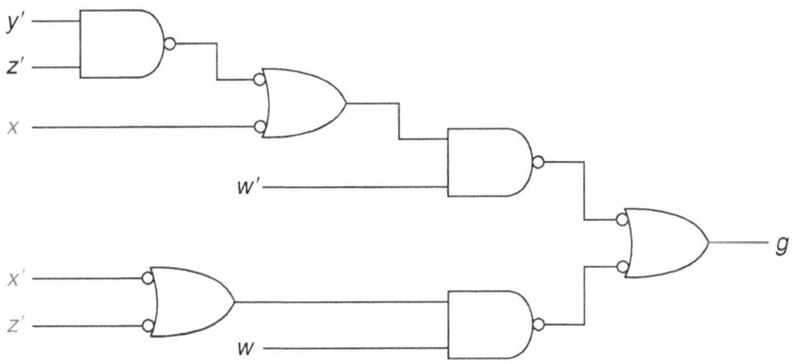

7. a. $f = (b'd' + b'cd') + (bc'd + bcd) + ab'd$
$= b'd' + bd + ab'd$
$= b'd' + d\,(b + b'a) = b'd' + bd + ad$
$= b'(d' + ad) + bd = b'd' + ab' + bd$

b. $g = (xy'z' + xy'z) + yz + wxy + xz$
$= xy' + yz + wxy + xz = x\,(y' + yw) + yz + xz$
$= xy' + wx + yz + xz$
$= xy' + wx + yz$ (consensus)

8. a. $a'b'c' + a'b'c + a'bc' + a'bc + ab'c + abc$

b. $w'x'y' + x'y'z' + wyz$

9.

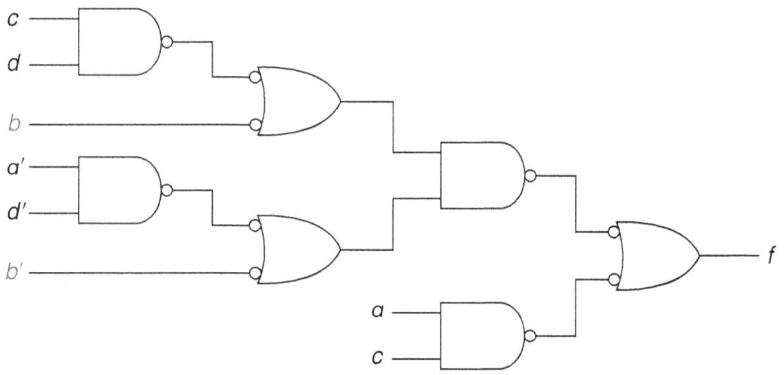

10.

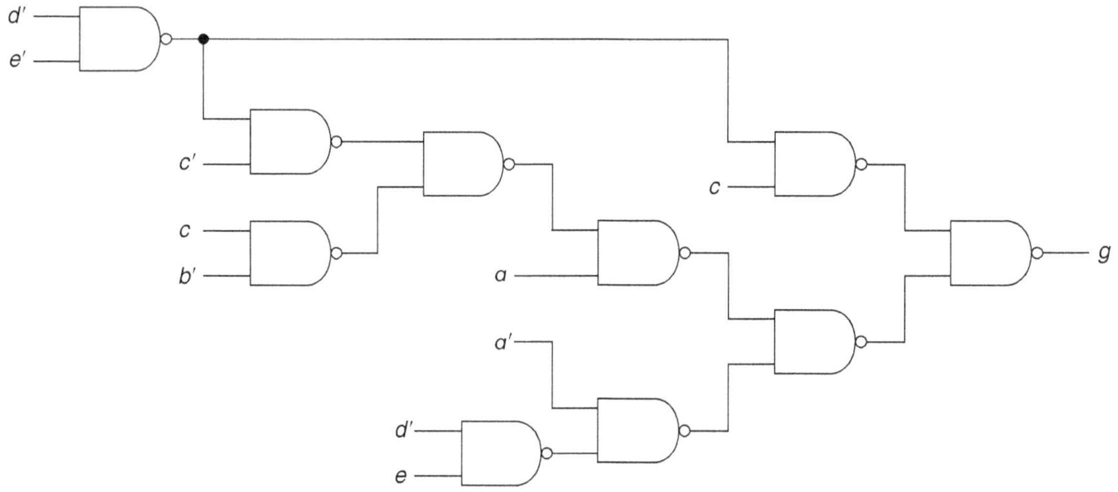

C.3 Chapter 3

1. a. $f(x, y, z) = \Sigma m\,(1, 2, 7) + \Sigma d(4, 5)$

b. $g = a'c + ab'c'd + a'bd + abc'$

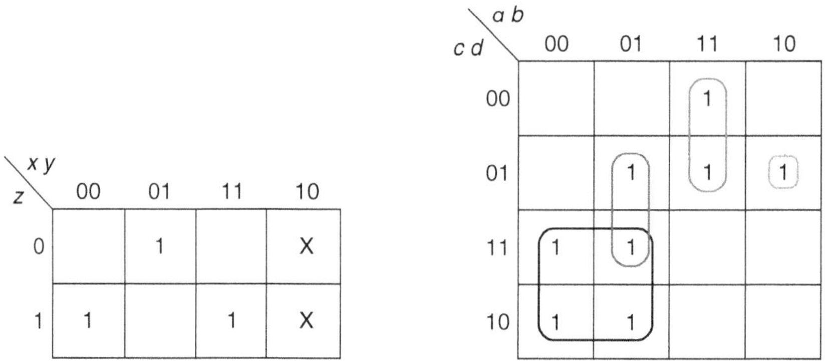

2. a. $wx'y'z' + wyz + w'x$ b. $acd + a'c' + a'd' + ab$

3. $b'd + bd' + ac + \{ab \text{ or } ad\} + \{a'b'c' \text{ or } a'c'd'\}$

4. $wz' + \{x'z \text{ or } wx'\} + \{xy'z' \text{ or } w'xy'\}$

5. $f = a'd + \{c'd \text{ or } b'd\}$

$f = d(a' + b') = d(a' + c')$

6. $f = wx + \{xy'z \text{ or } w'y'z\} + \{wyz \text{ or } x'yz\}$

$f = (w + z)(x + y)\{(x + z) \text{ or } (y' + z)\}\{(x' + y') \text{ or } (w + y')\}$

7. $A'B'C' + ACE + ABC'D + BCD'E' + \{A'B'D'E \text{ or } B'CD'E\}$

8. $ACE' + CDE + A'C'E' + BC'E + AB'C'$

$ACE' + CDE + B'C'E' + A'BC' + AC'E$

9. a. $f = xy'z' + wx' + wz'$

$g = w'z + w'xy + x'z$

b. $f = xy'z' + wz' + wx'z$

$g = w'z + w'xy + wx'z$

10. a. $f = w'z + w'y + yz + wx'z'$

$g = w'yz' + xz' + wxy + wy'z'$

$h = w'z + w'x + xyz + wx'y'z'$

b. $f = w'z + w'yz' + wx'y'z' + wxyz + x'y$

$g = w'yz' + xz' + wx'y'z' + wxyz$

$h = w'z + wx'y'z' + wxyz + w'x$

C.4 Chapter 4

1. $w'x', x'y'z', w'yz', w'y'z, wy'z', wxyz$
2. $g = a'cd + bd' + ac' + \{a'b \text{ or } bc'\}$
3. terms for both: $x'yz', w'xz, wx'y$

   f: $w'y'z, wyz, xz$

   g: $w'xy', w'yz, x'z', y'z', x'y$
4. $f = a'd' + a'cd$

   $g = b'd' + bd + a'cd$

C.5 Chapter 5

1.

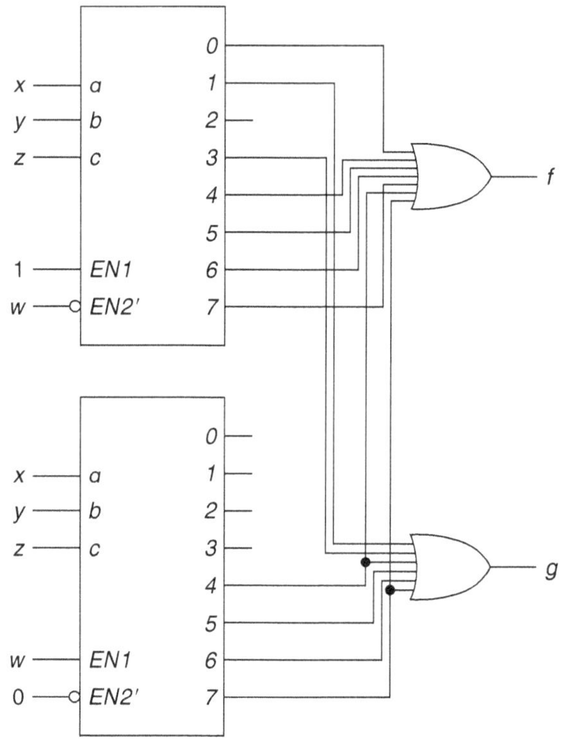

2.

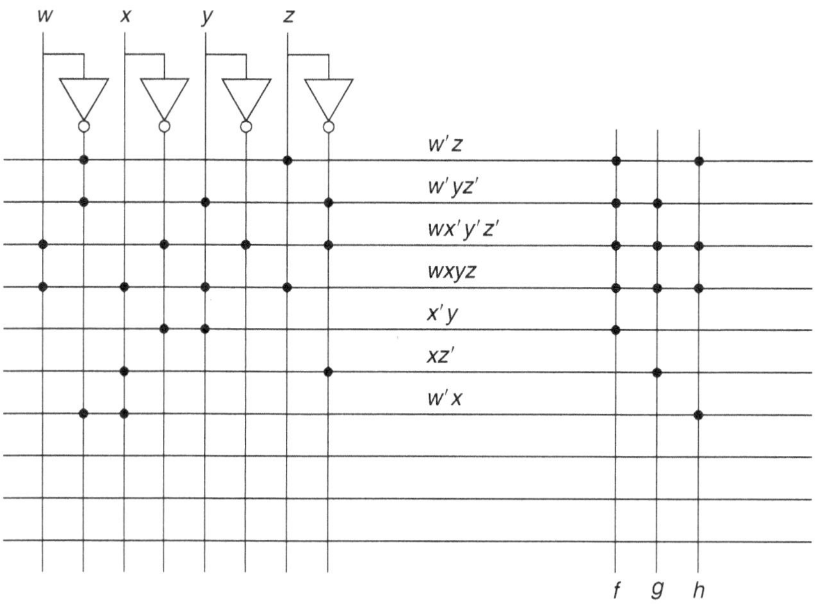

3.

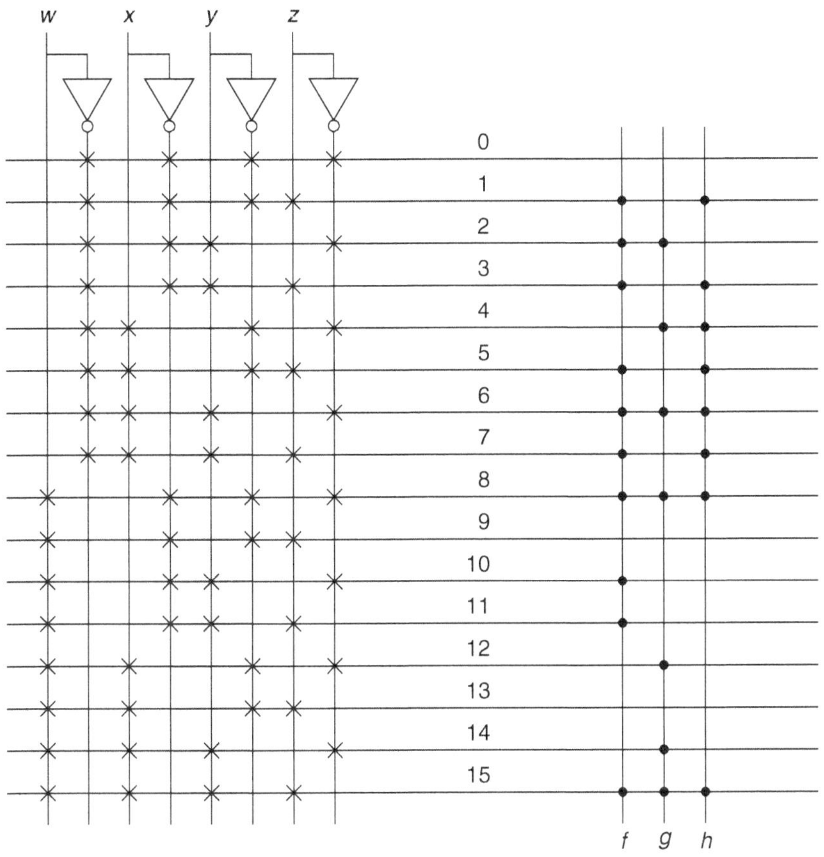

4.

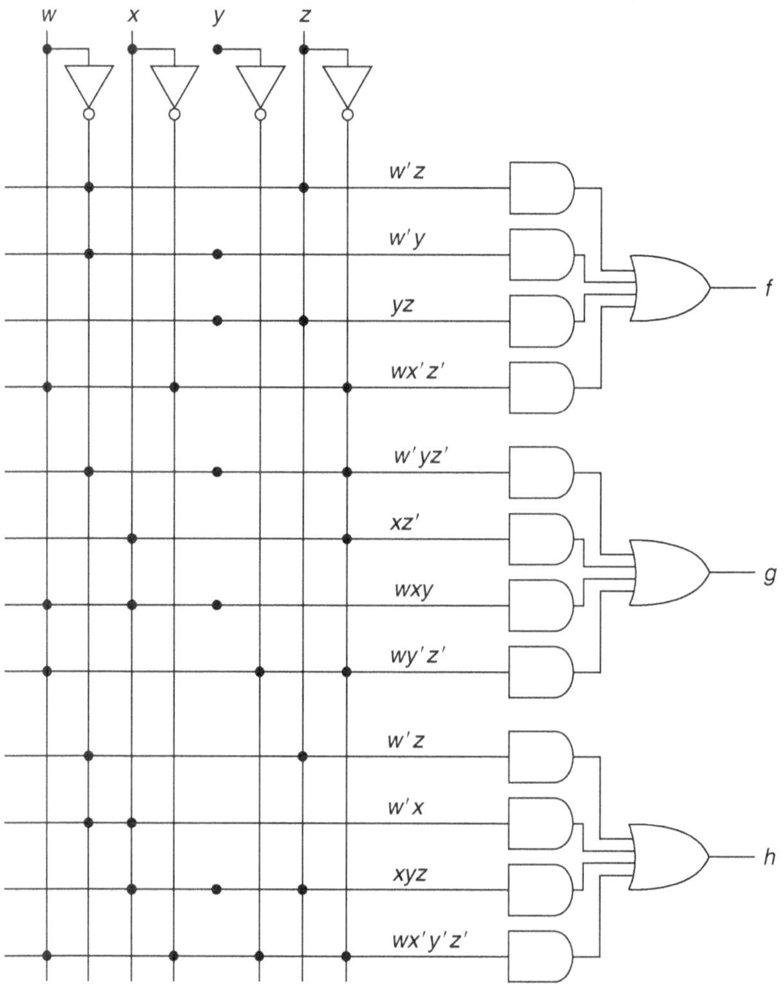

5.

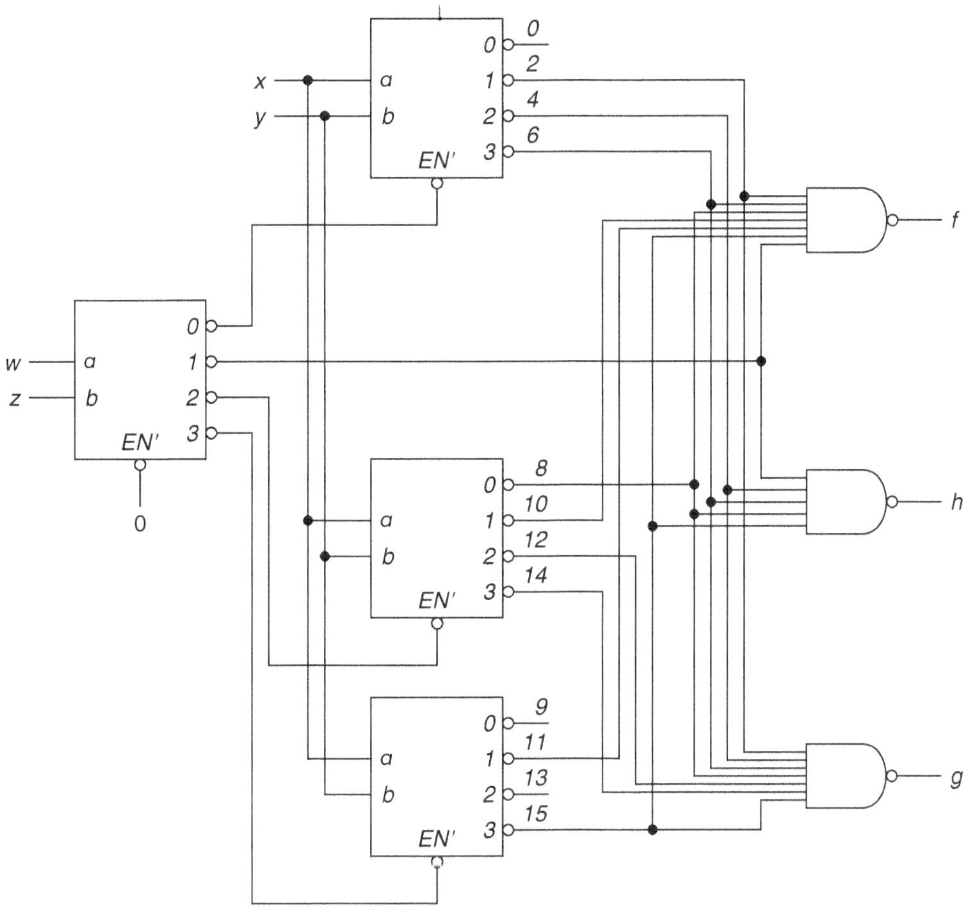

C.6 Chapter 6

1.

x	0	0	1	1	0	0	0	1	0	1			
q	A	C	B	D	B	A	C	B	D	B	D	B	
z	0	0	1	0	1	0	0	1	0	1	0	1	0

2.

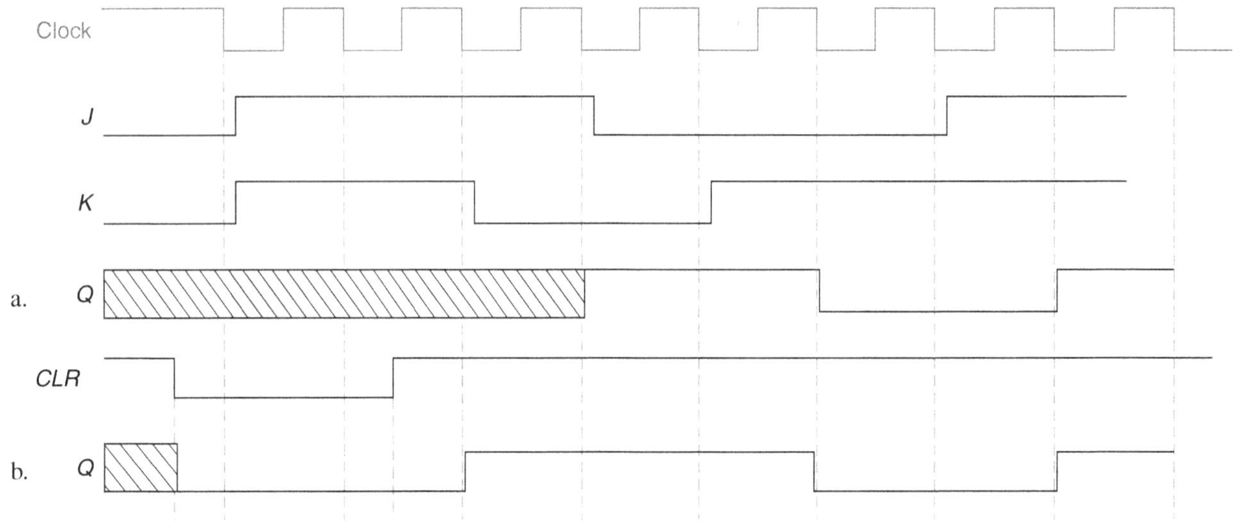

3. $D = xB + x'B'$ $T = A' + x$ $z = A' + B$

AB	$A^\star B^\star$ $x = 0$	$x = 1$	*z* $x = 1$
0 0	1 1	0 1	1
0 1	0 0	1 0	1
1 0	1 0	0 1	0
1 1	0 1	1 0	1

4. $D_A = xB' + x'B$ $D_B = x + A'$ $z = AB$

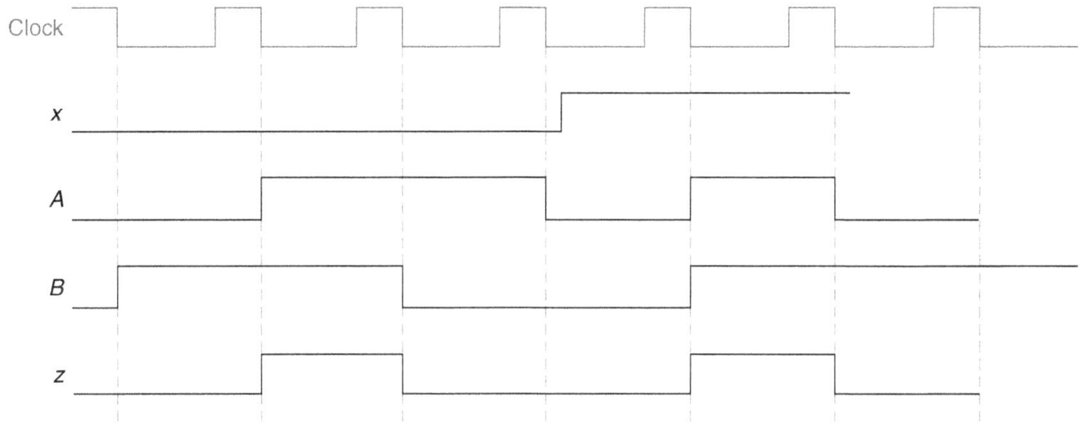

C.7 Chapter 7

1. $D_A = x'B' + xB$ $J_B = K_B = A' + x$ $z = x'A + xB'$
2. $S_1 = x$ $R_1 = x'q_2$ $J_2 = xq_1$ $K_2 = x'$ $z = q_2'$
3. a. $D_1 = x'q_1' + x'q_2 + q_1'q_2 + xq_1q_2'$
   $D_2 = x + q_1'q_2$ $z = q_1'q_2'$
   b. $D_1 = x + q_1q_2$ $D_2 = q_2'$ $z = q_1'q_2'$
   c.

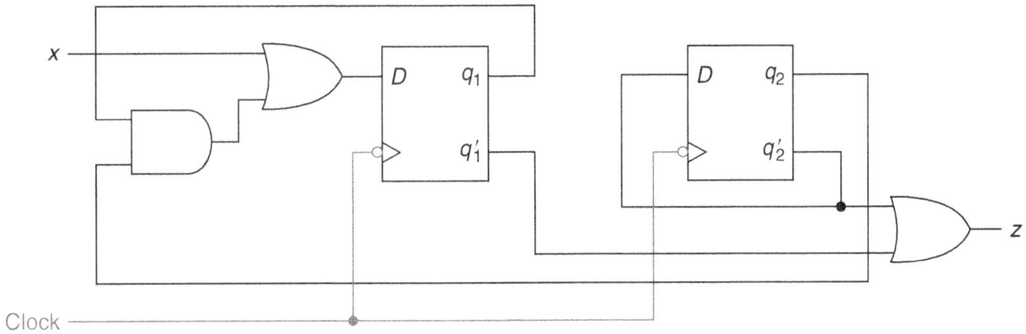

4. $D = A'$ $J = C'$ $K = A'C'$ $T = A' + B'C'$

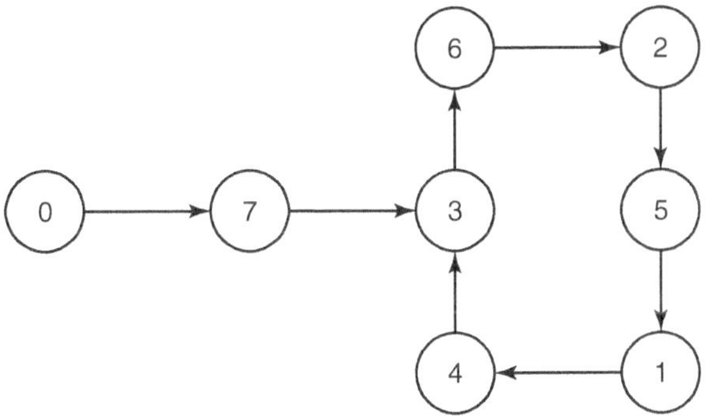

5. a. b.

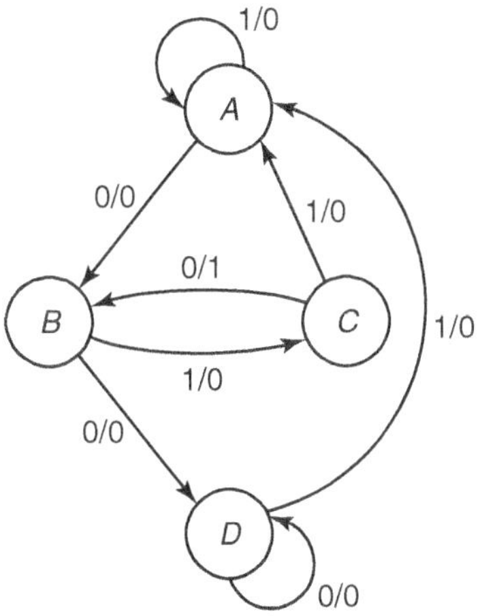

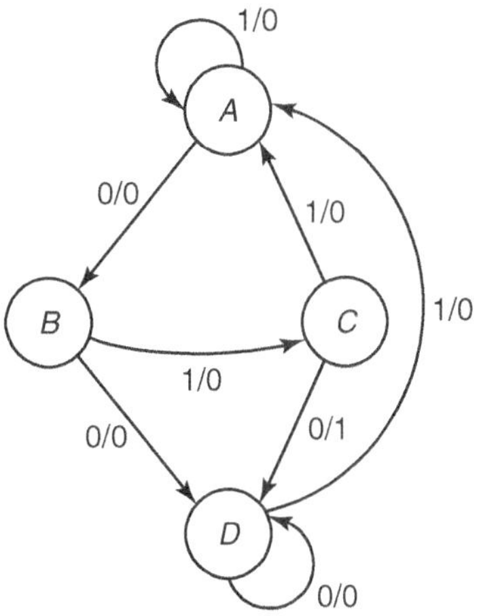

6.

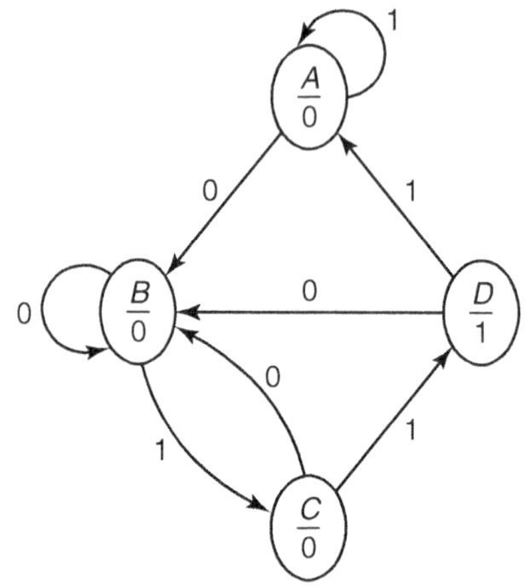

C.8 Chapter 8

1.

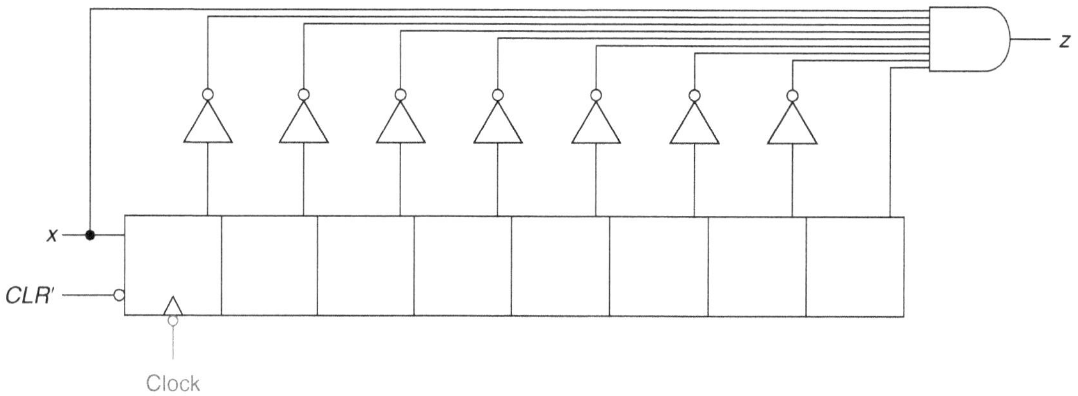

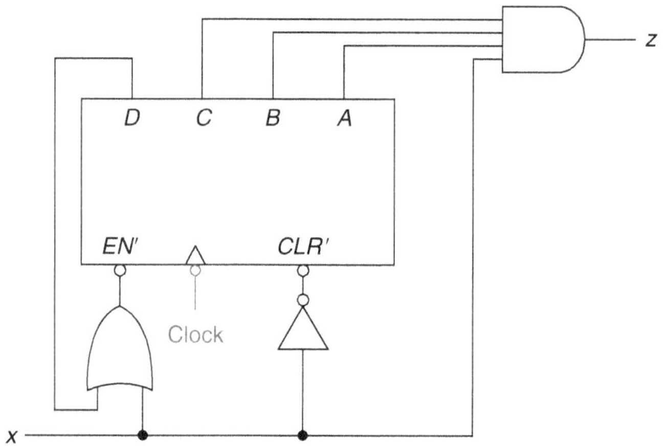

2.

$AB \backslash x$	0	1
00	1	
01	1	
11		1
10		1

D_A

$D_A = x'A' + xA$

$AB \backslash x$	0	1
00	1	1
01		1
11		1
10	1	1

D_B

$D_B = x + B'$

$AB \backslash x$	0	1
00	1	
01		
11		1
10	1	1

z

$z = x'B' + xA$

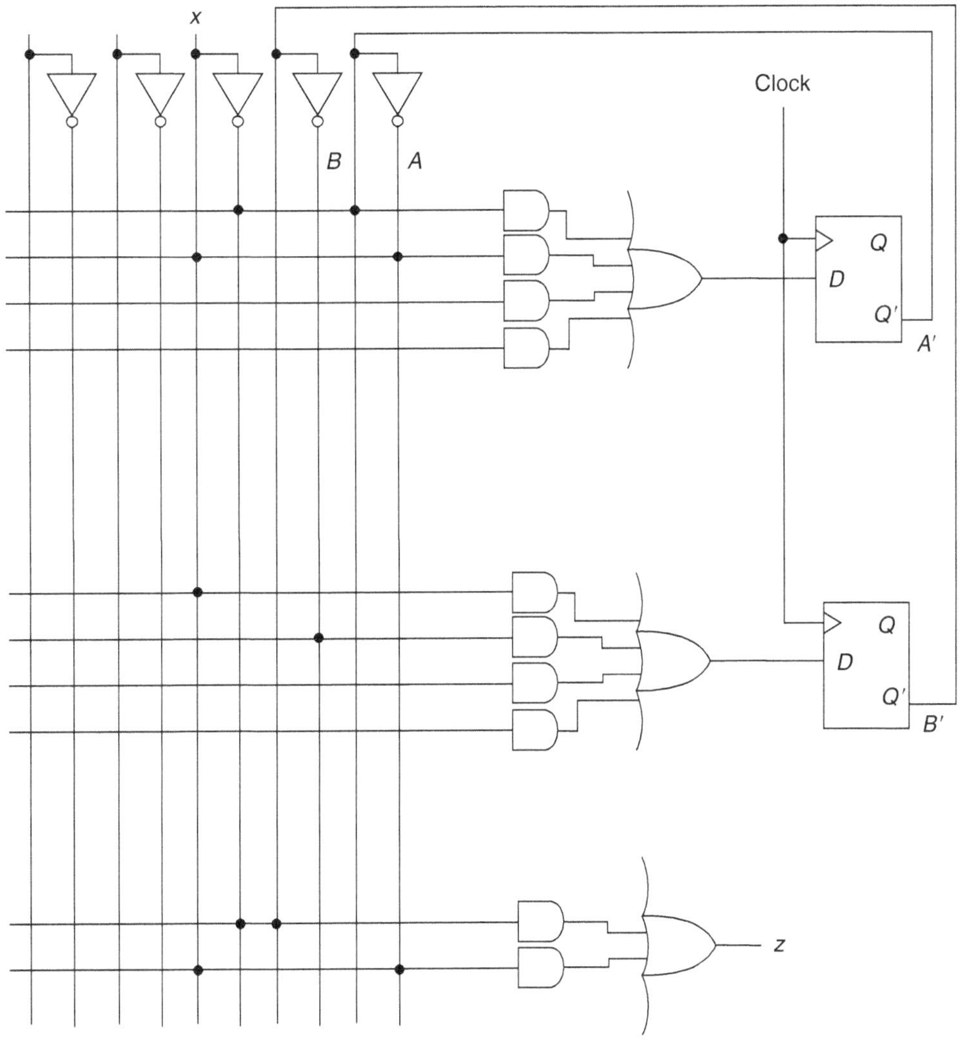

C.9 Chapter 9

1.

q	$q^\star$ $x = 0$	$x = 1$	z
A-B	C-D	A-B	0
C-D	E	A-B	0
E	C-D	A-B	1

2. a. P_1 = output consistent
   P_2 = SP
   P_3 = neither
   P_4 = SP, output consistent
   P_5 = SP
   P_6 = SP, output consistent

   b. P_4 allows us to reduce the system to that of Problem 1.

3. $P_1 = (AC)(B)(D)$
   $P_2 = (AD)(BC)$
   $P_3 = (A)(BD)(C)$
   $P_4 = (AC)(BD)$

4. Use P_3 for q_1 and $P_{OC} = (ACE)\ (BDF)$ for q_2. The product of these is $(AE)\ (BD)\ (C)\ (E)$. Using P_2, we keep A and F together, and B and C together. That gives either $(ADF)\ (BCE)$ or $(ABCF)\ (DE)$ as good partitions for q_3. Using the latter, we get

$$D_1 = x + q_1'$$
$$D_2 = x'q_1'q_3' + xq_1 + q_1q_2q_3' + xq_2'$$
$$D_3 = x'q_1'q_3' + xq_1 + \{q_1q_3 \text{ or } q_2q_3\}$$
$$z = q_2'$$

APPENDIX D: LABORATORY EXPERIMENTS

In the following sections, we will introduce three tools for implementing or simulating the circuits designed in the text. There will then be a variety of experiments, keyed to the material in the body of the text.

First, in D.1, we will describe a setup where integrated circuit packages will be wired and tested.

Second, in D.2, we will introduce a breadboard simulator that allows us to do the hardware experiments without requiring the laboratory equipment. The wiring of Section D.1 is done on a PC screen.

Next, in D.3, we will introduce LogicWorks, so that the behavior of circuits can be simulated, without actually building them. This will be particularly valuable to observe the timing behavior of the circuit, without the use of a logic analyzer.

We will then, in D.4, provide a set of experiments that can be accomplished with each of these systems.

The pin layout of all the integrated circuits referenced in the text is shown in D.5. Note that different manufacturers use different notations. We will follow the notation in the text.

D.1 HARDWARE LOGIC LAB

Logic circuits can be built and tested using a small breadboard that allows the user to plug in integrated circuit chips and wires (without making permanent solder connections). The additional equipment needed to perform most of these experiments are a 5-volt power supply (or battery), some switches, some LEDs (lights to display binary values), and a square wave generator with a 5-volt output (with variable speed capabilities). Some of the later experiments also use a pair of seven-segment displays and a pulser. The IDL-800 Logic Lab* provides a convenient way to build and test small and medium size digital circuits and includes all of the features described above and many others.

Circuits are wired on the breadboard, a small portion of which is shown in Figure D.1. (The breadboard in the next section [Figure D.6] is a computer simulation of this.) The main part of the breadboard has a

*Manufactured by K & H Mfg. Co., Ltd.

number of grooves, over which an integrated circuit chip fits, as indicated in Figure D.1. The chip fits in the first of a set of six holes, each of which is connected together internally. Thus, to connect something to a pin, the wire is inserted in one of those holes. (Do not put another chip over the groove next to the first one; the pins of the two chips would be connected. Immediately above and below the main section on many boards, there are two busses. One is usually used for ground. The other is usually used for +5 volts. On some boards, the various sections of the bus are connected internally; on others, they must be wired together. Some boards also have, on the bottom of the board, a set of pins in columns that are internally connected and used mostly for external signals that are to be connected to several places.

Figure D.1 Detail of the breadboard.

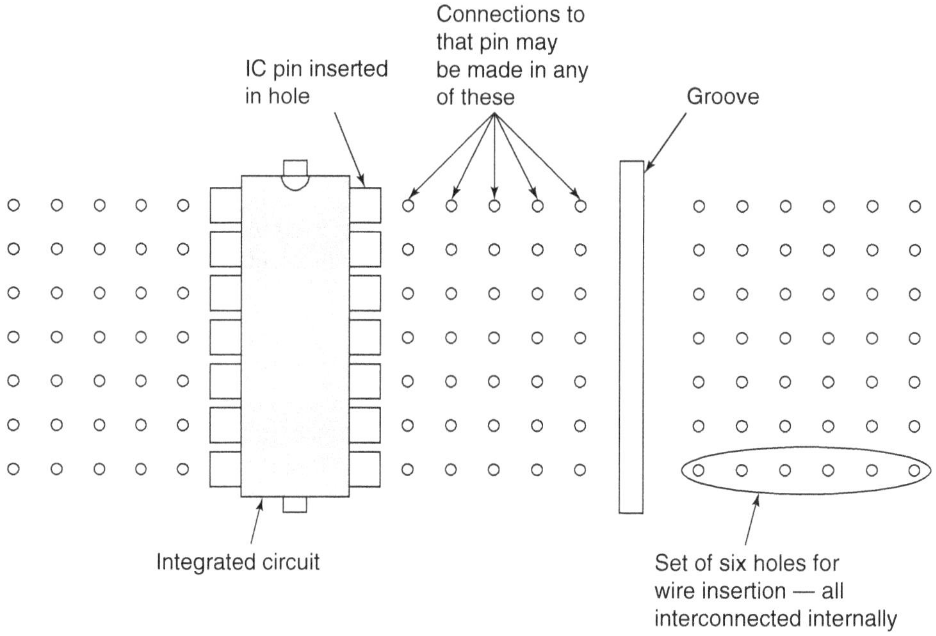

The integrated circuit package illustrated has 14 pins (as do all of them in the experiments in Chapter 2). The orientation of the chip is specified by the semicircle (at the top). Typically, that is just an indentation in the plastic shell of the chip. Pins are numbered from 1 (at the top, left of the semicircle) to 7 down the left side and then from 8 to 14 up the right side. (If there are more pins, the numbering is the same, starting at the upper left and continuing down the left side and up the right side.)

A closer look at the 7400 (with 4 two-input NAND gates) is shown in Figure D.2 in two formats:

Figure D.2 Layout of the 7400.

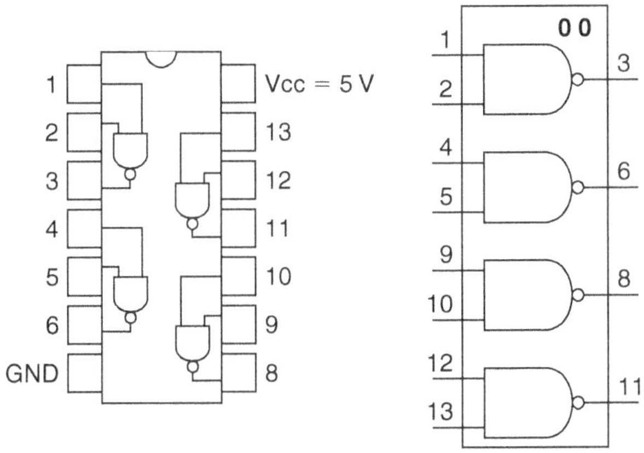

The first highlights the orientation of the pin connections; the second emphasizes the individual gates. From a wiring point of view, we are dealing with the first on the circuit board.

To illustrate the use of the system, consider the implementation of the function

$$f = ab' + bc$$

using NAND gates. The circuit for this is shown in Figure D.3.

Figure D.3 A NAND gate circuit.

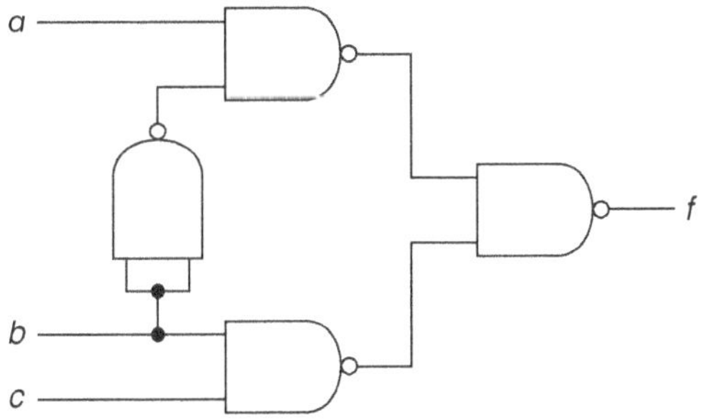

Since complemented inputs are often not available, b' was created using a NAND gate. (We could have done this with a NOT gate, but the 7400 has four NAND gates, and we can use the extra one as a NOT.)

In order to wire this, we need to associate each gate with one on the chip and find the pin numbers. The circuit is redrawn in Figure D.4 with the pin numbers indicated.

Figure D.4 NAND circuit with pins

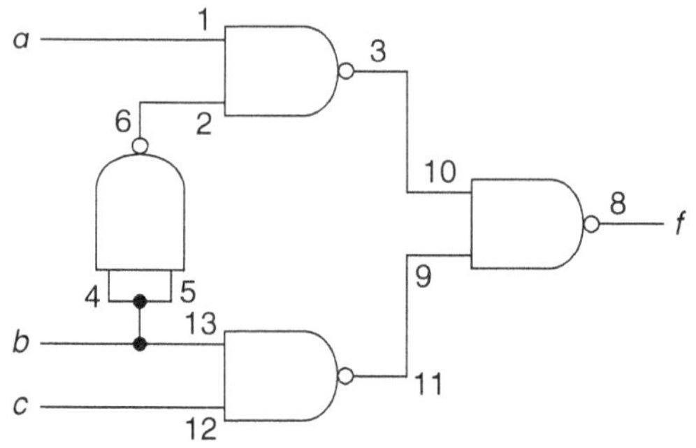

Now the connections can be made on the breadboard. The circuit of Figure D.5 shows the appropriate connections for this system. Note that it does not matter which of the five holes are used to connect something to a chip's pin. However, only one wire can fit in a hole; thus, when the same signal goes to several points, more than one of the holes is used (or one of the set of holes at the bottom of the board is used). Thus, for example, input *b* goes to pins 4, 5, and 13. In Figure D.5, it is connected directly to pin 4; then a wire is run from pin 4 to pin 5 and from pin 4 to pin 13. (It could have gone from pin 5 to 13.)

Figure D.5 Wiring for 7400 circuit.

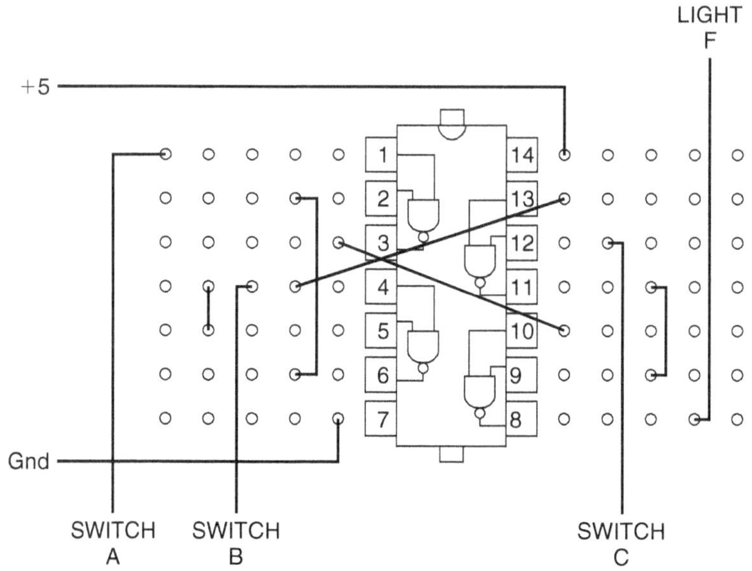

After the breadboard is wired (and before the power is turned on), connect the breadboard to the voltages, input switches, and output lights. The power can then be turned on and the system tested. (Caution: Do not insert or remove wires while the power is on.)

As an introduction to the system, build this circuit and test it. To test it, start with the three switches all in the 0 position and observe the output light. Repeat for each of the eight input combinations. Compare that with the truth table that was constructed based on the algebra.

Seven-segment displays are useful to output decimal results. A digit (in 8421 code) is input to a decoder/driver, the outputs of which provide the signals to light the display. The IDL-800 logic lab has two seven-segment displays. The BCD inputs to the decoder allow the connection of a BCD number (8421 code) to be displayed on either of the displays. Below each display, there is an active low enable input for that display. To use both displays, the inputs must be alternated. (The displays will look like they are lit even if the inputs are there only half of the time, as long as they alternate at a rate of about 60 Hz or higher.) If any code that does not correspond to a decimal digit (1010 and above) is entered, the display will remain blank. (There is also a P input that lights a decimal point on the right of the display.)

D.2 WINBREADBOARD™ AND MACBREADBOARD™*

The MacBreadboard, shown in Figure D.6, (also available for Windows as WinBreadboard) is a computer simulation of the logic laboratory described in Section D.1. A picture of the screen before building a circuit is shown in Figure D.6.

Figure D.6 Breadboard.

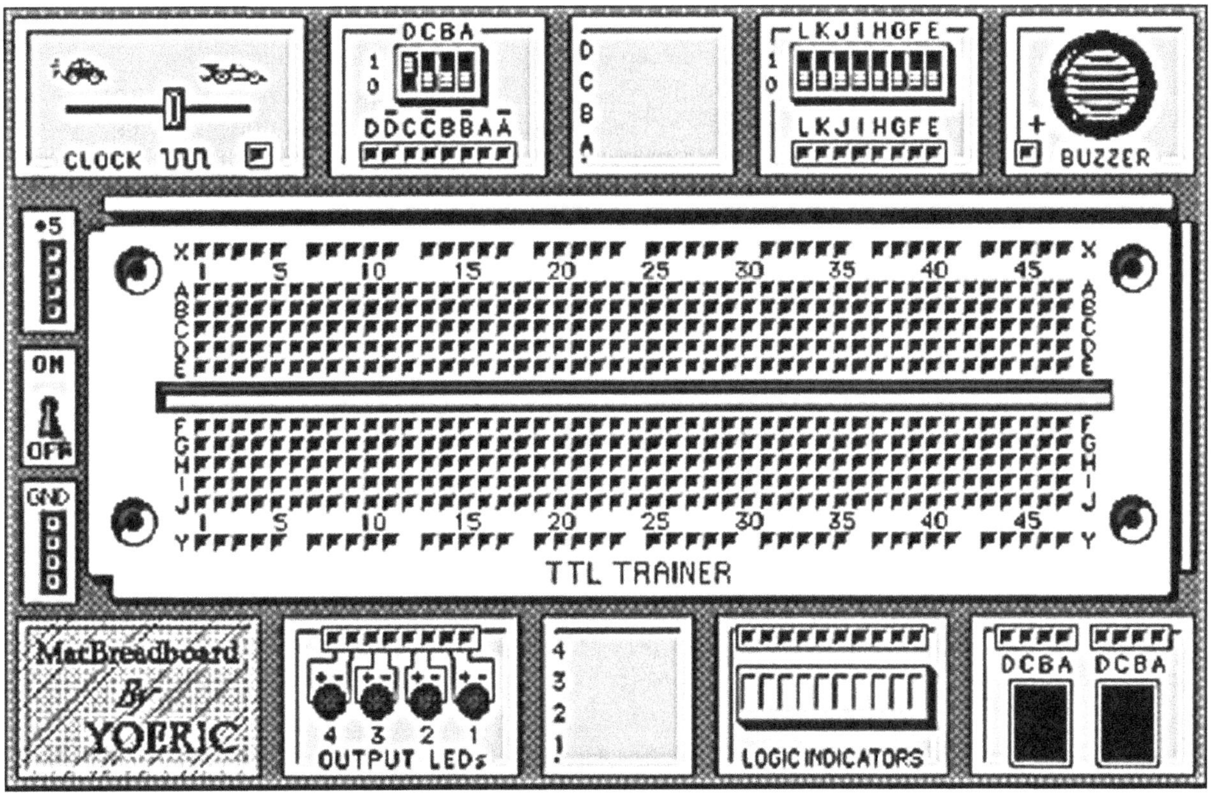

*Product of Yoeric Software, Chapel Hill, NC. The software can be purchased at http://www.yoeric.com/breadboard.htm.

This looks very similar to the hardware laboratory and has many of the same features. (Anyone who is not familiar with the hardware laboratory should review Section D.1 before proceeding). The pull-down menu "chips" provides a selection of more than 70 chips from the 7400 series. When a chip is selected, it is automatically placed* on the left end of the board. However, it can be moved to any position by clicking on and dragging it. When the chip is double clicked, the pin layout of that chip is displayed.

The top row of holes (labeled X) are connected together; they are usually connected to +5. Similarly, the bottom row (labeled Y) are connected and are used for ground. A wire connection must be made between one of the holes in these rows and +5 and ground. To connect a wire, click on a hole and drag to the other hole to which it is to be connected. Wires only run horizontally or vertically (not diagonally). If the pointer does not follow a straight line, the wire may zig zag across the board. To prevent this, hold down the shift key; the wire will then follow a straight line. On a color display, the wires can be made one of several colors. Either select the color before drawing the wire or click once on the wire and then select a color from the "color" pull-down list.

There are a set of four input switches (with uncomplemented and complemented outputs), labeled D, C, B, and A. There is also another set of eight switches (L to E) with only uncomplemented outputs. There is a set of four output LEDs (4 to 1). An active high signal can be connected to the + side and the other side to ground or an active low signal to the − side and the + side to 5 volts. There is also a set of 10 logic indicators (which are just active high output lights). The four switches and four LEDs can be labeled; those names will appear in the timing diagram.

A circuit with one NAND gate from a 7400 connected (with the inputs and outputs labeled) and a 7410 place on the board, but not connected is shown in Figure D.7.† If the system is turned on in this position, LED4 will be lit.

The breadboard has two seven-segment displays, each with a set of four inputs. It displays hexadecimal. (Of course, if the inputs are limited to the ten digits, the display is limited to 0 to 9, BCD in 8421 code.)

Some of the experiments, particularly in Chapters 6, 7, and 8, make use of the clock and pulser. The clock produces a square wave, the frequency of which can be controlled by the slide. (It has very low frequencies, from about 0.15 to 10 Hz; but that is all one can view.) The "clock" pull-down menu provides for pulses or steps, so that it is possible to follow the behavior of the system one clock pulse at a time. A timing diagram can be displayed (from the clock menu). The clock and all labeled switches and output LEDs will be displayed. The breadboard cir-

*The on/off switch must be in the off position to make any connections on the circuit board. Click on the switch to change it.

†As the diagrams get more complex, it is particularly important to draw the wires neatly and to use colors to signify meaning. For example, black is commonly used for ground and red for +5. (Colors are not obvious in this black and white picture.)

Figure D.7 7400 circuit.

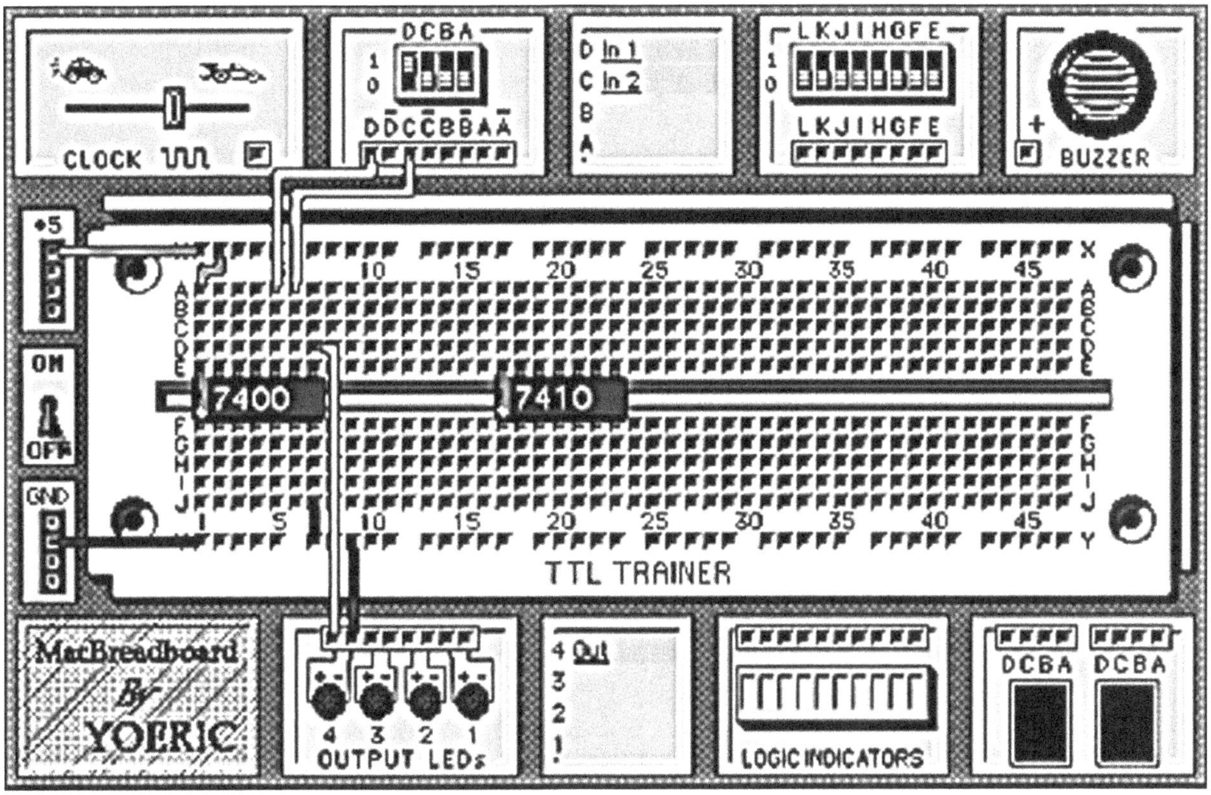

cuits do not have any delay built into the gates or flip flops; thus, all timing displays will correspond to the theoretical undelayed ones in the text.

D.3 INTRODUCTION TO LOGICWORKS

This appendix describes some of the basic features of LogicWorks, enough to begin using it with the experiments in this text. Version 5.0 for Windows also has additional features, including the ability to describe systems with a subset of VHDL.* The basic operation is the same on both the Windows and Macintosh platforms, but some of the detail differs. We will show the Windows variations in brown.

To start LogicWorks, double-click on its icon. That produces on the Macintosh five separate (but related) windows. The main window is the *Circuit Window*, where a block diagram of the circuit will be created. The *Tool Palette* is on the upper left corner of the screen; it allows us to draw and erase connections, add names, and probe the circuit. On the right is the *Parts Palette*; on that we can select from a variety of gates,

*LogicWorks is a product of Capilano Computing Systems, Ltd. The latest version (5.0) for Windows is sold exclusively through Prentice Hall Publishing. It is included with a book, giving full details of the software. The latest Macintosh version (4.5) is available at http://www.capilano.com/html/lwm.html.

integrated circuits, inputs, and displays. The bottom of the screen is the *Timing Window*, where a trace of the behavior of the circuit over time is displayed. Finally, in the upper left corner of that, is the *Simulator Palette*, that gives control of various features of the timing trace. In Windows, the Tool Palette and the Simulator Palette are replaced by a single Tool Bar (with basically the same functionality). We will use the word palette in the discussion below for both platforms.

We will first build and test a simple combinational logic circuit to implement

$$f = ab' + bc.$$

The block diagram of the circuit as we will construct it is shown in Figure D.8.

Figure D.8 LogicWorks example.

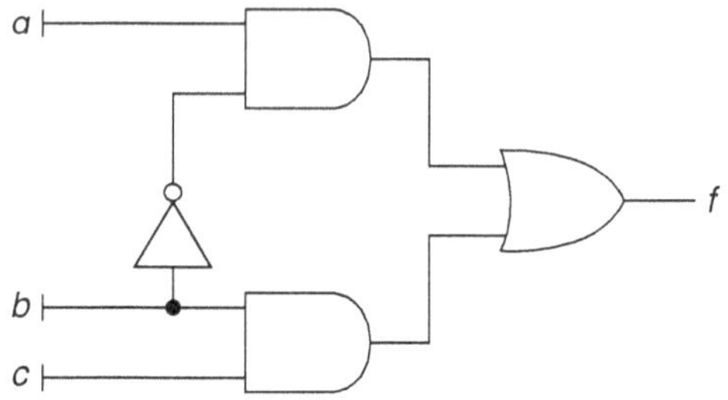

To build a model of this circuit with LogicWorks, first go to the parts palette, then click and drag the mouse on the title to highlight Simulation Gates.clf. A list of the types of gates that are available will appear. (Windows: All parts are merged into a single list; we will refer to Macintosh individual palettes in the text below.) For this problem, double-click on AND-2. When the cursor moves over the circuit window, a picture of the gate will appear. Move it to the center of the window and click. At that point, the gate will be fixed on the screen and another copy will appear. Since a second AND gate is needed, move it to a convenient spot and click again. When that type of gate is no longer needed, hit the space bar (or click on the arrow on the Tool Palette). Return to the Parts Palette, move down to the OR-2, and repeat the process. The final component is a NOT gate, obtained in the same way, except that we want it pointing up. To accomplish that, push the up arrow (↑) key while the gate is selected and then click it into position. Any gate may be highlighted by clicking on it, and then moved by dragging the mouse. (The orientation of a gate may be changed when it is highlighted by pulling down the left box on the Tool Palette and selecting the desired direction. (The side bubble is relevant only in three-state gates; it may be ignored for now.) (This can be accomplished in Windows by selecting the Orientation menu from the Schematic pull-down menu.) The screen should now look something like Figure D.9.

Figure D.9 Parts placed.

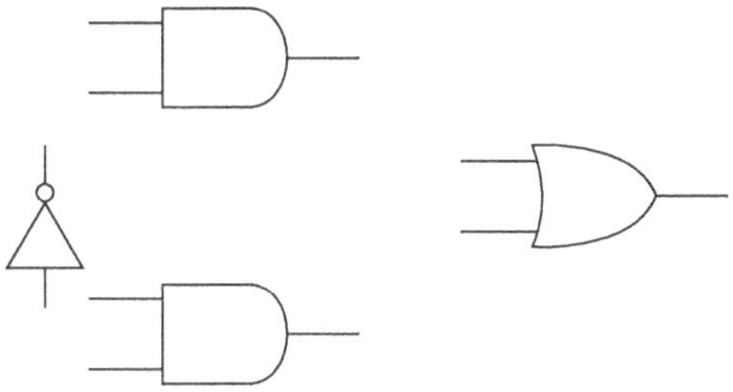

Now that all the gates are on the diagram, they need to be connected. Point to the end of any line and drag it to where it is to be connected. The path may be varied by depressing the key and/or the option key (CTRL and/or TAB key). If none of those paths are satisfactory, draw a line and release the mouse; then start again in another direction. Finally, a line can be drawn anywhere by clicking on the + cursor on the tool palette and dragging the mouse where the line is to go. At the end of the line click once to start a new line or double click to terminate line drawing. To remove a line (or a gate), select the Zap (lightning bolt) tool in the Tool Palette and point it to what is to be deleted. An alternative is to highlight the item and use the delete key. To get out of the zap mode, hit the space bar or the arrow on the Tool Palette.

Next, names can be added to the inputs and outputs (or any point in the circuit). To do this, use the Text Tool (the A on the Tool Palette). When that is highlighted, a pencil point is displayed. Move the point to the line that is to be named and click the mouse. An internal name will be displayed; just type over that. Move the name to wherever it is most convenient by clicking at the point to be named and then dragging to where the name is to be written. To exit text mode, use the arrow on the Tool Palette (or select some other tool); the space bar enters a space in the text.

To connect inputs, connect any point to ground or +5 volts, found on the CONNECT.CLF parts menu or the DemoLib.clf parts menu. There is also a binary switch (found on the DemoLib.clf parts menu). Clicking on that switch causes its value to change between 0 and 1. Finally, the probe tool (shown on the Tool Palette with a ?) can be used to test the value at any point. With that pointed and the mouse depressed, type in a 0 or 1 to set the value at that point. The probe will display a Z for an input that is not connected to anything and an X for a point whose value is unknown (for example, the output of a gate, the inputs of which are not specified). The output can be displayed permanently, using the *binary probe* from the DemoLib.clf parts menu.

The circuit, as completed, using switches for inputs and the binary probe for outputs, is shown in Figure D.10, first with all of the switches in the 0 position (producing a 0 output) and then with a in the 1 position and $b = c = 0$ (producing a 1 output).

Figure D.10 Completed circuit with input switches and output display.

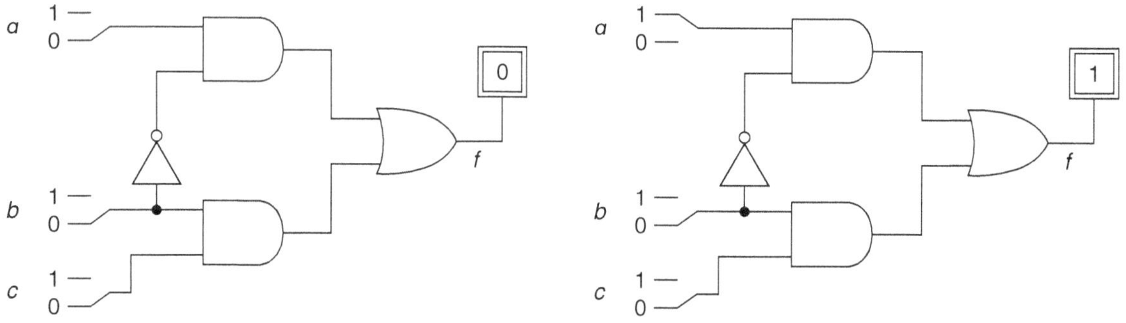

With switches and the probe in place, it is easy to complete the truth table for this function. As an introduction to LogicWorks, create this circuit and test it.

By selecting the 7400DEVS.CLF menu from the Parts Palette, a logic diagram for that chip appears on the Circuit window. (A large variety of 7400 series chips are available; we will reference many of them in the experiments that follow.) It can be clicked in place, just as any of the other components. Connections can then be made as before. The circuit for

$$f = ab' + bc$$

using 4 two-input NAND gates is shown in Figure D.11.

Figure D.11 Circuit using a 7400.

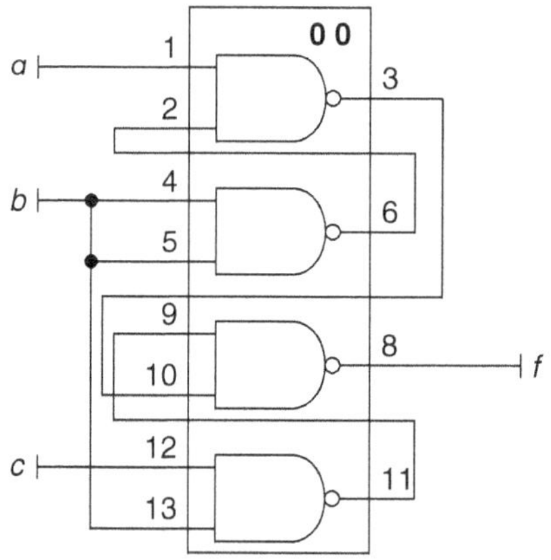

As before, it can be tested by connecting switches to the inputs or by connecting each to ground or 5 volts. Try this and see that it also works.

Finally, we will look at one other method of connection. If two points are given the same name, they are treated as if they are connected (even though no connection line is drawn). Thus, in the circuit of Figure D.12, all of the connections of the above diagram are made, switches are connected to each of the inputs, and a binary probe is connected to the output.

Figure D.12 Named connections.

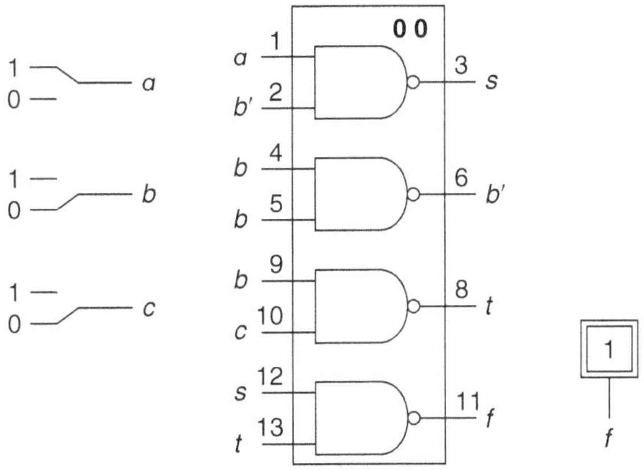

Parts of a circuit may be highlighted by clicking on them (in point mode). Hold the shift key down to highlight several parts. Also, by dragging the mouse from outside one corner of a circuit to outside the diagonal corner, a box is created such that, when the mouse is released, everything within the box is selected. To select the whole drawing, pull down Select All from the Edit menu. The Copy feature can be used to take this drawing and insert it in another document (perhaps a word processor). A drawing can also be printed directly from LogicWorks from the File menu. (All of these also work to copy or print a timing diagram when the Timing Window is highlighted.)

To examine some of the other ideas, we first need to look at the clock and the Timing Window. The clock is found on either the DemoLib.clf or Simulation IO.clf menu. It provides a square wave with a period of 20 units, unless modified (as described below). Any signal that is named will be displayed in the Timing Window. The speed of the display is controlled on the Simulator Palette (by buttons on the bottom row of the Tool Bar). By sliding the speed control bar to the left, the display can be slowed. At the left end, it stops. Click Step (symbol of man standing) to move from one event to the next. (An event is any point where a signal might change.) The display can be magnified by clicking on <> or shrunk by clicking on ><. The clock speed can be controlled by clicking on the clock (to highlight it) and pulling down Simulation Params . . . from the Simulate (Simulation) pull-down menu. Set the time the clock is low and the clock is high; then exit the menu by hitting return.

Every combinational logic device has a built-in delay of 1 time unit. That can be seen by connecting the clock to a device and observing the input and the output of that device. The delay can be changed using Simulation Params . . . with that device highlighted. To see the behavior, set up the circuit of Figure D.13 and set the clock to 40 units for both low and high. Set the delay to 10 units for each gate.

Figure D.13 Delay example.

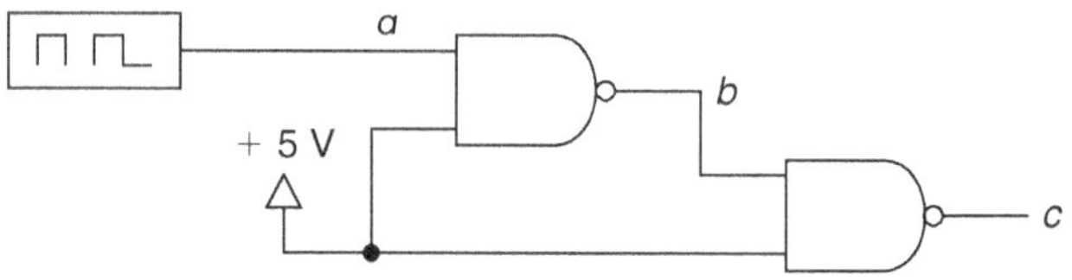

Stop the clock by moving the speed bar to the far left. Click on Restart (↻), which reinitializes the clock. Expand the display by clicking on <>. Then click once or twice on the right arrow of the speed bar to start the simulation. When it is stopped after 120 units, a display like the one of Figure D.14 is seen. Note that *c* is a duplicate of *a* delayed by 20 units (after the startup).

Figure D.14 Timing diagram.

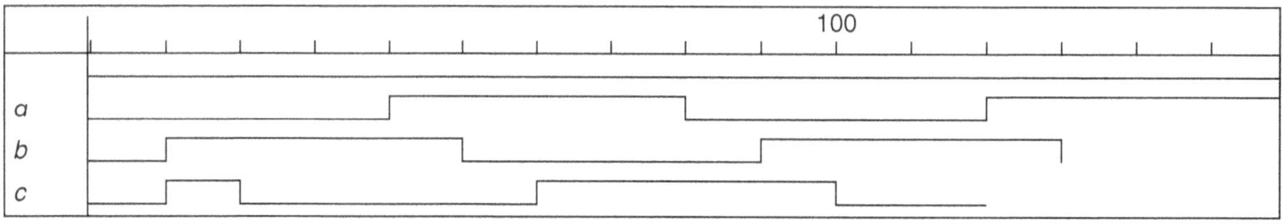

D.4 A SET OF LOGIC DESIGN EXPERIMENTS

Each of the experiments can be implemented on any of the systems with the modifications indicated. The notation below will be used to indicate the special needs.

HW: Hardware Logic Lab
BB: Breadboard Simulator
LW: LogicWorks

D.4.1 Experiments Based on Chapter 2 Material

■ **1.** For each of the following sets of functions, build each version using AND, OR, and NOT gates. Test them to show that each function in a set behaves the same as each of the others in that set.

a. $f = xy'z' + xy'z + xyz$
$g = xy' + xz$
$h = x(y' + z)$

b. $f = a'b'c' + a'b'c + abc' + ab'c'$
$g = a'b' + ac'$
$h = (a' + c')(a + b')$

c. $f = x'yz' + xyz' + xy'z$
$g = yz' + xz'$
$h = z'(x + y')$

d. $f = a'bc' + ab'c' + a'bc + ab'c$
$g = (a + b)(a' + b')$
$h = a'b + ab'$

e. $f = x'y'z' + x'yz' + xyz + xy'z$
$g = x'z' + xz$
$h = (x' + z)(x + z')$

f. $f = a'b'c + a'bc + abc$
$g = a'c + bc$
$h = c(a' + b)$

HW: Use one 7404 (NOT gates) to construct the complement of the variables. (Use the same 7404 outputs for all three versions.)

HW, BB: In addition, we have available 7411s (three-input AND gates), 7408s (two-input AND gates), and 7432s (two-input OR gates). There are no larger OR gates available and thus we must construct a multi-input OR gate from two-input gates. Each of the outputs should go to a different light, but the inputs come from the same three switches.

LW: Use individual gates (from Simulation Gates.clf).

2. Implement the systems of Experiment 1 using NAND gates for the sum of products expressions and NOR gates for the product of sums expressions.

HW, BB: Use 7400s, 7410s, 7430s, and 7402s (two-input NOR gates).

LW: Use individual gates.

3. Implement each of the following expressions (which are already in minimum sum of products form) using only 7400s (two-input NAND gates). No gate may be used as a NOT (except to form the complement of the inputs). Note that these are the functions of Exercise 25 in Chapter 2, where the number of two-input gates (not including the NOT gates) is shown in parentheses.

a. $f = wy' + wxz' + y'z + w'x'z$ (7 gates)

b. $ab'd' + bde' + bc'd + a'ce$ (10 gates)

c. $H = A'B'E' + A'B'CD' + B'D'E' + BDE' + BC'E + ACE'$ (14 gates)

d. $F = A'B'D' + ABC' + B'CD'E + A'B'C + BC'D$ (11 gates)

e. $G = B'D'E' + A'BC'D + ACE + AC'E' + B'CE$ (12 gates, one of which is shared) *f.* $h = b'd'e' + ace + c'e' + bcde$ (9 gates)

g. $F = ABE + AB'C' + A'D + CE' + B'D'E'$ (10 gates)

h. $g = a'c' + a'bd + acd' + ab'c + bce$ (8 gates if you share)

■ **4.** *a.* Build a full adder using NAND gates. Test it and save it to use with an experiment from Chapter 5.

b. Build the full adder using Exclusive-OR gates and NAND gates.

D.4.2 Experiments Based on Chapter 5 Material

■ **5.** Connect the 4-bit adder with one number (*A4 . . . A1*) to four data switches (with *A4* on the left switch) and the other number on the other four switches. Connect another switch to the carry input (*C0*). Connect the five outputs (*C4*, $\Sigma 4$, $\Sigma 3$, $\Sigma 2$, and $\Sigma 1$) to the right five indicators. Test the circuit by inputting any two 4-bit numbers plus a carry input and observe the result. Note that bit 4 is the high-order bit and bit 1 the low-order bit.

HW: Use the 7483 adder chip.

BB: Use the 74283 adder chip.

LW: Use the 7483 adder chip and nine data switches. Use binary probes for the outputs. Note that LogicWorks labels the bits 3 to 0 instead of 4 to 1.

■ **6.** In addition to the adder of Experiment 5, connect the 1-bit adder from Experiment 4 as the high-order bit of a 5-bit adder. Thus, connect *C4* to c_{in} of the adder from Experiment 4. There are now 11 inputs (two 5-bit numbers plus a carry in) and 6 outputs (the c_{out} and *s* outputs from the 1-bit adder plus the four sum outputs). Test the circuit by inputting various pairs of 5-bit numbers and a carry in of either 0 or 1; observe the result on the indicators.

HW: There are only 10 switches on the IDL-800 Logic Lab. Connect *C0* to ground or to 5 volts to input a 0 or 1.

■ **7.** HW: Take the adder from Experiment 5 and connect the four sum outputs to the decoder inputs for the seven-segment displays. Even though the inputs in the IDL-800 are labeled *A B C D* from left to right, the most significant bit is *D*. Thus, connect $\Sigma 4$ to *D*. Enable one of the displays by connecting its enable input to ground. (Note that in the IDL-800 there are switches between the decoder and the displays. They allow specific segments of the display to be disabled. They should all be in the ON position (to the right) for all of the experiments.)

BB: Connect the outputs from the adder of Experiment 5 to one seven-segment display. Try some addition problems such that the sum is 9 or less and observe the answer on the seven-segment display. The seven-segment display actually displays hexadecimal. You can connect both displays and show sums from 00 to 1F. (You need only connect input A to the high-order display.)

LW: Take the adder from Experiment 5 and connect the four sum outputs to a seven-segment display (found on the Simulation IO.clf menu) through a 7449 Display driver.

8. We have a 3-bit binary input number (on three of the switches) and wish to light one of eight output lights. Use a 74138 decoder to implement this. The decoder should always be enabled.

9. Use two 74138 decoders and two or three 7430s (eight-input NANDs) to implement the following functions:

a. $F(A, B, C, D) = \Sigma m(0, 1, 8, 9, 10, 12, 15)$
$G(A, B, C, D) = \Sigma m(0, 3, 4, 5, 7, 9, 10, 11)$

b. $F(A, B, C, D) + \Sigma m(1, 2, 3, 6, 9, 14, 15)$
$G(A, B, C, D) + \Sigma m(0, 1, 2, 8, 9, 12, 13, 15)$

c. $f(w, x, y, z) = \Sigma m(0, 1, 4, 5, 8, 15)$
$g(w, x, y, z) = \Sigma m(1, 2, 3, 7, 8, 10, 11, 14)$
$h(w, x, y, z) = \Sigma m(0, 1, 6, 7, 9, 10, 14, 15)$

d. $f(a, b, c, d) = \Sigma m(0, 3, 4, 5, 7, 8, 12, 13)$
$g(a, b, c, d) = \Sigma m(1, 5, 7, 8, 11, 13, 14, 15)$
$h(a, b, c, d) = \Sigma m(2, 4, 5, 7, 10, 13, 14, 15)$

HW, BB: Use switches for inputs and lights for outputs.

LW: Use switches for inputs and binary probes for outputs.

10. The 74161 counter* steps the three inputs through all combinations. The switch on the CLR input is there because the simulator requires the counter to be cleared; otherwise, the outputs will be indeterminate. The *P* and *T* enable inputs are active high, and the parallel load is disabled (+5 volts); thus, the inputs *A*, *B*, *C*, and *D* need not be connected.

*We will discuss counters and the 74161 in more detail in Chapter 8; for now, it is a handy tool to demonstrate some of the properties.

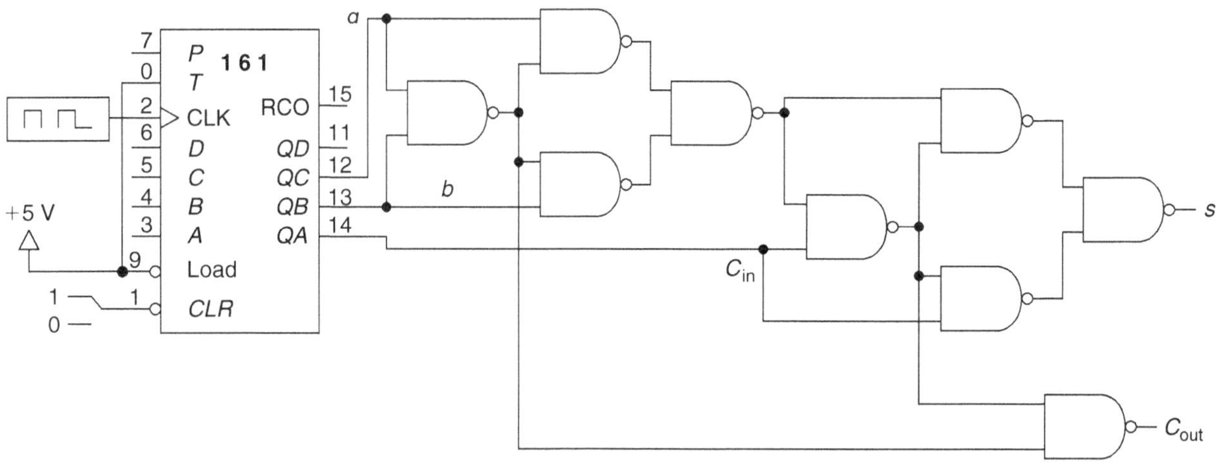

HW, BB: Set the clock frequency very slow.

LW: Try this with no delay and then with enough delay that its effect can be seen.

11. Implement the solutions to parts b and c of Exercise 23 (Chapter 5).

12. Build a 1-digit decimal adder. The inputs are the code for two decimal digits (in 8421 code) plus a carry in. Assume that none of the unused combinations exist. The outputs are the code for a decimal digit plus a carry. (The largest that the answer can be is 19.) See Section 4.8.1.

a. We will then display the result on five lights.

b. We will display the results on the two seven-segment displays.

HW: For the IDL-800, this requires a multiplexer and clock. A 74157 multiplexer is used to select one of the digits for BCD input to the displays. The same signal that selects is also used to select which display is enabled. Use the square wave from the function generator for this purpose. Remember that the displays are active low enabled, and one should be enabled when the wave is high and the other when it is low. (Note: The function generator output is not capable of driving the enable inputs; it must be connected to the enable through two inverters.)

LW: Two 7449 display drivers are needed.

13. Design a seven-segment display decoder using NAND gates for the second digit of the decimal adder of the previous problem such that segment *a* is lit for 6, segment *f* is lit for 7, and segment *d* is lit for 9 (the alternate display for each of these digits).

14. Use two 74151 multiplexers and a NOT gate to implement

$$f(a, b, c, d) = \Sigma m(0, 3, 4, 5, 7, 8, 12, 13)$$

D.4.3 Experiments Based on Chapter 6 Material

■ **15.** Connect the following circuit, using one half of a 7474 leading-edge triggered *D* flip flop.

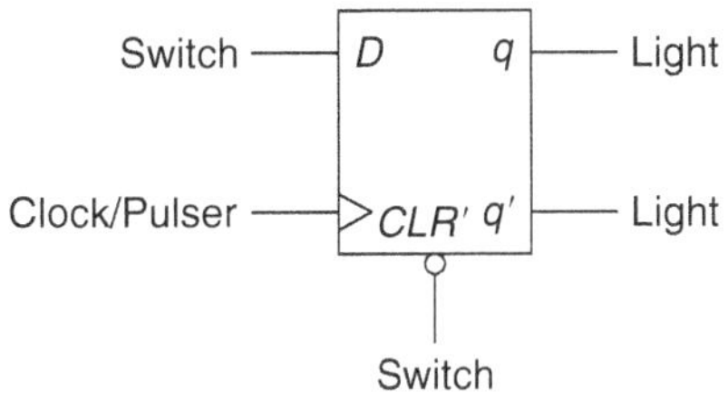

HW, BB: (a) Follow the sequence of steps listed below and record what is displayed on the two lights.

BB: Pull down the clock menu and set it to positive pulse.

1. Switch *D* -> 0
2. Switch *CLR'* -> 0
3. Pulse
4. Switch *CLR'* -> 1
5. Pulse
6. Switch *D* -> 1
7. Switch *CLR'* -> 0
8. Pulse
9. Pulse
10. Switch *CLR'* -> 1
11. Pulse
12. Pulse
13. Switch *D* -> 0
14. Pulse

HW: (b) In place of the pulser, connect the clock input to the square wave generator output, where it is set to the lowest frequency. Repeat the patterns for the two switches and observe what happens.

BB: (b) Set the clock speed fairly slow and change the clock to Free Run. Reset the timing diagram and try the switches in various positions. Notice when the outputs change relative to when the inputs change and when the clock changes.

LW: Note that the preset input must be connected to logic 1 (+5 volts) or to a switch if it is not used. Set the clock at a very slow speed and observe the behavior of the outputs as the two switches are changed.* Label the clock, *CLR'*, *D*, *Q*, and *Q'* and observe the display as the two switches are manipulated.

■ **16.** *a.* Connect a trailing-edge triggered *JK* flip flop from a 7473, using one switch for *J* and another for *K*. Devise a test sequence comparable to the one in Experiment 14 and observe the outputs.

*For the switches to work, the clock must be running or step must be clicked, even if there is nothing labeled and being displayed.

LW: Be sure that clear is connected and that the flip flop is initialized.

b. Connect the outputs of one of the *JK* flip flops (on the 7473) to the inputs of the next as shown below.

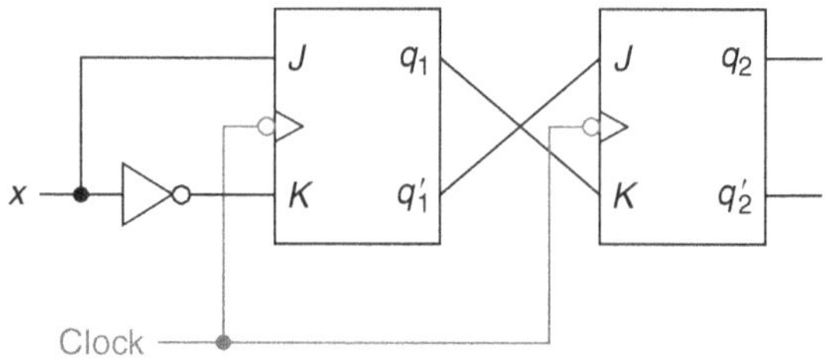

Devise a test sequence and observe the outputs.

■ **17.** Construct the circuit below using a 7473, a 7404, and a 7408.

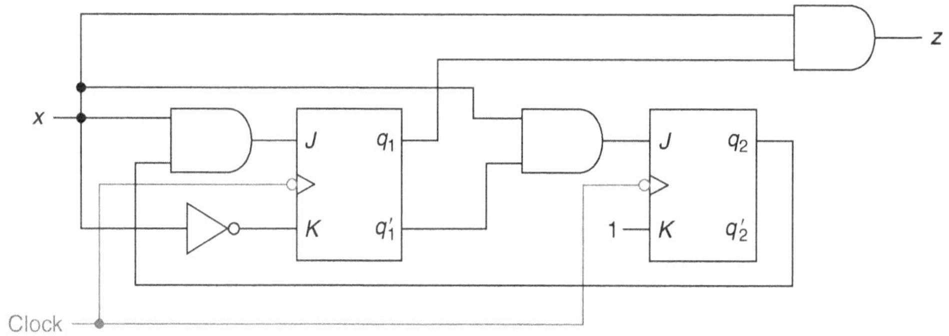

Follow the input pattern below.

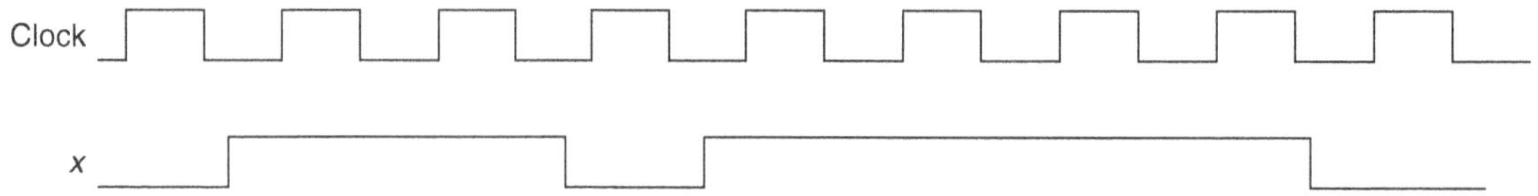

HW: Use the pulse switch for the clock, holding it down for a few seconds. (In that way, what happens on the leading edge is seen as the pulser is pushed and on the trailing edge as it is released. Be careful to hold it solidly down; otherwise, it may go back and forth between 0 and 1.)

BB: Try it both with the clock set on Step and on Free Run at a slow speed.

LW: Connect a switch to x and set the clock to the slowest speed. Label the clock, x, q_1, and q_2 so that the behavior can be displayed. Manipulate the switch so that the input pattern described in the problem is obtained. Stop the display when the end is reached and print out the timing diagram.*

18. *a.* Construct the circuit of Exercise 8a (at the end of Chapter 6) and test it.

b. Construct the circuit of Exercise 8b (at the end of Chapter 6) and test it.

D.4.4 Experiments Based on Chapter 7 Material

19. For each of the state tables in the following exercises of Chapter 7, design, build, and test a circuit using NAND gates and

i. *D* flip flops
ii. *JK* flip flops

a. 7.2a
b. 7.2d
c. 7.2f
d. 7.3c
e. 7.3e

20. Construct a synchronous base-12 counter using *JK* flip flops and a NAND gate.

21. Construct a synchronous counter using *D* flip flops and NAND gates that goes through the sequence

i. 1 3 5 7 6 4 2 0 and repeat.
ii. 1 3 4 7 2 6 0 and repeat.
iii. 6 5 4 3 2 1 and repeat.
iv. 1 3 4 7 6 and repeat.
v. 1 2 4 5 0 6 and repeat.
vi. 1 4 0 3 5 2 and repeat.

Set the clock at its lowest speed.

a. Display the results on three lights.

b. Connect the outputs to one of the seven-segment displays. (Of course, the first bit of the display input is 0. Be sure to connect the enable input for that display.)

HW: In the IDL-800, the clock speed cannot be made slow enough. Add a *JK* flip flop that is connected to change state every clock period. The output of that flip flop will be a square wave at half the frequency of the input. Use that to drive the display.

---

*To print, click on the timing display and choose Print Timing from the File menu. It is also possible to Select All and copy the timing to another document.

■ **22.** Build an asynchronous decade counter using *JK* flip flops and NAND gates.

HW, BB, LW: Display the results on a seven-segment display.

LW: Connect a switch to the *CLR′* input to reset the counter; that must be done at the beginning. Set the delay through each of the flip flops at 3. (Do this by highlighting all of them, pulling down Simulation Params from the Simulate menu, and changing the delay from 1 to 3. Watch the timing trace and see that the counter reaches its state well into the clock period. Also, the counter reaches 10 and remains there for a short period.

Magnify the display (by clicking <> on the Simulator Palette two or three times) and determine when the answer is stable relative to the trailing edge of the clock and how long the system stays in state 10. (Note that by clicking on the timing display, a vertical line will appear at that point. That will help measure the timing more accurately.)

D.4.5 Experiments Based on Chapter 8 Material

■ **23.** Using a 74164 shift register and a minimum number of AND, OR, and NOT gates, design and build a system that produces an output of 1 when the last nine inputs were 0.

HW, BB, LW: Use a pulser for the clock and a switch for the input.

■ **24.** Design a serial adder to add two 4-bit numbers. Each number is stored in a 7495 shift register.

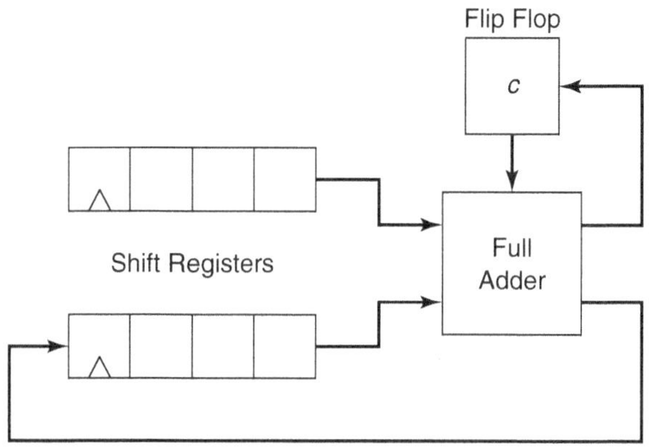

Load them using the parallel load capability. You must clear the carry storage flip flop before starting. Use a pulser for the clock and a switch to control whether it is loading or shifting. Display the contents of the lower shift register and the carry flip flop, which will have the result after four pulses.

■ **25.** Design a counter that goes from 0 to 59 and display the count on the two seven-segment displays.

HW: Since the displays need a clock to alternate between the digits much faster than the count clock, there are two alternatives:

a. Use the pulser to check the counting.

b. Set the frequency of the clock fast enough to get a good display and then use additional counters to reduce the frequency. (Remember that the OV output on the binary counter gives you an output for every 16 clock inputs.)

■ **26.** Build the solution to Exercise 12a in Chapter 8.

D.5 LAYOUT OF CHIPS REFERENCED IN THE TEXT AND EXPERIMENTS

Gates

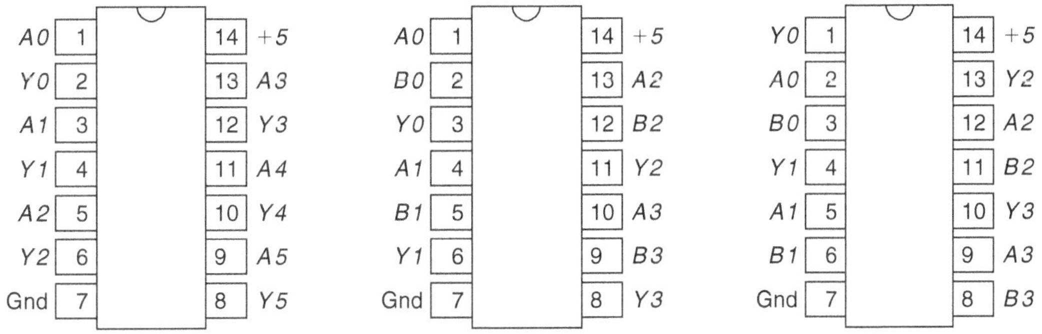

7404 NOT

7400 NAND
7408 AND
7432 OR
7486 XOR

7402 NOR

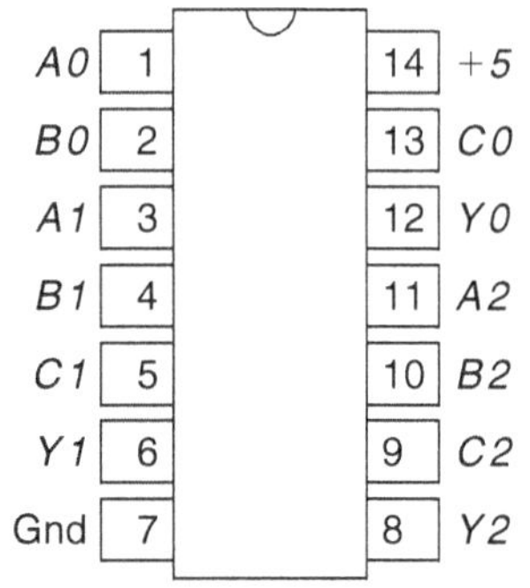

7410 NAND
7411 AND
7427 NOR

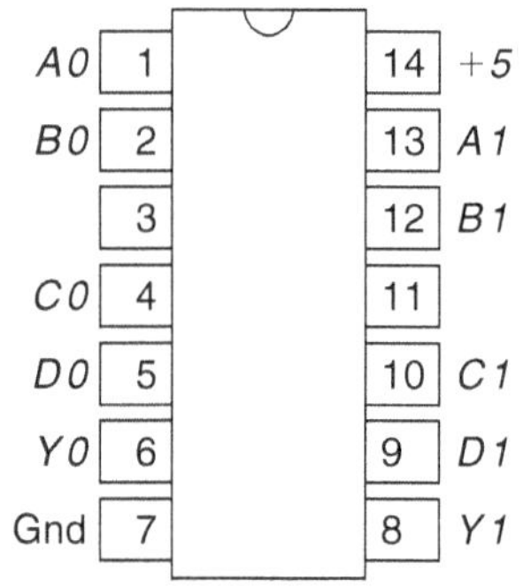

7420 NAND
7421 AND

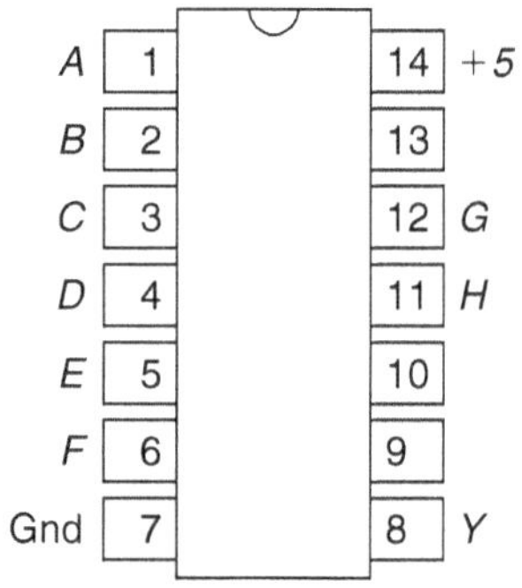

7430 NAND

A1 is one input to gate 1, *B1* is the second input, . . . ; *Y1* is the output.
Unlabeled pins are not connected.

Adders

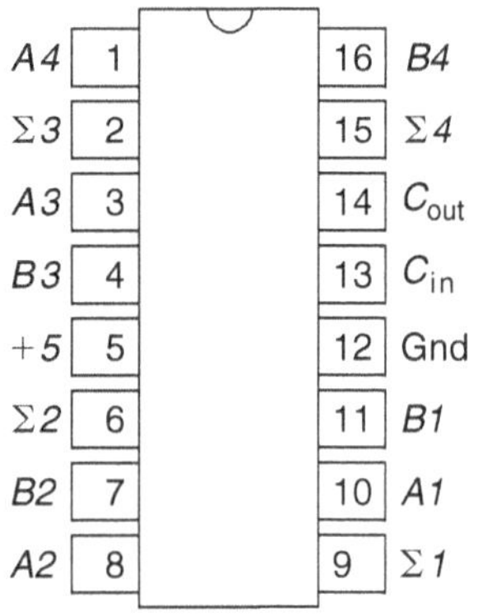

7483

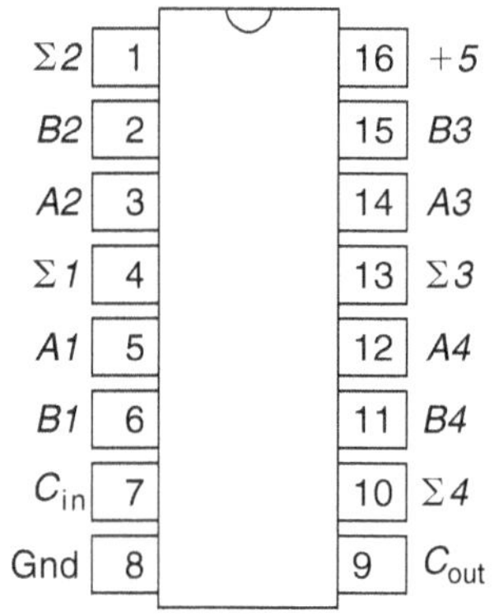

74283

Comparator

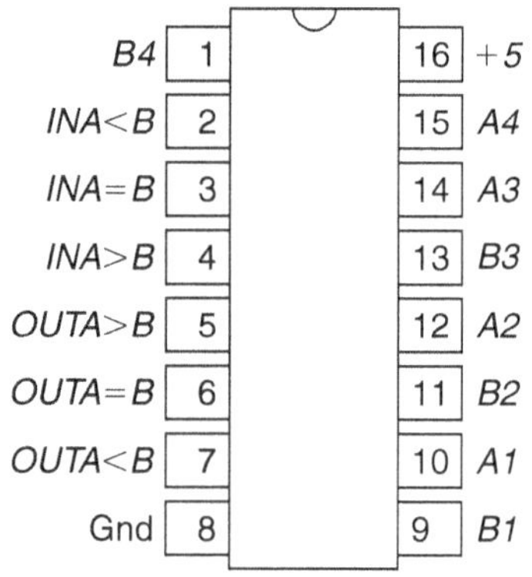

7485

Decoders

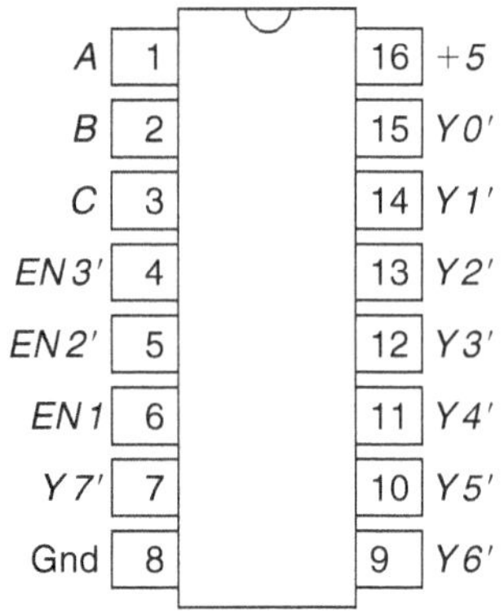

74138

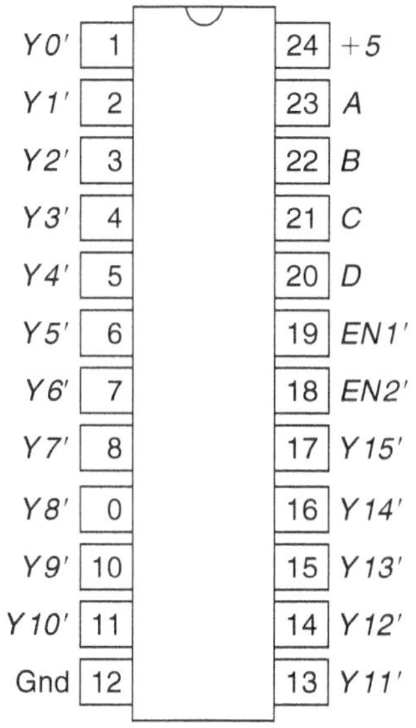

74154

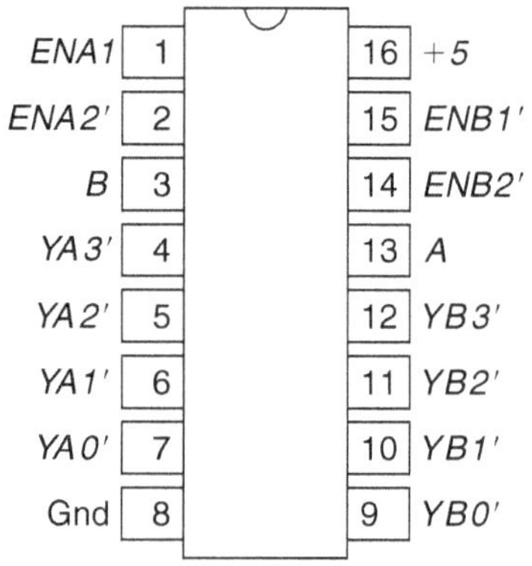

74155

D.5 Layout of Chips Referenced in the Text and Experiments

Priority Encoder

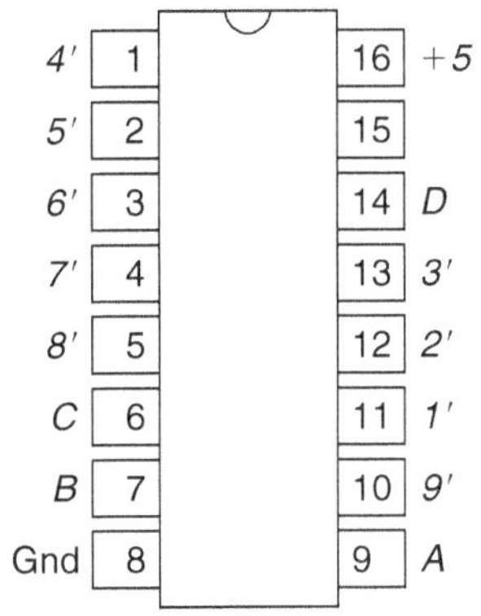

74147

Seven-Segment Decoder/Driver

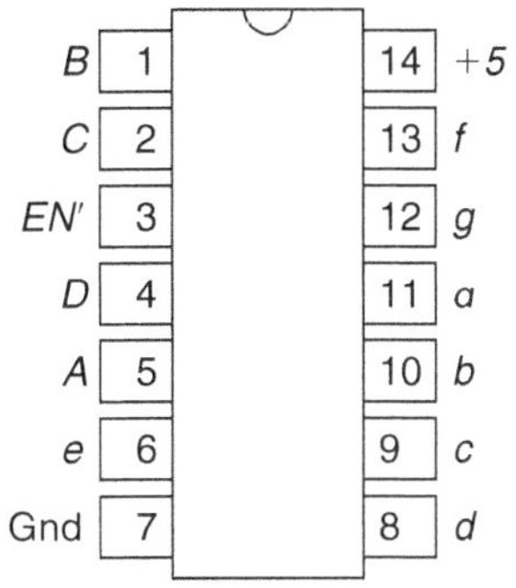

7449

Multiplexers

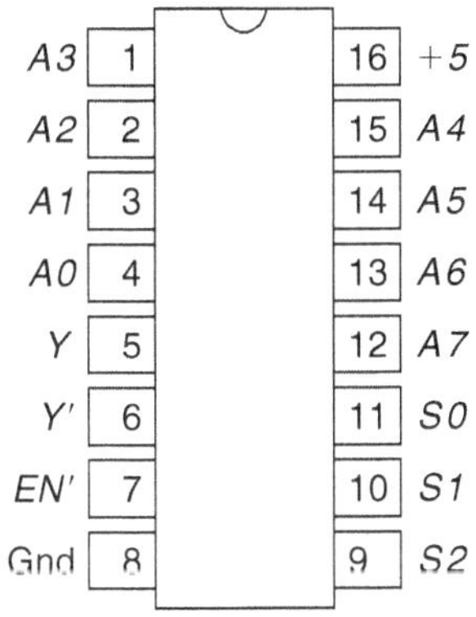

74151

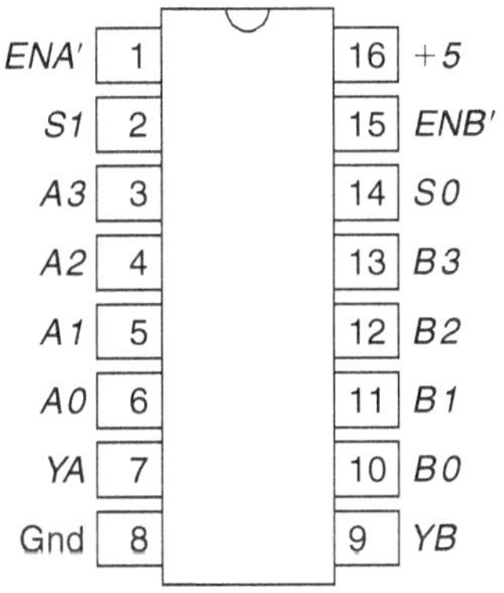

74153

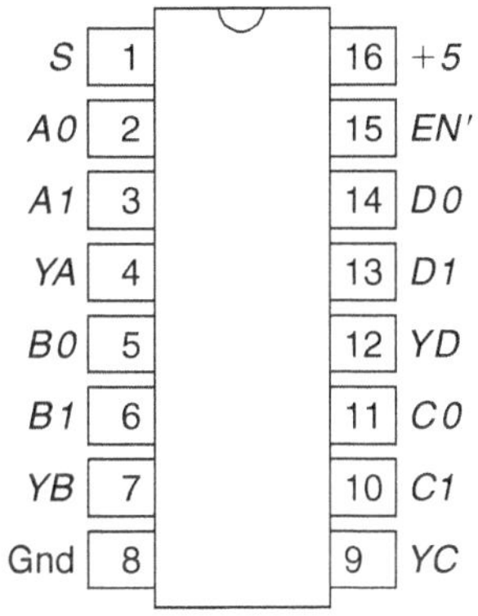

74157

Flip Flops

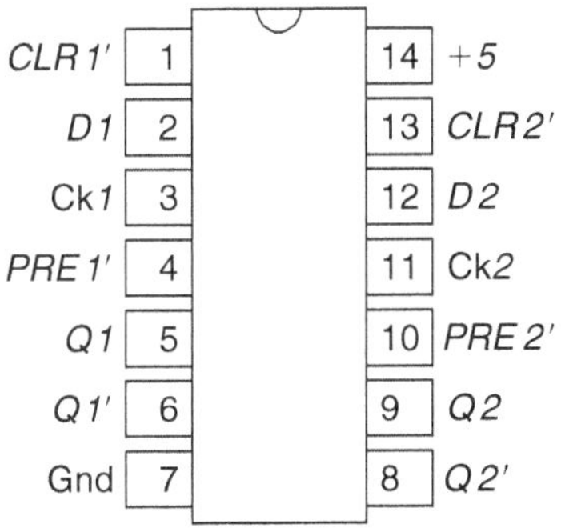

7474

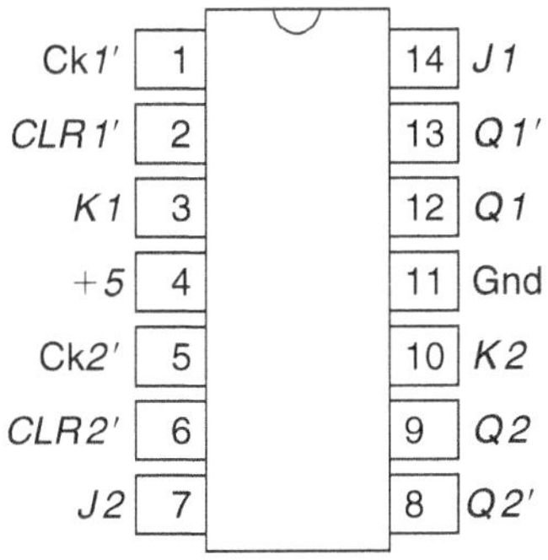

7473*

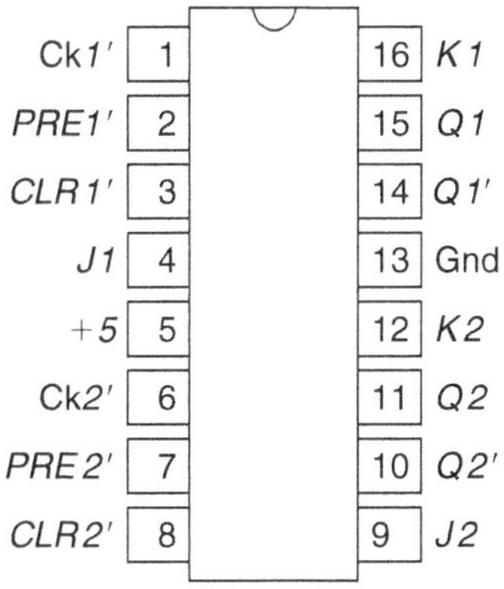

7476

*WinBreadboard includes the 7473A, for which the connections for *J1* and *K1* are interchanged, as are those for *J2* and *K2*.

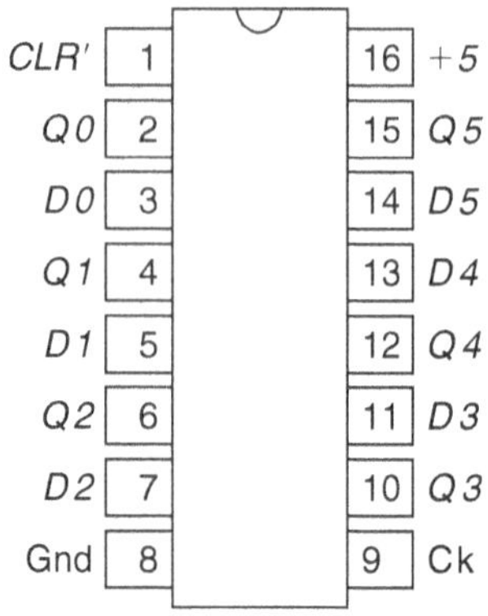

74174

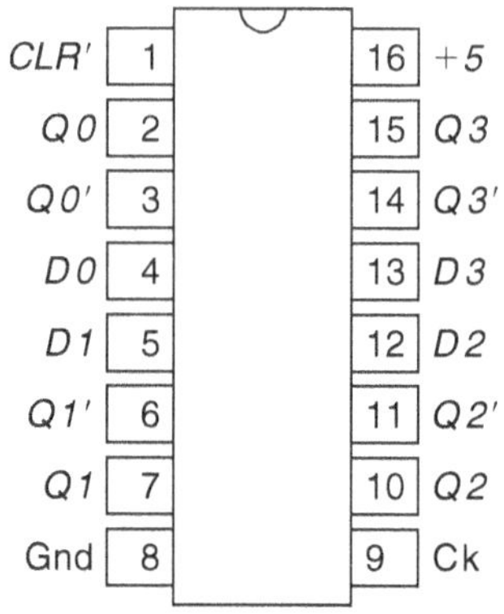

74175

Shift Registers

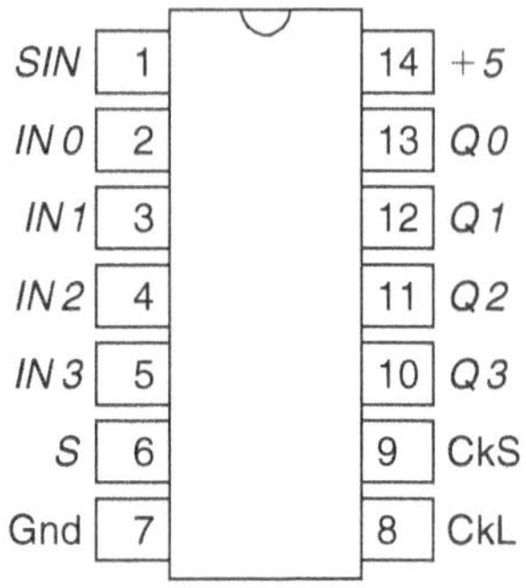

7495

S = 0: Shift, *S* = 1: Load
CkS: Shift clock
CkL: Load clock
SIN: Serial left bit Input

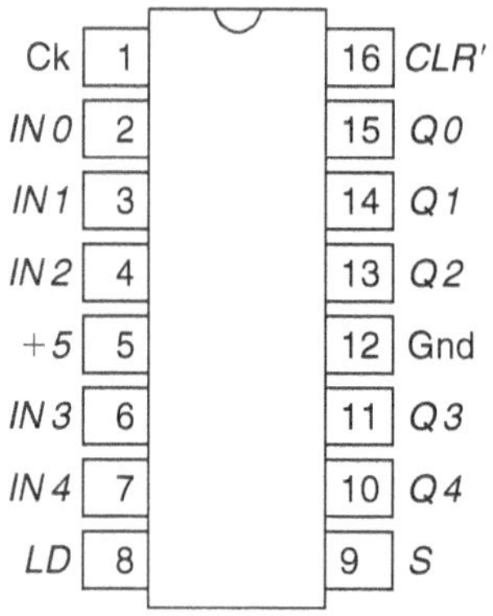

7496

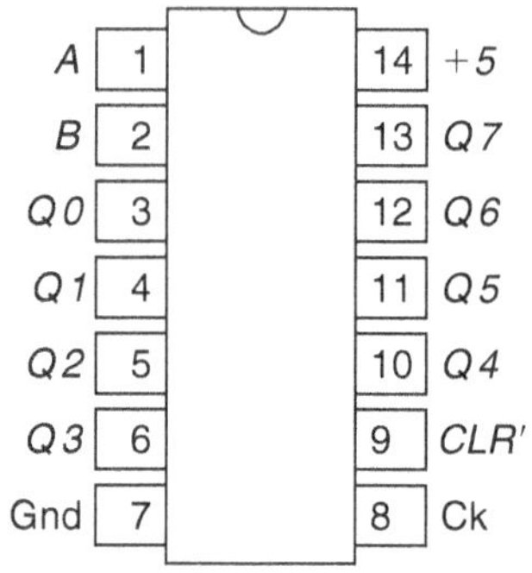

74164

Shift Registers

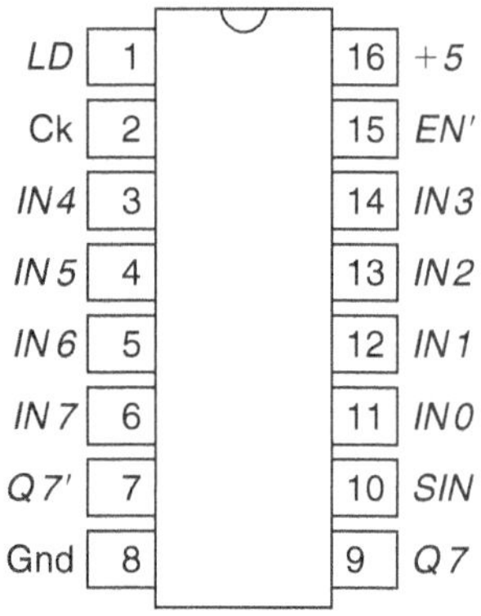

74165

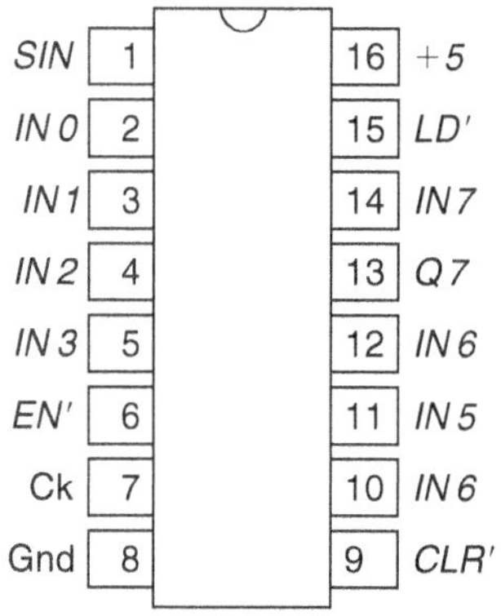

74166

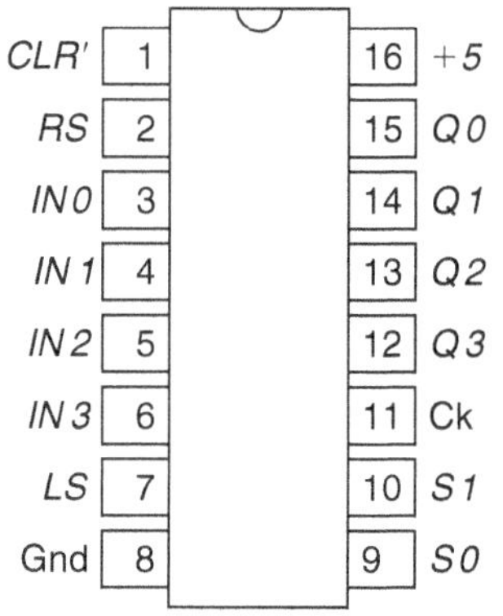

74194

D.5 Layout of Chips Referenced in the Text and Experiments

Synchronous Counters

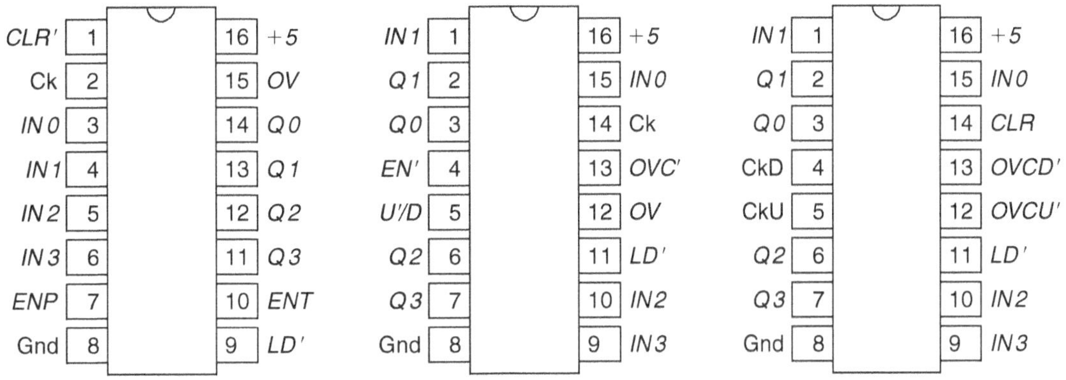

74160 – 74163

74190, 74191
OVC′: Clocked OV

74192, 74193

Asynchronous Counters

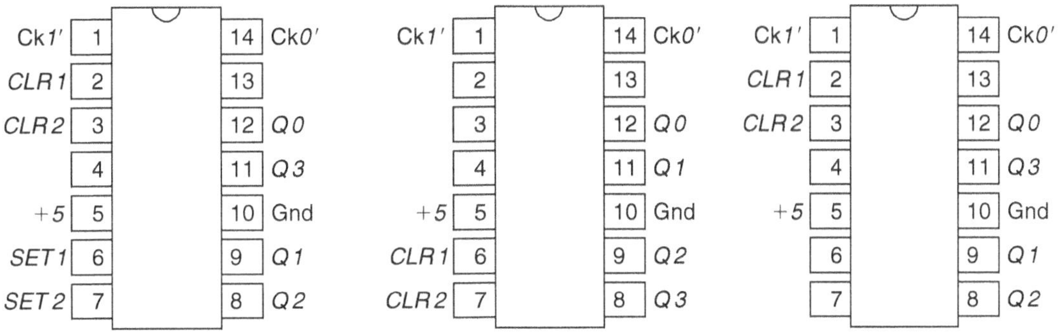

7490 7492 7493

CLR1 and *CLR2* must both be 1 to clear. *SET1* and *SET2* both 1 set to 1000.

APPENDIX E: COMPLETE EXAMPLES

E.1 COMBINATIONAL EXAMPLES

EXAMPLE E.1

The inputs, *w*, *x*, *y*, and *z* represent a positive binary integer. The output, *f*, is 1 iff the input is a prime or a perfect square but is 0 if the input is 0. A prime number is a positive integer divisible (with no remainder) only by 1 and itself. (Although 0 is a perfect square, we have specifically excluded that case.) Design this system using a minumum number of NAND or NOR gate packages.

The following is the truth table:

w	*x*	*y*	*z*	*f*
0	0	0	0	0
0	0	0	1	1
0	0	1	0	1
0	0	1	1	1
0	1	0	0	1
0	1	0	1	1
0	1	1	0	0
0	1	1	1	1
1	0	0	0	0
1	0	0	1	1
1	0	1	0	0
1	0	1	1	1
1	1	0	0	0
1	1	0	1	1
1	1	1	0	0
1	1	1	1	0

Shown next are maps for both *f* and *f*′.

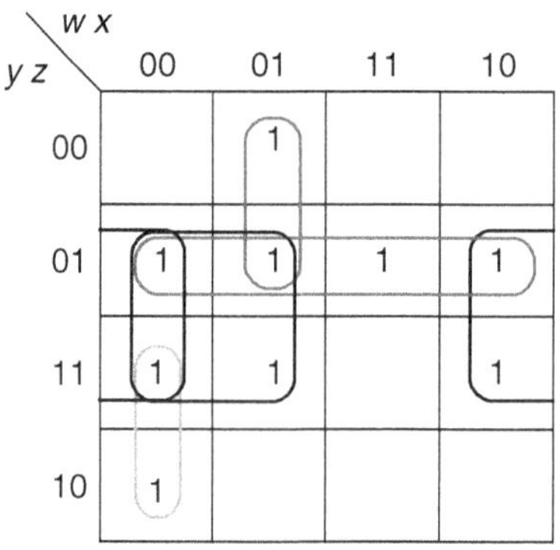

f

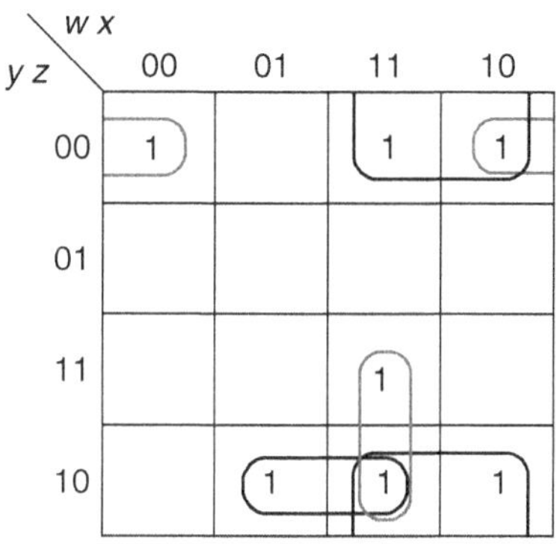

f′

$$f = w'z + x'z + y'z + w'xy' + w'x'y$$
$$f' = wz' + xyz' + wxy + x'y'z'$$
$$f = (w' + z)\,(x' + y' + z)\,(w' + x' + y')\,(x + y + z)$$

The two-level NAND gate implementation requires 3 two-input gates, 2 three-input gates, and 1 five-input gate, three packages. The two-level NOR uses 1 four-input gate, 3 three-input gates, and 1 two-input gate, only two packages (since the two-input gate uses the leftover four-input one).

The NOR implementation is

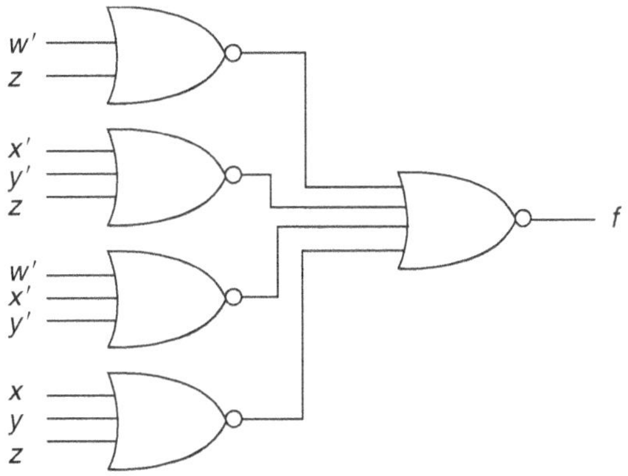

We could reduce the number of packages using NAND gates to two by factoring z from the second and third terms and w' from the others

$$f = z\,(x' + y') + w'\,(z + xy' + x'y)$$
$$= z\,(x' + y') + w'\,[z + (x + y)\,(x' + y')]$$

That results in the following circuit, which uses only 7 two-input NAND gates (two packages).

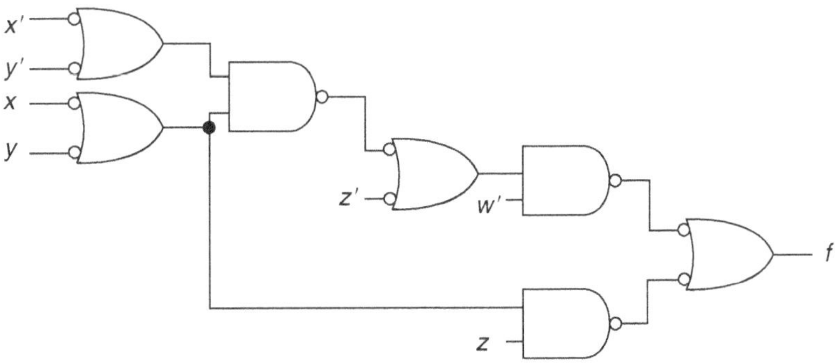

EXAMPLE E.2

The inputs represent a decimal digit in 2421 code (See Table 1.7). In that weighted code, each of the unused combinations also represent one of the decimal digits. Design a system with two outputs, *f* and *g*, such that *f* is 1 iff the digit represented is a multiple of 2 or 3 (or both) and *g* is 1 if this is not the normally used code. For example, 7 is normally coded 1101 (2 + 4 + 0 + 1) and the code 0111 (0 + 4 + 2 + 1) is unused. Thus, *f* = 0 in both rows, but *g* = 0 for row 1101 and *g* = 1 for row 0111.

A truth table for these functions is shown next.

w	*x*	*y*	*z*	Digit	*f*	*g*
0	0	0	0	0	0	0
0	0	0	1	1	0	0
0	0	1	0	2	1	0
0	0	1	1	3	1	0
0	1	0	0	4	1	0
0	1	0	1	5	0	1
0	1	1	0	6	1	1
0	1	1	1	7	0	1
1	0	0	0	2	1	1
1	0	0	1	3	1	1
1	0	1	0	4	1	1
1	0	1	1	5	0	0
1	1	0	0	6	1	0
1	1	0	1	7	0	0
1	1	1	0	8	1	0
1	1	1	1	9	1	0

We will start by getting sum of products representations, leading toward NAND gate solutions. The functions *f* and *g* are mapped below.

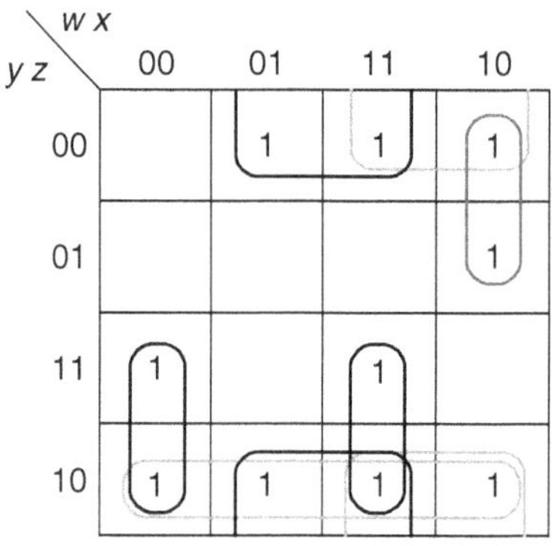

f

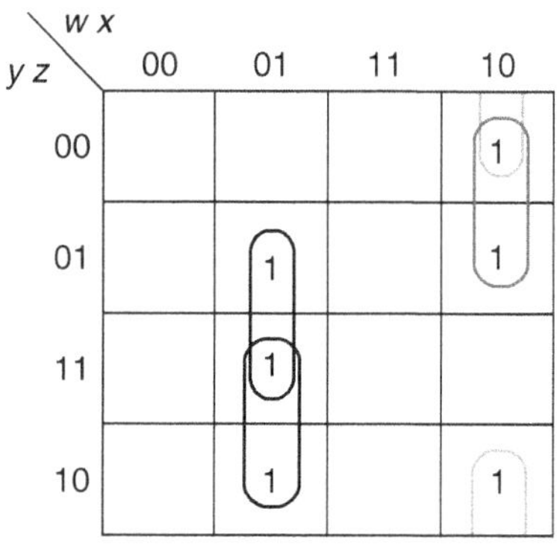

g

The minimum sum of products expressions for f and g are

$$f = xz' + w'x'y + wxy + wx'y' + \{wz' \text{ or } yz'\}$$
$$g = w'xy + w'xz + wx'y' + wx'z'$$

A two-level solution would require 2 two-input gates, 6 three-input gates (since we could share the gate producing $wx'y'$), 1 four-input gate, and 1 five-input gate. That would require five packages.

We could take advantage of sharing, by using $wx'z'$ instead of the last term in f. That would save a two-input gate, reducing the package count to four, since the two-input gate could be implemented using the extra four-input one.

Each function could be implemented with only two-input gates, sharing two, but requiring a total of 17 gates (five packages):

$$f = z'(x + y) + [w' + (x + y')(x' + y)][w + x'y]$$
$$g = w'(xy + xz) + w(x'y' + x'z')$$

Another approach, using two- and three-input gates comes from the following equations:

$$f = xz' + y(w'x' + wx) + wx'(y' + z')$$
$$g = w'x(y + z) + wx'(y' + z')$$

resulting in a circuit using 3 three-input gates and 8 two-input gates, only three packages. The circuit is shown below.

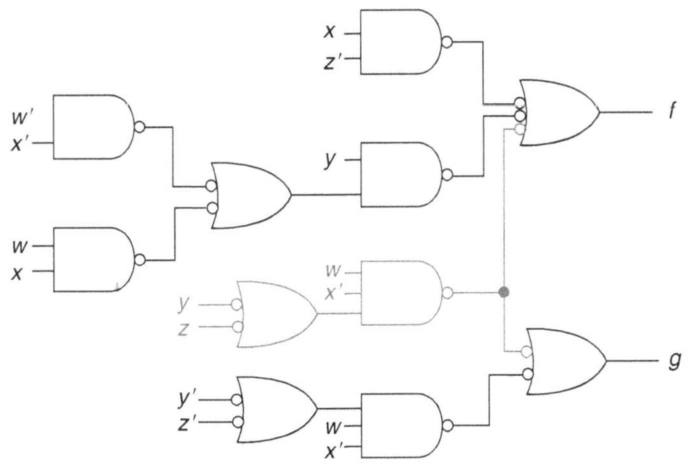

Next, we will look at product of sums expressions and NOR gate implementations. The maps of f' and g' are shown next.

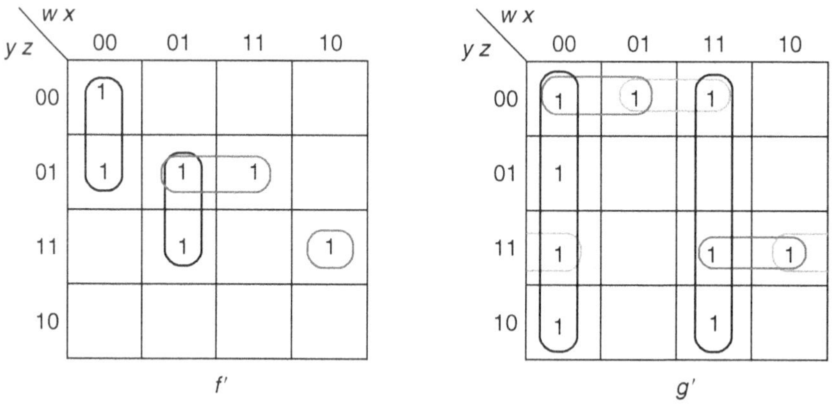

$$f' = w'x'y' + w'xz + xy'z + wx'yz$$
$$g' = w'x' + wx + \{w'y'z' \text{ or } xy'z'\} + \{wyz \text{ or } x'yz\}$$

or, choosing the first of the alternates,

$$f = (w + x + y)\,(w + x' + z')\,(x' + y + z')\,(w' + x + y' + z')$$
$$g = (w + x)\,(w' + x')\,(w + y + z)\,(w' + y' + z')$$

The two-level solution requires 2 two-input gates, 5 three-input gates, and 3 four-input gates, which could be implemented with four packages. There is no way to do it with all two-input gates or with less than four packages.

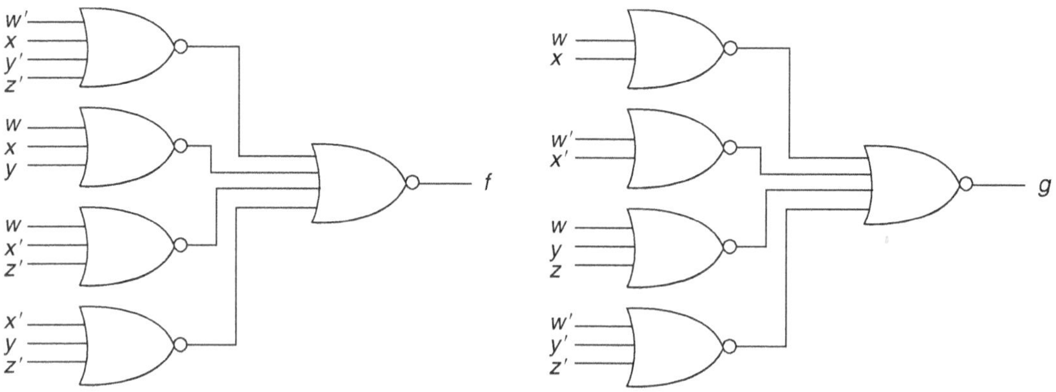

EXAMPLE E.3

The problem is to design a ball and strike counter for baseball. The inputs are how many balls (0, 1, 2, 3) before this pitch, how many strikes (0, 1, 2) before this pitch, and what happens on this pitch. The outputs are how many balls after this pitch (0, 1, 2, 3) or how many strikes after this pitch (0, 1, 2). In baseball, there are four outcomes of any pitch (from the point of view of this problem). It can be a strike, a foul ball, a ball, or anything else that will end this batter's turn (such as a hit or a fly out).

A foul ball is considered a strike, except when there are already two strikes, in which case the number of strikes remains 2. The output is to indicate the number of balls and strikes after this pitch unless the batter's turn is over. If the batter's turn is over for any reason, the output should indicate 0 balls and 0 strikes.

Show the code for the inputs (there should be 6—2 for the what happened on that pitch, 2 for the number of balls, and 2 for the number of strikes) and for the outputs (there should be 5—3 for balls and 2 for strikes). Then show maps and an implementation using NAND gates.

Comment: A more complete problem would include the number of outs, but that would involve two more inputs for the number of outs before the pitch and at least one more input column for pitch outcome, since we would need to differentiate between hits and outs, as well as double plays and players out stealing.

We will use the first two inputs, *a* and *b*, to indicate the number of balls, the next two, *c* and *d*, to indicate the number of strikes (which is never 3), and the last two, *e* and *f*, to indicate the outcome of the pitch, as follows:

e	*f*	Outcome
0	0	Strike
0	1	Foul
1	0	Ball
1	1	Anything else

The outputs, *w* and *x*, are the number of balls after the pitch, and *y* and *z* are the number of strikes after the pitch.

The six variable maps are shown next. The layers correspond to the number of balls; the columns are the number of strikes. Since there are never three strikes before a pitch, the 11 column is all don't cares.

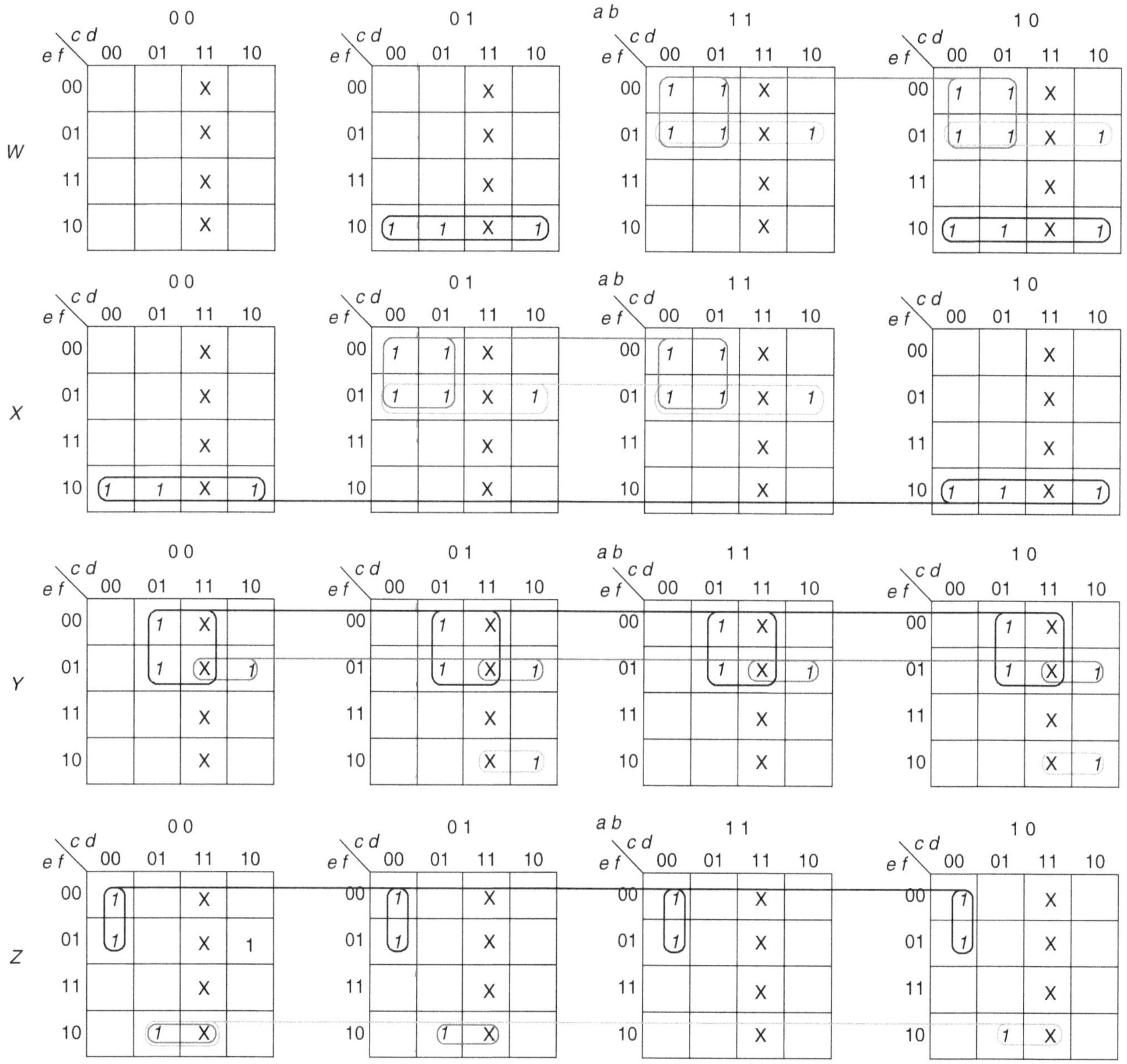

The resulting minimum sum of product equations are

$w = a'bef' + ab'ef' + ac'e' + ae'f$

$x = b'ef' + bc'e' + be'f$

$y = de' + ce'f + a'bcef' + ab'cef'$

$z = c'd'e' + a'def' + b'def'$

There are no common prime implicants that take advantage of sharing (as in Section 3.8). Implementing them directly requires

	Gates	Packages
Five-input	2	2
Four-input	6	3
Three-input	9	3
Two-input	1	1

for a total of nine packages.

Taking advantage of what is common in the first two terms of w and the last two terms of y, and also factoring literals in x and z, we can manipulate them to

$$w = (a'b + ab')\,ef' + ae'\,(c' + f)$$
$$x = b'ef' + be'\,(c' + f)$$
$$y = de' + ce'f + (a'b + ab')\,cef' = de' + c\,[e'f + (a'b + ab')\,ef']$$
$$z = c'd'e' + def'\,(a' + b')$$

Noting that the $(a'b + ab')\,ef'$ and $(c' + f)$ terms are shared, this requires only six packages (where either the extra three- or four-input gate is used for the 13th two-input one).

	Gates	Packages
Four-input	1	1
Three-input	5	2
Two-input	13	3

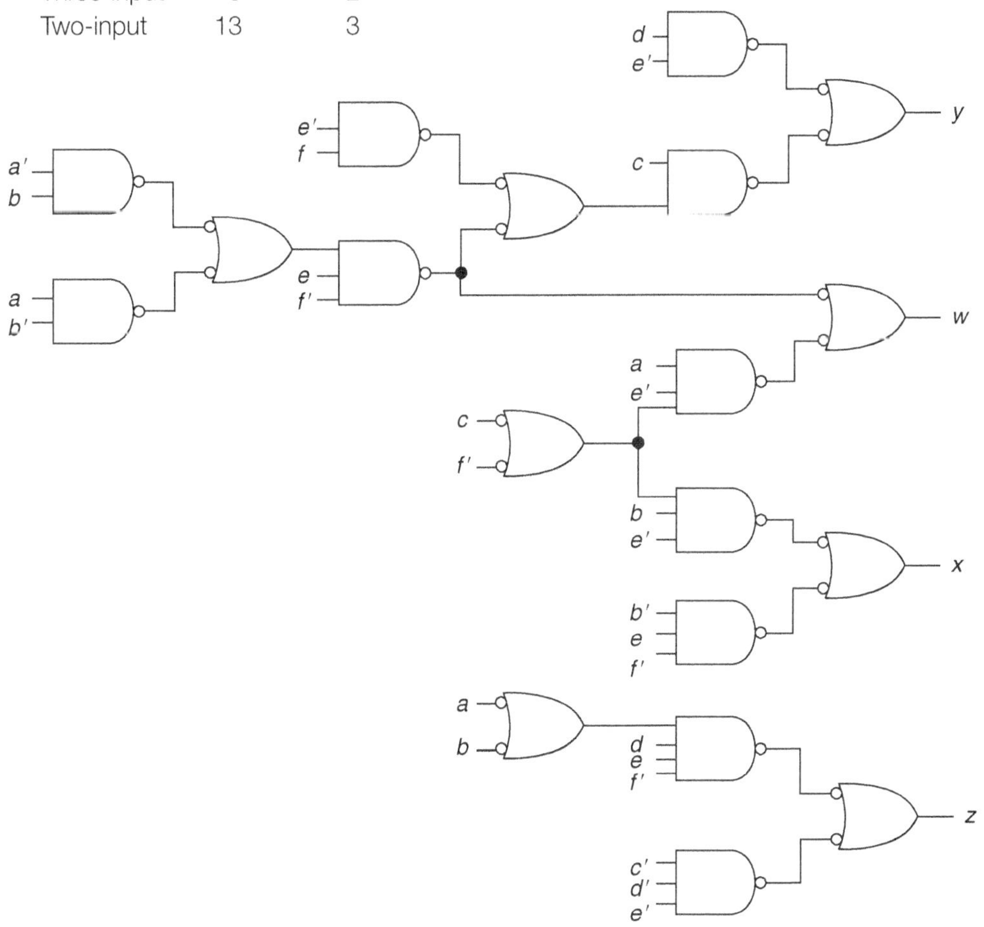

E.2 SEQUENTIAL EXAMPLES

EXAMPLE E.4

Design a Moore system with one input, *x*, and one output, *z*, such that *z* changes whenever there have been two consecutive 0 inputs. The system output is initially 0. Implement it with *JK* flip flops and NAND.

Sample
x 1 1 0 0 1 0 0 1 0 0 0 1 0 0 1 0 1 0 0 0 0 0
z 0 0 0 0 1 1 1 0 0 0 1 0 0 0 1 1 1 1 1 0 1 0 1

From the sample timing trace, it is clear that when there are more than two consecutive 0 inputs, the output keeps changing.

There are two nowhere states, *A* where the output is 0 and *B* where the output is one. In either of these states, a 1 input leaves the state unchanged, and a 0 input moves ahead. The other two states are *C*, where the output is still 0, but there has been a 0 input and *D*, where the output is still 1. This leads to the following state diagram.

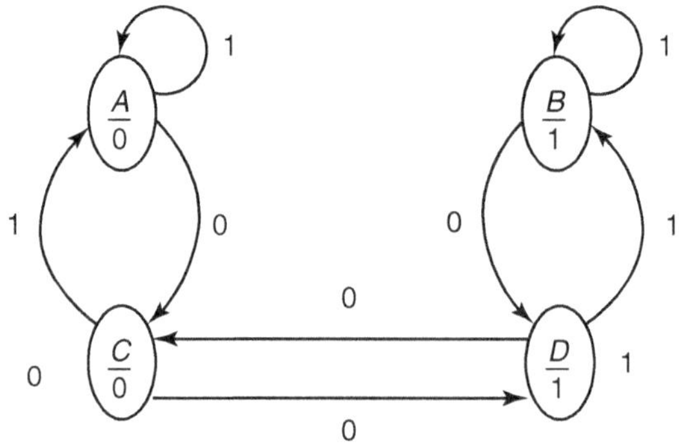

With consecutive 0 inputs, we go back and forth between states *C* and *D*. The state table for this is

Q	Q★ x = 0	Q★ x = 1	z
A	C	A	0
B	D	B	1
C	D	A	0
D	C	B	1

There are three state assignments that we might consider.

a.

Q	Q_1	Q_2
A	0	0
B	0	1
C	1	0
D	1	1

b.

Q	Q_1	Q_2
A	0	0
B	0	1
C	1	1
D	1	0

c.

Q	Q_1	Q_2
A	0	0
B	1	1
C	0	1
D	1	0

The first and third assignments require no output logic; $z = Q_2$ for assignment *a* and $z = Q_1$ for assignment *c*. For assignment *b*, $z = Q_1' Q_2 + Q_1 Q_2'$, requiring three gates. We will complete the design using assignments *a* and *c*.

			a.		c.	
x	Q_1	Q_2	$Q_1^\star$	$Q_1^\star$	$Q_1^\star$	$Q_2^\star$
0	0	0	1	0	0	1
0	0	1	1	1	1	0
0	1	0	1	1	0	1
0	1	1	1	0	1	0
1	0	0	0	0	0	0
1	0	1	0	1	0	0
1	1	0	0	0	1	1
1	1	1	0	1	1	1

For assignment *a*, the maps are

$Q_1 Q_2$ \ x	0	1
00	1	
01	1	
11	1	
10	1	

$Q_1^\star$

$Q_1 Q_2$ \ x	0	1
00		
01	1	1
11		1
10	1	

$Q_2^\star$

$J_1 = x'$ $\quad K_1 = x$ $\quad J_2 = K_2 = x' Q_1$ $\quad z = Q_2$

This requires 1 two-input NAND and two inverters.*

For assignment *c*, the maps are

$Q_1 Q_2$ \ x	0	1
00		
01	1	
11	1	1
10		1

$Q_1 Q_2$ \ x	0	1
00	1	
01		
11		1
10	1	1

$J_1 = K_1 = x' Q_2'$ $\quad J_2 = x' + Q_1$ $\quad K_2 = x' + Q_1$ $\quad z = Q_1$

*In Chapter 9, we will see that this assignment for Q_1 will produce the simplest inputs for that *JK* flip flop.

This requires 3 two-input NANDs and two inverters. (Assignment *b* would require 4 two-input NANDs and one inverter).

The circuit for assignment a becomes

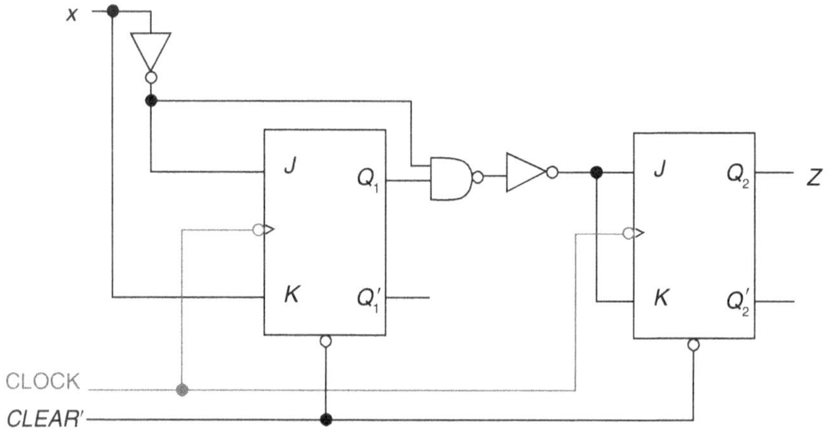

where the NOT gate is needed for the inputs to Q_2 to create an AND. Also, a *CLEAR'* signal is shown to initialize the system to state 00.

EXAMPLE E.5

We are designing an automatic light controller for a small room, one that holds a maximum of three people. There is a signal that is 1 for one clock period on line x_1 whenever someone enters the room and a similar signal on line x_2 when someone leaves. When the room is empty, the light in the room is off; when anyone is in the room, the light is on. Output z_1 controls that light. If the room is full, a red light, controlled by output line z_2, outside the room is lit.

We need an up/down counter, *AB*, initialized to 0, to keep track of the number of people in the room. It is somewhat different from the one discussed in Example 7.8 because there are separate inputs for counting up and counting down.

The state table is thus

AB	x_1x_2	$A^\star B^\star$			z_1z_2
	00	01	10	11	
00	00	XX	01	00	00
01	01	00	10	01	10
10	10	01	11	10	10
11	11	10	XX	11	11

The counter goes up when someone enters (the 10 column) and down when someone leaves (the 01 column). We assume that no one enters when the room is full and no one leaves when it is empty (accounting for the don't cares). The first output is 1 whenever the count is not 0, and the second is 1 when the count is 3. (This is a Moore system.)

The equations for the outputs can read from the state table.

$$z_1 = A + B \qquad\qquad z_2 = AB$$

The maps for the next state, with the *J* sections shaded, are shown next.

AB \ $x_1 x_2$	00	01	11	10
00		X		
01				1
11	1	1	1	X
10	1		1	1

A★

AB \ $x_1 x_2$	00	01	11	10
00		X		1
01	1		1	
11	1		1	X
10		1		1

B★

$J_A = x_1 x_2' B$ $\quad K_A = x_1' x_2 B'$ $\quad J_B = K_B = x_1' x_2 + x_1 x_2'$

The circuit is shown next, with a *CLEAR'* to initialize it.

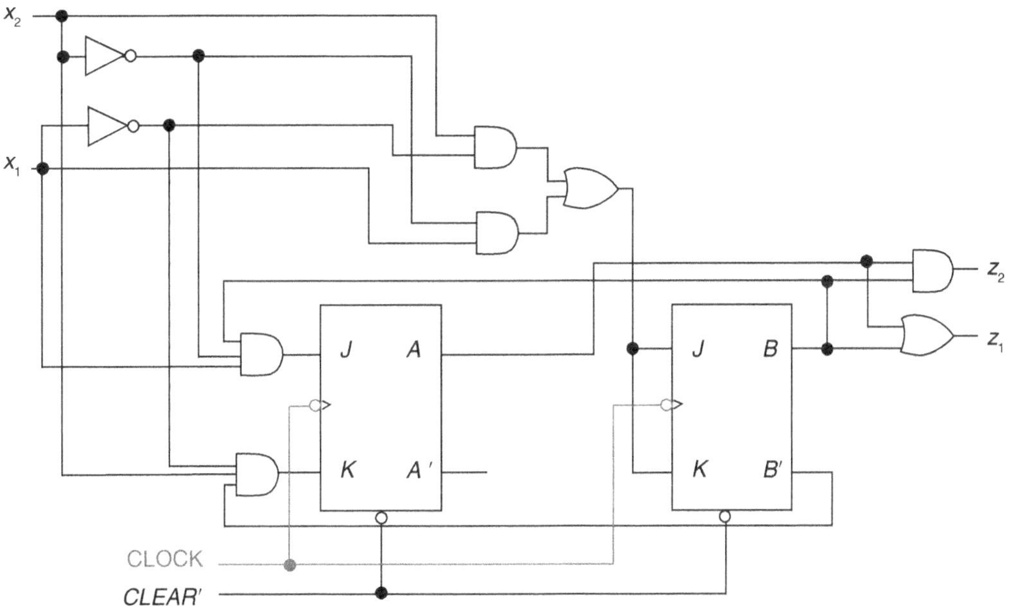

EXAMPLE E.6

Design a Moore system using *JK* flip flops that produces a 1 output if the input pattern has been 1 0 1 1

a. If overlapping is NOT allowed (5 states).
b. If overlapping is allowed (5 states).
c. Once the output is 1, it remains 1 as long as the pattern is continuing (7 states).

Samples

x	0 0 1 0 1 1 0 1 1 1 0 1 1 0 1 1 0 0
z_a	? 0 0 0 0 0 1 0 0 0 0 0 0 1 0 0 0 0 0 0 0
z_b	? 0 0 0 0 0 1 0 0 1 0 0 0 1 0 0 1 0 0 0 0
z_c	? 0 0 0 0 0 1 1 1 1 0 0 0 1 1 1 1 1 0 0 0

All three start out the same way, where state *A* is nowhere, looking for the first 1, state *B* is reached with the first 1, *C* is reached with the 0, *D* on the second 1, and *E* is reached when the pattern is complete and the output is 1. The first state diagram shows the answers for parts a and b.

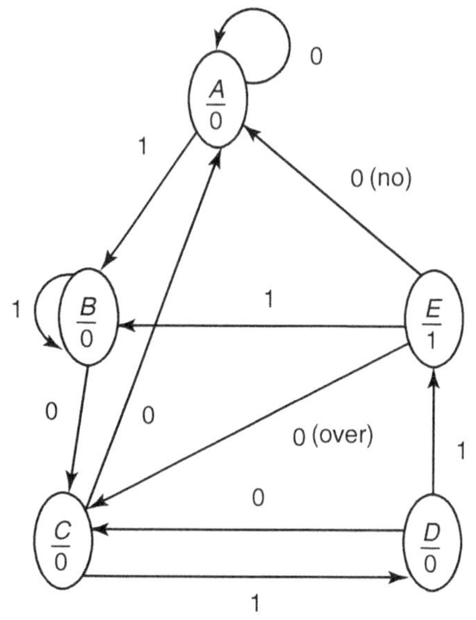

After getting to state *E*, a 1 input would be the first 1 in a new sequence (state *B*). If overlapping is not allowed, a 0 input leaves us nowhere, back in state *A*. If overlapping is allowed, we now have the 10 of a new pattern and go to state *C*.

For part c, we need two new states. From *E*, a 0 input continues the pattern and should thus produce a 1 output. Then a 1 input keeps it going (to state *G*). Finally, another 1 gets us back to state *G* as shown below.

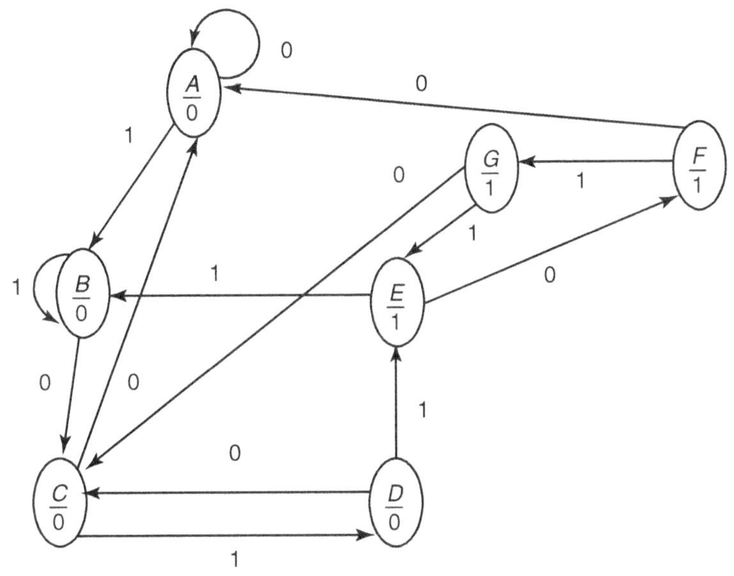

We will next look at the implementation of this system using *JK* flip flops. We will consider two state assignments:

a.

Q	$q_1\,q_2\,q_3$
A	0 0 0
B	0 0 1
C	0 1 0
D	0 1 1
E	1 0 0
F	1 0 1
G	1 1 0

b.

Q	$q_1\,q_2\,q_3$
A	0 0 0
B	0 1 0
C	0 0 1
D	0 1 1
E	1 1 0
F	1 0 1
G	1 1 1

The first just assigns the states in numerical order. The second uses some information from Chapter 9. First, we will convert the state diagram to a state table and then create the truth table using the first assignment.

Q	$Q^\star$ $x = 0$	$x = 1$	z
A	A	B	0
B	C	B	0
C	A	D	0
D	C	E	0
E	F	B	1
F	A	G	1
G	C	E	1

The design truth table has 16 rows:

	$x\ q_1\ q_2\ q_3$	$q_1^\star$	$q_2^\star$	$q_3^\star$	$J_1\ K_1$	$J_2\ K_2$	$J_3\ K_3$
A	0 0 0 0	0	0	0	0 X	0 X	0 X
B	0 0 0 1	0	1	0	0 X	1 X	X 1
C	0 0 1 0	0	0	0	0 X	X 1	0 X
D	0 0 1 1	0	1	0	0 X	X 0	X 1
E	0 1 0 0	1	0	1	X 0	0 X	1 X
F	0 1 0 1	0	0	0	X 1	0 X	X 1
G	0 1 1 0	0	1	0	X 1	X 0	0 X
—	0 1 1 1	X	X	X	X X	X X	X X
A	1 0 0 0	0	0	1	0 X	0 X	1 X
B	1 0 0 1	0	0	1	0 X	0 X	X 0
C	1 0 1 0	0	1	1	0 X	X 0	1 X
D	1 0 1 1	1	0	0	1 X	X 1	X 1
E	1 1 0 0	0	0	1	X 1	0 X	1 X
F	1 1 0 1	1	1	0	X 0	1 X	X 1
G	1 1 1 0	1	0	0	X 0	X 1	0 X
—	1 1 1 1	X	X	X	X X	X X	X X

After mapping these, we get

$J_1 = x\, q_2\, q_3$ $\qquad K_1 = x'\, q_2 + x'\, q_3 + x\, q_2'\, q_3'$

$J_2 = x'\, q_1'\, q_3 + x\, q_1\, q_3$ $\qquad K_2 = x'\, q_1'\, q_3' + x\, q_1 + x\, q_3$

$J_3 = q_1\, q_2' + x\, q_1'$ $\qquad K_3 = x + q_1 + q_2$

$Z = q_1$

This requires 8 two-input gates and 8 three-input gates plus the NOT for x'.

Using the second assignment, we get the following design truth table:

	$x\ q_1\ q_2\ q_3$	$q_1^\star$	$q_2^\star$	$q_3^\star$
A	0 0 0 0	0	0	0
C	0 0 0 1	0	0	0
B	0 0 1 0	0	0	1
D	0 0 1 1	0	0	1
—	0 1 0 0	X	X	X
F	0 1 0 1	0	0	0
E	0 1 1 0	1	0	1
G	0 1 1 1	0	0	1
A	1 0 0 0	0	1	0
C	1 0 0 1	0	1	1
B	1 0 1 0	0	1	0
D	1 0 1 1	1	1	0
—	1 1 0 0	X	X	X
F	1 1 0 1	1	1	1
E	1 1 1 0	0	1	0
G	1 1 1 1	1	1	0

We will map these and use the quick method.

q_2q_3 \ xq_1	00	01	11	10
00		X	X	
01			1	
11			1	1
10		1		

$Q_1^\star$

q_2q_3 \ xq_1	00	01	11	10
00		X	X	1
01			1	1
11			1	1
10			1	1

$Q_2^\star$

q_2q_3 \ xq_1	00	01	11	10
00		X	X	
01			1	1
11	1	1		
10	1	1		

$Q_3^\star$

The *J* sections of each of the maps are shaded, producing the equations

$$J_1 = x\,q_2\,q_3 \qquad K_1 = x\,q_3 + x'\,q_3'$$
$$J_2 = x \qquad K_2 = x'$$
$$J_3 = x'\,q_2 \qquad K_3 = x'\,q_2' + x\,q_2$$
$$Z = q_1$$

This assignment requires only 7 two-input gates and 1 three-input gate plus the NOT for x' (no three-input gates).

INDEX

Note: Page numbers having the format *9-x* indicate material in Chapter 9, which can be found online at http://www.mhhe.com/marcovitz.

D

R

S

T

U

V

W

FLIP FLOPS

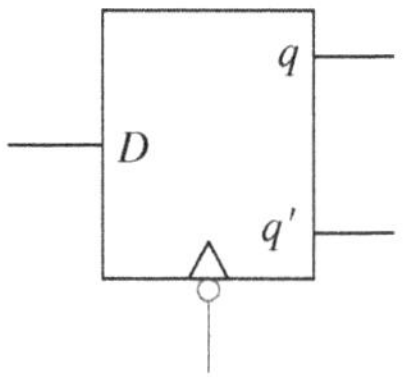

D	q	$q^\star$
0	0	0
0	1	0
1	0	1
1	1	1

$$q^\star = D$$

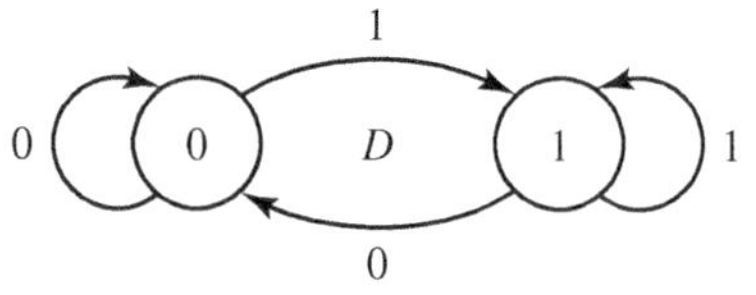

q	$q^\star$	D
0	0	0
0	1	1
1	0	0
1	1	1

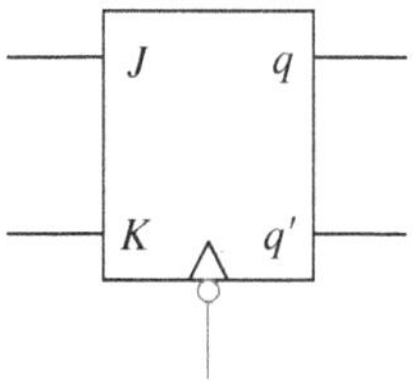

J	K	q	$q^\star$
0	0	0	0
0	0	1	1
0	1	0	0
0	1	1	0
1	0	0	1
1	0	1	1
1	1	0	1
1	1	1	0

$$q^\star = Jq' + K'q$$

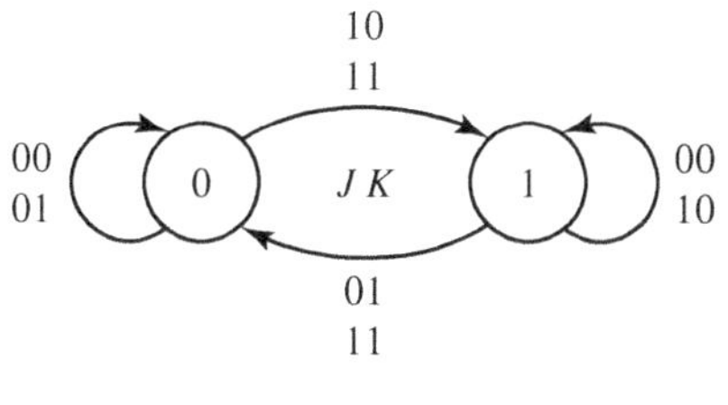

q	$q^\star$	J	K
0	0	0	X
0	1	1	X
1	0	X	1
1	1	X	0

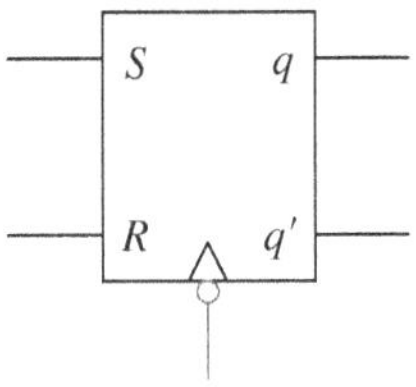

S	**R**	**q**	**q★**	
0	0	0	0	
0	0	1	1	
0	1	0	0	
0	1	1	0	
1	0	0	1	
1	0	1	1	
1	1	0	—	not
1	1	1	—	allowed

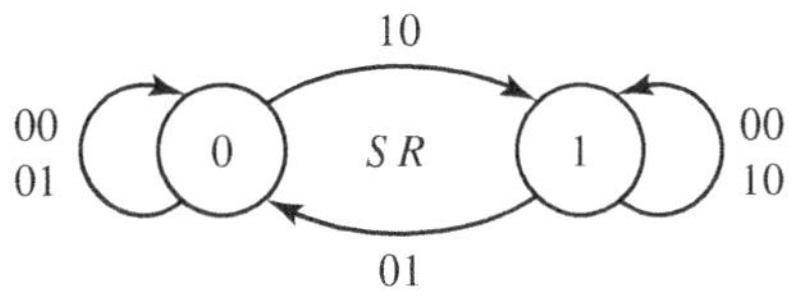

q	**q★**	**S**	**R**
0	0	0	X
0	1	1	0
1	0	0	1
1	1	X	0

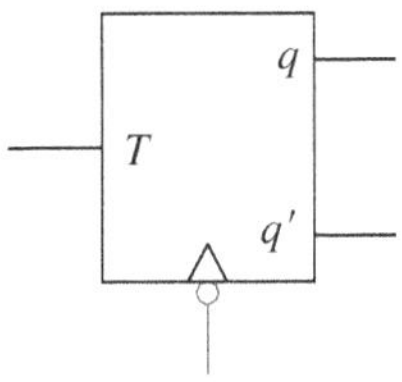

T	**q**	**q★**
0	0	0
0	1	1
1	0	1
1	1	0

$$q^\star = T \oplus q$$

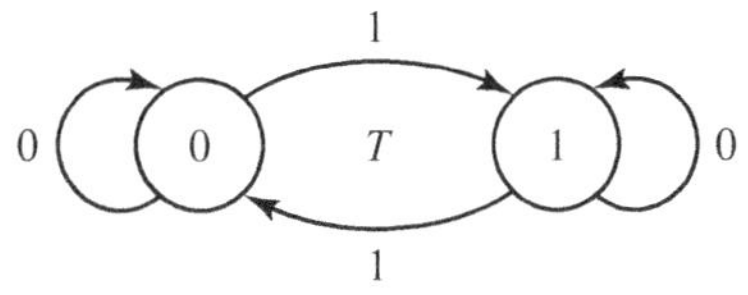

q	**q★**	**T**
0	0	0
0	1	1
1	0	1
1	1	0

Credits